UNDERSTANDING INFORMATION RETRIEVAL SYSTEMS

MANAGEMENT, TYPES, AND STANDARDS

UNDERSTANDING INFORMATION RETRIEVAL SYSTEMS

MANAGEMENT, TYPES, AND STANDARDS

Edited By
MARCIA J. BATES

CRC Press
Taylor & Francis Group
Boca Raton London New York

CRC Press is an imprint of the
Taylor & Francis Group, an **informa** business
AN AUERBACH BOOK

CRC Press
Taylor & Francis Group
6000 Broken Sound Parkway NW, Suite 300
Boca Raton, FL 33487-2742

Printed in the United States of America on acid-free paper
Version Date: 20111110

International Standard Book Number: 978-1-4398-9196-4 (Hardback)

Library of Congress Cataloging-in-Publication Data

Understanding information retrieval systems : management, types, and standards / editor, Marcia J. Bates.
pages cm
Includes bibliographical references and index.
ISBN 978-1-4398-9196-4
1. Information storage and retrieval systems. I. Bates, Marcia J., editor of compilation.

Z667.U53 2012
025.5'24--dc23 2011042159

Visit the Taylor & Francis Web site at
http://www.taylorandfrancis.com

and the CRC Press Web site at
http://www.crcpress.com

Contents

Introduction

UNDERSTANDING INFORMATION RETRIEVAL SYSTEMS: MANAGEMENT, TYPES, AND STANDARDS

Information retrieval systems, especially those accessed over the Internet, are ubiquitous in our globalizing world. Many are wonderfully easy to use, and it is therefore easy to assume that the design and implementation of information systems is a simple and straightforward process. However, systems need to be designed specifically for their intended functions in order to provide optimal support for the people who use them. It turns out that it is not always obvious what needs to be done to produce a really well-functioning information system. In addition, information systems are almost always part of a much larger infrastructure that is designed to support business, government, and other activities. All parts of that infrastructure need to mesh into a single well-functioning social and technical system, containing and optimizing the information systems within. Consequently, information systems are seldom stand-alone. They need to be made interoperable with other systems of many types, and at many levels of functionality.

Chapters on different types of information systems, on managing information systems, both as collections of data and as part of a larger social and administrative system, and on the technical standards that are required in order for the systems to inter-operate with other systems and networks in this volume are gathered together. World Wide Web–based systems are emphasized. Collectively, the chapters in this book provide an excellent introduction to the various aspects of developing and managing information retrieval systems in the context of real-world demands.

Emphasis is given to information systems that operate on relatively unstructured data, such as text, images, and music. This is the domain of what is commonly called *information retrieval (IR) systems.* ("Information systems" is the more general term, and includes systems working with highly structured data, such as payrolls. IR systems generally deal with the less structured kinds of data, which therefore introduce the complexities of natural language processing, image analysis, etc.) The chapters are drawn from the recently published *Encyclopedia of Library and Information Sciences, 3rd Ed.*[1] That encyclopedia might have been more accurately titled *Encyclopedia of the Information Disciplines,* as the entries are written by experts in many information-related fields: information systems, information retrieval, informatics, knowledge management, library and archival sciences, museum studies, and records management, among others.

Part I of this book, "General" (Chapters 1 through 7), provides an introduction at the broadest level to information retrieval systems. The core concepts of "information systems" (Chapter 1) and "information retrieval systems" (Chapter 2) are introduced. Next, what is known about how people search for information is described (Chapter 3), and theories and models of IR (Chapter 4) are laid out. The techniques for designing systems around user needs and preferences are presented in Chapter 5. Finally, ethical issues are discussed in Chapter 6, and careers and educational opportunities and requirements in the information systems field are presented in Chapter 7.

In Part II, "Management of Information Retrieval Systems" (Chapter 8 through 21), management issues are presented, and the decision process around likely information system solutions is elaborated. The term "management" is most often associated with the management of people or finances, but "information management" has an extra dimension of meaning. Even digitized information has to be managed both physically and within an administrative structure, is embedded in various possible technical systems and networks, and brings socially complex issues to the fore, such as piracy, version control, preservation, and meeting legal standards and requirements. An information manager has to understand and integrate all these issues and then generate effective solutions for the organization or institution holding the information.

Part III, "Types of Information Retrieval Systems" (Chapters 22 through 43), illustrates the rich variety of types of information retrieval systems in use today, and discusses the technical, operational and administrative issues surrounding each type. Everything from geographic information systems to interactive multimedia in museums to Web mining is addressed, in chapters on twenty-two different information system types and functions.

Finally, in Part IV, "Standards for Information Retrieval Systems" (Chapters 44 through 51), a number of the most important organizational and technical standards needed for successful information retrieval are presented and discussed. At the broadest level is the Open Archival Information System (OAIS) Reference Model (see Chapter 51), which maps out the various components and relationships involved in the management of archived information. At the middle level are standards such as the Text Encoding Initiative (TEI) (see Chapter 49), which describes the preferred approaches to marking up original resources, especially in the humanities, for later retrieval and research use by scholars and students. At the most detailed level is the Digital Object Identifier (DOI®) system (see Chapter 44), which makes possible the unique identification of each digital object.

Altogether, the contents of this volume introduce the reader—whether computer scientist, information professional, or student—to the key elements needed for understanding, designing, and implementing information retrieval systems in contemporary organizations.

REFERENCE

1. Bates, Marcia J.; Maack Mary Niles, Eds. *Encyclopedia of Library and Information Sciences, 3rd Ed.*; CRC Press, 2010.

Editor

Marcia J. Bates is professor emerita in the Department of Information Studies, Graduate School of Education and Information Studies, at the University of California at Los Angeles. She has researched, published, and taught in many areas of library and information sciences, including user-centered design of information systems, subject access, online search techniques, and information seeking behavior. She has authored over eighty publications, including some of the most highly cited articles in the field. She has also served as associate dean and department chair. Dr. Bates has consulted for a wide variety of organizations, including government, foundation, and private industry clients, as well as "dot-com" companies. Dr. Bates is a fellow of the American Association for the Advancement of Science, and has won numerous awards, including the Award of Merit, the highest award of the American Society for Information Science and Technology (ASIST), and the Frederick G. Kilgour Award for Research in Library and Information Technology. ASIST has also awarded her its "Best Journal of ASIST Paper of the Year Award" twice. (Web site: http://www.gseis.ucla.edu/faculty/bates/)

List of Contributors

Ricardo Baeza-Yates
Barcelona Media Innovation Centre
Yahoo! Research
Barcelona, Spain
Chapter 23: Web Retrieval and Mining, p. 313

David Bearman
Archives & Museum Informatics
Pittsburgh, Pennsylvania, U.S.A.
Chapter 43: Museum Web Sites and Digital Collections, p. 589

Kevin Butterfield
Wolf Law Library, College of William and Mary
Williamsburg, Virginia, U.S.A.
Chapter 38: Online Public Access Catalogs (OPACs), p. 529

Paul D. Callister
Leon E. Bloch Law Library, University of Missouri-Kansas City School of Law
Kansas City, Missouri, U.S.A.
Chapter 16: Digital Content Licensing, p. 211

Nicholas Carroll
Hastings Research, Inc.
Las Vegas, Nevada, U.S.A.
Chapter 13: Search Engine Optimization, p. 171

Vittorio Castelli
IBM T.J. Watson Research Center
Yorktown Heights, New York, U.S.A.
Chapter 28: Still Image Search and Retrieval, p. 381

Carlos Castillo
Yahoo! Research
Barcelona, Spain
Chapter 23: Web Retrieval and Mining, p. 313

Kevin S. Clarke
Appalachian State University
Boone, North Carolina, U.S.A.
Chapter 47: Extensible Markup Language (XML), p. 645

James E.P. Currall
University of Glasgow
Glasgow, United Kingdom
Chapter 10: Digital Asset Management, p. 135

Kimiz Dalkir
Graduate School of Library and Information Studies, McGill University
Montreal, Quebec, Canada
Chapter 8: Knowledge Management, p. 111

Gordon B. Davis
Carlson School of Management
University of Minnesota
Minneapolis, Minnesota, U.S.A.
Chapter 21: Information Systems Failure, p. 285

Brian Detlor
DeGroote School of Business
McMaster University
Hamilton, Ontario, Canada
Chapter 9: Information Management, p. 125

Marek J. Druzdzel
School of Information Sciences and Intelligent Systems Program, University of Pittsburgh
Pittsburgh, Pennsylvania, U.S.A.
Chapter 33: Decision Support Systems, p. 461

Emily Gallup Fayen
MuseGlobal, Inc.
Boston, Massachusetts, U.S.A.
Chapter 37: Integrated Library Systems (ILS), p. 513

Roger R. Flynn
School of Information Sciences and Intelligent Sciences Program, University of Pittsburgh
Pittsburgh, Pennsylvania, U.S.A.
Chapter 33: Decision Support Systems, p. 461

Chuan Heng Foh
School of Computer Engineering
Nanyang Technological University
Singapore
Chapter 45: Data Transmission Protocols, p. 615

Christopher Fox
Department of Computer Science
James Madison University
Harrisonburg, Virginia, U.S.A.
Chapter 20: Data and Data Quality, p. 269

Nicholas Gibbins
School of Electronics and Computer Science, University of Southampton
Southampton, United Kingdom
Chapter 48: Resource Description Framework (RDF), p. 659

Paul Gray
School of Information Systems and Technology, Claremont Graduate University
Claremont, California, U.S.A.
Chapter 7: Careers and Education in Information Systems, p. 91

Jill E. Grogg
University of Alabama Libraries
Tuscaloosa, Alabama, U.S.A.
Chapter 15: Version Control, p. 203

Kathleen Hall
Leon E. Bloch Law Library, University of Missouri-Kansas City School of Law
Kansas City, Missouri, U.S.A.
Chapter 16: Digital Content Licensing, p. 211

Wendy Hall
Intelligence, Agents, Multimedia Group, University of Southampton
Highfield, Southhampton, United Kingdom
Chapter 24: Semantic Web, p. 325

Derek L. Hansen
University of Maryland
College Park, Maryland, U.S.A.
Chapter 31: Recommender Systems and Expert Locators, p. 435

Randolph Hock
Online Strategies
Vienna, Virginia, U.S.A.
Chapter 22: Search Engines, p. 301

Nik Honeysett
J. Paul Getty Museum
Los Angeles, California, U.S.A.
Chapter 42: Interactive Multimedia in Museums, p. 575

Peter Ingwersen
Royal School of Librarianship and Information Science
Copenhagen, Denmark
Chapter 4: User-Oriented and Cognitive Models of Information Retrieval, p. 47

David Jank
Racanelli Learning Resources Center
Dowling College Library
Oakdale, New York, U.S.A.
Chapter 34: Collaborative Systems and Groupware, p. 473

Kalervo Järvelin
Department of Information Science
University of Tampere
Tampere, Finland
Chapter 4: User-Oriented and Cognitive Models of Information Retrieval, p. 47

Tapan Khopkar
University of Michigan
Ann Arbor, Michigan, U.S.A.
Chapter 31: Recommender Systems and Expert Locators, p. 435

Scott L. Klingler
School of Library and Information Science, University of Southern Mississippi
Hattiesburg, Mississippi, U.S.A.
Chapter 18: Information Storage Technologies, p. 245

Mounia Lalmas
Department of Computing Science
University of Glasgow
Glasgow, United Kingdom
Chapter 25: XML Information Retrieval, p. 345

Ray R. Larson
School of Information, University of California, Berkeley
Berkeley, California, U.S.A.
Chapter 2: Information Retrieval Systems, p. 15

Hady W. Lauw
Microsoft Search Labs
Mountain View, California, U.S.A.
Chapter 30: Web Social Mining, p. 419

Christopher A. Lee
School of Information and Library Science
University of North Carolina at Chapel Hill
Chapel Hill, North Carolina, U.S.A.
Chapter 51: Open Archival Information System (OAIS) Reference Model, p. 699

Kjell Lemström
Department of Computer Science
University of Helsinki
Helsinki, Finland
Chapter 29: Music Information Retrieval, p. 409

Timothy F. Leslie
Department of Geography and Geoinformation Science
George Mason University
Fairfax, Virginia, U.S.A.
Chapter 35: Geographic Information Systems (GIS), p. 485

Anany Levitin
Department of Computing Sciences
Villanova University
Villanova, Pennsylvania, U.S.A.
Chapter 20: Data and Data Quality, p. 269

Ee-Peng Lim
School of Information Systems
Singapore Management University
Singapore
Chapter 30: Web Social Mining, p. 419

William Moen
Texas Center for Digital Knowledge
University of North Texas
Denton, Texas, U.S.A.
Chapter 46: Information Retrieval Protocols: Z39.50 and Search & Retrieve via URL, p. 629

Reagan W. Moore
San Diego Supercomputer Center
University of California, San Diego
La Jolla, California, U.S.A.
Chapter 12: Management of Very Large Distributed Shared Collections, p. 161

Michael S. Moss
Humanities Advanced Technology and Information Institute, University of Glasgow
Glasgow, United Kingdom
Chapter 10: Digital Asset Management, p. 135

Douglas W. Oard
College of Information Studies
University of Maryland
College Park, Maryland, U.S.A.
Chapter 27: Multilingual Information Access, p. 373

Kieron O'Hara
Intelligence, Agents, Multimedia Group
University of Southampton
Highfield, Southampton, United Kingdom
Chapter 24: Semantic Web, p. 325

Lorne Olfman
School of Information Systems and Technology, Claremont Graduate University
Claremont, California, U.S.A.
Chapter 7: Careers and Education in Information Systems, p. 91

Norman Paskin
Tertius Ltd.
Oxford, United Kingdom
Chapter 44: Digital Object Identifier (DOI®) System, p. 605

Daniel V. Pitti
Institute for Advanced Technology in the Humanities
University of Virginia
Charlottesville, Virginia, U.S.A.
Chapter 50: Encoded Archival Description (EAD), p. 685

Thomas C. Redman
Navesink Consulting Group
Little Silver, New Jersey, U.S.A.
Chapter 20: Data and Data Quality, p. 269

Victor Rosenberg
School of Information
University of Michigan
Ann Arbor, Michigan, U.S.A.
Chapter 40: Personal Bibliographic Systems (PBS), p. 545

Robert J. Sandusky
Richard J. Daley Library
University of Illinois at Chicago
Chicago, Illinois, U.S.A.
Chapter 11: Network Management, p. 149

Chris Sauer
Said Business School, University of Oxford
Oxford, United Kingdom
Chapter 21: Information Systems Failure, p. 285

Dirk Schoonbaert
Institute for Tropical Medicine Antwerp
Antwerpen, Belgium
Chapter 40: Personal Bibliographic Systems (PBS), p. 545

Nigel Shadbolt
School of Electronics and Computer Science, University of Southampton
Southampton, United Kingdom
Chapter 48: Resource Description Framework (RDF), p. 659

Robert P. Spindler
Department of Archives and Manuscripts
Arizona State University
Tempe, Arizona, U.S.A.
Chapter 19: Electronic Records Preservation, p. 259

Dick Stenmark
Department of Applied IT
IT University of Gothenburg
Gothenburg, Sweden
Chapter 32: Knowledge Management Systems, p. 449

Perian Sully
Judith L. Magnes Museum
Berkeley, California, U.S.A.
Chapter 41: Collection Management Systems, p. 559

Lynn Sutton
Z. Smith Reynolds Library
Wake Forest University
Winston-Salem, North Carolina, U.S.A.
Chapter 39: Internet Filtering Software and Its Effects, p. 533

E. Burton Swanson
Anderson School of Management, University of California, Los Angeles
Los Angeles, California, U.S.A.
Chapter 1: Information Systems, p. 3

Elaine G. Toms
Dalhousie University
Halifax, Nova Scotia, Canada
Chapter 5: User-Centered Design of Information Systems, p. 65

Jennifer Trant
Archives and Museum Informatics
Toronto, Ontario, Canada
Chapter 43: Museum Web Sites and Digital Collections, p. 589

George Tzanetakis
Department of Computer Science
University of Victoria
Victoria, British Columbia, Canada
Chapter 29: Music Information Retrieval, p. 409

Ron Van den Branden
Centre for Scholarly Editing and Document Studies, Royal Academy of Dutch Language and Literature
Gent, Belgium
Chapter 49: Text Encoding Initiative (TEI), p. 671

Edward Vanhoutte
Centre for Scholarly Editing and Document Studies, Royal Academy of Dutch Language and Literature
Gent, Belgium
Chapter 49: Text Encoding Initiative (TEI), p. 671

Stephanie Walker
Brooklyn College, City University of New York
Brooklyn, New York, U.S.A.
Chapter 17: Piracy in Digital Media, p. 227

Nigel M. Waters
Department of Geography and Geoinformation Science, George Mason University
Fairfax, Virginia, U.S.A.
Chapter 35: Geographic Information Systems (GIS), p. 485

Jeff Weddle
School of Library and Information Studies
University of Alabama
Tuscaloosa, Alabama, U.S.A.
Chapter 15: Version Control, p. 203

Bradley J. Wiles
Hill Memorial Library
Louisiana State University
Baton Rouge, Louisiana, U.S.A.
Chapter 14: Records Compliance and Risk Management, p. 197

Iris Xie
School of Information Studies
University of Wisconsin-Milwaukee
Milwaukee, Wisconsin, U.S.A.
Chapter 3: Information Searching and Search Models, p. 31

Yiyu Yao
Department of Computer Science
University of Regina
Regina, Saskatchewan, Canada

and

International WIC Institute
Beijing University of Technology
Beijing, China
Chapter 26: Information Retrieval Support Systems, p. 363

Yi Zeng
International WIC Institute, Beijing University of Technology
Beijing, China
Chapter 26: Information Retrieval Support Systems, p. 363

Jun Zhang
Pitney Bowes
Shelton, Connecticut, U.S.A.
Chapter 31: Recommender Systems and Expert Locators, p. 435

Kai Zheng
Department of Health Management and Policy
University of Michigan
Ann Arbor, Michigan, U.S.A.
Chapter 36: Clinical Decision-Support Systems, p. 501

Ning Zhong
Department of Life Science and Informatics
Maebashi Institute of Technology
Maebashi-City, Japan

and

International WIC Institute
Beijing University of Technology
Beijing, China
Chapter 26: Information Retrieval Support Systems, p. 363

Vladimir Zwass
Gildart Haase School of Computer Sciences and Engineering, Fairleigh Dickinson University
Teaneck, New Jersey, U.S.A.
Chapter 6: Ethical Issues in Information Systems, p. 77

Part I

General

This section consists of overviews, providing an introduction to key broad-based aspects of information retrieval systems. In Chapter 1, E. Burton Swanson, a senior faculty member of the Anderson School of Management at the University of California, Los Angeles, provides the broadest introduction of all, presenting the whole area of "Information systems" as a discipline and as a subset of business processes. He writes of the origins of the field, and on the varieties of information systems studied and developed in the business world. He addresses the major areas of professional knowledge needed by the practitioner of information systems, and surveys the major social issues that pertain to information systems.

Ray R. Larson, of the School of Information at the University of California, Berkeley, homes in on the focus of this volume, that large subset of information systems known as "Information Retrieval Systems" (Chapter 2). As Larson notes in his abstract, information retrieval systems "aim to select relevant material from large collections of information in response to user queries." The information in IR systems is generally not as formally structured as that in the databases used in business processes, such as payroll and transaction records. Historically, the most common form is, simply, text in database collections, such as book records, article abstracts, and full text, though IR principles have been tested with images, music, and other media as well. Larson, a major researcher in the IR area, describes the components of IR systems, then presents the three classical IR models, Boolean, Vector, and Probabilistic. These models, first elaborated about 50 years ago, formed the original underpinnings of Web-based search engines used today.

Good information retrieval system design should be based on an understanding of the searching done by the people using those systems. Iris Xie, in "Information Searching and Search Models" (Chapter 3), surveys what is known about people using information systems. She reviews the research and theoretical models regarding the way people think about information needs, translate them into search queries, and then actually search on IR systems.

Kalervo Järvelin and Peter Ingwersen, two major European researchers in the information retrieval world, take IR theory to the next level in their chapter on "User-Oriented and Cognitive Models of Information Retrieval" (Chapter 4). Here, they blend an understanding of IR theory with theory about human searching and retrieval, and present several models that encompass the whole user-system complex.

People come into the picture in another way in Elaine G. Toms' chapter. She is Canada Research Chair in Management Informatics at Dalhousie University. In Chapter 5, "User-Centered Design of Information Systems," she addresses user-centered design (UCD), the process of designing information systems to work well with their human users. All too often, people have had to adapt to the design of information systems, and it should be the other way around. Needless to say, the human mind does not work the same way as a computer does; we process language differently, we articulate information needs slowly and often prefer to express those needs only in the process of exploring information resources. She describes the techniques that have been developed to structure an information system to support the natural human processes of needing information and searching for it.

We tend to think of technology as neutral and untroubled by ethical and political issues. However, information technology is a part of the information society; the human beings developing and implementing information systems encounter questions with ethical implications all the time in their work lives. Vladimir Zwass, in "Ethical Issues in Information Systems" (Chapter 6), reviews these matters in an interesting way. Throughout the chapter he follows three scenarios that highlight information system ethical issues. He discusses four major ethical areas in particular, privacy, accuracy, property, and access. There is much more to this area than might first be thought.

For those interested in a career in information systems, Paul Gray and Lorne Olfman, of the School of Information Systems and Technology of the Claremont Graduate University, provide an extensive introduction to the nature of information systems education in "Careers and Education in Information Systems" (Chapter 7). They explain the different learning areas and types of courses required in such programs, and provide a very helpful description of the kinds of job titles and career pathways available to people with an information systems background.

1 Information Systems

E. Burton Swanson

CONTENTS

INTRODUCTION

An information system is commonly a computer-based system for providing information to an organization to help guide its actions.[1] The term "information system" is also sometimes used in information science to refer to information retrieval systems based more on documents than on data, an application domain familiar to libraries, in particular. The term is sometimes also used very generally and informally, without reference to either computers or organizations. People sometimes refer to their own personal information systems, for instance. In this entry, we take the organizational perspective, which has its origins in business, but applies to organizations of every kind, including libraries.

In an organization, an information system typically features people working interactively with computers to accomplish a particular task. Human-computer interaction (HCI) enables both people and their machine extensions to be informed via the system. Where decisions are routine and highly structured, they may sometimes be automated and relegated to the machine.[2] Often, the information provided serves to coordinate workers' specialized but necessarily collective efforts. The varieties of information systems are many, reflecting the diversity of organizations and tasks to be accomplished. A typical large business firm has information systems to support its accounting and finance, operations, supply chain management, sales and marketing, customer service, human resource management, and research and development. But information systems are found everywhere, in organizations of all kinds and sizes, public as well as private.

This entry discusses information systems both as a subject and as a field of study and practice. In the sections to follow, information systems are first described in terms of their: 1) origins; 2) varieties; and 3) practices. As information systems also constitute: 4) an evolving field of study and practice with; 5) attendant social issues, these aspects too are considered.

ORIGINS

Modern information systems emerged with the rise and spread of digital computing in the 1950s, although punched card tabulating equipment was in use for data processing in organizations before then. The stored-program computer itself was initially viewed as a high-powered calculating device, suitable primarily for numerical and other sophisticated analyses. Such "scientific computing" was distinguished from what was termed "electronic data processing" (EDP), which emerged about the same time to support the more prosaic work of business, such as accounting.[3] In the 1960s, computers came to be designed and marketed specifically for business purposes, eventually displacing the tabulating equipment. Notably, a high-level programming language for business applications, Common Business-Oriented Language (COBOL), was also developed, which emphasized data and file structures, and deemphasized the computational features found in FORmula TRANslation (FORTRAN), the language most commonly used in scientific computing. COBOL ultimately became the most widely used programming language for the development of application software for information systems on mainframe computers. As much of this code remains in use, the language persists even today.

Beyond business-oriented application software, the emergence of data base technology in the late 1960s was central to the rapid rise and spread of large-scale information systems among firms. A data base is an organized collection of related data files.[4] A data base management system (DBMS) is system software that enables data bases to be managed as integrated wholes, where relationships among files are clearly delineated. With a DBMS, data can be defined via a data dictionary and managed separately from the different software which access it. Finally, the articulation of the relational data model as a foundation for data bases spurred the development of relational data bases in the 1970s, which came to dominate the field.[5] Today, Oracle provides the leading relational data base software for medium to large firms, while Microsoft's Access is well established among small businesses.

Together, application software and a related data base have come to form the digital content around which any modern information system is now built. Typically, the application software incorporates the "business rules" to be followed, while the data base incorporates the "business facts" that shape the data processing, for instance, in processing a business payroll, or in selling seats to a concert, or in managing the circulation of a library's holdings, or in almost any other endeavor in which carefully informed organizational actions are routinely taken. While the business facts and data base will typically be specific to the enterprise, the business rules and application software may be either specific or generic, i.e., commonly used, as with accounting systems that incorporate professionally mandated rules and principles. Where the business rules and application software is specific to the organization, it may underpin the unique capabilities of the enterprise, in which case it may be strategic.[6] Today, people in a wide variety of occupations and in organizations large and small are likely to work interactively with information systems to accomplish much of their work. Through networks and the Web and Internet, in particular, and through the use of laptops and mobile devices they engage in this HCI from wherever they happen to be and at whatever times they choose or are called upon to be available.

VARIETIES

Information systems come in a wide variety, reflecting the diversity in the organizations that employ them. Among business firms, some information systems will be characteristic of the industry, in particular, as with process control systems in chemical and refining enterprises, or electronic funds transfer (EFT) systems in banks and other financial services firms. However, certain basic types are found in enterprises of all kinds, reflecting both their historical origins based in then-new technologies and the nature of organization itself. These include transaction-processing systems; management information systems (MIS); decision support systems (DSS); group support systems; and enterprise systems. These are not pure types; actual systems may combine features of two or more basic types.

Transaction-Processing Systems

Transaction-processing systems support an enterprise in its transactions with others, such as customers, suppliers, and employees.[7] Every business transaction involves an exchange of goods, services, money, and information in some combination between the parties. Transaction-processing systems exist to ensure the integrity of these transactions. In today's world, each time a consumer makes a purchase with a credit card, withdraws cash from an account, or books an airline ticket, the consumer likely engages the other party's transaction-processing systems. Increasingly, a consumer does this directly, by swiping a bank card at a point-of-sale (POS) device or employing an automated teller machine (ATM) or initiating a purchase from the Web.

Beyond their primary function, transaction-processing systems also enable a business to coordinate its internal operations among units, especially in the making of goods, where parts are withdrawn from inventory and a manufactured item is assembled in a series of operations, and the final product eventually distributed from one location to another, for instance. Here and elsewhere, transaction-processing systems are basically event-driven, and are often engaged to authorize formal actions, such as accepting a customer order or authorizing a credit purchase. The business rules for such data processing may be quite sophisticated, as in credit authorization which incorporates rules aimed at fraud detection, for instance. The data pertaining to these events will ultimately serve to update a data base that is typically drawn upon in processing and is relied upon to give the current status of the organization's affairs. Where the data base is immediately updated as events happen, the system is said to operate in "real time." In the case of firms, basic transaction data will further feed the accounting systems that provide a formal financial picture of the ongoing business.

Where firms do business with each other, for instance, within a supply chain, their transaction-processing systems are also sometimes tied together by means of an interorganizational system that enables them to communicate directly with each other.[8] For such machine-to-machine communication, this necessitates resolution of disparities in how the data themselves are defined by the communicating parties. The interorganizational system may be based on electronic data interchange (EDI) arrangements or increasingly on eXtensible Markup Language (XML) standards for exchange over the Web. The concept of Web services envisions a world of business services and firm transactions seamlessly tied together via standards for business data of all kinds.[9]

Management Information Systems

Management information systems support an organization's hierarchical structure and are targeted to management at all levels. MIS aim to support every manager's need to know within his or her scope of responsibility, typically by extracting important performance information from data gathered from the organization's transaction-processing and operational systems and presenting it efficiently in tabular or graphical form. The concept of an MIS emerged in the 1960s and signaled an important transition in information systems, from traditional EDP to systems that served more sophisticated purposes.[10] In the United States, both practitioners and educators embraced the MIS concept and many business schools originated programs of study under this banner. Today the term continues to be widely used, although the more generic term "information systems" has become more common.

Executive information systems (EIS) were founded in the 1980s as a new form of MIS aimed at top management.[11] The early EIS featured access to news external to the business, in addition to traditional performance metrics, and further employed new graphics and communications technologies. Most recently, executive support systems have been developed which provide a personalized Web page and "executive dashboard" of up-to-the-minute information with which the manager is to engage and steer the enterprise. These systems are now also popularly referred to as "business intelligence systems," reflecting the sophisticated analytics that may lie behind the dashboard metrics.[12]

Decision Support Systems

Decision support systems emerged in the 1970s as interactive systems that supported managers and other "knowledge workers" in tasks that were semi-structured, where decisions could be aided by analytical computer-based means.[13] These systems shifted the original MIS focus from information to decisions. Early DSS featured innovative HCI employing graphics, formal models, and heuristics or algorithms as means of support. A pioneering example was IBM's Geodata Analysis and Display Systems (GADS), which supported organizational decisions related to urban geography, such as arranging police beats and assigning school district boundaries.[14] Today, the concept of geographical information systems (GIS) continues in this tradition as a major area of application supported by new technologies such as remote sensing, geographical positioning, graphical analytics, and visualization. The firm ESRI is the leading provider of GIS software.

The concept of group decision support systems (GDSS) extended the basic DSS concept in the 1980s. Substantial research led to the development of decision rooms equipped with systems that facilitated complex, interactive group decision making in a particular location.[15] The early focus was typically on largely unstructured problems, with tools provided to support collective brainstorming and idea evaluation, for instance, while further capturing a record of the group meeting. With advances in communications technologies, the GDSS concept soon evolved into one that supported group work more broadly, where group members could be at multiple locations and could also meet asynchronously as needed.

Group Support Systems

Beyond the informational and decisional needs of managers, it is well understood that communication and cooperation more broadly in the organization is required to coordinate the work undertaken within and across units. Certain of this communication and cooperation can be built into the work systems themselves; however, other organizational means such as cross-functional teams can also facilitate lateral communication, cooperation, and coordination, thus moderating the burden on the management hierarchy.[16] Not surprisingly, given the ubiquity of group work in organizations, a wide variety of systems have in recent years been originated to support group work, in particular.

The concept of computer-supported collaborative work (CSCW) originated in the 1980s to characterize designs for computer-enabled group work, understood to require substantial communication and coordination, typically over time and across locations.[17] Lotus Notes exemplified the software then deployed in these new systems and remains in wide use today. Current groupware in support of group work is diverse and includes, e.g., that which provides for electronic meetings, electronic mail and messaging, calendar management, project and document management, knowledge sharing, workflow management, and collaborative design. Today, group work can also be organized and conducted on the Web, making use of a commercially available service.

Enterprise Systems

Enterprise systems emerged in the 1990s with the rise of enterprise resource planning (ERP), a concept for integrating the major functional systems of the enterprise, in particular, the organization's financial, human resource, and operational systems around a common data base.[18] The principal means of integration was typically a software package provided by a vendor such as SAP or Oracle. Firms sought to replace their older and disparate home-grown legacy systems, which required high maintenance, with standard off-the-shelf software that promised an integrated solution to relieve them of this burden. ERP basically incorporated the firm's major transaction-processing and operational systems. Its adoption was further given a large boost by concerns related to the millennium bug and the threat it posed at the time to vulnerable legacy systems. Today, most large firms have adopted and implemented ERP in the form of packaged software provided by one or more leading suppliers.

A second type of enterprise system termed customer relationship management (CRM) has more recently also become popular, focusing on the "front office" of a firm, beyond the already heavily computerized "back office."[19] A central CRM aim is to provide the firm with a "unified view" of its customers, who might otherwise engage in separate transactions with different business units, each in the absence of full customer information. Just as it promises better customer service, CRM also typically supports a firm's sales force and enables it to be better managed. Still another CRM aim is to help the firm assess the profitability of its different customer segments, in the interest of focusing marketing and customer retention initiatives on achieving higher overall profits.

PRACTICE

Information systems practice rests on four closely intertwined bodies of professional knowledge: 1) application knowledge; 2) technology knowledge; 3) development knowledge; and 4) management knowledge. Each is associated with job specialties in the field.

Application Knowledge

Application knowledge refers to the domain in which the information system supports work within the organization. The system's users are of course expected to be knowledgeable in this domain, first and foremost. So too are the systems analysts who aid in specifying the requirements for any new system. The required knowledge may be relatively broad or narrow, shallow or deep, according to the work supported, which often involves multiple individuals in different roles. The purpose of the information system is typically to inform its various users within such a work system, in support of their decisions and actions.[20] Beyond their domain knowledge, users are typically trained in their interactive use of any new system, such that they understand how to navigate it, interpret its displays or other output, and provide needed data or other input. Ease of use is a major issue in successful implementation.

Notwithstanding such training, research suggests that new information systems are unlikely to deliver full value to organizations and their users until they have been assimilated into the work practices they support.[21] Repeated "learning by doing" is needed before users "appropriate" a system into their preferred work practices. Moreover, with such assimilation, certain application knowledge will be tacit on the part of users, demonstrated primarily in their competently doing the needed work. Users will also typically find new uses of information systems, beyond those envisioned by system designers. Systems are thus substantially "reinvented" through their use. Importantly, then, application knowledge is ultimately inseparable from the work practice that gives it meaning.

Technology Knowledge

Technology knowledge pertains to the computer-based platforms on which applications are built. This includes the computers, communications, storage and other devices, and the system software that operates these resources. Among the jobs associated with building and maintaining these platforms are those of the system programmer, the network manager, the data base administrator, and the Web master. Technology knowledge also pertains to basic tools and resources drawn on by those engaged directly in application development; these are sometimes integrated and provided in the form of a "work bench."

The most basic aspects of a computer-based platform are its suitability, capacity, and reliability in supporting applications. Growth in firms and their information systems makes capacity planning a vital task. Also important are standards.[22] Where the platforms are in wide use by organizations, the associated technology knowledge is similarly widespread and more easily acquired in the marketplace when needed. Even more significantly, widely used platforms attract their own extensions, as vendors build new features for them roughly according to the potential market reached. This advantage extends to the application software employed in system building, where a wider variety of packaged systems will be readily available for standard platforms.

Development Knowledge

Development knowledge pertains to the application software, data model, Web or other interface, and human procedures that are specified, built or otherwise acquired, documented, tested, installed, and maintained over the life of an information system. It pertains further to the methodology used in this particular work.[23] Principal jobs include those of the systems analyst, who in collaboration with prospective users specifies the functional requirements for the system, and the applications programmer, who in consultation with the systems analyst designs and codes the software to meet these specifications. Within the user community, "lead users" often represent the interest of their peers in the development activity, helping in particular with system implementation and needed training.

Project management knowledge for guiding implementation of systems is especially important, as system development work tends to be organized as projects. Senior developers of individual systems often work as project managers. Projects are typically managed according to their associated deliverables, schedule, and budget. Because of characteristic pressures on schedule and budget, a particularly important aspect of project management is attention to the quality of the deliverables as well as the avoidance of their expensive elaboration through "feature creep." While these issues have long been well known among professionals, they continue to bedevil most of those engaged in the work.[24]

Management Knowledge

Management knowledge pertains to the management of information systems activities within the enterprise. Depending on the size of the organization, managers may include: the data center or operations manager, the network manager, the applications development manager, the applications maintenance manager, and the executive in charge of the function as a whole, who in a large organization sometimes has the title of chief information officer (CIO). A primary responsibility of the CIO is the alignment of the information systems strategy with the broader firm strategy.[25] Another is the staffing and organization of the function and the building of its expertise, as well as setting policy and contracting for external services. A third is the building of a reliable and adaptable network and technological infrastructure.[26] Still another is the management of the application systems portfolio, and the allocation of resources between maintenance of existing systems and the development of new or replacement systems.[27]

One highly visible issue in recent years has been the outsourcing of the information systems function, in whole or in part. "Off-shoring" is much discussed, in particular. Much system development work in the most developed nations is now carried out in countries with more attractive wage rates and growing technical competencies, such as India and China, and certain eastern European states. Exactly which work should be outsourced and which should not remains controversial.[28] The data center itself is a prime candidate for outsourcing. In general, programming is more easily outsourced than is systems analysis, which requires a deep grasp of the work context. The long-run implications of this shift in work are globally significant for the world economy, beyond the immediate challenges and choices faced by today's managers.

AN EVOLVING FIELD

Today, the information systems field of study and practice remains an evolving one marked by continuous change. Notwithstanding its accomplishments to date, the field faces numerous challenges. Its various professional associations, publications, and research firms and consultancies will play important roles in guiding future information systems developments.

Professional Associations

The International Federation for Information Processing (IFIP), founded by 13 national computer societies in 1960, established Technical Committee 8 (TC8) on Information Systems in 1966. TC8's aims are "to promote and encourage interactions among professionals from practice and research and advancement of investigation of concepts, methods, techniques, tools, and issues related to information systems in organizations."[29] TC8 now includes eight working groups, the first of which, WG8.1, Design and Evaluation of Information Systems, was established in 1976, and the second of which, WG8.2, The Interaction of Information Systems and the Organization, was established in 1977.

The International Conference on Information Systems (ICIS) is the premier academic research conference in the field, held annually since 1980. The Association for Information Systems (AIS) is the leading academic association, established in 1994 to bring IS academics together from around the world. It sponsors ICIS and three regional conferences annually: the Americas Conference on Information Systems (AMCIS); the European Conference on Information Systems (ECIS); and the Pacific Asia Conference on Information Systems (PACIS). Among its other activities, AIS publishes the *Journal of AIS* and *Communications of AIS*, and sponsors AIS World, an important Web resource for IS scholars.

The IS field today also maintains its important roots in the allied fields of computer science, operations research, and management. The Association for Computing Machinery (ACM), founded in 1947, claims to be the world's oldest educational and scientific computing society and now serves professionals in more than 100 countries. Its many publications include the widely read *Communications of the ACM*, which features many articles of interest to IS professionals. Its interest groups include the Special Interest Group on Management Information Systems (SIGMIS). Among ACM's most important contributions has been its issuance since 1972-1973 of curriculum recommendations for academic programs of study in information systems.[30]

The Institute for Operations Research and Management Science (INFORMS), formed in 1995 from two earlier societies, is now an umbrella association of operations for research-oriented academics and practitioners that includes an Information Systems Society among its 10 societies. It also publishes the leading journal, *Information Systems Research*, started in 1990.

The Academy of Management includes an Organizational Communications and Information Systems Division among its some two dozen interest groups and divisions.

Among practitioners, the Society for Information Management (SIM), originally founded as the Society for Management Information Systems (SMIS) in 1969, serves IS executives and professionals through a series of chapters located primarily in North America. In its early years, SIM was instrumental in advancing the MIS concept among executives.[31] It also established the leading journal, *MIS Quarterly*, in 1977, in cooperation with the Management Information Systems Research Center (MISRC) of the University of Minnesota, which now publishes it exclusively, while SIM members receive it as a membership option.

Publications

Today, a wide variety of publications reaching both general and specialized audiences feature articles on information systems. Business periodicals such as *The Economist*, *Business Week*, and the *Wall Street Journal* provide good coverage for the general reader. In addition to those already mentioned, other notable academic journals devoted to information systems include the *Journal of Management Information Systems*, the *Journal of Information Technology*, *Information and Organization*, and the *European Journal of Information Systems*. Practitioners in the field find the periodicals *Information Week*, *CIO Magazine*, and *Computerworld* important for following current events in the fast changing technology industry.

Research Firms and Consultancies

Practitioners are also served by a number of market research and analysis firms such as Gartner Group and Forrester Research, which offer assessments of new technologies and their markets, as well as international consultancies such as Accenture, Deloitte, Tata Consulting, and IBM Business Services, which are widely engaged in "system integration" activities, and which further help to spread "best practices" in information systems among firms. These research firms and consultancies also serve as "thought leaders" in the institutional environment within which "organizing visions" for the application of new technologies originate and serve to guide adoption and diffusion.[32]

SOCIAL ISSUES

Information systems are associated with several ethical and social issues inherent to their nature, design, and use.[33] The authors Kenneth and Jane Laudon identify five moral dimensions to the Information Age: information rights and obligations; property rights and obligations; accountability and control; system quality; and quality of life.[34] We consider each briefly.

Information Rights and Obligations

Every information system poses questions of information rights and obligations, often for both persons and organizations. Rights to individual privacy are particularly salient in an age where much organizational data are gathered about customers, employees, and others, and too where those who do business on the Internet can easily gather individual data generated through Web site visits, for subsequent use in targeted advertising, for instance. Throughout the world, businesses thus now operate under various laws intended to safeguard individual privacy. In Europe, privacy protection is stronger than in the United States, as businesses there are generally prohibited from using information about persons without their prior consent. In the United States, most businesses make their privacy policy known to their customers, who must typically then "opt out" if they wish to avoid having certain of their data shared with others for marketing purposes. As many U.S. customers do not take this opt-out step, nor do many probably even consider it, their individual data are widely shared in marketing.

Privacy concerns are of course also inherent to surveillance schemes which employ information systems. Firms may closely monitor the work of their employees, sometimes stepping over the line into private lives. Governments of all kinds are notoriously tempted to keep more than close track of their citizens as well as others, as they seek to repel threats both real and imagined.

Property Rights and Obligations

Information systems also pose challenges to certain intellectual property, which increasingly is represented in digital form, and which a firm may seek to protect as a trade secret, or through copyright or patent. Both the software and the data associated with information systems are likely to be associated with property rights, as are other digital products such as music or video or text recordings that offer entertainment and education, and which are commonly organized, managed, and distributed via information systems. An interesting illustration today is Apple's i-Tunes business, which is entirely digital in nature, and which distributes music for download by consumers on demand, much of it under protection of Apple digital rights management (DRM) software that is itself a protected asset, with several different parties sharing in the resulting revenues.[35]

Accountability and Liability

Information systems also pose new issues of accountability as well as liability, where harm results from their employment. When things go massively wrong, e.g., when an operating error at a bank results in failure to automatically deposit customer paychecks in a timely manner, it may be difficult to disentangle the reasons behind the debacle. Often we are told that a software bug was the problem, and indeed this is often the case. But because information systems are based substantially in HCI, whether it was human error or a software bug or a problem in data exchanged or the interaction itself, or more broadly a problem in the design or execution of the work being carried out, or a failure in the oversight and management of overall system quality, blame can be difficult to fix and hence may sometimes be misplaced to avoid accountability and in some cases liability.

System Quality

As just suggested, system quality is a broader issue than one of minimizing the bugs in software. Organizations bear a responsibility to attend to the broader quality of their information systems. Research suggests that notwithstanding this responsibility, few firms systematically assess the quality of the data associated with their systems, for instance, even though data errors are known to be rather commonplace.[36] One area where attention to data quality is typically enforced is in business accounting, where external auditors provide independent oversight. However, even here, where the financial stakes may be high, system quality may be compromised through inattention or misguided cost cutting measures. The reality is that system quality is achieved only at the cost of means that ensure it.

Quality of Life

Lastly, information systems have long been associated with a variety of quality of life issues, especially as they pertain to system users.[37] Among ongoing issues are the extent to which power is centralized or decentralized through systems, the increased difficulty in maintaining a balance between individuals' working and private lives, new vulnerabilities to crime and abuse such as spam, the reengineering of work and its consequences for job skills needed, characteristic health problems such as repetitive stress injury (RSI), the problem of electronic trash disposal, and social inequities in access to technology, as illustrated by the much discussed problem of the "digital divide" in U.S. schools. In short, information systems have come to have pervasive consequences for the quality of our individual and social, and private and public lives.

CONCLUSION

In the relatively short span of several decades, information systems have emerged to be a dominant feature of modern organizational life, with broad implications for people everywhere. The future promises to extend this story. Currently, organizations throughout the world are rapidly building their presence on the Web, and moving from merely offering certain published content, sometimes disparagingly referred to as "brochure ware," to engaging in basic transactions with their customers, suppliers, and other partners. In short, more organizations are doing everyday business on the Web, popularly termed "electronic commerce," underpinned by information systems that make this possible. New businesses are at the same time originating everywhere on the Web to provide the basic infrastructure for doing this business (Google, eBay, and Amazon.com are widely known examples), as well as to offer new distribution for digital content in the realms of education and entertainment, in particular, attracting more traffic to the Web and thus broadening and deepening its user base, making it more appealing for social networking and advertising. As of this writing, the concept of "Web 2.0" as a social space that enables new forms of organizing is the latest new vision to capture the fancy of the field.[38]

ACKNOWLEDGMENTS

I have benefited from several excellent textbooks in preparing this entry and have incorporated them in the references section. They provide good resources for additional reading. I am also grateful to Ephraim R. McLean and an anonymous reviewer for their comments on an earlier prepared version.

REFERENCES

1. Langefors, B. Information systems theory. Inform. Syst. **1977**, *2*, 207–219.
2. Simon, H. *The New Science of Management Decision*; Harper & Row: New York, 1960.
3. Canning, R. *Electronic Data Processing for Business and Industry*; Wiley: New York, 1956.
4. Date, C.J. *An Introduction to Data Base Systems, 3rd Ed.*; Addison-Wesley: Reading MA, 1981.
5. Codd, E.F. A relational model of data for large shared banks. Commun. ACM **1972**, *13* (6), 377–387.
6. Porter, M.E.; Millar, V.E. How information gives you competitive advantage. Harvard Bus. Rev. **1985**, *63* (4), 149–160.
7. Zwass, V. *Foundations of Information Systems*, Chapter 9; Irwin/McGraw-Hill: Boston, 1998.
8. Johnston, R.; Vitale, M.J. Creating competitive advantage with interorganizational information systems. MIS Quart. **1988**, *12* (2), 153–165.
9. Hagel, J. III; Brown, J.S. Your next IT strategy. Harvard Bus. Rev. **2001**, *79* (10), 105–113.
10. Dickson, G.W. Management information systems: Evolution and status. Adv. Comput. **1981**, *20* 1–37.
11. Watson, H.J.; Rainer, K.; Koh, C. Executive information systems: A framework for development and a survey of current practice. MIS Quart. **1991**, *15* (1), 13–30.
12. Gray, P. *Manager's Guide to Making Decisions about Information Systems*, Chapter 8; Wiley: New York, 2006.
13. Keen, P.G.W.; Scott Morton, M.S. *Decision Support Systems: An Organizational Perspective*; Addison-Wesley: Reading MA, 1978.
14. Sprague, R.H., Jr.; Carlson, E.D. *Building Effective Decision Support Systems*; Prentice-Hall: Englewood Cliffs NJ, 1982, 41–54.
15. Dennis, A.R.; George, J.F.; Jessup, L.M.; Nunamker, J.F., Jr.; Vogel, D.R. Information technology to support meetings. MIS Quart. **1988**, *12* (4), 591–624.
16. Galbraith, J. *Designing Complex Organizations*; Addison-Wesley: Reading MA, 1973.
17. Grudin, J. Computer-supported cooperative work: Its history and participation. IEEE Comput. **1994**, *27* (5), 19–26.
18. Davenport, T.H. Putting the enterprise into enterprise systems. Harvard Bus. Rev. **1998**, *76* (4), 121–131.
19. Winer, R.S. A framework for customer relationship management. Calif. Manage. Rev. **2001**, *43* (4), 89–105.
20. Alter, S. *Information Systems, 4th Ed.*; Prentice-Hall: Upper Saddle River NJ, 2002.

21. Orlikowski, W.J. Improvising organizational transformation over time: A situated change perspective. Inform. Syst. Res. **1996**, *7* (1), 63–92.
22. Shapiro, C.; Varian, H.R. *Information Rules*; Harvard Business School Press: Cambridge MA, 1999.
23. Davis, G.B. Olson, M.H. *Management Information Systems*, Chapter 18; *2nd Ed.*; McGraw-Hill: New York, 1985.
24. Keil, M.; Robey, D. Blowing the whistle on troubled software projects. Commun. ACM **2001**, *44* (4), 87–93.
25. Luftman, J.N., Ed. *Competing in the Information Age: Strategic Alignment in Practice*; Oxford University Press: New York, 1996.
26. Weill, P.; Broadbent, M. *Leveraging the New Infrastructure: How Market Leaders Capitalize on IT*; Harvard Business School Press: Boston, 1998.
27. McFarlan, F.W. Portfolio approach to information systems. Harvard Bus. Rev. **1981**, *59* (5), 142–150.
28. Lacity, M.C.; Willcocks, L.P.; Feeny, D.F. IT outsourcing: Maximize flexibility and control. Harvard Bus. Rev. **1995**, *73* (3), 84–93.
29. Information bulletin. International Federation for Information Processing, January 2007, No. 37, 82.
30. Nunamaker, J.F., Jr.; Couger, J.D.; Davis, G.B. Information systems curriculum recommendations for the 80s: Undergraduate and graduate programs. Commun. ACM **1982**, 25 781–805 (11).
31. Society for Management Information Systems. What is a management information system? Research report no. 1 Society for Management Information Systems: Chicago, 1970.
32. Swanson, E.B.; Ramiller, N. The organizing vision in information systems innovation. Organ. Sci. **1997**, *8* (5), 458–474.
33. Mason, R.O. Four ethical issues of the information age. MIS Quart. **1986**, *10* (1), 5–12.
34. Laudon, K.C.; Laudon, J.P. *Essentials of Business Information Systems*, *7th Ed.*; Prentice-Hall: Upper Saddle River, NJ, 2007; 405.
35. iTunes: How copyright, contract, and technology shape the business of digital media—A case study. Digital Media Project. The Berkman Center for Internet & Society at Harvard Law School, March 2004.
36. Strong, D.M.; Lee, Y.W.; Wang, R.Y. Data quality in context. Commun. ACM **1997**, *40* (5), 103–110.
37. Mumford, E.; Weir, M. *Computer Systems in Work Design—The ETHICS Method*; Wiley: New York, 1979.
38. McAfee, A. Enterprise 2.0: The dawn of emergent collaboration. MIT Sloan Manage. Rev. **2006**, *47* (3), 21–28.

2 Information Retrieval Systems

Ray R. Larson

CONTENTS

INTRODUCTION

Information Retrieval (IR) is concerned with the storage, organization, and searching of collections of information. It has been part of significant part human technological development since the development of writing (or even earlier, since the mnemonic systems probably developed in prehistoric times can also be considered a form of mental IR). The earliest IR systems were the organization schemes of ancient archives and libraries, such as early Sumerian archives, or the "Pinakes" developed by Callimachus for the library of Alexandria. In the twentieth century the largest impetus to development of automated IR systems was the need to manage increasing larger quantities of information in business and scientific development. Early attempts at automating search capabilities for document collections involved techniques based on punched cards, as well as machines using optical sensing of codes on microfilmed documents.[1] The concept of using machine-based systems for storage and retrieval of information was popularized by Vannevar Bush's article "As We May Think" in 1945.[2] The term "information retrieval" was coined by Mooers in 1950.[3]

The goal of any IR system is to select the informational items (texts, images, videos, etc. which we will refer to as "documents") that are expected to be relevant for a given searcher (or user) from a large collections of such items. Today these collections range from small sets of items on an individual's personal computer to the vast resources of the World Wide Web. In all cases the task is the same: to extract some set of items that searchers *wants to have* from all of those they *do not want.*

This is not a simple task, and involves not only the technical aspects of constructing a system to perform such selection, but also aspects of psychology and user behavior to understand what differentiates the desired items from the nondesired from the particular user's point of view. In this entry, we focus on the technical aspects of the system and leave the many issues of user interaction in search systems to the entry "User-Oriented and Cognitive Models of Information Retrieval." We also do not consider, except in passing, the specific aspects of collections or of measuring relevance and search effectiveness. The entries "Information Retrieval and Evaluation," "Test Collections," "Web Information Retrieval," and "TREC (Text Retrieval Evaluation Conference)" cover these aspects of IR in detail. We also note that that we will focus on computer-based IR systems and will not attempt to cover other types (indexes, catalogs, etc.), nor will we spend time discussing the related field of database management. Note also that this entry does not attempt to cover *all* of the myriad variations of approaches to IR that have been tested over the years, but only those we consider to be of interest and that have been shown to be effective in IR evaluations.

In this entry, and in much of the history of IR research, the focus has been on the system and how to obtain the best possible results using some collection of documents with predefined set of "correct" answers (known as a *test collection*). This is sometimes referred to as the laboratory model of IR, where the system and its algorithms are the primary foci of the research and user aspects of the system are considered hardly at all. There are many critiques of this laboratory approach, but it has the advantage of allowing comparability between IR systems in terms of standardized measures of effectiveness for a given collection and set of queries.

This entry describes the common components that go into the design of IR systems. The major classes (or models) of retrieval algorithms (Boolean, vector, and probabilistic) are then described along with formal definitions of the basic form of these algorithms and the variations in common use in IR research. This section is an expansion and update of a similar description appearing in Larson.[4] We then examine query expansion techniques, and in particular *relevance feedback*, and how they are used in IR systems. Finally, we conclude with a short discussion of experimental IR systems and their relation to commercial and public IR systems.

INFORMATION RETRIEVAL SYSTEM COMPONENTS

Information retrieval systems are made of a number of software components (varying in details from system to system) that are concerned with the primary functions of the system. These are: 1) accepting input in the form of documents, extracting information from those documents and storing that information in a form that can be quickly accessed for matching to user searches; and 2) accepting user queries and converting those to a form that can be compared to the stored information about documents. These two processes are often referred to as "indexing" and "retrieval." In this section, we describe the common processes for indexing and retrieval, and indexes for matching the content of queries and documents. The retrieval models for ranking the results are discussed in the following section.

Text Processing

Figure 2.1 shows an abstract representation of an IR system. All IR systems rely on two interdependent processes to make their stored items (*records*, *documents*, or *document representatives*) accessible to users: *indexing* and *retrieval*. Although IR systems need not be computer-based (e.g., printed indexes and card catalogs can also be considered forms of IR systems), this entry focuses on computer-based systems.

The indexing process in IR systems (right-hand side of Figure 2.1) is concerned with deriving a representation of a document according to the rules and processes set up for the particular system. One of simplest forms would be to extract all of the words occurring in each document and store them in an index along with an indication of which document they came from. This is commonly known as *binary indexing*, that is, a given word is either associated with a document, or it is not. Alternatively, an IR system may use some form of *weighted indexing*, where words are assigned to documents with an associated numerical weight indicating the importance or significance of that

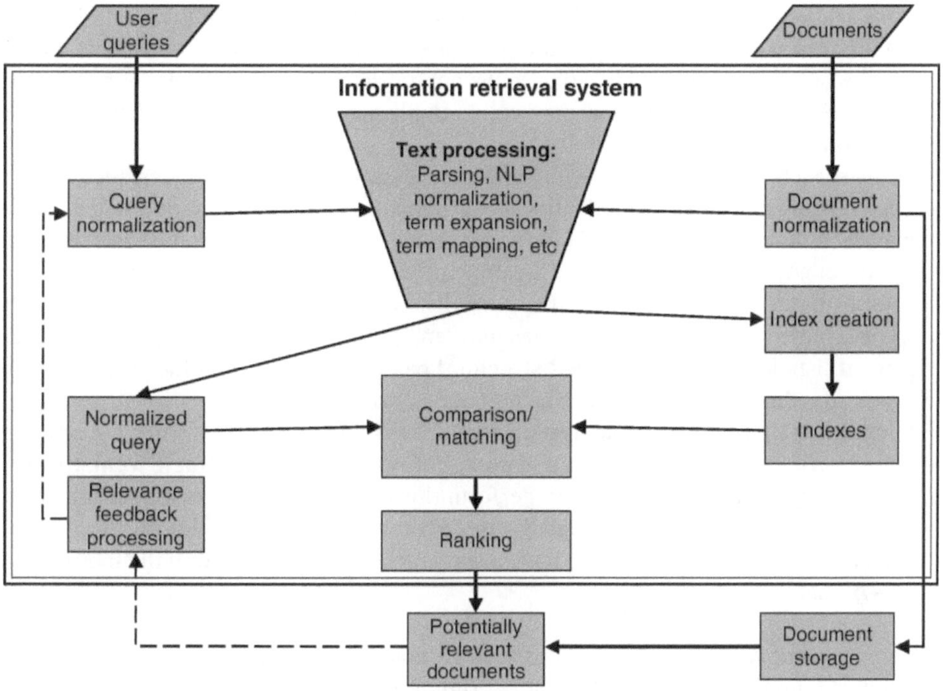

FIGURE 2.1 Structure of an information retrieval system.

term to the document.[5] Indexing will often also identify word position within a document, sometimes with enumeration of paragraph, sentence, and word position within a sentence. Such indexing can be used to determine proximity constraints for a query in a Boolean system (e.g., words in the query must occur in the same sentence or paragraph), or proximity weighting in ranked systems.

More commonly, the document normalization and index creation involve more complex text processing of the document contents than simple word extraction (the central trapezoid in Figure 2.1). In the rest of this entry, we will use "terms" to indicated elements of a document stored in the index. Terms may be words, or phrases, or some mapping of document content words to controlled vocabularies. The typical stages of text processing for document indexing may include

1. Structural identification: Recognition and selection of document elements based on document structure (e.g., selecting the title or author of the document). Because the structured document markup XML is now commonly used for the majority of documents available online, it has become relatively simple to identify and extract the significant structural elements of documents. Indexing may also store indications of the source of extracted terms in the index itself, permitting searches for both content and structure.
2. Tokenization: Individual "tokens" in the content are extracted. Tokens are portions of the content, typically sequences of alphabetic and numeric characters. Typically this involves ignoring spacing, page boundaries, and punctuation. The result is a set of tokens which may become terms in the index, or go through further processing. When individual words are extracted, their original positions in the content may also be retained in the indexes so that, for example, words near each other in the original text can be identified.
3. Token pattern recognition: Tokens may be examined to identify particularly meaningful or useful patterns. These may include such things as recognition of URLs or identifying sequences of capital letters (or capital letters with periods following them) as potential acronyms.

4. Normalization of tokens: This typically involves changing the capitalization of tokens to a single form (all lower case, for example). In some systems diacritics (accents, umlauts, etc.) may be removed and replaced with the appropriate base letter alone, or have multiple letters substituted. Some system may create duplicate tokens normalized in this fashion while retaining the original as well.
5. Part of speech tagging: Natural language processing (NLP) techniques such a part of speech tagging may be used to identify the different parts of speech in the content. Because the most common type of search is for nouns and noun phrases, this can be used to identify and extract noun phrases for special treatment.
6. Stopword processing: IR systems may have lists of words considered to be worthless in retrieval (these typically include articles like "an," "the," "a"). Some systems have different stopword lists for each of identified structural elements, or for each index. Stoplists may also specify classes of tokens (such as numbers) or parts of speech.
7. Stemming or morphological analysis: Many IR systems use some form of stemming to collapse various inflected forms of a word (e.g., cat and cats) into a single form. Stemming uses simple rule-based processing to perform this task and often does a poor job on some words. Morphological analysis typically uses a combination of exception dictionary lookup and rules. The intent of either is to have a single form of a word used in the indexes for all forms of that word.

Systems may include various combinations and variants of these processes. For example, some systems include both the "stemmed" form and original forms of terms, generating a table of original forms for each stem encountered during indexing and then using all forms during search. One advantage of this approach is that searches may be constrained to the original forms when needed, such as when the stemmed form is too inclusive.

As indicated in Figure 2.1, both document indexing and query processing require similar or identical text processing steps. This is to ensure that the tokens from the users query are comparable with the tokens extracted during document indexing.

Indexes and Query Matching

The results of text processing on incoming documents are stored in the indexes of the IR system. These indexes provide a fast lookup mechanism for each token extracted by the text processing, along with other information including some identifier for the document(s) that the token came from, and usually other information, such as statistical information about the frequency of occurrence of the token in each document, and in the collection as a whole, and possibly information about the location that each token came from in each document.

The specific file structures used for the indexes vary from system to system, but the most common are some form of "inverted file," where the data on all occurrences of a token in a collection are organized by a single instance of the token itself. This allows all of the data for resolving most queries to be fetched by a single lookup in the index for each token. The "comparison/matching" part of the processes shown in Figure 2.1 is responsible for this task. This tends to be fairly common across a wide variety of IR systems, regardless of their type or "model." The result of matching (or index lookup) is an unordered set of tokens and their associated information from the indexes, that were also in the *normalized query* (i.e., the results of applying the same text processing steps to the content of query that were applied to the stored documents).

INFORMATION RETRIEVAL MODELS AND RANKING

The true differentiation between IR systems occurs in the variations in the Text Processing and Ranking portions of Figure 2.1. The different approaches to deriving a ranked list of potentially relevant documents from the index matching results are often referred to as the "IR model." In this section, we will examine the main IR models and how they obtain this ranking of potentially relevant documents.

There are three main classes of retrieval models: Boolean, vector, and probabilistic. In addition there are many systems that are hybrids of two or more of these models (e.g., a vector system with Boolean result limiting features). We begin with some formal definitions of system elements that are common to all of the models, and then examine each model in turn.

In an IR system, we have a collection, **D**, of N documents, indexed by a set, **T**, of M unique index terms or attributes. An individual document in the collection, D_i, may be represented as a vector of index term weights:

$$D_i = (w_{i1}, w_{i2}, w_{ij}, \ldots ,w_{iM})$$

The value of each w_{ij} term weight is determined by the indexing function applied. These values may represent binary indexing, (where $w_{ij} = 1$ if term T_j occurs in document D_i, and $w_{ij} = 0$ otherwise), simple term frequency weights (where each w_{ij} represents the number of times index term T_j occurs in document D_i), to more complex probabilistic weighting schemes (where w_{ij} is based on an estimation of the conditional probability that users would consider D_i to be relevant given that their query contains the term T_j).

The set of index terms, **T**, consists of any searchable attribute associated with the documents in the collection. These may be word stems, words, phrases, or other elements (such as class numbers) that occur in the text of the document or derived during text processing. They may also include associated elements that are not index terms in a conventional sense, such as related terms or cross-references from a thesaurus, citation information, or references to other documents (e.g., hypertext links). These index terms may be formally represented by an *inverted file*, where each index term, T_j has an associated vector of weights, I_j such that:

$$I_j = (w_{1j}, w_{2j}, w_{ij}, \ldots,w_{Nj})$$

The document and index term vectors can be seen as a $N \times M$ matrix of w_{ij} weights. Thus, the collection of documents can be viewed as a matrix where the rows are individual document vectors and the columns the individual term vectors. In some systems the inverted file may also include positional information on the occurrence of the terms, and even include weights for the document, paragraph, and sentence level.

In virtually all IR systems, the inverted file is commonly used in retrieval operations instead of the document vectors.

Each query Q_k from the set of queries, **Q**, submitted to the system may be represented as a vector of index term weights:

$$Q_k = (y_{k1}, y_{k2}, y_{kj}, \ldots,y_{kM})$$

where y_{kj} is the weight assigned by the user or system to term T_j in the kth query.

The Boolean Model

The earliest retrieval model was the Boolean model based on Boolean logic. Systems using the Boolean model include most of the earliest commercial search services (like DIALOG or LEXUS/NEXUS), many online library catalogs, and many local search systems on individual Web sites. The Boolean model is a set-oriented model, where sets of documents are defined by the presence or absence of an individual index term. Using our formal definitions above, a single inverted file vector I_j can be considered as Boolean set, were each nonzero document weight in the vector defines a member of the set. In processing Boolean queries the sets representing the different search terms can be combined using the Boolean set operations intersection, union, and negation. These are usually expressed in a user's query as the *Boolean operators* AND, OR, and NOT.

- **AND:** Set intersection generates a new output set from two input sets where the members (documents) shared by both sets become the members of the output set.
- **OR:** Set union generates a new output set from two input sets where the members of either (or both) of the input sets are combined to become the new output set.
- **NOT:** Set negation operates on a single input set, and generates a new set that contains all members (documents) that are not in the input set.

All of these operations can be performed using a simple binary inverted file, or more complex weighted inverted files. Note, however, that the unary NOT operation can be very expensive to process in inverted files, since the result set would be all documents in the system not included in the set. As a result most Boolean IR systems restrict the use of NOT to the binary "ANDNOT" operation which excludes any members of the right-hand set from the left-hand set.

In Boolean IR systems, the user is typically responsible for formulating a combination of terms and Boolean operators that will, it is hoped, select the relevant documents for the user's information need. Boolean systems are commonly extended by inclusion of other operators usually providing additional restrictions on set intersection operations. For example, term proximity operations restrict a intersection to those documents that not only have both terms, but also have those terms within a specified distance from each other.

Pure Boolean IR systems have no inherent ordering of the result of Boolean query processing. Any order presented to the searcher is applied after the final Boolean result set is obtained. Many systems use some assumed useful ordering of the result set using document information (such as the date or author name of books in a library online catalog).

Many IR researchers have pointed out the major drawbacks with Boolean IR systems. These include

1. Boolean logic requires that the users be trained in construction of queries, because it is not intuitively obvious, and differs from common natural language usage. (e.g., a user seeking books on "cats and dogs" probably wants books on either, not just those that treat both.)
2. Boolean AND operations tend to be too restrictive. A search for "A AND B AND C" will eliminate any records that do not have all these terms. Those that have one or two of the three terms are rejected along with those that have none of the terms.
3. Boolean OR operations tend to be too inclusive. A search for "A OR B OR C" will retrieve any record with at least one of the terms, but no priority is given to those that include more than one of the terms.
4. Due to steps 2 and 3, the result of AND operations is often search failure, and the result of OR operations is often information overload.
5. Boolean logic treats each term equally, giving no priority to those that may be more important to the user's need.
6. Boolean logic requires that the user's query and the document indexing use the same terminology for matching to succeed.
7. Boolean logic does not permit the retrieved documents to ranked in any significant fashion, documents are either retrieved or rejected with no "middle ground."

Various extensions to Boolean systems have been proposed and tested over the years to allow result ranking based on applying weights to the terms and/or the Boolean operations. Examples include the use of "fuzzy sets," where set membership is weighted instead of binary, and the "AND" operator returns the minimum of the two input weights, while the "OR" operator returns the maximum. The final result set is ordered by the weights.

Vector Model

The vector space model[6] considers each document vector as described above to be a vector in an M-dimensional space (i.e., one dimension for each term in the collection). Vector space IR systems base their ranking on how close together the document vectors and query vector are in this M-dimension space. This can be seen as calculation of a similarity measure based on the terms used in the query and in the documents in the collection. In practice, the inverted file is used to ensure that the processing considers only documents with at least one term in common with the query (otherwise in typical collections vast amounts of computation would be needed to process all document vectors even when they have no terms in common with the query).

In retrieval, partial match techniques based on the vector space model[7] may be used to rank the documents in the collection in decreasing order of their similarity to the query. The simplest similarity function is the *inner product* of the document and query vectors:

$$\text{INNER}(D_i, Q_k) = \sum_{j=0}^{M} w_{ij} y_{kj}$$

A variety of other vector similarity measures normalize the value of the similarity to range between 0 and 1. Probably the most commonly used is the *cosine correlation*:

$$\text{COSINE}(D_i, Q_k) = \frac{\sum_{j=0}^{M} w_{ij} y_{kj}}{\sqrt{\sum_{j=0}^{M} w_{ij}^2 \cdot \sum_{j=0}^{M} y_{kj}^2}}$$

This is angular separation of the two vectors in the M-dimensional *vector space*.

The partial match techniques based on the vector model are distinguished by the different term weights and similarity measures used in calculating the *document weight* used to rank the retrieval. Some basic vector approaches are

1. *Coordination-level matching.* In coordination-level matching the term weights for documents (w_{ij}) and queries (y_{kj}) are binary and the inner product similarity function is used. The document weight calculated is simply the number of terms in common between the document and the query.
2. *Cosine correlation with binary weights.* This approach uses binary term weights and the cosine correlation to calculate the document weight.
3. *Cosine correlation with frequency weights.* This approach uses the term weights consisting of simple term frequencies, f_{ij}. That is, each w_{ij} is the number of times term T_j occurs in document D_i, and each y_{kj} is the number of times term T_j occurs in query Q_k. The cosine correlation between these weighted vectors is calculated to yield the document weight.
4. *Term frequency–inverse document frequency (TFIDF) weights.* In TFIDF matching, term weights are calculated as follows:

$$w_{ij} = f_{ij} \cdot \log \frac{N}{n_j}$$

where n_j is the number of documents that contain term T_j. This gives the highest weights to terms that occur frequently in a given document, but relatively infrequently in the collection as a whole, and low weights to terms that occur infrequently in a given document, but are very common throughout the collection. Query terms are weighted by simple term frequency, as above, and the document weight is calculated as the inner product of the query and document vectors.

The TFIDF approach is the most common form of vector space weighting, although there are a very large number of variants for it. Most of the variants include some form of normalization of term frequency. Well-known IR systems that use the vector space model are Salton's SMART system,[8] and more recently the open source Apache Lucene IR system originally developed by Doug Cutting.

Probabilistic Retrieval Methods

In the vector model there is an underlying assumption that documents which are similar to a query will be considered *relevant* to the information needs of the user who submits that query. Relevance is usually defined as a subjective assessment by a given user of the value or utility of a particular document in satisfying a particular need for information. We can say that for a particular search of an IR system, each of the documents in the collection either contains information that the individual wants, or it does not. If it does, then it is considered relevant, otherwise it is nonrelevant. The *document retrieval problem* is to select all of the records in the database that the user would find to be relevant, and reject all those that would be considered nonrelevant, that is, *all* and *only* the relevant documents should be retrieved.[9]

Given the individual nature of relevance judgements, we can assume that there are no purely deterministic relationships between the terms used in indexing documents and the relevance of a given document, or between the terms used in searching for a document and the relevance of that document. Instead, these relationships are *probabilistic* in nature. This suggests that there are no perfect solutions to the document retrieval problem, but there may be approximate solutions. According to a significant body of theoretical work in IR, the appropriate approach to IR is to rank each document in the database in descending order of its *probability of relevance* for a given user and query. This has been called the *probability ranking* principle.[10]

There were originally two competing schools of thought on probability of relevance that have come to be known as Model 1[5] and Model 2.[11] These models were subsequently unified into a unified higher-level Model 3 and lower-level Model 0.[12]

In discussing these probabilistic models we will assume that the set of all (present and future) documents in the collection, **D**, and the set of all (present and future) queries, **Q**, are described by binary vectors representing the presence or absence of index terms (although it should be noted that Robertson et al. (1982) make no such assumptions regarding representation). All possible document/query pairs (D_i, Q_j), define a $\mathbf{D} \times \mathbf{Q}$ probabilistic event space. Within this event space we can define relevance as a relation which holds between certain document/query pairs:

$$R = (D_i, Q_j)\ D_i \in \mathbf{D}, Q_j \in \mathbf{Q}$$

where document D_i is judged to be relevant by a user submitting query; Q_j Nonrelevance, $\overline{R}$, is the complement of this relation.

We also define a subset of documents, $\mathbf{x} \subseteq \mathbf{D}$, such that all documents in x are represented by identical binary vectors, i.e., those that are indexed by the same set of terms). Similarly, we have a subset, $\mathbf{y} \subseteq \mathbf{Q}$, of identical queries.

The notion of probability of relevance has a different interpretation under the four probabilistic models discussed in Robertson, Maron, and Cooper.[12] In Model 1, first formulated in a somewhat different form by Maron and Kuhns,[5] probability of relevance is seen as the relationship between a class of users (those submitting the same query) and a particular document:

$$P(R|\mathbf{y}, D_i)$$

Model 2, on the other hand, defines probability of relevance as a relationship between a class of documents and a particular user and use (or query):

$$P(R|Q_k, \mathbf{x})$$

The higher-level Model 3, proposed by Robertson, Maron, and Cooper,[12] defines the probability of relevance as the relationship between an individual use (query) of the system and an individual document:

$$P(R|Q_k, D_i)$$

The lower-level Model 0, also proposed by Robertson, Maron, and Cooper[12] and expanded by Wong and Yao,[13] defines the probability of relevance as a relationship between a class of queries and a class of documents:

$$P(R|\mathbf{y}, \mathbf{x})$$

Most experimental and operational IR systems based on probabilistic principles have used forms of Model 2 for their implementation. For retrieval in a Model 2 system, the probability of relevance is used to define a Bayesian decision function, that is, for any particular query, documents with a given description **x** should be retrieved if

$$P(R \mid Q_k, \mathbf{x}) > P(\bar{R} \mid Q_k, \mathbf{x})$$

That is, documents should be retrieved if the probability of relevance is greater than the probability of nonrelevance.

This decision rule commonly takes the form of a discriminant function:

$$g_{Q_k}(\mathbf{x}) = \log \frac{P(R \mid Q_k, \mathbf{x})}{P(\bar{R} \mid Q_k, \mathbf{x})}$$

These probabilities are difficult to calculate directly, but Bayes theorem can be applied to convert them to the more convenient form:

$$g_{Q_k}(\mathbf{x}) = \log \frac{P(\mathbf{x} \mid R, Q_k)}{P(\mathbf{x} \mid \bar{R}, Q_k)} + \log \frac{P(R \mid Q_k)}{P(\bar{R} \mid Q_k)}$$

where $P(\mathbf{x}|R, Q_k)$ is the probability that if, for a given query, a particular query/document pair is judged relevant, then the document would have description **x**. Since we are considering only a single query, we can define a subset, $\mathbf{D} \times Q_k$, of the $\mathbf{D} \times \mathbf{Q}$ event space, and the relevance relation:

$$R_{Q_k} = (D_i, Q_k) \mid D_i \text{ is relevant to } Q_k$$

where $R_{Q_k} \subseteq R$. If we define $P(R_{Q_k}) = P(R, Q_k)$, $P(\bar{R}_{Q_k}) = P(\bar{R}, Q_k)$, and assume that index terms are stochastically independent with respect to the relevance or nonrelevance of a document then

$$P(\mathbf{x} \mid R_{Q_k}) = P(w_1 \mid R_{Q_k})P(w_2 \mid R_{Q_k})...P(w_M \mid R_{Q_k})$$

$$P(\mathbf{x} \mid \bar{R}_{Q_k}) = P(w_1 \mid \bar{R}_{Q_k})P(w_2 \mid \bar{R}_{Q_k})\ldots P(w_M \mid \bar{R}_{Q_k})$$

where the w_i represent the individual index terms of the binary vector x. We also define the symbols, $p_i = P(w_i = 1 \mid R_{Q_k})$, and $q_i = P(w_i = 1 \mid \bar{R}_{Q_k})$. Under these assumptions:

$$P(\mathbf{x} \mid R_{Q_k}) = \prod_{i=1}^{M} p_i^{x_i}(1-p_i)^{1-w_i}$$

$$P(\mathbf{x} \mid \bar{R}_{Q_k} = \prod_{i=1}^{M} q_i^{x_i}(1-q_i)^{1-w_i}$$

By taking logs and substituting into the discriminant function, we get

$$g_{Q_k}(\mathbf{x}) = \sum_{i=1}^{M} w_i \log \frac{p_i(1-q_i)}{q_i(1-p_i)} + \sum_{i=1}^{M} w_i \log \frac{1-p_i}{1-q_i}$$

$$+ \log \frac{P(R \mid Q_k)}{P(\bar{R} \mid Q_k)} = \sum_{i=1}^{M} a_i w_i + K_1$$

where

$$a_i = \log \frac{p_i(1-q_i)}{q_i(1-p_i)}$$

and K_1 is a constant for any given query.

The Model 2 probabilities p_i and q_i can be calculated, or estimated, from frequency data. If there are N documents in the database and R′ of them are relevant for a given query, and the ith term occurs in n_i of the documents of which r_i are relevant, then a_i can be calculated as

$$a_i = \log \frac{r_i(N - n_i - R' + r_i)}{(n_i - r_i)(R' - r_i)}$$

Notice that this assumes that relevance is known, or can be estimated, in order to provide the frequency data that are used to estimate the probabilities. In practice, what is usually done is to estimate the frequencies based on a sample of documents evaluated by the user, or when such information is not available this formula reduces to the inverse document frequency described above. Thus Model 2 is most effective applied in a secondary search, or *relevance feedback*[14] situation, where documents retrieved in an initial search, often ranked according to a matching function based on rough estimates of the probabilities, are evaluated and the user's relevance judgments used to estimate Model 2 weights for a second search and re-ranking of the collection.

Okapi BM-25 Algorithm

The most widely used form of a probabilistically based IR algorithm is known as the Okapi BM-25 algorithm developed by Robertson.[15] The basic form of the Okapi BM-25 algorithm is

$$\sum_{j=1}^{|Q_c|} w^{(1)} \frac{(k_1+1)tf_j}{K + tf_j} \frac{(k_3+1)qtf_j}{k_3 + qtf_j}$$

where (in addition to the variables already defined)

$|Q|$ is the total number of terms in Q

$|Q_c|$ is the number of terms in Q that also occur in the document

tf_j is the frequency of the jth term in a specific document

qtf_j is the frequency of the jth term in Q

K is $k_1((1 - b) + b \cdot \text{dl/avdl})$

k_1, b and k_3 are parameters (set by experimentation for a given collection)

avdl is the average document length

$w^{(1)}$ is the Robertson–Sparck Jones weight[11]:

$$w^{(1)} = \log \frac{\left(\dfrac{r+0.5)}{R-r+0.5}\right)}{\left(\dfrac{n_{t_j}-r+0.5}{N-n_{t_j}-R-r+0.5}\right)}$$

n_{t_j} is the number of documents containing the jth term

r is the number of relevant components of a given type that contain a given term

R is the total number of relevant components of a given type for the query

The Robertson–Sparck Jones weights, when no relevance information is available, resolve to the inverse document frequency like the a_i measure above.

Logistic Regression Algorithm

Another approach to estimating probability of relevance uses the *Logistic Regression* (LR) algorithm originally developed by Cooper, Gey, and Dabney.[16] The LR model of probabilistic IR attempts to estimate the probability of relevance for each document based on a set of statistics about a document collection and a set of queries in combination with a set of weighting coefficients for those statistics. The statistics to be used and the values of the coefficients are obtained from regression analysis of a sample of a collection (or similar test collection) for some set of queries where relevance and nonrelevance has been determined. More formally, given a particular query and a particular document in a collection $P(R|Q_k,D_j)$ is calculated (or estimated) and the documents or components are presented to the user ranked in order of decreasing values of that probability. To avoid invalid probability values, the usual calculation of $P(R|Q_k,D_j)$ uses the "log odds" of relevance given a set of S statistics, s_i, derived from the query and database, such that

$$\log O(R \mid Q_k, D_j) = b_0 + \sum_{i=1}^{S} b_i s_i$$

where b_0 is the intercept term and the b_i are the coefficients obtained from the regression analysis of the sample collection and relevance judgements. The log odds form can be used to rank results directly or be simply converted to probabilities:

$$P(R \mid Q_k, D_j) = \frac{e^{\log O(R|Q_k,D_j)}}{1 + e^{\log O(R|Q_k,D_j)}}$$

The form of the LR algorithm used in the Cheshire II IR system[17,18] is

$$\log O(R \mid Q,C) = b_0 + \left(b_1 \cdot \left(\frac{1}{|Q_d|} \sum_{j=1}^{Q_d} \log qtf_j \right) \right)$$
$$+ \left(b_2 \cdot \sqrt{|Q|} \right)$$
$$+ \left(b_3 \cdot \left(\frac{1}{|Q_d|} \sum_{j=1}^{|Q_d|} \log tf_j \right) \right)$$
$$+ \left(b_4 \cdot \sqrt{\mathrm{dl}} \right)$$
$$+ \left(b_5 \cdot \left(\frac{1}{|Q_d|} \sum_{j=1}^{|Q_d|} \log \frac{N - n_{t_j}}{n_{t_j}} \right) \right)$$
$$+ b_6 \cdot \log |Q_d|$$

where (in addition to the variables alread defined above)
dl is the document length measured in bytes
N is the number of documents in the collection
b_i are the coefficients obtained though the regression analysis

The LR approach to IR is one of a class of approaches that attempt to "learn" how to rank based on collected previous results. Other approaches use methods ranging from machine learning to genetic algorithms to learn the best ways of ranking results, usually for specific collections.

Language Models

A rather different approach to probabilistic IR is based on language modeling originally developed for applications such as automatic speech recognition, machine translation, and OCR correction. A "language model" as used in IR systems is simply the statistical distribution of terms in documents and the collection as a whole. In language model-based IR instead of attempting to estimate probability of relevance, the system attempts to estimate the probability that a particular query was (or could have been) generated from language model for a given document. The results are then ranked according to this probability. The assumption is that if the query could have come from the document, then that document is likely to be relevant.

In the original description of language modeling, Ponte and Croft[19] define the probability estimates used to rank a document in the search results as

$$P(Q_k|M_d)$$

where Q_k is a query (as above) and M_d is the language model for a given document. A simple approach to estimating this model would calculate

$$p_{\mathrm{ml}}(T_j \mid M_d) = \frac{tf_j}{\mathrm{dl}_d}$$

This is simply the *Maximum likelihood estimate* of the probability of term T_j in document d where tf_j is the raw term frequency in document d and dl_d is the length of document d (in tokens). The simplest ranking function is then the product of the individual term probabilities:

$$P(Q_k \mid M_d) = \prod_{T_j \in Q_k} p_{\mathrm{ml}}(T_j \mid M_d)$$

The obvious problem with this ranking function is that it will be zero for any document that does not contain all of the query terms. Various approaches have been taken to normalize and *smooth* this basic model to avoid both the problem of going to zero and the implicit assumption that all documents with a given term share a common language model. Most implementations use much more sophisticated smoothing and model expressions than the simple unigram language model outlined here.

Language models have been quite effective in IR evaluation exercises like TREC (q.v.). The open source Lemur toolkit[20] makes language modeling algorithms available to researchers and students.

Inference Network Models

Inference networks are a form of probabilistic model that uses networks of known probabilities of events (such as the a priori probability of a term occurring in a document) to infer the probability of unknown events (such as the probability of relevance for a given document and query). Inference networks were developed by Turtle and Croft,[21] and are used in the INQUERY IR system. Inference networks can include nodes that are the results of Boolean operations into the probabilistic inference network.

Similar to inference networks are the IR application of neural networks where the probabilities of relevance given particular inputs are estimated by training the network, which involves adjusting the low-level probabilities of activation from one node to any connected nodes. The major difference is that in an inference net the inferential information is pre-encoded in the model (both as structure and parameters), while in neural nets nothing is encoded a priori, but instead a "blank" network is extensively trained on data and the inferences discovered based on this training.

Hybrid Models

Many IR systems combine two or more of the basic models discussed above in a single system. The most common combination is to permit some form of Boolean operations or restrictions on a ranked result set. This may involve use of explicit Boolean or extended Boolean operations (such as proximity processing) to restrict a ranked result set to those items that satisfy the Boolean constraint. Other hybrid systems may use "data fusion" methods to combine results from different retrieval algorithms.[22,23]

Combining probabilistic and (strict) Boolean elements, as well as operators to support various merging operations have been used in many systems as well. In implementation, strict Boolean operators and probabilistic searches (such as OKAPI BM-25 or LR) can be performed using the same inverted file structures, and they can be seen as as two parallel *logical* search engines. Each logical search engine produces a set of retrieved documents. When a only one type of search strategy is used then the result is either a probabilistically ranked set or an unranked Boolean result set. However, both can be combined in a single query and the search results are evaluated using the assumption that the Boolean-retrieved set has an estimated $P(R|Q_{\mathrm{bool}}, D)$=1.0 for each document component in the set, and 0 for the rest of the collection. The final estimate for the probability of relevance used for ranking the results of a search combining strict Boolean and probabilistic strategies is simply

$$P(R|Q, D) = P(R|Q_{\mathrm{bool}}, C)\, P(R|Q_{\mathrm{prob}}, C)$$

where $P(R|Q_{prob}, C)$ is the probability of relevance estimate from the probabilistic part of the search, and $P(R|Q_{bool}, C)$ is the Boolean. In practice the combination of strict Boolean "AND" and the probablistic approaches has the effect of restricting the results to those items that match the Boolean part, with ranking based on the probabilistic part. Boolean "NOT" provides a similar restriction of the probabilistic set by removing those document components that match the Boolean specification. When Boolean "OR" is used the probabilistic and Boolean results are merged (however, items that only occur in the Boolean result, and not both, are usually reweighted to the lower range of probabilistic results).

QUERY EXPANSION AND RELEVANCE FEEDBACK

In many IR tasks the queries submitted by a searcher are often very short and sometimes ambiguous. The goal of query expansion is to create a larger query from the searcher's initial expression and to use that to obtain (it is hoped) more relevant results. Some forms of query expansion take place in the initial text processing of the query (as discussed above) but the most effective methods involve obtaining relevance judgements on a sample of documents obtained using the initial query expression, and performing *relevance feedback* processing on those documents (shown as the dashed lines in Figure 2.1).

Relevance feedback has been shown to be remarkably effective in improving the result of a query. The Vector Space and Probabilistic models take somewhat different approaches to relevance feedback. However, the main idea is to modify the existing query based on the judged relevant and nonrelevant documents, usually extracting terms from the relevant documents and adding them to the query and also adjusting the weights for terms already in the query.

The most widely used Vector Space algorithm for relevance feedback is the Rocchio Method.[24] The Rocchio method is defined by

$$Q_{new} = \alpha Q_{old} + \frac{\beta}{n_1}\sum_{i=1}^{n_1} R_i - \frac{\gamma}{n_2}\sum_{i=1}^{n_2} S_i$$

where

Q_{old} is vector for the initial query
R_i is the vector for the judged relevant document i
S_i is the vector for judged nonrelevant document i
n_1 is the number of relevant documents chosen
n_2 is the number of nonrelevant documents chosen
α, β, and γ are parameters to tune the importance of the initial query and the relevant and nonrelevant terms; common settings are $\beta = 0.75$ and $\gamma = 0.25$

The probabilistic models commonly use some form of the Robertson–Sparck Jones weights for relevance feedback. This appears in the Okapi BM-25 Formula above. In relevance feedback the portions of that formula that need relevance information are filled in from the judged relevant and nonrelevant documents, and new weights are calculated for the query terms based on resulting weights. In the Cheshire II system the Robertson–Sparck Jones weights are calculated and used to select a number of most highly weighted terms from the judged relevant documents to add to the initial query and to reweight the initial query terms. This expanded query is then searched using the same LR algorithm as the initial query.

One interesting, and effective, technique that has been used in many retrieval evaluations with good results is the so-called Blind or Pseudo relevance feedback. In this approach there is no searcher involved nor actual relevance judgements made. Because many (if not most) IR systems tend to have relevant documents at the top of their rankings, this approach assumes that some arbitrary number of the top-ranked documents from the initial search are in fact relevant and applies relevance feedback processing to them (usually with a corresponding number of assumed nonrelevant documents from the bottom of the initial ranking). Even though there is no user judgement involved in this process, it has on average improved the results for systems using this method. Generally, however relevance feedback is most effective when the searcher is directing the relevance choices.

CONCLUSION

Information retrieval systems aim to select relevant material from large collections of information in response to user queries. The approaches used to accomplish this have been the focus of much research and development over the past 50 years, and have led to the algorithms underlying many commercial and Web-based search engines today. The article on Web Search Engines goes into more detail on the approaches taken by the various Web search companies. Even though the specific algorithms of any particular search engine are considered proprietary "trade secrets," we can safely say that all existing Web search engines use some combination of the models outlined above, usually with the addition of Web-specific ranking algorithms (such as Google's PageRank that ranks Web pages based on the numbers of ingoing HTML links for that page, as well as other "reputation-based" metrics). Effective search is considered to be one of the critical requirements of the Web, and is also an essential requirement in corporate and academic databases, digital libraries, and library catalogs. Information retrieval systems, as described here, provide proven effective search capabilities to these important services of the digital age.

REFERENCES

1. Buckland, M.K. *Emanual Goldberg and His Knowledge Machine*; Libraries Unlimited: Westport, CT, 2006.
2. Bush, V. As we may think. Atlantic Mon. **1945**, *176* (1), 101–108.
3. Mooers, C.N. Information retrieval viewed as temporal signalling. In *Proceedings of International Conference of Mathematicians*, Cambridge, MA, August 30–September 6 1950; AMS: Providence, RI, 1952; 572–573.
4. Larson, R.R. Evaluation of advanced retrieval techniques in an experimental online catalog. J. Am. Soc. Inform. Sci. **1992**, *43* (1), 34–53.
5. Maron, M.E.; Kuhns, J.L. On relevance, probabilistic indexing and information retrieval. J. ACM **1960**, 7 (3), 216–244.
6. Salton, G.; Wong, A.; Yang, C.S. A vector space model for information retrieval. Commun. ACM **1975**, *18* (11), 613–620.
7. Salton, G.; Buckley, C. Term weighting approaches in automatic text retrieval. Inform. Process. Manage. **1988**, *24* (5), 513–523.
8. Salton, G. *SMART Retrieval System: Experiments in Automatic Document Processing. Prentice-Hall Series in Automatic Computation*; Prentice-Hall: Upper Saddle River, NJ, 1971.
9. Maron, M.E. Probabilistic design principles for conventional and full-text retrieval systems. Inform. Process. Manage. **1988**, *24*, 249–255.
10. Robertson, S.E. The probability ranking principle in IR. J. Doc. **1977**, *33*, 294–304.
11. Robertson, S.E.; Sparck Jones, K. Relevance weighting of search terms. J. Am. Soc. Inform. Sci. May–June **1976**, 129–146.
12. Robertson, S.E.; Maron, M.E.; Cooper, W.S. Probability of relevance: A unification of two competing models for document retrieval. Inform. Technol.: Res. Develop. **1982**, *1*, 1–21.
13. Wong, S.K.M.; Yao, Y.Y. A probabilistic inference model for information retrieval. Inform. Syst. **1991**, *16* (3), 301–321.
14. Salton, G.; Buckley, C. Improving retrieval performance by relevance feedback. J. Am. Soc. Inform. Sci. **1990**, *41*, 288–297.
15. Robertson, S.E.; Walker, S. On relevance weights with little relevance information. In *Proceedings of the 20th Annual International ACM SIGIR Conference on Research and Development in Information Retrieval*, ACM Press: New York, 1997; 16–24.

16. Cooper, W.S.; Gey, F.C.; Dabney, D.P. Probabilistic retrieval based on staged logistic regression. In *15th Annual International ACM SIGIR Conference on Research and Development in Information Retrieval*, Copenhagen, Denmark, June 21–24; ACM: New York, 1992; 198–210.
17. Larson, R.R.; McDonough, J.; O'Leary, P.; Kuntz, L.; Moon, R. Cheshire II: Designing a next-generation online catalog. J. Am. Soc. Inform. Sci. **1996**, *47* (7), 555–567.
18. Larson, R.R. A logistic regression approach to distributed IR. In *SIGIR 2002: Proceedings of the 25th Annual International ACM SIGIR Conference on Research and Development in Information Retrieval*, Tampere, Finland, August 11–15, 2002; ACM: New York, 2002; 399–400.
19. Ponte, J.M.; Bruce Croft, W. A language modeling approach to information retrieval. In *SIGIR '98: Proceedings of the 21st Annual ACM SIGIR conference on Research and Development in Information Retrieval*, August 24–28, 1998; Melbourne, Australia. ACM: New York, 275–281.
20. The Lemur Project. The Lemur Toolkit for Language Modeling and Information Retrieval. http://www.lemurpr oject.org (accessed March 11, 2008).
21. Turtle, H.; Bruce Croft, W. Inference networks for document retrieval. In *Proceedings of the 13th International Conference on Research and Development in Information Retrieval*, Vidick, J.-L., Ed.; Association for Computing Machinery: New York, 1990; 1–24.
22. Lee, J.H. Analyses of multiple evidence combination. In *SIGIR '97: Proceedings of the 20th Annual International ACM SIGIR Conference on Research and Development in Information Retrieval*, July 27–31, 1997; Philadelphia, PA. ACM: New York, 1997; 267–276.
23. Larson, R.R. A fusion approach to XML structured document retrieval. Inform. Retriev. **2005**, 8, 601–629.
24. Harman, D. Relevance feedback and other query modification techniques. In *Information Retrieval: Data Structures & Algorithms*; Frakes, W., Baeza-Yates, R., Eds.; Prentice Hall: Upper Saddle River, NJ, 1992; 241–263.

3 Information Searching and Search Models

Iris Xie

CONTENTS

INTRODUCTION

The emergence of the Internet has created millions of end-users who search for information themselves. Information searching can be defined as users' purposive behaviors in finding relevant or useful information in their interactions with information retrieval (IR) systems. Despite their different foci, information searching can also be used as synonymous for IR, information-seeking, and information access.[1] While information-seeking refers to purposive behavior involving users' interactions with either manual or computer-based information systems in order to satisfy their information goals, information-searching refers to the microlevel of behavior when interacting with different types of information systems.[2] IR is also a broad concept similar to information seeking, but is more limited to users' interactions with computer-based information systems. Since research on information-seeking and IR has contributed significantly to research on information searching, some of the associated works are also reflected here.

Information searching can be characterized at different levels including tactics/moves, strategies, usage patterns, and models. Tactics or moves are the microlevel behaviors that users exhibit in their search process. Specifically, a tactic is a move that advances the search process. In some studies, a move can be defined narrowly by researchers. For example, a move is termed as any changes made in formulating a query.[3] Searching strategies are a combination of tactics or moves. According to Bates,[4] "A search strategy is a plan for the whole search, while a tactic is a move made to further a search" (p. 207). A search strategy involves multiple dimensions, such as intentions, resources, methods, and so on. Usage patterns identify patterns of query formulation and reformulation based on analysis of transaction logs submitted to electronic IR systems. Search models are illustrations of patterns of information searching and the search process. Some of the models also identify the factors that influence the search process.

Users and online IR systems are partners in the information search process (ISP). Online IR systems can be characterized as IR systems that allow remote access with searches conducted in real time.[5] Users generally search information from four types of online IR systems: online databases, online public access catalogs (OPACs), Web search engines, and digital libraries. Information searching can be categorized into intermediary information searching and end-user information searching. In intermediary searching, information professionals serve as intermediaries between users and the IR system in the search process, whereas in end-user searching, users directly search for information themselves.

This entry starts with the definitions of key terminologies in the Introduction, and follows by providing the overview of the historical context portraying the history of the four digital environments. The focus of the entry is on the identification of levels of search strategies ranging from search tactics/moves, types and dimensions of search strategies and usage patterns to the factors that influence the selection and application of search strategies. More important, this entry presents ten search models that illustrate the dynamic search process and a variety of variables that define the search process. Finally, future research for information searching and search models is discussed.

HISTORICAL CONTEXT

In order to discuss information searching and search models, we have to first provide a historical context, in particular the evolution of the four major digital environments that users interact with. The emergence of online databases and OPACs indicates a new era for information searching from manual information systems to computer-based IR systems. The availability of OPACs and CD-ROM databases enabled users to search for information themselves. Later, the Web and the array of information resources to which it provided access made end-user searching of IR systems much more widely available. As partners of information searching, the development and evolution of online IR systems to some extent affects how users search for information. That is why it is important to offer a historical context for information searching before presenting a discussion of information searching and search models.

OPACs hold interrelated bibliographic data of collections of a library that can be searched directly by end users. In the 1960s, library automation projects started in university libraries. Computer-based library systems were implemented in large universities by commercial vendors in the 1970s. OPAC systems designed for public access started in the 1980s. Four generations of OPACs have evolved across time, from the first generation of OPACs that followed either online card catalog models emulating the familiar card catalog or Boolean searching models emulating online databases to the new generation of Web OPACs which incorporate advanced search features and new designs from other types of IR systems and allow users to search for information resources generated from libraries, publishers, and online vendors.

Online databases consist of full-text documents or citations and abstracts accessible via dial-up or other Internet services. Several dial-up services were offered in the 1960s, and in 1972 commercial online services, such as Dialog and ORBIT, started. Traditionally, online searchers were information professionals who acted as intermediaries between users and online databases. After the creation of the World Wide Web, online vendors began to design Web versions of online services to help end users to search for information themselves more easily. Characteristics of the new online database services include easy access, customization and interactivity.

The emergence of the Web enabled millions of users to search for information without the assistance of intermediaries. Web search engines allow users to mainly search for Web materials. Four types of search engines have been developed to enable users to accomplish different types of tasks:

- Web directories with hierarchically organized indexes facilitate users' browsing for information.
- Search engines with a database of sites assist users' searching for information.
- Meta-search engines permit users to search multiple search engines simultaneously.
- Specialized search engines create a database of sites for specific topic searching.

Many of the Web search engines also offer users the opportunity to search for multimedia information and personalize their search engines. Now, Web search engines also extend their services to full-text books and articles in addition to Web materials. The popularity of Web search engines influences the way that users interact with other types of online IR systems.

Digital libraries collect, organize, store and disseminate electronic resources in a variety of formats. The availability of online access to digital libraries began in the 1990s. Digital libraries allow users to search and use multimedia documents, and can be hosted by a variety of organizations and agencies, either for the general public or for a specific user group. Digital libraries also pose challenges for end users to interact with multimedia information in different interface designs without the same support as of physical libraries.

SEARCH TACTICS AND SEARCH MOVES

Research on information searching has focused on four levels: tactics/moves, strategies, usage patterns, and models. Tactics are moves that users apply in the search process. Different types of tactics play different roles in assisting users who are searching for information. Based on their functions in the ISP, information tactics can be classified into monitoring tactics, file structure tactics, search formulation tactics, and term tactics. While monitoring tactics and file structure tactics are tactics used to track the search and explore the file structure to find desired information, a source, or a file, search formulation tactics and term tactics are tactics applied to assist in the formulation and reformulation of searches as well as to help select and revise terms in search formulation.[4] In addition to search tactics, idea tactics assist users in identifying new ideas and resolutions to problems in information searching. While idea generation tactics include think, brainstorm, meditate, etc., pattern-breaking tactics consist of catch, break, breach, and others.[6] Focusing on topic management, knowledge-based search tactics are anther type of tactic that broadens the topic scope, narrows the topic scope, and changes the topic scope.[7]

Similar to tactics, search moves directly illustrate how users interact with online IR systems. Search moves in general relate to query formulation and reformulations. They can be classified based on whether the meaning of a query has changed. When operational moves that keep the meaning of query components remain unchanged, conceptual moves change the meaning of query components. Conceptual moves are highly associated with search results. The objectives of these moves are to reduce the size of a retrieved set, enlarge the size of a retrieved set, or improve both precision and recall.[3] Search moves can also be grouped depending on whether the moves are related to conceptual or physical moves. Cognitive moves refer to moves that users conceptually make in order to analyze terms or documents, while physical moves refer to moves that users make in order to use system features.[8]

TYPES AND DIMENSIONS OF SEARCH STRATEGIES

Search strategies consist of combinations of tactics or moves, and can be characterized by types and dimensions. In online databases and OPAC environments, search strategies can be classified by different types: concept-oriented, system-oriented, interactive, plan and reactive strategies. Concept-oriented strategies refer to strategies that manipulate concepts of search topics. The majority of the most-cited search strategies belong to this type. Building-block, pearl-growing, successive-fractions, most-specific-facet-first, and lowest-postings-facet-first[9] represent concept-oriented strategies. Unlike concept-oriented strategies, system-oriented strategies focus on making good use of different system features: the known-item instantiation strategy, the search-option heuristic strategy, the thesaurus-browsing strategy, and the screen-browsing strategy.[10] The trial-and-error strategy is also a popularly applied strategy because people generally are not willing to use help features of IR systems.

Search strategies can also be defined by how and to what extent users interact with IR systems and information objects embedded in the systems. Search and browsing are the main strategies users employ when they interact with IR systems. Browsing strategies require more interactions than analytical search strategies.[11] Active and reactive strategies specify another approach to classifying search strategies. By applying plan strategies, users make decisions about how to search for information before the first move, such as author, title, concepts, external support, system features, etc. By applying reactive strategies, users make decisions by following one move after another, such as focus shifts, search term relationships, error recovery and so on.[12]

Search strategies in Web search engine environments have their own characteristics. Search strategies that concentrate on query reformulation were generated based on log analysis: specified, generalized, parallel, building-block, dynamic, multitasking, recurrent, and format reformulation.[13–15] Some of them are similar to search strategies in online database environments, such as specified, generalized, and building-block, but others show unique characteristics of search strategies in the Web search engine environment, such as multitasking, recurrent, dynamic, and others. In Web search engine environments, users sometimes perform different search tasks simultaneously; their searches are more dynamic, and they often apply the same search queries repeatedly. The Web environment also defines the unique design and features of the Web and Web searching. The ten problem-solving strategies[16,17] represent search strategies in Web searching: surveying, double-checking, exploring, link-following, back- and forward-going, shortcut-seeking, engine-using, loyal engine-using, engine-seeking and metasearching.

In order to further analyze the structure of strategies, researchers have explored dimensions of information-seeking strategies. A multifaceted classification of information-seeking strategies was first developed based on four behavioral dimensions consisting of the goal of the interaction (learn, select), method of interaction (scan, search), mode of retrieval (recognize, specify), and types of resources interacted with (information, meta-information). Each type of information-seeking strategy corresponded to a specific prototype of dialogue structure.[18,19] The underlying common dimensions of browsing—scanning (looking, identifying, selecting, and examining), resource (meta-information, whole object, and part of object), goal (locate, confirm, evaluate, keep up, learn, curiosity, and entertain), and object (specific item, common items, defined location, general, and none)—were identified to illustrate nine patterns of browsing.[20] Integrating research and empirical studies in different digital environments, dimensions of information-seeking strategies are further illustrated by intentions, methods, entities and attributes of interactions. Twelve types of intentions include identify, learn, explore, create, modify, monitor, organize, access, keep records, evaluate, obtain and disseminate. Eleven types of methods consist of scan, manipulate, specify, track, select, survey, extract, compare, acquire, consult, and trial-and-error. While entities refer to what users intend to acquire or work on, attributes specify the traits/elements of these entities. Entities contain knowledge, concept/term, format, item/object/site, process/status, location, system and human. Attributes are associated with entities; for example, specific, common, general, and undefined are attributes of data/information. Different combinations of the four dimensions represent a variety of information-seeking strategies that people engage in within an ISP.[21]

USAGE PATTERNS

Web searching adds new meaning to research on search strategies, in particular the analysis of transaction logs. Unlike studies on search strategies, usage patterns identified in Web search engine environments focus on patterns of query formulation and reformulation based on analysis of transaction logs submitted to search engines. Patterns of query formulation and reformulation in Web search environments can be characterized in five ways: 1) short queries; 2) short sessions with minimum reformulations; 3) minimum use of operators and search modifiers, not always used correctly; 4) minimum viewing results; and 5) search topics ranging from entertainment, recreation, and sex to e-commerce.[22–26] Log analysis is not limited to quantitative analysis; facets of query formulations were identified as well.

Usage patterns in different types of IR environments have also been compared. Both similarities and differences were identified. Short queries, short sessions, minimum view of search results, and similar unique queries were shown in Web search engine, Web page, and digital library environments. Search sessions vary in OPAC environments even though OPAC studies also exhibit short queries. More queries contain Boolean operators in digital library environments than in Web search engine environments.[27,28] Wolfram and Xie[29] defined the context of digital libraries as representing a hybrid of both "traditional" IR, using primarily bibliographic resources provided by database vendors, and "popular" IR, exemplified by public search systems available on the World Wide Web. Usage of online databases in digital libraries reveals that users' search topics were close to online databases and digital libraries but their search behaviors were more similar to searching Web search engines. In general, users engage in more extensive searching in more traditional IR environments, such as OPAC and online database environments.

FACTORS AFFECTING INFORMATION SEARCHING

Information searching is affected by different types of factors, in which four main types determine the selection and application of different search strategies: 1) user goal and task; 2) user knowledge structure; 3) design of IR systems; and 4) the social and organizational context.

As to task, complexity of task and stages of task play major roles in influencing search strategies. Task complexity has systematic relationships with the types of information, information channels and sources needed. As the level of task complexity increases, more information channels and resources are required.[30,31] The task stages, such as initiation, selection, exploration, formulation, collection, and presentation, on one hand, affect physical actions, cognitive thoughts, and affective feelings and appropriate tasks.[32] On the other hand, task stages such as prefocus, formulation, and postfocus decide changes in search tactics, term choices, and types of information, as well as relevance criteria.[33,36] When users move to a more focused stage, they apply more specified search terms, additional operators, and additional tactics. The types of information they search range from background information, theories and models to methods, specific information and empirical research results. In addition, the familiarity of tasks, timeframe, and types of tasks affect how users plan and apply different types of information-seeking strategies in the IR process.[37] Research has also demonstrated that different types of search tasks lead to the application of different types of information-seeking strategies.[38,40]

Three types of knowledge are required for effective information searching: 1) IR knowledge; 2) domain knowledge; and 3) system knowledge. While domain knowledge helps users to develop an in-depth understanding of the search task and what they want, IR knowledge assists users to develop conceptual and procedural strategies.[41] No doubt, experienced users apply better strategies and perform better than novice users in the ISP.[42,45] Domain expertise was proved to affect search behaviors and strategies and search performance.[46,49] Users in different disciplines have their unique characteristics in searching for information. For example, compared with scientists, humanities scholars engage in more searching for individual names, geographical and chronological terms, and unique terms in humanities.[50] There are also intertwining relationships among different types of knowledge. For example, domain knowledge only influences search tactics of experienced searchers. Simultaneously, domain knowledge of users determines whether their retrieval knowledge has an impact on their search tactics.[51] In addition to users' knowledge structure, their cognitive abilities as part of personal information infrastructure, unavoidably, also control their search strategies.[11] Cognitive styles and searching styles have been demonstrated as the main personal traits that influence search behavior and search performance.[52,55] Simultaneously, cognitive styles and users' knowledge structure are interrelated with search performance and search behavior. For example, cognitive styles have more impact on experienced users than on novice users in their interaction with Web search engines.[56]

The design of IR systems no doubt affects users in their selections of search strategies. Interfaces, computational mechanisms, and information objects are the main components of IR systems that guide or impede users in their application of different search strategies. As partners of users in the ISP, IR systems—in particular the design of interfaces—could direct users to more or fewer applications of certain strategies. At the same time, the availability or unavailability of certain features determines whether users could engage in certain strategies. Finally, the information objects that users interact with and the outcomes of interactions might influence their choices of next strategy. Many studies conducted in the Text Retrieval Conferences (TRECs) have compared IR systems with different designs, and the results demonstrate that the design of IR systems makes significant differences in users' application of search strategies and search performances. Researchers have enhanced their IR systems based on the results of the evaluation studies.

The social-organizational context also defines the environment that user–system interactions take place. Mainly, the work environment influences how users determine their search strategies in the search process. Dimensions of a working place, such as the goals and constraints, priorities, general functions, work processes, and physical objects, in particular priorities, constraints, and business/work cycles have an impact on users' choices of search strategies.[37,57] In addition, cultural dimensions shape how users interact with IR systems.[58]

SEARCH MODELS

Because it is difficult to differentiate search models and retrieval models, in particular interactive IR models as well as some of the information-seeking models that involve search components and process, ten models in relation to information searching regardless of what terms are used by their original creators are presented here. These search models can be classified mainly into two types. The first type, which mainly illustrates ISPs, includes Ellis' model of information-seeking behaviors, Bates' berry-picking approach, and Kuhlthau's model of the ISP. The second type, which emphasizes the factors that influence the process, consists of Fidel and Soergel's conceptual framework for online bibliographic retrieval, Vakkari's theory of the task-based IR process, Ingwersen and Järvelin's cognitive model, Belkin's episode model of interaction with texts, Saracevic's stratified interaction model, Xie's planned-situational interactive IR model, and Wang, Hawk, and Tenopir's multidimensional model of user–Web interaction. In order to avoid repetition, some of the search models are briefly discussed because they are also presented in other entries.

Ellis' Model of Information-Seeking Behaviors

Ellis[59,60] developed a behavioral model of the information-seeking behaviors of academic social scientists. This approach concentrates on the behavior instead of on cognitive activities. The six types of information-seeking characteristics are the key components of the model: 1) starting; 2) chaining; 3) browsing; 4) differencing; 5) monitoring; and 6) extracting. These characteristics cover the overall search process and indicate that users do engage in multiple types of information-seeking strategies. Ellis and Haugan[61] further modeled the information-seeking patterns of engineers and research scientists in relation to their research activities in different phases and types of projects. Similar behavior patterns were identified from this group of users: surveying, chaining, monitoring, browsing, distinguishing, extracting, filtering and ending. Ellis' model starts a new behavior approach to identify information-seeking patterns of users and cited widely by researchers who developed other search models.

Bates' Berry-Picking Approach

Continuing her work on search tactics, Bates[62] illustrated the dynamic search process that searchers went through in the berry-picking approach (Figure 3.1). It is one of the most cited approaches that not only identify the limitations of traditional IR models, but also characterize the complexity of the search process. It demonstrates that users engage in multiple information-seeking strategies in their search process. The berry-picking approach can be summarized with four characteristics: 1) searchers' queries evolve; 2) the search process is dynamic as people pick up berries instead of finding one retrieved set; 3) searchers apply multiple search strategies including footnote chasing, citation searching, examining journal runs, area scanning, performing subject and author searches in bibliographies and abstracting and indexing (A&I) services, and they shift their strategies during the search process; and 4) searchers access resources in different formats and content. The approach also outlines how to implement new search capabilities in the design of online search interfaces. Bates[63] further developed the cascade model that describes several design layers, which have to be taken into account in the process of system implementation. Design decisions at each layer have a cascading impact on subsequent layers; therefore, the information content, its database structure, and retrievable elements are essential for effective IR. Bates' berry-picking approach sets up the foundation for interactive IR that considers search process as user–system interactions.

Kuhlthau's Model of the ISP

The ISP model was created based on a series of studies of users searching for information in different information-seeking situations. The ISP model consists of six stages of ISP with feelings shown, cognitive thoughts, and physical actions taken in each stage. The six stages comprise:

1. Initiation
2. Recognition of a need to search for information

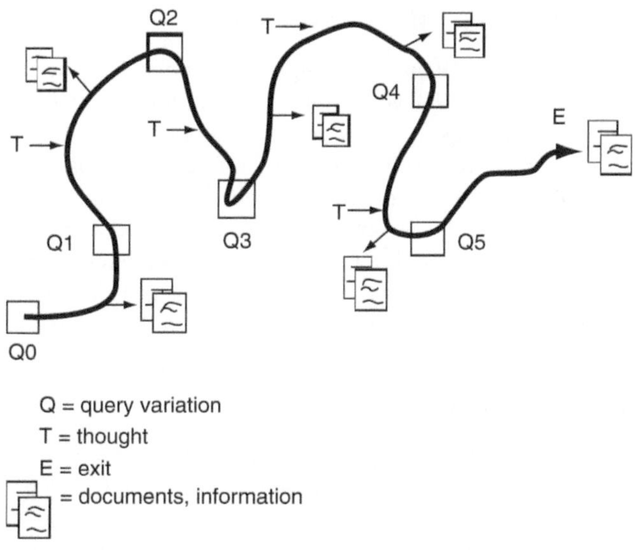

FIGURE 3.1 Bates' berry-picking approach. (From the design of browsing and berrypicking techniques for the online search interface, by M. Bates. In Online Rev., 13, 410, 1989.)

3. Selection and identification of an appropriate topic or approach
4. Exploration of relevant information on the topic
5. Formulation of a more focused topic
6. Collection of relevant information
7. Presentation and summarization of search results

Correspondently, feelings common to each stage change from uncertainty to relief, satisfaction or disappointment; thoughts shift from general or vague to more focused; actions range from seeking background information to seeking focused information; and tasks transform from recognition to completion. The ISP model has been widely tested and validated in a variety of digital environments.[33,34,64–66]

Fidel and Soergel's Conceptual Framework for Online Bibliographic Retrieval

Fidel and Soergel[67] presented a conceptual framework for online bibliographic retrieval. The framework highlights the main factors that affect the search process. Eight elements of the search process and interactions were identified including the setting, the user, the request, the database, the search system, the searcher, the searcher process and the search outcome. The variables associated with these elements were systematically collected and analyzed: 1) the setting (e.g., organization's orientation, organization affiliations, subject area of the organization, organization mission, etc.); 2) the user (cost behavior, education, prior experience, attitude, etc.); 3) the request (degree of specificity, degree of difficulty, etc.); 4) the database (coverage, update frequency, thesauri availability, cross-reference listings, cost, etc.); 5) the search system (search aids, search support capabilities, search capabilities, etc.); 6) the searcher (cost consciousness, personality traits, cognitive factors, demographic variables, etc.); 7) the search process (interaction with the user, database selection, query formulation, termination of the search, etc.); and 8) the search outcome (quality of retrieved results, precision, recall, etc.). This framework identifies the main factors affecting online bibliographic retrieval, and suggests possible relationships among the variables related to the search process. Although it is created specifically for the online bibliographic retrieval environment, it can also be applied to other digital environments.

Vakkari's Theory of the Task-Based IR Process

Vakkari's theory of the task-based IR process (Figure 3.2) considers the ISP as part of the task performance process. This theory is derived from a series of longitudinal studies that investigate students' information-seeking process in their research proposal-writing process for their master's theses.[33–35,68,69] Based on the results of a series of studies, this model illustrates how the task performance process in particular stages of ISP influences the information sought, search tactics applied, terms chosen, operators used, relevance judgments assessed, and documents obtained and used. It further enhances Kuhlthau's model of the ISP in terms of the relationships between stages of task and types of information searched for, changes in search tactics and terms, as well as relevance judgments. This theory systematically presents how tasks have impact on the search process.

Ingwersen and Järvelin's Cognitive Model

Ingwersen and Järvelin[70] developed a cognitive framework of interactive information-seeking, retrieval and behavioral processes (IS&R) (Figure 3.3) based on Ingwersen's original work[71,72] on the process of IR interactions. The new research framework places the cognitive actors or teams which bring their organizational, cultural, and social context to the interaction as the major components of the model instead of the searcher as the center of the interaction. The cognitive actors or teams include creators of information objects, indexers, designers of interfaces, designers of retrieval

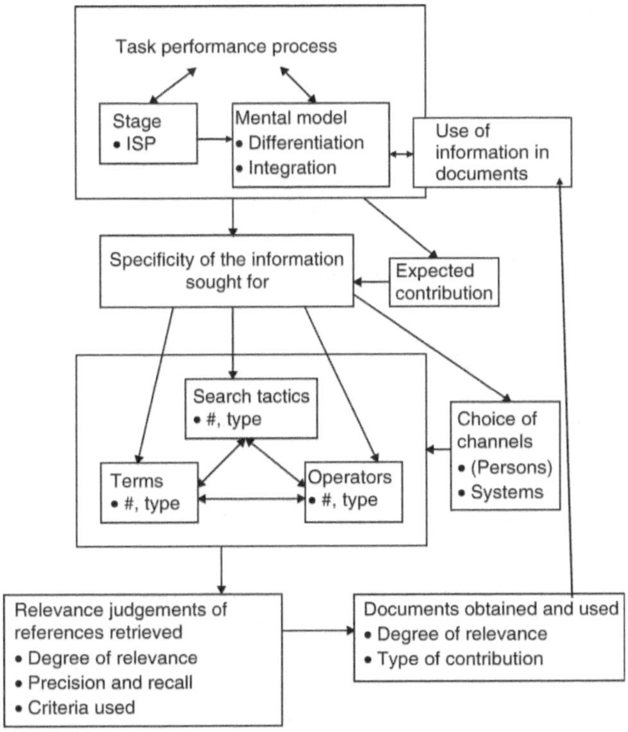

FIGURE 3.2 Vakkari's Theory of the Task-Based IR Process. (From A Theory of the task-based information retrieval process, by P. Vakkari. In J. Doc., 57, 58, 2001.)

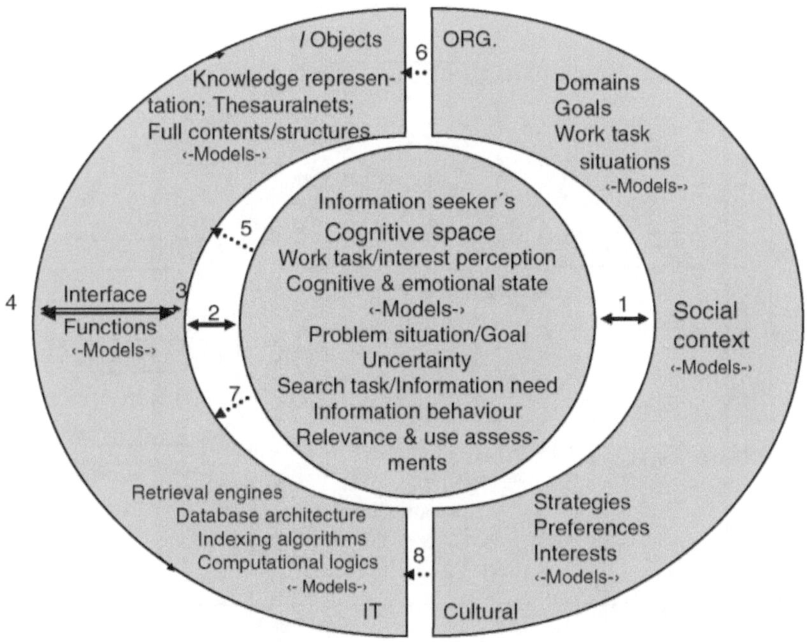

FIGURE 3.3 Modified version of Ingwersen and Järvelin's complex cognitive framework of interactive IS&R. (From *The Turn: Integration of Information Seeking and Retrieval in Context* (p. 274), by P. Ingwersen and K. Järvelin. In Springer, Heidelberg 2005. Modified by P. Ingwersen in 2007.)

mechanisms, gatekeepers, searchers, and communities representing different groups. While the first four arrows[1–4] present the interaction process, the rest of the four arrows[5–8] reflect the different types of generation and transformation of cognition or cognitive influence. An information seeker's cognitive space, interacting with both social context and IR systems, plays a central role. Interaction and perception are the central processes of the model. "Models" in each of the components reflect the perception of interpretation of their own contexts by any actor or component of the framework in a certain situation. All the participating cognitive structures are interrelated. This is one of the most comprehensive frameworks that reflect the dynamics and complexity of information-seeking and the retrieval process as well as associated factors.

Belkin's Episode Model of Interaction with Texts

Contrary to the traditional view of IR that people can specify their information needs and only engage in one type of information-seeking behavior, Belkin[73] pointed out that IR is interaction with texts. He[74] proposed the episode model interaction with texts (Figure 3.4), in which users' interaction with texts is the central process of IR. Belkin and his associates[18,19] further classified information-seeking strategies into four behavior dimensions (the goal of the interaction, method of interaction, mode of retrieval, and type of resource interacted with) and designed a dialog-based IR system that supports different types of information-seeking strategies. In this model, users' goals and tasks are the driving force for IR whereas representation, comparison, navigation, presentation, and visualization are the processes that facilitate users' interaction with texts. This model offers a theoretical framework for understanding how users interact with texts by applying multiple information-seeking strategies, and it further suggests how to design interactive IR systems to support multiple information-seeking strategies.

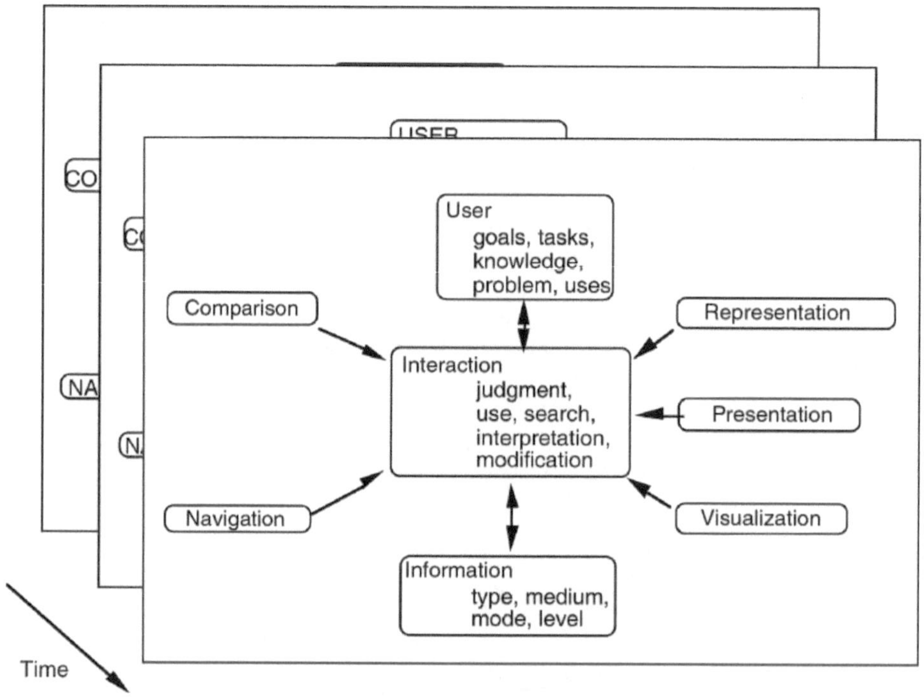

FIGURE 3.4 Belkin's episode model of interaction with texts. (From Intelligent information retrieval: Whose intelligence?, by N.J. Belkin. In ISI '96: Proceedings of the 5th International Symposium for Information Science (p. 29), Universtaetsverlag Konstanz, Konstanz, 1996.)

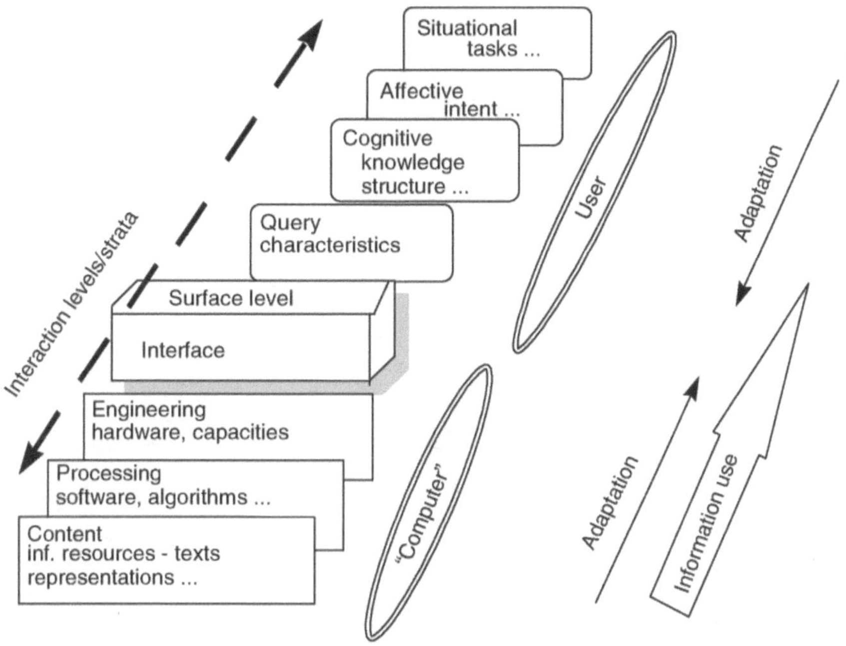

FIGURE 3.5 Saracevic's stratified model of IR interaction. (From The stratified model of information retrieval interaction: Extension and applications, by T. Saracevic. In Proceedings of the ASIS Annual Meeting (p. 316), Information Today, Medford, NJ, 1997.)

SARACEVIC'S STRATIFIED INTERACTION MODEL

Saracevic[75,76] proposed and enhanced the stratified interaction model (Figure 3.5) in which interaction of the interplay among different levels of users and systems is the central component. While users engage in cognitive, affective, and situational levels of interaction, system involvement includes engineering, processing, and content-level. On the cognitive level, the interaction takes place between the cognitive structure of users and texts. On the affective level, users interact with intentions, beliefs, and motivation. On the situation level, users interact with tasks and problems that lead them to look for information. On the engineering level, the process level, and the content level, the hardware, software, and information resources are the foci for analysis, respectively. Users interact with IR systems via interfaces on the surface level by searching, browsing, navigating, organizing, and viewing search results, providing feedback, and other activities. Interactions not only take place at the surface level, but also occur at the deeper levels, which might also lead to changes at the surface level. The complexity and dynamic interaction process requires changes and adaptations from both the user and system side. The main contribution of the stratified model is its identification of different levels of interactions from both the user and system side and their interplay.

XIE'S PLANNED-SITUATIONAL INTERACTIVE IR MODEL

Xie[21] enhanced her previous work[77,78] on the planned-situational interactive IR model derived from an empirical study. The planned-situational model of interactive IR (Figure 3.6) is developed to illustrate how plans and situations codetermine users' applying and shifting different information-seeking strategies in their search process. User goal and task are the driving forces for people to look for information. Four levels of user goals are constructed: 1) long-term goal; 2) leading search goal; 3) current search goal; and 4) interactive intention. Dimensions of the work task (stages, timeframe, and nature) and search task (origination, type, and domain) are identified to characterize

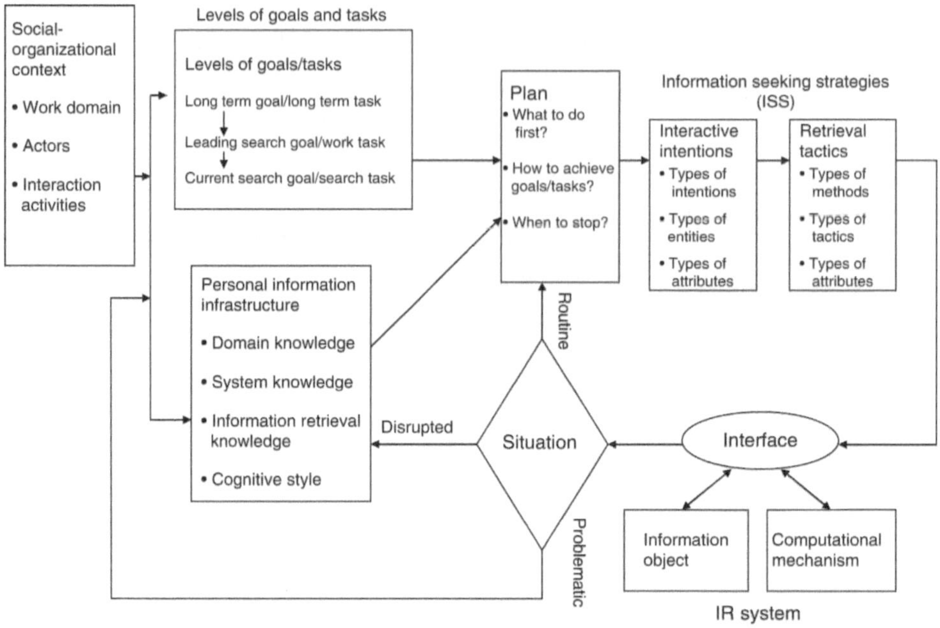

FIGURE 3.6 Planned-situational interactive IR model. (From Interactive Information Retrieval in Digital Environments (p. 216), by I. Xie. In IGI Publishing, Hershey, PA 2008.)

tasks. Higher levels of the goal/task impact lower levels of the goal/task. More important, levels of user goal and dimensions of tasks influence how users interact with IR systems. At the same time, information search requires users to apply different types of knowledge and skills into the search process. In addition, the social-organizational context defines the environment in which users interact with IR systems. Users and IR systems are the two partners of information searching. By interacting with the interfaces of IR systems, users interact with the information objects stored in these systems as well as with the computational mechanisms of the software and hardware of the systems.

Information-seeking strategies comprise interactive intentions and retrieval tactics, entities, and associated attributes. Planned and situational aspects codetermine the selection and shifts in information-seeking strategies. Three types of situations (routine, problematic, and disruptive) lead to different types of shifts in information-seeking strategies. In a routine situation, the situation can be determined sufficiently with the aid of habitual knowledge. In a problematic situation, after associating the elements of situations with a user's knowledge and plans, further clarification of the open elements of the situation is required. A third type of situation is a "disruptive situation," in which users do not encounter any problems, but they are distracted during the process of fulfilling their original current search goals/search tasks. The planned-situational model was tested and validated by empirical studies. This model not only identifies the macrolevel components for search and retrieval, but also uncovers shifts in information-seeking strategies and the factors that lead to the selection and shifts in information-seeking strategies at the micro-level.

Wang, Hawk, and Tenopir's Multidimensional Model of User–Web Interaction

Focusing on the Web environment, Wang, Hawk, and Tenopir[17] proposed a multidimensional model of user–Web interaction (Figure 3.7). The model consists of the user, the interface, and the Web space. Among them, the user is the key component. Users are influenced by situation factors, cognitive behavior, affective state, and physical skills. The interface facilitates users' interactions with Web spaces. Access methods, navigation tools, access results/objects, messages/clues, and

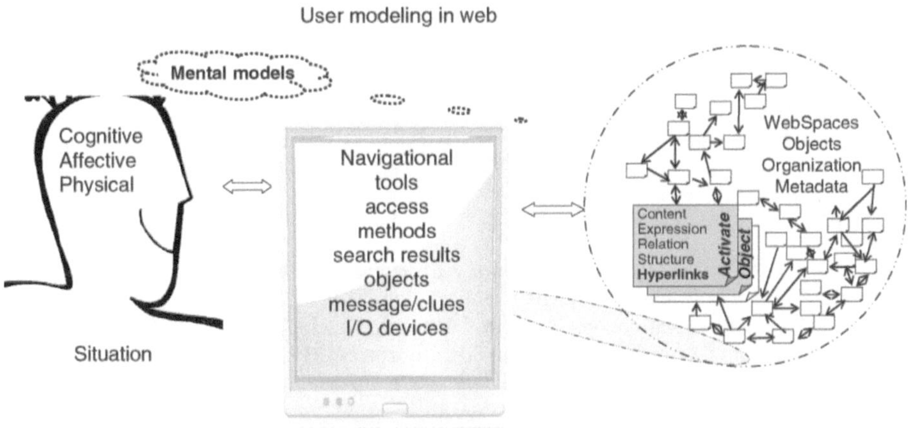

FIGURE 3.7 Modified version of Wang, Hawk, and Tenopir's multidimensional model of user–Web interaction in IR. (From Users' interaction with World Wide Web resources: An exploratory study using a holistic approach, by P. Wang, W. B. Hawk, and C. Tenopir. In Information Processing & Management, 36, p. 233. Modified by P. Wang 2008.)

input/output devices are the elements of the interface. The Web elements contain objects, activated objects, Web spaces, organization schemes, and metadata. This model is further tested and validated by an exploratory study of graduate students' interaction with a university Web site. Ten problem-solving strategies were identified. The findings show that cognitive factors define how users analyze questions, construct search statements and develop problem-solving strategies; affective factors affect how users adopt and use of strategies; and physical factors determine whether users can engage in efficient interactions. The multidimensional model of user–Web interaction defines how users search for information in the Web environment.

CONCLUSION

Information searching has evolved from searching for information using manual information systems to using electronic IR systems, as well as from intermediary search to end-user search. Recent research has revealed the limitation of traditional IR research: the assumption that information searching is static and people only formulate queries in their search process. Furthermore, research has shown that the ISP is a dynamic one in which people apply multiple types of search strategies. Different levels of information searching, from search tactics/moves to search strategies and usage patterns, have been identified, as well as factors associated with task, user knowledge structure, system design, and the social and organizational context influencing the search process. More importantly, search models have been developed to illustrate either the dynamic search process or major elements that affect the search process. These models also offer suggestions for IR system enhancement and design.

Unsolved problems in research on information searching and search models still exist, however. First, although research on information searching helps reveal the nature of how people interact with different types of IR systems, very few findings of user studies have been applied to the design of IR systems. There is a big gap between user-oriented study and system-oriented design. More collaborative research is needed to incorporate and implement the design principles derived from user studies into IR system design and evaluation. Second, a variety of search models have been developed; the problem is that we may not be able to find a one-size-fits-all model to account for all of the issues in the search process. Further research needs to examine how to integrate different types of search models and identify what is still missing. Third, the newer digital environments call for the need to search for multimedia information and information in different languages. More research is needed to identify search patterns in multimedia and cross-language retrieval. Finally, in order to facilitate users' easy adaptation to different digital environments, future research also needs to compare the similarities and differences of information searching in different digital environments and further transform research results into IR system design.

REFERENCES

1. Chu, H. *Information Representation and Retrieval in the Digital Age*; Information Today: Medford, NJ, 2003.
2. Wilson, T.D. Human information behaviour. Inform. Sci. **2000**, *3* (2), 49–56.
3. Fidel, R. Moves in online searching. Online Rev. **1985**, *9* (1), 61–74.
4. Bates, M.J. Information search tactics. J. Am. Soc. Inform. Sci. **1979**, *30* (4), 205–214.
5. Walker, G.; Janes, J. *Online Retrieval: A Dialogue of Theory and Practice*, 2nd Ed.; Libraries Unlimited: Englewood, CO, 1999.
6. Bates, M.J. Idea tactics. J. Am. Soc. Inform. Sci. **1979**, *30* (5), 280–289.
7. Shute, S.J.; Smith, P.J. Knowledge-based search tactics. Inform. Process. Manage. **1993**, *29* (1), 29–45.
8. Shiri, A.A.; Revie, C. The effects of topic complexity and familiarity on cognitive and physical moves in a thesaurus-enhanced search environment. J. Inform. Sci. **2003**, *29* (6), 517–526.
9. Markey, K.; Atherton, P. *ONTAP. Online Training and Practice Manual for ERIC Database Searchers*; ERIC Clearinghouse on Information Resources: Syracuse, NY, 1978.
10. Chen, H.; Dhar, V. Cognitive processes as a basis for intelligent retrieval system design. Inform. Process. Manage. **1991**, *27* (5), 405–432.
11. Marchionini, G. *Information-Seeking in Electronic Environments*; Cambridge University Press: Cambridge, 1995.
12. Soloman, P. Children's information retrieval behavior: A case analysis of an OPAC. J. Am. Soc. Inform. Sci. **1993**, *44* (5), 245–264.
13. Bruza, P.D.; Dennis, S. Query-reformulation on the Internet: Empirical data and the hyperindex search engine. In RIAO 97: Conference Proceedings with Prototype and Operational Systems Demonstrations: Computer-Assisted Information Searching on Internet, McGill University, Montreal, Quebec, Canada, 25th–27th June, 1997; RIAO 97, Ed.; CID: Paris, 1997; Vol. 1, 488–499.
14. Lau, T.; Horvitz, E. Patterns of search: Analyzing and modeling Web query refinement. In Proceedings of the 7th International Conference on User Modeling Banff, Canada, June 1999; Kay, J., Ed.; Springer-Wien: New York, 1999; 119–128.
15. Rieh, S.Y.; Xie, H. Analysis of multiple query reformulations on the web: The interactive information retrieval context. Inform. Process. Manage. **2006**, *42* (3), 751–768.
16. Hawk, W.B.; Wang, P. Users' interaction with the World Wide Web; problems and problem solving. In Proceedings of the 62nd ASIS Annual Meeting, Washington, DC, **1999**, *36*, 256–270.
17. Wang, P.; Hawk, W.B.; Tenopir, C. Users' interaction with World Wide Web resources: An exploratory study using a holistic approach. Inform. Process. Manage. **2000**, *36* (2), 229–251.
18. Belkin, N.J.; Marchetti, P.G.; Cool, C. BRAQUE: Design of an interface to support user interaction in information retrieval. Inform. Process. Manage. **1993**, *29* (3), 325–344.
19. Belkin, N.J.; Cool, C.; Stein, A.; Thiel, U. Cases, scripts and information seeking strategies: On the design of interactive information retrieval systems. Expert Syst. Appl. **1995**, *9* (3), 379–395.
20. Chang, S. *Toward a Multidimensional Framework for Understanding Browsing*; Unpublished doctoral dissertation, Rutgers University: New Brunswick, NJ, 1995.
21. Xie, I. *Interactive Information Retrieval in Digital Environments*; IGI Global Inc.: Hershey, PA, 2008.
22. Jansen, B.J.; Spink, A.; Saracevic, T. Real life, real users, and real needs: A study and analysis of user queries on the Web. Inform. Process. Manage. **2000**, *36* (2), 207–227.
23. Moukdad, H.; Large, A. Users' perceptions of the Web as revealed by transaction log analysis. Online Inform. Rev. **2001**, *25* (6), 349–359.
24. Spink, A.; Jansen, B.J. *Web Search: Public Searching of the Web*; Kluwer Academic Publishers: Boston, 2004.
25. Spink, A.; Wolfram, D.; Jansen, B.J.; Saracevic, T. Searching the Web: The public and their queries. J. Am. Soc. Inform. Sci. **2001**, *52* (3), 226–234.
26. Silverstein, C.; Henzinger, M.; Marais, H.; Morica, M. Analysis of a very large Web search engine query log. SIGIR Forum **1999**, *33* (1), 6–12.

27. Jones, S.; Cunningham, S.J.; McNab, R.; Boddie, S. Human–computer interaction for digital libraries: A transaction log analysis of a digital library. Int. J. Dig. Libr. **2000**, *3* (2), 152–169.
28. Wang, P.; Berry, M.; Yang, Y. Mining longitudinal Web queries: Trends and patterns. J. Am. Soc. Inform. Sci. Technol. **2003**, *54* (8), 743–758.
29. Wolfram, D.; Xie, H. Traditional IR for Web users: A context for general audience digital libraries. Inform. Process. Manage. **2002**, *38* (5), 627–648.
30. Byström, K. Information and information sources in tasks of varying complexity. J. Am. Soc. Inform. Sci. Technol. **2002**, *53* (7), 581–591.
31. Byström, K.; Järvelin, K. Task complexity affects information-seeking and use. Inform. Process. Manage. **1995**, *31* (2), 191–213.
32. Kuhlthau, C.C. Inside the search process: Information seeking from the user's perspective. J. Am. Soc. Inform. Sci. **1991**, *42* (5), 361–371.
33. Vakkari, P. eCognition and changes of search terms and tactics during task performance: A longitudinal study. In RIAO' 2000 Conference Proceedings, Content-Based Multimedia Information, Collège de France, Paris, France, April 12–14, 2000; RIAO, Ed.; CID: Paris, 2000; Vol. 1, 894–907. http://www.info.uta.fi/vakkari/Vakkari_Tactics_ RIAO2000.html (accessed July 15, 2008).
34. Vakkari, P. Relevance and contributory information types of searched documents in task performance. In Proceedings of the 23rd Annual International ACM SIGIR Conference on Research and Development in Information Retrieval, Belkin, N.J., Ingwersen, P., Leong, M.-K., Eds.; SIGIR forum; ACM Press: New York, 2000; Vol. 34, 2–9.
35. Vakkari, P.; Hakala, N. Changes in relevance criteria and problem stages in task performance. J. Doc. **2000**, *56*, 540–562.
36. Vakkari, P.; Pennanen, M.; Serola, S. Changes of search terms and tactics while writing a research proposal. Inform. Process. Manage. **2003**, *39* (3), 445–463.
37. Xie, H. Understanding human–work domain interaction: Implications for the design of a corporate digital library. J. Am. Soc. Inform. Sci. Technol. **2006**, *57* (1), 128–143.
38. Bilal, D. Perspectives on children's navigation of the World Wide Web: Does the type of search task make a difference. Online Inform. Rev. **2002**, *26* (2), 108–177.
39. Ford, N.; Miller, D.; Moss, N. Web search strategies and retrieval effectiveness: An empirical study. J. Doc. **2002**, *58* (1), 30–48.
40. Schacter, J.; Chung, G.K.W.K.; Dorr, A. Children's Internet searching on complex problems: Performance and process analyses. J. Am. Soc. Inform. Sci. **1998**, *49* (9), 840–849.
41. Marchionini, G.; Dwiggins, S.; Katz, A.; Lin, X. Information seeking in full-text end-user-oriented search-systems—The roles of domain and search expertise. Libr. Inform. Sci. Res. **1993**, *15* (1), 35–69.
42. Howard, H. Measures that discriminate among online users with different training and experience. Online Rev. **1982**, *6* (4), 315–326.
43. Lazonder, A.W.; Biemans, H.J.A.; Wopereis, I.G.J.H. Differences between novice and experienced users in searching information on the World Wide Web. J. Am. Soc. Inform. Sci. **2000**, *51* (6), 576–581.
44. Siegfried, S.; Bates, M.J.; Wilde, D.M. A profile of end-user searching behavior by humanities scholars: The Getty online searching project (Rep. No. 2). J. Am. Soc. Inform. Sci. **1993**, *44* (5), 273–291.
45. Sutcliffe, A.G.; Ennis, M.; Watkinson, S.J. Empirical studies of end-user information searching. J. Am. Soc. Inform. Sci. **2000**, *51* (13), 1211–1231.
46. Bhavnani, S.K. Important cognitive components of domain-specific search knowledge. In The Tenth Text Retrieval Conference, TREC-2001, Voorhees, E.M., Harman, D.K., Eds.; Information Today: Medford, NJ, 2002; 571–578.
47. Drabenstott, K.M. Do nondomain experts enlist the strategies of domain experts? J. Am. Soc. Inform. Sci. Technol. **2003**, *54* (9), 836–854.
48. Dumais, S.T.; Belkin, N.J. The TREC interactive tracks: Putting the user into search. In TREC: *Experiment and Evaluation in Information Retrieval*; Voorhees, E.M., Harman, D.K., Eds.; The MIT Press: Cambridge, MA, 2005; 123–152.
49. Wildemuth, B.M. The effect of domain knowledge on search tactic formulation. J. Am. Soc. Inform. Sci. Technol. **2004**, *55* (3), 246–258.
50. Bates, M.J.; Wilde, D.N.; Siegfried, S. An analysis of search terminology used by humanities scholars: The Getty Online Searching Project report no. 1. Libr. Quart. **1993**, *63* (1), 1–39.
51. Hsieh-Yee, I. Effects of search experience and subject knowledge on the search tactics of novice and experienced searchers. J. Am. Soc. Inform. Sci. **1993**, *44* (3), 161–174.
52. Bellardo, T. What do we really know about online searchers? Online Rev. **1985**, *9* (3), 223–239.

53. Fenichel, C.H. Online searching: Measures that discriminate among users with different types of experience. J. Am. Soc. Inform. Sci. **1981**, *32* (1), 23–32.
54. Fidel, R. Searchers' selection of search keys: I. The selection routine. II. Controlled vocabulary or free-text searching. III. Searching styles. J. Am. Soc. Inform. Sci. **1991**, *42* (7), 490–527.
55. Ford, N.; Wilson, T.D.; Foster, A.; Ellis, D.; Spink, A. Information seeking and mediated searching. Part 4. Cognitive styles in information seeking. J. Am. Soc. Inform. Sci. Technol. **2002**, *53* (9), 728–735.
56. Palmquist, R.A.; Kim, K.S. Cognitive style and online search experience on Web search performance. J. Am. Soc. Inform. Sci. Technol. **2000**, *51* (6), 558–567.
57. Fidel, R.; Pejtersen, A.M. From information behavior research to the design of information systems: The cognitive work analysis framework. Inform. Res. **2004**, *10* (1). http:// informationr.net/ir/10-1/paper210 .html (accessed July 10, 2008).
58. Callahan, E. Interface design and culture. Annu. Rev. Inform. Sci. Technol. **2005**, *39*, 257–310.
59. Ellis, D. *The Derivation of a Behavioral Model for Information System Design*; Unpublished doctoral dissertation, University of Sheffield: Sheffield, U.K., 1987.
60. Ellis, D. A behavioural approach to information retrieval system design. J. Doc. **1989**, *45* (3), 171–212.
61. Ellis, D.; Haugan, M. Modeling the information seeking patterns of engineers and research scientists in an industrial environment. J. Doc. **1997**, *53* (4), 384–403.
62. Bates, M.J. The design of browsing and berrypicking techniques for the online search interface. Online Rev. **1989**, *13* (5), 407–424.
63. Bates, M.M. The cascade of interactions in the digital library interface. Inform. Process. Manage. **2002**, *38* (3), 381–400.
64. Cole, C. Intelligent information retrieval: Part IV. Testing the timing of two information retrieval devices in a naturalistic setting. Inform. Process. Manage. **2001**, *37* (1), 163–182.
65. Hyldegard, J. Collaborative information behaviour: Exploring Kuhlthau's information search process model in a group-based educational setting. Inform. Process. Manage. **2006**, *42* (1), 276–298.
66. Kracker, J. Research anxiety and students' perceptions of research: An experiment: Part 1. Effect of teaching Kuhlthau's ISP model. J. Am. Soc. Inform. Sci. Technol. **2002**, *53* (4), 282–294.
67. Fidel, R.; Soergel, D. Factors affecting online bibliographic retrieval: A conceptual framework for research. J. Am. Soc. Inform. Sci. **1983**, *34* (3), 163–180.
68. Pennanen, M.; Vakkari, P. Students' conceptual structure, search process and outcome while preparing a research proposal. J. Am. Soc. Inform. Sci. **2003**, *54* (8), 759–770.
69. Vakkari, P. A theory of the task-based information retrieval process. J. Docu. **2001**, *57* (1), 44–60.
70. Ingwersen, P.; Järvelin, K. The *Turn: Integration of Information Seeking and Retrieval in Context*; Springer: Heidelberg, Germany, 2005.
71. Ingwersen, P. *Information Retrieval Interaction*; Taylor Graham: London, 1992.
72. Ingwersen, P. Cognitive perspectives of information retrieval interaction: Elements of a cognitive IR theory. J. Docu. **1996**, *52* (1), 3–50.
73. Belkin, N.J. Interaction with texts: Information retrieval as information seeking behavior. In *Information Retrieval '93: Von der Modellierung zur Anwendung*; Knorz, G., Krause, J., Womser-Hacker, C., Eds.; Universitaetsverlag Konstanz: Konstanz, Germany, 1993; 55–66.
74. Belkin, N.J. Intelligent information retrieval: whose intelligence? In Proceedings of the 5th International Symposium for Information Science (ISI '96): Humboldt-Universität zu Berlin, 17. -19. October 1996; Krause, J., Herfurth, M., Marx, J., Eds.; Universitätsverlag Konstanz: Konstanz, Germany, 1996; 25–31.
75. Saracevic, T. Modeling interaction in information retrieval (IR): A review and proposal. In Proceedings of the 59th ASIS Annual Meeting **1996**, *33*, 3–9.
76. Saracevic, T. The stratified model of information retrieval interaction: Extension and applications. In Proceedings of the 60th ASIS Annual Meeting **1997**, *34*, 313–327.
77. Xie, H. Shifts of interactive intentions and information-seeking strategies in interactive information retrieval. J. Am. Soc. Informa. Sci. **2000**, *51* (9), 841–857.
78. Xie, H. Patterns between interactive intentions and information-seeking strategies. Inform. Process. Manage. **2002**, *38* (1), 55–77.

4 User-Oriented and Cognitive Models of Information Retrieval

Kalervo Järvelin and Peter Ingwersen

CONTENTS

INTRODUCTION

The Laboratory Model of Information Retrieval (IR) has dominated IR research for half a century. The focus of this system-driven research is IR algorithms and their evaluation. Algorithms are evaluated for their capability of finding topically relevant documents.

Laboratory IR has recently been challenged by progress in research into "relevance," "interactive IR," and "information seeking." Recent work in analyzing the concept of relevance has resulted in identifying higher-order relevances, such as cognitive relevance and situational relevance, in addition to algorithmic and topical relevance. Real human users of IR systems introduce non-binary, subjective, and dynamic relevance judgments into interactive IR processes. Moreover, recent theoretical and empirical work in information seeking suggests that IR is but one means of information seeking which takes place in a context determined by, e.g., a person's task, its phase, and situation. For larger tasks one may identify multiple stages, strategies, tactics or modes of information access, and dynamic relevance. IR strategies, tactics, and relevance assessments are therefore affected by the stages of task performance.

Because of these empirical findings and theoretical arguments, the traditional Laboratory Model of IR evaluation has been challenged for its (lack of) realism. It has therefore been suggested that the developers of IR algorithms should consider how the algorithms are to be evaluated—in which frameworks and how to guarantee validity. Ingwersen and Järvelin[1] discuss the limitations of, and challenges to, the system-driven Laboratory IR.

User-oriented research on IR phenomena was (and is) not necessarily based on any specific epistemological perspective. It might be practice-related or very pragmatic in scope. On the other hand, since its start in 1977 the cognitive approach to IR could briefly be characterized as user- and intermediary-oriented, with an explicit epistemic approach underlying its scope. First during the past decade the approach has gained momentum and turned into a holistic view of "all" the interactive communication processes that occur during information transfer—including those associated with the retrieval engine. Simultaneously, user-centered IR research shifted focus from exploring traditional (scholarly) online interaction with the human intermediary as central actor to Web-based IR with the end-user as the player.

A cognitive turn took place in IR in the early 1990s. Robertson and Hancock-Beaulieu[2] see this turn to consist of three facets (or revolutions) that are crucial to understand in order to proceed toward a more integrated (holistic) theory of IR: the cognitive, the relevance, and the interactive revolutions. The cognitive and interactive revolutions combined entail the ideas that personal information needs ought to be treated as potentially dynamic, not static. They may change over time—probably due to learning and "cognition" in context during IR interaction. Relevance assessments hence also become dynamic and may take place in a variety of dimensions, so that the traditional topicality as a measure of relevance does not stand alone.

The present entry first discusses the domain of, and the kinds of models one may build for, user-oriented and cognitive IR. The focus of the entry is on the models, not on their empirical applications, and therefore we present several models with different emphases on user-oriented and cognitive IR—ranging from overall approaches and relevance models to procedural models, task-based models, and cognitive models.

THE DOMAIN OF USER-ORIENTED AND COGNITIVE IR

When the system-driven IR research could be seen to neglect information seekers in its modeling and experimentation, user-oriented IR research focused precisely on them. The complementary nature of these two areas may be seen in the light of Figure 4.1.

The system-driven IR research focused on the left side of the figure, on authors' texts, their representation, queries, and retrieval. The user-oriented and initial cognitive IR research focused on the right side, on users' problem spaces, information problems, requests, interaction with intermediaries, interface design, and query formulation but hardly on analyzing authors' texts, their representation, queries, or IR techniques. With the turn into a holistic view in the 1990s of "all" the interactive communication processes that occur during information transfer, the cognitive approach finally encompassed all the components of Figure 4.1 including the algorithmic and document areas.

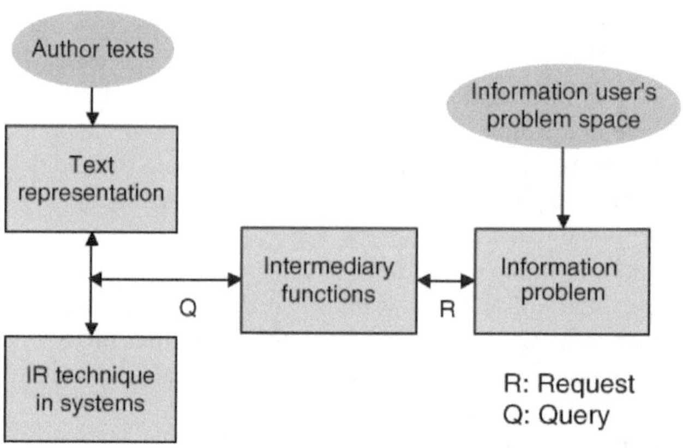

FIGURE 4.1 IR research areas. (From Means to improved subject access and representation in modern information retrieval, by P. Ingwersen and I. Wormell. In Libri **1988**, *38* (2), 95.)

The cognitive and user-oriented approaches differed from the systems-driven one in the following respects (pp. 193–194)[1]:

- *Concept of information.* Information is seen as a result of human interpretation processes and as related to human cognition; the understanding that formal systems contain data (or potential information) processed at low linguistic levels.
- *Nature of information need.* Needs are not always seen as well-defined and topical, but may be complex, muddled, verificative; and problem-based rather than topical.
- *Task dependency.* The perceived work task (or non-job related daily-life task or interest) situation is seen as the underlying reason for information need development.
- *IR system setting*
  - in the user-centered approach often assumed to be a hypertext supported, operational and Web-based Boolean IR system, increasingly with some best match properties, e.g., relevance ranking;
  - in the cognitive approach increasingly seen as also including best match systems in experiments and investigations;
  - the searcher and intermediary are seen as parts of the IR system, not just the technical components.
- *Role of intermediary.* The role of human intermediaries was originally much in focus but has declined in and after the 1990s; likewise, automatic intermediary systems were in focus in the 1980s, but this focus faded away in the 1990s; currently, end-user behavior and interaction is in focus.
- *Interaction.* is seen as the central process for cognitive IR; interaction has the purpose to benefit from the cognitive differences between various actors in the IR process; harmonizing such differences is regarded futile.
- *Relevance.* is seen as objective and subjective, multidimensional, dynamic and of non-binary nature.
- *Context.* IR is placed in context in a holistic way: all components/cognitive actors and structures of information seeking and IR are contextual to one another.
- *Conceptual relationships.* Strong relationships between the actors' contexts, situations, tasks/interests, information need development, relevance assessments, and perceptions of document representations during IR interaction.
- *Cognitive and user-oriented IR theory* focuses on the development of evaluation methods relevant to the user and his/her context rather than the matching performance of IR systems.

CONCEPTUAL MODELS IN IR

There are several different types of models in user-oriented and cognitive IR research. The terminology in the area varies—scholars discuss various models, paradigms, meta-theories, etc.—while often meaning the same or a very similar notion: socially shared "ontological" (what is out there to investigate?), "conceptual" (how to name that?), "factual" (what to take as givens?), epistemological (how can we possibly know about it?), and "methodological" (how can we learn about it?) assumptions in a research area. The present entry discusses them as "conceptual" models.

Functions of Conceptual Models: Conceptual models provide the conceptual and methodological tools for formulating hypotheses and theories. Thus they are, in fact, broader and more fundamental than scientific theories in that they set the preconditions of theory formulation. When they are also seen to represent schools of thought, chronological continuity, or principles, beliefs and values of the research community, they become paradigms.

The conceptual model of a research area is always constructed—it does not simply lie somewhere out there waiting for discovery. The construction of conceptual models in a research area often requires conceptual and terminological development. This may involve defining concepts better—regarding preciseness, accuracy, simplicity, generality, and suitability for expressing propositions. Moreover, good concepts represent essential features (objects, relationships, events) and classify central phenomena in ways that lead to interesting hypotheses. This means that the concepts should relate to each other explicitly and in systematic and fruitful ways.

Dimensions of Models: A single model does not exist that would cover all the aspects and phenomena of user-oriented and cognitive IR. Proposed conceptual models in the domain literature are varied. Below are some dimensions for classifying conceptual models.

- *Scope*: The range of phenomena that is covered. The scope of a model may cover, e.g., only online interaction or information need formation. Another model may cover the whole range from need formation to retrieval and document use.
- *Process orientation*: Some models are explicitly process models while others are static, not explicitly modeling an IR process as a sequence of stages.
- *Abstraction level*: Concrete models focus on actual concrete stakeholders in an IR interaction process, and their relationships, while abstract models focus on abstract phenomena or structures related to the stakeholders, and the relationships of the former.
- *Summary vs. analysis*: Summary models seek to summarize the central objects in an IR process and their gross relationships without classifying and analyzing either, whereas analytical models seek to classify the objects and relationships, and generate testable hypotheses.
- *Specificity*: Generic models claim validity over a range of empirical domains whereas a specific model only claims validity in a particular context. For example, a general model may be meant for any kind of document collection in any language and media whereas a specific one may represent image retrieval in a journalistic context.

In the following, models are grouped into generic models and relevance models (Sections on "Generic Models and Relevance Models"), process models (Section on "Online Interaction: Process Models"), models on cognitive structures and actors (Section on "Cognitive Structures and Actors"), and into task-based models (Section on Task-Based Models).

MODELS OF USER-ORIENTED AND COGNITIVE IR

GENERIC MODELS

To map out a research area, one needs a model of a broad scope. Often such models are, in addition to being broad, also summary models and generic models over a large domain. The Ingwersen–Wormell model, and Wilson's model, discussed below, are such examples.

The Ingwersen–Wormell model: The interaction model by Ingwersen and Wormell,[3] Figure 4.1, represents the components and the interactive processes in IR. The right-hand side presents the user's problem space, e.g., as part of a process of interest fulfillment or problem solving. If not solved by the user himself, this "problem space" may lead to an information problem or need that results in a request for information, often formulated for an IR system.

In the middle the intermediary functions consist of the entire system's capability to understand and support the information problem of the current searcher as well as the search possibilities and logic of the source system. These functions form part of the professional knowledge of the human intermediary (librarian/information specialist), or may be skillfully adapted to a front-end to the system as a user interface, in order to support retrieval. On the left-side components consist of author texts to be represented through indexing, and of IR techniques that determine the behavior of the IR system.

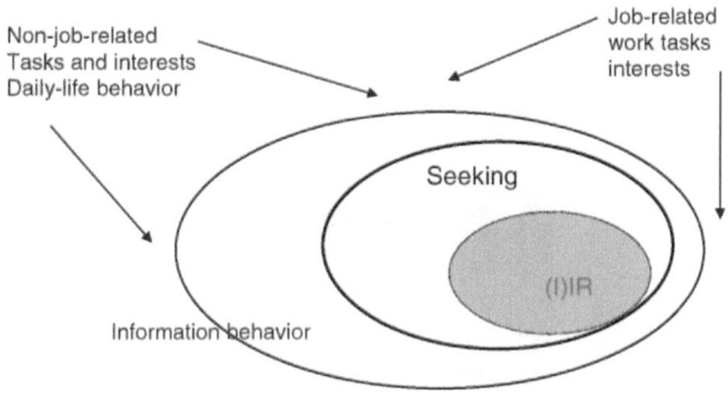

FIGURE 4.2 A nested model of information behavior. (Modified from Models in information behavior research, by T.D. Wilson. In J. Doc. **1999**, *55* (3), 249–270; in *The Turn: Integration of Information Seeking and Retrieval in Context*, by P. Ingwersen and K. Järvelin; Springer, Dortrecht, the Netherlands, 2005 (p. 198).)

Interaction takes place between an intermediary and an actor having a desire for information, whereby request formulation and reformulation (R) may occur. The query denotes reformulation or transformations (Q) of the request(s) for information, in the form required by the actual IR technique. At search time, the IR technique and user request and query (re)formulation interact.

The model reflects the typical pre-Web and pre-PC research situation strongly involving a human intermediary or an interface construct consisting of intermediary knowledge and functionalities—see also the MONSTRAT and Mediator models (Section on "Cognitive Structures and Actors"). The model points to a number of central variables involved in IR interaction most of which were studied intensively. The text representation component and processes were the least investigated—yet note the ASK-based studies (Section on "Cognitive Structures and Actors") and the THOMAS system,[4] which early on included this aspect.

Wilson's model: Wilson[5] summarized the central user-oriented or cognitive research models associated with information behavior studies, including interactive IR. His overall model, Figure 4.2, demonstrates the nesting of the central concepts, hereby also showing their contextual nature.

The central idea in Wilson's model is that interactive IR always takes place in the context of information seeking that again constitutes one of several information behavioral activities. As Wilson saw it, many IR models were basically confined to IR (the Laboratory Model) or IIR—not covering the information seeking process. A limitation of such models would be—as they contain strong elements of IR systems—that they do not explicitly point to softer seeking processes "not" involving formal information channels. The model points to ideas about which kind of behavioral processes that are distinctively "not" seeking processes as, for instance, communication and generation. Wilson's model depicted in Figure 4.2 contains, as an added feature, also the underlying situational reasons for information (seeking and IIR) behavior: the notions of "daily life interests" and "work task."

Relevance Models

The concept of relevance has been a difficult issue in information science and IR through the years. It received a lot of attention in the 1960s and 1970s—as reflected in Saracevic's[6] review. The main orientations in the notion of relevance were found early: on the one hand, one may speak about topical relevance; on the other hand about user-oriented relevance. After a decline of interest in relevance in the 1970s and 1980s, there was a revival of interest in the 1990s, producing several models of relevance based on a dynamic, multidimensional, and multigraded view of relevance. Here the models by Saracevic, Cosijn, Wang and Soergel, and Borlund are discussed.

Saracevic's stratified model: Saracevic's stratified model of interaction levels[7] was inspired by the idea of users placed in a context called the "environment." The model, Table 4.1, served dual

TABLE 4.1
The Saracevic Stratified Model in Tabular Form

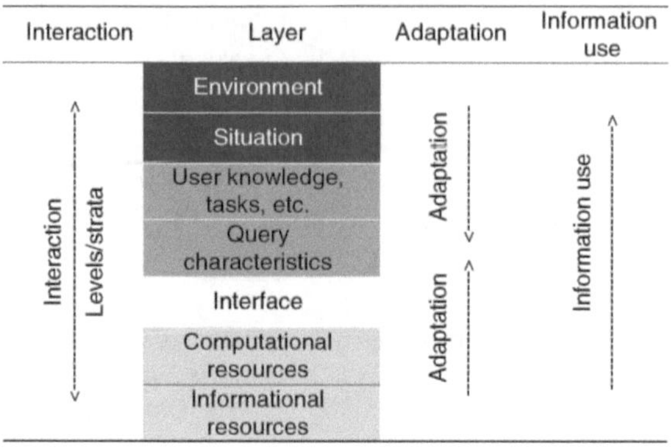

Source: Adapted from Saracevic (p. 218).

purposes: it pointed to three communication levels, and led to a revised view of the types of relevance involved in IR. The communication levels consisted of a "surface processing stratum" (light gray) dealing with data processing between sources and interface based on a query; this stratum is hence concerned with morpho-lexical and syntactic levels of information processing. The second stratum is the "interactive cognitive communication level" (gray) embracing the processes of perceiving information during human–machine interaction in relation to the perceived need for information. The third stratum is called "situational" (dark gray) and refers to information use with respect to a perceived work task in context. The latter two strata also rely on semantic and pragmatic levels of information processing.

Saracevic proposed a range of relevance types in IR interaction,[7] suggesting five increasingly subjective types of relevance: 1) "algorithmic" relevance, which is the basis for the ranked output by the search engine, and refers to the statistical and morpho-lexical relationships between request (or query) and retrieved objects; 2) "topicality," basically dealing with the aboutness relationship between document contents retrieved and request, as assessed by a person. Owing to the human assessment (interpretation) this type of relevance is not objective but rather of subjective emotional and intellectual nature; 3) "pertinence," which is associated between the nature of retrieved objects and the information need as perceived by the searcher at a given point in time; 4) "situational" relevance, corresponding to the relation between the retrieved objects and the work task (or daily-life) situation as perceived by the individual searcher; and "emotional/intentional" relevance. This stratified model became later extended to include graded relevance as an additional dimension by Spink, Greisdorf, and Bateman.[8]

The Cosijn model: Cosijn and Ingwersen[9] further developed the Saracevic model. They saw the emotional/intentional type as forming a natural part of "all" the subjective relevance categories (2–4); they also replaced it by a "socio-cognitive" relevance category referring to domain, context, and collective situational preferences. The socio-cognitive relevance by Cosijn and Ingwersen is objective and tangible. It signifies situational relevance assessments and interpretations made by "several" cognitive actors, simultaneously (like in a team or program committee) and/or temporally (citations, in-links).

Figure 4.3 integrates relevance types with the stages of an interactive IR process. Moving from the lower right-hand corner upwards signifies awareness and perception of the work task context that influences the information seeking processes turning into IR interaction and finally algorithmic IR. The opposite move implies feedback from the system and possible request and need modification as well as use of information for task performance, influenced by the simultaneous relevance

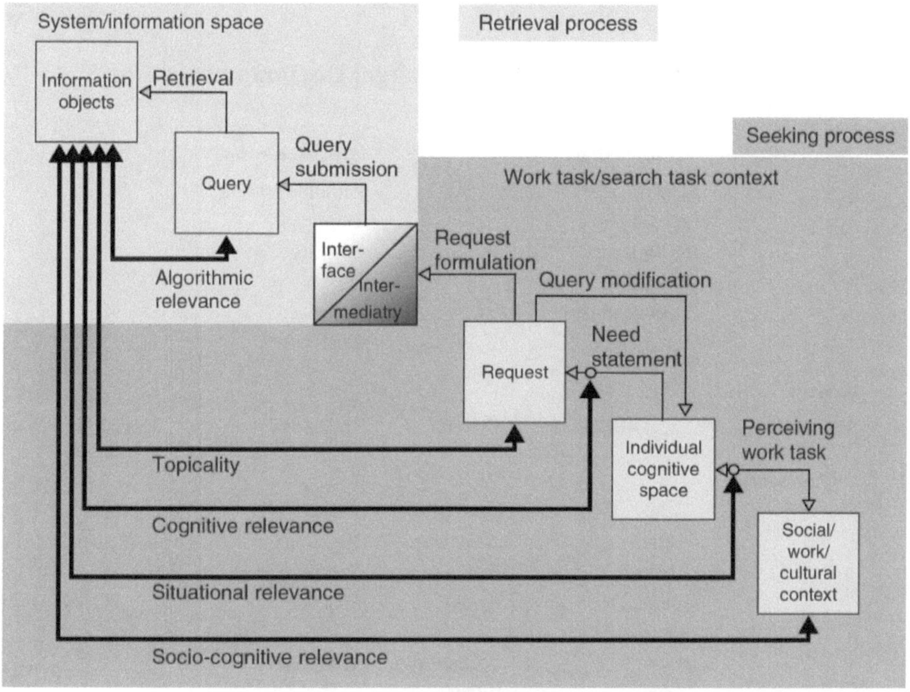

FIGURE 4.3 Integrating relevance types with the process stages of interactive IR. (Based on *Relevance Judgements in Information Retrieval*, by E. Cosijn; Ph.D. Thesis, University of Pretoria, Department of Information Science: Pretoria, South Africa, 2003 and Relevance judgements within the context of work tasks, by E. Cosijn. In *Information Interaction in Context*, Proceedings of the 1st IIiX Symposium on Information Interaction in Context, Copenhagen, Denmark, Oct 18–20, 2006; I. Ruthven et al., Eds.; Royal School of Librarianship: Copenhagen, Denmark, 2006; 20–29.)

judgments. Automatic query modification takes place in the upper left corner, based on algorithmic relevance assessment. This model suggests hypotheses on relationships between relevance types and criteria, and information seeking and retrieval processes and actions.

The Wang–Soergel model: Moving into the details of using information resulting from IIR, Wang and Soergel produced their document selection framework.[12] It was based on a longitudinal empirical study of 25 self-selected faculty and graduate students in Agricultural Economics. The framework, Table 4.2, was also a stage model. It presents in great detail the decision stages by applying 11 relevance criteria and 5 document value dimensions for the decision to select (and potentially later to use) retrieved documents. In addition, it succeeds in combining the criteria, values and decisions with the so-called "document information elements," that is, author-generated document structures and data elements as well as significant data connected to the "isness" of information objects. These are representations by additional cognitive actors responsible for the being of documents. It supplies highly interesting and novel possibilities of hypothesis generation on relationships between "structured" document "features," searcher knowledge, multiple relevance criteria, "and" perceived value(s) of documents. It supplements the Cosijn model by pinpointing to assessment variables at each point of subjective relevance judgment.

The Borlund model: Borlund summarized and discussed relevance research in Borlund.[13] Her model seeks to cover all the relevance types discussed above in an analytic manner, taking into account the temporal dimension too (Figure 4.4).

The double circle signifies that more than one actor (assessor or user) may be influenced by the same work task situation, also over time, and thus produce socio-cognitive relevance assessments. [11]

TABLE 4.2
A Tabular Representation of Wang–Soergel Document Selection Decision Stages

	Knowledge of		**Decision rules**	
	Topic		Multiple criteria	
	Person		Dominance	
	Organization		Scarcity	
	Journal			
	Document type		Satisfice	
	Elimination		Chain	
Process				
Document →	**DIEs →**	**Criteria →**	**Values →**	**Decision**
Components				
	Title	Topicality	Epistemic	Acceptance
	Author	Orientation	Functional	Maybe
	Abstract	Quality	Conditional	Rejection
	Journal	Novelty	Social	
	Series			
	Date	Availability	Emotional	
	Type	Authority		
		Relation		

Source: Adapted from Wang & Soergel (p. 118).
Note: DIEs = document information elements; Values = document values/worth.

Each actor may dynamically over time perceive the work task differently (CW–CW^n) and thus produce new versions of his or her information need (N–N^n). Algorithmic relevance (A) takes place in the real world and is objective, whereas intellectual topicality (IT), as Borlund calls "topicality," and pertinence (P) are seen as subjective manifestations of relevance. The IT curves into the actor to signify interpretation activities. The model may in addition point to other relationships

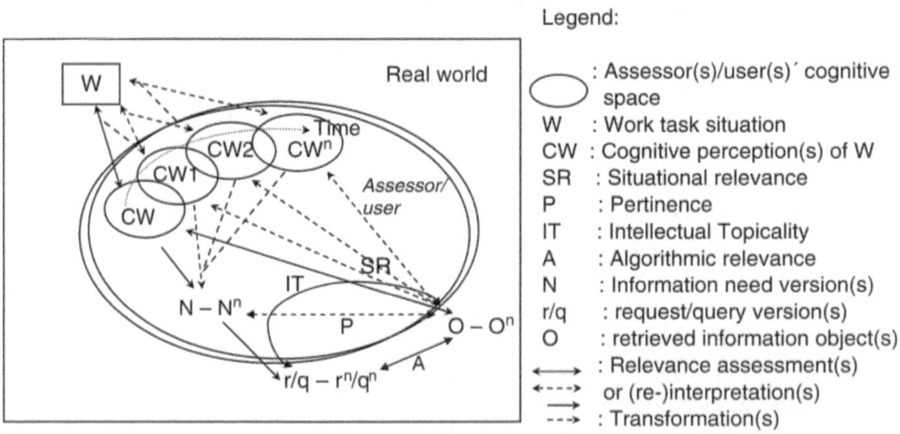

FIGURE 4.4 Types of relevance in a temporal setting. (Modified from *The Turn: Integration of Information Seeking and Retrieval in Context*, by P. Ingwersen and K. Järvelin; Springer, Dortrecht, the Netherlands, 2005 (p. 239) and Experimental components for the evaluation of interactive information retrieval systems, by P. Borlund. In J. Doc. **2000**, *56* (1), 71–90 (p. 31).)

and comparisons, for instance, between the real work task and formulated requests and queries or between the task, its fulfillment and the retrieved objects.

Online Interaction: Process Models

A number of models describe and analyze online searching, mainly in a Boolean real-life searching environment. Models by Fidel and Bates, discussed here, are representative and, owing to their generic nature, also still highly useful in the Web-IR context. They both focus on searcher's behavior in online interaction, especially on the acts (at various levels of conceptualization) that the searcher may choose to implement.

Fidel's models: Fidel and Soergel[15] developed a comprehensive model on factors affecting online bibliographic retrieval. They classified hundreds of searching variables into eight categories such as the "retrieval setting" (the organization, the status of online searching within it, the user group), the "user" (e.g., personality, education, and experience), the "request" (e.g., domain, complexity, and specificity), the "database(s)" used for searching (like coverage, structure, and cost), the "search system" (e.g., searching aids and output formats), the "searcher" (e.g., various personality features, education, and experience), the "search process" (e.g., interaction with the end-user and query formulation), and "search outcome" (recall, precision, and other measures). This model suggests a large number of variables and their possible relationships. The authors also noted that, taken individually, the variables seem to have little influence on search outcome. This model is abstract and analyzes to some degree the relationships of categories and their proposed variables. It is a specific model for all online (bibliographic) IR—but is easily usable in Web-IR environments.

In a range of empirical studies, Fidel investigated basic dimensions of online searching.[16–21] She first observed online searchers doing their regular job-related searches. This led to a characterization of "operationalist" and "conceptualist searchers" at presearch, search proper, and post-search stages (Figure 4.5). The former tended to use a large range of IR system capabilities in interaction (operational moves), focus on precision, but tended not to modify the specific meaning of requests. On the contrary, the latter tended to map requests into a faceted structure, focus on recall, and to use conceptual moves and thus modify the specific meaning of requests.

Subsequently, she analyzed the searchers' moves in interaction that are used to cut down or enlarge, or to move a search to better target it. Eighteen operational moves and a dozen conceptual moves were identified. The former keep the meaning of a search formulation intact but affect the result size or target, e.g., by limiting a search key to an index term field, adding a synonym, or by limiting by year of publication or language. The latter change the conceptual content of a search formulation, e.g., by intersecting the formulation with a new conceptual facet, by using broader or narrower index terms, etc.

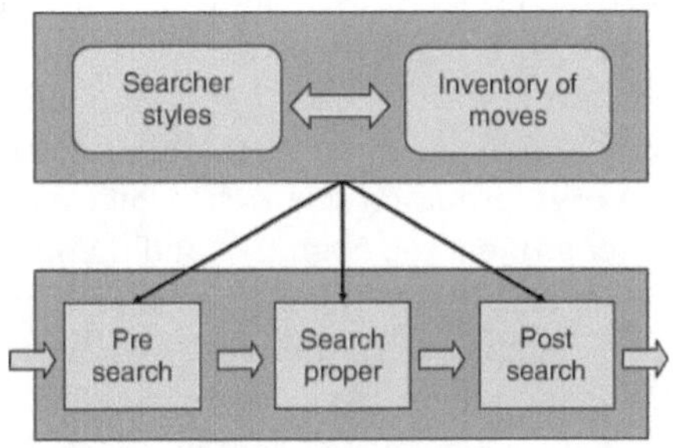

FIGURE 4.5 A simplified view of Fidel's model. (Based on Factors affecting online bibliographic retrieval: A conceptual framework for research, by R. Fidel and D. Soergel. In J. Am. Soc. Inform. Sci. 1983, *34* (3), 163–180.)

Lastly, Fidel analyzed searcher's selection of search keys and searching styles during operational online IR. Searching style was found to have a primary effect on retrieval behavior over three dimensions: level of interaction; preference for operational, or conceptual moves; and preference for text words or index terms. The "operationalist searcher" prefers to employ operational moves and is less concerned with recall than the "conceptualist" counterpart. The "free-text searcher" prefers to apply text keys and avoids consulting thesauri. In effect, Fidel's model is a model on the interaction process stages, possible searcher moves, search key selection, and searcher styles.

Bates' Berry-Picking: Bates[22,23] classified information search and idea tactics, which were intended for use in teaching and facilitating searching—seen as an interactive process using a (Boolean) IR system. In all, 29 search tactics in four categories, and 17 idea tactics were proposed. The tactics can be used to analyze what happens in a search process and to facilitate further steps in an on-going process related to Fidel's moves. The tactics themselves do not contain factors that would connect the search process to its context for analysis and explanation.

Later Bates[24] criticizes the narrow view of IR (traditional online and laboratory noninteractive) as searching based on a stable topical need. To Bates, real-life IIR was exploratory like "Berry-Picking." She developed Berry-Picking as a principle for searcher behavior that became very influential during the 1990s. The original[24] has a suggestive pictorial representation of a Berry-Picker's path leading from one patch of berries to another. In the following we describe this verbally. The principle entails that each new piece of information that searchers encounter provides them potentially with new ideas and direction to follow through interaction, and consequently a new conception of their information need. At each stage of the search, the user may identify useful information items leading her or him onwards. Therefore the user's requests and queries have several versions (Q0–Qn), which may change owing to the system feedback and user interpretation. Thus, we may here not simply talk of alternative versions of the request but also of more profound modifications. During the process the user may also repeat a query or revisit some earlier retrieved objects due to knowledge processes and cognition. Bates called this mode of retrieval an "evolving search." The information need situation is hence not satisfied by a single final retrieved set, but by a series of selections on the road, so to speak, of individual (elements of) information objects. Bates suggested several capabilities that might support users better in their various information seeking strategies than the IR systems of that time. In effect, Bates' model is an abstract descriptive model of IR interaction.

Cognitive Structures and Actors

The cognitive approach to IR produced several models of cognitive structures and actors and their interaction. The seminal ASK (Anomalous State of Knowledge) model by Belkin and colleagues, and the MONSTRAT and Mediator models by Belkin and colleagues, and Ingwersen are discussed below. The latter were part of the active development of intelligent intermediary systems for IR in the 1980s and early 1990s. Moreover, poly-representation is an important ingredient in, and a consequence of, the cognitive approach, so it is briefly presented.

The ASK model: Belkin[25–27] developed the ASK hypothesis and a concept of information for information science. The model in Table 4.3 is very general and abstract. Initially, it signified the cognitive communication system of information science[25]; later on it mapped the IR interaction at the two most important levels of cognition: the cognitive and the linguistic (surface) levels of communication.[26] In contrast to earlier and contemporary common beliefs in user studies and laboratory IR that an information need "jumps out of the blue"—is context-free—the ASK hypothesis attempted to explain "why" information need situations occur. The fundamental reason behind an ASK was the problematic situation the actor was facing if he/she could not manage to fulfill an issue or solve a problem at hand. In addition, ASK implies that the ensuing information (search) situation is dynamic and needs and requests may change with variation in cognition over retrieval session time. At the surface level of a message we have the texts (signs), which interact with the recipient. If

TABLE 4.3
The Communication System Of Information Science[25]

Linguistic Level of the System				
Generators	-->	Texts	<-->	Recipients
Cognitive Level of the System				
States of knowledge	-->	Information	<-->	ASK

Source: Adapted from Belkin.[25]
Note: Single-headed arrows (-->) denote transformations and double headed arrows (<-->) interaction.

he or she perceives the signs information is communicated at the cognitive level and the ASK is thus under change. This model led to more detailed cognitive communication models for information transfer, e.g., by Ingwersen (p. 33)[28] and further to the "bag"-models for interaction in Ingwersen (p. 33; 50).[1] Also, the ASK model led, through several empirical studies, to the MONSTRAT model by Belkin et al.[29]

The MONSTRAT and Mediator models: Belkin and colleagues followed up the work on the ASK hypothesis by a functional discourse analysis of pre-search user–librarian interactions. This led to an analysis scheme consisting of 10 categories and a number of sub-categories (Table 4.4). The meta-categories of the scheme correspond to the intermediary functions that constitute the analytic MONSTRAT model (MOdular functions based on Natural information processes for STRATegic

TABLE 4.4
Functions of the MONSTRAT Model

Name of the Function	Description
Dialogue mode (DM)	Determine appropriate dialogue type for situation, e.g., natural language, menu, form-based
Problem state (PS)	Determine position of user in problem treatment process, e.g., formulating problem for a paper (student)
Problem mode (PM)	Determine appropriate mechanism capability, e.g., reference IR or referral to institutions and persons
User model (UM)	Generate description of user type, goals, beliefs, e.g., graduate student, thesis or paper, R&D person, etc.
Problem description (PD)	Generate description of problem type, topic, structure, environment, wanted attributes in texts (doc.type)
Retrieval strategy (RS)	Choose and apply appropriate retrieval strategies to knowledge resource, e.g., exact match, best match
Response generator (RG)	Determine propositional structure of response to user appropriate to situation, e.g., list document titles
Input analyst (IA)	Convert input from user into structures usable by functional experts, e.g., parce request text, note option selection
Output generator (OG)	Convert response to a form appropriate to user and situation, e.g., display new menu, rank titles
Explanation (EX)	Describe mechanism operation, capabilities, etc. to user as appropriate

Source: Adapted from Belkin et al. (p. 399).

problem treatments) developed by Belkin et al.,[29] which, again, was the basis of active development of intelligent intermediary systems in the 1980s.[30]

Probably owing to its foundation in the analysis of search interviews the model encompasses the functionality of an interface for interactive IR but emphasizes strongly the searcher side of that device. Only the retrieval strategy, response generator and the output generator functionalities are associated with underlying IR engines and/or information sources. Hence, intelligent systems built on MONSTRAT (and similar expert system architectures) become stand-alone systems. The underlying document collection and the retrieval engine are integrated with the interface and hence not really modeled by MONSTRAT. This led Ingwersen to propose an extension to MONSTRAT, the Mediator model.[28] That model is based on 13 major functionalities and more than 50 minor ones. A rather symmetric cognitive view of the information transfer processes and knowledge types involved is reflected in the principle of the model. According to the Mediator methodology an intermediary mechanism must possess knowledge of the underlying "System Setting," including knowledge of documents, representation algorithms, database structures, etc. and the "IR processes," i.e., source selection and strategies. Symmetrically, it should contain knowledge of users and their potential preferences and expectations, IR know-how and domain knowledge (a preconditioned "User Model") and be able to carry out "Actual User and Request Model Building" during retrieval, based on the User Model. In order to be operational, it must consist of knowledge concerned with "Domains and Domain Tasks" (emotional/conceptual structures) and have "Intentionality," that is, means to store and use expectations based on past experiences and be able to plan its actions.

Ingwersen's interactive IR model: Both the MONSTRAT and the Mediator models were too early and too optimistic. In a future semantic Web context several of their functionalities may indeed work. We can probably observe some of the system-related functionalities, stressed by the Mediator model, in action in some current meta-search engines build independently on top of other remote systems and document collections, not under their direct control. This more symmetric perspective of IR interaction and transfer in general, centering on the interface–searcher interaction, is observable in the contextual models by Ingwersen,[28,31] which further explore the IR processes and components originally depicted in Figure 4.1.

Ingwersen[28,31] modeled IR interaction by incorporating the socio-organizational environment (context) of the current information searcher (Figure 4.6). That context includes the scientific or professional domain(s) with information preferences, strategies, and work tasks that influence the perception of the searcher. The model also emphasized poly-representation in documents, search engines and in the cognitive space of searchers at any point in time. Further, the model introduced the influence of context on the information and system spaces and the social interaction between socio-organizational factors and searchers. To the left the System Setting and Information Object space is also seen as context to the central interaction processes. It is in this model that cognitive actors appear for the first time, signified by the notion of "models" in each component. For instance, in the Information Object space, the variety of authors possess models of their future recipients (readers, viewers, listeners) and the Systems Setting component is intentionally geared toward information objects and searchers by models built into the algorithms. Searchers have (sometimes) models of systems and objects (expectations based on experiences) and interfaces must contain models of their potential IR systems and databases (left-hand side) and their searchers who, in turn, have models of interfaces and their socio-cultural and organizational contexts. However, the model did not explicitly demonstrate the relevance and information use dimensions of interactive IR.

Poly-representation: Ingwersen[28] developed the principle of poly-representation in close connection to cognitive models for IR. Document representation in IR systems typically supports subject access based on the contents of documents. In poly-representation, however, access to document contents is provided beyond subject matter—e.g., by form, colors, structural elements, reference, or out-link contents (anchors), citations or in-links, and a variety of metadata elements like author, employer or journal name—and sometimes supported by topical metadata added by humans. Therefore IR methods employing different representations retrieve different but overlapping results

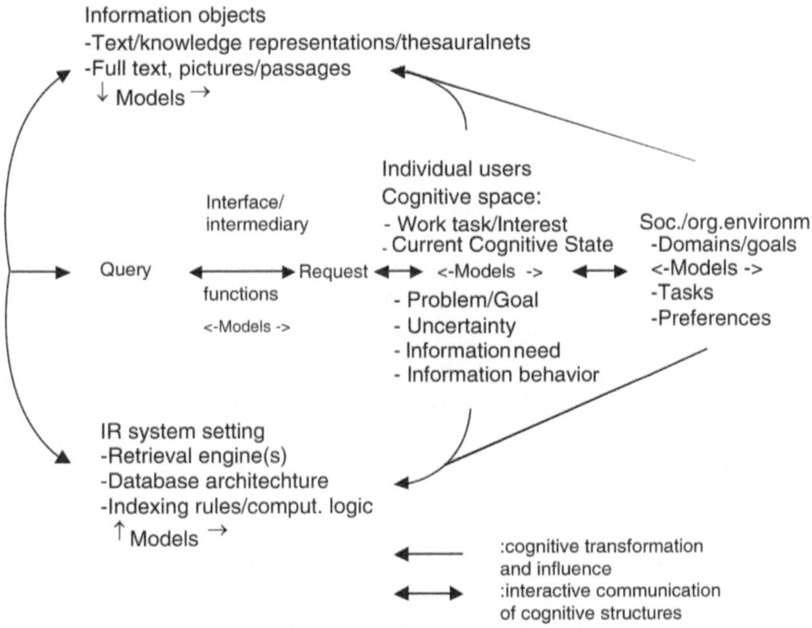

FIGURE 4.6 A cognitive model of IR interaction. (From *Information Retrieval Interaction*, P. Ingwersen; Taylor Graham, London, UK, 1992. (p. 16). Cognitive perspectives of information retrieval interaction: Elements of a cognitive IR theory, by P. Ingwersen, In J. Doc. **1996**, *52* (1), 3–50 (p. 9).)

(Figure 4.7). The overlaps may effectively be utilized for the benefit of increased precision or improved ranking of retrieval results.

Moreover, the principle of poly-representation may also be applied to the cognitive space of the information seeker in order to extract a richer context of statements to be used as search keys during IIR—not just problem and information need representations but also work task representations. Symmetrically, the poly-representation principle can be applied to data fusion by sets of

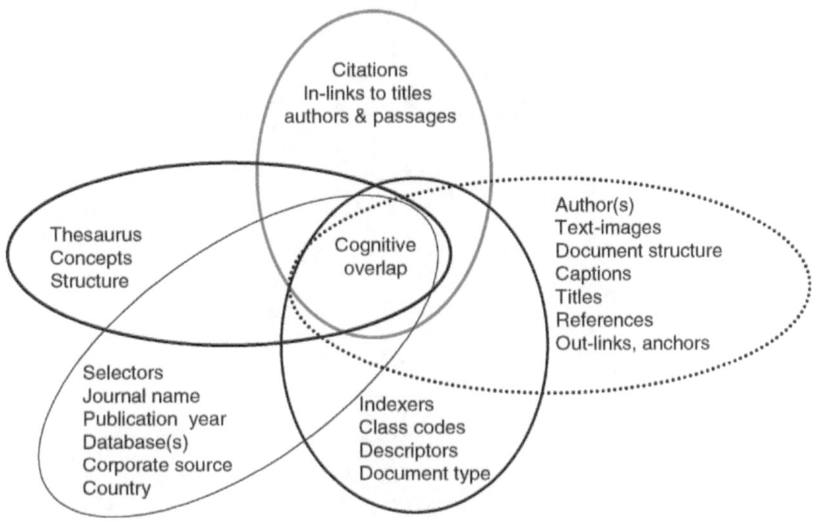

FIGURE 4.7 Principle of poly-representation of scholarly documents. Overlapping sets of information objects retrieved through different representations. (From *The Turn: Integration of Information Seeking and Retrieval in Context*, by P. Ingwersen and K. Järvelin; Springer, Dortrecht, the Netherlands, 2005 (p. 207).)

(cognitively) different but high performance search engines. The cognitive difference is signified by that the IR algorithms of the engines involved follow "very" different principles.[32]

Task-Based Models

Toward the end of the 1990s, the cognitive models of IR increasingly developed into explicitly task-based models. Vakkari[33,34] extended the Kuhlthau model of information seeking into the field of task-based IR. Ingwersen and Järvelin[1] further developed the model of Figure 4.6 into a genuine multidimensional research framework for IR and seeking studies.

Vakkari's model: Vakkari[33,34] extended the Kuhlthau Model of information seeking[35] in the field of task-based IR, based on a series of longitudinal empirical studies (Figure 4.8). His model explicates the relationships of task performance stages, kinds of information sought and its potential contribution, factors related to searching and relevance assessments and information use. In addition to the analysis explicated by the model, Vakkari showed that phases in task performance were systematically connected to the information searched for and the search tactics and usefulness of the information retrieved.

The strengths of the model include: 1) There is a clear-cut and necessary distinction between domain knowledge associated to (work) task performance, and IR knowledge; 2) Work task stages and use of information in work task performance are clearly separated from search task execution. The end product of the search task, that of relevance assessments, bridges back to the use of infor-

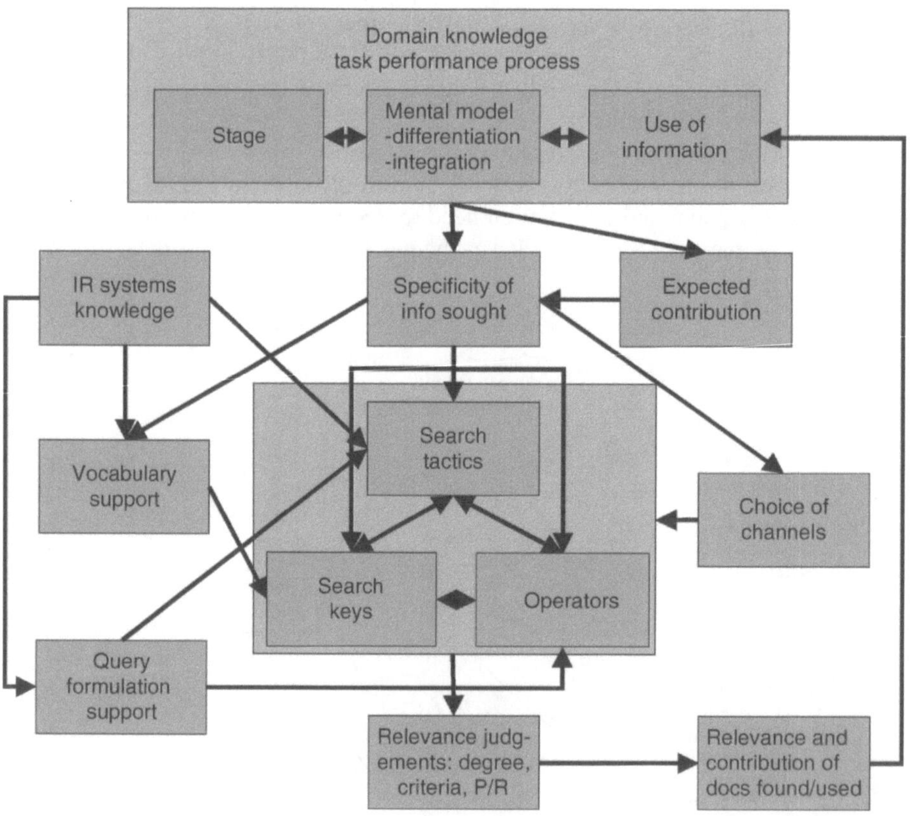

FIGURE 4.8 Stages in work and search task performance. Arrows represent the direction of impact. (Based on Changes in search tactics and relevance judgments in preparing a research proposal: A summary of findings of a longitudinal study, by P. Vakkari. In *Inform. Ret.* **2001**, *4* (3/4), 295–310 (p. 308).)

mation in task execution; 3) There exists the concept of "expected contribution," which refers to the experience gained by the actor in a historical sense.

The Ingwersen–Järvelin integrated model: Ingwersen and Järvelin (pp. 261, 274)[1] further developed and extended the cognitive and task-based IR models to a comprehensive model of information seeking and retrieval (IS&R) (Figure 4.9). Numbers on the model basically deal with processes of interaction,[1,4] such as social interaction,[1] or refer to different kinds of generation and transformation of cognition or cognitive influence.[5,8] They are explained below in more detail.

The model, Figure 4.9, emphasizes the information processes that are executed during IS&R in context over time: First, processes of social interaction[1] are found between the actor(s) and their past and present socio-cultural or organizational context. Social interaction may instigate IS&R activities, but may also form part of their fulfillment. Secondly, information interaction also takes place between the cognitive actor(s) and the cognitive manifestations embedded in the IT and the existing information objects via interfaces (2/3). The latter two components interact vertically (4) and constitute the core of an information system. This interaction only takes place at the linguistic sign level. Third, cognitive and emotional transformations and generation of potential information may occur as required by the individual actor (5/7) as well as from the social, cultural, or organizational context toward the IT and information object components (6/8) "over time." This implies a steady influence on the information behavior of other actors and hence on the cognitive–emotional structures representing them. The impact entails that actors may collaborate in teams—like in collaborative IR (CIR)—and collectively adapt to their surroundings.

The model emphasizes that all the participating cognitive structures are in context of all other cognitive components of the model. Hence, there exists a mutual dependency of context and actor or component, including intra-component structures. For instance, images in objects naturally act as context for the surrounding text and vice versa. At a more detailed level, depicted inside the nodes, the model develops further into the complexity of cognitive structures associated with its five components.

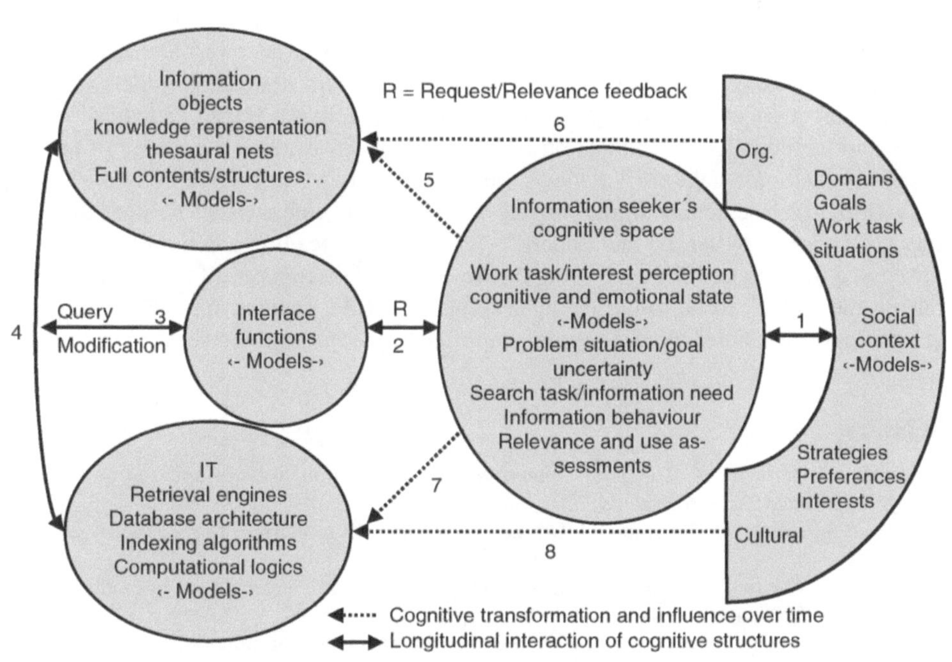

FIGURE 4.9 Cognitive framework of interactive information seeking, retrieval, and behavioral processes. (From *The Turn: Integration of Information Seeking and Retrieval in Context*, by P. Ingwersen and K. Järvelin; Springer, Dortrecht, the Netherlands, 2005 (p. 274).)

Each structure may take a different form depending on the type of information objects, media, and domain.

The framework suggests "empirical variables" that can be combined for research, and from which one may make hypotheses and predictions of potential solutions, for instance, for IR systems development or evaluation (pp. 274–275).[1] A more complete set of research variables categorized into nine dimensions extracted from this model, as well as suggestions for research designs, are discussed in Ingwersen, (pp. 313–376).[1]

CONCLUSION

In contrast to the laboratory IR model, there "must" exist several models for information seeking and interactive IR that complement one another. Which to use is dependent on the kind of IS&R processes one wishes to study, in particular via the involvement of seeking actors. The latter constitute a form and level of complexity not dealt with in system-driven information research and models.

The future may see the development of models and frameworks that increasingly encompass (task-based) context. It seems here important to stress that not only socio-cultural and organizational contexts are central to information interaction but that the system, network and information space—the systemic context—is vital for understanding such processes. Even relevant infrastructural features, like bandwidth or legislation, may necessarily form part of such contextual models.

FURTHER READING

Ingwersen and Willett[36] is an introduction to systems-oriented and cognitive approaches to IR. In addition there are early *ARIST* reviews on search techniques,[37] cognitive research,[38] and the user-oriented perspectives of IR research and analysis methods.[39] Further reviews and discussions of the cognitive approach to IR during the 1980s can be found in Belkin's overview,[40] Ellis's[41,42] critical essays on the cognitive paradigm, and in Ingwersen's[28] monograph. Belkin outlined the major contributions of analytic and empirical nature that have been rather explicitly based on the cognitive approach. The latest period sees the review on relevance research by Schamber,[43] while Efthimiadis[44] and Spink and Losee[45] provide in-depth discussions of models and empirical results of (human) query expansion and feedback issues, respectively. Harter and Hert[46] review the approaches and methods for the evaluation of information retrieval systems, also of relevance to user-oriented evaluations. Vakkari[47] reviews the issues addressed in research on task-based information searching. Web searching studies during the period and comparisons to more traditional (I) IR studies are reviewed by Jansen and Pooch.[48] Studies of the reading and use of academic literature is discussed by King and Tenopir.[49] Further reviews and discussions of the cognitive approach to IR during the 1990s can be found in Ingwersen's[50] ARIST chapter. Ingwersen and Järvelin[1] develop a synthesis of laboratory and cognitive approaches to information seeking and retrieval.

REFERENCES

1. Ingwersen, P.; Järvelin, K. *The Turn: Integration of Information Seeking and Retrieval in Context*; Springer: Dortrecht, the Netherlands, 2005.
2. Robertson, S.E.; Hancock-Beaulieu, M. On the evaluation of IR systems. Inform. Process. Manag. **1992**, *28* (4), 457–466.
3. Ingwersen, P.; Wormell, I. Means to improved subject access and representation in modern information retrieval. Libri **1988**, *38* (2), 94–119.
4. Oddy, R.N. Retrieving references by dialogue rather than by query formulation. J. Inform. Sci. **1977**, *1*, 37–53.
5. Wilson, T.D. Models in information behavior research. J. Doc. **1999**, *55* (3), 249–270.
6. Saracevic, T. Relevance: A review of and framework for the thinking on the notion in information science. J. Am. Soc. Inform. Sci. **1975**, *26* (6), 321–343.

7. Saracevic, T. Relevance reconsidered. In *Information Science: Integration in Perspective*, Proceedings of the 2nd International Conference on Conceptions of Library and Information Science (CoLIS 2), Copenhagen, Denmark, Oct 13–16, 1996; Ingwersen, P., Pors, N.O., Eds.; Royal School of Librarianship: Copenhagen, Denmark, 1996; 201–218.
8. Spink, A.; Greisdorf, H.; Bateman, J. From highly relevant to not relevant: Examining different regions of relevance. Inform. Process. Manag. **1998**, *34* (5), 599–621.
9. Cosijn, E.; Ingwersen, P. Dimensions of relevance. Inform. Process. Manag. **2000**, *36*, 533–550.
10. Cosijn, E. *Relevance Judgements in Information Retrieval*; Ph.D. Thesis, University of Pretoria, Department of Information Science: Pretoria, South Africa, 2003.
11. Cosijn, E. Relevance judgements within the context of work tasks. In *Information Interaction in Context*, Proceedings of the 1st IIiX Symposium on Information Interaction in Context, Copenhagen, Denmark, Oct 18–20, 2006; Ruthven, I. et al., Eds.; Royal School of Librarian-ship: Copenhagen, Denmark, 2006; 20–29.
12. Wang, P.; Soergel, D. A cognitive model of document use during a research project: Study I: document selection. J. Am. Soc. Inform. Sci. **1998**, *49* (2), 115–133.
13. Borlund, P. The concept of relevance in IR. J. Am. Soc. Inform. Sci. Technol. **2003**, *54* (10), 913–925.
14. Borlund, P. Experimental components for the evaluation of interactive information retrieval systems. J. Doc. **2000**, *56* (1), 71–90.
15. Fidel, R.; Soergel, D. Factors affecting online bibliographic retrieval: A conceptual framework for research. J. Am. Soc. Inform. Sci. **1983**, *34* (3), 163–180.
16. Fidel, R. Online searching styles: A case-study-based model of searching behavior. J. Am. Soc. Inform. Sci. **1984a**, *35* (4), 211–221.
17. Fidel, R. The case study method: A case study. Libr. Inform. Sci. Res. **1984b**, *6* (3), 273–288.
18. Fidel, R. Moves in online searching. Online Rev. **1985**, *9* (1), 61–74.
19. Fidel, R. Searchers' selection of search keys, I: The selection routine. J. Am. Soc. Inform. Sci. **1991**, *42* (7), 490–500.
20. Fidel, R. Searchers' selection of search keys: II: Controlled vocabulary or free-text searching. J. Am. Soc. Inform. Sci. **1991**, *42* (7), 501–514.
21. Fidel, R. Searchers' selection of search keys: III: Cearch-ing styles. J. Am. Soc. Inform. Sci. **1991**, *42* (7), 515–527.
22. Bates, M.J. Information search tactics. J. Am. Soc. Inform. Sci. **1979**, *30* (4), 205–214.
23. Bates, M.J. Idea tactics. J. Am. Soc. Inform. Sci. **1979**, *30* (5), 280–289.
24. Bates, M.J. The design of browsing and berrypicking techniques for the online search interface. Online Rev. **1989**, *13* (5), 407–424.
25. Belkin, N.J. Information concepts for information science. J. Doc. **1978**, *34* (1), 55–85.
26. Belkin, N.J.; Oddy, R.N.; Brooks, H.M. Ask for information retrieval: Part 1. J. Doc. **1982**, *38* (2), 61–71.
27. Belkin, N.J.; Oddy, R.N.; Brooks, H. ASK for information retrieval: Part 2. J. Doc. **1982**, *38* (3), 145–164.
28. Ingwersen, P. *Information Retrieval Interaction*; Taylor Graham: London, 1992.
29. Belkin, N.J.; Seeger, T.; Wersig, G. Distributed expert problem treatment as a model for information systems analysis and design. J. Inform. Sci. Prin. Pract. **1983**, *5*, 153–167.
30. Belkin, N.J.; Borgman, C.L.; Brooks, H.M.; Bylander, T.; Croft, W.B.; Daniels, P.J.; Deerwester, S.; Fox, E.A.; Ingwersen, P.; Rada, R.; Sparck Jones, K.; Thompson, R.; Walker, D. Distributed expert-based information systems: an interdisciplinary approach. Inform. Process. Manag. **1987**, *23* (5), 395–409.
31. Ingwersen, P. Cognitive perspectives of information retrieval interaction: Elements of a cognitive IR theory. J. Doc. **1996**, *52* (1), 3–50.
32. Larsen, B.; Ingwersen, P.; Kekäläinen, J. The polyrepre-sentation continuum in IR. In *Information Interaction in Context*, Proceedings of the 1st IIiX Symposium on Information Interaction in Context, Copenhagen, Denmark, Oct 18–20, 2006; Ruthven, I. et al., Eds.; Royal School of Librarianship: Copenhagen, Denmark, 2006; 88–96.
33. Vakkari, P. A theory of the task-based information retrieval process: A summary and generalization of a longitudinal study. J. Doc. **2001**, *57* (1), 44–60.
34. Vakkari, P. Changes in search tactics and relevance judgments in preparing a research proposal: A summary of findings of a longitudinal study. Inform. Ret. **2001**, *4* (3/4), 295–310.
35. Kuhlthau, C.C. *Seeking Meaning*; Ablex: Norwood, NJ, 1993.
36. Ingwersen, P.; Willett, P. An introduction to algorithmic and cognitive approaches for information retrieval. Libri **1995**, *45* (3/4), 160–177.
37. Bates, M.J. Search techniques. In *Annual Review of Information Science and Technology*; Williams, M.E., Ed.; Learned Information: Medford, NJ, 1981; Vol. 16, 139–169.

38. Allen, B.L. Cognitive research in information science: Implications for design. In *Annual Review of Information Science and Technology*; Williams, M.E., Ed.; Learned Information: Medford, NJ, 1991; Vol. 26, 3–37.
39. Sugar, W. User-centered perspective of information retrieval research and analysis methods. In *Annual Review of Information Science and Technology*; Williams, M.E., Ed.; Information Today: Medford, NJ, 1995; Vol. 30, 77–109.
40. Belkin, N.J. The cognitive viewpoint in information science. J. Inform. Sci.: Prin. Pract. **1990**, *16* (1), 11–15.
41. Ellis, D. A behavioural approach to information retrieval design. J. Doc. **1989**, *45* (3), 171–212.
42. Ellis, D. The physical and cognitive paradigms in information retrieval research. J. Doc. **1992**, *48* (1), 45–64.
43. Schamber, L. Relevance and information behavior. In *Annual Review of Information Science and Technology*; Williams, M.E., Ed.; Learned Information: Medford, NJ, 1994; Vol. 29, 3–48.
44. Efthimiadis, E.N. Query expansion. In *Annual Review of Information Science and Technology*; Williams, M.E., Ed.; Information Today: Medford, NJ, 1996; Vol. 31, 121–187.
45. Spink, A.; Losee, R.M. Feedback in information retrieval. In *Annual Review of Information Science and Technology*; Williams, M.E., Ed.; Information Today: Medford, NJ, 1996; Vol. 31, 33–78.
46. Harter, S.P.; Hert, C.A. Evaluation of information retrieval systems: Approaches, issues, and methods. In *Annual Review of Information Science and Technology*; Williams, M.E., Ed.; Information Today: Medford, NJ, 1997; Vol. 32, 3–94.
47. Vakkari, P. Task based information searching. In *Annual Review of Information Science and Technology*; Cronin, B., Ed.; Information Today: Medford, NJ, 2003; Vol. 37, 413–460.
48. Jansen, B.J.; Pooch, U. A review of Web searching studies and a framework for future research. J. Am. Soc. Inform. Sci. **2001**, *52* (3), 235–246.
49. King, D.W.; Tenopir, C. Using and reading scholarly literature. In *Annual Review of Information Science and Technology*; Williams, M.E., Ed.; Information Today: Medford, NJ, 2001; Vol. 34, 423–477.
50. Ingwersen, P. Cognitive information retrieval. In *Annual Review of Information Science and Technology*; Williams, M.E., Ed.; Information Today: Medford, NJ, 2001; Vol. 34, 3–52.

5 User-Centered Design of Information Systems

Elaine G. Toms

CONTENTS

INTRODUCTION

Rationale, Definition, and Scope

User-Centered Design (UCD) was founded on the premise that knowledge of users and their participation in the way systems are designed is essential.[1] User-centered design is a "multidisciplinary design approach based on the active involvement of users to improve the understanding of user and task requirements, and the interaction of user design and evaluation."[2] The emphasis is on "quality in use," the ultimate goal of a UCD process. This is not merely about pandering to the wants of the consumer (i.e., developing what sells), as the marketplace is littered with market flops; it is about understanding and uncovering the current and prospective needs of the user, and developing solutions that do not "frustrate, cost, confuse, irritate, and kill us."[3] It is not to be confused with making products "user friendly," a phrase that conjures up a rather pedantic notion of design, while at the same time making an implicit assessment about the "unfriendliness" of early systems.[4] The UCD approach was intended to make systems that are "easy to buy, easy to unpack, easy to set up, easy to upgrade, easy to learn, easy to use, engaging, intuitive, and integrated.[5]

As a result of this human-machine mix, UCD is inherently inter- and multidisciplinary, drawing from a blend of psychology, computer science, artificial intelligence, linguistics, anthropology, and sociology,[6] and in recent years particularly with web developments, graphic design, and animation as well as information science and business.

This entry first provides background on the genesis of UCD, following by a section on the philosophy and theoretical underpinnings of UCD, and then a description of the method as it is generally practiced.

Foundations

Traditionally systems design and development followed a system-centered, expert-driven methodology in which a set of requirements were defined at the beginning of a project, and the development process unfolded in a linear fashion from the list of specifications (i.e., what the system is supposed to be able to do) to the final product. This was adequate while systems were used by experts. With the emergence of end-user computing, users—the average people on the street—were unable to use products that resulted from such a process. The problems lay in the design of the user-interface, that part of the system that is visible to the user and with which the user interacts with the system. Users made mistakes, did not understand how to proceed, and could not figure out how to complete a task. The final assessment was that insufficient effort had been placed in understanding how users typically behave and perform the tasks for which the product was designed. In short, users were too much of an afterthought in the design process.

One of the earliest advocates of a focus on people first was Don Norman, a cognitive psychologist, who observed how people used many products including refrigerators, stoves, teapots, and doors as well as all sorts of electronic and digital devices.[7] Norman noted the mismatch between what the system expected the user to do, and what users typically do when faced with possible choices. Sometimes the product lacked an appropriate affordance, the property of a product which suggests what to do with it (compare a door knob which suggests twisting, with a lever-style handle). Sometimes there were no visible cues as to what to do next or a mismatch between what the user expected to do, and what appeared to be available (consider even today's cell phones, in which some phones are turned on by pressing "end," or turned off by pressing "start"). Sometimes the system provided no feedback as to whether anything had occurred when a user pressed a button, clicked on a menu choice, or issued a command (the "loading page" feedback mechanism within today's web browsers show the extent to which the browser has loaded the page). In those early days (and to a certain extent today), the user's conceptual model of the system, that is the user's notion of how the system should work, did not match how the system actually functioned. Emerging out of this understanding was the need for more UCDs. "Know thy user"[8] became the mantra, and often appended is the phrase "for they are not you," a statement directed at system developers.

User-centered design can be traced back to the 1960s when human factors started to address the way that scientists and engineers interacted with costly large mainframe computer systems; this was primarily but not solely related to the ergonomics of the hardware. The concept of the interface was limited in scope, as the interface was solely for command-line interaction, in which the system provided a prompt, and the user entered a response or command; the cost was strictly in programmers' time which was inexpensive when compared with the cost of the technology.

By the late 1970s to early 1980s, personal computers made word processing, spreadsheet manipulation, and simple graphics creation accessible to the person on the street. In 1981 IBM introduced its personal computer for home and small business users who had knowledge of the application domain, but no interest in the internal workings of the computer, unlike the typical computer users of the previous era. The concept of the graphical user interface or GUI (as in "gooey," as it was fondly called), emerged and, and with it, the demand for more user centered technologies.

The need to support the end user brought an increased awareness of the need to understand simply how people function: their cognitive processes, including motor learning, problem solving, semantic memory, and perception, and how these processes affect peoples' use of technologies. Human-computer interaction (HCI) emerged as a discipline and the Association of Computing

Machinery established the Special Interest Group on Computer-Human Interaction (SIGCHI) devoted to promoting human factors in the human-computer interaction process. UCD and HCI are sometimes used interchangeably, but UCD is a methodology of HCI.

Two core publications of the mid-1980s focused attention on the UCD problem. Norman and Draper's[6] edited monograph, *User Centered Systems Design* emerged out of a workshop at the University of California, San Diego in 1984 (and included a blue ribbon group of human-computer interaction pioneers). In the introduction, the two editors expressed their goals for the book, which have become the underlying foundation of UCD:

> We wish to . . . ask what the goals and needs of the users are, what tools they need, what kind of tasks they wish to perform, and what methods they would prefer to use. We would like to start with the users and to work from there.[9]

This was, at the time, a novel idea, but this book was the first consolidated synthesis to an emerging concept. At about the same time, Gould and Lewis outlined three core principles for design that included a focus on users, empirical measurement, and iterative design.[10] These have stood the test of time, and today serve as the basis for much of UCD practice. Emerging from this work was the concept of usability, and as already stated was not to be confused with user friendly. Making systems usable is a more complex construct that includes learnability, efficiency, memorability, being error-free, and subjectively pleasing.[11]

The 1980s also saw the emergence of a new type of information system for the information consumer. With the introduction of CD-ROM technology, large bibliographic databases which were formerly only accessible to expert intermediaries and domain experts willing to learn a cryptic code were now reachable by working domain professionals (e.g., scientists, lawyers, doctors, journalists) who had limited computer expertise within months, the former databases that contained abstracts and bibliographic citations to published newspaper, journals, and technical publications evolved into full-text systems, also available initially on CD-ROMs and later on mainframe systems with client-side graphical user interfaces.

At about the same time, how society, organizations, and culture shape the use of technology was being noticed. This introduced the importance of context: the situation in which the technology is being used affects that use and must be attended to within the design process. Suchman's groundbreaking study of the lowly photocopier identified how situatedness affected human social behavior in the context of technology use.[12] As a result, the need to integrate those influences called for more social and organizational analyses to be included in the design process. The concept of user incorporated more that the qualities of the individual.

By the 1990s, technology was not solely about transactional based technologies with structured data (e.g., numbers, codes) as its core; the emergence of the Internet and Web "informational" systems provided access to unstructured information (think text rather than numbers) that included ordinary homepages, newspapers, and the complete contents of books, journals, and videos. This placed new design needs on the concept of the user, the user's task, and the environment in which the user was situated. With the emergence of the Web, the custodians of information—from publishers to libraries, from government to the not-for-profit sector and e-commerce— had to re-think and transform their existing approaches to systems development.

Surprisingly, early technological developments did not match expectations in terms of increased productivity. Landauer claimed that the problem lay with inadequate engineering design for application software which was due to the lack of systematic testing of technologies in terms of their actual utility.[13] Instead he asserted that too much attention was focused on characteristics such as the speed of technology, its data storage capacity, the flawless operation of the technology, the number of features implemented, and its graphics quality. He argued for more testing of the ability of the technology to assist people in doing the work they needed to do. Despite the plethora of usability testing that was emerging at this time, Landauer claimed that too much of that testing was being devoted to aspects of the interface that would affect sales such as color and gadgetry, rather than addressing the formal functionality and usability of the system. Even today, customer satisfaction is considered the core success factor in assessing UCD processes internally.[14]

By the twenty-first century, the focus was all about the user or customer, as e-commerce entered the arena; the economic consequences of non-user oriented technologies now had a direct effect on a firm's economic survival. Users now "marched" with their mice from one non-usable Web site or e-commerce storefront to another. With the emergence of the Web, social computing enabled users to not just march with their mice, but also to complain, comment, and compliment technologies and services in listservs, blogs, wikis, and consumer-oriented Web sites.

Companies and organizations could no longer hide behind a poor technology. Today UCD is practiced by a range of systems developers including IBM, Microsoft, Google, Apple, and SAP. It has been a cornerstone of operations within IBM.[15] Within the information world, and libraries in particular, the concept of UCD came late, since most of the systems used by this group are produced by third-party vendors who have a limited marketplace for their products, and thus limited resources to apply to UCD. For example, it was not until 1990 that OCLC created its Usability Lab.

Emerging from this history was UCD as both a philosophy and a process. As a basic principle, UCD places the person—the user, and not the system at the center of systems development.

It is a process that considers cognitive factors (such as perception, memory, learning, problem-solving, etc.) as a core influence on a person's interaction with an object. This concept is as relevant to the design of teapots as it is to the computer mouse, word processors, search engines, and web-casting systems, and to the myriad of information appliances that are emerging in the marketplace.

PHILOSOPHY

Central to UCD is the conceptual foundation on which it is built. In this section, the three core concepts: information system, design, and user referenced by UCD, are defined and then integrated into the core theoretical perspective that underpins UCD.

Information System

Information system is a complex term. It is an application of computing and information technology developed to meet a defined need or purpose. The term is used to include the database and application programs as well as the procedures used to manipulate the database in concert with the application programs, and the hardware (e.g., computers, printers, telecommunication devices, and networks) used for processing data and information.

Information system is often identified with business applications, in particular, transaction processing systems such as payroll, book lending, and interlibrary loan systems. These could be classed as operational systems intended for planning and control within an organization. But the term information system is also used and continues to be used for both tactical and strategic information systems such as decision-support systems, executive information systems, and financial systems.

With the emergence of the Web in particular, information system is now used not just to reference transaction-based systems that manipulate structured data. When technology enabled mass storage and the ability to completely represent and present an information object (rather than just to access to its metadata), information systems enabled and facilitated many human information processes: finding, reading, synthesizing, evaluating, and so on of unstructured information. Now the range of tasks supported by information systems spans routine operations of, for example, automatic bank machines, to complex decision-making and problem-solving systems that require extensive backtracking and digressions.

This description above specifies the entire system, from a UCD perspective, the system begins with that aspect seen by the user—the user interface.

Design

User-centered design, as a philosophy, has its roots in industrial and architectural design. Design emerged around the fourteenth to fifteenth centuries, although there is no specific event to which this concept is attached.[16] Design arose with "the separation of thinking and doing"[16] after the work of master craftsmen, for example, was divided into architects and builders, and today that distinction can be used to separate designers from programmers in systems development.

The word design may be interpreted in multiple ways: on the one hand it specifies the process used, while on the other it references the arrangement of all of the components contained in the design. Design is imposed, and "only when the constituent parts of a whole have the unique end of contributing to the consummation of a conscious experience, do design and shape lose super-imposed character and become form."[17] Dewey was talking about art, but the same sentiment is true of systems design. Eames took a more pragmatic approach in referring to design as "a plan for arranging elements in such a way as to best accomplish a particular purpose."[18] The end product of a design is not purely a visual object, but a complex artifact that may support one or all of the senses depending on its purpose. From a systems design perspective, when all of the elements, procedures, and objects work in harmony, the system almost "disappears" as the user is "one" with the visible components.

In practice systems design stems from industrial design with a focus on the action and activities that define the purpose of the product. As such design involves a two-stage process: the first is a conceptual process to identify what the product is expected to do and how the action will unfold; and the second is the physical where the conceptual elements are rendered into real-world objects, such as layout, menu labels, icons, and buttons. The lines between the conceptual and physical are blurred in UCD.

User

Early users of information systems were experts who performed often routine and predictable actions with applications. They were technically trained and technically oriented, and more than willing to learn the arcane commands or procedures required to use an application. Over time, the user became anyone who applied a set of actions to a computing device, and the designer of a system was no longer comparable to the person who would subsequently use the application.

User as a concept has met with considerable discussion. Bannon pointed out very early in the development of UCD that a user was not necessarily a person who makes only casual use of a system.[19] A novice or naive computer user may be an expert in the application domain, for example, accounting, medicine; and, sometimes a novice in the application domain may be an expert computer user.

Instead, the word, user, is a generic concept that is intended to be replaced with a specific "job" or task function as in lawyers when speaking of legal information systems, or accountants when speaking of accounting systems. But a system might also have multiple levels of expertise as a citizen, mayor, or property inspector for municipal information systems. A typical user may be classed according to many attributes such as skill level (naive vs. expert, e.g., a law student vs. a partner, a history undergraduate student vs. a history professor); and by nature of use (ad hoc or daily). Nielsen characterizes users along three dimensions: computer expertise, computer experience, and knowledge about the task domain.[11] As a result, the concept of user is more complex than one imagines which somewhat explains the nature of UCD methodology (discussed later on).

Particularly within the engineering community, the term "stakeholders" is preferred to reflect the broader group from implicit to explicit consumers of the system. Lodge,[20,21] classed stakeholders into six types of users: governing body, sponsor, user specified, end user, input generator (the person who will enter data into a system) and the output receiver. This nomenclature tends not to be used within the human-computer interaction and information science communities.

Conceptual Foundation of UCD

How design, user and information system are blended is reflected in the early thinkers of UCD. In what is now considered a seminal work, Moran posited that "to design the user interface of a system is to design the user's model. The designer needs to understand . . . what knowledge goes into the user's conceptual model"[22] so that ultimately the user should not have to struggle to figure out what the designer intended. This led to thinking about how users act, behave, and perceive.

Card and colleagues[23,24] proposed a "model human processor" that could be used by the designer in contemplating how a person interacts with a computer at the interface. The model included three human systems, each with its own memories and processes: 1) a perceptual system that connects a person's sensations from the physical work to internal representations in the mind; 2) a motor system that translates human thought into physical actions; and 3) a cognitive system that retrieves facts, solved problems, and selects a suitable course of actions. Notably, for some tasks, the human behaves as a serial processor (clicking on a button in response to a display), while in others, the action requires integrated, parallel operations that engage the three human systems at once (reading from and selecting from, and finally resolving the information contained on a single webpage). In addition to describing how complex and dynamic a human is, Card and colleagues specified both the typical and range of values that could be expected in human performance. In doing so they provided a standard for the measurement concerns of Gould and Lewis.[10]

At about the same time, Norman described a "theory of action" to assist in understanding how users use systems[25] as illustrated in Figure 5.1. In general, a user approaches a system with a goal likely dictated by the task to be accomplished, but personal to the individual. The goal is converted into an intention which is acted upon, and subsequently executed using the system. The system is in a certain state of readiness; imagine a computer that has just been turned on. The user perceives, interprets, and evaluates the response from the system. Norman claimed that the users' goals and the perceived state of the system had to traverse two "gulfs" before users could make use of the system to achieve their goals. Thus, when the user approaches the system, the first challenge is what action can be taken to "bridge" the Gulf of Execution. When the system responds to a user's action, the user must now interpret that response to cross the Gulf of Evaluation. In using any system, this pairing of action and evaluation is a constant and continuous process.

Design needs to account for that process as the most elegantly designed systems fail when the user is uncertain about which action to take, or the system responds with a non-interpretable reply.

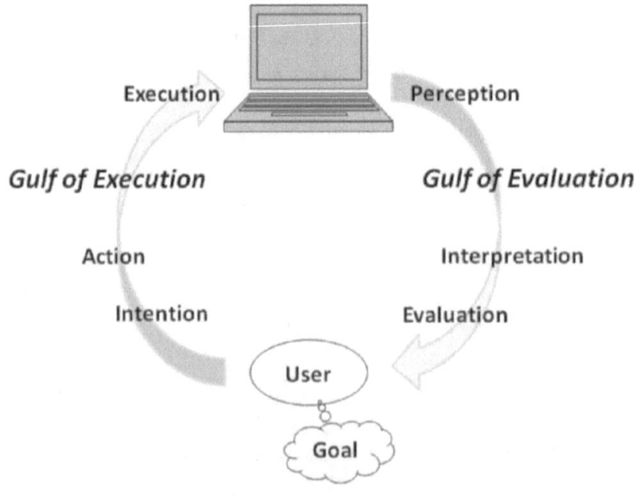

FIGURE 5.1 Norman's "Gulfs" embedded in his "theory of action" to describe how people interact with systems.[26]

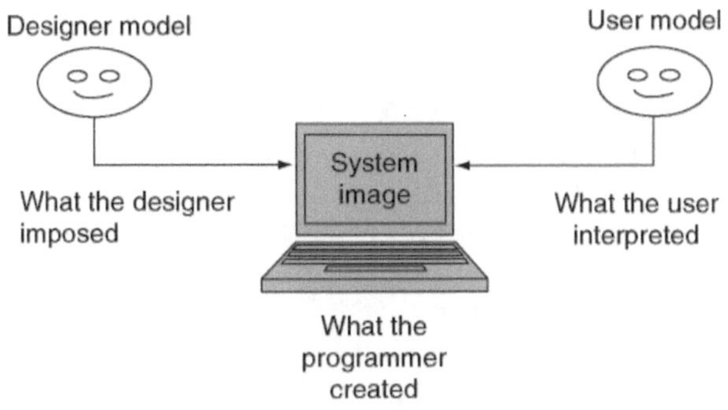

FIGURE 5.2 Designer, user, and programmers perspectives of the user.[29]

At the beginning of a project (see Figure 5.2), a designer envisions a conceptualization of the system, called the Designer Model, which is imposed on the system and is reflected in the System Image that is represented in the physical world by the user interface and represents the programmer's implementation of the designer's specifications.[27] The user approaches the user interface with a preconceived notion of what to expect; we consider this the User Model. Designers' models consist of the ideas that the designers attempt to embody in a system; the users' conceptual model is a mental representation that is formed by experience—experience with older technology, the physical world, related applications, and so on.[28,29] If the user's conceptual model is in line with the designer's model of the system, then the user is able to perform actions, and interpret responses made by the system. But when the two models are mismatched, the user is unable to bridge the Gulfs illustrated in Figure 5.1. The degree of discontinuity is directly related to how well the designer's model and the programmer's rendering of it actually match the user's model of the system. The user interface serves as the "bridge" between these two conceptual models. In general, when the designer fails to take user needs and requirements into account in the design process, the system is unlikely to succeed.

User-centered design emerged from this awareness of the tension between the designer's view of the world and the user's and is fundamentally the foundation for UCD practice. Over time, the focus on the user model morphed into the need for a full understanding of user in context— environmentally, socially, physically.[12] In more recent years, affect, the user's emotional response to systems has also emerged as a core factor in design; it is no longer sufficient for a system to be fully functional, but now needs to be "attractive" and perceived by its users as attractive as well.[29]

PROCESS

In addition to having a strong conceptual foundation, UCD defines a process—a practice or procedure—for the design of information systems. Back in 1985, Gould and Lewis[10] identified three principles that would lead to a UCD system:

1. Focus on users and their tasks early in the design phase.
2. Assess and evaluate through the design/development process.
3. Use an iterative design process so that the result can be improved over the developmental life cycle.

These have been modified and augmented over the years, and Shneiderman's principles[30] illustrated in Figure 5.3 is one of the most parsimonious examples of these.

What is believed to be the first example of UCD in practice is the 1984 Olympic Messaging System designed to provide voicemail and communication support for athletes at the Games.[31] The following brief synopsis of that work serves to illustrate the UCD process in practice.

1. Strive for consistency.
2. Enable frequent users to use shortcuts.
3. Offer informative feedback.
4. Design dialogs to yield closure.
5. Offer error prevention and simple error handling.
6. Permit easy reversal of actions.
7. Support internal locus of control.
8. Reduce short-term memory load.

FIGURE 5.3 Shneiderman's principles of UCD.[30]

At the beginning, an initial analysis of requirements was prepared and commented on by designers, managers, and prospective users. From this assessment, a number of functions that the system was expected to enable were modified, and some were removed. Simulations of these functions were tested and evaluated by the intended user groups: athletes and their friends and families. In addition, site visits to the Olympic village and interviews with those involved with the Olympics brought new information and data. Finally a prototype was build and tested with a wide range of people. Over the course of its development from the initial concept to the first prototype (and subsequently the final product), the design followed the three principles developed by Gould and Lewis.[10]

The UCD Process

Although practices may vary from organization to organization and from text to text, the International Standards Organization's standard, "Human-Centered Design Processes for Interactive Systems,"[32] describes the core elements. Written at a high conceptual level, the standard is not prescriptive, but provides guidance in the form of a five-stage model illustrated in Figure 5.4.

Plan the Human Centered Process

As suggested by the title, the intent of this stage is the development of a plan for the succeeding stages, and for how the UCD process fits within the entire systems development project. This is a living document that is updated over the life of the project.

The complexity of the plan will depend on whether the system is an innovation (i.e., nothing currently exists), replacement technologies for an existing product (e.g., word processor replaced the typewriter, and the online catalog replaced the card catalog), or a new version of an existing digital product. Thus, in some situations, the knowledge of users and their context may already be known, or the existing technology may place constraints on the design such as an application that works in

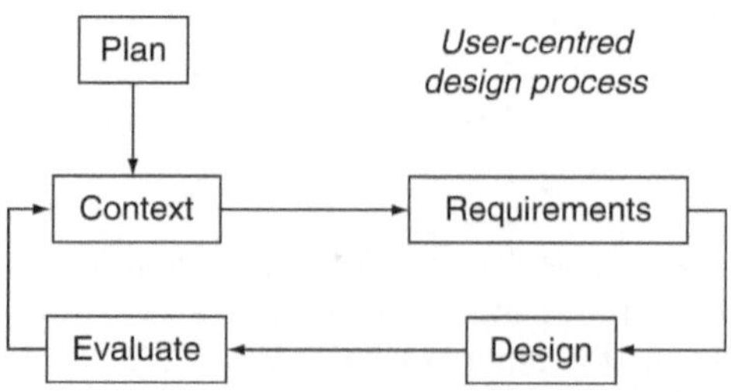

FIGURE 5.4 UCD process as described by ISO 13497.

a Windows environment rather than a Macintosh, or a technology that will be an added component to an existing application.

Understand and Specify the Context of Use

In this stage, understanding users and their tasks as well as the organizational and physical environment in which the system will be used are the core components. These will subsequently guide design rationale and additionally prescribe how evaluation—success of the product—will be measured. The context of use is described in terms of

1. Who the users are and what special characteristics they have
2. What work tasks users will need to perform, and how those tasks are interrelated, including the allocation of human and technological resources needed to complete a task
3. The matrix of user and task characteristics, so that specific scenarios of use can be described
4. The context or specific environment (including physical and social characteristics) in which the system will be used
5. The benchmarks that will be used to define both minimal and optimal requirements[32]

This stage identifies the range of intended users, the scope of their tasks and the contextual environment in which they operate. Central to this is an understanding of what the work is supposed to achieve; this is not about what the computer system is supposed to do, rather an explanation of the work task in isolation from the technology.

Specify User and Organizational Requirements

At this stage, the functional requirements of the system are specified with respect to users and the organization. What must the system do for it to be considered successful? This will describe

1. Required performance of the new system with respect to operational and financial objectives, and to relevant statutory or legislative requirements (including safety and health)
2. Task performance and its integration with work design and organization
3. Operations and maintenance feasibility[32]

This stage will document the design goals, guidelines and constraints, identify the priorities, and provide measurable criteria for testing the design, including usability criteria (e.g., efficiency, effectiveness, and satisfaction levels).

Produce Design Solutions

This stage includes devising the rough concept through to sketching and developing a complete design. This requires integrating existing knowledge and technological capability with knowledge of users and the context. It may include visual design, information architecture, and interaction design. Potential designs are

1. Created using existing standards, best practices, accepted guidelines and examples of other systems, etc.) to develop a proposed design solution
2. Rendered using simulations, low-fidelity prototypes, mock-ups, etc
3. Evaluated by users who are observed performing specified tasks, with or without the assistance of evaluators, and modified from feedback
4. Modified until design objectives (including usability objectives) are met[32]

This stage involves building a range of prototypes from low-fidelity paper prototypes, to high-fidelity prototypes that simulate the activity of the system.

Evaluate Designs against User Requirements

This stage evaluates the design with the user community using the application in a realistic environment. Depending on the number of iterations, this stage may be a formative evaluation intended to provide feedback to improve the design, or it may be summative to determine how well the system meets the criteria set out in the original plan.

These five stages are intended to be repeated as often as is required over the life of the project. Iteration and evaluation are considered critical to the success. In addition to the ISO approach, other variations have been well documented.[33–35]

Each of these five stages uses a variety of methodologies to collect the essential data required to fulfill the requirements of that particular stage. For example, in understanding context (Stage 2), a collection of formal and information techniques are used to find out what the system is intended to do. This stage usually involves a visit to the workplace and an observation of how things are currently being done, as the way work is performed is often not like the way that procedural manuals stipulate. Observation and interviewing (formal and informal) together with careful note taking and sometimes videotaping provides a wealth of data from which to identify the issues. Stage 5, the evaluation component, uses a variety of techniques depending on how many iterations of the process have been completed. Early evaluation techniques are more likely to be done with cognitive walkthroughs, and heuristic evaluation; later stages will do user testing with real users performing real tasks.

STANDARDS, PRINCIPLES, RULES, AND STYLE GUIDES

An international standard for UCD (previously discussed) specifies the design and development process, but is not the only standard relevant to UCD. ISO 16982 specifies usability methods that support "human"-centered design and is complementary to IS09241-11, *Guidance on Usability* which identifies how usability can be evaluated in terms of user performance (efficiency and effectiveness) and satisfaction. This is somewhat related to ISO 9126 which defines six categories related to software quality for the software engineering community: functionality, reliability, usability, efficiency, maintainability, and portability, as well as the overall goal of achieving quality in use. Other related standards recommend specifications for usability of consumer products (ISO 20282), icon symbols and functions (ISO 11581), pen-based interfaces (ISO 14754), mobile—PDAs—tools (ISO 18021), multimedia user interfaces (ISO 14915) (55) and documentation (ISO 15910) and a format for writing reports of usability test results (ISO 25062).

In addition to standards, a variety of principles such as the ones mentioned earlier are used. In the actual conduct of design, a number of rules or heuristics are applied such as number of items to use in menus, color and font combinations, and layout. In addition, individual organizations have developed "style guides" to prescribe how design is accomplished for products developed by that group. IBM, Microsoft, and Apple all have developed style guides for the development of software. As a result, UCD has some consistencies in practice, but could not be considered a standardized methodology.

USE AND VALUE OF UCD

The term UCD is not exclusive; some groups refer to it as customer-centered design, experience design, or usage-centered design. Raskin[36] distinguished between human centered and user-centered design. He claims a two-level design process in which the first stage is to ensure that the design relates to universal psychological attributes common to all humans, such as visibility of interface objects, amount of memorization that is acceptable, and human use of graphical elements. Once a system meets normal human physiological and psychological constraints, then the designers should attend to the task requirements of that particular user group. Raskin alleged that designers hand over responsibility for the human element to industry who is not always attuned to human capabilities.

The value of UCD is not universally understood or accepted. In a snapshot of UCD penetration among experienced practitioners, nearly three-quarters of respondents reported that UCD affected development within their organization and improved the usability of the final product.[37] However, it also provided a picture of a methodology that was not universally adopted. Often cited as a barrier to UCD practices are resources and organizational resistance, because there are no clear metrics about how to assess a UCD process. These findings result from a survey distributed in 2000 and 2001.[14] Undoubtedly with the growth in consumer digital products and the web, UCD now has greater penetration in organizations that produce consumer products. Ease of use for example, has been touted as the top factor contributing to conversion rates for Web sites, that is, getting customers to translate their visits into actions, or, in other words, purchases. Clearly in order to actually do that, one needs to adapt a UCD approach.

CONCLUSION

User-centered design is a process based on a strong conceptual foundation embedded in understanding how people function as human beings, and within the particular job function that a technology is intended to facilitate. The end product of such a process will provide a good fit between the user and the tasks that the user needs to accomplish, and the system that is intended to facilitate that activity. This is tightly integrated to a particular context that has social, political, and legal implications.

REFERENCES

1. Preece, J.; Rogers, Y.; Sharp, H.; Benyon, D.; Holland, S.; Carey, T. *Human-Computer Interaction: Concepts and Design;* Addison-Wesley: Wokingham, U.K., 1994.
2. Mao, J.-Y.; Vredenburg, K.; Smith, P.W.; Carey, T. The state of user-centered design practice. Commun. ACM **2005**, *48* (3), 105.
3. Cooper, A. *The Inmates are Running the Asylum;* SAMS: Indianapolis, IN, 1999; 17.
4. Winograd, T.; Flores, F. *Understanding Computers and Cognition: A New Foundation for Design*; Addison-Wesley: Reading, MA, 1987.
5. Vredenburg, K. Increasing ease of use. Commun. ACM **1999**, *42* (5), 67.
6. Norman, D.A.; Draper, S.W. (Eds.). *User Centered System Design: New Perspectives on Human-Computer-Interaction*; Erlbaum: Hillsdale, NJ, 1986.
7. Norman, D.A. *The Psychology of Everyday Things;* Doubleday: New York, 1988.
8. Hansen, W.J. User engineering principles for interactive systems. In Proceedings of the May 16–18, 1972, Spring Joint Computer Conference, Atlantic City, NJ, May 16–18, 1972, AFIPS '72; ACM: New York, 523–532.
9. Norman, D.A.; Draper, S.W. (Eds.). *User Centered System Design: New Perspectives on Human-Computer-Interaction*; Erlbaum: Hillsdale, NJ, 1986, 2.
10. Gould, J.D.; Lewis, C. Designing for usability: Key principles and what designers think. Commun. ACM **1985**, *28* (3), 300–311.
11. Nielsen, J. *Usability Engineering;* Academic Press: Boston, 1993.
12. Suchman, L. *Plans and Situated Actions: The Problem of Human Machine Communication*; Cambridge University Press: Cambridge, U.K., 1987.
13. Landauer, T.K. *The Trouble with Computers: Usefulness, Usability and Productivity*; MIT Press: Cambridge, MA, 1996.
14. Vredenburg, K.; Mao, J.-K.; Smith, P.W.; Carey, T. A survey of user-centered design practice. In Proceedings of the SIGCHI Conference on Human Factors in Computing Systems: Changing Our World, Changing Ourselves, Minneapolis, MN, April 20–25, 2002, CHI '02; ACM: New York; 471–178.
15. Vredenburg, K. Increasing ease of use. Commun. ACM **1999**, *42* (5), 67–71.
16. Cooley, M. Human-centered design. In *Information Design;* Jacobson, R., Ed.; MIT Press: Cambridge, MA, 2000; 59–81.
17. Dewey, J. *Art as Experience;* Penguin: New York, 1934, reprinted 2005; 122.
18. Eames, C. *Design Q&A;* (Color film directed by Charles Eames), 1972.

19. Bannon, L. From human factors to human actors: The role of psychology and human-computer interaction studies in systems design. In *Design at Work: Cooperative Design of Computer Systems;* Greenbaum, J., Kyng, M., Eds.; Lawrence Erlbaum Associates: Hillsdale, NJ, 1990; 25–44.
20. Lodge, L. A user led model of systems development. In *Participation in Systems Development;* Knight, K., Ed.; UNICOM Applied IT Reports, Kogan Page: London, 1989.
21. Smith, A. *Human Computer Factors: A Study of Users and Information Systems*; McGraw Hill: London, 1997.
22. Moran, T.P. The command language grammar: A representation for the use interface of interactive computer systems. Int. J. Man-Machine Stud. **1981**, *15*, 3–50.
23. Card, S.K.; Moran, T.P.; Newell, A. *The Psychology of Human-Computer Interaction;* Lawrence Erlbaum Associates: Hillsdale, NJ, 1983.
24. Newell, A.; Card, S.K. The prospects for psychological science in human-computer interaction. Hum-Comp. Interact. **1985**, *1* (3), 209–242.
25. Norman, D.A. Cognitive engineering. In *User-Centered System Design: New Perspectives on Human-Computer-Interaction;* Norman, D.A., Draper, S.W., Eds.; Erlbaum: Hillsdale, NJ, 1986; 31–61.
26. Norman, D.A. Cognitive engineering. In *User-Centered System Design: New Perspectives on Human-Computer-Interaction;* Norman, D.A., Draper, S.W., Eds.; Erlbaum: Hillsdale, NJ, 1986; 39, 40, 42.
27. Norman, D.A. Cognitive engineering. In *User-Centered System Design: New Perspectives on Human-Computer-Interaction;* Norman, D.A., Draper, S.W., Eds.; Erlbaum: Hillsdale, NJ, 1986; 46.
28. Carroll, J.M. Mental Models and Software human factors: an overview. Yorktown, NY: IBM Watson Research Centre, Research Report RC 10616, 1984.
29. Norman, D.A. *Emotional Design: Why We Love (or Hate) Everyday Things*; Basic Books: New York, 2004.
30. Shneiderman, B. *Designing the User Interface: Strategies for Effective Human-Computer Interaction*, 3rd Ed.; Addison Wesley: Menlo Park, CA, 1997.
31. Gould, J.D.; Boies, S.J.; Levy, S.; Richards, J.T.; Schoonard, J. The 1984 Olympic message system: A test of behavioral principle of system design. Commun. ACM **1987**, *30* (9), 758–769.
32. ISO/IEC. 13407, Human-centred design processes for interactive systems, ISO/IEC 13407; 1999.
33. Vredenburg, K.; Isensee, S.; Righi, C. *User-Centered Design: An Integrated Approach;* Prentice Hall: Upper Saddle River, NJ, 2002.
34. Rosson, M.B.; Carroll, J.M. *Usability Engineering. Scenario-Based Development of Human-Computer Interaction*; Academic Press: San Diego, CA, 2002.
35. Mayhew, D.J. *The Usability Engineering Lifecycle: A Practitioner's Handbook for User Interface Design*; Morgan Kaufman: San Francisco, 1999.
36. Raskin, J. *The Humane Interface: New Directions for Designing Interactive Systems*; Addison-Wesley: Boston, 2000.
37. Mao, J-Y.; Vredenburg, K.; Smith, P.W.; Carey, T. The state of user-centered design practice. Commun. ACM **2005**, *48* (3), 105–109.

6 Ethical Issues in Information Systems

Vladimir Zwass

CONTENTS

INTRODUCTION

Information technology offers potent tools that can serve to fulfill an individual's life, to further organizational goals, pursue national and international interest, or support environmentally sustainable regional development. The same technology can also be used to infringe on property in a digital form, invade individuals' private sphere, and to hold them in fear of omnipresent surveillance. The way the technology is deployed depends on our decisions as professionals and as users of information systems. It also depends on the enacted policies and legislation. All of us, therefore, should make the relevant decisions guided not only by the economic, organizational, and technological aspects of information systems, but also in consideration of their effects on individuals. Our knowledge of ethics helps us in making such decisions. Further, this knowledge can inform the evolution of the relevant public and organizational policies. What we may call infoethics is the application of ethical thinking to the development and use of information systems.

Ethics and Codes of Ethics

Ethics is a study of the principles of right and wrong that ought to guide human conduct. Ethics concerns itself with what values are worth pursuing in life and what acts are right. Therefore, ethics is a study of morality.

Human behavior and decision making fall into three domains, shown in Figure 6.1. The legal domain governs a variety of relatively well defined behaviors, specified by law enforceable in the courts of a given country or within a local jurisdiction. International bodies increasingly address legal issues that cross national borders. Computer crime and abuse, such as the destructive deployment of malware (e.g., computer viruses or worms) or misrepresentation of electronic identity toward financial gain, are the breaches of law and fall into this domain.

However, not every legal action is ethical. The domain of ethics is governed by the general norms of behavior and by specific codes of ethics. To see whether your decision making in a given case involves an ethical issue, you may apply the "sunshine test": "What if I read about my decisions and subsequent actions in tomorrow's paper?" Ethical considerations go beyond legal liability, and the breach of norms not punishable by law meets with social opprobrium. Only if the action is both legal and ethical, does it fall in the discretionary domain, where we properly act entirely according to our preferences.

Knowledge of ethics as it applies to the issues arising from the development and use of information systems, which we may call infoethics, helps us to make decisions in our professional life. Professional knowledge is generally assumed to confer a special responsibility in its domain. This is why the professions have evolved codes of ethics, that is, sets of principles intended to guide the conduct of the members of the profession. The principal code of ethics for information systems professionals is the Association for Computing Machinery (ACM) Code of Ethics and Professional Conduct, binding on the members of the ACM.[2] The code should be familiar also to all those whose professional life is affected by information systems. We have reproduced the fundamental statements of the ACM Code in Figure 6.2. In addition, corporations and other employers should establish their own codes of infoethics. Such corporate codes have been shown to influence the behavior of people who would otherwise not think that an important ethical issue was involved in their decision making.[3,4]

To select a course of action in an ethical dilemma, we turn to ethical theories.

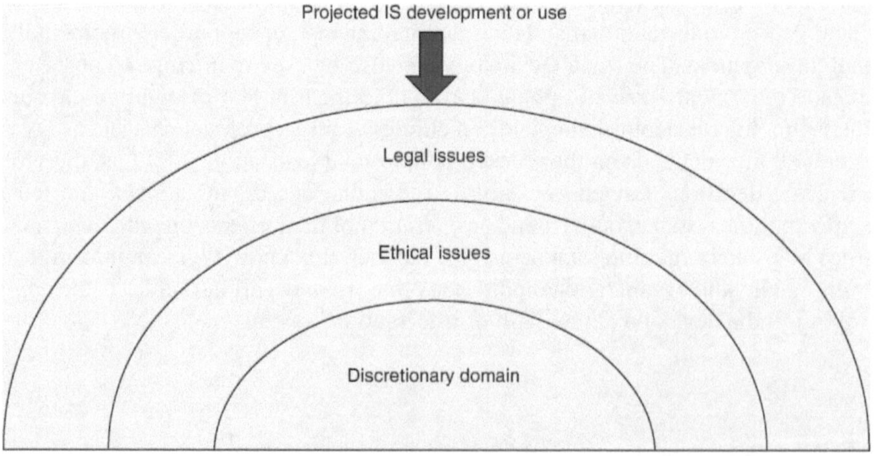

FIGURE 6.1 Domains of pursuit in problem solving or opportunity seeking with information systems. (From Zwass, V. *Foundations of Information Systems*; Irwin/McGraw-Hill: Boston, MA, 1998; 612, 616.)

1. **Contribute to society and human well-being.**
2. **Avoid harm to others.**
3. **Be honest and trustworthy.**
4. **Be fair and take action not to discriminate.**
5. **Honor property rights including copyrights and patents.**
6. **Give proper credit for intellectual property.**
7. **Respect privacy of others.**
8. **Honor confidentiality.**

FIGURE 6.2 General moral imperatives of the ACM Code of Ethics and Professional Conduct. (From ACM Code of Ethics and Professional Conduct; http://www.acm.org/about/code-of-ethics, (accessed February 28, 2008.)

Ethical Theories

Ethical theories give us the foundation for ethical decision making. Some of them are grounded in an individual's pursuit of virtue, such as justice or generosity. While important in the development of the moral sense of individuals, these lend themselves only to a limited degree to a reasoned decision-making process. There are two fundamental effective approaches to ethical reasoning:

1. Consequentialist theories tell us to choose the action with the best possible consequences. Thus, the utilitarian theory that prominently represents this approach holds that our chosen action should produce the greatest overall good for the greatest number of people affected by our decision. The difficulty lies in deciding what the "good" is and how to measure and compare the resulting "goods." The approach may also lead to sacrificing the rights of a minority. A social contract among the members of social groups implies the need to consider the lot of all these members. There are certain acts that are wrong in themselves and should be always avoided. These unethical acts interfere with the rights of others, the rights that may be derived from the other principal group of ethical theories.
2. Deontological theories argue that it is our duty to do what is right. Your actions should be such that they could serve as a model of behavior for others—and, in particular, you should act as you would want others to act toward you. Our fundamental duty is to treat others with respect—and thus not to treat them *solely* as a means to our own purposes.

Treating others with respect means not violating their rights. It is, therefore, vital that we recognize the rights of each human individual. The principal individual rights, enshrined in the United Nations' Universal Declaration of Human Rights and recognized in democratic societies, are

a. The right to life and safety;
b. The right of free consent—individuals should be treated as they freely consent to be treated;
c. The right to private property;
d. The right to privacy;
e. The right of free speech, extending to the right to criticize truthfully the ethics or legality of the actions of others;
f. The right to fair treatment—individuals who are similar in regards relevant to a given decision should be treated similarly;
g. The right to due process—individuals have a right to an impartial hearing when they believe their rights are being violated.

The emerging empirical moral psychology attempts to relate the actual human behavior in ethically challenging situations to the precepts of the ethical theories.[5] Thus, we learn empirically about the implicit or explicit use of ethical theories by information-systems professionals in their decision-making processes.[6] This helps us inculcate values and ethical decision-making modes. The application of ethical theories is best illustrated by considering practical cases, which we will now proceed to do.

SCENARIOS IN THE ETHICAL DOMAIN

Consider the following three scenarios, adapted from Parker.[7] We will come back to these scenarios after we discuss the tenets of infoethics.

Transactional Information on Smart Cards

The manager of the smart-card division of a financial institution has developed a new debit card as a smart card, containing a microprocessor chip and memory. Unbeknownst to its holder, not only the amount spent was debited, but also detailed data about every purchase transaction were stored on the card. As a result, any merchant presented with the card could evaluate the credit history of the cardholder. The financial institution was planning to allow the merchants to upload the data from the smart cards to their own servers. This would enable the retailers to use personal information about their customers for promotional purposes.

Consider these questions: Do you believe that there are any ethical issues involved? If so, what ethical principles were breached?

Who Owns E-Mail?

A firm had a policy allowing employees, upon approval, to use their personal computers (PCs), which were the property of the company, for personal purposes, including e-mail and Web access. When a possible acquisition of the company by another one was announced, a rising employee unrest was suspected. The president of the company ordered the security department to use specialized software to monitor all the PC activities of the employees, including the contents of their memos, e-mail messages, budgets in preparation, and so forth. Reports produced by the security department detailed what the employees produced both during their work and during private use of their PCs. The monitoring and reporting was done without employees' knowledge.

Was the action of the company management ethical or unethical in allowing personal use of corporate information technology by employees? How about the president's monitoring decision?

Let's Just Release This System

A project leader in the corporate information systems division was assigned by her manager, the vice president of sales for the company, a task to develop a new Internet-based billing system. When the work was being assigned, the project leader thought that the time and human resources provided were adequate to complete the project. However, due to an unexpected turnover of computing specialists, it became clear that the system could not be completed as designed within the available budget and time frame. The project leader warned her superior about the impending problem. She was forced to deliver a "bare bones" system, without adequate error detection, exception handling, security safeguards, and audit trail. When the system was fielded, it became a source of problems in customer service. Many customers were billed incorrectly and, following heated exchanges, switched suppliers. Cases of fraud were discovered, but proved impossible to trace. Business losses resulted and the project leader was blamed.

Was the action of the project leader ethical in knowingly implementing an inadequate system? How would you evaluate the actions of her superior in ordering an inadequate system into production?

The following general discussion of infoethics will allow us to discuss the issues involved in these cases.

ETHICAL ISSUES IN THE DEVELOPMENT AND USE OF INFORMATION SYSTEMS

The welfare of individuals and their specific rights, postulated by the ethical theories we discussed, need to be safeguarded in the environment of an information society. The principal ethical issues of concern with regard to information systems may be categorized as privacy, accuracy, property, and access.[8]

We have shown these principal ethical issues as the four circles in Figure 6.3. As shown in the figure, we can trace these issues to their sources: 1) the pervasive role and immense capabilities of systems for collecting, storing, communicating, and accessing information in our information society; 2) the complexity of information technology; and 3) the intangible nature of information and digital goods, such as digitized music or software. We also show in the figure the specific individual rights whose potential violation brings the issues to a head.

Tracing an ethical issue to its source and understanding the individual rights that could be violated help us understand the issue itself. For example, the intellectual property rights embodied in digital goods, such as software, are relatively easily violated because software is intangible and can be easily copied at a marginal cost close to zero. At the same time, the development costs of software are very high. Since information technology pervades so many aspects of our lives, particularly after the infusion of the Internet-Web compound, our privacy can be more easily violated than in the absence of this technology. Indeed, without computerized databases accessible over the Internet, fed by information systems that process our purchases, loan applications, insurance policies, and other transactions, it would hardly be possible to assemble the detailed record of our lives within seconds. At the same time, those bereft of access to the technology are impaired in many of the life's pursuits and their right to fair treatment is violated. An individual in a modern society who cannot make use of the World Wide Web is deprived of a principal source of information, transactions, and relationships. A handicapped person without access to an appropriate technology required to use a PC in a society where such use is needed to work is not treated fairly. We will now proceed to consider the four ethical issues in the following sections.

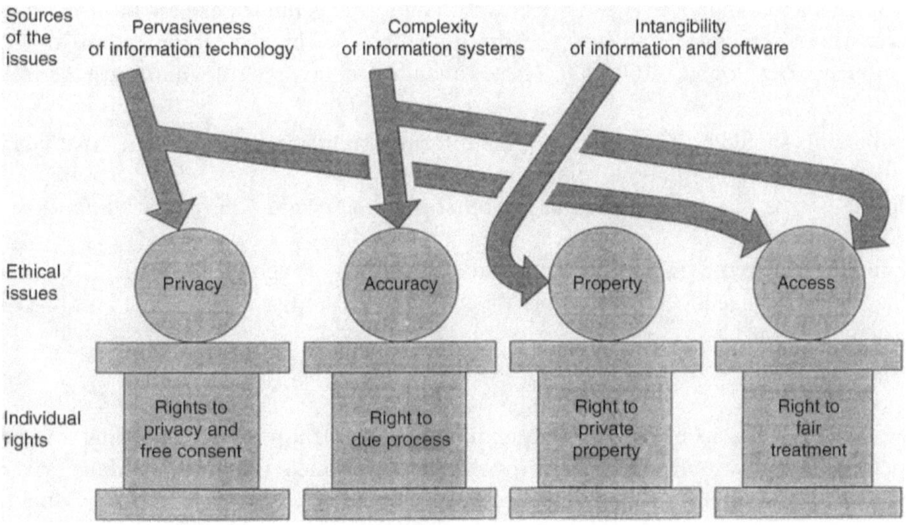

FIGURE 6.3 Ethical issues, their sources, and the underlying individual rights. (From Zwass, V. *Foundations of Information Systems*; Irwin/McGraw-Hill: Boston, MA, 1998; 612, 616.)

PRIVACY

Privacy is often considered the most important ethical issue raised by information systems. Privacy is the right of individuals to retain certain information about themselves without disclosure and to have any information collected about them with their consent protected against unauthorized access. When our privacy is invaded, we are embarrassed, diminished, and perceive a loss of autonomy—a loss of control over our lives. Invasion of privacy is a potent threat in an information society. Individuals can be deprived of opportunities to form desired professional and personal relationships or can even be politically neutralized through surveillance and gathering of data from the myriad databases that provide information about them. Most authorities agree that it is necessary to uphold the right to privacy as a basic individual right; Justice Louis Brandeis, over a century ago, called this right "the most valued by the civilized man." Even though this right is not guaranteed by the Bill of Rights in the United States, that constitutional document stresses that other rights, beyond those enumerated there, are retained by the people. The right to privacy is considered to be such a right.

Concern about privacy had existed for many years before computer-based information technology entered human affairs. Yet, computer-related technologies, and especially the massive use of the Internet-Web compound, create opportunities for privacy invasion that had not existed previously. Massive databases containing minute details of our lives can be assembled at low cost and can be made accessible anywhere and at any time. A Web search can be conducted at the behest of a governmental or business institution, or in a personal pursuit, to yield a large amount of private information about an individual, compiled from multiple sources.

Collection, storage, and dissemination of records concerning individuals from computerized databases are necessary to our business, government, indeed, to the very fabric of our lives. To balance this need with privacy protection, both legislation and ethical approach to the acquisition and use of these records are necessary. In the United States, privacy is protected by a variety of legislative acts, the most prominent of which is the amended Privacy Act originally enacted in 1974, which regulates the treatment of personal data by federal agencies. The handling of personal information by corporations has received far less legislative attention, and the essential legal mechanism in this case is the law of contract. A 1999 U.S. law requires financial institutions to send out their privacy policies to their customers. However, gaps in legislation and in its enforcement make it difficult to protect privacy through the legal system and leave much of the privacy issue in the domain of ethics.

The Privacy Act and the legislation that follows it specify the limitations on the data records that can be kept about individuals and are based on and what is known as Fair Information Practice Principles. These principles also underlie the guidelines set by the Organization for Economic Cooperation and Development (OECD). These fundamental privacy safeguards are the following:

- Individuals should be given notice of the information practices of the entity that wishes to collect personal information from them;
- No use can be made of the records for other than the original purposes without the individuals consent;
- Individuals have the right of inspection and correction of records about them;
- The collecting agency is responsible for the integrity and security of the record-keeping system;
- There is a mechanism in place to enforce the safeguards and offer redress.

Ensuring privacy in the face of rapidly expanding technological possibilities for its invasion is not easy. Controversies arise and the trade-offs involved test the ethical frameworks. Many privacy advocates favor an opt-in practice in soliciting personal information. In this case, the individual releasing the information needs to consent expressly to the information being used for the purpose specified by the requester. An alternative, the opt-out regime, favored by information collectors, makes the release of the information a default in the absence of an express prohibition by the individual.

The personalization of products and services acquired and sometimes also delivered over the Web requires personal information about the consumer. Effective m-commerce, that is, relationships and transactions conducted with wireless communications, indeed calls for consumer intimacy: the more information the system stores about the user, the higher is the speed and quality of the interaction.[9] Pervasive information systems that introduce ubiquitous computing and sensing technology into everyday objects magnify the exposure to potential intrusions on privacy.[10] Fair Information Practice Principles should serve as the essential decision-making guideline. Matching of the online profile with personally identifiable data is of particular concern. Privacy concerns should guide technological solutions in system fielding; such concerns are, for example, debated before the radio-frequency identification (RFID) tags are deployed on a wider scale.[11]

Privacy safeguards, such as privacy policies posted on the Web sites, even when audited by independent agencies (e.g., TRUSTe, http://truste.org), are insufficient to protect this information from abuse. A common loophole is the dissolution of the original firm that had collected the information under certain safeguards, for example, during a merger or an acquisition. Conflicts arise between an individual's right to privacy and the right of a larger community to protect itself.[12] Such issues include the rights of governments to decipher encrypted messages in the cases of suspected terrorism or crime, or the rights of parents to have access to the records of sex offenders who may endanger their children's welfare. In discharging their responsibility to enhance national security, governments may move to take away the ability of individuals to remain anonymous in a variety of situations, for example, by demanding identification in the airports.

Two database phenomena create specific threats of privacy invasion. The first, known as database matching, makes it possible to merge separate facts collected about an individual in several databases. If minute facts about a person are put together in this fashion in a context unrelated to the purpose of the data collection and without the individual's consent or ability to rectify inaccuracies, serious damage to the rights of the individual may result. The dispersion of personal data among several independent databases is one safeguard against invasion of privacy. The other concern relates to statistical databases that contain large numbers of personal records, but are intended to supply only statistical information (the U.S. Census database is the best example). A snooper, however, may deduce personal information by constructing and asking a series of statistical queries that would gradually narrow the field down to a specific individual. To prevent such disclosure, limitations on the allowed queries need to be placed (e.g., a query would not be answered if the answer would refer to fewer than 10 persons).

Information systems have made it possible to conduct systematic monitoring and surveillance of persons and groups. Among the technologies are the video-based systems that monitor city traffic for infractions or the systems that monitor the use of rental cars to account for excessive speed. The use of cookies and monitoring of the clickstream by many visited Web sites, while facilitating commercial transactions and marketing, is troubling to many. Monitoring an individual's whereabouts with a geographic positioning system, embedded in a cell phone, although useful in m-commerce, presents a danger to privacy. As stated in Figure 6.2, the ACM Code of Ethics obligates information systems professionals to "respect the privacy of others," and goes further to offer specific guidelines on how to do that.

Legislation and enforcement in the area of privacy in the United States are behind those in a number of other countries. Much is left to spotty self-regulation by business entities. Privacy statements to all clients by financial companies in the United States typically include such tropes: "We also may share information with other companies that are able to extend special offers we feel might be of value to you." Opt-out options are cumbersome. Online privacy policies have been found to aim at protecting the firms from litigation rather than reflect a commitment to fair data practices.[13]

The countries of the European Union (EU) offer particularly extensive legal safeguards of privacy. In the environment of business globalization this creates difficulties in transborder data flow, that is, transfer of data across national borders. Countries with more stringent measures for privacy protection object to a transfer of personal data into the states where this protection is more lax.

Therefore, a number of U.S. corporations have signed the so-called safe harbor agreement, complying with the EU privacy standards. The United Nations has stated the minimum privacy guarantees to be incorporated into national legislation.

While the Internet-Web compound enables manifold threats to privacy, it is also a medium for the management, or even manipulation, of one's public persona. Such reputation management often surrenders various aspects of the individual's privacy, to the individual's future regret. Social norms in that respect are in a state of flux.[14] Social networking companies on occasions introduce new features that open—without permission—the online behavior of individual participants to their online "friends."[15]

ACCURACY

Pervasive use of information in our societal affairs means that we have become more vulnerable to misinformation. Accurate information is error-free, complete, and relevant to the decisions that are to be based on it. Accurate information is grounded in high-quality, secure information systems, constructed by responsible professionals. Although stories about inaccurate information surface most frequently with regard to the credit-reporting industry, they reflect a generally low level of data quality control throughout the public and private sectors of the economies.

Inaccurate information can prevent an applicant from obtaining a credit card—or a job. When people rely on inaccurate information, other people may be deprived of their right to due process. An incorrect medical record can threaten your life. A weather report that incorrectly forecast the trajectory of a storm because the data from a failed buoy were unavailable to the computerized model sent a sailor to his death.[8] French police officers, in hot pursuit of a car recorded as stolen in their database, opened fire and wounded a law-abiding driver. The records of the car recovery by the legitimate owner and of the subsequent sale of the car were missing from the database. Multiple accidents involving massive radiation overdose administered by the radiation-therapy system Therac-25 have been traced to imperfectly tested software.[16]

Is the development of information systems that provide accurate information just the question of professional competence? In the third scenario presented in "Scenarios in the Ethical Domain," a "bare-bones" system was knowingly forced through by a firm's executive and knowingly implemented by a project leader. Similar events could have been behind any of the systems that led to the loss of individual welfare—or life—in the cases we just described. Beyond that, there exist various sources of possible bias in information systems—and the information system developers should be aware of that. The bias of concern to infoethics represents a persistent discrimination against certain categories of individuals and groups reflected in the design of an information system, which negatively affects the accuracy of information provided.[17] Professional integrity is an essential guarantor of information accuracy.

An ethical approach to information accuracy calls for the following:

- A professional should not misrepresent his or her qualifications to perform a task.
- A professional should indicate to his or her employer the consequences to be expected if his or her judgment is overruled. The ACM Code of Ethics and Professional Conduct speaks of the professional's obligation to "avoid harm to others" by carefully assessing potential impacts of an information system to be implemented.
- System safeguards, such as the controls and audits, are necessary to maintain information accuracy. Regular audits of data quality should be performed and acted upon.
- Individuals should be given an opportunity to correct inaccurate information held about them in databases. The sources of inaccuracies should be tracked down and eradicated.
- Contents of databases containing data about individuals should be reviewed at frequent intervals, with obsolete data discarded.

Regrettably, some information-systems professionals are likely to choose implementing a system with quality problems in the conditions known as moral hazard, that is when they have an incentive to act in their own interests and against the interests of their employer, while being able to hide this.[18] The same research has also shown that the ethical climate of an organization can influence these actions in the positive direction.

Accuracy problems have wider societal implications. A claim has been made that the absence of proper controls in some computerized election systems may threaten basic constitutional rights. An independent assessment of the e-voting systems certified for use in the State of California, as one example, showed serious security vulnerabilities.[19] Democratic process will require substantive information-accuracy safeguards before a wide move to electronic voting.

PROPERTY

The right to property is largely secured in the legal domain. However, intangibility of information is at the source of dilemmas that take clarity away from the laws, passing many problems into the domain of ethics. At issue are primarily the rights to intellectual property (IP): the intangible property that results from an individual's or a corporation's creative activity. The Web, which has become a uniquely valuable medium for legitimate distribution of data, information, and knowledge in a digital form, has also become a common means for breaching the rights to this property.

Intellectual property, such as software or other digital content, is protected by three legal mechanisms: copyright, patent, and trade secret. These means serve to protect the investment of creators and to ensure public good by encouraging disclosure so that further innovations can be made by others. Indeed, the copyright and patent laws are designed to assist in the public disclosure and thus further technological progress. Copyright registration, which is easy to obtain, protects the form of expression (e.g., a given program) rather than the idea itself (e.g., an algorithm). Because the underlying problem solution is more valuable than its coded expression, this is a limited protection. Patents, which are more difficult to secure, protect novel and nonobvious discoveries that fall in the United States within the subject matter of the U.S. Patent Act. Many patent applications for software failed to prove that they qualify under this "subject-matter" criterion. However, a U.S. Federal Appeals court has affirmed in 1994 the patentability of sufficiently innovative software. Because of the limitations of copyrights and patents with respect to intangible products, software developers most often rely on trade-secret protection. Trade-secret law protects the confidentiality of intellectual property through licenses or nondisclosure agreements.

An elaborate software system is expensive to create. The same software, or another digital product, can be copied at a negligible cost. Such is the nature of IP, which includes software, books, video, and music. Piracy in the form of selling illegally reproduced software has become a serious problem in international trade. In a number of countries, far more than the three-quarters of the sales of U.S. software packages are illegal copies. Worldwide software piracy costs the U.S. software industry many billions of dollars annually. Because the legal system trails the pace of technology and because ethical guidance is sought in framing the legal issues, many controversies spill over into the ethical domain. To "honor property rights" is one of the eight general moral imperatives of the ACM Code of Ethics.

The legal system and ethicists are grappling with many unresolved issues, such as

- To what extent can information and knowledge be considered property?[20]
- How to reconcile the public's right to access with the rights to IP and to privacy?
- What makes one digital product distinct from another?
- Would computer-generated works have a human author? If not, how would the property rights be protected?

In the case of property rights to electronic collections of data, such as directories, the U.S. courts have ruled that the copyright law protects only collections that display some creativity in the selection or arrangements of the data and does not protect such labor-intensive but nonoriginal collections as telephone white pages. Yet, the distinctions are often too fine to make a difference.

The industrial ecosystems producing digital goods, such as the music industry, have been transformed by the arrival of the Web as a mass medium. Owing to the compression of the content and to the broadband telecommunications technologies, high-quality music and video can be streamed and played directly over the Web. Music and video producers and sellers can be bypassed by consumers communicating in peer-to-peer mode and propagating copies of digital products. The technological domain offers, if only temporarily, a variety of methods of protecting this property, such as digital watermarks, as well as a broad encryption-based technology of digital rights management (DRM). The Digital Millenium Property Act, promulgated in 1998 to protect digital property, has made it illegal to circumvent a technological measure that controls access to a protected digital property. Taken together with the DRM technologies, the act goes beyond the preexisting copyright law and is likely to be challenged—justifiably, in much credible opinion.[21] As we may conclude, many legal issues regarding intellectual property remain unresolved. This is why it is particularly important to approach this property from an ethical standpoint to ensure that our decisions do not violate property rights of others.

ACCESS

It is a hallmark of an information society that access to information and knowledge is mediated by information technology, notably the Internet-Web compound, most of the workforce is employed in the processing of information and transformation of knowledge, and most of the goods and services available for consumption are information-related. To gain full access to the benefits of such a society, an individual must possess at least four things: 1) the intellective skills to deal with information; 2) access to information technology and media, including the Internet-Web compound; 3) access to information; and 4) access to a free expression over the digital media. If we consider these issues on national and global scales, we see that inequalities persist. Because each of us in a human society draws an economic benefit from the equality of opportunity and because each of us is ethically concerned about fairness, the issue of capable access to information and information technology redefines our concern for literacy.

Information technology does not have to be a barrier to opportunities. Quite the contrary, when deployed purposefully, it can *provide* opportunities not previously accessible. Internet access can bring the contents of the world's libraries, participation in the world's markets, and the advice of the world's experts to a remote location. Intensive work is being done on developing assistive technologies that enhance access of the handicapped to the information technology, and, thus, in many cases, to the social and economic mainstream. Assistive technologies for the blind include screen displays that work in an auditory mode through screen-reading software and speech synthesizers, and screens that work in a tactile mode with the use of a Braille display. Access to trustworthy electronic virtual communities, designed with ethical principles in mind, is a great source of support to people bearing afflictions.[22]

Indeed, with the phenomenal growth of shared computational resources, PCs, smart mobile devices, and of the Internet-Web services, the accessibility of information technology has grown vastly. But it has not grown equally. Access to the Internet is necessary to participate in the benefits of an information society and economy. Yet, several regions of the world, notably most of the countries of sub-Saharan Africa, remain with limited access. Significant digital divide persists between the developed and poor countries both in the information technologies and complementary assets, such as qualified professionals.[23] Various digital divides also exist in developed countries. Action to eradicate these divides and expand the domain of inclusion in the Internet benefits is an important ethical concern.

Another ethical concern is the expansion of access to digitized information. The claims of IP have to be balanced by the needs of expanding the commonwealth of accessible knowledge and information.[24] The One Laptop per Child global initiative brings low-cost laptop computers, connected to the Web, within the reach of children in poor countries. The Digital Commons initiative provides open access to the knowledge contributed by scholarly journals, as well as to the books not protected by copyright. The movement toward open source and free software makes both the digital products and the tools for their further development accessible to all. A broad understanding of access is gaining worldwide support. The cooperation of Yahoo with a government wishing to restrict the access of the citizens of its country to the riches of the Web's information and communication has met with an opprobrium that set an example.

MAKING ETHICAL DECISIONS

Let us consider how to make decisions applying ethical principles in the information-related domains—and then apply them to the scenarios presented above. The following decision-making sequence can be adopted:

1. Examine the issues to see whether they fall in the ethical domain. Seek appropriate professional guidance if the issues seem to be in the legal domain. Apply the "sunshine test" to see whether the issue is ethical or discretionary: Would your decision withstand public disclosure?
2. If you believe that ethical issues are involved, would a course of action you are considering violate individual rights? Would the action violate a professional code of ethics?
3. Choose the course of action that would not result in an ethical breach.

Let us now view, in this light, our three scenarios presented earlier:

Transactional Information on Smart Cards

The ethical issue of privacy is involved. The legality of the action can be challenged. However, it is obvious that the developers and the users of the system invaded privacy of the debit-card holders with the system that gathered and released data about them without their knowledge. People may consent to their personal data being stored for a specific purpose; however, no such consent was sought. The individuals were also deprived of their right to inspect and, if appropriate, correct their personal data. Furthermore, the financial institution's prospective plans imply an even broader breach of privacy by indiscriminate, uncontrolled release of transactional information to third parties, and should not be pursued. A breach of ethics may have financial consequences. A possible consumer outcry may render the system useless. Such an argument may indeed carry the day, if you need to defend your recommendation to not go ahead with developing a similar system.

Who Owns E-Mail?

Certainly, the management decision to allow employees the use of the company-owned computers and systems for private purposes violates no ethical principles. We could judge this to be a discretionary action and not an ethics issue. An employee stands in a different relationship to a workplace than a consumer does to a marketplace. But the monitoring action was taken without employees' knowledge and clearly it is a violation of their right to privacy and, thus, highly unethical if there was a justified presumption of privacy. However, employers have a right to set policy—and an obligation to make the employees aware of their terms of employment. Should you, as an employer, wish to pursue this course of action, such acceptable use policy has to be drawn up. Perhaps the employees should be able to label certain communications as private, with the employer undertaking an obligation to respect their rights. The least invasive forms of computer-based work monitoring should be adopted. Thus, monitoring of performance, rather than of behaviors or personal characteristics is preferred.

Let's Just Release This System

The vice president not only made a poor business decision (that would place the issue in the discretionary domain). By knowingly forcing the development of a defective system, he violated his duty to do what is right. What about the action of the project leader? The ACM Code obligates a professional to "give comprehensive and thorough evaluations of computer systems and their impacts, including analysis of possible risks."[2] The project leader failed to do so in this case by agreeing to implement a defective system and by failing to call her superior's action to the attention of higher authorities.

These three scenarios show that ethical decision making protects not only professional integrity and upholds the social contract. The expediency of "cutting ethical corners" often produces adverse business results.

CONCLUSION

Information technologies have the power to affect significantly the quality of our personal and working lives. Therefore, all knowledge workers and system users, and particularly computing professionals, face information-system-related problems whose solution involves ethical considerations. Purely technological or legal means of protecting individual rights affected by information systems are insufficient in separation from the tenets of infoethics.

The four principal infoethical issues, privacy, accuracy, property, and access, are subjects of professional and organizational codes of ethics, which should be familiar to computer professionals. In the workplace, the use of information technology may have positive or negative impacts on the worker, depending on the way the technology is deployed. Potential positive impacts include the increased ability to develop and exercise individual skills, and integration of work into meaningful tasks that can be performed with a large degree of autonomy. Potential negative impacts include reducing skills, routinization of work, and excessive monitoring of workers. Computer-based performance monitoring should be made the least invasive and should be organized in accordance with ethical principles. Infoethical principles should be inculcated in the workplace as a component of the corporate culture. Our moral lives, in turn, require reexamination in the face of the new technologies that confront our ethical principles.[25]

An information society both drives and is driven by incessant innovation. Emerging technologies present threats to the ethical uses of information systems, as well as the means to deal with these threats.[26] Beyond that, they offer the promise of a better life in an increasingly more inclusive global society. The proper deployment of emerging technologies has to be informed by the decision-making processes keeping in view the ethical issues raised by information systems.

REFERENCES

1. Zwass, V. *Foundations of Information Systems*; Irwin/ McGraw-Hill: Boston, 1998; 612, 616.
2. ACM Code of Ethics and Professional Conduct; http://www. acm.org/about/code-of-ethics (accessed February 28, 2008).
3. Pierce, M.A.; Henry, J.W. Computer ethics: The role of personal, informal, and formal codes. J. Bus. Ethics **1996**, *15*, 425–437.
4. Kreie, J.; Cronan, T.P. Making ethical decisions. Commun. ACM **2000**, *43* (12), 66–71.
5. Appiah, K.A. *Experiments in Ethics*; Harvard University Press: Cambridge, MA, 2008.
6. Thong, J.Y.L.; Yap, C.-S. Testing an ethical decision-making theory: The case of soft-lifting. J. Manage. Inform. Syst. **1998**, *15* (1), 213–237.

7. Parker, D.B.; Swope, S.; Baker, B.N. Ethical Conflicts in *Information and Computer Science, Technology and Business*; QED Information Sciences: Wellesley, MA, 1990.
8. Mason, R.O. Four ethical issues of the information age. MIS Q. **1986**, *10* (1), 5–12.
9. Zwass, V. Electronic commerce and organizational innovation: Aspects and opportunities. Int. J. Electron. Comm. **2003**, *7* (3), 7–37.
10. Kourouthanassis, P.E., Giaglis, G.M. (eds.); *Pervasive Information Systems, Advances in Management Information Systems*; M.E. Sharpe: Armonk, NY, 2008, Vol. 10.
11. Garfinkel, S.; Rosenberg, B. RFID: *Applications, Security, and Privacy*; Addison-Wesley: Upper Saddle River, NJ, 2006.
12. Etzioni, A. *The Limits of Privacy*; Basic Books: New York, 1999.
13. Pollach, I. What's wrong with online privacy policies? Commun. ACM **2007**, *50* (9), 103–108.
14. Solove, D.J. The *Future of Reputation: Gossip, Rumor, and Privacy on the Internet*; Yale University Press: New Haven, CT, 2007.
15. Vara, V. It's hard to hide from your friends. The Wall Street Journal January 30, 2008, Dl and D4.
16. Neumann, P.G. *Computer-Related Risks*; ACM Press: New York; Addison-Wesley: Reading, MA, 1995.
17. Friedman, B.; Nissenbaum, H. Bias in computer systems. ACM Trans. Inf. Syst. **1996**, *14* (3), 330–347.
18. Turtle, B.; Harrell, A.; Harrison, P. Moral hazard, ethical considerations, and the decision to implement an information system. J. Manage. Inform. Syst. **1997**, *13* (4), 7–28.
19. Bishop, M.; Wagner, D. Risks of e-voting. Commun. ACM **2007**, *50* (11), 120.
20. Branscomb, A.W. *Who Owns Information? From Privacy to Public Access*; Basic Books: New York, 1994.
21. Lessig, L. *Code and Other Laws of Cyberspace*; Basic Books: New York, 1999.
22. Leimeister, J.M.; Ebner, W.; Krcmar, H. Design, implementation, and evaluation of trust-supporting components in virtual communities for patients. J. Manage. Inform. Syst. **2005**, *21* (4), 101–135.
23. Shih, E.; Kraemer, K.L.; Dedrick, J. IT diffusion in developing countries. Commun. ACM **2008**, *51* (2), 43–48.
24. McFarland, M.C. Intellectual property, information, and the common good. In *Readings in Cyberethics*, 2nd Ed; Spinello, R.A., Tavani, H.T., Eds.; Jones and Bartlett: Sud-bury, MA, 2004; 294–304.
25. Cavalier, R.J., Ed.; *The Impact of the Internet on Our Moral Lives*; State University of New York Press: Albany, NY, 2005.
26. Rundle, M.; Conley, C. *Ethical Implications of Emerging Technologies: A Survey*; UNESCO: Paris, 2007. http://unes-doc.unesco.org/images/0014/001499/149992E.pdf (accessed March 22, 2008).

7 Careers and Education in Information Systems

Paul Gray and Lorne Olfman

CONTENTS

INTRODUCTION

Managing the vast stores of information and knowledge in libraries, in databases, and in knowledge repositories involves deep understanding of information systems (IS). This entry discusses the nature of IS and the educational opportunities and careers in the field.

University education in IS is centered principally in schools of business whose research objectives are to improve the application of IS in (usually profit-maximizing) organizations. Libraries are considered a specific field of application. IS studies in business schools and other departments such as computer science generally cover the fundamentals, but they do not emphasize the role of IS in library and information science (LIS). The uses of IS in LIS are taught principally in schools of information or informatics that emerged from schools of LIS. These schools usually offer full degrees or minors in IS specifically directed to libraries. Their emphasis is on the creation, processing, storing, and retrieval of information and knowledge.

A way of thinking about the use of computers in libraries is that it is similar to electronic commerce (e-commerce), the conducting of business over the Internet or over private networks. Many current library activities are forms of e-commerce. At the customer level, if you or I want a paper or a book or a question answered, we interact with the library in a way that is similar to e-commerce—ask for something and it is delivered electronically. On the supply side, libraries buy information electronically from JSTOR and other database providers such as LexisNexis, and obtain copies of books and journal articles from other libraries by e-order. E-mail is universal. All these activities depend on design and management of the IS behind them. In short, IS are at the core of how twenty-first century libraries really operate.

In keeping with the authors' backgrounds, this entry provides a view of IS in general. It covers the following topics:

- Differences among IS, computer science, computer engineering, and LIS
- Education in IS: B.S., M.S., and Ph.D. level curricula
- Schools of Information and Informatics
- Training and continuing education
- The IS industry (vendors, service providers, outsourcers, internal IS groups, and consultants)
- Specializations and job categories in IS (including total employment nationally and internationally)
- Careers in IS (in internal groups in institutions; in external vendors; working with user groups; "verticals" such as health, communications, technology vendors, education; joint projects between firms, departments; and global teams)
- Professional associations in IS
- Strategic use of IS
- Future of IS

INFORMATION SYSTEMS VS. LIBRARY AND INFORMATION SCIENCE VS. COMPUTER SCIENCE VS. COMPUTER ENGINEERING

While IS, LIS, computer science, and computer engineering are all concerned with managing information and knowledge, they are studied (and consider themselves) as different disciplines. In this subsection we consider the similarities and differences among them.

Library and Information Science (LIS) is defined in Prytherch[1] as

> the study and practice of professional methods in the use and exploitation of information, whether from an institutional base or not, for the benefit of users. An umbrella term, abbreviated LIS, is used to cover terms such as library science, librarianship, information science, information work etc.

In terms of IS, LIS focuses on such areas as document and records management and knowledge.

Computer Science (also called computing science) involves studying the foundations of information and computation and their application in computers. It is also concerned with computer languages and computer software.

Computer Engineering (also called electronic and computer engineering) combines computer science and electrical engineering. It focuses on software design, computer hardware design, and the integration of hardware and software.

Information Systems (IS) involves the study of the "(1) acquisition, deployment, and management of information technology resources and services ... and (2) development, operation, and evolution of infrastructure and systems for use in organizational processes."[2] Information systems differ from computer science and computer engineering in that the latter two are concerned with the creation of hardware and software rather than with their organizational implications. Information systems as a whole is a superset of IS within LIS.

EDUCATION IN IS

Table 7.1 summarizes the educational enterprise in IS.

Degrees in IS are availbale at the

- Undergraduate
- Masters
- Ph.D.

TABLE 7.1
Information Systems Education

Academic Level	Model Curriculum	Depts/schools in Universities	Delivery of Offerings
Undergraduate	IS2002[2]	Schools of Business	Full time
M.S.	MSIS 2006[3]	Schools of Business, Schools of Information	Full time, part time, remote via Internet or video
Ph.D.		Schools of Business, Schools of Information	Full time, part time, remote via Internet or video
Training and continuing education		Short courses, certificates	In class, on site, and remote (e.g., via the Internet)

levels. Model curricula and accreditation are available in the United States at the bachelor's and M.S. levels. Ph.D. programs are not standardized in this way. The most recent model curricula are published respectively in Gorgone, Davis et al.[2] for the undergraduate degree and in Gorgone, Gray et al.[3] for the master degree.

In the United States, these degree programs are housed in

- Schools of Information and Schools of Informatics
- Schools of Business
- Schools and Departments of Computer Science
- Schools of Liberal Arts

Many, but not all of the Schools of Information and the Schools of Informatics are descendants of Schools of Library Science that changed their name and expanded their offerings and their faculty to include IS (see discussion below).

UNDERGRADUATE MODEL CURRICULUM

The undergraduate curriculum[2] is based on the following image of the IS professional with a bachelor's degree:

1. Has a broad real-world perspective
2. Has strong analytical and critical thinking skills
3. Has interpersonal communication and team skills and strong ethical principles
4. Designs and implements information technology solutions that enhance organizational performance

The curriculum is directed to people studying in business administration programs but is tailorable to students studying in other disciplines such as LIS. Specifically, it contains:

1. General courses in IS suitable for all students regardless of their majors or minors
2. Specialized information technology and application design courses for both majors and minors in IS
3. Specialized application development, deployment, and project management courses for majors in IS

The output desired for IS majors, is shown in Figure 7.1.[2] The course structure is shown in Table 7.2.

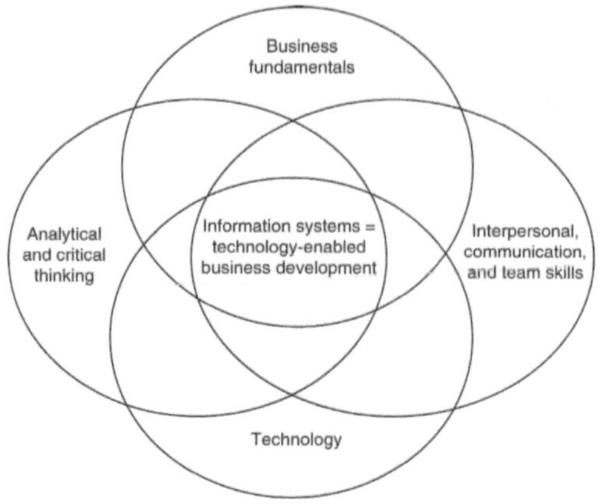

FIGURE 7.1 High-level categorization of IS graduate exit characteristics.

TABLE 7.2
IS2002 Course Structure for Undergraduates

Prerequisite	IS 2002.P0 Personal Productivity with IS Technology
Information systems fundamentals	IS 2002.1 Fundamentals of Information Systems
	IS 2002.2 Electronic Business Strategy, Architecture and Design
Information systems theory and practice	IS 2002.3 Information Systems Theory and Practice
Information technology	IS 2002.4 Information Technology Hardware and Software
	IS 2002.5 Programming, Data, File and Object Structures
	IS 2002.6 Networks and Telecommunications
Information systems development	IS 2002.7 Analysis and Logical Design
	IS 2002.8 Physical Design and Implementation with DBMS
	IS 2002.9 Physical Design and Implementation in Emerging Environments
Information systems deployment and management processes	IS 2002.10 Project Management and Practice

Source: IS 2002 model curriculum and guidelines for undergraduate degree programs in information systems.[2]

MSIS CURRICULUM

The M.S. model curriculum[3] is directed to create graduates who are prepared to provide leadership in the IS field. M.S. graduates should have the same skills, knowledge, and values as B.S. or B.A. graduates (Figure 7.2[3]) but at a higher level.

The M.S.I.S. course set recommended for IS professionals is listed in Table 7.3.

To be eligible to take these courses at the M.S. level, students are expected to have completed four prerequisite courses—two in IS:

- IS fundamentals
- Programming, Data, Files, and Object Structure

and a two-course sequence in business functions and processes.

All four prerequisite courses are usually already completed by students with an undergraduate degree in IS. However, students coming from other majors, such as LIS, may be required to take some or all of these prerequisites if they did not take them as undergraduates.

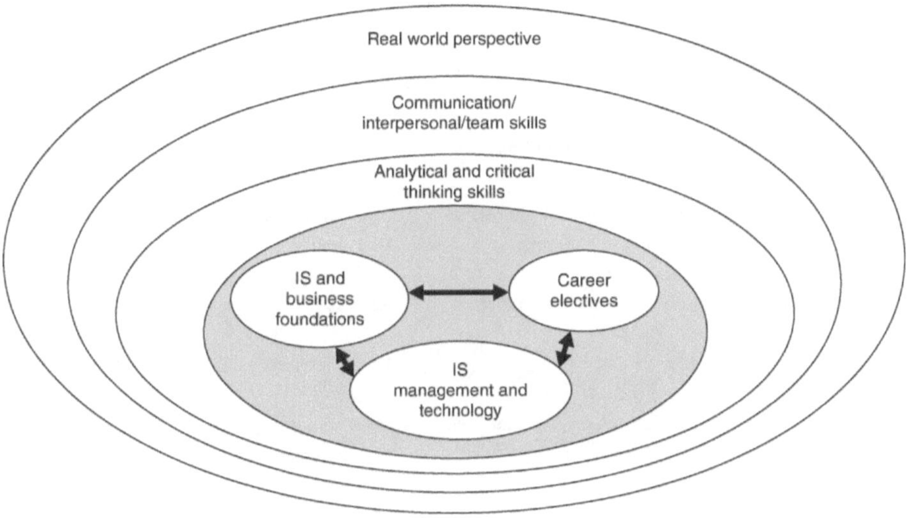

FIGURE 7.2 M.S. level output model.

The M.S.I.S. program shown in Table 7.3 consists of 12 courses divided into three parts, each consisting of four courses.

- IS technology
- Managing IS
- A coherent sequence in a specialization area

IS technology. The IS technology courses, shown in Table 7.4, focus on the broad range of technology-based topics that an M.S. student needs to know. Some topics appear in several courses because they are discussed from different viewpoints. The amount of time devoted to topics varies; for example, the discussion of human–computer interaction is extensive in the analysis, modeling, and design course because of the importance of the human factor in that subject.

Managing IS. No matter what the size of the organization, successful operation requires a working, and preferably highly efficient IS. IS management turns out to be one of the more complex problems organizations face. In libraries, as in most business organizations, IS are viewed as overhead that is necessary but whose costs should be minimized. Yet minimizing cost requires a trade-off with service.

Table 7.5 shows the suggested content of the management courses.

TABLE 7.3
M.S. Courses

IS Technology	Managing IS	Specialization Tracks
IT infrastructure	Project and change management	Four courses in depth in a particular subject area including, where possible, a practicum course involving experience in an organization
Analysis, modeling, Design, including Human–Computer Interaction Enterprise Systems	Strategy and policy Implication of digitization	
Emerging technologies and issues	Integrated capstone	

TABLE 7.4
Contents of the Technology Courses

IT Infrastructure	Analysis, Modeling, and Design	Data and Data Management	Emerging Technologies and Issues
IT architecture	Human–computer interaction	Information content	Data mining
Enterprise Information Infrastructure	Systems development methodologies	Distribution	Sourcing
Servers and Web services	Requirements determination	Process management	Web services and business processes
Layered network architecture	Team organization and communications	Data warehousing/data marts	Technology convergence
Internet protocols	Feasibility and risk analysis	Data mining	Security
Global WAN services	Design reviews	Managing storage area networks	Organizational intelligence
Enterprise network design	System development life cycle	Large systems (ERP)	Knowledge management
Wireless technologies	Conceptual and logical data modeling	E-commerce	Mobile computing
Network management	Database implementation	Content management	Ubiquitous computing
	Data organization		
Server architectures	Software and systems metrics		
Storage management and networks	Software package evaluation		

Source: MSIS 2006: model curriculum and guidelines for graduate degree programs in information systems.[3]

Specialization track. The purpose of the specialization track is to teach students about the specific field they want to work in and to provide field experience through a practicum. IS programs, given the need for economies of scale and the available skills of their faculty, usually can offer only three to five different specialization tracks. The tracks are usually technical, organizational, human factors, or tailored to specific industries that are prevalent in an area (e.g., software in Seattle, financial institutions in New York). Typically, the specialization tracks involve selection from among elective courses. Note that specialization tracks can be lockstep or custom tailored to individual students by mixing and matching electives.

In schools of information (see next subsection) that offer both library science and IS degrees, one of the specialization tracks is based on issues paramount in LIS (e.g., courses in databases, data retrieval, information issues, knowledge management, and more specialized issues such as geographic IS). In M.S. programs located in schools that do not offer library science, the specialization track requires selection of appropriate electives.

The conclusion from this brief survey is that potential students and faculty with interests in both library science and IS should read school descriptions carefully if their interest spans the two disciplines.

TRAINING AND CONTINUING EDUCATION

Because of the rapid changes in information technology and software, even highly educated practitioners require updates to their skill sets. As a result, a large number of training offerings are available commercially or through universities. These offerings typically span from 3 to 5 days. Vendors offer courses at multiple locations on a weekly or monthly basis. Moreover, they produce online

TABLE 7.5
Suggested Content of the Managing IS Courses

Project and Change Management	Implications of Digitization	Policy and Strategy	Capstone
Project life cycle	Ethics	Relationship between IS and the business	The enterprise as a system of integrated business processes
Project stakeholders	Privacy	IS and competitive position	Relationships with suppliers and customers
Project planning	Govt. regulations	Aligning IT goals and strategy	Strategic alignment of IT with the business
Software cost estimation	Globalization and sourcing	Creating IT values, vision, and mission	IT organization and governance
Work module design, assignment, version control	Intellectual property	IT strategic planning, infra-structure planning and budgeting	The value of IT
Role of repository, project library	Virtual work and telecommuting	IS implementation	Role of the CIO
Contingency planning	Implications of artificial intelligence	Inter-organizational systems	Sourcing
Reporting and controls	Security measures and planning	Outsourcing versus insourcing	Compliance
Testing and testing plans: alpha and beta	E-commerce	Globalization	Integrated enterprise architecture
Project Manager skills	Digital divide	Risk management	Platform choices
	IT workforce	Virtual organization	Impact of standards
			Vendor strategies

Source: MSIS 2006: model curriculum and guidelines for graduate degree programs in information systems.[3]

training (CDs, DVDs, and Internet accessible) for many software and hardware products, including the most popular ones produced by Microsoft, Oracle, and Cisco. These companies offer certifications that claim that the person who obtains them is qualified to install and maintain the related products. Many information-related jobs call for such certifications, although the value of these certificates seems to be declining.[4] Leading-edge libraries offer training for software that supports specialist areas such as geographic IS, statistical analysis systems, databases, and bibliographic systems. Information professionals who want to manage information departments and resources often attend one of the part-time, evening M.S. programs in IS available in most urban areas. Community colleges also offer courses and associate degree programs in IS.

THE IS INDUSTRY

Information systems pervade American organizations, including libraries. To create and service these organizations, a large number of

- Equipment manufacturers
- Software firms
- Service providers and outsourcers
- Internal IS organizations
- Consultant organizations

were created over the years. The stories of vast wealth accumulated by the founders of many of these organizations are part of the folklore. In this section we describe the role of each of these types of organizations and their relation to libraries.

Equipment (hardware) manufacturers. When computers first came on the scene commercially in the 1950s and 1960s, the focus was on building computers and peripheral equipment such as displays and printers. The machines were large, horribly expensive, and designed for medium and large firms and government agencies that could afford them. Following the introduction of the IBM PC Model 51 in 1981, personal computing became generally available and is now pervasive.

The technology broadened so that it now includes telecommunications that allows computers to be networked together. Telecommunications, in turn, made it possible to connect to the Internet. Where previously connection to the electric power grid was required, computer equipment is moving to wireless. Miniaturization led to ever less space being required and less heat generated.

Computer prices dropped from millions of dollars in 1960 to thousands today and computer user skills are nearing universality. The result is a computer-literate population that is accustomed to the digital life. The drop in costs made it possible for libraries and information repositories to use the technology to improve service and capabilities. However, recognize that while individual personal computers are cheap (prices under $1000/unit for the hardware are common), the large number of individual units required, as well as the cost of servers, networking, and peripherals still makes the total cost of ownership considerable for an organization. The term servers, as used here, refers to dedicated computers that provide software and other services to computers on a network. In some arrangements, a server can also be used to do local computations.

Software firms. In the early years of computing, software was literally given away with the hardware, since programmers were few and programming computers was a highly complex, skilled art. By the early 1960s, firms sprang up that offered software commercially with different versions compatible with the major mainframe types. The software was high priced and was almost exclusively rented. That is, ownership did not pass to the purchaser. Rather, the software firm charged an initial price and then an annual maintenance fee, typically equal to 15% of the initial price. The result was lock-in. That is, once a particular piece of software was acquired, it became quite expensive to switch to another vendor. An annual maintenance fee was charged by the software firm to cover its cost of revising and updating the software as the hardware changed and additional features were added. For PCs, the policy is different in that its copies of software are cheap and it is possible to own the software. However, upgrades of the software must be purchased, often at or near the same price as the original. Maintenance requires separate contracts.

The range of software available expanded over the years. Typical office suites offer word processing, spreadsheets, presentation graphics, small databases, and more. Specialized software is required for large databases for data warehousing, for knowledge management and other subjects of interest to libraries.

The Internet is a separate issue. Software for access (i.e., browsers) is currently free, but hardware is required for connection. The major problems of the Internet deal with content. In addition to viruses, worms, spyware, and other "malware" directed toward ruining or interfering with content, spam is a major concern. Spam refers to unsolicited, unwanted advertising, most of it for dubious products. For libraries, be they public or in a corporation, access to pornography over the Internet needs to be avoided. Software to deal with these issues is available, but it is not perfect. In fact, there is an arms race between providers and preventers of improper information, with one side or the other ahead at any particular time. Another content aspect is copyright protection where computer users want access to copyrighted material to which they are not entitled. Liability issues on copyright were still in contention when this entry was written in 2008.

Service providers and outsourcers. Libraries are faced with a classic "make or buy" problem. Although they can create their own computing environment, most purchase all or part of it from vendors such as catalog and database providers. Vendors include application service providers

(ASPs) and outsourcers. ASPs provide computer-based services to customers over a network. A classic example is the Internet Service Provider (ISP) who offers connections to the Internet.

Outsourcers are contractors who perform computer work ranging from internal production to managing a firm's operations to providing call centers. The movement of such work is called outsourcing and offshoring. Offshoring refers to contracting beyond the boundaries of the country whereas outsourcing usually refers to moving work domestically. Domestic outsourcing, of course, simply shifts jobs from an organization to a firm that specializes in some aspect of IS but still employs domestic workers. Although newspapers and magazines are filled with stories about moving jobs from high-wage western countries to low-wage countries such as India and China, only a small portion of IS jobs have moved overseas. For example, a 2008 survey shows that approximately 1.1% of IS jobs were offshored and that the trend is toward less offshoring and more domestic outsourcing in the future.[5] Although small in percentage of jobs, offshore software outsourcing still involves large sums of money. For example, a study published in November 2007[6] estimates revenues of near &55 billion alone for India, China, Malaysia, and the Philippines.

A growing number of firms provide "Software As A Service." That is, work is sent electronically to the ASP either over the Internet or on a private network. The ASP provides the computers and software that performs contracted tasks. The advantage is that the library does not need to perform that work internally at the cost of giving up some control over the work and how it is performed.

Internal IS organizations. Where a library system (usually with multiple locations) is a government service, their information operations may either be outsourced to a centralized information group that provides services to a number of government agencies or may be served by its own IS organization. Internal organizations, like those in businesses often have the advantage that they are part of the organization and know its needs. They can be more responsive in terms of both time and resources made available. This characterization assumes that the internal organization is not dysfunctional as internal IS operations sometimes can be. With an internal IS function, the library system is locked into its organization. If the internal organization is dysfunctional, outsourcing is one way of attempting to resolve the dysfunctionality.

Consultant IS organizations. IS consultants are called in when a specific problem needs to be solved and the organization does not have the skills or the personnel needed within their internal organization. Consultants do not come cheap. They are experienced, quality people and operate in a high overhead environment since they need to cover not only their costs while employed by a client but also their costs when between engagements.

Hiring consultants is, in effect, renting knowledge. It is a speculation. It is not possible to predict whether the consultants' work will pay off. They are hired based on the reputation of their organization and people, their past success, and their potential. Knowledge rentals involve knowledge transfer from the consultant to the client. Even though consultants are temporary hires, some knowledge will stay after they leave. Some consultants offer training as part of their service. Although libraries seek their help in solving specific problems, it is wise to write the consulting contract to include knowledge transfer.

SPECIALIZATION AND JOB CATEGORIES IN IS

The United States Bureau of Labor Statistics (BLS) provides a classification and comprehensive description of information-related jobs and requirements, the number of persons (currently) employed in these jobs, and a forecast of the expected growth in the number of these jobs. The statistics presented in this section are from the 2008–2009 version of the *BLS Handbook*. Libraries typically keep only the latest annual version of the *BLS Handbook*. Thus, the data presented in Table 7.6 are, in some cases, obsolete in years beyond 2008. However, it is our experience that the categories and numbers change slowly. Thus, the categories and the data will remain indicative over the next several years.[7]

TABLE 7.6
BLS Occupations in Information Fields

Occupation	Job Description	Employment 2006 and 2016	Salary Median (2006)[a] ($)
Computer Programmers	Write, test, and maintain the detailed instructions called programs that computers follow to perform their functions. Conceive, design, and test logical structures for solving problems by computer. With the help of other computer specialists, they figure out which instructions to use to make computers do specific tasks.	435,000 declining to 417,000	65,510
Computer and Information Scientists, Research	Work as theorists, researchers, or inventors. Their jobs are distinguished by the higher level of theoretical expertise and innovation they apply to complex problems and the creation or application of new technology. The areas of computer science research range from complex theory to hardware design to programming language design. They may work on design teams with electrical engineers and other specialists.	25,000 increasing to 31,000	93,950
Computer Software Engineers, Applications	Develop, create, and modify general computer applications software or specialized utility programs. Analyze user needs and develop software solutions. Design software or customize software for client use with the aim of optimizing operational efficiency. May analyze and design databases within an application area, working individually or coordinating database development as part of a team.	507,000 increasing to 733,000	79,780
Computer Software Engineers, Systems Software	Research, design, develop, and test operating systems-level software, compilers, and network distribution software for medical, industrial, military, communications, aerospace, business, scientific, and general computing applications. Set operational specifications, formulate and analyze software requirements. Apply principles and techniques of computer science, engineering, and mathematical analysis.	350,000 increasing to 449,000	85,370
Computer Systems Analysts	Solve computer problems and use computer technology to meet the needs of an organization. They may design and develop new computer systems by choosing and configuring hardware and software. They may also devise ways to apply existing systems' resources to additional tasks. Analysts who specialize in helping an organization select the proper system software and infrastructure are often called *system architects*. Analysts who specialize in developing and fine-tuning systems are often known as *systems designers*.	504,000 increasing to 650,000	69,760
Computer Specialists	Includes a variety of jobs such as Telecommunications Specialists, who focus on the interaction between computer and communications equipment; Webmasters, who are responsible for all technical aspects of a Web site, including performance issues such as speed of access, and for approving the content of the site; and Web Designers/Developers, who are responsible for day-to-day site creation and design.	136,000 increasing to 157,000	Not available

Database Administrators	Work with database management systems software and determine ways to organize and store data. They identify user needs and set up new computer databases. In many cases, database administrators must integrate data from outdated systems into a new system. They also test and coordinate modifications to the system when needed, and troubleshoot problems when they occur. An organization's database administrator ensures the performance of the system, understands the platform on which the database runs, and adds new users to the system.	119,000 increasing to 154,000	64,670
Network Systems and Data Communications Analysts	Design, test, and evaluate systems such as local area networks (LANs), wide area networks (WANs), the Internet, intranets, and other data communications systems. Network systems and data communications analysts perform network modeling, analysis, and planning, often requiring both hardware and software solutions. Analysts also may research related products and make necessary hardware and software recommendations.	262,000 increasing to 402,000	64,600
Computer and Information Systems Managers	Includes Chief Technology Officers, who evaluate the newest and most innovative technologies and determine how these can help their organizations; MIS/IT Directors, who manage computing resources for their organizations; and Project Managers, who develop requirements, budgets, and schedules for their firms' information technology projects.	264,000 increasing to 307,000	101,580
Network and Computer Systems Administrators	Design, install, and support an organization's computer systems. They are responsible for LANs, WANs, network segments, and Internet and intranet systems. They work in a variety of environments, including professional offices, small businesses, government organizations, and large corporations. They maintain network hardware and software, analyze problems, and monitor networks to ensure their availability to system users. Administrators also may plan, coordinate, and implement network security measures.	309,000 increasing to 393,000	62,130
Librarians	Often called information professionals, increasingly combine traditional duties with tasks involving quickly changing technology. Help people find information and use it effectively for personal and professional purposes. Manage staff and develop and direct information programs and systems for the public and ensure that information is organized in a manner that meets users needs. Librarians with computer and IS skills can work as automated-systems librarians, planning and operating computer systems, and as information architects, designing information storage and retrieval systems and developing procedures for collecting, organizing, interpreting, and classifying information.	158,000 increasing to 164,000	49,060

Source: BLS Handbook.[7]

[a] Note that the data are based on 2006. Add at least a 3% annual increase for each year after 2006.

Categories of taxonomies almost always overlap; job taxonomies are no different. The BLS does not directly classify jobs as information-related. The BLS classifications do not map one-to-one into the educational categories discussed previously. The differences, however, are not significant. BLS lists most information-related jobs in its professional occupations. However, some are included in the Business and Financial, Administrative, and Management occupation categories. Except for Computer Programmers and Librarians (both classified as professional), job growth through 2016 is predicted to be faster or much faster than average. Table 7.6 lists 11 BLS information-related categories that require at least a bachelor's degree along with a job description, current and expected employment figures; and median salary.

CAREERS IN IS

While the BLS classification provides a tool for understanding the current and future employment possibilities for the main groups of information-related jobs, a more direct description of jobs available to graduates of information programs can be inferred from job advertisements. A search of jobs advertised on Monster.com[8] in eight major urban areas in the United States (within a radius of 50 mi from Los Angeles, San Francisco, Denver, Dallas, Chicago, New York, Philadelphia, and Atlanta), as of mid-July 2008 show a wide variety of job titles. Some of the titles vary by levels (e.g., Network Analyst and Network Manager), showing the natural career paths in many information-related jobs from entry level jobs (typically analysts and technicians) to senior positions (such as Manager or Chief Technology Officer). Job titles can be classified into domains (e.g., administrator, architect, analyst). Table 7.7 shows selected job titles by domain from the Monster.com search.

Table 7.8 maps the BLS occupational categories to job title domains and application areas (e.g., business systems, database, network). Salaries range from &50,000 to well over &100,000 with any specific job spanning a wide dollar amount depending on qualifications and experience. Jobs in the Information Technology field are classified into 12 different areas in Monster.com, including Computer/Network Security, Database Developer/Administrator, Enterprise Software, Information Technology/Software Development, Information Technology Project Management, Network/Server Administrator, Software/System Architect, Software/Web Developer, Systems Analysis, Telecommunications Administration/Management, and Usability. A search within these categories using a set of standard keywords for job titles provided the set of available jobs within the eight urban areas noted above. There is some overlap in available jobs using this method of search (see Table 7.9). While this table includes only a fraction of all jobs listed, it provides a fair distribution of jobs across different cities and job types. The highest paying jobs are more typically available in New York, Los Angeles, and San Francisco.

Within a traditional Information Systems department in a large organization, the normal hierarchy includes a senior manager (or Chief Information or Technology Officer); directors of the key IS functions, including database systems, systems development, systems maintenance, telecommunications and security, and user support. A typical career path for a specialist in database might lead from an entry level position to a database administration position, to a director of database systems, and then possibly to manager. IS managers need leadership and administration skills. They are typically experts in one of the department functions as the following discussion of career paths explains.

It is more likely that a career path would include lateral movement from one organization to another rather than lateral movement within organizations. For example, a database administrator may find a job at the same level in another company that may pay better or that will include use of a different database system, rather than move to a role in systems development in the same company. That is, people become specialized in their skills. Experience in particular technologies counts a great deal in developing a career path. Most job advertisements ask for specific experience. Specialization makes it difficult to begin a career in the IS field at other than the entry level. For example, a typical career can begin at a consulting firm that specializes in particular technologies. After gaining expertise in that technology, the next step might be to take a job in the organization

TABLE 7.7
Job Domains and Job Titles

Job Domain	Job Titles
Administrator	Information Systems Administrator, Information Systems Database Administrator, Network Administrator, Senior Database Administrator, Systems Administrator
Analyst	Applications Systems Analyst, Business Analyst, Business Applications Analyst, Business Intelligence Data Analyst, Business Systems Analyst, Data Analyst, Help Desk Analyst, Information Security Analyst, Information Systems Analyst, Information Technology Analyst, Programmer Analyst, Quality Assurance Analyst, Senior Data Analyst, Senior Information Assurance Analyst, Senior Information Systems Analyst, Systems Analyst
Architect	Data Architect, Enterprise Architect, Information Architect, Information Systems Architect, Senior Information Architect, Software Architect, Web Information Architect
Auditor	Information Technology Auditor, Information Technology Senior Internal Auditor
Consultant	Business Systems Consultant, Implementation Consultant, Information Technology Consultant, Network Consultant, Senior Consultant Systems Domain, Storage Consultant
Designer	Application Designer, User Interface Designer, Web Designer
Developer	Application Developer, Database Developer, Information Technology Developer/Consultant, Senior Java Developer, Senior Software Developer, Senior Web Developer, Technical Developer, Web Developer, Web Developer/Image Librarian
Director	Director Clinical Information Systems, Director Information Systems, Director Information Technology, Global Information Technology Director, Information Technology Director
Engineer	Information Assurance System Engineer, Information Security Engineer, Information Security Network Engineer, Senior Engineer Information Systems, Senior Information Security Engineer, Senior Network Engineer, Senior Network Security Engineer, Software Engineer/Programmer, Systems Engineer, Technical Support Engineer
Librarian	Acquisitions and Collection Librarian, Corporate Librarian, Electronic Resources Librarian, Reference Librarian, Research Librarian, Technical Services Librarian
Manager	Information Security Manager, Information Services Manager, Information Systems Manager, Information Technology Manager, Manager Development, Manager Information Technology, Network Manager, Project Manager, Senior Information Security Manager, Senior Information Technology Project Manager, Senior Project Manager
Officer	Chief Technology Officer, Information Security Officer, Information Technology Disaster Recovery Officer
Professional	Information Technology Professional, System Administrator Professional
Programmer	Information Technology Programmer, Senior Application Programmer
Specialist	Application Specialist, Information Systems Specialist, Information Systems Support Specialist, Information Technology Specialist
Trainer	Business Application Trainer, Software Trainer, Web Product Support Specialist
Vice President	Chief Solutions Specialist, Chief Technology Officer, VP Business Solutions, VP Information Systems Technology
Writer	Report Writer, Senior Technical Writer, Technical Writer

Source: Monster.com[8] and BNET Dictionary.[9]

that previously hired the individual as part of the consulting team to install its software system. Many IS jobs require certifications for using and applying specific technologies offered by companies such as Microsoft, Sun, and Cisco. Certification requires training but results in higher salaries, although the premium has been decreasing.[4]

In small organizations, however, with only a small IS staff, each staff member is expected to have the skill needed to perform multiple functions. It is possible to move laterally and vertically back and forth between small and large organizations.

TABLE 7.8
Occupations, Application Areas, and Job Title Domains

Occupation	Application Area	Job Title Domain
Computer and Information Systems Managers	Director	Applications
		Information Systems
	Manager	Information Technology
Computer Programmers	Internet/Web	Analyst
		Developer
	Software	Programmer
Computer Security Specialists	Information Systems	Administrator
		Analyst
		Director
	Information Technology	Specialist
	Security/Data Security	
Computer Software Engineers, Applications	Applications	Analyst
		Architect
	Business Systems	Consultant
		Developer
		Engineer
	Software	Programmer
Computer Systems Analysts	Business Systems	Analyst
		Consultant
		Engineer
	Information Systems	Programmer/Analyst
	Information Technology	Specialist
Database Administrators	Database	Administrator
		Analyst
		Manager
	Information Systems	Programmer
Network and Computer Systems Administrators	Information Systems	Administrator
		Director
	Information Technology	Engineer
		Manager
	Network	Specialist
Network Systems and Data Communications Analysts	Information Systems	Administrator
		Consultant
	Network	Engineer
		Manager
		Programmer
		Specialist

Source: Monster.com.[8]

TABLE 7.9
Number of Available Jobs by Keyword in Monster.com

	Atlanta	Chicago	Dallas	Denver	LA	NY	Phila.	SF	Total
Database	12	26	13	14	27	54	27	41	214
Librarian	4	7	5	2	8	2	6	4	58
Network	54	77	64	60	92	174	86	78	685
Programmer	35	84	56	36	122	225	105	62	725
Security	25	43	29	23	44	85	28	39	316
Software Engineer	75	72	45	54	202	157	85	346	1036
System Administrator	19	43	34	33	65	129	52	69	444
Systems Analyst	31	42	32	12	63	112	50	45	387
Total	255	394	278	234	623	958	439	684	3865

Source: BNET Dictionary. Business Definition.[9]
Note: LA = Los Angeles, NY = New York, Phila. = Philadelphia, SF = San Francisco.

PROFESSIONAL ASSOCIATIONS

Whereas the American Library Association is the principal professional association for librarians, IS people typically belong to one or both of the following two groups: The Association for Information Systems (AIS) and the Association for Computing Machinery (ACM). AIS consists almost exclusively of people who teach IS in universities and colleges whereas ACM (the much larger of the two associations) consists of both academics and practitioners with a focus on computer science rather than IS. AIS produces two electronic journals, *Communications of AIS* (*CAIS*) and the *Journal of AIS* (*JAIS*). The flagship journal of ACM is *Communications of the ACM.* ACM also publishes a large number of specialty journals that deal with specific areas of computers and computer science.

STRATEGIC USE OF IS

The concept of strategic use of IS in libraries is used in two senses:

1. The creation of specific IS that provides a way of differentiating a library system from others.
2. A multiyear plan for operations into the future.

Differentiation. The goal of a strategic information system is to differentiate the organization by improving the organization's position. A strategic information system supports and shapes the organization's strategy, often leads to innovation in the way the organization conducts its work, creates new opportunities, or develops services based on information technology.[9] In library systems, differentiation can be achieved by introducing new technologies (e.g., geographic IS, data warehouse), new services (e.g., adding an electronic data source), new analysis methods (e.g., data mining capabilities) and more.

Multiyear strategic planning. Library systems typically create their own multiyear strategic plan. A large number of such plans are found by using a search engine such as Google (e.g., Table 7.10 considers seven such plans). In examining these plans, the use of information technology is featured both for providing services and administrative support.

Whereas the strategic plans shown in Table 7.11 are concerned with the library system as a whole, IS departments also create their own strategic plan. To be effective, the department's and

TABLE 7.10
Some Library Strategic Systems Plans

Institution	Title
Emory University	An Overview of the Five Year Strategy for the Emory Libraries, 2007
MIT	MIT Libraries Strategic Plan 1999
New York State Library	2006–2007 Strategic Plan: Improving Library Services for All in the New Century
The Saskatchewan Multitype Library Board	Strategic Plan Update, 2003
U.S. Library of Congress	The Mission and Strategic Priorities of the Library of Congress FY 1997–2004
University of Wisconsin Libraries	Strategic Directions 2005–2007
Wisconsin Department of Public Instruction	Wisconsin Library Technology Strategic Plan, Updated 2007

Source: Google search on: strategic systems and libraries (Accessed August 2007).

TABLE 7.11
Effects of Changing Technology on IS

From	To	From	To
Standardization	Commoditization	Data management	Knowledge management
Technological continuity	Technology integration	User friendly	Usability standards
Proliferation of hardware types	Synergy among hardware types	Access security	Protection against terrorism

the system's plans should be aligned with one another. That is, they must be designed to achieve the same goals. However, in addition to supporting the system's goals, the department's work includes responsibilities that are unique to its operation, ranging from creating the needed infrastructure to selecting new equipment and software to specifying personnel capabilities.

THE FUTURE OF INFORMATION SYSTEMS

Since the first commercial computer systems were installed in 1957, much changed in IS and even more changes can be expected. In this section, we present five of the many scenarios about the future of IS being discussed in 2008. The first four scenarios are based on a special issue on the IS Organization of the Future published in *Information Systems Management*.[10]

1. *The future organization of the IS function.* As noted above, IS organizations tend to be hierarchial, with a Chief Information Officer (CIO) at the top reporting to a senior officer of the firm and supervising departments for technology, design, internal operations, computer security, and service to other departments and outsiders (such as through call centers). We use CIO to refer to the person in charge of information systems. The actual title may vary from one organization to another. With the trends to divesting many of these functions (e.g., through outsourcing and Software As A Service), the IS organization could well morph into a small group of technical and business experts managing the evolution of the organization's technology and a larger on-site group providing only maintenance-level services.[11] However, in this case, IS career paths are not likely to change in that the same roles and functions are necessary for providing IS services by either insourcing or outsourcing.
2. The IT talent challenge. In response to the perceived trend to offshoring and as a result of the end of the stock market bubble in technology stocks in 2001, the number of students

that chose to major in IS, computer science, and related fields has declined. That decline was starting to turn around in 2008. Nonetheless, the combination of a reduced demand for IS education at the college level and an aging baby boomer IS workforce results in concern for the recruitment and retention of IS professionals because as the demand for professionals exceeds the supply, wages escalate.[12] Therefore, IS becomes a valuable career with a long-term future.

3. *A move to Wi-Fi and telecommuting.*[13] With the proliferation of portable technology (e.g., portable PCs, cell phones) and the continuing increase in the capabilities of these devices in a world without wiring, the current computer infrastructure is replaced by a wireless infrastructure that is able to provide large masses of data, information, and knowledge. Concomitant with the technology change, the workforce also becomes mobile and telecommuting[14] is the dominant way people work. This virtual workforce is supported anytime, at anyplace, including library services. The combination of Wi-Fi and telecommuting makes it more likely that some IS professionals, particularly those involved in geographically dispersed projects do not have to move their home as their assignments change.
4. *Harnessing the Technology.*[15] Table 7.11, shows how changing technology leads to changes in IS.

   Note that in Table 7.11 as well as in each of the five scenarios, the focus is much more on technology and human factors than it is on the content being managed. The strength of people trained in both library science and IS is that they view issues in terms of content as well as technology.
5. *Carr's "IT Doesn't Matter" hypothesis.* In May 2003, the *Harvard Business Review* carried an article titled "IT Doesn't Matter" by Nicholas G. Carr.[16] In this article and in a subsequent book,[17] Carr argues that IS, like railroads and electric power, is an infrastructure technology that became a commodity. Initially strategic, IS is now a commodity, no longer offering advantage. Thus, something that everyone had would no longer matter as a way of distinguishing organizations from one another. Carried to its extreme, Carr's notion implies the death of organizational computing. Developments such as outsourcing and Software As A Service are viewed as omens of Carr's vision.

Which of these five alternative scenarios will play out in the years ahead? We expect that the predominating viewpoint will be some combination of these scenarios.

The foregoing represents visions of IS in general. When we turn to library IS, the future seems bright. These systems are coming into full flower compared to their role in business in general where IS are already in an advanced state of maturity. The general coming shortage in people skilled in IS implies that people trained in library IS will continue to be in demand and, if their interests change, they will have the skills they need to be able to transfer their talents to many other applications.

One of the key trends in libraries is convergence, streamlining, and synergy. Instead of requiring users to go through multiple steps in research, including visiting library databases and online library catalogs, libraries are investigating ways to reduce the complexity of access such as federated search engines that combine databases, the online catalog, Web sites, and Open URL link resolvers (which provide links from non-full text citation/abstract databases to full text content). Libraries are also investigating innovative ways to market services and allow library users to match their tastes and research needs with library content in the Web 2.0[18] environment. Examples include

- Second generation catalogs with subject tag clouds and suggestions for similar reading.
- Podcasts.
- The use of social software such as blogs, Myspace, Facebook, and Second Life.

ACKNOWLEDGMENTS

We are indebted to Adam Rosencrantz of the Claremont University Center libraries for his in-depth discussions of this paper and for the example of the future of computing in libraries in the Conclusions section. We also thank the editor and an anonymous reviewer for valuable comments and suggestions.

REFERENCES

1. Prytherch, R. *Harrod's Librarians' Glossary and Reference Book: A Directory of Over 9,600 Terms, Organizations, Projects, and Acronyms in the Areas of Information Management, Library Science, Publishing, and Archive Management*; Ashgate Publishing Limited: Gower, UK, 2000; 242.
2. Gorgone, J.T.; Davis, G.B.; Valacich, J.S.; Topi, H.; Feinstein, D.L.; Longeneckr, H.E., Jr. IS 2002 model curriculum and guidelines for undergraduate degree programs in information systems. Commun. Assoc. Inform. Syst. **2002**, *11* (1), 1–53, http://cais.aisnet.org/articles/11-1/ default.asp?View=pdf&x=51&y=11 (accessed July 2007).
3. Gorgone, J.T.; Gray, P.; Stohr, E.A.; Valacich, J.S.; Wigand, R.T. MSIS 2006: Model curriculum and guidelines for graduate degree programs in information systems. Commun. Assoc. Inform. Syst. **2006**, *17* (1), 1–63, http:// cais.aisnet.org/articles/17-1/default.asp?View=pdf&x=72&y=12 (accessed July 2007).
4. Perelman, D. IT certifications declining in value, http://www.eweek.com/c/a/Careers/IT-Certifications-Declining-in-Value/?kc=EWKNLCSM061008FEA (accessed June 10, 2008).
5. Dubie, D. Outsourcing pummels offshoring in IT budget plans, Network World, http://www.network world.com/news/ 2007/101507-outsourcing-tops-offshoring.html (accessed June 10, 2008).
6. Analyst firm issues results of study on global outsourcing. Business World November 8, **2007**, S2/8.
7. BLS Handbook. In *Occupational Outlook Handbook (OOH), 2008–2009 Edition*; U.S. Department of Labor, Bureau of Labor Statistics: Washington, DC, 2008, http:// www.bls.gov/oco/ (accessed July 2008).
8. Monster.com http://www.monster.com (accessed July 2008).
9. *BNET Dictionary. Business Definition: Strategic Information Systems*, http://dictionary.bnet.com/defini tion/strate-gicþinformationþsystems.html (accessed August 2007).
10. Brown, C.V., Ed., Inform. Syst. Manag. **2007**, *24* (2), 101–102.
11. King, W.R. The IS organization of the future: Impacts of global sourcing. Inform. Syst. Manag. **2007**, *24* (2), 121–128.
12. Luftman, J.; Kempaiah, R. The IS organization of the future: The IT talent challenge. Inform. Syst. Manag. **2007**, *24* (2), 129–138.
13. Scott, J.E. Mobility, business process management, software, sourcing, and maturity model trends: propositions for the is organization of the future. Inform. Syst. Manag. **2007**, *24* (2), 139–146.
14. Nilles, J.; Carlson, R.; Gray, P.; Hanneman, G. *Substituting Communications for Transportation: Options for Tomorrow*; Wiley: New York, 1975.
15. Hoving, R. Information technology leadership challenges—Past, present, and future. Inform. Syst. Manag. **2007**, *24* (2), 147–154.
16. Carr, N.G. IT doesn't matter. Harvard Business Rev. **2003**, *81* (5), 41–49.
17. Carr, N.G. *Does IT Matter? Information Technology and the Corrosion of Competitive Advantage*; Harvard Business School Press: Boston, 2005.
18. O'Reilly, T. *What is Web 2.0: Design Patterns and Business Models for the Next Generation of Software*, http:// www.oreillynet.com/pub/a/oreilly/tim/news/2005/09/30/what-is-web-20.html (accessed June 2008).

Part II

Management of Information Retrieval Systems

Effective management of information systems requires the integration of various different bodies of expertise and knowledge. This section pulls together several of the most important kinds of management that are involved in producing and maintaining an excellent information systems ecology. First, several specific types of management involved are reviewed: Knowledge management, information management, digital asset management, and network management.

Addressed next are several specific issue areas of information management that often require planning and decision-making—resources stored in a distributed fashion, search engine optimization, records compliance and risk management, version control, digital content licensing, and piracy of digital media. The final portion of this section addresses the nitty-gritty, but vital, heart of information retrieval, namely, the quality of the resources—the nature of the storage technologies themselves, long-term preservation of electronic records, data and data quality, and how to avoid information systems failure.

The first two chapters, "Knowledge Management" (Chapter 8), by Kimiz Dalkir of McGill University, and "Information Management" (Chapter 9) by Brian Detlor of the DeGroote School of Business, McMaster University, address two closely related but nonetheless distinct concepts. Knowledge management is the broader concept, involving the "deliberate and systematic coordination of an organization's people, technology, processes, and organizational structure in order to add value through reuse and innovation," according to Dalkir. The focus is on knowledge as it exists in many forms throughout an organization: the skills and expertise of individuals and departments, as well as all forms of recorded knowledge. Knowledge management mobilizes all the informational resources of an organization when those resources are viewed as an invaluable part of the organization's brand and unique DNA. Information management has a somewhat narrower focus on the mobilization, collection, and organization of information resources for the better good of the parent organization.

In "Digital Asset Management" (Chapter 10), James E. P. Currall and Michael S. Moss, of the Humanities Advanced Technology and Information Institute, University of Glasgow, discuss the management issues that arise in association with digital resources, in particular the integration of analog and digital resources into a single effective information organization.

Today, information resources are routinely embedded a network; management of the network is a vital part of the larger task of providing effective service and resource access. Drawing on the Open System Interconnection model for communications systems, Robert J. Sandusky explains the five functional areas of "Network Management" in Chapter 11: fault, configuration, performance, accounting, and security management. Reagan W. Moore is one of the pioneers in managing the very large digital data sets arising in scientific research in seismology, high-energy physics, and other areas. He explains how these vast collections can be managed as data grids for sharing data, as well as serve as data archives, in Chapter 12, "Management of Very Large Distributed Shared Collections."

Digital resources are always embedded in a social, economic, and legal context. Several chapters address those larger issues in relation to technical characteristics of digital information stores, each in a different way. Nicholas Carroll, of Hastings Research, provides a masterly summary of the numerous means by which website owners have attempted to optimize the ranking for retrieval of their websites on search engines in Chapter 13, "Search Engine Optimization." Legal requirements and issues often have a major impact on what needs to be done with the records themselves. Bradley J. Wiles' chapter, "Records Compliance and Risk Management" (Chapter 14), lays out the legal and customary requirements that are associated with organizational records.

Documents are not all stand-alone; in many cases a dozen or more different versions for a given document may exist, and need to be related to each other and flagged for their function in the publication and distribution processes. Jill E. Grogg and Jeff Weddle address this issue in Chapter 15, "Version Control," with particular emphasis on scholarly communication.

A vital part of the information *about* a record, that is, of its "metadata," is the legal standing of the record with respect to its copyright and ownership status. In turn, it is the responsibility of owners of information resources to ensure their legal standing through proper licensing and distribution practices. Paul D. Callister and Kathleen Hall, of the University of Missouri School of Law, address the numerous legal issues associated with "Digital Content Licensing" (Chapter 16).

The other side of licensing is piracy. Stephanie Walker, of the City University of New York, reviews the controversial issue of piracy ("Piracy in Digital Media," Chapter 17) as it has erupted in the areas of software, audio files and music, video, and published works, and makes crucial distinctions among types of usage that are not always recognized in the popular press.

Turning now to questions of maintaining quality and accuracy in data, we first develop an understanding of the physical media of digital storage. Digitized information is often spoken of as though it were not corporeal, and existed in some intangible form somewhere "out there." But an understanding of the physical substrate of digital resources is a necessary basis for developing the entire technical, legal, and social superstructure that rests upon that substrate. Scott L. Klingler provides that explanation in Chapter 18, "Information Storage Technologies." Robert P. Spindler addresses a related issue in his discussion of "Electronic Records Preservation" (Chapter 19).

In the rush to take full advantage of the opportunities afforded by cheap online-accessible information resources, the importance of maintaining and improving data quality should not be overlooked. Thomas C. Redman and colleagues explain how to think about "Data and Data Quality" (Chapter 20), and review the methods and planning needed to ensure good quality data.

Chris Sauer and Gordon B. Davis, one of the founders of the field of information systems, address the ultimate worry in information system management: "Information Systems Failure" (Chapter 21). This topic has been studied as a small scientific subfield in and of itself, and Sauer and Davis provide the necessary understanding to enable an information systems manager to gain the upper hand in the matter of preventing failure and optimizing system performance.

8 Knowledge Management

Kimiz Dalkir

CONTENTS

INTRODUCTION

This entry provides an overview of knowledge management (KM), both as a scholarly discipline and a professional field of practice. Key terms such as "knowledge" and "knowledge management" are defined. Core concepts such as intellectual capital, lessons learned, best practices, and value-added knowledge reuse are introduced and defined. Key stages in the knowledge processing cycle are defined and described. A brief historical chronology of KM is outlined to show the multidisciplinary roots and the evolution that has taken place to date. The emerging roles for information professionals in KM are presented and the links to information studies are emphasized. The primary goal of this entry is to illustrate how KM that rests on a solid foundation of information management emerges as a stronger and more rigorous field of study and practice.

DEFINITION OF KNOWLEDGE MANAGEMENT

There is no universally accepted definition of KM. Part of this stems from the fact that there is a lack of consensus in defining knowledge. A sample dictionary definition of knowledge is

> The fact or condition of knowing something with familiarity gained through experience or association; acquaintance with or understanding of a science, art, or technique; the fact or condition of being aware of something; the range of one's information or understanding (e.g. answered to the best of my *knowledge*); the circumstance or condition of apprehending truth or fact through reasoning; the sum of what is known: the body of truth, information, and principles acquired by humankind; cognizance, awareness, learning.[1]

It is useful to view the knowledge in KM as being composed primarily of experiential knowledge that is highly subjective in nature. This can be contrasted with information that, although subject to different interpretations, is typically thought of as having a more neutral and verifiable nature. The same dictionary defines information as

> Knowledge obtained from investigation, study, or instruction; intelligence, news data or facts; the attribute inherent in and communicated by one of two or more alternative sequences or arrangements of

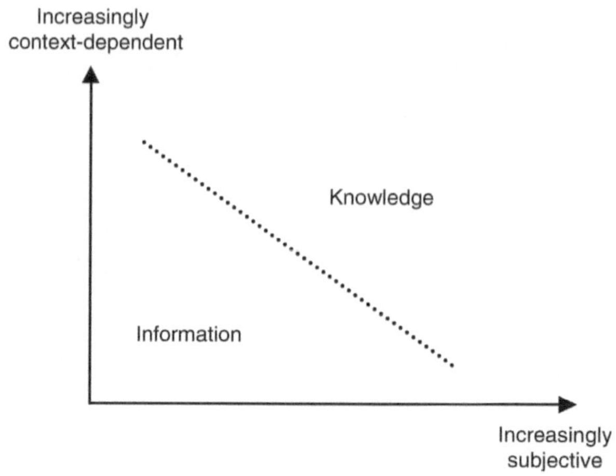

FIGURE 8.1 Key attributes of knowledge assets.

> something (as nucleotides in DNA or binary digits in a computer program) that produce specific effects **c** (1): a signal or character (as in a communication system or computer) representing data (2): something (as a message, experimental data, or a picture) which justifies change in a construct (as a plan or theory) that represents physical or mental experience or another construct.[1]

Other definitions from the KM literature include

> Knowledge is a subset of information: it is subjective; it is linked to meaningful behaviour; and it has tacit elements born of experience (p. 113).[2]
>
> Knowledge is always recreated in the present moment. Most of us cannot articulate what we know. It is largely invisible, and often comes to mind when we need it to answer a question or solve a problem.[3]
>
> Knowledge is a fluid mix of framed experience, values, contextual information, and expert insight that provides a framework for evaluating and incorporating new experiences and information. It originates and is applied in the minds of those who know. In organizations, it often becomes embedded not only in documents or repositories but also in organizational routines, processes, practices and norms (p. 5).[4]

A typical example of information would be to read the listings of movies being shown on a given week, reading the reviews, and consulting the times and places the film will be showing at. An example of knowledge would be calling on a friend who has, in the past, demonstrated an uncanny inverse relationship with respect to likes and dislikes: if this person liked a movie, experience has shown that one would hate it and vice versa. Knowledge is also brought into play in making a decision to drive or take public transport, given the time of year, possibility of inclement weather, and the rapid trend analysis that concludes that it has never been possible to find parking in time to see a movie being shown downtown.

A key point is that not all information is of value to a given individual, group, or organization. A knowledge asset is defined as knowledge that is of value, which is more context dependent and more subjective in nature, as illustrated in Figure 8.1.

The Multidisciplinary Nature of KM

There is a great diversity to be found in KM definitions. This is due to the multidisciplinary nature of the field. In fact, most definitions appear to provide only one piece of the KM definition puzzle, as they are heavily influenced by their particular discipline. Table 8.1 lists some of the different disciplines and specialties that have contributed to and that make use of KM.

TABLE 8.1
Diverse Disciplines that Contribute to Knowledge Management

1.	Organizational development, organizational science, and organizational learning
2.	Cognitive science, individual learning, and mental models
3.	Linguistics and computational linguistics
4.	Design of information technologies such as knowledge-based systems, document and information management, electronic performance support systems, and database technologies
5.	Information and library science, classification, and taxonomy
6.	Technical writing and journalism
7.	Anthropology and sociology, sociograms, and social network analysis
8.	Education and training
9.	Storytelling and communication studies
10.	Collaborative technologies such as Computer Supported Cooperative Work (CSCW) and groupware as well as intranets, extranets, portals, and other Web technologies

Here are a few sample definitions from the business perspective:

> Knowledge management is a business activity with two primary aspects: treating the knowledge component of business activities as an explicit concern of business reflected in strategy, policy, and practice at all levels of the organization; and, making a direct connection between an organization's intellectual assets – both explicit (recorded) and tacit (personal know-how) – and positive business results.[5]
>
> Knowledge management is a collaborative and integrated approach to the creation, capture, organization, access and use of an enterprise's intellectual assets.[6]
>
> There is much more to knowledge management than technology alone. Management is a business process (p. 95).[7]

Some definitions from the cognitive science or knowledge science perspective:

> Knowledge—the insights, understandings, and practical know-how that we all possess—is the fundamental resource that allows us to function intelligently.
>
> Over time, considerable knowledge is also transformed to other manifestations – such as books, technology, practices, and traditions – within organizations of all kinds and in society in general. These transformations result in cumulated expertise and, when used appropriately, increased effectiveness. Knowledge is one, if not THE, principal factor that makes personal, organizational, and societal intelligent behavior possible.[8]

Some sample definitions from the process/technology perspective:

> Knowledge Management (KM) was initially defined as the process of applying a systematic approach to the capture, structuring, management and dissemination of knowledge throughout an organization to work faster, reuse best practices, and reduce costly rework from project to project.[9–12]

American Productivity and Quality Center (APQC)[13] defines knowledge management as

> . . . the managing of knowledge through systematic sharing. Even in highly sophisticated modern knowledge organizations, the most valuable knowledge—the know-how in terms of what really gets results and what mistakes to avoid—often resides mainly in people's minds. Knowledge Management works towards migrating that knowledge from one person to a wide-range of individuals within an organization.

Some "people-oriented" definitions:

> Knowledge management is not seen as a matter of building up a large electronic library, but by connecting people so they can think together (p. 104).[3]

> Most executives seem to understand that knowledge is highly people-based, but they are stuck with an investment model that is geared primarily toward technology implementations (p. 86).[12]

Knowledge management and its varied definitions need to achieve a balance: there cannot be an overemphasis on any one of the key dimensions, such as technology.[14] Effective KM (and comprehensive KM definitions) should include people, process, technology, culture and measurable organizational objectives.[15,16]

Wiig[8] also emphasizes that given the importance of knowledge in virtually all areas of daily and commercial life, two knowledge-related aspects are vital for viability and success at any level. These are knowledge *assets* that must be applied, nurtured, preserved, and used to the largest extent possible by both individuals and organizations; and knowledge-related *processes* to create, build, compile, organize, transform, transfer, pool, apply, and safeguard knowledge. They must be carefully and explicitly managed in all affected areas. According to Wiig[6]

> Historically, knowledge has always been managed, at least implicitly. However, effective and active knowledge management requires new perspectives and techniques and touches on almost all facets of an organization. We need to develop a new discipline and prepare a cadre of knowledge professionals with a blend of expertise that we have not previously seen. This is our challenge!

The Intellectual Capital Perspective

The focus of intellectual capital management (ICM), on the other hand, is on those pieces of knowledge that are of *business value* to the organization—referred to as intellectual capital or assets.[17] While some of these are more visible (e.g., patents, intellectual property), the majority consists of know-how, know-why, experience, and expertise that tend to reside within the head of one or a few employees.[18,19]

Knowledge management is often characterized by a "pack rat" approach to content: "save it, it may prove useful some time in the future." Many documents tend to be warehoused, sophisticated search engines are then used to try to retrieve some of this content, and fairly large-scale and costly KM systems are built. Knowledge management solutions have proven to be most successful in the capture, storage, and subsequent dissemination of knowledge that has been rendered explicit—particularly lessons learned and best practices.

Intellectual capital management is characterized by less content—because content is filtered, judged, and only the best are inventoried (the "top ten" for example). Intellectual capital management content tends to be more representative of peoples' real thinking (contextual information, opinions, stories) due to its focus on actionable knowledge and know-how, with the result that less costly endeavors and a focus on learning (at the individual, community, and organizational level) results, rather than on the building of systems.

It is essential to identify that knowledge which is of value and is also at risk of being lost to the organization, through retirement, turnover, and competition. The best way to retain valuable knowledge is to identify intellectual assets and then ensure legacy materials are produced, and subsequently stored in such a way as to make their future retrieval and reuse as easy as possible.[20] These tangible by-products need to flow from individual to individual, between community of practice (CoP) members and, of course, back to the organization itself, in the form of lessons learned, best practices, and corporate memory.

The knowledge capture and transfer approaches described here help to

- Facilitate a smooth transition from those retiring to their successors who are recruited to fill their positions.
- Minimize loss of corporate memory due to attrition and retirement.

- Identify critical resources and critical areas of knowledge so that the corporation "knows what it knows and does well—and why."
- Build up a toolkit of methods that can be used with individuals, with groups, and with the organization to stem the potential loss of intellectual capital.

Knowledge management is often mistakenly perceived as a process of documenting knowledge held in people's minds, then storing or archiving this knowledge.[21] In fact, it is better to view KM in a broader context, one that encompasses all the processes used to generate value from knowledge-based assets. Knowledge management is facilitated by technology and by the culture of an organization. A good way of defining KM is

> . . . the deliberate and systematic coordination of an organization's people, technology, processes and organizational structure in order to add value through reuse and innovation. This is achieved through the promotion of creating, sharing and applying knowledge as well as through the feeding of valuable lessons learned and best practices into corporate memory in order to foster continued organizational learning (p. 3).[22]

CORE KM CONCEPTS

Kransdorff[23] coined the term "corporate amnesia" to refer to the loss of accumulated expertise and know-how due to employee turnover as people take what they know with them when they leave. The costs of employee turnover to the organization have been well documented (e.g., separation costs, recruitment and selection costs, training of replacements, initial lack of productivity of new hire, and the loss of productivity of coworkers during the transition). Far less research attention has been paid to the cost to the firm of losing know-how that resides within the minds of individual employees who depart. In an era of knowledge workers, learning organizations and service economies individuals are increasingly responsible for value creation. Although many organizations have succession plans in place, the process usually involves transferring know-how from the departing employee to their successor but the whole process has to be repeated again for the next departure. Organizations need to "capture" this know-how and transfer it to a stable, easily accessible, cumulative knowledge base—an organizational memory—to retain and make accessible valuable knowledge gained through the experiences of all knowledge in a continuous and uninterrupted manner.

Organizations need to effectively manage their organizational memory in order to prevent the loss of essential knowledge, particularly knowledge that resides predominantly in the heads of their knowledge workers ("tacit knowledge") and less in documents, procedures, and other tangible forms ("explicit knowledge").[24] More often than not, it is this difficult-to-articulate "know-how" that is of greatest value in organizational competitiveness and viability and which represents the vast majority of experiential know-how. Figure 8.2 shows how the metaphor of an iceberg is often used to depict tacit and explicit knowledge forms.

The National Aeronautics and Space Administration (NASA), for example, has publicly admitted that the knowledge of how to put a man on the moon has been lost.[25] The lessons that were learned and the innovations that were sparked cannot be found in the collective organizational memory of NASA. This means that NASA's organizational memory cannot be used as a resource to plan a more effective mission to send another manned flight to the moon or to Mars. A well-designed and well-managed organizational memory does not only combat corporate amnesia, but it ensures knowledge continuity—the effective transfer of know-how amongst peers and to future generations of knowledge workers. A better understanding of the nature of organizational memory, what it should include (content), how it can best be retained (technological containers), and how the accumulated lessons learned and best practices can be used by newcomers (connections), will help mitigate the cost of lost, forgotten, or un-transferred knowledge and know-how.

FIGURE 8.2 The iceberg metaphor used to show the respective proportions of tacit and explicit knowledge.

Organizations today face escalating risks of losing strategic knowledge and know-how and face incredible difficulties in recruiting and retaining skilled employees. Many industries face astounding rates of high and constant turnover. In addition, we are experiencing a demographic pressure as baby boomers rapidly approach retirement age, which means that a "critical mass" of knowledge will literally walk out the door over the next five to ten years. Approximately 11,000 baby boomers are turning 50 years old every day.[26] Over 80% of Canadian government federal executives will be eligible to retire by 2010 and 53% of U.S. federal civil servants will be eligible to retire within the next two years.[27] The number of workers age 55 and over is expected to increase by 47% the year 2010.[28] Other vulnerable organizations include high technology companies with very high turnover rates and the military or banking, where constant turnover is the norm given rotational postings.

Most successful organizations will state that their two greatest assets are the people who work for them and the knowledge they possess. The imminent turnover signals a potential for the loss of valuable accumulated knowledge and know-how in the form of the competence and expertise possessed by the departing individuals. This valuable knowledge and know-how exists in both formal or tangible forms, such as documents, but also in less visible forms—often referred to as tacit or difficult-to-articulate knowledge. Particular emphasis must be placed on the tacit form as this often resides within a given individual or group and is therefore more easily and completely lost when the people leave the organization.[29]

The typical technological tools used in KM are some form of centralized database system an intranet or Web portal to access the database content as well as other organizational knowledge, some type of messaging system (typically e-mail and discussion groups), some content management tools to organize the knowledge resources (e.g., content management software, taxonomy software) and some form of collaborative software (e.g., virtual meeting tools, groupware).

The essential elements that go into organizational memory include best practices, which are innovations or improved practices, processes, and so forth; together with the flip side of the coin: lessons learned, outcomes that were not desirable, or errors that should not be repeated. By carefully capturing, documenting, organizing, and making available accumulated experiential knowledge in the form of best practices and lessons learned, KM can provide a framework within which we can process knowledge throughout its useful life cycle.

Knowledge management typically addresses three levels within an organization: the individual, the group, and the organization. Organizational memory resides at the level of the organization and this is the preservation layer of KM. Innovation and knowledge creation occurs at the individual level while knowledge dissemination and sharing occur at the group level. In KM, groups of a particular nature, called "communities of practice" (CoPs) are often key elements in ensuring that valuable knowledge flows or moves around appropriately. These CoPs are essentially thematic networks of like-minded individuals who share a common purpose, a common professional zeal, and agree to mutually help out one another to achieve some strategic goals for the organization.[30,31]

Szulanski[32] introduced the notion of knowledge "stickiness" to refer to knowledge that was difficult to move around, and thus could provide little in the way of value to individuals, groups, or the organization as a whole. The knowledge processing cycle is used to describe the various stages a particular knowledge resource goes through during the course of its "lifespan" within an organization.

THE KNOWLEDGE PROCESSING CYCLE

Nonaka and Takeuchi described how knowledge was disseminated and transformed as it made its way around an organization in their Knowledge Spiral Model.[9] Essentially, knowledge is created by an individual, (an innovative idea for example), but remains initially tacit. This innovation or idea is typically shared only with trusted friends and colleagues at first ("socialization"). With time, others may be aware of the innovation and the knowledge may be transformed from its tacit state to an explicit one ("externalization"), by documenting it in the form of text, audio, or other formats. Once explicit, it is easier to disseminate more widely and to preserve in an organizational memory system. At this stage ("combination"), the content may be organized and reworked (e.g., addition of an abstract or executive summary). In the final stage ("internalization"), explicit knowledge once again becomes tacit as an individual learns, understands and "buys into" a knowledge resource (e.g., sees its value and decides to apply this new knowledge). The knowledge resource then continues cycling through the four quadrants in a "knowledge spiral." Figure 8.3 outlines the major stages in the Nonaka and Takeuchi KM model, as knowledge is transformed, disseminated and applied within an organization.

As knowledge resources circulate throughout an organization, value can be added at each step. A more detailed view of what happens to knowledge as it undergoes transformation from tacit to explicit and back again is provided in the form of a knowledge life cycle. The first stage is to either capture existing knowledge (e.g., already existing in tangible form such as project reports, conference reports, or other documents), or to create knowledge that does not yet exist in documented form (e.g., by interviewing subject matter experts to document a particular procedure). This knowledge resource can then be contributed to or made available for reuse by others. Knowledge is then codified by the addition of sufficient descriptive information about both the content and the format it is in (e.g., metadata describing theme, whether it is a text or also available as a short video clip). At this point, knowledge is further refined by sanitization (removing all sensitive information that may

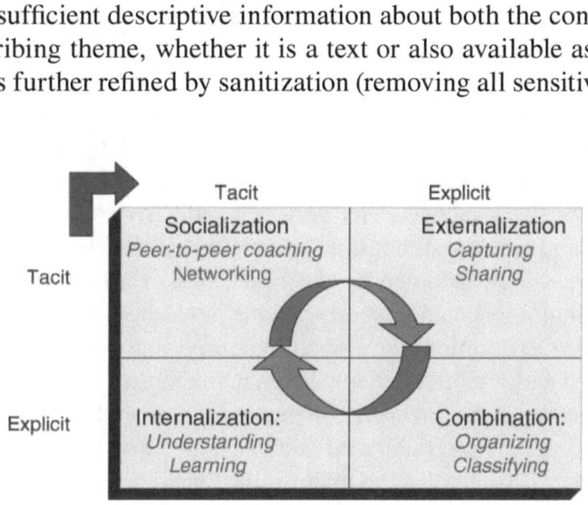

FIGURE 8.3 The Nonaka and Takeuchi knowledge spiral model of knowledge management.

TABLE 8.2
Key Steps in Knowledge Processing Cycle

Step Number	Description
1.	Knowledge capture
2.	Knowledge creation
3.	Knowledge contribution
4.	Knowledge codification
5.	Knowledge refinement (including sanitize) and reconstruction (e.g., synthesis)
6.	Knowledge selection—filter contributions
7.	Knowledge sharing and pooling
8.	Knowledge organization and access
9.	Knowledge learning and application
10.	Knowledge evaluation and reuse or divest (e.g., destroy, archive)

identify a person, place, or event, or other confidential content) and reconstruction (e.g., recombining or synthesizing in a new version). Contributions that have been refined and reconstructed are then subjected to a selective filtering process and those that are deemed to be valuable are made available for knowledge sharing.

Knowledge sharing involves the pooling and distribution of valuable content, either globally (e.g., a "broadcast" mode) or selectively (e.g., targeted to specific users, communities, or based on user profiles, subscriptions, etc.). The knowledge is better organized (classified using a taxonomic scheme) and access is typically provided through an intranet or portal interface. These valuable knowledge resources are then learned and applied by knowledge workers. Each knowledge resource is evaluated periodically in order to ensure continued relevance and to decide whether to discard or to archive at the appropriate time. Table 8.2 lists the key phases in knowledge processing that occurs during the useful life cycle of a knowledge resource, such as a best practice or lesson learned.

HISTORY AND EVOLUTION OF KM

Knowledge and management are concepts that have obviously been around for some time—the combination, "knowledge management," however, is fairly recent. The emergence of communication technologies that create real-time networks such as the Internet, intranets, e-mail, and so forth have made KM easier to implement.[33]

A number of management theories have contributed to definition of KM. Two KM gurus were responsible for establishing the field as a serious target for scholarly study: Peter Drucker,[34] who coined the term "knowledge worker" and who wrote about KM from a management perspective in the 1970s and Nonaka and Takeuchi, who wrote the seminal book *The Knowledge Creating Company* in the 1990s.[9] Others such as Peter Senge[35] and Chris Argyris[36,37] have focused on the "learning organization" and cultural dimensions of managing knowledge. The notion of knowledge as an asset became more widely adopted by the mid 1980s. Early pioneers in information technologies from artificial intelligence and expert systems at Carnegie Mellon University (CMU) and DEC (Digital Equipment Corporation) developed hypertext and groupware tools that allow information to be better shared and organized. Knowledge management-related articles began appearing in prestigious journals such as the *Harvard Business Review* and *Organizational Science* and a number of foundational books were published such as *The Fifth Discipline* and *The Knowledge-Creating Company*. Table 8.3 illustrates the major milestones in KM history.

In 1989, the International Knowledge Management Network (IKMN) was founded in Europe and was joined by the U.S.-based Knowledge Management Forum in 1994.

TABLE 8.3
Major Milestones in KM History

Year	Source	Event
1980	DEC, CMU	XCON Expert System
1986	Dr. K. Wiig	Coined KM concept at UN
1989	Consulting firms	Start internal KM projects
1991	HBR article	Nonaka & Takeuchi
1993	Dr. K. Wiig	First KM book published
1994	KM network	First KM conference
Mid-1990s	Consulting firms	Start offering KM services
Late 1990s	Key vertical industries	Implement KM and start seeing benefits
2000–2003	Academia	KM courses/programs in universities with KM texts

Businesses began implementing KM solutions in earnest in the 1990s. At first, projects tended to be technological implementations, mostly portals and knowledge repositories. This was followed by a wave of "people not technology" emphasis that led to the popularity of thematic networks or CoPs. A third wave emerged as knowledge workers, much like information workers, found themselves faced with "content overload" which in turn led to a number of content management, knowledge organization, or taxonomic classification projects to make the knowledge more readily accessible to users.

With the new millennium, KM faded a bit from public view, likely due to disappointment, the result of expectations having been raised too much by "KM hype" and focusing too much on technologies that were largely left untouched. Practitioners and researchers came to the realization that converting theory into practice was more challenging than previously thought. Among the missing elements were ensuring that KM was not being done for KM's sake but that there was a clear link to organizational objectives and that all participants saw value in KM (incentives for knowledge sharing, for example). By 2004, the field had finally shaken its burden of being yet another management fad. Organizations appreciated the holistic nature of KM and paid attention not only to tools but also to organizational culture requirements for successful KM solutions.

In parallel, the nature of work evolved, with collaboration becoming the default rather than the exception, not only for our professional lives but social interactions and learning objectives. Knowledge sharing with a group of trusted peers has become the de facto way of working, learning and living. Knowledge management found itself in tune with these changes that greatly facilitated its adoption as a philosophy, a mindset, a strategic perspective, and a way of interacting to create, share, and use valuable content.

Knowledge management today is being taught in universities around the world, typically in business, computer science, education, and information studies departments. Doctoral students are completing Ph.D. theses on KM topics. International conferences are being held around the world, with both practitioner and researcher tracks. A number of consortia and KM professional organizations have been established. The number and type of KM journals have also changed. While at first publications were primarily authored by KM tool vendors and practitioners, and in more general management, computer science and organizational science journalists, there has been a significant shift to more scholarly venues and publications that represent KM research rather than KM project mandates. Along with the proliferation in the number of journals, there has also been increasing specialization (e.g., *International Journal of Nuclear Knowledge Management*), more interdisciplinary journals (e.g., *Interdisciplinary Journal of Information, Knowledge and Management*), and more emphasis on international KM (e.g., *International Journal of Knowledge Management*). Up until about the year 2000, only non-peer reviewed journals were available (e.g., *KM World, KM*

TABLE 8.4
Major Peer-Reviewed KM Journals

Journal Title	Year Founded
IBM Systems Journal	1962
Journal of Managerial and Organizational Learning	1970
Journal of Management Information Systems	1984
Journal of Organizational Change Management	1989
Knowledge and Process Management	1996
Journal of Knowledge Management	1997
Journal of Management Studies	1997
Journal of Knowledge Management Practice	1998
Journal of Intellectual Capital	2000
E-Journal of Organizational Learning and Leadership	2002
Journal of Information and Knowledge Management (JIKM)	2002
Electronic Journal of Knowledge Management	2003
International Journal of Knowledge, Culture and Change Management	2003
Knowledge Management Research and Practice	2003
Interdisciplinary Journal of Storytelling Studies	2004
International Journal of Nuclear Knowledge Management (IJNKM)	2004
International Journal of Knowledge Management	2005
Knowledge Management for Development Journal	2005
International Journal of Knowledge Management Studies	2006
Interdisciplinary Journal of Information, Knowledge and Management (IJIKM)	2007

Review). Some of the major peer-reviewed KM journals available today are shown in Table 8.4, ordered by first year of publication.

Knowledge management is found in all vertical industry sectors (e.g., banking, pharmaceutical); in all sizes of organizations (including volunteer-run associations with less than 10 full-time employees); profit and nonprofit organizations and organizations with a strong hierarchical structure (for example, the U.S. military was one of the early pioneers of KM). Organizations today are defining and staffing KM positions. Knowledge management is increasingly perceived as an element that cuts across organizational structures, projects, and silos—it enjoys a status similar to that of "quality assurance" or "ethics" and it has become a critical element of organizational viability. Knowledge management is no longer something interesting to explore—it has become subsumed in the way in which individuals, groups, and organizations work, learn, and remember.

EMERGING ROLES FOR INFORMATION PROFESSIONALS

The KM field has transformed from one led primarily by consultants and other KM practitioners to a bona fide discipline, with a distinct body of knowledge. This has been paralleled by the growing number of academic programs that offer KM as compared to the predominately private sector training that had been the only way to learn about KM up until now.[38] TFPL[39] is a specialist recruitment, advisory, training, and research services company with offices in London focusing on KM, library and information management, records management, and Web and content management. Since 1987, TFPL has worked with organizations in both public and private sectors to help them develop and implement knowledge and information strategies and to recruit and train information and knowledge leaders and their teams. TFPL has drafted a KM skills and competencies guide to provide a clear and practical overview of KM skills and competencies that draws on the practical experience of organizations in a wide range of sectors and with varying approaches to KM.

In general, these KM skills include

- Time management to use their time and energy effectively for acquiring knowledge (spending all day surfing the Net is probably counterproductive).
- Use of different learning techniques to absorb key knowledge and learning quickly.
- Effective skills of advocacy and inquiry to present knowledge to, and gather knowledge from, others.
- Informal networking skills to build influence to gain access to people with knowledge.
- Resource investigation skills.
- Effective IT skills for recording and disseminating information.
- Skills of cooperative problem solving.
- Open dialogue skills.
- Flexibility and willingness to try new things and take educated risks.
- Active review of learning from mistakes, risks, opportunities, and successes.

The TFPL KM skills inventory[40] is based on an extensive international research. The project team contacted over 500 organizations involved in implementing KM, and identified the roles that they had created, the skills that were needed in those roles, and the additional skills that were required across the organization. These key skills included an understanding of the KM concept—the philosophy and theory—and an awareness of the experience of other organizations in developing KM solutions and approaches; an understanding of, and the ability to, identify the business value of KM activities to the organization; an appreciation of the range of activities, initiatives, and labels which are employed to create an environment in which knowledge is effectively created, shared, and used to increase competitive advantage and customer satisfaction.

Knowledge management roles are quite diverse and include such categories as senior and middle management roles—Chief Knowledge Officer (CKO) who ensures that KM goals are in line with organizational strategies and objectives; Chief Learning Officer (CLO) who ensures that the organization acts like a learning organization, improving over time with the help of accumulated best practices and lessons learned; Knowledge Managers who are typically responsible for the acquisition and management of internal and external knowledge. Other roles include

- Knowledge navigators, responsible for knowing where knowledge can be located, also called knowledge brokers.
- Knowledge synthesizers, responsible for facilitating the recording of significant knowledge to organizational memory, also called Knowledge Stewards.
- Content editors, responsible for codifying and structuring content, also called content managers; roles involving capturing and documenting knowledge—researchers, writers, editors.
- Web developers, electronic publishers, intranet managers, content managers.
- Learning-oriented roles such as trainers, facilitators, mentors, coaches—including those with responsibility for developing information and knowledge skills.
- Human resources roles with specific responsibility for developing programs and processes that encourage knowledge-oriented cultures and behaviors.
- Knowledge publishers, responsible for internal publishing functions, usually on an intranet, also called Webmasters, knowledge architects, Knowledge editors.
- Coaches and mentors, responsible for assisting individuals throughout the business unit or practice to develop and learn KM activities and disciplines.
- Help desk activities, including the delivery of KM and information related to training, also called Knowledge Support Office (KSO).

Knowledge management professionals require a multidisciplinary skill-set that consist of such competencies as finding, appraising, and using knowledge, beginning to be able to reformulate questions, navigating through content, evaluating the relevance of content, filtering out what is not needed, and synthesizing from diverse sources in order to apply the knowledge (e.g., to make a decision). Last but not least, they must contribute to the recording of such valuable experiences to organizational memory systems.[41]

CONCLUSION

Knowledge management has assumed a greater priority due to the demographic pressures created by retiring baby boomers. Retirement en masse means a loss of valuable knowledge and know-how that has been accumulated by experience over the years. All organizations, regardless of type of industry, size, country, and so forth will have to face the issue of knowledge continuity. Knowledge continuity is analogous to business continuity: while the latter targets data loss prevention due to disasters, the former targets knowledge loss due to turnover in personnel. Valuable knowledge must not only be preserved and transferred to future workers, but also transferred across geographical and temporal boundaries due to the fact that work today is spread out over networks that may extend beyond organizational boundaries. Knowledge management is the discipline and field of practice that will equip us with the necessary tools, processes, and skill-sets to ensure that knowledge reaches all knowledge workers so that they can carry out their work more efficiently and more effectively.

REFERENCES

1. Merriam-Webster Dictionary Online. http://www.m-w.com/ dictionary/knowledge (accessed November 20, 2008).
2. Leonard, D.; Sensiper, S. The role of tacit knowledge in group innovation. Calif. Manage. Rev. **1998**, *40* (3), 112–132.
3. McDermott, R. Why information technology inspired but cannot deliver knowledge management. Calif. Manage. Rev. **1999**, *41* (4), 103–117.
4. Davenport, T.; Prusak, L. *Working Knowledge*; Harvard Business School Press: Boston, 1998.
5. Barclay, R.; Murray, P. What is knowledge management? Knowledge Praxis. http://www.mediaccess.com/whatis. html, 1997 (accessed November 20, 2008).
6. Grey, D. What is knowledge management? Knowl. Manage. Forum March **1996**.
7. Sarvary, M. Knowledge management and competition in the consulting industry. Calif. Manage. Rev. **1999**, *41* (2), 95–107.
8. Wiig, K. *Knowledge Management Foundations*; Schema Press: Arlington, TX, 1993.
9. Nonaka, I.; Takeuchi, H. *The Knowledge-Creating Company: How Japanese Companies Create the Dynamics of Innovation*; Oxford University Press: New York, 1995.
10. Pasternack, B.; Viscio, A. *The Centerless Corporation*; Simon and Schuster: New York, 1998.
11. Pfeffer, J.; Sutton, R. *The Knowing-Doing Gap: How Smart Companies Turn Knowledge into Action*; Harvard Business School Press: New York, 1999.
12. Ruggles, R.; Holtshouse, D. *The Knowledge Advantage*; Capstone Publishers: Dover, NH, 1999.
13. APQC (The American Productivity and Quality Centre). What is KM? From the APQC knowledge base: http://www.apqc.org/portal/apqc/ksn?paf_gear_id=contentgear-home&paf_dm=full&pageselect=detail&docid=101261 (accessed November 20, 2008).
14. Hibbard, J. Knowledge tools debate. Information Week March 16, 1998. http://www.informationweek.com/673/ 73iudeb.htm (accessed November 20, 2008).
15. Frappaolo, C. Knowledge management: A 2001 perspective. http://www.kwork.org/Stars/KM_perspective.pdf (accessed November 20, 2008).
16. Levinson, M. The ABCs of knowledge management. CIO Magazine http://www.cio.com/article/40343/ABC_An_ Introduction_to_KM/40343/40343/1#1 (accessed November 20, 2008).
17. Bontis, N.; Nikitopoulos, D. Thought leadership on intellectual capital. J. Intel. Capital **2001**, *2* (3), 183–191.

18. Klein, D. *The Strategic Management of Intellectual Capital*; Butterworth-Heineman: Oxford, U.K., 1998.
19. Stewart, T. *Intellectual Capital*; Doubleday: New York, 1997.
20. Stewart, T.A. Software preserves knowledge, people pass it on. Fortune **2000**, *142* (5), 390–392.
21. Rothberg, H.; Erickson, G. *From Knowledge to Intelligence. Creating Competitive Advantage in the New Economy*; Butterworth-Heinemann: Boston, 2005.
22. Dalkir, K. *Knowledge Management Theory and Practice*; Butterworth-Heinemann: Boston, 2005.
23. Kransdorff, A. *Corporate Amnesia: Keeping Know-How in the Company*; Butterworth-Heinemann: Oxford, U.K., 1998.
24. Polanyi, M. *The Tacit Dimension*; Peter Smith: Gloucester, MA, 1966.
25. Glesinger, J. The not-so-hidden cost of lost knowledge. Energy Press J. September 2, **2008**. http://energy .pressand journal.co.uk/Article.aspx/800114/?UserKey= (accessed November 20, 2008).
26. Hutchison, L. Phased retirement saves intellectual capital. St. Louis Commerce Magazine **2001**. http:// www.stlcomm ercemagazine (accessed November 20, 2008).
27. Liu, S.; Fidel, R. Managing aging workforce: Filling the gap between what we know and what is in the system. In Proceedings of the 1st International Conference on Theory and Practice of Electronic Governance, Macao, China, December 10–13, 2007; (ICEGOV '07) ACM: New York, 2007; Vol. 232, 121–128. http://doi.acm.org/10.1145/ 1328057.1328084.
28. Liebowitz, J. Bridging the knowledge and skills gap: tapping federal retirees. Public Personnel Manage. **2004**, *33* (4), 421–447.
29. LaBarre, P. People go, knowledge stays. Fast Company **2001**, *17* (4). http://www.fastcompany.com/ magazine/17/ wyp17.html (accessed November 20, 2008).
30. Wenger, E.; Snyder, W. Communities of practice: The organizational frontier. Harvard Bus. Rev. January–February **2000**, 139–145.
31. Wenger, E.; McDermott, R.; Snyder, W. *Cultivating Communities of Practice: A Guide to Managing Knowledge*; Harvard Business School: Cambridge, MA, 2002.
32. Szulanski, G. *Sticky Knowledge—Barriers to Knowing in a Firm*; Sage: Thousand Oaks, CA, 2003.
33. Alvesson, M.; Karreman, D. Odd couple: Making sense of the curious concept of knowledge management. J. Manage. Stud. **2001**, *38* (7), 995–1018.
34. Drucker, P. *Management: Tasks, Responsibilities, Practices*; Harper & Row: New York, 1973.
35. Senge, P. *The Fifth Discipline: The Art and Practice of the Learning Organization*; Doubleday: New York, 1990.
36. Argyris, M.; Schön, D. *Theory in Practice. Increasing Professional Effectiveness*; Jossey-Bass: San Francisco, 1974.
37. Argyris, C. *Knowledge for Action. A Guide to Overcoming Barriers to Organizational Change*; Jossey-Bass: San Francisco, 1993.
38. Al-Hawamdeh, S. *Knowledge Management: Cultivating Knowledge Professionals*; Chandos Publishing: Rollinsford, NH, 2003.
39. TFPL website: http://www.tfpl.com.
40. TFPL Skills for knowledge management, a briefing paper by TFPL Ltd: Based on research undertaken by TFPL on behalf of the Library and Information Commission; TFPL Ltd.: London, 1999.
41. Henzcel, S. Supporting the KM environment: The roles, responsibilities, and rights of information professionals; Constructive thoughts on knowledge management. Information Outlook **2004**, (1), 14–19.

9 Information Management

Brian Detlor

CONTENTS

INTRODUCTION

Information management (IM) is a broad conceptual term that has various meanings and interpretations among different constituencies. Often the term is used interchangeably with others. For instance, information management is often equated with the management of information resources, the management of information technology (IT), or the management of information policies or standards.[1] Some suggest that information management draws upon ideas from both librarianship and information science.[2] The purpose of this entry is to clarify the meaning of the term "information management," to showcase its major perspectives, and to illustrate how it relates to associated terms.

What is information management (IM)? Information management is the management of the processes and systems that create, acquire, organize, store, distribute, and use information. The goal of information management is to help people and organizations access, process, and use information efficiently and effectively. Doing so helps organizations operate more competitively and strategically, and helps people better accomplish their tasks and become better informed.

This entry adopts a process orientation toward information management where IM is viewed as the control over the information life cycle. Various models of information processes exist; some of the major processes involved in information life cycle concern those that create, acquire, organize, store, distribute, and use information.

Importantly, this entry recognizes three major perspectives of information management: the organizational, library, and personal perspectives. By far, the organizational perspective is the most predominant and popular. In a nutshell, this perspective deals with the management of all information processes involved in the information life cycle with the goal of helping an organization reach its competitive and strategic objectives. A variety of information resources are managed by organizations. These include transactional information stored in databases, summarized information found in data warehouses, and unstructured information content found in documents and reports. From the organizational perspective, the management of IT is a major component of any IM plan. It is with this perspective where associated terms like information systems management,

IT management, data management, business intelligence, competitive intelligence, content management, and records management have relevance.

The library perspective of information management recognizes the unique role of information provision organizations, such as libraries, whose central mandate is to provide their clientele with access to information resources and services. As such, these types of organizations view information management primarily as the management of information collections, such as books and journals. With respect to information collections, libraries are neither the creators nor the users of this information. As such, this perspective deals with the management of a subset of information processes involved in the information life cycle with the goal of helping library patrons access and borrow information items held in the collection. It is with the library perspective where associated terms like knowledge organization, classification, cataloging, digital libraries, indexes, and information retrieval systems have relevance.

The personal perspective of information management, though not strong, is similar to the organizational perspective in that it involves the management of all information processes in the information life cycle. The major difference, however, is that the organizational perspective concerns the management of information of interest to the success and well-being of an organization, while the personal perspective deals with the management of information of relevance and concern to the individual.

In terms of this entry's organization, the remainder is structured to further explain the major points just described. First, description is given on the information life cycle and the process view of information management. This is followed by a detailed discussion on each of the three major perspectives of information management: the organizational, library, and personal perspectives. Finally, concluding remarks are made.

A PROCESS VIEW OF INFORMATION MANAGEMENT

Leading information management scholars and organizations purport a process-driven view of IM. For example, Wilson defines information management as "the application of management principles to the acquisition, organization, control, dissemination and use of information relevant to the effective operation of organizations of all kinds."[3] Similarly, Choo defines IM as the management of processes that acquire, create, organize, distribute, and use information.[1] Likewise, the U.S. Government Accountability Office defines information management as "the planning, budgeting, manipulating, and controlling of information throughout its life cycle."[4]

The conceptualization of information management from a process perspective emerged in the early 1990s.[5,6] Advocates of this approach stress that a process model of information management should encompass all or some parts of the information value chain or life cycle. Choo proposes six discrete information-related processes or activities that need to be managed: 1) identification of information needs; 2) acquisition of information to address those needs; 3) organization and storage of information; 4) design and development of information products; 5) distribution of information; and 6) information use.[1] Wilson positions the creation and use of information outside the information management rubric and purports the following six information-related processes pertaining to IM: 1) acquisition; 2) organization; 3) storage; 4) retrieval; 5) access/lending; and 6) dissemination.[7] Not all information management frameworks include information needs identification and information use as processes to be managed. However, many see the most critical issue facing information managers is eliciting information requirements and matching those information needs in the design and delivery of information systems to promote effective and efficient information use.[1,8,9]

With respect to this entry, the following are considered to be the predominant information processes to be managed in IM: information creation, acquisition, organization, storage, distribution, and use. Information creation is the process where individuals and organizations generate and produce new information artifacts and items. Information acquisition is the process where information items are obtained from external sources. Information organization is the process of indexing or classifying information in ways that support easy retrieval at later points in time. Information storage is the process of physically housing information content in structures such as databases or file systems. Information distribution is the process of disseminating, transporting, or sharing information. Information use is the process where individuals and organizations utilize and apply information made available to them. Effectively managing these information processes helps get the right information to the right people in the right forms at the right times and at reasonable costs.[1,10]

THE ORGANIZATIONAL PERSPECTIVE

The organizational perspective is the most predominant perspective of information management. Under the organizational perspective, IM concerns the management and control over the full life cycle of information processes ranging from creation to use for the betterment of the organization itself. In this sense, the management of information processes is seen as a strategic advantage that affords four kinds of benefits to an organization: 1) a reduction of costs; 2) a reduction of uncertainty or risks; 3) added value to existing products and services; and 4) the creation of new value through the introduction of new information-based products and services.[11]

Information as a Resource

Fundamental to the organizational perspective of information management is the view and treatment of information as a strategic resource—one that needs to be managed like any other critical organizational resource, such as people, equipment, and capital. Many organizations recognize the potential value of information and the need to be aware of what information resources exist in an organization, and the costs associated with acquiring, storing, processing, and using that information. Forward-looking companies consider information as a strategic asset that can be leveraged into a competitive advantage in the markets served by the company.[8]

The concept of managing information as an organizational resource emerged in the late 1970s with the creation of the US Paperwork Reduction Act that was established to resolve the huge costs of managing and handling information by bidders for government contracts.[12] It was at this time, that the term information resources management (IRM) became popular and was used to signify the management of both information and information technologies.[13,14] In reality though, the IRM concept was more about the management of data than it was about the management of other types of information, such as documents or reports. Case in point, an empirical assessment of the IRM construct defines IRM as "a comprehensive approach to planning, organizing, budgeting, directing, monitoring and controlling the people, funding, technologies and activities associated with acquiring, storing, processing and distributing data to meet a business need for the benefit of the enterprise"—not other types of information.[15]

This entry suggests that within the organizational perspective of information management, IM is more than just the management of data (e.g., raw facts stored in transactional databases). Rather, information management in organizations involves the management of a varied set of information resources, ranging from data to information.[16]

Data can be considered as "raw facts" that reflect the characteristics of an event or entity. Examples of data items held in an organization would be a customer name, an order quantity, or a unit price. The management of data in organizations traditionally belonged to the "Data Management" function or "Data Resource Management" department. Data management deals with the storage and processing of low-level data items found in transaction processing systems. The focus of data management is to maximize the speed, accuracy, and efficiency of processing and maintaining transactions or records.[1] Data management is concerned with the creation and "acquisition of data, its storage in databases, its manipulation or processing to produce new (value-added) data and reports via application programs, and the transmission (communication) of the data or resulting reports."[8]

Information can be viewed as "meaningful data" where data have been converted into a meaningful and useful context, such as in the identification of a best-selling or worst-selling product item from historical sales data for a company. Examples of information items managed in a company would be summarized information pulled from transactional database systems and stored in data warehouses and/or data marts. Such "business intelligent" systems support decision-making, and allow for the slicing-and-dicing of summarized transactional information to find patterns and trends in operational data (e.g., sales data, supplier data, customer profile data) of importance and relevance to the organization. For example, the mining of summarized transactional data stored in a data warehouse could be used to justify the promotion of a product or service to an untapped market segment, or to measure the effectiveness of a marketing campaign in a certain geographical area.[16]

Though more emphasis in organizations is placed on the management of data and information that is structured and formalized (i.e., data neatly contained within a transactional database or summarized information stored in a data warehouse), the amount of unstructured information that is created, acquired, organized, stored, distributed, and used within an organization usually far exceeds the amount of structured data and information an organization manages.

Unstructured information is the type of information that can be found in reports, documents, e-mail messages, and PowerPoint presentations, among others. This includes reports and documentation generated internally with a company and outside the enterprise as well. For example, managing information concerning industry trends, legislative regulations, competitor happenings, news bulletins, etc. is key to helping an organization stay abreast and react to competitor threats and environmental concerns. This is where information management intersects with a company's "competitive intelligence" initiatives and "environmental scanning" activities. Competitive intelligence refers to the analysis of information about competitors and competitive conditions in particular industries or regions.[17] Environmental scanning refers to the analysis of information about every sector of the external environment that can help an organization plan for its future.[18,19]

Often document management systems, also known as content management systems, help manage unstructured information that is created, acquired, organized, stored, distributed, and used within an organization. These systems support the electronic capture, storage, distribution, archiving, and accessing of documents. These systems typically provide a document repository where documents can be housed, indexed, and accessed. In these repositories, metadata information is maintained about each document that tracks each document's editorial history and relationships to other documents. Indexing of documents within these systems, through both manual keyword classifications and automatic indexing techniques, facilitates easy document retrieval by organizational workers at later points in time.[16]

Unstructured information also includes records of transactional information processing such as invoices, contracts, order requisitions, bills of lading, and financial statements. The actual data may be resident in a transaction database and managed elsewhere, but the entire record of the event, often with signatures, are handled as a complete entity that must be generated, stored, processed, retrieved, and archived. The management of such information is referred to as "records management" and involves the application of systematic and scientific control to all recorded information that an organization needs to do business.[20]

Managing Information Processes

A good information management program in an organization will manage the full life cycle of information ranging from creation to use. For example:

- When generating transactional data, steps will be taken to ensure that the data will be stored following database "normalization rules" to promote data integrity, the single sourcing of data, the reduction of wasted database space, and fast transaction processing.

- When acquiring information, such as the purchase of market research data or competitor intelligence information, steps will be taken to reduce duplicate purchases and to increase the accessibility of any purchased data and information across the enterprise.
- Any data or information that is stored will be adequately protected against unauthorized access, as security, privacy, and copyright concerns exist.
- Data and information stewardship programs will be set up to identify those organizational workers or units who are responsible for the quality and management of certain data and information items.
- Data and information will be regularly backed up for recovery purposes.
- Duplicate or mirror copies of data and information items will be created to facilitate access, and reduce network congestion and/or an overload of requests on the servers on which the data and information reside.
- Old data and outdated information will be archived and/or deleted.[16]

Information Technology's Role

Information technology plays a critical role in the management of information in organizations. However, having said that, it should be understood that IT is the technical medium upon which information is housed, accessed, retrieved, distributed, and used, and not the primary entity that is being managed under the information management rubric. Information processes are.

Nevertheless, much confusion exists over the role IT plays in the management of information in organizations, with some equating information management primarily to the management of IT itself. For example, the mission of the Society for Information Management (SIM), a professional society for chief information officers and senior IT leaders based in the United States, is "to provide international leadership and education in the successful management and use of IT to achieve business objectives."[21] Likewise, Davis and Hamilton define information management as "the management of information systems and information resources by an individual, a group, or an organization" and describe IM as a "new business function with responsibility to define organizational informational requirements, plan, and build an information infrastructure and information systems applications, operate the system, and organize, staff, and manage these activities."[22]

This entry suggests that such descriptions of the information management function in organizations are inappropriate and are better served by alternate terms such as information systems management or IT management. Information systems management refers to the control over the development, design, rollout, and support of information systems applications that support business processes and workflow. Information technology management refers to the management and control over IT (e.g., hardware, software).

A variety of factors need to be considered when managing technology in organizations. The appropriate hardware and software needs to be installed and implemented. Repair and maintenance of hardware and software systems must be done. Licensing concerns must be taken into consideration. Information systems professionals (e.g., programmers, network specialists, database administrators, systems analysts) need to be hired and trained.[16]

Information technology is very important to how information is managed in organizations, and the management of IT should be an integral part of any IM plan.[11] After all, IT facilitates the ability to support information creation, acquisition, organization, storage, distribution, and use in both efficient and effective manners.

Organizational Information Processing

Information management is concerned with organizational information processing. Two broad orientations exist in the organizational information processing literature that have implications on information management.[23]

The first, mainly developed at Carnegie Mellon University and represented by Herbert Simon, James March, and Richard Cyert, sees an organization's ability to process information as the core of managerial and organizational competencies and organizations as bounded, rational systems.[24] Here, strategies to improve information processing capabilities concern increasing an organization's information processing capacity and reducing an organization's need for information processing.[25]

The second, represented by Karl Weick and Richard Daft, sees organizations as loosely coupled systems where individual participants collectively develop shared interpretations of the environment and then act on the basis of this interpretation. In this sense, information processing is about reducing the equivocality or ambiguousness of information about the organization's external environment.[26]

Taking these two orientations of organizational information processing together, information management then is about increasing an organization's information processing capacity and reducing both information processing needs and information equivocality.

THE LIBRARY PERSPECTIVE

Outside of the organizational context, information management also has meaning in the library world and to other information provision organizations whose central mandate is to provide clientele with access to information resources and services. Information management is of concern to all kinds of libraries, such as public libraries and academic and research libraries. This includes corporate libraries that manage serial subscriptions and electronic access to industry reports and electronic databases for workers and employees in their organizations.

From a library perspective, information management concerns the management of information collections, such as books and journals. The goal of information management from a library perspective is to help library patrons access and borrow information items held in the collection. A variety of activities surround the management of a library collection, including the development of collection policies and materials budgets, the selection of collection items, the analysis of collection usage and end user collection needs, training of collection staff, preservation of collection items, and the development of cooperative collections with other institutions.[27]

Since libraries are neither the creators nor the users of information, this perspective deals with the management of a subset of information processes involved in the information life cycle. For example, Wilson identifies six information-related processes pertaining to IM that are applicable to the library perspective: 1) acquisition; 2) organization; 3) storage; 4) retrieval; 5) access/lending; and 6) dissemination.[7]

Information acquisition involves the process of buying or securing information from sources external to the library for the collection. Care must be taken to ensure that the correct information items are acquired (those that match the information needs of end users) and at reasonable costs.

Information organization pertains to the process of indexing or classifying information housed in the collection to support easy retrieval at later points in time. Today, this process is sometimes referred to as "knowledge organization" in the library world. For example, the International Society for Knowledge Organization (ISKO) utilizes the term "knowledge organization" to represent the process of how documents, document representations (such as bibliographic records), and concepts (keywords, constructs) are ordered and classified.[28] Likewise, Anderson defines knowledge organization as the "the description of documents, their contents, features and purposes, and the organization of these descriptions so as to make these documents and their parts accessible to persons seeking them or the messages that they contain" and describes how knowledge organization encompasses "every type and method of indexing, abstracting, cataloging, classification, records management, bibliography and the creation of textual or bibliographic databases for information retrieval."[29] In this sense, knowledge organization deals with both processes and systems.[30] With respect to information management, this entry suggests that the use of the "knowledge organization" label is misleading. In actuality, information items (such as documents and document representations) are being organized or ordered (i.e., indexed, classified, cataloged) rather than knowledge items (concepts, constructs) per se. As such, "information organization" is suggested to be a better label to use when talking about the indexing and classification of items held in a collection, at least from a library perspective of IM.

Information storage refers to physically housing items in the collection. This encompasses the housing of both paper and electronic documents (and their document representations). This could be accomplished by storing books and journals in physical stacks in the library or storing full-text electronic versions of documents in an electronic or digital library.

Information retrieval involves the process of searching and finding information in the collection. Typically end users will conduct a search query using electronic tools that are Web-based to find items of interest in the collection. In the information retrieval process, end users themselves, or information search intermediaries (librarians) working on the behalf of end users, "pull" the information that is needed from the collection.

Information access/lending involves the process of providing physical or electronic access to the collection and the ability to check out information items of interest. For paper-based documents, this may involve signing out and borrowing a physical information item. For information in electronic form, this may involve viewing the information item online and/or downloading a copy of the information item from the collection.

Information dissemination is the process of circulating physical information items of interest from the collection to end users. Traditionally, methods of dissemination involve the distribution of photocopied journal content pages, or the circulation of documents. Today, this has largely been replaced with electronic alert services that "push" information items in the collection of interest to specific users based on stored end user profiles.

The management of library information collections is a complex and ever-evolving process.[31] The extensive digitization of information resources has placed new pressures on libraries to respond to securing the requisite skills, resources, and competencies to successfully manage digital library collections.[32] In order to manage the transition and reliance on digital information collections, it is important more than ever for libraries to consider the expectations and needs of end users, as well as limitations in library staff and budget adaptability.[31] These are critical factors in rolling out any successful information management program from a library perspective.

THE PERSONAL PERSPECTIVE

Information management from the personal perspective refers to how individuals create, acquire, organize, store, distribute, and use information for personal purposes. This can concern the management of information for everyday use (e.g., personal calendars, schedules, diaries, news items) or work-related reasons (e.g., work schedules, things-to-do, project files). As such, personal information management involves the handling and processing of information over the entire information life cycle, just as in the case of the organizational perspective. However, the personal information management perspective differs from the organizational perspective of IM in that personal information management concerns items of interest to the individual, not the organization.

Central to the personal perspective of IM is the need to manage the information processes of information creation, acquisition, organization, distribution, and use so that the right information is accessible and available in the right place, in the right form, and of sufficient completeness and quality to meet personal information needs. A variety of information items are created, acquired, organized, stored, distributed, and used by people for personal purposes. These include personal notes, personal journals, Web pages, e-mail messages, news articles, address books, calendar dates, reminders, fax communications, etc.

Technologies and tools, such as electronic personal information managers like PDAs, help people carry out these processes more efficiently and effectively.[33] Cheap and fast search and storage technologies bring stability and order to people's often chaotic and messy personal information environments, and facilitate making the most of people's personal information collections.[34] Despite the benefits of these technological tools, there is some evidence to suggest that technological advances are less important in determining how individuals organize and use information than are the tasks that people perform.[35]

It is interesting to note that the phrase "personal information management" was first used in the 1980s with the advent of personal computers and their capacity to process and manage information.[36] However, the concept of "personal information management" was most likely first implied back in 1945 by Vannevar Bush when he envisioned using the "Memex" machine for personal information management—a machine that allowed an individual to store all his or her books, records, and communications and consult those personal information sources with great speed and flexibility.[37]

As the proliferation of personal computing devices and the explosion of the amount of information that is created, generated, and used continues to increase, the relevance of information management from the personal perspective will likely gain more attention and importance from both researchers and practitioners alike.

CONCLUSION

This entry provided a review and discussion of the information management concept. Importantly, a process-oriented definition of IM was proposed and three distinct perspectives of information management were described: the organizational, library, and personal perspectives. It was suggested that the organizational perspective was the most predominant, though the other two were shown to have relevance and meaning in today's world.

This entry emphasized the importance of information management. IM allows organizations to reach strategic goals and make sound decisions. IM enables libraries and other information provision organizations to manage information collections effectively and efficiently. IM helps people manage their own personal information collections.

This entry also described how IM is not so much about the management of technology, but rather more about the management of the processes of IM, specifically the creation, acquisition, organization, storage, distribution, and usage of information.

According to the current scope of the *International Journal of Information Management*, the challenge for information management now is less about managing activities that collect, store, and disseminate information, and more about placing greater focus on managing activities that make changes in patterns of behavior of customers, people, and organizations, and information that leads to changes in the way people use information.[38] This may not be such an easy task. People and their information behaviors are hard to change. So are organizational cultures.[11] IM is less about solving technical problems and more about addressing the human side of information management. Humans add the context, meaning and value to information, and it is humans who benefit and use this information. As such, "mastering information management is an essentially human task."[39]

REFERENCES

1. Choo, C.W. *Information Management for the Intelligent Organization: The Art of Environmental Scanning*, 3rd Ed.; Learned Information: Medford, NJ, 2002.
2. Macevičiūtė, E.; Wilson, T.D. The development of the information management research area. Inform. Res. **2002**, *7* (3). http://InformationR.net/ir/7-3/paper133.html (accessed July 2008).
3. Wilson, T.D. Information management. In *International Encyclopedia of Information and Library Science*; Routledge: London, 2003; 263–278.
4. http://www.GAO.gov (accessed July 2008).
5. Davenport, T.H. *Process Innovation: Reengineering Work Through Information Technology*; Harvard Business School Press: Boston, 1993.
6. McGee, J.V.; Prusak, L. *Managing Information Strategically*; John Wiley & Sons: Toronto, ON, 1993.

7. Wilson, T.D. 'The nonsense of knowledge management' revisited. In *Introducing Information Management*, Macevičiūtė, E., Wilson, T.D., Eds.; Facet Publishing: London, 2005; 151–164.
8. Karim, N.S.A.; Hussein, R. Managers' perception of information management and the role of information and knowledge managers: The Malaysian perspectives. Int. J. Inform. Manage. **2008**, *28* (2), 114–127.
9. Detlor, B. *Towards Knowledge Portals: From Human Issues to Intelligent Agents*; Kluwer Academic Publishers: Dordrecht, the Netherlands, 2004.
10. Robertson, J. Ten principles of effective information management. KM Column **2005**, November. http://www.steptwo.com.au/papers/kmc_effectiveim/index.html (accessed July 2008).
11. http://choo.fis.utoronto.ca/Imfaq/ (accessed July 2008).
12. Commission on Federal Paperwork, *Information Resources Management*; US Government Printing Office: Washington, DC, 1977.
13. Horton, F.W. *Information Resources Management: Concept and Cases*; Association for Systems Management: Cleveland, OH, 1979.
14. Horton, F.W. *The Information Management Workbook: IRM Made Simple*; Information Management Press: Washington, DC, 1982.
15. Lewis, B.R.; Snyder, C.A.; Rainer, R.K., Jr. An empirical assessment of the information resource management construct. J. Manage. Inform. Syst. **1995**, *12* (1), 199–223.
16. Baltzan, P.; Phillips, A.; Detlor, B. *Business-Driven Information Systems*, 1st Canadian Ed.; McGraw-Hill Ryerson: Whitby, ON, 2008.
17. Sutton, H. *Competitive Intelligence*; The Conference Board Inc.: New York, 1988.
18. Aguilar, F.J. *Scanning the Business Environment*; MacMillan Co.: New York, 1967.
19. Choo, C.W.; Auster, E. Scanning the business environment: Acquisition and use of information by managers. In *Annual Review of Information Science and Technology*, Williams, M.E., Ed.; Learned Information: Medford, NJ, 1993.
20. Robek, M.F.; Brown, G.F.; Wilmer, O.M. *Information and Records Management*, 3rd Ed.; Glencoe Publishing: Encino, CA, 1987.
21. http://www.simnet.org (accessed July 2008).
22. Davis, G.B.; Hamilton, S. *Managing Information: How Information Systems Impact Organizational Strategy*; Business One Irwin: Homewood, IL, 1993.
23. Choo, C.W. Towards an informational model of organizations. Can. J. Inform. Sci. **1991**, *16* (3), 32–62.
24. Simon, H. *Administrative Behavior: A Study of Decision-Making Processes in Administrative Organization*, 3rd Ed.; The Free Press: New York, 1976.
25. Galbraith, J.R. *Organization Design*; Addison-Wesley: Reading, MA, 1977.
26. Weick, K.E.; Daft, R.L. The effectiveness of interpretation systems. In *Organizational Effectiveness: A Comparison of Multiple Models*, Cameron, K.S., Whetten, D.A., Eds.; Academic Press: New York, 1983; 71–93.
27. Branin, J.J., Ed. *Collection Management in the 1990s*; American Library Association: Chicago, 1993.
28. http://www.isko.org/ko.html (accessed July 2008).
29. Anderson, J.D. Organization of knowledge. In *International Encyclopedia of Information and Library Science*, Feather, J., Sturges, P., Eds.; Routledge: London, 1996; 336–353.
30. http://www.db.dk/bh/lifeboat_ko/CONCEPTS/knowledge_organization.htm (accessed July 2008).
31. Branin, J.; Groen, F.; Thorin, S. The changing nature of collection management in research libraries. Libr. Resour. Tech. Serv. **2000**, *44* (1), 23–32.
32. Sreenivasulu, V. The role of a digital librarian in the management of digital information systems (DIS). Electron. Libr. **2000**, *18* (1), 12–20.
33. Jones, W. *Keeping Found Things Found: The Study and Practice of Personal Information Management*; Morgan Kaufmann Publishers: Burlington, MA, 2008.
34. Teevan, J.; Jones, W.; Bederson, B.B. Personal information management. Commun. ACM **2006**, *49* (1), 40–43.
35. Barreau, D. The persistence of behavior and form in the organization of personal information. J. Am. Soc. Inform. Sci. Technol. **2008**, *59* (2), 307–317.
36. Lansdale, M. The psychology of personal information management. Appl. Ergon. **1988**, *19* (1), 55–66.
37. Bush, V. As we may think. The Atlantic Monthly July **1945**, *176* (1), 101–108.
38. http://www.elsevier.com/wps/find/journaldescription.cws_ home/30434/description#description (accessed July 2008).
39. Davenport, T. Putting the I in IT. In *Mastering Information Management*; Pearson Education: London, 2000.

10 Digital Asset Management

James E.P. Currall and Michael S. Moss

CONTENTS

INTRODUCTION

There is a tendency to suggest that managing digital assets is radically different from the management of traditional stock in archives and libraries and therefore requires the establishment of separate units with specialist technical staff. While it is true that there are technical challenges and that digital assets behave differently from their analogue equivalents, stock selection and collection building remain constant. The specialist skills of curators of different types of assets continue to be needed. This is not just because they have different semantic and technical metadata, but because, just as in the analogue, they require specialist knowledge in their conservation and use. In any strategic approach to digital asset management the relationship of the content to organizational goals must be given priority over the technical, just as in any established archive or library environment. What at present sets the digital apart from the analogue is the scale of resources required for hardware, software, and technical support. When confronted by the digital and technical experts that call themselves information specialists, archivists and librarians need to remember that is what they are and that they have centuries of experience behind them.

WHERE TO START?

On the subject of preserving digital content there is a "bewildering array of essays, reports case studies, conference proceedings, workshops, and training venues with an equally confusing ranges of recommendations, proposals, predictions, and procedures" with major initiatives in many parts of the world. Some examples are Digital Preservation (Library of Congress) that is home to The National Digital Information Infrastructure and Preservation Program established in 2000,[1] the InterPARES project based at the University of British Columbia,[2] Preserving Access to Digital Information at the National Library of Australia,[3] Ryukoku University's Digital Archives Research

Center in Japan,[4] Digital Preservation Europe supported by the European Commission,[5] and the Digital Preservation Coalition in the United Kingdom established in 2001.[6] In January 2008 OCLC announced the formation of a "Task Force on Sustainable Digital Preservation and Access" "to explore dimensions of the sustainability challenge that have never been addressed before, and make the societal and institutional cases for supporting data repositories."[7] Although we all create information for our individual needs, the information that mostly concerns these initiatives is produced in an institutional or organizational context. Much of the literature and most projects take as their starting point "the complexity of preservation and long-term retrieval" of digital content,[8] rather than the processes involved in its creation and the business needs that might drive such investment, the traditional point of departure of the information professions in the analogue. This has consequences for both the analysis of the problem and any recommendations that may result.

MANAGING ASSETS

Much of the established literature concerns itself with preserving objects, where the objects are encoded in file formats that have technical properties and require processes of "life support" to remain accessible and therefore (presumably) useful. More recently there is a growing body of literature and initiatives around aggregations of objects in what are termed "repositories" and the processes that should be in place for a repository to be regarded as "trusted"[9] [*sic*] or perhaps better described as "trustworthy." Such discussion, which is centered on the question "How" is of course necessary, but it is a long way downstream of the really important issues which all begin, as they always have done, with "W"—What?, Why?, Who?, Where?, When? Central to any management task in any setting is the purpose for which it is taking place. This is often lost in the excitement of processes and technicalities. The Research Roadmap Working Group of Digital Preservation Europe recently examined the challenges of preservation from five vantage points: digital object level, collection level, repository level, process level, and organizational environment.[10] Only the last of these is concerned with creation and use and none are really centered on information content or purpose.

An instance of what happens if a narrow technical process view of management is taken is the treatment of risk in relation to digital material. It is invariably viewed as a set of threats to the integrity, renderability, or understandability of files, in other words downstream risks that require formalized process to mitigate. For example such risks involve server failure, fire, and flood—threats not opportunities. As Ross avers

> where preservation is concerned, the "risk amplifiers" have taken the high ground from "risk attenuators," as is evident from the growth in the number of publications, conferences, and conference presentations during the past ten years that stress how essential it is that we overcome the obstacles to the longevity of digital objects.[11]

As Harvey points out this rhetoric "is lamentably short on supporting specifics and evidence."[12] Such an approach both exaggerates the curatorial imperative and gives the impression that all digital objects, whatever their provenance and purpose, have more in common than the fact that they are represented as bit patterns (1s and 0s). This is fundamentally different from experience of the analogue paper world where no one would claim that all printed matter or manuscript material shared a common ontological status or an imperative to preserve. This confusion has been compounded by the development of mass storage devices that appear to offer the opportunity to keep "everything" irrespective of its current or likely future value and a pervasive postmodernism that problematizes the dominant discourse thereby suggesting that every information object has equivalent value.[13] As Greene puts it "who has the objectivity necessary to identify with certainty what is a turd and what is a 'critically important record?' "[14]

If we think of all information in the digital world as "objects," with no thought as to what information they contain or of the fact that they have more or less, rather than equal value then we are not so much managing assets as commodities. The purpose of this entry is to explore the issues that are important in Asset Management, with an eye to the fact that the assets are Digital, rather than the issues surrounding the Management of the Digital with the fact that they are Assets being incidental. It would be rather like managing a Wal-Mart store and forgetting that the stock all has different shelf lives and patterns of demand.

A Suggested Approach

Information has always been generated by processes that involve technology whether it be a stylus to write on slivers of bark on the frontier of the Roman empire in the first century AD[15] or a PC to generate a bit pattern in the twenty-first century. The relationship between process, available technologies, and societal change has been much researched by those interested in the history of material culture, particularly the printed book, who warn against a techno-deterministic presentism.[16–21] Heeding such advice and by investigating workflow, commentators are beginning to advance a different approach with the emphasis firmly on business needs and what are termed "artful processes [that] depend on the skills, experience, and judgment of the primary actors."[22] Those responsible for the creation and use of information objects, in turn, determine curation and preservation strategies and policies rather than these being imposed by technologists and records managers. Established practice in the analogue information world, accumulated over hundreds of years, is being restated in part by Web 2.0 technologies with Really Simple Syndication (RSS) and Atom feeds. This runs counter to the determination of information and Information and Communications Technology (ICT) professionals to formalize process and maintain control of information distribution, in ways that do not map well onto the needs and expectations of users. As long ago as 1997, the Effective Records Management (ERM) Project at the University of Glasgow in Scotland studied how information might best be managed in the digital world, with an emphasis on the information content and the needs and practices of those creating and using it. Using a demonstrator system, the ERM Project showed that such an approach to information handling effectively integrates technology and addresses the "risk amplifiers" in the creation and curation of digital information.[22] Gilland-Swetland reached much the same conclusion in a study in 2000.[23] If the goal is no longer to work towards rigidly integrated and formalized information assets but towards "looser and more dynamic couplings between service providers and consumers," then the individual characteristics and purposes of information objects becomes easier to describe.[24]

An approach to Digital Asset Management based on content and its value (What? and Why? questions) immediately raises the prospect of selection which clearly has to be based on some sort of rationale. This will vary from one setting to another; perhaps business need or collection policy and development or in the case of an individual acting in a private capacity; this may be purely sentiment. For all the talk of the emergence of a new preservation paradigm defined by the digital, this is the way it is in the analogue where information professionals have always had to work in a variety of institutional contexts and collaborate with "collectors."[25]

Managing assets has a cost associated with it and compared to paper information objects, digital information objects are less likely to survive being dumped on a shelf and forgotten about for years—in other words, benign neglect is unlikely to be a good strategy. This suggests that management of digital assets requires management of costs and inputs also. It is essential to grasp that preservation of any information object is an investment in order to realize future benefits from it. There is clearly an art to this in order to ensure that what is preserved does in fact bring benefits that justify the costs that have been incurred in preserving it, even if these do not become apparent for a very long time and are difficult to calculate.

CHALLENGES

One of the challenges for information professionals in the management of digital assets in relation to their nature as objects is that their very ontology appears to sweep away the curatorial boundaries that have separated libraries from archives, archives from museums, museums from galleries. A pattern of bits is relentlessly the same, whether it represents a new installation or an old master, a most secret report from the security services to an e-mail to a lover, a book, or this entry. The technical actions required by curatorial staff to preserve the pattern of bits are precisely the same, even if there is as yet no clear agreement about precisely what these should be. The reaction of the curatorial professions has been to attempt to translate their difference into the digital often by insisting on different standards of metadata or different approaches to appraisal or privileging that will be discussed later, rather than by focusing on the characteristics of the objects themselves and then concentrating on the actions required to preserve them. The other challenge is, paradoxically, almost the reverse and is based on the notion that precisely because all the objects are composed of 1s and 0s, that a single repository with a single metadata description framework is equally suitable for all types of object, whether they represent motion picture, sound, still image, engineering drawing, or character-based text, or whether they are records of banking transactions, minutes of meetings, art works, computer games, or state secrets. Such a technical approach ignores any underlying ontological characteristics that require different approaches to their curation and management. In the analogue a music score may be held in the same repository as a medieval manuscript, but the each require quite different curatorial approaches.

It is their status as information objects that determines their selection, description, and management as assets, whilst their status as digital objects determines how they are managed at a technical level. The former requires recognition of their difference, whilst the latter requires an acknowledgment of their sameness. We will distinguish between these two sorts of management as "Asset Management" and "Technical Management."

Digital Objects

There are broadly two origins of digital objects that lead to different approaches to their value as assets and the way in which they are managed: those that are born digital and those that are digitized from an analogue original that already forms part of a collection. From a technical management perspective, this is often confused and for convenience they are treated as if they have the same status from the perspective of asset management. This is largely because archives, libraries, and museums have or are investing heavily in digitization, often with the encouragement of external agencies with other agendas, for example, the Japanese Government is committed to make publicly available all the documents relating to the Second World War in an attempt to seek closure with their neighbors for wartime atrocities.[26]

The digitized object is a surrogate for an analogue original that has been appraised, privileged, or selected to form part of an institutional or private collection. Even if the digital surrogate permits exploration of features of the object not visible in the original, for example, in the *Beowulf* manuscript[27] or the Durham *Liber Vitae*,[28] it is not the original, and it may be that in the future with further technical development we will be able to see even more. Colin Webb, Director of Preservation Services at the National Library of Australia, warned "we shouldn't assume we can automatically convert handwritten, or even printed text with a variety of type faces in poor condition, into highly accurate searchable text."[29] Some digitization projects are the equivalent of analogue microfilming projects that sought to conserve heavily used originals by making the contents available in an alternative media, census returns and newspapers are good examples. If the digitization process involves either manual indexing, as with census returns, or optical character recognition, or old newspapers, it will be much more expensive and problematic than microfilming. Others and possibly the majority are not. They are usually conceived as learning resources that contain selected objects from collections that are situated in semi-structured environments to provide online users with a range of learning opportunities. The management of the assets in such projects can easily become haphazard, if care is not taken from the outset to ensure that preservation-quality images are made usually in Tagged Image File Format (TIFF) with appropriate technical metadata and, as importantly, they are properly referenced and cross-referenced to the analogue original.[30]

An essential criterion for all digitization projects is good project planning that includes a sustainability strategy and above all does not abandon the editorial controls familiar in the analogue. Digital objects still need to be described and cataloged in exactly the same way as their analogue equivalents, particularly where their context is within a learning resource. It is often tempting to reduce the budget for such management processes, as inevitably it drives up the unit cost, and to assume wrongly in most cases that income generation will cover at least part of the outlay. This is only true for a very small fraction of projects, where the digitized objects themselves have to be paid for by the customer, as is usually the case with census returns. Much also is made of the potential of repurposing digital surrogates in other learning environments, but there is little evidence to suggest this happens except perhaps on a very limited scale, partly because of advances in digitizing and distribution technologies, and partly because digital objects used in different settings have different metadata requirements.

The born digital object is "original" in that there is no version available on other media to fall back on if it becomes damaged and, since vast quantities of these are produced as a product or by-product of daily work in organizations, they have usually not been subject to selection for a collection. In managing such assets it is important to recognize that the process of selection from the moment of creation can work in reverse to the analogue. The retention of an object in an e-mail folder, for example, is often automatic and requires deliberate intervention to remove it, albeit sometimes with warning barriers, whereas in the analogue the decision to file rather than throw in the wastepaper basket demands a deliberate decision by the creator or recipient or their agents. Born digital objects have existed since the mid-1950s and with the advent of the PC from the 1970s information migrated rapidly into the digital.[31] A result of these developments was that processes familiar in the analogue world disappeared. For example, printed text was no longer "set" by a compositor, but simply converted into type from a word processed file and as a result often established editorial processes were abandoned. With the development of client–server architecture, from the 1980s and later Web-based architecture distribution of information objects was radically transformed and instead of copies being made, as for example in the printing of books, users viewed a single instantiation many times from a multiplicity of sites. This development finally demolished the intellectual distinction, which was already being eroded by technology, between archives that held unique objects and libraries that held multiple copies. There were now increasingly only unique objects, differentiated by the degree of intermediation—an online journal can be expected to have processes for quality review and refinement, whereas a personal Web site is unlikely to. This in a sense was the Gutenberg revolution the other way round, instead of copies of original being made available in print and widely distributed, the original itself could be viewed many times from many places.

Characteristics

Digital information assets, whilst having a great deal in common with their analogue cousins, have a number of characteristics that set them apart, and present challenges for their management and in particular for their long-term survival.[32] The most obvious is that individual objects are internally dynamic and inherently unstable in ways that their analogue equivalents could only be partially so.[33] A book or journal article used to have a critical apparatus that referred to other stable analogue resources that could be discovered usually in libraries, archives, museums, and research institutes. Now, as in this entry, they include "hot links" to Web sites and blogs that we can expect to be dynamic and in some cases to disappear. This is the problem that Brewster Kahle has sought to address in the Internet Archive.[34] Although a useful tool, in itself it is full of such broken links.

Other types of dynamic "behaviors" are often embedded in digital documents such as macro code or graphics that depend on specific versions of rendering software to function correctly. For the library community it is now difficult, if not impossible, to distinguish between editions or versions and, as anyone who has used track changes knows, to observe with any clarity the gestation of the "original." Wikipedia, for example, is edited continuously with little of the process of an analogue equivalent, although in this case there is at least a mechanism to cite a particular instantiation of an article. As problematic is the rendition of an "original" in a browser, word processing or other type of program that depends on the user settings, software version, screen size, printer configured for the system, and perhaps, the speed of an Internet connection. These may seem trivial problems to a technologist, but to those responsible for asset management, they present intellectual, technical, logical, and management challenges. In the analogue they are of vital importance, where we might describe this as a beautiful edition and that as a cheap edition or where we want to know precisely what an artist intended or the precise process of gestation of a literary work. This is why, although we may place a wide range of material in a digital repository, curatorial practice and user needs must continue to be differentiated.

It is often asked if all digital information assets share characteristics sufficient to make the idea of a single digital repository for a wide variety of assets a feasible proposition. In essence this question is about whether the management needs of music files are the same as committee papers, or whether the needs of scientific data files are the same as video. In-so-much as these are all files containing bit patterns of 1s and 0s, they might superficially appear to require the same treatment. Such an analysis fails to take account two very important characteristics of digital assets: the two differing types of metadata required adequately to describe them. Basic Dublin Core[35] metadata superficially appears to provide a simple level of description that can be applied to a wide range of digital assets, but whilst it tackles basic description, it does not deal with technical attributes that are essential for rendition, calibration, and the physical context of the object. Consider the 40–50 attributes detailed in the JPEG images stored automatically by digital cameras or the similar number of attributes that can be stored in an MP3 file on a MP3 player. Dublin Core represents just the attributes that file types may have in common, but the considerable number of attributes (stored within the file itself or externally) that differentiate formats may require very different treatment. In this context, it should be remembered that the purpose of information assets revolves around their intellectual content rather than their technical attributes and different types of content need different curation and management regimes, irrespective of differences in media type, file format, and such like.

The file formats used for storing digital information have an intimate relationship with both their intellectual content and the software required for their rendition. The management needs of file types vary in relation to the ownership of the format, quite apart from the content or the medium of the file. For example, the "shelf life" of files that are in proprietary formats (and thus under the control of a single commercial organization)[36] is significantly different from those that are nonproprietary[37] or proprietary,[38] but can be rendered and edited by a range of different pieces of software written by different organizations or individuals. Paper documents left in boxes in a storeroom decay relatively slowly (unless the environmental conditions are particularly unfavorable) and gradually, so that inspection will reveal when action needs to be taken to preserve them. Digital material, which needs hardware and software to render it, is very different. The media on which digital material is recorded are relatively unstable and a programme of transfer to new media is an essential management action. File formats suffer from technical obsolescence as hardware and software is developed and the environments that once rendered the file disappear from everyday use. This tends to happen more quickly for proprietary formats, as commercial pressures require constant change to ensure that products continue to produce healthy revenue streams.

Collections

Harvey in his useful treatment of the subject in a digital environment is unequivocal in declaring "Selection decisions are essential in managing collections of heritage materials."[39] Not everyone would agree that selection to form collections is desirable. Lynch claims "in the humanities scholars are using the digital medium to circumvent the haphazard historical gerrymandering of knowledge into institutional collections belonging to communities."[40] He believes that objects simply by being available on the Web will "find their own unexpected user communities" and there is, therefore, no need to select.[41] Although it is difficult to quarrel, this approach implies a keep everything "for ever" mentalité that is expensive and almost certainly unrealistic, and also that search engine algorithms are value free. Over a decade ago Miksa corrected the mistaken impression that even then the whole content of the web could be thought of as akin to a giant library or archive, preferring instead to see it from a library perspective as just an extension of the bibliographic universe from which to choose. [42] Selection of content to form collections depends on the survival and availability of material that accord with the intentions of the collector that may not of course be consistent over time. It is often assumed by information professionals that they are the sole arbiters in the process of selection rather than being, as it were, the bar tenders in the "Last Chance Saloon." The survival of all objects depends on chains of decisions that, even if haphazard, are rarely accidental. Such intentions are more often than not the context from which the object is chosen by a library, an archive or museum or even individuals to form part of their collections. For example a library that specializes in the French language will buy books about French not Afrikaans, an archive that collects business papers will be unlikely to acquire papers of bishops or imams, and an individual who collects broadsheets will not buy encyclopedias. We must never lose sight of the fact that collections are about content, something that enthusiasts for digital repositories sometimes seem to fail to grasp in trying to build up their holdings as part of a numbers game or a quest for a genre with unusual technical features.

The very concept of a collection is not straightforward and is open to a number of interpretations.[43] A library might call the whole of its holdings a collection or identify separate collections of significant material as special collections. An archive will invariably define collections in its holdings. Such differences often reflect ownership or provenance or typology or combinations of them. In the analogue the curator can simply point to the shelves that contain a collection and the same applies even when a collection is distributed. In the digital, boundaries are much more fluid and single objects can be selected from any source to form a collection and never need to be physically assembled in a library, archive, or museum let alone a single digital repository. This may benefit users, but only serves to complicate asset management. The virtual collection will inevitably be worth more than the parts, but there will always be a risk that some parts may disappear at the flick of a switch. It is easy to magnify such risks. They were there in the analogue, particularly when collections were in private hands. In 1972 the Earl Fitzwilliam burnt 19 tons of family papers on a bonfire at Wentworth Woodhouse in Yorkshire in northern England that lasted 3 weeks.[44] Famously Honoré Jaxon's huge collection of papers about Louis Riel's Resistance in Canada in 1885 became landfill after his eviction from his New York home in 1952.[45] Data loss, like so much else, depends on the context in which it was created and held. It would be reprehensible if data that supported an important scientific advance that was funded by external agencies was deliberately destroyed, whereas a poet or artist has every right to destroy or never to keep their working notes or drawings. This may be regretted and efforts may be made to persuade them otherwise; but every individual or organization has a perfect right to destroy data providing they are not contravening regulation or have assessed the risk of so doing.

A fundamental purpose of libraries is to provide access to information that has been collected and preserved. In the paper world and the early years of the digital world, the best way to achieve this was by owning copies of the relevant material and lending this to patrons or allowing them reference access within the library. Increasingly in the digital world, libraries are negotiating access agreements to digital assets on the servers of publishers, aggregators, and other types of collection owners or agents, and which members can access on their desktops.[46] The collections are becoming (at least partly) virtual and there is increasing concern as to what happens to access at the termination of agreements. In the paper world when subscription to a journal series is terminated, patrons can still obtain access to the issues subscribed to, but this is not guaranteed in the e-journal world. There are a number of projects and services that are being developed to try to address this problem. One such is the open source LOCKSS (Lots Of Copies Keeps Stuff Safe)[47] project that provides a mechanism for libraries to cache copies of journal content if their contract with the publisher permits this and furthermore to compare the cached content with other participating libraries and, if necessary, repair it to take care of problems that may result from corruption of the files. Another approach is being taken by the Portico service which "provides a permanent archive of electronic scholarly journals," to which libraries can subscribe.[48] The former approach gives libraries a type of ownership of the bit patterns representing the e-journals, but is designed to be a very low maintenance system which requires a low level of technical expertise, and therefore cost. The latter "outsources" the maintenance to the Portico service, but does not give the library any direct form of ownership of the bit patterns.

In the academic world, libraries have become increasingly interested in institutional digital repositories as a means to "own copies of" and manage the research output of their institutions. There is an interesting debate as to whether academics see their institution as the natural route for publishing their work or if discipline-based repositories fit more naturally with their culture and content. Davis and Connolly found that faculty at Cornell University showed relatively little interest in the institutional repository, tending towards a disciplinary culture rather than an institutional one.[49] It will be intriguing to see whether or not institutional repositories become established within academic culture and libraries continue to have an "ownership" role for institutional content as part of the development of their collections in the digital age. Attempts to force members of the academy to deposit research outputs and core data are unlikely to succeed as they immediately raise questions about academic freedom and intellectual property rights. There is no shortage of open source software for the creation of such repositories, for example, e-prints, Fedora, and DSpace are readily available.[50] Although these systems are intended to make the management of digital assets relatively easy and cost-effective, much time, effort, and resource is required to master them and put them to use and this is really only practicable in large, well-resourced organizations where a clear payback can be demonstrated.

In developing digital collection policy digital asset managers need to establish, as information managers have always had to, who the most appropriate custodians of the material under consideration are. Is this collection a place where such material should be housed? Such questions are never easy and the long-term issues around cost and management of digital material make the consequences of such decisions ever more involved. This is, of course, how it has always been and digital storage and access does not change this. What does change is the ability of third parties to discover material that may be held by a library or archive either illicitly or more commonly being made available without permission of copyright holders. This is particularly true of any performing arts data that by their very nature embody a maze of subsidiary rights where even the best intentioned curators may have trouble tracing ownership. Such complex IPR issues increasingly extend to all types of media, for example, a Web site will incorporate graphic design and images with associated rights as will any document with embedded behaviors that depend on licensed software. Creators of content, including supporting software, and their professional associations and advisers are becoming much more adept at recovering revenue for its use and in policing abuse. Curators who call for some distinction to be made in international copyright law between popular and academic content fail to grasp both how difficult it might be to draw the boundary and the sensitivities of the academic community about IPR and freedom of expression.

MANAGEMENT

The management of digital assets, like that of any other asset, cannot be separated from the overall management of an organization, whether it be a library, museum, archive, a university, or a commercial organization. This means that the senior management of the organization is responsible for the management of digital information assets just as much as they are for other types of asset. With the widespread introduction of the International Financial Supporting Standards (IFRS) organizations are required to declare such assets in their balance sheets, particularly if there is an associated revenue stream, for example, the sale of digital copies, depreciate them and report any contingent liabilities, such as the ownership of content by third parties.[51] For the digital asset manager, this is both an opportunity and a challenge. The opportunity derives from the fact that digital information assets have potential "value" for the organization, the challenge is to be able to present the opportunities to senior management in a way that enables the managers to understand the potential and the risks of not managing them well. In these circumstances auditors can be helpful both in determining "value" for accounting purposes and putting in place appropriate curatorial practices.

Information assets are normally classified in a balance sheet as intangible if they are tangential to an organization's primary goals. Valuing intangibles is tricky, because there has always been a reluctance on the part of accountants to attribute more than a nominal value to them even if a great deal of investment has been made in them, particularly since the dot-com bubble of 1995–2001 which attributed unrealistically large values to such assets. The *espida* project at the University of Glasgow developed a methodology that is widely applicable for this purpose and places emphasis on business need and by extension artful processes.[52]

The priority management gives to managing its digital assets will depend on organizational goals. A university research library that subscribes to many digital resources is likely to take it more seriously than a public library whose principal activity is to lend books. A company in the financial services sector will give it the highest priority if it wishes to remain in business. The ICT community assured management that the problems of storage, access, and preservation that were becoming acute in the analogue environment could be easily resolved by developments in technology. At the most extreme this could be expressed as "digitize the lot and destroy the analogue originals."[53] In some parts of the commercial world, particularly financial services, this strategy was pursued with success, albeit at a cost as much in workflow and data analysis as technology, whereas it led to very heated debates amongst librarians, especially about newspaper collections that were often printed on fragile paper that was both expensive and difficult to conserve and access.[54]

Digitization programs may no longer be so radical, but they often are predicated on the use of cheap off-site storage of the analogue originals. Such an equation can only apply where the analogue objects are already heavily used, as would be case with census returns, or where information can be more easily unlocked from a "machine readable" digital resource such as local newspapers. Initiation costs for making digital copies is expensive and it is often easy to overlook the potential costs of maintenance and exaggerate revenue streams.[55] Increasingly digitization projects result in the provision of online resources as part of a suit of digital services, for example, in the Digital Collections and Programs in the Library of Congress[56] and the Catalogues et Bibliothèque Numérique at the Bibliothèque Nationale de France.[57] Evidence suggests that, as in these two examples, where digital objects are in active use, their curation will be guaranteed as long as they are considered to be mission critical, but the same is true of the analogue. Where there is a business need to keep data alive human resourcefulness and investment will be found.[58]

Problems arise when information objects cease to be needed for current business. This is where a clear distinction needs to be drawn between the content of different objects. A library may be quite happy to delete an online book or cancel a subscription in the confidence that an exact copy will be held elsewhere, for example, in a copyright library, whereas in other contexts there may be requirements to retain noncurrent data for long periods, for example, under the 2002 Sarbanes–Oxley Act in the United States or the introduction in many jurisdictions of the UNECE Århus Convention on Access to Environmental Information.[59] It is no longer possible to assume that such controls only apply in a corporate context, particularly if a research library is in receipt of original electronic data that will need to be reviewed on a case by case basis, and in the United States where libraries and archives are subject to the Patriot Act. The degree to which any organization complies with the regulatory environment is a matter of balancing the risk of noncompliance against the costs of complying. If the penalties for noncompliance are relatively trivial, there is little incentive to invest in the retention of noncurrent information for such purposes. Regulation very rarely requires permanent retention (records relating to fissile material are one instance) and normally stipulates a period after which information assets can be destroyed. These will vary between categories and jurisdictions, and over time. All strategies for the management of digital assets must include procedures for secure destruction that are not as technically straightforward as they may seem. Where assets are retained beyond stipulated retention periods, any contingent liabilities that may reside in them remains and there have been several high profile cases where records that could have been destroyed have been discovered by the courts resulting in heavy penalties.[60] If, however, the noncurrent information has an identifiable ongoing "value" to an organization and the contingent liability arising from retention is considered low then a case may be made to the management to invest in long-term preservation.

In some instances, such as observational data from the solar system or the global environment or digital art, advancing a case for complete permanent retention as a business need is relatively straightforward. This does not mean arguments do not have to be advanced for costs to be subsumed within the overall resource allocation. In the majority of instances long-term, let alone permanent retention, will involve appraisal, privileging, or selection, principally to avoid any contingent liability and to remove objects considered of little value. This is much more complex than appraisal in the analogue because of the very granularity of many digital resources and associated IPR issues. Although there has been much discussion of macro and automated appraisal, the weakness of both approaches is that they embed the formulization of business process by information professionals; for example: "Macro-appraisal asserts that archivists not researchers or creators are society's professional agents appointed by law to form its collective memory."[61] Even for government records it is hard to envisage how this could be the case and in the private sector such an approach would be incredible. What it overlooks is the long tail of intentionality that underpins all information objects from the instant of their creation to their ultimate disposal. In rejecting any "scientific formula" for appraisal decisions Greene was unequivocal in stating that just because it is "localized and contingent"; "Appraisal is messy and complex, and its results are neither predictable nor uniform."[14] Nevertheless management will need to be confident that the process respects the due diligence that stakeholders expect.

A final challenge of the management of digital information assets is to ensure that they are managed in a secure way, such that they are not accidentally lost or fall into the wrong hands. Digital asset managers needs to have in place systems and processes that provide an appropriate level of surety that deposits entrusted to their care will be managed in a way that is commensurate with their value. What this means is not that there is a single defined standard for digital asset management, but that the effort and cost expended on management should be proportionate and that depositors have realistic understanding of what to expect. There is no such thing as an absolute guarantee that a digital asset will be available, accessible, and interpretable for all time. Some assets are required for a set period of time and this is followed by another, perhaps longer period, during which they have value but their survival is less "critical." Such distinctions should be reflected in management practices.

Logistics

Increasingly the tasks involved in digital information asset management are complex and require access to specialist services such as file type identification, format conversion, normalization, encryption/decryption, digital signatures, bit-pattern validation, persistent identifiers, and so forth. There are clear trends toward managing assets through a collection of loosely coupled services over the Internet, rather than via monolithic applications.[62] This trend toward Service Oriented

Architectures is described in a very readable article by Barbara Reed.[63] Whilst this article is written in the context of records management, it applies equally in other areas of information science. Digital asset managers will need to design environments that are appropriate to their needs from such tools and services or contract out this work to specialist consultants. Systems must be designed to suit the type of assets to be managed, and the objectives of the parent organization, providing

- Adequate storage media of appropriate types
- Context, metadata, and finding aids
- Access mechanisms
- Management and preservation services

taking account of regulation and compliance and both management and user perspectives.

Once a business case has been established for preservation, accepted and resources allocated, the capture of digital assets is not as straightforward as the analogue equivalent. There are those who argue that preservation requires intervention by librarians and archivists as the ultimate curators in the design of information systems. There are attendant dangers in confusing these two functions. Publishers may not welcome interference or advice from librarians, preferring to continue to control their digital assets so that they can be repurposed and repackaged, either in part or in whole, in the future. In an academic context it is for senior management and funding bodies to negotiate rights of access to and the deposit of assets that they have financed. This is contested territory that, as we have discussed, raises issues of IPR and freedom of expression that are difficult to resolve. In both the public and private sector the task of records managers is to manage current and noncurrent information within the context of corporate objectives. Sometimes this will result in either the creation of an archive or the transfer of assets to an archive, but often it will not and in these circumstances deposit will be a matter for negotiation. Since the constant is the information object, there needs to be consultation, but neither the records manager nor the archivist or librarian can dictate processes that must fulfill the business needs of the organization and not their own expectations in the way much of the literature on digital preservation suggests.

CONCLUSION

The best advice to a librarian or archivist confronted with the management of digital assets is to remember that it is the content that matters, not the technology. It is salutary to remind those who proclaim that the digital environment represents an information paradigm shift that there have been other revolutions in the management and distribution of information and knowledge with accompanying enabling technologies, such as printing in the fifteenth century and photography in the nineteenth. Librarians and archivists learned to deal with the far-reaching implications of these changes without losing sight of their core objectives to manage, curate, and make available information for the benefit of user communities. They have regularly had to reform their intellectual framework and the ways in which they curate, organize, and reference their collections to accommodate technical change and to match societal expectations which in themselves are constantly modified by technologies. With such a pedigree there is no reason to suppose they will not be a match for the challenge of the digital.

ACKNOWLEDGMENTS

The authors would like to thanks their colleagues and the doctoral students in the Humanities Advanced Technology and Information Institute at the University of Glasgow, particularly Dr. Susan Stuart, and successive students on the M.Sc. Information Management and Preservation programme for their help and inspiration.

REFERENCES

1. http://www.digitalpreservation.gov/ (accessed November 2007).
2. http://www.interpares.org/ (accessed November 2007).
3. http://www.nla.gov.au/padi/ (accessed November 2007).
4. http://www.afc.ryukoku.ac.jp/english/english.html (accessed November 2007).
5. http://www.digitalpreservationeurope.eu/about/ (accessed November 2007).
6. http://www.dpconline.org/graphics/index.html (accessed November 2007).
7. http://www.oclc.org/uk/en/news/releases/200692.htm (accessed March 2008).
8. 'Importance of Digital Preservation' Digital Preservation (Library of Congress) website, http://www.digitalpreservation.gov/importance/ (accessed November 2007).
9. See for example: *Trusted Digital Repositories: Attributes and Responsibilities*; An RLG-OCLC Report. Mountain View, CA, May 2002, http://www.oclc.org/programs/ourwork/past/trustedrep/repositories.pdf (accessed March 2008).
10. http://www.digitalpreservationeurope.eu/publications/dpe_research_roadmap_D72.pdf.
11. Ross, S. *Digital Preservation, Archival Science and Methodological Foundations for Digital Libraries*; keynote address at Ubiquitous Digital Libraries—11th European Conference on Research and Advanced Technology for Digital Libraries, Budapest 2007, author's draft available at: http://www.ecdl2007.org/sross_draft_ECDL_paper.pdf (accessed November 2007).
12. Harvey, D.R. *Preserving Digital Material*; Saur: München, 2005; 25.
13. Himmelfarb, G. Revolution in the library. Libr. Trends **1999**, *47* (4), 612–619.
14. Greene, M.A. Not magic, not science, but art: Comment on 'archival appraisal alchemy' (response to Richard Cox). Choices & Challenges, Collecting by Museums and Archives 2002, http://www.hfmgv.org/research/publications/ symposium2002/papers/greene.asp (accessed November 2007).
15. 'Vindolanda on Line' http://vindolanda.csad.ox.ac.uk/ (accessed November 2007).
16. Burke, P. *A Social History of Knowledge from Gutenberg to Diderot*; Polity Press: Cambridge, U.K., 2000.
17. Headrick, D. *When Information Came of Age: Technologies of Knowledge in the Age of Reason and Revolution 1700–1850*; Oxford University Press: Oxford, U.K., 2000.
18. Levy, D.M. *Scrolling Forward: Making Sense of Documents in the Digital Age*; Arcade: New York, 2001.
19. McLuhan, M. *The Gutenberg Galaxy: The Making of Typographic Man*; University of Toronto Press: Toronto, ON, 1962.
20. Webster, F. *Theories of The Information Society*; Routledge: London and New York, 1995.
21. McKitterick, D. *Print, Manuscript and the Search for Order 1450–1830*; Cambridge University Press: Cambridge and New York, 2003.
22. This work is described in: Currall, J.; Johnson, C.E.; Johnston, P.; Moss, M.S.; Richmond, L.M. *"No Going Back?" The Final Report of the Effective Records Management Project*; Project funded under the JISC Technology Applications Programme JTAP—375, 2001, http://www.gla.ac.uk/infostrat/ERM/Docs/ERM-Final.pdf. (accessed November 2007).
23. Gilliland-Swetland, A.J. *Enduring Paradigm, New Opportunities The Value of the Archival Perspective in the Digital Environment*; Council on Library and Information Resources: Washington, DC, 2000.
24. Hill, C.; Yates, R.; Jones, C.; Kogan, S.L. Beyond predictable workflows: Enhancing productivity in artful business processes. IBM Systems Journal – Business Collaboration **2006**, *45* (6), 674, http://www.research.ibm.com/journal/sj/454/hill.html (accessed November 2007).
25. Harvey, D.R. *Preserving Digital Materials*; Saur: München, 2005; 22–23.
26. http://www.jacar.go.jp/english/ (accessed March 2008).
27. Kiernan, K. Electronic Beowulf; British Library: London, 2004.
28. http://www.dlv.org.uk/ (accessed November 2007).
29. Webb, C. *Limitations and Pitfalls of Digitisation*; National Library of Australia, Staff Papers, 2000, http://www.nla.gov.au/nla/staffpaper/2000/webb5.html (accessed November 2007).
30. See for example Carpenter, J.; Antonowicz, L. *Digitisation of Learning Materials and Community Grids for Learning: Final Evaluation Findings*; Big Lottery Fund, 2006; http://www.biglotteryfund.org.uk/er_eval_digi_final.pdf (accessed March 2008), No.26.
31. A useful timeline, admittedly with a US perspective can be found in the Digital Preservation Management tutorial compiled by Cornell University at http://www.library.cornell.edu/iris/tutorial/dpm/timeline/index.html (accessed November 2007).
32. An overview of some of these characteristics may be found in Currall, J.; Johnson, C.E.; Johnston, P.; Moss, M.S.; Richmond, L.M. *"No Going Back?" The Final Report of the Effective Records Management*

Project; Project funded under the JISC Technology Applications Programme JTAP—375, 2001, http://www.gla.ac.uk/infostrat/ERM/ Docs/ERM-Final.pdf (accessed November 2007).
33. Allison, A.; Currall, J.; Moss, M.; Stuart, S. Digital identity matters. JASIST **2005**, *56* (4), 364–372.
34. The Internet Archive can be accessed via the 'Way Back Machine' at: http://www.archive.org/index.php and a good description of it philosophy and how it operates is given in Wikipedia at: http://en.wikipedia.org/wiki/Internet_Archive (accessed March 2008).
35. The Dublin Core Metadata Initiative (DCMI) is described at: http://dublincore.org/ "The Dublin Core Metadata Initiative provides simple standards to facilitate the finding, sharing and management of information."
36. The file formats used by the Microsoft Office Suite of products. http://www.microsoft.com/ is a good example. (accessed March 2008).
37. LaTeX. http://www.latex-project.org/ (accessed March 2008) is a non-proprietary document preparation system that has maintained stable file formats over a period of two decades having been first developed in 1985 by Leslie Lamport.
38. The Portable Document Format (PDF) belongs to Adobe Systems (http://www.adobe.com/), but its definition is published and there are many tools that have been written that can read, write and edit the format.
39. Harvey, D.R. *Preserving Digital Materials*; Saur: München, **2005**, *55*, 53–75.
40. Lynch, C.A. Colliding with the real world: Heresies and unexplored questions about audience, economics, and control of digital libraries. In *Digital Library Use: Social Practice in Design and Evaluation*; Bishop, A., Butterfield, B., House, N., Van., , Eds.; The MIT Press: Cambridge, MA, 2003.
41. Lynch, C. Digital collections, digital libraries and the digitization of cultural heritage information. First Monday **2002**, *7* (5). http://www.firstmonday.org/issues_7/lynch/ (accessed November 2008).
42. Miksa, F.L.; Doty, P. *Intellectual Realities and the Digital Library*; University of Texas: Austen, TX, 1994; 16. http://www.csdl.tamu.edu/DL94/paper/miksa.html (accessed November 2008).
43. Lee, H.-L. What is a collection? J. Am. Soc. Inform. Sci. **2000**, *51* (12), 1106–1113.
44. The mansion of mystery and malice. The Sunday Times February 11, 2007.
45. Smith, D.B. *Honoré Jaxon: Prairie Visionary*; Coteau Books: Regina, SK, 2007.
46. Kane L.T. Access versus Ownership.
47. LOCKSS, in Encyclopedia of Library and Information Science, 2nd Ed., p. 50. http://www.lockss.org/lockss/Home (accessed March 2008).
48. Portico, http://www.portico.org/ (accessed March 2008).
49. Davis, P.M.; Connolly, M.J.L. Institutional Repositories: Evaluating the Reasons for Non-use of Cornell University's Installation of DSpace. Dlib Magazine March/April **2007**, *13* (3/4), http://www.dlib.org/dlib/march07/davis/03davis.html (accessed March 2008).
50. Eprints – http://www.eprints.org/, Fedora – http://www.fedora-commons.org/, DSpace – http://www.dspace.org/ (accessed March 2008).
51. http://www.icaew.co.uk/library/index.cfm?AUB=TB2I_ 25594. (March 2008).
52. http://www.gla.ac.uk/espida/ (accessed November 2007).
53. Baker, N. *Double fold: libraries and the assault on paper*; Random House: New York, 2001.
54. McKitterick, D. *Do we want to keep our newspapers*? Office for Humanities Communication Publication: London, 2002.
55. Moss, M.; Currall, J. Digitisation: taking stock. J. Soc. Archivists **2004**, *25* (2), 123–137, (accessed March 2007), from http://eprints.gla.ac.uk/1059/.
56. http://www.loc.gov/library/libarch-digital.html (accessed November 2007).
57. http://www.bnf.fr/pages/catalogues.htm (accessed November 2007).
58. Waller, M.; Sharpe, R. *Mind the gap—Assessing digital preservation needs in the U.K.*; Digital Preservation Coalition: London, 2006, http://www.dpconline.org/docs/reports/uknamindthegap.pdf (accessed November 2007).
59. Buckley, J.W. *New Life for Dead Storage Technologies*; Storage Networking Solutions (SNS): Europe, 2007, http://www.snseurope.com/snslink/news/printer-friendly.php? newsid=5759 (accessed November 2007).
60. FDA V. Brown & Williamson Tobacco Corp. (98–1152) 529 U.S. 120 (2000) 153 F.3d 155, affirmed, and British American Tobacco Documents Archive (2004), http://bat.library.ucsf.edu/ (March, 2004).
61. Cook, T. *Appraisal Methodology: Macro-Appraisal and Functional Analysis*; Library and Archives of Canada: Ottawa, 2001. http://www.collectionscanada.ca/information-management/007/007007-1035-e.html#tphp (accessed November 2007)
62. Kim, Y.; Ross, S. Genre Classification in Automated Ingest and Appraisal Metadata. In *Proceedings UK e-Science All Hands Meeting 2006: Achievements, Challenges, and New Opportunities, Nottingham*, Cox,

S.J., Ed.; National e-Science Centre; Glasgow and Edinburgh, 2006, http://eprints.erpanet.org/110/01/genre_extraction_KIM_ROSS_2006_ ECDL.pdf (accessed November 2007).
62. A good example are the services provided by the UK National Archives based on its PRONOM file format registry (http://www.nationalarchives.gov.uk/pronom/), which can be accessed via the DROID (digital record object identification) tool http://droid.sourceforge.net/wiki/index.php/Introduction (accessed March 2008).
63. Reed, B. Service-oriented architectures and recordkeeping. Records Management Journal **2008**, *18* (1), 7–20.

11 Network Management

Robert J. Sandusky

CONTENTS

INTRODUCTION

Network management includes activities related to the design, construction, and operation of communications networks, which are one type of distributed infrastructure. Network management activities are performed by a network management organization (NMO). An NMO is one of many types of information technology service organizations and, as discussed here, is responsible for the design, monitoring, and evolution of distributed infrastructure (an assemblage of hardware, software, and services) in its particular organizational context. The network itself is the primary object of the NMO's work and the NMO generally has little influence over how the network is used by other members and affiliates of the organization. An NMO may be a single organization but will typically interact with multiple organizations including customers, peer organizations collaborating to provide network services, and vendors. Network management, in all but the simplest cases such as a home or small single-site local area network (LAN), is inherently a distributed activity: a network usually includes equipment distributed in multiple locations. At the smaller end of the scale, equipment may be located in multiple rooms or on multiple floors of a building (referred to as a LAN). In more complex cases, the equipment may be located in multiple buildings (on a campus or across a metropolitan area, often referred to as a MAN, or metropolitan area network), in multiple cities, or even multiple countries (a WAN, or wide area network). This entry will assume, for purposes of illustration and discussion, a MAN or WAN unless otherwise noted.

This entry begins with a brief description of the types of components that make up a MAN or WAN and are the network components that require management. The five major dimensions of network management, as defined by the International Standards Organization (ISO) as part of the Open Systems Interconnection model, are used to introduce the range of activities associated with management of complex networks. Next, how design work is approached in NMOs is discussed in terms of the classic "waterfall" software development life cycle. The dynamic and collaborative nature of work within an NMO is described in terms of two interrelated modes of working: design work and real-time supervisory control work. Finally, the critical role of information management is described in the context of a disaster recovery/business continuity test.

WHAT IS MANAGED IN A NETWORK?

Networks, including the Internet, closed or private networks built by organizations, and smaller-scale LANs, are composed of several classes of components. Applications (e.g., Web sites, enterprise databases, digital libraries, e-mail systems) made accessible to remote users, messages carried by the network (i.e., frames, packets), end-user computers (i.e., client computers), server computers (e.g., Web servers, file servers, proxy servers), routers, switches, hubs, equipment racks, link signaling devices (i.e., link encryptors, digital signaling units/digital "modems"), access lines (e.g., the Ethernet cabling from client computers to a local switch, router, or hub), wireless access points, and long-distance telecommunications circuits (e.g., the higher-capacity, leased digital line between network locations usually connecting routers to each other).[1] All of these network components, except the cables, contain software and configurable parameters and all must be managed in order to provide effective network services that evolve to meet demand and keep pace with technical innovations. Vendor-provided software for configurable components must be tested and implemented to fix bugs, patch security holes, and to add functionality. The NMO also monitors the network in real-time for failures, errors, traffic bottlenecks, etc., and corrects problems by issuing commands to change component state and by swapping failed components with replacements. The NMO also monitors actual usage patterns and takes requests for new services into account as part of its network design and provisioning work.

The NMO must have the means to organize information about all the elements of the network in order to manage these components. The NMO must also have a set of operating parameters that, in combination with the network components, can enable the NMO to create appropriate standard operating procedures (SOPs) and ancillary support systems such as trouble ticket, configuration management, test scheduling, and reporting systems.

DIMENSIONS OF NETWORK MANAGEMENT

A conceptual framework associated with the ISO's Open Systems Interconnection model for communications systems is used to organize the full range of network management activities.[2] While originally focused on network management, this framework may be used to characterize the management of distributed computing systems more generally. The OSI framework is broken down into five functional areas: fault management, configuration management, performance management, accounting management, and security management.

Fault management is the detection, diagnosis, and correction of problems, or faults, in a network. Network components asynchronously generate fault data as messages, referred to as alarms, which are categorized as major, minor, and informational depending upon their significance or impact. Major alarms are generated when a network component fails due to hardware failure, software failure, or because the component can no longer be contacted by the network management systems (i.e., it has become isolated from the rest of the network). Minor alarms are generated when less critical events are detected, such as a performance threshold being exceeded, a burst of transmission errors is detected, or a failure of a subcomponent (e.g., a single interface card failure on a large router). Informational messages are generated for a variety of reasons, do not require direct attention by the real-time supervisory control (RTSC) staff, but are logged and available if needed (e.g., an anomalous but automatically recoverable condition, such as a communications protocol error). As alarms are generated, they are propagated to the NMO via both a real-time and an archival path. Alarms are sent to network management workstations that are continuously monitored by RTSC staff and to databases for long-term alarm storage. Propagation of alarms to the network management workstations supports the real-time work of isolating and correcting faults requiring direct intervention by NMO staff. Examples of faults requiring real-time intervention include failures that do not automatically recover or large-scale failures that trigger the performance of a SOP. Propagation of alarms to databases provides comprehensive historical data for postevent, trend, or long-term fault analysis.

Faults are logged in a database using a record format that includes date, time, location, fault codes, and other information of potential use in diagnosis, correction, or to support subsequent, long-term analysis. To support fault diagnosis, NMO staff use diagnostic test tools and component status query commands to retrieve real-time component status, and various component activation/deactivation commands to alter component status or component operating parameters. NMO staff are trained in troubleshooting procedures, and have access to SOPs for monitoring the network, documenting fault conditions in trouble tickets, and problem escalation (i.e., when to contact next-level expertise and/or management if a fault cannot be corrected in a timely manner). Trouble tickets are created for all faults requiring intervention. The trouble ticket is a locus for a textual narrative of the situation as it unfolds, providing capabilities to combine descriptions of evidence, activity, causal hypotheses, as well as a record of interpersonal, intra-, and inter-organizational communications. To correct faults that have been diagnosed, the NMO staff use commands to alter physical configurations (e.g., to replace a failed component with a backup component), manually activate a deactivated component, or to modify the operating parameters of affected components.

Configuration management is the set of capabilities that allow the NMO to set up and modify the network's physical and logical configurations. Following initial implementation the network's physical and logical configurations will change "to alleviate congestion, isolate faults or meet changing user needs."[2] Configuration changes may be unplanned, caused by network faults, or as a result of NMO staff action in response to a fault or changing, real-time network conditions, or as part of a preplanned configuration change. Faults often cause spontaneous network reconfigurations, such as removal of a long-distance telecommunications link from the network topology. Networks must be fault-tolerant: their internal complexity (the large number of varied and interconnected components) and reliance on long-distance telecommunications links result in frequent (e.g., several per day) single component failures. Therefore, networks must be designed to tolerate all single-component failures in order to be considered minimally reliable. In order to provide availability on the order of 99.9% or higher, the design must tolerate the simultaneous failure of any two components. In some situations, networks are designed to tolerate all dual-component failures as well as a subset of three-component failures. Network components are designed to attempt automatic recovery following failures, and many failures are corrected automatically. In a significant percentage of cases, NMO diagnosis and correction are required to either effect component recovery (e.g., manually reactivating a component) or to temporarily reconfigure the network so connections and traffic flow around the failure (e.g., moving a LAN's connection from its failed default router to an available connection on an alternate router). Planned network reconfigurations take two forms: predesigned modifications that are intended to be permanent, such as changes made to address new requirements, and predesigned modifications that are intended to be temporary, such as those that are part of disaster recovery/business continuity plans. Adding, modifying, or removing routers, interface cards to a router, or telecommunications circuits between routers are examples of common planned permanent configuration management activities. Network planning and design work is required prior to implementation of either a new network or a significant revision to an existing network. One of the implications of designing a fault-tolerant system is the need to preplan the organization's responses to a range of anticipated fault events including normal, single-component failures (e.g., loss of a long-distance telecommunications link) or high-impact failures (e.g., complete loss of connectivity for a network site, whether it is caused by natural disaster, massive telecommunications link failure, fire, simultaneous failure of both primary and backup routers, etc.). Preplanning work is complex, and results in the creation of SOPs that guides NMO reconfigurations in response to classes of failures (see discussion below in the section on "Perspectives on Network Management Work").

Performance management refers both to the capabilities in the network that support measurement of network use and the expertise within the NMO to analyze data, justify recommendations for change, and plan the configuration changes needed to support emerging or anticipated network uses. NMOs are interested in understanding and documenting past usage patterns, comparing current usage patterns to historical patterns, and using both historical and current data to support the capacity planning process. While performance monitoring occurs in real-time as the RTSC staff continuously monitor utilization of network components like routers and long-distance telecommunications links, the bulk of performance management activities are performed "off-line" by design staff. Network components periodically—every few minutes—log levels of usage by writing data to network management servers for later analysis. Network components may also generate fault messages or alarms when utilization levels exceed certain thresholds to enable real-time supervisory staff to respond with network configuration changes. Networks and their protocols are designed to be tolerant of fluctuations in network traffic or topology, so real-time intervention is not usually required. Performance management is part of the longer-term network design process and involves analysis of the logged performance data in order to detect changes in usage patterns that lead to modifications in the network's configuration. For example, increasing network traffic between two locations may lead to installation of higher capacity routers, telecommunications links, reconfiguration of the network topology, or a combination of the three.

Accounting management is the set of capabilities that allows the NMO to collect and manage usage and configuration data, track costs, and charge network users according to the tariffs, service level agreements, or contracts that are in place. Several network components may be capable of generating and transmitting usage data that may be fed into an off-line accounting or billing system (e.g., routers and servers running shared applications may generate data that are fed into a billing system). Costs of other components, such as cables, routers, or equipment racks, may have their costs allocated on some other basis (such as employee head count or a count of connections), or may be factored into usage-sensitive charges. NMOs evaluate the costs, benefits, and complexity of collecting and correlating large amounts of data and negotiating customer agreements in order to produce detailed bills against other approaches that don't require detailed usage-based calculations (e.g., simpler, flat-rate or percentage-allocated cost-recovery arrangements). The simpler approaches are particularly useful for networks built to support the internal operations of an organization. NMOs providing services to the public, such as land-line and mobile telecommunications organizations, are more likely to develop usage-sensitive procedures.

Security management is concerned with control of physical access to network components, end-point authentication, user authentication, key management for encryption, end-to-end data encryption, security log management, monitoring emerging security threat vectors and developing organizational responses, and firewall management. Security management has two objects in the network management context: first, the network itself must be secured (e.g., control the access to router management ports which are used to issue reconfiguration commands to the router; ensure that physical access to network equipment at all locations is controlled; manage NMO staff authentication and access); second, the network must support the security requirements of the users and applications transmitting data across the network (e.g., providing encryption of telecommunications circuits; end-to-end encryption of data streams; management of encryption keys). In environments with high security needs, including financial institutions, health care organizations, and commercial organizations in highly competitive markets, security management responsibilities are concentrated in an independent part of the organization, with a management chain distinct from the RTSC and technical staffs. A separate management chain encourages, enforces, and makes a high degree of transparency possible through establishment of arms-length relationships between different parts of the NMO. NMOs with these types of stringent needs will also employ a comprehensive internal auditing process, augmented by recurring external audits. Security logs, like fault logs, identify date, time, location, and diagnostic information. Security logs should be reviewed regularly in order to identify unusual usage patterns or to correlate successful and unsuccessful access attempts by users and intruders alike. Several of the activities included in security management, including encryption key management and developing responses to emerging security threats, are complex management challenges in a distributed environment.[3]

PERSPECTIVES ON NETWORK MANAGEMENT WORK

Network management depends upon the blending of actions performed by people with a range of skills and expertise, and these actions depend upon information management practices. Design and RTSC work patterns are defined, and the central role of information management in network management is described. These two work patterns are discussed in the context of the five dimensions of network management. The section concludes with a description of a complex yet typical activity, a disaster recovery test (DRT), which illustrates the relationship between information and activity in distributed infrastructure management.

PATTERNS OF WORK

Network management combines patterns of both design and RTSC work. Research has shown that design work and RTSC work have different rhythms and patterns that, in network management, are coordinated to perform fault, configuration, performance, accounting, and security management. RTSC work is event driven, dynamic, and involves the interaction of multiple workers with complex systems.[4] Malfunctions in the operation of these systems can result in serious consequences such as the loss of human life or financial loss. Signs of malfunction must often be recognized and responses formulated within minutes or seconds in order to prevent adverse consequences. By contrast, design work has different patterns and rhythms than RTSC work and is characterized as being self-paced (as opposed to being event-driven), reflective (as opposed to being time-constrained), and creative.[4–6] The object of design work is usually to iteratively create, study, or revise some artifact like a document, a set of specifications, a product, or a system, such as a data communications network. In network management, there are frequently occasions when workers who usually do design work join the RTSC staff to perform event-driven and time-constrained work, particularly with regard to fault and configuration management. This section will first describe how an NMO for a WAN is organized. How new network implementations are managed is described next, followed by a description of the role of information management in network management work. Finally, the five dimensions of network management (above) are discussed in terms of design work and RTSC work.

The NMO for a large network, such as a national-scale WAN, includes a staff of technical specialists who provide depth of knowledge in particular technologies, the RTSC staff, budget, accounting, and administrative support staff, and executive management. Categories of technical specialists include network hardware engineers, network software engineers, data security specialists, and circuit/topology experts. Network hardware engineers are specialists in network equipment, signaling equipment, electrical requirements, lower-level network protocols, and troubleshooting. The most skilled network hardware engineers will have degrees in computer or electrical engineering. Network software engineers are more likely to be trained in computer science, and will have expertise in higher level network protocols, software debugging, software development, and software engineering processes (e.g., the waterfall systems development life cycle discussed below). Circuit/topology experts manage the leased long-distance telecommunications circuits and the relationships with the vendor or vendors from whom they are leased, and are responsible for managing the network topology. Security specialists may have backgrounds in either engineering or computer science, but will focus on authentication, authorization, dedicated security hardware (e.g., link encryptors and firewalls) and encryption key management processes. In large NMOs, the security experts will be in a separate group and report to a different manager than do the hardware and software engineers in order to maintain arms-length relationships and help ensure that security procedures and standards are not compromised by expediency (e.g., cost or schedule pressures). In total, these technical experts are referred to here as "members of the technical staff."

The RTSC staff is organized into three shifts, with shift supervisors who report to the supervisory control manager. The RTSC staff are the people who work most directly and most often with the network itself, monitoring the network's health and configuration (fault and configuration management). The RTSC staff also act as the human interface between the network and the NMO's internal and external customers. The RTSC staff work in one or more centralized network control rooms. RTSC staff backgrounds are likely to vary from some who have university degrees in a variety of technical and nontechnical fields, to those who have experience in real-time operations but little or no postsecondary education.

The budget and accounting staff rely upon information generated by and about the network to manage billing, budgeting, and financial planning. The executive managers often have backgrounds that include a degree in a technical field and experience as a member of the technical staff. As managers, they will have a well-developed model of the technology and the ability to perform cross-community coordination with the various NMO groups (members of the technical staff, RTSC staff, accountants), internal and external customers, and vendors.

Network design and software engineering processes have many parallels, and can be described by well-known life cycle models such as the "waterfall" model of software development (Figure 11.1). In both situations, the goal is to create a new object: the network or piece of software. The life cycle begins with the identification and documentation of *requirements*. Given a set of relatively stable requirements, one or more *design* alternatives can be produced to satisfy the requirements. Given agreement on a design, *implementation* of the object can begin. As the object is created, each discrete piece undergoes *testing*, and the object is ultimately tested as a whole. After successful testing, the object is released and goes into *maintenance* (software) or goes into *production operation* (network). The life cycle is repeated as new requirements emerge. Each of these subsequent iterations can be managed using the same life cycle model: new requirements are documented, a network design revision is created, and the changes are implemented, tested, and made operational. The NMO is responsible for managing the entire implementation/revision life cycle for its network, and the cycle can be reiterated many times throughout the useful life of the network. Typical types of new requirements for a network include expanding the network into new locations, increasing capacity, or adding support for new data transmission protocols.

In order to design a new network (or modify an existing network), requirements must be gathered to inform the network design (network locations, traffic patterns and types, security and reliability requirements, service level requirements, cost parameters, etc.). During the network design process, engineers use a combination of formal, algorithmic, and professional heuristic processes. For example, given a certain expected traffic load, algorithmic tools can be used to define the number, arrangement, and sizes of routers and the circuits connecting them. The arrangement of routers and circuits is referred to as the network topology. WANs are never designed as a completely interconnected mesh (i.e., each site linked directly to each other site, Figure 11.2), so the topology must be

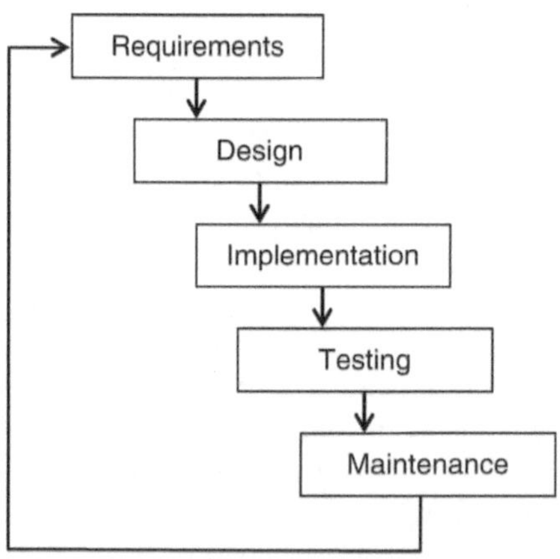

FIGURE 11.1 The "waterfall" systems development life cycle.

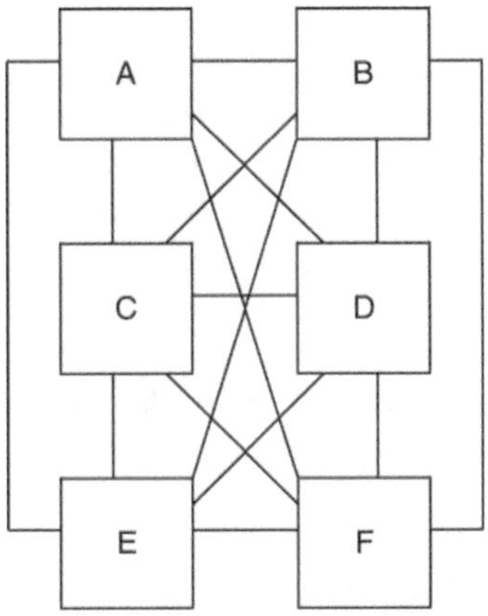

FIGURE 11.2 Full mesh topology, where A, B, C, D, E, and F are network sites.

carefully designed to provide adequate support for the traffic patterns and service-level expectations while minimizing operating costs: long-distance circuits between cities are often leased from a telecommunications provider and have recurring monthly costs (Figure 11.3). The set of equipment and services needed can then be acquired, installed, and tested. Any moderately complex network is, when built, an ecosystem comprised of a wide variety of equipment and services, including cables, equipment racks, signaling devices (e.g., encryptors and digital "modems"), routers, and network management servers and workstations. Each type of equipment (e.g., routers) can be thought of as a species within the ecosystem. Engineers plan and manage installation and testing of hardware and services at each site (the routers, link signaling devices, switches, hubs, racks, long-distance telecommunications circuits, wired and wireless access points, and cables). Software engineers define and test connection parameters and system options within routers, link signaling devices, and any other software-configurable network components. RTSC staff monitor and control the systems as they are installed and tested, perform routine tasks (on both a daily and per-shift basis) and respond to faults. Documentation, policies, and SOPs are developed and refined throughout the planning, implementation, and testing phases. Customer endpoints (LANs, hosts, servers, and applications) are connected to the network, tested, and the new network is in production operation and maintenance mode. Following initial implementation of a network, configuration change tends to be

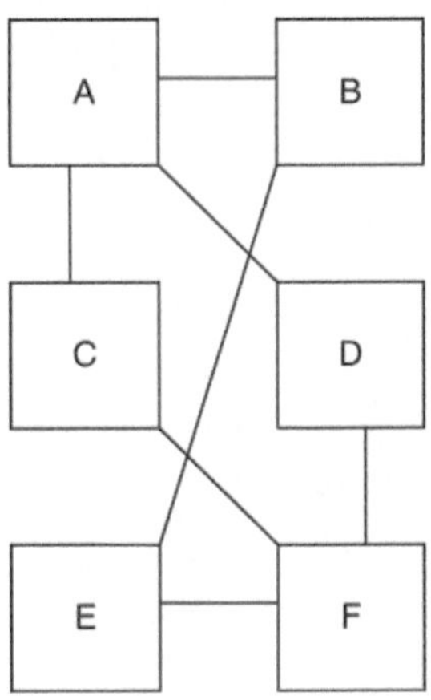

FIGURE 11.3 Optimized network topology, where A, B, C, D, E, and F are network sites.

gradual, to replace failed equipment, replace a species (e.g., routers) with an upgraded version, or to make modifications in response to changing user or organization needs. Whether initial installation or incremental upgrade, network reconfigurations include both physical changes (replacing a hardware component), software changes (modifying software parameters related to the component, also known as provisioning), and changes to the documentation.[7]

Management of distributed infrastructure, including network management, is information-intensive work. Each kind of equipment included in the network is managed by its own workstation-based suite of applications tailored to manage that layer of technology. Each of these systems contains a database (the Management Information Base, or MIB) that provides a representation of the configuration of that layer of the network, providing an accurate, one-to-one correspondence to the physical network configuration. Information in each MIB is, however, isolated and few tools exist to provide effectively merged views of data from all layers of the network. SOPs are created, using an iterative process of proposal, negotiation, and testing, in order to define preplanned and vetted operational sequences for use in routine and nonroutine but anticipated situations. SOPs are organization and context specific, reflecting organizational values and priorities as well as the combinations of technology that make each WAN unique (e.g., kinds of equipment and locations). Some (SOPs) are so commonly used that the RTSC staff has them memorized and the paper documents are only used by newcomers or as referents during discussion. Other procedures, like disaster recovery procedures, are hopefully never actually used. Versions of these types of procedures are often modified into test scripts, which are used once and then discarded.

The NMO staff creates formal databases and other information management tools to serve the specific needs of the NMO, such as trouble ticket, configuration management, and test scheduling systems. Other formal information systems include the vendor provided MIBs and the NMO's own SOPs. Other more situated and less formal information systems included are handwritten notes and collections of information assembled by individuals, created spontaneously by the NMO staff in order to allow them to do their work more effectively. The informal systems often combine information drawn from one or more formal information sources. The combination of information from multiple sources results in new information compounds[8] that highlight, through processes of extraction, juxtaposition, and integration of domain semantics, what is salient in a domain rich with information.[9] People from all parts of the organization spend a great deal of time seeking and gathering bits of formal data, adding the organization-specific stuff of meaning and context, and producing useful, but often difficult to find and manage collections of information. These informal information compounds are often expressed in tabular format in order to represent relationships between physical and logical objects. The relationships of logical objects (like the symbolic or mnemonic name of a network device) to physical objects (like a port on a router or a cable) are enormously important during troubleshooting or in planning for network changes. These information compounds are a means by which the members of the NMO can introduce the organization-specific data about customers, purpose, and meaning into both the real-time supervisory control and design environments. However, maintaining the integrity of these informal representations over time is difficult due to the high rate at which changes are made to the network configuration.

Schematic drawings of relationships between network devices are another common information compound useful in highlighting important relationships between discrete elements in the network. These, too, are prone to problems caused by change and poor document maintenance.

Patterns of Work and Dimensions of Network Management

The degree to which members of the technical staff, who are primarily responsible for network design work, and the RTSC staff, who are responsible for monitoring and controlling the network in real-time, share and coordinate the work associated with the five dimensions of network management varies by dimension, and is influenced by the values, priorities, and other characteristics of the NMO. The work patterns described below are based upon network management work as practiced in a large financial institution,[10] but are typical of any NMO operating a WAN in a context where high security, reliability, and availability are expected.

In terms of fault management, members of the technical staff will be engaged in the requirements definition and implementation of equipment and software related to fault management. Software engineers may develop or customize systems for managing alarm data in either real-time or for fault diagnosis or post hoc fault analysis. Members of the technical staff do not participate routinely in fault monitoring activities: this is the responsibility of the RTSC staff. However, under certain conditions, such as during real-time troubleshooting, members of the technical staff merge with the RTSC staff—usually joining together in the network control room—to isolate and resolve a difficult problem as quickly as possible.

Faults requiring intervention occur frequently in large networks, often because of the complex hardware and software configurations located at each network site or because of problems with the telecommunications circuits that connect network locations to each other. An NMO creates procedures (SOPs) that define the canonical responses to typical fault situations. RTSC staff use the SOP as a reference when responding to typical faults, which should result in rapid service recovery performed in a standardized manner. If the standard response does not work, the RTSC staff moves into troubleshooting mode in order to restore service to affected users (by perhaps reconfiguring the network so that redundant or alternate components can be used by the affected users), isolate and characterize the outage, document the outage in a database (by creating a trouble ticket that serves as a collection point for alarms, actions taken, actors involved; a trouble ticket created in response to nonroutine events becomes a narrative of the NMOs collective actions), and escalate the situation (i.e., notify management and next-level technical support, including hardware and software engineers who are responsible for network design and are typically expert in relatively narrow areas such as circuits, routers, or security; or possibly equipment or service providers).

Configuration management is primarily performed by members of the technical staff using a reflective, self-paced, and creative design process, although the RTSC staff are involved for the implementation, testing, and ongoing maintenance. A standard implementation process, such as the waterfall process described above, is typically used to manage preplanned, permanent configuration changes. The RTSC staff may make temporary configuration changes in response to network faults, or as part of the execution of a SOP (e.g., see the description of a DRT below).

Performance management is almost entirely done by members of the technical staff in a reflective process where data collected by the network is compiled and analyzed. In rare cases, real-time network congestion may bring RTSC and design staff together in the control room for real-time analysis and intervention. These rare real-time situations are likely to cause a network capacity review by members of the technical staff.

Accounting management is also almost entirely a post hoc, off-line activity. RTSC have little to do other than ensure that the accounting data is being collected continuously. Accounting data is usually important to the NMO even in cases where detailed usage tracking is not done; usage information is still likely to be used to demonstrate NMO and network relevance as well as to help apportion network costs to customer organizations.

Security management involves members of the technical staff most directly and includes managing access control, user accounts and passwords, and encryption key management procedures. The RTSC staff does get involved, particularly in diagnosing suspected link encryption or data encryption problems. In a 24-hour, high-security environment, additional control procedures are required to manage access to "superuser" passwords that may need to be accessed from a secure location, such as a safe, when required for fault resolution.

Information and Activity in Network Management

An example of how an NMO plans and conducts a disaster recovery, or business continuity, test (DRT) is indicative of the ways the design and RTSC staffs interact and of the reliance of the

NMO on effective information management. The DRTs in a WAN are complex. The DRT scenario assumes that the entire network site, its servers, and LANs at that the site have all been disabled (e.g., due to a fire, flood, etc.). A private network with high standards for availability would set as a network design requirement the ability to survive the complete loss of any network site by providing connectivity at an alternate, backup site. This requirement directs many other decisions and activities. For example, the need to redirect huge flows of data from a failed site to a backup site has an impact on the initial design of the network and its topology, as well as the way recovery mechanisms within the network are customized. The NMO also commits significant human resources from the technical and RTSC staff to create SOPs that will support this sort of recovery within the target times, which require complete network and server recovery within a few hours of the outage. The SOP likely contains scores of steps that are to be performed in a preplanned sequence, often by multiple organizations working in coordination. Such a complex document must be created and reviewed by both RTSC and technical staffs: the members of the technical staff are subject matter experts with deep knowledge of a narrow technical specialty, while the RTSC staff have broad working knowledge of the range of network technologies, but with less technical depth. The RTSC staff's "big picture" view of the network and the organizational environment allows them to contribute information about how activities should be sequenced and coordinated, both within and across the participating sites. People from multiple organizations and sites must be familiar with the procedures and rehearse them regularly. Backup data must be transmitted regularly, often on a continuous transaction-by-transaction basis, or by using daily data transfers. In either case, these data transfers become part of the RTSC staff's ongoing responsibilities.

The planning for a DRT begins a couple of months before the test date. A DRT director, usually a manager, is assigned responsibility for planning and running the test. Draft test scripts are distributed, which are modified versions of the SOP. The modifications reflect the goals and exceptions for the current test. (It is, as a practical matter, nearly impossible to take a major site out of the network for the 18–24 hours it takes to run a disaster simulation and test all of the recovery and fallback procedures. The tests are invariably limited to some degree to accommodate other competing requirements.) Conference calls are held where the site being tested, the NMO, and any other sites involved in recovery of servers "walk through" the script, looking for errors, sequencing problems, negotiating modifications, and inserting proper articulation and control points (e.g., periodic management conferences to review progress and status when the test is executed). Members of the technical staff and RTSC staff are present at all of the planning meetings and participate in the discussions and negotiations. The SOP is designed to serve as a canonical text in that it embodies the actions to be taken in the event that an "ideal" disaster occurs: a complete, total disaster at the site that would render it unusable. As such, the SOP embodies a "best practice" approach to dealing with a disaster, providing guidance on the most reliable way to effect the recovery of each piece of the failed environment at the backup sites. At the start of the test, the disaster itself is simulated, and how the simulation is to be performed is part of the test script. Specific dates and times are included in the test script to provide a rough sense of what it means to be on or behind or ahead of schedule during the test, values which are not included in the canonical SOP.

As the test date nears, it is discussed during the normal change and scheduling meetings to ensure the readiness of the NMO and other direct participants, to allow new information to be integrated into the schedule and plan, and to ensure awareness by a wider range of people and organizations who may be conducting other activities that overlap with the DRT. The day before the test begins, a final meeting is held, attended by representatives from all locations with responsibility for conducting the DRT. This meeting is the last opportunity for cancellations, late modifications to the test script, discussion of resource conflicts, times, etc.

The DRT begins a couple of hours before dawn, and RTSC staff from the NMO are responsible for many of the first steps to reconfigure the network to support movement of servers and other systems from the site under test to various recovery sites at other locations across the network. The third shift NMO staff cannot participate in daytime planning meetings that have occurred during the past week, and so they rely upon the written test schedules and scripts, plus any information passed verbally to them by the previous shift staff. They are also likely to have other network reconfigurations to perform during the same time period, near the end of their shift. If this part of the day goes well, the NMO will be in good shape for the entire weekend. If not, the political fallout could last for weeks. The site disaster will be simulated by disabling all of the network connections from other network sites to the site under test, in effect isolating that site from the rest of the network. The NMO RTSC staff issue status commands to ensure that the circuits are inactive. Alarms printers and displays record the disables as well as hundreds of other, cascading events. Network elements, represented by icons, change from green to red on many of the workstations. The NMO RTSC staff contact the test director to report that their current task is completed.

Contingencies are bound to arise in any event this complex. One site may get a late start; there may be problems reading a tape when trying to restore a software image at the backup site. The NMO is also likely to be dealing with normal problems, such as circuit problems that are causing high error rates and affecting network performance. In real time, processes move forward at the many participating sites. Some parts of the process get stuck and require intervention; some succeed; others simply fail, and the test script is modified on the fly in a continuous series of phone calls and negotiations. When the reality of the test day proves problematic, people can refer to the plan and make on-the-spot decisions about how to work around the difficulty: steps may be done in the "wrong" order, certain steps skipped, or certain steps repeated. These variations must be noted at the NMO as they occur, both to keep track of the test status in real time and as information to be used to modify the underlying SOP and subsequent similar test scripts.

The duration the DRT and other tests may span shift boundaries, making it necessary for accurate status to be passed from shift to shift. Managers from the NMO need status and may be on site or at home. The technical staff members supporting this and other simultaneous tests need to be aware of the status of the major test and adjust their weekend activities accordingly. The NMO must coordinate its activities through the DRT manager. As the test runs, problems may occur which must be resolved. Some parts of the test may be omitted in response to unexpected problems to avoid compromising the entire test.

The final event associated with a DRT is the postmortem held the following week. The participants in the postmortem are the same as those who participated in the many pretest meetings. The DRT director in effect grades the performance of the participants. The NMO and other organizations are held responsible for problems arising during the test. Responsibility for resolving each problem is publicly assigned. Resolution of problems assigned to the NMO may involve modifying the SOP or making configuration changes to the network. Even though problems occur during the DRTs, they are, due to the careful preplanning and test-day coordination, almost always considered successful.

CONCLUSION

Network management is not exclusively a technical issue of routers, telecommunications links, servers, applications, and the interconnections of LANs via metropolitan or WANs. Effective network management depends upon the blending of design and RTSC work to support all dimensions of network management: fault, configuration, performance, accounting, and security management. Effective organization and control of complex, dynamic information is also important to the NMO, as it enables the recording and communication of large amounts of information in forms that incorporate the values of the NMO and the larger organization within which it is embedded. While the five dimensions of network management form a common basis for organizing network management across a wide variety of organizations, the details of network management practice are situated and influenced by security requirements, available technical expertise, and budget. The concerns of network management apply as well to other situations in which distributed infrastructure must be managed.

Standards published by the Internet Engineering Task Force (IETF) have come to dominate network management practice. The most important of these are the Simple Network Management Protocol Version 3 (SNMPv3), defined in Requests for Comment 2571–2575.[11–15] Further information about the technical aspects and best practices of network and infrastructure management, including how SNMPv3 is used in practice, can be found in a number of works, including Limoncelli–Muller.[16–19]

REFERENCES

1. Panko, R.R. *Business Data Networks and Telecommunications*, 6th Ed.; Pearson Prentice Hall: Upper Saddle River, NJ, 2007.
2. Klerer, S.M. The OSI management architecture: An overview. Network **1988**, *2* (2), 20–29.
3. Millman, D. Authentication and Authorization. In *Encyclopedia of Library and Information Sciences*, 3rd Ed.; Taylor & Francis: New York, 2009; 413–419.
4. Jones, P.M. Cooperative work in mission operations: Analysis and implications for computer support. Comput. Support. Coop. Work Int. J. **1995**, *3* (2), 103–145.
5. Bucciarelli, L.L. An ethnographic perspective on engineering design. Des. Stud. **1988**, *9* (3), 159–168.
6. Schön, D.; Bennett, J. Reflective conversation with materials. In *Bringing Design to Software*; Winograd, T., Ed.; ACM Press: New York, 1996; 171–184.
7. Wang, H.H. *Telecommunications Network Management*; McGraw-Hill: New York, 1999.
8. Paepcke, A. Information needs in technical work settings and their implications for the design of computer tools. Comput. Support. Coop. Work J. Collab. Comp. **1996**, *5* (1), 63–92.
9. Goodwin, C. Professional vision. Am. Anthropol. **1994**, *96* (3), 606–633.
10. Sandusky, R.J. Infrastructure management as cooperative work: Implications for systems design. Comput. Support. Coop. Work J. Collab. Comput. **2003**, *12* (1), 97–122.
11. Harrington, D.; Presuhn, R.; Wijnen, B. *An Architecture for Describing SNMP Management Frameworks*, RFC 2571; Internet Engineering Task Force, 1999, http://www.ietf.org/rfc/rfc2571.txt (accessed August 7, 2008).
12. Case, J.; Harrington, D.; Presuhn, R.; Wijnen, B. *Message Processing and Dispatching for the Simple Network Management Protocol*, RFC 2572; Internet Engineering Task Force, 1999, http://www.ietf.org/rfc/rfc2572.txt (accessed August 7, 2008).
13. Levi, D.; Meyer, P.; Stewart, B. *SNMP Applications*, RFC 2573; Internet Engineering Task Force, 1999, http://www.ietf.org/rfc/rfc2573.txt (accessed August 7, 2008).
14. Blumenthal, U.; Wijnen, B. *User-based Security Model (USM) for Version 3 of the Simple Network Management Protocol (SNMPv3)*, RFC 2574; Internet Engineering Task Force, 1999, http://www.ietf.org/rfc/rfc2574.txt (accessed August 7, 2008).
15. Wijnen, B.; Presuhn, R.; McCloghrie, K. *View-based Access Control Model (VACM) for the Simple Network Management Protocol (SNMP)*, RFC 2575; Internet Engineering Task Force, 1999, http://www.ietf.org/rfc/rfc2575.txt (accessed August 7, 2008).
16. Limoncelli, T.A.; Hogan, C.J.; Chalup, S.R. *The Practice of System and Network Administration*, 2nd Ed.; Addison-Wesley: Upper Saddle River, NJ, 2007.
17. Burke, J.R. *Network Management: Concepts and Practice, A Hands-on Approach*; Pearson Education: Upper Saddle River, NJ, 2004.
18. Morris, S.B. *Network Management, MIBs and MPLS*; Prentice Hall: Upper Saddle River, NJ, 2003.
19. Muller, N.J. *LANs to WANs: The Complete Management Guide*; Artech House: Boston, 2003.

12 Management of Very Large Distributed Shared Collections

Reagan W. Moore

CONTENTS

INTRODUCTION

Scientific data collections are being assembled that contain the digital holdings on which future research is based. The collections are assembled by researchers from multiple institutions, and then accessed by all members of a scientific discipline. The data collections are massive in size, comprising hundreds of terabytes of data (a terabyte is a thousand gigabytes) and tens of millions of files. The software infrastructure that manages these collections must provide not only traditional digital library services, such as indexing, discovery, and presentation, but also preservation services to ensure authenticity and integrity. The types of material in the collections range from digital simulation output generated by scientific applications, to observational data taken by experiments, to real-time sensor data streams from thousands of sensors. Thus the management of scientific data collections requires the integration of capabilities from multiple disparate communities: data grids for sharing data, digital libraries for publishing data, persistent archives for preserving data, and real-time sensor systems for automating the creation of collections.

The challenge is made more difficult by the fact that large data collections are inherently distributed. The collections may reside on multiple storage systems with a copy on disk for interactive access and a backup copy on tape for long-term preservation. Their assembly may involve collaborators from multiple institutions, with both the sources of the collection coming from multiple sites and the users of the collection located at multiple sites. To effectively mitigate risk of data loss, data collections are distributed across multiple types of storage systems located at geographically separated locations. All of these reasons force scientific data collections to build upon software systems that are capable of managing distributed data.

In this entry, we give some examples of large scientific collections, examine the fundamental principles on which distributed shared collections are based, describe data management infrastructure that is in production use today, and close with a description of the next generation of data management software that is currently under development.

SCIENTIFIC DATA COLLECTIONS

Researchers that generate large scientific data collections include seismologists, high-energy physicists, astronomers, and educators. Seismologists manage observational data about the propagation of seismic waves through the earth crust, and generate very large simulation output data sets to predict the effect of earthquakes. An example is the Southern California Earthquake Center (SCEC),[1] which has stored over 165 TB of simulation output, comprising more than 3.5 million files, with more than 70 researchers collaborating on the creation of the SCEC collection.[2] The SCEC project is now proposing the generation of more than a petabyte of data (a petabyte is a thousand terabytes) from higher resolution simulations of seismic waves generated by an earthquake on the San Andreas Fault in Southern California.

The BaBar high-energy physics project[3] replicates experimental data taken at the Stanford Linear Accelerator in Palo Alto, California to researchers in Lyon, France at the Institut National de Physique Nucleaire et de Physique des Particules. The project has replicated more than 700 TB of data, moving up to 5 TBs of data per day between the sites. When the CERN accelerator becomes functional, related high-energy physics projects will generate a petabyte of data per year.[4]

The largest data sets in the future may come from the astronomy community. The Large Synoptic Survey Telescope[5] will take images of the sky every 3 days to detect near-earth objects such as asteroids, starting in 2013. More than 100 PB of images will be archived. Current astronomy sky surveys are measured in the tens of terabytes in size. The 2-Micron All Sky Survey comprises 12 TB of images aggregated across 6 million 2 MB files.[6]

The National Science Digital Library[7] organizes scientific educational material that is posted on Web sites. The URL of each item is registered into a central repository at Cornell University. An archive, comprising over 70 million Web pages, has been assembled by crawling the Web sites. The archived Web pages are aggregated into containers and stored on both tape and disk to provide an alternate retrieval location when the original Web site is not available.

The Real-time Observatories, Applications, and Data management Network (ROADNet)[8] manages real-time sensor data streams from more than 4000 sensors. Data is streamed from seismic sensors, environmental sensors, coastal lidar systems, remote cameras, and oceanographic sensors into object ring buffers, and then archived for later use. The sensor streams can be queried to identify relevant data, and then correlated with other data streams. The 4000 sensor data streams come from multiple independent projects, but rely upon common software infrastructure to facilitate use by researchers.

Each of these collections is distributed across multiple storage systems, located at different institutions, with the local infrastructure managed by local administrators. The fundamental underlying principle that is used to manage the data is that of a shared collection. Software infrastructure is installed at each site that makes it possible to name, organize, and access the data as if it were stored on a local resource. The software infrastructure has to provide a uniform name space for identifying the files, manage access controls across multiple independent institutions, manage replication of the files onto multiple types of storage systems, manage checksums to ensure data integrity, manage descriptive information about each file, and provide uniform access mechanisms to data stored on multiple types of storage systems (disk, tape archives, binary large objects in databases, database tables, and object ring buffers for sensor data). The software technology that does this is called a data grid.[9]

DISTRIBUTED DATA MANAGEMENT PRINCIPLES

The preservation community bases their data management on the principles of authenticity and integrity.[10] Authenticity is an assertion that the provenance (attributes about the creation of the data) is preserved. This includes the concept of "chain of custody"; that operations on the data have only been performed by authorized archivists. Integrity is an assertion that the preservation environment has not compromised the data; that the bits have not changed. It is not sufficient to show that the data are uncompromised, one must also show that the data correspond to the original deposition into the collection with an unbroken chain of control, and that the data can be interpreted and manipulated even after the original creating application is gone. The latter implies the need to manage technology evolution. A preservation environment insulates the records from changes occurring in the technology used to support the collection.

The same principles apply when assembling distributed shared collections. The origin of the scientific data must be tracked to assign academic credit, provenance information is needed to guide the use of the data, and the integrity of the data must be maintained. Shared collections use descriptive metadata organized in a central catalog to manage provenance information. However, management of integrity in a distributed environment is much harder. There are multiple risks that must be mitigated: media corruption such as a disk crash or broken tape; operator error such as data overwrites on both disk and tape; systemic vendor error such as bad microcode in a tape drive; natural disaster such as fire or flood; and malicious users. These are compounded by the unavailability of systems due to network outages and remote maintenance periods. Any problem that occurs in the distributed environment is treated as a problem of the data grid, instead of the remote resource.

The additional principle that is needed is the concept of infrastructure independence.[11] The properties of the shared collection are managed independently of the capabilities of the storage systems where the data reside. The three main categories of properties that must be managed for shared collections are data virtualization, trust virtualization, and management virtualization. Data virtualization manages the naming, access, and manipulation of data independently of the type of storage system. Trust virtualization manages authentication and authorization independently of the remote administrative domains. Management virtualization characterizes and automates the application of management policies independently of the remote institutions. Through these three virtualization mechanisms, one can access distributed data, control who is allowed to use the data, and verify that the authenticity and integrity have been preserved even for data located on another continent on a storage system managed by a separate institution. Because the virtualization mechanisms are automated by software infrastructure, very large collections can be maintained with a minimal amount of labor support. The goal is software that can evaluate assessment criteria, track whether each file in the system has been correctly managed, and initiate recovery procedures while maintaining audit trails of all operations applied to each file. Such an environment can institute management policies that mitigate the risk of data loss through replication and synchronization within a data grid, and federation between independent data grids.

Note that infrastructure independence implies the ability to add new technology over time, and migrate a collection from obsolete technology onto new technology. The ability to manage data distributed across multiple types of storage systems is the same ability that is needed to manage technology evolution for preservation environments.

Data Virtualization

Data grids implement logical name spaces that are used to identify not only the files, but also the users of the system and the components of the system. Typically, three name spaces are controlled by data grids:

1. Distinguished name space for users. The identity of the archivists, or curators, or users is managed independently of the remote storage system or administrative domain. Users of the system authenticate their access based upon the authentication system implemented by the data grid.
2. Logical name space for files or digital entities. The digital entities that are registered into the shared collection may be files, binary large objects, database tables, URLs, SQL

command strings, or remote directories. Any organization that is imposed on the distributed data is expressed as a structure on the logical file name space such as a collection hierarchy.

3. Logical name space for storage systems. Multiple physical storage systems may be identified through a single logical storage resource name. This makes it feasible to support collective operations across storage systems, such as automated data replication (writing to a logical resource name causes a copy to be made at each of the associated physical storage systems), load leveling (a copy is made at the storage system with the most space left), or caching (a copy is made on a disk cache associated with a tape archive).

Given these three logical name spaces, access controls can be asserted as constraints between the logical user name space, the logical storage name space, and the logical file name space. When data is migrated onto new resources within a data grid, neither the file name nor the access controls change. The data grid associates provenance information with the logical file name, ensuring that authenticity can be preserved. The data grid associates system-level metadata such as checksums, audit trails, replica location, access controls, file size, and creation time with the logical file name, ensuring that integrity can be tracked over time. Data grids use a central metadata catalog to hold both the provenance and system-level metadata.

Data grids are implemented as peer-to-peer software servers, with a software server installed at each storage system where the data reside. The software server manages the mapping from the logical file name to the physical file residing on the storage system for access, and the mapping from the access protocol desired by the user to the access protocol used by the storage system. Part of infrastructure independence is the ability to use your preferred access protocol to retrieve data from legacy systems that are unable to process modern protocols. Data grids support access by C library calls, Unix shell commands, Perl/Python/Windows load libraries, workflow systems, grid portals, Web browsers, digital libraries such as DSpace[12] and Fedora,[13] and Web service description languages (WSDL) across all storage systems where the software servers reside.

Data grids act as middleware, enabling the execution of the file-based and metadata-based operations required by data management applications. It is not sufficient to provide just the POSIX I/O operations supported by disk file systems (open, close, read, write, seek, stat, sync, etc.). Operations required for authenticity and integrity assurance, and network latency management are also needed. Since data grids manage distributed data, multiple levels of aggregation are needed to minimize the impact of the network latency caused by the finite speed of light. This is done by aggregating files before movement over the wide area network, aggregating metadata before movement and loading into a metadata catalog, and aggregating I/O commands into remote procedures that are executed at the remote storage system. In each case, the number of messages that are sent over the wide area network is minimized. This not only improves response time, but also improves scalability, enabling the manipulation of 1000 files at a time.

Trust Virtualization

The management of access controls at remote sites is possible if the data grid owns the data that are stored at each remote site. This means that data are written onto the remote storage system under an account that corresponds to the data grid. Persons accessing the data grid authenticate their identity to the data grid system. The data grid then checks whether they are authorized to perform the desired operation. If so, the data grid accesses the remote storage system on behalf of the user and performs the operation. Thus the data grid software servers must also map from requests made by a user to allowed operations on data that are stored under a data grid account. The trust virtualization mechanisms provide an additional level of authentication beyond the security mechanisms employed at each site. A desired impact is the ability to create a single sign-on environment. Once the user has authenticated their identity to the data grid, they can perform authorized operations on data anywhere within the data grid. They do not need to authenticate their identity at each remote storage system.

The data grid technology used to support each of the above application examples is the Storage Resource Broker (SRB), developed at the San Diego Supercomputer Center (SDSC).[14] Each of the capabilities listed above is supported by the SRB, and is in production use. SRB data grids are typically implemented as federations of multiple independent data grids. Each data grid manages a local metadata catalog and multiple storage systems. Federation is the controlled sharing of name spaces between two or more data grids. A trust relationship is established between two data grids and the data grid administrators decide which of the name spaces will be shared. Different types of federation are then possible:[15]

- Peer-to-peer data grids. None of the name spaces are shared. Instead a person can only access public data within the remote data grid.
- Central archive. Each data grid replicates a copy of their data onto the central archive, including both the files and the provenance metadata.
- Master–slave data grids. All data that reside in a slave data grid are distributed from the master data grid.
- Chained data grids. A data grid administrator pulls data and metadata successively from one data grid in a chain to the next. This is typically used in international collaborations that are managing replicas on different continents.
- Deep archives. The goal is to build a preservation environment that cannot be seen or accessed from a publicly accessible data grid. The approach requires the creation of a staging data grid between the public data grid and the deep archive. The administrator of the staging data grid pulls data from the public data grid to the staging data grid. The administrator of the deep archive then pulls data from the staging data grid into the deep archive. The result is that the identity of the deep archive administrator, the location of the deep archive, and the content of the deep archive cannot be seen from the public data grid.

Management Virtualization

The ability to automate the application of management policies in a distributed environment is critical to the ability to manage very large collections. As the size of collections grow, the validation of integrity and authenticity becomes onerous. Since a data grid is composed of storage systems in which failures might occur at any point in time, both authenticity and integrity must be periodically reassessed, and recovery operations implemented to correct identified problems. Examples include replacement of a replica if a remote storage system crashes, validation of audit trails to prove that only the authorized administrators performed selected operations, and verification of checksums. Each time a problem is identified, the data grid should initiate the required management policy for recovery.

The automation of management policies is an active area of research. The approach taken by the integrated Rule-Oriented Data System (iRODS) under development UNC and UCSD[16] is to differentiate between institutional policies, the management infrastructure needed to implement the policies, and the underlying data grid infrastructure that interacts with the remote storage system.[17] Table 12.1 shows the additional levels of virtualization that are required.

Each community specifies the assessment criteria they use to validate properties about their data collections. Assessment criteria might be driven by measures of trustworthiness such as those proposed by the Research Libraries Group and the National Archives and Records Administration.[18] The assessment criteria are mapped onto sets of persistent state information that can be compared to desired values. An example is assessment of risk mitigation against data loss, by requiring at least two copies of each file be stored on two different storage systems. The persistent state information for each file would need to include the number of copies and the location of each copy.

TABLE 12.1
Characterization of Management Policies and Corresponding Infrastructure

Data Management Environment	Conserved Properties	Control Mechanisms	Remote Operations
Management functions	Assessment criteria	Management policies	Capabilities
Data management infrastructure	Persistent state	Rules	Remote microservices
Software infrastructure	Database	Rule engine	Storage system

Each assessment criterion is maintained by management policies that control what can be done with the files. The management policies are mapped onto sets of rules that control the execution of the remote operations at each storage system. An example is a rule that automatically creates a replica of any file written to a specified collection. The capabilities needed to implement the management policies are mapped onto a set of remote microservices. Each microservice corresponds to a set of operations performed at the remote storage system. The rules are executed by a rule engine, and the resulting persistent state information is stored in a database. Data grid technology provides the infrastructure independence needed to deal with multiple types of databases and storage systems.

The choice of rules to apply is driven by a combination of the identity of the person requesting an operation, the collection that is being manipulated, and the storage system where the data resides. The ability to apply different rules for each operation means that operations required by the data grid administrator can be controlled independently of the operations that might be performed by a public user. The rules can be applied at the time of the requested operation, or deferred for later execution, or executed periodically to validate an assessment criterion.

Management virtualization requires the definition of three more logical name spaces. Within the iRODS system, logical name spaces are also provided for

- Rules—new versions of rules can be added
- Microservices—new versions of microservices can be added
- Persistent state information—additional persistent state information attributes can be added

By adding simultaneously the triplet of {rule, microservice, persistent state}, it is possible to control the evolution of the rule management system itself. New capabilities can be added and executed in parallel with old capabilities, since each new capability can reference a different set of rules, microservices, and state information. A metarule can be written that controls the migration of a collection from an old set of management policies to a new set of management policies.

A second desired capability is improved control of federations of data grid. Under the SRB data grid, authentication was done by the home data grid, but authorization was done by the remote data grid. In a rule-based environment, when data is replicated onto a second data grid, the controlling rules and microservices can also be replicated, implying that it is possible to build a federation environment in which the home data grid remains in control of how their files may be used, even then they are shared with other data grids.

Rule-based systems are optimized by minimizing the number of rules that are applied. This in turn requires defining the correct level of aggregation of remote operations into microservices, and the correct set of microservices for aggregation into capabilities. Microservices that only implement the basic POSIX I/O operations are too low a level for use by a data grid administrator. The number of commands that would need to be executed for a file-level operation become excessive. Fortunately, the operations supported by data grids provide a strong template for deciding how to aggregate operations. Within the SRB data grid, multiple levels of aggregation are used within each of the logical name spaces:

- Users {Single user, group, federation}
- Resources {Single storage system, compound resource, cluster}
- Files {Single file, container, directory}
- Metadata {Single attribute, hierarchical table, collection}
- Management policies {Single capability, set of capabilities, nested rules}

The SRB data grids support identification of users as an individual entity, as a member of a group, or as a member of a data grid within a federation. Storage resources can be referenced as single storage systems, or as a compound resource such as a disk cache in front of a tape archive, or as a cluster across which load leveling is done. Files can be manipulated as individual files, or after aggregation into a physical container, or recursively in a logical directory hierarchy. Metadata attributes can be manipulated as single attributes defined by a user, or through a hierarchical table structure that implements a snowflake schema, or as a collection containing multiple files. Management policies also have multiple levels of aggregation as rules controlling a single microservice, or a set of microservices, or in a recursive-nested hierarchy of rules and microservices.

By building microservices that manipulate each level of granularity, it becomes easier to map operations within the data grid to management policies. Analyses have been made of the capabilities required for the NARA Electronic Records Archive,[19] and their mapping onto rules that can be implemented in the iRODS environment.[20] The mapping identified over 170 rules that would be used to control either operations on records, or the manipulation of structured information. More than 200 persistent state information attributes were identified that were needed to express the results of applying the rules. A similar mapping has been made of the RLG/NARA assessment criteria for trusted digital repositories to iRODS rules and microservices. The assessment criteria comprised about 105 rules for the tracking of trustworthiness. Together, these two assessments provide a definition of the minimal rule set needed to manage distributed shared collections.

A second approach toward quantifying the required management policies for distributed shared collections is to examine the policies requested by production users of the SRB data grid technology. A generic set of 15 rules were identified that would allow each data grid administrator to implement the specific control policies they desired. These rules are primarily for the management of shared collections and include

- Administration—controlling the creation and deletion of users and collections
- Storage selection—controlling how physical resources are selected within a given logical resource name
- Data access—controlling the additional steps performed when data is read from a collection
- Data write—controlling the additional steps performed when data is added to a collection
- Transport—controlling the number of parallel I/O threads to use when moving data
- Deletion—controlling the operations performed when data is deleted

Thus it is possible to build the simple rule environments that meet the needs of today's production shared collections.

DATA MANAGEMENT TECHNOLOGIES

Many of the multiple data management systems currently under development have made explicit choices for the integration of management policies into their software systems. It is worthwhile to examine how their management policies have been implemented, and whether it is possible to integrate each of the approaches into a common system. Three notable systems are the Logistical Distribution Network,[21] LOCKSS—Lots of Copies Keep Stuff Safe,[22] and the Semantic Grid.[23]

The Logistical Distribution Network uses the Internet Backplane Protocol to manage data at the block level. A file is broken up into multiple blocks, with the blocks distributed to multiple remote storage systems. The blocks are migrated between storage systems based on demand to keep the data close to the user. The blocks can also be replicated to support load balancing. A Logistical Distribution Network is designed to make very efficient use of the network bandwidth, and move data at rates approaching the network bandwidth using a single data stream. An interesting integration effort is the porting of data grid technology on top of a Logistical Distribution Network, with the data grid providing interoperability with archives and databases.

The LOCKSS system replicates data at the file level, assuming an authoritative source for the original ingestion of data into the system. The system is used to support data downloaded from publishers. Access control policies are implemented as modules controlling access for data received from each publisher. Integrity is managed by federating with preferably at least six other sites that have also downloaded the same files. A voting protocol between sites that have downloaded the same material is used to verify that each site's copy is authentic. This minimizes risk that operations by a local administrator have compromised the integrity and authenticity of files in a collection. Again, a research topic is the integration of a LOCKSS system with rule-based systems for automating application of additional management policies.

The Semantic Grid uses logical relationships between semantic terms to reason on inferred attributes about independent data collections. The logical relationships are organized in ontologies for each scientific domain. Semantic Grids apply the reasoning to data stored in multiple data grids to improve discovery of the desired data. An example of this is the integration of inference engines with SRB data grids, in a product called S-SRB.[24]

SUMMARY

Data management systems are rapidly evolving from single site collections into distributed environments in which the data are stored across multiple systems. The initial SRB data grid technology supported shared data collections and provided the essential virtualization mechanisms needed to manage and manipulate distributed data for digital libraries and persistent archives.[25] The next generation of rule-based data management systems will automate the application of management policies, minimizing the amount of labor needed to build and maintain a shared collection. Rule-based systems have the attraction of being able to manage their own evolution, directly associate allowed operations (microservices) with individual files or collections, and apply access controls even in federated environments. Given the expected emergence of data format description languages that will characterize structures in data, rule-based systems will be able to apply access controls on structures within files, enabling the automated redaction of data files. The drive for the creation of rule-based systems is coming from the massive collections that will appear in the next 5–10 years. Without rule-based data management systems, the labor requirements for assessing integrity and authenticity will not be possible to sustain.

ACKNOWLEDGMENTS

The principle developers of the SRB and iRODS technology are Michael Wan (UCSD), Arcot Rajasekar (UNC), and Wayne Schroeder (UCSD), of the San Diego Supercomputer Center. This work was supported in part by the NSF ITR grant on Constraint-based Knowledge Systems for Grids, Digital Libraries, and Persistent Archives, the NSF SCI0438741 (National Archives and Records Administration research prototype persistent archive supplement), and the Lawrence Livermore National Laboratory project with UCSD on Scientific Data. The views and conclusions contained in this entry are those of the authors and should not be interpreted as representing the official policies, either expressed or implied, of the National Science Foundation, the National Archives and Records Administration, or the U.S. government.

REFERENCES

1. http://www.scec.org (accessed February 2007).
2. Faerman, M.; Moore, R.; Minster, B.; Maechling, P. Managing large scale data for earthquake simulations. J. Grid Comput. **2007**, *5* (3) 295–302.
3. http://www.slac.stanford.edu/BFROOT/ (accessed February 2007).
4. http://public.web.cern.ch/Public/Welcome.html (accessed February 2007).
5. http://www.lsst.org/lsst_home.shtml (accessed February 2007).
6. http://www.ipac.caltech.edu/2mass/ (accessed February 2007).
7. http://nsdl.org/ (accessed February 2007).
8. Rajasekar, A.; Vernon, F.; Lindquist, K.; Orcutt, J.; Lu, S.; Moore, R. Accessing sensor data using meta data: A virtual object ring buffer framework. In *Proceedings of the 2nd International Very Large Data Base Workshop on Data Management for Sensor Networks*, Trondheim, Norway, August 29, 2005.
9. Moore, R. Data intensive computing. In *The Grid: Blueprint for a New Computing Infrastructure*, 1st Ed.; Foster, I., Kesselman, C., Eds.; Morgan Kaufmann: San Francisco, 1999; 105–129.
10. Moore, R. Building preservation environments with data grid technology. Am. Archivist **2006**, *69* (1), 139–158.
11. Moore, R.; Baru, C.; Rajasekar, A.; Ludascher, B.; Marciano, R.; Wan, M.; Schroeder, W.; Gupta, A. *Collection-Based Persistent Digital Archives—Parts 1 & 2. D-Lib Magazine*; April/March 2000. http://www.dlib.org/.
12. http://www.dspace.org/ (accessed February 2007).
13. http://www.fedora.info/ (accessed February 2007).
14. http://www.srb.diceresearch.org (accessed February 2007).
15. Rajasekar, A.; Wan, M.; Moore, R.; Schroeder, W. Data grid federation. In *Proceedings of the 2004 International Conference on Parallel and Distributed Processing Techniques and Applications—Special Session on New Trends in Distributed Data Access*, Las Vegas, NV, June 21–24, 2004.
16. http://irods.diceresearch.org (accessed February 2007).
17. Rajasekar, A.; Wan, M.; Moore, R.; Schroeder, W. http://irods.diceresearch.org. A prototype rule-based distributed data management system. In *Proceedings of High Performance Distributed Computing Workshop on Next Generation Distributed Data Management*, Paris, France, June 20, 2006.
18. http://www.rlg.org/en/pdfs/rlgnara-repositorieschecklist.pdf (accessed November 2006).
19. http://www.archives.gov/era/pdf/requirements-amend0001.pdf (accessed November 2006).
20. Smith, M.; Moore, R. Digital archive policies and trusted digital repositories. In *Proceedings of the 2nd International Digital Curation Conference: Digital Data Curation in Practice*, Glasgow, Scotland, November 21–22, 2006.
21. http://loci.cs.utk.edu/ (accessed February 2007).
22. http://www.lockss.org/lockss/Home (accessed February 2007).
23. http://www.semanticgrid.org/index.html (accessed February 2007).
24. http://www.itee.uq.edu.au/~eresearch/projects/dart/workpackages/si3.php (accessed February 2007).
25. Moore, R.; Rajasekar, A.; Wan, M. Data grids, digital libraries and persistent archives: An integrated approach to publishing, sharing and archiving data. Proc. IEEE Grid Comput. **2005**, *93* (3), 578–588 [special issue].

13 Search Engine Optimization

Nicholas Carroll

CONTENTS

INTRODUCTION

Search engine optimization (SEO) is the craft of elevating Web sites or individual Web site pages to higher rankings on World Wide Web (WWW) search engines through programming, marketing, or content acumen. The definition often includes specifications for increased traffic to a given Web site, improved quality of traffic, increased profits, or brand awareness.

In a typical online search on a topic, anywhere from hundreds to millions of articles may be extracted and ranked by probability of relevance on a search engine results page (SERP). From the earliest appearance of Web search engines, creators of Web sites realized that ranking high was vital for visits to their Web sites, since users seldom look on even second or third screens of rankings, let alone the hundredth screen. The numbers of Web sites on the Web increased so rapidly from the beginning that the competition for the most desirable top positions developed rapidly.

In this entry, we move through several key aspects of SEO. First, we define "rankings," and review the origins and history of SEO. Then we discuss what is known as "Black Hat" and "White Hat" SEO, as the competition for rankings can lead to distortions and misleading rankings, depending on what techniques are used.

The heart of the entry concerns SEO methods. We review keyword selection and then attend to various aspects of the content of the Web pages, such as keyword density, placement, and consistency. We then go on to the technical aspects and review techniques such as keyword stuffing, meta tags, and cloaking, as well as strategies for boosting page rank through links from and to other Web sites, with brief discussion of combined strategies and the analytic methods applied to track results.

The entry expands into more general issues such as broad vs. narrow targeting, page longevity and rank, geographic targeting, and increasing competition. Trends in SEO practices are described from early to present time, as are external trends affecting SEO.

We conclude with a description of SEO regulation, mostly in the form of search engines policing their listings, and an overview of typical behavior patterns of search engine users.

All the methods described have been or continue to be effective SEO to some degree. Changes in search engine indexing protocols as well as their methods for displaying search results mean that no strict description of the best method or methods can remain entirely accurate indefinitely. This entry does not cover pay-per-click, other forms of online advertising, or the resale of Web site traffic or links.

Because the discipline originated in the mid-1990s, terminology is still in flux. General references at the end of this entry point to the more authoritative Web sites and definitions.

DEFINITION OF HIGHER RANKINGS

"Higher rankings" in the popular press or lay discussion generally equates with the goal of having a Web page appear in the first 10 or 20 search records for a particular search term, as it is broadly established by tracking that few search engine users will click through to any link beyond the 20th record. SEO professionals usually discuss rankings in terms of SERP position (Figure 13.1).

Before search engines accepted paid advertisements, SEO was considered a unique form of promotion, radically different from all traditional forms of advertising. It is now more often considered a subset of search engine marketing (SEM), and is sometimes referred to as "organic search" or "natural SEM," as opposed to paid advertisements placed on the pages of search engines or their affiliates.

Online commerce was the originating force behind search engine promotion and remains the primary driving force behind SEO. Nonprofits and government bodies apply some SEO methods but tend to rely on their unique identity to assure them a prominent SERP position, e.g., the Red Cross, Amnesty International, the Vatican, the New York Department of Motor Vehicles, or the Peoria Public Library.

ORIGINS AND HISTORY OF SEO

The term "search engine optimization" came into popular use in 1997–1998 and is frequently attributed to Danny Sullivan,[1] then operating "Search Engine Watch," though Sullivan states he is uncertain who coined it. Previous terms included "search engine placement," "search engine ranking," "search engine positioning," and "search engine promotion," the latter attributed to Jim Rhodes,[2]

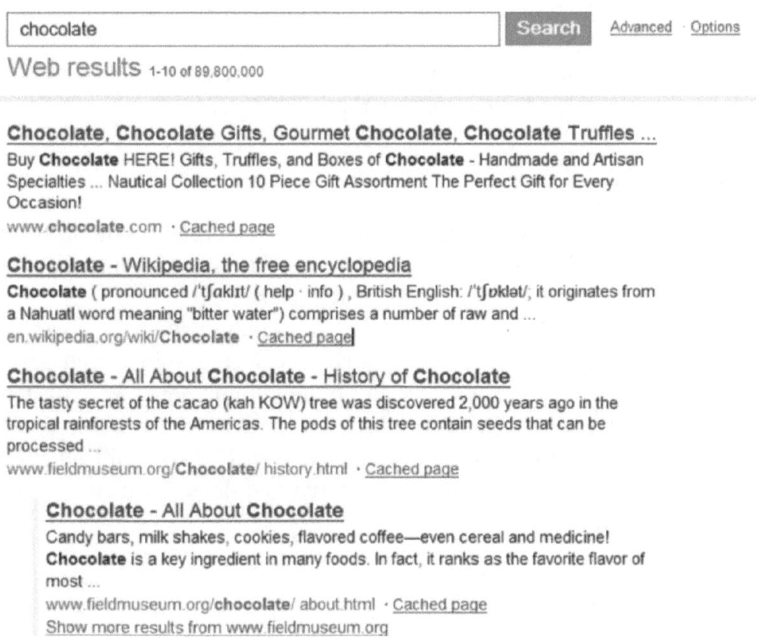

FIGURE 13.1 Typical SERP in search for chocolate, showing the first four results.

author of "The Art of Search Engine Promotion." Predecessors such as Heath[3] in his 1995 article "Pointers on how to create business Web sites that work" did not have a formal name for SEO.

The period from the mid-1990s to about 2000 was characterized by broad experimentation on the part of both search engines seeking a business model and Web site creators intent on promoting themselves. Search engines were relatively under-powered and minimally staffed; their primary focus was on keeping pace with the growth in new Web sites. SEO quickly became part of the American "wild, wild Web" metaphor, with more active Web site owners engaging in a huge variety of methods to gain higher rankings, as described in "SEO Methods." In a period when many multinational organizations did not have Web sites at all, smaller and more nimble organizations and individuals aggressively practiced SEO to establish a beachhead on the WWW.

The early days of search engines were in some ways a struggle against pornography. Visitors who started using search engines after 2000 have little conception of how pervasive the online sex industry was at one time, with their records appearing among search results for cooking, art, quilting, travel, and other innocuous subjects.

As search engines have grown and become more sophisticated, and the number of Web sites has increased more than tenfold, aggressive maneuvering to rank well in the SERPs has to some extent given way to a focus on ranking well in particular niches, and executing well on fundamentals rather than exercising brilliance in manipulating search engines.[4]

PRACTITIONERS AND SOFTWARE

Early Search Engine Promoters and Reporters

Early SEO innovation was an individualistic endeavor, primarily developed by small-to-midsize businesses ranging from small hotels to makers of custom sports equipment. Several such niche and popular products were financially successful, demonstrating that SEO was a path to profit.

Web sites with forums for exchange of SEO strategies began to appear by 1996, including still-existing Web sites such as http://virtualpromote.com, http://www.searchengineforums.com, and the archived http://www.deadlock.com/promote.

Web sites reporting on search engines and optimization began about the same time, including http://www.wilsonweb.com, http://www.searchenginewatch.com, and http://www.webmasterworld.com. More recent additions include http://www.seobook.com/blog, http://www.searchengineland.com, and http://www.toprankblog.com/search-marketing-blogs.

The Current SEO Industry

Whether offered as a subset of SEM services or sold alone as organic search, SEO has become a niche industry with its own sales forces and conventions. The service may be sold as a one-time audit or on an ongoing basis with monthly billing and performance reporting.

Pure SEO consulting firms now number in the thousands, primarily concentrated in North America and the United Kingdom. Tens of thousands more Web designers and developers offer the service as ancillary to building Web sites, and an unknown number of Webmasters and Web site owners apply SEO methods to their own Web sites.

Gross expenditures on SEO in 2006 were estimated at over USD one billion, with steady annual growth anticipated. This figure describes organic search and does not include paid advertising or most in-house work in smaller companies.[5]

SEO Software (Automating the Process)

Automated Web page submission tools came into being in the mid-1990s soon after search engines began indexing the WWW. For some years, they were a vital part of SEO strategy for large Web sites, as manually entering thousands of URLs into the submission pages of a dozen search engines was extremely time-consuming. Submission tools fell into disuse as search engines became more adept at "deep crawling" (following links into the lower levels of Web sites' file hierarchies). The ones currently in use typically offer additional features such as help in choosing keywords and automated reporting on SERP positions.

Web analytics tools move beyond automated reporting to features such as tracking visitors' paths through Web sites, and integrating the data with financials.[6]

Most content management systems, originally focused on intranets, now include management features for Web sites, and many are programmed to allow a significant modification of variables important to SEO.[7] Likewise most blogging software includes features that encourage users to add keywords to the title tags, the Web page body, and the filename of a given Web page.

SEO Worldwide

While search engines are now used worldwide, most SEO reporting is about the United States, Canada, and the United Kingdom. Activity in other countries must be inferred. Australia, Ireland, and Russia in particular have significant indications of entrepreneurial SEO, including blogs on the subject.[8]

BLACK HAT VS. WHITE HAT SEO

"White Hat" SEO typically refers to strategies and tactics that are in concordance with the policies of online search engines, in a loose tacit agreement to provide Web surfers with "relevant content." "Black Hat" SEO describes tactics that ignore generally accepted conventions of ethical WWW behavior to advance an agenda or commercial interest. The focus on search engine policies before other interests flows from the pervasive position of search engines, at the mid-point in the process of aggregating Web page data and delivering it to users. The tilted point of view is buttressed by the oligopoly of major search engines, with a small number of them processing the vast majority of searches, while millions of Web sites vie for high rankings.

Technically sophisticated tactics are often equated with Black Hat SEO, and a focus on high-quality content with White Hat SEO. However, there is substantial overlap; few if any tactics can be inherently classified as good or evil. From the perspective of a user, the main criteria of legitimate SEO is whether a given search return is relevant to their interests, regardless of how it achieved its ranking. Most experienced SEO practitioners consider intent to be the defining factor.

Typically, methods considered Black Hat SEO develop high page rankings faster, while those known as White Hat SEO tend to create longer-lasting rankings. A preference for one approach or the other is not entirely a matter of the SEO practitioner's personal preferences; it also depends on the business model. Web sites or pages promoting products and services with short life cycles are suited to Black Hat methods, as they do not suffer from being "burned," meaning they have drawn the attention of search engine administrators and been banned from that search engine's index entirely. (This has also happened to sites of long-view organizations such as auto manufacturers when SEO subcontractors acted with an excess of zeal.)

White Hat SEO is better suited to Web sites that offer products with long life cycles. It is also suited to academic or government Web sites, where there is likely to be a consistent focus over decades—such Web sites often gain high and enduring SERP rankings simply by publishing high-quality content about a particular subject.

SEO METHODS

In describing SEO it is necessary to distinguish between automated search engines and manually created directories such as Yahoo! Directory (http://dir.yahoo.com) or the Open Directory Project (ODP) (http://www.dmoz.org), where listings are added by human editors rather than automated protocols.

SEO describes strategies and tactics for influencing page rank on search engines that use "robots" (http://www.robotstxt.org/wc/faq.html) or "spiders" to "crawl" Web pages, traveling from page to page through hyperlinks, and indexing those pages by algorithms and protocols. While directories such as the original Yahoo! Directory can be searched from within Yahoo!, and the ODP pages can frequently be found in SERPs, it is the manner of creating the index that differentiates search engines and directories.

Elements of a Web Page to Be Optimized

The following example of HTML (Hypertext Markup Language) is referred to throughout this entry. The markup language and page structure used are explained in Table 13.1 below the example. (Web page structure can be viewed in almost all Web browsers by selecting the "View > Source" or "View > Page Source" option.)[9]

```
<html>
<head>
<title>ELIS—Encyclopedia of Library and Information Sciences 2008-2009</
title>
<meta name="description" content="The definitive reference to library and
information sciences.">
<meta name="keywords" content="encyclopedia, marcia, bates, mary, niles,
maack, mack, optimise">
</head>
<body>
<h1>ELIS—Encyclopedia of Library and Information Sciences</h1>
<img src="images/ELIS-cover.gif" alt="ELIS encyclopedia cover" />
<p>Body content written for SEO is rich in keywords and also readable.
Proper nouns such as "encyclopedia" are used instead of pronouns.
Initializations such as "SEO" are spelled out as "search engine
optimization," both to include alternate search terms and to increase
keyword density in the Web page. To target both sophisticated and lay
searchers, common terms such as "acronym" are used in addition to precise
terms such as "initialization." Concepts are described by all likely
variants, such as "SERP," "search engine position," or "ranking."</p>
<h2>Further Encyclopedia Resources</h2>
<p>See the <a href="http://informationr.net/ir/12-4/colis/colis29.
html">encyclopedia description</a> for further information on ELIS.</p>
<p><font size="-1">Keywords: encyclopaedia, taylor, francis, marcia,
bates, mary, niles, maack, mack, optimise</font></p>
</body>
</html>
```

Choosing Keywords to Target—The Core of SEO

Regardless of preferred methods, White Hat or Black Hat, content or technical, the most critical part of effective SEO is deciding which keywords to target for high rankings. While search engines continually work to improve their ranking algorithms, they are not clairvoyant; targeting the right keywords is still the foundation of reaching the right audience.[10]

A self-centric viewpoint will usually lead an organization to aim at high rankings for its own name, services, agendas, or products. For example, the Raffles Hotel or the band U2 might focus on targeting searches for their own name, in a reasonable belief that most potential customers are specifically seeking them, rather than hotels in Singapore or rock music in general.

TABLE 13.1
Tags and Text in a Simple Web Page

Tags and Text in a Simple Web Page, as Seen Through an HTML Editing Tool	Explanation of HTML Tags and Structure
<html>	Flag to user's browser: Begin parsing for HyperText Markup Language
<head>	Begin the head content (which is not visible in a browser)
<title>ELIS: Encyclopedia of Library and Information Sciences</title>	The page title is the single most important part of Web page text for search engine ranking. While not shown in the body text in a Web browser, it can be seen in the title bar at the top, and is shown as the title of the Web page in almost all search engine listings
<meta name="description" content="The definitive reference to library and information sciences.">	Most search engines will use the meta description as the default description in SERPs. SEO practitioners consider this tag a minor influence on SERP position, and usually orient the text towards readers rather than search engines
<meta name="keywords" content="encyclopedia, marcia, bates, mary, niles, maack, mack, optimise">	The meta keywords tag, originally intended as a field for general metadata, was widely abused by SEO practitioners and is now a minor or irrelevant element of SEO
</head>	End of the Head section
<body>	Begin the text visible in a browser
<h1>ELIS: Encyclopedia of Library and Information Sciences</h1>	Headings tags, from H1 down to H6, are the equivalent of chapter and section headings in books, and are usually considered influential in SEO
<img src="images/ELIS-cover.gif" alt="ELIS encyclopedia cover" />	IMG tags define what image to display as part of a Web page. The "alt" attribute is used to store a brief description, typically keywords
<p>Body content written for SEO is rich in keywords. . . [etc.]"</p>	The paragraph tag is the fundamental "container" for body content
<h2>Resources</h2>	The second-level heading tag may have influence on SERP position, as well as significance for metadata and document readability
<p>See the <a href="http://informationr.net/ir/12-4/colis/colis29.html">encyclopedia description</a> for further information on ELIS.</p>	An outbound link where the "anchor text" contains the relevant keyword "encyclopedia"
<p>Keywords: encyclopaedia, taylor, francis, marcia, bates, mary, niles, maack, mack, optimise</p>	This is an unsightly but often necessary addition to the body content, displaying related keywords in the body text, where the search engines will read and index them. This practice evolved when search engines stopped indexing meta keywords
</body>	End of the body element
</html>	Flag to user's browser: end of HTML file

Further information on HTML is available at http://www.w3.org/MarkUp/Guide/.

While this may be a successful strategy for broadly known organizations or people, it is considered poor-quality SEO when an unknown product, service, or agenda is being advanced. Products and agendas without name recognition are better served by targeting a generic search term such as "stainless steel ball bearings" than a term like "Smith Ball Bearing Company." A multinational company such as General Electric or Hitachi—that manufactures a huge variety of products—might likewise target searches for the products rather than its own company name.

Regardless of whether the focus is on the organization or the products, SEO can fail when names are chosen without forethought to online search, particularly when they compete with long-established names. Two examples:

1. Any product named "Guardian" must compete in the SERPs with dozens of well-established newspapers throughout the English-speaking world.
2. Organizations using initializations that might be unique in a local telephone directory frequently face obscurity when competing for recognition in a global medium—"ABC" is not only an initialization for the American Broadcasting Company, but hundreds or thousands of other organizations throughout nations that use the Roman alphabet.

This leads to a fundamental truth about the limits of SEO as a promotional avenue: it can only succeed if people are searching for relevant keywords. If an idea or product is beyond the public's conception, it cannot be promoted through search engines—in contrast to promotion through traditional untargeted media such as radio, TV, or print. This usually makes SEO a poor method for promoting radically new ideas. For example, "anti-gravity belts" is a search only used by 10-year-old boys.

When possible, experienced SEO practitioners perform keyword analysis before a Web site is built, expanded, or redesigned, using paid or free online tools such as http://www.keyworddiscovery.com, http://www.wordtracker.com, http://inventory.overture.com/d/searchinventory/suggestion/ or https://adwords.google.com/select/KeywordToolExternal to view aggregated searches conducted on search engines.

Content

At its simplest, the content-focused approach to SEO is to tell the story thoroughly and precisely, in hopes that the words (content) will find a fit with search engine indexing algorithms, and rise in the rankings for particular search terms. The presumption in this strategy is that the writer's words will also find harmony with the terms used by searchers, and if the writer does have the same interests—and frame of reference—as the target audience, this by itself can result in highly successful SEO. (Conversely, Web pages written in ignorance of either subject matter or audience may achieve high SERP positions, but not necessarily for the keywords that draw the desired audience.)[11]

A highly content-oriented strategy is often seen in Web sites that were conceived and designed by an individual or small group. Content-oriented Web sites or sub-sites may also come into being in an organization with no SEO strategy at all, such as a department of a university, where the authors are discussing the same or related subjects.

Density

Keyword density receives attention because it is easy to understand and simple to calculate through online density-checkers such as http://www.keyworddensity.com. (Such tools are easily found through search engines with the term "keyword density analyzer.")

Though the effectiveness of intentionally repeating keywords throughout a Web page is debated by SEO practitioners, a search for highly promoted products such as "loans," "chocolate," or "discount shoes" will return numerous high-ranking Web pages with the core keyword repeated dozens of times, and keyword densities reaching up to 7% or higher of the page's content. (However, exceptionally high-density pages can suddenly plummet in the SERPs or be dropped from the index entirely if search engines classify them as examples of "keyword spamming," described in the Technical strategies section below.)

Conversely, using a set of keywords only once in a Web page usually results in SERP obscurity, even if the set is extremely precise. For example, even "dodo bird nesting" returns tens of thousands of Web pages, and of the first few dozen search engine records, almost all will have the three keywords used several times.

Many SEO practitioners and analysts favor well-written content over keyword density, as search engines become better at differentiating between conventional prose and deliberately enhanced Web pages. This school of thought says that content should be primarily aimed at humans, not search engines, and that good writing not only entices users to read and act, but is better search engine bait in the first place. The belief is often expressed as "Content is king."

Placement

The placement of keywords in a Web page is a significant factor in SEO, since search engine algorithms accord more weight to certain positions, whether visible or within tags (see Table 13.1). Notable areas for placement include

Visible in Web page
Inside heading tags `<h1, h2, h3. . . .>`
Placed at the beginning (top) of a Web page.
Within outbound links, i.e., "anchor text" (example in Table 13.1).
Placed NEAR other keywords (generally within 10 words).
Visible in SERPs and browser title bar
Inside the HTML <title> tag.
As part of the URL

Competition over search terms and SERP positions has expanded the use of keywords to the point that they are now routinely made part of file names (e.g., http://www.mysite.com/used-software-for-sale.html), or may even form the domain name itself, e.g., http://www.usedsoftwareforsale.com.

The title tag is almost universally agreed to be highly important by SEO practitioners. Most other placements are debated. The `<meta="keywords">` tag is largely considered of no importance. The "alt" content in image tags `<img src alt="[image description]">` is considered significant in image SERPs, less so in the overall ranking of a Web page.[12]

Inclusion of Related Keywords

Due to the unpredictability of user search behavior, many SEO practitioners include synonyms, cognates, tangential terms, and misspellings in Web pages. In the mid-1990s, SEO practitioners placed such related keywords in the meta keywords field (see Table 13.1), but massive abuse and misuse of that field led virtually all search engines to stop indexing meta keywords. As a result, SEO practitioners reluctantly turned to placing them as a visible footer on the Web page, though this compromises the esthetics of page design. Some examples of keyword (or "tags") line listings:

Synonyms, cognates, and closely related terms for a medical page about trigeminal neuralgia, formerly called tic douloureux:
"Keywords: tic douloureux, neuropathy, facial pain, face pain."
Tangential terms (statistical outliers) for a site on vegetarian diet:
"Keywords: low sodium, low fat, organic."
Variants on the author's name for a Web page written by Jon Smythe:
"Keywords: John, Smith, Smyth."
Common misspellings for a travel Web site about Colombia:
"Keywords: accommodation, Columbia."
(However, when a keyword tag is used to repeat words already in the body content, it simply becomes "keyword stuffing"—see "Keyword Loading" below.)

Consistency

Building a Web site with a consistent pattern of clearly related keywords is commonly known as creating a "theme."[13] A Web site with a clear theme stays on a single topic or closely related topics throughout its pages (barring such standard pages as "Contact Us"). This strategy builds the overall ranking of the Web site and, as a consequence, the SERP positions of the individual Web pages.

The concept "clearly related" restricts thematic rank-building to keyword relationships that search engines are capable of recognizing. Where "ship" and "marina" might begin to build a theme relating to recreational sailing, search engines would be less likely to recognize a theme in a Web page with the separate keywords "ship" and "space." Once combined into the more specific keyword "spaceship," the page becomes identifiable as related to science fiction or space exploration, and if the Web site also contains the words "galaxy" and "parsec," a theme begins to build.

The interest in themes peaked around 2004, alarmists suggesting that Web sites without a keyword theme would plummet in the SERPs.[14] However, there are exceptions to the rule: newspapers, encyclopedias, and many news blogs will never have a clear theme, yet they still can reach high SERP positions for a variety of keywords, based on meeting search engine criteria other than consistency of subject matter.

Technical

A technically oriented SEO strategy emphasizes programming skill or ingenuity over command of language, familiarity with the target audience, or interweaving related content. Tactics vary from the simple, which can be executed by anyone familiar with HTML, to the sophisticated, which require knowledge of programming, Web site servers, or WWW and Internet protocols.

Keyword Loading, Stuffing, and Spamming

Keyword density can be taken to an extreme. Efforts to increase keyword density or variety that involve excessive or awkward repetition are known as "keyword loading." An example would be replacing every instance of "it" in a page with the noun in question.

When this repetition reaches the level of incoherence, with the same word or words used dozens of times in the body, title, or tags of a Web page, it is usually called "keyword stuffing" (a.k.a. "cramming"), "spamming the index" ("index" referring to the search engines' databases of Web pages), or "spamdexing." One of the earliest SEO tactics, it began with simply repeating keywords hundreds of times, generally at the bottom of the page, and frequently with the font color the same as the background color, thus rendering the text invisible to humans. As search engine algorithms began to discount this tactic, keyword spamming evolved into a more precise metering of keyword density. This obsolete technique periodically sees a resurgence as search engine administrators let down their guard.

The Meta Keywords Tag

Located in the head section of a Web page's HTML (see Table 13.1) and invisible to users viewing a Web page in a browser, the meta keywords tag was created purely for metadata.

In the mid to late 1990s meta keywords were highly popular as a quick path to higher rankings, and indeed stuffing the meta keywords field showed some success when only a few million pages were being indexed. By the time the tactic became broadly known—with "keyword-jacking" lawsuits over copyright and trademark infringement—search engines were on their way to downranking the meta keywords tag contents, and usually not indexing the keywords in the field at all.

Entry Pages

"Entry page" is the broadest descriptor for the strategy of creating particular pages to rank well with search engines, sometimes finely tuned to rank well with a particular search engine. "Doorway page" and "gateway page" imply that a page contains some relevant content that has been tuned for high SERP position. "Bridge page" or "jump page" imply that a page may be little more than an uninformative landing page that either urges the visitor to click through to the rest of the Web site, automatically redirects them to the rest of the Web site, or redirects them to an entirely different

Web site.[15] Most media coverage of such pages classifies them as Black Hat SEO. However, there is no clear agreement on the definition of these pages or their relative level of deception. Many SEO practitioners observe that while bridge and jump pages may be technical and possibly Black Hat as well, all pages visible to search engines are in a real sense entry pages.

Cloaking

"Cloaking" is used to describe a broad range of tactics. The common element is that the human visitor and the search engine spiders "see" different content when visiting a Web page. In the simplest form, the SEO practitioner creates a page tuned for high SERP position, and replaces it with a human-readable page after the page has been indexed by search engines (of course the artificially high ranking only lasts until search engine spiders visit the page again).

Two of the more technical methods, which attempt to deceive search engines on a continuing basis:

1. *User-agent-specific page delivery*, in which the Web page server "sniffs" the incoming page request, extracts the data that identifies what browser the visitor is running (e.g., "googlebot" or "msnbot"), and delivers a special Web page tuned to gain higher SERP on that SE.
2. *IP-specific page delivery*, in which the Web page server delivers a special Web page based on the visitor's Internet Protocol address (e.g., "127.0.0.1").

Cloaking is broadly considered one of the most aggressive and sophisticated forms of Black Hat SEO, but search engine analysts point out that even cloaking has legitimate purposes, as when a Web site is migrating to a new domain name; the owners may want to keep the old Web site available to the public until the new one becomes established in SERPs.[16]

Linking

Links have become such an important determinant of SERP position that under some circumstances they may override all other elements of ranking, and catapult a Web page of little or no relevance to a top SERP position.

Link-Weighting Fundamentals

Since the mid-1990s, search engines have routinely tracked the links from (and to) Web sites, often assigning a relative value based on the links' source or destination. Links pointing to a Web site are generally called "inbound links," and links pointing to other Web sites "outbound links." (Inbound links are frequently called "backlinks," though the term has other technical meanings in computing.)[17]

"Link-weighting" is frequently described as "link popularity" or even "popularity" measurements by popular media. More accurately, search engine link analysis algorithms attempt to infer the value of a Web page or entire Web site based on four factors:

1. The number of inbound links.
2. The "quality" of the inbound links, based on the quality of the originating Web site. Assessing the quality of Web sites is where link-weighting moves into more sophisticated and sometimes arcane mathematics.[18,19] In simple terms, an inbound link from a major university has more value than a link from an obscure small business, and has a greater beneficial effect on SERP position.
3. The "relevance" of the inbound link. A Web site about a baseball team benefits more by inbound links from other baseball-oriented Web sites than by links from the personal pages of fans.

4. The keywords contained within inbound links (the linked text visible in a browser), known as "anchor text." The most famous example was the 2003 link manipulation of Google SERPs (known as "Google bombing") in which hundreds or more Web site owners inserted the link `<a href="http://www.whitehouse.gov/president/gwbbio.html">Miserable Failure</a>` into their pages, causing the U.S. White House biography of George W. Bush to rise to the top ranking for the term "miserable failure."[20] (The gwbbio.html page rose to #1 ranking on Google for that term even though it did not contain either of the keywords in question.)

The cumulative importance of these factors in SERP position has led to naming the collective effect of inbound links "link juice" (American "slang definition of" "juice": influence, clout, http://www.m-w.com.)

Web sites with many relevant or high-quality links pointing to them (inbound links) are known as "authority" Web sites; those with many links pointing to other relevant Web sites (outbound links) as "expert" or "hub" Web sites. The presumption built into the search engine algorithms is that a Web site with many inbound links from high-quality Web pages is an authoritative source, and that pages with many outbound links to authority Web sites serve as a WWW resource. (The mathematics can become circular and even self-reinforcing, as when http://www.wikipedia.org Web pages briefly started to dominate #1 SERPs positions for thousands of subjects.)

Strategies for Leveraging Links

Link-weighting was implemented to in effect create a weighted voting scheme and take some of the control of rankings away from a Web site's designer. Since weighting means that not all inbound links are of equal value to SERP position, the methodology also opened the door to SEO opportunities of bewildering complexity, in which Web sites buy, sell, and trade links to and from their Web sites in order to improve their SERP positions.

Always a factor in SEO, "link building" is now broadly considered a core element of strategy, and in some schools of thought the most important element.[21] Increasing media attention brought linking as a SERP ranking factor to the attention of Web site owners and the quickly growing number of SEO practitioners, and today organizations spend substantial time and effort on link building aimed at high rankings.

Non-reciprocal links (a.k.a. "generosity links") were the first evolution, in the mid-1990s. At that time Web site creators linked to almost any remotely related Web site, including their competitors. By the late 1990s "reciprocal links" had become the standard, though the exchange was offered with a view to a direct increase in traffic rather than SERP position.

Soliciting inbound links, at first done casually, now often means assigning employees or subcontractors to solicit links from high-ranking Web sites. The return on investment is questionable—high-ranking Web sites have little to gain by giving an outbound link, and the site owners may be concerned that linking to a low-quality Web site will harm their own rankings. (Soliciting links should not be equated with link building, a broader term that covers all strategies for gaining inbound links.)[22]

The practice of posting links in discussion groups also originated with the goal of direct traffic rather than influencing SERP positions. "FFAs" (Free For All Web sites), "link farms," and "link rings" were crude early link-exchange schemes, most variants indiscriminately exchanging thousands of links without regard to relevance. While such sites are still active, their value in SEO has largely been eliminated by increasing sophistication of search engine ranking protocols. Most SEO practitioners today consider participating in them to be useless at best, and at worst, possibly injurious to a Web site's SERP positions.

"Paid links"—inbound links that have been purchased, sometimes masking as editorial recommendations—existed before the WWW on Internet bulletin boards, always with the intent of publicity or direct financial gain. With the broadening awareness of SEO, using paid links to influence

SERP position has become both a business strategy and a source of contention between Web site owners and search engines.

Good content, the oldest link-building strategy of all, is a somewhat indirect way to build links. Coupled with even a modest amount of self-promotion beyond good SEO—or occasionally just with good content that perfectly targets a popular search—competent writing on a particular subject can generate hundreds or thousands of inbound links to a given Web page, often without any communication at all with the Web sites that are giving the links. Because content-inspired linking may produce results slowly (in months or years), and is often difficult to quantify, few organizations devote serious effort to the method.

Web Site and Web Page Structure

The directory (folder) structure of an SE-friendly Web site looks similar to a clearly and logically organized hard drive on a personal computer, with the additional proviso that every document is directly or indirectly linked from the home page or some other prominent Web page. Ideally the structure is "shallow" (three or fewer sub-directory levels), to make it easier for search engines to spider, though that has become less important as all major search engines now perform deep crawling.

Actual page structure of HTML pages is in theory dictated by an adherence to W3C standards. In practice, Web sites use almost any markup code that can be rendered by a Web browser and leave the difficulties of indexing to the search engines.

There are drawbacks to unorthodoxy where search engine rankings are concerned. Use of highly irregular Web site structure, page structure, or file naming conventions can seriously harm SERP position. In extreme cases, search engines simply do not add a Web site to their indexes; poor Web site structure can be as destructive to Web site rankings as the most extreme Black Hat tactics, and "site maps" generated specifically to aid search engines in indexing a Web site are not a substitute for logical Web site structure.[23]

Despite a broad disregard for standards among Web site owners, most SEO practitioners consider disciplined site and page structure fundamental good practice, though these are seen as a foundation for SEO rather than an SEO strategy in themselves.

Web Analytics

The most thorough SEO practitioners use "Web analytics" to analyze Web site traffic for patterns that can lead to enhanced SEO. While the term embraces areas more concerned with usability and user behavior while on a Web site, analytics sweeps in SEO functions such as keyword analysis and SERP position monitoring.

Data can be collected by "tagging" individual Web pages with Javascript and other programming, or by placing cookies on visitors' browsers.

"Keyword analysis" is often initiated at the server level through "log analysis." Because WWW communications protocols usually pass the full URL of the previously visited page to the destination Web site, the headers can be processed for search terms, and those terms then organized and further analyzed.

In either case, data is then analyzed manually, or with in-house programming, or with one of the many commercial Web analytics programs.

The data below is a sample of some of the information that can be extracted from Web site server logs: visitor's ISP, visitor's IP address, number of pages visited, time and date, visitor's browser and operating system, the Web site the visitor came from, the search terms they used, and the landing page.

A visitor from "dynamic.dsl.com" (88.104.65.226) was logged twice, starting at 12:46:36 on Sunday, October 14, 2007.

The initial browser was Firefox/2.0.0.7 (Windows XP; en).

This visitor first arrived from http://www.google.co.uk while searching "ecommerce business models 1–10" and visited "digitalenterprise.org/models/models.html."

There has been a general shift in Web analytics from log analysis to page tagging, in part due to the limits of log information compared with information gained by tagging, and in part driven by vendors of analytics software.

Combining Content, Technical, and Linking SEO

Strategies that combine all three forms of SEO may be the most effective in gaining high SERP positions. Combined strategies are uncommon because Web sites are normally designed without regard to SEO (although the most effective SEO is begun at the conceptual level), and because Web site owners and managers rarely allow significant changes to the structure or content of their Web sites after they are built and online.

An alternate way of viewing SEO is "on page" or "off page" SEO, the former being methods applied directly to Web sites and pages, the latter focusing on methods external to a Web site, such as link strategies.[24]

BROAD ISSUES IN SEO

A number of strategic issues that may affect a Web site go beyond fundamental SEO tactics or current "best practices."

Building Downwards vs. Outwards

Large or growing organizations face the question of whether to house all their Web pages under a single WWW domain, or to establish separate Web sites for different services, product lines, or agendas. An established organization with a strong brand will usually lean keyword targeting towards its own brand name in SERP positions, and thus benefit from housing all its Web pages under a single domain, whereas a newer organization with separate divisions would be more likely to establish separate Web sites for each product line or goal.

This is not strictly a business issue; a university establishing a new campus in a different city would probably create a new Web site for that campus, just as a business that sells to both architects and game designers might choose to divide its product lines into two separate Web sites. The university would certainly link its two Web sites for the link-weighting benefits; the company selling unrelated products might not link its Web sites at all.

Broad vs. Narrow Targeting and Long-Tail Terms

The potential benefits in targeting highly specific searches were known to SEO practitioners by 1995–1996. Bed and breakfasts were one of the earliest and most evident examples, showing how highly specific keywords (e.g., "bed breakfast Ireland Kilkenny") could reach precisely the right audience.

Since the Web was still sparsely populated, the more skilled practitioners were able to gain high SERP rankings for broad searches at the same time as they targeted narrow niches. For example, in 1997, it was possible for an Irish bed and breakfast's Web site to gain a high SERP position for both its own locale and Irish B&Bs in general. That grew more difficult with increasing competition, and today a search for "bed breakfast Ireland" will generally return a SERP dominated by bed and breakfast directories and associations.

The changing situation became somewhat better understood in 2003, when Zipfian distributions were mentioned in an article by Clay Shirky about "power laws" as applied to blogs.[25] Power laws were later popularized as "The Long Tail" by an article in *Wired* magazine.[26] With use of the term growing, many clients and SEO practitioners now refer to any three- to four-word term as a "long-tail term"; others use the description more correctly to describe an uncommon search term.

There are now indications that the pendulum of interest has swung too far towards uncommon terms, and that organizations are targeting long-tail terms without a clear view towards long-term benefits such as memberships or profits.[27]

Balancing Targeting and Serendipity

While some organizations have only one easily described product or agenda, for most organizations SEO can be too successful when it targets particular search terms so tightly that their Web pages can be found by little else. When virtually all traffic to a Web site comes from a small number of terms, analyzing incoming search terms becomes an exercise in analyzing what one already knows. Ideally, improvements in SEO create an increase in targeted traffic along with an increase in unanticipated search terms. While this can be analyzed in terms of Zipfian distributions, in proactive marketing it is better represented by the APUPA (Alien–Penumbral–Umbral–Penumbral–Alien) bell curve (Figure 13.2).

SEO can also be too successful when a Web page captures a high SERP position on a major search engine for an extremely broad term like "health." Where this might be satisfactory to a large organization like the U.S. National Institutes of Health, an organization focusing on a particular niche of health could be swamped with masses of unwanted Web site visitors and e-mail.[28] Web sites deluged by unwanted traffic sometimes convert a liability to an asset by "reselling" the traffic or the entire Web site.

Lead Time and Longevity

Search engines rarely assign top rankings to newly indexed Web pages. A Web site can take months or even years to reach its "natural" position in SERPs. This is sometimes called the "sandbox," referring to the period a new Web site may wait for a good SERP position or even to be listed at all by a search engine.

Equally, search engines assign value to longevity, and older well-ranked Web sites dating from the 1990s can be notoriously difficult to dislodge from their SERP positions by new competitors.

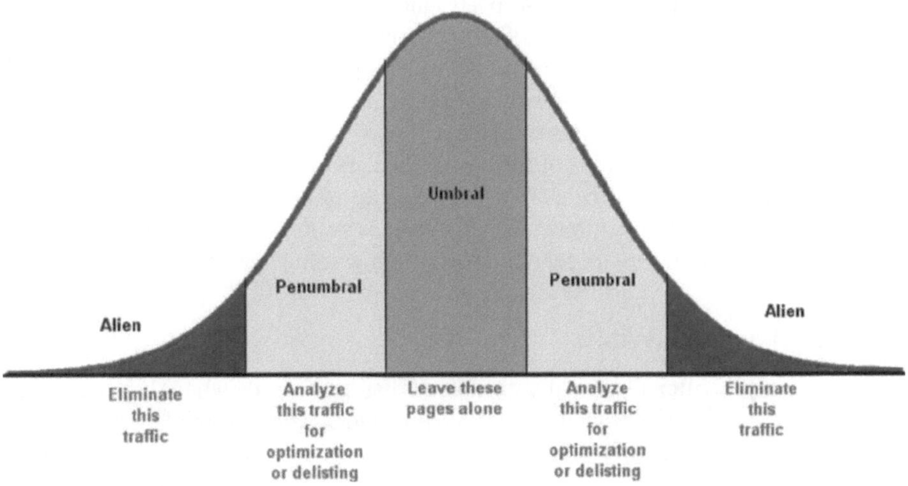

FIGURE 13.2 APUPA chart expressed in SEO terms. © Hastings Research, 2005.

Geographic Targeting

Geographic targeting through SEO had limited success through the mid-00s. Few early Web site designers made a diligent attempt to anticipate all the geographic keywords searchers might use, and those who did target searches with geographic keywords often used so many keywords (e.g., "London," "Pimlico," "Knightsbridge," "Belgravia," "Dulwich," "Stratford," "Paddington," "Fleet Street"—and every other village and neighboring town) that the pages were treated as index spam by search engines, and down-ranked to obscurity. Other designers created dozens or even thousands of "mirror pages" (pages with substantially similar content), each targeting a particular locale, with the result that the pages were down-ranked for "duplicate content."

In a cause-and-effect loop, users learned that searching by locale was nearly useless, and abandoned the effort (with the exception of specific travel destinations), leading most SEO practitioners to abandon their efforts at geographic targeting.

With the now-growing success of geographic targeting efforts by search engines—typically displaying maps showing physical locations—users have again started searching geographically, and most SEO practitioners advise making some effort to target searches containing geographic keywords, even though geographic searches may be defined by commercial databases rather than SEO efforts.

SEO Source Tracking

The wealth of data that accompanied visitors to Web sites led many ecommerce pioneers to think the perfection of marketing analysis had arrived. While this sometimes bordered on true for new businesses that were entirely WWW-based, the opposite turned out to be the case for large, established organizations already being marketed through advertising, mail, public relations, and retail outlets; the WWW added another layer of complexity to their market tracking. Due to its 24-hr availability, the WWW also creates a "smoothing" effect on response to promotional efforts, which can hinder analysis of event-driven spikes in visitor traffic.

Refinements in Web analytics have not entirely compensated for these factors, and in many ways Web site traffic source analysis remains less precise than that of traditional promotion and advertising.

Increased Competition

The continuing growth in the number of Web sites and Web pages means newly created Web sites have increasing difficulty gaining rankings for common keywords, so their approach is often to use a fanciful domain name and drive Web traffic via social networking or publicity instead of SEO.

Aside from the natural growth in Web sites, huge numbers of "made for ads" (MFA) Web sites have been created for no purpose other than to make money by hosting online advertisements—they have no products, services, or agendas of their own. Because advertising revenue indirectly comes from organizations that pay for online ads, MFA Web sites often specifically target keywords used by existing organizations. Nonprofit informational Web sites such as Wikipedia (http://www.wikipedia.org/) also compete directly for many search terms, often gaining very high search rankings.

Search Engines Only Index Words

While search engines are often technically capable of distilling words when they are represented in images, and in theory from audio tracks, in practice they index words from readable text documents, file names, or metadata attached to other forms of electronic files. There is a persistent failure to understand this aspect of SEO, with many Web site owners believing that if the human eye can read the words or grasp the meaning, the search engines will correctly index the files.

Further restricting SEO, search engines by choice index only certain types of text documents or metadata. At one time that meant pure text or HTML only. Most search engines are now willing to crawl and index file formats such as PDF (Portable Document Format), Microsoft Word and Excel, and in some cases Flash.

TRENDS

FADING TRENDS

"Meta keyword tags" were the first major chimera in SEO ("The meta keywords tag" earlier). They have been followed by other imaginary fast-tracks to high SERP position, all beginning with a grain of truth then blown out of proportion.

"Google PageRank" has been one of the most persistent areas of focus in SEO. Because of media attention and the easy access to the publicly visible PageRank via the Google Toolbar, the scale has commanded a great deal of interest from Web site owners, many of whom consider the published PageRank a practical scale for performance-based SEO contracts. Most SEO professionals now consider public PageRank in itself a minor factor in a Web site's actual SERP positions, more an effect than a cause. The latter opinion is to some extent corroborated by Google, Inc.[29] Over the course of 2007, countless Web sites saw their Google public PageRank drop significantly, which may further diminish interest in the measurement. ("PageRank" in popular usage should not be confused with "pagerank," an internal Google term.)

Web site "traffic"—whether measured in "hits" (requests for individual files, whether pages or images), "page views," "unique visitors," or the dot-com measure of "more eyeballs"—is slowly losing its popular connection to rankings, as organizations focus on conversion rate of users' visits to desired actions. (In extreme cases, traffic volume will have greater influence on SERP positions than relevance; however, this is uncommon and often results from a situation such as a major news event, where the boost in rankings may be due to a proliferation of inbound links, rather than traffic volume itself.)

CURRENT TRENDS

Link building previously described in "Link-weighting fundamentals"

Pursuing "long-tail" searches (previously described in "Broad vs. Narrow Targeting and Long-Tail Terms")

Bringing SEO in-house: Major companies in North America and Europe are increasingly bringing SEO in-house as their online sales grow to (USD) millions or hundreds of millions. Companies are hiring in consultants, training current employees, or both.[30]

Using best practices: Clients and employers are now commonly asking that practitioners follow "best practices." For SEO, the term describes such basic practices as prioritizing meta titles and heading tags, including keywords, and avoiding discredited (Black Hat) tactics.[31]

Tuning metadata for search engine interfaces: Increasingly, practitioners structure Web pages so that titles, descriptions, and filenames are presented appealingly on SERPs. Eye-tracking studies, where eye motion is represented by printed "heat maps," are currently the basis for most decisions in tuning metadata.[32]

Tagging Web pages: adding keywords or allowing visitors to add keywords to the visible text—is common on many social networking Web sites and some ecommerce and media Web sites, but has shown mixed results in improving SERP positions, possibly due to the indiscriminately chosen keywords selected by lay users, Web site owners, and bloggers. Tagging may benefit SERP position most for Web sites that encourage commentators to use "controlled vocabularies."[33] It may also boost SERP positions for "long-tail" search terms.

Web 2.0 designs: Web 2.0 methods have been criticized as being detrimental to SEO. This criticism has arisen with each evolution in Web site development, from "dynamic page delivery" (assembling Web pages from databases "on the fly") through Cascading Style Sheets and PDF files. In most previous instances, organizations' design preferences have won out over SEO considerations, and eventually the major search engines have adapted their protocols to classify new Web page structures and document formats.

Since search engines do not immediately retool for new forms of Web page markup and structure, Web sites that employ Web 2.0 methods such as AJAX (Asynchronous Javascript and XML) or that stream together content from different sources ("mashups") may drop in SERP positions until search engines decide how to interpret these new document structures.

Trends Affecting SEO

New Search Engine Presentation Methods

Clusters of search records such as those displayed by http://www.clusty.com or http://www.ask.com are likely to continue improving in relevance; if they increase in popularity, each cluster link will constitute a second-tier SERP, and SEO may begin targeting particular clusters.

Drop-down *contextual search suggestions* are now offered at http://www.ask.com and http://www.yahoo.com. Because users see contextual suggestions as they type, even before seeing the first SERP, "contextual position" may become a sought-after goal of SEO. Since contextual suggestions are all displayed on the first screen of a search engine's Web site, without the need for scrolling down, position is not likely to be as critical as SERP position, and "contextual inclusion" may prove to be the desired goal. (Contextual search flows from a given search engine's database of "most likely" requests; it should not be confused with the URL suggestions that Web browsers make by accessing a user's own search history.) (Figure 13.3).

With exceptions, such as the European search engine Kartoo (http://www.kartoo.com), interfaces such as topic maps and link maps show little sign of entering the mainstream of WWW search, and thus do not affect SEO.

Blended search—the blending into the primary WWW SERPs of news, images, maps, videos, and other types of records once considered niche searches—have now been instituted by major search engines.[34] This presents opportunities to the more aggressive SEO practitioners, some of whom are attempting to dominate blended SERPs with a mix of varied data formats. (Blended search has also been called "universal search.")

Specialized Searches

Specialized searches have been offered for decades through pre-Web online information providers. They are often called "vertical searches" (i.e., niche search). Specialized search could disrupt current SEO strategies, whether it is offered by major search engines or niche suppliers. First, if niche searches or tools proliferate in the GYM group (Google, Yahoo, Microsoft)—each with its own

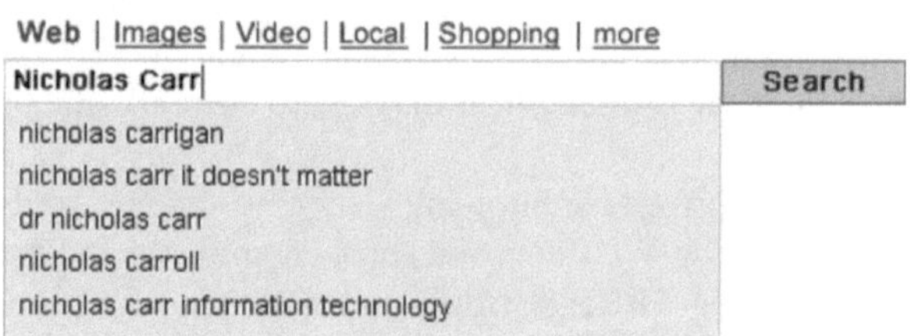

FIGURE 13.3 Example of drop-down contextual search suggestions.

classification protocols—they may dilute the value of SEO methods that address the GYM standard algorithms. Second, niche search engines such as http://www.vivisimo.com have entered the search race, and others such as http://www.northernlight.com (founded 1996) are reentering public search; these specialized search engines are usually less susceptible to technical methods, as they tend to use proportionately more human editing than broad reach search engines. Either trend could diminish the importance of technical- or link-based SEO.

"Personal search" has been a holy grail of the Internet industry since the mid-1990s. Early attempts at personal search included Yahoo! personalization features and numerous failures in "push technology" (Push technology: A means of automatically delivering information via the Internet to subscribers based on their choices for customized news, etc. *Webster's New Millennium Dictionary of English*, 2007. Described by H.P. Luhn as "SDI" (Selective Dissemination System), http://www.ischool.utexas.edu/~ssoy/organizing/l391d2c.htm, accessed February 2009). The current trend is towards analyzing individual users' search requests in the context of their previous searches (remembered by the server) and delivering customized results. Taken to an extreme, this could theoretically filter out a majority of available Web pages regardless of the SEO efforts invested, as search engines "learn" to focus on individual users' core interests.

"Local search" (geographic search) has become a serious goal for search engines. However other than travel destinations, few small retail businesses have Web sites, so search engines cannot easily find data for them by crawling the WWW. The primary solution to date has been to buy or barter for data such as traditional telephone book databases. Other new local search companies are aggregating local data for search engines, often crawling online local directories for source data search engines themselves are encouraging data entry from local organizations. Some trades with guilds such as law or medicine have niche Web sites with search functions; as yet few are comprehensive. Trades without guild organizations such as auto repair or beauty services may depend entirely on the success of aggregation if they are to be located through broad search. In few of these cases do current SEO methods provide a clear path into SERPs, and paid listings may vie with SEO in creating online exposure for local businesses.[35]

Alternate Search Channels

Alternate search channels could have an even more dramatic effect on SEO practices than blended or niche search services:

SEO for mobile communications devices: Analysis of users' WWW search behaviors on mobile devices has shown an emphasis on local retail search followed by entertainment. Coupling mobile search with GPS navigation feedback opens the prospect of delivering content or ads raises the prospect of directing mobile users to the nearest restaurant or a movie showing, thus both of these searches are potentially lucrative advertising venues—search engines are pursuing them, and SEO will follow. It is not yet certain whether search engines will convert conventional Web pages to mobile-friendly formats, or whether organizations will have to create new pages specifically targeting mobile devices.[36,37]

SMO (*Social Media Optimization*): It is arguable how much SMO involves "search" in the sense of users searching by keywords, because the spread of information on social networking Web sites is largely viral (self-promotion coupled with word-of-mouth). SMO is currently practiced by creating profiles on popular social media sharing and news Web sites, building a large base of "friends" and contributing unique promotional content with the option for other community members to vote in favor or against. Popular content that goes "hot" is placed on the high traffic home pages of the social media sharing and news sites, sometimes generating tremendous amounts of exposure, direct traffic, and secondary effect inbound links from bloggers that post about the content. SMO also involves using software to make posts automatically, this latter method being simply spamming. There may be a growing synergy between SEO and SMO, and SMO may become a parallel profession lumped under the umbrella of SEM.[38,39]

STANDARDS AND REGULATION IN SEO

The practice of SEO is marked by the absence of standards, other than those imposed by the willingness of major search engines to index Web pages, their level of effort in returning the most relevant Web pages, and punitive actions (down-ranking or de-listing) taken against what search engine administrators consider unacceptable manipulation of SERP positions.

HTML

Standard Web pages (HTML) are in theory defined by W3C standards—which are largely ignored by both Web developers and amateurs. Other formats now being indexed by search engines—including PDF, Microsoft Word and Excel, and still images and videos—follow even fewer standards.

Certification

Certification is in beginning stages. Some businesses have begun offering SEO credentials, and accredited colleges are now beginning to offer courses in SEO.

SEO Industry

The SEO industry may be loosely divided into SEO professionals of varying ability; Web designers and programmers who know the rudiments; and a much more visible group of low-cost SEO companies that operate through advertising and e-mail marketing.[40]

While there are no formal standards or regulation, informal standards are slowly evolving through consensus of trade associations and Web sites reporting on SEO. (See "Bibliography" at the end of this entry.)

Search Engines

Because it is difficult to mathematically determine whether a given Web page's content accurately reflects the page's relevance to visitors (much less the creator's true agenda), search engines have faced and continue to face an impossible task in down-ranking deceptive pages without penalizing legitimate ones. (In the classic if now simplistic example, a medical Web site can unwittingly trigger an algorithm aimed at filtering out pornography pages.)

Attempts to "game" (manipulate) search engine rankings have been so relentless, from the first significant appearance of online search engines, that many experts consider search engine administration to be equally a process of excluding Black Hat pages and elevating relevant pages.[41] While penalizing irrelevant content faces the same problem as returning relevant content—a struggle to develop artificial intelligence—most search engines strongly downgrade Web sites that are found to be using the more technically complex SEO tactics such as IP-specific page delivery (see "Cloaking" earlier).

This issue of controlling Black Hat SEO without penalizing White Hat SEO is a continued source of tension between search engine administrators and SEO practitioners. Search engines selling advertising space on their own SERPs has exacerbated the tension by raising the issue that pursues traditional media, of whether there is a true division between editorial and advertising departments (or search relevance and advertising, in the case of search engines).

Like the evolution of military tactics, regulation is a game of innovation and counter-measure. The counter-measures may make a given tactic so ineffective that it is completely forgotten by both attackers and defenders, at which point it may be reintroduced by the attackers. (A medical analogy would be the mutation of microorganisms in reaction to new antibiotics, accompanied by the resurgence of forgotten diseases when society no longer guards against them.)

Government Regulation

At present there is no hint of SEO regulation. As subcontractors, SEO consultancies are in a position similar to advertising agencies—with no actual control over organizations or distribution channels—so any government regulation is likely to flow indirectly from regulation of Web sites themselves (trade practices) or of search engines (particularly in the United States, where antitrust law may affect conglomeration of major search engines with software, hardware, or media companies).

USER BEHAVIORS IN SEARCH

User behavior while searching online shows more consistency than change in the period from 1995 to 2008. This section will briefly address the consistent behaviors and available research on the course of changes.

Users' search behavior has a strong effect on SEO, since many users click the first listing in a SERP. On the other hand, gaining a #1 SERP position for a particular search term does not guarantee that a user will click that link; they might click the #2 link or the #10 link if those page titles, descriptions, or URLs are more compelling.

In the same vein, there is no clear evidence that users who click the first record will take further action; many SEO practitioners believe the more motivated users will scan an entire SERP before deciding which link to click. Regardless, user behavior while visiting SERPs affects SEO decisions as well as the search engines' goal of relevance.

Research into specific behaviors has revealed a great deal about what users do in the specific environment of a search engine interface when tested in a laboratory setting. It leaves unanswered many questions about why users search the way they do—in part because most research has focused on what users do when looking at a SERP, without inquiring how or why they arrived at that particular SERP, or what actions they take after clicking a particular link. More research is required to develop consistent conclusions. Substantial research from information science has yet to be incorporated in SEO; when it is, it may transform strategies and tactics.

Variables that affect user search behavior:

- Users' level of subject knowledge
- Improvements in results returned by search engines
- Users' confidence in the quality of search results
- Degree of users' sophistication in search
- Presentation style of individual search results (title, description, URL, etc.)
- Motivation/curiosity/laziness
- Habituation among users (hardening behaviors)
- Search engine interface design
- Number of search engines available

Basic Behaviors

Few users methodically click search results in sequential order, from the first result to the bottom of the page. Typically they skip over unappealing titles or URLs, and may bounce back and forth between organic search listings and paid listings. (Depending on SERP design, users may not always know the difference between paid and organic listings.) If a relevant Web page is not found quickly, users may change search engines, change their search term, or migrate to a general information Web site such as a dictionary, encyclopedia, or user-fed Q&A Web site.

Searching Popular Subjects

Patterns of search seen on Wordtracker, Yahoo! search tool, or KeywordDiscovery continue to show a preponderance of searches for celebrities and popular news, as described since 1999 in the weekly "Lycos 50" listing of the most popular topical searches (http://50.lycos.com/archives.asp) with written analysis and opinion. Google Trends (http://www.google.com/trends), which shows the number of searches for chosen terms in chart format, is well-suited to display spikes in interest, relative interest in different subjects, or seasonal patterns in popular searches; like the Lycos 50, it demonstrates that a huge proportion of Web searches are for popular subjects rather than niche information.

Use of Boolean Syntax

In the 1990s, WWW search engines typically limited the use of search syntax to Boolean AND, OR, and NOT, with OR as the default. (With AND or NOT typically applied by +/– symbols.) Initially these options were only available by typing them into the search term entry box. HotBot search engine was one of the earliest to offer Boolean logic to untrained users, with the addition of a drop-down box offering AND as well as "exact phrase" options, but the options were rarely used.

In the late 1990s, search engines moved towards a default (or forced) Boolean AND; by early 2003, it was the default on all major search engines search engines.[42] Although this change narrowed search results, it also hugely increased the relevance of results, and, at the same time, reduced the average user's motivation to learn Boolean syntax. Some data samples suggest that Boolean search skills are known to a smaller percentage of users today than in 1997, though it is uncertain whether the decrease is due to a loss of interest in search syntax or an influx of less sophisticated users.[43]

Search Engine Loyalty

Available statistics strongly indicate that users are now more likely to refine or expand their search term than switch to another search engine.[44] The disinclination to switch is often called "loyalty" in a broad sense; motivating factors could be the generally improved quality of search returns over the last few years, or users' increased recognition of the value of using precise search terms. In terms of user behavior, this could be described as a slight shift from "berrypicking" (wandering about and collecting bits of information) to more linear search behaviors.[45]

Hardened User Behaviors

Users' search behavior search engines may have become "hardened," or fixed, by their expectations, in particular in the United States and Canada, because the majority of popular search engines have presented returns as linear lists since the mid-1990s. Current SEO is predicated on the idea that users type keywords into a box, click a "Search" button, and scan a list from top to bottom.[46] Because they represent a large conceptual shift, interfaces that present information in clusters, topic maps, or relationship maps face an entry barrier.

User Behavior Worldwide

Patterns of user behavior outside the United States and Canada do not show identical evolution. While less analysis has been done, in regions as disparate as England and China users are apparently more willing to examine entire SERP pages, as well as second and third pages, and less likely to click on the first or first few SERP positions.

CONCLUSION

Beginning in the mid-1990s, SEO evolved from placing random keywords in all possible parts of Web pages, to more focused doorway page strategies targeting particular keywords. By 2000, improvements in search engines were rendering most of such tactics obsolete, and SEO practitioners moved on to the integration of overall Web site structure, and then on to establishing a Web site's relationship with the WWW as a whole through linking.[47] For most, the reluctant and secondary focus of SEO was on users or quality of content. For others, a focus on user experience as well as SEO provided long term, sustainable results throughout the evolution.

SEO now faces broad changes in search and user behavior. The growth of online information is outpacing the indexing rates of all search engines. Search engines are struggling to deal with that overload, and in the process changing their strategies about what information to present and how to present it. Hardware—notably mobile communications devices—is redefining the technical limits of information presentation and also creating niches in user search behaviors.

ACKNOWLEDGMENTS

With thanks to Jim Rhodes, Jim Heath, Lee Odden, Guy Shalev, Paula Sheil, and Kelly Bryan.

REFERENCES

1. Sullivan, D. http://forums.searchenginewatch.com/showth read.php?t=78 (accessed February 2009).
2. Rhodes, J. Art of search engine promotion, 1997. http://www.deadlock.com/promote/search-engines (accessed February 2009).
3. Heath, J. *Pointers on How to Create Business Websites That Work*, Published online, 1995. Earliest available version at http://www.viacorp.com/pointers1995.html (accessed February 2009).
4. November 2006 Web Server Survey Netcraft **2006**, http://news.netcraft.com/archives/2006/11/01/november_2006_web_server_survey.html (accessed February 2009).
5. Search Engine Marketing Professional Organization (SEMPO), *The State of Search Engine Marketing 2006: Survey of Advertisers and Agencies*, 5. Search Engine Marketing Professional Organization (SEMPO): Wakefield, MA, 2007.
6. Web Analytics Association, http://www.webanalyticsassociation.org (accessed February 2009).
7. CMSWatch, http://www.cmswatch.com (accessed February 2009).
8. Wilsdon, N., Ed.; Global Search Report 2007, E3internet, 2007. http://www.multilingual-search.com/global-search-report-2007-released-free-pdf/15/10/2007 (accessed February 2009).
9. The Global Structure of an HTML Document, http://www.w3.org/TR/html401/struct/global.html (accessed February 2009).
10. Grappone, J.; Couzin, G. *Search Engine Optimization: An Hour A Day*; Sybex: Hoboken, NJ, June 2006; 46–47, 101. http://www.yourseoplan.com/book-inside-contents.html (accessed February 2009).
11. Whalen, J. Avoiding clueless-is as clueless-does SEO, http://searchengineland.com/070927–071933.php (accessed February 2009).
12. Stamoulis, N. The top 8 SEO techniques (A dispute), http://www.searchengineoptimizationjournal.com/2007/09/17/the-top-8-seo-techniques-a-dispute (accessed February 2009).
13. Seda, C. *How to Win Sales & Influence Spiders*; New Riders: Berkeley, CA, February 2007, 5.
14. Bradley, S. Using keyword themes to structure your site content, 2006, http://www.vanseodesign.com/blog/seo/keyword-themes-for-site-structure/ (accessed February 2009).
15. Sullivan, D. *What Are Doorway Pages?* Published online, 2007, http://www.searchenginewatch.com/showPage.html?page=2167831 (accessed February 2009).
16. Sherman, C. *In Defense of Search Engine Cloaking*; Published online, 2001, http://www.searchenginewatch.com/showPage.html?page=2157261 (accessed February 2009).
17. Nelson, T.H. *Literary Machines*; Mindful Press: Sausalito, CA, 1982. (This is the earliest specification of the term hyperlinking, ca. 1965.)
18. Langville, A.; Meyer, C. *Google PageRank and Beyond: The Science of Search Engine Rankings*; Princeton University Press: Princeton, NJ, 2006.

19. Kleinberg, J. *Authoritative Sources in a Hyperlinked Environment*, Proceedings of the 9th ACM–SIAM Symposium on Discrete Algorithms, San Francisco, 1998. Extended version in J. ACM **1999**, 46. Also appears as IBM Research Report RJ 10076, May 1997, http://www.cs.cornell.edu/home/kleinber/auth.pdf (accessed February 2009).
20. Sullivan, D. Google kills Bush's miserable failure search & other Google bombs; 2007. http://searchengineland.com/070125–230048.php (accessed February 2009).
21. Wall, A. *The SEObook*; 2007, 197–199. http://www.seobook.com.
22. Bodden, L. Making sense of linking and site promotion; 2007. http://www.toprankblog.com/2007/09/linking-site-promotion/ (accessed February 2009).
23. Thurow, S. The right way to think about site maps; 2007. http://searchengineland.com/070809–091501.php (accessed February 2009).
24. Off Page Optimisation VS On Page Optimisation, http://www.directtraffic.org/on_page_optimisation.htm (accessed February 2009).
25. Shirky, C. Power laws, weblogs, and inequality; 2003. http://www.shirky.com/writings/powerlaw_weblog.html (accessed February 2009).
26. Anderson, C. The long tail. Wired Mag. **2004**. http://www.wired.com/wired/archive/12.10/tail.html (accessed February 2009).
27. Brynjolfsson, E.; Hu, Y.; Smith, M.D. From niches to riches: the anatomy of the long tail. Sloan Manage. Rev. **2006**.
28. Carroll, N. The anti-thesaurus: A proposal for improving internet search while reducing unnecessary traffic loads; 2001. http://www.hastingsresearch.com/net/06-anti-thesaurus.shtml (accessed February 2009).
29. http://www.google.com/corporate/tech.html (accessed February 2009).
30. *Search Marketing Benchmark Guide 2008*, 2008, 43–50. http://www.sherpastore.com/Search-Marketing-Benchmark-2008.html (accessed February 2009).
31. Fusco, P.J. SEO Best Practices: 20 Questions; 2007, http://www.clickz.com/showPage.html?page=3624560 (accessed February 2009).
32. Whitepapers and videos on user eye tracking, http://www.enquiroresearch.com/ (accessed February 2009).
33. Tagging advisory from DailyKos.com political blog, http://www.dkosopedia.com/wiki/Standard_Tags_-_alpha_list (accessed February 2009).
34. Sullivan, D. Search 3.0: The Blended & Vertical Search Revolution, http://searchengineland.com/071127–091128.php (accessed February 2009).
35. Guide on how to get your business listed on major local search engines, yellow pages sites and social local networks. http://www.locallytype.com/pages/submit.htm (accessed February 2009).
36. Carroll, N.; McGraw, M.; Brahms, S.; Rodgers, D. Wireless usability 2001–2002 report, http://www.hastingsresearch.com/reports/62-wap-2001.shtml (accessed February 2009).
37. Holahan, C. The battle for mobile search. BusinessWeek **2007**, http://www.businessweek.com/technology/content/feb2007/tc20070220_828216.htm (accessed February 2009).
38. Bhargava, R. 5 Rules of Social Media Optimization (SMO), 2006. http://rohitbhargava.typepad.com/weblog/2006/08/5_rules_of_soci.html (accessed February 2009).
39. Seda, C. *How to Win Sales & Influence Spiders*; New Riders: Berkeley, CA, 2007; 58–74.
40. Seda, C. *How to Win Sales & Influence Spiders*; New Riders: Berkeley, CA, 2007; 16–22.
41. Price, G. Personal communication about gaming search engines, http://www.resourceshelf.com (accessed February 2009).
42. Sullivan, D. Search Features Chart; 2001, http://searchen ginewatch.com/showPage.html?page=2155981 (accessed February 2009).
43. Hastings Research proprietary databases of real-time searches and web server logs, 1995–2008.
44. Search Marketing Benchmark Guide 2008, 2007, 135, http://www.sherpastore.com/Search-Marketing-Benchmark-2008.html.
45. Bates, M.J. The Design Of Browsing And Berrypicking Techniques For The Online Search Interface, 1989, http://www.gseis.ucla.edu/faculty/bates/berrypicking.html (accessed February 2009).
46. Nielsen, J. Mental models for search are getting firmer, 2005, http://www.useit.com/alertbox/20050509.html (accessed February 2009).
47. Rhodes, J. Personal communication on early SEO practices.

BIBLIOGRAPHY

1. A timeline of SEO. http://blog.searchenginewatch.com/blog/060417-130526 (accessed February 2009).
2. http://www.searchengineland.com (accessed February 2009).
3. http://www.searchenginewatch.com (accessed February 2009).
4. http://www.seopros.org (accessed February 2009).
5. http://www.sempo.org/learning_center (accessed February 2009).
6. http://www.sempo.org/learning_center/sem_glossary (accessed February 2009).

USERS SECTION

1. Mezei, C. Website and search engine user behavior analysis, 2006, http://www.searchnewz.com/latest search/senews/sn-4-20061101WebsiteandSearchEngineUserBehaviorAnaly-sis.html (accessed February 2009).
2. Search Engine User Behavior Study, iProspect, 2006, http://www.iprospect.com/about/whitepaper_ seuserbehavior_-apr06.htm (accessed February 2009).

14 Records Compliance and Risk Management

Bradley J. Wiles

CONTENTS

INTRODUCTION

The concepts of *compliance* and *risk management* have been applied to various methods and strategies of business operations in a wide variety of industries over the past several decades.[1] This entry identifies banking, investment firms, and insurance companies as being particularly sensitive to managing risk and maintaining compliance to ensure sound business management. Minimizing risk and meeting various levels of statutory obligations are consistently perceived as necessary for stability, growth, and longevity. This is particularly relevant in the *archives and records administration* field, where securing the human record depends on evolving legal requirements, professional norms, and institutional standards. This entry will examine the place of compliance and risk management within the context of archives and records administration. It will provide separate definitions of each concept and evaluate these as related and complementary aspects of the creation, capture, and use of records.

Perhaps first it would be useful to provide a comprehensive definition for records management, simply because the principles it encompasses are generally applicable to a wide array of records and information activities. Records management is

> a professional discipline that is primarily concerned with the management of document-based information systems. The application of systematic and scientific controls to recorded information required in the operation of an organization's business. The systematic control of all organizational records during the various stages of their life cycle, from their creation or receipt, through their processing, distribution, maintenance, and use, to their ultimate disposition.[2]

The purpose of records management is, "to promote economies and efficiencies in recordkeeping, to assure that useless records are systematically destroyed while valuable information is protected and maintained in a manner that facilitates its access and use."[2]

Records management is also concerned with the analysis of any and all recorded information created, received, maintained, or used by an organization in accordance with its mission, operations, and activities.[3] Furthermore, records management deals with records regardless of age, type, or format, and is often an enterprise-wide undertaking that relies on cooperation at all levels of an organization.[4] Present-day records management is an outgrowth of traditional archival practice, but typically deals with contemporary recorded information and documents.[4] In the mid-twentieth century, a distinction was made between "historical" and "modern" documents, mostly because of the deluge of records flowing into traditional archives following World War II.[4] However, this distinction is no longer prevalent, and records management principles are applied to records produced by corporations, businesses, and governmental units (organizations using and retaining documents in the course of regular business), as well as those kept by historical societies, manuscript libraries, and other cultural institutions (organizations who hold collections for reasons of scholarship or posterity). In nearly all instances, the concepts of compliance and risk management factor significantly into the modern practice of archives and records administration.

RECORDS COMPLIANCE

It is somewhat difficult to comprehensively define compliance in the context of archives and records administration, simply because compliance measures are constantly in flux. In most instances, recordkeeping and reporting are part and parcel of other core compliance areas within organizations. These might include promoting fair and ethical business conduct, requiring proper environmental, health, and safety policies, or ensuring consumer protection,[5] and may or may not have a records component. In general, records compliance requirements derive from legislation, regulatory standards, codes of best practices, or community expectations (p. 10).[4] These requirements exist at all social, political, and organizational levels, might be explicit or implied, and incorporate any number or combination of requirements (pp. 38–39).[4] For example, explicit legal requirements for the creation and management of records in a particular industry could mandate the extended retention of certain types of records created in particular operational contexts. It might also dictate the form in which these records should be maintained, the rights of individuals or corporate bodies to have access to those records, and the protection of the intellectual property that the records contain (p. 38).[4]

Compliance requirements affect records at all stages throughout their life cycle and can be subject to multiple legal jurisdictions. A significant amount of legal research is often necessary for organizations to determine the legal requirements for retention, destruction, discovery, and disclosure. The first step is to verify which authoritative entities the organization falls under. The degree of regulation varies by the type of industry and while the majority of businesses and organizations are not subject to any recordkeeping guidelines, those that are (e.g., financial services and pharmaceuticals) tend to be heavily regulated by multiple entities.[6] In particular, those responsible for an organization's legal and regulatory records compliance in the United States should be familiar with the Uniform Rules of Evidence (which apply to state courts), the Federal Rules of Evidence (which apply to federal courts), the National Conference of Commissioners on Uniform State Laws (which helps interpret and standardize laws across jurisdictions), the Uniform Commercial Code, the Uniform Electronic Transactions Act, the Photographic Copies as Evidence Act, the Federal Paperwork Reduction Act, the Code of Federal Regulations, and the statutes of the National Archives and Records Administration.[6]

The notion of accountability factors heavily into an organization's need to maintain compliance with strictures set forth by internal and external forces. In order to support accountability the records management department or representative must initiate a multilateral assessment of business needs, evidentiary requirements, legal obligations, and recognized best practices (pp. 155, 158).[4] This will enable ready response to legal challenges, grievances, and complaints from within and outside of the organization. Typically, compliance is checked—and accountability is fostered—through any number of internal and external inspections and audits, which often consist of a close physical examination of an organization's recordkeeping system measured against whatever compliance issues are at hand (p. 159).[4] The most effective audit procedures are ones established at the founding of the vital records management program and that remain sensitive to changing compliance regulations (pp. 75–76).[3] Audits best support accountability through regular scheduling that matches other organizational troubleshooting efforts and through designating proper authority to carry out inspections, make assessments, and implement recommendations. Though records retention audits typically only consist of a sampling of an organization's records series, this is usually sufficient to determine that organization's appropriate level of need for records security, storage, duplication, and destruction (pp. 75–76).[3]

RISK MANAGEMENT

According to the Association of Records Managers and Administrators, or ARMA International, risk management is a process that ensures an organization does not assume an unacceptable level of risk and includes both risk analysis and risk assessment procedures as key components.[7] The level of risk is determined by the importance of the record. All records have relative value, but vital records—ones that are unique and irreplaceable—tend to take precedence over those that can be recreated or those that are not essential to normal business operations (p. 73).[2] Risk analysis involves the evaluation of exposure of vital records to specific risks and provides a basis for protection planning by identifying threats and vulnerabilities (p. 133).[3] There are several broad categories of threats, which include destruction, loss, corruption, and improper disclosure of records and information (p. 133).[3]

In any organization it is imperative to discern acceptable levels of risk and typically this is accomplished through qualitative or quantitative risk assessment. The qualitative approach is most useful at identifying and categorizing physical security problems and other vulnerabilities such as malicious destruction, warfare, terrorist attacks, civil insurrections, purposeful sabotage, vandalism, and theft, as well as natural disasters or man-made accidents, errors, negligence, and incompetence (pp. 133, 136).[3] Quantitative risk assessment is based on methodologies developed for product safety analysis and computer security applications (p. 136).[3] It initially relies on qualitative measures such as site visits, and focuses on group discussions, but also uses numeric calculations to determine the annualized loss expectancy of a given institution (p. 136).[3] This dollar amount is estimated by figuring the probability of a particular event (or events) occurring over a given time span (p. 137).[3] Ultimately, it factors in the cost of record or information restoration, the loss of business as a result of not being able to perform specific business functions, and the costs of any litigation that might ensue (p. 137).[3] Upon completion of the analysis and assessment, risk can be managed through a series of controls, protections, and preventative measures that include strategic location (or relocation) of facilities, limiting access to vital records storage areas, stringent personnel screening and training, effective physical and electronic security, maintenance of multiple copies of vital records and information, initiating disaster recovery and business continuity plans, and developing a system of internal audits to ensure structural integrity (pp. 138–141).[3]

Though risk management largely addresses the prospect of lost business or capital, it would be insufficient to consider records risk management strictly in financial terms. One of the main tools of managing risk is the development of records retention policies and schedules. A records retention plan helps prioritize value by determining the risks involved in not keeping or destroying a set of records against the costs of maintaining them (p. 161).[4] However, this often represents a convergence of competing interests between internal and external factors, which are not always financial. For example, cultural institutions such as archives repositories or special research libraries might feel justified spending an inordinate amount of resources to keep a certain records collection because of its social or historical importance, or because of the prestige it confers on the institution. Likewise, organizations that do not use records expressly for their scholarly or cultural value still might justify the expense of maintaining an historical archive because of its potential to provide materials for advertising, marketing, public relations, and in support of corporate memory (pp. 158–159).[4] The length and quality of any retention program can be radically contingent among the various types of organizations that use records and the functions that those records fulfill.[8] This entry identifies the traditional retention schedules as following along departmental and functional lines, which can cause a tremendous amount of overlap and duplication. It recommends a process-based retention schedule that documents the work flow and follows legal retention requirements and business needs. This duration is based on the operational needs of the institution and the multiple levels of risk that accompanies those needs.

Though risk management procedures are partially based on what *might* happen—the worst-case scenario, the probability of disaster—it also involves active management of records and information assets from the earliest stages of production. Increasingly this means following a legally viable records retention policy, after taking steps to ensure authenticity in the production of records and information to meet all legal and regulatory requirements (p. 103).[4] The possibility of litigation has emerged as a primary concern in the creation and capture of records, particularly in the digital age when most documents are not necessarily created, stored, and disseminated in static formats.[9] The types of records that withstand legal challenges are those created as part of a transaction (as opposed to those created *ad hoc* or retroactively) during the regular course of business and that comply with legal guidelines for content, medium, or layout (pp. 103–104).[4] Indeed, the landscape of records management, and thus the tools and procedures for managing risk, currently operate under a hyper-regulated atmosphere of compliance.

RECORDS COMPLIANCE AND RISK MANAGEMENT IN COMBINATION

According to a recent article in a financial services publication,

> In recent years . . . risk management and compliance have begun to converge in a new paradigm. In what amounts to a subtle but important shift in mindset, compliance requirements are now considered a major source of risk . . . Such thinking leads to a natural prioritization of compliance initiatives: Those risks that pose the greatest threat . . . are highest on the list. Strategies to eliminate and/or manage such risks become the primary focus of the compliance function. Since compliance requirements that relate to protecting client interests pose some of the greatest risks . . . taking a risk-oriented approach to compliance naturally aligns the firm's interests with client interests.[10]

The relationship of records compliance and risk management in archives and records administration is often one of reciprocity. The identification and management of risk is usually dictated by compliance measures that exist within and outside of an organization. Compliance measures—through legislation, best-practices initiatives, or organizational rules—are sensitive to business needs and generally reflect standards determined by industry-wide risk assessment. This reciprocal relationship is perhaps most fully embodied in the Australian National Archives, which adopted the Australian Standards for Records Management (AS-4390) in 1996.[11] AS-4390 approaches government records from a risk management perspective and seeks to ensure impartiality and accountability among the creators and keepers of state records.[11] AS-4390 also provides for a system of compliance audits and continual monitoring of documentary integrity (pp. 171–172).[4] In this sense, AS-4390 demonstrates how, when applied to an organization, the principles of risk management and compliance are interrelated and complementary. In 2001, it was adapted by the International Organization for Standardization (ISO 15489-1:2001) as the preferred model for electronic records produced and maintained by governmental bodies (pp. 27, 249).[4] The authors note that ISO 15489–1:2001 standard for sustainable records management is based on AS-4390, and these provide the "benchmark against which records management programmes and systems can be measured."

In some instances the confluence of risk management and compliance complicates the rubric under which an organization operate's. Risk often accompanies reward and sometimes the benefit of partial or noncompliance is perceived as outweighing the cost. For example, a multinational company may have branches in several jurisdictions that all require different retention periods for vital records. To keep all vital records in every jurisdiction for the longest possible period to cover all bases may be cost prohibitive. To irregularly schedule and follow several retention plans may be logistically impossible. In this instance, the organization will likely turn to whatever cost/benefit analysis its risk and compliance cohorts have formulated. They would consider which records were most abundant and valuable, where these records were located, and exactly what compliance requirements it was absolutely necessary to fulfill. In the event that the compliance measures did not specifically address records, the organization would factor in limitations on legal recourse against any action they might carry out (p. 159).[4] From there, it could be decided that the risk of less than full compliance of certain records (of relatively low value) in certain jurisdictions (with less punitive measures and enforcement) is acceptable. The likelihood of getting caught and receiving a fine, or of losing business and prestige, might be considered less than the cost of full compliance.

Though this may not present an ideal scenario, realistically the level of compliance becomes a matter of how an institution chooses to allocate its resources, particularly in a regulation-heavy climate.[12] This entry asserts that despite the billions of dollars spent to accommodate laws like Sarbanes–Oxley and HIPPA, one hundred percent compliance is "fundamentally impossible." However, compliance and risk management are increasingly no longer viewed as necessary evils or impediments to profitable business operations. More and more records are considered assets, whether they are used in everyday business transactions or for academic and cultural reasons. As a result, risk management and compliance are increasingly perceived as core operational functions, integral to the solvency and growth of an organization. In the wake of far-reaching banking, investment, and corporate accounting scandals of this decade, risk management and compliance in records administration should further gain cachet as necessary systemic enhancements. They should no longer merely serve as corrective measures only used after an organization gets caught doing something illegal or unethical.

CONCLUSION

This entry has attempted to identify the key elements of risk management and compliance in archives and records administration, both as individual concepts and as complementary components of recordkeeping. It should be reiterated that the management of risk requires an enterprise-wide assessment of threats and vulnerabilities increasingly aimed at securing dynamic documentary formats. As a result of greater reliance on digital mediums, the move toward more stringent regulation and standardization has found both support and controversy in the archives and records management world. It could safely be assumed that as governments, businesses, cultural institutions, and other organizations become more fully digitized, risk management and compliance will become even more closely connected.

ACKNOWLEDGMENTS

The author would like to thank the following: Dr. Ciaran Trace and Dr. Louise Robbins at the University of Wisconsin School of Library and Information Studies, and Dr. Peter Gottlieb at the Wisconsin Historical Society.

REFERENCES

1. Ludwick, K. Tackling risk-based compliance. J. Invest. Compl. **2006**, *7* (4), 61.
2. Robek, M.; Brown, G.; Stephens, D., Eds. *Information and Records Management: Document-Based Information Systems*, 4th Ed.; Glencoe/McGraw-Hill, Inc.: Woodland Hills, CA, 1995; 585.
3. Saffady, W. *Records and Information Management: Fundamentals of Professional Practice*; ARMA International: Lenexa, KS, 2004.

4. Shepherd, E.; Yeo, G. *Managing Records: A Handbook of Principles and Practice*; Facet Publishing: London, 2003.
5. Cellini, R.J. Compliance risk: A top-10 list. Directors Boards **2007**, *31*, 52–53.
6. Cogar, R.N. Legal 101 for RIM Professionals. Inform. Manag. J. **2005**, *39* (6), 49–56.
7. ARMA International, *Vital Records: Identifying, Managing, and Recovering Business-Critical Records*; ANSI/ ARMA International: Lenexa, KS, 2003; 6.
8. Torres, T. Creating a process-focused retention schedule. Inform. Manag. J. **2006**, *40* (5), 62–69.
9. Arnold, J.R. We're not in Kansas anymore. AIIM E-doc Mag. **2007**, *21* (1), 50–54.
10. Martin, D.; Manley, M.R. Linking compliance, risk management. Pensions Investments **2006**, *34* (18), 12.
11. Boles, F. *Selecting and Appraising Archives and Manuscripts*; Society of American Archivists: Chicago, 2005; 31–32.
12. Gincel, R. The awful truth about compliance. InfoWorld **2005**, *27* (50), 29.

BIBLIOGRAPHY

1. Allman, T.Y. Fostering a compliance culture: The role of the Sedona guidelines. Inform. Manag. J. **2005**, *39* (2), 54–61.
2. Kahn, R.A. Records management and compliance: Making the connection. Inform. Manag. J. **2004**, *18* (3), 28–35.
3. Lemieux, V.L. *Managing Risks for Records and Information*; ARMA International: Lenexa, KS, 2004.
4. Montana, J.C.; Dietel, J.E.; Martins, C.S. *Sarbanes–Oxley Act: Implications for Records Management*; ARMA International: Lenexa, KS, 2003.
5. St. Germain, R. Information security management best practice based on ISO/IEC 17799. Inform. Manag. J. **2005**, *39* (4), 60–66.
6. Swartz, N. Enterprise-wide records training: Key to compliance success. Inform. Manag. J. **2006**, *40* (5), 34–44.

15 Version Control

Jill E. Grogg and Jeff Weddle

CONTENTS

INTRODUCTION

For library and information science, version control is the activity of identifying and managing iterations of a document for archival and retrieval purposes. While version control can be problematic for documents and information objects of all types and formats, it is especially so for scholarly communication—particularly journal articles—distributed in electronic formats.

In all the many unforeseen challenges that electronic publishing has unleashed for the information profession, there exist two principle elements: political and technical. Version control is no exception. Many stakeholders in the information industry are shaping the version control discussion, and these discussions have resulted in recommended solutions and directions.

In 2002, a research team headed by Raymond Siemens produced a report entitled "The Credibility of Electronic Publishing" for the Humanities and Social Sciences Federation of Canada (HSSFC). This report attempted to define and assess the current state of affairs for scholarly electronic publishing as well as provide some recommendations for future action.[1] One of the sections of the report, "Archiving and Text Fluidity/Version Control," specifically addresses the unique situation that electronic publishing presents for text alteration. In this section, members of the HSSFC-appointed research team note:

> Texts can be adapted, abstracted, translated, edited, condensed, corrected, marked up, transcribed, annotated, amended, paraphrased, transliterated, illustrated, indexed, or abridged. They can be commented upon or referenced by other texts. They can be analysed or synthesized. These modifications, and any others that might be considered, produce distinct versions, all related to the original text.[2]

Indeed, what is important to note is that any alteration(s) to an original text produces a distinct version. Therefore, versions of a text need to be uniquely identifiable while simultaneously containing information that describes the relationships among the various versions. Version control, then, is the effort to "name the versions of the text" and to specify "the differences between the revision and the original text."[2] Moreover, version control endeavors to define what is meant by the original and authoritative text.

In 2005, the U.S. Government Printing Office (GPO) prepared a white paper on version control of documents within the purview of the Federal Depository Library Program. The GPO was particularly concerned with electronically disseminated documents. Government Printing Office concerns fall into seven broad categories. These include version definition, or "unique manifestation of a publication"; version control, which includes "acquiring, cataloging, storing, preserving, and retrieving different versions of publications"; version triggers, which are changes that exceed agreed upon limits; version detection, which deals with identifying and detecting alternate versions; version identifiers, which are metadata tags; version crosswalks, which are a subset of version identifiers and provide links to all other versions; and depository library responsibilities for superseded versions. While it focuses on government documents, the GPO report is extensible in that it offers parameters that can be applied to any discussion of version control.[3]

In April 2008, the National Information Standards Organization (NISO), in partnership with the Association of Learned and Professional Society Publishers (ALPSP), released a report that defines specific stages or iterations of a journal article. Similar to the GPO's seven broad categories, the NISO/ALPSP Journal Article Versions (JAV) Technical Working Group identified seven terms, or stages, of an article's development. According to members of the JAV Technical Working Group, the report is meant to offer recommended practices for the scholarly publishing community. The report summarizes the issue:

> Researchers, their institutions, and journal publishers are rapidly moving on from using static, single copies of research papers that are essentially "images" of a printed document. Changes in the way we create, edit, circulate, validate, publish, find, use, and update articles are producing multiple versions whose status and provenance is often unclear. Online searching now allows multiple versions to be found but rarely makes clear the relationships between them.[4]

Specific recommendations of the group are discussed in subsequent sections.

SCOPE AND HISTORY

Standards, rules, local practices, terminology, and definitions evolved over many years to ensure version control of printed matter. Even so, it has always been problematic to ensure that a published text is in complete agreement with all other versions of that text. Pirated or plagiarized editions, misreadings of manuscripts, and other issues have long clouded issues of text authenticity and authority. With the emergence of electronic publications, these rules, practices, and so forth face much greater challenges. Contemporary efforts to address long-standing problems of unique manuscript identification are addressed by Matthew J. Driscoll in "The MASTER Project: Defining Standards for Electronic Manuscript Catalog Records." The international Manuscript Access through Standards for Electronic Records (MASTER) Project's "document type definition" (DTD) standards and application of the closely associated Text Encoding Initiative's (TEI) *Guidelines for Electronic Text Encoding and Interchange* are applied to archived medieval manuscripts. TEI guidelines allow for description along several broad and flexible categories, including its physical location; title, place of origin, and language(s); contents; physical description; history; and administrative issues such as availability and custodial history.[5]

The shift from printed manuscripts to electronic documents greatly accelerated the appearance of document iteration. This acceleration becomes problematic when coupled with the fact that gatekeeping functions traditionally associated with scholarly and commercial publishing diminish when authors, or any other person, can, in some cases, disregard copyright law and change a text at will, store it on a server, and disseminate it via whatever scheme he or she chooses. Copyright becomes a tangled Web when one considers that the author may no longer hold copyright to his or her own work if he or she has agreed to transfer copyright to the publisher for a limited or unlimited amount of time. Therefore, he or she may not possess the legal permission to post particular versions—especially the final "published" version—of his or her own work by self-archiving on a personal Web site or in an institutional repository.

Self-archiving is usually the process of an author maintaining a document copy in electronic format. This electronic document may be made available to the author or anyone else designated by the author. The clear benefit of self-archiving is easy access and information dissemination within the scholarly community. One potentially negative consequence is that variant versions of a particular document may circulate in this way. An institutional repository is "defined to be a Web-based database (repository) of scholarly material which is institutionally defined (as opposed to a subject-based repository)."[6]

Issues of copyright and permission to disseminate work are usually negotiated between the author and the publisher at the time of publication; many publishers have specific policies and guidelines regarding how an author may alter and/or disseminate versions of his or her work after publication. For instance, some publishers allow authors to retain copyright to their work but negotiate from the author the one-time rights, exclusive for a given amount of time (e.g., 90 days), to be the first publisher of the work, and the right to distribute the work exclusively for a given amount of time (e.g., 90 days) after publication. After this predetermined period (e.g., 90 days), the author may distribute, reprint, etc., as he or she pleases. On the other end of the spectrum, some publishers have much stricter and more limited agreements with authors wherein the author transfers copyright to the publisher in perpetuity.

Regardless of the copyright issues involved and the myriad possibilities for agreements between the publisher and the author, it remains that many different versions of any given article do and can exist. To focus on the journal article for purposes of explication, one journal article can exist in multiple electronic versions. In 2005, Sally Morris offered a partial list of possible versions of one journal article:

1. Privately circulated early draft (could be >1 iteration)
2. Version presented at public event (again, could be >1)
3. Pre-submission version(s)
4. Version as submitted to journal x (may differ when resubmitted to journal y)
5. Version amended after peer review (may go through >1 round of amendment)
6. Version as accepted by journal x
7. Accepted version, with substantive editing by journal editor and/or publisher (again, may be multiple iterations)
8. Accepted version, with substantive editing and copyediting—ready for publication
9. Publication version (as above, formatted and paginated)—proof
10. Publication version corrected and passed for publication
11. Published version, not on publisher's site (e.g., PDF), thus potentially lacking some functionality
12. Published version (on publisher's site, with full functionality)
13. Post-publication version with errata/addenda (maybe on publisher's site, with functionality) or elsewhere without it[7]

VERSION OF RECORD AND OPEN ACCESS

While it is beyond the scope of this entry to explore the complicated world of open access (OA), it is impossible to discuss version control without addressing some of the major features of OA. Broadly, OA is the movement to make scholarly literature "digital, online, free of charge, and free of most copyright and licensing restrictions."[8] Morris does not explicitly refer to any particular publishing models in her list; she does not overtly refer to OA or toll-based models because version control issues prevail in both worlds. Indeed, journal articles published in the more traditional toll-based scholarly literature, or journal articles published in OA journals can be versions of record.

The NISO/ALPSP JAV Technical Working Group defines version of record (VoR): "a fixed version of a journal article that has been made available by any organization that acts as a publisher by formally and exclusively declaring the article 'published.'"[4] Furthermore, the notes to the VoR definition explain:

> The VoR may exist in more than one location (e.g., a publisher's Web site, an aggregator site, and one or more repositories). That is, there may be more than one *copy* of a VoR but there is only one *version* of a VoR. In Functional Requirements for Bibliographic Records (FRBR) terms, there may be more than one *manifestation* or *instance* of a VoR, but there is only one *expression* of it.[4]

In other words, VoR transcends notions of multiple copies. Yet, the increasing prevalence OA archives and repositories have ultimately complicated the issue of version control for the scholarly community. The mere existence of such OA material (and other toll-based copies such as those that exist in aggregator databases) requires the reliance on FRBR differentiation between manifestation and expression.

Version control faces two distinct sets of challenges: political and technological. OA itself is an increasingly political movement, especially in light of the Consolidated Appropriations Act, 2008, which includes a provision directing the National Institutes of Health (NIH) to require "scientists to submit final peer-reviewed journal manuscripts that arise from NIH funds to the digital archive PubMed Central upon acceptance for publication."[9] This Act was signed into law despite lobbying efforts of the Partnership for Research Integrity in Science and Medicine (http://www.prismcoalition.org), which is a coalition that has the support of the Professional and Scholarly Publishing Division of the Association of American Publishing.

In addition to the complexities that OA introduces, version control often resembles a Gordian knot because divergent groups have a vested interest in insuring that their voices are heard in any effort to create standardized solutions. Publishers, authors, researchers, vendors, aggregators, subscription agents, OA advocates, universities and other research centers, librarians, standards organizations—while there is some consensus of opinion among this variegated list, each group nonetheless represents a particular constituency with unique goals and interests. The JAV Technical Working Group's report lists the following stakeholders as important variables in identifying the dimensions of an article version: author, editor, referee, publisher, librarian, reader, and funder. Other dimensions articulated by the JAV Technical Working Group are time, added value, manifestation, and siblings.[4]

PEER REVIEW

In 2000, a working group of publishers acknowledged one outcome of the version control problem as changing the context within which peer-reviewed articles are perceived: "The peer-reviewed article will continue to play a crucial part in the certification, communication, and recording of scientific research. However, in the electronic environment it represents one point on a potential continuum of communication."[10] Peer review—in one form or another—has represented the bedrock of reputable scholarly output since at least the beginning of modern science in the seventeenth century, and any discussion of a potential change in its role in scholarly communication is significant.

The issue of peer review as it relates to OA and thus version control is a volatile one, with information industry stakeholders arguing many sides of this complicated issue. Some say that peer review in OA scholarly output is as rigorous and honest as it is within conventional toll-based publishing; others argue that peer review and thus quality of scholarship suffers in the face of OA. In her 2005 article, "Version Control of Journal Articles," Morris noted the emerging problem of definitive or authoritative versions of documents verses "good enough" versions and its implications for scholars. The problem, as described by Morris, is pernicious. As listed earlier, she identifies 13 basic variants, from privately circulated early drafts, through post-publication versions with errata and addenda and argues that a reader cannot easily discern differences between these versions.[11]

Steven Harnad addresses the worries of researchers, university administrators, and librarians in terms of version control and peer review. He notes that there is no need to be concerned about self-archiving because:

> There will be self-archived preprints, revised drafts, final accepted, published drafts (postprints), updated, corrected post-postprints, peer comments, author replies, revised second editions. OAI-compliant Eprint Archives will tag each version with a unique identifier. All versions will be retrieved by a cross-archive OAI search, and the 'hits' can then be identified and compared by the user to select the most recent, official or definitive draft, exactly as if they had all been found in the same index catalog.[12]

OAI is the Open Archives Initiative, and it "develops and promotes interoperability standards that aim to facilitate the efficient dissemination of content."[13]

APPROPRIATE COPY AND OPENURL

In addition to the implications for readers, Morris observed that version control is of great concern to libraries, which are faced with the multifaceted problems of tight budgets; appropriate copies based upon institutional affiliation; multiple, free online versions; and versions which are either self-archived or archived by independent institutions or other repositories. In response to some of these issues, libraries point users to their appropriate copy via link resolvers and the OpenURL framework. It is important to distinguish between the version control and the appropriate copy problem. The appropriate copy problem has two equal dimensions: 1) the multiple availability of any given resource from a variety of sources and 2) the subsequent challenge of pointing the reader to the copy of this resource appropriate for him or her, usually by virtue of his or her institutional affiliations.

If restricted to the toll-based universe, a given journal article might be available from the publisher or from a number of secondary aggregators (e.g., EBSCO, ProQuest, Gale). A researcher at a university may have access to only some of these article copies, and the library or information center wants to insure that the researcher reaches those copies which are appropriate for him or her. If expanded to include the OA universe of materials, the phrase "appropriate copy" then comes to "denote the copy of a resource to which a user has rightful access, usually by virtue of his or her institutional affiliations but perhaps also by virtue of an information object being *open access*."[14]

The OpenURL framework was developed to address the appropriate copy problem, and it is now a NISO standard, Z39.88, OpenURL v. 1.0. Via link resolvers, the OpenURL framework is widely used to point users to their appropriate copies. The appropriate copy problem and its solution in OpenURL/link resolvers primarily address a problem of access; version control, on the other hand encompasses issues of authority and management as well as defining the stages in the life cycle of an article. OpenURL also primarily focuses on pointing users to versions of record, which, again, can be in multiple locations. The other versions of an article—such as more ephemeral ones kept in an author's institutional repository, for example—are currently outside the technical capability of the OpenURL/link resolvers. With version control, many technological hurdles remain, including: a standardized schema to identify the VoR or authoritative version as well as an extensible model to identify and explain the relationships among the different iterations of a document.

TECHNOLOGICAL INITIATIVES

One such effort to clearly articulate the different stages in the life of an article as well as the relationships among those stages was released in an April 2008 report by a joint partnership between NISO and ALPSP, the JAV Technical Working Group. Perhaps the most definitive work to date on the issue of version control, the recommended practices released by the JAV Technical Working Group attempts to "provide a simple, practical way of describing the versions of scholarly journal articles that typically appear online before, during and after formal journal publication."[4] The working group builds upon earlier, previously mentioned efforts.

In September 2005, NISO and ALPSP charged the group with creating a plan that included:

1. Creation of use cases to identify the most common journal article life cycles.
2. Analysis of use cases to determine common life cycle stages.
3. Selection of preferred vocabulary for the most common life cycle stages.
4. Development of appropriate metadata to identify each variant version and its relationship to other versions, in particular the definitive, fully functional published version.
5. Establishment of practical systems for ensuring that the metadata is applied by authors or repository managers and publishers.[15]

Cliff Morgan, Vice President, Planning and Development and Director, John Wiley & Sons, Ltd., was the chair of the joint NISO/ALPSP working group. In an August 2007 interview, Morgan noted: "In the digital world, multiple versions of journal articles are often available online. This can cause confusion because there is no way of identifying the various versions by either a common terminology or identification scheme." Morgan went on to explain that the working group "will recommend terms and definitions for journal article versions and define the relationships between these versions. We're focusing on key stages rather than every possible iteration of an article from origination to publication."[16]

Critical to the working group's efforts is the notion that the group focuses on "key stages" of the version continuum rather than "every possible iteration." The group considered a variety of attributes in order to describe different versions: "Ownership, bibliographic context, identifiers [e.g., digital object identifier (DOI)], relationships, fixity, and peer review are explicitly stated in the terms and definitions that we recommend. They can be described by the article version names and some are already covered by standard metadata elements (e.g., bibliographic reference, date, and DOI)."[4] Of particular note is the attention paid to the version of record. Morgan elucidated the importance of this stage:

> The VoR constitutes the "minutes of science"—the formally certified record of a research project. It is this version that has been peer-reviewed, edited, composed, and verified by the author; it is this version that benefits from publisher investment in managing the above process, building the journal brand, and adding functionality such as linking and e-alerts, and for which the publisher takes legal responsibility. This is also the version that is most likely to be cited by other researchers.[16]

If the VoR is easily identifiable, then the problem of researchers questioning which version is the final, authoritative one is solved.

The seven stages identified by the working group are

1. Author's Original
2. Submitted Manuscript Under Review
3. Accepted Manuscript
4. Proof
5. Version of Record
6. Corrected Version of Record
7. Enhanced Version of Record

Each stage is accompanied by a full definition and note. Also included in the report are graphical representations of the relationships among formal and gray literature as well as a number of "use cases" to provide a clearer picture of how the recommended terms would apply in real-world situations.

What remains to be seen is to what extent the recommendations in the report will be implemented by publishers and other stakeholders in the information industry. Version control is still very much an issue in flux, and thus it presents interested parties with a moving target. Some publishers have already created and maintained internal practices for version control that may or may not be consistent with the group's recommended practices. If a publisher has invested significant capital in creating and maintaining an internal schema, then only time will tell if the said publisher will implement the NISO/ALPSP recommendations. Additionally, while the report explains some relationships among formal and gray literature, the group primarily concerned itself with a fairly narrow scope: journal articles. The continued evolution of the formally published journal article itself presents problems. If the electronic version with an assigned DOI is the version of record, then it begs the question about the necessity of assigning volume, issue, and page numbers for a journal article version of record. Questions of version control for other formal literature—book chapters, proceedings, etc.—remain. Moreover, an ocean of gray literature exists. With the advent of electronic publishing, gray literature and other informal publishing enjoy unprecedented accessibility. Such accessibility arguably leads to formerly "hidden" scholarship now occupying a more prominent place in our intellectual space and community of scholarship. Ultimately, many questions remain and while the group's work is essential, it is only one step toward an unknown future.

Version control is an international issue and as such, there are multiple initiatives underway to address its unique challenges. Two other programs created to study version control are the United Kingdom-based Joint Information Systems Committee Validating Repository Content project (VALREC, http://www.jisc.ac.uk/whatwedo/programmes/programme_rep_pres/tools/valrec.aspx and http://valrec.eprints.org/) and the London School of Economics VERSIONS Project (http://www.lse.ac.uk/library/versions/).

CONCLUSION

Version control remains a thorny issue with many technological and political barriers. The very nature of electronic information allows for an ease of replication and adaptation heretofore unheard of in scholarly communication. However, information industry stakeholders have recognized the issue and have formed a variety of international projects to study and recommend standardized solutions for identifying and managing iterations of a document for archival and retrieval purposes.

REFERENCES

1. Siemens, R.; Best, M.; Burk, A.; Grove-White, E.; Gue'don, J.-C.; Kerr, J.; Pope, A.; Rockwell, G.; Siemens, L. The Credibility of Electronic Publishing: A Report to the Humanities and Social Sciences Federation of Canada. 2002, http://web.mala.bc.ca/hssfc/Final/Credibility.htm (accessed December 2007).
2. Burk, A.; Kerr, J.; Pope, A. Section 4: Archiving and text fluidity/version control. In The Credibility of Electronic Publishing: A Report to the Humanities and Social Sciences Federation of Canada. 2002, http://web.mala.bc.ca/hssfc/Final/Archiving.htm (accessed December 2007).
3. United States Government Printing Office. Office of Information Dissemination, Program Development Service; Version control: Draft. 2005, http://www.access.gpo.gov/su_docs/fdlp/pubs/proceedings/05spring/cdqa/version_control_ white_paper.pdf (accessed December 2007).
4. National Information Standards Organization/Association of Learned and Professional Society Publishers, Journal Article Versions Technical Working Group. Journal Article Versions (JAV): Recommendations of the NISO/ALPSP JAV Technical Working Group. April 2008. http://www.niso.org/publications/rp/RP-8—2008.pdf (accessed November 2008).
5. Driscoll, M.J. The MASTER project: Defining standards for electronic manuscript catalogue records. In *Care and Conservation of Manuscripts 6*, Proceedings of the Sixth International Seminar, Royal Library, Copenhagen, Denmark, October 19–20, 2000; Fellows-Jensen, G., Springborg, P., Eds.; Museum Tusculanum Press: Copenhagen, Denmark, 2002, http://books.google.com/books?hl = en&id = iz17G5pKB1AC&dq = care + and + conservation + of + manuscripts + 6&printsec = frontcover&source = web&ots = G8zvpZ8zW0&sig = oI8B6q7UHIYC0p45QkN1FYU4C7w#PPP1,M1 (accessed December 2007).
6. Bailey, C.W., Jr. Institutional repositories, Tout de suite; 2008, http://www.digital-scholarship.org/ts/irtoutsuite.pdf (accessed January 2008).

7. Grogg, J.E. Linking users to open access. Searcher **2005**, *13* (4), 52–56.
8. Suber, P. Open access overview; 2007. http://www.earlham.edu/~peters/fos/overview.htm (accessed January 2008).
9. U.S. Department of Health and Human Services. National Institutes of Health Public Access. http://publicaccess.nih.gov/ (access November 2008).
10. Antelman, K. Self-archiving practice and the influence of publisher policies in the social sciences. Learn. Publ. **2006**, *19* (2), 85–95.
11. Morris, S. Version control of journal articles; 2005. http://www.niso.org/workrooms/jav/Morris.pdf (accessed November 2008).
12. Harnad, S. Open Access to peer-reviewed research through author/institution self-archiving. In Digital Libraries; Andrews, J., Law, D., Eds.; Ashgate: Hants, U.K., 2004; 63–98.
13. Open archives initiative. http://www.openarchives.org/ (accessed January 2008).
14. Grogg, J.E. Introduction linking and the OpenURL. Libr. Technol. Rep. **2006**, *42* (1), 5–7.
15. National Information Standards Organization. NISO/ ALPSP Working Group on Versions of Journal Articles. http://www.niso.org/workrooms/jav (accessed November 2008).
16. *Library Connect*, Editorial Office. Five quick questions with Cliff Morgan. Elsevier Libr. Connect Newsl. **2007**, *5* (3), 9. http://libraryconnect.elsevier.com/lcn/0503/lcn0503.pdf (accessed January 2008).

16 Digital Content Licensing

Paul D. Callister and Kathleen Hall

CONTENTS

INTRODUCTION

Content licensing primarily concerns the licensing of property, which itself consists of certain legal rights. Besides copyright law, content licensing takes place within the context of rights and obligations stemming from an array of local, national, foreign, and international laws. Such law may concern author or creator's "moral rights," "neighbor rights," lender's rights, defamation, privacy, publicity, pornography and obscenity, international trade, exports and technology transfer, privacy, trademark, commercial codes, and employment and contract law, etc.

To understand content licensing, copyright and other law must be juxtaposed with the law governing the formation, interpretation, warranties, and remedy for breach of contract. The issues are complicated by choice of applicable commercial law. While it is always prudent to consult an attorney with respect to negotiating, drafting, and litigating any contract, this is especially true with respect to the technical field of copyright law. Consequently, the topics and issues discussed in this entry are for informational purposes only and should not be relied upon in lieu of consultation with competent legal counsel.

WHAT IS A LICENSE?

A license is a contract, not necessarily in writing, in which one party (the licensor) transfers rights to use certain property to a user (the licensee) for some limited period of time or until some event. A permanent transfer of rights is an assignment or sale, even when the licensor retains other related rights (e.g., the transfer of rights to publish in print but not in any electronic medium). With respect to intellectual property, a licensor may, but need not be, the creator, or even the owner, of the work being transferred.

By entering into license agreements, the parties seek to establish a mutually beneficial relationship in which they exchange certain promises or consideration (payment), set forth their respective rights and obligations, and provide for redress in the event of breach (i.e., a failure of one or more of the parties to meet their obligations). Besides license to use property for a given term, the licensee may seek certain warranties (guarantees) from the licensor, that the person has title or the rights to the content being licensed, and that additional payments or liability to third parties will not result from licensee's use of the property. As used in this entry, content licensing refers to license agreements affecting informational content and the software necessary to access that content.

One principal difference between licensing content and purchasing information in a print publication is that the "first sale" doctrine generally does not apply.[1] The first sale doctrine cuts off the right of owners to seek additional remuneration each time a work is subsequently sold or lent to another.[2]

WHAT RIGHTS MAY BE ADDRESSED IN A LICENSE AGREEMENT?

Although it may be said that all property consist of rights, in the case of intellectual property[3] such property owes its existence to rights enumerated in the law, and often by statute. The right to license intellectual property interests may potentially originate in the law of copyright, neighboring rights, moral rights, and electronic rights, etc. Several of these respective sources of intellectual property rights frequently addressed in content licensing agreements are considered below.

COPYRIGHT LAW

In the United States, such rights are found in Title 17 of the United States Code (USC) § 106 and include rights to

1. Reproduction;
2. Adaptation (or "derivative works");
3. Distribution (including "sale or other transfer of ownership, or by rental, lease, or lending");
4. Public performance (limited to "literary, musical, dramatic, and choreographic works, pantomimes, and motion pictures and other audiovisual works");
5. Public display (limited to "literary, musical, dramatic, and choreographic works, pantomimes, and pictorial, graphic, or sculptural works, including the individual images of a motion picture or other audiovisual work"); and
6. Digital audio transmission (limited to sound recordings).

In addition, 17 USC § 201 (c), sets forth rights of publishers of "collective works" in relation to the rights of contributing authors. Specifically, publishers of collective works have the right to publish contributed articles in "revisions" of the original collected work (e.g., a second edition of the same encyclopedia) and in any "later collective work in the same series" (e.g., a subsequent reprint of an article in the *same* journal). In the European Union, the EU Database Directive provides protections for publishers of databases.[4]

Enumerated rights, such as those expressed in U.S. federal copyright law, form the basis for property rights assigned pursuant to licensing agreements. Similar rights may also be found in the common law of the various U.S. states and the law of foreign nations. Each of these rights may serve as the basis for an assignable property right and may further be limited in seemingly infinite variations by terms set forth in the licensing agreement (by time, jurisdiction, medium, types of uses, etc.).

Neighboring Rights

Besides copyright law, additional rights affecting licensing agreements stem from other law, including state law and the laws of foreign nations. For instance, many civil law jurisdictions such as France (and California, alone among U.S. jurisdictions), provide for neighboring rights (*droit de suite*), or rights designed to compensate artists for subsequent resale and reproduction of their works (traditionally, the law presumed that the reproduction rights to the works of fine artists had been transferred to the buyer of that painting, sculpture, etc., whereas the rights to literary works had not).[5] In California, *droit de suite* is applied through the California Resale Royalties Act.[6] The Berne Convention, which was adopted by the United States in 1989, recognizes *droit de suite.* Unlike many other rights protected by the treaty, *droit de suite* requires that an author's country recognizes the right. In addition the convention's provision recognizing the right may not be "self-executing" under U.S. law (i.e., applicable without enabling legislation).[7]

As a result of neighboring rights, licensees often seek express warranties in licensing agreements whereby the licensor warrants that the person not only has the right to lease or title to the licensed property, but that licensed use (or acquisition) of such property by the licensee (or purchaser) will not result in liability as the result of neighboring rights that any third (noncontracting) party may have. In addition, licensees often require an indemnification clause in the agreement whereby the licensor agrees to fully compensate the licensee as a result of liability to third parties.

Moral Rights

In many countries, under the Berne Convention, and to some extent in the United States, but only with respect to visual artists, there is a distinctive category of rights known as "moral rights" or *le droit moral.* This bundle of rights varies by legal jurisdiction, but can generally be enumerated:

1. Attribution or paternity (including the rights to be identified as the author, free from false attribution, and to publish anonymously or pseudonymously);
2. Integrity (to prevent derogatory substantive changes to the work);
3. Disclosure (or nondisclosure), reconsideration, and withdrawal (from circulation); and
4. Association (or disassociation of the work from products or institutions distasteful to the author or artist).[8]

In many jurisdictions, moral rights are noneconomic rights. Whether or not such rights in property can be alienated, waived, or can survive their authors and creators depends upon the law of the jurisdiction being applied. The Berne Convention recognizes rights of attribution and integrity, but it leaves it up to signatory members how to protect such rights. Furthermore, the convention does not require such rights to be inalienable, "unwaivable," or to survive the death of the author or creator.[9] Under the convention, foreign authors and artists enjoy the same rights as native citizens in nations adhering to the convention.

Under the U.S. Visual Artists Rights Acts of 1990, now 17 USC § 106A, moral rights are addressed with respect to "visual art," but only with respect to rights of attribution and integrity. In addition to U.S. federal law, several states have adopted moral rights, but to the extent such rights concern the attribution and integrity rights of visual artists, state law is preempted by the federal statute.[10]

France and Germany each represent yet two different conceptions of moral rights (in addition to the U.S. viewpoint). In France, moral rights are separate from economic rights, and consequently, cannot be alienated, and have no set term.[11] In Germany, the duality of rights (economic and moral) is not recognized. Rather the approach is to prohibit the complete assignment or transfer of rights, and the term of the rights is set by statute.[12]

The impact of moral rights on licensing agreements, to some extent, depends upon whether such rights may be waived, assigned, or limited under applicable law. Regardless of the validity of such limitations, however, licensees seek warranties that the licensor has not infringed upon any third party's rights and that the intended use per the agreement will not infringe upon such rights. In addition, the licensor may seek similar assurances that the licensee will not infringe upon any third party's moral rights (e.g., by removing attribution information, etc.). Per an indemnification clause, each party may also seek compensation for any liability resulting from infringements by the other.

E-Rights

With the development of the Internet and other information technologies, some have questioned whether "e-rights" constituted a new class of rights. While the U.S. Supreme Court decision in *New York Times v. Tasini* found that e-rights (in that case rights to republish the work of freelance journalists in a searchable database) do not automatically vest with print publishers, a closer reading reveals the real issue decided by the Court. That issue was whether, in that instance, the electronic database constituted a revision of the earlier collective, print work (which would favor the publisher, as an exception to infringement for "collective works" under 17 USC § 201(c)), or a new work (which would favor the freelance journalists). Under 17 USC § 201(c), publishers of "collective works" acquire the right to reproduce and distribute a "particular collective work, any revision of that collective work, and any later collective work in the same series." The Supreme Court found that the database, which included many collective works (and not just a digital version of the original collective work), and provided access to each freelance article individually and separately, was indeed a new work.[13] Thus, under *Tasini*, the issue is not whether e-rights are distinctive, but whether a database is considered a "revision," or falls within another exception for publishers of previous collective works under 17 USC § 201(c).

The Second, Ninth, and Eleventh Circuits have followed *Tasini*'s lead in utilizing traditional copyright analysis to determine rights in e-content. For example, in *Faulkner v. National Geographic Enterprises, Inc.*,[14] plaintiff authors sued National Geographic when it published a compilation of all previous issues in CD-ROM format, through which the original content appeared in its original context, albeit in a different medium. Like the *Tasini* court, the Second Circuit focused on whether the CD-ROM constituted a compilation, or a revision of a compilation, within the meaning of § 201(c) of the Copyright Act. Because the CD-ROM presented the "underlying works . . . in the same context as they were presented . . . in the original versions," which had not been the case in *Tasini*, the Second Circuit held that the CD-ROM was a "privileged revision."[15] In similar litigation also involving National Geographic, the Eleventh Circuit very recently reached the same result using a § 201(c) analysis.[16] The Ninth Circuit looked to §§ 101 and 106 of the Copyright Code in *Perfect 10 v. Amazon.com*, which involved slightly different, but similar, issues arising out of thumbnail images and redirected access to copyrighted images through Google's Image Search feature.[17] Using traditional analysis, the court found that thumbnail images were "fair use." Thus, these post-*Tasini* courts have not treated e-rights as separate or distinct, but have continued to apply traditional copyright analysis.

E-rights, to the extent that they represent rights in media created by new technologies, serve as a reminder of the importance of carefully identifying (with the assistance of competent legal counsel) what rights are subject to a licensing or assignment agreement. Careful attention needs to be given to new and unforeseen media that may result from new technologies. It follows that the greater the breadth of rights being licensed or assigned, the greater the compensation that may be expected. To assure the rights are being discretely bargained for, and thus do not include non-enumerated rights, each right or use should be identified with corresponding consideration, and a statement as to who holds the unnamed rights (including rights in any new media) should be included.[18]

APPLICATION OF COMMERCIAL LAW

In addition to law governing the creation of intellectual property rights (such as copyright), licensing transactions are governed by commercial law (i.e., law governing contracts). Other law may apply as well, such as consumer protection statutes, labor relations codes, professional codes of conduct, bankruptcy and debtor–creditor law, and trade law. Because it is generally in the interest of commercial transactions to promote predictability and uniformity, uniform and model commercial codes are important as sources for law governing licensing transactions.

What Law Applies

In the United States, state law largely governs contract and commercial law through a series of uniform acts known as the Uniform Commercial Code (UCC), promulgated by the National Conference of Commissioners of Uniform State Laws (NCCUSL). For transactions involving "computer information," a special uniform or model act was prepared in 1999, known as the Uniform Computer Information Transactions Act (UCITA). Amendments to UCITA were introduced and considered in 2000 and 2001; in 2002, NCCUSL approved the final revisions and amendments to UCITA and recommended it for enactment in all the states.[19] As of summer 2007, only Maryland and Virginia have adopted the act.[20] UCITA is controversial, and Iowa, North Carolina, West Virginia, Idaho, Vermont, and New York have passed or introduced legislation refusing to apply UCITA to contracts with their citizens.[21] In addition, a committee of the ABA has recommended that UCITA be rewritten.[22] In spite of UCITA's widespread rejection, given the need for a uniform law and the impact of the UCC, not only in the United States, but also on commercial codes throughout the world, UCITA (or its progeny) may yet become an important source for the construction and interpretation of digital licensing agreements throughout the world. If nothing else, UCITA represents an important effort to address the multitude of issues pertaining to content licensing and computer information transactions.

To the extent that a U.S. state has not adopted UCITA, then often UCC Article 2 applies. In varying degrees, state courts in Connecticut, Kansas, Massachusetts, Georgia (applying Michigan law), Nebraska, New York, and Tennessee have applied UCC Article 2 to computer software licenses. Likewise, federal courts in California, Florida, New Hampshire, New Jersey, and Pennsylvania have interpreted the laws of their respective states to apply UCC Article 2, and federal courts in Michigan and Kansas have applied Illinois and Wisconsin UCC law, respectively.[23] Because many software licenses involve the licensing of both goods (the software product) and services (technical, customer support, and client-specific programming), many courts weigh whether the services or the goods predominate.[24] The question of whether software has been designed as a service (to which UCC Article 2 has been found not to apply)[25] or whether it is a product customized for a particular user or includes installation and other services (to which the UCC has been applied)[26] is one that requires careful weighing of all the pertinent facts. In addition to UCC Article 2, Article 2A, governing leases, has been adopted in 49 states and the District of Columbia. The sole state yet to adopt Article 2A is Louisiana, which has also declined to adopt Article 2.[27] Because of the similarity of leases to licenses in terms of transfers of rights or use and possession, but not ownership, one may speculate that UCC Article 2A will become the dominant law governing content licensing agreements (assuming UCITA is not widely adopted).

In August of 2002, proposals to amend Articles 2 and 2A of the UCC to exclude "information" from the definition of "goods" were submitted to the NCCUSL.[28] Such a definition of "goods" would mean that neither Article 2 nor 2A would apply to most information transactions. Somewhat surprisingly given the historical resistance of UCC Article 2 to amendment, the proposed changes were adopted in 2003. Currently, in defining "goods," Articles 2 and 2A both specify that "[t]he term does not include information."[29] The Official Comment to Article 2 acknowledges, however, that transactions often include both goods *and* information, and that it will ultimately be up to courts to determine whether, and to what extent, Article 2 should apply.[30] As of summer 2007, Oklahoma is the only state that has incorporated this change into its commercial code.[31]

At present there is no treaty or convention expressly addressing computer information transactions in the same manner as UCITA. The European Union's EC Legal Advisory Board has expressed considerable hesitation and reluctance to fashion their own law after UCITA. Principally, concern has been expressed over whether UCITA, even if adopted, will be done so on a uniform basis because of some of its controversial provisions and approach: acceptance of click-wrap agreements (via electronic agents), choice of law, focus on software (rather than other forms of intellectual property), and the acceptance of denial of access and electronic self-help as remedies for breach.[32]

The UNCITRAL Model Law on Electronic Commerce addresses admissibility of electronic documents, electronic signatures, and "data messages" pertaining to the sale of goods, but not on the licensing of copyright. Another law that may apply is the Convention on Contracts for the International Sale of Goods (CCISG) (however, unlike the UCC, the convention does not apply to "goods purchased for consumer purposes" meaning for "personal, family, or household use").[33] In addition, the European Directive on Unfair Terms in Consumer Contracts,[34] the European Data Directive,[35] and the European Directive on Legal Protection of Databases may also apply.[36]

Writing Requirement and Requirements of Formation

Under UCITA § 201, the licensing of digital rights for transactions involving payment of $5000 or more generally requires written agreement. With respect to transfers in ownership, U.S. federal copyright law under 17 USC § 204(a) requires written contracts. UCITA § 201 provides for exceptions to the written requirement, which exceptions are common to commercial contract law. Generally, no writing is needed when

1. The contract term is one year or less;
2. Performance has been tendered and accepted;
3. Such agreement has been admitted under oath;
4. Written confirmation of a contract is received between merchants and no objection is made within a reasonable time.

In addition to the requirement that certain contracts be in writing, there are other requirements to the formation of a valid license agreement:

1. Parties intent and basis for remedy[37]
2. Agreement as to material terms[38]
3. When applicable, a valid offer and acceptance[39]

Official Comment 5 of UCITA § 202 clarifies that if there is disagreement as to the "scope" of the license, there is no contract.

Because of the utilization of "shrink-wrap" and "click-wrap" agreements" (i.e., agreements that are accepted by clicking "yes" on prompted display of a license agreement as part of the loading or use of software or a computer service), UCITA devotes considerable attention to the use of "electronic agents" to manifest acceptance of an agreement. Sections 107, 112, 207, and 208, recognize shrink- or click-wrap agreements. Click-wrap agreements are recognized through electronic agents, which are defined under § 102(a)(27) as "a computer program, or electronic or other automated means, used independently to initiate an action, or to respond to electronic messages or performances, on the person's behalf without review or action by an individual at the time of the action or response to the message or performance." In other words, it is possible to manifest assent or acceptance of an agreement through automated means without written signature. An example of acceptance by electronic agent is found in Official Comment 4 of UCITA § 206: "Officer dials the telephone information system using the company credit card. A computerized voice states: 'If you would like us to dial your number, press "1"; there will be an additional charge of $1.00. . . .'"

Shrink-wrap or click-wrap agreements are permitted under UCITA §§ 112, 113, 208, and 209 under the following conditions:

1. The parties had reason to know at the outset that terms would be proposed for later agreement.
2. There is an opportunity to review the terms before assent is given (this may be after payment is tendered).
3. There will be assent involving acts or inaction taken with reason to know that it will create an inference of assent.
4. If the party does not assent, it has a right to a return and refund of any price paid, which right is cost free in a mass-market case.
5. In a mass-market case, the terms are produced and assented to at or before the time of initial use of the software.

Notwithstanding the validity of shrink-wrap and click-wrap agreements or acceptance by electronic agents, UCITA § 206(a) does grant courts discretion to fashion a remedy where the acceptance resulted from "fraud, electronic mistake, or the like."

Some state consumer protection statutes may differ from UCITA in terms of their signature or record-keeping requirements. UCITA does not alter these requirements, but rather provides states the latitude to specify which such statutes are to prevail over UCITA provisions in case of a conflict.[40] State consumer laws enjoy special status (for preempting terms of licensing agreements) under UCITA.

Other laws may also recognize shrink- or click-wrap agreements. While UCC § 2-204(1) provides that "a contract for sale of goods may be made in any manner sufficient to show agreement, including . . . conduct by both parties which recognizes the existence of such a contract . . .," U.S. courts are divided as to whether shrink-wrap agreements are enforceable.[41] UCC § 2A-204(1), governing leases, contains an almost identical provision to Article 2. The CCISG permits electronic agreements (without a writing) unless one of the contracting states specifically mandates a writing requirement by excluding the applicable provision of the convention.[42]

Finally, although yet to be ratified by any country, the Hague Convention for Choice of Court Agreements (CCCA), provides a liberal standard of contract formation: "by any . . . means of communication which renders information accessible so as to be usable for subsequent reference."[43] Under this standard, almost any "click-" or "shrink-wrap agreement" concluded pursuant to the law of a signatory nation would be enforceable.[44] However, the CCCA exempts contracts entered into for personal or household purposes.[45]

Enforceability of Contractual Terms against a Fundamental Public Policy or Conflicting with Other Law

The Eighth, Ninth, and Federal circuits have recently looked at the enforceability of "no reverse engineering" clauses included in shrink-wrap or click-wrap agreements. Faced with claims that such terms violate public policy in that they prohibit fair use, courts have generally held that those who agree to such license terms are bound by them.[46] Courts have also rejected the argument that "no reverse engineering" clauses are preempted by the Copyright Act, finding that the mutual assent and consideration required by a contract claim provide an "extra element" that makes the right asserted qualitatively different from the rights protected under the Copyright Act.[47] Absent a license term that prohibits it, however, the Ninth Circuit has held that reverse engineering constitutes fair use, privileged under § 107, when "there is good reason for studying or examining the unprotected aspects of a copyrighted computer program."[48]

Under UCITA, a license agreement (or other contract) in which any term "violates a fundamental public policy" may result in the court finding that the contract is unenforceable or limiting enforcement to the remainder of the contract.[49] In Official Comment 3 to UCITA §

105, a "shrink-wrap license" prohibiting the licensee from ever criticizing the software is seen as problematic. On the other hand it is expressly noted that such a provision might be accepted in a negotiated license where the license pertained to software in the early stages of development, which had not been released to the general marketplace.[50] In addition, courts may refuse to enforce or limit the enforcement of contracts or terms that are unconscionable (generally, terms that are very "one-sided").[51]

Besides considering public policy, UCITA provides for the preemption of federal law and state consumer protection statutes.[52] Other state law does not preempt private license agreements (unless explicitly considered by the state when it enacts UCITA). This is important because copyright and other rights contained in state law, which may be broader than federal copyright law, consequently do not preempt contractual agreements under UCITA.

Of particular concern is whether licensors of digital content can extend their rights that would otherwise be limited with respect to applicable federal copyright law (state law, except for consumer law, is granted a lesser standing to preempt terms of the license agreement under UCITA § 105). The act attempts to balance a fundamental policy of contract law to enforce contractual agreements with "public interest in assuring that information in the public domain is free for all to use from the public domain and in providing access to information for public purposes such as education, research, and fair comment."[53] Having said this, there is no question that UCITA fundamentally advocates the enforceability of license agreements. "[I]t is clear that limitations on the information property rights of owners that may exist in a copyright regime, where rights are good against third parties, may be inappropriate in a contractual setting where the courts should be reluctant to set aside terms of a contract."[54] Indeed, courts are particularly reluctant to set aside negotiated (as opposed to "mass-market," "shrink-" or "clip-wrap") agreements.[55]

With respect to "mass-market" transactions, Official Comment 3 of UCITA § 105 suggests that license terms prohibiting the making of multiple copies, use of information for commercial purposes, limiting the number of authorized users, or modification of the software or content are generally enforceable.[56] However, terms in a "mass-market" agreement that "prohibit persons from observing the visible operations or visible characteristics of software and using the observations to develop noninfringing commercial products, that prohibit quotation of limited material for purposes of education or criticism, or that preclude a nonprofit library licensee from making an archival (backup) copy would ordinarily be invalid in the absence of a showing of significant commercial need."[57] Additional provisions are suggested for the circumvention of technical measures protecting copyright for purposes of checking security and to provide for the "interoperability of computer programs." Finally, "to the extent that Congress has established policies on fair use, those can be taken into consideration under [UCITA § 105]."[58] Consequently, policy articulated in the legislative history of the fair use provisions of 17 USC § 107 may have bearing on the enforceability of terms in license agreements that otherwise restrict the application of "fair use."

Like UCITA, UCC Article 2 has a section addressing "unconscionable contracts."[59] It does not, however, have a specific section addressing conflict with fundamental public policies or consumer protection statutes. However, the UCC does not necessarily restrict claims of aggrieved parties to breach of contract under the UCC. For example, it is possible to bring a claim for breach of warranty under the UCC in the same action as claims based upon violation of a consumer protection statute provided that the consumer protection claim is not simply a restatement of the breach of warranty claim.[60] Likewise, UCC Article 2A, governing leasing, and now adopted in 49 states, addresses consumer protection statutes but does not conflict with "fundamental public policy."[61] Article 2A also addresses "unconscionable" leases and terms.[62] The CCISG, unless otherwise noted therein, expressly does not address the "validity of the contract or any of its provisions . . . ."[63] Consequently, enforceability of terms that may be in violation of a fundamental public policy or unconscionable is a matter to be determined under national or local law pursuant to choice of law rules.

Choice of Law and Forum

Choice of law and forum matter because the outcome of a particular dispute may rest on the discrepancies of the law between jurisdictions. Under UCITA § 109, the law governing any agreement is generally the law selected by the parties per the agreement. However, this does not apply to "consumer contracts" (i.e., between a licensed merchant and consumer) to the extent that this would affect the application of any state law (such as consumer law) pursuant to choice of law rules under UCITA (assuming the absence of agreement as to choice of law).

If the parties have not specified what law applies by agreement, then the law of the licensor's jurisdiction applies if the contract called for electronic delivery of the product or information, and the law of the licensee's jurisdiction applies if a delivery was designated by a tangible medium. In any other instance, the law of the jurisdiction with the "most significant relationship to the transaction applies." As a final caveat, for an international transaction in which choice of law has not been determined per the agreement, the law of a jurisdiction outside the United States only applies if a party located in the United States would have "substantially similar protections and rights" to those found under UCITA. As indicated in Official Comment 5, this does not mean "merely that the foreign law is different," but rather the "differences must be substantial and adverse." Under UCITA § 110, choice of forum, the place where litigation of a dispute will take place, is also left up to the parties unless the choice is "unreasonable and unjust." Official Comment 3 indicates:

> Terms may be unreasonable in that they have no commercial purpose or justification . . . and their impact may be unjust if the term unfairly harms the other party . . . . On the other hand, an agreed choice of forum based on a valid commercial purpose is not invalid simply because it adversely affects one party, even if bargaining power was unequal.

In essences valid commercial purposes, such as a party's location, will justify choice of a particular forum.

For those states that do not adopt NCCUSL's recently changed definition of "goods," which now excludes "information,"[64] UCC Article 2 applies Article 1, § 1-301, to determine choice of law for digital content agreements. Like UCITA, the UCC distinguishes consumer from other types of transactions, but otherwise gives deference to the choice of the parties regardless of whether the jurisdiction selected has a "reasonable relation" to the transaction. However, for consumer transactions, the selected jurisdiction must bear a "reasonable relation" to the transaction, and may not deprive a consumer of any protection under their applicable consumer protection law. Regardless of whether the transaction is a consumer transaction, per § 1-301, a choice of law clause is "not effective to the extent that application of the law of the State or country designated would be contrary to a fundamental policy of the State or country" whose law would otherwise apply.

In the absence of UCITA, and once again assuming that "information" is not excluded from the definition of "goods," UCC Article 2A may become the preferred uniform law for interpreting content licenses. Under Article 2A, choice of law and forum clauses for consumer leases are limited:

1. If the law chosen by the parties to a consumer lease is that of a jurisdiction other than a jurisdiction in which the lessee resides at the time the lease agreement becomes enforceable or within 30 days thereafter or in which the goods are to be used, the choice is not enforceable.
2. If the judicial forum chosen by the parties to a consumer lease is a forum that would not otherwise have jurisdiction over the lessee, the choice is not enforceable.[65]

Consequently, under either UCC Article 2 or 2A, applicable consumer law of the party who is a consumer will generally always apply. Indeed, under Article 2A, the law of the party who is a consumer will always apply.

Although only applying to commercial (and not consumer) transactions, the CCISG, applies if both of the parties (which must be in different countries) are located in contracting states (to the CCISG), or if the law of a contracting state applies through choice of law rules.[66] Having said this, parties may, per the agreement, elect out of the application of the convention.[67] Since the convention neither applies to consumer transactions nor addresses the validity or enforceability of contractual terms,[68] choice of law rules of the jurisdiction where the dispute is adjudicated have to be applied for many issues relating to international transactions. For U.S. courts, choice of law questions are increasingly decided based upon "significant relationship" of the jurisdiction to the transaction (even if the UCC is not considered). Certain factual contacts are weighed to determine if such a relationship exists:

- The place of contracting;
- The place of negotiation of the contract;
- The place of performance;
- The location of the subject matter of the contract; and
- The domicile, residence, nationality, place of incorporation, and place of business of the parties.[69]

In addition several policy considerations are weighed:

- Maintenance of interstate and international order;
- Relevant policies and government interests of the forum;
- Relevant policies of other interested states;
- Relevant interests of those states in the determination of the particular issue;
- Protection of justified expectations (of the parties);
- Basic policies underlying the particular field of law;
- Certainty, predictability and uniformity of result;
- Simplification of the judicial task; and
- Application of the better rule of law.[70]

For EU countries, the issue of choice of law is governed by the Convention on the Law Applicable to Contract Obligations (adopted in 1960), which generally honors the choice of the contracting parties.[71] If no choice has been made by the parties, the law of the country "most closely connected" which usually defaults to the domicile or place of business of the party "who is to effect the performance" (i.e., deliver the licensed product).[72] Once again, certain exceptions are made for consumer contracts (defined as pertaining to goods or services outside of the buyer's profession.[73]

Warranties

Warranties are additional promises made by the parties, usually pertaining to ownership of/or rights to the property being licensed, capacity to contract, outstanding claims for infringement, etc. Warranties may be specified by contract, but there are always certain warranties addressed in the applicable governing law on contracts. Under UCITA § 401(a), a licensor, who is "a merchant regularly dealing in information of the kind warrants that the information will be delivered free of the rightful claim of any third person by way of infringement or misappropriation . . . ." For other licensors (although also applying to merchants who deal in information), the warranty is limited: "no person holds a rightful claim to, or interest in, the information which arose from an act or omission of the licensor, other than a claim by way of infringement or misappropriation, which will interfere with the licensee's enjoyment of its interest. . . ."[74] Additional warranties (that the information is not in the public domain and that no other party shares in rights to the information) are made in the event that an exclusive license is granted.[75] Warranties are not made with respect to the infringement of rights pertaining to collective administration (e.g., rights obtained through collective bargaining), or with respect to compulsory rights (certain limitations on copyright under U.S. law).[76] Neither do UCITA's § 401 warranties apply to informational rights arising under foreign law (unless the contract expressly provides for warranties under the laws of other countries *and* the rights originate in countries "under a treaty or international convention to which the country and the United States are signatories").[77]

The warranties set forth in UCITA § 401 can be waived or modified by agreement, but only if by "specific language or by circumstances that give the licensee reason to know that the licensor does not warrant that competing claims do not exist or that the licensor purports to grant only the rights it may have."[78] In an electronic or automated transaction, the language has to be "conspicuous."[79] Merchants have the option of "quitclaiming" rights without any warranty.[80]

UCITA also applies for express warranties (additional promises made by the licensor)[81] and, with respect to software, an implied warranty of merchantability (i.e., "fit for the ordinary purpose for which programs of that description are used").[82]

For content licensing agreements, a key issue is always whether there is a warranty as to the accuracy of information. UCITA § 404 distinguishes between licensors who are merchants "in a special relationship of reliance with a licensee," who collect and compile previously non-published information, and other kinds of licensors (editors or "conduits" for informational content). Essentially, the former are required to exercise "reasonable care." In determining whether a "special relationship of reliance" exists, several requirements are articulated in the Official Comments to § 404, which comments attempt to capture doctrines already set forth in U.S. case law:

- Licensor possesses "unique or specialized expertise";
- Licensor is in a "position of confidence and trust with the licensee such that reliance on the inaccurate information is justified";
- Licensor is in the business of providing the type of information that is the subject of the transaction;
- Information is personally tailored to the needs of the licensee.[83]

In addition, to the UCITA warranties for accuracy, other duties may be imposed on professionals (lawyers, physicians, etc.) based upon the law of the respective jurisdictions of their practice. The exclusion from warranty under § 404(b)(1) is for "published informational content," which is "informational content made available to the public as a whole or to a range of subscribers on a standardized, not a personally tailored, basis."[84] The policy behind this exclusion is discussed on Official Comment 3.b. Regardless of UCITA or the UCC, claims brought against information and news services have been made under negligence rather than contractual warranty theory, and courts have found First Amendment reasons for not imposing liability.[85]

Published informational content is the subject matter of general commerce in ideas, political, economic, entertainment or the like, whose distribution engages fundamental public policy interests in supporting and not chilling this distribution by creating liability risks. This Act treats published informational content that is computer information analogously to print newspapers or books which are not exposed to contractual liability risks based on mere inaccuracy; treating the computer informational content differently would reject the wisdom of prior law. Creating greater liability risk in contract would place an undue burden on the free flow of information. Once again, UCITA attempts to capture existing law as defined in the courts.[86]

In addition to warranties concerning noninfringement, express warranties, and accuracy of information, UCITA also addresses implied warranties for compatibility with computer systems dependent upon whether the licensor "has reason to know any particular purpose for which the computer information is required . . . ."[87]

Like UCITA, both UCC Articles 2 and 2A provide for warranties from infringement, express warranties and implied warranties of merchantability. Instead of providing for an implied warranty addressing system integration, UCC Articles 2 and 2A each have an implied warranty for a "particular purpose."[88] However, there is a material difference with respect to UCC Articles 2 and 2A pertaining to warranties from infringement. Generally, Article 2 just warrants "rightful" title, and freedom from security interests, encumbrances, and liens.[89] Article 2A, pertaining to leases grants freedom from interference with enjoyment (otherwise known as "the warranty of quiet enjoyment") resulting from "a claim to or interest in the goods not attributable to the lessee's own act or omission . . ."[90] The distinction is that "quiet enjoyment" includes the right to *use* and possess property without infringing upon third parties, whereas good title only refers to infringement as a result of the transfer of ownership (e.g., a transfer of title to a car may legitimately transfer ownership without guaranteeing that the car may be driven on state roads). This is a clear instance in which UCC Article 2A favors licensees. One can imagine litigation over whether Article 2A should apply to a transaction because the licensee argues that a particular use of the licensed information is covered under § 2A-211's warranty of enjoyment. Like UCC Article 2, the CCISG requires transfer of good title (for intellectual property this warranty is limited to infringements of which the licensor knew or should have known),[91] but there is no reference to a warranty for quiet enjoyment.

Like UCC Article 2A, UCITA warrants the "enjoyment" of the licensee's interest from competing interests or claims "which arose from an act or omission of the licensor . . . ."[92] Merchants who "regularly deal[] in information" have an unrestricted warranty of delivery that is free of third party claims for infringement or misappropriation (i.e., the infringement does not have to result from acts or omissions of the licensor). However, this higher standard for certain merchants does not encompass warranties of quiet enjoyment (which, for such merchants, still requires acts or omissions on their part).[93]

However, since UCITA does not limit the warranty on merchants who "regularly deal[] in information" to their infringements resulting from *their own acts and omissions*, it provides better protection in some instances for licensees than Article 2A, but without explicit reference to enjoyment. Consequently, whether UCITA, the CCISG, UCC Article 2, or UCC Article 2A applies can have significant impact on the outcome of a dispute.

To illustrate this difference, imagine that a business subscribes to a database of fine art images from a commercial vendor who regularly sells databases of images from art museums and galleries. The license agreement says nothing about permissible uses of the images, and the initial subscription or access to images does not constitute infringement. The subscribing business uses an image as a background for the Web pages of its Web site. The owner of the image, a museum, informs the subscribing business that it is infringing on the museum's rights by using the image on its Web site. Apparently, the museum had licensed the images to the database vendor for educational purposes only, and the vendor was expressly obligated under its agreement with the museum to place a statement as to the educational limitation in any sublicense agreements, such as the one with the business (but failed to do so). The subscribing business to the database seeks redress from the database vendor for breach of implied warranty. Under UCITA § 401(b) and UCC § 2A-211(a), the database vendor may be held in breach of his warranty for quiet enjoyment. However, under both UCC § 2-312 and the CCISG Article 42, the database vendor is only in breach if it does not have good title, and it is unclear in this instance whether the database vendor's failure to notify the subscribing business of any limitations for "educational purpose" constitutes failure of good title, especially since there are other permissible uses for the database. Since this section of UCC Article 2 has been applied to software,[94] a legitimate issue is raised as to the potential for disparate treatment under the different uniform laws. This disparity may lead to "forum shopping" and greater use of contractual provisions that select the applicable law.

Remedies—Electronic Self-Help and Denial of Access

Although UCITA generally avoids functioning as a consumer protection statute, it does, in its final draft, completely ban the licensor's use of electronic disabling devices or "self-help."[95]

Termination of access for access contracts is permissible upon "material breach" of the agreement or "if the agreement so provides" without any other limitation under UCITA.[96] Other remedies are available under UCITA including damages, cancellation, withholding payments, discontinuing access (for access contracts), repossession of all copies of the licensed information, etc.[97]

UCITA's use of electronic "self-help" (in early drafts where it was permitted) is really a reflection of UCC Article 9, pertaining to secured transactions, specifically the repossession of collateral.[98] However, no analogous provision exists in UCC Article 2 or 2A or the CCISG. The propriety of such action is uncertain under case law. For example, a Minnesota case on the subject discusses claims (or counterclaims) against those invoking electronic deactivation of software; the court basically found that deactivation was appropriate because it comported with license terms to which the parties had agreed.[99] In another case (although unpublished), claims based upon breach of warranty and the Computer Fraud and Abuse Act (CFAA)[100] survived a summary judgment motion to dismiss.[101] Subsequent case law ruled that the CFAA applies not just to hackers but to computer manufacturers as well.[102] In yet another instance, a "drop dead" software device was found "void as a matter of public policy."[103]

Without the blessing of a uniform law such as UCITA, utilization of electronic self-help remedies such software deactivation and "drop dead" devices may subject licensors to liability. Even with UCITA, a significant legal issue is raised as to whether federal statutes such as CFAA or state or federal consumer protection statutes are superseded by UCITA with respect to electronic self-help.

As a kind of self-help remedy, termination of access, as provided for under UCITA § 814, does not have the same stringent requirements for exercise as electronic measures embedded in software under UCITA § 816. However, even the exercise of this remedy may be problematic if it conflicts with federal statutes or state consumer law.[104] Nonetheless, the apparent greater latitude available for the termination of access remedy may propel vendors into exclusively providing content via online services.

CONCLUSION

Content licensing is a complex legal subject necessitating review of the applicable law both creating intellectual property rights and governing contractual agreements and licensing. In addition, consumer protection and other law may impact the transaction. Because of the nature of information transactions to involve a wide array of jurisdictions, choice of law has to be carefully considered with respect to international, foreign, and domestic (both state and federal) law. To add yet an additional layer of complexity, UCITA, a uniform law governing computer information transactions has evoked widespread opposition, and significant disharmony among jurisdictions. Nonetheless, UCC Articles 2 and 2A (and potentially, on a limited basis, the CCISG) may, on an increasing basis, fill some of the void left by UCITA. This is especially true of Article 2A, governing leases, assuming UCITA fails and that states decline to redefine their codifications of Article 2A to exclude information transactions.

Principal among the issues addressed by the various commercial codes and conventions are issues of formation, unenforceability, warranties, and available remedies in the event of breach. Particularly noteworthy (and worthy of scrutiny) are the attempts of such uniform laws to resolve issues surrounding shrink-wrap, click-wrap, mass-market transactions, and the validity of provisions conflicting with copyright law (including the interest of the public in "fair use"); other state and foreign intellectual property rights (which may be broader than, for instance, U.S. federal law); and state consumer laws. In addition, the enforceability and desirability of choice of law and forum provisions, the scope and validity of both implied and explicit warranties, and the potential for abuse and disruption potentially caused by remedies such as denial of access and electronic self-help through means such as disabling devices in software need to be resolved.

NOTES

1. *U.S. v. Wise*, 550 F.2d 1180, 1190 (9th Cir. 1977).
2. *Black's Law Dictionary* 651 (7th ed. 1999).
3. *Id.* at 813.
4. Nimmer, R.T. *1 Information Law*—§ 3.45 (available through WL Infolaw, database updated May 2007) (citing Directive on Legal Protection of Databases, 96/9/EC, O.J. 77 (March 27, 1996)).
5. Nimmer, M.B.; Nimmer, D. 2 *Nimmer on Copyright*, § 8C.04[A][1](August 2004).
6. Cal. Civ. Code § 986 (West Supp. 2007).
7. 2 *Nimmer on Copyright*, *supra* note 5, at § 8C.04[A][2] (August 2004).
8. Harris, L.E. *Digital Property: Currency of the 21st Century*; 1998; 127–129.
9. 3 *Nimmer on Copyright*, *supra* note 5, at § 8D.01[B] (August 2004).
10. *Id.*, at § 8D. [02][A] and [B] (August 2004), and § 8D.06[F][1] (December 1999).
11. Geller, P.E.; Nimmer, M.B. 1 *International Copyright Law and Practice*; France § 1[3] (available through LexisNexis, database updated regularly).
12. 2 *International Copyright Law and Practice*, *supra* note 11 at § 7[1] and [3] (available through LexisNexis, database updated regularly).
13. *NY Times Co. v. Tasini.*, 533 U.S. 483, 121 S.Ct. 2381, 150 L. Ed. 2d 500 (2001).
14. 409 F.3d 26, *cert. den. sub nom. Faulkner v. National Geographic Soc.*, 546 U.S. 1076 (2005).
15. *Id.* at 38.
16. *Greenberg v. National Geographic Society*, 533 F.3d 1244 (9th Cir. 2008), *cert. denied*, 129 S. Ct. 727 (2008) (freelance photographer sued over an electronic collection of past magazine issues in which plaintiff's copyrighted photographs had appeared).
17. 487 F.3d 701 (9th Cir. 2007).
18. Harris, *supra* note 8, at 103–104.
19. The final version of UCITA may be viewed at http://www.law.upenn.edu/bll/archives/ulc/ucita/2002final.htm.
20. Md. Code Ann. Com. Law. § 22-101 (2000), Va. Code Ann. § 59.1-501.1 (2001)
21. Iowa Code § 554D.125 (2004), (transferred from § 554D.104 4. (2002) (act amended indicating intention to consider adoption of UCITA, see 2001 IA HF 2446), N.C. Gen. Stat. § 66-329 (2001), W. Va. Code § 55-8-15 (2001), Idaho Code Ann. § 29-116 (2007), Vermont Stat. Ann. Comm. and Trade, § 2463a (2004), A.B. 7902, 224th Sess. (NY 2001). Similar legislation has been introduced in Ohio and Washington. H.B. 287, 124th Gen. Assem., Reg. Sess. (OH 2001) and SB 6314, 57th Leg., 1st Reg. Sess. (WA 2002).
22. American Bar Association Working Group Report on the Uniform Computer Information Transactions Act ("UCITA") (2002), http://www.abanet.org/leadership/ucita.pdf
23. Sand, S.J. *Validity, Construction, and Application of Computer Software Licensing Agreements*, 38 ALR 5th, 20–21 (1996 and Supp. 2007). See also *Micro Data Base Sys. v. Dharma Sys., Inc.*, 148 F.3d 649, 654–55 (7th Cir. 1998)(applying New Hampshire law), *NMP Corp. v. Parametric Tech. Corp.*, 958 F. Supp. 1536, 1542 (N.D. Okla. 1997)(applying Massachusetts law) and *Systems Design & Mgmt. Info, Inc. v. Vogel*, 1991 U.S. Dist. LEXIS 10079, at *17-*20 (W.D. Mich. 1991)(applying Illinois law).
24. *Micro Data Base Systems, Inc. v. Dharma Systems, Inc.*, 148 F. 3d 649, 654–655 (7th Cir. 1998), *NPM Corp. v. Parametric Technology Corp.*, 958 F. Supp. 1536, 1542 (N.D. Okla. 1997), *Colonial Life Ins. Co. v. Electronic Data Sys. Corp.*, 817 F. Supp. 235 (D.N.H. 1993), and *Dahlmann v. Sulcus Hospitality Technologies, Corp.*, 63 F. Supp. 2d 772, 775 (E.D. Mich. 1999).
25. *Micro-Managers, Inc. v. Gregory*, 434 N.W. 2d 97 (Wis. Ct. App. 1988), *State v. Lockheed Martin IMS*, 2002 WL 99554 (Cal. Ct. App. 2002) (non-published, non-citable).
26. *Micro Data Base Systems, Inc. v. Dharma Systems, Inc.*, 148 F. 3d 649, 654 (7th Cir. 1998) and *RRX Industries, Inc. v. Lab-Con, Inc.*, 772 F. 2d 543, 546–547 (9th Cir. 1985).
27. Uniform Commercial Code Reporting Service, State UCC Variations, Thomson-West, Louisiana 1 (2007).
28. Draft for Approval Proposed Amendments to Uniform Commercial Code Article 2 Sales § 2-103(l) (July 26-August 2, 2002 annual meeting), at http://www.law.upenn.edu/bll/archives/ulc/ucc2/annual2002.htm; Draft for Approved Proposed Amendments to Uniform Commercial Code Article 2A Leases § 2A-103(o) (July 26–August 2, 2002 annual meeting), http://www.law.upenn.edu/bll/archives/ulc/ucc2a/annual2002.htm.
29. U.C.C. § § 2-103(1)(k) and 2A-103(1)(n) (2007).
30. U.C.C. § 2-103 cmt. 7.
31. Okla. Stat. Ann. tit. 12A, § 2-105(1)(West 2007), Okla. Stat. Ann. tit. 12A, § 2A-103(1)(h)(West 2007).
32. Legal Advisory Board, Directorate-General Information Society, European Commission, Agenda Brussels, 7–9, May 18, 2000, http://europa.eu.int/ISPO/legal/en/lab/000518/LAB180500-3.pdf.

33. *2 Information Law*, *supra* note 4, § 12.12 (citing Convention Article 2(a))(available through Westlaw Infolaw, database updated May 2007).
34. Council Directive 93/13/EEC of 5 April 1993 on unfair terms in consumer contracts, 1993 O.J. (L95) 29–34; available online at http://eur-lex.europa.eu.
35. Directive 95/46/EC of the European Parliament and of the Council of 24 October 1995 on the protection of individuals with regard to the processing of personal data and on the free movement of such data, 1995 O.J. (L 281) 31–50; available online at http://eur-lex.europa.eu.
36. Directive 96/9/EC of the European Council and of the Council of 11 March 1996 on the legal protection of databases, 1996 O.J. (L 77) 20–28; available online at http://eur-lex.europa.eu.
37. UCITA § 202(c) (amended 2002). All citations to UCITA herein are to the 2002 amendment. See *supra* note 19.
38. UCITA § 202(d).
39. UCITA § 202 (a), § § 203-206.
40. UCITA § 105 cmt. 6.
41. *ProCD, Inc. v. Zeidenberg*, 86 F. 3d 1447 (7th Cir. 1996) (shrink wrap contract is enforceable under UCC), *Hill v. Gateway* 2000, Inc., 105 F. 3d 1147 (7th Cir. 1997) (followed ProCD), *Klocek v. Gateway, Inc.*, 104 F. Supp. 2d 1332 (D. Kan. 2000) (declined to follow ProCD), *Specht v. Netscape Communications Corp.*, 150, F. Supp. 2d 585 (S.D.N.Y. 2001) (declined to follow ProCd).
42. United Nations Convention on Contracts for the International Sale of Goods (hereinafter CCISG), April 11, 1980, S. Treaty Doc. No. 9, 98, 19 I.L.M. 668 (1980), Articles 11, 12, and 96, available at http://fletcher.tufts.edu/multi/texts/BH775.txt.
43. Hague Convention for Choice of Courts Agreements, concluded June 30, 2005, Art. 3(c)(ii) available at http://www.hcch.net/index_en.php(follow the "conventions" hyperlink; then follow "all conventions"; then follow "Convention of 30 June 2005 on Choice of Court Agreements").
44. Hague Convention, *supra* note 43, Art. 8.
45. *Id.*, at Art. 2(1).
46. *Davidson & Assoc. v. Jung*, 334 F. Supp.2d 1164, 1180–81 (E.D. Mo. 2004), *aff'd* 422 F.3d 630 (8th Cir. 2005)(defendants waived their "fair use" right to reverse engineer by agreeing to the license terms); *Bowers v. Baystate Tech., Inc.*, 320 F.3d 1317, 1325–1326 (Fed. Cir. 2003), *cert. denied*, 539 U.S. 928 (2003)(parties are free to contractually forego the limited ability to reverse engineer a software product under the exemptions of the Copyright Act).
47. *Meridian Project Sys., Inc. v. Hardin Constr. Co.*, 426 F. Supp.2d 1101, 1109 (E.D. Cal. 2006)(to the extent that the license agreement prohibits reverse engineering, breach of contract claim is not pre-empted because the contract protects a qualitatively different right than those protected by the Copyright Act). See also *Information Law*, *supra* note 4, at § 2:18, and 4 *Nimmer on Copyright*, *supra* note 5, at § 13.05[D][4] (August 2005).
48. *Sega Enter., Ltd. v. Accolade, Inc.*, 977 F.2d 1510, 1520 (9th Cir. 1993). The Ninth Circuit has followed its own precedent in regards to reverse engineering cases where no license terms are involved. See *Sony Computer Entm't, Inc. v. Connectix Corp.*, 203 F.3d 596 (9th Cir. 2000). In *DSC Communications Corp. v. DGI Technologies, Inc.*, 898 F. Supp. 1183, 1189 (N.D. Tx. 1995), the Northern District of Texas followed *Sega* in holding that reverse engineering, when engaged in for purposes of studying unprotected aspects of a copyrighted program, constitutes fair use; as in *Sega*, no license terms prohibited reverse engineering.
49. UCITA § 105 (b).
50. UCITA § 105 cmt. 3.
51. UCITA § 111 (including cmt. 2).
52. UCITA § 105 (a) and (e).
53. UCITA § 105 cmt. 1.
54. UCITA § 105 cmt. 1.
55. *Man O War Restaurants, Inc. v. Martin*, 932 S.W. 2d 366 (Ky. 1996.). See also UCITA § 105 cmt. 3 ("Where parties have negotiated terms in their agreement, courts should be even more reluctant to set aside terms of the agreement.").
56. UCITA § 105 cmt. 3.
57. UCITA § 105 cmt. 3.
58. UCITA § 105 cmt. 3.
59. UCC § 2-302 (as amended 2003).
60. *Winter Panel Corp. v. Reichhold Chemicals, Inc.*, 823 F. Supp. 963 (D. Mass. 1993).
61. UCC § 2A-104 (as amended 2003).
62. UCC § 2A-108 (as amended 2003).

63. CCISG, *supra* note 42, Article 4a.
64. See *supra* note 28 and accompanying text.
65. UCC § 2A-106 (as amended 2003).
66. CCSIG, *supra* note 42, Article 1.
67. CCISG, *supra* note 42, Art. 6.
68. CCISG, *supra* note 42, Arts. 2(a) and 4(a).
69. *Restatement (Second) of Conflict of Laws* § 188(2) (1969) and 16 *Am. Jur* 2d § 87 (1998).
70. 16 *Am. Jur 2d* § 88 (1998).
71. Convention on the Law Applicable to Contract Obligations, June 19, 1980, Art. 3, available at http://fletcher.tufts.edu/multi/texts/BH784.txt.
72. *Id.*, at Art. 4.
73. *Id.*, at Art. 5.
74. UCITA § 401(b)(1).
75. UCITA § 401(b)(2) and cmt. 4.
76. UCITA § 401(c)(1).
77. UCITA § 401(c)(2).
78. UCITA § 401(d).
79. UCITA § 401(d).
80. UCITA § 401(e).
81. UCITA § 402.
82. UCITA § 403 and cmt. 3(a).
83. UCITA § 404, cmt. 3(a)(citing *Restatement (Second) of Torts* § 552 (1965), *Murphy v. Kuhn*, 90 N.Y. 2d 266, 682 N.E. 2d 972 (N.Y. 1997), *A.T. Kearney v. IBM*, 73 F. 3d 238 (9th Cir. 1997), and *Picker International, Inc. v. Mayo Foundation*, 6 F. Supp. 2d 685 (N.D. Ohio 1998)).
84. UCITA § 404 cmt. 3(b) (citing *Cubby, Inc. v. CompuServe, Inc.*, 3 CCH Computer Cases 46,547 (S.D.N.Y. 1991), *Daniel v. Dow Jones & Co., Inc.*, 520 N.Y.S. 2d 334 (N.Y. City Ct. 1987), and *Great Central Insurance Co. v. Insurance Services Office, Inc.*, 74 F. 3d 778 (7th Cir. 1997)). See also *Ginsberg v. Agora, Inc.* 915 F.Supp. 733 (D.Md. 1995), *Gutter v. Dow Jones*, Inc. 490 N.E. 2d 898 (S.Ct. Ohio 1986).
85. See *Daniel*, 520 N.Y.S. 2d 334, *Ginsberg*, 915 F.Supp. 733, and *Gutter*, 490 N.E. 2d 898. However, for instance where liability was found based upon futures trading regulations, see *R&W Technical Services Ltd. v. Commodity Futures Trading Commission*, 205 F.3d 165 (5th Cir. 2000).
86. UCITA § 404 cmt. 3(b)(citing *Cubby*, 3 CCH Computer Cases 46,547 (S.D.N.Y. 1991), *Daniel*, 520 N.Y.S. 2d 334, and *Great Central Insurance Co.*, 74 F. 3d 778).
87. UCITA § 405.
88. *Compare* UCC § 2-315 *with* § 2A-213.
89. UCC § 2-312 (1).
90. UCC § 2A-211 (as amended 2003 and 2005).
91. CCISG, *supra* note 42, Art. 42.
92. UCITA § 401(b) and (b)(1).
93. UCITA § 401(a) and (b).
94. *Camara v. Hill*, 596 A. 2d 349, 157 Vt. 156 (Vt. 1991).
95. UCITA § 816(b).
96. UCITA § 814.
97. UCITA §, § 802, 808, 809, 810, 814, and 815.
98. UCC § 9-609.
99. *American Computer Trust Leasing v. Jack Farrell Implement Co.*, 763 F. Supp. 1473 (D. Minn. 1991), *aff'd American Computer Trust Leasing v. Boerboom Intern., Inc.*, 967 F. 2d 1208 (8th Cir. 1992)(this case presented many claims, which unsuccessfully incorporated a variety of legal theories including fraud, RICO conspiracy, extortion, consumer debt protection statutes, trespass, nuisance, violations of the federal wiretapping statute, violations of the Electronic Communications Decency Act, breach of contract, fraud, and theft).
100. 18 U.S.C. § 1030 (2002).
101. *North Tex. Preventive Imaging v. Eisenberg*, 1996 U.S. Dist. LEXIS 19990 (C.D. Cal. 1996).
102. *Shaw v. Toshiba Am. Info. Sys.*, 91 F. Supp. 2d 926 (E.D. Tex. 1999). See also In re AOL, Inc. Version 5.0 Software Litig., 168 F. Supp. 2d 1359 (S.D. Fl. 2001).
103. Franks & Sons v. Information Solutions, 1988 U.S. Dist. LEXIS 18646 (N.D. Okla.) (order clarified in 1988 U.S. Dist. LEXIS 19356 (N.D. Okla)).
104. UCITA § 105(a) and (c).

17 Piracy in Digital Media

Stephanie Walker

CONTENTS

INTRODUCTION

Piracy, when used in discussions of digital media, refers to the unauthorized copying, usage, and often sale or distribution of copyrighted materials (or materials for which some party has other intellectual property rights) in digital form, excluding materials which have been created or are distributed either specifically as fully "open access" materials, or those which have been licensed under some form of "open access" license (such as, for example, that offered by Creative Commons—see http://creativecommons.org/). Also excluded are materials or portions of materials deemed to have been utilized under "fair use" provisions of copyright law (though "fair use" is, in the digital world, sometimes a disputed concept). A full discussion of "fair use" is beyond the scope of this entry; the interested reader is referred to Section 107 of the U.S. Copyright Act (title 17, U.S. Code, online at http://www.copyright.gov/title17/92chap1.html#107), or to a discussion of fair use on the Web site of the U.S. Copyright Office, at http://www.copyright.gov/fls/fl102.html, and the topic has been discussed at length in legal, technical, and library literature.

Any discussion of piracy in digital media must necessarily encompass several major categories of digital media. There are common issues in discussing piracy across various types of digital media, but there are also specific considerations for various categories of media. Media and issues are outlined briefly here, but will be discussed in greater detail in the following section. Major types of digital media for which piracy is an issue include software (including various business applications), audio files/music, and video-based materials, including movies and television shows. Publishers who have ventured into e-books also have concerns about piracy. Indeed, digital intellectual property of any kind, from e-books to online lectures and classes to full-length creative works such as music albums or movies, is vulnerable to piracy. Piracy can be accomplished through a variety of means, from simple copying of material to a portable media device such as a "flash" drive or CD to much more elaborate schemes. Piracy is a global phenomenon; where there are computers, Internet access, and digital materials, there is piracy at some level, though its prevalence varies greatly from one country to another. There are a number of factors that have been identified or posited as contributing to the likelihood of piracy being widespread, including economic factors, cultural factors, and more, along with factors which inhibit widespread piracy. Piracy of digital media can cause economic harm to producers and inhibit development of new software or artistic creations. However, digital hosting, sharing, or transmission of files can also provide a means by which lesser known or previously unknown content creators can gain exposure for their work, and potentially attract future sales. Some well-known musicians (including highly popular bands such as Radiohead, Oasis, and Nine Inch Nails, to mention just a few) have also utilized digital sharing of files or offered portions of their work at low or reduced prices or even at no cost, or have offered to allow users to pay what they wish. There are strong arguments that such sharing increases music fan bases and in some cases frees musicians from restrictive contract agreements.[1] However, as has also been extensively reported in the media, major associations for the software, music, movie, and publishing industries have been taking aggressive (and frequently controversial) legal action to fight back against piracy.

PIRACY OVERVIEW: MEANS, PREVALENCE, AND COSTS

Software

Software can be quite vulnerable to piracy. Common business productivity software, especially, is often purchased by a single person, who then shares his one legal copy with friends, family, or colleagues.[2] There are also numerous sites where unlicensed or illegally copied software is available for free or greatly reduced costs, either by downloading or by placing an order for a copy which is then delivered or sent to the user upon receipt of payment. In some countries, the rates of software piracy exceed 90%—meaning that for every 100 copies of software, only 10 (or fewer) have been legally purchased and installed (see below). The rest are illegal copies, sometimes known as warez.[3] This affects software publishers' revenues, and many publishers claim this leaves a lower level of funds available for investment and research in new or updated software applications. As long ago as the year 2000, Ram D. Gopal and G. Lawrence Sanders (who have written extensively on piracy-related issues) provided some specific and surprising details on the widespread and dramatic problems associated with software piracy. They reported that as early as 1997, the Software Publishers Association estimated that losses due to piracy for business application software in the United States alone reached $2.8 billion, and that worldwide, the revenue losses were estimated at $11.4 billion, and in some countries, including Kuwait, Pakistan, Indonesia, Bulgaria, China, Turkey, Egypt, Bolivia, and El Salvador, the rate of piracy was estimated to approach or exceed 90%.[2] Furthermore, because of a number of unique characteristics, software and other digital goods are particularly vulnerable to piracy: it is expensive to produce the first copy, but inexpensive to reproduce and distribute additional copies, and it is easy to share without impacting the value of the original product. "These idiosyncratic traits of software and related digital products," they write,

> have facilitated their illegal distribution worldwide. Several countries in the world are referred to as "one-legitimate-copy" countries, where one legal copy of a software package is sufficient to meet the demands of an entire nation. The advent of the Internet has amplified the problem. There are numerous warez (colloquial reference to pirated and cracked software) Web sites that permit customers to select from a menu of pirated software up to the 650 MB capacity of a CD. For around $30–$60, payable via credit card, the warez vendor will burn the CD and deliver it to the customer's doorstep.[3]

In the intervening years, there have been some changes in copyright law and there have been efforts by the U.S. government and by professional and business organizations to persuade other countries to take measures to lessen piracy rates, but they have met with mixed success, and in some cases with none. (It should also be noted that the Software Publishers Association merged with the Information Industry Association to become the SIIA—the Software and Information Industry Association.) "Many countries, particularly those without a viable local software industry, find it counterproductive to thwart piracy," Gopal and Sanders argue.

> While the threats of trade sanctions have arm-twisted many countries to enact copyright laws, they are rarely enforced . . . . China, for example, has recently cranked up raids against CD factories that manufacture bootlegged copies of software and confiscated the CD presses (each worth as much as $1 million). The suspicion, however, is these presses are put back into service in government-owned factories to manufacture CDs containing pirated software.[4]

Meanwhile, the costs of piracy continue to rise. In 2006, the Business Software Alliance (BSA) estimated total costs of software piracy worldwide at $40 billion, and reported that piracy rates have discouraged investment by software producers in some countries, such as the Philippines, where the BSA reports a piracy rate of 71% since 2004.[5] However, in the same article, representatives of such major software publishers as Symantec, Alcatel-Lucent, and Adobe Systems are quoted as providing statements to the effect that piracy is a concern, but does not determine strategic direction and is not the primary concern, and that they have made various adaptations to fight piracy and continue to do so.[5] Doubtless, piracy has an effect on revenue and on product distribution and development strategies; how much of an effect seems difficult to determine, and dependent on sources and methods.

Audio Files/Music

Piracy of audio files (especially music) is probably the best known area of digital piracy, due to heavy publicity surrounding court cases and activities by the RIAA and various music companies directed at stopping piracy, and due to statements by many artists on both sides of the file-sharing issues. The issues of pirated music, the services and tools which facilitate music file sharing and downloading, and the industry and legislative responses to such activities, have been widely reported in newspapers, magazines, and professional journals. Certainly not all shared music is pirated music; as aforementioned, many musicians support file-sharing or make portions of their music available for free or at reduced costs via various methods. As well, many users remember the days in the 1970s when the music industry claimed vociferously that home taping was killing music, and tried to discourage people from taping songs from the radio or sharing a homemade mixed cassette tape with a friend. It didn't work, and in reality, music sales grew. "Before the advent of home taping," writes Peter Martin, Economics Editor of the Canberra Times,

> Americans bought around 2.5 long-playing records a year. After two decades of home taping, they were buying 4.5 recorded cassettes and LPs a year. Stan Liebowitz, a Professor of Economics at the University of Texas, argues forcefully that the explosion in recorded music sales wasn't accidental. It was caused by the introduction of the cassette. Before then, music listening was limited to one room in each house—the one with the record player. The advent of the cassette made it possible to listen in the car, while jogging, in the garden, practically anywhere.[6]

Today, one commonly hears stories about the decline of the recorded music industry. In a 2007 Washington Post article, Frank Ahrens reported that

> The music industry experienced the greatest one-year loss in sales of compact discs last year, and rising revenue from songs and albums bought on the Internet failed to offset the consumer flight from CDs. Revenue from CD sales was down 13 percent last year compared with 2005, the Recording Industry Association of America reported yesterday. The drop-off exceeds that of any year during the Napster era of 2001 to 2004, when the file-sharing service and its descendants—such as Kazaa and Grokster—allowed users to download music for free. Meanwhile, online sales of singles from services such as Apple's iTunes were up 60 percent last year. However, because online sales remain a small percentage of all music sales, the industry's total revenue—for tangible and online products—was down 6.2 percent compared with 2005, the RIAA reported . . . . The music industry has blamed piracy for the dive in CD sales and began suing downloaders and the file-sharing services in retaliation in 2003.[7]

A lengthier discussion of legislative responses is included later in this entry; however, it is worth noting at this point that on December 22, 2008, an Associated Press report confirmed that the RIAA

> . . . has abandoned its policy of suing people for sharing songs protected by copyright and will work with Internet Service Providers (ISPs) to cut abusers' access if they ignore repeated warnings. The move ends a controversial program that saw the RIAA sue about 35,000 people since 2003 for swapping songs online. Because of high legal costs for defenders, virtually all of those hit with lawsuits settled, on average for around $3,500. The RIAA's legal costs, in the meantime, exceeded the settlement money it brought in.

This applies to individuals only; there is no current indication that organizations will no longer be sued.[8]

Yet even in claims that music sales are being "destroyed" by illegal downloading, there appears to be conflicting information. Again in the Canberra Times, in response to a request by the Australian Recording Industry Association to have the Minister of Communications enact a "three strikes and you're out" law which would ultimately allow users to be cut off from Internet access if they were caught three times illegally downloading material, Peter Martin reported that according to the Australian Recording Industry Association's own sales figures, in 1982, sales of recorded music were at the level of 29 million units, and have risen steadily; now, ". . . after the most recent five years of sustained CD-burning, intensive file swapping, the introduction of the iPod, wringing by the industry, we bought 99 million— easily an all-time record and an impressive jump of 23 per cent on the year before."[6] This includes not only 44 million units of physical CDs sold in that year, but also sales of new formats for music, including ring tones, digital albums, single tracks, music videos, and more. "The industry," Martin argues,

> will argue that it would be selling even more if it wasn't for illegal downloading. It's hard to prove. Certainly it would be selling less if it turned back the clock to before illegal downloads began. And it is highly likely that illegal downloads stimulate sales. That used to be the function of CD-singles—loss-making samplers that would introduce consumers to new music and new bands. CD singles are all-but extinct. At the start of the decade the industry sold 12 million. It now sells just 2.5 million, having ceded the promotional business to the file sharing sites it claims to hate. Without those sites we would be exposed to a lot less new music and we might buy less . . . . In the face of zero evidence that illegal downloads are hurting music sales or drying up the supply of music, the industry wants the Minister for Communications to empower our ISPs cut us off from the web if it finds we have been downloading something it does not want us to.[6]

Again, we find conflicting reports from various sources on the effects which downloading (whether illegal or not) is having on the music industry, and thus on the effects of piracy on digital music.

However—to return to basics, including procedures and methods, and a brief history of music downloading—how precisely are music files shared? Music files are widely shared in many ways, including peer-to-peer networks which allow users to permit access a portion of their computer; networks and services which host files and allow for storage on their site; file-sharing services which allow users to post a file and notify a friend that the file is there for them to retrieve; or simple e-mailing of compressed files.

In some peer-to-peer networks, one must apply for "membership" to the network. One example of a way to apply for membership might be to offer to share rare or desirable files; this was the model followed by a service known as Hotline. If your application is approved by the site organizers, then you can access other files available through the network. But you must upload the promised files, or permit network members to access a secured portion of a server where these files are located. Many files shared via such services were not illegally obtained or even copyright protected, and often materials were not uploaded to servers owned by the company, but naturally, copyrighted and pirated materials were sometimes available. However, the idea was that responsibility for copyright clearance would fall upon the users, as would liability for infringements. There were many such networks and services that facilitated file sharing, and many persist. Such services, however, never obtained the notoriety or popularity of later incarnations such as Napster.

Napster was started by Shawn Fanning, a young programmer and student at Northeastern University in Boston, MA, and ultimately released by Fanning and two friends, Jordan Ritter and Sean Parker. It was the first well-known (and wildly popular) peer-to-peer file-sharing service. The service was unveiled broadly in 1998. The difference between Napster and many earlier peer-to-peer sites was that users could upload music files to, and download music files from, Napster itself, and the files were hosted on Napster servers. Users liked the cost (free), the ease of use, and the ability to download only songs they liked and create their own compilation CDs. Musicians could also post their own songs on Napster, and many did so in hopes of stimulating growth in their audience; it was a means of marketing their material and hopefully stimulating radio play and future sales. However, music industry players soon launched multiple lawsuits against Napster, claiming that Napster's actions and services were illegal and facilitated theft; certainly, some of the material that users posted on Napster was copyrighted, non-open access material, for which permission to post had not been sought. The RIAA launched a lawsuit against Napster in December 1999. The band Metallica was infuriated that some of their work was circulating on Napster, and shortly thereafter being played on radio stations, even before it was even released for commercial sale. Dr. Dre, Madonna, and other artists soon followed suit. In 2000, A & M Records sued Napster under the Digital Millennium Copyright Act (DMCA). The plaintiff's lawyers contended that Napster's users were directly infringing copyright, that Napster was liable for contributory copyright infringement, and that Napster was liable for vicarious copyright infringement.[9]

Napster argued that it was not liable for users' breaches of copyright, and that it could be used for many noninfringing purposes as well. Many users also contended that file sharing would help sales by allowing users to hear music and decide if they liked it before purchasing. However, the court found Napster guilty on all counts. Napster appealed to the Court of Appeals for the 9th Circuit but lost, though the appeals court recognized that Napster could be used for many purposes which did not constitute or facilitate copyright infringement. Napster was ordered to block access to infringing materials, but found this technologically and practically unfeasible; they shut down in July 2001 and eventually filed for bankruptcy. The service was restarted some time later under new ownership as Napster 2.0, a service offering legal copies of music files for sale, but it has never regained the popularity it had enjoyed as a free service.

Today, there are numerous services which offer legal copies of music. One popular example is the iTunes music store, which sells songs to be played on its popular iPod music players. Microsoft offers a similar service, as do many other companies. There are also still many copyright-infringing sites and services, both better and lesser known; some will be briefly discussed later in this entry. Lawsuits continue as each one is discovered by the music industry, and the music industry and other industries continue to lobby government for changes to legislation and harsher penalties for copyright infringement and theft of intellectual property. But it is difficult to keep up with the sheer volume of such sites, and some are better than others at hiding their activities from unwanted eyes.

Currently, BitTorrent is one popular technology used for downloading files. There are near-innumerable sites which make use of BitTorrent technology, for legal purposes or otherwise. While some such sites (such as the now-defunct Oink) have been shut down, others proliferate. It is impossible, in any practical way, to keep up with the sheer volume of sites which offer material (both legal and in violation of copyright) for downloading. In BitTorrent sites, the site acts as an organizer and indexer, and does not provide files for downloading. Rather, BitTorrent sites offer metadata giving the location of files being offered for downloading, and checksums which can be used to verify the integrity of the file once a download is completed. Pirate Bay, one popular BitTorrent tracker (as systems offering BitTorrent technology, file metadata and locations, and checksums are called), offers indexes to sites where one can download music, movies, games, and software. Pirate Bay has been the subject of repeated legal actions, but the founders assert that they are not participating in copyright violation. Peter Sunde Kolmisoppi, speaking on behalf of Pirate Bay to *Wired* magazine, compared Pirate Bay to Google, saying "We're just a general purpose search engine and torrent-tracking system. You can put whatever you want on the Pirate Bay. We don't participate in how the people communicate with each other. We only participate in bringing the possibility to communicate and share files."[10] Lawyers for various plaintiffs disagree.

As well, some sites are located in other countries, and therefore not bound by U.S. law; many countries (notably Russia) refuse to recognize many international copyright agreements or restrictions. Other sites have relocated to, or are located in, countries where they feel they are less likely to be prosecuted for copyright infringement. Pirate Bay moved to a double-blind distributed server model; the founders provided servers to other people without telling them the content included Pirate Bay, and those people rented space for the material without telling the founders where the servers were.[10]

Another way in which music files (and many other types of files) can be shared is through file-sharing services which allow users to post a file and notify a friend that the file is there for them to retrieve. These function in a manner somewhat analogous to a post office. One person uploads a file to the site, specifying a single person or a group of addressees to whom notification should be sent. One such service is known as YouSendIt. The recipient receives a notice via e-mail, much like the slip that the post office puts in your mailbox to tell you that a large parcel has been delivered to your local post office and is awaiting pickup. The addressee then clicks on the link in the e-mail or goes to the appropriate URL and enters specific information, and then retrieves the file. YouSendIt and similar services are popular as a means of avoiding the file size restrictions on attachments which are common to many e-mail systems. This avoids any issue of posting a file to a server and making it widely available, and there is nothing illegal about offering services such as YouSendIt provides, but there are still no guarantees that the file being sent is legally obtained or copied or perhaps is open access.

A similar type of service allows you to upload a file to a server and leave it there, and then tell other people, by e-mail or by posting a notice on a blog or wiki, or in any number of other ways, to go to a certain link and download the file. Many music blogs provide links to uploaded files, and a wide array of search tools is available for use in locating such blogs. Finally, users can simply compress or zip files and send them directly to friends and colleagues as well. Such services are a highly convenient means of sharing information, and certainly not inherently illegal in any way; the question of illegality would arise only when considering the contents of a file attachment and whether permission to copy or share any materials for which such permission was even required had been granted.

One more way in which material is made widely available is through the creation and sale of pirated, illegal copies of CDs. This is an issue for software and for music alike, and for movies, there are pirated copies of videos, DVDs, or Blu-ray discs. This is an international concern, deeply disturbing to the associated industries—music companies, software producers, film companies, and others. In many countries, one can easily find the latest CDs from popular recording artists selling for a fraction of the price that would be charged in the United States, often before the official release dates. Pirated music or movies are not necessarily of the same quality as those that are legitimately produced: quality can vary widely, depending on a number of factors. Some copies are created from original tapes or files or other original materials that have been leaked to counterfeiters; some movies are copied simply by a person who sits through a viewing of a legitimate copy of a movie in a theater, with an illegal handheld video device, and then sells copies of the resulting movie. Similarly, copies of downloaded audio files may vary. RealAudio files purportedly were of poorer quality than purchased, legitimate CDs; however, with the advent of the MP3 standard, there have been considerable improvements in quality. Many people claim the quality of MP3 audio files remains inferior to legitimate CDs, but the popularity of downloading (whether legal or illegal) attests to the fact that many users consider it adequate. Pirated copies of music and movies are also not limited to foreign countries: one need only walk down the streets of New York (to use just one example) to find street vendors selling CDs and DVDs for far less than one would expect. Some may be legal, but police have frequently cracked down on pirated and counterfeit copies being sold.

Video: Movies, TV Shows, and More

Video sharing sites are among the most popular destinations on the Web. YouTube, Yahoo! Video, and many others offer users the opportunity to upload videos to their servers, and make them publicly available. Many people upload perfectly legal materials—home videos or other materials for which they own the copyright or for which they have obtained permission, or open access materials. Libraries have posted training and orientation videos, promotional videos, and much more on YouTube, sometimes as a way to avoid the bandwidth restrictions in place at their institutions, or simply as a way to ensure widespread distribution of their materials. One simple example of a YouTube video explaining how to use the library catalog of Brooklyn College is located at http://www.youtube.com/watch?v=zLq1BzASsGU; many libraries have posted extensive orientation and training videos. Companies post materials: to provide just one example, ARTStor, an art image database, has posted a video showing people how to register with and use their service at http://www.youtube.com/watch?v=oAIQsiINIAA. Political campaigns and political action groups post videos highlighting the achievements and purported virtues of some candidates, or pointing out the alleged deficiencies of others; the 2008 U.S. Presidential Election saw an explosion of material from individual voters and advocates, action groups, and even the campaigns of the candidates themselves; there were even "YouTube" debates, where during a number of the official debates, candidates took questions from voters who had posted their questions via their own YouTube videos. But there are also many instances of copyrighted materials being posted without permission having been obtained, in violation of the policies of the host site. These can be subject to takedown, but by the time the offending material is removed it may have been further copied or distributed.

YouTube has received a number of takedown notices under the DMCA. Several entertainment companies claimed that the site contained full-length versions or long clips from a number of popular TV programs, and that these had been posted by users who had not obtained permission from rights holders.[11] YouTube was also sued by private individuals such as Robert Tur, who captured on tape the beating of trucker Reginald Denny during the 1992 riots in Los Angeles, and noted that this footage appeared on YouTube without his permission. Interestingly, "Tur did not claim that the site violated the DMCA. Instead, he invoked the 2005 Supreme Court decision in *MGM v. Grokster* and accused YouTube of building a network through the promotion of copyright infringement—i.e., piracy."[11]

However, YouTube had one advantage which had previously been unavailable to Napster. Congress has since added a provision to the DMCA, known as the Online Service Provider Safe Harbors provision (Section 512(c)). Under this provision, YouTube is not liable for the actions of its users if it has posted a clear notice and takedown provision, which indicates that if copyright-infringing material is found and YouTube is notified that material on its site infringes copyright, it will remove the material. YouTube has such a posting, and removes infringing material when it is notified. This has not entirely stopped lawsuits: in July 2008, a lawsuit in the amount of $779 million (USD) was filed against YouTube (owned by Google since 2006) by the Italian broadcaster Mediaset.[12] In 2007, a $1 billion copyright infringement lawsuit was filed against Google itself; the plaintiff was Viacom, which owns MTV networks and Paramount Pictures.[12]

There are also a number of smaller sites that offer content which potentially infringes on copyright (presuming permission to post/distribute has not been sought). In 2007, Michael Arrington, coeditor of the popular Techcrunch weblog, wrote that

> Full length copies of well known TV shows and/or movies are readily available on a number of YouTube competitors. Watch, for example, *The Office* on DailyMotion, *Scrubs* on GoFish, or *South Park* on Veoh (update: GoFish and Veoh have apparently removed the shows . . .). And if searching for the shows on

> these sites is just too much work, there are other sites that aggregate and organize this content, and embed it on their own sites. Watch any episode from any of the 11 seasons of *South Park* on Allsp.com. And new site VideoHybrid is in a class of its own, with dozens of full length movies and virtually every popular TV show. VideoHybrid even gives statistics showing exactly how many times copyrights have been violated.[13]

The MPAA and various entertainment companies and television producers have been watching YouTube, Yahoo! Video, and many other sites, but not all well-known sites have yet been targeted. "It's not clear if the MPAA and networks just aren't focusing on these smaller video sharing sites yet," Arrington also states, "or if DMCA notices are simply being ignored. These sites aren't hiding out and trying to evade the law—they're funded by well known venture capitalists and, in Veoh's case, copyright holders. And GoFish is actually a public company."[13]

As noted, the sale of pirated counterfeit DVDs and Blu-ray discs of movies, whether internationally or locally, is of great concern to the motion picture industry. Companies get no revenue from pirated movies, and many claim that the sometimes poor quality of the counterfeit materials could damage the movie producers' reputations and standards. But again, it appears to be nearly impossible to determine or even estimate with any degree of certitude how much piracy is taking place. The entertainment industry claims that "piracy costs the United States between $200 and $250 billion annually in lost sales, and 750,000 jobs."[14] However, there does not appear to be independent verification of these figures.

Published Works

Creators and distributors of other published works, such as book publishers and authors, are also concerned about issues of piracy. If the published works are normally in electronic form, the potential piracy issues and opportunities are similar to those for other digital materials. If the published works are in print, digitized copies of the original print works are at issue. (Of course, book "piracy" can also be accomplished by making additional print copies of print volumes, via such means as obtaining books and creating copies or additional print runs for sale. However, since this entry focuses on piracy in digital media, this will be excluded from discussion.)

One example of controversy surrounding digitized copies of print works is the Google Print Library Project. When Google announced in late 2004 that it would be working with the University of Michigan, Harvard University, Stanford University, the New York Public Library, and Oxford University to scan all of or portions of their collections (Harvard, for example, provided only a portion of their vast collections, and included no books which were in copyright), the reaction was swift. The Authors Guild, which is the largest society of published writers in the United States, termed this project a "brazen violation of copyright law"[15] and promptly sued Google. The Association of American Publishers (AAP) and their president, former Democratic congresswoman Patricia Schroeder, agreed, arguing that Google's business model for this project was to "take everything you create, for free, and sell advertising around it."[16] Five major publishers (McGraw-Hill Cos., Pearson Education Inc., Penguin Group (United States) Inc., Simon & Shuster Inc., and John Wiley & Sons Inc.) filed suit as well, and the French Publishers Association (representing over 400 French publishers) and La Martiniere Group also filed suit. Google argues that only material which is out of copyright will be freely available to all users; that books which are indexed in this project and which are still under copyright will be held to a limited display of "snippets" of text; and that creation of an index such as they avow the Google Print Library Project to be constitutes fair use under copyright law. As well, they state that any publishers who do not wish their books included can request removal of individual titles by contacting Google. Some authors support the lawsuits, but others have opposed it, arguing that it can only help them if potential readers find it easier to discover their books, even in "snippet" form. Several additional university libraries later joined the Google Print Library Project. The entire project, including other stakeholders in addition to libraries, became known as the Google Book Search project.

On October 28, 2008, Google announced that it had reached a settlement with U.S. publishers and authors, for $125 million.[17] The settlement agreement runs to approximately 300 pages, not all questions have been resolved, and reactions have been decidedly mixed. Harvard University Librarian Robert Darnton asserted that potential limitations on access to and use of materials could make it impossible for Harvard to continue to participate; Paul Courant of the University of Michigan wrote that the agreement changed Google from a "universal digital library" to a "universal digital bookstore" because of fees which would be charged to access more than small portions of books in copyright.[18] Other reactions, positive and negative abound. A discussion of the settlement could be fodder for an entire book in itself, and is beyond the scope of this entry, but it is worth noting that issues of fair use were not resolved for one and all. Writing a legal analysis for the Electronic Frontier Foundation (EFF), Fred von Lohmann asserts that

> . . . this outcome is plainly second-best from the point of view of those who believe that Google would have won the fair use question at the heart of the case. A legal ruling that scanning books to provide indexing and search is a fair use would have benefited the public by setting a precedent on which everyone could rely, thus limiting publishers' control over the activities of future book scanners. Instead, only Google gets to rely on this settlement, and the agreement that makes many concessions that a fair user shouldn't have to make.[19]

By contrast, the Open Content Alliance, a book scanning project sponsored by Microsoft and Yahoo and working with a number of other academic libraries, including libraries from Columbia University and the University of Toronto among others, deals only with books currently in the public domain. Google News Search was also entangled in a lawsuit in Belgium, where Copiepresse, an organization managing a number of Belgian newspapers, was objecting to its use of content, including headlines, in Google News Belgium. The decision in that case went against Google, and Google was ordered to remove Copiepresse articles. Other legal action is still pending.

Another example of a controversy surrounding books and journals is the lawsuit against Georgia State University (GSU), launched in 2008 by the American Association of University Publishers (AAUP). GSU made available, through electronic reserves and its password-protected course management system, digital copies of articles in journals to which they subscribed. The AAUP claims as well that professors linked directly to some of the resources through open Web pages; however, at the time of this writing, it is unclear whether or not specific examples of this latter practice were available. The lawsuit alleges widespread copyright infringement; GSU counters that these practices are permissible under fair use. The case remains before the courts. Many universities and colleges have made deals with publishers to permit e-reserves, either in response to threatened lawsuits or in efforts to avoid them; Cornell University, in particular, was an early player, and developed a set of comprehensive electronic course content guidelines, available online at http://www.copyright.cornell.edu/policy/Copyright_Guidelines.pdf.[20]

LEGISLATIVE FRAMEWORK

Before 1964, laws relating to piracy of intellectual property covered only printed works; in 1964, the U.S. Copyright Office began including software for registration. In 1974, the National Commission on New Technological Uses (CONTU) began to try to determine whether new technology growth was out-pacing existing copyright law, and what protection should be extended; in 1980, the Copyright Act was amended to explicitly include computer programs. In 1990, Congress approved the Software Rental Amendments Act, which "prohibits the commercial rental, leasing or lending of software without the express written permission of the copyright holder. An amendment to Title 18, of the United States Code, was passed by congress in 1992. This amendment, known as Public Law 102-561, made software piracy a federal offence and instituted criminal penalties for copyright infringement of software."[21]

In 1998, the DMCA became law. The reasoning behind this law was that copyright holders needed better laws to protect their rights and combat piracy.

> DMCA provided those tools – and also created a whole new class of crime that causes unfortunate side effects. The Electronic Frontier Foundation (http://www.eff.org) posted *Unintended Consequences: Three Years Under the DMCA* in May. The executive summary argues that DMCA's anti-circumvention provisions (Section 1201) have not been used as Congress envisioned. Congress was after pirates and wanted to ban black boxes, but the provision has been used to stifle legitimate activities. According to EFF's report, Section 1201 chills free expression and scientific research, jeopardizes fair use, and impedes competition and innovation. The summary provides examples of otherwise-legitimate activities made impossible by Section 1201 (e.g., fast-forwarding through commercials before a DVD movie), real-world examples of the harm done by DMCA, including self-censorship for fear of violating the act, scientists unwilling to come to the U.S., the assault on fair use represented by copy-protected pseudo-CDs, and more.[22]

As one media education professor complains, "The DMCA trades the broad fair use doctrine for a series of narrowly defined exemptions"[23] and there is no exemption for media education; theoretically, for every usage of media work for educational purposes, a media education professor would need to research the rights holders and obtain written, explicit permission—a tiresome and lengthy process. Also in 1998, shortly after the passage of the DMCA, the *Sonny Bono Copyright Term Extension Act* was passed into law. This law extended copyright terms by 20 years, causing many materials to take much longer to become available in the public domain.

In May, 2008, the U.S. District Court in Seattle ruled in favor of a man named Timothy S. Vernor who had posted a copy of Autodesk software on the Internet auction site eBay for resale. Autodesk had requested summary judgment against Vernor for contributory copyright infringement, but the Court ruled in his favor, and stated that the first sale doctrine of copyright law applied. The Court found that first sale applied.[24] This is the same principle as that by which used book stores operate: the publisher of a book gets nothing when a reader resells his copy of a novel to a used book store, as the publisher has already benefited from revenues received from the first sale. The case may be appealed, though, and there is much remaining confusion as to what constitutes legal or illegal practice regarding resale of technology. It is confusing, because contributory copyright infringement is essentially that with which Pirate Bay was charged. Pirate Bay charges nothing (and various materials loaded on its servers may not be under copyright, or may be open access), and Mr. Vernor was reselling a piece of software. Yet each was charged similarly, in very different environments. The legislative framework for copyrighted, non-open access software is often still unclear—as is indeed the case for other copyrighted materials. Additionally, the legislative structure in which intellectual property exists and operates varies widely depending on the country in which the property is created or utilized. Laws can be quite different from one country to the next, and international law is not accepted everywhere.

Pirate Bay is currently facing charges that it is "promoting other people's infringement of copyright laws"[10] and there is a movement by Swedish Culture & Justice ministers to give Swedish courts the power to force ISPs to reveal the Internet Providers (IPs) of their subscribers, in order to charge the subscribers themselves for copyright infringement.[25] Pirate Bay continues to face charges in Swedish courts, and people and organizations continue to appeal to the Swedish government to address the issues raised by Pirate Bay, even though they have ostensibly moved all of their servers out of Sweden.

According to some reports, in China, "bootleggers selling 75 cent DVDs dominate 95 per cent of the market"[26] and in an effort to combat this trend (which the studios claim cost them up to $3.8 billion a year), some companies have begun slashing the prices of legitimate DVDS. For example, "Time Warner is reducing the price further, to $1.50 or less, and releasing movies in as little as 15 days after theater runs."[26]

The Software Industry Association of America (SIAA) monitors auction sites, and insists that pirated materials be removed, "either the DMCA's notice-and-takedown process or eBay's VeRO

(Verified Rights Owner) program."[27] Microsoft has launched several lawsuits against vendors using auctions sites to sell pirated software; "suits were brought in the U.S., Germany, the Netherlands, France, and Britain, as well as Argentina, Australia, Belgium, Korea, Mexico, and Poland."[28] FileMaker, Symantec, and other companies have also launched similar suits.

In the European Union (EU), however, the top court (the European Court of Justice) recently ruled, in a dispute between the Spanish music rights holders association Promuiscae and Spain's top telecom operator Telefonica, that EU countries were permitted to refuse to disclose names of file sharers on the Internet in civil cases. Telefonica argued that it was only required to disclose subscriber information in criminal cases, and the court said that "Community law does not require the member states, in order to ensure the effective protection of copyright, to lay down an obligation to disclose personal data in the context of civil proceedings."[29] In Belgium, Copiepresse won its lawsuit against Google news; in Italy, the lawsuit against YouTube proceeds. Requirements of service providers to reveal information about customers vary widely, and legal decisions regarding fair use and copyright continue to vary as well from country to country.

In the United States, various commercial ISPs have been accused of BitTorrent throttling—refusing to allow access to known BitTorrent sites, regardless of whether material being accessed is legal or copyright-free, or of choking access to such an extent as to reduce download speed to a crawl, in hopes of limiting or discouraging user access. ISPs generally deny this practice is occurring, but some are currently under investigation for the practice. Notably, Comcast has been cited for BitTorrent throttling, and the Federal Communications Commission (FCC) asserts that this practice violates Net Neutrality rules. However, it is unclear whether the FCC has authority to actually do anything about BitTorrent throttling, or take any action against Comcast.[30] ISPs have also sometimes been asked to turn over subscriber information, especially when there are allegations of piracy or other illegal practices, and some have complied, while others have refused and taken the issue to court, with varying results. In some countries, notably China, the Internet is filtered, and many sites cannot be accessed; Pirate Bay is apparently among those blocked by the Chinese government.

Universities and colleges have in many cases become perplexed not just about what they can legally provide in terms of electronic course reserves, but also about what professors may do in terms of excerpting materials for their classes. How large a clip from a film can they show to their class, for example, without having to obtain public performance rights? Will they risk being accused of piracy, or potentially charged, if the clip is too large? With so much still before the courts and the government, and many laws and regulations still unclear, many potential users of materials are afraid of risking a lawsuit, and claims of a "chilling effect" are common. In an attempt to alleviate this, the Center for Social Media of the School of Communication of American University has created a set of guidelines for copyright and fair use in documentary film, available online at http://www.centerforsocialmedia.org/resources/fair_use.[31] However, especially in the digital world, the exact parameters of fair use remain difficult to ascertain. A number of organizations which dispute the strong actions of many copyright holders or organizations representing copyright holders claim that not only does strict enforcement infringe upon fair use and cause a chilling effect, it also infringes upon free speech, as writers and artists and filmmakers may be unwilling to risk being sued.[32]

The legislative structure in which music, TV, and motion picture companies attempt to protect their material from unauthorized distribution or piracy is also somewhat unclear. The DMCA seems to lean heavily toward support for rights holders (some claim to the detriment of other stakeholders) but the Online Provider Safe Harbor clause does protect sites and their owners from unauthorized behavior by their users, if they have a clear "notice and takedown" policy. And yet, video and music sharing sites proliferate, and many offer free and easy access to copyrighted material. Is the MPAA not focusing on smaller sites? Or are the sites getting takedown notices, and ignoring them? Why, as aforementioned, are some of the sites public companies, or "funded by well known venture capitalists and, in Veoh's case, copyright holders"[13] if there is fear of legal reprisals? As well, the RIAA in particular has focused strong efforts on targeting universities and colleges, asserting that students are heavy users of pirated music. On May 3, *Wired* magazine noted "universities in the US are experiencing a '20-fold increase' in the number of takedown notices from the RIAA in the last ten days. Indiana University reports 80 notices a day, but they say their traffic hasn't increased significantly over the same time period."[32] There have been mixed responses from the universities and colleges that have been thus targeted; various responses and recent changes to RIAA actions will be discussed in the next section.

Finally, there is also a lack of clarity surrounding access to and distribution of electronic copies of journals, journal articles, and books. Back in the days when all books and journals were published in print form, libraries had long-established and clear policies and procedures. They might vary from library to library—but you knew what to do, whether you were a publisher, a librarian, or a researcher. Books and journals were published and sold in print form. Libraries purchased the materials (whether outright or via a standing order or subscription), and processed them according to whatever procedures they had established. Materials were made accessible to library patrons—again, according to whatever policies the library had established. Some institutions had "open stacks" and patrons could browse; others had closed stacks and library staff would retrieve requested materials. When photocopiers came into existence and became commonly used in libraries, researchers might copy articles or chapters they needed. Hopefully they would follow fair use principles as to the amount of material that could be copied, but whether they did or not, the principles and legal issues were generally fairly clear, and libraries frequently posted signs informing patrons of any restrictions. Interlibrary loan departments receiving article requests knew how much they could copy and send.

In a digital world, the legislative issues are again somewhat murky, and many questions have arisen. Articles in electronic form are much more easily transferred, copied, and shared. This is perfectly legal in many circumstances, but often there are disputes. For example, some licenses for electronic journals and databases refuse to permit libraries to use articles within these databases for interlibrary loan purposes, or they may place a variety of restrictions on the usage of the articles. Some will permit a library to print a copy of an article from an e-journal and use the printed copy to fill the request, but will not permit an electronic copy to be e-mailed. There are many possible permutations of restrictions that can be imposed. Some publishers wish to restrict access to their e-journals and databases by imposing such restrictions as limiting access to a single terminal or a set number of terminals within a library; some publishers refuse to permit remote access. As well, some publishers require institutions, including libraries, to sign agreements which require them to keep the terms of particular licenses confidential—so theoretically, you cannot even compare the deal your library has signed with that signed by another library.

As for e-books, procedures and restrictions vary by publisher here as well. Many publishers place restrictions on how much of a book can be saved, downloaded, and/or printed by a particular user or from a particular computer IP address. Some put restrictions on the number of simultaneous users for each item. Some object to e-books being used by entire classes unless multiple copies or user licenses are purchased. Some attempt to restrict access to e-books or e-journals in course management systems or online course systems such as Blackboard.

Again, one need only look to the aforementioned lawsuit against GSU for one example of a dispute between publishers and an academic institution as to how electronic materials may be used for online courses; many institutions (such as Cornell University and its libraries, for example) have worked out detailed agreements. Publishers are concerned about potential lost sales if their product is copied or shared—and this is much easier to accomplish when the material in question is in electronic format.

The recent settlement in the Google Book Search seems to impose a number of restrictions on access to and usage of works in their database, and reactions have been mixed. Many people have praised the increased overall access to digital copies of books. However, in an editorial written for the online *Library Journal*, Editor in Chief Francine Fialkoff criticizes restrictions that will affect libraries and their patrons:

> One public access terminal per public library building. Institutional database subscriptions for academic and public libraries that secure once freely available material in a contractual lockbox, which librarians already know too well from costly e-journal and e-reference database deals. No remote access for public libraries without approval from the publisher/author Book Rights Registry, set up to administer the program. And no copying or pasting from that institutional database, though you can print pages for a fee. Of course, you can always purchase the book, too. Those are just a few of the choice tidbits from the 200-page settlement in the Association of American Publishers (AAP) and Authors Guild three-year-old suit against Google, drawn from Jonathan Band's "Guide for the Perplexed: Libraries and the Google Library Project Settlement."[33]

Fialkoff emphasizes that the settlement document does include provisions and specifications that outline what libraries are and are not permitted to do, and that in many instances, access to materials should become more widespread. However, she continues by stating that

> ultimately, it is the restrictions that scream out at us from the miasma of details. Even the libraries that were initial partners (or those that become partners) in the Google scan plan don't fare well. They get a single digital copy of each book from their collection—mind you, they've paid for these books already—and can print a replacement copy only if a new copy isn't available at a "fair price." They can allow faculty and students to "read, print, download, or otherwise use five pages of any book in its LDC" (library digital copy set) for books "not commercially available," but they can't use the LDC for interlibrary loan or e-reserves. There are all kinds of potentially costly, nightmarish administrative minutiae, including a security plan and annual audits of usage and security.[33]

Intellectual property and the rights of creators, publishers, vendors, and users are all tied in closely with issues of piracy and other (sometimes arguably) unauthorized or illegal access to and usage of digital materials of all types.

A related controversy is the issue of whether research which is accomplished and published partially or wholly with the assistance of public funding, such as grants, should be free of charge, either immediately or after a period of time. One interesting, and ongoing, case in point is the controversy surrounding the National Institutes of Health (NIH) Public Access Policy. In December 2007, the United States Congress and President George W. Bush authorized the NIH to require that any articles which were a result of research that had received public funding (such as an NIH grant, for example) be deposited, after a period of one year, in the PubMed Central archive. Articles need not be deposited immediately; a lag period of one year from time of publication was granted. This allowed publishers of the scientific journals which had accepted and printed the articles to continue to have sales of their journals, but researchers who were willing to wait a year would ultimately be able to obtain free access to the specific articles containing research results which had been supported by public funding. The American Association of Publishers fiercely opposed the NIH Public Access Policy. Subsequently, on September 9, 2009, Representative John Conyers (then Chairman of the House Judiciary Committee) introduced a bill (H.R. 6845, the Fair Copyright in Research Works Act) "designed to strike down the NIH Public Access Policy and prevent other federal agencies from implementing similar policies. According to the text of the bill, 'No Federal agency may, in connection with a funding agreement, impose or cause the imposition of any term or condition that requires the transfer or license to or for a Federal agency of any right provided under' copyright law."[34] Of course, if the Public Access Policy is struck down, then articles resulting from publicly funded research would be treated as any other articles, and "piracy" of such materials (or any other unauthorized action) would be subject to the same laws and penalties.

In December 2007, the Prioritizing Resources and Organization for Intellectual Property Act (variously shortened and referred to as PROIPA or PRO IP Act or PRO-IP Act) was introduced. In May 2008, it passed the House Judiciary Committee; this is the first step, though, and if the bill fails to pass both the House and the Senate before the end of the year, it would need to be brought forward anew in 2009. The bill is cosponsored by many legislators, including the Chair of the

House Judiciary Committee, Representative John Conyers, Jr. and the Chair of the Subcommittee on Courts, the Internet, and Intellectual Property, Representative Howard Berman. Some of the provisions of PROIPA include massive reforms to copyright and patent enforcement. Statutory damages would be raised, and there would be a lower threshold for prison terms for copyright offenses.

In its initial form, the bill included a controversial rule which allowed litigants to stop treating compilations of copyrighted works as a single work. Thus, a music label could seek many times the normal statutory damages if they sued someone for copyright violation involving copying an album: every song would be treated separately. Similarly, for magazines or newspapers, every article would be treated separately. This rule, Section 104, was removed by Representative Berman before the bill went to the full Committee, after hearings during which proponents of the section argued that allowing works to be treated as compilations devalued individual articles or songs or other portions of a compilation. Opponents of the provision argued that statutory provisions for damages were already high, and that there was no proof any rights holder had ever been injured by insufficient compensation due to the existence of the compilations rule. Accordingly, the provision was removed.[35] The bill also provides for the establishment of an Intellectual Property Enforcement Division in the U.S. Justice Department.

Issues of copyright, intellectual property, piracy, and related issues (such as the issue of whether open access to publicly funded research shall be mandated or optional) continue to be issues of hot debate and ongoing interest to a wide variety of stakeholders.

RESPONSES

Library associations, intellectual property scholars, technology associations, and many others are unified in opposition to the PROIPA legislation and to various provisions of the DMCA. The Library Copyright Alliance, the Computer & Communications Industry Association, and the EFF, among others, have all written to Congress to express this opposition and dispute various claims made (such as claims about how widespread piracy is, and how great its costs are). In an essay on the difficulties created by raising the bar on getting permissions for usages that were clearly previously considered fair use, Peter Decherney argues that "If you are a documentary filmmaker, insurance companies and distributors have raised the permission bar to an impossibly high level. Documentary filmmakers are frequently expected to clear every use of copyrighted and trademarked material even when those uses are plainly allowed by the law."[23] He also goes on to describe the difficulties now inherent when professors wish to show clips of movies for classes; in many cases, they risk being in violation of copyright, though usage of portions of work for nonprofit, educational purposes had generally been considered to fall within the range of fair use in predigital times. As previously mentioned, GSU is battling the AAUP, which claims that copyright was infringed by the way in which GSU made electronic course reserve materials available.

Some ISPs are also unhappy—and not just those who have been accused of BitTorrent throttling. In the United States, to date, ISPs have generally not been held responsible when copyrighted materials are illegally made available via their servers. They must comply with takedown notices, but are not held responsible for the behavior of their users in posting the infringing materials in the first place. But this is not the case everywhere. In February 2008, *Business Week* reported that proposed legislation in Britain could turn ISPs into a different kind of ISP—Internet Service Policemen. ISPs would be held responsible for the behavior of their customers, ISPs who failed to halt illegal downloads would be sanctioned, and ISPs could be compelled to turn over information about customers who infringed intellectual property rights.[36] These proposals are still in their early stages. However,

> the tough ISP stance has already set off alarms. Industry analysts and legal experts warn the proposals could hurt legitimate downloading of Internet content and saddle ISPs already suffering from thinning margins with much higher costs. Equally important, the proposal raises privacy and free-speech issues.

> Under long-standing common carrier principles, communication companies aren't legally responsible for the content of the traffic they carry over their wires and wavelengths even if it's a conversation between robbers planning a crime or somebody downloading child porn. Britain's ISP plan could upend this bedrock principle by turning carriers into cops.[36]

At present, it is not technologically possible to distinguish between legal and illegal content being carried across the ISPs; imposing such restrictions could lead to extensive content monitoring by ISPs, jeopardizing user privacy. And even if the content of every file was monitored, who is to say that a user transmitting a file containing a research article, a scanned chapter of a book, a song, a video, or any other digital material, has not obtained permission to do so?

Universities and colleges are themselves ISPs, to their large communities of faculty, staff, and students. The RIAA has targeted postsecondary educational institutions, claiming that music piracy is rampant among students. Tactics espoused by the RIAA have included sending letters to university administrators demanding that the university reveal the identities of students using computers with various IP addresses; demanding that universities filter their Internet access to exclude peer-to-peer sites; and sending notices to universities asking them to pass along to individual students pre-litigation letters demanding that they pay up to $3000 or face prosecution in court. Since February 2007, the RIAA "has provided some 4000 such letters to more than 150 colleges and universities. The letters offer the students what they call bargain settlements if they act fast, by punching in a credit card number at http://www.p2plawsuits.com."[32] The RIAA is also "backing legislation in states such as Illinois and Tennessee that would require schools that get a certain number of notices to begin installing deep packet monitoring equipment on their internet and intranets."[32] As well, the RIAA had hired a company called MediaSentry to gather information about students and other potential music copyright infringers. MediaSentry would "troll the Internet in search of people who upload large amounts of music. The information that MediaSentry collected became an integral part of the RIAA's aggressive litigation strategy."[37]

However, MediaSentry was the cause of considerable controversy, including allegations by lawyers acting (for students and for some academic institutions opposing the RIAA in court) of invasion of privacy. In a report in the *Wall Street Journal*, Ray Beckerman, a lawyer who "maintains the Recording Industry vs. the People blog and who has represented more than a dozen clients fighting the RIAA"[37] was quoted as citing "MediaSentry's practice of looking for available songs in people's file-sharing folders, downloading them, and using those downloads in court as evidence of copyright violations. He says MediaSentry couldn't prove defendants had shared their files with anyone other than MediaSentry investigators."[37] Other tactics MediaSentry allegedly employed included "scan[ning] for anyone downloading files through LimeWire and Ares."[38] In 2008, the RIAA ended its agreement with MediaSentry, without disclosing its reasons, switching instead to Danish firm DtecNet Software ApS. Officially, the RIAA stood by the methods MediaSentry used, "citing University of Washington research released last year that concluded the company's methodology incorporates ';best practices.' "[37]

Responses (to RIAA actions) from colleges and universities have varied widely. In some cases, the university in question has simply immediately turned over all student information. Of course, this is easier if the student is always using the same computer, i.e., in a dorm room. Even in these cases, though, if there are two students sharing a dorm room, the RIAA has been known to sue both students, though only one may be guilty of infringement. This was the case when, in 2004, the RIAA sued two students attending Portland State University. The University responded to the subpoena from the RIAA by providing personal identifying information about two roommates. It could not determine which student was using the computer in the room, so it provided information on both students. One student, Delaney Conway, was not the person using the computer at all, yet the record company lawyers insisted that she pay $4500. She refused, and determined to fight the case. The case against Ms. Conway was finally dropped, and her roommate paid a settlement fee. Other universities have refused to provide any identifying information, citing either student privacy issues or, in some cases, the impossibility of telling which student was using which computer. The latter is particularly difficult to determine when the computers are public, or available to many people, as is the case in a computer lab or library.

Some universities have fought back on behalf of their own students, or, in one case, on behalf of non-students accused of piracy. The University of Maine's Cumberland Legal Aid Clinic has fought back against the RIAA on behalf of its students. In Oregon, the University of Oregon, with support from the State Attorney General, filed a motion to quash the RIAA's subpoena demanding student identities, explaining that

> it is impossible to identify the alleged infringers from the information the RIAA has presented: 'Five of the seventeen John Does accessed the content in question from double occupancy dorm rooms at the University. With regard to these Does, the University is able to identify only the room where the content was accessed and whether or not the computer used was a Macintosh or a PC . . . The University cannot determine whether the content in question was accessed by one occupant as opposed to another, or whether it was accessed instead by a visitor.'

The AG's motion further argues that "Plaintiffs' subpoena is unduly burdensome and overbroad. It seeks information that the University does not readily possess."[39] The University of San Francisco School of Law has taken action against the RIAA even further, and attorneys-in-training from its Intellectual Property Law Clinic, under the supervision of law professors, are helping clients outside of their own community, pro bono. "They reached out 3000 miles to get involved in *Elektra v. Torres and Maverick v. Chowdhury*, two cases going on in Brooklyn, NY, against non-college defendants."[40] Some additional complications include the fact that the Family Education Rights Protection Act (FERPA) makes it illegal to reveal most private information about students; that IP addresses of individual computers may be dynamically allocated, rather than static, and thus it can be impossible to identify with any certainty who used what computer at what time, and for what purpose; and that IP addresses can be falsified by clever people wishing to hide their identities and actions.

Results to such cases have been mixed. In some cases, various privacy arguments have not held; in others, judges have strenuously objected to some RIAA tactics and actions, even to the extent where some judges have threatened to fine RIAA lawyers. There have been allegations in court that MediaSentry violated privacy and engaged in unlicensed data mining to gather information about defendants or those suspected of engaging in illegal downloading. A defendant named Tanya Anderson filed an amended complaint against the RIAA, seeking to stop them from "continuing to engage in criminal investigation of private American citizens."[41] Again, this case is ongoing; it had begun as a the countersuit to the lawsuit where "RIAA lawyers tried to grill a 10-year-old girl, only later to drop their case for lack of evidence and have the mother sue them for malicious prosecution."[41] In a case involving four Boston University students, the EFF filed a brief in support of the students, who were represented by other lawyers. In that case, the *Boston Globe* reported on April 4, 2008 that

> US District Judge Nancy Gertner ruled this week that the university cannot turn over the names of students to several major record companies that sued for the information until she can do a more in-depth review. The ruling, for the moment, quashes the companies' efforts to hold the students liable for copyright infringement, which could have resulted in thousands of dollars in fines. Laywers who supported the students said the decision would make it harder for record companies to win some 20,000 similar cases they have brought nationwide.[38]

Judge Gertner's ruling forbade Boston University from "turning over names until it shows her its Internet service agreement with students so that she can review what privacy protections, if any, it affords."[38] One recent development in the RIAA strategies is especially interesting. In December 2008, the RIAA decided to cease filing lawsuits against individuals engaging in downloading, though it plans to continue with cases currently filed; instead, it will continue its discussions with ISPs to attempt to reach agreements on file monitoring.

FUTURE DIRECTIONS AND CONCLUSIONS

Illegal downloading of music, software, visual images, videos, films, electronic books, electronic journal articles, or any digital material is theft. But what constitutes "illegal" downloading? This is, in many instances, unclear. "Fair use" has long been part of copyright law, and some allegations of piracy are met with a defense that the copying or usage or sharing falls within fair use. What, in a digital environment, constitutes fair use? There are many complications to various cases, and many debates about the appropriateness of various responses and actions. Arguments have become quite heated on all sides, in the courts and in the popular press. There are many details to be worked out by the courts, and it is likely that these battles will continue for some time.

Many technological solutions have been attempted, including copy protection added to DVDs and CDs; thus far, all solutions seem to have been vulnerable to hacking, and none appears to have succeeded. It may indeed be illegal to circumvent such protective technology; that does not mean it is not possible, and once a means to circumvent the protection is devised, one can be fairly well assured that it will be posted all over the Internet within hours.

Solutions have been proposed that would see ISPs held legally responsible for the content of what is posted on their services; arguments made against this include considerations such as privacy rights or freedom of speech. There have been suggestions that persons caught illegally downloading music or films should lose access to their Internet service; some schools have instituted such policies, and there are proposals being floated to have commercial ISPs follow suit. Alternatively, there have been proposals to have ISPs levy monthly fees on broadband customers and turn these fees over to the RIAA, the MPAA, the SIIA, the BSA, and/or other groups. Fees have been proposed on blank media, such as recordable CDs, as well. In some cases, reducing the prices of software, music, and movies is being attempted; the success of this strategy has not been fully documented to date. The only certainty appears to be that digital piracy (and even the definition of what constitutes digital piracy) will remain a controversial subject for many years to come.

REFERENCES

1. Bands rushing to ditch labels and embrace free: Are the floodgates opening? October 8, 2007 issue. http://www.techdirt.com/articles/20071008/154529.shtml (accessed January 6, 2009).
2. Gopal, R.D.; Sanders, G.L. Global software piracy: You can't get blood out of a turnip. Commun. ACM **2000**, *43* (9), 84.
3. Gopal, R.D.; Sanders, G.L. Global software piracy: You can't get blood out of a turnip. Commun. ACM **2000**, *43* (9), 85.
4. Gopal, R.D.; Sanders, G.L. Global software piracy: You can't get blood out of a turnip. Commun. ACM **2000**, *43* (9), 86.
5. Ramos, M.G.S. Investors discouraged by rampant software piracy, says group. Bus. World October 23 2007, S1–S3.
6. Martin, P. Music industry's false note. Canberra Times (Final Edition) April 1, 2008, 11.
7. Ahrens, F. Despite drop in CD sales, music industry is upbeat. Washington Post (Suburban Edition) April 18 2007, D01.
8. Associated Press. No more file-sharing suits for RIAA. Daily Variety December 22, **2008**, 5.
9. *A&M Records, Inc. v. Napster, Inc.*, 239 F.3d 1004, 1013, 1020 (9th Cir. 2001).
10. Kravets, D. Pirate bay says it can't be sunk, servers scattered worldwide. Wired Blog Network, http://blog.wired.com/27bstroke6/2008/02/the-pirate-bay.html (February 1, 2008 issue, accessed March 28, **2008**).
11. Decherney, P. From fair use to exemption. Cinema J. **2007**, *46* (2), 126.
12. Day, M. Mediaset logs lawsuit vs. YouTube. Daily Variety July 31, **2008**, 6.
13. Arrington, M. Forget YouTube: Go to these sites if you want hard core copyright infringing content. Techcrunch, April 4, 2007. http://www.techcrunch.com/2007/04/04/forget-youtube-go-to-these-sites-if-you-want-hard-core-copyright-infringing-content/ (accessed December 2007).
14. Library Journal Academic Newswire, May 6, 2008. http://www.libraryjournal.com/info/CA6562808.html (accessed May 20, 2008).

15. Mills, E. Authors Guild sues Google over library project. C-Net News.com, http://business2-cnet.com/2102-1030_3-5875384.html?tag=st.util.print (September 21, 2005 issue, accessed November 2007).
16. Bray, H. Publishers battle Google book index: Suit joins action filed by authors over copyright. Boston Globe (online), October 20, 2005. http://www.boston.com/business/technology/articles/2005/10/20/publishers_battle_google_book_index.html (accessed October 2007).
17. Bray, H. Google search starts new chapter with $125M deal. Boston Globe October 29, 2008, B5.
18. Albanese, A. Harvard slams Google settlement; others react with caution. Libr. J. Acad. Newswire, October 30, http://www.libraryjournal.com/article/CA6610115.html?nid=2673&rid=reg_visitor_id&source=title (accessed January 8, 2009).
19. Von Lohmann, F. Google book search settlement: A reader's guide. Electronic Frontier Foundation, http://www.eff.org/deeplinks/2008/10/google-books-settlement-readers-guide (accessed January 8, 2009).
20. http://www.copyright.cornell.edu/policy/Copyright_Guidelines.pdf (accessed August 2008).
21. Hamade, S.N. Piracy and terrorism in the Arab world. Dig. Middle E. Stud. **2006**, *15* (2), 2.
22. Crawford, W. Copyright out of whack II: Control run amok. October 2002, 42–43.
23. Decherney, P. In focus: Fair use and film. Cinema J. **2007**, *46* (2), 119.
24. *Vernor v. Autodesk*, No. 07-1189 (W.D. Wash. May 20, 2008), http://www.scribd.com/doc/3077102/Vernor-v-Autodesk-No-071189-WD-Wash-May-20-2008 (accessed January 8, 2009).
25. *Sweden to Give Courts New Power to Hunt IP Infringers*; Slashdot.org, http://yro.slashdot.org/article.pl?sid=08/03/16/0046228 (March 16, 2008 issue, accessed March 2008).
26. Berretta, D. Pirate tactics. Foreign Policy 2006, 115, 92.
27. Kupferschmid, K. SIIA gets tough on software piracy. Inform. Today **2007**, *24* (7), 52.
28. Kupferschmid, K. SIAA gets tough on software piracy. Inform. Today **2007**, *24* (7), 54.
29. *EU Court Says File Sharers Don't Have To Be Named*; Slashdot.org, http://yro.slashdot.org/article.pl?sid=08/01/29/2025257 (January 29, 2008 issue, accessed January 2008).
30. McCullagh, D. FCC probably can't police Comcast's Bit-Torrent throttling. C-Net News.com, http://news.cnet.com/8301-13578_3-10000821-38.html (accessed July 2008).
31. American University School of Communications Center for Social Media. *Fair Use and Free Speech Resources*; http://www.centerforsocialmedia.org/resources/fair_use (accessed August 2008).
32. *Massive Increase in RIAA Copyright Notices*; Slashdot. org, http://yro.slashdot.org/article.pl?sid=08/05/02/0350227 (May 2, 2008 issue, accessed May 2008).
33. Fialkoff, F. Google deal or rip-off? Librarians need to protect the public interest. Library Journal.com, December 15, 2008. http://www.libraryjournal.com/article/CA6618842.html (accessed January 9, 2009).
34. Peek, R. The battle over PubMed central continues. Inform. Today November **2008**, *25* (10), 17.
35. Anderson, N. Rep. Berman pulls controversial "compilations" rule from PRO-IP Act. Ars Technica, http://arstechnica.com/news.ars/post/20080306-rep-berman-pulls-controversial-compilations-rule-from-pro-ip-act.html (March 6, 2008 issue, accessed October 30, 2008).
36. Scott, M. Anti-piracy plan threaten free speech: Proposed legislation in Britain aimed at curtailing illegal web downloads would turn ISPs into "internet service policemen." Business Week Europe (online), February 22, 2008. http://www.businessweek.com/globalbiz/content/feb2008/gb20080222_084238.htm?chan+globalbiz_europe+index+page_top+stories (accessed February 2008).
37. McBride, S. Changing tack, RIAA ditches MediaSentry. Wall Street Journal, (online), January 5, 2009. http://online.wsj.com/article/SB123109364085551895.html (accessed January 9, 2009).
38. Levenson, M. Music downloaders win round in court. In Boston Globe. April 4, **2008**, A1.
39. Dawson, K. *Arizona Judge Shoots Down RIAA Theories*; Slashdot.org, April 30, 2008. http://news.slashdot.org/arti-cle.pl?sid=08/04/29/1840250 (accessed April 2008).
40. *University of San Francisco Law Clinic Joins Fight Against RIAA*; Slashdot.org, February 29, 2008. http://yro.slashdot.org/article.pl?sid=08/02/29/0120224&tid=123 (accessed February 2008).
41. *Lawsuit against RIAA Tries to Stop Them All*; Slashdot. org, April 1, 2008. http://news.slashdot.org/article.pl?sid=08/04/01/0731209 (accessed April 2008).

18 Information Storage Technologies

Scott L. Klingler

CONTENTS

INTRODUCTION

According to a study by the School of Information Management and Systems at the University of California, Berkeley, the world produced about 5 exabytes of new information in 2002. An exabyte is 2^{60} bytes or approximately 1,000,000,000 gigabytes. All storage capacities in this entry are approximate because storage is measured in a binary (base 2) numbering system. For example, there are 1024 bytes in a kilobyte, not the 1000 bytes normally associated with a kilobyte. A terabyte is 1,099,511,627,776 bytes, not 1,000,000,000,000 bytes. The approximations are much easier to work with. Five exabytes of information is roughly equivalent to 500,000 digital copies of the print collections of the Library of Congress. According to the same study over 90% of this new information was stored on magnetic media. Less than 10% was stored in analog format such as paper or film.[1] In 2007, Horison Information Strategies estimated that more than 12 exabytes of information were created worldwide annually.[2] IDC analysts estimated that in 2006 all digital data totaled 261 exabytes and that by 2011 it will increase tenfold. In 2007 there was less storage available than that required for new data.[3]

Since the advent of the modern electronic computer, information storage technologies, technologies used to keep digital data for current or future use, have experienced rapid improvements. Typically, each new generation of data storage has been smaller in relative size and larger in capacity. In libraries and other information organizations or centers, digitization of materials is relatively new when compared to the long history of books and libraries. This entry discusses information storage technologies that are used in a wide variety of information organizations including libraries.

The scope of this entry is to provide an orientation to some information storage technologies and their utilization. First, specific storage technologies are described: magnetic tape, automated tape, disk, virtual storage, storage networks, and Solid State Disk (SSD). Optical storage (CD-ROMs and DVDs) is only discussed because of its widespread use, but only briefly because the growing consensus is that optical storage is not an archival medium. Then, a storage technologies hierarchy is presented along with a description of how the hierarchy can be used for Information Lifecycle Management (ILM). Media obsolescence and data migration are described next. Last, archival preservation is discussed in the context of the inevitability of media obsolescence.

STORAGE TECHNOLOGIES

Citius. Altius. Fortius. Swifter. Higher. Stronger. Translated into slightly different words this familiar motto could aptly describe the continual improvements being made to storage technologies: faster data movement; larger capacities; more reliable storage of data.

Magnetic media hold over 90% of the world's new information annually.[1] Magnetic tapes and disks are the mainstay of information storage technologies. Inventive minds seeking ways to increase capacity and speed up data transfer rates developed disk arrays, automated tape libraries, and virtual tape and disk systems. The magnetic media discussed in this section include the following: magnetic tape, automated tape, disk, virtual storage and storage networks. Although not magnetic media, SSD and optical disk (CD-ROM and DVD) are also included. SSD is discussed because of its increasing use to supplement and supplant magnetic media. Optical disk is discussed briefly because of its widespread use, but there is a growing consensus that optical storage is not an archival medium. One common thread among all of these media types is the rapid technological changes that are occurring in the data storage industry.

Magnetic Tape

An overwhelming majority of the world's digital information is stored on magnetic tape. Tape technology is the longest lived and most durable magnetic media available today. The ability to read and write more bits of data per square inch (called Areal Density), and therefore the capacity of storage media, has doubled approximately every 18 months. This relates to the magnetic properties of magnetic tapes, disks, and read/write heads—not entirely unrelated to Moore's Law for the number of components on and cost of semiconductors. (Moore's Law, named after its originator, Gordon Moore, predicted that the number of components on an integrated circuit would double approximately every two years for approximately the same production cost.)[4] Tape was originally produced on spools or round reels, but as data densities (and tape capacities) increased and tape thicknesses decreased, the spools were placed in rectangular cartridges. The end of the tape in a single spool cartridge is specially fitted so the tape drive can capture the end and wind it on a take-up spool in the tape drive. Tape cassettes and some tape cartridges have both supply and take-up spools integrated inside.

There are two basic types of magnetic tape: linear and helical scan. Linear tape drives record data longitudinally by track. Linear tape has been produced in 7-track to 576-track or greater formats and in multiple densities. The IBM 3480, 3490, and 3590 (Magstar) cartridges are high performance linear tape for archiving and backup of data with capacities of 200 megabytes (200 million bytes) to 10 gigabytes (10 billion bytes). Each of these IBM formats were, in-turn, once regarded as the industry standard for mainframe magnetic tape and all are still widely used today. The 3490 drive was backward-compatible and could read 3480 tapes. The 3590 (Magstar) drive was also sold into non-mainframe operations. Other manufacturers produced compatible tape cartridges and drives. Digital Linear Tape (DLT) is a proprietary tape format, introduced by Digital Equipment Corporation in the early 1970s, for non-mainframe computer systems (formerly called Open Systems). Quantum purchased the rights to DLT technology in 1994 and in the late 1990s produced the most recent version of DLT, Super Digital Linear Tape (SDLT), an increased capacity variant of DLT. SDLT drives and tapes can store up to 800 gigabytes of uncompressed data. An accepted rule of thumb is that the average compression ratio used for planning purposes is 2:1. Using compression techniques, approximately twice the amount of native or uncompressed data can be stored in the same space occupied by the uncompressed data. Of course, this ratio is dependent on the type of data being stored. For example, some files are already in a compressed form like MP3 audio, JPEG image, MPEG video, and some database files. These files will not compress much. In some cases, the further compressed file would have a compression ratio of slightly over 1:1. It's even possible to end up with a larger file than the original. Another linear tape technology, Linear Tape-Open (LTO) Ultrium, is a linear tape format also developed for non-mainframe systems. Multiple vendors manufacture LTO-compatible drives and media. The most recent version of LTO drives and tapes, the LTO-4, stores a native (uncompressed) 800 gigabytes of data. Currently, the largest capacity linear tape drives and tapes are the proprietary format Sun StorageTek T10000B with a native storage capacity of 1 terabyte. The Sun StorageTek T10000B was announced in July 2008. While all of these are linear tape technologies, they are mostly incompatible with different formats offered by other manufacturers.

Helical scan tape drives record data diagonally on the magnetic tape. This offers faster data transfer rates and increased capacity over linear tape. In the past, helical scan tape has been viewed by some as less reliable than linear tape. Sony's Advanced Intelligent Tape (AIT) and Super AIT (SAIT) are proprietary high capacity helical scan tape formats that are currently available for non-mainframe computer systems. StorageTek offered a helical scan tape drive for mainframe computer systems, known as Redwood, which was discontinued in 2002. DV/MiniDV and Mini (digital video), VHS videotapes (analog), 4 mm DAT (digital audio tape), and 8 mm (digital data) are also common helical scan formats.

Since many corporate policies and government regulations require stored digital data to be preserved in its original and unalterable binary form, storage equipment and media manufacturers produce tape drives and tape cartridges that limit cartridges to a single write. This technology is referred to as WORM—Write Once Read Many. Much of the data saved on WORM technology are infrequently or never read resulting in the technology often being called Write Once Read Seldom-if-Ever or WORSE. Some also call it Write Once Read Never (WORN).

Automated Tape

Magnetic tape is the workhorse of data storage. When it is used manually it is remarkably slow. A simplified description of the manual tape process is as follows: A person is alerted that a tape cartridge needs to be mounted on a tape drive. A person retrieves the cartridge and places it in the designated drive. The tape drive loads the tape, writes to or reads it, unloads and then ejects it. A person then removes the tape and returns it to its designated place in the tape library.

Automated tape libraries speed up tape operations by positioning the cartridges closer together and by replacing the human element with precision robotics. Robots, unlike humans, can perform multiple tasks in rapid succession—almost simultaneously. For example, after a tape has been loaded in a drive, the robot can return another tape to its storage cell or library position on its way to get and load yet another tape. Multiple tasks can be queued for completion by the robot. The robots in automated tape libraries work relentlessly and don't complain about working overtime. There are numerous manufacturers of automated tape libraries, but all libraries perform similarly. Adding autoloaders, devices that allow multiple tape cartridges to be prepositioned in the tape drives, can also speed up the process in an automated library. Multiple cartridges that are to be mounted sequentially, or blank tapes or scratch tapes (used tapes designated for reuse) can be placed in the autoloader by the robot as time permits leaving only the task of removing each cartridge as it is ejected from the drive.

Automated tape library software tracks tape drive status, storage cell occupancy, and the location of storage media in the library. Some automated tape library software is more sophisticated and will move frequently used storage media to library cells closer to a drive based on usage.

Automated tape libraries can hold from fewer than 100 to tens of thousands of tape cartridges and can store a few gigabytes to petabytes of data. A petabyte is approximately 1000 terabytes. Any tape technology or format imaginable can be placed in a library, including VHS, Betamax, or commercial videotapes. Even CD-ROMs and DVDs can be put in an automated tape library. Automated tape library technology is well-suited for large, active digital libraries or digital archival collections.

Disk

Just as for magnetic tape, the size, cost, and reliability of disk storage have improved over time. In 1956, IBM's 5 megabyte hard drive sold for $50,000. Today, 1 terabyte (1000 gigabytes) of disk can be purchased for under $200.[5] In the desktop and small server environments, the price of 100 megabytes (100 million bytes) of disk storage purchased in the early 1990s will buy a terabyte of disk today. The largest hard disk now available has a data storage capacity of 3/4 to 1 terabyte. The cost of storage per gigabyte has decreased steadily. Where once tape storage systems were significantly less expensive than using disk to store data, the cost of disk storage per gigabyte is so close to that of tape as to make the decision to use disk storage for backup very attractive. Unfortunately, large disk capacities in a single disk drive have caused concern because of the potential to lose more data in a single drive failure. That risk is somewhat mitigated since disk drives are becoming more reliable. Another consideration is the limited bandwidth over which to transfer data. While disk drive capacities are growing, the interface bandwidth is growing slower. Adding to the complexity of disk storage, disk drives and disk arrays are manufactured with many different interfaces and protocols.

A disk drive has several rigid disks or platters that vary in size from less than one in. to 3.5 in. Figure 18.1 depicts the physical layout of a disk drive. The platters are coated with a thin layer of magnetic material upon which to record the data and are physically attached to a common spindle that is driven by a motor. The fastest disk drives rotate around the spindle at 15,000 revolutions per minute (rpm). Typical desktop computer disk drives operate at 5400 or 7200 rpm. Read and write heads are placed on both sides of each of the platters and move in unison over the same relative position of the platters. A common misconception is that there is a vacuum inside a disk drive assembly

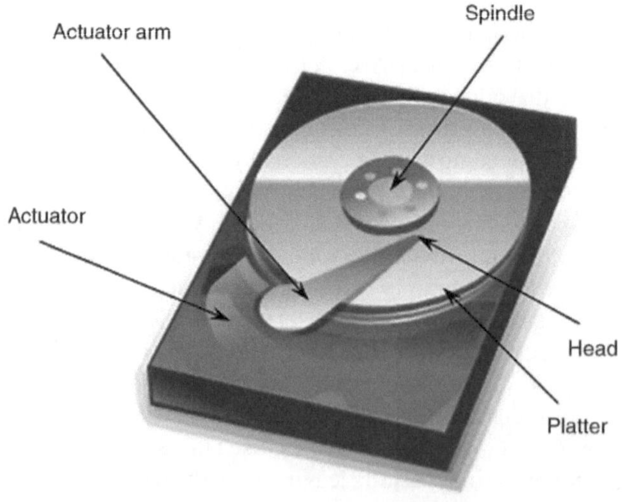

FIGURE 18.1 Physical disk drive layout.

when, in fact, a layer of air is essential to keep the heads above the surface of the platters. If a head touches the surface of a platter it can result in a head crash or failure rendering the drive unusable.

Logically, each platter is arranged in tracks or concentric circles (see Figure 18.2). There are tens of thousands of tracks on a modern disk drive. Tracks are further divided into sectors. Early generations of disk drives had the same number of sectors per track. Disk drives currently manufactured use a method called zoned bit recording that provides more sectors on the longer tracks towards the outer edge of the platter. A cylinder is a set of tracks on all platter surfaces where the read/write heads are simultaneously positioned. One way to visualize a disk drive cylinder is to imagine a hollow cylinder centered on the spindle that goes through every platter surface. The combination of all of the single tracks where the cylinder touches each platter surface is a disk cylinder. The read/write heads are attached to the ends of the actuator arms which are moved by the actuator.

The properties of disk drives are specified through several measurements. Of course, the *capacity* of the drive is the amount of data in bytes that can be stored on the disk drive. Another common measurement is the *spindle or rotation speed* which is the speed of the spindle in revolutions per minute. The *data transfer rate* indicates how much data can be transferred by the drive and controller per second. Other measurements are related: seek time, rotational latency, settle time, and command overhead time. *Seek time* is the average time it takes to find a specific piece of data on the disk with the actuator arm moving between the center and edge of the platters. Seek time is measured in milliseconds. *Rotational latency* is the time it takes to move the platter to the location of a piece of data. Best case rotational latency is when the disk head is right over the data. The worst case rotational latency is when the disk head is just beyond the data location and the disk must go around almost a complete revolution to read the data. *Settle time or settling time* is the time required for the head to stabilize after it has been moved and can read data. *Command overhead time* is the time from when a command is given to the disk drive and the disk drive begins to perform the command. *Access time* is the time it takes to begin retrieving data and is a combination of seek time, rotational latency, data transfer rate, and command overhead time—the latter two being very small contributors. There are also three related density measurements that are a factor of the read/write heads and the magnetic surface of the platters. *Areal density* is the number of bits per square inch that can be stored on the disk drive. *Track density* is the number of tracks per inch measured perpendicularly to the tracks. There are thousands of tracks per inch in today's disk drives. *Linear or recording density* expresses how much data can be stored on an inch of a track. Since each track is a different length and has a different number of sectors, the tracks closer to the outer edge of the platter will have

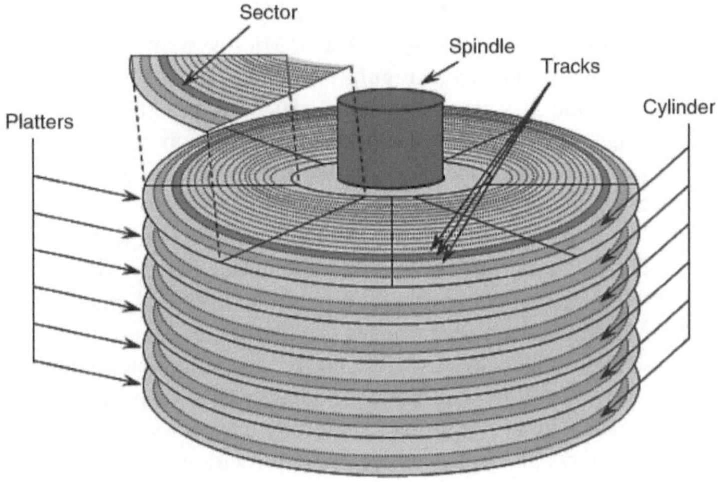

FIGURE 18.2 Simplified logical disk drive.

higher linear densities than those closer to the spindle. Manufacturers usually report the maximum linear density.

Disk drives can be attached to each other in arrays of disks to provide large storage capacities. Redundant Arrays of Inexpensive Disks (RAID) schemes are frequently implemented and can offer increased protection from data loss resulting from failure of one or more disk drives. RAID levels are numbered 0 through 7. RAID 0 distributes data across the disks in the array through data striping (portions of the data are written to different disks) providing improved data access, but not data redundancy. RAID 1 is disk mirroring—providing two physically identical copies of the data on the disks. Mirroring data by itself does not protect against data corruption. Disk mirroring can be accomplished using hardware or software. The hardware implementation of disk mirroring often uses a single disk controller to write the data to two identical disk drives. A software disk mirroring implementation typically sends two copies of the data to different drives, not necessarily simultaneously. RAID levels 2 through 7 combine data striping and parity to allow recovery of data if a disk drive fails. In the case of RAID levels 2 through 7, when a disk drive fails, the drive is reconstructed from the data and parity information that is striped on the remaining drives. Parity is a method used for error detection and, in some cases, error correction. Common forms of parity are even and odd parity in which the bits that make up a byte of data are summed and an additional bit or bits is added to make the sum of the byte plus the added bit(s) either even or odd. This simple parity scheme provides for error detection and would not be used for error correction. More complex parity schemes have multiple parity bits. Some have multiple parity bits located on a drive separate from the original data allowing correction and re-creation of data. There are also combinations of RAID levels, such as 5 + 1, that provide data striping and parity with mirroring. The data striping and two parity of RAID 6 allow recovery from the loss of up to two disk drives in the array.

A newer disk array technology is the Massive Arrays of Idle Disks (MAID). MAID are similar to RAID except the inactive or idle disks are powered down by the MAID controller until they are needed. This can reduce energy consumption and heat generation and will extend the life of the disk drives.

Emerging disk technologies are increasing media capacities further by recording data perpendicularly or vertically in relation to the plane of the disk instead of in parallel or horizontally (see Figure 18.3). This is possible due to improvements in both read/write heads and magnetic material deposited on the platter surface.[6]

Virtual Storage

It is not uncommon for actual disk drive utilization to be below 80% for mainframe disk storage and 60% or lower for non-mainframe disk storage.[7] A Sun Microsystems study found non-mainframe disk utilization even lower at around 30%.[8] Figure 18.4 illustrates the typical levels of utilization in mainframe and non-mainframe disk storage.[7] Tape cartridges are utilized at low levels, too.

Virtualization of storage allows increased utilization of space on both disks and tape cartridges. Storage virtualization can look like either disk drives or tape drives. In virtual storage solutions a collection of disk drives or a combination of disk drives and tape drives appear as disk or tape to the computer system. In some cases the storage devices may be a collection of dissimilar capacities and technologies. Disk is better utilized in virtual disk (see Figure 18.5) because of better disk space management. Virtualized tape, shown in Figure 18.6, uses disk drives as though they were very fast tape drives. Whole tape cartridge images or volumes are stored using only the amount of storage needed instead of using the capacity of an entire tape volume (cartridge), thereby eliminating the empty space at the end of the tape. For example, unutilized space becomes very important when only 200 megabytes of data are written to a 1 terabyte capacity tape cartridge. The controller or computer system reorganizes disk space to optimize utilization. Virtual tape with a tape library, illustrated in Figure 18.7, functions like virtual tape except tape cartridge images are automatically moved to and recalled from physical tape using algorithms or management policies based on

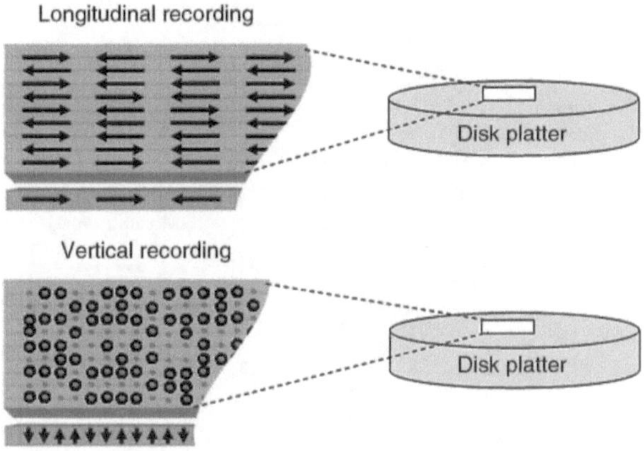

FIGURE 18.3 Longitudinal and vertical recording on disk. (Adapted from *Storage Spectrum*, by F. Moore, Horison Information Strategies, Boulder, CO, 2007.[6])

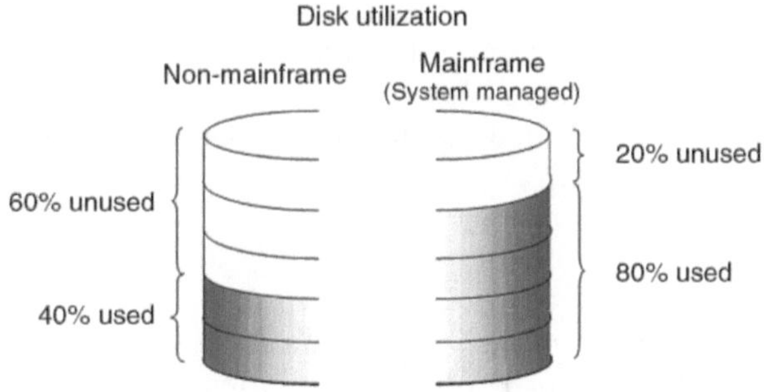

FIGURE 18.4 Disk utilization. (Adapted from *Storage Spectrum*, by F. Moore, Horison Information Strategies, Boulder, CO, 2007.[8])

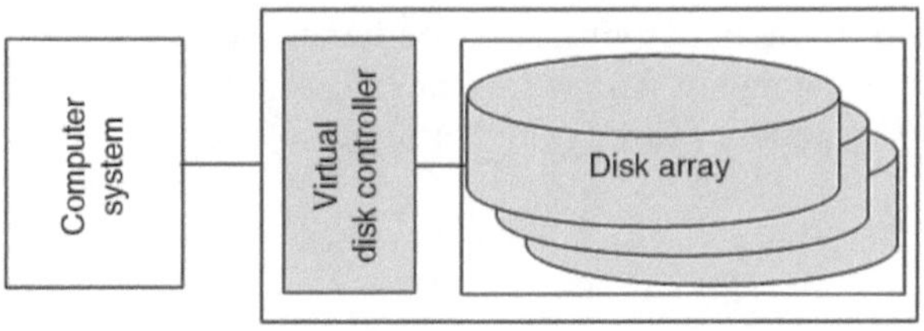

FIGURE 18.5 Virtual disk.

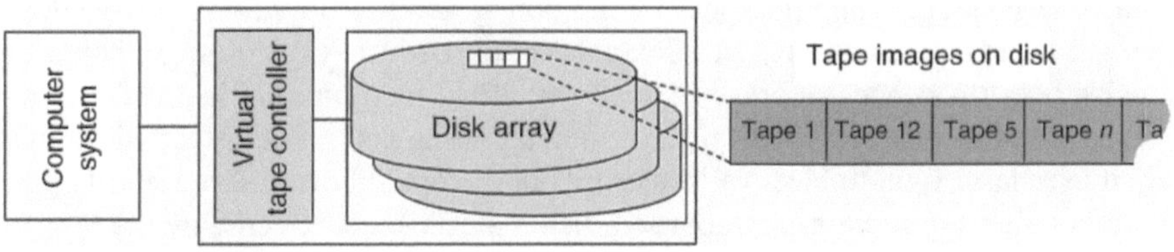

FIGURE 18.6 Virtual tape.

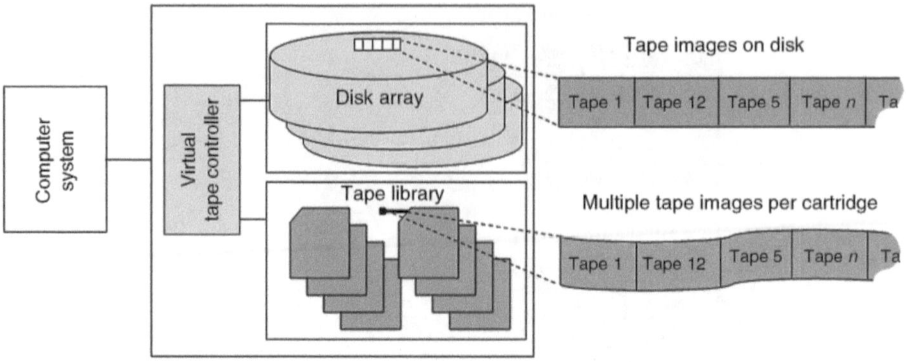

FIGURE 18.7 Virtual tape with tape library.

creation date and time, usage, or need for access of the tape images, or other criterion. These management policies can range from simple ones, such as moving the tape cartridge image immediately from disk to physical tape, or more complex ones, such as retaining the tape cartridge image on disk for 48 hr then moving it to a physical tape cartridge with other virtual tape images in an automated tape library. Tape volumes are moved from disk to tape either directly through the virtual disk or tape controller, or through the computer system.

The power of virtual technology is in the management policies and optimization routines of the software.

SSD

SSD, devices that use semiconductors such as Random Access Memory (RAM), Electronically Programmable Memory (EPROM), or Flash memory instead of magnetic media, is not a new storage technology but has been available in one form or another since the late 1970s. A well-known form of SSD is the USB drive or thumb drive. SSD is faster than tape or disk drives because there are no read/write heads, media, or other parts that must move. The cost per gigabyte of SSD today is only a fraction of its cost in the 1970s and is more widely accepted as a disk replacement, particularly in notebook computers, because of improvements in reliability, physical size, capacity, and speed of the underlying semiconductor technology.[9,10] The largest size SSD currently available is 128 gigabytes. The maximum capacity is continuing to increase. Smaller drives (approximately 64 gigabyte capacity) are being installed in notebook computers to replace the disk drives.

Optical Storage

Optical disk is ubiquitous. As an example of the ubiquity of CD and DVD technology consider this anecdotal story: A computer user calls the Information Technology help desk and asks for a technician to come and repair their computer. It seems the *cup holder* (CD drive) on their computer was broken. Today everyone has one regardless if they know what to do with it. CD-ROM and DVD technologies are everywhere and are useful for short- to medium-term storage; however, there is a growing consensus that optical storage is not an archival medium. Optical disk storage is very similar to other storage technologies that use circular, spinning disks, but instead of using magnetics to store data it uses laser light to burn valleys or pits in the optical disk. Representing data bits, the valleys (and non-valleys or remaining unburned disk material) are detected by the laser reader. Of course, there are other formats of optical media besides red laser-based CD and DVD. Blu-Ray Disc (BD) and Ultra Density Optical (UDO) are two examples of blue-violet laser technology that store much more data per disk (50 gigabytes by BD and 60 gigabytes by UDO) than double-sided, double-density DVD technology (8.5 gigabytes). With the use of the smaller wavelength blue-violet laser and a larger numerical aperture the laser beam is focused more narrowly and records more data in roughly the same amount of space as a DVD. The numerical aperture is related to the refractive index of the medium the light is passing through and the angle of the beam being emitted from the laser—a discussion of which is beyond the scope of this entry.[11] The Optical Storage Technology Association (OSTA) asserts that the media for these advanced technologies will last 50 years and longer.[12] One manufacturer of UDO media and drives states that the media will last over 50 years while another claims a media life of more than 100+ years.[13,14] Two of the reasons optical media is losing confidence is media decay and the rapid technology obsolescence of the supporting hardware, a discussion of which comes later in this entry.

Networked Storage

Thus far we have been discussing storage that is connected directly to the computer system or server, also known as Direct Attached Storage (DAS). There are ways of making storage accessible to multiple users or systems at the same time through networking—a concept introduced in the 1990s. Two common architectures used for networked storage are Network Attached Storage (NAS) and Storage Area Networks (SAN). Don't be confused by the deceptively similar names. Although there are advantages to both, the major difference between NAS and SAN is how the storage is networked. NAS uses the same network as applications (Ethernet), so the data to and from storage devices compete with applications for network bandwidth. There are exceptions. It is possible to use NAS over a SAN. SANs use networks that are solely dedicated to transporting storage data. As would be expected, SANs are normally more expensive to implement. Not only must another network be installed, but the network is also built using expensive Fibre Channel equipment and fiber-optic cable. NAS products are appliance- or server-centric and SANs are storage- or network-centric. These are not opposing technologies. Both SANs and NAS products can be used in the same organization at the same time to access different pools of storage.

Having looked at types of storage, let us now look at combining the types of storage in a storage hierarchy based on technology, cost, and speed of the devices.

STORAGE HIERARCHY AND ILM

Rephrasing a television commercial from the 1960s: "Do you know where your data are?" Most of us expect our data/information stored on our computer systems to always be available. Yet, how much of the data we save is rarely used or never used again? Should the rarely or never used data occupy the same type of storage space as the active data? The storage hierarchy shown in Figure 18.8 provides a tiered framework for storing and managing data. The three tiers of the storage hierarchy are primarily differentiated by technology, cost, and speed of the storage drives and media. The top tier is often referred to as the online storage tier (disk or SSD), the middle tier is the nearline storage tier (automated tape robotics or virtual storage), and the bottom tier or offline storage tier consists of magnetic tape and non-digital or analog data.[15]

ILM (also called Digital Lifecycle Management or DLM) is the practice of using the best tier of the storage hierarchy or best storage technology (as defined by the organization's requirements) to store data. ILM is based on the concept that the lifecycle of information can and should be managed through judicious use of policies governing the utilization of different tiers of storage technology. Management policies are based on items such as the importance of the data, and performance, accessibility, and equipment and media reliability requirements. Data that are frequently used or that must always be available are usually stored on media that have quick retrieval and fast data transfer, such as hard disks or SSD (online storage). Less frequently used data might be stored on slower, less costly technology such as automated or virtual tape systems (nearline storage). Data that

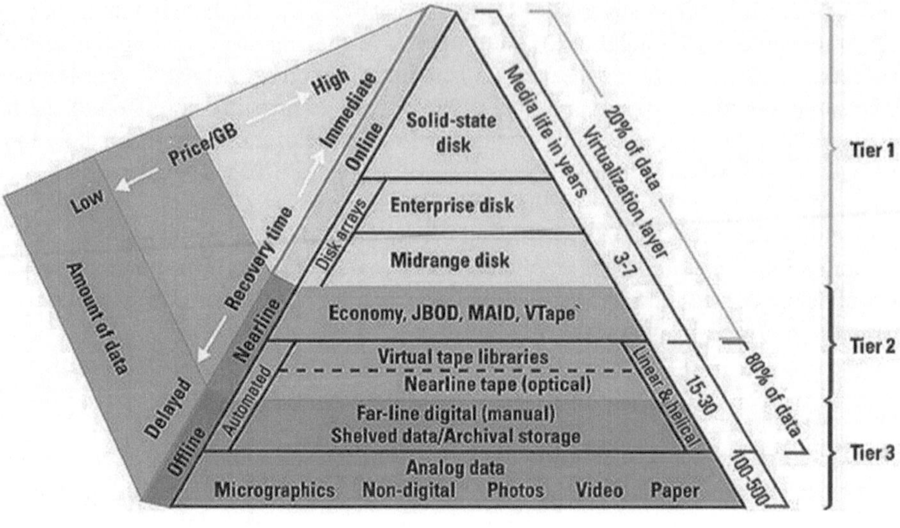

FIGURE 18.8 Storage hierarchy. Acronyms: JBOD, Just a Bunch of Disk; MAID, Massive Arrays of Idle Disks; VTape, Virtual Tape. (From *Storage Spectrum*, by F. Moore, Horison Information Strategies, Boulder, CO, 2007.[15])

are seldom or never used but must be retained might be stored on the least expensive technology available, such as tape systems (off-line storage).[15]

The importance and frequency of use of digital data files change over time. When the importance or usage of data files moves above an established threshold, the files are migrated to a higher tier of storage in the hierarchy. Similarly, when data files are less frequently accessed or when another measure, such as file size, moves below an established threshold, the files are migrated to a lower hierarchy of storage allowing its previously occupied, more valuable storage space to be reallocated for use by a more important or more frequently used file.

MEDIA OBSOLESCENCE, DATA MIGRATIONS, AND ARCHIVAL PRESERVATION

Each new generation of data storage has necessitated migration from earlier generations. In the large-system or mainframe world there were migrations from magnetic core storage to large disk platters to smaller hard disk drives to disk arrays and SSD. There were also migrations from tape reels to tape cartridges to virtual tape. Within generations there have been many improvements in size and speed, as well. These technological advances necessitate the migration of data from obsolete, or nearly so, digital media to current digital media. Table 18.1 shows the lifespans of various media.[16] Note that even though optical disks and SSD have long lifespans given, there are examples of media decay and obsolescence even with those technologies. No digital media lifespan approaches that of archival acid-free paper and film. A discussion on technology obsolescence follows which should also be considered when choosing any storage technology or media.

Technological obsolescence requires ongoing management. This is different from ILM in that the data movement is based on changes in technology rather than the importance, frequency of use, or other characteristics of the data. The following examples provide a glimpse at the potential impact of technological obsolescence.

Between 1987 and 2007, over 5400 CD-ROM and DVD-ROM titles were created and distributed through the Federal Depository Library Program (FDLP). During that period the Federal government worked to provide information via Web sites instead of on CD-ROM or DVD-ROM.[17] While Web site access replaces the optical media and its distribution, it does not obviate issues of media

TABLE 18.1
Media Lifespans

Media		Lifespan
Digital media		
Hard disks	Hard disks consist of magnetic platters that spin at high speeds while reading or writing data. Due to the velocity, hard disks tend to suffer from a physical degradation within a period of three years or so.	3 to 6 years
Magnetic tape	Magnetic tape drives are the chosen backup media for enterprise storage. Their resilience, large storage capacity (1 TB or more) and fast writing speeds make them suitable for archiving large amounts of data quickly.	10 to 30 years
Optical disks	The durability of CD-ROM, CD-R, DVD-ROM, and DVD-R varies due to differences in their protective coating. CD-Rs tend to have a shorter lifespan of 10 years while the denser, more expensive DVDs usually last anywhere from 70 to 100 years.	10 to 100 years
Static memory	Devices like thumb drives and CompactFlash cards utilize static, nonmoving RAM for storing data. Protection from constant wear-and-tear effects also makes them less prone to physical degradation than movable media, giving them a longer product life.	50 to 100 years
Analog media		
Newspaper	Paper is cheap, readily available, and doesn't require electricity. No worms or viruses. Requires the most physical storage space.	10 to 50 years
Archival-grade acid-free paper	Longest life non-digital media.	100 to 250+ years
Film	Longest life for non-digital film storage with a high media cost and low density.	10 to 500 years

Source: *Storage Spectrum*, by F. Moore, Horison Information Strategies, Boulder, CO, 2007.[16]

obsolescence and the necessity for data migration. It merely moves these storage problems to a different location, the hosting Web server disk, and usually ignores archival preservation of the data. Centralization of the archival preservation effort is probably the best approach to migration and long-term availability of the data on these CD-ROMS and DVD-ROMs.

In 1986, the National Archives of the United Kingdom participated in the 900 years anniversary celebration of the Domesday Book of 1086. Using advanced technology, the National Archives created a couple of videodisks with recordings of researchers and other citizens. In 2000, just 14 years later, obsolescence of the hardware and software made the videodiscs unreadable.[18]

Obsolescence and media migration combine to become a technological tightrope. The trick is in balancing the obsolescence of the technology, the decision of which replacement technology is the best for long-term storage, and the migration of the data. This is especially important if we intend to preserve our digital data for any long duration. According to Baker, Keeton, and Martin, "the goal of long-term archival storage applications is to preserve and provide read access to stored content for however long it is valuable—perhaps forever."[19]

Today, there exists no digital media that allow 100-year digital preservation.[3] Even 100 years is considerably less than the goal of forever. Unfortunately, there aren't any certain predictions as to what a 100-year digital preservation technology might be or when it might be developed, if at all. In fact, data saved to digital archival media 50 years ago and not migrated to newer technology exist in one, and maybe more, of the following four general states:

1. The data are unreadable because of deterioration of the media. Even if they are maintained in optimal conditions, disk platters and magnetic tapes deteriorate over time. Bad disks or tapes usually mean bad data at best and unrecoverable data at worst.
2. The equipment needed to read the media/data is no longer available. Rapid advances in technology result in frequent equipment replacement. Even if the media from 50 or 100 years ago were still usable, it would be difficult or impossible to find the equipment required to read it. This inevitable obsolescence of storage technology requires that data be migrated to newer technology before the older technology becomes obsolete.
3. The software application to read and use the data is no longer available.
4. The file format cannot be understood.

The third and fourth states above are interrelated. If the software that created the files on the media is no longer available, the files may not be usable because the file format is unknown or cannot be used by any other software.

Rhyno suggests there are five processes or systems pertaining to digital archival preservation. They are: 1—Data migration; 2—Emulation; 3—Encapsulation; 4—Multiple strategic backups; and 5—Universal coding.[20] While all of these are important, migration and multiple strategic backups deal directly with our topic of information storage technologies. We have already discussed data migration so let us move on to talk about data backups.

Just like the realtor's anecdote about location, there are three things that are key to preserving digital data: backup, backup and backup. Some information professionals think you can never have too many copies of your data. But, there is a real cost associated with that philosophy. Nothing comes without a price. While backups must be made often, they also must be made strategically. The primary strategic questions are: What data do you have, how is it organized, and what needs to be preserved? In other words, you must manage your data.[21] Of course, it is critical to maintain a copy of essential and archival data. This is necessary because of the very real threat of someone modifying or deleting your data, perhaps even inadvertently by someone in your organization. There are many backup schemes to consider, such as taking daily backups or at other time intervals, replacing the backup media periodically, and using software and hardware capabilities to provide copies, snapshots, or mirrors of your digital files,[22] A reliable process must be established and tested to help assure up-to-date copies of your data. Also, there are other methods that can be used with backups to maintain the integrity or trustworthiness of your files. One such method is the Lots of Copies Keep Stuff Safe (LOCKSS) project.

Stanford University and Sun developed, tested, and implemented the LOCKSS project, a process that checks distributed copies of files to insure they are not being modified or deleted by unwanted processes or events. Systems with a copy or copies of a file are polled to determine if the file is the correct version. Files with requests for replacement or deletion are checked against versions of the file at other repositories. A majority of repositories, with a weighted history of correct poll responses, determine which version is correct and should be retained.[23,24]

There are several models or frameworks that address the whole digital archival process. The OAIS reference model is one such framework developed to manage and preserve space research data. OAIS not only provides the framework or reference model, it provides information on how an archive will successfully meet its mission to preserve and provide access to data. The introductory guide to the reference model explains three distinct levels or parts of the model. The first part is about the environment in which an OAIS archive operates. The second describes the functions or services that the archive uses to accomplish its job of preserving and making available data. The third part describes the objects or information packages that go through the archival process. The model can be envisioned as a high-level road map or plan. It gives general direction or the big picture, but not the specifics of how to get there or to implement an archive.[25]

The Open Archives Initiative Protocol for Metadata Harvesting (OAI-PMH) was developed from the OAIS reference model and gives specific guidelines and best practices for implementing and managing an archival repository.[26]

CONCLUSION

Technologies change, and like many other technologies, information storage technologies have undergone rapid changes. The results have been smaller physical sizes, faster data movement, greater capacity and more reliable data storage. Magnetic media, primarily tapes and disk drives, are the mainstay of digital storage. With storage capacities of up to 1 terabyte on a tape or disk, it is possible to store more data than ever before. In fact, it has been estimated that the 261 exabytes that comprise all of the world's digital data in 2006 will increase tenfold by 2011. This enormous amount of data will require more automation and better management capabilities, including better management of data migrations caused by media obsolescence, technology to support long-term preservation for 100 years or more, and improved backup and data protection methodologies. Whatever digital storage technology you choose, it will eventually become obsolete, need to be replaced, and require data to be migrated to a new technology. Though analog paper and film can be preserved for hundreds of years, at present there is no digital storage technology that will allow 100-year preservation. It is unknown what a 100-year digital preservation technology might be or when it will be developed, if at all. What is known is that information storage technologies are getting better and more advancements are yet to come.

ACKNOWLEDGMENT

I wish to acknowledge the assistance of Fred Moorc, President, Horison Information Strategies and his significant lifetime contributions to the knowledge and understanding of storage technologies.

REFERENCES

1. http://www2.sims.berkeley.edu/research/projects/how-much-info-2003/ (accessed July 2008).
2. Moore, F. *Storage Spectrum*; Horison Information Strategies: Boulder, CO, 2007; 9.
3. *The Diverse and Exploding Digital Universe: An Updated Forecast of Worldwide Information Growth through 2011*; IDC: Framingham, MA, March 2008. http://www.emc.com/collateral/analyst-reports/diverse-exploding-digital-universe.pdf (accessed July 2008).
4. Moore, G.E. Cramming more components onto integrated circuits. Electronics **1965**, *38* (8), 114–117.
5. http://www.pcmag.com/article2/0,2817,2184654,00.asp (accessed July 2008).
6. Moore, F. *Storage Spectrum*; Horison Information Strategies: Boulder, CO, 2007; 16.
7. Moore, F. *Storage Spectrum*; Horison Information Strategies: Boulder, CO, 2007; 29.
8. Preimesberger, C. 10 biggest storage challenges. eWeek October 8, **2007**, 26.
9. The solid state of storage. *PC Mag*. November 6, **2007**, *26* (21), 19.
10. Beard, B. The TCO of solid-state drives. Network World January 16, **2008**, 25.
11. http://www.blu-ray.com/info/ (accessed January 2009).
12. *Critical Data Retention: Archiving Reference Data and Business Critical Information*; Optical Storage Technology Association, 2008. http://www.osta.org/technology/pdf/ archive.pdf (accessed January 2009).
13. http://h18006.www1.hp.com/products/quickspecs/11931_na/11931_na.pdf (accessed January 2009).
14. http://www.plasmon.com/archive_solutions/media.html (accessed January 2009).
15. Moore, F. *Storage Spectrum*; Horison Information Strategies: Boulder, CO, 2007; 46.
16. Moore, F. *Storage Spectrum*; Horison Information Strategies: Boulder, CO, 2007; 42.
17. Gano, G.; Linden, J. Government information in legacy formats: Scaling a pilot project to enable long-term access. D-Lib Mag. **2007**, *13* (7/8). http://www.dlib.org/dlib/july07/linden/07linden.html (accessed July 2008).
18. *Your Data at Risk: Why You Should Be Worried about Preserving Electronic Records*; The National Council of Archives: Richmond Surrey, U.K., 2005. http://www.ncaonline.org.uk/materials/yourdataatrisk.pdf (accessed August 2008).

19. Baker, M.; Keeton, K.; Martin, S. *Why Traditional Storage Systems Don't Help Us Save Stuff Forever*. http://www.hpl. hp.com/techreports/2005/HPL-2005-120.pdf (accessed August 2008).
20. Rhyno, A. *Using Open Source Systems for Digital Libraries*; Libraries Unlimited: Westport, CT, 2004.
21. *Your Data at Risk: Why You Should Be Worried about Preserving Electronic Records*. The National Council of Archives: Richmond Surrey, U.K., 2005. http://www.ncaonline.org.uk/materials/yourdataatrisk.pdf (accessed August 2008).
22. Moore, F. *Storage Spectrum*; Horison Information Strategies: Boulder, CO, 2007; 40.
23. Lesk, M. Collections and preservations. In *Understanding Digital Libraries*; Elsevier: San Francisco, 2005; 248–258.
24. Reich, V.; Rosenthal, D.S.H. LOCKSS: A permanent Web publishing and access system. D-Lib Mag. **2001**, *7* (6).
25. Lavoie, B.F. *The Open Archival Information System Reference Model: Introductory Guide*; Digital Preservation Coalition Technology Watch Series Report 04-01, 2004. http://www.dpconline.org/docs/lavoie_OAIS.pdf (accessed August 2008).
26. Lagoze, C.; *The Open Archives Initiative Protocol for Metadata Harvesting*. http://dx.doi.org/10.1108/07378830310479776 (accessed August 2008).

BIBLIOGRAPHY

1. Friedlander, A. The National Digital Information Infrastructure Preservation Program: Expectations, realities, choices and progress to date. D-Lib Mag. **2002**, *8* (4). http://www.dlib.org/dlib/april02/friedlander/04friedlander.html (accessed August 2008).
2. Jackson, J. Digital longevity: The lifespan of digital files. Digital preservation Coalition **2002**. http://www.dpconline. org/graphics/events/digitallongevity.html (accessed August 2008).
3. Jantz, R.; Giarlo, M.J. Architecture and technology for trusted digital repositories. D-Lib Mag. **2006**, *11* (6). http://www.dlib.org/dlib/june05/jantz/06jantz.html (accessed August 2008).
4. Jantz, R.; Giarlo, M.J. *LOCKSS*; Stanford University Libraries. http://www.lockss.org/lockss/Home (accessed August 2008).
5. Lynch, C. Canonicalization: A fundamental tool to facilitate preservation and management of digital information. D-Lib Mag. **1999**, *5* (9). http://www.dlib.org/dlib/september99/09lynch.html (accessed August 2008).
6. Moore, F. *Storage: Infinite Disruption*; Storage Technology Corporation: Louisville, CO, 2001.
7. Rosenthal, D.S.H.; Robertson, T.; Lipkis, T.; Reich, V.; Morabito, S. Requirements for digital preservation systems: A bottom-up approach. D-Lib Mag. **2005**, *11* (11). http://www.dlib.org/dlib/november05/rosenthal/11rosenthal.html (accessed August 2008).
8. Rothenberg, J. *Avoiding Technological Quicksand: Finding a Viable Technical Foundation for Digital Preservation*; Council on Library and Information Resources: Washington, DC, 1999. http://www.clir.org/pubs/reports/rothenberg/pub77.pdf (accessed August 2008).
9. Rothenberg, J. What the library is doing. The Library of Congress. http://www.digitalpreservation.gov/library/ (accessed August 2008).

19 Electronic Records Preservation

Robert P. Spindler

CONTENTS

WHAT IS AN ELECTRONIC RECORD?

Electronic records can include information originally created in an electronic format or information created in hard copy or analog format and subsequently digitized through use of digital imaging, optical character recognition technologies or direct analog to digital conversion for audio and video information. Electronic records can include digital image files, audio files, and geographic information system files, as well as the more common documents produced by word processing or e-mail. Compound documents may include several of the above technologies in a single product.

An electronic record is a form of information produced in the course of an event or a routine activity by an individual or an organization. Electronic records are created and retained as specially designed output from an information system or personal computer. They may be selected for retention because of their comprehensiveness and portability, or they may not be retained since other forms of the same information (e.g., hard copy, microfilm) may be preferable for personal use, acceptable as evidence, or retained at lower cost. Most files output or saved from information systems or personal computers are not electronic records. Simple backups or downloads usually do not contain sufficient contextual information to authenticate and verify the accuracy of the content.

CONNECTING CONTENT AND CONTEXT

For many years, archivists have struggled to understand and explain the difference between an electronic record and electronic information or data. Archivists have made important distinctions between the content of information and its context, since elements of the context of information creation can certify the accuracy and authenticity of information content. Context is also essential for documenting how and when content changes have been made over time. Electronic records must have content *and* context in order to successfully document an event, an activity, or a business transaction.

Electronic publications often serve as a record of an activity or transaction since they generally are presented with attributions of authorship and sources. They are often granted the status of records because authors, footnotes, and bibliographies provide sufficient context for readers to have confidence in the accuracy and authenticity of the information presented. Other electronic information products such as specially formatted output from a large information system are intended to serve as records, but often that output does not include the contextual information necessary to be considered a reliable record of an event or transaction. Much of the research in electronic record preservation has centered on identifying the contextual information necessary to authenticate the content of an electronic record.

HISTORY OF ELECTRONIC RECORDS PRESERVATION

Early attempts to collect and preserve electronic records began with the establishment of data libraries that supported social science research in the 1970s. These projects generally concentrated on retaining textual and numeric research data in a software-neutral form for access and reuse. Although certain quality control tests were conducted and error logs were investigated, it was the mission of these institutions to retain data derived from specific research projects to facilitate subsequent reuse and research replication. Contextual information about the data was generally retained in separate data dictionaries and codebooks that described the functions and allowable data values for specific pieces or fields of information.

The U.S. National Archives received its first accession of electronic records in 1970, and this function was retained through several reorganizations to this day. The current Center for Electronic Records physically acquires and preserves similar textual and numeric data sets produced by government agencies and does not generally retain electronic records in software-dependent formats. The center and its predecessors developed and implemented standards for selecting and accessioning electronic records, conducting quality control tests, and establishing public access services.

As more electronic content was produced with the advent of inexpensive personal computers and mainframes in the 1980s, computing professionals established facilities and routines for system backups. They generally did not consider long-term retention other than content presented in computer output microfilm (COM). Quite often the labeling on COM sets and backup tapes was not sufficient to describe the scope or age of the content within. At the end of this decade, electronic reformatting technologies such as digital imaging became widely available and many institutions implemented imaging to reduce paper record storage costs. Legal standards were soon established for certifying the accuracy of digitally reformatted content, but these standards generally focused on documenting imaging and quality control as routine business practices for litigation defense support.

In the 1990s, e-mail and word processing became essential features of business and personal life, and questions of the accuracy and authenticity of electronic records began to emerge in highly publicized cases of fraud and unauthorized system security breaches.

The landmark 1993 U.S. Court of Appeals decision in Armstrong versus Executive Office of the President highlighted the challenges of increasing government efficiency through technology, while retaining citizens' right to access government records. The decision confirmed that, in this case, e-mail did constitute a federal record that must be retained or destroyed in accordance with the Federal Records Act. The court also ruled that printouts of White House e-mails did not contain sufficient structural and contextual information to authenticate the communications and that the electronic version of the communications needed to be retained to satisfy federal record-keeping requirements.

In the next few years, widespread availability of digitization technologies and production of electronic books, journals, and indexes enabled the development of digital libraries that presented locally owned and commercially licensed content made accessible through the Internet. The opportunity for development of digital libraries caused librarians to take a more active interest in preservation for electronic publications and establishment of metadata standards to support Internet resource discovery.

In 1997, the Virginia Institute of Technology (Virginia Tech) initiated the first university program to accept electronic theses and dissertations. This project highlighted the similarities between librarians' concerns for preserving electronic publications and archivists' interest in preserving electronic records. Theses and dissertations are simultaneously considered a publication and also a student record. As a result of the Virginia Tech initiative and in response to the 1996 Research Libraries Group report *Preserving Digital Information*, archivists and librarians began to study the relationships between content and context. Academic research on these issues emerged with the support of the National Historical Publications and Records Commission, a division of the National Archives and Records Administration that made electronic records research a funding priority throughout the 1990s.

Beginning in 1989, Luciana Duranti of the University of British Columbia published a series of articles in the journal *Archivaria* that examined the applicability of diplomatics for modern record-keeping practices. Diplomatics was a mid-seventeenth-century discipline that viewed the character and content of individual documents, as well as the organizational context of document production, as indicators of document integrity and authenticity. Intrinsic and extrinsic elements of particular documentary forms are cataloged and used as tests of authenticity. Extrinsic elements included medium used, script, language, seals, and annotations, while intrinsic elements included document protocol, actions taken or described in the document, and final responsibility for the content.

In 1994, Duranti's interest in diplomatics and document authentication led her and colleague Terry Eastwood to establish the "University of British Columbia (UBC) Project," which defined requirements for creating, handling, and preserving reliable and authentic electronic records in active record-keeping systems. Duranti and Eastwood then collaborated with the U.S. Department of Defense to set standards for record management system requirements that are used for certifying software vendors and their products. A planned second phase of the UBC Project was intended to address long-term preservation of inactive electronic records, but the scope of such a project required a larger and more diverse research team. As a result, the "InterPARES" (International Research on Permanent Authentic Records in Electronic Systems) project was launched in 1999, an international research initiative in which archivists, computer engineers, national archival institutions, and private industry representatives are working to develop the theoretical and methodological knowledge required for the permanent preservation of authentic electronic records.

Meanwhile, in 1991, the Minnesota Historical Society hosted the "Working Meeting on Research Issues in Electronic Records," which established the National Historical Publications and Records Commission's research agenda for electronic record keeping. In response to this agenda, Richard Cox of the University of Pittsburgh launched a three-year project, beginning in 1993, to establish functional requirements for record keeping in electronic information systems. The project also investigated several related topics including organizational culture, technical capabilities of existing software, utility of standards and policies for satisfying archival requirements, and evaluation of technology and policy strategies.

The "Pittsburgh Project" resulted in dissemination of lists of functional requirements for record keeping, an analysis of tactics for implementing record-keeping systems, and an assessment of variables that may affect the use and implementation of those systems. In 1994, project consultant David Bearman of *Archives and Museum Informatics* and project researcher Ken Sochats asserted that the functional record-keeping requirements could be converted into formal requirements for specific metadata elements. In 1995, Philip Bantin of Indiana University began testing this model in an analysis of records systems for the Financial Management Support and Enrollment Services offices at that institution. More recently, the Australian Recordkeeping Metadata Research Project has made substantial progress on metadata issues, with record-keeping metadata standards issued by the Commonwealth, Victorian, and New South Wales governments between 1998 and 2001.

The search for electronic record preservation strategies also led to attempts to enunciate the competencies necessary for archivists, records managers, and librarians to participate in electronic preservation projects. In 1993, the Committee on Automated Records and Techniques of the Society of American Archivists established the Automated Records and Techniques Curriculum Project, and this work also resulted in the publication of a special edition of *The American Archivist* dedicated to electronic records case studies.

In addition, two annual national conferences on electronic records preservation were established. Cohasset Associates, a Chicago consulting firm established the MER: Managing Electronic Records conference in 1993, which serves as a forum for presentation of emerging preservation strategies that is widely attended by corporate and government organizations. In 1999, Arizona State University established ECURE: Preservation and Access for Electronic College and University Records, which focuses on the special record-keeping needs of colleges and universities and is dedicated to the critical analysis and dissemination of practical strategies for electronic records access and preservation.

Advanced technologies are now being applied to electronic preservation issues. In 1999, the Distributed Object Computation Testbed project was established as a partnership between the U.S. Patent and Trademark Office, the National Archives and Records Administration, and the San Diego Supercomputer Center. The test bed was developed to store complex documents on geographically distributed data archives and systems using the processing power of supercomputers to implement preservation strategies from the digital library, archival, and computing communities. Brewster Kahle's Internet Archive established technology that finds and stores snapshots of websites from around the world in an attempt to comprehensively document the Internet. Both the National Archives and the Library of Congress recently implemented programs to collect archival snapshots of selected web pages, but none of these projects have fully addressed the potential software incompatibility and proprietary markup issues related to websites.

At the beginning of the twenty-first century, implementation of new technologies continues to advance as archivists, librarians, and technology professionals continue to work on several aspects of the electronic records preservation challenges. The Government Paperwork Elimination Act of 1998 and the Electronic Records and Signatures in Global and National Commerce Act of 2000 (known as E-Sign) mandated widespread implementation of electronic government services and electronic signatures. Similar legislation has been adopted in several state governments.

Interactive Internet technologies and the advent of virtual reality and desktop videoconferencing are increasing the complexity of electronic record keeping. Electronic content is increasingly software dependent so that long-term retention of products may require continued support for obsolete software and operating systems, active migration of records to new software, or development of emulation hardware and software. Increasing data storage capacities and the fast development and implementation of proprietary compression and backup technologies are hastening the obsolescence and increasing the incompatibility and interoperability of data storage media and systems. Widely distributed computing facilities and multi-institutional or multinational collaborations make retention and appropriate deletion of electronic records much more difficult than before. Distributed computing places greater pressure on policy, procedure development, and oversight since file maintenance is no longer centralized.

PRESERVING ELECTRONIC INFORMATION

Thirty years of work in acquiring and retaining electronic content has not resulted in complete solutions for electronic record preservation, but researchers have started to identify and catalog the major barriers to successful electronic record keeping. A successful electronic record preservation strategy requires attention to seven major challenges (Table 19.1).

Storage Media

Storage media is often used to support backups, off-line storage, or distribution of electronic content. These challenges have received a great deal of attention in the popular media and the professional literature, but they are the easiest to manage since estimates of the reliable shelf life of various media and interoperability of certain media formats like CD-R are available. We can project the expected physical life of the media, track changing format standards for media players, and plan to move the information to new media based on the expected physical shelf life and availability of new formats and players. The generally accepted reliable shelf life of compact discs for example is 5–100 years, depending on several factors, including manufacturer, production materials used, storage conditions, level of use, etc. However, many experts believe that physical obsolescence and incompatibility and noninteroperability of storage media occur faster than the media can physically degrade. One source reports that media players are becoming obsolete every 2 to 5 years. It is critically important to move electronic content from old storage media to newer media before the old media player fails or becomes unavailable. Commercial data conversion and recovery services and some archival repositories retain and maintain some obsolete media players, but the usable life of this equipment is unknown.

TABLE 19.1
Seven Challenges of Electronic Record Preservation

Challenge	Example
1. Physical degradation of storage media	CD does not read anymore since the recording surface has been degraded by air pollutants.
2. Physical obsolescence of storage media	5.25 inch floppy disc does not fit in CD-R drive.
3. Incompatibility/noninteroperability of storage media	One manufacturer's DVD disc will not play in DVD players produced by a different manufacturer.
4. Software, operating system, or encoding incompatibility/noninteroperability	New software release will not run file from old release.
	New software release opens old file, but contents are corrupted.
	Software is not compatible with operating system.
	Product designed for display with one Internet browser does not look the same in a different browser.
	Proprietary backup software and storage format not compatible with new release or other backup software.
	Proprietary codes from HTML editing packages do not convert to XML.
5. Human error/vandalism	Accidental or malicious deletion.
	Website is vandalized.
6. Backups and snapshots	Backups lost or overwritten.
	Wrong files backed up.
	Incomplete snapshot: Video server backed up, Web server not backed up.
	Snapshots of different servers not contemporaneous.
7. Metadata	Insufficient context to verify source and authenticate content.

Software and Document Encoding Issues

Software incompatibility or noninteroperability results in files that will not open at all or documents that are corrupted and must be repaired if possible (usually through comprehensive manual reentry or manual editing and correction of content). The two major strategies for addressing software incompatibility and noninteroperability issues are known as emulation and migration.

The emulation concept proposed by Jeff Rothenberg of the Rand Corporation involves writing new software that mimics the appearance and functionality of old software. Recently, experts in this area have challenged emulation, suggesting that efforts to write emulation software solutions have not resulted in exact reproductions of appearance or function. Approximate reproductions of appearance or function might be sufficient for some record-keeping applications, provided that the information content is accurate and can be authenticated.

Migration tends to be the more widely accepted preservation strategy, in which files are regularly saved to new releases of the same software as they become available or are converted to new software produced by another manufacturer. Migration is not always successful, as conversion programs do not always have full "backward compatibility" that results in "clean" conversions between old and new software releases. Many electronic document managers are selecting ubiquitous software packages, relying upon a large "installed base" in the hope that that the manufacturer will survive for many years and that future releases will have complete backward compatibility. In addition, software manufacturers have not always supported "interoperability" by including reliable conversion programs for moving files between their own products and those of other manufacturers without corruption. Manufacturers are increasingly including backward compatibility and limited interoperability into their product designs, but, for now, migration cannot be considered a fully reliable preservation strategy.

When electronic information is encoded to support electronic publication or display on the Internet, the selection of encoding syntax or language is an important issue. Although standards for encoding electronic documents such as SGML (standard generalized markup language), HTML (hypertext markup language) and XML (extensible markup language) have been established, software developers have not always complied with the standard, introducing proprietary codes in their document-editing software. These are codes that may be misinterpreted or cannot be read by other software packages, resulting in data-processing errors or changes of document color or formatting. Color or formatting may not be essential elements of a textual electronic record but may be significant components of multimedia presentations that incorporate graphic or video content. Proprietary codes can sometimes be replaced with their standardized equivalents but the appearance and functionality of the document could be changed as a result.

Human Error and Vandalism

Human interaction with electronic information presents important challenges for electronic records preservation. At a very basic level, the culture of technology transfer, adoption, and implementation makes preservation more difficult since our faith in new technology sometimes precludes critical analysis of its effectiveness. Those who would champion system design changes that support effective record keeping often are met with resistance since record keeping is often not valued as highly as fast implementation. One result of our culture is that although sound data management practices are available, systems managers for large enterprise level systems or users of desktop personal computers do not always rigorously follow them.

Electronic records can also be intentionally compromised through actions of individuals who have access to the content or have learned to circumvent data security measures. Records can also be corrupted as an intended or unintended consequence of a computer virus infection. An individual can compromise any encryption and security technology with access to specialized expertise and high-performance computing facilities. Often, violations of system security are undetected until damaged content or other evidence of the violation is subsequently discovered. These threats to electronic record keeping can be minimized through the retention and maintenance of off-line backups.

Backups and Snapshots

Reliable backups of electronic records are essential for successful short-term retention since data can easily be deleted or corrupted with the push of a button. Redundancy has always been a very successful preservation strategy and inexpensive data storage can make redundancy cost effective. Backups are intended to support recovery from disasters, system failures, or human error, but many data losses can be attributed to improperly managed backups.

Backup failures can result from of improper backup system configuration, lack of quality control, failure to migrate the content before backup system failure, incompatibility with new backup systems, or simple operator command error. Most backup systems use proprietary compression and software that has a very high degree of noninteroperability and incompatibility. In addition, the rapid increases in storage technology capacity and the increasing frequency of new backup software releases make long-term survival of backups unlikely. Accurate file backups must be made to a nonproprietary and compressionless environment, and they must be effectively migrated or emulated for successful long-term preservation. The timing and scope of backups should be established in advance, rigorously followed, and tested for accuracy and completeness. Many experts believe that given the risks, backups are not effective for record keeping. Migration of records to a specially designed record-keeping system or redundant live-server storage may be more reliable, especially for long-term retention.

Specially designed downloads of websites known as "snapshots" are key issues for preserving a record of an interactive website since their scope and timing are critical for capturing a "record" of the changing content. Many complex Web products are now stored on a number of different servers to facilitate efficient retrieval and display. The products themselves only exist for a moment in time on a patron's computer screen, but the sources of the content are distributed. All the source files of product components must be included in the snapshot so that the record of the website is complete, unless certain parts of the content are deemed "nonrecord," such as the chat room attached to an electronic college course.

The timing of snapshots is also important since an interactive website may have certain components that are static and others changing. Snapshot timing needs to be established with some attention to the rate and nature of change in the website. Ideally, the snapshot of the record components across a series of servers should be done contemporaneously so an accurate record of the components and their relationships can be retained.

Metadata and Retention of Context

The essential difference between data or electronic information and an electronic record is that electronic records have information content *and* specific pieces of contextual information that authenticate or explain the content. This contextual information is called "metadata."

In general, metadata tags or "metatags" are elements of textual information inserted into the header of an electronic file to enable automated searching, retrieval, and use of the content within the file. In the record-keeping context, metadata is divided into two types: descriptive metadata and administrative metadata.

Descriptive metadata is generally used for describing or indexing the content of an electronic file. The Dublin Core is recognized as the most commonly used structure for presenting metadata, and the development of this standard and other descriptive metadata standards is driven by the need to support Internet commerce or other business applications. Dublin Core does contain elements that support retention of some but not all of contextual information necessary for effective record keeping.

Administrative metadata addresses more of the contextual information necessary to understand the accuracy and authenticity of the content. It also can facilitate management and preservation of the electronic file over time. Administrative metadata can document such attributes as document version, software and hardware requirements, location and availability of other metadata such as software documentation, location and availability of backup files, and migration history. Establishing and implementing administrative metadata standards would greatly improve the prospects for electronic record preservation in the future.

BIBLIOGRAPHY

General Research Reports

1. CENSA, *Titanic 2020 (Press Release and Research Report)*; 1999. http://www.censa.org/html/Press-Releases/Titanic2020.htm (accessed February 9, 2001).
2. Research Libraries Group, *Preserving Digital Information: Report of the Task Force on Archiving of Digital Information*; Research Libraries Group: Mountain View, CA, 1996. http://lyra.rlg.org/ArchTF/tfadi.index.htm (accessed February 9, 2001).

Electronic Signatures

1. National Archives and Records Administration, *Records Management Guidance for Agencies Implementing Electronic Signature Technologies*; 2001. http://www.nara.gov/records/policy/gpea.html (accessed February 9, 2001).

Encoding/Markup Standards

1. World Wide Web Consortium Homepage with links to HTML standard and verification service. http://www.w3.org (accessed February 9, 2001).

Metadata and Authentication

1. Dublin Core Metadata Initiative Homepage. http://purl.org/dc/ (accessed February 9, 2001).
2. Gilliland-Swetland, A. In *Introduction to Metadata (Presentation Abstract and Bibliography)*. ECURE: Preservation and Access for Electronic College and University Records, Tempe, AZ, October 7–8, 1999; http://www.asu.edu/it/events/ecure/ecure1999/gilliland-swetland-present.html (accessed February 9, 2001).
3. InterPARES Project Homepage. http://www.interpares.org/ (accessed February 9, 2001).
4. State Records, New South Wales, *New South Wales Record-keeping Metadata Standard (draft)*; 2001. http://www. records.nsw.gov.au/publicsector/erk/metadata/rkmetadata.htm (accessed February 9, 2001).
5. University Archives, Indiana University Bloomington Libraries, Indiana University Electronic Records Project, *Metadata Specifications*; 1998. http://www.indiana.edu/~libarche/metadataspecifications.html (accessed February 9, 2001).

Migration and Preservation Cost Analyses

1. Balough, A. The true cost of electronic documents. Rec. Inf. Manag. Q. **1998**, *14* (1), 1.

Recordkeeping System Design Projects

1. San Diego Supercomputer Center, Distributed Object Computation Testbed Homepage. http://www.sdsc.edu/ DOCT/ (accessed February 9, 2001).

Software Migration/Emulation Strategies

1. Bearman, D. Reality and chimeras in the preservation of electronic records. D-Lib Mag. April **1999**, *5* (4). http://www.dlib.org/dlib/april99/bearman/04bearman.html (accessed February 9, 2001).
2. Rothenberg, J. *Avoiding Technological Quicksand: Finding a Viable Technical Foundation for Digital Preservation*; Council on Library and Information Resources: Washington, DC, 1999. http://www.clir.org/pubs/reports/rothenberg/contents.html (accessed February 9, 2001.)

Web Site Preservation

1. National Library of Australia, *Safeguarding Australia's Web Resources: Guidelines for Creators and Publishers;* 2001. http://www.nla.gov.au/guidelines/2000/webresources.html (accessed February 9, 2001).
2. Spindler, R. In *Preserving Web-Based Records*. ECURE: Preservation and Access for College and University Electronic Records Conference, Tempe, AZ, 1999. http://www.asu.edu/it/events/ecure/ecure1999/spindler-presentation. html (accessed February 9, 2001).

20 Data and Data Quality

Thomas C. Redman, Christopher Fox, and Anany Levitin

CONTENTS

THE NATURE OF DATA

Of the triumvirate of concepts *data, information*, and *knowledge* at the conceptual foundations of the information age, data is by consensus regarded as the most basic. Like the other two, however, the concept of data is not well understood. Although it is basic, the notion of data is surprisingly multifaceted and complex. One reason for this is that the word is used in so many different ways in conversation. For example, one hears comments such as the following:

1. The data on this graph prove my point.
2. The data point is six.
3. See, here are the data we need.
4. I cannot get the data out of the database.
5. When you get some data like that, you know it is time to do something drastic.
6. The data misled us because they were wrong.

Some of these uses of the word treat data as tangible measurements, as in comments 1 and 2. In other uses, the term seems less tangible, but is a motivator for action, as in comments 3 and 5. Some uses seem to treat data as something abstract or conceptual, as in comment 2, and others seem to deal more with physical representations for data, as in comments 1 and 4. In some cases data are treated as factual, and in others, like comment 6, the data may not be correct. This variety of uses of the word data raises many questions about what data are, and how we should understand the term.

A thorough treatment of data quality must be based on a clear understanding of the meaning of the term data. In developing this understanding in this section, we first explore the data life-cycle, the sequence of phases through which data pass as they progress from creation to storage and use. Data's life-cycle model is, in effect, a formal way of looking at "the social life of information."[1] The life-cycle model helps account for the different uses of the term data because, at different stages in their life, data change in subtle ways. Based on the lifecycle, we consider definitions of data and select the definition that encompasses the most critical features and advances our objective of quality assessment, control, and improvement.

The Data Life Cycle

As noted, the data life cycle is the sequence of activities that create and populate a *data bank* in which data are stored, find and extract data from a data bank, and manipulate and use extracted data (Figure 20.1).[2] The data life cycle includes the following activities:

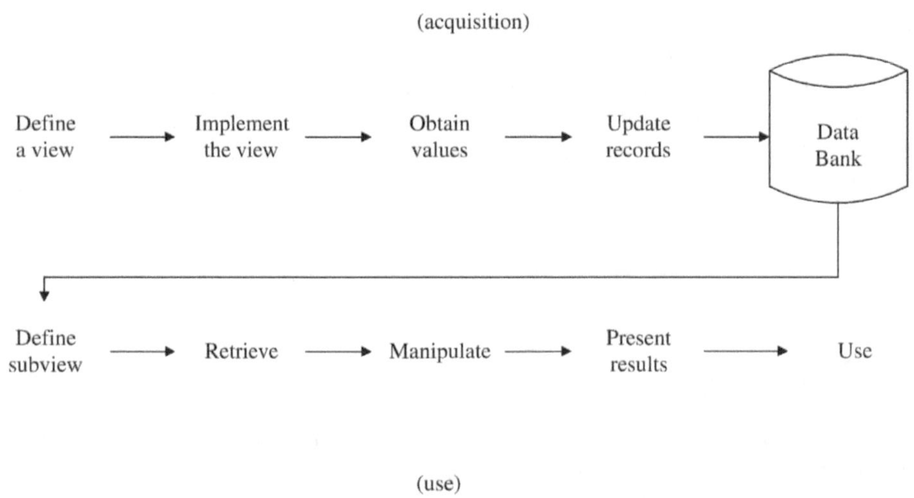

FIGURE 20.1 The Data Life Cycle. (© Navesink Consulting Group.)

1. *Defining a model*—The portion of the real world to be described by the data is defined, and the detailed mechanism of description is specified. This involves defining entity types, their attributes, and attribute domains, all discussed further below.
2. *Implementing the model*—An empty data bank, or physical data repository, is created. In a small organization, the data bank may be a sheet of paper, and implementing the model may involve laying out columns for recording data. For electronic databases, the model must be described in the language of the database management system.
3. *Obtaining values*—Data values are collected for the part of the world modeled in the data bank. Common ways of obtaining data values are measuring, surveying, observing, and copying another source. Poor data values are a principal issue in data quality and are discussed throughout this article.
4. *Storing values*—Data values are recorded in the data bank according to the conventions established in the data model.

   The result of these *data acquisition* activities is data stored in a data bank. Subsequent *data usage* activities put the data to use in the following ways.
5. *Define a view*—Typically a data customer or application requires only a subset of the data available in a database. A *view* describes the portion of the data to be used. By convention, in quality management, we call those who use data, products, or services *customers*. Technologists often refer to the same people as *users*.
6. *Retrieve*—Data (values) of interest are retrieved from the data bank.
7. *Manipulate*—Data are processed in one or more of four principal ways: classification, analysis, manipulation, and synthesis. This step is sometimes bypassed when the sole intention is to present data to a customer.
8. *Present results*—The data are formatted (graphed, listed, etc.) and given to the customer. The appropriate form of presentation depends on many factors, including the results of retrieval and presentation, the presentation medium, and the customer. (People need one form of presentation, application software, another.)
9. *Use*—Data may be used on presentation to the customer.

This simplified version of the model does not include activities to access the quality of data and make adjustments. (The reader interested in such details should see Levitin).[2]

Criteria for a Definition of Data

The data life cycle suggests that data must be defined in a way that will account for the fundamental operations of defining models and views, collecting and updating values, storing, retrieving, and manipulating data, and presenting data and using them for a variety of purposes. The following criteria are also important in a good definition of data.[3]

- *Clarity and simplicity*—This criterion holds for any good definition.
- *Nonreliance on the term information*—This criterion avoids circular definitions.
- *Agreement with common usage*—We want to understand the term data, not to create a new meaning for a common term.
- *Inclusion of conceptual and representational aspects of data*—Both are too important to leave out.
- *Wide applicability*—The definition should include data as diverse as meter readings and the contents of databases and document information systems.
- *Suggestive of quality dimensions*—The definition should lead to practical data quality improvements.

Data Defined

Many definitions of data have been suggested in the literature; the one that best meets the criteria discussed in the previous section is based on the classic definition of the term accepted in the database community. (For an in-depth discussion see Whtimore).[4] This definition is really a collection of definitions of several related terms.

A *conceptual model* or a *data model* is an abstract description of some part of the world, called the *universe* or *enterprise*, that associates, or maps, objects in the world to abstract objects in the model, called *entities*. The portion of the world modeled may include both physical and abstract objects. Characteristics of the modeled real-world objects and relationships between them are captured in the model as attributes. An *attribute* is a property of an object that can assume values from a set called the *domain* of the attribute. There are no restrictions on the elements of a domain; they may be numbers, strings, entities, sets of entities and so forth. An entity is said to have an attribute when the attribute applies to the entity. Entities in a conceptual model that share a set of attributes are grouped together as an entity type.

To illustrate these definitions, consider two conceptual models used to define the reader. Consider first the conceptual model employed by his/her employer. The entities in this conceptual model consist of all past or present employees. The attributes of interest include name, employee ID, status, department, and so forth. Each attribute has well-defined domains of permissible values, for example, the domain for the attribute department includes all departments (Human Resource, Finance, Operations, etc.) of the employer's organization (note that the domain may change as the organization changes). Besides indicating the properties of entities, attributes may be used as entity identifiers. For example, this conceptual model might use the Employee ID attribute as an entity identifier.

Within this framework, we define a *datum* or *data item*, as a triple $<e, a, v>$, where e is an entity in a conceptual model, a is an attribute of entity e, and v is a value from the domain of attribute a. A datum asserts that entity e has value v for attribute a. *Data* are the members of any collection of data items. Returning to the example, a datum in the collection is <John Doe, Department, "Legal">, indicating that the department assigned to the employee John Doe is "Legal."

Note that the Internal Revenue Service (IRS) may also take an interest in the reader. The conceptual model it uses may overlap the employer's. For example, both include Name. But the employer's model may not include Year 2000 dividend income. Likewise the IRS's model need not include Department.

To complete this characterization of data, the mechanism of data representation must be included. A *data representation* is a set of rules for recording data triples on some medium. A *data recording* is a physical object interpretable (via a data representation) as a listing of data items. Representation of data values is accomplished via a *format*, or convention for recording data values using *symbols*, or representational elements. Publications data might be recorded in a paper index, a card catalog, or a computer database. A typical mechanism places all data values for a particular entity together in a *record* consisting of a *field* for every attribute in which the value for the attribute is stored. In many cases, the representations for values in fields will follow traditional formats. For example, author attribute values are typically recorded in a "last-name-first" format using the Roman alphabet.

This definition of data satisfies the criteria discussed in the section above in the following ways:

- The definition is set in the context of conceptual modeling, so it accounts for the data life-cycle activities of defining models and views. It also matches the standard conceptual foundations in the database literature.[5]
- The definition distinguishes data values, attributes, and entities, which are necessary to make sense of the data life-cycle operations of defining a model, of collecting and updating values, and of storing, retrieving, manipulating, and presenting data.
- The definition is simple; if necessary, it can be stated in precise mathematical terms so it is clear.

- The definition does not mention information, so information can be defined in terms of data without circularity.
- This definition of data accords with everyday uses of the word. For example, a water meter reading can be understood as a recording, using a certain data representation, of the value of an attribute (WaterConsumption) of an entity (the CUSTOMER).
- This definition accounts for both the conceptual and representational aspects of data.
- This approach is applicable in all studies of data in systems, including database systems, document information systems, and manual data systems.
- This definition of data lends itself to the study of all salient quality dimensions of data, as we will discuss below.

In summary, the ordered triple view of data meets all requirements for an adequate definition of data, and provides the necessary basis for a thorough consideration of data quality.

QUALITY AND QUALITY CONTROL

The most basic idea in quality is to "create and keep a customer."[6] One collection of data that satisfies customer needs better than a second collection is of higher quality. It follows that the most important measure of quality is customer satisfaction and that a key component of any good approach to quality is determining who the customers are and understanding their needs. Although this is simple in principle, it is complicated enormously by a dynamic world: customer needs change continuously, new competitors enter the market, new offerings appear, and so forth. And data customers can have a stunning array of needs. A simplifying notion is that of "fitness for use," as illustrated in Figure 20.2, below.

Although data quality must ultimately be defined by the data's customers, several characteristics stand out as important to most customers. These characteristics are called *data quality dimensions*. Given the definition of data above, quality dimensions can be classified according to three major quality concerns: quality of a conceptual model, quality of data values, and quality of data representation[7]; alternative approaches developed by Massachusetts Institute of Technology's (MIT) Total Data Quality Management Research Program can be found in.[8–10] Finally, one can also take the point of view that customers should not be required to separate their requirements of data from those of database systems and that data quality dimensions should be viewed as a subset of all requirements. (See Redman[7] for a comprehensive list of dimensions).

QUALITY OF A CONCEPTUAL MODEL

A *conceptual model* provides a framework for a data set by specifying entity classes, their attributes, and attribute domains. In addition, various constraints, often called *business rules*, can be

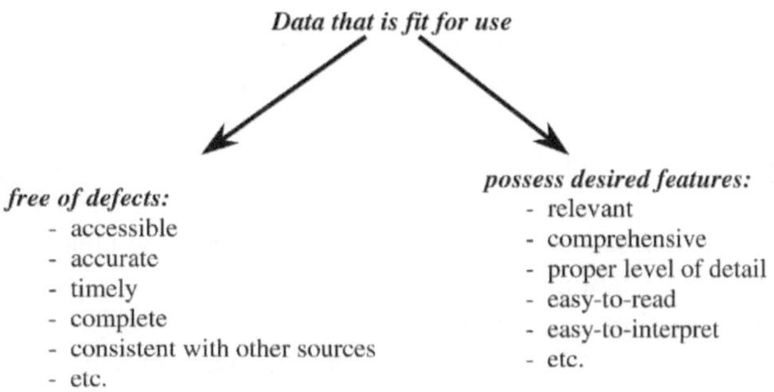

FIGURE 20.2 Data Quality Defined. Data are of high quality if they are fit for their intended uses (by customers) in operations, decision making, and planning (after Juran). (© Navesink Consulting Group.)

included in the model. Quality dimensions of a conceptual model can be grouped into six categories: content, scope, level of detail, composition, consistency, and reaction to change. (This grouping follows Levitin and Redman[11]; see Flavin[12] and Fidel[13] for alternative views. See also Brackett[14] for an in-depth discussion of a good data modeling practice).

Content

This category includes characteristics of the facts represented by the data. The most important of them is *relevance*: the degree to which a model's components are pertinent for the intended applications. Although the importance of data relevance seems obvious, lack of relevance has been singled out by several authors as among the most important issues in data quality.[15,16] Another concern is that all model components have *unambiguous definitions*. The necessity and difficulty of achieving clear definitions is discussed by Brackett,[14] Kent,[17] and Thompson.[18] The lack of clear definitions continues to plague many important databases (see Sy[16] and Gardner[19]) Finally, the *obtainability of values* for entities and attributes must be considered. Obtainability of values can meet various obstacles. For example, including gender information in a database may be illegal because it may lead to job discrimination. Obtaining blood types for all employees or citizens may not be affordable.

Scope

This characteristic involves the breadth of coverage of a model. A model should be both *comprehensive* and *essential*. In other words, a model must be broad enough to satisfy all the needs of its intended customers but not include unnecessary information. In practice, identifying the needs of even a single customer poses serious challenges for a data modeler. Integrating different sets of requirements to allow data sharing by several customers or applications as required for modern database management systems adds additional issues and difficulties.

There are several reasons for choosing a model broader than the one minimally necessary. First, the designer must usually create a model to accommodate both current and future applications. Second, redundancy can be introduced as a way to check data values. For example, a census form may ask for both the number of children in a household and a list of their names. Third redundancy speeds up some queries. For example, even though the number of employees in a DEPARTMENT can be calculated by checking the department attribute of all EMPLOYEEs, it will be available more quickly as the value of the (redundant) attribute NumberOfEmployees. Unless justified for one of these reasons, the expense of obtaining, storing, and maintaining unnecessary data should be avoided.

Level of Detail

Choosing the proper level of detail for a conceptual model has two aspects. The first is exemplified by the choice of size of geographic regions for recording sales. Data might be recorded for a city, a county, a state, and so forth. This characteristic is called *attribute granularity*. Lower levels of granularity provide more detail and the opportunity of keeping more data (e.g., subtotals) for finding and correcting errors. On the other hand, a lower level of granularity leads to a larger volume of data. Detailed data may be harder to obtain and usually increase costs. Customers may also be annoyed when presented with data more detailed than needed.[20]

The other aspect of level of detail is called *domain precision*, the measurement or classification detail used in defining an attribute's domain. For example, measurements in inches are more precise than measurements in feet. Similarly, having 20 distinct values in a color attribute's domain is more precise than having 7. (See a realistic example in Sy and Robbin's[16] discussion of the Standard Industrial Classification).

Composition

This characteristic concerns the structuring or grouping of facts represented by data. Each entity type of data model should be *natural*; that is, it should be a natural grouping of natural attributes with natural domains. This requirement can be met if each entity type has a sensible counterpart in the part of the world being modeled, and each attribute captures a single fact about entities and their relationships. Such an attribute typically represents some property (e.g., the gender of an employee) or it used for identification (e.g., the Social Security number of an employee). Unnatural "multifact" attributes are often introduced to satisfy outdated implementation constraints. For example, an attribute may be defined to hold a code for both age bracket and gender in an effort to save storage space. Date[21] discusses other examples and their consequences. Although multifact attributes should be avoided, some well-established classification schemes incorporate secondary information. For example, room numbering schemes often code the floor into the number. It is hard to call this familiar scheme unnatural. (Things have a tendency to become natural when we get used to them.) Secondary facts may also be incorporated into values for redundancy and security.

In a well-composed conceptual model, each type must have a mechanism for distinguishing individual entities. This requirement, called *occurrence identifiability*, is often incorporated into the definition of an entity type. Usually, occurrence identification is accomplished with a *primary key*, one or more attributes whose value(s) uniquely identify individuals. For example, SocialSecurityNumber can serve as a primary key for an EMPLOYEE entity type.

A good model should also promote *homogeneous* types. This means that each attribute should apply to all individuals of the type. This does not preclude using values for "none," "exists but unknown," or even "existence is unknown" (each of these may apply, e.g., to TelephoneNumber).

Consistency

There are two aspects of this quality dimension. The first is *semantic consistency*, which requires consistency of definitions among related components of a model. Problems often arise with definitions from different databases. For example, Whitmore[22] cites a serious discrepancy in oil import figures reported by the U.S. Bureau of the Census and the Department of Energy caused by the differing definitions of "petroleum," "U.S.," and "month." Sy and Robbin[16] discuss many examples of problems with U.S. government data. The second aspect of consistency is *structural consistency*, which requires consistency in combining a model's components. For examples, such commonly used attributes as PersonName, Address, Date, and TimeOfDay should have the same structure across all entity types. Tasker[23] has suggested standard structures for such attributes.

Reaction to Change

A conceptual model provides a framework for representing information about a part of the world, but both the world and customers' requirements change over time. A good model *must accommodate change*. We classify changes into four categories: addition or deletion of an entity (e.g., hiring or firing an employee), changing a value (e.g., changing a salary), changing a domain (e.g., introducing a new car model), and introducing a new attribute or entity type. The first two kinds of changes, called *updates*, are routinely performed in any computer-based database management or document information system without any change in the underlying model; the other two require changes in the model.

Most authors mention "flexibility" as the only design characteristic for accommodating change. In practice, changing a model is usually a serious and expensive task and the ability to accommodate change without redesign is an important practical need. We define a model's *robustness* as its ability to reflect changes in the world and its customer's requirement without design changes. The first step toward design robustness is to select attributes that will not change or whose changes can be easily accommodated. For example, SocialSecurityNumber is a more robust identifier of people in the United States than a Name (even if a name's uniqueness could be guaranteed) because it is easier for a person to change names than social security numbers. Another avenue to robustness is to anticipate changes and provide for them in the original design. For example, a company that currently produces sweaters with sizes "small," "medium," and "large" may produce other sizes in the future. No matter how robust a model may be, some design changes will have to be made eventually. A model's *flexibility* is its capacity to change to meet unanticipated demands. A good model is flexible as well as robust.

Quality Dimensions of Data Values

We group dimensions of data quality involving data *values* into four categories: accuracy, currency, completeness, and consistency.

Accuracy

The *accuracy* of a datum $<e, a, v>$ is the degree of closeness of v to some value v' in the domain of attribute a considered correct for the entity e. Sometimes v' is referred to as the *standard*. If the value v is identical to the correct value v', the datum is said to be *accurate* or *correct*. To illustrate, consider an EMPLOYEE entity identified by the EmployeeNumber 314159, and the attribute YearOfBirth. If the value of YearOfBirth for employee 314159 is the year the employee was born, the datum is correct.

Accuracy is most easily measured in terms of inaccuracy. Inaccuracy for a single datum may be computed as the absolute difference between the correct value v' and datum's value v. For the example above, inaccuracy may be quantified as the absolute difference between the year of birth v' and the value v for the attribute YearOfBirth. The (in)accuracy of a database can be measured in two ways. *Field (in)accuracy* is the fraction of triples in the database with (in)correct data values. *Record (in)accuracy* is the fraction of entities in the database whose records are error-free; that is, the fraction of all entities in the database all of whose attributes have correct data values. Records are usually composed of several fields, so record accuracy is much lower than field accuracy. Furthermore, errors in different fields may be unimportant or disastrous. These last two observations suggest caution when judging database quality on the basis of error rate.[24]

Accuracy and correctness are not as simple as they seem, especially when it comes to evaluation. It is often difficult to determine the standard. Sometimes there is not an obvious single correct value for an attribute, as is often the case in spelling, especially names. Sometimes the correct value is undefined, as when an entity identifier is wrong. In the example above, there may be no correct value for YearOfBirth if there is no employee 314159. It may also be difficult to quantify inaccuracy, even if the correct value is known, because the attribute in question may resist quantification, as do label, category, and description data. In summary, measuring data inaccuracy is often not easy when it is possible, and it is not always possible.

Currency

The ordered triple definition of data treats data as snapshots of part of the world. Most objects change with time, introducing opportunities for data to become incorrect or inaccurate. A datum is *current* or *up-to-date* at time t if it is correct at time t, and *out-of-date* at time t if it is incorrect at t but was correct at some time before t. Currency may be quantified by measuring how far out-of-date a value is. Database currency can be measured as the fraction of out-of-date triples in the database. As an example, suppose the annual salary of an EMPLOYEE can only change at the start of a calendar year, and that some employee's salary was \$36,000 in 1992, \$39,000 in 1993, and \$43,000 in 1994. If during 1994 a datum shows the salary as \$43,000, it is up-to-date; if it shows \$36,000, it is two years out-of-date; if it shows \$42,000, it is simply incorrect.

Completeness and Duplication

The degree to which a data collection has values for all attributes of all entities that are supposed to have values is its *completeness*. A data collection may be incomplete because of missing values in the triples present or because some triples are missing entirely. In the case of missing values, the completeness of a single datum may be measured by whether or not it has a required value; a completeness measure for an entire data collection is then the fraction of triples in the collection with missing values. When a triple is missing a value, a special "null" value may be assigned for it. The meaning of null is different, depending on whether the attribute is mandatory, optional, or inapplicable. For mandatory attributes, the null value means value unknown. For optional attributes, the null value may mean that the attribute applies but we lack its value, or that the attribute does not apply, or that we do not know whether the attribute applies. For an inapplicable attribute, like NameOfSpouse for an unmarried person, the null value signifies that the attribute does not apply. In theory, these cases could be distinguished with different kinds of null values; in practice, having even one kind of null value causes problems for database systems.[25,26]

A data collection may also be incomplete because some triples that should be included are missing. Missing record incompleteness can be measured by finding the fraction of records missing from the data collection.

Consistency and Integrity

Data are said to be *consistent* with respect to a set of conceptual model constraints if they satisfy all the constraints in the set.[27] One measure of the consistency of a datum is a binary indication (Yes or No) of whether the datum satisfies all constraints. A measure for an entire data collection is then the fraction of inconsistent triples in the collection. Correct data must be consistent. The converse statement (consistent data are correct) need not be true. Said differently, consistency is necessary but not sufficient for correctness. Nevertheless, it is important to distinguish consistency as a special dimension because checking consistency is usually much easier and cheaper than checking corrections. Data integrity is sometimes used as a synonym for consistency, but sometimes it means data accuracy or correctness and, sometimes, security and concurrency control in database management systems.[28–30]

Quality Dimensions of Data Representation

From a customer's perspective, the most important data representation issue is the means chosen to represent data values by symbols on a recording medium, called the *format*. The following are the four major formats[31]:

- *String formats* represent values by character strings over some alphabet, including alphanumeric strings, and bitstrings. This category includes numeric coding schemes, most computer storage mechanisms, and most textual representations of data.
- *Positional/marking formats* specify values by marking a particular spot on a recording medium. This category includes coding sheets used in questionnaires and graphical methods.[32–35]
- *Icon formats* use pictorial symbols to represent values.
- *Color formats* represent data values by colors.

The first two formats are the most widely used, but there are several applications in which the last two appear as well.[36]

The most important quality dimension of a format is its *appropriateness*, both for meeting customer needs and using the recording medium effectively. Customers deal with representations of data, not data triples themselves, and their needs are of primary importance. They depend on two factors: the type of customer (human, mechanical, optical, etc.), and the task the customer is to perform (communication, analysis, storage, etc.). Reliable and convenient use of recording media is obviously of practical importance.

A format should result in a correct interpretation of values represented; that is, the format should be unambiguous. For example, a format representing three ratings with the digits 1, 2, and 3 is more ambiguous (to a human) than the one using the strings "worst," "average," and "best." Ambiguity may also arise when a format does not specify a unit of measurement for quantitative data. Special care is needed with icon and color formats because there is not wide agreement about their meaning.

A third quality dimension of formats is *universality* or *portability*, which is the degree to which a format can be used by a wide range of customers. In this respect, specifying numbers with words of a natural language is inferior to using arabic digits. Similarly, representing telephone numbers without area codes is inferior to including area codes. When using a color format, colors must be chosen bearing in mind that color-blind people can distinguish some colors but not others.

A good format must also be sufficiently *precise*, which means that there must be distinct representations for any two values in an attribute's domain. For example, formats for quantitative data must provide means for specifying numbers as precisely as required. A fifth quality dimension is *flexibility*, which is the ability of a format to accommodate changes in the domain of values represented. This issue has arisen in many information systems struggling to adapt to real-world change.[36,37] A sixth quality of a good format is its *ability to represent null values*. A good format should represent null values in a way clearly understood by customers; Celko[36] retells the tale of the motorist who got thousands of traffic tickets because his license plate read "none." Finally, a format should *make efficient use of the recording medium*.

DATA QUALITY MANAGEMENT

Over the last several decades, any number of quality techniques have been developed and applied. The greatest penetration has occurred in the manufacturing sector, where any number of industries now produce far better products at far lower cost. The service sector has recently begun to apply quality techniques, also with good success. And some organizations have begun to extend quality techniques to data.

Perhaps the most important lesson learned is that, more than anything else, an organization's leadership dictates the quality of its products, services, and data. While technical excellence is important, consistent, sustained management effort is essential.

Quality Systems

The totality of an organization's efforts that bear on quality define its quality system. Thus, the quality system includes leadership, management, and the application of tools to understand customer needs, measure quality, find and fix defects, and so forth. And while literally thousands of techniques have been tried, all support one of three basic quality management philosophies:

- So-called *first-generation* philosophy and techniques provide quality through inspection and rework of final products, hopefully, before they are passed on to customers.
- So-called *second-generation* philosophy and techniques provide quality by minimizing root causes of defects in the processes that produce final products. Here the term *process* means the sequence of work activities that produce and deliver products or services to customers.
- So-called *third-generation* philosophy and techniques aim to design processes so that defects cannot be produced.

Each of these approaches is discussed briefly in the following sections.

First Generation: Inspection and Rework

In this approach to quality, a product or service is inspected for conformance to needs before delivery to a customer. Products or services that fail inspection are either reworked or discarded. In the simplest case, everything is inspected, but more sophisticated acceptance sampling procedures can reduce inspection costs.[38]

The strength of this approach is that it usually improves outgoing quality. Its major drawbacks are that inspections are often difficult and expensive, and reworking or discarding products or services is always expensive. Further, process quality levels tend not to improve beyond a limiting level. Inspection and rework is the first step that an organization takes to achieve quality.

Second Generation: Process Quality Management

The fundamental tenet of process quality management is that process performance can be made predictable within limits. A process operating within expected limits is in a state of *statistical control*. For such processes, statistical and other methods can identify process weaknesses and then changes can be made to improve process performance. For example, suppose a process for collecting and filling service orders is measured and found to be out of control. After study, several problems with ill-defined procedures are identified and eliminated. The process then operates in a state of statistical control with an average error rate of 0.1%. Further study of the process then reveals error-prone activities that can be improved, thereby reducing its average error rate to 0.05%. The net results of these activities are that: 1) they make the output of the process predictable and known and 2) they produce measurable improvements in process performance. (For a fuller account of this approach see Ishikawa,[39] Wadsworth).[40,41]

Process quality management requires some investment, but as processes are brought under control and improved, total costs go down (inspecting and reworking defects is simply much more expensive than preventing them). Furthermore, process quality management can produce sustainable quality improvements as necessary to satisfy customer needs.

Third Generation: Process Design

This approach attempts to make large improvements quickly by designing or redesigning a process from scratch rather than letting it evolve through process quality management. This goal can be reached by making the process simpler and less error-prone, often by incorporating higher technology in both the process and its design.[42] A third-generation philosophy and supporting techniques are required to meet 6σ (six-sigma) quality levels; today, symbolic of world-class quality (6σ equates to 3.4 defects per million).

Combining Quality Management Approaches

All three approaches to quality management discussed above have proven effective in countless instances, especially in manufacturing settings. The two process-based approaches are more advanced and more effective than inspection and rework for the following reasons:

- Defects are expensive to find and fix; detecting and removing a defect can cost up to 10 times as much as preventing it.
- Defects that customers find have a direct impact on customer satisfaction, the ultimate measure of quality.
- Experience has shown that world-class quality levels cannot be achieved solely through inspection and rework.

Despite their weaknesses, inspection and rework have their place alongside process quality management and process design, and mature quality systems combine all three approaches. For example, an organization may have carefully designed a process to minimize errors and may be managing it actively to steadily improve and optimize its performance. Nevertheless, a bad product or service may still find its way to a customer, where it must be replaced or fixed. A mechanism for inspection and rework may thus need to be present in even the most sophisticated environments.

Although quality approaches have been pioneered in manufacturing enterprises, they have also been effective in service industries.[43] And experience over the last 10 to 15 years confirms that they work for data as well. More specifically, experience confirms that the first two approaches work well. (See English,[44] Loshin[45] and Redman[46] for examples). The next subsection reviews specific methods for applying these three general approaches to data quality.

QUALITY CONTROL APPROACHES APPLIED TO DATA

While all dimensions of data quality are important (at least to some customers), in this section, we focus only on data accuracy. It is important to all customers and is a good vehicle for illustrating the application of quality approaches to data.

First Generation: Error Detection and Correction

The most prevalent method for controlling and improving data accuracy is to detect and correct inaccurate values. The simplest procedure is to compare data values to the world and fix those that are wrong. For example, consider an employee database containing data on work and home addresses. It is common for the administrators of such databases to survey employees regularly to verify and correct their addresses. Depending on how cooperative employees are (and whether or not the address verification and correction form reaches them), this procedure can work very well. It is costly, however, and yields no sustained improvement in data quality over time; after a survey, the accuracy of data will deteriorate steadily until the next survey is done.

A second technique, called *database bashing*, is also used frequently when data values are stored in two or more databases. Corresponding values in the databases are compared, and when a disagreement is detected, an investigation finds the correct value, and the databases are fixed. This technique has several advantages over comparing all values to the real world. It is easier to manage and tends to cost less, especially when the databases can be compared using a computer, but, like all techniques based on inspection and rework, it does not yield sustained quality improvement.

A third technique, called *data editing*, involves computerized checking of data values against constraints. These constraints may be simple or sophisticated and typically involve the following:

- *Checks of a single field.* For example, a field whose domain is {0, 1, 2, . . . , 10} may have its values checked against this set.
- *Checks of several fields.* The checked fields could be in a single record or in several records. For example, a field recording the NumberOfEmployees of a DEPARTMENT might be checked by examining the department field of all EMPLOYEE records and counting the EMPLOYEEs in the DEPARTMENT.
- *Probabilistic field checks.* For example, a record with a gender field value of female and a height field value of 78 in. is unlikely.

Such constraints are often called business rules. See Ross[47] for further details. Once a record is found to be in error, further investigation locates and corrects the offending field(s). This technique may be used in the data life cycle during the activities of storing data values, retrieving data values, and manipulating data values, or as part of special data cleanup activities.

Data editing is popular because it is (apparently) computationally cheap. It is often difficult to generate an effective and complete list of edits, however.[14,48] Once errors are found, it is still expensive to investigate and correct them. Finally, data editing provides no lasting quality improvements.

In summary, inspection and rework methods are not very effective for improving data quality because they are conducted downstream of data-value creation, usually either during a storage activity or during usage activities of the data life cycle. Although these methods result in short-term data quality improvements to specific data values, they cannot provide lasting improvements because they do not attack the sources of errors.

Second Generation: Prevent Errors at their Sources

An alternative to error detection and correction is to focus on processes that create data values. Conceptually, this is simple. As in manufacturing, one must first achieve a state of statistical control. Errors are then reduced by identifying where and how they occur and changing the process to prevent them. Improvements made this way require more effort than inspection and rework but are sustainable and, therefore, cheaper in the long run.

But there are many practical problems. One problem stems from the fact that data move around the organization so quickly. Data created to satisfy a customer's order one day are used to manage inventory, to track sales, to plan next year's marketing campaign, and so forth, the next day. Data customers are harried in doing their current jobs, be it managing inventory, tracking sales, or planning next year's marketing campaign. When confronted with inaccurate data, they are simply more inclined to correct them or compensate for poor quality in some other way, than they are to seek out the sources of incorrect data.

That said, many organizations have made substantial improvements. And they have lowered costs and sped up their business processes and decision-making (error detection and correction takes time and costs money) as a result. Ten "best practices" have been observed.[7] These are summarized as follows:

1. Senior management recognizes the importance of high-quality data and has mobilized the organization to improve. And they have focused data quality efforts on the most important data.
2. The organization holds those who create data responsible for the quality of data they create. This includes both internal and external data sources.
3. The organization identifies and actively manages its most important data suppliers.
4. The organization identifies and actively manages its most important internal business processes.
5. The organization recognizes "social issues" around data (such as that noted above) and actively manages data. It attaches value (often monetary) to data.
6. The organization understands "the most important needs of the most important customers." Data quality efforts are thus focused on the most important data.
7. The organization measures data quality levels. Measurement can be difficult. After all, data do not have physical properties such as size, weight, and impedance. Fortunately, good measurement information can often be obtained cheaply. One simple method piggybacks process measurement on data-editing activities: failed edits can be classified and counted, and these measurements used for quality control and improvement. AT&T has developed a useful technique called *data tracking*[49] for better process measurement and error detection and localization. Data tracking follows data through a process to determine where data are corrupted. Subsequent investigation identifies the root cause(s) of errors and removes them.
8. Statistical control of data sources is achieved. Control implies that data quality levels will be predictable into the future. And controlled processes are more easily improved.
9. Organizations with the best data are good at defining and conducting improvement projects that get to the root causes of error and eliminate (or at least mitigate) them.
10. Organizations with the best data set and meet aggressive targets for improvement. Indeed, they focus less on actual quality levels than on the rate of improvement.

Third Generation: Process Design for Data Quality

The third data quality improvement approach is to design or redesign processes to minimize errors. This approach is usually initially more expensive than either inspection and rework or process quality management, but, when successful, it yields large gains in a short time and may be cheaper than either one in the long run. Typically, process design introduces new information technologies. For example, an automatic bar-code reader may be introduced into a process because it reads product codes faster and more accurately than a person can.

Limited experience in designing processes confirms that the following ideas[7] can work well:

1. Replace humans with automation in repetitive tasks in which people are likely to make errors, such as data input, data transcription or reformatting, and data searching. More generally, automating well-defined tasks and processes yields gains in speed, productivity, and quality. Conversely, automating poorly defined tasks and processes rarely works.
2. Design processes to optimize end-to-end performance, not the performance of subprocesses.
3. Capture data as close as possible to its original source. Minimize duplication, data transcription, data transformation, and redundant data storage.
4. Employ a "just-in-time" philosophy to data creation.
5. Design data editing and handling of exceptions into the process.
6. Employ simple data codes and extensive, easy-to-access data dictionaries.
7. Data quality measurement should be designed into processes that create data from the beginning. This provides nonintrusive mechanisms that can be used for quality improvement and control, especially when measurement can be built into the software that supports a process.

Process design for data quality is a promising area for further work in the future.

DATA QUALITY AND THE INTERNET

Even a casual glance confirms that the importance of data, and, hence, data quality, has grown enormously over the past decades. Many factors are involved, including the transition to the information economy, the tremendous gains in all sorts of information technologies, and the thirst for ever-more detail to support decision makers. As the importance of data has grown, so too has the need for data quality. And there is no end in sight.

The Internet, thus, is the latest in this series of technological advances and social changes. While the impact will evolve as the Internet evolves, a few points about data quality and the Internet are pertinent.

The first observation is that the Internet creates new data customers. Organizations are publishing data on the Internet that they had previously held as proprietary. Those who view these data almost certainly have different needs than internal customers. They have not been trained on how to interpret data, making clear definition and ease of interpretation more important. They are not familiar with the nuances inherent in the data and could be more easily misled, making accuracy more important. Their native language may be different, making dimensions associated with data presentation more important. Perhaps most importantly, they have different needs and they themselves are different. Some, such as those seeking medical advice relevant to a particular condition, may be focused and discerning but not technically sophisticated. Some, such as college students desiring to complete a report, may be technically advanced but in a hurry and not too careful about what they accept as fact, and so forth.

The second change involves the use of the Internet to conduct business operations. Supply chain management is a good but, by no means, only example. Supply chain management involves using the Internet to order goods and services, arrange and make payment, coordinate deliveries, and so forth. Without the Internet, organizations spend an enormous amount of time and money on supply chain management. Supply chain management works reasonably well, and the Internet offers the opportunity to do so at far lower cost. But only if the data are of high quality.

Third, the Internet makes things possible that are currently not. We do not wish to enter the debate about whether or not "the Internet changes everything." See Porter[50] for a compelling, though not proven, viewpoint that it does not. But it does appear that opportunities to replace standard or commodity products and services with products and services tailored specifically to the individual may indeed become realities. Certainly health care providers are beginning to talk about drugs formulated specifically for individual patients. "Markets of size one" form part of the hope of customer resource management, and so forth. All share the following characteristics:

- They require vast quantities of individual-specific data.
- The impact of poor data is much greater.

CONCLUSION

To summarize, data quality is a subject of primary importance in the twenty-first century. Many factors, including the Internet appear to be making high-quality data more important than ever. Improvement must be based on preventing errors at their sources.

REFERENCES

1. Brown, J.S.; Duguid, P. *The Social Life of Information*; Harvard Business School Press: Boston, 2000.
2. Levitin, A.V.; Redman, T.C. A model of the data (life) cycle with application to quality. Inf. Softw. Technol. **1993**, *35* (4), 217–223.
3. Fox, C.; Levitin, A.V.; Redman, T.C. The notion of data and its quality dimensions. Inf. Process. Manag. **1994**, *30* (1), 9–19.
4. Fry, J.P.; Sibley, E.H. Evolution of data-base management systems. ACM Comput. Surv. **1976**, *8* (1), 7–42.
5. Fleming, C.; von Halle, B. *Handbook of Relational Database Design*; Addison-Wesley: New York, 1989.
6. Levitt, T. *The Marketing Imagination*; The Free Press: New York, 1986.
7. Redman, T.C. *Data Quality: The Field Guide*; Butterworth-Heinemann: Boston, 2001.
8. Wang, R.Y.; Strong, D.M.; Guarascio, L.M. Data Consumers' Perspectives of Data Quality. In *Technical Report TDQM-94-01, Total Data Quality Management (TDQM) Research Program*; Sloan School of Management, MIT: Cambridge, MA, 1994.
9. Wand, Y.; Wang, R.Y. Anchoring Data Quality Dimensions in Ontological Foundations. In *Technical Report TDQM-94-03, Total Data Quality Management (TDQM) Research Program*; Sloan School of Management, MIT: Cambridge, MA, 1994.
10. Wang, R.Y.; Ziad, M.; Lee, Y.W. *Data Quality*; Kluwer Academic Publishers: Boston, 2001.
11. Levitin, A.V.; Redman, T.C. Quality dimensions of a conceptual view. Inf. Process. Manag. **1995**, *31* (1), 81–88.
12. Flavin, M. *Fundamental Concepts of Information Modeling*; Yourdon Press: New York, 1981.
13. Fidel, R. *Database Design for Information Retrieval*; John Wiley: New York, 1987.
14. Brackett, M.H. *Data Resource Quality*; Addison Wesley: New York, 2000.
15. Loebl, A.S. Accuracy and Relevance and the Quality of Data. In *Data Quality Control: Theory and Pragmatics*; Liepins, G., Uppuluri, V.R.R., Eds.; Marcel Dekker: New York, 1990; 105–143.
16. Sy, K.J.; Robbin, A. Federal Statistical Policies and Programs: How Good Are the Numbers?. In *Annual Review of Information Science and Technology*; Williams, M.E., Ed.; Elsevier Science Publishers: Amsterdam, 1990; Vol. 25, 3–54.
17. Kent, W. *Data and Reality*; Elsevier Science Publishers: Amsterdam, 1978.
18. Thompson, J.P. *Data with Semantics: Data Models and Data Management*; Van Nostrand Reinhold: New York, 1989.
19. Gardner, E. UB-82 forms offer wealth of information, misinformation. Mod. Healthc. September 24, **1990**, 18–29.

20. Rockart, J.F. Chief executives define their own data needs. Harv. Bus. Rev. **1979**, *57* (2), 81–93.
21. Date, C.J. Don't Encode Information into Primary Keys! In *Relational Database Writings 1989–1991*; Date, C.J. Ed.; Addison-Wesley: Reading, MA, 1992; 461–466.
22. Whtimore, T. Computers take rap for bad data. Computerworld, August 29, **1988**, *21*.
23. Tasker, D. *Fourth Generation Data*; Prentice-Hall: Englewood Cliffs, NJ, 1989.
24. Intner, S.S. Much ado about nothing: OCLC and RLIN cataloging quality. Libr. J. February 1, **1989**, 38–40.
25. Date, C.J. *An Introduction to Database Systems*, 4th Ed.; Addison-Wesley: Reading, MA, 1987; Vol. 1.
26. Imielinski, T.; Lipski, W. Incomplete information in relational databases. JACM, **1984**, *31* (4), 761–791.
27. Elmassri, R.; Navathe, S.B. *Fundamentals of Database Systems*; Benjamin/Cummings: Redwood City, CA, 1989.
28. Brodie, M.L. Specification and Verfication of Data Base Semantic Integrity. In *Doctoral Dissertation*; University of Toronto: Canada, 1978.
29. Tsichritzis, D.C.; Lochovsky, F.H. *Data Models*; Prentice-Hall: Englewood Cliffs, NJ, 1982.
30. Date, C.J. *An Introduction to Database Systems*, 4th Ed.; Addison-Wesley: Reading, MA, 1983; Vol. 2.
31. Levitin, A.V. *Formats for Data Representation: A Taxonomy and Quality Dimensions*; Working Paper, AT&T Bell Laboratories: Holmdel, NJ, 1992.
32. Bertin, J. *Semiologie Graphique*, 2nd Ed.; Mouton-Gautier: The Hague, 1973. (English translation by W. Berg & H. Wainer, published as Semiology of Graphics, University of Wisconsin Press, Madison, 1983.).
33. Cleveland, B. *The Elements of Graphing Data*; Wadsworth: Monterey, CA, 1985.
34. Tufte, E.R. *The Visual Display of Quantitative Information*; Graphics Press: Cheshire, CT, 1983.
35. Tufte, E.R. *Envisioning Information*; Graphics Press: Cheshire, CT, 1990.
36. Celko, J. Make or brake your system. Database Program. Des. **1989**, *2* (3), 19–20.
37. Newmann, P.G. The clock grows at midnight. Commun. ACM **1991**, *34* (1), 170.
38. Schilling, E.G. Acceptance Sampling. In *Juran's Quality Control Handbook*, 5th Ed.; Juran, J.M., Ed.; McGraw-Hill: New York, 1999.
39. Ishikawa, K. *Introduction to Quality Control*; 3A Corporation: Tokyo, 1990.
40. Wadsworth, H.; Stephens, K.S.; Godfrey, A. *Modern Methods for Quality Control and Improvement*; John Wiley: New York, 1986.
41. *AT&T, Process Quality Management and Improvement Guidelines*; AT&T: Indianapolis, IN, 1988. Issue 1.1.
42. Phadke, M.S. *Quality Engineering Using Robust Design*; Prentice-Hall: Englewood Cliffs, NJ, 1989.
43. Rosander, A.C. *Applications of Quality Control in the Service Industries*; Marcel Dekker: New York, 1985.
44. English, L.P. *Improving Data Warehouse and Business Information Quality*; John Wiley & Sons: New York, 1999.
45. Loshin, D. *Enterprise Knowledge Management: The Data Quality Approach*; Academic Press: Boston, 2001.
46. Redman, T.C. *Data Quality for the Information Age*; Artech House: Boston, 1996.
47. Ross, R.G. *The Business Rule Book*; The Database Research Group, Inc.: Boston, 1997.
48. Svanks, M.I. Integrity analysis: Methods for automating data quality assurance. Inf. Softw. Technol. **1988**, *30* (10), 595–605.
49. Huh, Y.U.; Keller, F.R.; Redman, T.C.; Watkins, A.R. Data quality. Inf. Softw. Technol. **1990**, *32* (8), 550–565.
50. Porter, M.E. Strategy and the internet. Harv. Bus. Rev. **2001**, *79* (3), 62–78.

21 Information Systems Failure

Chris Sauer and Gordon B. Davis

CONTENTS

INTRODUCTION

Information systems (IS) failure has been a focus for study and action for both practitioners and academics since the late 1960s.[1–3] Most organizations have struggled to deliver systems that work and deliver benefits. Practitioners have wrestled with these difficulties in their workplace and the public has experienced systems' shortcomings in trying to use them. Nobody seriously doubts that failure has been and continues to be a problem to be tackled.

The focus on failures does not mean that there are two classes of applications—those that succeed and those that fail. There is a continuum of results ranging from clear and utter failure to very high success. There are applications that are barely acceptable but survive, and there are applications that are mildly successful and fail.

This entry reviews only one end of the spectrum of results: applications that are failures. The meaning of "information system success" is a significant issue[4] in itself and is not the purpose of this entry. Information system failure and information system success are not simply opposites.[5] To achieve success, it is necessary to remove causes of failure, but doing so may not be sufficient for a successful outcome. More broadly, the study of failure is justified by the belief that, just as the study of cognitive malfunction can help us understand good mental functioning, it casts light on what it takes to achieve success. Understanding "information system failure," therefore, represents one but only one part of what needs to be understood for the effective design, implementation, management, and exploitation of an information system.

Where once "failure" was viewed as an almost objectively identifiable state, today there is wide recognition that it is an evaluation based on an assessment of some dimension or dimensions of performance relative to goals, targets, or expectations. Failure in one dimension, say a budget overrun, may be more than compensated for by success in another dimension, say timely implementation. And, as what is regarded as performance has itself changed, so the domain of failure studies has evolved. For this reason, it is appropriate for this entry to take an historical approach.

In this entry, the study of failure is treated as one important branch of the study of IS performance. Our overall objective is to provide a rigorous basis by which to understand what may be meant by "IS failure" and a set of signposts to appropriate analytical approaches by which to develop greater insight into the phenomenon.

We start with a review of recent performance data. We examine the various changes that have affected perceptions of IS performance. We identify a number of cognate subliteratures that have developed over recent years and which signal a growing maturity of analysis. We provide a framework by which to understand the historical development of academic research in this field.

THE SCALE OF IS FAILURE

Prior to 1995, most assessments of the scale of IS failure were informal in nature and anecdotally derived. In 1995, the Boston-based consulting group, Standish, published its findings under the banner headline, *Chaos*![6] Based on data about more than 3000 IS projects, it reported that 31% were abandoned without being completed. These it dubbed failures. Some 53% failed to meet at least one of its budget, schedule, and scope targets. These were dubbed challenged projects. The remaining 16% that hit all three targets were deemed successes. These have since become the most widely cited failure statistics.

Every 2 years since 1995, the Standish Group has released updates on these figures. Figures released for 2004 revealed 29% hit all targets, 53% were challenged in missing at least one target and 18% were classified as failures.[7] In summary according to the Standish Group figures there has been sustained improvement but there remains continuing cause for concern. While some question the Standish survey and analysis methodology,[8] raising questions about the accuracy of the detailed findings, in 1995 few doubted the broad conclusion that most IT projects seriously underperformed. Subsequent surveys reinforced the point (e.g., Taylor).[9] Likewise today, more than a decade later, the improving trend they identify is commonly acknowledged.

Less clear is the extent of the improvement and therefore the extent of the outstanding problem. To measure this, it is better to use percentage variance from targets.[10] Otherwise we cannot tell whether "challenged" projects are more or less challenged over time. Sauer et al.[10] also argue that an absolutist definition of success by which any variance however small assigns a project to the challenged category is too strict. In most cases a small budgetary or schedule overrun is of negligible significance. Using statistical clustering techniques, they show that there is a significant gap between the majority of projects that miss their targets by just a small percentage margin and those that are clearly failing on a more substantial scale and that therefore it is worth tolerating some small margin of variance. However, even on this more optimistic assessment, at least one-third of all projects fall well short of delivering on all their targets.

THE EVOLUTION OF IS PERFORMANCE

In the previous section we saw that IS performance has changed over time and that the metrics by which performance in general and failure specifically are identified are not definitively agreed. In this section we explain how the phenomenon itself has changed and explore the implications for the measurement and identification of failure.

We start with a distinction between systems and systems projects. In the 1960s and 1970s, the system and the project were often conflated. If a system failed, say because it did not deliver the functionality its users wanted, it was usually the case that the project had been troubled too and vice-versa. This was also a period in which computer malfunctions were common resulting in breakdowns ranging from the everyday experience of the computer being "down" to catastrophic loss. Such malfunctions have been extensively cataloged by Peter Neumann in his Inside Risks column in the Communications of the Association for Computing Machinery over many years.[11] While more reliable hardware and standardized and re-usable software have removed many causes of such malfunctions, they remain a continuing hazard (e.g., Hodgson)[12] but today are rarely such as to cause abandonment of a system.

With the advent of rigorous project management disciplines it has become normal to detail precise targets, in terms of budget, schedule, quality, and scope. These are essentially internal measures that in principle are within a project manager's capacity to control. It has become apparent therefore that a project may be successful in meeting its internal targets yet not deliver beneficial business outcomes. More recently, as the role IT plays in organizations has become critical to their functioning as exemplified by the widespread adoption of e-business for front office business functions, there have been cases of projects failing to hit budget and schedule targets but nevertheless delivering highly desirable business outcomes. The distinction between the system and the project is therefore both conceptually sensible and practically relevant.

What counts as an information system and therefore what is involved in an IS project has changed over time and this has affected the measure of performance. Purpose-built systems have given way to standard packages (so-called enterprise software). Projects are therefore more about system integration than software development. This has led to two important consequences. First, it has engendered more ambitious, more complex projects that combine packaged functionality to an extent that was previously unimaginable. Second, because the software is prewritten, it has encouraged organizations to direct project managers' efforts to implementation, business process change, and value harvesting. This latter has extended project scope considerably and turned managers' attention to an external target, the business value achieved by investment in an information system.

This shift in emphasis from internal to external targets, from assessing performance against process to performance on outcomes, is appropriate from a commercial investment perspective. It is, however, problematic to measure because IT systems do not deliver value on their own, they do so through organizational and business process change.[13] Even if the value itself is measurable and measured, and it often is not, the extent to which that value derives from the information system may not be possible to determine. Further problems include the question of when to measure value outcomes. Often immediately after implementation, organizational performance suffers[14] before recovering and improving. But the longer the lag between implementation and outcome measurement, the more space there is for extraneous variables to affect the value outcome.

Thus far in this section, we have examined how IS performance has evolved in practice. We now turn to how its conceptualization has evolved academically. A significant breakthrough came with the explicit recognition that "failure" is an evaluation not an objective description. Lyytinen and Hirschheim[15] developed a new pluralist concept of expectations failure which explicitly recognized that failure was a judgement relative to expectations and that expectations vary among stakeholders. This pluralism opened the way to the possibility that a single system or project could be a failure relative to one set of stakeholders and a success relative to others. It also triggered discussion of whether some stakeholders' expectations might weigh more in arriving at a single overarching evaluation—this is "on balance" a failure notwithstanding some less important stakeholders viewing it as a success. Several responses have emerged. Some have tried to identify apparently unequivocal failures such as abandoned projects (e.g., Johnson[6] and Ewusi-Mensah[16]) though it has been argued that even an abandoned project might be viewed by some stakeholders as a success if an objective was to learn about a new technology, test customer responses, or experiment in some other way.[17] Sauer[17] advanced an uneasy compromise that recognized the plurality of stakeholders but recognized that a distinction should be made between supporters of a project and those who were uninvolved or active opponents. Others have finessed the issue by focusing on specific dimensions of performance such as budget and schedule variance without using explicitly evaluative terminology.[18–20] In doing so, by the very nature of their choices of performance dimensions to study including the recent introduction of business value as an outcome measure, they can be argued to implicitly favor the expectations of traditional stakeholders such as the owners and managers of businesses. By contrast, others have embraced pluralism and absorbed it into new theoretical approaches such as Actor-Network Theory, which we discuss below.

We can summarize this section by saying that the conceptualization of failure has evolved and matured in three ways. The first has been the distinction between systems and projects. The second has been the expansion of the legitimate scope of IS projects with consequences for what dimensions of performance are assessed. The third has been recognition of the evaluative nature of "failure." This has surfaced disagreement as to which stakeholders' expectations should receive priority. This is a political disagreement rather than one of facts or data. Those who believe that owners and manager as the agents of owner matter more will adopt a more traditional view of failure whereas those who believe that employees, the public, and others have just as much right to their interests and expectations being respected will take a more egalitarian and pluralist position.

EMERGING COGNATE LITERATURES

A further manifestation of the maturation of our understanding of IS failure has been the emergence of several cognate literatures. We briefly discuss in turn risk, partial abandonment, expectation management, escalation, and drift.

Risk as discussed in the extensive IS and software engineering literatures relates to failure by seeking to identify what may be conducive to failure, how to assess its probability and impact, and how to manage it. It is about the probability of failure in some shape or form. It has typically been strongest at identifying sources of risk such as starting conditions or behaviors that give rise to failure.[21] Such studies usually result in extensive lists. The usual suspects thus identified typically include: unclear objectives, uncertain requirements, inadequate project management, too little user involvement, and shortage of top management support. The literature has been less convergent in its focus on risk assessment. While there is an in-principle agreement that risk consists of two elements (the probability of some outcome and its impact), the determination of what the actual risk amounts to has proved problematic. Some have focused on the impact of total failure as represented by abandonment,[22] while others have looked at specific dimensions of performance such as running over schedule or budget. Some studies while recognizing that impact is an element of risk focus principally on the probability of underperformance.[10] The management of risk, and therefore the prevention of failure, has principally consisted of attending to risk factors to prevent their occurring or mitigating their effect when they do occur.

A further set of cognate studies is that on partial abandonment.[23,24] This recognized that a common strategy for coping with underperformance, such as projected schedule or budget overruns, or unanticipated events is to descope, which is to say abandon, some elements of a project. It advanced our thinking by showing that what might simplistically be viewed as a symptom of failure can also be an instrument for preventing failure or further failure. Failure is not a simple cut and dried function of any single indicator.

The focus on expectations failure brought into focus the idea that success and failure are a function of the targets as well as the delivery and performance of a system. That is to say that one way of preventing failure is to manage expectations closer to what is realistically achievable. Ginzberg[25] pioneered this notion. It has received limited attention subsequently[26] although, influenced by Danish research,[27] the United Kingdom's Office of Government Commerce today mandates that all projects control for "strategic optimism," the tendency to set expectations unduly high.

A more abundant cognate literature has been that on escalating commitment to a failing course of action. It addresses the key question of why organizations do not cut their losses sooner.

Inspired by a substantial corpus of work in Organizational Behavior,[28–32] and recognizing that many IS projects have been characterized by sponsors pouring in good money after bad to projects that would ultimately fail, researchers have explored the applicability of existing theory and sought to adapt it to the IS failure phenomenon.[33–35] While escalation of resourcing is indeed a common feature of projects and existing research enriches our understanding of why it occurs, its practical value is limited by the question of whether we can adequately recognize failure in advance and the extent to which escalation often genuinely sustains a project that would have collapsed without it.

Finally, the "drift" literature introduces a further recognizable phenomenon associated with project performance and which may often either result in failure or substitute for it. Instigated by Ciborra,[36] the idea is that objectives are not immutable fixtures in a project but are subject to organizational politics that often neutralizes them without radically reviewing the case for the project or system. The resultant drift leaves organizations with IS investments that do not meet their real needs but which are not subjected to the scrutiny that might lead to their redevelopment or abandonment. Empirical exploration and development of this phenomenon is in its infancy.[37,38]

So, while risk research has worked to connect failure to management practice with a view to reducing its probability, the other cognate literatures have functioned to situate failure within a more sophisticated understanding of organizational contexts and what counts as success within them. Specifically, partial abandonment recognizes that failure on one dimension of performance, namely scope, may be sacrificed to achieve better performance on another such as budget. Expectation management extends this more realistic approach to what will count as good or bad performance by recognizing that targets in the form of stakeholder expectations are legitimately subject to influence and change. Escalation theory is an inverse of partial abandonment in that it shows why larger and larger overruns on resourcing such as budget may be promoted in the interests of achieving scope and outcome expectations, and how this can be dysfunctional. The focus on drift brings a recognition that not all systems and projects are subject to clear-cut evaluations on a continuing basis and that over time objectives and expectations may be diluted through organizational political processes without any re-evaluation occurring. Failure studies if they are to embody a realistic and sympathetic understanding of the richness and complexity of organizational life must embrace the insights that these cognate studies have brought to the table.

APPROACHES TO UNDERSTANDING IS FAILURE

As our understanding of the concept of IS failure has evolved, so too have our approaches to analyzing the causes of failure. We can distinguish three broad approaches. At one extreme, we have static analyses based on the identification of factors that predispose to failure. At the other extreme, the emphasis is on dynamic analysis and the explication of processes by which failure comes about. Bridging the two is the interactionist approach.

Static Approaches

Static, factor-based approaches were at their most popular in the early days when failure was seen more as an objective phenomenon. It was easy then to ask what caused failure and to look for factors that "determined" failure. What were seen in retrospect as common features of failures rapidly became accepted as causes which if rectified would lead to improved performance and outcomes. Research was undertaken to validate this view (see Larsen[39] for a compendious review of factors identified in the research).

Within this class of approaches, several versions developed emphasizing different perspectives and therefore different failure factors. We identify three here: the technological perspective, the organizational/cultural perspective, and the political perspective.

The Technological Perspective

A distinguishing feature of the technological perspective has been its strong focus on the technology elements as the most important considerations for an information system (and often the only components to consider in building the system). The efficient processing of data and the efficient operating of hardware and software provide the goals around which people and procedures are to be organized. Studies in this perspective have often embodied two important assumptions. The first is that technology in all its forms (including hardware, software, and databases) is considered to be "good." The "imperative" in technological imperative refers to the inevitability of technology to "compel" acceptance, use, and conformity to it.[40] Any resistance to a given technology is regarded as merely an irrational, impermanent phenomenon. The second is that implementation of technology alone is sufficient to secure organizational benefits. Together these assumptions conspire to exclude other factors as relevant to success and failure.

The technological perspective therefore implies a dominant focus on formal development procedures for systems analysis and design, the purpose of which is to build or upgrade an information system. There are four major phases in the development cycle. The first phase consists of requirements determination to identify the output of the hardware–software system and the data to be input and processed. The second phase is conceptual design to create a "logical" or conceptual blueprint for the system. The third phase is the "physical" or implementation design for specific software and hardware needed in the information system. Building or upgrading the hardware–software system follows. All formal system development methodologies, as well as the tools of computer-aided software engineering that implement them, involve these four phases or variations of them. The technological perspective tends to underlie not only most development methodologies but also most textbooks on programming, systems analysis, systems design, database management systems, and telecommunications.

In the technological perspective, the diagnosis of an information system failure focuses on a hardware failure, a software failure, a data failure, or any combination of these. The chosen hardware platform may have defects in its manufacture or configuration. The software may suffer from poor design or error-prone construction. The database may harbor inconsistent, incomplete, or outdated data. Since the technological perspective assumes that users can correctly and completely define processing requirements, a failure in the system may also arise because the requirements were specified incorrectly or incompletely. For instance, the information system could lack the capacity to support the processing load if this were not specified correctly.

In general, the remedy for a potential information system failure based on the technological perspective view is for people to conform to the development cycle procedures and to follow processes specified for operation of the system with its hardware, software, and database. The technological perspective requires that people (analysts, designers, managers, programmers, end users, etc.) do or redo the steps of the systems analysis and design correctly. Any failure by people to respond appropriately (e.g., users who do not willingly participate in the requirements determination step, users who resist using the installed system, designers who neglect to install adequate backup procedures, or designers who themselves resist using computerized tools) is seen as a failure of developers and users and not a failure of technological solutions to organizational problems.

The Organizational/Cultural Perspective

By contrast with the technological perspective, in the organizational/cultural perspective it is technology that must adapt to people and to organizations. An organization, in this view, is more than a collection of people. An organization is a structure of roles and rules in which the rules delimit the aims, resources, prerogatives, actions, and behaviors allowed to the person occupying a role. The "culture" in organizational culture refers to the organizational members' shared knowledge or shared understanding of the structure of roles and rules. As successive generations of participants enter, pass through, and leave an organization, its structure of roles and rules continues to exist and to evolve slowly. Upon entering an organization, an individual becomes subject to the organization's structure of roles and rules. Different individuals, when placed in the culture, tend to display similar actions and behaviors. Thus, the culture is the ongoing realization, albeit often partial, of the formal organizational design. An information system application that reflects the desires of one person or a group of people but ignores organizational culture is unlikely to fit the way the organization works.

Preceding the installation of a new information system or the upgrading of an existing one, the organizational/cultural perspective emphasizes the existence of beliefs and assumptions shared among the organizational members, about what computers do, how technology affects jobs, why the current information system is being upgraded or replaced, and so forth. When held by people in contemporary organizations, these beliefs and assumptions operate much like myths, metaphors, and magic among "natives" in preliterate societies.[41] In this view, an information system is but one among many artifacts crafted by organizational natives for use in their daily activities and rituals. Hence, in the organizational/cultural perspective, an information system failure is a failure of this artifact to serve and be compatible with the activities and rituals of the organizational natives.

In the organization culture of information technology, a poor fit between an information system (the hardware, software, and data) and the organizational culture is conducive to an information system failure. A framework useful for identifying a poor fit between information system and organizational culture specifies seven categories of shared beliefs and assumptions that can be violated by systems:[42,43]

1. Shared beliefs and assumptions about innovation and action (e.g., Are original and creative behaviors "good?")
2. Risk taking (e.g., Is the norm to be proactive and take responsibility for one's own actions, or to be reactive and avoid responsibility?)
3. Integration (e.g., How much importance is placed on communicating and cooperating with other organizational members?)
4. Top management contact (e.g., Does top management customarily relate to subordinates by being affirming or openly critical?)
5. Autonomy in decision making (e.g., Are organizational members allowed, encouraged, expected, or trusted to make decisions on their own?)
6. Performance orientation (e.g., Are the criteria for compensation, job security, and job promotion concretely established, explicitly known, and actually used?)
7. Reward orientation (e.g., Do rewards take the form of a "carrot" or "stick?")

In this framework, the failure potential for an information system increases with the number of categories of cultural assumptions with which the information system is incompatible, as well as the extent of the respective incompatibilities. For instance, consider an information system that makes an assumption that there is open sharing of data across the organization's different divisions (integration) and that new users of the system will take responsibility for the decisions that they make with the help of the information system (risk taking). If the organizational members share a norm in which each division guards its data as a valued resource and if the organizational members share, as an accepted practice, the custom of "blaming the computer" for their bad decisions, there is a significant threat of failure for the new system. Any additional incompatibilities between the information system and other shared beliefs and assumptions would increase the threat of an information system failure.

To prevent or to remedy an information system failure, the organizational/cultural perspective requires that the information system be designed and adjusted to respect the constraints that the organizational culture imposes. A strong proponent of this view will maintain that an information system is an artifact crafted to serve the activities of an organization, and therefore the information system should always conform to the organization, rather than vice versa. In other words, a proponent of the organizational culture view may take the position that altering an organizational culture to fit an information system, even if possible in the long run, is a dangerous course of action.

The organizational/cultural perspective extends the technological perspective by bringing in organizational/cultural factors. It also introduces the idea of a fit between the technology and the organization/culture. However, it continues to assume that the important challenge is to establish the right conditions in terms of getting two sets of factors aligned with each other.

The Political Perspective

The political perspective extends the organizational/cultural perspective by introducing power as the real basis by which organizations work. Power is the ability of a person, group, or organizational unit to overcome resistance or opposition to achievement of its ends; politics is the exercise of this ability.[44–46] In this view, activities that accompany the development, implementation, and use of an information system provide an arena in which a person, group, or organizational unit can exercise power, whether or not the ends for which the power is exercised bear any relevance to the purposes that the information system is ostensibly said to serve. Success or failure of the information system relative to these ostensible purposes is secondary to the achievement of the power objectives.

In a classic case study of an information system implementation,[47] a new information system threatened to alter the power between the corporate accounting group and divisional accounting personnel. The system was designed to allow the accounting group at corporate headquarters immediate access to data belonging to the accounting group in each of the company's different divisions. In the existing procedures, each division controlled its own data (stored in thick manual ledger books), and corporate accounting could only obtain it through reports prepared by division accountants. Built into the design of the new information system was a presumption that there should be a different distribution of power relative to the division data. This design was contrary to the existing power over the data. In the technological imperative view and the organizational culture view, resistance to the proposed system could be explained as opposition to a more efficient system or opposition to changes in the culture of corporate versus division roles. In the political perspective, the efficiency considerations or role changes were secondary; the main objective of the system for the corporate accountants was political. They wanted to disrupt the existing balance of power in the organization and introduce a new balance of power based on data access that favored the corporate group.

In the political perspective, the failure potential for an information system application increases if it violates the constraints imposed by the organizational distribution of power. In some cases, an application will be allowed to succeed only if it supports the political agenda of a powerful group within the organization. IS may be used explicitly to change the distribution of power in an organization; in such cases, the design of the system is a secondary factor in success or failure. The major issue is the effectiveness of change agents in negotiating redistribution or organizational power.

To prevent or remedy an information system failure due primarily to strong political opposition, the political considerations must be surfaced and negotiated. Political considerations may be somewhat hidden; surfacing them through high-level discussions allows the effect of the system to be dealt with in the context of high-level goals of the organization. An explicit understanding of the effect of the system on the relative power of the organizational participants may allow negotiations and compromise. In the absence of such compromise, political opposition to a system may be sufficient to cause failure.

The political perspective has sometimes been operationalized in research in terms of the fit between an information system or project and the power structure. Such operationalizations fall under the factor approach. Others however have recognized that power can be renegotiated and as such the processes by which IS are treated affect their success or failure.

Interactionist Approaches

Interactionist approaches bridge the step from factors to processes. In accepting that factors may influence each other, they implicitly introduce a temporal element to the analysis of failure. For example, a factors analysis might identify inadequate involvement of business users in requirements specification and user resistance as critical causes of failure. The interactionist recognizes that the user resistance may be a function of the lack of involvement. In turn, perceived user resistance may deter technologists from consulting the users. The causes of failure develop and harden over time. Implicitly, such approaches recognize that the different factor approaches embody important elements that may contribute to a comprehensive analysis of failure. We briefly describe two such approaches: the sociotechnical perspective and the exchange perspective.

The Sociotechnical Perspective

In the sociotechnical systems view, an information system is more than a technical system of hardware and software. An information system is a social system that uses information technology.[48,49] Failure is not a failure of the information technology alone or the organization alone, because there is a strong interaction between the two. The same information technology will exhibit different properties when used in different organizational contexts. Sociotechnical theory[50] predicts that optimizing only the technical system or optimizing only the social system will lead to information system failure. To avoid failure, neither system can be managed separately from the other.

The interactive effects between the social system and the information technology have a parallel in the chemical difference between mixtures and compounds. The properties of a mixture are simply a combined set of the respective properties of the individual elements that constitute the mixture. The reason is that the elements in a mixture do not react to one another; their respective properties remain intact. However, the properties of a chemical compound are different from the respective properties of the constituent elements. The reason is that the elements react to one another; their respective properties are replaced by the new properties of the compound entity. In this analogy, an information system is more like a compound than a mixture. Its constituent social system and information technology react to one another, so that their properties in combination are different from their properties in isolation.

In the sociotechnical view, failure potential is increased by development processes and procedures that do not integrate both social and technical considerations. In sociotechnical development, the future users of the system specify important job and work design considerations. There is a joint effort involving both users and technical personnel to consider alternative information system technical designs and select one that achieves a reasonable trade-off between job design and technical efficiency. Dominance of technical considerations increases the probability of failure due to user resistance. The sociotechnical approach recognizes the fact that user resistance can cause a technically well designed system to fail and user enthusiasm can cause a somewhat mediocre technical design to succeed. These dynamics are the basis for a process that looks for the best combination of technical and social factors.

To prevent or remedy an information system failure, the sociotechnical view specifies a sociotechnical requirements and development process. Users are empowered with sufficient information to be effective participants in design discussions and decisions. Obtaining commitment by users to make the system succeed is an essential part of the process.

The Exchange Perspective

The exchange perspective[17] develops the sociotechnical perspective in one specific direction. It emphasizes one critical basis of interaction, viz. the creation and sustaining of a balanced exchange between a project team or those who manage an information system and the key supporters of that project or system. It argues that projects and systems fail if two conditions obtain[1]: there are insufficient resources to continue developing or operating the system, and[2] key supporters are dissatisfied.

This perspective sees systems and projects as needing a range of different forms of support from a range of stakeholders. Support can include material resources such as funds, equipment, space, practical support such as involvement in project processes, problem-solving, and management attention, psychic support such as publicly observable commitment, as well as organizational support in terms of politics and working the organizational system. Stakeholders who may be key supporters include senior management sponsors, operational users, end customers, the project team, and the supply chain. As supporters' levels of satisfaction may ebb and flow over time, the task of IS management and project management is one of maintaining sufficient levels of satisfaction to ensure a continuing flow of needed resources. Thus, for example, the project process can be seen as the challenge of marshalling the right resources to deliver sufficient progress and expectation of benefit that supporters will continue to provide those resources. If progress stalls, resources needed to overcome a hurdle may not be forthcoming resulting in further difficulties for the project and further damage to supporters' expectations. The project team may be able to break out of this vicious circle by actions that restore confidence such as bringing forward the delivery of some benefits or by actively managing supporters' perceptions. If on the other hand it is unable to break out of this vicious circle, the project will be set for failure. Projects can be seen as an ongoing complex interactive process where exchange is at the heart of the interactions.

Process Approaches

Since the mid-1990s failure analyses have emerged that focus more on a detailed examination of process and the search for patterns in process. They have tended to view success and failure outcomes as not determined by factors or even by interactions but as a function of a yet more complex account of the processes by which multifarious influences affect projects and systems over time. As yet no single perspective has come to dominate the field. However, we shall give special attention to Actor-Network Theory because it has been widely employed in social studies of IS including failures, and because it encompasses ideas from numerous other perspectives.

From within the IS discipline, Newman and Robey[51] enabled process analyses of failure through their more general articulation of the elements of process analysis, and Newman has applied it in his failure research.[52,53] Outside the discipline, in the broad area of social studies of technology, a number of case studies have been published that have cast light on IS failure through detailed accounts of IS processes.[54] This has then been brought back into the discipline by critical theory–oriented researchers such as Howcroft, Wilson, and Mitev adopting a social shaping of technology perspective and applying it to failures.[55,56]

Actor-Network Theory

Actor-Network Theory has recently become a popular tool for analyzing IS failure.[36–38,57–59] Actor Network Theory has a number of attractions. First, it is the first approach in many years to take a balanced position in relation to technology. That is, where for most researchers over the last 15–20 years it has been accepted that technology is subservient to human/organizational objectives, Actor-Network Theory places technology on a par with other stakeholders. It then views the object of study, say a project failure, through the lens of the actor-network in which it is embedded. Humans, institutions, and technologies are among the stakeholders who populate the network and propagate influences through its nodes. In this manner, the complexity of the contexts within which IS failures occur is well represented. Further, one of the core ideas of the theory is that of breakdown. The essence of this insight is that when something appears to be functioning well we treat it as a black box. Only when it begins to fail do we start to unpack it to understand what is going on. Thus, for example, we can understand "drift" in these terms.

The limitations of Actor-Network Theory are that it is still evolving a set of concepts for general use. Early analyses using it have tended to be very complex and not productive of readily practical conclusions.

Conclusion: The Future of Failure

Ten years ago, the question arose as to whether the increased commodification of IT would lead to standard solutions to such an extent that the problem of failure might dissolve.[60] The alternative scenario was that the strategic benefits of IT would be such that organizations would continue to seek to differentiate themselves and would therefore continue to pursue distinctive, non-commodity solutions. The improvements in performance are noted earlier in this entry but the continued difficulties in achieving expectations suggest that elements of both scenarios have occurred. This suggests that the issues associated with understanding and preventing failure will continue to be highly relevant for the foreseeable future.

The challenge for research is to strike a balance between analyses that embody every causal constituent in a failure but where it is difficult to see the wood for the trees, and those that are simpler but which promise too much to the practitioner because they suggest that a relatively simple intervention will be sufficient to prevent failure. Having developed over the last 20–30 years a growing maturity in our understanding it is easy for research to fall into the former category. It is this trick that Actor-Network Theory or alternatives will have to master if it is to be both academically successful and practically useful.

CONCLUSION: SUMMARY OF LESSONS ABOUT FAILURE FOR PRACTITIONERS

The entry has lessons for scholars and researchers. It also has lessons for practitioners. These can be summarized as follows:

1. The evaluation of success or failure for a project is not usually a simple "success" or "failure" or identification of a single reason for the result. Success or failure depends on the criteria being used, the stakeholders being considered, and the level of expectations.
2. Organizations respond to perceptions of failure in various ways. One response is abandonment. Other possible responses include escalation and revision of expectations.
3. The ideal lessons for practitioners would be a set of simple prescriptions to prevent failure and ensure success. The analysis of the failure research provides guidance but no simple list of prescriptions. A thoughtful practitioner seeking to reduce the potential for failure should consider both static factors that predispose to failure and the interaction of factors that may lead to failure.
4. Static causes. Three types of causes that predispose to failure and therefore should be considered as part of prevention measures are
   a. Technological. The focus in failure prevention and failure analysis is on correct and complete hardware, software, or data (or a combination of these technological elements). Today, these are the least common causes of failure.
   b. Organization/culture. The focus is on a good fit between the system and the activities, rules, roles, rituals, and culture of an organization.
   c. Political. The focus is on incorporating the effect of political power on design, acceptance, and use of a system.
5. Interaction causes. The focus on static causes may not be sufficient. Factors may influence each other. Two approaches to understanding and analyzing failure based on interactions are
   a. Sociotechnical. This analysis is based on the view that an information system is a social system that uses information technology. To avoid failure, the interaction of the two systems must be considered in the designs of both.
   b. Exchange perspective. Systems and projects need forms of support from a range of stakeholders. Critical to avoiding failure is creating and sustaining a balanced exchange between a project team and key supporters.
6. An emerging view that is perhaps not ready for widespread practitioner use is to analyze the process by which a complex set of influences affect the way projects and systems develop over time.

ACKNOWLEDGMENT

This entry adds to and develops aspects of the entry on Information Systems Failure by Gordon B. Davis, Allen S. Lee, and Kathryn Nickles in the previous edition of the Encyclopaedia of Library and Information Sciences.

REFERENCES

1. Naur, P.; Randell, B. *Software Engineering: Report on a Conference Sponsored by the NATO Science Committee*; Garmisch: Germany, October 7–11, 1968. http://homepages.cs.ncl.ac.uk/brian.randell/NATO/nato1968.PDF (accessed January 11, 2007).
2. Colton, K.W. Computers and police: Patterns of success and failure. Sloan Manage. Rev. **1972**, winter, 75–98.
3. Lucas, H.C. Jr. *Why Information Systems Fail*; Columbia University Press: New York, 1975.
4. DeLone, W.H.; McLean, E.R. Information systems success: The quest for the dependent variable. Inform. Syst. Res. **1992**, *3* (1), 60–95.
5. Hirschheim, R.; Smithson, S. A critical analysis of information systems evaluation. In *Information Systems Assessment: Issues and Challenges*; Bjørn-Andersen, N., Davis, G.B., Eds.; Elsevier (North-Holland): Amsterdam, 1988; 17–37.
6. Johnson, J. Chaos: The dollar drain of IT project failures. Appl. Dev. Trends **1995**, January, 41–47.
7. Johnson, J. *My Life is Failure*; Standish Group International: West Yarmouth, MA, 2006.
8. Jørgensen, M.; Moløkken-Østvold, K.J. How large are software cost overruns? Critical comments on the Standish Group's CHAOS reports. Inform. Softw. Technol. **2006**, *48* (4), 297–301.
9. Taylor, A. IT projects: Sink or swim. Comput. Bull. **2000**, *42*, January, 24–26.
10. Sauer, C.; Gemino, A.; Reich, B. Managing projects for success: The impact of size and volatility on IT project performance. Commun. ACM **2007**, *50* (11), 79–84.
11. Neumann, P. CACM inside risks, 2007, http://www.csl.sri.com/users/neumann/insiderisks.html#menu2 (accessed January 11, 2007).
12. Hodgson, M. Computer error keeps airport on summer time. Guardian Newspaper; Monday October 29, 2007.
13. Markus, M.L. Technochange management: Using IT to drive organizational change. J. Inform. Technol. **2004**, *19* (1), 4–20.
14. Ross, J.W.; Vitale, M. The ERP revolution: Surviving vs. thriving. Inform. Syst. Front. **2000**, *2* (2), 233–241.
15. Lyytinen, K.; Hirschheim, R. Information systems failures: A survey and classification of the empirical literature. Oxf. Surv. Inform. Technol. **1987**, *4*, 257–309.
16. Ewusi-Mensah, K.; Przasnyski, Z.H. On information systems project abandonment: An exploratory study of organizational practices. MIS Quart. **1991**, 67–86.
17. Sauer, C. *Why Information Systems Fail: A Case Study Approach*; Alfred Waller: Henley-on-Thames, 1993.
18. Faraj, S.; Sproull, L. Coordinating expertise in software development teams. Manage. Sci. **2000**, *46* (12), 1554–1568.
19. Nidumolu, S. The effect of coordination and uncertainty on software project performance: Residual performance risk as an intervening variable. Inform. Syst. Res. **1995**, *6* (3), 191–219.
20. Gemino, A.; Reich, B.H.; Sauer, C. A temporal model of information technology project performance. J. Manage. Inform. Syst. **2008**, *24* (3), 9–44.
21. Schmidt, R.; Lyytinen, K.; Keil, M.; Cule, P. Identifying software project risks: An international delphi study. J. Manage. Inform. Syst. **2001**, *17* (4), 5–36.
22. Barki, H.; Rivard, S.; Talbot, J. An integrative contingency model of software project risk management. J. Manage. Inform. Syst. **2001**, *17* (4), 37–69.
23. Sauer, C. Partial abandonment as a strategy for avoiding failure. In *Information Systems Development: Human, Social and Organizational Aspects*; Proceedings of IFIP WG8.2 Working Conference, Noordwijkerhout, May 17–19, 1993; Avison, D.E., deGross, J., Kendall, J., Eds.; Elsevier (North Holland): Amsterdam; 143–167.
24. Martin, A.; Chan, M. Information systems project redefinition in New Zealand: Will we ever learn? Aust. Comput. J. **1996**, *28* (1), 27–40.
25. Ginzberg, M.J. Early diagnosis of MIS implementation failure: Promising results and unanswered questions. Manage. Sci. **1981**, *27* (4), 459–478.

26. Sauer, C.; Willcocks, L.P. Unreasonable expectations: NHS IT, Greek choruses and the games institutions play around mega-programmes. J. Inform. Technol. **2007**, *22* (3), 195–201.
27. Flyvbjerg, B.; Bruzelius, N.; Rothengatter, W. *Megaprojects and Risk: An Anatomy of Ambition*; Cambridge University Press: Cambridge, 2003.
28. Brockner, J.; Rubin, J.Z. *Entrapment in Escalating Conflicts: A Social Psychological Analysis*; Springer-Verlag: New York, 1985.
29. Brockner, J. The escalation of commitment to a failing course of action: Toward theoretical progress. Acad. Manage. Rev. **1992**, *17* (1), 39–61.
30. Ross, J.; Staw, B.M. Expo 86: An escalation prototype. Admin. Sci. Quart. **1986**, *31*, 274–297.
31. Ross, J.; Staw, B.M. Organizational escalation and exit: Lessons from the Shoreham nuclear power plant. Acad. Manage. J. **1993**, *36* (4), 701–732.
32. Staw, B.M.; Ross, J. Behavior in escalation situations: Antecedents, prototypes, and solutions. In *Research in Organizational Behavior*; Staw, B.M., Cummings, L.L., Eds.; JAI Press: Greenwich, CT, 1990; Vol. 9, 39–78.
33. Keil, M. Pulling the plug: Software project management and the problem of escalation. MIS Quart. **1995**, December, 420–447.
34. Keil, M.; Mann, J.; Rai, A. Why software projects escalate: An empirical analysis and test of four theoretical models. MIS Quart. **2000**, *24* (4), 631–664.
35. Drummond, H. *Escalation in Decision Making: The Tragedy of Taurus*; Oxford University Press: Oxford, 1996.
36. Ciborra, C. and Associates, *From Control to Drift: The Dynamics of Corporate Information Iinfrasructures*; Oxford University Press: Oxford, 2000.
37. Holmstrom, J.; Stalder, F. Drifting technologies and multipurpose networks: The case of the Swedish cashcard. Inform. Organ. **2001**, *11*, 187–206.
38. Elbanna, A.R. The inertia of ERP projects: Diffusion or drift. In *Organizational Dynamics of Technology Based Innovation: Diversifying the Research Agenda*, Proceedings of the IFIP TC 8 WG 8.6 International Working Conference, June 14–16, 2007; McMaster, T., Wastell, D., Ferneley, E., DeGross, J., Eds.; Manchester, U.K., 2007; 253–266.
39. Larsen, K.R.T. A taxonomy of antecedents of information systems success: Variable analysis studies. J. Manage. Inform. Syst. **2003**, *20* (2), 169–246.
40. Markus, M.L.; Robey, D. Information technology and organizational change: Causal structure in theory and research. Manage. Sci. **1988**, *34* (5), 583–598.
41. Hirschheim, R.; Newman, M. Symbolism and information systems development: Myth, metaphor and magic. Inform. Syst. Res. **1991**, *2* (1), 29–62.
42. Romm, T.; Pliskin, N.; Weber, Y.; Lee, A. Identifying organizational culture clash in MIS implementation. Inform. Manage. **1990**, *21* (2), 99–109.
43. Pliskin, N.; Romm, T.; Lee, A.; Weber, Y. Presumed versus actual organizational culture: Managerial implications for implementation of information systems. Comput. J. **1993**, *36* (2), 143–152.
44. Pfeffer, J. *Power in Organization*; Ballinger: Cambridge, MA, 1981.
45. Markus, M.L.; Pfeffer, J. Power and the design and implementation of accounting and control systems. Account. *Organ. Soc.* **1983**, *8* (2/3), 205–218.
46. Robey, D. Power and politics. In *Designing Organizations*; Robey, D., Irwin: Homewood: Illinois, 1991; 347–382.
47. Markus, M.L. Power, politics and MIS implementation. Commun. ACM **1983**, *26* (6), June, 430–444.
48. Land, F.; Hirschheim, R. Participative systems design: Rationale, tools and techniques. J. Appl. Syst. Anal. **1983**, *10.*
49. Davis, G.B.; Lee, A.S.; Nickles, K.R.; Chatterjee, S.; Hartung, R.; Wu, Y. Diagnosis of an information system failure. Inform. Manage. **1992**, *23* (5), 293–318.
50. Cherns, A. The principles of sociotechnical design. Hum. Relat. **1976**, *29* (8), 783–779.
51. Newman, M.; Robey, D. A social process model of user-analyst relationships. MIS Quart **1992**, *16* (2), June, 249–266.
52. Newman, M.; Noble, F. User involvement as an interaction process: A case study. Inform. Syst. Res. **1990**, *1*, 1.
53. Pan, S.L.; Pan, G.S.C.; Newman, M.; Flynn, D. Escalation and de-escalation of commitment to information systems projects: Insights from a project evaluation model. Eur. J. Operat. Res. **2006**, *173* (3), 1139–1160.
54. Bloomfield, B.; Coombs, R.; Knights, D.; Littler, D., Eds. *Information Technology and Organizations: Strategies, Networks and Integration*; Oxford University Press: Oxford, 1997.

55. Mitev, N.N. More than a failure? The computerised reservation systems at French Railways. Inform. Technol. People **1996**, *9* (4), 8–19.
56. Howcroft, D.; Mitev, N.; Wilson, M. What we may learn from the social shaping of technology approach. In *Social Theory and Philosophy of IS*; Mingers, J., Willcocks, L., Eds.; John Wiley and Sons: Chichester, 2004; 329–371.
57. Vidgen, R.T.; Mc Master, T. Black boxes, non-human stakeholders, and the translation of IT through mediation. In *Information Technology and Changes in Organizational Work*; Proceedings of the IFIP WG 8.2 working conference on information technology and changes in organizational work. Orlikowski, W.J., Walsham, G., Jones, M.R., DeGross, J.I., Eds.; Chapman and Hall: London, 1995; 250–271.
58. Sarker, S.; Sarker, S.; Sidorova, A. Understanding business process change failure: An actor-network perspective. J. Manage. Inform. Syst. **2006**, *23* (1), 51–86.
59. Bartis, E.; Mitev, N.N. A multiple narrative approach to information systems failure: A successful system that failed. In *Relevant rigour, rigorous relevance*; Proceedings of 15th European Conference on Information Systems, June 7–9, 2007; St. Gallen University, Switzerland.
60. Sauer, C. Deciding the future for IS failures: Not the decision you might think. In *Re-Thinking Management Information Systems*; Galliers, R.D., Currie, W., Eds.; Oxford University Press: Oxford, 1999.

Part III

Types of Information Retrieval Systems

In this section, we proceed to review many different types of information retrieval systems, with an emphasis on Web-based systems. Though some common internal mechanisms are used within IR systems, such systems also have to be adapted to the hugely varying circumstances of their use. One size does not fit all, and great improvements in performance can be attained through design for specific uses and audiences.

Randolph Hock, of Online Strategies, introduces "Search Engines" (Chapter 22), the key type of IR system used on the World Wide Web. Carlos Castillo and Ricardo Baeza-Yates, of Yahoo! Research, apply and adapt core concepts of information retrieval to the Web context in Chapter 23, "Web Retrieval and Mining." Kieron O'Hara and Dame Wendy Hall, a Fellow of the Royal Society, and one of the early developers of the Semantic Web, describe the "Semantic Web" in Chapter 24, of that name. The purpose of the Semantic Web is to provide structure and links among heterogeneous information sources to enable automatic computation and other forms of automatic processing on the underlying information. "XML Information Retrieval" (Chapter 25), described by Mounia Lalmas, of the Department of Computing Science, University of Glasgow, deals with the marking up of documents to enable targeted retrieval from portions of documents.

Yiyu Yao and colleagues, of the Beijing University of Technology, provide a model for IR systems that includes several kinds of support for the system and user, in order to improve overall performance, in Chapter 26 "Information Retrieval Support Systems." About these "IRSS" they say: "By moving beyond browsing, navigating, and retrieval, IRSS focus on a wide range of supporting functionalities, including summarization, exploration, analysis, knowledge discovery, results organization, retrieval strategy recommendation, and so on."

Each of the next three chapters addresses a major extension of conventional IR system design, making retrieval possible beyond the historical emphasis on monolingual text. Douglas W. Oard addresses "Multilingual Information Access" (Chapter 27); Vittorio Castelli, of IBM, lays out "Still Image Search and Retrieval" (Chapter 28); and Kjell Lemström and George Tzanetakis present "Music Information Retrieval" (Chapter 29).

Each of the remaining chapters in Section 3 addresses what could be called application areas—systems developed for particular environments. These areas, however, are in most cases so large themselves that they constitute their own research and development arenas. Whole conferences, professional associations, and grants programs exist to develop IR systems in these areas, and the ongoing research continually improves the efficiency and effectiveness of information storage and retrieval, as well as our understanding of the human-system interface in a wide range of human situations.

The general importance of human contact and the explosive growth of online social media have generated their own research and development areas. Hady W. Lauw, of Microsoft Search Labs, and Ee-Peng Lim, of the School of Information Systems, Singapore Management University, explore "Web Social Mining" (Chapter 30) and Derek L. Hansen and colleagues drill in on "Recommender Systems and Expert Locators" (Chapter 31).

In the broad context of business and other organizational environments, Dick Stenmark presents "Knowledge Management Systems" (Chapter 32). He discusses the dimensions that are important in distinguishing and designing various types of knowledge management systems. A specific class of knowledge management systems, one at the heart of organizational performance, is covered in Chapter 33, "Decision Support Systems," as explained by Marek J. Druzdzel and Roger R. Flynn. Still another class of system supporting organizational performance, in this case by teams, is to be found in Chapter 34, "Collaborative Systems and Groupware," by David Jank.

Because of the value of geographical information to many business, government, and other institutions, geographic information has itself become a major research and development area. Timothy F. Leslie and Nigel M. Waters, of the George Mason University Department of Geography and Geoinformation Science, introduce the reader to this large area in "Geographic Information Systems (GIS)" (Chapter 35). Another area drawing vast sums of research and development money is medical information systems. In this context, Kai Zheng, of the University of Michigan Department of Health Management and Policy, introduces "Clinical Decision-Support Systems" (Chapter 36).

The section ends with several chapters on information systems in library, academic, and museum contexts. Libraries were, of course, the original information institutions, and, in the developing digital age, museums have joined libraries in needing to process and retrieve large amounts of digital information and images for their staff and for public users of museum Websites.

"Integrated Library Systems (ILS)," described in Chapter 37 by Emily Gallup Fayen, have been under development for over 40 years, helping libraries integrate the processing necessary to order materials, catalog them, provide an end-user catalog, manage circulation records, and de-accession resources, all in a single system reducing redundancy. The chief library information systems seen by library users, both in-house and remotely online, are the "Online Public Access Catalogs (OPACs)" (Chapter 38), described by Kevin Butterfield. These were one of the earliest information retrieval systems available to the general public, developed in the early 1980's, and they pioneered many IR innovations.

Public libraries have the added issue to deal with of ensuring that children not be exposed to unsuitable websites while searching the public computers online in libraries. Internet filtering is a kind of reverse IR system, identifying retrievals to *exclude*. Lynn Sutton, of the Reynolds Library of Wake Forest University in North Carolina, describes these systems and the social issues surrounding them in Chapter 39, "Internet Filtering Software and Its Effects."

For academics and students, the development of bibliographies and citation lists becomes a major information processing and retrieval issue when references grow into the hundreds or thousands. Dirk Schoonbaert and Victor Rosenberg review the history and state of the art of this class of small, but vital information retrieval systems in "Personal Bibliographic Systems (PBS)" (Chapter 40).

The section closes with three chapters on museums-related information systems. Museums need to keep IR systems of their sometimes vast collections, and each record within the system requires unusually extensive description—of the item itself, its provenance and legal standing, its history of curation, conservation, loans, etc. This special kind of database requires many kinds of retrieval capabilities and field types. Perian Sully, of the Judah L. Magnes Museum, and an expert in these "Collection Management Systems" (Chapter 41), describes them for the reader. Museums have been innovative in developing "Interactive Multimedia in Museums" (Chapter 42) for visitors. Nik Honeysett, of the J. Paul Getty Museum, describes this type of information system. Finally, David Bearman and Jennifer Trant, major originators and players in the world of museum informatics, describe the development and management of "Museum Web Sites and Digital Collections" (Chapter 43).

22 Search Engines

Randolph Hock

CONTENTS

INTRODUCTION

Web search engines, for the public at large, have come to be perhaps the most frequently used computer services for locating information. To some degree the same is true for many researchers, information professionals, and others. To most effectively and efficiently utilize these services, some understanding of the structure, make-up, content, features, and variety and breadth of these services is essential. This entry addresses those various aspects including just what is meant by "search engines," the components of a search engine, and typical search features, and it provides a profile of the major general Web search engines and a look at specialty search engines, visualization engines, and metasearch engines.

WHAT IS MEANT BY "SEARCH ENGINES"?

The term "search engines" can have a variety of meanings, in the broadest sense referring to any computer program that facilitates the searching of a database. In the context of library and information science, however, the term has come to primarily refer to "Web search engines," that is, those services on the Web that allow searching of a large database of Web pages and other Web content by word, phrase, and other criteria. (For this discussion, hereafter, "search engines" will be taken to refer to "Web search engines.") A certain level of ambiguity becomes apparent, however, when it is realized that what is often referred to as a "search engine" is often a reference to the overall service that is provided, beyond just a search of Web sites. ("Google" is thought of not as just the searching part of the Google enterprise, but the many added features and content as well.) It is often impossible and unproductive to discuss the narrower "searching" part without discussing the broader range of services. That ambiguity in terminology is a result and artifact of the history of search engines but recognition of the ambiguity is necessary for an understanding of the current nature of such services.

Search engines vary in a number of ways and most could be considered to fall into one of four categories: General Web Search Engines (which have the purpose of searching a large portion of all pages that exist on the Web), Specialty Search Engines (which focus on searching a specific kind of document, file type, or sources from a particular subject or geographic region), Visualization Search Engines (which furnish diagrams, images, or other "visuals" to show relationships among the items in a particular set of retrieved items), and Metasearch Engines (which gather together the search results on a specific topic from multiple search engines).

COMPONENTS OF A SEARCH ENGINE

General Web search engines and specialty search engines can be considered to have four major components that correspond to the steps required to create the service: 1) the identification and gathering of the material (Web pages, etc.) to be included in the engine's database; 2) an indexing program and the corresponding generated indexes; 3) the searching and ranking algorithms; and 4) the user interface.

Identifying Material to Be Included

Search engines identify those Web pages (and other items) to be included in the service's database by two means: "crawling" and submissions of pages. The first, "crawling" consists of having programs ("crawlers" or "spiders") that on an ongoing basis scan the Internet to identify new sites or sites that have changed, gather information from those sites, and feed that information to the search engine's indexing mechanism. The crawlers start by examining pages that the service already knows about and looking there for "new" links (links that the service does not already know about). When such links are identified, the pages to which the links led are likewise examined for "new" links, and so on. More popular Web sites (such as those that have lots of links to them) may be crawled more thoroughly and more frequently than less popular sites.

The second way search engines identify new items to be added to the database is by having Web site owners (or others) "submit" sites or pages. Most engines provide a form by which this can be done. Search services maintain their own policies as to whether submitted (or for that matter, pages identified by crawling) will indeed be added to the database, particularly looking to exclude unacceptable content (spam, sexually explicit material, etc.)

Search Engine's Index and Indexing Program

After a new or changed page is identified by the search engine's crawler, the page will typically be indexed under virtually every word on the page (up to some usually undisclosed limit). In addition to text words, other parts or characteristics of the page may also be indexed, including the URL (Uniform Resource Locator, the "Web address"), parts of the URL, links, metadata found in the "head" of the document, the URLs of links on the page, image filenames, words in linked text, etc. By identifying and indexing these pieces of data (pieces or characteristics of the Web page or other type of indexed document, such as an Excel file), they become searchable "fields," thereby allowing users to use those fields to increase the quality of their search. The search system may also "derive" additional fields, such as language, by analysis of the document.

The Search Engine's Retrieval and Ranking Algorithms

By narrow definition, the actual search "engine" is the search service's retrieval program, that is, the program that identifies (retrieves) those pages in the database that match the criteria indicated by a user's query. That identification function is necessarily supplemented by another important and more challenging program that is used to determine the order in which the retrieved records should be displayed, based on measures that try to identify which retrieved records (pages, etc.) are likely to have the highest relevance in respect to the user's query.

This "relevance-ranking" algorithm usually takes many factors into account.

Exactly what factors go into the relevance ranking process varies, but they include: use of keywords in titles, text, headings, etc.; popularity of the sites (how many and which sites link to the site.); words used in anchors (clickable text); internal links (how many and what kind of links within the larger site point to the page); quality of links leading out to other pages (whether they point to high quality pages); etc.[1]

The success or the failure of the relevance ranking algorithm is critical to the user's perception of the search engine, the user's continued use of that system, and the commercial success of the engine.

The Interface Presented to the User for Gathering Queries

This interface the user typically sees includes the home page of the search service and other pages (such as an advanced search page) that present search options to the users and accept the users' search queries, as well as the search results page. The search service can choose to have their page focus almost exclusively on "search" (as with Google) or be a more general, wide-reaching "portal" page, providing much more than just searching capabilities. (The "portal" dilemma for search services will be discussed in more detail later.)

Regardless of what other services and information are provided on the service's homepage, the "searching" part usually consists of a single search box plus links to an advanced search page and to other searchable databases that are made available by the service (images, video, news, etc.) Usually there are also links to "help" screens, etc. While the simplicity of a single search box appeals to the less experienced user, it also usually provides substantial, but not obvious, capabilities for extensive searching sophistication, such as the potential for using Boolean logic and "prefixes" (e.g., "title:")

to perform field searching and other functions. The advanced search page much more explicitly lays out the possibilities to the user, providing a menu-based approach to utilization of features.

The Portal Dilemma

From the early days of search engines, search engine providers have wrestled with the decision as to whether to make their home page one that focuses almost exclusively on "search" or one that provides a variety of added services such as news, weather, etc., the latter approach often referred to as a "portal." From its beginning, before it was even a "search engine" and was just a directory, Yahoo! preferred the portal approach. AltaVista, a leading search engine in the 1990s, went back and forth between the two extremes, a situation which may have contributed to its demise. Google was, from the beginning, almost purely "search engine" and the simplicity of its interface was undoubtedly one factor in its rapid rise in popularity. Search services tend to "cover their bets" however, by providing alternatives. Yahoo! provides a Google-like option at search.yahoo.com and Google provides a personalizable Yahoo-style page with its iGoogle portal page.

Searching Options Typically Provided

All leading search engines provide a range of user accessible options that permit the user to modify their search queries in ways that can improve both the precision and the recall of their search results. Which specific options are provided varies from engine to engine, but there are several that are fairly typical (and some that are unique to a particular engine.) The most typical options include Boolean operations, phrase searching, language specification, and specifying that only those pages are retrieved for which the search term appears in a particular part (field) of the record such as the title, URL, or links. Since engines now cover other document types beyond just pages written in HyperText Markup Language (HTML), with several engines users can also narrow their search to a specific file format (Web pages, Adobe Acrobat files, Excel files, etc.). Most engines also provide an option to filter "adult content" material.

Boolean Logic

In the context of Web searching, "Boolean logic" refers to the process of identifying those items found in the database that contain a particular combination of search terms. It is used to indicate that a particular group of terms must all be present (the Boolean "AND"), that any of a particular group of terms is acceptable (the Boolean "OR"), or that if a particular term is present, the item is rejected (the Boolean "NOT").[2]

Engines usually provide two different ways to qualify a query with Boolean operations (1): the option of applying a syntax directly to what is entered in the search box and (2); menu options on an advanced search page. Using the menus can be thought of as "simplified Boolean" and, depending upon the structure of the advanced search page, may or may not provide the precision achievable by the use of syntax in the main search box (For example, the ability to apply "OR"s to more than one of the concepts included in the query may be done in the main search box but may not be allowed for on the advanced search page.)

The exact syntax used varies with the search engine. All major engines currently automatically apply an "AND" between your terms, so when the following is entered:

prague economics tourism

what will be retrieved is what more traditionally would have been expressed as: prague AND economics AND tourism.

Very precise search requirements can be expressed using combinations of the operators along with parentheses to indicate the order of operations. For example:

```
(grain OR corn OR wheat) (production OR harvest) oklahoma 1997
```

At various times, search engines have allowed the use of symbols (+, &, –, etc.) instead of words (AND, OR, NOT) and indeed, for the "NOT" most search engines currently suggest the use of a minus sign in front of the term. Some search engines require the use of parentheses around "nested" (OR'ed) terms, some do not.

For details on Boolean syntax for any search engine, the help pages for that engine should be consulted. There are also Web sites, such as Search Engine Showdown from Greg Notess (http://www.searchengineshowdown.com) that summarize the syntax (and other features) for all major engines.

The alternative to using syntax to apply Boolean is the use of menus on an advanced search page. There, for example, you may find a pull-down menu, where, if you choose the "all the words" option, you are requesting the Boolean AND. If you choose the "any of the words" option from such a menu, you are specifying an OR. There is usually also a box for excluding terms ("NOT").

Phrase Searching

Phrase searching is an option that is available in virtually every search engine, and almost always uses the same syntax, the use of quotation marks around the phrase. For example, searching on "Red River" (with the quotation marks) will assure that you get only those pages that contain the word "red" immediately in front of the word "river." Of all search engine techniques, this is widely regarded as one of the most useful and easiest for achieving higher precision in a Web search. It is also useful for such things as identifying quotations and identifying plagiarism.

Title Searching

Title searching, that is, limiting your retrieval to only those items (pages) that have a particular term or combination of terms in their title, is one example of "field searching," as referred to earlier. It is also another example of a technique that can yield very high precision in a search. Most search engines use the "intitle:" prefix and/or the "allintitle:" prefix for the syntax for title searching. ("allintitle:" allows specifying that more than one term be included in the title, not necessarily in any particular order.)

URL, Site, and Domain Searching

Search engines typically index Web pages (and other document types) by both the overall URL and by the segments of the URL. This facilitates the finding of any document that comes from a particular domain or part of a domain (also a specific site or part of a site). Doing a search in which results are limited to a specific site allows one, in effect, to perform a search of that site. Even for sites that have a "site search" box on their home page, more complete results can often be found by using this technique than by using the site's own search feature. "inurl:", "allinurl:," and "site:" are the prefixes commonly used.

The term, "Domain searching" is sometimes used to refer to the above process and the use of the term, "Domain," points out that this approach can be used to limit retrieval to sites having a particular top-level domain, such as: gov, edu, uk, ca, or fr. This could be used, for example, to identify only Canadian sites that mention tariffs, or to only get educational sites that mention biodiversity.

Link Searching

There are two varieties of "link" searching. In the more common variety, one can search for all pages that have a hypertext link to a particular URL, and in the other variety, one can search for words contained in the linked text on the page. In the former, you can check, for example, which Web pages have linked to your organization's URL. In the second variety, you can see which Web pages have the name of your organization as linked text. Either variety can be very informative in terms of who is interested in either your organization or your Web site. Also, if you are looking for information on an organization, it can sometimes be useful to know who is linking to that organization's site.

This searching option is available in some search engines on their advanced page and/or on the main page with the use of prefixes. (usually "link:"). Engines may allow you to find links to an overall site, or to a specific page within a site.

Language Searching

Although all of the major engines allow limiting retrieval to pages written in a given language, they differ in terms of which languages can be specified. The 40 or so most common languages are specifiable in most of the major engines. Though some engines provide a prefix option for searching for languages, more typically one would go to the engine's advanced search page to narrow to a language.

Date Searching

Searching by the date of Web pages is an obviously desirable option, and most major engines provide such an option. Unfortunately, because of lack of clear or reliable information on a page regarding when the page itself was initially created, the date on which the content of the page was created, or even when the content on the page was significantly modified, it is often impossible for a search engine assign a truly "reliable" date to a Web page. As a "workaround," engines may take the date when the page was last modified or may assign a date based on when the page was last crawled by the engine. For searching Web pages, users should be aware of this approximation and its effect on precision when using the date searching option that is offered by most search engines (usually on their advanced search page). (On the other hand, for some of the other databases an engine may provide, such as news, the date searching may be very precise.)

Searching by File Type

For most of the 1990s, most search engines only indexed and allowed searching of regular HTML pages. In the crawling process (or for submitted pages) when the engine's indexing program encountered a link that led to another type of document, such as an Adobe Acrobat (pdf), or Excel (xls) file, the link was ignored. Starting with Adobe Acrobat files, other file types were fairly rapidly added to the corpus of "indexable" pages. This not only increased the breadth of resources available to the searcher, but also provided the capability for the searcher to limit retrieval by type of file. Limiting to Adobe Acrobat files provides documents more suited to printing. Narrowing to PowerPoint files can provide convenient summaries of a topic. Limiting to Excel files can often enable a greater focus on statistics.

Search Results Pages

As well as providing enhanced searching capabilities, search engines also enhance the content of results pages, beyond presenting just a listing of the Web page results that match the user's query. At the same time they search their Web database, they may automatically search the other databases they have, such as news, images, and video, and on search pages may automatically provide links to the matching items from those additional databases. Some search engines may search additional "reference" resources, such as dictionaries, encyclopedias, maps, etc., and likewise display matching content from those sources.

As well as displaying such supplemental content on results pages, search engines may also provide suggestions for ways in which the user might further qualify search criteria. This is done by suggesting related, narrower, or broader topics. Some engines also provide links to narrow the search by file type, language, or type of site (weblog, forum, commercial or noncommercial, etc.)

Specific options may also be offered on results pages for each retrieved item. Some engines keep a copy of each page they have indexed and provide a link to that "cached" page. This is particularly useful if, in the time since the page was indexed, the page was removed, is not available because of a server problem, or has changed in a way such that the term the user searched for is no longer on the page.

With records for pages that are not in the language of the search engine interface, there may be an option to translate the record (for example, if the user is using an English language version of Google and a page is in French or if the user is using the French version and the page is in English). Click on the "translate" link to receive a machine translation of the page. As with other machine translations, what you get may not be a "good" translation, but it may be an "adequate" translation, adequate in that it will give you a good idea of what the page is talking about. Also keep in mind that only "words" are translated. The translation program cannot translate words you see on a page that are actually "images" rather than "text."

One feature offered on search results pages by all of the major engines is a spell-checker. If you misspelled a word, or the search engine thinks you might have, it graciously asks something like "Did you mean?" and gives you a likely alternative. If it was indeed a mistake, just click on the suggested alternative to correct the problem.

Search results pages will usually display links labeled as "Sponsor Results," "Sponsored Links," etc.—These are "ads" for Web sites and are there because the Web site has paid to appear on the search engine's results pages. Major engines keep these sponsor sites clearly identifiable by, for example, putting them in a blue background, or to the side of the page. Searchers should remain aware that it is the presence of these ads that makes the existence of search engines possible.

The Search Engine Leaders—Post-2000

Popularity of various search engines can change fairly quickly. In the early and mid-1990s a list of the most popular engines included, among others, AltaVista, Hotbot. Excite, InfoSeek, and Lycos, (Yahoo! was still a primarily a directory, and though it had a search engine function, for that function it made use of, at various times, AltaVista's and Google's databases.)

By the latter part of the 2000s the following were the leaders: Google, Yahoo!, MSN/Windows/ Live Search, AOL, and Ask. (in that order). Those five search engines represented 94% of all (U.S.) searches.[3] (Brief profiles of the engines just mentioned are given below.)

Google

Google, which emerged as a company in 1998, grew very rapidly, its growth attributed largely to the simplicity of its interface, the lack of advertisements on the home page, and the quality of its relevance ranking (that fact significantly affected by Google's patented PageRank program.)[4] Google rather quickly went beyond "search" and began providing additional features and content, some of the enhancements emerging from within the Google organization and some (such as its e-mail service, Gmail) being patterned after such services already offered by its competitors. By the late 2000s, Google claimed more of the search market than all of its competitors combined and was offering a broad range of search services and a number of services not directly related to search

For its Web search offerings, Google provides all of the typical search options (Boolean, field searching, etc.) plus some unique searching features, the latter including numeric range searching (e.g., china history 1850 . . . 1890), and synonym searching (e.g., ~cars). As well as the searching of Web pages, Google also offers searches of databases of images, maps, news, products, video, groups, books (Google Book Search), journal articles (Google Scholar), and blogs. Some of these search offerings are very similar to corresponding services offered by Google's competitors, but some, such as "Google Book Search," were original and regarded by many as "ground-breaking" and even in some cases, controversial. (Google Books Search is a major book digitalization project, in cooperation with major publishers and libraries.) The search features provided with each of these databases is typically tailored to the specific nature of that kind of content.

Many of Google's Web search features are features that were already found on other search engines, but for which Google provided significant enhancements. One example is Google Language Tools. Many search engines have provided a translation option that allows retrieved items from a number of non-English languages to be translated, using programs such as SYSTRAN's Babel Fish. In 2007, Google enhanced its own translation feature by allowing the user not just to translate a specific result, but to input a search in the user's own language, then have Google automatically translate the search terms, perform the search, and then deliver results in both languages. Translations are done using Google's own statistical translation technology.

As it grew, Google rather rapidly redefined itself to be much more than a "search engine," adding services that went beyond "search" and even beyond usual Web site content. Some services had a direct relationship to "search," such as Google News Alerts, Google's financial portal ("Google Finance"), the Google Toolbar for Web browsers, a desktop search tool for searching the content of one's own computer, and Google's own Web browser ("Chrome"). Some of the services Google began to offer included types of things that already existed as "portal" features in other search services. These offerings included a customizable portal page (iGoogle) with Google's own calendar and notebook and links to a variety of other content such as newsfeeds. Among other services are Gmail (a Web-based e-mail service), Google Earth (imagery and related geospatial content for the entire Earth, as well as the Moon and the sky) and Google Talk (an instant messaging service). One of the manifestations of "Web 2.0" is availability of user-accessible software that is resident on the Web, rather than on the user's own computer. (The term, "Web 2.0," refers not to an actual "version" of the Web, but to the fact that the nature of the Web, by the middle of the first decade of the twentieth century, had changed from being primarily a place to go to find information to being a place that was much more personal, interactive, and collaborative, with the Web as a "platform" where programs are provided, used, and shared.) Google has moved very much in the Web 2.0 direction, providing Picasa (a photo-sharing and editing service), SketchUp (a computer-aided design, CAD, program), Google Docs (a collaborative spreadsheet, word-processor, and presentations program), and Sites (for creating Web sites). Google also offers "mobile" services (including mobile search, maps, text messaging, Gmail, etc.), an enterprise version of Google's search engine, and a custom search engine that allows a user to have a search box (on their own Web site or as a page on Google) that delivers a search of only the user's own selection of Web sites.

Yahoo!

Yahoo! was among the earliest Web sites that had the purpose of leading users to specific content on the Web. In the beginning, Yahoo! was exclusively a "Web directory," a categorized list of selected Web sites. By 2000, however, it had begun a transformation to a portal site, having, in addition to the directory, over three dozen links to news, services, and other resources provided by Yahoo and its affiliates, including pages for shopping, auctions, phone numbers, a calendar, and more. From its earliest days, the Yahoo! homepage contained a search box, but results for that search came from a search of the directory, and later a search of Web databases from other search providers.

Yahoo!'s directory function became less and less central and in 2004 Yahoo! created its own database of Web pages. Though emphasis on "search" continued to increase and the emphasis on the directory declined significantly, Yahoo!'s main image continued to be that of a portal, with the emphasis on the wide range of other services provided by Yahoo! and its partners, including Yahoo!'s highly popular e-mail service and its sections on autos, finance, games, groups, health, job listings, maps, real estate, travel, and over 50 other content areas.

In the area of Web search, Yahoo! currently provides typical Web search features such as Boolean and field searching, though a continued absence of a link on its main page to its advanced search page reinforces the impression of Yahoo!'s preference for a portal focus over search focus. It's personalized portal page, My Yahoo!, is judged by some to be the most popular portal on the Web.[5]

In addition to Web search, Yahoo! offers searching of the following databases: news, images, video, maps, local (businesses), shopping, audio, jobs, Creative Commons, people (phone numbers and addresses), and travel reservations search.

MSN/Live Search

Microsoft has made several attempts since the mid-1990s to produce a Web search engine that is competitive with Google and Yahoo!. The attempts, made available primarily through Microsoft's MSN portal, have gone by a variety of names, including Microsoft Search, MSN Search, Windows Live, and, in 2008, Live Search (live.com). Search features have varied considerably and have at times been less robust than those of its competitors. Live Search presented some innovative features such as a design that allowed continuous scrolling through search results, but it, like some other features in the MSN search products, was short-lived. The 2008 version provided the typical Boolean and field searching options, plus some additional options such as "prefer:" by which the user can adjust the ranking weight for search terms, and "feed:" and "hasfeed;" which identify Web sites that contain RSS links on the user's chosen topic. In addition to the search for Web pages, Live Search also offers searches for images, video, news, maps, health information, local (businesses), products, and travel.

AOL

AOL Search is the search engine found on AOL's main portal page and is also available at search .aol.com. The search is provided in conjunction with Google and Web search results come from the Google database (but are typically fewer in number than when the search is done on Google itself. AOL Search also provides options for searching images (using Google), video ("Powered by TRUVEO"), news, shopping, jobs, maps, movies, music, personals, travel, and yellow pages.

Ask

Ask, which was formerly AskJeeves, underwent a number of significant changes as it changed from the "question and answer" format of the original AskJeeves. Ask created a substantial Web database with fairly typical search functionality, though missing some features such as an OR Boolean function. In 2008, the company underwent a reorganization which produced some doubts among those who watch search engines as to Ask's commitment to "search." As well as its Web search, with Ask you can also search databases of images, news, maps, businesses, shopping, TV listings, events, videos, recipes, and blogs. Results pages for Web searches automatically incorporate results from multiple databases and provide a "binoculars" icon for previewing results without leaving the results page.

Other General Search Engines

There are a number of other general Web search engines, including GigaBlast, Exalead, and others. Exalead (http://www.exalead.com/search), from France, incorporates a number of features unavailable in other current search engines, including truncation ("words starting with"), phonetic spelling, approximate spelling, and NEAR. These are important to note because they are reflective of a level of sophistication of search techniques a bit closer to those found in commercial search services such as Lexis/Nexis, Factiva, and DIALOG, but not found in Web search engines.

Specialty Search Engines

Over the years, a variety of search engines have appeared that could be classified as "specialty" search engines. Among these there have been attempts to create search engines that focus on a particular topic or geographic location. In most cases, an examination of these showed that what was provided was more of a "directory" of selected sites than a broad ranging crawler-based search of Web pages for the specific topic or locality. On the other hand, there have been many successful attempts to produce search engines that provide searching for a particular format or type of document, such as images, video, blogs, forums, etc.

News

Searching of news databases is available from all of the general Web search engines. There are numerous other Web sites that specialize in searching news content. Each of these have varying degrees of searchability, and from the research perspective it is important to note that the coverage can vary significantly, especially in regard to the number of news sources included, the time span for the content of the database, and the languages covered. Among the better-known news search engines are: NewsNow, Silobreaker, NewsExplorer, RocketNews, Topix.net, World Press Review Online, and NewsTin.

Images

The most commonly encountered image search engines are those that are included as databases provided by the general Web search engines, including Google, Yahoo!, Live Search, AOL, and Ask. As well as subject searching, most of these engines allow for Boolean, and narrowing by size, coloration, site, and adult-content filtering. On Google's advanced image search page you can also narrow to news or photo content, or those that appear to include faces. Flickr (flicker.com), an image sharing Web site, has also gained extensive popularity as an image search engine. The extensive tagging of photos by Flickr users makes millions of images searchable. PicSearch provides an extensive collection of images from the Web and in addition to the above search criteria also allows narrowing to animated images. There are also image search engines such as Corbis, Fotosearch, and Stock.XCHNG which enable users (for a fee) to have use of photos from commercial photographers and photo archives.

Video

As with image searching, searching for video is available from major search engines, including Google, Yahoo!, Live Search, and AOL. Extensive searching of videos produced by individuals, as well as commercial video, is available from YouTube, the leading video-sharing site. Depending upon the search engine, options are provided for searching by Boolean, language, duration, domain/site/source, format, popularity, aspect ratio, and resolution, plus filtering for adult-content. Some video search engines specialize in video from TV, including news programs, interviews, etc. These include Blinkx (free) and TVEyes (fee-based). Both of these utilize voice-recognition technologies to create searchable transcripts for their video content.

Forums

Content found in forums (discussion groups, groups, newsgroups, etc.) can be utilized for a number of applications, ranging from hobbies to tracking terrorist activities, and there are search engines that specialize in finding this category of document. Among the search engines that provide such access to forums from multiple sources across the Web are BoardReader and OMGILI. (There are a number of other places where groups can be searched, such as Google, Yahoo!, Topica, Delphi Forums, but those sites focus on searching only the content that is hosted on their own Web sites.)

Other Specialty Search Engines

There are still other categories of specialty search engines, including those for searching blogs and RSS feeds (examples: Technorati, IceRocket, Bloglines, and Google Blog Search), for searching podcasts (examples: Podcastdirectory.com, Podcast.com), and for searching for information on people (examples: pipl Search, Infobel, Yahoo People Search, Intelius, PeopleFinders).

Visualization Engines

Visualization search engines are Web sites (or programs) that provide a very different "look" (literally) at search results. Instead of the traditional linear, textual list of retrieved items, results are shown on a map that spatially shows conceptual connections. Most current visualization engines utilize not a database of their own, but borrow one from other engines (Google, Yahoo!) or other sites such as Amazon.com. Visualization has been, and continues to be, an area of extensive research and there are several sites that demonstrate various visualization approaches. The type of conceptual and visual mapping done by these sites can be especially useful for quickly exploring the concept possibilities, directions, and terminology for a particular search. It presents a "connect the dots" approach, enabling understanding relationships among the concepts found in various search results—rather than just browsing lists of results. Among the leaders in this area are Kartoo, TouchGraph, and Grokker, and Quintura.

Metasearch Engines

The term "metasearch engine" (or "metasearch site") usually refers to Web sites that search multiple search engines in a single search. The degree of overlap (or lack thereof) between search engine results is something that professional searchers frequently consider and allow for as they search and searching more than one engine is a widely encouraged technique. Metasearch engines have been available since the 1990s and include sites such as Dogpile, Clusty, Ixquick, Mamma. Search.com, and many others. Each of these may provide additional benefits beyond just a compilation of results from more than one engine, for example, the "clustering" (categorization) of retrieved results, a feature that may not be provided by the target engines themselves. However, users should be aware of several shortcomings that may be encountered with these tools: 1) most of the current metasearch engines do not cover the largest major engines, particularly Google and Yahoo!, which tend to block queries from metasearch engines; 2) metasearch engines typically only return the first 10–20 results from any of the "target" engines; 3) metasearch engine results often discard useful and search-relevant information found on the actual search engine's results pages; 4) metasearch sites, even if they do cover the largest engines, may be required by those engines to show paid listings first; and 5) metasearch engines typically do not allow application of many of the search features available in the target engines themselves.

Metasearch engines should be distinguished from "comparison search" sites, such as Zuula.com and Twingine (twingine.no) which provide more of a side-by-side comparison of actual results from the target engines.

CONCLUSION

Web search engines have evolved significantly since they were first introduced in the early 1990s. The basic concept has remained the same, but the quality of results, the size of their databases, and the types of material that they include have increased dramatically. The total number of general Web search engines "in the race" has decreased and at present is dominated by one service, Google. Where the field of players has expanded is in the area of specialty search engines which focus on a specific type of Web "document." What has evolved even more dramatically is the "mission" of search services, which particularly in the case of Google, has gone far beyond "search." With advancing technologies, increasing interactiveness of the Web, and a more and more Internet-centered society, users can expect continued, fast-paced innovation.

REFERENCES

1. Sullivan, D. Ranking the SEO ranking factors. *Search Engine Land*; searchengineland.com/ranking-the-seo-ranking-factors-10890.php (accessed April 2009).
2. Bednarek, A.R. Boolean Algebras [ELIS Classic]. *Encyclopedia of Library and Information Sciences*, 3rd Ed.; Taylor & Francis: New York, 2009; 660-665..
3. Nielsen//Netratings Announces August U.S. Search Share Rankings. New York, September 19, 2007. NetRatings, Inc. http://www.nielsen-netratings.com/pr/pr_070919.pdf (accessed April 2009).

4. Vise, D.; Malseed, M. *The Google Story*; Bantam Dell: New York, 2005; 37–40.
5. About.com. Web Trends: The Top Ten Most Popular Portals on the Web. February 25, 2008. http://webtrends.about.com/od/webportals/a/topten_portals.htm (accessed April 2009).

BIBLIOGRAPHY

1. Search Engine History. http://www.searchenginehistory.com.
2. Search Engine Showdown. http://www.searchengineshow-down.com.
3. Vise, D.; Malseed, M. *The Google Story*; Bantam Dell: New York, 2005.

23 Web Retrieval and Mining

Carlos Castillo and Ricardo Baeza-Yates

CONTENTS

INTRODUCTION

Information retrieval is the area of computer science concerned with the representation, storage, organization, and access to documents.

Documents, in this definition, are understood in a broad sense, and include Web pages and other contents available on the Web. The Web is an unique medium for information dissemination, characterized by low entry barriers, low publishing costs, high communication speeds, and a vast distribution network.

Most methods for information retrieval were developed in the 1970s and 1980s for relatively small and coherent collections, such as the ones found in traditional libraries. The Web poses significant challenges to these methods, being massive, dynamic, and distributed.[1]

Web information retrieval (Web IR) or Web search, differs significantly from traditional information retrieval. The two main differences are the scale and nature of the collections being processed. Web search includes topics such as Web crawling, indexing and querying, adversarial Web IR issues, and Web distributed systems and evaluation metrics. Another relevant topic is Web data mining, which includes the analysis of the content, structure, and usage of the Web. In the following, we focus on these two topics, Web search and Web data mining. Our coverage of details and bibliography is by no means complete, and the interested reader is referred to Baeza-Yates and Ribeiro-Neto[2] and Chakrabarti.[3]

WEB SEARCH

Web search is the main application of Web IR, and a very successful one. From the user's point of view, a short query consisting of a few keywords is written in a search box, and the search engine

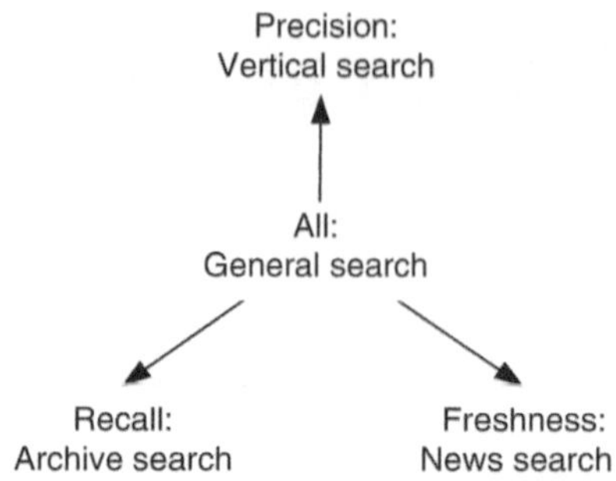

FIGURE 23.1 Trade-offs of different search engines.

displays in return a short list, typically of 10–20 Web pages that are considered relevant to the query issued and expected to be high-quality documents.

The two main goals in search are precision and recall, and they are, to a certain extent, competing goals.

Precision is defined as the fraction of relevant results contained in the result set, or in a part of the result set. For instance, if 3 out of 10 results for a query are relevant, the precision is 30%.

Recall is defined as the fraction of relevant results in a set, compared with the total number of pages on the Web that would be relevant for this query. Of course, the total number of pages on the Web relevant for a particular query is an unknown quantity, but for popular query terms it can be estimated using sampling techniques.

An information retrieval system can have high recall at the expense of precision, simply by returning more results, and high precision at the expense of recall, by removing results for which the algorithm is unsure about their relevance. The design of effective algorithms for search seeks a balance among these two extremes, and in the Web the focus is on precision as recall cannot be measured, only estimated.

In the case of Web search there is a third goal that is freshness. The Web changes continuously and the copy of the Web that the search engine has can become stale very quickly. The three goals: precision, recall, and freshness are sometimes mutually exclusive and introduce three-way trade-offs,[4] as depicted in Figure 23.1. These trade-offs create the possibility of several niche markets apart from general Web search, including: vertical search, over a particular subset of pages; archive search, over several snapshots of the Web; and news search, over Web sites that change with very high frequency.

An additional consideration in search engine design is efficiency. Large Web search engines have to deal with a large volume of queries and search huge data collections, so even large amounts of computational resources can be insufficient. Successful algorithms for Web search avoid consuming too many resources per query or per document.

From the point of view of the search engine, Web search occurs in two main phases. The first phase is off-line, with a certain periodicity or by permanent incremental maintenance. It includes crawling the Web to download pages and then indexing them to provide fast searches. The second phase is done online, and corresponds to the process of querying and ranking, which consists in building a ranked list of results using the index for a particular query. These phases are depicted in Figure 23.2 and explained in more detail in the rest of this section.

Web Crawling

A Web crawler is a system that automatically downloads pages from the Web following a set of predefined rules. A Web crawler receives as input a starting set of URLs that constitutes a "seed set," and a set of rules to follow. The crawler first downloads the pages from the seed set, extracts the links found in such pages, and then follows those links recursively while certain criteria are met. Crawling the Web is a required step for many Web IR applications.

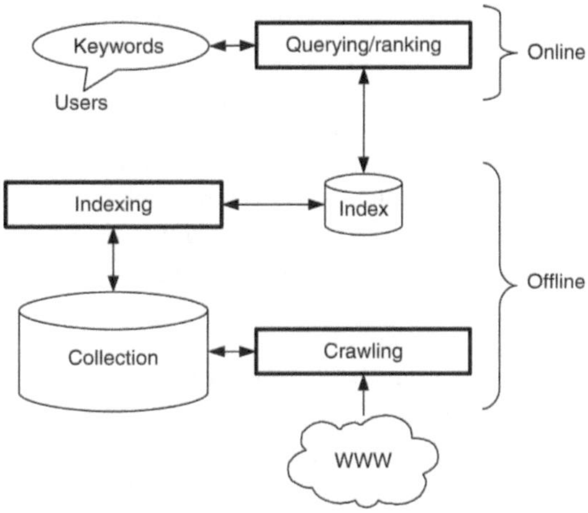

FIGURE 23.2 Phases of Web search.

Aside from Web search, Web crawlers are multipurpose systems that can be used for a variety of tasks, including finding and reporting "broken links" or other coding errors, and computing statistics about the Web.

The most important design constraint of Web crawlers is that they must avoid disrupting the Web servers they interact with. While downloading Web pages, the crawler is using the resources of others, and thus it must keep its resource consumption as low as possible. Web crawler designers and operators must take every possible step to control the frequency of visits to sites and keep them to a minimum. Also, the authors of Web sites have to ultimately decide which part, if any, of their sites can be visited by crawlers. This is done by using the robots exclusion protocol.[5]

After downloading the pages, they have to be processed to be used by the search engine or other application. HTML is the main language for coding documents on the Web, but there are many other formats present, including PDF, plain text, plus the document formats used by popular text-processing software such as Microsoft Word or OpenOffice. These formats have to be converted to a single representation before they can be used.

The importance of freshness is another aspect of the crawler's operation. The Web is very dynamic, and it changes continuously; this means that by the time the crawler has finished collecting a set of pages, many of the pages it has downloaded have already changed.[6] Crawling the Web, to a certain extent, resembles watching the sky at night[2]: the light we see from the stars has often taken thousands of years to reach our eyes. Moreover, the light from different stars has taken different amounts of time, so what we see is not a snapshot of the sky at any given moment, present or past. It is a combination of images from different times. The same happens with the collection of Web pages crawled by a search engine.

The Web pages that are not directly accessible by following links, but require the user to enter a query in an online form (e.g., enter an author's name to retrieve bibliographic data), constitute the "hidden Web."[7] Searching this content is challenging for search engines. In most cases, large information providers generate "crawler-friendly" pages for better indexing by search engines, but other forms of collaboration may arise in the future, including exposing an interface for querying the local database to the search engine.

Indexing

After collecting pages, the next step is to create an index to enable fast searches over the downloaded pages. The first step toward indexing a large collection is to consider an appropriate logical view of the content. The most used logical view for this task is the "bag of words" model,[8] in which each document is represented as a multiset containing all its keywords, disregarding the order in which they appear.

To produce this logical view, text normalization operations are applied to the original texts. These operations include tokenization, stopword removal, and stemming.

Tokenization is the process by which a text is separated into words. This is trivial in Western languages, but harder to do in other languages such as Chinese.

Stopwords are functional words that do not convey meaning by themselves, such as articles and prepositions. The removal of stopwords reduces the amount of data processing and the size of the index, and also improves the retrieval accuracy of information retrieval systems.

Stemming is the extraction of the morphological root of a word. This allows us to search for "housing" and retrieve results that include "house" or "houses."

After the text normalization operations have been applied, most search systems build an index, a data structure designing to accelerate the process of retrieving documents containing a given query. The most prevalent type of such structure is an inverted index. In Figure 23.3, an example of an inverted index for a collection of five toy documents (each of them having two words) is shown.

An inverted index is composed of two parts: a vocabulary, containing all the terms in the collection, and a posting list, which contains references to the documents(s) in which each word of the vocabulary appears. An inverted index is a powerful tool for the search engine, enabling very fast response times. In the example of Figure 23.3, if we search for "global AND climate" in the inverted index, the task is basically to intersect the set of pages containing "global" {1, 2, 5} with the set of pages containing "climate" {2, 3, 4}, obtaining as a result the set {2}. If these lists are sorted, their intersection can be computed very quickly. This is how a basic inverted index works. There are many techniques for providing faster search or reducing the space occupied by the index. For example, if phrase or proximity search is needed, the exact positions where the term appears in a document must be also encoded in the posting list. The interested reader is referred to Baeza-Yates and Ribeiro-Neto[2] and Witten, Moffat, and Bell[9] for an overview of indexing techniques.

Another aspect is that large search engines achieve high response times by means of parallelization. In this case, the index has to be divided in some way, and each piece of the index has to be given to a different physical computer. There are two main strategies for this partitioning. One is to give each machine a set of documents, the other one is to give each machine a set of terms.[10]

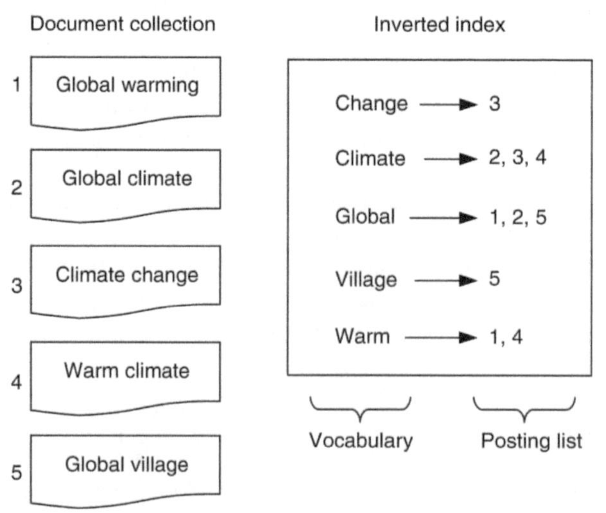

FIGURE 23.3 Example of an inverted index.

Querying and Ranking

Most search engines receive queries expressed as a set of keywords. Scalable question answering systems, in which users express their information need by means of a question, have remained elusive to researchers in particular because many natural language processing algorithms still require a prohibitive amount of computational power for Web-scale collections.

Typical queries are very short, between two and three keywords each. After receiving a query, the search engine uses its inverted index (or indexes) to build a page with results that is shown to users. To a certain extent, the problem of finding a set of pages that are related to the query is the "easy" part, given that for most broad queries there are thousands or millions of documents that are potentially appropriate. The most difficult challenge is to find among those documents, a small subset of the best 10 or 20. This is the problem of ranking.

Ranking has two main aspects: relevance and quality. The dimension of relevance indicates how related is the retrieved document to the user intention. The dimension of quality indicates how good is the document by itself. Search engines try to produce results for a given query that are both relevant for the query and have high quality. One of the main techniques to do fast ranking is to use partial evaluation techniques, such that only the top ranked answers are computed, and the rest of the answer is computed incrementally as the user demands it.

Relevance

Given that the search engine cannot understand the meaning of the queries nor of the documents, it must resort to statistical methods to compare queries to documents. These statistical methods allow the search engine to provide an estimation on how similar the query is to each document retrieved, which is used as an approximation of how relevant is the document for the query.

The vector space model[8] is the most used framework for measuring text similarity. It represents each document as a vector in a high-dimensional space, in which each dimension is a term, and the magnitude of each component of the vector is proportional to the frequency of the corresponding term, and inversely proportional to the document frequency of the term in the collection.

Differences in document size have to be taken into account for the similarity measure between documents, so the angle between documents is used instead of, for instance, the Euclidean distance between them. For instance, the angle between the documents "global warming" and "warming warming global global" is zero (so the documents are equivalent according to this metric), the angle between the documents "global warming" and "global climate" is 45° (under a simple weighting scheme), and the angle between the documents "global warming" and "climate change" is 90°. For normalization purposes, the cosine of such angle is the standard way of expressing this similarity metric.

Information retrieval systems usually do not apply the vector space model naïvely, as it has significant weaknesses. By itself the vector space model does not take relationships among terms into account.[11] For instance, strictly speaking the cosine similarity between the "global warming" and "climate change" is zero, and the cosine similarity between "global warming" and "strawberry ice cream" is also zero; but clearly the first pair of concepts have a closer relationship than the second pair. Two methods that can be applied to overcome this problem are query expansion and latent semantic indexing.

Query expansion consists in adding related words to the queries, and the same technique can be applied to documents. For instance, this could convert automatically "global warming" into "global world warming climate" and "climate change" into "climate warm cold change global." The specific words that are added can be obtained from different sources, including cooccurrence in the collection. In the case of the Web, there are rich sources of information to obtain words related to a document. The main one is anchor text, that is, the text contained in the links pointing to the current document. This is a very important feature in the ranking computed by most modern search engines. A second source of information are social book-marking sites that allow users to associate tags to documents.

Latent semantic indexing[12] consists in projecting the vectors representing queries (and documents) into a different, and usually smaller, space. This technique is based on principal component analysis and attempts to group automatically terms into the main "concepts" representing multiple weighted terms.

Quality

Search engines are designed to extract a set of features from the documents they index, and use those features to assert what is the quality of a given document. Quality is hard to define and of course hard to estimate using statistical measures. However, certain textual features from documents, including content length, frequencies of some words, features about the paragraphs, etc. tend to be correlated with human assessments about document quality.[13]

Apart from the content of the pages themselves, on the Web a rich source of information for inferring quality can be extracted from links. Links on the Web tend to connect topically related pages,[14] and they often imply that the target document has an acceptable or high level of quality. Thus, they can be used for finding high-quality items in the same way as academic citations can partially characterize the importance of a paper. The same considerations as for academic citations apply: not all of the links imply endorsement,[15] some pages attract many citations for other reasons aside from quality, and citation counts can be inflated by self-citations or citations that point to errors; among other problems.

There are two classic link analysis algorithms to obtain quality metrics for Web pages: PageRank and HITS. For a survey of their variants, and other methods, see Borodin, et al.[16]

The PageRank algorithm[17] defines the importance of a page in a recursive manner: "a page with high PageRank is a page referenced by many pages with high PageRank." Despite the definition being recursive, it is possible to compute PageRank scores using results from Markov chain theory. In brief, the wanderings of a "random surfer" are simulated, in which a person browses the Web by following links at random. The PageRank score of a page is roughly proportional to the amount of expected visits the random surfer will do to each page.

The HITS algorithm[18] is another method for ranking Web pages. It starts by building a set of pages related to a topic by querying a search engine, and then expands this set by using incoming and outgoing links, by crawling the Web or by querying a search engine again. Next, two scores for each page are computed: a *hub score* and an *authority score*.

As shown in Figure 23.4, a page with a high hub score is a page that links to many pages with a high authority score. A page with a high authority score is a page linked by many pages with high hub score. Again, despite the apparent circularity of the definition, both hub and authority scores can be computed efficiently by an iterative computation.

Another source of information for ranking pages on the Web is usage data. A page that is visited frequently and/or for long periods by users may be more interesting than a page that is not. This information can be obtained by the search engine by providing a client-side add-on such as a toolbar, or by instrumenting the search engine result pages to capture click information.

Ranking Manipulation

Visits from search engines are an important source of traffic for many Web sites. Given that in the case of commercial ventures on the Web, traffic is strongly correlated with sales volume, there is a significant economic incentive for obtaining high rankings on search engines. These incentives may lead Web page authors to use deceptive techniques for achieving high rankings.[19] These deceptive techniques are known as a whole as search engine spam.

There are many types of search engine spam: inserting many keywords on Web pages, linking nepotistically among pages, providing different contents to the search engine than to users (also called "cloaking"), among others; for a survey of these methods, see Gyöngyi.[20]

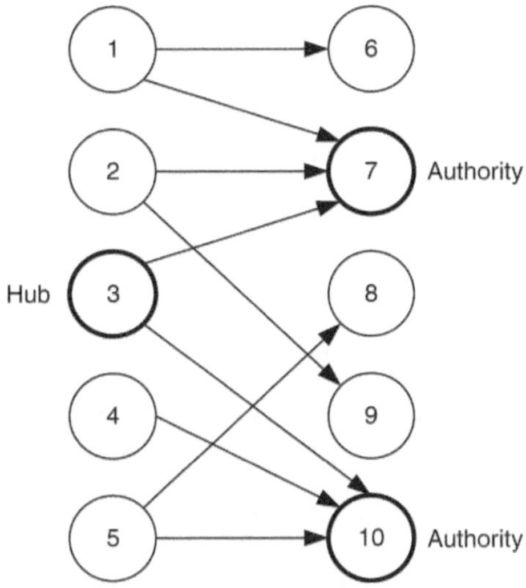

FIGURE 23.4 A graph with one page with high hub score (number 3) and two pages with large authority scores (numbers 7 and 10).

Search engine spam has been an important issue for search engines for a number of years, and it is not likely to be solved in the near future. Web spam damages search engines' reputation as it exploits and weakens the trust relationship between users and search engines.[20] Spamming has become so prevalent that without countermeasures to identify and remove spam, the quality of search engine results would be very poor.[21]

WEB MINING

Web mining is the application of data mining techniques to find patterns on data downloaded from the Web. Based on the main source of data they use, these techniques can be broadly classified as Web content mining, Web link mining, and Web usage mining.

Content Mining

Web content mining is the extraction of knowledge from the textual content of Web pages. The main challenge here is that HTML, while designed initially to be a language for logical formatting, is actually used as a language for physical formatting. Logical formatting describes document structure, such as paragraphs and headings, while physical formatting describes visual attributes like font sizes, colors, and spacings. With logical formatting, it would be easier to extract information than with the current physical formatting.

In general, the Web sites that are rich in information are built using "dynamic pages" that are generated on demand, in response to a user click or query. These pages are created by querying a local database, formatting the results as HTML, and then displaying such results to the user.

For example, let us consider a Web site about movies being shown in theaters. This Web site may present the movies on a tabular form with the titles, ratings, and show times, for instance. A Web search engine or other information provider interested on doing Web information extraction must read this table and reconstruct the original schema based on it. For example, it must find out that the first column contains the movie title, the second column the rating, and the third column the show times. This is easy for a human but it is hard to do it automatically. Most of the time, some information is lost, as depicted in Figure 23.5.

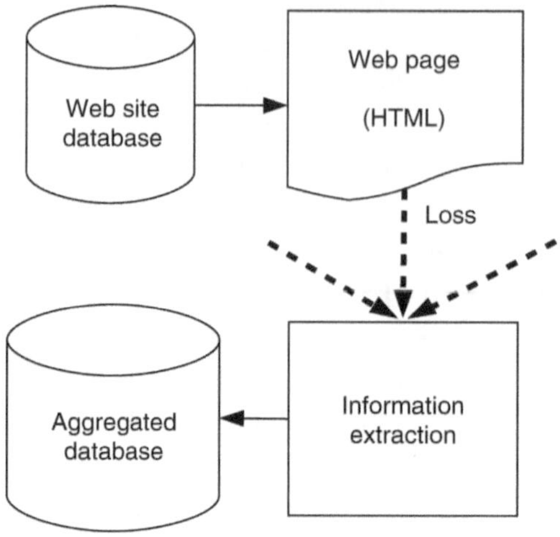

FIGURE 23.5 Information loss when extracting content from the Web.

Information extraction systems use clues from the page's formatting and structure, domain knowledge, and training examples, among other sources of information, to map HTML fragments to tuples in relations. They can also use methods for detecting the page template and isolating navigational areas that do not contribute content. The systems that do this task are informally known as "content scrapers" and they can be quite accurate, specially when restricted to particular domains. For a survey of information extraction methods, Kayed and Shaalan.[22]

Other aspects of content mining besides information extraction are content classification, sentiment analysis, and duplicated pages detection.

Content classification in general looks at statistics obtained from the Web pages to classify their contents. In many cases, this is done to find out what is the topic the contents are about. In other cases, content classification is used to extract document properties such as the genre of the document, or whether it expresses more opinions or more facts, or to evaluate how well-written a document is. In all cases, a statistical description of the document is created, and then a machine learning algorithm takes that description and a set of training labels to construct a model able to separate automatically the classes.[23,24]

Sentiment analysis, including "intention mining," is the task of finding what is the sentiment or intention of the author of a document. Specifically, it can be used to determine if a certain fragment is expressing a negative or positive opinion. This is very important given the large amount of product and service reviews available on Web pages, blogs, or forums. These reviews are typically very short, usually no more than a few paragraphs. The techniques of sentiment classification include the analysis of the frequency of certain terms,[25] with the aid of part-of-speech taggers or other natural language processing tools.

Finally, there is a significant amount of duplicate content on the Web. According to Broder, et al.,[26] roughly one-third of the pages on the Web are duplicates or near duplicates of another page, and recent studies have confirmed this trend. Finding near-duplicate content[27] is important for efficiency reasons, to avoid downloading and indexing many times the same pages. It is also important to filter out plagiarism, so that the original page gets ranked high, and not the copies.

Link Mining

The overall structure of the Web differs significantly from the one exhibited by random networks. The most salient difference is that, while on a random network most of the nodes have a degree

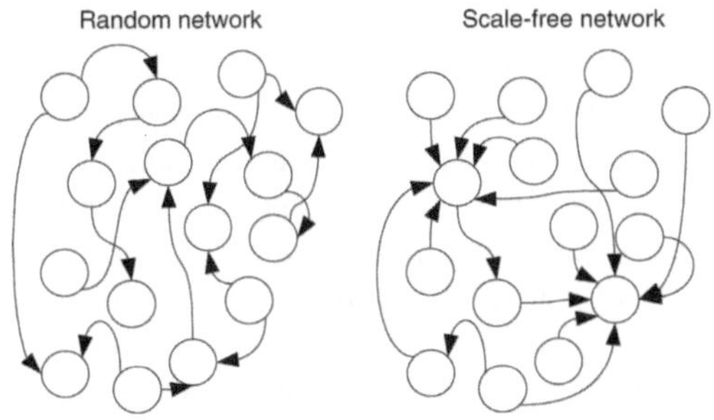

FIGURE 23.6 Difference between a random network and a scale-free network.

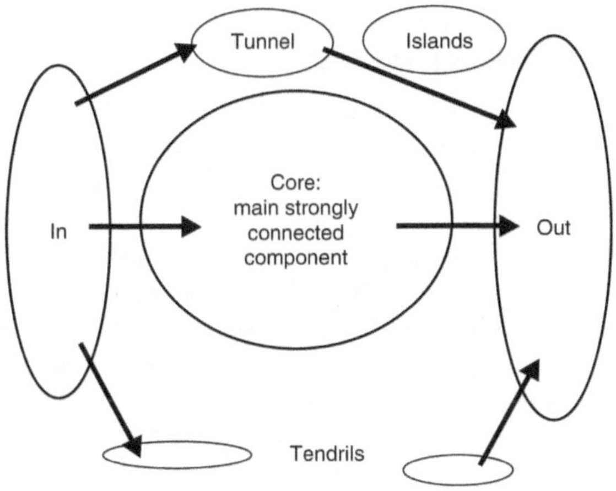

FIGURE 23.7 Bow-tie structure on the Web.

(number of connections) close to the average, in networks such as the Web, the distribution of the degree is very skewed. The networks that have this property are called scale-free networks.

Figure 23.6 depicts a random network and a scale-free network with the same number of nodes and edges. In a scale-free network, a few nodes attract more of the in-links. This can be explained by "rich-get-richer" processes[28] in which having many links gives a better chance of attracting new links, increasing the disparity in the number of connections over time.

At a macroscopic level, looking at the properties of the network as a whole, we can describe the Web in terms of the strongly connected components on it. A strongly connected component is a part of a graph in which all pairs of nodes can reach each other (in both directions) by following links. The Web exhibits a very large strongly connected component (CORE), other components that are reachable to/from it by directed links (IN and OUT, respectively), and pages that cannot be reached at all from the CORE, which are called ISLANDS. Minor components such as TENDRILS and TUNNEL can also be identified. This description is called the bow-tie structure of the Web[29] given its shape, depicted in Figure 23.7.

PageRank and HITS could be considered simple link mining techniques. More elaborated link analysis can be used for finding similar pages, communities, or detection of Web spam based in links.

Usage Mining

Usage data on the Web is abundant and valuable. Web site administrators can capture usage data by enabling logging on their Web servers, and they can enrich such data by instrumenting their internal links. There are several free software packages available that can do sophisticated analysis of access logs and can discover, for instance, typical browsing paths. This is of particular importance for retailers and other e-commerce Web sites that can use this information to drive the design of their Web sites, improving the user experience and/or increasing their sales volume.

Search engines have access to the queries written by the users, and the pages they selected after seeing the list of results (and the pages they did not select). Data from user search sessions can be used to increase the relevance of the results.[30] Interesting relationships can be inferred by looking at users, queries, and pages. We can observe, for instance, that similar users tend to issue similar queries, that similar pages show up as results for related queries, and so on.

Usage data is increasingly valuable for search engines. Privacy issues arise in the confluence of the legal and technical aspects associated to this data collection, and both users and search engine have incentives for maintaining and enforcing the secrecy of this data.

CONCLUSIONS AND CURRENT TRENDS

As we have seen, Web retrieval methods differ from standard information retrieval methods, and can adapt to the large-scale, open, and distributed nature of the Web. For the future, two topics that are attracting a significant research effort are the mobile Web and the semantic Web.

The Mobile Web is the Web that is accessible and used through portable devices. Today, the capabilities of most mobile cell phones are well beyond just making phone calls. Many include Web-browsing software, and a growing fraction of the activity on the Web is carried through these devices, including browsing, searching, and even producing content (e.g., in the case of cell phones equipped with a camera). A challenge here is to provide users of portable devices with an experience that takes into account their geographical location and their current activity.

The Semantic Web[31] is a vision of the future of the Web, in which the Web contents can be read and understood by both humans and software agents. This will enable information integration and sharing without losing information. Several technologies enable the semantic Web, ranging from simple markup languages as the Extensible Markup Language (XML) to other languages that describe relationships among objects, classes, and properties. On top of these layers, applications will be able to analyze and, later, to reason about the contents and to extract knowledge from them.

REFERENCES

1. Arasu, A.; Cho, J.; Garcia-Molina, H.; Paepcke, A.; Raghavan, S. Searching the web. ACM Trans. Internet Technol. **2001**, *1* (1), 2–43.
2. Baeza-Yates, R.; Ribeiro-Neto, B. *Modern Information Retrieval*; Addison-Wesley: New York, 1999.
3. Chakrabarti, C. *Mining the Web: Analysis of Hypertext and Semi Structured Data*; Morgan Kaufmann: San Francisco, 2002.
4. Kobayashi, M.; Takeda, K. Information retrieval on the web. ACM Comput. Surv. **2000**, *32* (2), 144–173.
5. Koster, M. A standard for robot exclusion, http://www. robotstxt.org/wc/robots.html, 1996.
6. Ntoulas, A.; Cho, J.; Olston, C. What's new on the web?: The evolution of the web from a search engine perspective. In *Proceedings of the 13th conference on World Wide Web*; ACM Press: New York, 2004; 1–12.
7. Raghavan, S.; Garcia-Molina, H. Crawling the hidden web. In *Proceedings of the 27th International Conference on Very Large Data Bases*; Morgan Kaufmann: Rome, Italy, September 2001; 129–138.
8. Salton, G. *Introduction to Modern Information Retrieval (McGraw-Hill Computer Science Series)*; McGraw-Hill: New York, 1983.
9. Witten, I.H.; Moffat, A.; Bell, T.C. *Managing Gigabytes: Compressing and Indexing Documents and Images*; Morgan Kaufmann: San Francisco, 1999.
10. Tomasic, A.; Garcia-Molina, H. Performance of inverted indices in shared-nothing distributed text document information retrieval systems. In *PDIS '93: Proceedings of the Second International Conference on Parallel and Distributed Information Systems*, IEEE Computer Society Press: Los Alamitos, CA, 1993; 8–17.

11. Sahami, M.; Mittal, V.; Baluja, S.; Rowley, H. The happy searcher: Challenges in web information retrieval. In *8th Pacific Rim International Conference on Artificial Intelligence, volume 3157 of Lecture Notes in Computer Science*, Auckland, New Zealand, August 2004; Springer: Berlin/Heidelberg, 3–12.
12. Deerwester, S.; Dumais, S.T.; Furnas, G.W.; Landauer, T.K.; Harshman, R. Indexing by latent semantic analysis. J. Am. Soc. Inform. Sci. **1999**, *41* (6), 391–407.
13. Richardson, M.; Prakash, A.; Brill, E. Beyond pagerank: Machine learning for static ranking. In *Proceedings of the 15th international conference on World Wide Web*, ACM Press: Edinburgh, Scotland, May 2006; 707–715.
14. Davison, B.D. Topical locality in the web. In *Proceedings of the 23rd annual international ACM SIGIR Conference on Research and Development in Information Retrieval*, ACM: Athens, Greece, July 2000; 272–279.
15. Haas, S.W.; Grams, E.S. Page and link classifications: Connecting diverse resources. In *Proceedings of the third ACM conference on Digital libraries*, ACM Press: Pittsburgh, PA, June 1998; 99–107.
16. Borodin, A.; Roberts, G.O.; Rosenthal, J.S.; Tsaparas, P. Link analysis ranking: Algorithms, theory, and experiments. ACM Trans. Internet Technol. **2005**, *5* (1), 231–297.
17. Page, L.; Brin, S.; Motwani, R.; Winograd, T. The page-rank citation ranking: Bringing order to the Web, Technical report, Stanford Digital Library Technologies Project, 1998.
18. Kleinberg, J.M. Authoritative sources in a hyperlinked environment. J. ACM **1999**, *46* (5), 604–632.
19. Gori, M.; Witten, I. The bubble of web visibility. Commun. ACM **2005**, *48* (3), 115–117.
20. Gyöngyi, Z.; Garcia-Molina, H. Web spam taxonomy. In *First International Workshop on Adversarial Information Retrieval on the Web*, Chiba, Japan, May 2005; 39–47.
21. Henzinger, M.R.; Motwani, R.; Silverstein, C. Challenges in web search engines. SIGIR Forum **2002**, *36* (2), 11–22.
22. Kayed, M.; Shaalan, K.F. A survey of web information extraction systems. IEEE Trans. Know. Data Eng. **2006**, *18* (10), 1411–1428.
23. Dumais, S.; Chen, H. Hierarchical classification of web content. In *Proceedings of the 23rd annual international ACM SIGIR conference on Research and development in information retrieval*, ACM Press: Athens, Greece, July 2000; 256–263.
24. Chakrabarti, S.; Dom, B.; Agrawal, R.; Raghavan, P. Scalable feature selection, classification and signature generation for organizing large text databases into hierarchical topic taxonomies. VLDB J. **1998**, *7* (3), 163–178.
25. Pang, B.; Lee, L.; Vaithyanathan, S. Thumbs up?: Sentiment classification using machine learning techniques. In *EMNLP '02*: Proceedings of the ACL-02 conference on Empirical methods in natural language processing, Association for Computational Linguistics: Philadelphia, PA, July 2002; 79–86.
26. Broder, A.Z.; Glassman, S.C.; Manasse, M.S.; Zweig, G. Syntactic clustering of the web. Comput. Netw. ISDN Syst. **1997**, *29* (813), 1157–1166.
27. Fetterly, D.; Manasse, M.; Najork, M. Detecting phrase-level duplication on the world wide web. In *SIGIR '05*: Proceedings of the 28th annual international ACM SIGIR conference on Research and development in information retrieval; ACM Press: New York, 2005; 170–177.
28. Barabási, A.L.; Albert, R. Emergence of scaling in random networks. Science **1999**, *286* (5439), 509–512.
29. Broder, A.; Kumar, R.; Maghoul, F.; Raghavan, P.; Rajagopalan, S.; Stata, R.; Tomkins, A.; Wiener, J. Graph structure in the web: Experiments and models. In *Proceedings of the Ninth Conference on World Wide Web*; ACM Press: Amsterdam, Netherlands, May 2000; 309–320.
30. Baeza-Yates, R. Applications of web query mining. In *Proceedings of the 27th European Conference on IR Research, ECIR 2005, volume 3408*; Springer: Santiago de Compostela, Spain, March 2005; 7–22.
31. Berners-Lee, T.; Hendler, J.; Lassila, O. The semantic web. Scientific American **2001**, *284* (5), 34–43.

BIBLIOGRAPHY

1. Information Retrieval methods, in general, and Web search, in particular, is discussed in the book by Baeza-Yates and Ribeiro-Neto [2, Chapter 13]. A textbook by Chakrabarti[3] deals with several topics related to Web Mining.

24 Semantic Web

Kieron O'Hara and Wendy Hall

CONTENTS

INTRODUCTION

The semantic web (SW) is an extension, in progress, to the World Wide Web (WWW), designed to allow software processes, in particular artificial agents, as well as human readers, to acquire, share, and reason about information. Whereas the WWW consists largely of documents, which are generally created for human consumption, the SW will be a web of data, making them more amenable for computers to process.[1] The data will be processed by computer via semantic theories for interpreting the symbols (hence: *semantic* web). In any particular application, the semantic theory will connect terms within a distributed document set logically, and thereby aid interoperability.

For instance, people use a lot of data in daily interactions, viewing bank statements, or digital photographs, or using diaries or calendars. But this does not constitute a web of data, because the data are neither exported from the applications in which they are stored or were created, nor linked to other relevant data. In a genuine web of data, such data could be used seamlessly in a number of applications. For example, one could view one's photographs (which will contain a time stamp) in one's calendar, which would then act as a prompt to suggest what one was doing when they were taken. The data which one uses would be to some extent freed from the constraints of particular applications, and instead could be interlinked and reused creatively.

As another example, Web services can currently be accessed and executed via the Web, but because the Web does not provide much information-processing support, services must be specified using semiformal languages and as with information retrieval humans need to be kept in the loop. Web services described using SW techniques should provide support for autonomous agents and automatic systems.[2]

The world of linked information is a very unstructured, "scruffy" environment. The amounts of information that systems need to deal with are very large indeed. Furthermore, systems must pull together information from distributed sources, where representation schemes can be expected to be highly heterogeneous, information quality variable, and trust in information's provenance hard to establish. SW technology needs to be based on standards that can operate in this heterogenous information world.

The SW therefore requires two types of information standard to operate. First, it requires common formats for integrating information from these diverse sources. And second, it needs a language to express the mapping between the data and objects in the real world, in order to allow a seamless understanding of a distributed set of databases. Hence, for instance, we could signal that a database containing a column *zip code* and another database with a column labeled *ZC*, were actually both referring to the same concept with their different labels, and by creating such a semantic link, we could then start to reason over both databases in an integrated fashion. Such semantic links are often obvious to humans, but not to computers. A key formalism here is the *ontology*, which defines the concepts and relationships that we use in particular applications. Ontologies are central to the SW vision, as providing the chief means by which the terms used in data are understood in the wider context.[1,3]

THE AIM OF THE SEMANTIC WEB

The aim of the SW is to shift the emphasis of reasoning from documents to data, for three reasons. First, it will facilitate data reuse, often in new and unexpected contexts. Second, it will help reduce the amount of relatively expensive human information processing. Third, it will release the large quantity of information, not currently accessible, that is stored in relational databases (RDBs) by making it directly machine-processable.[4]

This implies that RDB objects must be exported to the Web as first-class objects, which in practice entails mapping them onto a consistent system of resource identifiers—called Universal Resource Identifiers (URIs—see below). The SW itself is a suite of languages and formalisms designed to enable the interrogation and manipulation of representations which make use of URIs.[1]

It is hoped that the SW will exhibit the same *network effects* that promoted the growth of the WWW. Network effects are positive feedback effects connected with *Metcalfe's law* that the value of a network is proportional to the square of the number of users/members. The more people share data that can be mapped onto URIs, the more valuable that data is. As value increases, more agents join the network to get the benefits, and include information that they own in the network which further increases its value. This, like the WWW model, is radically different from other models of the value of information, wherein value is dictated by *scarcity* (copyright, intellectual property restrictions, etc). In decentralized networks like the Web the value of information is dictated by *abundance*, so it can be placed in new contexts, and reused in unanticipated ways.

This is the dynamic that enabled the WWW to spread, when the value of Web documents was seen to be greater in information-rich contexts. One initiative to support the development of the SW is the creation of a discipline of *web science*, which is intended to exploit study of both technical and social issues to predict such matters with more accuracy.[5,6]

If the SW is to grow in an analogous way, more data has to be exposed to the Web that can be mapped onto URIs. In practice, this means that the data must be exposed in the resource description framework (RDF), an agreed international standard whose role in the SW is described below[7]; in particular, it can be used not only to assert a link between two resources, but also to name (and therefore make explicit) the relationship that links them. RDF is the language of choice for reuse, because it is a relatively inexpressive language compared to other formalisms used in the SW (see Figure 24.1 for a pictorial representation of the layers of formalisms required for the SW vision—expressivity increases as we ascend the diagram). The importance of RDF in this model is dictated by the so-called principle of least power, which states that the less expressive the representation language, the more reusable the data.[8]

The importance of growth is such that a stage can be reached when reuse of data—one's own or that of other people—is facilitated. There would ideally be so much information exposed in RDF that the contexts into which one's own data can be placed would be rich enough and numerous enough to increase its value significantly. RDF (as described below) represents information as a subject–predicate–object triple each of whose component parts is a URI. If the objects, resources, or representations referred to by the URIs are defined in ontologies, then this enables the interoperability at which the SW aims.

Hence another vital component in the SW is the development and maintenance of ontologies. These must be endorsed by the communities that use them, whether they are large-scale, expensive ontologies developed as a result of a major research effort, or relatively ad hoc creations intended to support small-scale collaboration.

Ontologies can also play an important role in bringing (representatives of) two or more communities together for a common purpose, by expressing a common vocabulary for their collaboration, onto which the terms of each discipline can be mapped. Such collaborative efforts are extremely important for reuse of content.[3]

This is not to say that search and retrieval on the current Web is not of high quality; the methods pioneered by Google and others work very well. Nevertheless, keyword-based search techniques are vulnerable to a number of well-known flaws. Individual words can be ambiguous. A document can refer to a topic of interest without using the keyword. Keywords are language-dependent. Information distributed across several documents cannot be amalgamated by keyword search. And even though PageRank and related algorithms for search produce impressive results, the user still

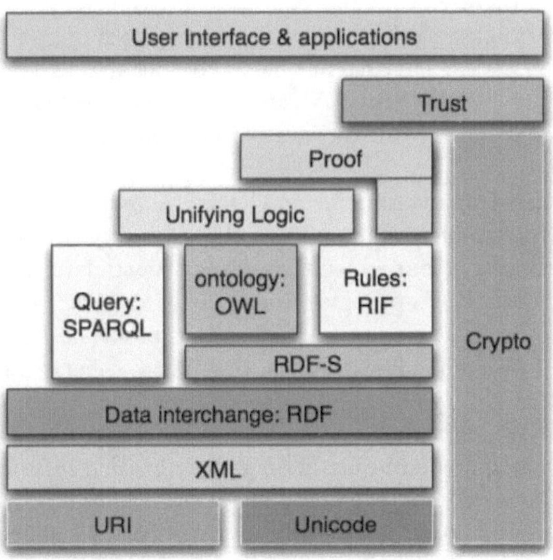

FIGURE 24.1 The layered view of the semantic web. (From A framework for Web Science, by T. Berners-Lee, W. Hall, J.A. Hendler, K. O'Hara, N. Shadbolt, D.J. Weitzner, Found. Trends Web Sci. 2006, *1* (1), 1–134.)

needs to read manually through the ordered list of retrieved pages, and inspect their content to determine relevance to his/her inquiry. This involvement of the user is a hindrance to scalability.

The SW should make more accurate querying possible, using ontologies to help with problems of ambiguity and unused keywords, and data linking to query across distributed datasets. Furthermore, it should be able to go beyond current search with respect to the three issues of reuse, automation, and exploitation of RDBs. And as well as search and retrieval, the addition of information processing support to the Web will help promote other functions such as Web services and knowledge management.

COMPONENTS OF THE SEMANTIC WEB

At one level, the SW is a complex of formalisms and languages each doing a different job in the representation of information, as shown in Figure 24.1. Each formalism is an internationally agreed standard (see below), and the composition of the functions these formalisms serve supports semantically enabled reasoning on data.

At the bottom of this diagram stands the URIs which identify the resources about which the SW provides reasoning capabilities.[9] The universality of URIs is extremely important—i.e., it is vital that whatever naming convention is used for URIs is adopted globally, so as to create the network effects that allow the SW to add value. Interpretation of URIs must also be consistent across contexts. In other words, when we *dereference* URIs (i.e., when we locate the resource to which the URI refers), we should always get the same object. If these conditions about URI naming schemes are met, then making an association between a URI and a resource means that different people can refer or link to it consistently in their conversations. The other basic formalism, Unicode, is an industry standard that allows computers to represent text in different writing systems.

The next layer up, eXtensible Markup Language (XML), is a language to mark up documents, and a uniform data exchange format between applications.[10] It allows the insertion of user-defined tags into documents that provide information about the role that the content plays. So, for instance, XML allows one to write a document describing a book, and also to *annotate* the document with machine-readable *metadata* to indicate e.g., who the authors of the book are.

RDF[7] is a very minimal knowledge representation framework for the Web, which uses a basic subject–predicate–object structure, with the twist that it assigns specific URIs to its individual fields—including in the predicate position, thereby identifying a relationship between the entities identified by the connected nodes. This use of URIs allows us to reason not only about objects but also about the relationships between them. XML is a metalanguage that provides a uniform framework for markup, but it does not provide any way of getting at the *semantics* of data; RDF is the first step toward semantics.

The resource description framework schema (RDFS, sometimes known as RDF(S)[11]) gives greater scope for sharing information about individual domains; whereas RDF is a data interchange language that lets users describe resources using their own vocabularies, and makes no assumptions about the domains in question, RDFS provides a basic set of tools for producing structured vocabularies that allow different users to agree on particular uses of terms. An extension of RDF, it adds a few modeling primitives with a fixed meaning (such as class, subclass and property relations, and domain and range restriction).

A key component for SW applications is the *ontology*. Ontologies[3] are shared conceptualizations of a domain which are intended to facilitate knowledge and information sharing by coordinating vocabulary and allowing basic inference of inheritance and attributes of objects. Several initiatives are developing ontologies, particularly in a number of sciences, which means that the scientists are likely to be among the important early adopters of SW technology (see below). RDFS is an important step toward the SW vision, as the addition of modeling primitives makes it a basic ontology representation language.

However, greater expressivity is likely to be required in the development of more complex ontologies, and the World Wide Web Consortium (W3C) has issued a Web Ontology Language (OWL[12]) in multiple versions that allows ontologies to be not only represented but also checked for logical properties such as consistency. The three species of OWL are: 1) OWL Full, containing all the OWL primitives, allowing arbitrary combination of those primitives with RDF and RDFS (allowing changes in meaning even of predefined OWL or RDF primitives), but also providing so much expressive power as to make the language undecidable (i.e., it cannot be guaranteed that a computation using the full expressive power of OWL Full will be completed in a finite time); 2) OWL DL, which restricts application of OWL's constructors to each other, and corresponds to a decidable *description logic*, but which is not fully compatible with RDF; and 3) OWL Lite, which sacrifices even more expressive power to facilitate implementation and reasoning.[12] This set of relations affects the downward compatibility of the SW layer diagram—the only version of OWL that is downward compatible with RDF and RDFS (i.e., so that any processor for that version of OWL will also provide correct interpretations of RDFS) is OWL Full, which is undecidable (pp. 113–115).[13,14]

All varieties of OWL use RDF for their syntax, and use the linking capabilities of RDF to allow ontologies to be distributed—ontologies can refer to terms in other ontologies. Such distributivity is a key property for an ontology language designed for the SW.[15]

OWL supports some kinds of inference, such as subsumption and classification, but a greater variety of rules and inference is needed. Hence, work is currently ongoing on the Rule Interchange Format (RIF), which is intended to allow a variety of rule-based formalisms, including Horn-clause logics, higher order logics, and production systems, to be used.[16] Various insights from Artificial Intelligence (AI) have also been adapted for use for the SW, including temporal (time-based) logic, causal logic, and probabilistic logics.[1]

Having represented data using RDF and ontologies, and provided for inference, it is also important to provide reliable, standardized access to data held in RDF. To that end, a special query language SPARQL (pronounced "sparkle"), which became a W3C recommendation in January 2008, has been designed.[17] Logic and proof systems are envisaged to sit on top of these formalisms, to manipulate the information in deployed systems.[1]

A very important layer is that of *trust*.[18] If information is being gathered from heterogeneous sources and inferred over, then it is important that users are able to trust such sources. The extent of trust will of course depend on the criticality of the inferences—trust entails risk, and a risk-averse user will naturally trust fewer sources.[19,20] Measuring trust, however, is a complex issue.[21] A key parameter is that of provenance, a statement of: 1) the conditions under which; 2) the methods with which; and 3) the organization by which, data were produced. Methods are appearing to enable provenance to be established, but relatively little is known about how information spreads across the Web.[22]

Related issues include respect for intellectual property, and the privacy of data subjects. In each case the reasoning abilities of the SW can be of value, and initiatives are currently under way to try to exploit them.[23] Creative commons[24] is a way of representing copyright policies and preferences based on RDF to promote reuse where possible (current standard copyright assumptions are more restrictive with respect to reuse). And research into the policy aware web is attempting to develop protocols to allow users to express their own privacy policies, and to enable those who wish to use information to reason about those policies.[25] Cryptography protocols to protect information will also play an important role, as shown in Figure 24.1.

ADDITIONAL FACTORS IN SEMANTIC WEB DEVELOPMENT

INFRASTRUCTURE

Another important part of SW development is the infrastructure that supports it. In particular, if data is to be routinely published to the Web in RDF format, there must be information repositories that can store RDF and RDFS. These *triple stores* (so-called because they store the RDF triples) must provide reasoning capabilities as well as retrieval mechanisms, but importantly must be *scalable*. Examples of triple stores include JENA,[26] 3store,[27,28] and Oracle 11*g*.[29] OWLIM is a repository which works as a storage and inference layer for the Sesame RDF database, providing reasoning support for some of the more expressive languages of the SW, RDFS, and a limited version of OWL Lite.[30,31]

Reasoners

As representation in the SW is more complex than in previous technologies, so is reasoning. The area of SW reasoning has been the focus of much research, in order to infer the consequences of a set of assertions interpreted via an ontology. In such a context, inference rules need clear semantics, and need to be able to cope with the diverse and distributed nature of the SW.

There are a number of important issues of relevance in this area: 1) Under what conditions is negation monotonic (i.e., the addition of new facts does not change the derivation of not-p), or nonmonotonic (including negation as failure, deriving not-p from the failure to prove p)?; 2) How should we handle conflicts when merging rule-sets?; 3) "Truth" on the Web is often dependent on context—how should a reasoner represent that dependence?; 4) How should scalability be balanced against expressivity?; 5) Logic often assumes a static world of given "facts," but how should it be adapted to the SW, a much more dynamic space where propositions are asserted and withdrawn all the time?; and 6) The heterogeneous nature of the SW means that data in the SW is of varying trustworthiness; how should a reasoner deal with variable reliability? None of these questions has a "correct" answer, but any SW reasoning system needs to address them.

There has been a lot of research on SW reasoning, but an important desideratum is that a reasoner should support the W3C recommended formalisms, in particular supporting OWL entailment at as high a level as possible, and SPARQL querying. Examples include: Jena, an open source SW framework for Java, with a rule-based inference engine[32]; Pellet, a sound and complete OWL-DL reasoner[33]; and KAON2, an infrastructure for managing ontologies written in OWL-DL and other SW rule languages.[34] For a short review of the problems and prospects for SW reasoning, see Fensel.[35]

Bootstrapping

Bootstrapping content for the SW is one more important issue. Sufficient content is required for the hoped-for network effects to appear. There are initiatives to generate data in RDF and to expose it on the Web as a vital first step. The DBpedia[36] is based on the Web 2.0 community-created encyclopedia Wikipedia, and is intended to extract structured information from Wikipedia allowing much more sophisticated querying. Sample queries given on the DPpedia Web site include a list of people influenced by Friedrich Nietzsche, and the set of images of American guitarists. DBpedia uses RDF, and is also interlinked with other data sources on the Web. When accessed in late 2007, the DBpedia dataset consisted of 103 million RDF triples. Other examples of linked data applications include the DBLP bibliography of scientific papers,[37] and the GeoNames database which gives descriptions of millions of geographical features in RDF.[38]

Even if RDF began to be published routinely, there is still a great deal of legacy content on the Web, and to make this accessible to SW technology some automation of the translation process is required. Gleaning Resource Descriptions from Dialects of Languages (GRDDL) allows the extraction of RDF from XML documents using transformations expressed in Extensible Stylesheet Language Transformations (XSLT) an extensible stylesheet language based on XML. It is hoped that such extraction could allow bootstrapping of some of the hoped-for SW network effects.[39]

Annotating documents and data with metadata about content, provenance, and other useful dimensions (even including relevant emotional reactions to content[40]) is also important for the effort to bring more content into the range of SW technologies.[41] Multimedia documents, such as images, particularly benefit from such annotation.[42] Again, given the quantities of both legacy data, and new data being created, methods of automating annotation have been investigated by a number of research teams in order to increase the quantity of annotated data available without excessive expenditure of resources.[41,43,44]

The Social Context: Web Science

The SW vision has been delineated with some care by the W3C, and as has been seen involves an intricate set of connections between a number of formalisms, each of which is designed to do a certain job. As we will describe in the next section, that vision has altered and gained complexity over time.

In general, there are severe complications in the mapping between the microlevel engineering of Web protocols, and the macrolevel social effects that result from large-scale use of the Web. The combination of scales, effects, and phenomena involved is too large to be easily covered by a single discipline, even computer science. The social interactions enabled by the Web place demands on the Web applications underlying them, which in turn put requirements on the Web's infrastructure. However, these multiple requirements are not currently well-understood.[45] Social studies tend to regard the Web as a given, whereas the Web is rather a world changeable by alterations to the protocols underlying it. Furthermore, the Web changes at a rate that is at least equal and may be faster than our ability to observe and analyze it.

The SW is a development bringing the Web vision to a new level of abstraction, yet the current state of our knowledge of the Web and its relation to off-line society leaves a number of questions unanswered about how it will impact at a large scale. In particular, it is unknown what social consequences there might be of the greater public exposure and sharing of information that is currently locked in databases. Understanding these consequences is important partly because the developers of the SW want to build a technology that is not harmful to society thanks to emergent social effects, and partly because it is important that the SW goes with the grain of society, in order that it be effective in real-world situations.[5]

To this end, in 2006 the Web Science Research Initiative (WSRI) was set up as a joint venture by the Massachusetts Institute of Technology and the University of Southampton to foster the interdisciplinary study of the Web in its social and technical context. WSRI's role includes crafting a curriculum for study across the various relevant disciplines; Berners-Lee.[6] is a detailed review of the wide range of scientific and social-scientific research that is likely to be relevant, including graph and network theory, computer science, economics, complexity theory, psychology, law, etc.

HISTORY AND INTELLECTUAL BACKGROUND

The vision of a web of data was always implicit in the ideas underlying the development of the WWW, and was articulated by Sir Tim Berners-Lee at the first WWW conference in 1994. Berners-Lee is well known as the inventor of the WWW in 1989–1991, and has been a leading figure in the development of the SW. As well as holding chairs at the Massachusetts Institute of Technology, United States, and the University of Southampton, United Kingdom, Berners-Lee is the director of the W3C, which he founded in 1994.

A key moment in the development, and public perception, of the SW was an entry written for *Scientific American* by Berners-Lee, James A. Hendler, and Ora Lassila in 2001.[46] This entry postulated the next stage of the WWW explicitly as one where data and information, as well as documents, are processed automatically, and envisaged a world where intelligent agents were able to access information (e.g., from calendars, gazetteers, and business organizations) in order to undertake tasks and planning for their owners.

This vision of automation of a series of routine information processing tasks has not emerged at the time of writing (2008). The article's agent-oriented vision distracted attention from the main point of the SW, the potential of a web of linked *data* (as opposed to documents) with shared semantics. Hence, in 2006, Berners-Lee, together with Nigel Shadbolt and Wendy Hall, published another article in the IEEE journal *Intelligent Systems*, which made that point explicitly, and argued that the agent-based vision would only flourish with well-established data standards.[1]

The *Scientific American* article painted a very enticing picture, but its key message was less to do with the agents and more to do with the semantic information infrastructure that Berners-Lee et al. were advocating. Indeed, the infrastructure will be used for many knowledge management purposes, not only in allowing agents to communicate. The agent-focused rhetoric of the article has prompted some to argue that the SW is a restatement of the program of AI in the 1960s and 1970s, and will share its perceived failures. We address this question below, in the section entitled "Controversies."

In 2001 (and before), the conceptualization of the various formal layers of the SW was as shown in Figure 24.2, with a fairly straightforward cascade up from URIs to XML and namespaces, to RDF and RDFS, through ontologies to rules, logic, proof and trust (the diagram has been widely distributed, but see e.g., Berners-Lee).[47] Comparison with Figure 24.1 shows how the details of the SW layers have had to be amended over time as implementation has continued. The requirements for expression of ontology-related information has led to an extra complexity from that envisaged in 2001, while the criticism of the SW vision based on the *Scientific American* article has led to a realization that not only the expressive formalisms need to be in place, but also tools and methods need to be created to allow use of SW technologies to integrate smoothly into organizations' standard information workflows (e.g., Shadbolt, Vargas-Vera, Golbeck and Alani[1,44,48,49]). This led to a top layer, User Interface, being added to the Figure 24.2 structure at a later date.

Where intelligent agency has appeared—and there are currently several applications, including shopbots and auction bots—it has tended to be handcrafted and unable to interact with heterogeneous information types. This is largely because of a lack of well-established scalable standards for information sharing; however, progress is being made toward that goal, especially via the painstaking committee-based standards development processes instituted by the W3C. These standards are crucial for the SW to "take off," and for the hoped-for network effects of a large number of users to emerge.[1]

The SW vision has been implemented by standard bodies, such as the Internet Engineering Task Force (IETF) as well as the W3C (the W3C is responsible for standards specific to the WWW), which have orchestrated efforts together with the user community to develop the languages at various levels to share meaning. Once standards are set by the W3C, they are called *recommendations*, acknowledging the reality that with the decentralization of the Web, and a lack of a central authority, standards cannot be enforced. The first RDF standard was specified in 1997 and became a W3C recommendation in 1999, thereby providing a minimal knowledge representation language for the Web with the clear backing of the nascent SW community.

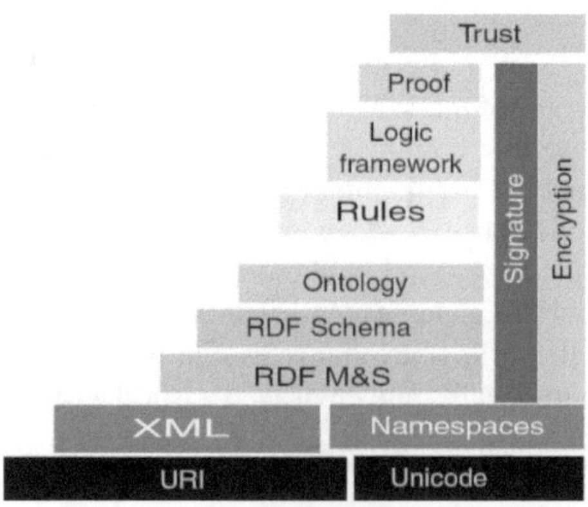

FIGURE 24.2 The early layered view of the Semantic Web.

Fixed standards for expressing ontologies appeared later in the process, with RDFS and OWL becoming recommendations in 2004. OWL evolved from other ontology language efforts, including Ontology Inference Layer (OIL)[50] and DARPA Agent Markup Language (DAML)[51] whose merged product, DAML+OIL, was the most important predecessor to OWL.[52] In January 2008, the query language SPARQL became a W3C recommendation, while the RIF was under development in mid-2008.

Figure 24.3, created in 2003, illustrates Berners-Lee's vision of the pattern of SW development using the visual metaphor of a tide flowing onto a beach (this diagram is widely available, but see Connolly).[53] From top to bottom in the diagram are the various layers of the SW diagram, from trust and proof down to data exchange and markup. From left to right come the various stages in a rough lifecycle from research to deployment: the first stage is a blue-sky research project; the second is the production of a stable system or formalism that is not a standard; the best aspects of these systems are then used as the bases for W3C standards, and the final stage is one of wide deployment. Hence, for instance, early ontology efforts like Cyc and description logics led to efforts such as DAML and OIL, which in turn helped create OWL. Wide deployment of OWL then results in a so-called web of meaning.

The "sea" of research and deployment approaches from the bottom left of Figure 24.3 to the top right, as the "tide" comes in. Hence in 1998, various formalisms were in place for all the various levels of representation of the SW, but only XML was a Web standard and beginning to be used widely. By 2003, OWL and RDFS were close to their final forms, and RDF was beginning to be used widely for cross-application interoperability. At the time of writing, the "tide" has advanced further to the right, so work is ongoing on rule language RIF, and query language SPARQL became an official W3C recommendation in 2008. Meanwhile OWL is being used more frequently by ontology builders.

The SW's history to date is largely one of standard-setting. However, it has also been argued that, analogous to other systems which have spread quickly and grown exponentially, what is needed is a "killer app" (i.e., an application that will meet a felt need and create a perception of the technology

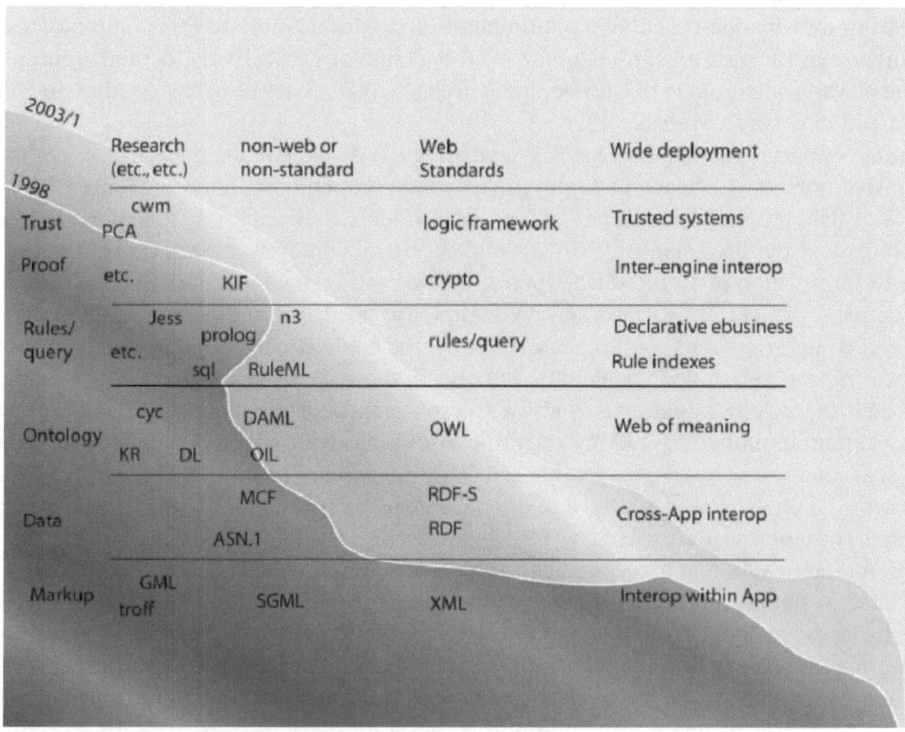

FIGURE 24.3 A representation of the progress of semantic web development.

as "essential"). Less ambitiously, the SW's spread depends not only on having an impressive set of formalisms, but also software tools to use information represented in those formalisms.[49] The SW is clearly not, at the time of writing, an information resource in routine use. Nevertheless, there are some applications where SW technologies are serving valuable purposes, and we review some of these in the next section.

APPLICATIONS AND SYSTEMS

Properties of Systems

In general, SW projects tend to exhibit a few constant features. They generate new ontologies for the application domain (for example, art, or computer science), and use them to interrogate large stores of data, which could be legacy data or freshly harvested. Hence a body of evidence is building up that ontologies have an important role in mediating the integration of data from heterogeneous sources.

Furthermore, the results of SW projects are generally presented using custom-built interfaces. This hints at a very important research area, which is the development of scalable visualizers capable of navigating the graph of connected information expressed in RDF. As can be seen, the importance of applications and user interfaces was made clear in the latest version of the layered SW diagram (Figure 24.1).

In this section we will look at active SW successes, focusing on application areas and types, then commercial/real-world systems, before finally looking at some of the more successful academic efforts as judged by the SW development community itself.

Application Areas

There are areas where the SW is already an important tool, often in small focused communities with pressing information-processing requirements and various more or less common goals. Such communities can function as early adopters of the technology, exactly as the high energy physics discipline played a vital role in the development of the WWW. A series of case studies and use cases is maintained in w3.org's Web site.[54]

The most important application for SW technology is *e-science*, the data-driven, computationally intensive pursuit of science in highly distributed computational environments.[55] Very large quantities of data are created by analyses and experiments in disciplines such as particle physics, meteorology, and the life sciences. Furthermore, in many contexts, different communities of scientists will be working in an interdisciplinary manner, which means that data from various fields (e.g., genomics, clinical drug trials, and epidemiology) need to be integrated. Many accounts of distinct and complex systems (e.g., the human body, the environment) consist of data brought from disciplines varying not only in vocabulary, but also in the scale of description; understanding such systems, and the way in which events at the microscale affect the macroscale and *vice versa*, is clearly an important imperative. Many scientific disciplines have devoted resources to the creation of large-scale and robust ontologies for this and other purposes. The most well-known of these is the *gene ontology*, a controlled vocabulary to describe gene and gene product attributes in organisms, and related vocabularies developed by open biomedical ontologies.[56] Others include the protein ontology, the cell cycle ontology, Medical Subject Headings (MeSH, used to index life science publications), systematized nomenclature of medicine (SNOMED), and AGROVOC (agriculture, forestry, fisheries, and food).

E-government is another potentially important application area, where information is deployed widely, and yet is highly heterogeneous. Government information varies in provenance, confidentiality, and "shelf life" (some information will be good for decades or even centuries, while other information can be out-of-date within hours), while it can also have been created by various levels of government (national/federal, regional, state, city, and parish). Integrating that information in a timely way is clearly an important challenge (see for instance a pilot study for the United Kingdom's Office of Public Sector Information, exploring the use of SW technologies for disseminating, sharing, and reusing data held in the public sector.[57])

Commercial Activity

There is an increasing number of applications that allow a deeper querying of linked data. We have already discussed DBpedia,[36] DBLP,[37] and GeoNames.[38] Commercial applications are also beginning to appear. Garlik[58] is a company seeking to exploit SW-style technologies to provide individual consumers with more power over their digital data. It reviews what is held about people, harvesting data from the open Web, and represents this in a people-centric structure. Natural Language Processing is used to find occurrences of people's names, sensitive information, and relations to other individuals and organizations. Declaration of interest: Wendy Hall is chair of the Garlik Advisory Board. Twine[59] is intended to enable people to share knowledge and information, and to organize that information using various SW technologies (also, like Garlik, using Natural Language Processing). Twine's developer Nova Spivack has coined the term "knowledge networking" to describe the process, analogous to the Web 2.0 idea of "social networking."

The increasing maturity of SW technology is being shown by the growing number of successful vendors of SW technology. We have already seen OWLIM,[31] which was developed by Ontotext, a semantic technology lab focused on technologies to support the SW and SW services based in Sofia, Bulgaria, and Montreal, Canada; Ontotext has been and is a partner in a number of major SW research projects.[60] Ontoprise, based in Karlsruhe, Germany, is a software vendor for implementing SW infrastructure in large, distributed enterprises; its products include OntoBroker, which provides ontology support using the W3C recommended languages OWL, RDFS and SPARQL, and Semantic MediaWiki+, a collaborative knowledge management tool.[61] Asemantics, with offices in Italy, Holland, and the United Kingdom, uses a combination of Web 2.0 paradigms with SW technologies such as XML and RDF. The SW technologies are powerful representational tools but are often perceived as hard to use and search, so Asemantics attempts to exploit the perceived usability of Web 2.0 to present data in more widely accepted formats.[62]

Academic Work: The Semantic Web Challenge

Much of the major work in the SW has been carried out in the academic sphere, and in funded research projects between academic and commercial partners, and is reported in journals and conferences (see end of entry for a list of the more importance conferences). Any review of academic work in this field will inevitably be selective; for the purposes of this entry we will focus on a particular effort to nurture applications, the *Semantic Web Challenge*.

The SW Challenge was created in 2003, and associated with the International Semantic Web Conference (ISWC) of that year. Since then it has become an annual competition to create an application that shows SW technology in its best aspects, and which can act as a "benchmark" application. Hence the SW Challenge gives us a series of illustrative applications thought by researchers' peers to constitute best SW practice.[63]

To meet the criteria for the Challenge, a tool or system needs to meet a number of requirements,[64] which provide a useful characterization of the expectations governing an SW system, and are suggestive of the expected properties of SW applications. For instance, it should use information from sources that are distributed and heterogeneous, of real-world complexity and with diverse ownership. It should assume an open world, and that the information is never complete, and it should use some formal description of the meaning of the data. Optional criteria include a use of data in some way other than the creators intended, use of multimedia, and use of devices other than a PC. Applications need not be restricted to information retrieval, and ideally the system would be scalable in terms of the amount of data used and the number of distributed components cooperating. All these criteria indicate areas where SW systems would be expected to have an advantage.

The winners of the SW Challenge to date are as follows:

- 2003: CS AKTive Space (University of Southampton), an integrated application which provides a way to explore the U.K. Computer Science Research domain across multiple dimensions for multiple stakeholders, from funding agencies to individual researchers, using information harvested from the Web, and mediated through an ontology.[65]
- 2004: Flink (Vrije Universiteit Amsterdam), a "Who's Who" of the SW which allows the interrogation of information gathered automatically from Web-accessible resources about researchers who have participated in ISWC conferences.[66]
- 2005: CONFOTO (appmosphere Web applications, Germany), a browsing and annotation service for conference photographs.[67]
- 2006: MultimediaN E-Culture Demonstrator (Vrije Universiteit Amsterdam, Centre for Mathematics and Computer Science, Universiteit van Amsterdam, Digital Heritage Netherlands and Technical University of Eindhoven), an application to search, navigate, and annotate annotated media collections interactively, using collections from several museums and art repositories.[68]
- 2007: Revyu.com (Open University), a reviewing and rating site specifically designed for the SW, allowing reviews to be integrated and interlinked with data from other sources (in particular, other reviews).[69]

CONTROVERSIES

The SW vision has always generated controversy, with a number of commentators being highly skeptical of its prospects. Let us briefly review some of the disputed issues.

The Semantic Web as "Good Old-Fashioned Artificial Intelligence"

One view holds that the SW is basically a throwback to the project to program machine intelligence which was jokingly christened by John Haugeland "GOFAI" (good old-fashioned AI). This proved impossible: so much of human intelligence is implicit and situated that it was too hard a problem to write down everything a computer needed to know to produce an output that exhibited human-like intelligence. For instance, if a human is told about a room, further explanations that a room generally has a floor, at least three walls, usually four, and a ceiling, and some method of ingress that is generally but not always a door, are not required. But a computer needs to be told these mundane facts explicitly—and similarly every time it is introduced to a new concept.[70]

One attempt to work around this problem is the Cyc project, set up in 1984, which aims to produce a gigantic ontology that will encode all commonsense knowledge of the type about the room given above, in order to support human-like reasoning by machines.[71] The project has always aroused controversy, but it is fair to say that over two decades later, GOFAI is no nearer. The implicit nature of commonsense knowledge arguably makes it impossible to write it all down.

Many commentators have argued that the SW is basically a re-creation of the (misconceived) GOFAI idea, that the aim is to create machine intelligence over the Web, to allow machines to reason about Web content in such a way as to exhibit intelligence.[72,73] This, however, is a misconception, possibly abetted by the strong focus in the 2001 *Scientific American* article on an agent-based vision of the SW.[46] Like many GOFAI projects, the scenarios in that article have prominent planning components. There is also continuity between the AI tradition of work on formal knowledge representation and the SW project of developing ontologies (see below).

The SW has less to do with GOFAI as with context-based machine reasoning over content (and the provision of machine-readable data on the Web). The aim is not to bring a single ontology, such as Cyc, to bear on all problems (and therefore implicitly to define or anticipate all problems and points of view in the ontology definition), but rather to allow data to be interrogated in ways that were not anticipated by their creators. Different ontologies will be appropriate for different purposes; composite ontologies can be assembled from distributed parts (thanks to the design of OWL); and it is frequently very basic ontologies (defining simple terms such as "customer," "account number," or "account balance") that deliver large amounts of content. It is, after all, a matter of fact that people from different communities and disciplines can and do interact without making any kind of common *global* ontological commitment.[1,6,74]

Indeed, we can perhaps learn from the experience of hype and reaction that accompanied the development of AI. There has been a great deal of criticism of AI, but much has been learned from AI research and some AI methods and systems are now routinely exploited in a number of applications. The same may be expected of the SW. We should not expect to wake up one morning with the SW implemented and ready for use. Rather, a likelier model is that SW technologies will be incorporated into more systems "behind the scenes" wherever methods are needed to deal with signature SW problems (large quantities of distributed heterogeneous data).

Arguments for and Against Ontologies

The importance of ontologies for the SW has been another point of friction with those who believe the program unrealistic. Ontologies are seen as expensive to develop and hard to maintain. Classification of objects is usually done relative to some task, and as the nature of the task changes, ontologies can become outdated. Classifications are also made relative to some background assumptions, and impose those assumptions onto the resulting ontology. To that extent, the expensive development of ontologies reflects the world view of the ontology builders, not necessarily the users. They are top-down and authoritarian, and therefore opposed to the Web ethos of decentralization and open conversation. They are fixed in advance, and so they don't work very well to represent knowledge in dynamic, situated contexts.[75–77]

Furthermore, say the critics, the whole point of the Web as a decentralized, linked information structure is that it reflects the needs of its large, heterogeneous user base which includes very many people who are naïve in their interactions. The infrastructure has to be usable by such people, which argues for simplicity. The rich linking structure of the current Web, combined with statistically based search engines such as Google, is much more responsive to the needs of unsophisticated users. The SW, in contrast, demands new information markup practices, and corporations and information owners need to invest in new technologies. Not only that, but current statistical methods will scale up as the number of users and interactions grows, whereas logic-based methods such as those advocated by the SW, on the other hand, scale less well (cf., e.g., Zambonini).[78]

Folksonomies

One development as part of the so-called Web 2.0 paradigm (of systems, communities, and services which facilitate collaboration and information-sharing among users) that has drawn attention in this context is that of the "folksonomy." Folksonomies have arisen out of the recent move to allow users to "tag" content on Web 2.0 sites such as the image-sharing site Flickr, and the video-sharing site YouTube. Having seen content, users are allowed to tag it with key words, which, when the number of users has become large enough, results in a structure of connections and classifications emerging without central control. Their promoters argue that folksonomies "really" express the needs of their users (since all the structure has arisen out of their user-based classifications), whereas ontologies "really" express the needs of authorities who can "impose" their views from the top-down.[76]

However, folksonomies are much less expressive than ontologies; they are basically variants on keyword searches. A tag "SF" may refer to a piece of science fiction, or to San Francisco, or something else from the user's private idiolect. Indeed, that ambiguity arises even if we make the unrealistic assumption of a monoglot English user community. Once we realize speakers of other languages will use a system, then there are further possible ambiguities—for instance, in German "SF" might refer to the Swiss television station Schweizer Fernsehen.

Resolving This Controversy

When a community is large enough and the benefits clear, then a large-scale ontology building and maintenance program is justified. In a recent note, Berners-Lee argues that such conditions will be perhaps more frequently encountered than skeptics believe. On the very broad assumptions that the size of an ontology-building team increases as the order of the log of the size of the ontology's user community, and that the resources needed to build an ontology increase as the order of the square of community size, the cost per individual of ontology building will diminish rapidly as user community size increases. Of course these assumptions are not intended to be deeply realistic, so much as indicative of how the resource implications diminish as the community increases in size. Berners-Lee's moral: "Do your bit. Others will do theirs."[74]

Even so, not all ontologies need to be of great size and expressive depth. Certainly the claim that has been made that the SW requires a single ontology of all discourse on the model of Cyc, but this is not backed up by the SW community. Such an ontology, even if possible, would not scale, and in a decentralized structure like the Web its use could not be enforced. We should rather expect a lot of use of small-scale, *shallow* ontologies defining just a few terms that nevertheless are widely applicable.[74] Experience in building real-world SW systems often shows that expectations about the cost and complexity of the ontologies required are overblown, and the ontology-building process can be relatively straightforward and cheap.[79]

For example, the machine-readable friend-of-a-friend (FOAF) ontology is intended to describe people, their activities, and their relations to other people. It is not massively complex, and indeed publishing a FOAF account of oneself is a fairly simple matter of form-filling (using the FOAF-a-matic tool).[80] But the resulting network of people (showing their connections to other people) has become very large indeed. A survey performed in 2004 discovered over 1.5 million documents using the FOAF ontology.[81]

With respect to Folksonomies, it is important to note that ontologies and folksonomies serve different purposes. Folksonomies are based on word tags, whereas the basis for ontology reference is via a URI. One of the main aims of ontology definition is to *remove* ambiguity—not globally, for this may well be impossible, but rather within the particular context envisaged by the developer (see the section on "Symbol Grounding" below). Folksonomies will necessarily inherit the ambiguity of the natural language upon which they are based. And while folksonomies emerge from data-sharing practices, it is not necessarily the case the ontologies are authoritarian; rather, the latter should ideally be *rationalizations* of current sharing practice. This does entail departure from current practice, but not necessarily of great magnitude. Indeed, a strong possibility is to use cheaply gathered folksonomies as starting points for ontology development, gradually morphing the Web 2.0 structures into something with greater precision and less ambiguity.[82]

Symbol Grounding

An important aspect of the SW is that URIs must be interpreted consistently. However, terms and symbols are highly variable in their definitions and use through time and space. The SW project ideally needs processes whereby URIs are given to objects, such that the management of these processes is by communities and individuals, endorsed by the user community, who ensure consistency. This URI "ownership" is critical to the smooth functioning of the SW.[1]

But the process of *symbol grounding* (i.e., ensuring a fixed and known link between a symbol and its referent) is at best hard, and at worst (as argued by Wittgenstein, for instance) impossible.[83,84] Meanings do not stay fixed, but alter, often imperceptibly. They are delineated not only by traditional methods such as the provision of necessary and sufficient conditions, but also by procedures, technologies and instrumentation, and alter subtly as practice alters.

Any attempt to fix the reference of URIs is a special case of symbol grounding, and is consequently hard to do globally. It is certainly the case that attempting to resist the alteration in community practices and norms, and reformulation of meanings of terms, would be doomed.

Yorick Wilks has argued that since much knowledge is held in unstructured form, in plain text, automatic Natural Language Processing techniques, statistically based, can be used to "ground" meanings of terms for the SW.[73] Berners-Lee, on the other hand, maintains that the SW is necessarily based on logic and firm definitions (even if those definitions were imperfect, or highly situated and task-relative), not words, use patterns and statistics. Wilks' point is that the aim of defining terms in logic is too idealistic, and anyway depends on false assumptions about ordinary word meaning. Berners-Lee's counterargument is, in effect, that though meanings are not stable, they can be stable *enough* relative to individual applications and in particular contexts to allow the SW approach to work.

CONCLUSION

The SW has been somewhat misunderstood in some commentaries. Its aim is not to force users to accept large ontologies remote from data-sharing practice imposed by shadowy authorities. Neither is it intended to produce a theory of all discourse, or to reproduce GOFAI. Rather, it is intended to shift the emphasis of the Web from being a web of documents to a web of linked *data*. It is the development of formalisms and technologies facilitating the creation, sharing, and querying of linked data using sharable ontologies to establish common interpretations. For this reason, an alternative name for the SW is the *web of linked data*.

The SW is a work in progress. As it stands, the "buy in" to the SW has not yet produced the desirable network effects, although several disciplines are enthusiastic early adopters of the technology (e.g., the e-science community). And there are still several important research issues outstanding. It is not yet known how best to: 1) query large numbers of heterogeneous information stores at many different scales; 2) translate between, merge, prune, or evaluate ontologies; 3) visualize the SW; and 4) establish trust and provenance of the content.

As complex technologies and information infrastructures are developed, there is a dynamic feedback between requirements, analysis, engineering solutions, and hard-to-predict global behavior of human, machine, and hybrid systems. Understanding how basic engineering protocols governing how computers talk to each other can result in social movements at a very different level of abstraction is very hard, yet essential to realizing the SW vision. Indeed, such understanding, the defining purpose of the discipline of *Web Science*, is essential to ensuring that *any* Web-based information structure is beneficial.[5]

ACKNOWLEDGMENTS

The authors would like to thank Tim Berners-Lee, Nigel Shadbolt, James A. Hendler, Daniel J. Weitzner, Harith Alani, Marcia J. Bates, and an anonymous referee for helpful comments and discussions.

REFERENCES

1. Shadbolt, N.; Hall, W.; Berners-Lee, T. The Semantic Web revisited. IEEE Intell. Syst. **2006**, *21* (3), 96–101.
2. Fensel, D.; Bussler, C.; Ding, Y.; Kartseva, V.; Klein, M.; Korotkiy, M.; Omelayenko, B.; Siebes, R. Semantic Web application areas. In *7th International Workshop on Applications of Natural Language to Information Systems (NLDB 2002)*, Stockholm, Sweden, June 27–28, 2002, http://www. cs.vu.nl/~ronny/work/NLDB02.pdf, 2002 (accessed July 2008).

3. Fensel, D. *Ontologies: A Silver Bullet for Knowledge Management and Electronic Commerce*, 2nd Ed.; Springer: Berlin, 2004.
4. Berners-Lee, T. Relational databases on the Semantic Web, http://www.w3.org/DesignIssues/RDB-RDF.html, 1998 (accessed December 2007).
5. Berners-Lee, T.; Hall, W.; Hendler, J.; Shadbolt, N.; Weitzner, D. Creating a science of the Web. Science **2006**, *313* (5788), 769–771.
6. Berners-Lee, T.; Hall, W.; Hendler, J.A.; O'Hara, K.; Shadbolt, N.; Weitzner, D.J. A framework for Web Science. Found. Trends Web Sci **2006**, *1* (1), 1–134.
7. Klyne, G.; Carroll, J.J.; McBride, B. Resource Description Framework (RDF): Concepts and abstract syntax, 2004 http://www.w3.org/TR/rdf-concepts/ (accessed December 2007).
8. Berners-Lee, T. Principles of design, 1998, http://www.w3.org/DesignIssues/Principles.html (accessed December 2007).
9. Berners-Lee, T.; Fielding, R.; Masinter, L. Uniform Resource Identifier (URI): Generic syntax, 2005, http://gbiv.com/proto-cols/uri/rfc/rfc3986.html (accessed December 2007).
10. Bray, T.; Paoli, J.; Sperberg-McQueen, C.M.; Maler, E.; Yergeau, F. *Extensible Markup Language (XML) 1.0*, 4th Ed.; 2006, http://www.w3.org/TR/xml/ (accessed December 2007).
11. Brickley, D.; Guha, R.V.; McBride, B. RDF vocabulary description language 1.0: RDF Schema, 2004, http://www.w3.org/TR/rdf-schema/ (accessed December 2007).
12. McGuinness, D.L.; van Harmelen, F. OWL Web Ontology Language overview, 2004, http://www.w3.org/TR/owl-features/ (accessed December 2007).
13. Antoniou, G.; van Harmelen, F. *A Semantic Web Primer*; MIT Press: Cambridge MA, 2004.
14. Dean, M.; Schreiber, G.; Bechhofer, S.; van Harmelen, F.; Hendler, J.; Horrocks, I.; McGuinness, D.L.; Patel-Schneider, P.F.; Stein, L.A. OWL Web Ontology Language Reference, 2004, http://www.w3.org/TR/owl-ref/ (accessed December 2007).
15. Smith, M.K.; Welty, C.; McGuiness, D.L. OWL Web Ontology Language guide, 2004, http://www.w3.org/TR/owl-guide/ (accessed December 2007).
16. Boley, H.; Kifer, M. RIF basic logic dialect, 2007, http:// www.w3.org/TR/rif-bld/ (accessed December 2007).
17. Prud'hommeaux, E.; Seaborne, A. SPARQL query language for RDF, 2007, http://www.w3.org/TR/rdf-sparql-query/ (accessed December 2007).
18. Golbeck, J. Trust on the World Wide Web: A survey. Found. Trends Web Sci. **2006**, *1* (2), 1–72.
19. Bonatti, P.A.; Duma, C.; Fuchs, N.; Nejdl, W.; Olmedilla, D.; Peer, J.; Shahmehri, N. Semantic Web policies—a discussion of requirements and research issues. In *The Semantic Web: Research and Applications*, 3rd European Semantic Web Conference 2006 (ESWC-06), Budva, Montenegro, 2006; Sure, Y., Domingue, J., Eds.; Springer: Berlin, 2006.
20. O'Hara, K.; Alani, H.; Kalfoglou, Y.; Shadbolt, N. Trust strategies for the Semantic Web. In *Workshop on Trust, Security and Reputation on the Semantic Web*, 3rd International Semantic Web Conference (ISWC 04), Hiroshima, Japan, 2004, http://eprints.ecs.soton.ac.uk/10029/ (accessed December 2007).
21. Golbeck, J.; Hendler, J. Accuracy of metrics for inferring trust and reputation in Semantic Web-based social networks. In *Engineering Knowledge in the Age of the Semantic Web*, Proceedings of 14th International Conference, EKAW 2004, Whittlebury Hall, U.K. 2004; Motta, E.; Shadbolt, N.; Stutt, A.; Gibbins, N.; Eds.; Springer: Berlin, 2004; 116–131.
22. Groth, P.; Jiang, S.; Miles, S.; Munroe, S.; Tan, V.; Tsasakou, S.; Moreau, L. An architecture for provenance systems, http://eprints.ecs.soton.ac.uk/13216/1/ provenanceArchitecture10.pdf, 2006 (accessed December 2007).
23. O'Hara, K.; Shadbolt, N. *The Spy in the Coffee Machine: The End of Privacy As We Know It*; Oneworld: Oxford, 2008.
24. http://creativecommons.org/about/ (accessed December 2007).
25. Weitzner, D.J.; Hendler, J.; Berners-Lee, T.; Connolly, D. Creating a policy-aware Web: Discretionary, rule-based access for the World Wide Web. In *Web and Information Security*, Ferrari, E.; Thuraisingham, B.; Eds.; Idea Group Inc: Hershey, PA, 2005.
26. http://jena.sourceforge.net/ (accessed December 2007).
27. http://sourceforge.net/projects/threestore (accessed December 2007).
28. Harris, S.; Gibbins, N. 3store: Efficient bulk RDF storage. In *Proceedings of the 1st International Workshop on Practical and Scalable Systems*, Sanibel Island, FL, 2003, http://km.aifb.uni-karlsruhe.de/ws/psss03/proceedings/harris-et-al.pdf (accessed December 2007).
29. http://www.oracle.com/technology/tech/semantic_technolo gies/index.html (accessed December 2007).
30. http://www.ontotext.com/owlim/ (accessed July 2008).

31. Kiryakov, A.; Ognyanov, D.; Manov, D. OWLIM: A pragmatic semantic repository for OWL. In *Web Information and Systems Engineering–WISE 2005 Workshops*, Proceedings of the Workshop on Scalable Semantic Web Knowledge Base Systems at WISE 2005, New York, November 2005; Dean, M.; Guo, Y.; Jun, W.; Kaschek, R.; Krishnaswamy, S.; Pan, Z.; Sheng, Q.Z.; Eds.; Springer: Berlin, 2005; 182–192, http://www.ontotext.com/publica tions/ssws_owlim.pdf (accessed July 2008).
32. McBride, B. Jena: Implementing the RDF model and syntax specification. In *Proceedings of the 2nd International Workshop on the Semantic Web: SemWeb 2001*, World Wide Web Conference 2001, Hong Kong, May 2001; Decker, S.; Fensel, D.; Sheth, A.; Staab, S.; Eds.; CEUR-WS, Vol. 40, 2001, http://sunsite.informatik.rwth-aachen. de/Publications/CEUR-WS/Vol-40/mcbride.pdf (accessed July 2008).
33. Sirin, E.; Parsia, B.; Cuenca Grau, B.; Kalyanpur, A.; Katz, Y. Pellet: A practical OWL-DL reasoner. J. Web Semant. **2007**, *5* (2), 51–53.
34. http://kaon2.semanticweb.org/ (accessed July 2008).
35. Fensel, D.; Van Harmelen, F. Unifying reasoning and search to Web scale. IEEE Internet Comput. **2007**, *11* (2), 96, 94–95 (sic).
36. Auer, S.; Bizer, C.; Kobilarov, G.; Lehmann, J.; Cyganiak, R.; Ives, Z. DBpedia: A nucleus for a Web of open data. In *Proceedings of the 6th International Semantic Web Conference 2007*, Busan, South Korea, 2007, http://iswc2007. semanticweb.org/papers/715.pdf (accessed December 2007).
37. http://www4.wiwiss.fu-berlin.de/dblp/ (accessed December 2007).
38. http://www.geonames.org/ (accessed December 2007).
39. Connolly, D., Ed. Gleaning Resource Descriptions from Dialects of Languages (GRDDL), 2007, http://www.w3. org/TR/grddl/ (accessed December 2007).
40. Schröder, M.; Zovato, E.; Pirker, H.; Peter, C.; Burkhardt, F. W3C emotion incubator group report, 2007, http://www.w3.org/2005/Incubator/emotion/XGR-emotion/ (accessed December 2007).
41. Handschuh, S.; Staab, S.; Eds. *Annotation for the Semantic Web*; IOS Press: Amsterdam, 2003.
42. Troncy, R.; van Ossenbruggen, J.; Pan, J.Z.; Stamou, G.; Halaschek-Wiener, C.; Simou, N.; Tsouvaras, V. Image annotation on the Semantic Web, 2007, http://www.w3.org/ 2005/Incubator/mmsem/XGR-image-annotation/ (accessed December 2007).
43. Handschuh, S.; Staab, S.; Ciravegna, F. S-CREAM—Semi-automatic Creation of Metadata. In *Knowledge Engineering and Knowledge Management: Ontologies and the Semantic Web*, Proceedings of 13th International Conference, EKAW 2002, Siguënza, Spain, 2002; Gómez-Pérez, A.; Benjamins, V.R.; Eds.; Springer: Berlin, 2002; 358–372.
44. Vargas-Vera, M.; Motta, E.; Domingue, J.; Lanzoni, M.; Stutt, A.; Ciravegna, F. MnM: Ontology-driven semiautomatic and automatic support for semantic markup. In *Knowledge Engineering and Knowledge Management: Ontologies and the Semantic Web*, Proceedings of 13th International Conference, EKAW 2002, Siguënza, Spain, 2002; Gómez-Pérez, A.; Benjamins, V.R.; Eds.; Springer: Berlin, 2002; 379–391.
45. Hendler, J.; Shadbolt, N.; Hall, W.; Berners-Lee, T.; Weitzner, D. Web Science: An interdisciplinary approach to understanding the World Wide Web. Commun. ACM **2008**, *51* (7), 60–69.
46. Berners-Lee, T.; Hendler, J.; Lassila, O. The Semantic Web. Sci. Am. May **2001**, http://www.sciam.com/article. cfm?articleID=00048144-10D2-1C70-84A9809EC588EF21 (accessed December 2007).
47. Berners-Lee, T. Foreword. In *Spinning the Semantic Web: Bringing the World Wide Web to its Full Potential*; Fensel, D.; Hendler, J.; Lieberman, H.; Wahlster, W.; Eds.; MIT Press: Cambridge, MA, 2003; xi–xxiii.
48. Golbeck, J.; Grove, M.; Parsia, B.; Kalyanpur, A.; Hendler, J. New tools for the Semantic Web. In *Knowledge Engineering and Knowledge Management: Ontologies and the Semantic Web*, Proceedings of 13th International Conference, EKAW 2002, Siguënza, Spain, 2002; Gómez-Pérez, A.; Benjamins, V.R.; Eds.; Springer: Berlin, 2002; 392–400.
49. Alani, H.; Kalfoglou, Y.; O'Hara, K.; Shadbolt, N. Towards a killer app for the Semantic Web. In *The Semantic Web*, Proceedings of the International Semantic Web Conference 2005, Hiroshima, Japan, 2005; Gil, Y.; Motta, E.; Benjamins, V.R.; Musen, M.A.; Eds.; Springer: Berlin, 2005; 829–843.
50. Fensel, D.; Horrocks, I.; van Harmelen, F.; Decker, S.; Erdmann, M.; Klein, M. OIL in a nutshell. In *Knowledge Engineering and Knowledge Management: Methods, Models and Tools*, Proceedings of 12th European Knowledge Acquisition Workshop (EKAW 2000), Juan-les-Pins, France, October 2000; Dieng, R.; Corby, O.; Eds.; Springer: Berlin, 2000; 1–16, http://www.cs.vu.nl/~onto-know/oil/downl/oilnutshell.pdf (accessed July 2008).
51. http://www.daml.org/about.html (accessed July 2008).
52. Patel-Schneider, P.; Horrocks, I.; van Harmelen, F. Reviewing the design of DAML + OIL: An ontology language for the Semantic Web. In *Proceedings of the 18th National Conference on Artificial Intelligence*

(AAAI02), Edmonton, Canada, 2002, http://www.cs.vu.nl/~frankh/postscript/AAAI02.pdf (accessed December 2007).
53. Connolly, D. Semantic Web update: OWL and beyond, 2003, http://www.w3.org/2003/Talks/1017-swup/all.htm (accessed December 2007).
54. http://www.w3.org/2001/sw/sweo/public/UseCases/ (accessed December 2007).
55. Hendler, J.; de Roure, D. E-science: The grid and the Semantic Web. IEEE Intell. Syst. **2004**, *19* (1), 65–71.
56. http://www.geneontology.org/ (accessed July 2008).
57. Alani, H.; Dupplaw, D.; Sheridan, J.; O'Hara, K.; Darlington, J.; Shadbolt, N.; Tullo, C. Unlocking the potential of public sector information with Semantic Web technology. In *Proceedings of the 6th International Semantic Web Conference 2007*, Busan, South Korea, 2007, http://iswc2007.semanticweb.org/papers/701.pdf (accessed December 2007).
58. https://www.garlik.com/index.php (accessed December 2007).
59. http://www.twine.com/ (accessed December 2007).
60. http://www.ontotext.com/index.html (accessed July 2008).
61. http://www.ontoprise.de/index.php?id=134 (accessed July 2008).
62. http://www.asemantics.com/index.html (accessed July 2008).
63. http://www.informatik.uni-bremen.de/agki/www/swc/index. html (accessed December 2007).
64. http://challenge.semanticweb.org/ (accessed December 2007).
65. Schraefel, M.M.C; Shadbolt, N.R.; Gibbins, N.; Glaser, H.; Harris, S. CS AKTive Space: Representing computer science on the Semantic Web. In *Proceedings of WWW 2004*; New York, 2004, http://eprints.ecs.soton.ac.uk/9084/ (accessed December 2007).
66. Mika, P. Flink: Semantic Web technology for the extraction and analysis of social networks. J. Web Semant. **2005**, *3* (2), http://www.websemanticsjournal.org/papers/20050719/ document7.pdf (accessed December 2007).
67. Nowack, B. CONFOTO: A semantic browsing and annotation service for conference photos. In *The Semantic Web*, Proceedings of the International Semantic Web Conference 2005, Hiroshima, Japan, 2005; Gil, Y.; Motta, E.; Benjamins, V.R.; Musen, M.A.; Eds.; Springer: Berlin, 2005; 1067–1070.
68. Schreiber, G.; Amin, A.; van Assem, M.; de Boer, V.; Hardman, L.; Hildebrand, M.; Hollink, L.; Huang, Z.; van Kersen, J.; de Niet, M.; Omelayenko, B.; van Ossenbruggen, J.; Siebes, R.; Taekema, J.; Wielemaker, J.; Wielinga, B. MultimediaN e-culture demonstrator, 2006, http://www.cs.vu.nl/~guus/papers/Schreiber06a.pdf (accessed December 2007).
69. Heath, T.; Motta, E. Revyu.com: A reviewing and rating site for the Web of data. In *Proceedings of the 6th International Semantic Web Conference 2007*, Busan, South Korea, 2007, http://iswc2007.semantic-web.org/papers/889. pdf (accessed December 2007).
70. Haugeland, J. Understanding natural language. J. Philos. **1979**, *76*, 619–632.
71. Lenat, D.B. Cyc: A large-scale investment in knowledge infrastrcture. Commun. ACM **1995**, *38* (11), 32–38.
72. Jones, K.S. What's new about the Semantic Web? Some questions. SIGIR Forum **2004**, *38* (2), http://www.sigir. org/forum/2004D/sparck jones_sigirforum_2004d.pdf (accessed December 2007).
73. Wilks, Y. The Semantic Web: Apotheosis of annotation, but what are its semantics? IEEE Intell. Syst. **2008**, *23* (3), 41–49.
74. Berners-Lee, T. The fractal nature of the Web, 2007, http://www.w3.org/DesignIssues/Fractal.html (accessed December 2007).
75. Pike, W.; Gahegan, M. Beyond ontologies: Toward situated representations of scientific knowledge. Intl. J. Hum. Comput. Stud. **2007**, *65* (7), 674–688.
76. Shirky, C. Ontology is overrated: categories, links and tags, 2005, http://www.shirky.com/writings/ontology_o-verrated.html (accessed December 2007).
77. Stevens, R.; Egaña Aranguren, M.; Wolstencroft, K.; Sattler, U.; Drummond, N.; Horridge, M.; Rector, A. Using OWL to model biological knowledge. Intl. J. Hum. Comput. Stud. **2007**, *65* (7), 583–594.
78. Zambonini, D. The 7 (f)laws of the Semantic Web, 2006, http://www.oreillynet.com/xml/blog/2006/06/the_7_flaws_of_the_semantic_we.html (accessed December 2007).
79. Alani, H.; Chandler, P.; Hall, W.; O'Hara, K.; Shadbolt, N.; Szomsor, M. Building a pragmatic Semantic Web. IEEE Intell. Syst. **2008**, *23* (3), 61–68.
80. http://www.ldodds.com/foaf/foaf-a-matic (accessed December 2007).
81. Ding, L.; Zhou, L.; Finin, T.; Joshi, A. How the Semantic Web is being used: An analysis of FOAF documents. In *Proceedings of the 38th International Conference on System Sciences, 2005*, http://ebiquity.umbc.edu/_file_ directory_/papers/120.pdf (accessed December 2007).

82. Mika, P. Ontologies are us: A unified model of social networks and semantics. J. Web Semant. **2007**, *5* (1), 5–15.
83. Harnad, S. The symbol grounding problem. Physica D **1990**, *42*, 335–346. http://users.ecs.soton.ac.uk/harnad/Papers/ Harnad/harnad90.sgproblem.html (accessed December 2007).
84. Wittgenstein, L. *Philosophical Investigations*; Basil Blackwell: Oxford, 1953.

BIBLIOGRAPHY

1. Antoniou, G.; van Harmelen, F. *A Semantic Web Primer*; MIT Press: Cambridge MA, 2004.
2. Berners-Lee, T. *Weaving the Web: The Past, Present and Future of the World Wide Web by Its Inventor*; Texere Publishing: London, 1999.
3. Berners-Lee, T.; Hall, W.; Hendler, J.A.; O'Hara, K.; Shadbolt, N.; Weitzner, D.J. A framework for web science. Found. Trends Web Sci. **2006**, *1* (1), 1–134.
4. Berners-Lee, T.; Hall, W.; Hendler, J.; Shadbolt, N.; Weitzner, D. Creating a science of the Web. Science **2006**, *313* (5788), 769–771.
5. Berners-Lee, T.; Hendler, J.; Lassila, O. The Semantic Web. Sci. Am. May **2001**. http://www.sciam.com/article. cfm?articleID=00048144-10D2-1C70-84A9809EC588EF21 (accessed December 2007).
6. Fensel, D. *Ontologies: A Silver Bullet for Knowledge Management and Electronic Commerce*, 2nd Ed.; Springer: Berlin, 2004.
7. Fensel, D.; Hendler, J.; Lieberman, H.; Wahlster, W. *Spinning the Semantic Web: Bringing the World Wide Web to its Full Potential*; MIT Press: Cambridge, MA, 2003.
8. Shadbolt, N.; Hall, W.; Berners-Lee, T. The Semantic Web revisited. IEEE Intell. Syst. **2006**, *21* (3), 96–101.
9. There are several important annual conferences for the SW community, including: the World Wide Web Conference (WWW); the International Semantic Web Conference (ISWC—pronounced Iss-wick); the European Semantic Web Conference. These conferences preserve their proceedings online.
10. The World Wide Web Consortium's Semantic Web activity page is at http://www.w3.org/2001/sw/, and contains references to interviews, manifestos and statements by key SW developers. It also maintains a useful site of case studies and use cases at http://www.w3.org/2001/sw/sweo/ public/UseCases/. For Web Science, see http://webscience.org/.

25 XML Information Retrieval

Mounia Lalmas

CONTENTS

INTRODUCTION

Documents can be structured or unstructured. Unstructured documents have no (or very little) fixed predefined format, whereas structured documents are usually organized according to a fixed predefined structure. An example of a structured document is a book organized into chapters, each with sections made of paragraphs and so on. Nowadays, the most common way to format structured content is with the W3C standard (http://www.w3.org/XML/) for information repositories and exchanges, the eXtensible Mark-up Language (XML).

Much of the content available on the Web is formatted in HTML. Although HTML imposes some structure on a Web content, this structure is mainly for presentation purposes and carries little meaning. In contrast, XML is used to provide meaning about the stored content. More precisely, in the context of text documents, with which this entry is concerned, XML is used to specify the logical, or tree, structure of documents, in which separate document parts (e.g., chapter, section, abstract) and their logical structure (e.g., a chapter made of sections, a section and its title, an article and its abstract) are explicitly marked-up. As an increasing number of documents are being made available in XML format, effective means to access them are needed. As for standard (unstructured) documents, this requires appropriate query languages, representation methods, and ranking algorithms.

Approaches for accessing logically structured documents were first proposed in the 1990s.[1–4] In the late 1990s, as XML was adopted as the standard document format, approaches for what became known as XML information retrieval were being developed.[5–7] Research in XML information retrieval was then further boosted with the set-up in 2002 of the Initiative for the Evaluation of XML Retrieval (INEX),[8] a yearly evaluation campaign that provides a forum for the evaluation of approaches specifically developed for XML information retrieval. INEX provides test collections and evaluation measures, which make it possible for organizations worldwide to evaluate and compare their XML information retrieval approaches.

By exploiting the logical structure of XML documents, the goal of an XML information retrieval system is to implement so-called focused retrieval strategies, which aim at returning document components, i.e., XML elements, instead of whole documents in response to a user query. These focused retrieval strategies aim to break away from the traditional retrieval unit of a document as a single large (text) block. This is believed to be of particular benefit for information repositories containing long documents, or documents covering a wide variety of topics (e.g., books, user manuals, legal documents), where the users effort to locate relevant content within a document can be reduced by directing them to the most useful parts, i.e., the most useful XML elements, in the document.

To identify the most useful XML elements to return as answers to given queries, XML information retrieval systems require:

- Query languages that allow users to specify the nature of relevant components, in particular with respect to their structure
- Representation strategies providing a description not only of the content of XML documents, but also their structure
- Ranking strategies that determine the most relevant elements and rank these appropriately for a given query

In this entry, we provide an overview of "Query Languages," "Representation Strategies," and "Ranking Strategies" developed for XML information retrieval. The representation and ranking strategies presented in this entry were evaluated within the INEX evaluation campaigns.[9–14] The entry finishes with some conclusions on XML information retrieval research, and some references to early work related to XML information retrieval.

QUERY LANGUAGES

XML documents are organized into a logical structure, as provided by the XML mark-up. For example, a scientific article, such as those forming the IEEE test collection used in INEX (see Figure 25.1), consists of a front matter (<fm>), a body (<bdy>), and a back matter (<bm>). The front matter contains the article's metadata, such as title, author, publication information, and abstract. Following it is the article's body, which contains the actual content of the articles, and is structured into sections (<sec>), subsections (<ss1>), and sub-sub-sections (<ss2>). These logical units start with a title, followed by a number of paragraphs. The back matter contains a bibliography and further information about the article's authors.

Users may want to specify conditions to limit the search to specific XML elements. For example, a user may want sections discussing "XML retrieval evaluation," whereas another user may look for paragraphs about "effectiveness measures" contained in sections about "XML retrieval evaluation." Here we have a combination of content constraints, "XML retrieval evaluation" and "effectiveness measures," typical to information retrieval, and structural constraints, "section," "paragraph," and "paragraph within section." XML query languages have been developed with the aim to express various levels of content and structural constraints. They can be classified as content-only or content-and-structure query languages.

```
<article>
  <fm>
  ...
   <ti>IEEE Transactions on...</ti>
     <atl>Construction of...</atl>
     <au>
        <fnm>John</fnm>
        <snm>Smith</snm>
        <aff>University of...</aff>
     </au>
     <au>...</au>
  ...
   </fm>
   <bdy>
     <sec>
        <st>Introduction</st>
        <p>...</p>
        ...
   </sec>
   <sec>
     <st>...</st>
     ...
     <ss1>...</ss1>
     <ss1>...</ss1>
   ...
   </sec>
   ...
  </bdy>
  <bm>
   <bib>
     ...
   </bib>
</bm>
</article>
```

FIGURE 25.1 Sketch of the structure of a typical article in the INEX test collection.

Content-only queries make use of content constraints only, i.e., they are made of words, which is the standard form of input in information retrieval. They are suitable for XML retrieval scenarios where users do not know, or are not concerned, with the document logical structure when expressing their information needs. Although only content conditions are being specified, XML information retrieval systems must still determine what are the best fragments, i.e., the XML elements at the most appropriate level of granularity, to return to satisfy these conditions. For example, the best answer for a query "XML retrieval evaluation" may be a subsection and not a section, as the section, although relevant, may be less specific to the query than the subsection. An XML information retrieval system task is to determine this appropriate level of granularity for any given query.

Content-and-structure query languages provide a means for users to specify content and structural information needs. It is toward the development of this type of queries that most research on XML query languages lies. We can distinguish between three main categories of content-and-structure XML query languages, namely in sections "Tag-Based Languages," "Path-Based Languages," and "Clause-Based Languages." For the latter two types, we provide a brief description, mainly through examples, of current languages, namely XPath and Narrowed Extended XPath I (NEXI), and XQuery and XQuery Full-Text, respectively.

Tag-Based Queries

With tag-based queries, words in the query are annotated with a single tag name, which specifies the type of desired result elements, e.g., a section, an abstract. For example, the information need "retrieve sections about XML retrieval evaluation" would be expressed as `section:XML retrieval evaluation`. An example of a tag-based query language is XSEarch.[15]

Tag-based queries are intuitive, and have been used in domains outside XML information retrieval (e.g., faceted search, Web search). However they only express simple, although important and likely common, structural constraints. They cannot express, for instance, relationship (structural) constraints, e.g., "a paragraph contained in a section," which may be needed for complex retrieval scenarios.

Path-Based Queries

Path-based queries are based upon the syntax of XPath (XML Path language, http://www.w3.org/TR/xpath), which has been defined by the W3C to navigate to components of an XML document. The most important concept in XPath is the location path, which consists of a series of navigation steps characterizing movements within an XML document.

For example, `chapter/section` is a location path, where `chapter` and `section` are steps that navigate to elements of types "chapter" and "section," respectively. The fact that the steps are separated by "/" means that the location path selects section elements directly below chapter elements. Section elements are referred to as children of chapter elements. The navigation steps can be separated by "//". For example, `chapter//section` navigates to all section elements that are directly or indirectly below a chapter element. Section elements are referred to as descendants of chapter elements. Special steps include the self step denoted "." and parent step "..". For example, `.// section` returns all section elements contained directly or indirectly in the currently navigated element.

At each step, predicates can be specified between "[" and "]", which must be satisfied for elements to be navigated into. For example, the following XPath query `//article[@year=2002]/title` selects the "titles" of "articles" published in 2002, and only those.

An important function in XPath for the purpose of XML information retrieval is the function `contains()`. For example, the query `//section [fn : contains (. /title, "XML retrieval")]` will return all section elements with a title containing the string "XML retrieval". The result of this XPath query is a set of section elements, and not a ranked list of section elements. Thus XPath is not an XML query language that can be directly used in XML information retrieval. Nonetheless, it is used by, or has inspired, other path-based query languages, some of which allowing the ranking of results, e.g., XXL,[16] XIRQL,[17] and NEXI.[18] We discuss the last one, NEXI.

The NEXI query language was developed by INEX, as a simple query language for XML information retrieval evaluation. NEXI consists of a small but enhanced subset of XPath. The enhancement comes from the introduction of a new function, named `about()`, which requires an element to be about some specified content criteria. It replaces the XPath `contains()` function, to reflect that an element can be relevant to a given query without actually containing any of the words used in the query.

A small subset of XPath was chosen because NEXI was not developed to test the expressiveness of a query language for XML information retrieval, but to evaluate XML information retrieval effectiveness. For instance, the parent/child navigation step "/" was considered particularly problematic as it was open to misinterpretation by assessors, and hence was dropped. We recall that in information retrieval evaluation, assessors are used in the process of building a test collection. Their task is to judge the relevance of the information returned to them as answers to given queries. All result elements must have at least one `about()` function. This is because for the purpose of evaluating retrieval effectiveness, what matters is that the relevant elements are actually returned. For instance, the following query `//section [about(., XML retrieval)]//title`, which requests titles of sections about "XML retrieval evaluation," is not allowed in NEXI; it is indeed a mechanical process to return the title of a section deemed relevant to "XML retrieval."

We finish with an example of a NEXI query:

```
//article [about(. //bdy, XML retrieval)]//
section [about(., evaluation)]
```

This query is asking for section elements about "evaluation" contained in articles that have a body that discusses "XML retrieval."

NEXI was developed by INEX for the purpose of evaluating XML information retrieval effectiveness. It remains the task of the XML information retrieval system to interpret a NEXI query, where the interpretation is with respect to the `about()` condition as implemented by the retrieval model, and the structural constraint as implemented by the query processing engine, used by the XML information retrieval system. Sections "Scoring Strategies" and "Combination Strategies" describe approaches used to implement the `about` conditions, whereas section "Processing Structural Constraints" describes approaches used to process structural constraints, for the purpose of ranking XML elements for given queries.

Clause-Based Queries

Clause-based queries for XML information retrieval can be compared to SQL, the standard query language for (relational) databases. These queries are made of nested clauses to express information needs. The most prominent clause-based query languages for XML information retrieval are XQuery (http://www.w3.org/TR/xquery/) and XQuery Full-Text (http://www.w3.org/TR/xpath-full-text-10/).

XQuery is an XML query language that includes XPath as a sublanguage, but adds the possibility to query multiple documents and combine the results into new XML fragments. The core expressions of XQuery are the FLWOR expressions, which we illustrate with an example. The following query is a FLWOR expression that lists the authors, ordered by their last name, that have written at least 100 articles:

```
for $aut in (doc ("aut.xml")//author)
      let $c:=
            count (doc("article.xml")/article
                  [author=$aut])
                  where $c>100
                  order by $aut/lastname
                  return
                  <author> {$aut/lastname, $c} </author>
```

The `for` (F in FLWOR) clause binds the variable $aut so that it iterates over the author elements in the document "aut.xml" in the order that they appear. For every such binding, the `let` (L) clause binds the variable $c to the number of articles from author $aut (from the document "article.xml"). Those author elements for which the condition in the `where` (W) clause is true are selected, i.e., number of articles is above 100. The resulting bindings are sorted by the `order by` (O) clause on the author last name. Finally, the `return` (R) clause creates for each binding $aut and $c in the result of the preceding clause a new author element that contains the last name element of the author, and the associated number of articles.

XQuery is a powerful XML query language. However, its text search capabilities are limited and, in addition, the result is a set of (new) XML fragments; no ranking is performed. Thus its usefulness in XML information retrieval is limited. This has led to the development of XQuery Full-Text.[19]

XQuery Full-Text has been inspired by earlier query languages for searching structured text, e.g., ELIXIR,[20] JuruXML,[21] XIRQL.[17] The added text search capabilities come with the introduction of the *FTContainsExpr* expression, as shown in the following example:

```
//article[./title ftcontains {"XML", "retrieval"}
       all] // author
```

which returns the authors of articles whose title contains the words "XML" and "retrieval." XQuery Full-Text defines primitives for searching text, such as phrase, word order, word proximity, etc. For example, the following XQuery Full-Text expression:

```
//article[./title ftcontains {"XML", "retrieval"}
all window 6 words]//author
```

restricts the proximity of the matched words to appear within a window of six words in title elements.

To support the ranking of results, *FTScoreClause* expressions have been introduced to allow for the specification of score variables. For instance, the following query:

```
for $b score $s in //article [.//section ftcontains
       {"XML", "retrieval"} all]
              order by $s descending
              return <article title= "{$article/title}"
       score= "{$s}"/>
```

iterates over all articles whose sections contain both "XML" and "retrieval", where the $b variable binds the score of each such article to the score variable $s. These variables are used to return the titles of the articles and their scores in order of decreasing relevance.

XQuery Full-Text does not implement a specific scoring method, but it allows an implementation to proceed as it wishes. In other words, each XQuery Full-Text implementation can use a scoring method of its choice. Therefore, an appropriate implementation of XQuery Full-Text can allow ranking of results. From a user perspective, XQuery Full-Text may be viewed as far too complex, which is one of the reasons the INEX community developed NEXI, a path-based query language with less expressiveness than a clause-based query language, as its query language. A second one was to keep the construction of the test collections manageable, for instance during the assessment task (see explanation on "assessors" earlier in the entry). Nevertheless, XQuery Full-Text is needed in applications involving expert users, e.g., medical domain, patent industry, law.

REPRESENTATION STRATEGIES

To retrieve documents relevant to a query, the first task of an information retrieval system is to index all documents forming the searched collection. The indexing task aims to obtain a representation of the content of documents (i.e., what each document is about), which can then be used to score each document according to how relevant it is to a given query. Classical indexing strategies in information retrieval make use of term statistics, the most common ones being the within-document term frequency, *tf*, and the inverse document frequency, *idf*. *tf* is the number of occurrences of a term in a document and reflects how well a term captures the topic of a document; a term that occurs frequently in a document can be considered a good description of the document content (apart from common words, referred to as stop words, e.g., "the," "every" in the English language). *idf* is the inverse number of documents in which a term appears and is used to reflect how well a term discriminates between relevant and non-relevant documents; a term that appears in all documents of the collection is not good at discriminating between the content of two documents, and hence their relevance or nonrelevance.

With these term statistics, an index is build, for instance in the form of an inverted file, which gives for each term in the collection its *idf*, and for each document containing that term, the corresponding *tf*. Indexing algorithms for XML information retrieval require similar terms statistics, but at element level, i.e., they require so-called within-element term frequency, *etf*, and inverse element frequency, *ief*. The indexing of a collection of documents involves other steps than calculating term statistics. These include tokenization, stop word removal, stemming, etc.[22] In XML information retrieval, the same steps are applied, and other steps such as parsing the XML format, which are not discussed in this entry. Also not discussed in this entry is that an index of the structure is build in order to record the relationships between elements.

In XML information retrieval, there are no a priori fixed retrieval units. The whole document, a part of it (e.g., one of its sections), or a part of a part (e.g., a paragraph in the section), that is, elements at all levels of granularity, all constitute potential answers to a given query. The simplest approach to allow the retrieval of elements at any level of granularity is to index all elements. Each element thus corresponds to a document, and conventional information retrieval representation techniques can be used. Term statistics (*etf* and *ief*) for each element are then calculated exactly in the same way as for *tf* and *idf* but based on the concatenation of the text of the element and that of its descendants.[23]

This is the most common approach. It however raises an issue because of the nested nature of the units forming an XML document: the *ief* value of a term will consider both the element that contains that term and all elements that do so in virtue of being ancestors of that element. For instance, for a section element composed of two paragraph elements, the fact that a term appears in the paragraph implies that it also appears in the section. This "double" occurrence may have an adverse effect with respect to using *ief* to discriminate between relevant and nonrelevant elements.

As a consequence, alternative means have been used to calculate *ief*. For instance, *ief* has been estimated across elements of the same type[24] or across documents.[25] The former greatly reduces the impact of nested elements on the *ief* value of a term, but does not eliminate it if elements of the same type are nested within each other (as it is the case with the Wikipedia test collection used at INEX[26]). The latter is the same as using inverse document frequency, which completely eliminates nested elements. Experimental results[27] indicate that estimating *ief* across documents shows slight improvement over using elements. However, other experimental results[28] show that better performance was obtained estimating *ief* across all elements than across elements of the same types. As of today, it is not yet clear what is the best way to estimate *ief*, whether the estimation strategy depends on the retrieval model and its artifacts used to rank elements, or whether the issue of nested elements actually matters. Further research is needed here.

An alternative to using the concatenated text in an element to estimate term statistics is to derive them through the aggregation of term statistics (both *etf* and *ief*) of the element's own text, and those of each of its children elements.[29,30] Aggregated-based ranking, discussed in section "Aggregation," uses the aggregated representation of elements to rank elements.

A second alternative approach is to only index leaf elements. A leaf element is one at the bottom of the document tree structure, i.e., an element with no children elements, or an element that is considered the smallest possible unit of retrieval. This implies that term statistics will only be calculated for leaf elements, which can then be used to rank the leaf elements themselves. With such strategy, the ranking of non-leaf elements requires propagation mechanisms (discussed in section "Propagation") that combine the score of their children elements into that of the element.[31] Both this and the above (aggregation) strategies overcome the issue of nested elements with respect to the calculation of *ief*.

It has also been common to discard elements smaller than a given threshold (usually expressed in terms of number of words),[23] which are often considered not meaningful retrieval units (they are too small to make much sense as results). It was however argued[32] that although the small elements should not be returned, they might still influence the scoring of enclosing elements, so they should still be indexed, in particular when a propagation mechanism for scoring non-leaf elements is used.

A final strategy,[25,33] referred to as selective indexing, is to only index those element types with the highest distribution of relevant elements in past relevance data. With this strategy, a separate index is built for each selected element type (e.g., for a collection of scientific articles, these types may include article, abstract, section, subsection, and paragraph). The statistics for each index are then calculated separately. Since each index is composed of terms contained in elements of the same type (and likely comparable size), more appropriate term statistics are generated. In addition, this approach greatly reduces the term statistics issue arising from nested elements, although it may not eliminate it. At retrieval time, the query is then run in parallel on each index, and the list results (one for each index) are merged to provide a single list of results, as discussed in section "Merging."

It is not yet clear which indexing strategy is the best, as obviously which approach to follow would depend on the collection, the types of elements (i.e., the DTD), and their relationships. In addition, the choice of the indexing strategy has an effect on the ranking strategy. An interesting research would be to investigate all indexing strategies within a uniform and controllable environment to determine those leading to the best performance, across, or depending, on the ranking strategies.

RANKING STRATEGIES

Given an indexed collection of XML documents, the next task of an XML information retrieval system is to return for each submitted query, with or without structural constraints, a list of XML elements ranked in order of their estimated relevance to that query. In information retrieval, retrieval models are used to calculate what is called a retrieval score (usually a value between 0 and 1), which is then used as a basis to rank documents. Many of the retrieval models developed for unstructured text (document) retrieval have been adapted to XML information retrieval to provide such a score at element level (section "Scoring Strategies"). These scores may be used to directly generate the ranked list of elements, or as input to combination strategies required for some indexing strategies in order to rank elements at all levels of granularity (section "Combination Strategies"). For content-and-structure queries, in the context of INEX as expressed by the path-based query language NEXI (see section "Path-Based Queries"), the structural constraints must be processed to provide results that not only satisfy the content, but also the structural criteria of such queries (section "Processing Structural Constraints"). Finally, not all relevant elements should be returned as results, as they may contain overlapping content. This is because of the nested nature of XML documents, which often means that a parent and its child element may both be estimated as relevant, although to a different extent. Some processing is needed to deal with overlapping elements in result lists (section "Removing Overlaps").

Scoring Strategies

Whatever the representation strategy, i.e., whether all elements or only a subset of them are indexed, a scoring function is used to estimate the relevance of these elements for a given query. With the propagation strategy (discussed in section "Propagation"), the scoring function is applied to leaf elements only, whereas in other cases, it is applied to all potentially retrievable elements. Scoring functions used in XML information retrieval have been based on standard information retrieval models, such as the vector space, BM25, language models, to name a few. These have been adapted to incorporate XML-specific features. As an illustration, we describe a scoring function defined upon a language modeling framework inspired by Sigurbjornsson, et al.[23]

Given a query $q = (t_1, t_2, \ldots, t_n)$ made of n terms t_i, given an element e and its corresponding element language model θ_e, the scoring function expressed by $P(e|q)$ is defined as follow:

$$P(e|q) \propto P(e)P(q|\theta_e)$$

$P(e)$ is the prior probability of relevance for element e and $P(q|\theta_e)$ is the probability of a query being generated by the element language model θ_e, and can be calculated as

$$P(t_1,\ldots,t_n \mid \theta_e) = \prod_{i=1}^{n} \lambda P(t_i \mid e) + (1-\lambda)P(t_i \mid C)$$

$P(t_i|e)$ is the probability of term t_i in element e, $P(t_i|C)$ is the probability of query term t_i in the collection, and λ is the smoothing parameter. $P(t_i|e)$ is the element model based on element term frequency (modeling *itf*), whereas $P(t_i|C)$ is the collection model, for example, based on inverse element frequency (modeling *ief*).

One important XML feature is the length of an element. Indeed, it was shown[34] that considering element length is necessary in XML information retrieval to cater for the wide range in element sizes. This can be incorporated by setting the prior probability $P(e)$ as follows:

$$P(e) = \frac{\text{length}(e)}{\sum_C \text{length}(e)}$$

where length(e) is the length of element e. Examples of other XML-specific features used in XML information retrieval include the path length,[35] the type of an element (its tag),[36] and the number of topics discussed in an element.[37]

The size of elements forming XML documents varies greatly. For example, compare a paragraph to a section in a 10-page scientific article. There are likely to be fewer terms indexing the paragraph than the section, leading to a higher chance of a vocabulary mismatch between a paragraph (or any small elements) and a query than between a section (or any large elements) and the same query. In addition, the fact that a paragraph element does not contain all query terms, but is contained in a section element that contains all query terms, is likely to be more relevant than if contained in a section element that does not contain all query terms.

More generally, the context of an element, i.e., the parent, all or some of its ancestors, or the entire document, can provide more evidence on what an element is or is not about. To incorporate the selected context(s) in estimating relevance, the score of an element is modified to include that of its (selected) context(s). The most common technique is to use the document containing the element as context (the document is also an element, albeit a large one, and corresponds to what is being referred to as the root element). This means combining the score of the element to that of the XML document containing that element, where the element and the document retrieval scores are estimated by an XML information retrieval model. The combination can be as simple as the average of the two scores.[38] A scaling factor can be used to emphasize the importance of one score compared to the other.[33] This technique (using element and document scores) has been shown to increase retrieval performance, in particular for long documents, and has been widely used in XML information retrieval.

Combination Strategies

Three of the representation strategies described in section "Representation Strategies" require combination strategies to provide a rank list of all potentially retrievable elements. These combination strategies are propagation (section "Propagation"), aggregation (section "Aggregation"), and merging (section "Merging").

Propagation

The propagation strategy is needed with the representation strategy that only indexes leaf elements. The relevance of the leaf elements for given queries is estimated on this indexing, resulting in retrieval scores for leaf elements. The relevance of non-leaf elements is estimated through a propagation mechanism, where the retrieval score of a non-leaf element is calculated on the basis of the retrieval scores of its descendant elements. The propagation starts from the leaf elements and moves upward in the document tree structure.

The most common propagation mechanism consists of a weighted sum of retrieval scores. For instance, the number of children elements of an element has been used as a weight[31]:

$$\text{score}(e,q) = D(m)\sum_{e_c} \text{score}(e_c q)$$

where score(e,q) is the retrieval score of an element with respect to query q, e_c is a child element of e, m is the number of retrieved children elements of e, $D(m) = 0.49$ if $m = 1$ (e has only one retrieved child element), and 0.99 otherwise. The value of $D(m)$, called the decay factor, depends on the number of retrieved children elements. If e has one retrieved child then the decay factor of 0.49 means that an element with only one retrieved child will be ranked lower than its child. If e has several retrieved children, the decay factor of 0.99 means that an element with many retrieved children will be ranked higher than its children elements. Thus, a section with a single relevant paragraph would be considered less relevant than the paragraph itself, as it is simply better to return the paragraph as returning the section does not add anything more. On the other hand, a section with several retrieved paragraphs will be ranked higher than any of the paragraphs, as it will allow users to access these several paragraphs through the returned section.

This approach, known as the GPX model, has been very successful within INEX, across test collections and retrieval scenarios. Another successful approach, implemented in the XFIRM system,[32] is to define the weight used in the propagation based on the distance between an element and its retrieved leaf elements.

Aggregation

This combination strategy is applied when the representation of an XML element is defined as the aggregation of the representation of its own content (if any) and the representations of the content of its children elements (if any). Retrieval is then based on these aggregated representations. The representation of the element's own content is generated using standard indexing techniques, whereas an aggregation function is used to generate the representation of the non-leaf elements. The aggregation function can include parameters (referred to as, e.g., augmentation factor[29]) specifying how the representation of an element is influenced by that of its children elements (a measure of the contribution of, for instance, a section to its embedding chapter). Aggregation is to be contrasted to propagation; in the former, the combination is applied to representations, whereas in the latter, it is applied to retrieval scores.

To illustrate aggregation, we describe an approach based on the language modeling framework inspired from Ogilvie and Callan.[30] There, each element e is modeled by a language model θ_{eown} based on its own content. Now assume that e has several children, e_j, each with their own language model θ_{ej}. Let $P(t|\theta_{eown})$ and $P(t|\theta_{ej})$ be the probability of query term t being generated by the language models θ_{eown} and θ_{ej}, respectively. The language model, called θ_e, modeling the element e based on its own content and that of its children, is defined as a linear interpolation of language models:

$$P(t \mid \theta_e) = \lambda_{\text{own}} P(t \mid \theta_{e_{\text{own}}}) + \sum_{e_j} \lambda_j P(t \mid \theta_{e_j})$$

where

$$\lambda_{\text{own}} + \sum_{e_j} \lambda_j = 1$$

The λ parameters model the contribution of each language model (i.e., element) in the aggregation, here implemented as a linear combination. The ranking of the elements is then produced by estimating the probability that each element generates the query (e.g., similarly to the formulation described in section "Scoring Strategies"). The effectiveness of the aggregation, however, depends heavily on the appropriate settings of the λ parameters, whose values are usually estimated through learning methods.

Merging

The last combination strategy is that of merging, which is needed when a selective indexing strategy is used. With this indexing strategy, a separate index is created for each selected type of elements (e.g., article, abstract, section, paragraph, etc.). A query submitted to the XML information retrieval system is run against each index separately, resulting in separate ranked lists of, e.g., article elements, section elements, paragraph elements, etc. These lists need to be merged to provide a single ranking, across all element types.

In Mass and Mandelbrod,[33] the vector space model is used to rank elements in each index. Let e be an element and q a query. The following scoring function is used:

$$\text{score}(e,q) = \frac{\sum_{t \in q} w(t,q) \times w(t,e) \times ief(t)}{\|q\| \times \|e\|}$$

where $w(t,q)$ is the term weight based on within-element (etf)/query term frequency, and $ief(t)$ is the inverse element frequency. To merge the lists, normalization is performed to take into account the variation in size of the elements in the different indices (e.g., paragraph index vs. article index). For each result list, the element scores are normalized with score(q, q), which corresponds to the score of the query as if it was an element in the collection run against the corresponding index. This ensures that scores across indices are comparable. The lists are then merged based on the normalized scores.

Processing Structural Constraints

We described so far approaches that were developed and evaluated during the INEX campaigns to rank elements given the content condition of a query. Given a query consisting of terms, these approaches deliver a list of elements ranked according to how they have been estimated relevant to that query. As discussed in section "Query Languages," content-and-structure query languages have been developed to allow users to specify structural constraints, e.g., "give me a section in an article about XML technology that also discusses in one of its section book search."

Within INEX, structural constraints are viewed as hints as to where to look to find relevant information. The reasons for this view are twofold. First, it is well-known that users of information retrieval systems do not always, or simply cannot, properly express the content criterion (i.e., select the most useful query terms) of their information need. It is very likely that this also holds for the structural criterion of the information need. For instance, a user asking for paragraph components on "XML retrieval evaluation measures" may not have realized that relevant content for this query is scattered across several paragraphs, all of them contained within a single section. For that user, it may make more sense to return the whole section instead of individual paragraphs. Second—and to some extent as a consequence of the first reason above—there is a strong belief in the XML information retrieval community that satisfying the content criterion is, in general, more important than satisfying the structural criterion. For instance, even if a user is looking for section components on a particular topic, returning to that user abstract components would still be satisfactory, as long as the content criterion is satisfied.

Two main approaches have been developed to process structural constraints in XML information retrieval following this so-called vague interpretation of the structural constraints in content-and-structure queries. A first approach is to build a dictionary of equivalent synonyms. If, for example, `<p>` corresponds to paragraph type and `<p1>` corresponds to the first paragraph in a sequence of paragraphs, it would be quite logical to consider `<p>` and `<p1>` as equivalent tags.[39,40] The dictionary can also be built from analyzing past relevance data.[41] If in such a data set, for example, a query asked for `<section>` elements, then all types of elements assessed relevant for that query can be considered equivalent to the `<section>` tag. Thus with this approach, if the structural constraint refers to, e.g., `<section>`, then any element that is of type considered equivalent to `<section>`, will satisfy that structural constraint.

A second technique is that of structure boosting. There, the retrieval score of an element is generated ignoring the structural constraint of the query, but is then boosted according to how the structural constraint is satisfied by the element. The element structure and the query structure are compared and a structure score is generated. This structure score can be based on comparing the paths,[21,24] and/or the tags in the paths.[42] An important issue here is to determine the appropriate level of boosting, i.e., how much the initial content-based score should be boosted by the structure score.

The above techniques and their variants are mostly used to determine the relevance of an element according to the content condition and tag-based like structural constraints, e.g., "retrieve sections about XML retrieval." For more complex structural constraints, as allowed by a path-based language such as NEXI, e.g., "retrieve paragraphs about ranking algorithms contained in sections about XML retrieval," a first step is usually applied, which is to divide the query into two tag-based like subqueries, e.g., "retrieve paragraphs about ranking algorithms" and "retrieve sections about XML retrieval." Each subquery is then processed according to its content condition, and its tag-based like structural condition as described in the previous two paragraphs. Each subquery results in a ranked list of elements. To generate a ranked list for the whole query, the two ranked lists are compared, e.g., only elements returned for the "paragraph" subquery whose ancestors are contained among the elements returned for the "section" subquery are then retrieved. The final score depends on the implementation of the contain operation, e.g., a simple set containment, or using fuzzy operators.[43]

Techniques for processing structural constraints were evaluated in the context of INEX, where the relevance of an element was assessed based on content only. In other words, there was no assessment of whether, for instance, a section element was a better element type to return than another element type (if both were relevant according to their content). Also, considering the structural constraints did not usually increase retrieval performance, apart maybe at very early ranks.[44] This result may however be due to the evaluation methodology. More research is needed regarding the usefulness and the impact of structural constraints for XML information retrieval.

Removing Overlaps

We recall that the aim of an XML information retrieval system is to return the most relevant elements for a given query. Because of the nested structure of XML documents, when an element has been estimated relevant to a given query (by any of the XML ranking strategies presented in this entry), it is likely that its ancestors will also be estimated as relevant, although likely to a different extent. This is because the same text fragment can be contained in several elements along a same path (e.g., a paragraph, its enclosing subsection, the enclosing section, etc). Thus the element itself, its ancestors, and a number of its descendants may be contained in the result list, eventually leading to a considerable amount of redundant information being returned to users, which may not be acceptable to them.[45]

The outcome of any of the ranking strategies described so far in section "Ranking Strategies" is a list of elements ranked according to their estimated relevance to a given query, without looking at the overlap issue. XML information retrieval systems may have to decide which elements should be returned from a list of relevant but overlapping elements. Several approaches have been proposed to generate overlap-free result lists. Their starting point usually consists of the list of elements returned as results to a query, which they then process.

The most common approach, referred to as brute-force filtering, selects the highest ranked element from the result list and removes any ancestor and descendent elements from lower ranks. The process is applied recursively. This approach relies on the provision of ranking strategies that rank, among overlapping elements, those that should be selected at higher ranks. However, the ranking may not be appropriate for the purpose of returning the list of the most relevant non-overlapping results. This has led to a number of alternative approaches, where the tree structure of the XML documents has been considered to decide which elements to remove from a list of overlapping results.

In the first such approach,[41] a notion of the usefulness of an element is introduced to decide which elements to remove. Usefulness is modeled through a utility function defined upon the retrieval score of an element, its size, and the amount of irrelevant information contained in its children elements (implemented as the "amount" of text contained in the non-retrieved children elements). An element with an estimated utility value higher than the sum of the utility values of its children is selected and its children are removed. Otherwise, the children elements whose utility values exceed some set threshold are selected and the element is removed.

An alternative approach[46] looks at the distribution of retrieved elements in the XML document's tree structure, in addition to their score, to select the elements to retain. For instance, an element that has many of its descendants retrieved, but which are evenly distributed in the corresponding subtree structure, and in addition has a similar score to the parent element, is selected. This is because already from that selected element, all its descendants, many of which are being estimated as relevant, can be accessed. Otherwise, its descendants are selected to be themselves further processed.

A third approach[47] calculates a new score for each element on the basis of the retrieval scores of its (if any) descendent elements. This is done through a bottom-up propagation mechanism, using for instance the maximum or average operation to recalculate the scores. These scores are used to generate a new ranked list, which is then filtered by selecting the highest ranked elements, and then removing either all ancestors or all descendants of that selected element from the list (e.g., brute-force filtering). The best performances were obtained using the maximum function and removing the descendants.

Techniques that explicitly considered the document logical (tree) structure to remove overlaps usually outperformed those that did not. There is, however, the issue of speed, as the removal of overlaps is done at query time, thus requiring efficient implementations. An interesting question would be to investigate the effect of the original result list (how good it is, and how we define "goodness") on the overlap removal strategy. There are indications that a good initial result list, where good depends on the definition of relevance in the context of XML information retrieval, leads to better overlap-free result list than a less good one.[48]

DISCUSSION

XML information retrieval research is related to work on structured document retrieval. The term "structured document retrieval," which was introduced by the information retrieval community, refers to "passage retrieval" and "structured text retrieval." In passage retrieval, documents are first decomposed into passages (e.g., fixed-size text-windows of words,[49] fixed discourses such as paragraphs,[4] or topic segments through the application of a topic segmentation algorithm[50]). Passages are then retrieved as answers to a query (and have also been used to rank documents as answers to the query). Since 2007, INEX has a passage retrieval task.[51]

Structured text retrieval is concerned with the development of models for querying and retrieving from structured text,[52] where the structure is usually encoded with the use of mark-up languages, such as SGML, and now predominantly XML. Examples of pre-XML/NEX approaches include.[1,3,53] Most of the early structured text retrieval models, however, do not return a ranked list of results. Approaches that were specifically developed for XML retrieval, but still pre-INEX include.[54–57] A survey on indexing and searching XML retrieval is from Luk, et al.,[58] and two workshops on XML retrieval held at the SIGIR (http://www.sigir.org/) conference were reported.[5,7] A recent overview on XML retrieval research is from Amer-Yahia and Lalmas.[59]

Research on XML retrieval significantly flourished since the set-up of INEX, as the latter allowed the evaluation and comparison of XML information retrieval approaches. Nowadays, XML retrieval is almost a synonym for structured document retrieval, or structured text retrieval. In this entry, we described many of the strategies used for representing and ranking XML elements, which were experimented on the INEX test collections. We also described query languages that were developed to access XML documents with respect to both content and structural conditions.

It is not yet possible to state which approaches, whether for querying, representing, or ranking, or their combination, work best, since many factors are involved when deciding how relevant an element is to a given query (e.g., the size of an element, the type of element, the relevance of structurally related elements, the interpretation of the structural constraint, etc.). Indeed, XML information retrieval can be regarded as a combination problem, where the challenge is to decide which evidence to combine and how to combine it for effective retrieval. We can however postulate that considering the context of the element, the size of the element, and the element's own content (directly or using a propagation or aggregation strategy) to estimate that element relevance to a given query has been shown to be beneficial for XML information retrieval. An open research question is the processing of structural constraints, as so far, only limited improvement in retrieval performance has been observed with structure-and-content queries.

The querying, representation, and ranking strategies described in this entry have been developed with the purpose of estimating the relevance of an element for a given query, which is only one retrieval scenario. This may not necessarily be the end task in XML information retrieval. Returning overlap-free results is another retrieval scenario, one where users do not want redundant information (approaches developed for this purpose were described in section "Removing Overlaps"). Another retrieval scenario investigated at INEX is the relevant in context task.[60] This task is concerned with returning the most relevant documents for a given query, and within each document, identifying the most relevant elements. Such a retrieval scenario was identified as important, if not expected, in a user study carried out within a software company regarding the benefit of focused retrieval.[61]

In the relevant in context task, elements from the same documents are grouped together. A system could also create so-called "fictitious" documents, i.e., new documents made from some intelligent aggregation of elements coming from different documents, which is another retrieval scenario, currently receiving increasing attention in information retrieval research.[62] XQuery Full-Text would be an appropriate language for this task, as it allows the specification of new XML fragments to return as results.

Another retrieval scenario, also investigated at INEX, is the best in context task.[60] There, the aim is to identify the one and only best entry point in a document, i.e., the XML element, from where one could start reading relevant content. Such a retrieval scenario makes sense with a collection of relatively medium size documents (e.g., Wikipedia documents used at INEX since 2006[26]).

Although not discussed in this entry, two important issues in XML information retrieval are interface and interaction. Appropriate interfaces are needed to cater for the richer and likely more complex interaction between users and XML information retrieval systems, for example, with respect to expressing content-and-structure queries.[63] Since 2004, INEX runs an interactive track (iTrack) that looked at interaction issues in XML information retrieval.[64] One outcome of iTrack is that users did not like being returned (at least too much) redundant information (overlapping results). This led to the development of algorithms specifically dedicated to remove or reduce overlaps (see section "Removing Overlaps"). A second outcome was that users expected to have not only access to relevant elements, but also the context of these elements (e.g., the document containing, or the parent element of, a retrieved element). This led to the proposal of a table of a content shown in conjunction to the element being accessed[65] or the use of heatmap highlighting relevant elements within a retrieved document.[66]

Information retrieval approaches developed for querying, representing, or ranking are relevant to applications concerned with the effective access to repositories of documents annotated in XML, or similar mark-up languages. XML retrieval is becoming increasingly important in all areas of information retrieval, and in particular in the area of so-called focused retrieval.[67] Current applications of XML information retrieval technologies already exist.[68] An example is that of book search,[69] which is a research track being investigated at INEX since 2007.[70]

ACKNOWLEDGMENTS

This entry is based on two other entries on XML information retrieval cowritten by the author, a book chapter on "Structured Text Retrieval" to appear in the second edition of Baeza-Yates and Ribeiro-Neto,[71] and an entry on "XML Retrieval"[72] to appear in the Encyclopedia of Database Systems.[73] The author would like to thank Benjamin Piwowarski and Anastasio Tombros for their comments on this entry.

REFERENCES

1. Burkowski, F. Retrieval activities in a database consisting of heterogeneous collections of structured text. In 15th Annual International ACM SIGIR Conference on Research and Development in Information Retrieval, Copenhagen, Denmark, 1992; 112–125.
2. Clarke, C.A.; Cormack, G.; Burkowski, F. An algebra for structured text search and a framework for its implementation. Comput. J. **1995**, *38* (1), 43–56.
3. Navarro, G.; Baeza-Yates, R. Proximal nodes: A model to query document databases by content and structure. ACM Trans. Inform. Syst. **1997**, *15* (4), 400–435.
4. Wilkinson, R. Effective retrieval of structured documents. In *Proceedings of the 17th Annual International ACM SIGIR Conference on Research and Development in Information Retrieval*; Springer-Verlag: New York, Inc., 1994; 311–317.
5. Baeza-Yates, R.; Fuhr, N.; Maarek, Y. Second edition of the "XML and information retrieval" workshop held at SIGIR' 2002, Tampere, Finland. SIGIR Forum **2002**, *36* (2), 53–57.
6. Blanken, H.; Grabs, T.; Schek, H.-J.; Schenkel, R.; Weikum, G., Eds. *Intelligent Search on XML Data, Applications, Languages, Models, Implementations, and Benchmarks*; Springer: New York, 2003; Vol. 2818.
7. Carmel, D.; Maarek, Y.S.; Soffer, A. XML and information retrieval: A SIGIR 2000 workshop. SIGIR Forum **2000**, *34* (1), 31–36.
8. Gövert, N.; Kazai, G. Overview of the initiative for the evaluation of XML retrieval (INEX) 2002. In First Workshop of the INitiative for the Evaluation of XML Retrieval (INEX), Schloss Dagstuhl, Germany; 2002; 1–17.
9. Fuhr, N.; Go¨vert, N.; Kazai, G.; Lalmas, M., Eds. *INitiative for the Evaluation of XML Retrieval (INEX).* In Proceedings of the First INEX Workshop. Dagstuhl, Germany, December 8–11, 2002, Sophia Antipolis: France, 2003. ERCIM Workshop Proceedings, ERCIM.
10. Fuhr, N.; Kamps, J.; Lalmas, M.; Malik, S.; Trotman, A., Eds. Focused Access to XML Documents, 6th International Workshop of the Initiative for the Evaluation of XML Retrieval, INEX 2007, Dagstuhl Castle, Germany, December 17–19, 2007, Selected papers, 2008.
11. Fuhr, N.; Lalmas, M.; Malik, S., Eds. INitiative for the evaluation of XML retrieval (INEX). In *Proceedings of the Second INEX Workshop*, Dagstuhl, Germany, December 15–17, 2003, 2004.
12. Fuhr, N.; Lalmas, M.; Malik, S.; Kazai G., Eds. Advances in XML information retrieval and evaluation. In Fourth Workshop of the INitiative for the Evaluation of XML Retrieval (INEX 2005). 2006; Vol. 3977 of Lecture Notes in Computer Science Springer-Verlag.
13. Fuhr, N.; Lalmas, M.; Malik, S.; Szlavik, Z., Eds. Advances in XML information retrieval. In Third International Workshop of the Initiative for the Evaluation of XML Retrieval, INEX 2004, Dagstuhl Castle, Germany, December 6–8, 2004, Revised selected papers, 2005; Vol. 3493 of Lecture Notes in Computer Science, Springer.

14. Fuhr, N.; Lalmas, M.; Trotman, A., Eds. Comparative evaluation of XML information retrieval systems. In 5th International Workshop of the Initiative for the Evaluation of XML Retrieval, INEX 2006, 2007; Vol. 4518 of Lecture Notes in Computer Science, Springer-Verlag.
15. Cohen, S.; Mamou, J.; Kanza, Y.; Sagiv, Y. XSEarch: A semantic search engine for XML. In 29th International Conference on Very Large Data Bases, Berlin, Germany; 2003; 45–56.
16. Theobald, A.; Weikum, G. The index-based XXL search engine for querying XML data with relevance ranking. In EDBT, 2002; Springer-Verlag: London; 477–495.
17. Fuhr, N.; Grossjohann, K. XIRQL: An XML query language based on information retrieval concepts. ACM Trans. Inform. Syst. **2004**, *22* (2), 313–356.
18. Trotman, A.; Sigurbjornsson, B. Narrowed extended Xpath I (NEXI). In Advances in XML Information Retrieval, Third International Workshop of the Initiative for the Evaluation of XML Retrieval, INEX 2004, Dagstuhl Castle, Germany, Revised selected papers, 2005; 16–40.
19. Amer-Yahia, S.; Botev, C.; Dörre, J.; Shanmugasundaram, J. Full-text extensions explained. IBM Syst. J. **2006**, *45* (2), 335–352.
20. Chinenyanga, T.T.; Kushmerick, N. Expressive retrieval from XML documents. In 24th Annual International ACM SIGIR Conference on Research and Development in Information Retrieval, New Orleans, LA, 2001; 163–171.
21. Carmel, D.; Maarek, Y.; Mandelbrod, M.; Mass, Y.; Soffer, A. Searching XML documents via XML fragments. In 26th Annual International ACM SIGIR Conference on Research and Development in Information Retrieval, Toronto, ON, Canada, 2003; 151–158.
22. Manning, C.; Raghavan, P.; Schutze, H., Eds. *Introduction to Information Retrieval*; Cambridge University Press: Cambridge, 2008.
23. Sigurbjornsson, B.; Kamps, J.; de Rijke, M. An element-based approach to XML retrieval. In Proceedings INEX 2003 Workshop, Schloss Dagstuhl, Germany, 2004; 19–26.
24. Theobald, M.; Schenkel, R.; Weikum, G. TopX and XXL at INEX 2005. In Advances in XML Information Retrieval and Evaluation, 4th International Workshop of the Initiative for the Evaluation of XML Retrieval, INEX 2005, Dagstuhl Castle, Germany, Revised selected papers, 2006; 282–295.
25. Clarke, C. Controlling overlap in content-oriented XML retrieval. In 28th Annual International ACM SIGIR Conference on Research and Development in Information Retrieval, Salvador, Brazil, 2005; 314–321.
26. Denoyer, L.; Gallinari, P. The Wikipedia XML corpus. SIGIR Forum **2006**, *40* (1), 64–69.
27. Ramírez, G. Structural features in XML retrieval, Ph.D. thesis, University of Amsterdam, Amsterdam, 2007.
28. Broschart, A.; Schenkel, R.; Theobald, M.; Weikum, G. TopX @ INEX 2007. In Focused access to XML documents, 6th International Workshop of the Initiative for the Evaluation of XML Retrieval, INEX 2007, Dagstuhl Castle, Germany, Selected papers, 2008.
29. Gövert, N.; Abolhassani, M.; Fuhr, N.; Grossjohann, K. Content-oriented XML retrieval with HyRex. In First Workshop of the INitiative for the Evaluation of XML Retrieval (INEX), Schloss Dagstuhl, Germany, 2002; 26–32.
30. Ogilvie, P.; Callan, J. Hierarchical language models for XML component retrieval. In Advances in XML Information Retrieval, Third International Workshop of the Initiative for the Evaluation of XML Retrieval, INEX 2004, Dagstuhl Castle, Germany, Revised Selected Papers, 2005; 224–237.
31. Geva, S. GPX—gardens point XML IR at INEX 2005. In Advances in XML Information Retrieval and Evaluation, 4th International Workshop of the Initiative for the Evaluation of XML Retrieval, INEX 2005, Dagstuhl Castle, Germany, Revised selected papers, 2006; 240–253.
32. Sauvagnat, K.; Hlaoua, L.; Boughanem, M. XFIRM at INEX 2005: Ad-hoc and relevance feedback tracks. In Advances in XML Information Retrieval and Evaluation, 4th International Workshop of the Initiative for the Evaluation of XML Retrieval, INEX 2005, Dagstuhl Castle, Germany, Revised selected papers, 2006; 88–103.
33. Mass, Y.; Mandelbrod, M. Component ranking and automatic query refinement for XML retrieval. In Advances in XML Information Retrieval, Third International Workshop of the Initiative for the Evaluation of XML Retrieval, INEX 2004, Dagstuhl Castle, Germany, Revised selected papers, 2005; 73–84.
34. Kamps, J.; de Rijke, M.; Sigurbjörnsson, B. Length normalization in XML retrieval. In 27th Annual International ACM SIGIR Conference on Research and Development in Information Retrieval, Sheffield, U.K., 2004; 80–87.
35. Huang, F.; Watt, S.; Harper, D.; Clark, M. Compact representations in XML retrieval. In Comparative Evaluation of XML Information Retrieval Systems, 5th International Workshop of the Initiative for the Evaluation of XML Retrieval, INEX 2006, Dagstuhl Castle, Germany, Revised and selected papers, 2006; 64–72.

36. Gery, M.; Largeron, C.; Thollard, F. Probabilistic document model integrating XML structure. In INEX 2007 Pre-Proceedings, 2007; 139–149.
37. Ashoori, E.; Lalmas, M.; Tsikrika, T. Examining topic shifts in content-oriented XML retrieval. Int. J. Dig. Libr. **2007**, *8* (1), 39–60.
38. Arvola, P.; Junkkari, M.; Kekäläinen, J. Generalized contextualization method for XML information retrieval. In ACM CIKM International Conference on Information and Knowledge Management, Bremen, Germany, 2005; 20–27.
39. Mass, Y.; Mandelbrod, M. Retrieving the most relevant XML Components. In INEX 2003 Proceedings, 2003; 53–58.
40. Sauvagnat, K.; Boughanem, M.; Chrisment, C. Answering content and structure-based queries on XML documents using relevance propagation. Inform. Sys. **2006**, *31* (7), 621–635.
41. Mihajlovic, V.; Ramírez, G.; Westerveld, T.; Hiemstra, D.; Blok, H.E.; de Vries, A. TIJAH scratches INEX 2005: Vague element selection, image search, overlap, and relevance feedback. In Advances in XML Information Retrieval and Evaluation, 4th International Workshop of the Initiative for the Evaluation of XML Retrieval, INEX 2005, Dagstuhl Castle, Germany, Revised selected papers, 2006; 72–87.
42. van Zwol, R. B^3-SDR and effective use of structural hints. In Advances in XML Information Retrieval and Evaluation, 4th International Workshop of the Initiative for the Evaluation of XML Retrieval, INEX 2005, Dagstuhl Castle, Germany, Revised selected papers, 2006; 146–160.
43. Vittaut, J.-N.; Piwowarski, B.; Gallinari, P. An algebra for structured queries in Bayesian networks. In Advances in XML Information Retrieval, Third International Workshop of the Initiative for the Evaluation of XML Retrieval, INEX 2004, Dagstuhl Castle, Germany, December 6–8, 2004; Revised selected papers, 2004; 100–112.
44. Trotman, A.; Lalmas, M. Why structural hints in queries do not help XML retrieval. In 29th Annual International ACM SIGIR Conference on Research and Development in Information Retrieval, Seattle, WA, 2006; 711–712.
45. Tombros, A.; Malik, S.; Larsen, B. Report on the INEX 2004 interactive track. SIGIR Forum **2005**, *39* (1), 43–49.
46. Mass, Y.; Mandelbrod, M. Using the INEX environment as a test bed for various user models for XML retrieval. In Advances in XML Information Retrieval and Evaluation, 4th International Workshop of the Initiative for the Evaluation of XML Retrieval, INEX 2005, Dagstuhl Castle, Germany, Revised Selected Papers, 2006; 187–195.
47. Popovici, E.; Ménier, G.; Marteau, P.-F. SIRIUS XML IR system at INEX 2006: Approximate matching of structure and textual content. In Comparative Evaluation of XML Information Retrieval Systems, 5th International Workshop of the Initiative for the Evaluation of XML Retrieval, INEX 2006, Dagstuhl Castle, Germany, Revised and selected papers, 2007; 185–199.
48. Ashoori, E. Using topic shifts in content-oriented XML retrieval, Ph.D. thesis, University of London, Queen Mary, 2009.
49. Callan, J. Passage-level evidence in document retrieval. In Proceedings of the 17th Annual International ACM SIGIR Conference on Research and Development in Information Retrieval; Springer-Verlag: New York, Inc., 1994; 302–310.
50. Hearst, M. TextTiling: Segmenting text into multi-paragraph subtopic passages. Comput. Linguist. **1997**, *23* (1), 33–64.
51. Kamps, J.; Pehcevski, J.; Kazai, G.; Lalmas, M.; Robertson, S. INEX 2007 evaluation metrics. In Focused Access to XML Documents, 6th International Workshop of the Initiative for the Evaluation of XML Retrieval, INEX 2007, Dagstuhl Castle, Germany, Selected papers, 2008.
52. Baeza-Yates, R.A.; Navarro, G. Integrating contents and structure in text retrieval. SIGMOD Rec. **1996**, *25* (1), 67–79.
53. Macleod, I. Storage and retrieval of structured documents. Inform. Process. Manage. **1990**, *26* (2), 197–208.
54. Chiaramella, Y.; Mulhem, P.; Fourel, F. A model for multimedia information retrieval, Tech. rep, University of Glasgow, Glasgow, 1996.
55. Lalmas, M. Dempster-shafer's theory of evidence applied to structured documents: Modelling uncertainty. In 20th Annual International ACM SIGIR Conference on Research and Development in Information Retrieval, Philadelphia, PA, 1997; 110–118.
56. Rölleke, T.; Lalmas, M.; Kazai, G.; Ruthven, I.; Quicker, S. The accessibility dimension for structured document retrieval. In Advances in Information Retrieval, 24th BCS-IRSG European Colloquium on IR Research, Glasgow, U.K., 2002; 284–302.
57. Schlieder, T.; Meuss, M. Result ranking for structured queries against xml documents. In DELOS Workshop: Information Seeking, Searching and Querying in Digital Libraries, Zurich, Switzerland, 2000.

58. Luk, R.P.; Leong, H.V.; Dillon, T.; Chan, A.S.; Croft, W.B.; Allan, J. A survey in indexing and searching XML documents. J. Am. Soc. Inform. Sci. Technol. **2002**, *53* (6), 415–437.
59. Amer-Yahia, S.; Lalmas, M. XML search: Languages, INEX and scoring. SIGMOD Rec. **2006**, *35* (4), 16–23.
60. Malik, S.; Trotman, A.; Lalmas, M.; Fuhr, N. Overview of INEX 2006. In Comparative Evaluation of XML Information Retrieval Systems, 5th International Workshop of the Initiative for the Evaluation of XML Retrieval, INEX 2006, Dagstuhl Castle, Germany, December 17–20, 2006; Revised and selected papers, 2007; 1–11.
61. Betsi, S.; Lalmas, M.; Tombros, A.; Tsikrika, T. User expectations from XML element retrieval. In 29th Annual International ACM SIGIR Conference on Research and Development in Information Retrieval, Seattle, WA, 2006; 611–612.
62. Lalmas, M.; Murdock, V., Eds. ACM SIGIR Workshop on Aggregated Search. Singapore, 2008.
63. Zwol, R.; Baas, J.; van Oostendorp, H.; Wiering, F. Bricks: The building blocks to tackle query formulation in structured document retrieval. In Advances in Information Retrieval, 28th European Conference on IR Research, ECIR 2006, London, 2006; 314–325.
64. Tombros, A.; Larsen, B.; Malik, S. The interactive track at INEX 2004. In Advances in XML Information Retrieval, Third International Workshop of the Initiative for the Evaluation of XML Retrieval, INEX 2004, Dagstuhl Castle, Germany, Revised selected papers, 2005; 410–423.
65. Szlávik, Z.; Tombros, A.; Lalmas, M. Feature- and query-based table of contents generation for xml documents. In Advances in Information Retrieval, 29th European Conference on IR Research, ECIR 2007, Rome, Italy, April 2–5, 2007; 456–467.
66. Kamps, J.; Koolen, M.; Sigurbjörnsson, B. Filtering and clustering XML retrieval results. In Comparative Evaluation of XML Information Retrieval Systems, 5th International Workshop of the Initiative for the Evaluation of XML Retrieval, INEX 2006, Dagstuhl Castle, Germany, Revised and Selected Papers, 2006; 121–136.
67. Trotman, A.; Geva, S.; Kamps, J. Report on the SIGIR 2007 workshop on focused retrieval. SIGIR Forum **2007**, *41* (2), 97–103.
68. Pharo, N.; Trotman, A. The use case track at INEX 2006. SIGIR Forum **2007**, *41* (1), 64–66.
69. Kantor, P.B.; Kazai, G.; Milic-raylying, N.; Wilkinson, R., Eds. Proceedings of the 2008 ACM Workshop on Research Advances in Large Digital Book Repositories, Books-Online 2008, Napa Valley, CA, October 30, 2008, 2008, ACM.
70. Kazai, G.; Doucet, A. Overview of the INEX 2007 book search track (BookSearch '07). SIGIR Forum **2008**, *42* (1), 2–15.
71. Baeza-Yates, R.A.; Ribeiro-Neto, B. *Modern Information Retrieval*; ACM Press/Addison-Wesley: New York, 1999.
72. Lalmas, M.; Trotman, A. XML retrieval. In *Encyclopedia of Database Systems*; Ozsu, M.; Liu, L., Eds. Springer, 2009.
73. Ozsu, M.; Liu, L., Eds. *Encyclopedia of Database Systems*; Springer, 2009.

26 Information Retrieval Support Systems

Yiyu Yao, Ning Zhong, and Yi Zeng

CONTENTS

INTRODUCTION

With the advances of information and Web technologies, everyone faces a great challenge of information overload. One may feel lost in the overwhelming volume of information, and in many cases misinformation. For example, a scientist can have a real difficulty in keeping up with current research and figuring out what has been done by using Information Retrieval Systems (IRS) and search engines.[1,2] One is no longer satisfied with retrieval systems that provide limited supports of browsing, navigation, and retrieval. There is a great demand on retrieval systems and search engines with a great variety of new functionalities and supports.[3]

We can observe a few trends in the new, or latest versions of, retrieval systems and search engines that attempt to address the above-mentioned problems. For example, some recent retrieval systems provide better user interface that allows more user control[4] in the search process and retrieval-results refinement and reorganization. Some search engines provide more utilities that support user exploration of a collection of information items. There are more domain-specific and narrow-scope search engines that make more effective use of domain knowledge and structures of a collection of information items. In addition, results from machine learning, data mining, intelligent agents, and other fields are being incorporated into retrieval systems and search engines to increase their performance. However, there is still lack of a commonly agreed label for those research efforts, and there seems to be a need of a framework so that we can study them systematically. The recently proposed notion of Information Retrieval Support Systems (IRSS) may serve this purpose.[5–7] IRSS may be used as a subsystem of a research support system (RSS).[7–9] They may also be considered a step toward knowledge retrieval systems (KRS).[10,11]

By introducing IRSS as a new field of study, we may be able to draw the attention of researchers working on the related topics. Many related, but isolated and scattered studies, techniques, tools, and systems can be unified under an umbrella term of IRSS. The benefits are the convergence of new generation retrieval systems, search engines, and Web services that aim to provide a variety of utilities, tools, and languages to support a user to find what they really need, including data, information, and knowledge.

Three fundamental issues are investigated in this entry. We examine the evolution process of retrieval systems, from data retrieval to information retrieval, and from information retrieval to information retrieval support. We outline the conceptual architecture of IRSS and discuss the basic concepts, characteristics, and functionalities of these types of systems. We comment on implementation issues of IRSS with reference to related fields and suggest a technical foundation based on granular computing. The materials of this entry are based on our preliminary studies.[5–7]

EMERGENCE OF IRSS

There are several factors that affect the evolution of retrieval systems, namely, the characteristics of information items, the characteristics and demands of users, and available technologies. It can be said that retrieval systems evolve from simple and specific task to intelligent and multiple tasks. We are now entering a stage when IRSS are necessary and technologically feasible.

From Data Retrieval to Information Retrieval

Van Rijsbergen provided a comparative study of data retrieval systems (DRS) and IRS regarding their common features and differences.[12] Both DRS and IRS focus on storage-and-retrieval functionality, with very limited support for other functionalities.

In traditional DRS, data items can be precisely described by using well-understood representation schemes, and user needs can be formally represented by query languages (e.g., SQL). The model is deterministic in the sense that the relationships between data items and user needs are well and objectively defined and consequently exact match and deductive inference can be used. The intolerance of uncertainty of data retrieval had motivated many researchers to search for generalized data retrieval models, such as fuzzy databases and extended Boolean queries.[13]

The stringent requirements of data retrieval made it unsuitable for the case of documents storage and retrieval where a collection of natural language documents is involved. Information retrieval was evolved from data retrieval by considering the following issues. Documents and user needs cannot always be precisely described, and their relationships are ill and subjectively defined. The model is nondeterministic in the sense that partial or best match and inductive inference are used. The results of an IRS are typically a list of ranked information items. They are documents or paragraphs containing keywords in queries. One needs to read those documents in order to find the required information. In other words, IRS and search engines are reference systems that indirectly meet the user requirements.

From Information Retrieval to Information Retrieval Support

The limited functionalities of IRS and search engines is insufficient to meet the demands of users in the Web age. IRSS have emerged as the next generation in the evolution of retrieval systems that focus on more supporting functionalities at a higher intelligence level.

The emergence of information retrieval support can be seen from several important trends in the search community. One of them is the separation of vertical search and horizontal search. While traditional horizontal search deals with general purpose search needs, vertical search handles domain-specific needs. Vertical search[14] plays a daily-increasing important role on the Web.[15–18] For example, Google Scholar, CiteSeerX, DBLP, MSRA Libra, etc., are specialized retrieval systems for academic literature search; Amazon, Google product search, Microsoft Live product search, etc., are for product retrieval online; Zoominfo is a vertical search engine for company, people network, and job information. All of these vertical search systems provide various ways to better support specific groups of users in particular domains. Another trend is the study of exploratory search systems for users with insufficient domain and contextual knowledge to formulate effective retrieval queries.[10,19] Many related workshops and special issues have emerged during these years. They include HCIL SOH 2005 Workshop on Exploratory Search Interfaces, SIGIR 2006 Workshop on Evaluating Exploratory Search Systems, SIGCHI 2007 Workshop on Exploratory Search and Human Computer Interaction, a special issue on "Supporting Exploratory Search" in *Communications of the ACM* (49(4), 2006), a special issue on "Evaluating Exploratory Search Systems" in *Information Processing and Management* (44(2), 2008). Exploratory search systems support users through information visualization and multimedia presentation and allow users to browse and explore an information collection to refine queries.[20,21] The third trend is that retrieval systems and search engines start to provide more tools for users to manipulate retrieval results, so that they may make better use of retrieved items. It becomes evident that these trends have a common goal of providing more and better supports to users by increasing the functionality and flexibility of traditional IRS.

By moving beyond browsing, navigating, and retrieval, IRSS focus on a wide range of supporting functionalities, including summarization, exploration, analysis, knowledge discovery, results organization, retrieval strategy recommendation, and so on.[5–7,22] The objective of an IRSS is to support many different types of user tasks in finding and utilizing information, in a similar way that a decision support system (DSS) assists managers in decision making.[23]

Characteristics of IRSS

As the next generation retrieval systems, IRSS are extensions of IRS. In order to provide more supporting functionalities by IRSS, we need to design and implement new models, languages, utilities, and tools to assist a user in investigating, analyzing, understanding, and organizing a document collection and search results. These tools allow a user to explore both the semantic and structural information of each individual document, as well as the entire collection. An IRSS is a user-oriented system in the sense that a user plays a more central role, and the system plays a supporting role. First, the system should be very flexible so that a user can perform a wide range of tasks. In some sense, an IRSS is a platform that allows a user to work on tasks in information and knowledge search. A user can make decisions at various stages. Second, instead of being a passive system waiting for user queries, the system may actively support a user by providing useful information without being explicitly asked. Third, an IRSS is adaptive to a user by collecting implicit and explicit feedback through user–system interaction. Thus, an IRSS must have learning capacity. From the performance point of view, an IRSS emphasizes accuracy and effectiveness more than efficiency and online processing. Fourth, the results from an IRSS must be more than a simple ranked list of information items. Moreover, a user should be allowed to visualize, reorganize, and compare various search results from different perspectives.

An IRSS needs to manage a large class of models of data, information, and knowledge. Three related types of models need to be considered. Documents in a document collection serve as the raw data of IRSS. The document models deal with representations and interpretations of documents and the document collection. The retrieval models deals with search. The presentation/recommendation models deal with the representation and interpretation of results from search. A single document model, retrieval model, or presentation model may not be suitable for different types of users. Therefore, IRSS must support multiple models, and provide tools for users to manage various models.

The document models allow multirepresentation of documents. Granular computing will play an important role in the construction of document models.[6,24,25] One can use hierarchical granulation for a document, namely, a layered and multiresolution representation of documents. The same document is represented in less detail at a higher level than at a lower level. With multimodel capability, a user can create different logical views of a document and logical links between documents, as well as compare and investigate various views. The resulting in-depth knowledge can help the user locate and infer useful information. The recent development of XML enables us to describe both the structural and semantic information of a document. Such information makes the construction of multirepresentation document models an achievable goal.

The retrieval models provide languages and tools to assist a user in performing tasks such as searching and browsing. IRSS should provide multistrategy retrieval. A user can choose different retrieval models with respect to different document models. The retrieval process of IRSS is no longer just keyword matching. Instead, it must consider different types of inference methodologies. Thus, an IRSS provides different inference models to meet various needs from different users. Both deductive inference and inductive inference are considered. Recently, several models were proposed for inference on Web scale, and can be considered as possible choices for IRSS. For example, associative inference and analogical inference can help find relevant results more effectively.[26] Variable precision logic can be used to develop reasoning method based on incomplete information source and under time constraints.[27] Based on Simon's theory on rational choice,[28] combining reasoning and search on the Web scale is proposed.[29] which may also be related to the study of IRSS.

The presentation/recommendation models allow a user to view and arrange search results, as well as various document models. The same results can be viewed in different ways by using distinct presentation/recommendation models. Moreover, a user can analyze and compare results from different retrieval models.

An IRSS also needs to build various models of users to provide better and personalized support. An IRSS may actively collect user information, user–system interaction information, and various other logs to build user profiles. With deep knowledge of users, an IRSS may provide more intelligent support. For example, user models may help an IRSS to select the best combination of document, retrieval, and presentation models. The full function of an IRSS is achieved by managing these models, as well as the associated languages, tools, and utilities.

THE CONCEPTUAL ARCHITECTURE OF IRSS

Many retrieval systems are starting to provide more supporting functionalities to users. They are typically implemented by simply adding components to existing IRS. There is still a lack of conceptual framework that allows us to have a more systematic study. And one cannot expect great progress without such a framework. For this reason, we consider here a conceptual architecture of IRSS.

Our interpretation of IRSS draws extensively from the related field of Decision Support Systems (DSS).[23] While DSS focus on supporting and improving decision making, IRSS focus on supporting and improving retrieval. The philosophy, principles, and techniques from DSS are applicable to IRSS by substituting the tasks of "decision making" for the tasks of "information retrieval." This view of IRSS is particularly reasonable if one considers the fact that it is necessary to obtain useful information in order to make intelligent and rational decision.[5]

Gorry and Morton[30] define DSS as "interactive computer-based systems, which help decision makers utilize data and models to solve unstructured problems." Turban and Aronson[23] compare different definitions of DSS and suggest that DSS are "computer-based information systems that combine models and data in an attempt to solve unstructured problems with extensive user involvement through a friendly user interface." From these definitions, we want to stress two important

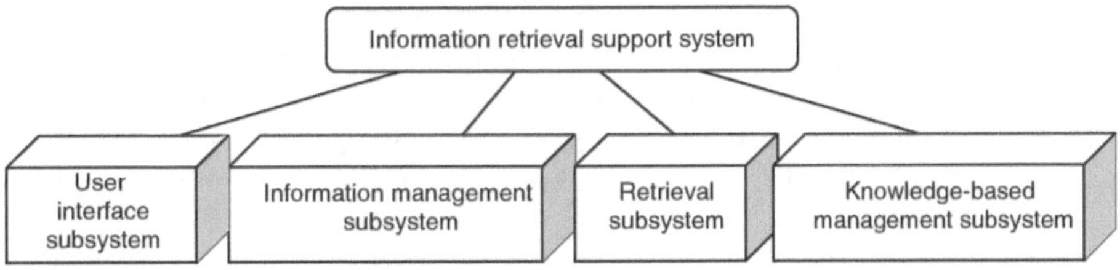

FIGURE 26.1 The conceptual architecture of IRSS.

features of DSS pertinent to our interpretation of IRSS. One feature is the combination of data and models. Data are raw and uninterpreted facts. In order to make sense of raw data, one needs to construct various models. Therefore, a DSS deals with both data and their interpretations. The other feature is the emphasis on the user involvement.[5]

A simple conceptual architecture of IRSS is shown in Figure 26.1, consisting of a user interface subsystem, an information-management subsystem, a knowledge-based management subsystem, and a retrieval subsystem. Their main functionalities are summarized below

- User interface subsystem: provides a friendly interface for user–system interaction (containing different functionalities, and tools to support retrieving and postprocessing)
- Information management subsystem: collects and manages data, information, and knowledge of a collection of information items
- Knowledge-based management subsystem: manages various models (e.g., document models, retrieval models, presentation/recommendation models, and user models) to support other subsystem
- Retrieval subsystem: performs the retrieval and inference tasks, and analyzes retrieval results from multiple perspectives and provides the results to users through user interface

The four subsystems work together to provide retrieval support to users. The main concern of this architecture is based on a combination of the traditional architecture of IRS and DSS.

IMPLEMENTATION OF IRSS

In this section, we look at the implementation of IRSS by mentioning results from related fields and giving the granular computing basis of IRSS.

Fields Related to IRSS

To build a relatively new discipline, we need to draw ideas, techniques, results, and lessons from many other fields. A few related fields are summarized below, in addition to previously mentioned DSS.[5]

Expert Systems

A well-established practice in expert systems is the separation of knowledge and inference engines. While the inference engine is logic-based and problem-independent, the knowledge base is domain-specific. Expert system shells that implement an inference engine can be used to build many different domain-specific expert systems. Similarly, we can build a knowledge-based IRSS by separating knowledge-base and management subsystems. An IRSS shell can be built that provides a set of domain- and user-independent tools. Another feature of expert systems is the explanation functionality. An expert system not only provides a solution, but can also give reasons to justify the solution. It is reasonable to insist on the explanation functionality of an IRSS.

Machine Learning and Data Mining

By applying algorithms of machine learning, data mining, and especially text mining to documents stored in an IRSS, one may discover patterns and extract knowledge useful to a user. Such functionalities are particularly useful to users who are interested in exploratory searching and browsing. For example, a user can track trends in a particular area or discover emerging topics from the constantly changing document collection. A user may also discover links between different documents or research areas.

Computer Graphics and Information Visualization

In many cases, a user may not want the details about particular documents. A user may want to have a general feeling before going to a more in-depth analysis. This can be accomplished with a granulated view, in which details are omitted. Most current IRS present search results in the form of ranked list of individual documents. In an IRSS, a user should be able to use graphics and visualization tools to view a particular document model and retrieval results. Graphics and visualization techniques may enable users easily to perform qualitative inference and analysis at multiple levels.

Intelligent Information Agents

Intelligent information agents have been used by many IRS to collect information and interact with users. The potential of agents needs to be further explored in IRSS. In particular, a user should be allowed to construct a personalized agent to interact with an IRSS. The autonomy and learning capabilities of agents make them attractive to both IRSS and users.

Granulation in IRSS

An important task of an IRSS is the management of various models. Typically, these models provide multiview and multilevel representations of the information items and users. In order to obtain such representations, the recently proposed theory of granular computing may provide the required theoretical and technological basis.[31]

Document space, user space, term space, and retrieval-results space can be granulated respectively, to achieve multilevel and multiview representations. The four types of space granulation are related to each other. To provide retrieval results for different types of users, user space is granulated. A user granule may require a specific type of retrieval-result granule. Term space is granulated to support document-space and query-space granulations. An IRSS can recommend relevant terms to users for refining a query based on different levels of term granulation. Document space is granulated to different categories and the document granules can be retrieved based on relevant-term granules.

Document-Space Granulation

Traditional IRS focus more on documents, and the associated granulations are always document clusters based on the contents of documents.[1,12] This single view may not fully explore information and knowledge about a document collection. In general, a document collection can be granulated in at least three views: content view, structure view, and usage view.[32]

From the content view, document-space granulation may reveal the relationships among different documents or relationships between a specific document and a given topic. From the structure view, citations and links among different documents can be considered as implicit connections, which provide a different kind of granulation.[33] From the usage view, documents that are accessed together can be put into the same document granule.[32]

User-Space Granulation

Different types of users have different needs, and hence they should be classified into different user granules. User-space granulation is mainly based on user profiles and user access logs. Based on Web-usage mining, we can find interesting rules for certain types of users.[34] User-space granulation is necessary for personalized retrieval support. The granulated user space will be useful for locating relevant retrieval-results granules.

Term-Space Granulation

In IRSS, terms are granulated into a hierarchical structure based on relationships among them. For example, some terms may be very specific and belong to a more general term, and some terms may be synonyms, etc. Manual and automatic thesauri (such as co-occurrence analysis and grammatical analysis) are concrete methods for one-level term-space granulation.[35,36] In general, one may consider hierarchical classification methods for multiple-level granulations. A granule network of domain knowledge can be built based on term-space granulation.[7,32] Document granulation can be based on this granule network of terms, and a document can be associated with term granules. For example, gene and protein names are used for building domain-knowledge structures for biomedical literature classification.[37] In the retrieval process, if query terms are too general, an IRSS could suggest users to refine the query terms using the granulated term space. On the other hand, if user terms are too specific, the system could suggest users with synonyms, co-occurring words, or more general terms. The term-space granulation also can be used for retrieval-results granulation. Retrieval results can be organized into a granule network based on term-space granulation.

Retrieval-Result–Space Granulation

In order to have an in-depth understanding of the retrieval results, one may granulate them to form a multilevel view. One way to achieve this is through the use of user-space granulation and term-space granulation. For example, by using term-space granulation, retrieval results may be organized to reflect different levels of generality of terms, which may meet the user needs at different level of details. Depending on user-space granulation, one may choose the right level of term-space granulation for presenting retrieval results. Retrieved documents can also be presented based on document-space granulations.

CONCLUSION

With the advance of any technology, we need to find new applications that realize its benefits. The introduction of IRSS is to take advantage of recent achievements in information and Web technologies on one hand, and to maximize the potential values of the Web on the other. A search engine equipped with more supporting functionalities will enable users to make full and wise use of the Web. The main feature of an IRSS is to expand the functions of current retrieval systems beyond search, navigation, and browsing. Such systems will play an important role in the next generation of the World Wide Web and the study of WI.

This entry briefly discusses the fundamental issues of IRSS. We demonstrate that IRSS represents the next generation in the evolution of retrieval systems, from DRS to IRS, and from IRS to IRSS. A conceptual architecture of IRSS is proposed. Regarding the implementation of IRSS, we examine a few related fields. Granular-computing theory is used to obtain multiview and multilevel representations through term-space, user-space, document-space, and retrieval-results-space granulations. These multiple representations may enable an IRSS to support users more intelligently.

REFERENCES

1. Baeza-Yates, R.; Ribeiro-Neto, B. *Modern Information Retrieval*, 1st Ed.; Addison Wesley: New York, 1999.
2. Dominich, S. *Mathematical Foundations of Information Retrieval*, 1st Ed.; Kluwer Academic Publishers: Dordrecht, 2001.
3. Solso, R.L.; MacLin, O.H.; MacLin, M.K. *Cognitive Psychology*, 8th Ed.; Allyn & Bacon, Inc.: Boston, 2007.

4. Bates, M.J. Where should the person stop and the information search interface start? Inform. Process. Manage. Int. J. **1990**, *26* (5), 575–591.
5. Yao, Y.Y. Information retrieval support systems. Proceedings of the 2002 IEEE World Congress on Computational Intelligence, Honolulu, Hawaii, May 12–17, 2002, 773–778.
6. Yao, Y.Y.; Song, K.; Saxton, L.V. Granular computing for the organization and retrieval of scientific XML documents. Proceedings of the 6th Joint Conference on Information Science, North Carolina, March 8–13, 2002, 377–381; Caulfield, H.J., Chen, S.H., Cheng, H.D., Duro, R.J., Honavar, V., Kerre, E.E., Lu, M., Romay, M.G., Shih, T.K., Ventura, D., Wang, P.P., Yang, Y.Y., Eds.; 2002.
7. Yao, Y.Y. Granular computing for the design of information retrieval support systems. *In Information Retrieval and Clustering*, 1st Ed.; Wu, W., Xiong, H., Shekhar, S., Eds.; Kluwer Academic Publishers: Dordrecht, 2003.
8. Yao, Y.Y. A framework for web-based research support systems, Proceedings of the 27th Annual International Computer Software and Applications Conference, November 3–6, Dallas, TX, 2003, 601–606; IEEE Computer Society, 2003.
9. Yao, J.T.; Yao, Y.Y. Web-based information retrieval support systems: Building research tools for scientists in the New Information Age, Proceedings of the 2003 IEEE/WIC International Conference on Web Intelligence, Halifax, Canada, October 13–17, 2003, 570–573; IEEE Computer Society, 2003.
10. Yao, Y.Y.; Zeng, Y.; Zhong, N.; Huang, X.J. Knowledge retrieval (KR), Proceedings of the 2007 IEEE/WIC/ACM International Conference on Web Intelligence, Silicon Valley, November 2–5, 2007, 729–735; IEEE Computer Society.
11. Zeng, Y.; Yao, Y.Y.; Zhong, N. Granular structure based knowledge retrieval. Comput. Sci. **2008**, *35* (3), 194–196, 224 (in Chinese).
12. Van Rijsbergen, C.J. *Information Retrieval*, 1st Ed.; Butter-worths: London, 1979.
13. Takahashi, Y. Fuzzy database query languages and their relational completeness theorem. IEEE Trans. Knowl. Data Eng. **1993**, *5* (1), 122–125.
14. Chau, M.; Chen, H.C. Comparison of three vertical search spiders. IEEE Comput. **2003**, *36*, 56–62.
15. Nie, Z.Q.; Ma, Y.X.; Shi, S.M.; Wen, J.R.; Ma, W.Y. Web object retrieval, Proceedings of the 16th International World Wide Web Conference, Banff, AB, Canada, May 8–12, 2007, 81–90.
16. Nie, Z.Q.; Wen, J.R.; Ma, W.Y. Object-level vertical search, Proceedings of the Third Biennial Conference on Innovative Data Systems Research, Asilomar, CA, January 7–10, 2007, 235–246.
17. Wang, Y.; Geng, Z.H.; Huang, S.; Wang, X.L.; Zhou, A.Y. Academic web search engine: Generating a survey automatically, Proceedings of the 16th International World Wide Web Conference, Banff, Alberta, Canada, May 8–12, 2007, 1161–1162.
18. O'Brien, P.; Abou-Assaleh, T. Focused ranking in a vertical search engine, Proceedings of the 30th ACM SIGIR Conference, Amsterdam, the Netherlands, July 23–27, 2007, 912.
19. White, R.W.; Kules, B.; Drucker, S.M.; Schraefel, M.C. Supporting exploratory search. Commun. ACM **2006**, *49* (4), 37–39.
20. Marchionini, G. Exploratory search: From finding to understanding. Commun. ACM **2006**, *49* (4), 41–46.
21. Schraefel, M.C.; Wilson, M.L.; Russell, A.; Smith, D.A. MSPACE: Improving information access to multimedia domains with multimodal exploratory search. Commun. ACM **2006**, *49* (4), 47–49.
22. Brajnik, G.; Mizzaro, S.; Tasso, C.; Venuti, F. Strategic help in user interfaces for information retrieval. J. Am. Soc. Inform. Sci. Technol. **2002**, *53* (5), 343–358.
23. Turban, E.; Aronson, J.E. *Decision Support Systems and Intelligent System*, 1st Ed.; Prentice Hall: Englewood Cliffs, NJ, 2001.
24. Wong, S.K.M.; Yao, Y.Y.; Butz, C.J. Granular information retrieval. In *Soft Computing in Information Retrieval: Techniques and Applications*; Crestani, F., Pasi, G., Eds.; Physica-Verlag: Heidelberg, 2000; 317–331.
25. Zadeh, L.A. Towards a theory of fuzzy information granulation and its centrality in human reasoning and fuzzy logic. Fuzzy Set. Syst. **1997**, *19*, 111–127.
26. Berners-Lee, T.; Hall, W.; Hendler, J.A.; O'Hara, K.; Shadbolt, N.; Weitzner, D.J. A framework for web science. Foundation. Trend Web Sci. **2006**, *1* (1), 1–130.
27. Michalski, R.S.; Winston, P.H. Variable precision logic. Artif. Intell. **1986**, *29* (2), 121–146.
28. Simon, H.A. A behavioral model of rational choice. Quart. J. Econ. **1955**, *69* (1), 99–118.
29. Fensel, D.; van Harmelen, F. Unifying reasoning and search to web scale. IEEE Internet Comput. **2007**, *11* (2), 96, 94–95.
30. Gorry, G.A.; Morton, M.S.S. A framework for management information systems. Soloan Manage. Rev. **1971**, *13*, 55–70.

31. Yao, Y.Y. The art of granular computing, Proceedings of the International Conference on Rough Sets and Emerging Intelligent Systems Paradigms, Lecture Notes in Artificial Intelligence 4585, Warsaw, Poland, 2007, 101–112; Springer, 2007.
32. Yao, Y.Y.; Zeng, Y.; Zhong, N. Supporting Literature Exploration with Granular Knowledge Structures, Proceedings of the 11th International Conference on Rough Sets, Fuzzy Sets, Data Mining, and Granular Computing, Lecture Notes in Artificial Intelligence 4482, Toronto, ON, Canada, May 14–16, 2007, 182–189; Springer, 2007.
33. Salton, G. *Dynamic Information and Library Processing*, 1st Ed.; Prentice-Hall: Englewood Cliffs, NJ, 1975.
34. Wong, S.K.M.; Yao, Y.Y. Query formulation in linear retrieval models. J. Am. Soc. Inform. Sci. **1990**, *41* (5), 334–341.
35. Morita, K.; Atlam, E.; Fuketa, M.; Tsuda, K.; Oono, M.; Aoe, J. Word classification and hierarchy using cooccurrence word information. Inform. Process. Manage. **2004**, *40* (6), 957–972.
36. Tokunaga, T.; Iwayama, M.; Tanaka, H. Automatic thesaurus construction based on grammatical relations, Proceedings of the 1995 International Joint Conference on Artificial Intelligence, Montreal, QC, Canada, 1995, 1308– 1313; Morgan Kaufmann, 1995.
37. Hoffman, R.; Valencia, A. Implementing the iHOP concept for navigation of biomedical literature. Bioinformatics **2005**, *21*, 252–258.

BIBLIOGRAPHY

The references below are all available online (accessed December 20, 2008).

1. Yiyu Yao's page on publication related to "Information Retrieval Support Systems": http://www2.cs.uregina.ca/~yyao/research/IRSS.html.
2. Web-based Support Systems (WSS): http://www2.cs.uregina.ca/~wss.
3. 2008 International Workshop on Web Information Retrieval Support Systems: http://uxlab.cs.mun.ca/wirss2008/.
4. Proceedings of the SIGIR 2006 workshop on evaluating exploratory search systems: http://research.microsoft.com/en-us/um/people/ryenw/eess/EESS2006_Proceedings.pdf.
5. Proceedings of the 2008 Information Seeking Support Systems Workshop: http://ils.unc.edu/ISSS/papers.
6. Special issue on supporting exploratory search. Commun. ACM **2006**, *49* (4). http://portal.acm.org/citation.cfm?id=1121949.1121978.
7. Special issue on evaluating exploratory search systems. Inform. Process. Manage. **2008**, *44* (2).http://www.sciencedirect.com/science/journal/03064573/44/2

27 Multilingual Information Access

Douglas W. Oard

CONTENTS

INTRODUCTION

The central thesis of Tom Friedman's book *The World is Flat* is that we now live in a world in which technological innovation is creating opportunities for more seamless global interaction than has heretofore been possible.[1] It is important to recognize that "technological innovation" encompasses far more than mere technical innovation—equally important is our ability as a society to learn to productively use the technical capabilities that we can create. This entry examines one such technology: helping users to find information in ways that "flatten" language barriers. In keeping with what is emerging as common usage, we refer to this challenge as Multilingual Information Access (MLIA).

This word "multilingual" can be used in many ways, so let us start by saying what we mean. A multilingual collection is a collection of documents that contains more than just a single language (e.g., English and Chinese). These documents may each contain just one language, or some of the documents might contain words from more than one language. Our interest is in helping a searcher to find the documents that they seek, regardless of the language in which they are expressed. For simplicity, we will assume in this entry that documents are expressed in writing and stored as e-text (i.e., as digital sequences of character codes), but similar approaches have been applied to scanned documents and spoken word collections, and might in the future also be applied to visual languages (e.g., American Sign Language).

Who needs MLIA? We can envision at least two user groups. Perhaps the most obvious is so-called polyglots—people who are able to at least read (and perhaps write) more than one language. For example, more than one billion people who know at least some English are native speakers of some other language. Polyglots can benefit from MLIA in at least three ways: 1) they can find documents in more than one language with a single search; 2) they can formulate queries in the language(s) for which their active vocabulary is largest; and 3) they can move more seamlessly across languages over the course of an information-seeking episode than would be possible if documents written in different languages were available only from different information systems.

Monoglots (those who know only a single language) form a second important group. For example, many Americans can read only English, while many citizens of China can read only Chinese. Those populations essentially live in different worlds, worlds that MLIA can help to bridge.

MLIA always involves Cross-Language Information Retrieval (CLIR), in which queries in one language are used to find documents in another. When the user cannot read the document language, some form of translation service will usually be needed. This might be as simple as automatic translation of short snippets, or as complex as on-demand translation by a subject matter expert. There are, however, also cases in which adequate results might be presented without translation. For example, someone who knows only Japanese might search a collection of newspaper photographs that are indexed using only English terms and still easily recognize which of the resulting photographs would best meet their needs.

The remainder of this entry is organized as follows. The next section places MILA in historical perspective and explains (or at least interprets) how and why modern techniques for MLIA evolved in the way that they did. The section "Cross-Language Information Retrieval" then describes the present state of the art for CLIR, the key technical capability in all MLIA applications. The section "The Rest of the Story" builds on that, broadening the coverage to address interaction design and information-seeking processes. Finally, "the entry" concludes with a brief survey of the present state of practice and elucidation of some important open questions.

A BRIEF HISTORY OF MULTILINGUAL INFORMATION ACCESS

Gaining access to information in unfamiliar languages has always been an important problem. The intense technological competition that was emblematic of the Cold War in the second half of the twentieth century created a substantial demand on both sides for translation of scientific and technical papers. After some early, and rather disappointing, experiments with automatic translation, the United States National Research Council recommended in 1966 that basic research continue, but that the work of people, rather than machines, provide the principal means for making foreign-language information accessible for the foreseeable future.[2] This recommendation fostered the development of a part of the information industry that focused on translating scientific and technical literature and indexing those translations. Journal articles and so-called gray literature (e.g., technical reports) were translated either prospectively or on demand by a number of organizations, and the World Translations Index (and its predecessors) evolved to provide the needed indexing service for speakers of English.

The economic growth and linguistic diversity of Europe in the second half of the twentieth century provided the impetus for the second major innovation, the development of multilingual thesauri. Oard and Diekema surveyed the genesis of this work, from the first published report (in 1964 from Germany) through publication of the current (1985) version of ISO Standard 5964, which recommends techniques for construction of multilingual thesauri.[3]

Substantial reliance on human translation and thesaurus-based indexing were good choices at the time, but three key events dramatically changed the opportunity space. The most obvious was the end of the Cold War, which resulted in substantial changes in national investment strategies. The International Translations Centre ceased operations in 1997 with the publication of the last volume of the World Translations Index, citing declining demand for their services that resulted from increasing adoption of English as a lingua franca for scientific communication and from declining funding for information science more generally.

The second key event was the rise of the World Wide Web, and in particular the widespread adoption of Web search engines such as Lycos, AltaVista, and Google. Furnas et al. had remarked on what they referred to as the "vocabulary problem" in human–system interaction, observing that "new or intermittent users often use the wrong words and fail to get the actions or information they want."[4] Although the fuzzy-match full-text search capabilities of the 1990s-era Web search engines were far from perfect, experience with that technology began the process of incrementally shifting expectations away from intermediated thesaurus-based search and toward end-user "natural language" search.

The third event, which attracted far less attention at the time, was a remarkable payoff from the investments in basic research that the National Research Council had recommended. Earlier approaches, based on hand-coded rules, had proven to be problematic because the rules could interact in ways that were difficult to anticipate. As a result, at some point adding additional rules in an effort to improve things could actually reduce translation quality. In 1990, a group at IBM Research first published a radical new technique based on one simple idea: machines can learn to translate by using statistical analysis to identify regularities in large collections of translations that were generated by people.[5] Importantly, as more examples are provided, translation quality improves. This "data-driven" approach, which came to be called statistical Machine Translation (MT), is thus well matched to a networked world in which assembling ever-larger collections is increasingly tractable.

These three events, unfolding together in the last decade of the twentieth century, came together to transform both the need for, and the opportunities to provide, automated techniques to support multilingual information access by end users. The spark that ignited the process was a 1996 workshop at an information retrieval conference in Zurich.[6] Early techniques were limited by their reliance on online bilingual dictionaries, but techniques based on statistical machine translation were soon introduced. As described in the next section, this ultimately yielded fuzzy-match full-text search capabilities that accommodate language differences between the queries and the documents remarkably well. End-user search requires more than just accurate ways of finding documents that may be useful, however. Equally important, the user must be able to recognize those useful documents, understand their contents, and (sometimes) draw on that understanding to progressively improve their queries; the section "Conclusion" addresses those issues.

CROSS-LANGUAGE INFORMATION RETRIEVAL

The core capabilities that enable MLIA are indexing and query processing for CLIR. Indexing proceeds in three stages: 1) language and character set identification; 2) language-specific processing; and 3) construction of an "inverted index" that allows rapid identification of documents which contain specific terms. Sometimes the language in which a document is written and the character set used to encode it can be inferred from its source (e.g., *New York Times* articles are almost always written in English, and typically encoded in ASCII) and sometimes the language and character set might be indicated using metadata (e.g., the HTML standard used for Web pages provides a metadata field for specifying the character set). In other cases (or to confirm an initial guess), a very simple form of content analysis can be used to identify those boundaries languages and character sets. The usual approach is to count the frequency of character sequences, and then to guess the language based on similarity to counts computed in the same way for documents written in a known language. For example, the first sentence in this paragraph would yield the following 3-byte sequences: "the", "he", "e c", "co", "cor", "ore", etc. The technique is easily extended to accommodate multibyte character encodings by counting bytes rather than characters. Language and character set classification using this technique is remarkably accurate (typically well over 95%) for any text that is at least as long as a typical paragraph, so language switching within a single document can sometimes also be detected using this technique.

Once the language and character set are known, the character set can be converted to a standard representation (often Unicode) and two types of language-specific processing are then typically applied: 1) tokenization to identify the terms that could be indexed; and 2) stopword removal to identify terms that need not be indexed (for efficiency reasons). For English, tokenization typically involves splitting on white space and then using rule-based techniques to remove common endings (so-called "stemming"). Identifying "word" boundaries is more complex in "freely compounding" languages such as German, Finnish, and Tamil, and in "unsegmented" languages such as Chinese. Of course, the spoken form of every language exhibits this same tendency to run words together without pauses, so techniques similar to those used in speech recognition for identifying words can be used to identify. The basic idea is to draw on two sources of evidence: we can know most of the words that exist in the language (using a dictionary), and we can guess which word sequences might make sense (e.g., from statistical analysis of word usage). Using these ideas together would tell us that the word "Washington" found in a German document might (from the dictionary) be segmented as "was," "hing," and "ton," but (from usage statistics) that such a segmentation would be unlikely to be correct—in this case we would therefore index the unsegmented word "Washington."

The inverted index used in CLIR is similar in structure to an inverted index used in any information retrieval system, but the information stored in that index may be different. Conceptually, an inverted index includes two parts: 1) a lookup table stored in fast main memory that can be used to rapidly find the "postings" for a specific term (i.e., identifiers for all documents containing that term); and 2) The postings file, which (because of its size) must be stored on the (much slower) hard disk. One of the most important advances in information retrieval system design in the past decade was the widespread introduction of automatic compression techniques for the postings file. Because these techniques are tuned to achieve the greatest compression for the most common terms, stopword removal is no longer essential as an efficiency measure in monolingual applications. In CLIR, however, deficiencies in the translation technique can sometimes yield inappropriate results for translation of very common words. Stopword removal is therefore still common in CLIR applications.

The most obvious distinguishing feature of CLIR is that some form of translation knowledge must be embedded in the system design, either at indexing time or at query time. Essentially, three approaches are possible: 1) translate each term using the context in which that word appears to help select the right translation; 2) count the terms and then translate the aggregate counts without regard to the context of individual occurrences; or 3) compute some more sophisticated aggregate "term weight" for each term, and then translate those weights. Somewhat surprisingly, while the first two of these work about equally well in many cases, term weight translation is typically not competitive.

If the user will ultimately require a machine-generated translation, and if that translation is always into the same language, then a strong case can be made for translating every term in context at indexing time. In its simplest form (which is often adequate), this essentially amounts to simply running a full machine translation system as a preprocessing step prior to building the inverted index. Efficiency arguments against this approach would be hard to make: a translation system fast enough for responsive interactive use at query time would also be fast enough to process every document in all but the very largest collections at indexing time.

When full translation is not needed (e.g., for polyglot users), or when translations into many different languages may be needed to serve a linguistically diverse population, indexing documents using the terms in their original language is typically the preferred system architecture. In this case, considerable efficiency improvements can be obtained by translating term counts rather than term occurrences. The basic approach, first discovered by Pirkola[7] (SIGIR, 1998), is to count every possible query-language translation of each term as having been found in the document. Subsequent refinements resulted in further improvements from using translation probability for individual terms to estimate partial counts[8] and from aggregating translation probabilities for synonymous terms.[9] Regardless of the details, the key idea is to compute "term weights" in the query language rather than in the document language. Many of the commonly used term weighting formulae give more weight to rare terms than to common terms, which comports well with the way professional searchers are trained to enhance the precision of their search using terms that they expect will be highly specific. Since specificity is a feature of the query, it makes sense that computing term weights in the query language would work well.

Among all of the advances in CLIR, none has had anywhere near as large an effect as accurate translation probabilities. The best reported results for systems that lack any notion of translation probability (often called "dictionary-based" techniques) are in the range of 70–80% of what would have been achieved using queries written in the same language as the documents. (These results are normally reported as an average across many topics. The most commonly reported search quality statistics in the CLIR literature is "average precision," which is designed to emphasize the density of relevant documents near the top of a ranked list where most searchers are expected to focus their attention.) The best reported results for systems that use translation probabilities well is closer to 100% of what would have been achieved using same-language queries.[9] It is worth taking a moment to consider what that means—today, we can build systems to search French documents that work (approximately) equally well regardless of whether the query is written in French or in English! Of course, for any specific query the system might do better with French or with English, but on average over repeated use the best systems that can be built today do about equally well in CLIR or monolingual applications.

The key question, therefore, is how to obtain sufficiently accurate translation probabilities. It turns out that this problem was solved for us as one part of statistical MT.[5] The key idea behind statistical MT is that a machine that knows very little about language (e.g., just how to recognize a word) can learn to recognize (and later replicate) patterns of language use by counting what happens in very large collections of examples of language use. Specifically, we give our machine an enormous collection of examples of actual translations (e.g., "man in the moon" and "l'homme dans la lune") and ask it to find the most common alignments of individual terms (e.g., "man" and "l'homme" in this case, but "l'humanite" for "man" in "the evolution of modern man"). If the examples from which the machine learns are representative of the cases to which it will later be applied, the translation probabilities learned by the machine can be quite useful. A full MT system contains additional processing stages, but for CLIR it is often sufficient to simply use the learned translation probabilities directly (with some pruning to suppress the effect of relatively rare random alignments).

THE REST OF THE STORY

There is, however, quite a bit more to the search process than simply automatically creating best-first rankings of documents that the user might wish to examine. Three key questions arise: 1) can people learn to formulate effective queries?; 2) can people recognize useful documents in the result set?; and 3) can people adequately understand the contents of those documents to meet their information needs? Research on these topics is still in its infancy, and moreover we can reasonably expect that as translation technology improves the answers to these questions may change. There will be, therefore, substantial scope for important Library and Information Science research on these questions for some time to come.

The most tractable of these questions at present turns out to be the second one: people seem to be remarkably good at recognizing useful documents using even relatively poor translations. In 2001, the Cross-Language Evaluation Forum (CLEF) started an annual interactive track (iCLEF) to foster research on these questions. In that first year, the focus was on interactive assessment of topical relevance using machine translation. Representative users (in this case, university students) were presented with a written topic statement in a language they knew well (e.g., English) and a set of news stories in some other language that they did not know at all (e.g., Spanish) that had been ranked by a CLIR system and then automatically translated back into the language of the topic statement. Topical relevance judgments made by native speakers of the language in which the news stories were written were used as a gold standard. On average (over several users, each working on several topics), the searchers who did not know the document language agreed with the native speakers about as often as two native speakers would be expected to agree with each other.[10]

Together, those studies indicate that recognizing relevant documents using automatic translation of short summaries or of entire documents is usually not a particularly difficult task. Considerable scope remains, however, for future research on optimally combining the technology for summary generation and translation, for analysis of specific cases in which present technology is not meeting user needs well, and for determining how best to present those results to the user (e.g., as several lists or as a single integrated list).

The third challenge, translating documents well enough that the user can understand their contents, is exactly the goal for which automatic systems for machine translation are optimized. Translation quality can be measured in two ways: 1) an "intrinsic" evaluation in which we ask how similar an automatic translation is to something that a human translator would actually create; or 2) an "extrinsic" evaluation in which we ask how well the reader can accomplish some task using the translation. Intrinsic evaluations provide an important way of assessing incremental progress in the design of machine translation systems, but extrinsic evaluation sheds more light on the ability of present translation technology to meet user needs in multilingual information access applications.

The iCLEF 2004 user studies provided an initial extrinsic evaluation of translation quality, measuring the user's ability to answer factual questions when searching a large collection of news stories in an unfamiliar language. The results of those studies indicated that (on average, across users) only about 70% of the questions could be answered at all, and that (on average, across users and answered questions) only about 70% of those answers were correct. Considering both factors together, those factual questions were answered correctly about half the time.[11]

Jones et al. took this approach further, measuring the utility of an improved machine translation system across four source types (newspaper stories, text-only discussion groups, automatically transcribed news broadcasts, and automatically transcribed talk shows) using a reading comprehension test. They reported about 80% accuracy for answers to factual questions, but only about 50% accuracy for answers to questions that called for some degree of abstract reasoning.[12] From this we can conclude that present machine translation technology can satisfy some user needs, but that further improvements in translation quality will be needed before broadly useful multilingual access applications can be fielded.

The first of the questions posed at the start of this section, whether people can learn to formulate effective queries, is at this point the one we know the least about. The reason for this is simple—to learn very much about this would require long-term studies of real users performing real tasks. But before that can happen we must develop and field real systems capable of supporting those tasks, and those systems don't yet exist. Some insights have begun to accumulate from anecdotal reports of user experiences during structured user studies that have implications for system design. For example, sometimes searchers will recognize a useful term in a translated document and add it to their query, which will only work well if translation of documents and queries are implemented in a consistent manner (which was not the case in early systems). It also seems to be a good idea to inform users when no translation is known for a query term. It is not yet clear how far to take this idea of informing the user—should we show them the translated query? All possible translations for each query term? Alternate translations for some of the terms in a summary or a full document? Perhaps soon we will begin to see studies using Google's new MLIA capability (described below) that will begin to shed light on some of these questions.

CONCLUSION

Adoption of MLIA capabilities in deployed systems seems to have been far slower than the progress on the underlying CLIR technology would support. Deficiencies in current MT systems are undoubtedly a limiting factor in many cases, although applications intended for use by polyglot users would naturally be less affected by those deficiencies. Some cases may reflect a chicken-and-egg paradox: MLIA is needed only for large multilingual collections, but collection development policies in many cases predate the availability of these techniques. Web search would seem to be a natural first mover in MLIA (after all "World-Wide" is the Web's first name!), but there too adoption has been slower than the technology base would support. One commonly cited limiting factor for Web search engines has been the challenge of developing a suitable business model for monetizing MLIA. Regardless of the cause, it seems clear that developing a broader experience base with MLIA techniques will be an important next step.

In May, 2007, Google introduced a rudimentary MLIA capability by coupling query translation (to search Web pages in a different language) with document translation (to translate the result list, and individual results). Such an approach can be easily "bolted on" to any Web search engine since Web search engines typically already include automatic language identification and language-specific processing. (Indeed, Yahoo announced a similar service for German users in 2005, although apparently without much success.) Similar techniques have been used for CLIR research by modifying freely available information retrieval systems that had originally been designed for monolingual applications (e.g., Lucene), and at least one freely available system includes provisions for easily incorporating translation probabilities (Indri's "weighted structured queries"). Some degree of adoption is now also becoming evident among commercial providers of search services. For example, Autonomy now offers cross-language search capabilities (e.g., for enterprise search by multinational corporations).

These emerging capabilities are first steps in the direction of developing a richly multilingual information ecology that could support the next generation of research on information-seeking behavior in such settings. The few studies that have been conducted in recent years have typically focused on single information systems, relatively narrowly scoped collections, and, of necessity, users who have no prior experience with any MLIA application. As more users gain access to a broader range of increasingly capable systems, richer and more nuanced study designs will become possible.

Some open issues remain with regard to the technology base as well. For example, development costs for language-specific processing depend on the number of languages that must be accommodated, but the overall value of processing a specific language varies with the importance to the user of the languages that might be written in that document. With hundreds of written languages in use around the world, a point of diminishing returns may be reached beyond which the development costs for language-specific processing can no longer be justified. In such cases, a simple alternative is to count character sequences (in the same way as for language identification) and then simply index those character sequences. While this works reasonably well for monolingual applications in which the query and the document are written in the same language, how best to integrate translation capabilities into such an architecture is presently less clear.

Another open research question in MLIA is how best to present results from different languages. The challenge in this case arises because present systems for ranking documents in decreasing order of probable utility rely on relative relevance" scores that lack an absolute meaning. The consequence is that we can reasonably hope to determine whether one French document is a better match to the query than another French document, but determining whether an English document is a better match to that query than some French document requires that we create some way of comparing English scores with French scores. Progress on this problem has to date been rather disappointing, with merged result lists often being far less satisfactory than the best single-language result set. Presenting several ranked lists, one per language, is possible, but that approach does not scale well as the number of languages grows.

Result set presentation is a special case of the more general issue of interaction design, for which the research to date has just started to scratch the surface. When first introduced, things that are new are often patterned on things that are already well understood. Newspapers, for example, initially resembled the pamphlets that had preceded them. Later, when newspapers first started providing content on the Web, it resembled a printed newspaper. So it should be no surprise that Google's first try at MLIA looks like, well, Google. New capabilities tend to create their own dynamics, however, with new users bringing new needs, which drives development of new technologies, sometimes ultimately resulting in something that would have been difficult to imagine at the outset. MLIA has progressed far enough at this point for us to begin on that path, but not nearly far enough for us to yet predict where that path will lead us.

ACKNOWLEDGMENTS

The author is grateful to Noriko Kando for initial discussions that led to this entry. This work has been supported in part by DARPA contract HR0011-06-C-0022 (GALE).

REFERENCES

1. Friedman, T.L. *The World is Flat: A Brief History of the Twenty-First Century*; Farrar, Straus and Giroux: New York, 2005.
2. Pierce, J.R., et al. *Languages and Machines—Computers in Translation and Linguistics, ALPAC Report*, National Academy of Sciences; National Research Council: Washington, DC, 1966.
3. Oard, D.W.; Diekema, A.R. Cross-language information retrieval. Ann. Rev. Inform. Sci. Technol. **1998**, *33*, 223–256.
4. Furnas, G.W.; Landauer, T.K.; Gomez, L.M.; Dumais, S.T. The vocabulary problem in human-system communication. Commun. ACM **1987**, *30* (11), 964-971.
5. Brown, P.F. et al. A statistical approach to machine translation. Comput. Linguist. **1990**,*16* (2), 79-85.
6. Grefenstette, G., Ed. *Cross-Language Information Retrieval*; Kluwer Academic: Boston, 1998.
7. Pirkola, A. The effects of query structure and dictionary setups in dictionary-based cross-language information retrieval. In *21st Annual ACM SIGIR Conference on Research and Development in Information Retrieval (SIGIR 1998)*, Melbourne, Australia, August 24-28, 1998; Croft, W., et al., Eds.; ACM, New York, 1998; 55–63.
8. Xu, J.; Weischedel, R. TREC-9 cross-lingual retrieval at BBN, The 9th Text Retrieval Conference (TREC-9), Gaithersburg, MD, November 13–16, 2000; 106–115.
9. Wang, J.; Oard, D.W. Combining bidirectional translation and synonymy for cross-language information retrieval. In *Proceedings of the 29th Annual International ACM SIGIR Conference on Research and Development in Information Retrieval (SIGIR 2006)*, Seattle, WA, August 6–11, 2006; Efthimiadis, E.N. et al., Eds.; ACM, New York, 2006; 202–209.
10. Oard, D.W. et al. Interactive cross-language document selection. Info. Retrieval **2004**, *7* (1-2), 205-228.
11. López-Ostenero, F.; Gonzalo, J.; Peinado, V.; Verdejo, F. Cross-language question answering: Searching pasajes vs. searching documents. In *Multilingual Information Access for Text, Speech and* Images, Fifth Workshop of the Cross-Language Evaluation Forum (CLEF 2004), Bath, U.K., September 15–17, 2004; Peters, C. et al., Eds.; LNCS, Vol. 3491, Springer-Verlag, Berlin, 2005; 323–333.
12. Jones, D. et al. ILR-based MT comprehension test with multi-level questions, Human Language Technologies 2007: The Conference of the North American Chapter of the Association for Computational Linguistics (HLT-NAACL 2007), Companion Volume, Short Papers, Rochester, NY, April 22–27, 2007; 77–80.

BIBLIOGRAPHY

1. Excellent sources for the latest work on CLIR include the proceedings of the Cross-Language Evaluation Forum (CLEF), (http://www.clef-campaign.org) in Europe, the NACSIS/NII Test Collection Information Retrieval (NTCIR) evaluations (http://research.nii.ac.jp/ntcir) in Japan, and the Forum for Information Retrieval Evaluation (FIRE) (http://www.isical.ac.in/~clia) in India. Contemporaneous reports on earlier CLIR research are also available from the Text Retrieval Conference (TREC) (http://trec.nist.gov) and the Topic Detection and Tracking (TDT) evaluations (http://www.nist.gov/speech/tests/tdt/).
2. For a historical perspective on the developments in MLIA, see the Annual Review of Information Science and Technology, volume 33 (1998). For a broad forward-looking treatment of the subject, see the papers and presentations from the SIGIR 2006 workshop on New Directions in Multilingual Information Access (http://ucdata.berkeley.edu:7101/projects/sigir2006/program.htm).

28 Still Image Search and Retrieval

Vittorio Castelli

CONTENTS

INTRODUCTION

During the first decade of the twenty-first century digital images have rapidly supplanted traditional film-based images in many application areas. The most visible example is consumer photography, where, due to technological advancements, the digital medium has overtaken the traditional film. Digital cameras with high-quality optics and high-resolution sensors are much smaller than old 35 mm cameras. Cellular phones often have built-in digital cameras with resolutions that match that of a typical mid-range computer monitor. External USB hard disks with 1 Tb of capacity or more are available at a fraction of the cost of a personal computer, allowing consumers to store large numbers of digital pictures. Distributing digital images is also very easy: telecommunication companies offer services to share images acquired via cellular phone cameras, while social networking sites provide intuitive interfaces for posting personal photographs on the Internet. Accessing images over the Web has become almost instantaneous, thanks to the widespread availability of broadband connectivity for home use, over the phone lines (using DSL, i.e., Digital Subscriber Line, technology), or over the cable-television networks.

Digital imagery has quickly supplanted traditional imagery in scientific fields, particularly in radiology. Several types of radiological images have always been acquired through electronic sensors—magnetic resonance imaging (MRI), TAC, and Positron emission tomography (PET), for example. The availability of high-resolution sensors and especially of high-resolution, high-contrast computer displays has made it possible in many cases to replace traditional, film-based x-ray imagery with digital images. Technological advances are making digital radiography appealing even in applications where high-resolution images are required, such as for mammography.

Advances in imaging techniques have also enabled the reproduction of precious documents, historical artifacts, and figurative art masterpieces with sufficient wealth of details to be usable not only by the general public, but even by scholars. This trend was pioneered in the mid-1990s, for example, by the Vatican Digital Library initiative[1]; more recent development include the digital rendering of Michelangelo's David statue.[2]

Quite interestingly, techniques for *retrieving* digital images from large collections or from the Internet have only partially kept up with the pace of the digital imagery explosion. The most widely used search engines can retrieve images through keyword-based searches and build image indexes based on the HTML tags of the images and on keywords that appear in the text in the proximity of the images. Specific scientific fields have developed metadata standards to describe information on how images are acquired and on their content. However, the ultimate goal, the ability of retrieving images by specifying the desired content, is still a research topic and, despite the numerous advances in the field, has proven, so far, to be an elusive achievement.

In this entry, we provide an overview of still-image retrieval by content. We start section "Introduction" by discussing how images are represented in digital format. In section "Image Formats and Data Compression" we introduce the concept of content-based retrieval of still-image data (CBIR, for content-based image retrieval). Section "Query Specification" introduces the definition of *objects* as the building blocks for content representation within an image. In section "Content Representation and Objects" we identify different abstraction levels at which objects can be specified. We discuss how simple objects can be defined as connected regions that are homogeneous with respect to pixel-level, feature-level, semantic-level, and metadata-level characteristics. We describe how information can be efficiently represented at these different levels, how a user can specify content, and what mechanisms can be used to perform the search. Simple objects can also be defined simultaneously at multiple abstraction levels, and aggregated to form composite objects. The semantics of both types of objects, and the techniques required to search for them are the subject of section "Defining Content at Multiple Abstraction Levels."

In section "Progressive Search at Multiple Abstraction Levels" we briefly introduce a different perspective on image retrieval, affective image retrieval, where the image is treated as a signifier and the user specifies the desired signified. For example, a user could ask the system to retrieve images that convey "happiness," that describe "democracy," or that illustrate "Memorial Day."

In section "Effective Image Retrieval" we then discuss specific applications of the techniques described in the entry to Digital Libraries. We analyze specific examples of digital libraries of scientific data: medical image databases, repositories of remotely sensed images, and databases used by the oil industry.

IMAGE FORMATS AND DATA COMPRESSION

Data compression techniques are commonly used in image databases to reduce the required storage space. As we shall see in later sections it is sometimes possible to use properties of the compression algorithms for indexing and retrieval purposes. Hence, we briefly review some fundamental concepts of image compression.

The goal of source coding (data compression) is to produce a representation of the original signal which requires fewer bits. Compression is accomplished by reducing the redundancy present in the original data, and possibly by selectively discarding some information. Methods that discard information are called *lossy*, and the remaining ones are called *lossless*. In (gray scale) images, there are two main sources of redundancy: the similarity of spatially close pixels, and the nonuniformity in the overall intensity distribution.

Neighboring pixels commonly have similar brightness (intensity), and it is often possible to rather accurately estimate a pixel value from those of the surrounding ones. Hence, only the difference between the predicted and the original values needs to be encoded, and this difference in general can be represented by fewer bits than the original grayscale value. Two main classes of approaches exist to reduce spatial redundancy. The first operates in the *spatial domain*, by exploiting local redundancy. A typical example is the lossless mode of JPEG standard: here, the image is scanned line by line from left to right, the value of each pixel is predicted using the values of the closest previously scanned pixels and the difference between predicted and actual values is computed (this approach is also known as predictive coding). The second class of approaches operates in a *transform domain*. Natural images have higher energy in the lower frequencies of the spatial spectrum, that describe slower intensity variations, than in the higher frequencies. The *two-dimensional Fourier transform* [[3], Chapter 8] hence concentrates most of the image energy in a few low-frequency coefficients. Each Fourier coefficient is generated from the entire image, and is not easily predicted from neighboring coefficients, hence the transform effectively reduces spatial redundancy. The *two-dimensional block discrete cosine transform* (DCT), used in the JPEG standard[4] is closely related to the Fourier transform, but is more local in nature: the image is first blocked into 8×8 squares, and each block is transformed separately. Again, most of the energy is concentrated in a small subset of coefficients, and coefficients cannot be effectively predicted from the values of their neighbors because their statistical dependence is weak. The *wavelet transform*,[5] used in the JPEG2000 standard,[6] relies on a high-pass filter (H) and a low-pass filter (L). The image rows are filtered separately, and the result is filtered column by column. This operation produces a subband, which is commonly identified by the used filters: for instance, if rows are filtered with the high-pass filter and the columns with the low-pass filter, the resulting subband is denoted by HL. Hence, there are four possible subbands, LL, HL, LH, and HH, depicted in Figure 28.1. Subbands are downsampled by retaining each other row and each other column. A ℓ level wavelet transform repeats the described operation on the LL subband $\ell - 1$ times. The transform yields both spatial and spectral information. The lower-frequency subband (LL at level ℓ) is well localized in frequency and each coefficient depends on a large number of image pixels. The higher-frequency subband (HH at level 1) is well localized in space, but contains information on roughly the top half of the frequency spectrum. Most transform coefficients at the higher levels have values close to zero, while most of the energy is in the lower-frequency subbands. Figure 28.1 illustrates this concept. The LL subband is a smaller version of the original image, the LH subband captures edges aligned with the

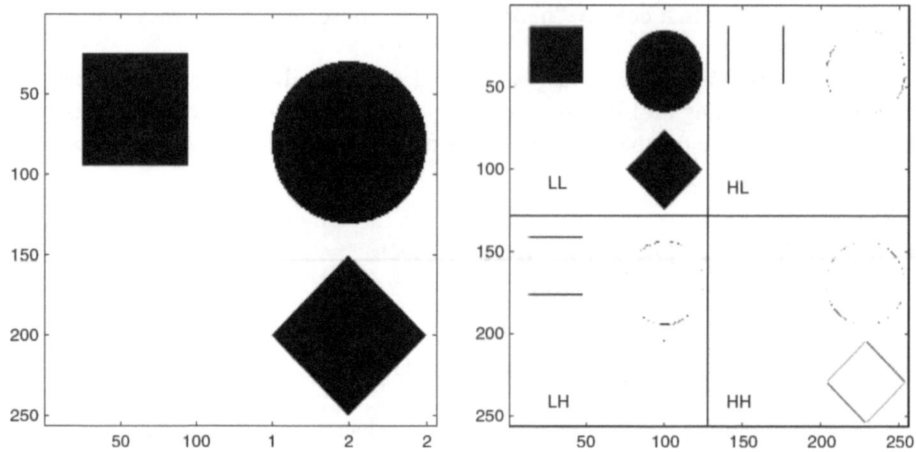

FIGURE 28.1 A simple image (left) and its two-dimensional wavelet transform (right).

horizontal axis, the LH subband captures edges aligned with the vertical axis, and the HH subband captures diagonal edges.

From both wavelet transform and block DCT it is easy to obtain a multiresolution representation of the image, that is, a sequence of increasingly smaller and coarser approximations to the original. As we shall see in subsequent entries, this property can be advantageously used during search.

The second cause of redundancy is present in most images: some of the intensity values are more common than others, and data compression can be achieved by encoding them with shorter codewords. Numerous techniques exist to accomplish this task, such as Shannon coding, Huffman coding, Arithmetic coding, and Lempel-Ziv-like codes, etc. An introduction can be found in Cover.[7] In general, higher intensity redundancy results in better compression. Spatial redundancy reduction almost invariably yields a significant increase in the intensity redundancy, and for this reason favors compressibility.

With lossless techniques, images typically compress by a factor of 2–3. If higher compression ratios are desired, information must be selectively discarded to improve compressibility. Two mechanisms are available, thresholding and quantizing,[8] which are usually applied after the spatial redundancy reduction and always before the intensity redundancy reduction. Thresholding changes to zero all values that are close to it. For example, in predictive coding, all small prediction errors could be set to zero. Quantizing (via *scalar quantization*, SQ) means reducing the number of allowed intensity values, by partitioning the intensity scale into regions (bins), assigning a representative intensity value to each bin, and changing each pixel to the representative value of the bin into which it falls. Both thresholding and quantization can be used simultaneously.

A substantial amount of research has been devoted to a general class of quantization schemes, called *vector quantization* (VQ).[8,9] VQ has its root in the well-known result in Information Theory that states that quantizing *independent* Gaussian random variables together yields lower distortion at the same rate than quantizing them separately (see, e.g., Problem 13.1 in Cover and Thomas[10]). Further improvements can be achieved if the random variables are not independent, as it is typically the case for neighboring image pixels. VQ compression of an image consists of: tessellating the image into groups of neighboring pixels having the same size, say d (e.g., dividing the image into 2×2 pixel regions); partitioning the d-dimensional space of pixel groups into bins; selecting a representative group of d pixels for each bin; and mapping each group of pixels from the image to the representative group of the bin into which it falls.

If thresholding, VQ, or SQ are used, either on the image or on its transform,[11,12] it is generally not possible to recover the original data from its compressed version. To select the thresholding and quantization parameters, often a measure of similarity between the original and reconstructed image is used, such as the mean squared error. Compression ratios of 10 to 1 or better are possible with lossy schemes, without appreciable deterioration of the image quality. However, since these techniques nevertheless introduce visual artifacts, their application to scientific data is rare, and essentially limited to remote browsing of the images over slow networks. By combining a lossy scheme with lossless encoding of the difference between the original and reconstructed image, it is possible to obtain a lossless scheme which can also be used for image retrieval.

SEARCHING IMAGE REPOSITORIES BY CONTENT

In traditional relational databases, queries are expressed using a highly structured language, such as SQL. This is possible because the information managed by the database is itself highly structured and can be stored, for instance, in one or more tables. Images, like many other types of multimedia data, are by nature unstructured. Therefore, they are difficult to organize using relational or object-relational databases and to retrieve using a structured query language. No universal solution exists to the problem of organizing and searching data in image databases: information retrieval from image repositories is a field of research that is currently in the process of reaching maturity.

Ideally, multimedia repositories should be searched by allowing the user to specify the desired content of the data to be retrieved. However, the old proverb "a picture is worth a thousand words" describes well the difficulties that a user encounters when attempting to specify exactly what the retrieved images should contain. The almost universal approach to overcome this difficulty is to rely on similarity-based search. The large class of heterogeneous methodologies developed for searching multimedia databases is commonly known in the field as *content-based retrieval* (CBR).[13] The main challenges posed by content-based search are automatic extraction and indexing of the content (to which this entry is devoted), query specification, and display of the results. In practice, however, the problem is very hard. In particular, a chasm exists between what search features can be extracted by existing systems from the user's query, and what content the user is actually interested in. This is called *semantic gap*,[14] and was well characterized by Smeulders et al.,[15] as the "lack of coincidence between the information that one can extract from the visual data and the interpretation that the same data have for a user in a given situation." Most of the research in CBR has been devoted to map information that can be extracted automatically from images, from associated metadata, and from context information (such as text near images embedded into documents) to user's semantic.

QUERY SPECIFICATION

There are numerous query specifications styles that are appropriate for image databases. The early CBR systems, such as QBIC,[13] VisualSeek,[16] and Virage,[17] used an example-based interface where the user would construct queries by supplying one or more examples. Graphical Query Languages offer an appealing alternative; however they have a steep learning curve and limited support for multimedia datatypes and relationships. A drag-and-drop interface supporting a quasinatural query language that combines English-like sentences with multimedia data, such as images, has been proposed in Bergman, et al.[18] and used in conjunction with the SPIRE system[19] in a variety of application scenarios. This interface supports the composition of the type of queries described in this entry. Intelligent user interfaces for CBIR are described in Vermilyer.[20]

Many CBR systems rely on a paradigm for interaction with the user called *Relevance Feedback*.[21] In relevance feedback, the user issues a query and, upon receiving a set of results, inspects them, selects those that are most relevant and submits them to the system. The system appropriately modifies the query based on the user's feedback. The turn-taking dialog between user and system continues until the user is satisfied with the results.

CONTENT REPRESENTATION AND OBJECTS

In this entry, we define the content of images in terms of *objects*. We distinguish between simple objects, which can be thought as the building blocks of an image, and composite objects, collections of simple objects grouped by spatial (or temporal) relations. Therefore, we will not distinguish between a "scene" and the image of a complex object with multiple parts: our concept of composite object encompasses both.

SIMPLE OBJECTS AND ATTRIBUTES

A *simple object* is a connected region of an image which is homogeneous with respect to some specific characteristics. An entire image and any connected portion of an image are therefore simple objects, defined by constraints on pixel locations.

Objects have *attributes*. We distinguish *defining* attributes, that are used in the definition of a particular type of object, from *non-defining* attributes, that do not characterize the type of object. For example, a forested area can be defined as a region of a remotely sensed image having specific spectral reflectance and textural characteristics: in this case texture and spectral reflectance are defining attributes, while the location of the forest and its size in pixels are not.

Attributes can be *numerical* or *categorical*. Surface area and location are examples of numerical attributes. The type of a lesion observed in a MRI scan of the brain is a categorical attribute. Categorical attributes can be further characterized as *sharp* or *fuzzy*. An attribute of a geological stratum in a formation microscanner imager (FMI) is its thickness. Thickness can be defined as a sharp attribute, and measured for instance in feet, or as a fuzzy attribute, taking fuzzy values such as "thin," "medium," and "thick." A stratum 4 ft thick could also be characterized by membership values of .6 to the "thin" category, .4 to the "medium" category and 0 to the "thick" category. Attributes can also be either *deterministic* or *probabilistic*. Consider measuring the area of a lake in square meters (thus, we define it as a numerical, sharp attribute) using a remotely sensed image: while some pixels clearly fall entirely within the lake, some contain both dry land and water. Hence, the lake surface cannot be measured exactly, and only an estimate can be produced. This estimate can be treated as a random variable, and confidence intervals can be constructed from the image, for example by counting the number of pixels containing both water and dry land. Similarly, consider classifying automatically a forested area using a remotely sensed image, and assume that the statistical classifier decides that with probability .9 the forest is an evergreen forest, and with probability .1 is deciduous. Here the class label (a categorical attribute) is probabilistic rather than deterministic.

It is important to note the distinction between fuzzy attributes and probabilistic attributes. In the forest example, the classifier is telling us that of all forested areas looking like the one being analyzed, 90% are evergreen forests, and 10% are deciduous forests. This is different from saying that 90% of the trees in the patch of vegetation are evergreen and the remaining 10% are deciduous. The former characterization is probabilistic, the latter is fuzzy.

Finally, we note that attributes can be either *scalar* or *vector-valued*. The size (in number of pixels) of an object is an example of scalar attribute, its color histogram (section "Color Descriptors and Color Matching") is a vector-valued attribute.

COMPOSITE OBJECTS

Simple objects are not sufficient to characterize the content of images. A *composite object* or *compound object* is a collection of simple objects that satisfy a set of spatial or temporal relations. A river delta as seen in a FMI image can be defined as a group of well-defined strata, arranged in a specific order.

Like attributes, spatial and temporal relations can themselves be sharp (for instance, "within *n* pixels") or fuzzy (for instance, "near"). Composite objects provide a powerful paradigm for specifying the content of images, especially those used in scientific applications.

Examples of object-based image representations are the paradigm adopted in SPIRE,[19,22] described in this entry, the *blobworld* representation,[23,24] and the framework used in VisualSEEk.[16] The blob-world approach, based on segmenting images with an Expectation-Maximization (EM) algorithm[25] applied to combined color and texture features, is well-tailored toward identifying objects in photographic images, provided that they stand out from the background. Each object is efficiently represented by replacing it with a "blob"—an ellipse identified by its centroid and its scatter matrix. In VisualSEEk, the query is specified in terms of color regions and their spatial organization.

DEFINING CONTENT AT MULTIPLE ABSTRACTION LEVELS

Attributes of image objects, or, more generally, of multimedia data, can be represented, described and searched at different levels of abstraction. We can readily identify four such levels, namely raw-data, feature, semantic, and metadata level. Simple objects can be defined at each level, or simultaneously at multiple levels.

Searching Images at the Raw Data Level

Digital images are two-dimensional arrays of pixels. Each pixel is represented as one or more numeric values denoting the intensities in different bands of the electromagnetic spectrum at its specific location. A pixel-level object can be defined as a connected portion of an image. Two pixel-level objects are equal if they have the same size and shape, and if the pixels in the corresponding positions have identical values.

Similarity between two pixel-levels objects having the same size and shape is defined in terms of similarity between the values of the pixels in corresponding positions. A pixel-level object having n pixels can be represented as a n-dimensional point, by making each pixel correspond to a different coordinate. The difference between two pixel-level objects can then be defined in terms of the Euclidean distance between the corresponding points. Alternatively, a pixel-level object can be represented as an n-dimensional vector, starting at the origin and ending at the above defined n-dimensional point. In this case, the similarity between two objects can be defined using their inner product.

The SPIRE system[19] supports image search at the numerous levels, including the raw-data level.

Progressive Pixel-Level Retrieval

Computing the Euclidean distance (or the inner product) between a query object and all the subsets having identical shape and size, of all the images in the database, is a very expensive operation. Matching can be based on cross-correlation, or the correlation coefficient.[3] Here, image representation can significantly reduce the computational complexity. Cross-correlation is still an expensive operation in the pixel domain. However, multiplying the Fourier transforms of two images (a much faster operation) is equivalent to computing the cross-correlation in the pixel domain. In Vaidyanathan,[26] the author notices that cross-correlating the corresponding subbands of two images and adding the results produces a subsampled version of the cross-correlation. By noticing that the wavelet transform concentrates most of the energy in the lower-frequency subbands, and that a similar property holds for the low-frequency components of block-DCT, Li, Turek and Feig[27] and Castelli, et al.[28] concluded that the results of Vaidyanathan,[26] can be well approximated by just considering the cross-convolution of the lower-frequency subbands (or DCT coefficients). Local maxima in this approximation suggest possible location of matches. Once candidate locations are identified, the search can be refined by computing and adding contributions from higher-frequency subbands. Large computational savings are achieved by refining the search only around candidate matches rather than on the entire image.

Rather than being a general mechanism, raw-level search has specific applications. It is extremely useful to identify distinctive objects across a time series of images or of images acquired from different instruments, hence it is useful for coregistration purposes. For example, remotely sensed images of the same region acquired by the same instrument vary over time because of slight differences in the orbit, altitude, and orientation of the platform. To coregister the images, ground control points are identified, using pixel-level techniques, and their positions used to compute the warping mapping between the images. Analogously, in medical imaging, distinctive anatomical features must be precisely identified to compute the exact position of the tissues or organs of interest.

Features

The term *feature* denotes an aspect of an image that can be captured by a numeric or, more rarely, categorical quantity (called a descriptor) computed from the raw data. By definition, features do not have an immediate semantic meaning. In the literature, the term feature is often used to denote the descriptor.

Typical image features describe color, texture, and spatial properties, such as shape. We distinguish between *global features*, that represent an image in its entirety, and *local features* that capture localized properties. Global feature descriptors are often used for photographic images, but have in general poor retrieval qualities. It is likely that the use of global features originated with one of the early CBR systems, QBIC,[13] which represented each image with a color feature vector, a texture feature vector, and a shape feature vector. In reality, when a new image is ingested in QBIC, the operator is supposed to manually outline a region of interest, from which the feature descriptors are extracted, and that becomes the subject of the image. Local feature descriptors are much more useful for indexing purposes. They are either extracted by first segmenting the image into homogeneous regions and computing features for each region (as in the blobworld,) or by dividing the image into a large number of small, overlapping windows (e.g., overlapping), and computing features for each window.[28] The advantages of the first approach are that it produces a smaller data volume, and that an appropriate segmentation scheme often produces results that are acceptable from the viewpoint of the user. The advantage of the second approach is the increased flexibility, since objects are not predefined and can be extracted to better match the query.

We now discuss two of the most commonly encountered classes of features in image databases: color and texture. In each subsection, we briefly describe how the category is used, what descriptors are commonly used and how similarity is captured. We conclude each subsection with remarks on specific applications, and, when appropriate, on how to speed up the search by relying on properties of image compression schemes.

Color Features

The Use of Color for Retrieval

Color is commonly used to index images,[29] and is one of the main features used in early CBIR systems, such as QBIC[13] and Virage.[17] It is a very important feature for photographic images and works of art, and histological images. It has limited applicability to radiological imaging, which is almost universally displayed in gray scale (and only rarely using false-colors, which are not useful in indexing), in oil-exploration imagery (where, again, false coloring is used), and in satellite imagery, where the multispectral information is used to extract semantics and not used directly as a low-level property.

Color Descriptors and Color Matching

Color features for similarity retrieval are usually variations of the color histogram. The first step in the feature computation is a selection of the color space. For typical digital photographs, where each pixel is represented as the superposition of three basic colors, red, green, and blue, the RGB space is the most natural choice. Here, each pixel value corresponds to a point in a three-dimensional space, whose coordinates are the red, green, and blue intensity. Pixels of images compressed with the JPEG image compression standard can be immediately represented in the YCrCb space. The natural color space for television data (such as newscasts, sport events, movies, etc.) depends on the standard: NTSC uses the YIQ space, PAL and SECAM use the YUV standard. None of the mentioned color spaces is perceptually uniform, in the sense that Euclidean distances between points in the color space do not capture well the subjective similarity between colors. Hence, numerous other color spaces have been used with moderate success by different authors, such as the hue-saturation-value (HSV) space,[29] the Munsell color space,[30] the opponent-axis space,[31] or the CIE-LUV space.[32]

The second step in the color histogram computation is quantization: the color space is subdivided into cells, a representative color is selected for each cell, and all the pixel values falling in a specific cell are replaced by the representative value. The quantized color space usually contains anywhere from 64 to 4096 different colors.

The color histogram of an image is finally computed by counting how many pixels fall in each cell of the quantized color space. The counts can be normalized (divided by the size of the image), in which case they sum to 1. A non-normalized color histogram having b bins can be represented as a point in a b-dimensional space, the ith coordinate of which is equal to the number of counts in the ith bin. If the color histogram is normalized, it lies on a b-dimensional simplex, which is a $(b - 1)$-dimensional surface.

Different functions on the color histogram spaces have been proposed to capture similarity between images. These functions are usually distances between the points representing the histograms. While the choice of the color space and of the number of quantization bins appear to affect the quality of the retrieval, the choice of the similarity function is less important, and most commonly used ones are essentially interchangeable.

Image representation can be combined with color feature extraction. For instance, research has been done on how to approximate the histograms of images compressed with the JPEG standard with the color histogram of the DC components.[33]

Further Uses of Color

Color is a powerful means for conveying meaning and emotions. Itten[34] codified a psychological theory on the use of the color in art to convey semantics. It is unsurprising, then, that color has been used to retrieve images of paintings from collections of art works. Colombo, Del Bimbo, and Pala[35] analyze the color content of photographs of paintings, and derive measures of harmonic accordance, contrast of luminance, contrast of saturation, and contrast of warmth. As a response to a query, the system returns the most similar paintings with respect to one or more of the listed color quantities. Del Bimbo, et al.[36] extract color and shape using a multiresolution representation of the image. By using a low-resolution approximation (which can be easily obtained from the wavelet transform or the block-DCT), the system can make judgments about the overall color composition of the painting and use them during retrieval.

Texture Features

Definition and Use

Texture describes the local intensity variations in an image. In natural images, texture is a property of individual surfaces, and is an important visual cue especially for categorizing materials and substances: water, wood, grass, snow, cloth, fur, brick walls, sand, etc. are just few examples of entities that humans can identify even in black and white pictures based on texture.

Texture is extremely important in scientific imagery, where commonly expert use textural characteristics to interpret the data. For example, in remotely sensed images, erosion patterns, types of tree associations, and types of crops can be analyzed in terms of texture. In well-bore and core images, the stratigraphical analysis is exquisitely textural in nature. In some types of medical images, such as mammograms, texture is a powerful indicator of pathology.

Texture Descriptors

Texture descriptors are generally extracted from grayscale images. For color images, descriptors are computed from the overall intensity map (computed by adding the square of the pixel values in each color band), from each individual color band, or from selected color bands. Color textures have been the subject of rather few studies.[37–39]

There are three main classes of texture descriptors.

1. **Spatial-domain** descriptors are computed directly from the image (or the intensity map). Several feature sets belong to this class, and here we describe the most common ones.
   a. The *gray-level differences histogram*[40] counts how many times the differences between pixel values in a window and the value at the center occur within an image or a region. Statistical properties of the histogram, such as its mean, variance, central moments, entropy, etc., are used to represent texture properties, such as overall brilliance, intensity variations, etc.
   b. The *co-occurrence matrix* counts how many times a pair of intensity values occurs in pixels having a fixed distance in a predefined direction. Corresponding texture descriptors[41–43] are derived properties of the matrix, such as the entropy or the moments, and have been related to visual properties, such as regularity, homogeneity, directionality, and periodicity of the texture.
   c. *Tamura's features*[44] were selected to capture specific characteristics of the human visual system, and describe texture in terms of coarseness, directionality, roughness, regularity, contrast, and line-likeness. Studies show that, in practice, coarseness, contrast, and directionality alone yield most of the discriminatory ability of the feature set, and that adding the remaining three features improves retrieval results only marginally. Tamura's features capture very well high-level characteristics of texture, but fail to provide fine-level discrimination.
2. **Transform-domain** descriptors are computed from a transform of the image. When an image is compressed with a transform-based method, the corresponding texture descriptors can be obtained at a very moderate computational cost.
   a *Wavelet-based* descriptors[45] capture the local spatial frequency content of the image. $2^k \times 2^k$ portion of an image is described to a good degree of approximation by $3d + 1$ subblocks of a d-levels wavelet transform: one in each of the three high-frequency subbands (HL, LH, HH) at each level, and one in the low frequency subbands at level d. A block at level ℓ has size $2^{k-\ell} \times 2^{k-\ell}$. Smith and Chang[45] suggest computing the wavelet transform of the image, conceptually dividing the image into nonoverlapping square blocks, and considering for each block the corresponding $3d + 1$ portions of the transform. The mean value and the variance of the coefficients within each transform portion are then computed, and concatenated to produce a texture feature vector. The authors also suggest an algorithm for merging adjacent image blocks to segment the image into regions of homogeneous texture.
   b. *Gabor-based* features[46] are among the most discriminating texture descriptors available. The (even, symmetric) Gabor filters are uncorrelated Gaussians with variances σ_x and σ_y in the x- and y-directions, modulated by a sinusoid of frequency ϕ varying along the x-axis, and rotated by an angle θ, hence they are defined by four parameters. In the spatial frequency domain, they correspond to two Gaussians having variances $1/(2\pi\sigma_x)$ and $1/(2\pi\sigma_y)$, centered at ϕ and $-\phi$ respectively, in a reference frame rotated by θ. Their main property is that they trade off optimally localization in the spatial domain and in

the frequency/orientation domain. Hence, the magnitudes of the Gabor coefficients give a good indication of directionality and periodicity of the texture. A texture feature vector is constructed by selecting a group of filters at various orientations, scale (variances), and frequencies, computing the corresponding Gabor coefficients, and concatenating them. Experiments show that Gabor features are competitive with other texture descriptor sets in a wide variety of application domains,[45,47,48] and have been successfully used for texture discrimination and classification[49] and image segmentation.[50]

3. **Random-field** models describe texture as a spatial stochastic process. Technically, in this context a spatial stochastic process is a probability measure on the collection of possible images.[51] Practically, a random field is a probability distribution over sets of neighboring pixels. Markov random fields (MRF) are a special class of processes specified through the conditional distribution of the value of a pixel given the values of specific neighbors. Due to their effectiveness, they have been used for a long time for description and representation,[52–54] classification,[55–57] synthesis,[58,59] compression,[59] and segmentation of texture.[60–64] Gaussian MRF are particularly appealing, due to the simplicity of the model: here pixel values can be written as the sum of a linear combinations of the values of their neighbors and of a correlated Gaussian noise. Simultaneous autoregressive models (SAM), where the Gaussian noise is white (i.e., uncorrelated), are even simpler, and have been widely used for image retrieval field. Typical texture features obtained from random field models are the parameters of the model itself: for example, a SAM texture descriptor would consist of the vector of coefficients used in the linear combination and of the variance of the white Gaussian noise. It is also possible to simultaneously fit different models to the data (characterized, for instance, by different neighborhoods), and use the index selected model a further descriptor.

Texture Similarity and Texture-Based Retrieval

Similarity (or better, dissimilarity) between texture feature vectors is usually measured by means of a distance function. Let **x** and **y** denote two such vectors. The most commonly used metric is the Euclidean distance, defined as

$$D^{(2)}(\mathbf{x},\mathbf{y}) = \sqrt{\sum_{i=1}^{d} (\mathbf{x}[i] - \mathbf{y}[i])^2}$$

It is rotationally invariant and weights all the features equally. This last property is undesirable when the ranges of the different feature descriptors vary significantly. For example, the variance of the gray scale difference histogram is often much larger than the mean, and would have a significantly bigger effect in determining similarity. Furthermore, additional flexibility is required when the system is allowed to learn the relative importance of different features from the user input and feedback. Metrics that can be used to satisfy both requirements are the weighted Minkowsky distances and the generalized Euclidean distance. The former is defined as

$$D^{p}(\mathbf{x},\mathbf{y}) = \left[\sum_{i=1}^{d} w_i \left|\mathbf{x}[i] - \mathbf{y}[i]\right|^{p}\right]^{1/p}$$

where

p is a positive number
w_i are weights
d is the length of the feature vector

The latter is defined as

$$D(\mathbf{x}, \mathbf{y}) = [(\mathbf{x} - \mathbf{y})^{\mathrm{T}}\mathbf{K}(\mathbf{x} - \mathbf{y})]^{1/2}$$

where **K** is a positive definite matrix having determinant equal to 1. Further details on similarity measures for retrieval can be found in Santini and Jain.[65]

Progressive Texture Retrieval

As previously described, several texture features can be extracted from image transforms, and therefore are easily computed when the images are compressed using a transform-based scheme. Texture features extracted from different levels of the multiresolution pyramid can also be used to speed up search.[40] Here, an optimal starting level in the pyramid is identified using the examples provided with the query. Pruning of the search space is then performed by texture matching at this starting level: note that higher starting levels are characterized by fewer homogeneous regions within images, and hence yield faster matching. However, a higher starting level introduces a larger approximation in the matching, as details are lost, and therefore the selectivity threshold for the pruning must be relaxed accordingly. Since the two effects are contrasting, there is always an optimum starting level from the speed viewpoint. Only the regions that pass the pruning stage are retained and further analyzed at the immediately finer level of the multiresolution pyramid. The process is repeated until the full-resolution level is reached. Tenfold increase in retrieval speed have been observed with this technique.

Shape Features

At a first glance, searching images repositories by specifying the shape of desired contained objects appears to be a natural and intuitive approach to CBR. In reality, however, it is a problematic endeavor at best. First, most animate objects are not rigid and their shapes can vary substantially as they move. Even for rigid objects, perspective and angle of view can radically change the shapes recorded in an image. Additionally, shape is not invariant with respect to rotations of the image. In spite of these difficulties, shape-based image retrieval has been an active and often successful field of investigation. Another difficulty with shape features is that they rely heavily on accurate images segmentation, which is largely unsolved. If objects cannot be precisely segmented, shape features can be misleading or even meaningless. In contrast, color or texture features are not so sensitive to inaccurate segmentation. For example, if an object is segmented into two pieces, the colors from the two pieces still reflect the object, but the partial shapes can be arbitrary and dramatically different from the true shape.

Indexing images by shape requires solving three separate classes of problems. The first is *shape extraction*: images must be analyzed to extract shapes of objects. The literature in this field is very large, and image retrieval has borrowed techniques from other disciplines, such as robotic vision. The wide spectrum of approaches to shape extraction range from accurate segmentation, to approximate representation of shape regions, to extraction of low-level features that capture aspects of shape, such as edges.

The second problem is *shape representation*: the shape must be described by numeric quantities that can be used for retrieval. Numerous descriptors have been proposed in the literature, which can be classified along several dimensions. A first distinction is between *global* and *local* descriptors. Global descriptors capture properties of the shape as a whole, for example its elongation or the overall smoothness of the contour. Local descriptor capture properties of selected regions of the shape, for example, the presence of sharp angles in the contour. A second distinction is between *complete* and *partial* descriptors. Complete descriptors attempt to retain all properties of the shape, while partial descriptor capture only characteristics that are deemed salient for retrieval. A third distinction is between *interior* and *boundary* representations. Interior methods describe a shape, for example, by means of approximations or using a sequence of approximations. Boundary methods describe properties of the contour line, for example, by means of piecewise polynomial lines. Other dimensions distinguish between *rotationally invariant* and *rotationally variant* features, *single-scale* and *multi-scale* features, *composition-of-part* and *deformation* methods.

The third problem is *shape matching*. This is typically accomplished by means of an appropriate distance function. Unfortunately, there is no universal shape similarity metric: different feature are matched with different, specific similarity functions. A detailed discussion of these metrics, a more in-depth view of the categorization reported in this section can be found in Kimia,[66] which is an excellent introduction to shape-based retrieval.

Shape-based techniques have had only limited application in photographic image retrieval, where often segmented shapes are associated with texture- and color-based representations of the interior.[67] In contrast, shape has been successfully used in several specialized application areas, such as medical imaging[68]; biometric identification[69]; and retrieval of logos, trademarks, and watermarks.[70] A survey on recent advances in CBR of three-dimensional shapes can be found in Icke.[71]

Searching Images at the Semantic Level

Semantic Content Characterization

Searching images at the semantic level is one of the most difficult tasks faced by CBIR systems. The main challenges are representing semantics, extracting it automatically from the images, and indexing it. These problems are particularly severe in databases of photographic image, where the subjectivity of the user perception plays a major role. For example, a specific image could be described as "an outdoors scene," "a picture from an outdoors sport event," "a picture from a golf tournament," or "a picture of the 18th hole at the St. Andrews golf club in the year 2000, taken while Tiger Woods is putting to win the tournament and the golf grand slam." Scientific data, however, is often more amenable to automatic extraction of semantic content. We first discuss photographic images, and later scientific imagery.

Jaimes and Chang[72] proposed a scheme to represent multimedia content which uses 10 abstraction levels, divided into two groups. The first group contains levels related to percept, corresponds to the pixel and feature levels, and divides into different levels global and local content. The second group, containing six levels (generic object, generic scene, specific object, specific scene, abstract object, abstract scene,) provides a very good framework for describing semantic content in photographic images and video, and can be successfully used as guideline for constructing indexes. Referring to the example of the previous paragraph, the first two descriptions would be indexed at the generic scene, while the last belongs to the specific scene level.

Semantic Content Extraction

While researchers have proposed solutions on how to organize semantic content for search purposes, the automatic extraction of semantic content from photographic images and video is still an unsolved problem and will remain such at least for the next few years. Some of the difficulties encountered are very similar to those raised by the automatic object recognition problem, to which the computer vision discipline has devoted decades of efforts. Specific algorithms exist to identify particular classes of objects within images, such as deciduous trees,[73] naked people and horses[74]; specific types of scenes, such as sunsets, outdoors, and indoors images[75]; and some very high level semantics such as warmth, and harmony of a painting.[35] Automatic image annotation is a form of semantic context extraction: Li and Wang[76,77] propose methods for automatically associating a collection of labels to images.[78]

Still-image retrieval at the semantic level can pose challenges beyond those related to object recognition: users, for example, might look for images with a specific purpose in mind, for example, to evoke desired emotions (e.g., images that evoke sadness, images with dramatic effect, etc.), which is discussed in the section "Affective Image Retrieval."

Following Liu, et al.[79] we classify the technical approaches to semantic content extraction into five categories:

1. *Defining high-level concepts through object ontology.* Methods of this class rely on small-size vocabularies of simple descriptors and a mechanism for mapping low-level features extracted from the image into the vocabulary. An example of such descriptor could be "bright-green region." High-level semantic concepts are expressed in terms of the descriptors: a "lawn" could be described as a "bright-green region located in the bottom half of a photograph." The main limitation of the approach lies in how to appropriately design ontologies for specific tasks.
2. *Using supervised or unsupervised learning.* In the case of supervised learning, a training set consisting of examples labeled with high-level semantic labels is used to train a classifier. The classifier learns to associate low-level features with semantic concepts. In unsupervised learning, the low-level features representations of a large collection of images are partitioned into similar groups, and groups are associated to semantic concepts. The similarity measure is defined on the feature space, or on the space of probability distributions over the feature space, such as in Li and Wang.[77]

   The main limitation of supervised learning methods is their reliance on large manually labeled training sets. The main limitation of unsupervised learning methods is that the correspondence between groups and semantic concepts is incidental.
3. *Interacting with the user via relevance feedback.* Semantic concepts are learned on the fly by a classifier through an iterative refinement process. During a turn of the iterative refinement process, the user is shown candidate examples picked by the classifier, marks some as positive (in some cases, as negative); the classifier then updates its internal model using the user feedback. The main limitation of the approach lies in the limited number of examples that a user can reasonably label.
4. *Matching content through semantic templates.* A semantic template is the "signature" of a semantic concept extracted from a collection of representative images. Unlike when using supervised learning, the designer of semantic concepts must often have a good understanding of the underlying features.
5. *Combining image features and features from surrounding text.* This approach is well suited for retrieval of images from the World Wide Web, which are embedded within HTML pages. Currently, the analysis of the surrounding text is often limited to keyword selection, but advances in natural language processing make the approach increasingly appealing. An important challenge arises from the difficulty of determining whether the surrounding text is actually descriptive of the image content.

Scientific data offers numerous opportunities for automatic semantic content extraction. Experts often interpret the imagery by relying on low-level visual cues, which might be captured by a computer. Additionally, a great deal of the semantic content can be described in terms of objects and their spatial relations, there are no scenes, and the abstract levels of Jaimes and Chang are irrelevant. We briefly discuss three cases: remotely sensed images, oil well-bore images, and medical images.

One of the main uses of multispectral remotely sensed images is to identify and distinguish different types of land cover. The applications are numerous: from management of forestry to the identification of diseases in crops, to crop yield prediction, to environmental monitoring. Different types of land cover have different spectral reflectance: for instance, vegetation reflects in the green part of the spectrum, absorbs in the red (hence, leaves and grass look green), and is highly reflective in the near infrared; barren terrain, on the other hand, has moderate to high reflectance in all the visible and near-infrared spectrum. Automatic classifiers can be constructed to label the individual pixels, identify connected regions and produce semantic objects such as "forests," "urban areas," "bodies of water," etc. These classifiers are usually specific to an instrument, a particular geographical region and a given time of the year.

Well bore data for the oil industry contain both image-like information (acquired, for instance, by the FMI instrument) and one-dimensional data, acquired by appropriate log instruments. Bulk lithology (the type of rock) can be inferred from the log data, and classifiers can automate the task. The well can then be partitioned into labeled strata and rock formations, defined as associations of strata satisfying relative position constraints, can easily be searched.

Radiological imagery has recently received substantial attention as a prime candidate for automatic extraction of semantic content. In addition to the data acquired by the medical instrument, each image is analyzed by a trained radiologist, who produces a reading containing semantic information. This reading is then stored in the medical information system and linked to the image, together with additional metadata, as mandated by the standards with which the repository complies. An ontology based approach for retrieving semantic content from medical image repositories is reported in by Wei and Barnaghi,[80] while Lehmann, et al.[81] describes a strategy for automatic image categorization according to a large number of semantic classes. An overview of recent results related to CBIR from medical images can be found in Müller, et al.[82]

Progressive Semantic Retrieval

Progressive techniques that rely on properties of compression schemes exist to speed up the daunting task of labeling the tens of gigabytes produced daily by an instrument. Progressive classification[83] analyzes the multiresolution pyramid. It uses a different classifier for each level of the pyramid. Starting from an appropriate level, the appropriate classifier decides whether each pixel corresponds to a semantically homogeneous region at full resolution, in which case it labels the entire region, or not, in which case it marks the pixel. The marked pixels are then analyzed at the immediately finer resolution level, using an analogous classifier. The process terminates when the full-resolution level is reached and all marked pixels are labeled. This approach is not only several times faster than pixel-wise classification, but, under general condition, it is also more accurate.

Metadata

Metadata is the highest content abstraction level. It corresponds to information that cannot be inferred or extracted from the image itself, or that is associated to the image in a manual fashion. The date and time of a photographic image, the names of the people appearing in it, the author of a painting and his biography, the location of a well, the name and medical history of a patient, the satellite used to acquire an image are examples of metadata.

Metadata is either structured, and is characterized by the presence of predefined fields whose values have well-specified types, or unstructured, for example textual captions of images. Standards exist or are emerging to regulate structured metadata. They are always specific to a particular application domain, such as medicine, geographical information, remotely sensed data, etc.

Structured metadata is amenable to management using a traditional database. Unstructured metadata can be indexed using information retrieval methodologies. Both cases are beyond the scope of this entry.

PROGRESSIVE SEARCH AT MULTIPLE ABSTRACTION LEVELS

Only the simplest multimedia queries are expressed in terms of a single attribute. These queries are called *atomic* by Fagin.[84] They retrieve the simplest simple objects. For example, one could ask a photographic database for pictures of the current president of the United States (semantic query), a museum digital catalog for paintings by Renoir (metadata query), a fashion archive for fabric having a certain mix of colors (feature-level query). The repository would probably answer the query by returning a large number of results. More specific queries that return a smaller, better defined set of images, are expressed in terms of multiple attributes. For instance, the user might want to retrieve images of paintings by Renoir having as subject scenes from "la Grenouillère," or images of a tumor (metadata-level) having specific size and contour characteristics (feature level).

To support multiple-attribute queries, an image repository has to solve several problems, related to both the semantics of the query and its execution. In this section we discuss these classes of problems and describe solutions proposed in the literature.

The Semantics of Combining Multiple Attributes

Image and multimedia databases must support approximate queries: the user can only provide an approximate description of the desired content, and ask the repository to return the images that best match the specification. It is acceptable to ask for images of gray cars, and have the system return a ranked list of three images, containing respectively a gray sedan, a "metallic silver" convertible and a "silver frost" SUV. The similarity search paradigm yields a significant amount of flexibility, but at the same time complicates the interpretation of queries. Consider asking a photographic image database for pictures of "red cars." In a traditional database, this query would be expressed in SQL as `select image_id where subject='car' and color='gray'`, and the result would be a list of image identifiers containing gray cars. In the example, only the gray sedan would be returned.

In a multimedia database, the equalities in the constraints are substituted by similarity functions, and the "and" connective becomes a function that combines the similarity values of the two constraints. Early CBIR systems, such as QBIC, allowed the user to combine similarities with respect to color, texture, and shape. The user selects the importance of the three features using a graphical user interface, the similarity of images to the query is then computed separately for each feature, and the three resulting scores are combined by means of a weighted average with coefficients proportional to the importance of the features. This approach is simple, but lacks flexibility.

The query framework implemented in the Garlic system[85,86] solves the problem by treating similarity scores as fuzzy membership functions.[84,89] Scores obtained from matching individual constraints are normalized between 0 (no match) and 1 (perfect match), and combined using fuzzy Boolean connectives. The simplest forms of fuzzy AND and OR are respectively, the minimum and the maximum of the connected scores, while the negation (NOT) corresponds to subtracting the score from 1. Hence, if the color "silver frost" matches gray with a score of .8 and an SUV matches a car with a score of .9, the silver frost SUV matches the query for a gray car with an overall score of .8, the minimum of the two.

This framework can conceptually be extended to composite objects,[90] by noting that relations between simple objects produce sharp or fuzzy scores that can be treated in the same way as the object attribute scores.

Searching at Multiple Levels of Abstractions

Fagin[84,89] proposes an algorithm that executes queries containing m constraints on attributes. The algorithm assumes that the search engine can return the top k results in response to atomic queries, and that can compute the score of a database item with respect to an atomic query. The algorithm first evaluates in parallel the m atomic queries, returning for each the smallest set of top results such that there are k distinct database items that appear in each result set. Clearly, when the atomic queries are combined with the minimum function, or with a function which is monotonic in the scores, these k database items constitute the result set L. The algorithm then combines, for each item of L, the scores of the individual atomic query, to produce its score. The scored results are finally sorted in decreasing order and returned to the user.

A sequential processing algorithm for retrieving composite objects is described by Li et al.[90] and consists of three procedures. The first procedure consists of linearizing the description of a composite object into a set of subgoals. The ordering is a function of the dependence between simple objects and of the availability of precomputed indexes for executing atomic queries. The result of the step is a chain of subtasks. The second procedure manages the computation of sets of L results from each subtask. The first time the procedure is invoked on a subtask, it produces the best L matches, the second time it produces the next best L matches, etc. The third procedure controls the execution flow in a dynamic programming fashion: it starts from the first task in the chain, and retrieves the best k matches (out of the block of L items retrieved by the second procedure), then it executes the second task, and retrieves the best k matches for the subproblem consisting of the first and second task. The computation continues by subsequently adding tasks, and keeping track of the scores of the individual subtasks and of the current set of results. It is possible that the score of the kth partial result be smaller than the scores of the worst result currently produced by a particular subtask: if this is the case, the algorithm might be ignoring relevant database items, and a backtracking is invoked, that retrieves further objects from the offending subtask.

Further enhancements of the algorithm are presented in by Li et al.[91] where several fuzzy relations are discussed, and details are given on the execution flow control.

When ordering the subtasks, it pays to consider the abstraction level at which they operate. Metadata atomic queries are usually faster to execute and more restrictive than queries at any other level. They are in general followed by semantic queries, feature-level queries, and raw-data queries in the order. Further optimization can be performed in a query-dependent fashion: the system can collect statistics on how effective different types of queries are at pruning the search space, and use the information while staging the query execution.[92]

AFFECTIVE IMAGE RETRIEVAL

Up to this point, we have concerned ourselves with the problem of describing the visual content of images for the purpose of search and retrieval. However, since the early days of mankind, imagery has been used as a powerful way of describing concepts that transcend the pictorial representation. The image acts as a signifier and refers to a signified which could be an emotion (e.g., sadness, tranquility, etc.), an abstract concept (e.g., portrait paintings often convey information on the personality of the sitter), an event or a recurrence (e.g., the Vietnam War, the Declaration of Independence, etc.). Paintings have also been used to convey philosophical or theological teaching (e.g., the background of the *Mona Lisa* captures Leonardo's view of a dynamic, ever changing nature, and contains clear references to the author's fascination with hydrodynamics and hydraulics). Affective image indexing and retrieval is a discipline that lies at the intersection of affective computing[93] and CBIR; its goal is to support queries containing the specification of the emotions evoked by the desired images.

Most approaches to affective image indexing and retrieval rely on the correlation between low-level perceptual cues and the emotions they cause.[35] For example Li et al.[94] map texture features to a thesaurus of affective concepts; Wu et al.[95] analyze the usefulness of color, text, shape, and their combination for affective image retrieval, while Bianchi-Berthouze and Kato[96] describe a system that interactively creates a Kansei user model based on low-level features extracted from Web images.

IMAGE REPOSITORIES AND DIGITAL LIBRARIES

Early research in still-image retrieval was often pursued in connection with the field of *multimedia digital libraries*. Digital libraries are organized collections of multimedia data, providing storage, retrieval, and transmission functionalities. They are used to manage text,[97] music and audio,[98] images,[30] video,[99] and other forms of electronic content. During their development, early digital libraries posed numerous challenges in all fields of computer science. At the hardware and system software levels, new computer architectures have been invented to efficiently store and transmit large amount of data; requirements have been imposed on operating systems to provide the desired quality of service and data integrity; and new assumptions on how data is accessed and modified have guided the design of file systems that efficiently manage multimedia files. At the application level, new systems for acquiring digital content have been developed; novel content representation models have been devised; algorithms for efficiently searching large collections of data have been explored; and simple, yet powerful user interfaces have been investigated to specify the desired content and to represent the returned results.

In recent years, efforts have been pursued in different directions that often depend on the application field. For example, in remote sensing the focus has shifted from creating large repositories containing data from a large variety of sources to supporting federations of data as service providers. For example, the Federation of Earth Science Information Partners, or ESIP (http://www.esipfed.org/), originated from a NASA grant, is composed of distributors of satellite and ground-based data sets, providers of data products and technologies, organizations that develop tools for Earth Science, and strategic funding partners. As a consequence, problems of metadata standardization and of interoperability of data sets and data products derived from the data sets have taken the precedence over the original still-image retrieval problems. Other fields of investigation include collaborative learning,[100] data fusion, digital library federation, leveraging new computation paradigms such as grid computing,[101] supporting e-Science,[102] all of which are beyond the scope of this entry. The present section contains an overview of the early work in the area of digital libraries for image data, where a substantial emphasis was devoted to image retrieval.

The ground work in the general area of digital libraries was sponsored by the Digital Libraries Initiative (DLI). The first studies were conducted at Carnegie Mellon,[99] U.C. Berkeley,[103] U.C. Santa Barbara,[104] University of Illinois at Urbana–Champaign,[97] University of Michigan,[105] and Stanford University.[106] The field of research has since seen a proliferation of projects. Early image digital libraries organized photographic images, catalogs of museums and art galleries,[107] fingerprints,[69] medical data,[108,109] geographically referenced data,[104] satellite images,[28] etc. We briefly review some of these applications.

Medical Image Databases

Medical imaging[110] is one of the most powerful diagnostic tools available. X-ray radiographs are essentially the only radiological images acquired using film, in analog format: most other modalities acquire data in digital format, hence can be managed by a digital library. Digital radiography and digital mammography are becoming increasingly popular, and we will see in the near future filmless radiology departments. Enabling technologies in digital radiology include: advances in sensor quality (resolution, signal-to-noise ratio), which make the quality of digital images comparable to that of film-based images; improvements in high-resolution, high-contrast flat-panel displays, which increase the productivity of radiologist; and high-speed connections to the Internet, that enable teleradiology, whereby a specialist can diagnose images acquired in multiple hospitals or imaging clinics.

Medical imaging is characterized by a variety of modalities, which are suited to investigating different types of properties, and yield data in different formats. Anatomy, physiology, biochemistry, and spatial properties of the body and its organs can be studied with appropriate radiological instruments.

X-ray radiography is the most common form of medical imaging. It directly measures the opacity of the body or of contrast media to electromagnetic radiation having wavelengths in the 100 Å to 0.01 Å range. The part of the body to be imaged is placed between a source that produces a large, non-diverging beam of x-rays and a sensor array, which records the intensity of the transmitted radiation. A digital radiograph is large: for example, a digital mammogram is a gray-scale image whose typical size is 4000×4000 pixels, and where each pixel is represented as a 12 or 14 bit number: hence, a single mammogram corresponds to 32 megabytes of data.

Computed tomography (CT) produces indirectly images of slices of the body. A series of digital radiographs of the same thin area of the body are acquired from different angles. The resulting set of projection is then analyzed by a computer which reconstructs a slice, whose typical size is

512×512 pixels, each represented by 2 bytes. During an examination, several slices are acquired, and about 20 megabytes of data are generated.

MRI measures the amount of water present in tissues, by aligning the spins of the hydrogen atoms in a thin slice of the body to a strong magnetic field, tilting them, and measuring the variations in magnetic field while the spins realign. A computer analyzes the signal and produces a 256×256 ixels image, where each pixel requires one or two bytes. Numerous slices are typically acquired during a single examination, and 10–20 megabytes of data are generated. Functional MRI is a novel technique that measures activity of organs, typically the brain. Angiographic MRI is used to image blood vessels. Diffusion MRI images the diffusion of liquids in tissues, and is used in the diagnosis of ischemic strokes.

PET measures positrons emitted by radioactive dies which are injected in the body and distribute themselves within the target organ in proportion to the physiological activity of its various parts. PET therefore measures the distribution of the source of radiation within the body.

Ultrasounds are extremely useful for imaging soft tissues, but cannot penetrate bones. Their use is mostly limited to the abdomen and the heart. During an ultrasound examination, the apparatus measures the reflectance (rather than the transparency) of the tissues to the ultrasounds emitted by a source. Doppler ultrasound is a special technique that allows to measure the blood flow within desired organs, such as the liver, and is the only type of medical image to be displayed in color for diagnostic purposes.

Several other diagnostic imaging techniques exist, including single photon emission computed tomography (SPECT), magnetic source imaging (MSI), digital subtraction angiography (DSA), electrical impedance tomography (EIT), electrical source imaging (ESI), etc.

A typical radiology department can easily generate several gigabytes of data a day. The data is heterogeneous in nature: even within the same modality, scanners produced by different manufacturers generate data with different characteristics and formats. The two main problems in this field are dealing with the large number of different equipment types (from scanners, to display workstations, to communication networks, large storage subsystems, database management systems, etc.) that form a picture archiving and communication system (PACS), and managing the sheer volume and the different formats of the data. Recently the ARC-NEMA Digital Imaging and Communications in Medicine (DICOM) standard has specified a non-proprietary digital image format, a specific data file structure and protocols for the interchange of biomedical images and associated medical information.

Medical image databases have an incredible potential in diagnostic medicine, in medical research, and in education; however, their use in such applications is still limited. For example, we can envision that future medical image databases will be powerful differential diagnosis tools: the radiologist, facing an unclear case, will be able to retrieve and consult all the images containing a similar lesion stored in the data repository, but there still are no commercial systems supporting this capability. In medical research, we auspicate that image features will be widely included in clinical studies. Education is probably the application where image databases are starting to realize their potential: for example, the Uniformed Service University of Health Sciences, the U.S. federal government health sciences university, operates an online medical image database called MedPix™, which incorporates peer-reviewed radiological teaching files. MedPix contains images with associated textual information and provides image and textual search tools. MedPix is a prominent example of the radiological resources available on the World Wide Web. A survey of these Web-based resources can be found in Schiller and Fink.[111]

Query-by-content from medical image databases has mostly relied on metadata, texture, and shape features, since most medical images are typically in gray scale. In a recent study,[81] the authors investigate the use of the combination of texture features with scaled representation of the images to categorize medical images for CBR purpose. They report that, even with global features and with a large number of categories,[81] they were able to achieve 85% classification accuracy and the correct class was within the top ten guesses in 98% of the cases. Specialized applications of texture in the medical domain include the analysis and enhancement of mammograms. A mammogram is essentially a texture image that rarely contains objects with a well-defined contour. Digital enhancement of mammographical images should increase the visual difference between normal tissue and abnormalities,[112] and filters that match the specific texture of abnormalities should be used.[113] Similarly, texture features are extremely valuable inputs to automatic classifiers of medical images.[114] We conclude this section by directing the reader interested in CBIR in the medical domain to Müller et al.[82] which contains a broad overview of the topic as well as an extensive bibliography.

Remotely Sensed Image Databases

Remotely sensed images provides us with a wealth of information that find applications in meteorology, earth sciences, environmental studies, urban planning, forestry management, agriculture, education, and, of course, law enforcement and defense.[115]

Instruments are carried on satellites (platforms) that orbit the earth. Often several instruments are carried on a single platform. Geostationary satellites are on an equatorial orbit, while lower-altitude platforms are usually on a quasipolar orbit. An instrument consists of one or a few parallel rows of sensors. Each row contains from a few dozens to a few tens of thousands sensors, each of which acquires a pixel of data, requiring one or two bytes. For polar-orbiting satellites, the rows are parallel to the surface of the earth and perpendicular to the direction of motion of the platform. At predefined intervals, each row of sensors acquires data from a long and narrow strip of the surface of the earth, and produces a line in the image. Between intervals, the platform moves along its orbit, and at different acquisition times the field of view of the instrument covers a different strip. The imaging process is therefore somewhat analogous to that of a desktop scanner.

Satellite images represent different quantities. Most instruments acquire data reflected data in one or more spectral bands. Instrument having long sensor rows usually acquire data in few spectral bands. The LANDSAT Thematic Mapper (TM), for example, acquires data in 6 spectral bands from blue to mid-infrared and in one thermal band, at 30 m resolution, and has more than 6000 pixels per line. Spectrometers, on the other hand, acquire data simultaneously in hundreds of narrow spectral bands, but typically have shorter sensor rows. For example, the CASI instrument has 288 spectral channels and 512 pixels per line.

Few instruments image emissions in the far infrared portion of the electromagnetic spectrum, and essentially measure the temperature of the surface of the earth, of the oceans, or of strata in the atmosphere. Synthetic aperture radars (SARs) measure the reflectance of the surface to microwave or short wave emissions generated on the satellite, as well as the distance between the surface and the satellite, and they yield images that can be used to produce elevation maps or to study certain types of land covers, such as ice.

Satellite instruments image the surface at a wide variety of resolutions. In some meteorological satellites, a pixel corresponds to several square miles on the surface. The NOAA AVHRR instrument acquires data having resolution of about 1 km. The LANDSAT Multi-Spectral Scanner is a medium resolution instrument with resolution of 79 m on the ground. The French SPOT 1 and 2 have resolutions of 10 m. Until recently, satellites capable of acquiring high-resolution images have had only military applications. More recent commercial satellites can acquire images with impressive details: for example the QuickBird satellite owned by DigitalGlobe is capable of 60 cm (roughly 2 ft) resolution in panchromatic mode and of 240 cm in multispectral mode. Images from QuickBird form part of the high-resolution images available via the popular Web-based application Google Earth mapping service. Some images from the Google Earth mapping service have an even higher resolution; at the time of this writing these images are actually aerial photos, rather than satellite images.

Numerous properties of satellite imagery pose challenges to the image database technology. Orbiting instruments generate data at an impressive rate: for example, the Earth Observing System satellites produce about 300 gigabytes a day. The data is collected at few sites, and its distribution in electronic format is difficult due to its sheer volume. The image content is extremely dense, and different information is useful in different application fields: hence satellite data management requires powerful indexing methodologies.

Image Databases for the Oil Industry

The oil industry is a major producer and user of image and volumetric data. Using seismic techniques, large three-dimensional models of geological formations are constructed. From the types of strata and their formations, it is possible to infer the presence of oil, the extension of the reservoir, and to determine the best strategies for drilling. The resolution of such three-dimensional data is in the order of meters or of tens of meters, and each model corresponds to a surface area of tens or hundreds of square km, and to depths of several km.

The relatively poor resolution of such data makes it inadequate for fine-tuning the drilling process. In some occasions, the stratum containing oil is only a few feet deep, and the drill has to be steered right into the stratum. Different types of images are used for this purpose. During the drilling process, it is possible to extract portions of the core, which are then cut, polished, and photographed. Similarly, packs of instruments are lowered to the bottom of the well and slowly retrieved. Some of the instruments measure global properties of the surrounding strata every few feet, such as the gamma ray emission, while others have arrays of sensors that are pressed against the walls of the well, and produce high-resolution measurements of properties such as electric conductivity. The formation FMI has 196 such sensors that measure the electrical resistivity along the circumference of the bore at depth intervals of 0.1 in. FMI data is usually represented as a false-color image having 196 columns and tens of thousands (or more) rows.

In some cases, microphotographs of core samples are used to assess the yield potentials of an oil field.

Besides the large amount of data, image databases for the oil industry face the challenge of data fusion: three-dimensional data, well-bore images, and microphotographs are often used in conjunction to make operative decisions. Powerful indexing techniques are also needed: for example, when combining three-dimensional seismic data (which provides a global, low-resolution view of the oil field) with images from the different well bores (which provide a sparse, highly localized, and high-resolution characterization), the analyst is often interested in determining the exact depths of specific geological formations at all well locations, to improve the accuracy of the model. This is currently a slow, labor-intensive process that requires manually matching hard copies of FMI images, tens of meters long. Automatic extraction and indexing of the data can substantially simplify the task.[48,116]

CONCLUSIONS

We have defined a framework for defining, representing, and searching the content of image repositories at different abstraction levels. We have discussed how raw-data, feature, and semantic level descriptions can be extracted from the images and automatically indexed. We have noted how the combination of image representation (compression) and processing yield significant speedups in content extraction at each abstraction level.

Simple objects, defined as connected image regions which are homogeneous with respect to specific characteristics, form the atomic unit of content retrieval. They can be defined and searched at one or more abstraction levels. Composite objects are sets of simple objects satisfying spatial or temporal constraints. We have discussed the semantics of simple and composite objects and described appropriate retrieval methodologies.

There are numerous open problems in the field. The automatic extraction of semantic content from photographic images is probably the most complex. The investigation of new high-dimensional indexing structures supporting flexible metrics is also an open area of research. Improvements in the interaction between the user and the system where the system learns how individual users tend to formulate queries are needed to make large digital libraries easier to use. Standards need to be defined, to allow a search engine to simultaneously query multiple repositories, and combine the contained information. Finally, a better infrastructure, with faster communication lines, is needed to remotely query large image repository.

ACKNOWLEDGMENTS

The author would like to thank Dr. Chung-Sheng Li, Dr. Lawrence D. Bergman, Dr. Yuan-Chi Chang, Dr. John R. Smith, and Dr. John J. Turek for the years of cooperation that led to the development of the SPIRE system, Dr. Ian Bryant, Dr. Peter Tilke, Dr. Barbara Thompson, Dr. Loey Knapp, and Dr. Nand Lal, for their comments and suggestions, and for defining applications scenarios for our technology.

REFERENCES

1. Mintzer, F. et al. Toward on-line, worldwide access to Vatican library materials. IBM J. Res. Dev. **1996**, *40* (2), 139–162.
2. Koller, D. et al. Protected interactive 3D graphics via remote rendering. In *Proceedings of the 31st International Conference on Computer Graphics and Interactive Techniques, SIGGRAPH2004*, New York; ACM Press: New York, 2004; 695–703.
3. Pratt, W.K. *Digital Image Processing*, 2nd Ed.; John Wiley & Sons: New York, 1991.
4. Pennebaker, W.; Mitchell, J.L. *JPEG Still Image Data Compression Standard*; Van Nostrand Reinhold: New York, 1993.
5. Shensa, M.J. The discrete wavelet transform: Wedding the Á trous and Mallat algorithms. IEEE Trans. Sig. Proc. **1992**, *40* (10), 2110–2130.
6. Lee, D.T. JPEG 2000: Retrospective and new developments. Proc. IEEE **2005**, *93* (1), 32–41.
7. Cover, T.J.; Thomas, J.A. *Elements of Information Theory*, 2nd Ed.; John Wiley & Sons: New York, 2006.
8. Gray, R.M.; Neuhoff, D.L. Quantization. *IEEE Trans. Info. Theory Commemorative Issue* October **1998**, *44* (5), 2325–2383.
9. Gersho, A.; Gray, R.M. *Vector Quantization and Signal Compression*; Kluwer: Boston, 1992.
10. Cover, T.J.; Thomas, J.A. *Elements of Information Theory*; John Wiley & Sons: New York, 1991.
11. Cosman, P.; Gray, R.M.; Vetterli, M. Vector quantization of image subbands: A survey. IEEE Trans. Image Process. **1996**, *5* (2), 202–225.
12. Shapiro, J.M. Embedded image coding using zerotrees of wavelet coefficients. IEEE Trans. Signal Process. **1993**, *41* (12), 3445–3462.
13. Niblack, W. et al. The QBIC project: Querying images by content using color texture, and shape. In *Proceedings of the SPIE—The International Society for Optical Engineering, Storage and Retrieval for Image and Video Databases*, 1993; Vol. 1908, 173–187.
14. Hare, J.S. et al. Bridging the semantic gap in multimedia information retrieval: Top-down and bottom-up approaches. In *Mastering the Gap: From Information Extraction to Semantic Representation*, 3rd European Semantic Web Conference; Bouquet, P., Brunelli, R., Chanod, J.-P., Niederée, C., Stoermer, H., Eds.; 2006.
15. Smeulders, A. et al. Content-based image retrieval at the end of the early years. IEEE Trans. Pattern Anal. Mach. Intell. **2000**, *22* (12), 1449–1380.
16. Smith, J.R.; Chang, S.-F. VisualSeek: A fully automated content-based image query system. In *Proceedings of the ACM Multimedia* '96, Boston, November 18–22, 1996; 87–98.
17. Bach, J.R. et al. The Virage image search engine: An open framework for image management. In *Storage and Retrieval for Still Image Video Databases*, Proceedings of the SPIE—The International Society for Optical Engineering, 1996; Vol. 2670, 76–87.
18. Bergman, L.D. et al. Drag-and-drop multimedia: An interface framework for digital libraries. IJODL **1999**, *2* (2/3), 170–177, (Special Issue on User Interfaces for Digital Libraries).
19. Bergman, L.D. et al. SPIRE, a digital library for scientific information. IJODL **2000**, *3* (1), 85–99, (Special Issue on Tradition of Alexandrian Scholars).
20. Vermilyer, R. Intelligent user interface agents in content-based image retrieval. In *Proceedings of the 2006 IEEE SoutheastCon*, Memphis, TN, 2006; 136–142.

21. Zhou, X.S.; Huang, T.S. Relevance feedback in image retrieval: A comprehensive review. Multimedia Syst. **2003**, *8* (3), 536–544 (Special Issue on Content-Based Image Retrieval).
22. Castelli, V. et al. Search and progressive information retrieval from distributed image/video databases: The SPIRE project. In *Proceedings of the ECDL '98*, Crete, Greece, September 1998.
23. Belongie, S. et al. Color- and texture-based image segmentation using EM and its application to content-based image retrieval. In *Proceedings of the Sixth International Conference on Computer Vision*, January 1998.
24. Carson, C. et al. Region-based image query. In *Proceedings of the IEEE CVPR '97 Workshop on Content-Based Access of Image and Video Libraries*, Santa Barbara, CA, 1997.
25. Dempster, A.P.; Laird, N.M.; Rubin, D.B. Maximum likelihood from incomplete data via the EM algorithm. J. Roy. Stat. Soc. B **1977**, *39* (1), 1–38.
26. Vaidyanathan, P.P. Orthonormal and biorthonormal filter banks as convolvers, and convolutional coding gain. IEEE Trans. Signal Process. **1993**, *41* (6), 2110–2130.
27. Li, C.-S.; Turek, J.J.; Feig, E. Progressive template matching for content-based retrieval in earth observing satellite image databases. Proc. SPIE Photonic East **1995**, *2606*, 134–144.
28. Castelli, V. et al. Progressive search and retrieval in large image archives. IBM J. Res. Dev. March **1998**, *42* (2), 253–268.
29. Smith, J.R.; Chang, S.-F. Tools and techniques for color image retrieval. In *Proceedings of the SPIE Storage and Retrieval for Still Image Video Databases*, San Jose, CA, February 1996; Vol. 2670, 426–637.
30. Niblack, W. et al. The QBIC project: Querying images by content using color texture, and shape. IBM Res. J. **1993**, *9203* (81511).
31. Swain, M.J.; Ballard, D.H. Color indexing. Int. J. Comput. Vis. **1991**, *7* (1).
32. Gray, R.S. Content-based image retrieval: color and edges; Technical Report 95-252, Department of Computer Science, Dartmouth University: Dartmouth, MA, 1995.
33. Feig, E.; Li, C.-S. Computing image histograms from compressed data. In *Proceedings of the SPIE Electronic Imaging and Multimedia Systems*, Beijing, China, 1996; Vol. 2898, 118–124.
34. Itten, J. *Kunst der Farbe*; Otto Maier Verlag: Ravensburg, Germany, 1961 (in German).
35. Colombo, C.; Del Bimbo, A.; Pala, P. Semantics in visual information retrieval. IEEE Multimedia **1999**, *6* (3), 38–53.
36. Del Bimbo, A. et al. Visual querying by color perceptive regions. Pattern Recogn. **1998**, *31* (9), 1241–1253.
37. Gagalowicz, A.; Ma, S.D.; Tournier-Lasserve, C. Efficient models for color textures. In *Proceedings of the IEEE International Conference on Pattern Recognition, ICPR '86*, 1986; 412–414.
38. Hernandez, O.J.; Khotanzad, A. An image retrieval system using multispectral random field models, color, and geometric features. In *Proceedings of the 33rd Applied Imagery Pattern Recognition Workshop*, October 2004; 251–256.
39. Yu, H.; Li, M.; Zhang, H.; Feng, J. Color texture moment for content-based image retrieval. In *Proceedings of the IEEE Int. Conf. Image Processing, ICIP '02*, Rochester, NY, June 2002; 929–932.
40. Li, C.-S.; Chen, M.-S. Progressive texture matching for earth observing satellite image databases. In Proceedings of the SPIE on Multimedia Storage and Archiving Systems, Boston, November 18–19, 1996; Vol. 2916, 150–161.
41. Davis, L.S.; Johns, S.; Aggarwal, J.K. Texture analysis using generalized co-occurrence matrices. IEEE Trans, Pattern Anal. Mach. Intell. July **1979**, *1* (3), 251–259.
42. Haralick, R.M.; Shanmugam, K.; Dinstein, I. Texture features for image classification. IEEE Trans. Syst. Man. Cybernet. **1973**, *3*, 610–621.
43. Parkkinen, J.; Selkainaho, K.; Oja, E. Detecting texture periodicity from the co-occurrence matrix. Pattern Recogn. Lett. **1990**, *11*, 43–50.
44. Tamura, H.; Mori, S.; Yamawaki, T. Texture features corresponding to visual perception. IEEE Trans. Syst. Man. Cybern. **1978**, *8* (6), 460–473.
45. Smith, J.R.; Chang, S.-F. Quad-tree segmentation for texture-based image query. In *Proceedings of the ACM Multimedia '94*, San Francisco, October 15–20, 1994; 279–286.
46. Jain, A.K.; Farrokhnia, F. Unsupervised texture segmentation using Gabor filters. Pattern Recogn. **1991**, *24* (12), 1167–1186.
47. Li, C.-S.; Castelli, V. Deriving texture feature set for content-based retrieval of satellite image database. In *Proceedings of the IEEE International Conference on Image Processing, ICIP '97*, Santa Barbara, CA, October 26–29, 1997; 567–579.
48. Li, C.-S.; et al. Comparing texture feature sets for retrieving core images in petroleum applications. In *Proceedings of the SPIE Storage and Retrieval for Image and Video Databases VII*, San Jose, CA, January 1999; Vol. 3656, 2–11.

49. Ma, W.Y.; Manjunath, B.S. Texture features and learning similarity. In *Proceedings of the IEEE Computer Vision and Pattern Recognition, CVPR '96*, San Francisco, June 18–20, 1996; 425–430.
50. Ma, W.Y.; Manjunath, B.S. Edge flow: A framework of boundary detection and image segmentation. In *Proceedings of the IEEE Computer Vision and Pattern Recognition, CVPR '97*, 1997; 744–749.
51. Guyon, X. *Random Fields on a Network: Modeling, Statistics, and Applications*; Springer Verlag: New York, 1995.
52. Chen, C.C.; Dubes, R.C. Experiments in fitting discrete Markov random fields to textures. In *Proceedings of the IEEE Computer Vision and Pattern Recognition, CVPR '89*, 1989; 298–303.
53. Hassner, M.; Sklansky, J. Markov random field models of digitized image texture. In *Proceedings of the IEEE International Conference on Pattern Recognition, ICPR '78*, 1978; 538–540.
54. Hassner, M.; Sklansky, J. The use of Markov random fields as models of texture. Comput. Graphics Image Process. **1980**, *12*, 357–370.
55. Chellappa, R.; Chatterjee, S. Classification of textures using Gaussian Markov random fields. IEEE Trans. Acoust., Speech Signal Process. **1985**, *33*, 959–963.
56. Cohen, F.S.; Fan, Z.; Attali, S. Automated inspection of textile fabrics using textural models. IEEE Trans. Pattern Anal. Mach. Intell. **1991**, *13* (8), 803–808.
57. Solberg, A.H.S.; Taxt, T.; Jain, A.K. A Markov random field model for classification of multisource satellite imagery. IEEE Trans. Geosci. Remote Sens. **1996**, *34* (1), 100–113.
58. Chellappa, R.; Chatterjee, S.; Bagdazian, R. Texture synthesis and compression using Gaussian-Markov random field models. IEEE Trans. Syst. Man Cybernet. March **1985**, *15* (2), 298–303.
59. Chellappa, R.; Kashyap, R.L. Texture synthesis using 2-D noncausal autoregressive models. IEEE Trans. Acoust. Speech Signal Process. **1985**, *33*, 194–203.
60. Bouman, C.A.; Shapiro, M. A multiscale random field model for Bayesian image segmentation. IEEE Trans. Image Process. March **1994**, *3* (2), 162–177.
61. Chen, J.L.; Kunda, A. Automatic unsupervised texture segmentation using Hidden Markov Model. In *Proceedings of the IEEE ICASSP '93*, 1993; 21–24.
62. Goktepe, M.; Yalabik, N.; Atalay, V. Unsupervised segmentation of gray level Markov model textures with hierarchical self organizing maps. In *Proceedings of the IEEE International Conference on Pattern Recognition, ICPR '96*, Vienna, Austria, 1996; D7M.3.
63. Hansen, F.R.; Elliott, H. Image segmentation using simple Markov field models. Comput. Graphics Image Process. **1982**, *20*, 101–132.
64. Noda, H.; Shirazi, M.N.; Kawaguchi, E. A MRF model-based method for unsupervised textured image segmentation. In *Proceedings of the IEEE International Conference on Pattern Recognition, ICPR '96*, 1996; B94.2.
65. Santini, S.; Jain, R. Similarity measures. IEEE Trans. Pattern Anal. Mach. Intell. **1999**, *21* (9), 871–883.
66. Kimia, B.B. Shape representation for image retrieval. In *Image Databases, Search and Retrieval of Digital Imagery*; Castelli, V., Bergman, L.D., Eds.; John Wiley & Sons: New York, 2002; Chap. 13, 345–372.
67. Carson, C. et al. Blobworld: A system for region-based image indexing and retrieval (long version); Technical report UCB/CSD-99-1041; EECS Department, University of California: Berkeley, CA, 1999.
68. Antani, S.; Lee, D.J.; Longa, L.R.; Thoma, G.R. Evaluation of shape similarity measurement methods for spine x-ray images. J. Vis. Commun. Image Repres. September **2004**, *15* (3), 285–302.
69. Jain, A.; Lin, H.; Bolle, R. On-line fingerprint verification. IEEE Trans. Pattern Anal. Mach. Intell. **1997**, *19* (4), 302–314.
70. Eakins, J.P.; Boardman, J.M.; Shields, K. Retrieval of trade mark images by shape feature-the ARTISAN project. In *Proceedings of the IEE Colloquium on Intelligent Image Databases*, May 1996; 1–6.
71. Icke, I. Content based 3d shape retrieval a survey of state of the art. Pattern Recognition Laboratory, The Graduate Center, City University of New York (http://www.cs.gc.cuny.edu/icke/academic/2ndexam.pdf), November 2004.
72. Jaimes, A.; Chang, S.-F. A conceptual framework for indexing visual information at multiple levels. In *Proceedings of the SPIE—The International Society for Optical Engineering, Internet Imaging*, San Jose, CA, January 2000; Vol. 3964, 2–15.
73. Haering, N.; da Vitoria Lobo, N. Features and classification methods to locate deciduous trees in images. Comput. Vis. Image Und. July/August **1999**, *75* (1/2), 133–149.
74. Forsyth, D.A.; Fleck, M.M. Body plans. In *Proceedings of the IEEE Computer Vision and Pattern Recognition*, CVPR '97, 1997.
75. Vailaya, A. et al. Content-based hierarchical classification of vacation images. In *Proceedings of the IEEE International Conference on Multimedia Computing and Systems*, Florence, Italy, June 7–11, 1999; 518–523.

76. Li, J.; Wang, J.Z. Automatic linguistic indexing of pictures by a statistical modeling approach. IEEE Trans. Pattern Anal. Mach. Intell. **2003**, *25* (9), 1075–1088.
77. Li, J.; Wang, J.Z. Real-time computerized annotation of pictures. IEEE Trans. Pattern Anal. Mach. Intell. **2008**, *30* (6), 985–1002.
78. Li, J.; Wang, J.Z. Alpir™ automatic photo tagging and visual image search. Online Demo.
79. Liu, Y. et al. A survey of content-based image retrieval with high-level semantics. Pattern Recogn. **2007**, *40* (1), 262–282.
80. Wei, W.; Barnaghi, P.M. Semantic support for medical image search and retrieval. In *BIEN'07: Proceeding of the Fifth IASTED International Conference*, Anaheim, CA, 2007. ACTA Press, Anaheim, CA, 2007; 315–319.
81. Lehmann, T. et al. Automatic categorization of medical images for content-based retrieval and data mining. Com-put. Med. Imag. Grap. **2005**, *29* (2–3), 143–155.
82. Müller, H. et al. A review of content-based image retrieval systems in medical applications—Clinical benefits and future directions. Int. J. Med. Inform. **2003**, *73* (1), 1–23.
83. Castelli, V. et al. Progressive classification in the compressed domain for large EOS satellite databases. In *Proceedings of the IEEE ICASSP '96*, May 1996; Vol. 4, 2201–2204.
84. Fagin, R. Fuzzy queries in multimedia database systems. In *Proceedings of the 17th ACM Symposium on Principles of Database Systems, PODS '98*, Seattle, WA, June 1–3, 1998; ACM Press: New York, 1998; 1–10.
85. Carey, M.J. et al. Towards heterogeneous multimedia information systems: The Garlic approach. In *Proceedings of the Fifth International Workshop on Research Issues in Data Engineering: Distributed Object Management*, 1995; 124–131.
86. Cody, W. et al. Querying multimedia data from multiple repositories by content, the Garlic project. In *Proceedings of the Third Working Conference on Visual Database Systems*, 1995.
87. Kilr, G.J.; Yuan, B. *Fuzzy Sets and Fuzzy Logic, Theory and Applications*; Prentice Hall: Upper Saddle River, NJ, 1995.
88. Zadeh, L.A. Fuzzy sets. Inform. Control **1965**, *8* (3), 338–353.
89. Fagin, R. Combining fuzzy information from multiple systems. In *Proceedings of the 15th ACM Symposium on Principles of Database Systems, PODS '96*, Montreal, Canada, June 3–5, 1996; ACM Press: New York, 1996; 216–226.
90. Li, C.-S. et al. Sequential processing for content-based retrieval of composite objects. In *Proceedings of the SPIE Storage and Retrieval for Image and Video Databases VI*, San Jose, CA, January 24–30, 1998; Vol. 3312, 2–13.
91. Li, C.-S. et al. Framework for efficient processing of content-based fuzzy Cartesian queries. In *Proceedings of the SPIE Storage and Retrieval for Media Databases*, 2000; Vol. 3972, 64–75. Also available as IBM Research Report RC21640, January 11, 2000.
92. Li, C.-S. et al. Progressive content-based retrieval of image and video with adaptive and iterative refinement. U.S. Patent 05,734,893, March 31, 1998.
93. Tao, J.; Tan, T. Affective computing: A review. In Affective Computing and Intelligent Interaction, *Lecture Notes in Computer Science*, Springer, Berlin/Heidelberg, 2005; Vol. 3784, 239–247.
94. Li, H.; Li, J.; Song, J.; Chen, J. Fuzzy mapping from image texture to affective thesaurus. In *Bio-Inspired Computational Intelligence and Applications, Lecture Notes in Computer Science*, Springer, Berlin/Heidelberg, 2007; Vol. 4688, 357–367.
95. Wu, Q.; Zhou, C.; Wang, C. Content-based affective image classification and retrieval using support vector machines. In Affective Computing and Intelligent Interaction, *Lecture Notes in Computer Science*, Springer, Berlin/Heidelberg, 2005; Vol. 3784, 239–247.
96. Bianchi-Berthouze, N.; Kato, T. K-dime: An adaptive system to retrieve images from the web using subjective criteria. In DNIS '00: Proceedings of the International Workshop on Databases in Networked Information Systems, London, Springer-Verlag, 2000; 157–172.
97. Schatz, B. et al. Federating diverse collections of scientific literature. IEEE Comput. Mag. **1996**, *29* (5), 28–36.
98. Li, V.O.K.; Wanjiun, L. Distributed multimedia systems. Proc. IEEE **1997**, *85* (7), 1063–1108.
99. Wactlar, H.D.; Kanade, T.; Smith, M.A.; Stevens, S.M. Intelligent access to digital video: Informedia project. IEEE, Comput. Mag. **1996**, *29* (5), 46–52.
100. Collins, L.M. et al. Collaborative eScience libraries. Int. J. Digit. Libr. **2007**, *7* (1), 31–33.
101. Candela, L. et al. Diligent: Integrating digital library and grid technologies for a new Earth observation research infrastructure. Int. J. Digit. Libr. **2007**, *7* (1), 59–80.
102. Digital Library Goes e-Science (DLSci06), Workshop Held in Conjunction with ECDL 2006, Alicante, Spain, September 17–22, 2006.

103. Wilensky, R. Towards work-centered digital information services. IEEE Comput. Mag. **1996**, *29* (5), 37–43.
104. Smith, T.R. A digital library for geographically referenced materials. IEEE Comput. Mag. **1996**, *29* (5), 54–60.
105. Atkins, D.E. et al. Toward inquiry-based education through interacting software agents. IEEE Comput. Mag. May **1996**, *29* (5), 69–76.
106. Paepcke, A. et al. Using distributed objects for digital library interoperability. IEEE Comput. Mag. **1996**, *29* (5), 61–68.
107. Mintzer, F. Developing digital libraries of cultural content for internet access. IEEE Commun. Mag. **1999**, *37* (1), 72–78.
108. D'Alessandro, M.P. et al. The Iowa Health Book: Creating, organizing and distributing a digital medical library of multimedia consumer health information on the internet to improve rural health care by increasing rural patient access to information. In *Proceedings of the Third Forum on Research and Technology Advances in Digital Libraries ADL '96*, 1996; 28–34.
109. Lowe, H.J. et al. The image engine HPCC project, a medical digital library system using agent-based technology to create an integrated view of the electronic medical record. In *Proceedings of the 3rd Forum on Research and Technology Advances in Digital Libraries, ADL '96*, Washington, DC, May 1996; 45–56.
110. Macowsky, A. *Medical Imaging Systems*; Prentice Hall, Englewood Cliffs, NJ, 1983.
111. Schiller, A.; Fink, G. Radiology resources on the net: So many images, so little time. Emerg. Med. News **2004**, *26* (3), 38–40.
112. Petrick, N. et al. An adaptive density-weighted contrast enhancement filter for mammographic breast mass detection. IEEE Trans. Med. Imaging **1996**, *15* (1), 59–67.
113. Strickland, R.N.; Han, H. Wavelet transform matched filters for the detection and classification of microcalcifications in mammography. In *Proceedings of the IEEE International Conference on Image Processing, ICIP '95*, Washington, DC, October 23–26, 1995; Vol. 1, 422–425.
114. Christoyianni, I.; Dermatas, E.; Kokkinakis, G. Neural classification of abnormal tissue in digital mammography using statistical features of the texture. In *Proceedings of the Sixth IEEE International Conference on Electronics, Circuits and Systems, ICECS '99*, September 1999; 117–120.
115. Richards, J.A. *Remote Sensing Digital Image Analysis, an Introduction*, 2nd Ed.; Springer-Verlag: New York, 1993.
116. Bergman, L.D. et al. PetroSPIRE: A multi-modal content-based retrieval system for petroleum applications. In *Multimedia Storage and Archiving System*, Boston, 1999; Vol. 3846.
117. Castelli, V.; Bergman, L.D., Eds. *Image Databases, Search and Retrieval of Digital Imagery*; John Wiley & Sons: New York, 2002.
118. Chen, Y.; Li, J.; Wang, J.Z. *Machine Learning and Statistical Modeling Approaches to Image Retrieval*; Springer, 2004.
119. Feng, D.D.; Siu, W.C.; Zhang, H., Eds. *Multimedia Information Retrieval and Management*; Springer: Berlin, 2003.
120. Marques, O.; Furht, B. *Content-Based Image and Video Retrieval (Multimedia Systems and Applications)*; Springer: Berlin, 2002.
121. Wilhelmus, A.; Smeulders, M.; Jain, R., Eds. *Image Databases and Multi-media Search*; World Scientific: Singapore, 1997.
122. Sagarmay, D., Ed. *Multimedia Systems and Content-Based Image Retrieval*; Idea Group, Inc., 2004.
123. Eakins, J.; Graham, M. Content-based image retrieval. http://www.jisc.ac.uk/publications/publications/contentimagefinalreport.aspx 39, JISC (October 1999).
124. Datta, R.; Joshi, D.; Li, J.; Wang, J.Z. Image retrieval: Ideas, influences, and trends of the new age. ACM Comput. Surv. April **2008**, *40* (2), 1–60.
125. Venters, C.C.; Cooper, M. A review of content-based image retrieval systems. http://www.jisc.ac.uk/publications/publications/contentreviewfinalreport.aspx, JISC, June 2000.
126. Kherfi, M.L.; Ziou, D.; Bernardi, A. Image retrieval from the World Wide Web: Issues, techniques, and systems. ACM Comput. Surv. **2004**, *36* (1), 35–67.

BIBLIOGRAPHY

We conclude this entry by listing additional resources for the interested readers. In recent years, several books have been published on the topic of still-image repositories, search, and retrieval.

A general introduction can be found in Chen,[117] while Feng[118] describes a Machine Learning approach to CBIR. Numerous books on multimedia repositories contain sections on image collections, including Marques[119] and Wilhelmus.[120] In addition to these publications, which can be used as introductions to the topic or as textbooks, several collections of selected papers have appeared in the literature.[121,122] Numerous articles review current results in CBIR,[123,24] CBIR systems,[125] shape-based retrieval,[71] semantic-level retrieval,[79] as well as for applications such as CBIR for medical imaging[82] and retrieval from the World Wide Web.[126]

29 Music Information Retrieval

Kjell Lemström and George Tzanetakis

CONTENTS

INTRODUCTION

The spread of the Internet and the creation of the World Wide Web have offered exciting real-world problems for existing and novel theories and methods. Among the large amount of digital documents publicly available, there is a large number of musical documents, in various formats, that should be retrievable in musically pertinent and user-friendly ways.

This entry focuses on content-based techniques, as opposed to the text-based methods, developed for retrieving music from large databases of polyphonic music. In a typical setting the query pattern to be searched for is a short musical excerpt that can be given, e.g., by humming or playing an instrument, or by recording a snippet from a sound recording. In this entry, we divide the techniques in two categories depending on whether they are based on symbolic or audio representation. In general, the symbolic methods are appropriate for a *query-by-humming* application, where an occurrence of a query forms only some portion of the whole polyphonic structure of the matching part in the database. The audio methods are used for *query-by-example* applications, where the query constitutes a possibly distorted snippet taken from the underlying database.

The symbolic techniques developed for content-based music retrieval are based either on string or on geometric representation. The "Symbolic Techniques" section gives an overview on techniques and results that are obtained by using these frameworks. In the section "Audio Techniques," we provide a survey of different content-based problems using audio representations that have been proposed. The survey is structured based on the type of query used, the information extracted and the specificity of the desired results. Finally in the section "Bridging Symbolic and Audio

Content-Based Music Retrieval," we conclude the entry by some ideas on how to bridge the gap between the symbolic and audio techniques.

SYMBOLIC TECHNIQUES

Symbolic music representations, such as the Western Common Music Notation (CMN) or Music Instrument Digital Interface (MIDI), are most often used for storage purposes: they include detailed information for artists or, in the case of MIDI for musical instruments, how to perform the stored music. Although performances differ from each other, the listener still perceives them as the same musical works. This justifies the use of symbolic representations for content-based music retrieval purposes. The advantage of performing retrieval in the syntax level (i.e., using a symbolic representation as opposed to audio) is the possibility to search for occurrences that are embedded in the music structure, such as a melody line in a polyphonic orchestration—the occurrence may even be distributed among several instruments of the orchestration.

Choosing the representation. There are several important, intrinsic features of music and the application that need to be taken into account to have effective retrieval results, the most important being

1. The inherent polyphony of real-world music
2. Location invariance to allow occurrences to reside anywhere in the database, not just in incipits (the "opening line" of the music; usually the first four bars of the melody)
3. Transposition invariance to allow matching music in different keys
4. Time scaling invariance to allow matching music in different tempi
5. Tolerance to "noise" caused by various sources (the database may contain unexpected musical embellishments, a conversion process may have caused errors, the hummed/played query pattern contains inaccuracies)

Together these five features form a complex problem field and they all have to be considered already when choosing a suitable representation.

Previously, the symbolic representations used for content-based music retrieval have been based either on string[1–4] or geometric representations.[5–10] Of the five aforementioned properties, the first one has the strongest impact on choosing an appropriate representation. As opposed to monophonic music, which is relatively naturally representable by using string representation, casting polyphonic music to linear strings[11–14] is often not effective.[15] However, string matching has been adopted to some restricted cases, as discussed below. When using the string matching framework, the properties (3) and (4) are dealt with at the representational level, the remaining ones by the methods solving the specific problems.

The geometric representations, on the other hand, accommodate equally and naturally to both monophonic and polyphonic music. This discrimination has led most of the recent studies on symbolic content-based music retrieval to focus on the geometric representations. With the geometric framework the properties (2–5) are typically dealt with the methods solving the problems.

USING STRING MATCHING FRAMEWORK

Problem Definition

When using the string matching framework, the polyphonic content-based music retrieval problem is casted to a slightly modified string matching problem. In this case the usual setting is such that the pattern to be searched for is monophonic while the database to be searched is polyphonic. To this end, let us represent both the musical pattern $P = P_1,\ldots, P_m$ and the database $T = T_1,\ldots, T_n$ as strings of sets of integers. Thus, in a string S (corresponding either to P or T) each S_i models a chord and is formally a subset of an integer alphabet Σ. Let us denote by q the size of the largest chord in S, i.e., $q = \max\{|S_i| \mid 1 \leq i \leq m, n\}$. The polyphonic structure may consist of K parallel monophonic voices. In such a case each Si consists of pairs $\langle k,h \rangle_i \in K \times \Sigma$ in order to be able to track the voicing information. Naturally, if $q = 1$, S is monophonic; otherwise it is polyphonic. Each S_i thus corresponds to a chord of notes, and is comprised of notes having their onsets simultaneously. This representation is also known as onset-based representation.[15]

The content-based music information retrieval (MIR) problem is as follows. Given a long database $T = T_1,\ldots,T_n$ and a relatively short music query pattern $P = P_1,\ldots,P_m$, the task is to find all locations in T where P occurs. Here an occurrence might mean an exact, transposed, or approximate occurrence.

We define that there is an *exact occurrence* of P at position j, if $P_i \in T_{j+i-1}$ holds for $i = 1,\ldots,m$. Furthermore, there is a *transposition invariant occurrence* of P at position j, if there is an integer d such that each $(P_i + d) \in T_{j+i-1}$.

When both P and T are monophonic, an exact and a transposition invariant occurrence means that $P_i = T_{j+i-1}$ and $(P_i + d) = T_{j+i-1}$ for each i, respectively. A k approximate occurrence of P is found if there is a subsequence P' of T, such that P' can be obtained from P by using k or fewer editing operations. An *approximate transposition invariant occurrence* is defined accordingly.

Results

When dealing with the polyphonic content-based music retrieval problem, in some limited cases it may suffice to heuristically reduce the polyphonic music structure in a monophonic one and then apply classical string matching algorithms. See, for instance Blackburn and DeRoure[16] and Uitdenbogerd and Zobel[17] for such reduction heuristics. The power of the onset-based representation becomes evident when searching for *distributed occurrences* of the pattern. In such a case the pattern appears in consecutive positions within the database but may jump across the voices (or the voicing information is simply absent).

If transposition invariance is not needed the edit distance framework can be used in a straitforward manner.[11,12,18] The combinatorial explosion in the transposition invariant case can be avoided by chopping the possibilities in n-grams (strings of length n).[19] When the degree of polyphony is high, however, this may prove not to be an efficient solution because of the large number of generated n-grams. Another possibility is to split the pattern to bare intervals that are searched individually.[13] This requires a two-pronged search: the candidates found in the first phase have to be examined in another phase to discard discontinuous patterns (the subsequent interval does not begin in the note where the former ends). When the voicing information is available, one can also look for a transposition invariant occurrence that minimizes the number of jumps across the voices.[14]

Using Geometric Framework

Problem Definition

Let us now introduce the geometric framework and consider the content-based music retrieval problems as point pattern matching ones. The points are real values in a d-dimensional real space $\mathbb{R}^d$; at times the space needs to be discretized to the integer space $\mathbb{Z}^d$ for efficiency purposes.[5,7] In a typical case, music is represented by using two dimensions: one (horizontal) dimension represents the note *onset time* (i.e., when the associated note is to be invoked), the other (vertical) gives the *pitch* (i.e., the perceived height of the note) information. To consider the note durations, several extensions to this basic point setting have been suggested[6,9,20] (see below).

In this way, the symbolic content-based music retrieval problems can be seen as special cases of point pattern matching (an excellent tutorial to point pattern matching can be found in Mäkinen and Ukkonen).[21] Let us consider this more formally. Given two point sets P and T, where typically

$|P| \ll |T|$, both being finite subsets of $\mathbb{R}^d(\mathbb{Z}^d)$, the general task is to search for pairs (f, τ) where f is a transformation ($f \in F$) and $\tau \subset T$, such that $f(P)$ matches τ. To take care of the properties (2) and (3) (cf. above), the set of allowed transformations includes *translations*, denoted by F_t, where a constant vector is added to each point in P. Time scaling invariance (property (4)) is obtained by including *scales*, denoted by Fs, in which case distances to a common origin are multiplied by a constant. Depending on the application, a *match* may be exact or approximate; in the latter case an appropriate similarity measure needs to be selected. Please note that by definition, as opposite to the string matching case, an exact match allows "extra intervening" elements in T.

The most typical problems are exact point pattern matching and largest common pointset matching under translations. In *exact point pattern matching under translations* the quest is to find $f \in F_t$ such that $f(P) \subset T$. The straightforward way to include approximation in this is to allow a minimum number of unmatched points of P. To that end, the *largest common pointset matching under translations* looks for the largest $\tau \in T$ where $\tau \subset f(P)$ for some $f \in F_t$. The respective problems including scalings are defined analogously.

Results

In the following we assume that P and T are lexicographically ordered. (Let $(a,b),(a',b') \in \mathbb{R}^2$. In a *lexicographic order* vector $(a,b) \leq (a',b')$ if and only if $a < a$ or ($a = a'$ and $b \leq b'$).) If that is not the case, they can be ordered in $O(|P| \log |P|)$ time and $O(|T| \log |T|)$ time, respectively. Moreover, recall that typically $|P| \ll |T|$.

Matching under translations. The exact point pattern matching problem under translations is solvable in $O(|P||T|)$ time and $O(|P|)$ working space.[6] However, the solution has an expected running time of $O(|T|)$. For deterministic point pattern matching algorithms quadratic running times seem to be the lower bound.

THEOREM 1: THE LARGEST COMMON POINTSET PROBLEM UNDER TRANSLATIONS IS 3SUM-HARD

If we assume that $|T| = n$ and $|P| = \Theta(|T|)$, according to Theorem 1 an $o(|P||T|)$ time algorithm for largest common pointset would mean that there is an $o(n^2)$ algorithm for the 3SUM problem, which would be an unexpected theoretic breakthrough. (Given n numbers, the 3SUM problem is to find whether there are three numbers a, b, and c among them for which $a + b + c = 0$ holds.)

A straightforward algorithm solving the largest point pattern matching under translations runs in $O(|P||T|\log(|P||T|))$ time.[22] The algorithm calculates translation vectors from each point in the pattern P to each point in T. The translations are subsequently sorted in order to find the translation giving the maximal occurrence. With a better sorting routine the running time can be improved to $O(|P||T|\log|P|)$.[6]

To date, no deterministic algorithm is known to solve the problem in a quadratic time. It may be that the largest point pattern matching under translations is also SORTING X + Y-hard, in which case Ukkonen et al.'s algorithm may already be an optimal solution. (Given two sets X and Y of n numbers, the SORTING X + Y problem is to sort the set $X + Y = \{x + y \mid x \in X, y \in Y\}$.)

By accepting that some of the true occurrences may not be found, faster solutions are obtainable. To this end one can either use subquadratic time approximation algorithms,[8,9] or a solution based on discretized values and an indexing schema similar to inverted files used for natural language information retrieval.[5]

Indexing. Exact solutions based on indexing face two major problems; let us assume an index T for T that is built in time $f(n)$. First, Theorem 1 implies that it is 3SUM-hard to create largest common pointset queries using T, working in $g(m)$ time and holding $f(n) + g(m) = o(n^2)$. Second, the number of the possible translation vectors is exponential in the length of T and, therefore, a total index would also require exponential space.

In addition to the inverted file approach, recently two more indexing schemes have been proposed. The first uses a *metric index* working under earth moving distance.[20] However, it seems difficult with this approach to support translations or partial matching with polyphony. Another method is to use a sparse index and a statistical filtering approach to search for promising areas in T. This approach relies heavily on the power of filtration but seems to be several orders of magnitude faster than the online (nonindexing) algorithms, both in the exact point pattern matching and in the largest common pointset problem.[10]

Note durations. There are several suggestions on how to equip symbolic representations with note durations. A natural idea is to replace the points (representing the note onsets) with horizontal line segments, where the length of the segment represents the duration of the corresponding note.[6] Then the task becomes to search for a translation so that the segment patterns, representing P and T, intersect as much as possible. Interestingly enough, this modified problem is solvable in $O(|P||T| \log (|P||T|))$ time, and if reduced to integer space, in $O(|P||T| \log |P|)$ time.[6] The space reduction also enables the use of a more general distance function considering consonance/dissonance aspects of the music in hand.[7] Other possibilities include the use of earth moving distance when the durations are represented as the weight of the points[20] or the use of a third dimension to represent the durational information.[9]

Matching under translations and scaling. For the moment, it has not been widely studied how to have both translation and scaling invariance at the same time. The problem in combining these two invariances is due to that the former is an additive, while the latter is a multiplicative property. Recall that the translation invariance actually captures two features: transposition and location invariances. The obvious way to achieve scaling invariance would be the use of a logarithmic encoding of the time axis. That way, however, only occurrences starting at the origin chosen for the logarithmic scale would be found thus losing the location invariance.

A naïve solution for solving largest common pointset problem under translations and scaling works in time $O(|P|^3 \; |T|^3)$. First, the translation vectors are calculated, in a lexicographical order, from each point in the pattern to each point in the database. This gives $|P|$ increasing sequences of vectors (pairs of real values) each of length $|T|$. Then, each possible time scaling value is selected by choosing two vectors from two distinct sequences; there are $O(|P|^2 \; |T|^2)$ possibilities in this choice. For each time scaling value, the maximum co-occurrence between pattern and database needs to be determined. This can be done by checking whether each of the remaining $|P| - 2$ sequences (each containing $|T|$ vectors) includes a vector that accords with the chosen scaling factor. This is feasible in $O(|P||T|)$ time. These found candidates are to be verified by checking that the associated pitch intervals also match.

In order to avoid the high polynomials in the running time, it has been suggested to consider only those scalings that appear within a window whose width is chosen independently of the size of P and T.[9]

AUDIO TECHNIQUES

A wide variety of different retrieval scenarios have been explored using audio-based techniques. In many cases they can be formulated as "query-by-example" applications in which the user provides a possibly distorted snippet and looks for similar music pieces in a large collection. Even for the cases where the "query-by-example" view is not a perfect fit it is a reasonable approximation. For example, genre or style classification can be formulated as a retrieval problem where given a piece of music or a genre label the system returns other pieces in the same genre or style. In addition even in the cases of systems with no notion of a query such as audio-based music browsing systems based on exploration many of the underlying techniques and algorithms are the same.

A rough taxonomy of audio-based MIR systems can be created along the following major "dimensions": query type, extracted information, and specificity. Although for presentation purposes we describe these various stages and types of information separately, successful MIR systems typically utilize multiple of these stages and representations. The citations provided are mainly representative of existing research and its diversity rather than being an exhaustive list.

Query Type

Probably the most common type of query is a piece of music in audio format (query-by-example). The goal of the MIR system is to retrieve other pieces of music from a large collections that sound "similar" to the example query. This problem is typically formulated as a nearest neighbor problem between audio content representations which are described in more detail below. Other query possibilities are based on metadata such as genre,[23] style,[24] mood,[25] or artist name.[26] These problems are typically formulated as classification problems and solved using a supervised learning approach. In such an approach the MIR system is "trained" to classify music pieces it has not encountered before by analyzing music pieces that have been labeled by a human. This is done in order to create statistical models that can predict the correct label with high accuracy for data that has not been encountered before. A variety of such "classifiers" have been proposed including Gaussian mixture models, decision trees, artificial neural networks (ANNs), and support vector machines (SVMs). More details can be found in textbook such as Theodoridis and Koutroumbas.[27]

Although not as explored as the previous two approaches to queries another interesting possibility is for the user to "perform" some aspect of the desired returned results. Examples of such "performed" queries include beat-boxing,[28] humming,[29,30] singing,[30] tempo by tapping, or even matching the retrieved music to the speed of jogging and more generally specific exercise goals.[31]

Representations and Extracted Information

A variety of different sources of information can be used as the basis for creating audio music retrieval systems. To some extent the traditional musical aspects of melody, harmony, rhythm, and instrumentation have inspired similar types of audio analysis. The most direct modeling is through sequences of feature vectors that statistically represent the time varying timbral characteristics of a music piece. Frequently features proposed for speech recognition such as the Mel-Frequency Cepstral Coefficients (MFCCs)[32] are utilized. MFCCs summarize spectral information (the energy distribution of different frequencies) by taking into account the characteristics of the human auditory system. Such features depend on the instrumentation of a piece, how the timbral "texture" changes over time as well as how humans perceive this information.

In other cases, for example in cover song identification or automatic chord detection, it is desired to have a representation that is related to the pitch content of the music rather than the specifics of the instruments and voices that are playing. Although a full music score generated by an automatic transcriptive system could be used, unfortunately current transcription technology is not robust enough to be used reliably. Instead the most common pitch content representation is the Pitch and Pitch Class Profile (other alternative names used in literature are pitch histograms and chroma vectors). The pitch profile measures the occurrence of specific discrete musical pitches in a music segment and the pitch class profile considers all octaves equivalent essentially folding the pitch profile into 12 pitch classes. The pitch profile and pitch class profile are strongly related to the underlying harmony of the music piece. For example, a music segment in C major is expected to have many occurrences of the discrete pitch classes C, E, and G that form the C major chord.

Automatically extracting information related to rhythm is also an important component of audio MIR systems and has been an active area of research for over 20 years. A number of different subproblems within this area have been identified and explored. The most basic approach is finding the average tempo of the entire recording which can be defined as the frequency with which a human would tap their foot while listening to the same piece of music. The more difficult task of beat tracking consists of estimating time-varying tempo (frequency) as well as the locations in time of each beat (phase). Rhythmic information is hierarchical in nature and tempo is only one level of the hierarchy. Other levels frequently used and estimated by audio MIR systems are tatum (defined as the shortest commonly occurring time interval), beat or tactus (the preferred human tapping tempo), and bar or measure. For some MIR applications such as automatic classification it is possible to use a representation that provides a "salience" value for every possible tempo—e.g., the beat histograms described in Lu, Liu, and Zhang.[23]

Beat analysis approaches can be characterized in different ways. The first and most important distinction is by the type of input: most of the earlier beat tracking algorithms used a symbolic representation while audio signals have been used more recently. Symbolic algorithms can still be utilized with audio signals provided an intermediate transcription step is performed—typically audio onset detection. Another major distinction between the algorithms is the broad approach used which includes rule-based, autocorrelative, oscillating filters, histogramming, multiple agent, and probabilistic. A good overview of these approaches can be found in Chapter 4 of Klapuri and Davy.[33]

In many modern pop and rock recordings each instrument is recorded separately and the final mix is created by a recording producer/engineer(s) who among other transformations add effects such as reverb or filtering and spatialize individual tracks using stereo panning cues. Information about this production process can be reverse-engineered from the recording and although not strictly musical in the traditional sense can be used to build more effective MIR systems. For example, the amount of stereo panning and placement of sources remains constant in older recordings that tried to reproduce live performances compared to more recent recordings that would be almost impossible to realize in a live setting. Stereo panning features have recently been used for audio classification.[34]

Specificity

Given a particular query as well as a representation that captures relevant musical content information the user expects to retrieve a set of results that are "similar" in some way to the original query. A variety of different "similarities" have been explored with varying degrees of specificity. The most specific type of retrieval is audio fingerprinting where the goal is to return other instances of the exact same recording possibly subject to noise, minor edits (such as hand clapping removal), and audio compression.[35] Audio fingerprinting can be used for discovering copyright violations as well as associating metadata with music pieces. Remixes also correspond to the same underlying recorded performance, however, with the addition of extra musical materials such as drum loops and beats. In cover song identification the goal is to find other recordings of the same song that are performed by different musicians and instrumentation.[36] Content-based features for cover song identification must capture higher level musical constructs such as chord progressions and not be sensitive to instrumentation changes. Pitch and pitch class profiles are frequently used for this purpose. Artist,[24] album and genre similarity[23] although to some extent artificial tasks have the advantage that it is relatively straightforward to obtain ground-truth using existing metadata associated with files and therefore provide qualitative comparisons between different feature sets for describing audio content.

Specificity also relates to the amount of relevant results returned by the system which has implications about the methods used for matching. High-specificity results typically only return few relevant objects and therefore typically require calculating some kind of similarity or matching function between the query and all items in the collection. For low-specificity queries such as, e.g., based on a genre label the number of retrieved objects is typically much larger and therefore amendable to a different type of approach. When there is sufficient label data supervised machine learning techniques can be used to "train" statistical models of the data that can directly "classify" a music piece with a discrete category. Retrieval can then be more efficiently performed by randomly selecting pieces and returning as relevant only the ones that have the correctly assigned label avoiding full comparisons of the query with the entire collection.

Evaluation

Music information retrieval is a new growing research area and one of the major challenges that researchers have to face is evaluation. A lot of the early work in MIR and still a large part of existing work is performed with in-house datasets which makes systematic comparison of different approaches and algorithms impossible. Since 2005 MIREX (the MIR Evaluation eXchange), (http://www.music-ir.org/mirex2007/index.php/Main_Page) has been an effort to address this problem and provide comparisons and evaluations on common datasets. It is a community-based formal evaluation framework coordinated and managed by the International Music Information Retrieval Systems Evaluation Laboratory (IMIRSEL) at the University of Illinois at Urbana–Champaign (UIUC). Every year based on interest by the community a set of different tasks are proposed and research groups around the world submit their algorithms for comparative evaluation. One of the challenges with MIREX is that the datasets used are not provided to the participants and therefore all submitted algorithms must be executed at UIUC. This to some extent also prevents "overfitting" of submitted systems to the particular data collection. Browsing the results for each task is a great way to see what the current state of the art is and which groups are active in each task. There are multiple metrics that can be used to evaluate different systems even for the same task. In order to provide a rough picture of the current state of the art we provide representative results of the "best" performing systems for some of the MIREX audio-based tasks: genre classification 68.29% (7000 30-sec clips, 10 genres, MIREX2007), audio mood classification 61.50% (600 30-sec clips, 5 moods, MIREX2007), and audio artist identification 48.14% (30-sec clips, x artists, MIREX2007). All these results show percentage of clips correctly classified using a threefold cross-validation scheme where one-third of the data is used for testing and two-thirds for training and the process is repeated three times. Other results include audio music similarity 0.568 (100 random queries from 7000 songs, evaluated by human graders with a fine score between 0 and 10, score is the normalized sum of fine-grained human similarity decisions, MIREX 2007) and audio tempo extraction 94.29% (percentage of at least one tempo correct, MIREX 2006).

User Interfaces

Ultimately any MIR system needs to be used by humans. Music listening is a personal, subjective, enjoyable experience which automation should enhance and support. Therefore, the interaction with the user is a critical and essential component of MIR research that has been gaining importance as the field matures. One of the interesting directions in this area is content- and context-aware user interfaces that rely on automatic audio analysis techniques to inform the visual presentation of music collections. Such interfaces typically employ content-based audio feature extraction as described previously followed by dimensionality/visualization techniques that map the extracted features into visual attributes or positions of objects. Self-organized maps (SOM) are used in the Islands of Music system to map audio feature vectors to positions in a two-dimensional grid which is colored using a map metaphor.[37] Musicream utilizes principal component analysis (PCA) to assign colors to disks that represent individual music pieces and to adjust the playlist composition by using a water tap metaphor.[38]

BRIDGING SYMBOLIC AND AUDIO CONTENT-BASED MUSIC RETRIEVAL

The obvious possibility for bridging symbolic and audio content-based music retrieval is to use an automatic polyphonic music transcription method for extracting a symbolic representation from an audio signal, and then to apply some of the methods described in the section "Symbolic Techniques." Nevertheless, automatic polyphonic transcription is a hard technical problem for which there is no current general-purpose and reliable solution, although there has been remarkable progress in this direction.[33]

In some cases it is possible to combine symbolic and audio content-based music retrieval approaches without requiring a full music transcription system. For example, it is possible to use the monophonic reduction (recall from the section "Using String Matching Framework") in order to use symbolic queries for audio databases[39] or to retrieve a symbolic score from a score collection by using a polyphonic audio query.[40] More generally, the polyphonic audio-score alignment can be used to discover the respective parts of an audio signal and a score.[41,42] An *off-line* application for such an alignment is in the back-end of a query-by-humming system: the back-end is needed in order to playback the part of an audio file that corresponds to the found occurrence, in a symbolic music file, of a hummed query. *Online* audio-score alignment is needed in computer accompaniment.[43]

ACKNOWLEDGMENT

Kjell Lemström was supported by the Academy of Finland (Grant #108547).

REFERENCES

1. Mongeau, M.; Sankoff, D. Comparison of musical sequences. Comput. Humanities **1990**, *24*, 161–175.
2. Ghias, A.; Logan, J.; Chamberlin, D.; Smith, B.C. Query by humming—Musical information retrieval in an audio database. In ACM *Multimedia 95 Proceedings*, San Francisco, 1995; 231–236.
3. McNab, R.J.; Smith, L.A.; Bainbridge, D.; Witten, I.H. The New Zealand digital library MELody inDEX. D-Lib Mag. **1997**. http://www.dlib.org/dlib/may97/meldex/05witten.html.
4. Lemström, K. *String matching techniques for music retrieval*; Ph.D. thesis, University of Helsinki, Department of Computer Science, 2000. Report A-2000-4.
5. Clausen, M.; Engelbrecht, R.; Meyer, D.; Schmitz, J. Proms: A web-based tool for searching in polyphonic music. In *Proceedings of the International Symposium on Music Information Retrieval (ISMIR'00)*, Plymouth, MA, October 2000.
6. Ukkonen, E.; Lemström, K.; Mäkinen, V. Sweepline the music! In *Computer Science in Perspective—Essays dedicated to Thomas Ottmann*; vol. 2598, of Lecture Notes in Computer Science; Springer-Verlag, New York, 2003, 330–342.
7. Lubiw, A.; Tanur, L. Pattern matching in polyphonic music as a weighted geometric translation problem. In *Proceedings of the 5th International Conference on Music Information Retrieval*, Barcelona, October 2004; 289–296.
8. Clifford, R.; Christodoulakis, M.; Crawford, T.; Meredith, D.; Wiggins, G. A fast, randomised, maximal subset matching algorithm for document-level music retrieval. In *Proceedings of the 7th International Conference on Music Information Retrieval*, Victoria, BC, October 2006; 150–155.
9. Romming, C.A.; Selfridge-Field, E. Algorithms for polyphonic music retrieval: The hausdorff metric and geometric hashing. In *Proceedings of the 8th International Conference on Music Information Retrieval (ISMIR'07)*, Vienna, Austria, October 2007; 457–462.
10. Lemström, K.; Mikkilä, N.; Mäkinen, V. Fast index based filters for music retrieval. In *Proceedings of the ninth International Conference on Music Information Retrieval (ISMIR'08)*, Philadelphia, PA, September 2008; 677–682.
11. Bloch, J.J.; Dannenberg, R.B. Real-time accompaniment of polyphonic keyboard performance. In *Proceedings of the 1985 International Computer Music Conference*, Vancouver, BC, 1985; 279–290.
12. Holub, J.; Iliopoulos, C.S.; Mouchard, L. Distributed string matching using finite automata. J. Automata Lang. Comb. **2001**, *6* (2), 191–204.
13. Lemström, K.; Tarhio, J. Transposition invariant pattern matching for multi-track strings. Nord. J. Comput. **2003**, *10* (3), 185–205.
14. Lemström, K.; Mäkinen, V. On minimizing pattern splitting in multi-track string matching. J. Discr. Algorithm. **2005**, *3* (2–4), 248–266.
15. Lemström, K.; Pienimäki, A. On comparing edit distance and geometric frameworks in content-based retrieval of symbolically encoded polyphonic music. Musicae Scien-tiae **2007**, *4a*, 135–152.
16. Blackburn, S.; DeRoure, D. A tool for content based navigation of music. In *ACM Multimedia 98 Proceedings*, Bristol, 1998; 361–368.
17. Uitdenbogerd, A.L.; Zobel, J. Manipulation of music for melody matching. In *ACM Multimedia 98 Proceedings*, Bristol, 1998; 235–240.

18. Dovey, M.J. A technique for "regular expression" style searching in polyphonic music. In *The 2nd Annual International Symposium on Music Information Retrieval (ISMIR'01)*, Bloomington, IN, October 2001; 179–185.
19. Doraisamy, S.; Rüger, S.M. An approach towards a polyphonic music retrieval system. In *The 2nd Annual International Symposium on Music Information Retrieval (ISMIR'01)*, Bloomington, IN, October 2001; 187–193.
20. Typke, R. *Music retrieval based on melodic similarity*; Ph.D. thesis, Utrecht University, the Netherlands, 2007.
21. Mäkinen, V.; Ukkonen, E. Point pattern matching. In *Encyclopedia of Algorithms*; Kao, M., Ed.; Springer-Verlag: New York, 2008; 657–660.
22. Wiggins, G.A.; Lemström, K.; Meredith, D. SIA(M)ESE: An algorithm for transposition invariant, polyphonic content-based music retrieval. In *Proceedings of the International Conference on Music Information Retrieval (ISMIR '02)*, Paris, France, October 2002; 283–284.
23. Tzanetakis, G.; Cook, P. Musical genre classification of audio signals. IEEE Trans. Acoust. Speech Signal Process. **2002**, *10* (5), 293–302.
24. Li, T.; Ogihara, M. Music artist style identification by semi-supervised learning from both lyrics and content. In *ACM Int. Conf. on Multimedia*, New York, 2004; 364–367.
25. Lu, L.; Liu, D.; Zhang, H.J. Automatic mood detection and tracking of music audio signals. IEEE Trans. Acoust. Speech Signal Process. **2006**, *14* (1), 5–18.
26. Ellis, D.P.W.; Whitman, B.; Berenzweig, A.; Lawrence, S. The quest for ground truth in music artist similarity. In *International Conference on Music Information Retrieval (ISMIR)*, Paris, France, 2002.
27. Theodoridis, S.; Koutroumbas, K. *Pattern Recognition*, 3rd Ed.; Academic Press: London, 2006.
28. Kapur, A.; Benning, M.; Tzanetakis, G. Query by beat-boxing: music retrieval for the DJ. In *Proc. Int. Conf. on Music Information Retrieval (ISMIR)*, Barcelona, Spain, 2004.
29. Ghias, A.; Logan, J.; Chamberlin, D.; Smith, B. Query by Humming: Musical Information Retrieval in an Audio Database. ACM Multimedia **1995**; 213–236.
30. Dannenberg, R.B.; Birmingham, W.P.; Tzanetakis, G.; Meek, C.; Hu, N.; Pardo, B. The MUSART test-bed for query-by-humming evaluation. Comput. Music J. **2004**, *28* (2), 34–48.
31. Oliver, N.; Kreger-Stickles, L. Papa: Physiology and purpose-aware automatic playlist generation. In *Proc. Int. Conf. on Music Information Retrieval (ISMIR)*, Victoria, BC, 2007.
32. Davis, S.; Mermelstein, P. Experiments in syllable-based recognition of continuous speech. IEEE Trans. Acoust. Speech Signal Process **1980**, *28*, 357–366.
33. Klapuri, A.; Davy, M., Eds. *Signal Processing Methods for Music Transcription*; Springer: New York, 2006.
34. Tzanetakis, G.; Jones, R.; McNally, K. Stereo panning features for classifying recording production style. In *Proc. Int. Conf. on Music Information Retrieval (ISMIR)*, Vienna, Austria, 2007.
35. Cano, P.; Battle, E.; Kalker, T.; Haitsma, J. A review of algorithms for audio fingerprinting. In *Proc. Int. Workshop on Multimedia Signal Processing(MMSP)*, Virgin Islands, 2002.
36. Ellis, D.; Poliner, G. Identifying cover songs with chroma features and dnamic programming beat tracking. In *Proc. Int. Conf. on Audio, Speech and Signal Processing (ICASSP)*, Hawaii, 2007.
37. Pampalk, E.; Dixon, S.; Widmer, G. Exploring music collections by browsing different views. Comput. Music J. **2004**, *28* (2), 46–62.
38. Goto, M.; Goto, T. Musicream: New music playback interface for streaming, sticking, sorting and recalling musical pieces. In *Proc. Int. Conf. on Music Information Retrieval (ISMIR)*, London, 2005.
39. Suyoto, I.S.H.; Uitdenbogerd, A.L.; Scholer, F. Searching musical audio using symbolic queries. IEEE Trans. Audio Speech Lang. Process. **2008**, *16* (2), 372–381.
40. Pickens, J.; et al. Polyphonic score retrieval using polyphonic audio queries: A harmonic modeling approach. In *Proc. Int. Conf. on Music Information Retrieval (ISMIR)*, Paris, France, 2002.
41. Hu, N.; Dannenberg, R.B.; Tzanetakis, G. Polyphonic audio matching and alignment for music retrieval. In *Proc. IEEE Workshop on Applications of Signal Processing to Audio and Acoustics (WASPAA)*, Mohonk, NY, 2003.
42. Fremerey, C.; Müller, M.; Kurth, F.; Clausen, M. Automatic mapping of scanned sheet music to audio recordings. In *Proceedings of the ninth International Conference on Music Information Retrieval (ISMIR'08)*, Philadelphia, PA, September 2008; 413–418.
43. Dannenberg, R.; Raphael, C. Music score alignment and computer accompaniment. Commun. ACM **2006**, *49* (8), 38–43.

30 Web Social Mining

Hady W. Lauw and Ee-Peng Lim

CONTENTS

INTRODUCTION

Web social mining refers to conducting social network mining on Web data. Here, we adopt a very broad interpretation of Web data which includes Web sites, Web pages, Web servers' and applications' log data, as well as user-generated data from Web 2.0[1] sites. As increasing amount of user data is made available on the Web, it opens up a new world of opportunities for the Web data to be mined for realizing new applications and making existing ones work more intelligently.

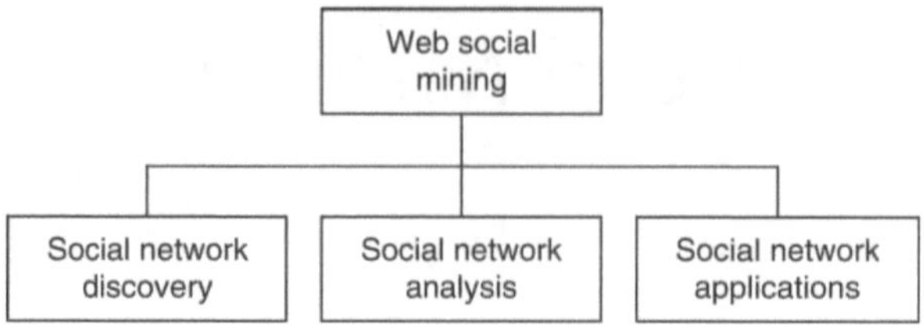

FIGURE 30.1 Web social mining topics.

As shown in Figure 30.1, Web social mining can be covered in three aspects, namely, *social network discovery, social network analysis*, and *social network applications*. Social network discovery refers to the construction of social networks linking users and sometimes other semantic entities together so as to study individual- or community-level properties in social network analysis. Patterns and knowledge about individuals and their communities are then incorporated into a wide range of social network applications.

While Web social mining poses more diverse opportunities for commercial applications, it has a deep root in social network analysis, a research discipline pioneered by social scientists. Hence, many of the models and techniques developed for social network analysis by social scientist are still applicable to Web social mining. On the other hand, Web social mining has added new challenges of automatically discovering social networks from the raw Web data which we call social network discovery.

The objective of this entry is to survey the essential concepts, problems, solution techniques, and applications of Web social mining. Hopefully, this will serve as a good introduction to Web social mining and a reference for future research and application development. In this entry, we give an overview of Web social mining by first examining the various forms of Web data available for social network mining. We then introduce a set of fundamental social network concepts. We review the Web social mining work in three subsequent sections, covering social network discovery, analysis, and application, respectively. Given that Web social mining covers a large set of concepts and topics, we shall only describe the key ones very briefly. Interested readers can refer to the provided references for more detailed information.

WEB DATA SOURCES

Web social mining can be conducted on a plethora of Web data embedding information about user–user and user–object links. Traditional Web data sources consists of Web pages from different sites, as well as the user browsing and search activity records logged by Web servers, Web applications (e.g., Web search engines, e-commerce sites, etc.), and Web browsers. Web page data are often regarded as unstructured content documents in which people, company, product, and other entity names may be found and their relationships can be extracted by text mining. In some Web sites, Web pages may be much more structured as the pages are directly generated from data maintained in relational or XML databases. An example of such Web sites is the DBLP Computer Science Bibliography (or simply DBLP, http://www.informatik.uni-trier.de/~ley/db/). DBLP provides bibliographic information of computer science publications organized by author, conference, journal, and subject. When Web sites contain structured content about semantic entities, their data can potentially be used for Web social mining. In the case of DBLP, there has been much social network mining research on coauthorships among researchers since one can easily extract the coauthors of publications.[2,3]

Web social mining actually begins to flourish when Web 2.0[1] becomes popular. Web 2.0 consists of Internet sites that offer Web users a range of services to interact with one another, sharing information, collaborating, and maintaining social relationships. As Web 2.0 sites attract huge population of users, there are also commercial incentives drawing upon the social relationships among users to further enhance user experiences at these sites, and/or to generate revenues from advertisement or product sales. This can be done by discovering the influence of users' opinions, providing new services to users (e.g., product recommendation), etc. In the following, we classify the existing Web 2.0 sites into four broad categories by the characteristics of their data.

1. ***Social networking sites.*** Examples of social network sites include Facebook (http://www.facebook.com), MySpace (http://www.myspace.com), and LinkedIn (http://www.linkedin.com). These are Web 2.0 sites allowing users to construct their personal profiles as well as to connect themselves with networks of friends. As the relationship links among users at these sites are user specified, they usually provide the ready social networks for further analysis. One can also correlate the network properties (e.g., authority) with the personal profile attributes.
2. ***Content sharing sites.*** Web 2.0 sites for content sharing include YouTube (http://www.youtube.com), Flickr (http://www.flickr.com), delicious (http://delicious.com), and many others. The content to be shared covers video, audio, photo images, social bookmarks, etc. Using these sites, users publish their content files making them easily accessed, commented, and rated by other users. These content sharing sites offer large set of content objects in addition to user data for constructing large social networks and determining the user interests and other properties in the networks.
3. ***Collaboration sites.*** There are several Web 2.0 sites offering collaboration services to users. Here we highlight two typical collaboration examples, namely Wikipedia and community question answering (QA) portals, e.g., Yahoo! Answers (http://answers.yahoo.com), askville (http://askville.amazon.com), and answerbag (http://www.answerbag.com). Wikipedia is currently the largest online encyclopedia with millions of articles collaboratively edited by millions of users. In community QA portals, users post questions and other users answer them. As multiple answers can be provided to the same questions, one can find collective efforts in answer contribution. At the collaboration sites, each user leaves a trace of his or her contribution (e.g., authored article content, questions, and answers) which can be used for Web social mining.
4. ***E-commerce sites.*** E-commerce sites such as eBay (http://www.ebay.com), yelp (http://www.yelp.com), and Epinions.com (http://www.epinions.com) are beginning to harness user participation to create new business models that create new revenues. For example, eBay relies on buyers rating sellers so as to derive the latter's reputation. Epinions and yelp, on the other hand, have users providing reviews and ratings on products. While e-commerce sites have tighter control over their data, they often provide rating and pricing information about products which can be used in Web social mining.

FUNDAMENTAL CONCEPTS

We review the basic terminology of social network that will be used for the rest of the entry.

- ***Actor.*** An actor is an entity whose relationships to other actors are mapped onto a social network. Examples of actors include people, objects, organizations, countries, etc.
- ***Link.*** A link directly relates a pair of actors. There could be diverse meanings attached to a link, including: *evaluation* (e.g., liking/disliking, respect, friendship), *affiliation* (e.g., person belonging to a club), *interaction* (e.g., communicating, collaborating), etc.

  A link is either directed from one actor to another or undirected if it is symmetrically shared between the two actors. A dichotomous link is either present or absent, while a valued link is weighted with a range of values, with higher values usually indicating stronger relationships. A valued link may also be unsigned, with positive link weights, or signed, where link weight may be positive or negative (e.g., liking or disliking).

- ***Path.*** A path connects a pair of actors through an unbroken chain of links. The length of a path is the number of links that make up the chain.
- ***Subgroup.*** A subgroup comprises a subset of actors in a social network, as well as all the links between them. The actors to be included in a subgroup are selected based on specific criteria, which will be discussed later.
- ***Relation.*** A social network may have several types of links. A relation is the set of all links of a specific type. For example, if we define two relations R_{friend} and R_{work}, then all links based on friendship make up R_{friend} and all links based on working relationship make up R_{work}.
- ***Mode.*** A social network may have several types of actors. Mode refers to the number of distinct types of actors. If all actors are of the same type (e.g., people), the network is a one-mode network. If there are two types of actors (e.g., people and organizations), it is a two-mode network.

SOCIAL NETWORK DISCOVERY

The problem of social network discovery can be expressed as follows: *given a finite set of actors, find out which pairs of actors have a link between them and, if applicable, what the weight of each link is.* The solution to this problem requires some criterion to decide whether there is sufficient evidence to infer a link between two nodes and to quantify the strength of that link. Below, we list four such criteria that have been used in prior work, namely: *self-reported*, *communication*, *similarity*, and *co-occurrence*. As shown by the taxonomy in Figure 30.2, the former two usually give rise to directed links; the latter two, to undirected links. Note that for each criterion, links can be inferred from either offline or online activities.

Self-Reported

Self-reported links refer to links discovered from the involved actors themselves. A directed link from actor a_i to another actor a_j exists if a_i has reported it. Such links are directed since a_j may not necessarily report a link to a_i. Even if a pair of actors mutually report links to each other, they may not attach equal weights to the link.

Classical social network research discovers self-reported links through carefully constructed procedures such as questionnaires, interviews, direct observations of interactions, manual sifting through archival record, or various experiments.[4] The discovery effort is time- and resource-intensive, covers a small number of actors, and is usually restricted to specific settings (e.g., people in a company/school).

Web settings lower the barrier and create incentives for a user to report links to others. Someone maintaining a homepage or a blog often lists hyperlinks to Web sites or blogs of friends (e.g., LiveJournal),[5] to increase their connectivity within the community, which helps to increase traffic

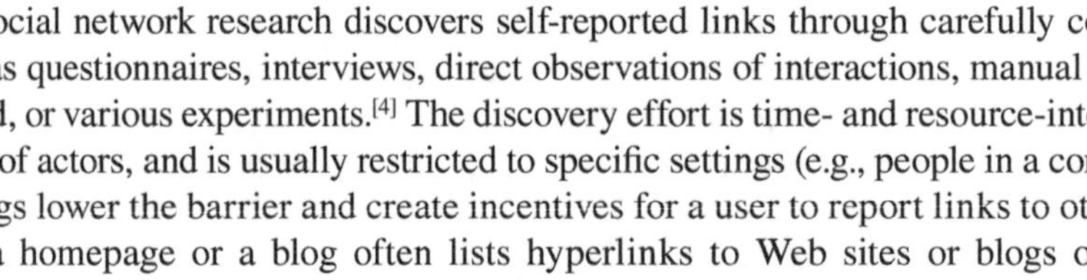

FIGURE 30.2 Taxonomy of social network discovery.

to their homepage or blog. Similarly, profile pages of community-centric sites such as Facebook or Friendster[6] commonly display a self-professed list of friends within the community. Consequently, there are voluminous and diverse self-reported links that can be harvested from these sources.

Communication

Communication, defined generally as transfer of information or resources, is commonly exhibited by socially related people. Communication-based links are usually directed from the originator to the recipient. If desired, an undirected link may be inferred from bidirectional links. Links are usually weighted by the frequency and intensity (e.g., conversation length) of the communication.

Evidence of communication can be drawn from direct observation of interactions or interviews, e.g., asking a group of people to give accounts of work communication.[7] Much of modern communication is computer-mediated, over the Internet, which often leaves a trail in the form of usage logs that can be mined for evidence of sustained communication. Sources of online communication include records of e-mail,[8,9] Instant Messaging (IM),[10–12] newsgroups,[13,14] phone logs,[15] etc.

Similarity

Similarity has its foundation on the well-received sociological idea that friends tend to be alike.[16,17] This leads to the premise that the more people have in common, the likelier it is that they are related. Similarity-based links are naturally undirected, since the notion of similarity is symmetric.

Prior work on similarity-based links involves identifying the relevant attributes of users that may indicate relationship, and a suitable similarity measure. Homepages with similar content and linkages may represent a group of related individuals.[18] Two people whose sets of communication partners overlap may be affiliated to a common group.[19] Other forms of similarity include sharing the same opinions or areas of interest,[20] or even sharing similar vocabulary choices in e-mail messages.[21]

Cooccurrence

Cooccurrence assumes that if several actors occur together more frequently than random chance alone would allow, they are likely associated in some way. Like similarity, it is also undirected by nature. Prior work on cooccurrence-based links can be organized into two streams: *transactional*, where there is a clear boundary within which two actors are said to cooccur, and *spatiotemporal*, where the boundary of cooccurrence is defined by space and/or time.

Transactional Cooccurrence

The term *transaction* is borrowed from work on frequent pattern mining.[22,23] It refers to a discrete instance within which a few items may cooccur, e.g., a supermarket transaction involving a number of product items. A frequent pattern involves a set of items that cooccur together in many transactions, and thus are likely to be associated with one another. Applied to social network discovery, a transaction in an off-line setting may refer to a party attended by a pair of actors,[4] a movie that a pair of actors act in,[15] or a publication which a pair of researchers coauthor.[24,25] In an online setting, a transaction may refer to a Web page where the names of a pair actors cooccur.[26]

Spatiotemporal Cooccurrence

The boundary of a transaction is not always clear-cut, especially when it involves continuous dimensions such as space and time. Suppose that we have a set of tuples $\{\langle a,s,t \rangle\}$, where each tuple records an actor a appearing at location s at time t, and we wish to infer links between pairs of actors based on cooccurrences. A transaction must then be defined in terms of space and/or time. For example, a spatial transaction can be derived by discretizing the space dimension using a sliding window.[27] A temporal transaction can be a time interval within which two IM users must be online together (and thus are more likely to engage in a conversation).[11,12]

In turn, a spatiotemporal cooccurrence is defined over both space and time. Spatiotemporal movement data is a possible indicator of social association.[28–30] Our work *STEvent* in Lauw, et al.[31] concerns social network discovery from spatiotemporal cooccurrences. STEvent focuses on the analysis of movement data and algorithm development to infer associations. It generalizes the spatiotemporal cooccurrence beyond movement over physical locations to include other location types such as cyber locations.

SOCIAL NETWORK ANALYSIS

Social network analysis attempts to find useful structures, patterns, or insights that exist within a social network. As shown in the taxonomy in Figure 30.3, such studies may look for "important" actors in the network (*actor analysis*), "important" paths connecting a subset of actors (*path analysis*), and subgroups that exist within a network (*subgroup analysis*).

Note that we do not distinguish between social networks derived from off-line or online activities. Most analytical methods simply assume a readily available social network. Neither do we distinguish between directed links or undirected links. Most analytical methods can be adapted to both types of links. The common workaround is to define analysis for directed links and treat undirected links as bidirectional links, or to define analysis for undirected links and ignore the direction of directed links.

ACTOR ANALYSIS

The problem of actor analysis can generally be expressed as follows: *given a social network, measure or rank the "importance" of every actor in the network.* There are various definitions of importance, which usually represents a certain property or behavior of an actor. As shown in the taxonomy in Figure 30.3, prior work in actor analysis has largely focused on the following definitions of importance: *centrality*, *influence*, *reputation*, and *anomaly*.

Centrality

Centrality equates importance of actors to occupying strategic or central locations in a network.[4] Such actors are more visible and are involved in more relationships with other actors. Social network researchers have developed the following measures of centrality that are mostly based on the structural properties of a graph.

Degree. The degree centrality of an actor is their number of links. The intuition is that central actors should be the most active, and should have the most connections to others in its vicinity. This

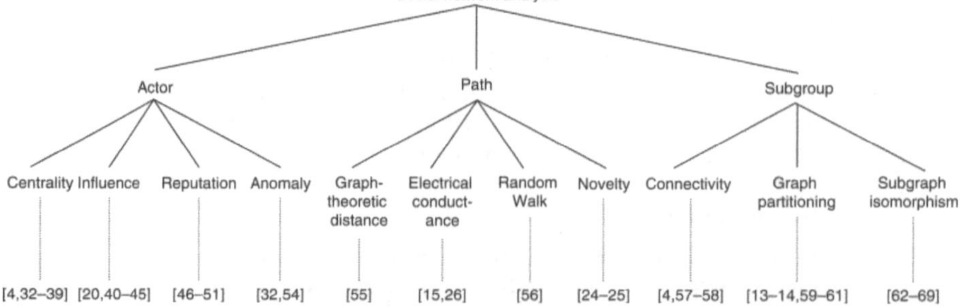

FIGURE 30.3 Taxonomy of social network analysis.

measure has been applied to law enforcement, where it is used to identify the key players in a price fixing conspiracy,[32] and the supposed ringleader of 911 terrorist network (Mohammed Atta).[33]

Closeness. The closeness centrality of an actor is the inverse of the average path length from the actor to all other actors in the network. The reasoning is that an important actor should have easy access to others members of the network.

Betweenness. The betweenness centrality of an actor is the number of distinct shortest paths (connecting any pair of actors) that pass through it. Actors with high betweenness values are in a position to control communication channels, either by impeding or accelerating or just by getting informed of such communication.

Eigenvector centrality. The eigenvector centrality of an actor is the sum of the eigenvector centralities of other actors with links to the actor.[34,35] This measure takes into account not just the number of links that an actor has, but also the quality of those links. Intuitively, a central actors is one whom many other central actors link to. The most well-known and successful application of eigenvector centrality is for ranking Web pages based on hyperlinks for Web search, e.g., PageRank,[36] HITS,[37] and various other link analysis algorithms.[38,39]

Influence

Influence equates importance of actors to ability to propagate the adoption of an idea or a product to other actors in the network. The mode of propagation could be through various channels such as word-of-mouth or persuasion. This measure found application in viral marketing, which depends on identifying high-influence individual to promote products and services to their acquaintances.[20,40–43]

The propagation framework is as follows.[41] Each actor is in one of two states: active or inactive. Initially, only one or a few *seed* actors are active, while the rest are inactive. The propagation of active state proceeds in discrete iterations. In each iteration, an inactive actor may get activated by its active neighbors. Actors that are active in the previous iterations remain active. The iterations terminate after a preset number of iterations, or when no further activation is possible. The influence of an actor (or a small subset of actors) is measured by using the actor(s) as seed actor(s) and counting the final number of active actors at the end of the iterations. The mechanism by which an actor is activated generally falls into either the *threshold model* or the *cascade model.*

Threshold model. In the threshold model,[44] each actor a_j has a threshold activation value of θ_j, and the link weight w_{ij} from a_i to a_j reflects a_i's degree of influence on a_j. Actor a_j is activated in the iteration when $(\Sigma_{\text{active } ai \in \text{neighbors}(aj)} w_{ij}) \geq \theta_j$.

Cascade model. In the cascade model,[45] the link weight w_{ij} from a_i to a_j reflects the probability that a_i can successfully activate a_j. In each iteration of the propagation process, each active actor a_i is given a chance to activate an inactive neighbor a_j with a probability of success equal to w_{ij}.

Reputation

Reputation is often equated with trustworthiness. In online settings, interaction between strangers is common. Thus, platforms that support such interactions (e.g., online auction sites) often institute a reputation system that allows users to evaluate how trusted an actor is by others in the network. All things being equal, one would rather transact with actors of higher reputation. There are two main criteria for inferring the reputation of an actor: *past behaviors* and *trust evaluation by others.*

Past behaviors. One way to determine how trustworthy an actor will be in the future is to see how trustworthy the actor has been in the past. The auction site eBay maintains a *feedback score* for each registered user. On completing a transaction, a buyer and a seller may give a feedback point to each other, which can be 1 (positive rating), 0 (neutral rating), or −1 (negative rating). The feedback score (reputation) of an actor is their running total of feedback points.[46] In product review site Epinions, a user may write product reviews and gets paid based on the number of people who read the reviews. Each review may also be rated by other users. The reputation of a user is a function of the rating scores received by the user's reviews.[47]

Trust evaluation by others. Some systems such as FOAF[48] and Epinions[49] maintain a social network, where each link denotes a trust relationship. Thus, another way to determine how trustworthy an actor is, is to see how many other actors in the network trust her.[50,51] For example, the work on EigenTrust[50] measures the reputation of an actor as the sum of the reputations of other actors with trust links to the actor (akin to eigenvector centrality applied on a network of trust relationship).

Anomaly

In contrast to centrality, anomaly equates importance to being different from or having few connections to other actors. For instance, key players (bosses) in a criminal network may intentionally keep a distance from others for fear of detection by the police and let their underlings carry out their wishes.[32] Finding anomalous actors is akin to outlier detection,[52,53] which is concerned with identifying data points that are situated at a distance from the majority of data points. In prior work, anomalous actors have been defined as those with low closeness centrality values,[32] or those least visited by random walks starting from other actors in the network.[54]

Path Analysis

The problem of path analysis can generally be expressed as follows: *given a social network and ≥2 seed actors, identify the set of "important" paths connecting the seed actors.* The important paths are those that are most likely undertaken from one seed actor to another. Prior work is organized based on how each defines what make up the important paths. As shown in the taxonomy in Figure 30.3, the four main criteria are: *graph-theoretic distance*, *electrical conductance*, *random walk*, and *novelty.*

Graph-Theoretic Distance

Several distance measures in graph theory that could serve to measure the importance of a path include *shortest path* and *maximum flow.*

Shortest path. The shortest path is the path with minimum number of links (for dichotomous links), or the path with maximum total weight (for valued links). This measure has been used to identify strongest association paths between entities in a criminal network.[55] For instance, if two criminals are known to be cooperating, they are likely to use the shortest path between them. Individuals along this association path are themselves potential suspects in the criminal activity.

Maximum flow. In the maximum flow approach, the social network is modeled as a flow graph. One seed actor is designated as the source node, and the other the sink node. Each link in the network is a channel for the flow of material, which is limited by the capacity (link weight). The maximum flow path allows the greatest flow of materials from the source to the sink.

Electrical Conductance

A social network could also be modeled as an electrical circuit. Each seed actor is assigned a potential (source node 1 V and sink node 0 V). Each link is like a resistor with a certain conductance value (link weight). The best path is the one that delivers the highest electrical current from the source node to the target node. The electrical conductance model for mining interesting connections between individuals in a social network was first proposed by Faloutsos et al.[26] and further improved upon by Koren et al.[15]

Electrical conductance is superior to graph-theoretic distance measures in two ways. Unlike the shortest path approach, this model takes into account the popularity of intermediate nodes in a path. Popular nodes allow greater leakage of electricity, corresponding to weaker and incidental connections to a popular person that a normal person would have. Unlike the maximum flow approach, this model takes into account the length of a path in determining interestingness. Longer paths accumulate resistance which impedes the flow of electricity, similar to weaker social relationship to be expected from a longer social path.

Random Walk

Another way to measure path importance is using the random walk mechanism. Random walk is a traversal of a social network graph, which starts from a seed actor and picks the next neighboring actor to visit randomly (either with uniform probability or with probability proportional to link weight). If we start independent random walks from each seed actor, intuitively the paths that are most commonly traversed by these random walks in aggregate are the most important paths connecting the seed actors. The work on center-piece subgraph[56] applies the random walk model to find interesting coauthorship connections. Unlike the electrical conductance model, the center-piece subgraph may also include good paths that connect only a subset of (not all) seed actors.

Novelty

Path importance may also be defined in terms of novelty or uniqueness. A given social network may consist of a few relations (e.g., friendship relation, work relation). Thus, a path may be constructed by links of a few different relations. The novelty of a path is how rarely the combination of relation types in its links can be found in other paths. A novel path captures a unique and exclusive relationship between the seed actors. For example,[24] discovered paths denoting student-teacher relationships based on their exclusive coauthorship with each other,[25] found that the only two mafia groups to be involved in a gang war in a simulated criminal database were connected by paths made up of novel combinations of evidence links (e.g., money transactions, meetings, killings).

Subgroup Analysis

In a social network, for every actor, there is a relatively small subset of other actors that the actor knows well; that small subset constitutes a subgroup. In general, members of a subgroup interact more frequently and intensively with other members than with nonmembers. A network consists of one or more subgroups, which may or may not overlap with each other. The subgroup analysis problem can be concisely stated as follows: *given a social network, identify the subgroups in the network.* In prior work, there are various definitions of what constitutes a subgroup. As shown in the taxonomy in Figure 30.3, these definitions fall into one of three categories: *connectivity*, *graph partitioning*, and *subgraph isomorphism.*

Connectivity-Based Subgroups

Connectivity-based subgroups are defined in terms of how connected members in a subgroup are.[4,57,58] Here we look at three such criteria: mutuality, reachability, and nodal degree.

Mutuality. Mutuality-based subgroups, called *cliques*, are maximal complete subgraphs of at least three actors. This definition captures the idea of cohesiveness, where everyone knows everyone else. However, due to its strictness, cliques are relatively rare in real-life data.

Reachability. Reachability only requires that any pairwise member of a subgroup is reachable from each other through a path of a length not more than n links. If the path may involve an actor outside the subgroup, the subgroup is called *n-clique*. A more restrictive version, *n-clan*, can be derived by rejecting those n-cliques that require a path involving a nonmember.

Nodal degree. Another way to relax the mutuality requirement is to allow each actor to have a lower degree than mutuality would have required. Given k and n, a subgroup of n members is termed a *k-plex* if at most k links can be missing from each actor to its neighbors, or a *k-core*, if at least k links must be present from each actor to its neighbors.

Graph Partitioning

Graph partitioning assumes that a social network consists of a set of disjoint subgroups. Finding those subgroups involves removing a set of links such that the social network graph is partitioned into disjoint subgraphs. This method has been used to find subgroups in networks with unsigned links as well as those with signed links.

Unsigned links. In a network of unsigned links, the objective is to partition the graph into components, such that each component is relatively dense, but the cut (the set of links to be removed) between any two components is relatively sparse. As there could be many possible cuts, the best cut is the one that maximizes the value of some goodness function. This method has been used to partition a collection of newsgroups[14] and Web pages[59,60] into subgroups consisting of newsgroups or Web pages of similar topics.

Signed links. In a network of signed links, the objective is to partition the graph into components, by removing negative links, such that each component consists of as many positive links as possible. For example,[13] split contributors of newsgroups on controversial issues (e.g., politics, abortion) into two camps: those who are for or against a particular issue.[61] Split a network of political parties and a network of tribes into subgroups of similarly aligned parties/tribes.

Subgraph Isomorphism

Subgraph isomorphism assumes that a subgroup has a nonrandom pattern of linking among its members (subgraph pattern), which is shared by a number of other subgroups. Hence, finding subgroups within a network is equivalent to finding subgraph patterns that have many isomophic instances in the network. Below, we review two approaches to derive such subgroups: *A priori–like algorithms* and *compression-based approach.*

A priori–like algorithms. A subgraph pattern is frequent if the number of isomophic instances meets the specified threshold value. To reduce the space of subgraph patterns whose frequencies have to be determined, most of the proposed algorithms[62–67] follow the general principle of the a priori algorithm that was first proposed by Agrawal and Srikant[23] for mining association rules from transaction databases. Adapted to graph data, the principle states that a subgraph pattern has a higher frequency than any of its supergraphs (other patterns that subsume the subgraph). If a subgraph pattern is not frequent, none of its supergraphs need to be considered.

Compression-based approach. Unlike the a priori–like algorithms that find all subgraph patterns whose frequencies meet the threshold, the compression-based approach employs a greedy algorithm to find a subset of subgraph patterns that together result in a good compression of the original graph.[68] Using the minimum description length (MDL) principle, compression is achieved by replacing all isomorphic instances of a subgraph pattern with a more concise representation called "concept." Mukherjee and Holder[69] used this approach to identify substructures in a terrorist network, revealing the chain-like communication channels used by terrorist cells.

SOCIAL NETWORK APPLICATION

Below, we list a number of applications (mostly online applications) with Web social mining aspects. While the list is by no means exhaustive, it sufficiently paints a picture of how the techniques reviewed earlier in this entry may be used in real-life applications.

Online Social Media

Online social media refers to online applications for disseminating and sharing information that also support socially oriented features. Examples of such applications include: blogs (e.g., LiveJournal, http://www.livejournal.com), wikis (e.g., Wikipedia), content sharing (e.g., Flickr for photos, YouTube for videos), online communities (Facebook,[70] Friendster,[6] MySpace[71]), and social bookmarking (e.g., delicious). Such applications often allow users to assign *tags* (textual annotations) to objects in order to collaboratively organize content, to assign *ratings* to collaboratively evaluate content, and to maintain one's *social network* in order to track the latest goings-on, activities, and interests of friends. The social aspects of these activities lend themselves to social network analysis. For example, by analyzing the pattern of hyperlinking among blog posts, we can identify the opinion leaders among bloggers.[72] By analyzing the edit history of Wikipedia articles, we can identify the most authoritative authors.[73]

Social Search

Social search refers to querying one's social network to look up interesting actors or paths. For instance, one may look for actors whose profiles fit the description given in a query, e.g., someone looking for potential dates.[70] Alternatively, one may look for actors holding a specific piece of information.[74,75] This is especially useful for information that is not widely available and may not be indexed in public databases. For example, the answer to the question "Which camera shop in my local neighborhood would offer a good deal to students of my university?" is probably known by a university friend who is an avid photographer. One may also search for interesting association paths. *ReferralWeb*[76] allows a user to explore the chains of referrals leading to a target actor. Users of such a system may be a businessman who wishes to get an introduction to a potential business partner or a graduating student who needs a reference letter from a well-known academician.

Recommender Systems

Recommender systems are online applications that generate personalized recommendations (e.g., which book to buy) based on information provided by the users.[77–79] Some recommender systems require the user to manually enter a personal profile of interests, preferences, or expertise. Others may infer this information implicitly from the user's past activities, e.g., user's purchasing history at Amazon (http://www.amazon.com) or user's ratings on movies at GroupLens (http://www.grouplens.org). A similarity-based social network can then be constructed based on this information. The system could then generate recommendations to an actor based on what other similar or related actors have purchased or rated highly.

Academic Peer Review

Peer review refers to the collaborative exercise in which academicians evaluate each other's work, in order to determine which papers should be accepted for publications in conference proceedings and journals, or which research proposals should be granted funding. Questions that often come up during the peer review process include how to identify the best papers or proposals taking into account the varying rating scores assigned by different reviewers,[80,81] and how to best assign reviewers to objects (papers or proposals) taking into account such factors as the match in topics between reviewers and objects and the workload of reviewers.[82–84]

Social network techniques would likely be useful in deriving the answers to these questions as many academic activities can be mapped onto social network representation. For example, there is a wealth of research on social networks based on coauthorship,[15,24,56,85] cocitation (being cited together in publications),[86–91] bibliographic coupling (citing common publications),[92] etc. Social network analysis can be employed to generate insights that would help to improve and inform the peer review process, e.g., identifying the authorities in specific fields,[91] or tracking which communities are growing or shrinking.[85]

CONCLUSIONS

Web social mining is a topic that sees the cross-fertilization of computing and social science leading to a wide range of interesting applications on the Web. This entry provides a brief survey of the essential concepts and techniques used in Web social mining. It covers social network discovery that allows social networks to be derived from Web and Web 2.0 data, social network analysis that find patterns and knowledge about actors, paths, and other structures in the social networks, and some example applications that can benefit from Web social mining. As new forms of Web data and applications emerges, new Web social mining models and techniques will be in demand thus inspiring more vibrant research in this area.

REFERENCES

1. O'Reilly, T. What is web 2.0: Design patterns and business models for the next generation of software. O'Reilly, **2005**.
2. Zaiane, O.R.; Chen, J.; Goebel, R. Dbconnect: Mining research community on dblp data. In *WebKDD/SNA-KDD '07: Proceedings of the 9th WebKDD and 1st SNA-KDD 2007 Workshop on Web Mining and Social Network Analysis*, San Jose, CA, 2007; 74–81.
3. Nascimento, M.A.; Sander, J.; Pound, J. Analysis of sigmod's co-authorship graph. SIGMOD Rec. **2003**, *32* (3), 8–10.
4. Wasserman, S.; Faust, K. *Social Network Analysis: Methods and Applications*; Cambridge University Press: Cambridge, U.K., 1994.
5. Kumar, R.; Novak, J.; Raghavan, P.; Tomkins, A. Structure and evolution of blogspace. Commun. ACM **2004**, *47* (12), 35–39.
6. Boyd, D.M. Friendster and publicly articulated social networking. In *Extended Abstracts of the Conference on Human Factors and Computing Systems*, Vienna, Austria, 2004; 1279–1282.
7. Garton, L.; Haythornthwaite, C.; Wellman, B. Studying online social networks. J. Comput. Med. Commun. June **1997**, *3* (1).
8. Chapanond, A.; Krishnamoorthy, M.S.; Yener, B. Graph theoretic and spectral analysis of Enron email data. In *Proceedings of the Workshop on Link Analysis, Counterter-rorism, and Security (in conj. with SIAM International Conference on Data Mining)*, Newport Beach, CA, 2005; 15–22.
9. Diesner, J.; Carley, K.M. Exploration of communication networks from the Enron email corpus. In *Proceedings of the Workshop on Link Analysis, Counterterrorism, and Security (in conj. with SIAM International Conference on Data Mining)*, Newport Beach, CA, 2005; 3–4.
10. Ahmad, M.A.; Teredesai, A. Modeling spread of ideas in online social networks. In *Proceedings of the 5th Australasian Conference on Data mining and Analystics*, Australian Computer Society, Inc.: Darlinghurst, Australia, 2006; 185–190.
11. Resig, J.; Dawara, S.; Homan, C.M.; Teredesai, A. Extracting social networks from instant messaging populations. In *Workshop on Link Analysis and Group Detection (in conj. with the 10th ACM SIGKDD International Conference on Knowledge Discovery and Data Mining)*, Seattle, WA, 2004.
12. Resig, J.; Teredesai, A. A framework for mining instant messaging services. In *Workshop on Link Analysis, Coun-terterrorism, and Privacy (in conj. with SIAM International Conference on Data Mining)*, Lake Buena Vista, FA, 2004.
13. Agrawal, R.; Rajagopalan, S.; Srikant, R.; Xu, Y. Mining newsgroups using networks arising from social behavior. In *Proceedings of the 12th International World Wide Web Conference*, Budapest, Hungary, 2003; 688–703.
14. Borgs, C.; Chayes, J.; Mahdian, M.; Saberi, A. Exploring the community structure of newsgroups. In *Proceedings of the 10th ACM SIGKDD International Conference on Knowledge Discovery and Data Mining*, ACM: New York, 2004; 783–787.
15. Koren, Y.; North, S.C.; Volinsky, C. Measuring and extracting proximity in networks. In *Proceedings of the 12th ACM SIGKDD International Conference on Knowledge Discovery and Data Mining*, ACM: New York, 2006; 245–255.
16. Feld, S.L. The focused organization of social ties. Am. J. Sociol **1981**, *86*, 1015–1035.
17. Carley, K. A theory of group stability. Am. Sociol. Rev. **1991**, *56* (3), 331–354.
18. Adamic, L.A.; Adar, E. Friends and neighbors on the Web. Soc. Netw. July **2003**, *25* (3), 211–230.
19. Schwartz, M.F.; Wood, D.C.M. Discovering shared interests using graph analysis. Commun. ACM **1993**, *36* (8), 78–89.
20. Richardson, M.; Domingos, P. Mining knowledge-sharing sites for viral marketing. In *Proceedings of the 8th ACM SIGKDD International Conference on Knowledge Discovery and Data Mining*, Edmonton, Alberta, Canada, 2002; 61–70.
21. Keila, P.S.; Skillicorn, D.B. Structure in the Enron email dataset. In *Proceedings of the Workshop on Link Analysis, Counterterrorism, and Security (in conj. with SIAM International Conference on Data Mining)*, Newport Beach, CA, 2005; 55–64.

22. Agrawal, R.; Imielinski, T.; Swami, A. Mining association rules between sets of items in large databases. In *Proceedings of the ACM International Conference on Management of Data*, Washington, DC, 1993; 207–216.
23. Agrawal, R.; Srikant, R. Fast algorithm for mining association rules. In *Proceedings of the 20th International Conference on Very Large Databases*, Santiago, Chile, 1994; 487–499.
24. Lin, S.; Chalupsky, H. Unsupervised link discovery in multi-relational data via rarity analysis. In *Proceedings of the 3rd IEEE International Conference on Data Mining*, Melbourne, FL, 2003; 171–178.
25. Lin, S.; Chalupsky, H. Issues of verification for unsupervised discovery systems. In *Workshop on Link Analysis and Group Detection (in conj. with the 10th ACM SIGKDD International Conference on Knowledge Discovery and Data Mining)*, Seattle, WA, 2004.
26. Faloutsos, C.; McCurley, K.S.; Tomkins, A. Fast discovery of connection subgraphs. In *Proceedings of the 10th ACM SIGKDD International Conference on Knowledge Discovery and Data Mining*, Seattle, WA, 2004; 118–127.
27. Shekhar, S.; Huang, Y. Discovering spatial co-location patterns: A summary of results. In *Proceedings of the 7th International Symposium on Spatial and Temporal Databases*, Redondo Beach, CA, 2001; 236–256.
28. Choudhury, T.; Pentland, A. Sensing and modeling human networks using the Sociometer. In *Proceedings of the 7th IEEE International Symposium on Wearable Computing*, IEEE Computer Society: Washington, DC, 2003; 216–222.
29. Eagle, N.; Pentland, A. Reality Mining: Sensing complex social systems. Pers. Ubiquitous Comput. **2006**, *10* (4), 255–268.
30. Terry, M.; Mynatt, E.D.; Ryall, K.; Leigh, D. Social Net: Using patterns of physical proximity over time to infer shared interests. In *Extended Abstracts of the ACM Conference on Human Factors in Computing Systems*, ACM: New York, 2002; 816–817.
31. Lauw, H.W.; Lim, E.-P.; Tan, T.T.; Pang, H. Mining social network from spatio-temporal events. In *Workshop on Link Analysis, Counterterrorism and Security at SDM'05*, 2005.
32. Xu, J.; Chen, H. Untangling criminal networks: A case study. In *Proceedings of the 1st Symposium on Intelligence and Security Informatics*, Tucson, AZ, 2003; 232–248.
33. Krebs, V.E. Mapping networks of terrorist cells. Connections **2002**, *24* (3), 43–52.
34. Bonacich, P. Technique for analyzing overlapping memberships. Sociol. Methodol. **1972**, *4*, 176–185.
35. Bonacich, P. Simultaneous group and individual central-ities. Soc. Netw. **1991**, *13* (2), 155–168.
36. Page, L.; Brin, S.; Motwani, R.; Winograd, T. The Page Rank citation ranking: Bringing order to the Web. In Stanford Digital Library Technologies Project; 1998.
37. Kleinberg, J.M. Authoritative sources in a hyperlinked environment. J. ACM **1999**, *46* (5), 604–632.
38. Borodin, A.; Roberts, G.O.; Rosenthal, J.S.; Tsaparas, P. Link analysis ranking: Algorithms, theory, and experiments. ACM Trans. Inter. Technol. **2005**, *5* (1), 231–297.
39. Haveliwala, T.H. Topic-sensitive PageRank: A context-sensitive ranking algorithm for Web search. IEEE Trans. Know. Data Eng. **2003**, *15* (4), 784–796.
40. Domingos, P.; Richardson, M. Mining the network value of customers. In *Proceedings of the 7th ACM SIGKDD International Conference on Knowledge Discovery and Data Mining*, San Francisco, 2001; 57–66.
41. Kempe, D.; Kleinberg, J.; Tardos, E. Maximizing the spread of influence through a social network. In *Proceedings of the 9th ACM SIGKDD International Conference on Knowledge Discovery and Data Mining*, Washington, DC, 2003; 137–146.
42. Leskovec, J.; Adamic, L.A.; Huberman, B.A. The dynamics of viral marketing. ACM Trans. Web **2007**, *1* (1), 5.
43. Ong, K.; Ng, W.; Lim, E. Mining relationship graphs for effective business objectives. In *Proceedings of the 6th Pacific-Asia Conference on Knowledge Discovery and Data Mining*, Taipei, Taiwan, 2002; 561–565.
44. Granovetter, M. Threshold models of collective behavior. Am. J. Sociol. **1987**, *83* (6), 1420–1443.
45. Goldenberg, J.; Libai, B.; Muller, E. Talk of the network: A complex systems look at the underlying process of word-of-mouth. Market. Lett. **2001**, *12* (3), 211–223.
46. Resnick, P.; Kuwabara, K.; Zeckhauser, R.; Friedman, E. Reputation systems. Commun. ACM **2000**, *43* (12), 45–48.
47. Chen, M.; Singh, J.P. Computing and using reputations for internet ratings. In *Proceedings of the 3rd ACM Conference on Electronic Commerce*, ACM: New York, 2001; 154–162.
48. Golbeck, J.; Hendler, J. Inferring binary trust relationships in Web-based social networks. ACM Transa. Internet Technol. **2006**, *6* (4), 497–529.

49. Guha, R.; Kumar, R.; Raghavan, P.; Tomkins, A. Propagation of trust and distrust. In *Proceedings of the 13th International Conference on World Wide Web*, ACM: New York, 2004; 403–412.
50. Kamvar, S.D.; Schlosser, M.T.; Garcia-Molina, H. The Eigentrust algorithm for reputation management in P2P networks. In *Proceedings of the 12th International Conference on World Wide Web*, ACM: New York, 2003; 640–651.
51. Xiong, L.; Liu, L. Peertrust: Supporting reputation-based trust in peer-to-peer communities. IEEE Trans. Knowl. Data Eng. **2004**, *16* (7), 843–857.
52. Arning, A.; Agrawal, R.; Raghavan, P. A linear method for deviation detection in large databases. In *Proceedings of the 2nd ACM SIGKDD International Conference on Knowledge Discovery and Data Mining*, ACM: New York, 1996; 164–169.
53. Knorr, E.; Ng, R. A unified notion of outliers: Properties and computation. In *Proceedings of the 3rd ACM SIGKDD International Conference on Knowledge Discovery and Data Mining*, AAAI Press: Menlo Park, CA, 1997; 219–222.
54. Sun, J.; Qu, H.; Chakrabarti, D.; Faloutsos, C. Neighborhood formation and anomaly detection in bipartite graphs. In *ICDM*; 2005; 418–425.
55. Xu, J.; Chen, H. Fighting organized crimes: Using shortest-path algorithms to identify associations in criminal networks. Decis. Support Syst. **2004**, *38* (3), 473–487.
56. Tong, H.; Faloutsos, C. Center-piece subgraphs: Problem definition and fast solutions. In *Proceedings of the 12th ACM SIGKDD International Conference on Knowledge Discovery and Data Mining*, ACM: New York, 2006; 404–413.
57. Freeman, L.C. The sociological concept of "group": An empirical test of two models. Am. J. Sociol. **1992**, *98*, 152–166.
58. Freeman, L.C. Cliques, galois lattices, and the structure of human social groups. Soc. Netw. **1996**, *18* (3), 173–187.
59. Flake, G.W.; Lawrence, S.; Giles, C.L. Efficient identification of web communities. In *Proceedings of the 6th ACM SIGKDD International Conference on Knowledge Discovery and Data Mining*, ACM: New York, 2000; 150–160.
60. Flake, G.W.; Lawrence, S.; Giles, C.L.; Coetzee, F.M. Self-organization and identification of Web communities. Computer **2002**, *35* (3), 66–71.
61. Yang, B.; Cheung, W.; Liu, J. Community mining from signed social networks. IEEE Trans. Know. Data Eng. **2007**, *19* (10), 1333–1348.
62. Chakrabarti, D.; Faloutsos, C. Graph mining: Laws, generators, and algorithms. ACM Comput. Surv. **2006**, *38* (1), 2.
63. Inokuchi, A.; Washio, T.; Motoda, H. An apriori-based algorithm for mining frequent substructures from graph data. In *Proceedings of the 4th European Conference on Principles of Data Mining and Knowledge Discovery*, Springer-Verlag: London, 2000; 13–23.
64. Kuramochi, M.; Karypis, G. Frequent subgraph discovery. In *Proceedings of the 2001 IEEE International Conference on Data Mining*, IEEE Computer Society: Washington, DC, 2001; 313–320.
65. Kuramochi, M.; Karypis, G. Discovering frequent geometric subgraphs. Inform. Syst. **2007**, *32* (8), 1101–1120.
66. Yan, X.; Han, J. gSpan: Graph-based substructure pattern mining. In *Proceedings of the 2002 IEEE International Conference on Data Mining*, IEEE Computer Society: Washington, DC, 2002, 721.
67. Yan, X.; Han, J. CloseGraph: Mining closed frequent graph patterns. In *Proceedings of the 9th ACM SIGKDD International Conference on Knowledge Discovery and Data Mining*, ACM: New York, 2003; 286–295.
68. Cook, D.J.; Holder, L.B. Graph-based data mining. IEEE Intell. Syst. March **2000**, *15* (2), 32–41.
69. Mukherjee, M.; Holder, L.B. Graph-based data mining on social networks. In *Workshop on Link Analysis and Group Detection (in conj. with the 10th ACM SIGKDD International Conference on Knowledge Discovery and Data Mining)*, Seattle, WA, 2004.
70. Lampe, C.; Ellison, N.; Steinfield, C. A Face(book) in the crowd: Social searching vs. social browsing. In *Proceedings of the 20th ACM Conference on Computer Supported Cooperative Work*, ACM: New York, 167–170.
71. Patil, S.; Lai, J. Who gets to know what when: Configuring privacy permissions in an awareness application. In *Proceedings of the SIGCHI Conference on Human Factors in Computing Systems*, ACM: New York, 2005; 101–110.
72. Song, X.; Chi, Y.; Hino, K.; Tseng, B. Identifying opinion leaders in the blogosphere. In *Proceedings of the 16th ACM Conference on Conference on Information and Knowledge Management*, ACM: New York, 2007; 971–974.

73. Hu, M.; Lim, E.-P.; Sun, A.; Lauw, H.W.; Vuong, B.-Q. Measuring article quality in Wikipedia: Models and evaluation. In *Proceedings of the 16th ACM Conference on Conference on Information and Knowledge Management*, ACM: New York, 2007; 243–252.
74. Yu, B.; Singh, M.P. Searching social networks. In *Proceedings of the 2nd Joint Conference on Autonomous Agents and Multiagent Systems*, ACM: New York, 2003; 65–72.
75. Zhang, J.; van Alstyne, M. SWIM: Fostering social network based information search. In *Extended Abstracts on Human Factors in Computing Systems*, ACM: New York, 2004; 1568–1568.
76. Kautz, H.; Selman, B.; Shah, M. Referralweb: Combining social networks and collaborative filtering. Commun. ACM **1997**, *40* (3), 63–65.
77. Adomavicius, G.; Tuzhilin, A. Toward the next generation of recommender systems: A survey of the state-of-the-art and possible extensions. IEEE Trans. Knowl. Data Eng. **2005**, *17* (6), 734–749.
78. Herlocker, J.L.; Konstan, J.A.; Terveen, L.G.; Riedl, J.T. Evaluating collaborative filtering recommender systems. ACM Trans. Inform. Syst. **2004**, *22* (1), 5–53.
79. Resnick, P.; Varian, H.R. Recommender systems. Commun. ACM **1997**, *40* (3), 56–58.
80. Riggs, T.; Wilensky, R. An algorithm for automated rating of reviewer. In *Proceedings of the 1st ACM/IEEE-CS Joint Conference on Digital Libraries*, Roanoke, VA, 2001, ACM: New York, 2001; 381–387.
81. Walker, H.M.; Ma, W.; Mboya, D. Variability of referees' ratings of conference papers. In *Proceedings of the 7th Annual Conference on Innovation and Technology in Computer Science Education*, ACM: New York, 2002; 178–182.
82. Dumais, S.; Nielsen, J. Automating the assignment of submitted manuscripts to reviewers. In *Proceedings of the 15th International ACM SIGIR Conference on Research and Development in Information Retrieval*, ACM: New York, 1992; 233–244.
83. Geller, J.; Scherl, R. Challenge: Technology for automated reviewer selection. In *Proceedings of the 15th International Joint Conferences on Artificial Intelligence*, Morgan Kaufmann, San Francisco, 1997; 55–61.
84. Hettich, S.; Pazzani, M.J. Mining for proposal reviewers: Lessons learned at the National Science Foundation. In *Proceedings of the 12th ACM SIGKDD International Conference on Knowledge Discovery and Data Mining*, Philadelphia, PA, 2006; 862–871.
85. Backstrom, L.; Huttenlocher, D.; Kleinberg, J.; Lan, X. Group formation in large social networks: Membership, growth, and evolution. In *Proceedings of the 12th ACM SIGKDD International Conference on Knowledge Discovery and Data Mining*, ACM: New York, 2006; 44–54.
86. Chen, C.; Carr, L. Trailblazing the literature of hypertext: Author co-citation analysis (1989–1998). In *Proceedings of the 10th ACM Conference on Hypertext and Hypermedia*, ACM: New York, 1999; 51–60.
87. Culnan, M.J. The intellectual development of management information systems, 1972–1982: A co-citation analysis. Manage. Sci. **1986**, *32* (2), 156–172.
88. Sullivan, D.; White, D.H.; Barboni, E.J. Co-citation analyses of science: An evaluation. Soc. Stud. Sci. **1997**, *7*, 223–240.
89. Small, H. Co-citation in the scientific literature: A new measure of the relationship between two documents. J. Am. Soc. Inform. Sci. **1973**, *24* (4), 265–269.
90. Small, H.G. A co-citation model of a scientific specialty: A longitudinal study of collagen research. Soc. Stud. Sci. **1977**, *7*, 139–166.
91. White, H.D.; McCain, K.W. Visualizing a discipline: An author co-citation analysis of information science, 1972– 1995. J. Am. Soc. Inform. Sci. Technol. **1998**, *49* (4), 327–355.
92. Kessler, M. Bibliographic coupling between scientific papers. Am. Doc. **1963**, *14*, 10–25.

31 Recommender Systems and Expert Locators

Derek L. Hansen, Tapan Khopkar, and Jun Zhang

CONTENTS

INTRODUCTION

Despite the abundance of recorded information, many information seekers turn to other humans for advice and recommendations. Humans, after all, can be quite adept at identifying and solving problems, summarizing relevant content, generating new ideas, and personalizing information. In addition, for some, interacting with other humans is far more socially enjoyable than interacting with static content. Thus, it is no surprise that the Internet is as much a platform for social interaction as it is a document repository.

System designers have taken advantage of the fact that so much social action is captured online by creating systems that extend traditional word-of-mouth exchanges. This entry discusses two such systems: *recommender systems* that provide personalized recommendations (e.g., movie suggestions) for items of potential interest, and *expert locator systems* that automatically identify experts on a particular topic of interest making it possible to obtain personalized advice from knowledgeable individuals outside of one's immediate social network. Expert locator systems can be thought of as a subset of recommender systems where experts are the "items" being recommended. We treat them separately in this entry because in practice there are often important distinctions between recommending items and people. The remainder of the entry defines these two types of systems, outlines their key characteristics, provides some historical and current examples, and identifies the key research questions related to them. It concludes with a discussion about the importance and potential of these techniques given the increased amount of activity that can be digitally captured.

RECOMMENDER SYSTEMS

People are often confronted with situations where they need to assess the potential value of something that they have never experienced before. We need to find a new book to read, choose a doctor, and know which business is credible. When confronted with these situations, we often turn to experts or peers for recommendations. Increasingly, people receive recommendations from automated tools called recommender systems. For example, people browsing a book at Amazon are presented with a list of related books of potential interest. The related books (listed under the "People who bought this book also bought" header) are identified by a recommender system that relies upon the historical purchasing patterns of Amazon customers. More generally, recommender systems suggest items of potential interest to individuals who do not have personal experience with the items.

Though recommender systems have gained visibility with the spread of the Internet, they are not confined to the Web. Better Business Bureaus, Zagat's restaurant reviews, and The Times Book Review are some examples of recommender systems that predate the Web. Two things make Web-based recommender systems fundamentally different. First, they are able to provide personalized recommendations tailored to individuals. In contrast to The Times Book Review that provides the same recommendations to every reader, recommender systems can recommend a book based on the other books you personally enjoy, while not recommending it to others with different tastes. Second, recommender systems are able to base recommendations on the data from the masses, not just a handful of reviewers and editors. The online environment has also made it easier to efficiently capture people's preferences and easily distribute recommendations.

Broadly speaking, recommender systems can be classified into two types: collaborative and content-based. Collaborative recommender systems make recommendations based on the prior experience of other users, while content-based systems make recommendations based on features or descriptions of the items themselves. There are also hybrid recommender systems that mix these two approaches. For simplicity, we present them independently in the following sections.

COLLABORATIVE SYSTEMS

Collaborative recommender systems draw on the historical experience, or preferences of some users to make recommendations to other users. These systems are also called "Collaborative Filters" or "Social Filters" and have been used in a variety of settings to recommend newsgroup articles (e.g., GroupLens), books (e.g., Amazon's "People who bought this also bought" feature), movies (e.g., MovieLens), music (e.g., Last.fm), and even people (e.g., eBay's feedback system and other expert locators systems discussed in the following section).

Last.fm is a good example of a collaborative recommender system that offers many different recommendations. The site is a music portal that allows users to listen to music, find new music they are likely to enjoy, and find people with similar music tastes. When a user logs into the site, he can enter in his favorite songs and bands and add them to his "playlist," one of the components of his user profile. The system then compares the user's profile with the profiles of other Last.fm users. This comparison makes it possible to identify users who have similar tastes (e.g., people who like and dislike the same music). These individuals are shown as "neighbors" and a user is presented with opportunities to view their music lists. In this way, the system recommends people based on the similarity of user profiles. The system also provides a user with the option of hearing songs that his neighbors as a collective enjoy. Furthermore, when visiting an artist's home page a user can have

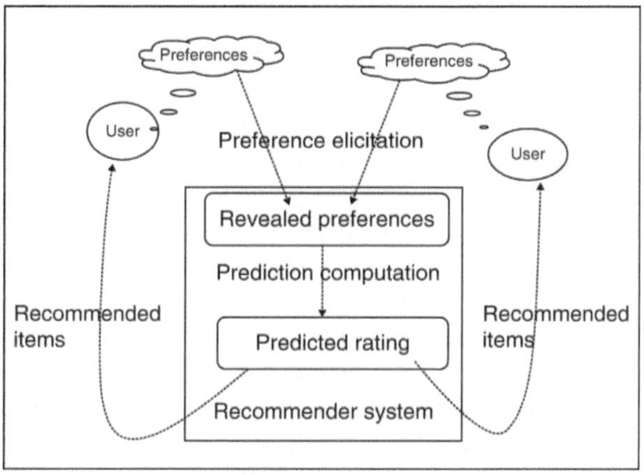

FIGURE 31.1 Schematic representation of a collaborative recommender system.

songs by "similar" artists recommended, where similarity is based on the collective preferences of people who listen to that artist.

To make recommendations like those at Last.fm, a collaborative recommender system must perform the following tasks:

1. Elicit Preferences: Learn about the users' preferences and store them in user profiles.
2. Compute Predictions: Predict how well a user would like an unfamiliar item based on the data from the user profiles.
3. Make Recommendations: Use the predictions to make recommendations.

Figure 31.1 provides a schematic representation of a recommender system, showing how these tasks relate to one another. Different recommender systems use different approaches to perform each of these tasks. We now discuss each of the tasks in turn.

Elicit Preferences

Recommender system can learn about the users' preferences by explicitly asking them to rate certain items; or by using implicit measures such as purchase history, search history, or time spent browsing an article. Most recommender systems that use the explicit method ask users to rate items in the database that they have experienced in the past. The systems use these ratings to form and periodically update a model of the user's preferences. Some recommender systems employ an alternative approach where they ask all users to rate items from the same "gauge" data set and model their preferences based on these ratings.[1]

Recommender systems can vary in the amount of detail that is captured with the ratings and the scale used to capture them (i.e., the dimensionality and granularity of ratings). A recommender system could obtain detailed ratings along multiple dimensions (e.g., quality and timeliness) or it could ask for a one-dimensional rating (e.g., overall satisfaction). Ratings could be on an all positive scale, all negative scale, or a positive and negative scale. The ratings can also vary on granularity. They may use a 1 to 5 scale like Amazon.com or a "thumbs up" and "thumbs down" scale like Digg. Each of these design choices has different implications for the accuracy of recommendations and also a user's privacy and the ease of entering ratings. They will also influence which prediction algorithms are possible to use.

Compute Predictions

Several alternative algorithms are used to make predictions and thus recommendations. Improving the accuracy of predictions is an area of active research, which has received additional impetus through Netflix's announcement in late 2006 of a $1 million prize for the first team that improves the predictions of Netflix's recommender algorithm by 10%.

Recommender algorithms can be classified into two types: (1) memory-based and (2) model-based.[2] Memory-based algorithms use data from all users to make predictions directly, while model-based algorithms use data from all users to formulate a single model of user preferences, and then use this model to make predictions. Recommender algorithms can also be classified based on whether they use correlations between users or between items.

In the user-user approach, correlation between two users is computed based on the scores of items that are rated (or used if the recommender system uses implicit measures) by both the users. The recommender system computes correlations between all such user pairs, which can be used in a variety of ways. One of the popular approaches is to use these correlations as weights when making predictions by taking a weighted average over the opinions of other users who have rated an item. Another approach is to use the user–user correlations to divide the user population into clusters of users, where users in the same cluster are considered to have similar preferences. Predictions for a user's hitherto unrated item are made by averaging the opinions of the other users in her cluster. Other approaches use statistical techniques such as Principal Component Analysis or Singular Value Decomposition and seek to identify latent factors in the data and make predictions based on those.

In systems that use the item–item approach (e.g., Amazon.com's "Users who bought this book also bought" feature), correlations between item pairs are computed instead of correlations between user pairs. Correlation between two items is computed using ratings of all the users who have rated both items. The system recommends items that are highly correlated with the items that are highly rated (or used) by the user.

When computing predictions, recommender algorithms usually perform some sort of normalization in order to account for systematic differences in the way people choose ratings. For example, if a person's average rating is 4.5 out of 5 and they give something a 3, the 3 rating is pretty bad. On the other hand, if a person has an average rating of 2.5 out of 5, a 3 rating is pretty good.

Make Recommendations

The objective of a recommender system is to present each user with items she is most likely to enjoy. To this effect, a recommender system can use the predictions in a variety of ways. As illustrated in the Last.fm example, the user can choose to have recommended songs play based on similar artists, neighbors, or her entire history.

System designers need to make several important design decisions in this phase. Besides the obvious design decisions about the interface, the system designer needs to determine what is the maximum permissible error. The error could be an error of commission (incorrectly recommending an item) or an error of omission (not recommending an item that should be recommended). The margin of permissible error for either type depends on the benefit of a correct recommendation and the cost of an incorrect recommendation. Consider a hypothetical Web site where medical treatment in discussed and recommended. Here a good recommendation not made or an incorrectly made recommendation could affect the health of a user. For video sharing, Web sites like YouTube, a recommendation is unlikely to have such important ramifications for the user, but it is still an important decision for the service provider. The service provider has an incentive to provide more recommendations if it leads to increased usage (or sale). At the same time the reduced usability due to poor recommendations may result in the user opting out of the system altogether, so there is still a need for an appropriate threshold.

The system designer needs to consider these issues when deciding the metrics for evaluating the predictions and the magnitude of permissible error. A good recommender system should continually seek feedback from the user and evaluate the accuracy of its predictions. Root Mean Square Error

(RMSE) and Mean Absolute Error are some of the evaluation metrics commonly used in recommender systems. The Netflix prize requires a 10% RMSE improvement in the predictions of Netflix's algorithm.

Content-Based Systems

Content-based systems recommend items based on features of the items themselves. Unlike collaborative systems, there is no need for data from other individuals. For a content-based system to work, a representation of each item must be generated. This can be done automatically, as when all of the words in a book or article are indexed. Or, it can be done manually as when a human cataloger associates a particular genre (i.e., romance) or subject heading to a book. An example of a very simple content-based system would be a news aggregation Web site that displays "related" articles that are textually "similar" to the one that a user is currently reading.

Many content-based systems provide personalized recommendations. In addition to having a representation of each item, this requires that individuals have a user profile that includes data about a user's likes and dislikes. As with collaborative systems, data for a content-based user profile can be explicitly entered or implicitly captured based on behavior (e.g., purchasing patterns).

This user profile is then compared with the representations of potential items and those that match closely are recommended. A variety of different techniques (i.e., algorithms) are used to compare user profiles and item representations in order to predict which items a user will like. These differ from those used in collaborative systems because the comparison is not between different ratings; it is between a user's profile and the representations of items. Common techniques are the use of information retrieval and machine learning algorithms (Hinshelwood[3] for a more complete list with examples).

Pandora is an example of a content-based system that recommends music. In contrast to Last.fm, it does not rely on any other user recommendations. Instead, it is based on a representation of each song, called a Music Genome, which is created automatically by a special software tool. A song's Music Genome consists of hundreds of musical attributes that describe qualities of melody, harmony, rhythm, form, composition, and lyrics. When a user enters a favorite song, Pandora recommends other songs with a similar Music Genome. Over time, users are presented with new songs which they rate. A user profile is automatically created that keeps track of the user's likes and dislikes. Additional songs are recommended taking into consideration the entire user profile.

Challenges of Recommender Systems

Designers and managers of recommender systems face several challenges. Some of these are dependent on the type of recommender system.

Content-based systems face two primary challenges:

1. Creating representations of certain items can be costly and time intensive. Although full-text, digital documents lend themselves well to automatic indexing, other items such as physical objects, small textual items such as quotes, and movies are difficult to automatically index in a satisfactory way.
2. Even when representations of items are available, they may not represent the characteristics that are most important to the user's enjoyment of the item. Jokes are a good example of this. While one could index the words used in a joke, the user's enjoyment of the joke has far less to do with the words than it does with the humor. In other words, knowing that a joke is about a chicken doesn't help a user know if she would enjoy the joke. One potential strategy for overcome this problem would be to add meta-data to items. However, for items like jokes or poems the meta-data would be so subjective that it would not likely produce accurate predictions for any particular user.[3]

Since collaborative systems are not based on the representation of an item, they can work for items that are costly or difficult to accurately represent, such as physical objects or jokes. However, they have their own set of challenges:

1. Eliciting enough user ratings to generate accurate predictions for all items is a constant source of concern for the designers and managers of recommender systems. Users need to be provided with sufficient incentives to participate.
2. New users and new items both suffer from the "cold-start" problem. New users do not get good recommendations until they have rated a sufficient number of items; and new items rarely get recommended until a sufficient number of users have rated (or used) them.
3. There may be entities that have an interest in manipulating the recommender system in order to promote certain items. An example of such a manipulation scheme called "sybil attack" or "shilling attack" involves creating a number of spurious users and providing ratings such that certain items get recommended more often. Preventing such manipulations or limiting the damage they cause, is an important consideration for recommender system designers and an active area of research.

To overcome some of these challenges, recommender systems may use a combined approach (both content-based and collaborative) or provide tools that allow people to use preexisting data (e.g., upload iTunes playlists all at once).

Recommender System Research

Online recommender systems have been developed and studied since the mid-1990s. Two related systems were simultaneously developed in the mid-1990s and were instrumental in showing the value of collaborative recommender systems:

1. GroupLens—a net news collaborative recommender system created by Resnick et al.[4] Resnick continued to study recommender systems as an editor for a special issue of *Communications of the Association for Computing Machinery (ACM)* on the topic in 1997[5] and as a contributor to numerous articles on the subject. Reidl has also remained highly active in recommender system research with his colleagues at the GroupLens research lab at the University of Minnesota. They have performed a number of studies of MovieLens, a recommender system for movies. Their Web site[6] is a good starting point for potential researchers with its list of publications and downloadable datasets.
2. Ringo—a music collaborative recommender system developed at MIT by Shardanand and Maes.[7] It was later made into a commercial product called Firefly, which was eventually bought out by Microsoft. Music recommender systems are now common and among the most advanced and popular (e.g., Last.fm, Pandora).

Research on recommender systems has continued to grow and doesn't show any signs of slowing down. Several special issues of well-respected journals have focused on recommender systems including the *Communications of the ACM*,[5] *ACM Transactions on Information Systems*,[8] *ACM Transactions on Computer–Human Interaction*,[9] and *IEEE Intelligent Systems*.[10] Research can also be found in conferences like ACM Special Interest Group on Information Retrieval, ACM Computer-Human Interaction, and ACM Electronic Commerce. Numerous workshops have been held over the years, and in 2007, the first annual ACM Recommender Systems[11] conference was held. Current research focuses on nearly every aspect of recommender systems from the recommendation algorithms, to interfaces design, to security, and privacy issues.

Summary

Recommender Systems are a powerful tool for recommending new items to individuals either based on content (content-based systems) or other users' experiences (collaborative systems). It is a highly active area of research that epitomizes the current social computing trends. While there are challenges with recommender systems (e.g., needing sufficient numbers of people and items rated before it works), they have already become widely used by corporations such as Amazon, NetFlix, Pandora, TiVo, Google, and others.

EXPERT LOCATOR SYSTEMS

Turning to experts for help is nothing new. We are all familiar with the ability of experts to diagnose a complex problem, clarify an issue, identify hidden structure, point us to a hard-to-locate resource, and perform a task that requires significant skill. Although some expert knowledge can be made explicit in the form of books, videos, diagrams, and knowledge-base entries, other knowledge is implicit and difficult to codify. Thus, it is often preferable to gain access to the source of the knowledge, the expert, in order to obtain the full benefit of the expertise. Unfortunately, it is not always easy to identify experts, especially within large organizations or distributed communities. Recently, systems have been developed to help locate individuals with needed expertise. These expert locator systems go by many names including expertise finders, expertise location engines, expert locators, and enterprise expertise management systems.

An expert locator system is a collection of technologies and social practices designed to help an individual find someone with the appropriate skills, knowledge, or expertise to meet a particular need. Some are stand-alone systems, but most are integrated into a more comprehensive knowledge management solution. While a basic organizational chart or an informal friendship-based network may be considered an expert locator system in the broadest sense, the term typically refers to more advanced systems that use implicitly or explicitly provided data to identify experts.

Researchers and practitioners have developed and examined expert locator systems since the early 1990s. Most empirical studies have taken place within large corporate settings, although more recent work has looked at expertise location among peer groups and virtual help-based communities. The most active research communities currently examining expert locator systems are the Computer Supported Cooperative Work (CSCW) and Knowledge Management communities. As a result, research on the topic is often published in conference proceedings in these areas (e.g., ACM–CSCW, ACM Conference on Information and Knowledge Management, ACM International Conference on Knowledge Discovery and Data Mining, ACM Recommender Systems) and information systems journals such as CSCW and KES (Knowledge-Based and Intelligent Engineering Systems). However, a considerable amount of research is scattered throughout publications on topics such as artificial intelligence, algorithms, Web personalization, and information systems more generally.

The following sections describe different subtypes of expert locator systems. The area is new enough that the vocabulary around them has not yet solidified. We group the systems into the following categories: *expert databases*, *automatic expertise finders*, *expertise recommenders*, and *expert referral systems*.

Expert Databases

Early expert locator systems were usually called expertise databases, knowledge directories, yellow pages, or knowledge maps. These systems consist of a searchable database of individuals along with data about their prior experience, expertise, organizational role, and contact information. Typical systems include Microsoft SPUD, HP CONNEX, and the NASA expertseeker. These systems are usually designed for identifying experts to help solve technical problems or to match employee competencies with company positions.

Inputting accurate and detailed enough data into these databases can be a significant challenge. Some organizations rely upon assessment interviews, skill inventories, and extensive surveys of employees, but such methods can be costly and labor intensive. In other cases, individual employees are expected to enter information about themselves. Although individuals are the most qualified to describe their own expertise, they often lack motivation to add content—an activity that has few immediate rewards. Furthermore, they may not recognize the potential value of some of their less obvious skills and fail to report them. No matter who contributes the data, expert database entries can suffer from being over-simplified, one-dimensional assessments of expertise that are not informative enough to help direct the fine-grained, context specific questions that lead people to seek out experts. Finally, some systems rely on taxonomies to describe and catalog people's knowledge and skills. While this may encourage consistency and point out areas that may not have been considered, developing, and implementing taxonomies requires considerable effort and are likely to be misapplied if individuals are entering their own data.

Another related challenge is maintaining content over time. People leave, new skills are developed, positions change. For those who rarely use expert locator systems, keeping their data current is not on their top list of priorities. As a result, some expert databases quickly become obsolete. Additionally, organizations may not initially recognize the full investment required to maintain these systems once they are created.

Automatic Expertise Finders

As more and more activity occurs in the digital environment, it has become possible to profile individuals' expertise based on their conversations (e.g., in discussion forums and e-mail exchanges) and the documents associated with them (e.g., publications). An *automatic expertise finder* is a type of expert locator system that takes advantage of the implicit data left behind in the form of digital traces and documents. Such systems typically build expertise profiles from the implicit data by using information retrieval techniques (e.g., indexing). A person's expertise is usually described as a term vector and is used later for matching expertise queries using standard IR techniques. This allows people to search for a relevant expert in much the same way that they might search for a relevant document.

Well-known systems in this category include Who-Knows,[12] ContactFinder,[13] and MITRE MII Expert Finder.[14] Who-Knows identifies experts across an organization by using Latent Semantic Indexing techniques on the project documents people produce. ContactFinder identifies experts based on their participation patterns and message content. Expert Finder identifies experts based on documents people produce, as well as some experience-related information including basic employment information (e.g., positions held) and projects in which they participated.

These systems solve many of the challenges of expert databases since there is no need to manually contribute and maintain expertise information, and the automatically generated profiles are considerably more developed than the simple keyword-based profiles. However, these systems also have limitations. First, some individuals have expertise that is not yet represented in their digital traces. This is particularly true of new employees, as well as individuals who rely primarily on telephone and face-to-face meetings. Second, from the technical perspective, we still need to improve ways of selecting and integrating different sources and types of data to better reflect people's expertise. We also need to improve the ways of matching information seekers' fine-grained information needs with the large and amorphous expertise profiles. These are active areas of research, and we can expect improvements in the techniques that are used.

Finally, and perhaps most importantly, these systems largely do not consider the social perspectives of expertise sharing. For instance, their results are usually ranked purely based on the computed information similarity between the query and profiles. However, there are many other criteria that people use to select experts in real life and many other social factors that contribute to individual's willingness to share information and have meaningful interactions. The following section discusses systems that were designed with these social considerations in mind.

Expertise Recommenders

Rooted in the field of CSCW, Ackerman and other researchers developed a series of systems that address both social and technical issues related to expertise location and sharing. In contrast to systems that only identify experts based on content overlap, these systems attempt to create a social and technical environment that encourages information sharing and recognizes the importance of social context.

Answer Garden (AG) is a system designed to help in situations like technical support, where there is a continuing stream of questions, many of which occur repeatedly, but some of which have never been seen before.[15] It has a branching network of diagnostic questions that helps users find answers. If there is no available answer, it automatically routes the question to the appropriate expert who can answer the user and record the answer into the branching network for future users. The design of AG addresses two important social issues in expertise finding. First, askers are anonymous to the experts. This decreases the asker's social costs related to status implications and the need for reciprocity, although it also loses some of the potentially helpful contextual information. Second, by continually adding questions and answers into the corpus, it decreases the expert's workload in answering the same questions repeatedly and grows the organizational memory incrementally.

Field studies of AG showed mixed results. Questioners appreciated the anonymity, but many of the answers they received were not at the appropriate level (e.g., an answer was too technical and lengthy). This finding suggests that expertise locator systems should route organizational members to individuals with the right level of expertise, not just to experts with the highest level of expertise. A future field study of an AG-like system highlighted some of the limitations of the system including frustration due to incomplete data and continually changing classification schemes.[16] The study also found that the AG approach is subject to the impact of the given division of labor and organizational micro-politics.

A new version of AG, AG2 was developed to overcome some of the original limitations.[17] Unlike AG, where the expert location occurred manually, an expertise location engine was developed for AG2. Various computer-mediated communication mechanisms are also added. One important social innovation was the fact that the AG2 expert locator algorithm prefers to "stay local" when selecting expertise to allow contextualization, a concept that was found useful in later systems as well. If a local expert is unavailable, the system supports an escalation process whereby the query is sent on to others until an answer is provided. Thus, the system helps gracefully overcome failures with initial expert recommendations. Another interesting change to AG2 is that the system tends to blur the dichotomy between experts and seekers, recognizing that individuals may be novices in some areas and experts in other areas.

Expertise Recommender (ER) is another system developed by McDonald and Ackerman in order to address issues identified from a field study of AG2.[18] The major contribution of this system is that it can select experts based on a range of social factors such as organizational closeness and workload, not just level of expertise. As more data about our actions and relationships become available online, many new possibilities for identifying an *appropriate* expert become viable.

It is important to recognize that the systems discussed in this section are research prototype systems that are not as widely used as those previously discussed. Although a framework for including additional factors into the expert identification algorithms has been developed, few modules have been implemented. Future research examining the social factors that should be considered (e.g., privacy considerations and motivational issues) when recommending experts seems promising. It short, this research shows that finding an expert is not enough. One must also understand the other social factors related to their willingness to participate and have enough contextual knowledge to help.

Expert Referral Systems

Another approach to identifying experts is to use a referral process, where an individual has his colleagues and friends introduce, or refer, an expert. This referral method has been used throughout time. However, as more information about our social relationships is made available in digital form, systems have been developed to augment our ability to get high quality referrals from our peers. We call these *expert referral systems.*

ReferralWeb was the first well-known system that utilized social network information to help individuals find and be introduced to experts on a particular topic.[19] In ReferralWeb, people's expertise are indexed based on individuals' publications. Social network information is extracted from the coauthorships or co-appearances in their Web pages. Experts are identified via traditional information retrieval techniques (as described in the *automatic expertise finders* section). Once identified, the information seeker is presented with visualizations of the network structure, and a list of referral chains that can be taken to get from your known peers to the desired expert. For example, it might show that my friend John knows Lucy who knows the expert Jack; likewise it would show other paths to Jack through different friends who know him.

Although not designed specifically for the purpose of finding experts, Yenta[20] helps individuals find others with similar interests—individuals who may be in the best position to provide expert advice. Yenta acts like a personal agent. It creates people's personal interest profiles by mining documents in their local machines. The profile is stored locally and uses inter-agent communication to find people who have information similar to the query, all the while protecting the actual content from being shared with others. Yenta also clusters people based on their shared interests to built social coalitions and provides tools to communicate with others in the same cluster. Thus, Yenta can be thought of as a recommender system as described earlier in this article. Other related systems include MARS[21] and SWIM.[22] Recently, with the advancement of social network theory research, there are increasing number of peer-to-peer applications designed to share knowledge and resources (e.g., files and contacts) through social networks, as well as commercial social network systems (e.g., spoke and visiblepath) that are designed to help people share contact information. As social networking sites such as Facebook and LinkedIn become ubiquitous, expert referral systems will be a natural fit.

These expert referral systems have several advantages and disadvantages. They support the age-old practice of finding information through social contacts that is familiar to all of us and socially acceptable. They provide added motivation for individuals to help those who seek them out; after all, an expert is more likely to provide help if they have been introduced by a mutual friend or perhaps even an automatic agent that has identified some hidden similarity. These systems are relatively easy to implement using basic peer-to-peer and information retrieval techniques. They also can provide contextual information about individuals based on their social network relationships, helping expert seekers make more educated decisions about whether or not it is worth contacting a particular expert. Unfortunately, systems like ReferralWeb increase the amount of time required to contact an expert; not only the information seeker's time but also the friends that are part of the referral chain. They may also decrease the pool of experts who are reachable in practice, since referral chains that are too long (or nonexistent) discourage contact with the expert. There is a need for more empirical studies of these systems to help reveal additional advantages and disadvantages.

Summary

In this section we have outlined a variety of different expert locator systems including expert databases, automatic expertise finders, ERs, and expert referral systems. Additional systems are described in Ackerman et al.[23] Because research on expert locator systems is still in its infancy, the specific terminology and categorization we provide is tentative and likely to change as new techniques are developed and integrated with other knowledge management and social software programs. However, many of the key principles, trends, and design considerations discussed above are enduring. In this summary, we address two of the most prominent.

One common trend is the use of implicit data rather than explicitly entered data in expert locator systems. This trend is likely to continue as more and more of our activities are recorded in a digital environment and can potentially be used to identify our expertise domains, our social network ties, and other factors of interest (e.g., availability). For instance, Zhang et al.[24] explored ways of using people's asking-answering histories in online forums to infer expertise levels. Further developing tools to integrate these various data sources will be vital to improving expert locator systems. These issues are also important for designing recommender systems more generally.

Another common theme is the need to consider the social implications of expert locator systems. The *expertise recommenders* and the *expert referral systems* emphasize that locating the most knowledgeable individual on a topic is not enough. After all, the most knowledgeable individual may not be able to present information at the right level for the information seeker or may be too far removed from the local context to be of benefit. Furthermore, the most knowledgeable individuals may not have sufficient incentives to participate, especially if they are bombarded with questions from strangers. Systems that take into consideration these social factors and align the incentives of the various parties are far more likely to succeed in the long run. In this sense, expert locator systems may be better labeled expertise sharing systems.

CONCLUSION

In this entry we have discussed two types of systems that facilitate learning from other people in a highly personal way. Recommender systems provide personalized recommendations for individuals about items that they have not yet experienced for themselves. Expert locators help identify people who are knowledgeable on a topic, so they can personally engage with those who seek their expertise. These systems provide nice alternatives and complements to traditional information retrieval techniques. When finding a relevant document is not enough, expert locators provide access to individuals with expertise and recommender systems provide additional pointers to resources that may not have been considered in the original search query. Research on these topics is growing rapidly and the methods for performing them are improving as a result. In addition, as more and more activity is implicitly captured online, it is increasingly possible to improve these tools and apply them in new domains.

REFERENCES

1. Goldberg, K.; Roeder, T.; Gupta, D.; Perkins, C. Eigentaste: A constant time collaborative filtering algorithm. Inform. Ret. **2001**, *4* (2), 133–151.
2. Breese, J.; Heckerman, D.; Kadie, C. Empirical analysis of predictive algorithms for collaborative filtering. In *Proceedings of the 14th Conference on Uncertainty in Artificial Intelligence*, Uncertainty in Artificial Intelligence, Madison, WI, July 24–26, 1998; Cooper, G., Moral, S., Eds.; Morgan Kaufman: San Francisco, 1998; 43–52.
3. Pazzani, M.J.; Billsus, D. Content-based Recommendation Systems. In *The Adaptive Web*; Brusilovsky, P., Kobsa, A., Nejdl, W., Eds.; Springer: Berlin/Heidelberg, Germany, 2007; 325–341. (http://www.springerlink.com/content/qq35wt68l6774261/for all info).
4. Resnick, P.; Iacovou, N.; Suchak, M.; Bergstrom, P.; Riedl, J. GroupLens: An open architecture for collaborative filtering of netnews. In *Proceedings of the 1994 ACM Conference on Computer Supported Cooperative Work*, Computer Supported Cooperative Work, Chapel Hill, NC, October 22–26, 1994; ACM Press: New York, 1994; 175–186.
5. Crawford, D., Ed. Commun. ACM **1997**, *40*, (3).
6. http://www.grouplens.org/ (accessed February 2008).
7. Shardanand, U.; Maes, P. Social information filtering: Algorithms for automating "word of mouth". In *Proceedings of the SIGCHI Conference on Human Factors in Computing Systems*, Conference on Human Factors in Computing Systems, Denver, CO, May 7–11, 1995; Association for Computing Machinery/Addison-Wesley: New York, 1995; 210–217.

8. Konstan, J.A., Ed.; Introduction to recommender systems: Algorithms and Evaluation. ACM Trans. Inform. Syst. (TOIS) **2004**, *22* (1), 1–4.
9. Riedl, J. Dourish, P. Introduction to the special section on recommender systems. ACM Trans. Comput.-Hum. Interact. (TOCHI) **2005**, *12* (3), 371–373.
10. Felfernig, A.; Friedrich, G.; Schmidt-Thieme, L. Guest editors'. Introduction: Recommender systems, IEEE Intell. Syst. **2007**, *22* (3), 18–21, doi: 10.1109/MIS.2007.52.
11. *Proceedings of the 2007 ACM Conference on Recommender Systems*, RecSys'07, Minneapolis, MN, October 19–20, 2007; ACM Press: New York, 2007.
12. Streeter, L.; Lochbaum, K. Who knows: A system based on automatic representation of semantic structure. In *Proceedings of the Conference on Computer-Assisted Information Retrieval*, RIAO'88 Program Conference, Cambridge, MA, March 21–24, 1988; CID: Paris, 1988; 380–388.
13. Krulwich, B.; Burkey, C. Contactfinder agent: Answering bulletin board questions with referrals. In *Proceedings of the 13th National Conference on Artificial Intelligence*, AAAI National Conference, Portland, OR, August 4–8, 1996; AAAI Press: Menlo Park, CA, 1996; 10–15.
14. Maybury, M.; D'Amore, R.; House, D. Automated discovery and mapping of expertise. In *Sharing Expertise: Beyond Knowledge Management*; Ackerman, M.S., Pipek, V., Wulf, V., Eds.; MIT Press: Cambridge, MA, 2003; 359–382.
15. Ackerman, M.S. Answer garden: A tool for growing organizational memory. Wirtschaftsinformatik **1995**, *37* (3), 320–321.
16. Pipek, V.; Wulf, V. Pruning the answer garden: Knowledge sharing in maintenance engineering. In *ECSCW 2003: Proceedings of the Eighth European Conference on Computer Supported Cooperative Work*, Computer Supported Cooperative Work, Helsinki, Finland, September 14–18, 2003; Kuutti, K., Karsten, E.H., Fitzpatrick, G., Dourish, P., Schmidt, K., Eds.; Kluwer Academic: Dordrecht, the Netherlands, 2003; 1–20.
17. Ackerman, M.S.; McDonald, D.W. Answer garden 2: Merging organizational memory with collaborative help. In *Proceedings of the 1996 ACM Conference on Computer Supported Cooperative Work*, Computer Supported Cooperative Work, Boston, November 16–20, 1996; ACM Press: New York, 1996; 97–105.
18. McDonald, D.W.; Ackerman, M.S. Expertise recom-mender: A flexible recommendation system and architecture. In *Proceedings of the 2000 ACM Conference on Computer Supported Cooperative Work*, Computer Supported Cooperative Work, Philadelphia, PA, December 2–6, 2000; ACM Press: New York, 2000; 231–240.
19. Kautz, H.; Selman, B.; Shah, M. Referral web: Combining social networks and collaborative filtering. Commun. ACM **1997**, *40* (3), 63–65.
20. Foner, L.N. Yenta: A multi-agent, referral-based matchmaking system. In *Proceedings of the 1st International Conference on Autonomous Agents*, International Conference on Autonomous Agents, Marina del Rey, CA, February 5–8, 1997; ACM Press: New York, 1997; 301–307.
21. Yu, B.; Singh, M.P. Searching social networks. In *Proceedings of the 2nd International Joint Conference on Autonomous Agents and Multiagent Systems*, International Conference on Autonomous Agents, Melbourne, Australia, July 14–18, 2003; ACM Press: New York, 2003; 65–72.
22. Zhang, J.; Van Alstyne, M. SWIM: Fostering social network based information search. In *CHI '04 Extended Abstracts on Human Factors in Computing Systems*, Conference on Human Factors in Computing Systems, Vienna, Austria, April 24–29, 2004; ACM Press: New York, 2004; 1568.
23. Ackerman, M.; Pipek, V.; Wulf, V., *Eds. Sharing Expertise: Beyond Knowledge Management*; MIT Press: Cambridge, MA, 2002.
24. Zhang, J.; Ackerman, M.S.; Adamic, L. Expertise networks in online communities: Structure and algorithms. In *Proceedings of the 16th International Conference on World Wide Web*, International World Wide Web Conference, Banff, Canada, May 8–12, 2007; ACM Press: New York, 2007; 221–230.

BIBLIOGRAPHY

1. Ackerman, M.S.; Halverson, C.A. Sharing expertise: The next step for knowledge management. In Social Capital and Information Technology; Huysman, M., Wulf, V., Eds.; MIT Press: Cambridge, MA, 2004; 273–300.
2. Ackerman, M.; Pipek, V.; Wulf, V., Eds. *Sharing Expertise: Beyond Knowledge Management*; MIT Press: Cambridge, MA, 2002.

3. Adomavicius, G.; Tuzhilin, A. Toward the next generation of recommender systems: A survey of the state-of-the-art and possible extensions. IEEE T. Knowl. Data. En., **2005**, *17* (6), 734–749.
4. http://www.grouplens.org/ (accessed February 2008).
5. *Proceedings of the 2007 ACM Conference on Recommender Systems*, RecSys'07, Minneapolis, MN, October 19–20, 2007; ACM Press: New York, 2007.
6. Resnick, P.; Varian, H.R. Recommender systems. Comm. ACM **1997**, *40* (3), 56–58.
7. Riedl, J.; Konstan, J. *Word of Mouse: The Marketing Power of Collaborative Filtering*; Warner Books: New York, 2002.
8. Terveen, L.; Hill, W. Beyond recommender systems: Helping people help each other. In *HCI in the New Millennium*; Carroll, J., Ed.; Addison Wesley: Boston, 2001.

32 Knowledge Management Systems

Dick Stenmark

CONTENTS

INTRODUCTION

Knowledge management systems (KMS) refers to a class of information systems (IS) that is used to enhance knowledge and information transfer within an organization and to manage organizational knowledge.[1] Although this statement seems straightforward, it is rather difficult to define what a KMS is, since it is still unclear exactly what should be included in the concept of knowledge management (KM). What is the difference between knowledge and information and can computer applications really deal with knowledge? Some have argued that computers can only process data, and certainly not knowledge.[2] What, then, is a KMS and what role does it play in KM work? Before we can talk about *systems* for KM, we need a shared view of KM itself.

Is KM an emerging new discipline of its own or is it a topic that runs across several existing scholarly discourses? Throughout the years, there have been advocates of both positions. There are also commentators arguing that organizations have always been practicing KM-related activities so there is essentially nothing new to KM. This is no uncommon phenomenon but something that happens whenever new terminology is introduced. In the 1980s, Cronin asked whether information management had something new to offer or if it was just a new label for librarianship.[3] Twenty or so years later, people ask the same thing about KM and KMS.

Whilst several voices claim that there is no consensus regarding what exactly knowledge management is or how it differs from information management, Davenport and Grover in their editorial comment on the 2001 Special KM issue of Journal of Management Information Systems (JMIS) concluded that KM as a *practical* phenomenon was here to stay but that *formal research* on the topic was lacking.[4] A couple of years have passed since Davenport and Grover made this observation and today it is fair to say that KM has established itself as a research topic, as reported elsewhere in this encyclopedia. Davenport and Grover continued by observing that IT support for KM, i.e., KMS, was seen as a useful but far from required resource by practitioners and scholars alike.

In the following text, we shall first look briefly at the history of KM and KMS before turning to the various theories underpinning this field. Thereafter, some of the most well-cited frameworks for KMS found in the IS literature are introduced to help the reader see what *types* of KMS are available. The ontological aspects of KMS are touched upon before finally discussing the challenges KMS are facing today.

ROOTS OF KM

It can be debated when and where KM started, since it depends on what discipline you examine. A large number of fields have clearly influenced the emerging KM discourse—e.g., sociology, human resource management, organization science, and IS research to name but a few. Many commentators would probably hold organizational learning as the one discipline that has had the perhaps most profound effect on the KM field.[5,6] When it comes to KMS, though, the IS discipline has taken a leading role, since the development, implementation, and use of systems to informate and automate are central to the IS field.[7]

Tiwana[8] places the roots of KM in the 1950s management literature, whereas Maier[6] traces the first instances of KM back to the studies of societal application of knowledge in the late 1960s and early 1970s. However, it was not until the late 1980s, through the writings of, e.g., Sveiby and Lloyd[9] and Wiig,[10] that the phenomenon started to receive more widespread attention. Nonaka and Takeuchis's book "The Knowledge Creating Company"[11] is also an early landmark in organizational KM literature and one of the most cited sources with almost 10,000 references in Google Scholar.

What propelled the development of KM as a new research discipline was the growing emphasis on knowledge work and knowledge workers as the primary source of productivity as opposed to assets such as land or capital.[11] This view paved way for the knowledge-based perspective of the firm[12] that suggests that the tangible resources of an organization generate value dependent on how they are combined and applied, which in turn depends on the organization's knowledge. This knowledge is deeply permeated in culture, procedures, routines, systems, and minds of the individual employees.

In the introduction of their 2001 paper, Alavi and Leidner note that it is not the existence of this knowledge per se that matters, but the ability to apply it and put it to use. To that end, advanced information technologies can be instrumental in effectuating the knowledge-based view of the firm by systemizing, enhancing, and expediting large-scale knowledge management.[13]

CRITIQUE OF KM

Knowledge management as a research discipline has also received critique. Some have argued that it is no more than yet another exemplar in a long list of management fads that have come and gone over the years.[2,14] In his critical analysis of KM, Wilson concludes:

> [Knowledge management] is, in large part, a management fad, promulgated mainly by certain consultancy companies, and the probability is that it will fade away like previous fads.[14]

Much of this skepticism stems from the fact that many consultancy firms and software vendors simply seemed to have renamed their old services and products, replacing the term "information" with the term "knowledge." Therefore, says Wilson:

> [T]he confusion of 'knowledge' as a synonym for 'information' is one of the most common effects of the 'knowledge management' fad.[14]

In addition to the fad debate, the KM discourse was also criticized for being "technology-driven." Comparing and contrasting the KM literature to that of organizational learning (OL), Swan et al. found that although the two disciplines are concerned with the improvement of organizational performance through knowledge development, i.e., human issues, only the OL literature focused on humans whereas the KM literature was predominantly occupied with tools and techniques.[5] The emphasis on information technology in the KM literature resulted in people being marginalized to either "inputs to KM [. . .] or as constraints on its effectiveness [. . .]" (p. 673).[5] Swan and colleagues argue that much of the richness of human relations is lost when KM is reduced to merely technology.

This distinction between technology-oriented and human-oriented approaches has a long tradition in organization science and goes back to at least the early 1980s. However, a more holistic understanding of KM that encompasses both these stances has developed, and much of the turf wars from the late 1990s have now abated.

THEORETICAL FOUNDATION

Much of the epistemology used in KM literature has been influenced by the separation of knowledge in a tacit and an explicit component. The notion of tacit knowing is attributed to philosopher Michael Polanyi but was introduced to the KM discourse by Nonaka and Takeuchi.[11] Interestingly, the commonly used tacit–explicit distinction is not directly derived from Polanyi's work. Most commentators see explicit knowledge as knowledge that has been captured and codified into manuals, procedures, and rules, and is easy to disseminate. Tacit knowledge, on the other hand, is then knowledge that cannot be easily articulated and thus only exists in people's hands and minds, and manifests itself through their actions. In contrast, Polanyi does not make such a distinction. Instead, he envisions tacit knowing as the backdrop against which all understanding is distinguished.

While Polanyi speaks of tacit *knowing*, i.e., the verb, as a backdrop against which all actions are understood, Nonaka and Takeuchi use the term tacit *knowledge*, i.e., the noun, to denote particular type of knowledge that is difficult to express. This view has been criticized but due to the strong influence of Nonaka and Takeuchi's writings on the knowledge management discourse, this interpretation has been widely adopted. Amongst the critics are Tsoukas, who argues that tacit knowledge is *not* explicit knowledge internalized. Instead, tacit knowledge is inseparable from explicit knowledge since "[t]acit knowledge is the necessary component of all knowledge" (p. 14).[15] According to Tsoukas the two are so inseparately related that to even try to separate the two would be to "miss the point." There had perhaps been less confusion had Nonaka instead used the term "implicit knowledge."

Tsoukas recognizes that the dichotomy between tacit and explicit knowledge and the taxonomies derived from this duality have advanced our understanding of organizational knowledge by showing its multifaceted nature. However, such typologies also limit our understanding by the inherent formalism that accompanies them. "The conceptual categories along which the phenomena are classified must be assumed to be discrete, separate, and stable. The problem is that they hardly ever are" (p. 14).[15]

The tacit–explicit dichotomy has also taken other expressions. Choo suggests a differentiation between tacit, explicit, and cultural knowledge,[16] and Spender suggests, in addition to tacit and explicit knowledge, individual and collective knowing.[12] Blackler speaks of embodied, embedded, embrained, encultured, and encoded knowledge.[17] Yet another derivative is the distinction between the community view and the commodity view. The community view sees knowledge as socially constructed and inseparable from the knower, whereas the commodity view holds knowledge as a universal truth, and as facts and collectable objects.[18] Though several other ways to classify knowledge exist and have been suggested, they all, more or less, build on the tacit–explicit dichotomy.

DEFINITION OF KM SYSTEMS

Whereas most people agree that data and information may exist outside humans, supporters of the community view of knowledge have argued that knowledge can never be separated from the knower and thus never stored digitally.[2,13] Computer support for knowledge management would thus be, in a sense, impossible. How can we then talk about KMS?

KMS is often employed as a catalyst or enabler of KM but such implementations should not be carried out without careful coordination with the required people-oriented activities needed. Alavi and Leidner note that while KM initiatives may not *require* tools, IT can certainly support KM in many ways, in particular in firms where the ratio of *knowledge workers* is high.[13] Schultze defines a knowledge worker as someone who interacts knowledgeable with information and sees information not only as something derived from knowledge but as something that changes knowledge.[19] There is thus a tight relationship between information and knowledge and it seems that any knowledge work needs to be supported by information technology.

As stated in the introduction, a KMS is an IS and IS and knowledge systems are thus not radically different; instead, there is a subtle yet important difference in the *attitude* towards and the *purpose* of the systems. Whereas an IS processes information without engaging the users, a KMS must be geared towards helping the users to understand and assign *meaning* to the information.[13] The value of any given piece of information resides in the relationship between the information and the user's knowledge. This means that design of KMS should be based on an understanding not only of the information per se, but also of the context where the user develops the information need, and the analysis of the usage of the same information once it has been obtained and interpreted by the user.[20]

Following Alavi and Leidner,[13] a KMS should thus be understood as a particular class of information systems developed specifically to support organisations in their attempt to create, codify, collect, store, integrate, share, and apply knowledge.

KMS THEORY

The theoretical foundation underpinning KMS vary considerably and are not easily detected but we can get a reasonably good picture by looking at Schultze and Leidner's classification of theoretical perspectives in KM-related IS research. Having reviewed six leading IS journals and thoroughly analyzed nearly 100 articles from 1990 to 2000, Schultze and Leidner showed that a vast majority or 70% belonged to the Normative Discourse, 25% could be labeled as Interpretative Discourse and only a handful of papers represented a Critical (or Dialogic) Discourse.[21]

According to Schultze and Leidner's analysis, the normative discourse, which is characterized by a strive towards consensus from an a priori understanding of what the research problems are, typically assumes progressive enlightenment and increasing rationalisation, management, and control. IS research representing the normative discourse are thus concerned with "codification, normalisation of experience and the search for law-like relationships" (pp. 216–217).[21] Much of the research focus on problem solving, and it creates "a problem space that can be decomposed in a logical, top-down fashion" (p. 221).[21] Although both the research topics and the way knowledge is operationalised show great diversity, a common metaphor used within the normative discourse is that of knowledge as an asset. Researchers in this category typically view knowledge as a key driver of organizational efficiency and performance. Amongst the theories underpinning normative research, Schultze and Leidner mention innovation diffusion theory, absorptive capacity theory, and management cognition theory (p. 222).[21]

The interpretative discourse, which also opts for consensus but from an emergent understanding of the organizational situation, emphasizes the social aspects of organizational life that has not been rationalized or systematized. IS research representing the interpretative discourse thus aims "to create a coherent, consensual, and unified representation of what the organisational reality is 'actually' like" (p. 217),[21] and is typically targeted on work situations and organizational practices. Knowledge is therefore studied indirectly via its role in organizational transformation and how it is supported by various types of KMS. In this discourse, knowledge, technology, and organisational practice are all seen as socially constructed and dynamic, and the theories upon which interpretative research rests include organisational learning, communities of practice, activity theory, and bricolage (pp. 224–225).[21]

It is evident that almost all KM-related IS research is consensus-oriented. There are, however, also those who apply a dissensus-oriented approach. Although Schultze and Leidner treat critical and dialogic as two separate discourses, I shall here use the critical discourse label to include both these perspectives, since both understand struggle, conflict, and tension as natural organizational states. Seen from this perspective, organizations are "sites of political struggle and fields of continuous conflict" (p. 217)[21] and the objective of the research is thus to show that there is no coherent reality but different forms of domination and distortions. KMS (and other IT tools) are thus not to be understood as neutral, according to this perspective, but should be seen as instruments to make invisible work visible or to actively change social conditions. Schultze and Leidner call for more research in the critical discourse since this perspective allows the highlighting of the social inequities underpinning the distinction between service and knowledge work and the examination of contradictions in managing knowledge.[21] The direct implications for KMS, however, are less obvious.

TYPES OF KMS AND THEIR APPLICATIONS

As we saw earlier, many vendors tried to repackage their applications under the KM label at the end of the last millennium and a list of different KMS can therefore be made arbitrarily long. Instead of presenting a list of software that not all would agree upon, and, in addition, soon would be dated, it is more useful to examine three of the most referenced classification schemes for KMS and let them define the *various types of applications* that are possible. The frameworks are Hansen et al.'s *Codification vs. Personalization* from *Harvard Business Review* in 1999,[22] Hahn and Subramani's *Knowledge Residence and Level of Structure* from ICIS 2000,[23] and finally Alavi and Leidner's scheme from MISQ in 2001.[13]

Codification vs. Personalization

An early framework for KM work (and hence for KMS to support that work) is found in Hansen et al.'s well-referred article from *Harvard Business Review*. Based on their studies of management consultancy firms, and implicitly building on Nonaka's dichotomy of explicit and tacit knowledge, Hansen et al. divide knowledge management efforts into two different strategies; codification and personalization.[22]

Companies where the KM strategy centers on codifying and storing knowledge into databases for easy dissemination and retrieval is said to follow a codification strategy. In such companies, computers have a central role in the strategy, as carriers of knowledge. Hansen et al. point to Ernst and Young as a company following a codification strategy. Knowledge is harvested and coded into documents or other "knowledge objects" as an informant called them (p. 108),[22] and these are thereafter stored in electronic repositories for later retrieval. Even though the codification process is laborious, Ernst and Young has dedicated staff members doing nothing else but codifying knowledge into documents—this approach allows for scaling up since the repositories are accessible for all employees worldwide and available around the clock. Once the object is put into the repository it can be used over and over again at a very low cost, provided it does not have to be modified. Companies using the codification strategy thus typically deal with problems where the same solution can be applied many times. The "economics of reuse" is what motivates the KM efforts in these companies, and the KMS used are typically document management systems and databases.[22]

In contrast, when knowledge is tied to the individual that developed it and thus cannot be stored in a database, it has to be shared through face-to-face interactions. The role of the computers is thus to facilitate communication between people. Companies with this approach are said to follow a personalization strategy, and Hansen et al. mention McKinsey as a company in this category. In their company, knowledge emerges out of dialogues between individuals and their IT focus is thus to enable interactions between employees. Part of McKinsey's KM strategy is to move people between offices to expand their networks. Even though face-to-face meetings are unequalled for sharing tacit knowledge, space and time distances may sometime prevent people from physical meetings. McKinsey thus engage e-mail and video conferencing equipment to communicate and allow employees tap into the expertise of their peers. Companies following a personalization strategy typically deal with unique problems that do not have clear solutions and where customized answers must be provided. In "experts economics" knowledge is tacit and cannot be systematized and made efficient. Instead, these companies charge much higher prices, and KMS used are expert finder systems and communications software.[22]

Hansen et al. stress that companies should not try to combine these two strategies but, based on their business strategy, select one as their main KM strategy and merely use the other as a complementary strategy.

Knowledge Residence and Level of Structure

Adding another dimension to the tacit–explicit dichotomy, Hahn and Subramani present a framework for KMS by looking on the one hand at where the knowledge is said to reside (i.e., in artifacts or in people) and on the other hand to the extent to which knowledge is said to impose or require an a priori structure. These axes form a two-by-two matrix hosting four different classes of KMS.[23]

- One is where the system manages knowledge artifacts that has an inherent structure or where the system imposes a structure on the artifacts. Formal document repositories and data warehouses belong to this class.
- A second class also requires an a priori structure but manages links to knowledgeable people. A competence database intended to let employees find colleagues with specific skills falls into this class.
- A third class does not impose any structure in particular and assumes that knowledge is codified into artifacts. Intranets where Web pages and documents are found through full-text indexing search engines belong to this class.
- Finally, a fourth class again requires no structure but provides means for employees to identify and communicate with local experts. Discussion forums and e-mail Listservs are systems in this class.

Hahn and Subramani identify three interesting challenges regarding KMS. First, balancing information overload and potential useful content involves the size and diversity of both the users and the content. When the knowledge resides in artifacts, more items means higher chances of being able to find what you need. Also when human resources are required, more users increase the possibilities of finding a knowledgeable coworker. The down side is that more information also means more unrelated or useless information, and more users typically generate more interactions and more e-mails, which blurs the picture. For the same reason is diversity useful, and no problem in highly structured environments, but when structures and shared vocabularies are lacking, diversity can easily get overwhelming.[23]

Second, balancing additional workload and accurate content addresses the issue of keeping KMS updated. Highly structured environments require considerable efforts to ensure the appropriateness of the structure, and this work often comes on top of the employees' ordinary work tasks. In more loosely structured systems motivation to share knowledge often comes in the form of higher social status. The downside is that those who contribute and earn a reputation may end up being occupied answering people's questions and helping colleagues instead of doing their jobs.[23]

Third, balancing exploitation and exploration means being aware of the fact that reliance on existing solutions only may result in a competency trap.[24] A system that supports the exploitation of existing knowledge may provide short-term benefits but in the long run be detrimental to the organization. At the same time, a system preoccupied with generating new knowledge may prevent organizational members from learning and adding to the collective experience that exists in the organization.

Hahn and Subramani suggest the KMS should consider including agent technology, collaborative filtering methods, advanced visualization tools, in order to address the above challenges.[23]

Alavi and Leidner's Scheme

Without suggesting an explicit framework, Alavi and Leidner in their review of the literature discussing applications of IT to knowledge management efforts, identify three common approaches: Coding and sharing of best practice, Creation of knowledge directories, and Creation of knowledge networks (p. 114).[13]

Coding and sharing of best practice is one of the most common applications of KMS, according to Alavi and Leidner. The term "best practice" is typically used to refer to a superior or exemplary practice that leads to superior performance. By collecting and codifying stories that mediate such practice, organizations can build KMS that stores and disseminates these experiences within the organization.

Creation of knowledge directories forms a second common class of KMS. Knowledge directories are also known as expert finder systems and aim at mapping the internal expertise of the organization. Alavi and Leidner report that 74% of the respondents in Gazeau's survey believed that their organization's most useful knowledge was not available in explicit form. When knowledge cannot be codified into artifacts, creating knowledge directories allows organizational members to benefit from the knowledge by being able to find and subsequently talk to the knowledgeable coworker.

Creation of knowledge networks is the third commonly used approach to KMS. Applications to first identify and then bring together (virtually or face-to-face) people from the same community of practice or those who share an interest has proven useful in many organizations. Ford Motor Company found that by sharing knowledge in networks the development time for cars was reduced by 33%. Online forums belong to the technology used in this approach.[13]

We have seen that KMS can either be used to support a commodity view of KM, where the explication of knowledge is assumed not only to be possible but also necessary, or a community view of KM, where the implicit nature of knowing puts people in focus. The success of KMS (as with most IS) depends on the extent of use, which in turn depends on a number of factors. In their concluding discussion, Alavi and Leidner point to a set of research questions concerning the application of IT to KM. In sum, they ask what effect an increased breadth and depth of knowledge via KMS would have on organizational performance; how to ensure that knowledge in an KMS can be modified (if necessary) prior to being used, and how these modifications too can be captured; how anonymized knowledge in a KMS can be trusted; and what are the quality and usefulness factors of KMS.[13] The answers to many of these questions are still pending.

ONTOLOGICAL ASPECTS

It has often been argued that only individuals can think and act—not organizations. At the same time, as human beings we are social creatures and we tend to seek, and benefit from, each other's company. Inputs from colleagues and the surrounding context greatly affect our ability to create and use knowledge because the individual and the collective interact in fruitful ways. Focusing primarily on how new knowledge emerges, Nonaka and Takeuchi stress the fact that knowledge creation initiates from the individual but is a process that moves through expanding communities of interaction, crossing group, division, and, finally, organizational boundaries.[11] Other scholars have made similar comments about other KM processes.

Still, IT support for KM has traditionally focused on organizational-wide systems, possibly due to the acknowledged fact that the usefulness of a KMS grows exponentially with the size of the organization. Much of the IS research has thus had a macro-level focus, but also applications supporting organizational learning and organizational memory are common in the KMS repertoire. The challenge associated with organizational KMS is that individuals often have to provide input without getting much back in return. This problem, often referred to as the maintenance problem seriously threatens the quality and usefulness of these systems.

Another category of KMS are the groupware systems targeting smaller subsets of the organization, typically aiming for management. This category includes various types of Decision Support Systems (DSS). Many KMS in this category can also be related to the field of Computer-Supported Collaborative Work (CSCW). Typical applications here include Helpdesk applications and expert finder systems within specific subgroups. The maintenance problem continues to be a challenge also at this level.

When it comes to the individual, there has—until recently—not been equally much support. Some argue that this situation is about to change. One of the problems here is that not all of the applications used at an individual level are officially labeled KMS. For example, the information retrieval (IR) field has provided the knowledge worker with search engines and other tools to help locate information, but not all would agree that a search engine is a KMS. Another noticeable trend is the growth of social media. These applications exploit the individual–collective relationship and are able to provide the individual with added value through the actions of the collective relationship and vice versa. It will be interesting to follow this development to see whether social media will provide a means to avoid, if not solve, the maintenance problem.

THE KMS CHALLENGES

A number of KMS challenges can be identified in the KM literature. One issue is that of dispersion of work. It is argued that knowledge workers are increasingly dispersed—spatial as well as contractual.[25] Organizational members work outside the physical boundaries of the firm and/or change positions within the firm, often including geographical changes. This, it is argued, makes them less exposed to colleagues with similar functional skills.

There is also the contractual dispersion, i.e., the provisional nature of employment and the higher level of partial or temporary involvement in the firm that many knowledge workers experience. In addition, many are engaged in virtual teams that often reorganize and have high turnover rates. This dispersion of work requires KMS that allows for effective sharing of the latest knowledge.[25,26]

Another issue is the shorter product and process life cycles in today's organizations.[26] This compresses the time window for capturing the lessons learned and knowledge created in the process and leaves the knowledge workers with little time to document and save their experiences. At the same time knowledge becomes obsolete much quicker. KMS need to be able to deal effectively with these circumstances.

The above concerns can be seen as aspects of a larger and overarching challenge, i.e., how to keep KMS updated and current. While many of today's organizations expect KMS to become major catalysts for innovations in terms of the ways in which businesses can be organized and conducted, there is plenty of IS research that indicate that such systems often fail when implemented in everyday knowledge work. In response, a distinguishable issue in KMS research is how to support knowledge work with IS in a successful way. It has been found that although the systems work technically and should function well in theory, they remain unused by the organizational members.[27] Following this, the development of systems with the capacity to bridge the knowing-doing gap in organizations has been recognized as a significant area of KMS research.

However, the imbalance between the desire for accurate content and the workload required to achieve this still appears to be a critical problem, leading to systems of little use for organizations in their knowledge application processes. It has been suggested that the problem stems from the fact that the requirements for KMS are fundamentally different from those of other types of IT and are thus not covered by existing IS design theories.

Markus et al. have identified three primary differences.[28] First, knowledge work processes requires that expert knowledge is adapted and/or contextualized to specific local conditions. Decision support systems and executive IS do not provide system features that can handle expert knowledge or contextualize translation rules. Resulting from this, DSS and expert systems inhibit creative problem finding and solution generation. While expert systems manage general expert knowledge, they fail to support contextual knowledge and the flexibility needed for process emergence. Second, these types of systems are all specifically designed for a known type of user, e.g., managers. Being designed for a particular type of user community, these systems are not well adapted to emergent work processes characterized by shifting user types having varying knowledge requirements. Third, knowledge workers have access to many different types of systems but since these systems often are isolated and not integrated into work practice, knowledge workers tend to manage their systems rather than getting the job done.

To circumvent these problems, it has been suggested that KMS should be integrated with or build into already existing applications since key to a successful KMS is to facilitate usage.[29] As knowledge work requires creativity in order to produce idiosyncratic and esoteric knowledge, knowledge work practice is untidy compared to operational or administrative business processes. Hence, KMS must be able to go beyond written instructions and official task descriptions, thus appreciating exceptions not only as something inevitable but as a necessity. Consequently, KMS must not be isolated but should be integrated into work practice. For the purpose of avoiding situations where knowledge workers manage their systems rather than getting the job done, developers must recognize sociotechnical issues associated with disparity in work and benefit. In this way, KMS capable of attracting a critical mass of users can be developed. In addition, paying attention to unobtrusive accessibility and the adoption process may deepen developers' understanding of how support systems can be better integrated with both the day-to-day tasks of knowledge workers and their performance of the tasks.

CONCLUDING SUMMARY

In the 1990s there was a rather heated debate whether or not KM was a fad but this seems to have abated. Now, there is consensus that KM—at least as a pragmatic issue—is here to stay. With knowledge replacing economy of scale as business driver and with increasing portion of knowledge workers in today's organizations, knowledge management, and the need for IT support for it, is not likely to go away.

The strong focus on technology that we witnessed in early KM work has been compensated for and practitioners and researchers alike now have acknowledged that knowledge cannot exist outside the mind of a human being. Cultures that encourage and motivate individuals to share, combine, and reuse knowledge are recognized as equal, if not more, important as IT, even amongst technologists. IT is still likely to continue to play an important part, not as driver and single success factor but as catalyst, facilitator and enabler of social networks, virtual meeting places, and new discussion forums. One of the general lessons learned is that technology is important and useful but it should not be the driving force in KM work.

Several commentators have pointed to the fact that KMS in the late 1990s were discrete, standalone systems not aligned with the organizations' business processes. Such systems had to be explicitly attended to on top of ordinary tasks, thus adding to—not facilitating—the work to be carried out.[29] Newer KMS appear to be better integrated with existing business infrastructure and enterprise applications, thereby allowing employees to seamlessly apply organizational knowledge in whatever work they are engaged. However, there is still a need for development and research in this area.

On the theoretical side, no core theory on knowledge management has yet been developed, and KM may still be understood as an "umbrella construct," i.e., a broad and somewhat unclear label that is used to contain a whole variety of loosely connected issues.[30] Without a clear theoretical focus, some commentators argue, the original concept risks being eroded until it has no value and collapses, as researchers explore divergent paths and build isolated islands of knowledge. Spender[31] has argued strongly that KM and KMS research need a core theory that distinguishes them from other fields but at the same time is narrow enough to allow laypeople to recognize and understand what is and what is not a KMS. Not much work is currently to be found along such lines.

In their editorial introduction to the 2003 special issue on KM and IT in *IT and People*, Gray and Meister argue that KMS researchers are facing a bigger problem than did researchers of earlier organizational phenomena, since knowledge is neither new nor physically present and there is thus nothing concrete to point to. An independent core theory of KM and KMS is therefore needed, they argue.[32]

However, several future scenarios are possible. If the development towards more knowledge work continues, we may end up in the scenario predicted by Davenport and Grover where "every industry will view itself as knowledge-intensive (p. 4).[4] If everything is KM, will the concept then still be meaningful, and if every application is a KMS, will the term be useful? At the other end of the spectrum lies a scenario where KM becomes so diversified and scattered that for this reason is pointless to talk about KM and IT support for it. Where we will end up remains to be seen.

REFERENCES

1. Voelpel, S.; Dous, M.; Davenport, T. Five steps to creating a global knowledge-sharing system: Siemens' ShareNet. Acad. Manage. Execut. **2005**, *19* (2), 9–23.
2. Galliers, R.; Newell, S. Back to the future: From knowledge management to data management. In *Proceedings of European Conference on Information Systems 2001*, Bled, Slovenia, June 27–29, 2001; 609–615.
3. Cronin, B. Introduction. *In Information Management: From Strategies to Action*; Cronin, B., Ed.; Aslib: London, 1985; vii–ix.
4. Davenport, T.H.; Grover, V. Editorial: Special issue on knowledge management. J. Manage. Inform. Syst. **2001**, *18* (1), 3–4.
5. Swan, J.; Scarbrough, H.; Preston, J. Knowledge management—The next fad to forget people. In *Proceedings of European Conference on Information Systems 1999*, Copenhagen, Denmark, June 23–25, 1999; 668–678.
6. Maier, R. *Knowledge Management Systems*, 2nd Ed.; Springer: Berlin, 2004.
7. Butler, T. From data to knowledge and back again: Understanding the limitations of KMS. Knowl. Process Manage. **2003**, *10* (3), 144–155.
8. Tiwana, A. *The Knowledge Management Toolkit: Practical Techniques for Building Knowledge Management Systems*; Pearson Education: Upper Saddle River, NJ, 1999.
9. Sveiby, K.E.; Lloyd, T. *Managing Know-How*; Bloomsbury: London, 1987.
10. Wiig, K.M. Management of knowledge: Perspectives of a new opportunity. In *User interfaces: Gateway or bottleneck?*; Bernold, T., Ed.; Gottlieb Duttweiler Institute: Zurich, 1988; 101–116.
11. Nonaka, I.; Takeuchi, H. *The Knowledge-Creating Company: How Japanese Companies Create the Dynamics of Innovation*; Oxford University Press: Oxford, 1995.
12. Spender, J.-C. Making knowledge the basis of a dynamic theory of the firm. Strateg. Manage. J. Winter Special Issue, **1996**, *17*, 45–62.
13. Alavi, A.; Leidner, D. Review: Knowledge management and knowledge management systems: Conceptual foundations and research issues. MIS Q. **2001**, *25* (1), 107–136.
14. Wilson, T.D. The nonsense of knowledge management. Inform. Res. **2002**, *8* (1), paper no. 144. http://informationr.net/ir/8–1/paper144.html (accessed December. 2008).
15. Tsoukas, H. The firm as a distributed knowledge system: A constructionist approach. Strateg. Manage. J. Winter Special Issue **1996**, (17), 11–25.

16. Choo, C.W. *The Knowing Organization*; Oxford University Press: Oxford, 1998.
17. Blackler, F. Knowledge, knowledge work and organizations: an overview and interpretation. Organ. Stud. **1995**, *16* (6), 1021–1046.
18. Swan, J.; Scarbrough, H. Knowledge management: Concepts and controversies. J. Manage. Stud. **2001**, *38* (7), 913–921.
19. Schultze, U. A confessional account of an ethnography about knowledge work. Manage. Inform. Syst. Quart. **2000**, *24* (1), 3–41.
20. Stenmark, D. Information vs. knowledge: The role of intranets in knowledge management. In *Proceedings of HICSS-35*, Hawaii, January 7–10, 2002.
21. Schultze, U.; Leidner, D. Studying knowledge management in information systems research: Discourses and theoretical assumptions. Manage. Inform. Syst. Quart. **2002**, *26* (3), 213–242.
22. Hansen, M.; Nohria, N.; Tierney, T. What's your strategy for managing knowledge? Harvard Bus. Rev. March–April **1999**, *77* (2), 106–116.
23. Hahn, J.; Subramani, M. A framework of knowledge management systems: Issues and challenges for theory and practice. In *Proceedings of International Conference on Information Systems 2000*, Brisbane, Australia, December 10–13, 2000, 302–312.
24. Levitt, B.; March, J.G. Organizational learning. Annu. Rev. Sociol. **1988**, *14*, 319–340.
25. Corso, M.; Martini, A.; Pellegrini, L.; Massa, S.; Testa, S. Managing dispersed workers: The new challenge in knowledge management. Technovation **2006**, *26* (5–6), 583–594.
26. Donnellan, B.; Fitzgerald, B. Developing systems to support organisational learning in product development organisations. Electron. J. Knowl. Manage. **2003**, *1* (2), 33–46.
27. Schultze, U.; Boland, R.J. Knowledge management technology and the reproduction of knowledge work practices. J. Strateg. Inform. Syst. **2000**, *9*, 193–212.
28. Markus, L.M.; Majchrzak, A.; Gasser, L. A design theory for systems that support emergent knowledge processes. Manage. Inform. Syst. Quart. **2002**, *26*, 179–212.
29. Stenmark, D.; Lindgren, R. System support for knowledge work: Bridging the knowing-doing gap. Intl. J. Knowl. Manage. **2006**, *2* (2), 46–68.
30. Hirsch, P.; Levin, D. Umbrella advocates versus validity police: A life-cycle model. Organ. Sci. **1999**, *10*, 199–212.
31. Spender, J.-C. Exploring uncertainty and emotion in the knowledge-based theory of the firm. Inform. Technol. People **2003**, *16* (3), 266–288.
32. Gray, P.H.; Meister, D.B. Introduction: Fragmentation and integration in knowledge management research. Inform. Technol. People **2003**, *16* (3), 259–265.

BIBLIOGRAPHY

General KM

1. Davenport and Prusak, *Working Knowledge: How Organizations Manage What They Know*; Harvard Business School Press: Boston, 1997.

Knowledge Management Systems

2. Barnes, S., Ed.; *Knowledge Management Systems: Theory and Practice*; Thomson learning: London, 2002.
3. Malhotra, Y. Why knowledge management systems fail? Enablers and constraints of knowledge management in human enterprises. In *Handbook on Knowledge Management 1: Knowledge Matters*; Holsapple, Ed.; Springer-Verlag: Berlin, 2002; 577–599.
4. Rubenstein, A.H.; Geisler, E. *Installing and Managing Workable Knowledge Management Systems*; Greenwood Publishing Group Inc.: Westport, CT, 2003.
5. Ruggles, R.L., Ed.; *Knowledge Management Tools*; Butter-worth Heinemann: Boston, 1997.

33 Decision Support Systems

Marek J. Druzdzel and Roger R. Flynn

CONTENTS

INTRODUCTION

Making decisions concerning complex systems (e.g., the management of organizational operations, industrial processes, or investment portfolios; the command and control of military units; the control of nuclear power plants) often strains our cognitive capabilities. Even though individual interactions among a system's variables may be well understood, predicting how the system will react to an external manipulation such as a policy decision is often difficult. What will be, for example the effect of introducing the third shift on a factory floor? One might expect that this will increase the plant's output by roughly 50%. Factors such as additional wages, machine weardown, maintenance breaks, raw material usage, supply logistics, and future demand also need to be considered, however, because they will all affect the total financial outcome of this decision. Many variables are involved in complex and often subtle interdependencies, and predicting the total outcome may be daunting.

There is a substantial amount of empirical evidence that human intuitive judgment and decision making can be far from optimal, and it deteriorates even further with complexity and stress. In many situations, the quality of decisions is important; therefore, aiding the deficiencies of human judgment and decision making has been a major focus of science throughout history. Disciplines such as statistics, economics, and operations research developed various methods for making rational choices. More recently, these methods, often enhanced by various techniques originating from information science, cognitive psychology, and artificial intelligence, have been implemented in the form of computer programs, either as stand-alone tools or as integrated computing environments for complex decision making. Such environments are often given the common name of *decision support systems* (DSSs). The concept of DSS is extremely broad, and its definitions vary, depending on the author's point of view. To avoid exclusion of any of the existing types of DSSs, we define them roughly as interactive computer-based systems that aid users in judgment and choice activities. Another name sometimes used as a synonym for DSS is *knowledge-based systems*, which refers to their attempt to formalize domain knowledge so that it is amenable to mechanized reasoning.

Decision support systems are gaining an increased popularity in various domains, including business, engineering, the military, and medicine. They are especially valuable in situations in which the amount of available information is prohibitive for the intuition of an unaided human decision maker, and in which precision and optimality are of importance. Decision support systems can aid human cognitive deficiencies by integrating various sources of information, providing intelligent access to relevant knowledge, and aiding the process of structuring decisions. They can also support choice among well-defined alternatives and build on formal approaches, such as the methods of engineering economics, operations research, statistics, and decision theory. They can also employ artificial intelligence methods to heuristically address problems that are intractable by formal techniques. Proper application of decision-making tools increases productivity, efficiency, and effectiveness, and gives many businesses a comparative advantage over their competitors, allowing them to make optimal choices for technological processes and their parameters, planning business operations, logistics, or investments.

Although it is difficult to overestimate the importance of various computer-based tools that are relevant to decision making (e.g., databases, planning software, spreadsheets), this entry focuses primarily on the core of a DSS, the part that directly supports modeling decision problems and identifies best alternatives. We briefly discuss the characteristics of decision problems and how decision making can be supported by computer programs. We then cover various components of DSSs and the role that they play in decision support. We also introduce an emergent class of *normative systems* (i.e., DSSs based on sound theoretical principles), and in particular, decision-analytic DSSs. Finally, we review issues related to user interfaces to DSSs and stress the importance of user interfaces to the ultimate quality of decisions aided by computer programs.

DECISIONS AND DECISION MODELING

Types of Decisions

A simple view of decision making is that it is a problem of choice among several alternatives. A somewhat more sophisticated view includes the process of constructing the alternatives (i.e., given a problem statement, developing a list of choice options). A complete picture includes a search for opportunities for decisions (i.e., discovering that there is a decision to be made). A manager of a company may face a choice in which the options are clear (e.g., the choice of a supplier from among all existing suppliers). She may also face a well-defined problem for which she designs creative decision options (e.g., how to market a new product so that the profits are maximized). Finally, she may work in a less reactive fashion, and view decision problems as opportunities that have to be discovered by studying the operations of her company and its surrounding environment (e.g., how can she make the production process more efficient). There is much anecdotal and some empirical evidence that structuring decision problems and identifying creative decision alternatives determine the ultimate quality of decisions. Decision support systems aim mainly at this broadest type of decision making, and in addition to supporting choice, they aid in modeling and analyzing systems (e.g., as complex organizations), identifying decision opportunities, and structuring decision problems.

Human Judgment and Decision Making

Theoretical studies on rational decision making, notably that in the context of probability theory and decision theory, have been accompanied by empirical research on whether human behavior complies with the theory. It has been rather convincingly demonstrated in numerous empirical studies that human judgment and decision making are based on intuitive strategies, as opposed to theoretically sound reasoning rules. These intuitive strategies, referred to as *judgmental heuristics* in the context of decision making, help us in reducing the cognitive load, but alas at the expense of optimal decision making. Effectively, our unaided judgment and choice exhibit systematic violations of probability axioms (referred to as *biases*). Formal discussion of the most important research results, along with experimental data, can be found in an anthology edited by Kahneman, Slovic, and Tversky.[1] Dawes[2] provided an accessible introduction to what is known about people's decision-making performance.

One might hope that people who have achieved expertise in a domain will not be subject to judgmental biases and will approach optimality in decision making. Although empirical evidence shows that experts indeed are more accurate than novices, within their area of expertise, it also shows that they also are liable to the same judgmental biases as novices, and demonstrate apparent errors and inconsistencies in their judgment. Professionals such as practicing physicians use essentially the same judgmental heuristics and are prone to the same biases, although the degree of departure from the normatively prescribed judgment seems to decrease with experience. In addition to laboratory evidence, there are several studies of expert performance in realistic settings, showing that it is inferior even to simple linear models (an informal review of the available evidence and pointers to literature can be found in the book by Dawes).[2] For example, predictions of future violent behavior of psychiatric patients made by a panel of psychiatrists who had access to patient records and interviewed the patients were found to be inferior to a simple model that included only the past incidence of violent behavior. Predictions of marriage counselors concerning marital happiness were shown to be inferior to a simple model that just subtracted the rate of fighting from the rate of sexual intercourse (again, the marriage counselors had access to all data, including interviews with the couples). Studies yielding similar results were conducted with bank loan officers, physicians, university admission committees, and so on.

Modeling Decisions

The superiority of even simple linear models over human intuitive judgment suggests that one way to improve the quality of decisions is to decompose a decision problem into simpler components that are well defined and well understood. Studying a complex system built out of such components can be subsequently aided by a formal, theoretically sound technique. The process of decomposing and formalizing a problem is often called modeling. Modeling amounts to finding an abstract representation of a real-world system that simplifies and assumes as much as possible about the system, and while retaining the system's essential relationships, omits unnecessary detail. Building a model of a decision problem, as opposed to reasoning about a problem in a holistic way, allows for applying scientific knowledge that can be transferred across problems and often across domains. It allows for analyzing, explaining, and arguing about a decision problem.

The desire to improve human decision making provided motivation for the development of various modeling tools in disciplines of economics, operations research, decision theory, decision analysis, and statistics. In each modeling tool, knowledge about a system is represented by means of algebraic, logical, or statistical variables. Interactions among these variables are expressed by equations or logical rules, possibly enhanced with an explicit representation of uncertainty. When the functional form of an interaction is unknown, it is sometimes described in purely probabilistic terms (e.g., by a conditional probability distribution). Once a model has been formulated, various mathematical methods can be used to analyze it. Decision making under certainty has been addressed by economic and operations research methods, such as cash flow analysis, break-even analysis, scenario analysis, mathematical programming, inventory techniques, and various optimization algorithms for scheduling and logistics. Decision making under uncertainty enhances the above methods with statistical approaches, such as reliability analysis, simulation, and statistical decision making. Most of these methods have made it into college curricula and can be found in management textbooks. Due to space constraints, we do not discuss their details further.

Components of Decision Models

Although a model mathematically consists of variables and a specification of interactions among them, from the point of view of decision making, a model and its variables represent the following three components: 1) a measure of preferences over decision objectives; 2) available decision options; and 3) a measure of uncertainty over variables influencing the decision and the outcomes.

Preference is widely viewed as the most important concept in decision making. Outcomes of a decision process are not all equally attractive, and it is crucial for a decision maker to examine these outcomes in terms of their desirability. Preferences can be ordinal (e.g., more income is preferred to less income), but it is convenient and often necessary to represent them as numerical quantities, especially if the outcome of the decision process consists of multiple attributes that need to be compared on a common scale. Even when they consist of just a single attribute but the choice is made under uncertainty, expressing preferences numerically allows for trade-offs between desirability and risk.

The second component of decision problems is available decision options. Often these options can be enumerated (e.g., a list of possible suppliers), but sometimes they are continuous values of specified policy variables (e.g., the amount of raw material to be kept in stock). Listing the available decision options is an important element of model structuring.

The third element of decision models is uncertainty. Uncertainty is one of the most inherent and most prevalent properties of knowledge, originating from incompleteness of information, imprecision, and model approximations made for the sake of simplicity. It would not be an exaggeration to state that real-world decisions not involving uncertainty either do not exist or belong to a truly limited class. As Benjamin Franklin expressed it in 1789 in a letter to his friend M. Le Roy, "in this world nothing can said to be certain, except death and taxes" (*The Complete Works of Benjamin Franklin*, John Bigelow (Ed.), G.P. Putnam's Sons: New York and London, 1887; Vol. 10, 1700).

Decision making under uncertainty can be viewed as a deliberation—determining what action should be taken that will maximize the expected gain. Due to uncertainty, there is no guarantee that the result of the action will be the one intended, and the best one can hope for is to maximize the chance of a desirable outcome. The process rests on the assumption that a good decision is one that results from a good decision-making process that considers all important factors and is explicit about decision alternatives, preferences, and uncertainty.

It is important to distinguish between good decisions and good outcomes. By a stroke of good luck, a poor decision can lead to a very good outcome. Similarly, a very good decision can be followed by a bad outcome. Supporting decisions means supporting the decision-making process so that better decisions are made. Better decisions can be expected to lead to better outcomes.

DECISION SUPPORT SYSTEMS

Decision support systems are interactive, computer-based systems that aid users in judgment and choice activities. They provide data storage and retrieval, but enhance the traditional information access and retrieval functions with support for model building and model-based reasoning. They support framing, modeling, and problem solving.

Typical application areas of DSSs are management and planning in business, health care, the military, and any area in which management will encounter complex decision situations. Decision support

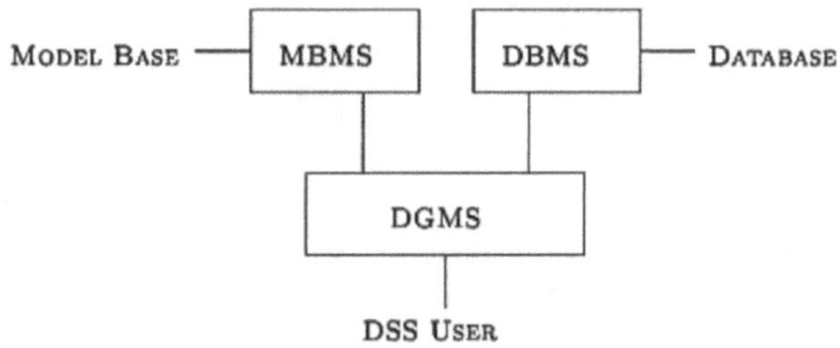

FIGURE 33.1 The architecture of a DSS. (From Sage, A.P. *Decision Support Systems Engineering*; John Wiley & Sons, Inc.: New York, 1991.[31])

systems are typically used for strategic and tactical decisions faced by upper-level management—decisions with a reasonably low frequency and high potential consequences—in which the time taken for thinking through and modeling the problem pays off generously in the long run.

There are three fundamental components of DSSs[3]:

- *Database management system* (*DBMS*). A DBMS serves as a data bank for the DSS. It stores large quantities of data that are relevant to the class of problems for which the DSS has been designed and provides logical data structures (as opposed to the physical data structures) with which the users interact. A DBMS separates the users from the physical aspects of the database structure and processing. It should also be capable of informing the user of the types of data that are available and how to gain access to them.
- *Model-base management system* (*MBMS*). The role of MBMS is analogous to that of a DBMS. Its primary function is providing independence between specific models that are used in a DSS from the applications that use them. The purpose of an MBMS is to transform data from the DBMS into information that is useful in decision making. Because many problems that the user of a DSS will cope with may be unstructured, the MBMS should also be capable of assisting the user in model building.
- *Dialog generation and management system* (*DGMS*). The main product of an interaction with a DSS is insight. Because their users are often managers who are not computer trained, DSSs need to be equipped with intuitive and easy-to-use interfaces. These interfaces aid in model building, but also in interaction with the model, such as gaining insight and recommendations from it. The primary responsibility of a DGMS is to enhance the ability of the system user to use and benefit from the DSS. In the remainder of this entry, we use the broader term user interface rather than DGMS.

Although various DSSs exists, the above three components can be found in many DSS architectures and play a prominent role in their structure. Interaction among them is shown in Figure 33.1.

Essentially, the user interacts with the DSS through the DGMS. This communicates with the DBMS and MBMS, which screen the user and the user interface from the physical details of the model base and database implementation.

NORMATIVE SYSTEMS

NORMATIVE AND DESCRIPTIVE APPROACHES

Whether one trusts the quality of human intuitive reasoning strategies has a profound impact on one's view of the philosophical and technical foundations of DSSs. There are two distinct approaches to supporting decision making. The first aims at building support procedures or systems that imitate human experts. The most prominent member of this class of DSSs are *expert systems*, computer programs based on rules elicited from human domain experts that imitate reasoning of a human expert in a given domain. Expert systems are often capable of supporting decision making in that domain at a level comparable to human experts. Although they are flexible and often able to address complex decision problems, they are based on intuitive human reasoning and lack soundness and formal guarantees with respect to the theoretical reliability of their results. The danger of the expert system approach, increasingly appreciated by DSS builders, is that along with imitating human thinking and its efficient heuristic principles, we may also imitate its undesirable flaws.[4]

The second approach is based on the assumption that the most reliable method of dealing with complex decisions is through a small set of normatively sound principles of how decisions should be made. Although heuristic methods and ad hoc reasoning schemes that imitate human cognition may in many domains perform well, most decision makers will be reluctant to rely on them whenever the cost of making an error is high. To give an extreme example, few people would choose to fly airplanes built using heuristic principles over airplanes built using the laws of aerodynamics enhanced with probabilistic reliability analysis. Application of formal methods in DSSs makes these systems philosophically distinct from those based on ad hoc heuristic artificial intelligence methods, such as rule-based systems. The goal of a DSS, according to this view, is to support unaided human intuition, just as the goal of using a calculator is to aid human's limited capacity for mental arithmetic.

Decision-Analytic DSSs

An emergent class of DSSs known as *decision-analytic DSSs* applies the principles of decision theory, probability theory, and decision analysis to their decision models. Decision theory is an axiomatic theory of decision making that is built on a small set of axioms of rational decision making. It expresses uncertainty in terms of probabilities and preferences in terms of utilities. These are combined using the operation of mathematical expectation. The attractiveness of probability theory, as a formalism for handling uncertainty in DSSs, lies in its soundness and its guarantees concerning long-term performance. Probability theory is often viewed as the gold standard for rationality in reasoning under uncertainty. Following its axioms offers protection from some elementary inconsistencies. Their violation, however, can be demonstrated to lead to sure losses.[5] Decision analysis is the art and science of applying decision theory to real-world problems. It includes a wealth of techniques for model construction, such as methods for elicitation of model structure and probability distributions that allow minimization of human bias, methods for checking the sensitivity of a model to imprecision in the data, computing the value of obtaining additional information, and presentation of results (see, e.g., von Winterfeldt[6] for a basic review of the available techniques). These methods have been under continuous scrutiny by psychologists working in the domain of behavioral decision theory and have proven to cope reasonably well with the dangers related to human judgmental biases.

Normative systems are usually based on graphical probabilistic models, which are representations of the joint probability distribution over a model's variables in terms of directed graphs. Directed graphs, such as the one in Figure 33.2, are known as Bayesian networks (BNs) or causal networks.[7] Bayesian networks offer a compact representation of joint probability distributions and are capable of practical representation of large models, consisting of tens or hundreds of variables. Bayesian networks can be easily extended with decision and value variables for modeling decision problems. The former denote variables that are under the decision maker's control and can be directly manipulated, and the latter encode users' preferences over various outcomes of the decision process. Such amended graphs are known as *influence diagrams*.[8] Both the structure and the numerical probability distributions in a BN can be elicited from a human expert and are a reflection of the expert's subjective view of a real-world system. If available, scientific knowledge about the system, both in terms of the structure and frequency data, can be easily incorporated in the model. Once a model has been created, it is optimized using formal decision-theoretic algorithms. Decision analysis is based on the empirically tested paradigm that people are able to reliably store

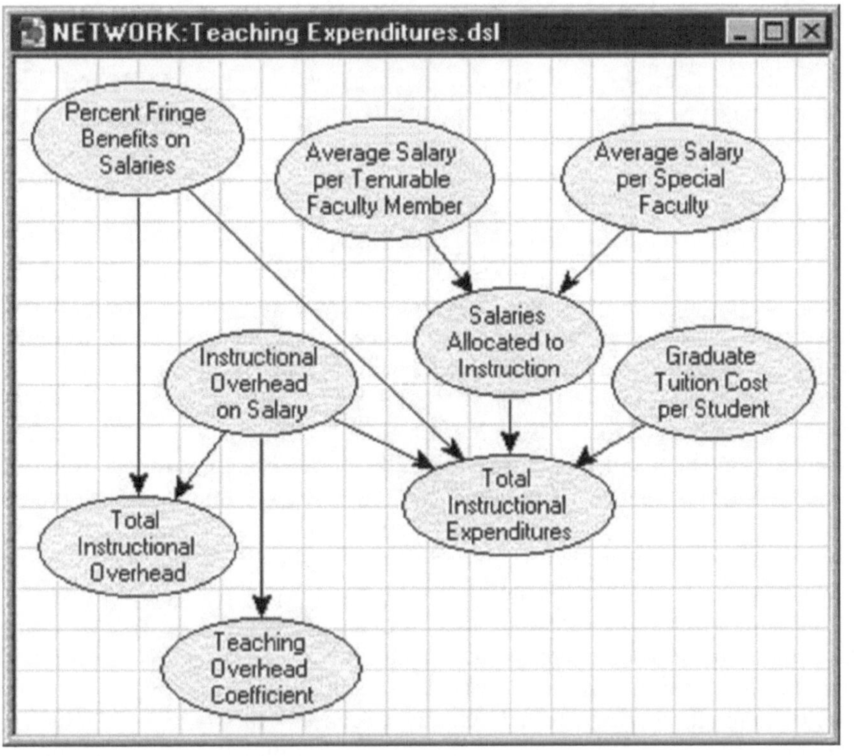

FIGURE 33.2 Example of a BN modeling teaching expenditures in university operations.

and retrieve their personal beliefs about uncertainty and preferences for different outcomes, but are much less reliable in aggregating these fragments into a global inference. Although human experts are excellent in structuring a problem, determining the components that are relevant to it and providing local estimates of probabilities and preferences, they are not reliable in combining many simple factors into an optimal decision. The role of a decision-analytic DSS is to support them in their weaknesses using the formal and theoretically sound principles of statistics.

The approach taken by decision analysis is compatible with that of DSSs. The goal of decision analysis is to provide insight into a decision. This insight, consisting of the analysis of all relevant factors, their uncertainty, and the critical nature of some assumptions, is even more important than the actual recommendation.

Decision-analytic DSSs have been successfully applied to practical systems in medicine, business, and engineering. Some examples of applications are described in a special issue of *Communications of the ACM* on practical applications of decision-theoretic methods (Vol. 38, No. 3, March 1995). We encourage the readers to experiment with GeNIe,[9] a development system for decision-analytic DSSs developed at the Decision Systems Laboratory, University of Pittsburgh, available at http://genie.sis.pitt.edu/. As these systems tend to naturally evolve into three not necessarily distinct classes, it may be interesting to compare their structure and architectural organization.

- *Systems with static domain models.* In this class of systems, a probabilistic domain is represented by a typically large network encoding the domain's structure and its numerical parameters. The network comprising the domain model is normally built by decision analysts and domain experts. An example might be a medical diagnostic system covering a certain class of disorders. Queries in such a system are answered by assigning values to those nodes of the network that constitute the observations for a particular case and propagating the impact of the observation through the network to find the probability distribution of some selected nodes of interest (e.g., nodes that represent diseases). Such a network can, on a case-by-case basis, be extended with decision nodes and value nodes to support decisions. Systems with static domain models are conceptually similar to rule-based expert systems covering an area of expertise.

- *Systems with customized decision models.* The main idea behind this approach is automatic generation of a graphical decision model on a per-case basis in an interactive effort between the DSS and the decision maker. The DSS has domain expertise in a certain area and plays the role of a decision analyst. During this interaction, the program creates a customized influence diagram, which is later used for generating advice. The main motivation for this approach is the premise that every decision is unique and needs to be looked at individually; an influence diagram needs to be tailored to individual needs.[10]
- *Systems capable of learning a model from data.* The third class of systems employs computer-intensive statistical methods for learning models from data.[11–15] Whenever there are sufficient data available, the systems can literally learn a graphical model from these data. This model can be subsequently used to support decisions within the same domain.

The first two approaches are suited for slightly different applications. The customized model generation approach is an attempt to automate the most laborious part of decision making, structuring a problem, so far done with significant assistance from trained decision analysts. A session with the program that assists the decision maker in building an influence diagram is laborious. This makes the customized model generation approach particularly suitable for decision problems that are infrequent and serious enough to be treated individually. Because in the static domain model approach, an existing domain model needs to be customized by the case data only, the decision-making cycle is rather short. This makes it particularly suitable for those decisions that are highly repetitive and need to be made under time constraints.

A practical system can combine the three approaches. A static domain model can be slightly customized for a case that needs individual treatment. Once completed, a customized model can be blended into the large static model. Learning systems can support both the static and the customized model approach. However, the learning process can be greatly enhanced by prior knowledge from domain experts or by a prior model.

Equation-Based and Mixed Systems

In many business and engineering problems, interactions among model variables can be described by equations that, when solved simultaneously, can be used to predict the effect of decisions on the system, and hence support decision making. One special type of simultaneous equation model is known as the structural equation model (SEM), which has been a popular method of representing systems in econometrics. An equation is structural if it describes a unique, independent causal mechanism acting in the system. Structural equations are based on expert knowledge of the system combined with theoretical considerations. Structural equations allow for a natural, modular description of a system—each equation represents its individual component, a separable and independent mechanism acting in the system—yet, the main advantage of having a structural model is, as explicated by Simon,[16] that it includes causal information and aids predictions of the effects of external interventions. In addition, the causal structure of a SEM can be represented graphically,[16] which allows for combining them with decision-analytic graphical models in practical systems.[16,17]

Structural equation models offer significant advantages for policy making. Often a decision maker confronted with a complex system needs to decide not only the values of policy variables, but also which variables should be manipulated. A change in the set of policy variables has a profound impact on the structure of the problem and on how their values will propagate through the system.

The user chooses which variables are policy variables and which are determined within the model. A change in the SEMs or the set of policy variables can be reflected by a rapid restructuring of the model and predictions involving this new structure.[18]

Our long-term project, the Environment for Strategic Planning (ESP),[19] is based on a hybrid graphical modeling tool that combines SEMs with decision-analytic principles. The ESP is capable of representing both discrete and continuous variables involved in deterministic and probabilistic relationships. The powerful features of SEMs allow the ESP to act as a graphical spreadsheet integrating numerical and symbolic methods, and allowing the independent variables to be selected at will without having to reformulate the model each time. This provides an immense flexibility that is not afforded by ordinary spreadsheets in evaluating alternate policy options.

USER INTERFACES TO DSSs

Although the quality and reliability of modeling tools and the internal architectures of DSSs are important, the most crucial aspect of DSSs is, by far, their user interface. Systems with user interfaces that are cumbersome or unclear or that require unusual skills are rarely useful and accepted in practice. The most important result of a session with a DSS is insight into the decision problem. In addition, when the system is based on normative principles, it can play a tutoring role; one might hope that users will learn the domain model and how to reason with it over time, and improve their own thinking.

A good user interface to DSSs should support model construction and model analysis, reasoning about the problem structure in addition to numerical calculations, and both choice and optimization of decision variables. We discuss these in the following sections.

Support for Model Construction and Model Analysis

User interface is the vehicle for both model construction (or model choice) and for investigating the results. Even if a system is based on a theoretically sound reasoning scheme, its recommendations will only be as good as the model on which they are based. Furthermore, even if the model is a very good approximation of reality and its recommendations are correct, they will not be followed if they are not understood. Without understanding, the users may accept or reject a system's advice for the wrong reasons and the combined decision-making performance may deteriorate even below unaided performance.[20] A good user interface should make the model on which the system's reasoning is based transparent to the user.

Modeling is rarely a one-shot process, and good models are usually refined and enhanced as their users gather practical experiences with the system recommendations. It is important to strike a careful balance between precision and modeling efforts; some parts of a model need to be very precise, whereas others do not. A good user interface should include tools for examining the model and identifying its most sensitive parts, which can be subsequently elaborated on. Systems employed in practice will need their models refined, and a good user interface should make it easy to access, examine, and refine its models. Some pointers to work on support for building decision-analytic systems can be found in.[21–24]

Support for Reasoning about the Problem Structure in Addition to Numerical Calculations

Although numerical calculations are important in decision support, reasoning about the problem structure is even more important. Often when the system and its model are complex, it is insightful for the decision maker to realize how the system variables are interrelated. This is helpful not only in designing creative decision options, but also in understanding how a policy decision will affect the objective.

Graphical models, such as those used in decision analysis or in equation-based and hybrid systems, are particularly suitable for reasoning about structure. Under certain assumptions, a directed graphical model can be given a causal interpretation. This is especially convenient in situations where the DSS autonomically suggests decision options; given a causal interpretation of its model, it is capable of predicting effects of interventions. A causal graph facilitates building an effective user interface. The system can refer to causal interactions during its dialogue with the user, which is known to enhance user insight.[25]

Support for Both Choice and Optimization of Decision Variables

Many DSSs have an inflexible structure in the sense that the variables that will be manipulated are determined at the model-building stage. This is not very suitable for planning of the strategic type when the object of the decision-making process is identifying both the objectives and the methods of achieving them. For example, changing policy variables in a spreadsheet-based model often requires that the entire spreadsheet be rebuilt. If there is no support for that, few users will consider it as an option. This closes the world of possibilities for flexible reframing of a decision problem in the exploratory process of searching for opportunities. Support for both choice and optimization of decision variables should be an inherent part of DSSs.

Graphical Interface

Insight into a model can be increased greatly at the user interface level by a diagram representing the interactions among its components (e.g., a drawing of a graph on which a model is based, such as in Figure 33.2). This graph is a qualitative, structural explanation of how information flows from the independent variables to the dependent variables of interest. Because models may become very large, it is convenient to structure them into submodels, groups of variables that form a subsystem of the modeled system.[2,6] Such submodels can be again shown graphically with interactions among them, increasing simplicity and clarity of the interface. Figure 33.3 shows a submodel-level view of a model developed in our ESP project. Note that the graph in Figure 33.2 is an expanded version of the *Teaching Expenditures* submodel in Figure 33.3. The user can navigate through the hierarchy of

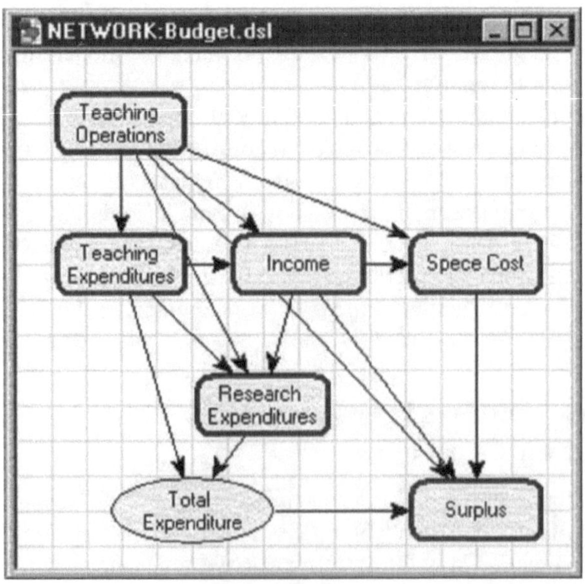

FIGURE 33.3 A submodel-level view of a decision model.

the entire model in her quest for insight, opening and closing submodels on demand. Some pointers to work on user interfaces of decision-analytic systems can be found in Wang,[24] Druzdzel[26,27] and Wiecha.[28]

CONCLUSION

Decision support systems are powerful tools integrating scientific methods for supporting complex decisions with techniques developed in information science and are gaining an increased popularity in many domains. They are especially valuable in situations in which the amount of available information is prohibitive for the intuition of an unaided human decision maker, and in which precision and optimality are of importance. Decision support systems aid human cognitive deficiencies by integrating various sources of information, providing intelligent access to relevant knowledge, aiding the process of structuring, and optimizing decisions.

Normative DSSs offer a theoretically correct and appealing way of handling uncertainty and preferences in decision problems. They are based on carefully studied empirical principles underlying the discipline of decision analysis, and they have been successfully applied in many practical systems. We believe that they offer several attractive features that are likely to prevail in the long run as far as the technical developments are concerned.

Because DSSs do not replace humans but rather augment their limited capacity to deal with complex problems, their user interfaces are critical. The user interface determines whether a DSS will be used at all and, if so, whether the ultimate quality of decisions will be higher than that of an unaided decision maker.

ACKNOWLEDGMENTS

Work on this entry was supported by the National Science Foundation under Faculty Early Career Development (CAREER) Program, grant IRI-9624629, by the Air Force Office of Scientific Research under grants F49620-97-1-0225, F49620-00-1-0112, and FA9550-06-1-0243 and by the University of Pittsburgh Central Research Development Fund. Figures 33.2 and 33.3 are snapshots of GeNIe, a general purpose development environment for graphical DSSs developed by the Decision Systems Laboratory, University of Pittsburgh, and available at http://genie.sis.pitt.edu/. We want to thank Ms. Nanette Yurcik for her assistance with technical editing.

REFERENCES

1. Kahneman, D.; Slovic, P.; Tversky, A., Eds. *Judgment Under Uncertainty: Heuristics and Biases*; Cambridge University Press: Cambridge, 1982.
2. Dawes, R.M. *Rational Choice in an Uncertain World*; Hartcourt Brace Jovanovich: San Diego, CA, 1988.
3. Sage, A.P. *Decision Support Systems Engineering*; John Wiley & Sons, Inc.: New York, 1991.
4. Henrion, M.; Breese, J.S.; Horvitz, E.J. Decision analysis and expert systems. AI Mag. Winter **1991**, *12* (4), 64–91.
5. Savage, L.J. *The Foundations of Statistics*, 2nd revised Ed.; Dover Publications: New York, 1972.
6. von Winterfeldt, D.; Edwards, W. *Decision Analysis and Behavioral Research*; Cambridge University Press: Cambridge, 1988.
7. Pearl, J. *Probabilistic Reasoning in Intelligent Systems: Networks of Plausible Inference*; Morgan Kaufmann Publishers, Inc.: San Mateo, CA, 1988.
8. Howard, R.A.; Matheson, J.E. Influence diagrams. In *The Principles and Applications of Decision Analysis*; Howard, R.A., Matheson, J.E., Eds.; Strategic Decisions Group: Menlo Park, CA, 1984; 719–762.
9. Druzdzel, M.J. SMILE: Structural Modeling, Inference, and Learning Engine and GeNIe: A development environment for graphical decision-theoretic models. In *Proceedings of the Sixteenth National Conference on Artificial Intelligence (AAAI-99)*, Orlando, FL, 1999; 902–903.

10. Holtzman, S. *Intelligent Decision Systems*; Addison-Wesley: Reading, MA, 1989.
11. Spirtes, P.; Glymour, C.; Scheines, R. *Causation, Prediction, and Search*; Springer Verlag: New York, 1993.
12. Pearl, J.; Verma, T.S. A theory of inferred causation. In *KR-91, Principles of Knowledge Representation and Reasoning*, Proceedings of the Second International Conference, Cambridge, MA, Allen, J.A., Fikes, R., Sandewall, E., Eds.; Morgan Kaufmann Publishers, Inc.: San Mateo, CA, 1991; 441–452.
13. Cooper, G.F.; Herskovits, E. A Bayesian method for the induction of probabilistic networks from data. Mach. Learn. **1992**, *9* (4), 309–347.
14. Glymour, C.; Cooper, G.F., Eds. *Computation, Causation, and Discovery*; AAAI Press: Menlo Park, CA, 1999.
15. Heckerman, D.E.; Geiger, D.; Chickering, D.M. Learning Bayesian networks: The combination of knowledge and statistical data. Mach. Learn. **1995**, *20* (3), 197–243.
16. Simon, H.A. Causal ordering and identifiability. In *Studies in Econometric Method. Cowles Commission for Research in Economics*; Monograph No. 14; Hood, W.C., Koopmans, T.C., Eds.; John Wiley & Sons, Inc.: New York, 1953; Chapter III, 49–74.
17. Druzdzel, M.J.; Simon, H.A. Causality in Bayesian belief networks. In *Proceedings of the Ninth Annual Conference on Uncertainty in Artificial Intelligence (UAI-93)*; Morgan Kaufmann Publishers, Inc.: San Francisco, 1993; 3–11.
18. Simon, H.A.; Kalagnanam, J.R.; Druzdzel, M.J. Performance budget planning: The case of a research university; 2000. Unpublished manuscript.
19. Druzdzel, M.J. ESP: A mixed initiative decision-theoretic decision modeling system. In *Working Notes of the AAAI-99 Workshop on Mixed-Initiative Intelligence*; Orlando, FL, 1999; 99–106.
20. Lehner, P.E.; Mullin, T.M.; Cohen, M.S. A probability analysis of the usefulness of decision aids. In *Uncertainty in Artificial Intelligence 5*, Henrion, M., Shachter, R.D., Kanal, L.N., Lemmer, J.F., Eds.; Elsevier Science Publishers: B.V.: North Holland, 1990; 427–436.
21. Druzdzel, M.J.; Díez, F.J. Criteria for combining knowledge from different sources in probabilistic models. J. Mach. Learn. Res. **2003**, *4* (July), 295–316.
22. Druzdzel, M.J.; van der Gaag, L.C. Building probabilistic networks: "Where do the numbers come from?" guest editors' introduction. IEEE Trans. Knowl. Data Eng. **2000**, *12* (4), 481–486.
23. Lu, T.-C.; Druzdzel, M.J. Causal mechanism-based model construction. In *Proceedings of the Sixteenth Annual Conference on Uncertainty in Artificial Intelligence (UAI-2000)*; Morgan Kaufmann Publishers, Inc.: San Francisco, 2000; 353–362.
24. Wang, H.; Druzdzel, M.J. User interface tools for navigation in conditional probability tables and elicitation of probabilities in Bayesian networks. In *Proceedings of the Sixteenth Annual Conference on Uncertainty in Artificial Intelligence (UAI-2000)*; Morgan Kaufmann Publishers, Inc.: San Francisco, 2000; 617–625.
25. Druzdzel, M.J. Probabilistic reasoning in decision support systems: From computation to common sense. Ph.D. thesis, Department of Engineering and Public Policy, Carnegie Mellon University: Pittsburgh, PA, 1992.
26. Druzdzel, M.J. Five useful properties of probabilistic knowledge representations from the point of view of intelligent systems. Fundamenta Informaticæ **1997**, *30* (3/4), 241–254. (special issue on knowledge representation and machine learning).
27. Druzdzel, M.J. Explanation in probabilistic systems: Is it feasible? Will it work? In *Proceedings of the Fifth International Workshop on Intelligent Information Systems (WIS-96)*, Deblin, Poland, 1996; 12–24.
28. Wiecha, C.F. An empirical study of how visual programming aids in comprehending quantitative policy models (Volumes I and II), Ph.D. thesis, Department of Engineering and Public Policy, Carnegie Mellon University: Pittsburgh, PA, 1986.

34 Collaborative Systems and Groupware

David Jank

CONTENTS

DEFINITION

Collaborative systems and groupware have evolved a great deal from their somewhat static roots as multifunctional technology platforms. They are now best viewed as dynamic technology environments designed to facilitate the completion of shared workgroup tasks. This evolution is significant as it provides evidence of the most important dynamics affecting shared technology systems today: the influence of the human user on the development of collaborative technology, and the emergence of cognitive science as a key contributor to online cooperative work. What distinguishes collaborative systems from groupware is their emphasis on recognizing and supporting the cognitive processes of individuals operating within workgroups in order to enhance the completion of shared workplace tasks. The term "groupware" generally refers to application software families that are utilized to facilitate task completion among groups, whether or not they are organizationally linked.[1]

Collaborative systems are the logical extension of groupware, which was initially developed to dynamically facilitate human interaction via shared usage of software applications in a networked environment.[2] Unlike groupware, collaborative systems are less standalone in nature, and more interactive in their shared workgroup functionality. While groupware essentially refers to shared application environments to facilitate information exchange, collaborative systems are best understood as a triadic relationship among the enhanced technological features of information technology (IT), the versatility of human–computer interaction (HCI), and the cognitive psychology principles that are at the heart of computer-supported cooperative work (CSCW).[3] Their value to the field of information management is evident both in the areas of enhanced data processing and real-time automation of cooperative work.

INTRODUCTION

The purpose of this entry is to highlight the evolution of both groupware and collaborative systems, and to emphasize how the latter has evolved as an information phenomenon separate from its antecedent groupware. Taxonomic breakdowns will itemize the key software components distinguishing each from the other. Finally, an ontology will be presented that illustrates how both groupware and collaborative systems have influenced IT developments in the area of library and information service (LIS).

While collaborative systems and groupware are best considered as independent entities, it is impossible to discuss one without considering the other. The driving force behind groupware was a desire to enable electronic information exchange between two or more users in a shared environment.[4] This genre of computer software allowed multiple users to dynamically share information, but did not account for their interactivity or the unique practices central to their work.[5] This awareness has been cited as the key driver of collaborative systems development.[6]

Research in the field of CSCW had established that both learning and work task completion in a shared environment were enhanced when individualized processes of cognition were accounted for by systems developers.[7] Such enhancements included improved work performance,[8] achieved operational efficiencies,[9] and an established sense of collaborative atmosphere through the recognition of cultural diversity in the workplace.[10] Ultimately, early groupware platforms were seen as not reflective of changes in the workplace dynamic of today[11]; thus, the cognitive principles now understood as inherent to collaborative work environments were not being adequately addressed by groupware processes that were less activity-centric.[12] Accounting for such variables has led collaborative systems to be viewed as bridges between the worlds of workplace IT and social computing at work.[13]

Figures 34.1 and 34.2 illustrate the conceptual topology of both groupware and collaborative technology platforms. In a traditional groupware environment, users are generally unaware of the presence of a system mediator who is dedicated to monitoring both the interface and the repository, and who exists outside of the immediate sphere of work. End-user interaction with information repositories is based entirely on what is viewed through the interface. The defining characteristic of collaborative systems, on the other hand, is autonomy within the workgroup. Though each workgroup shares access to varying numbers of information repositories, all mediative activities occur within the group and are shared among its members.

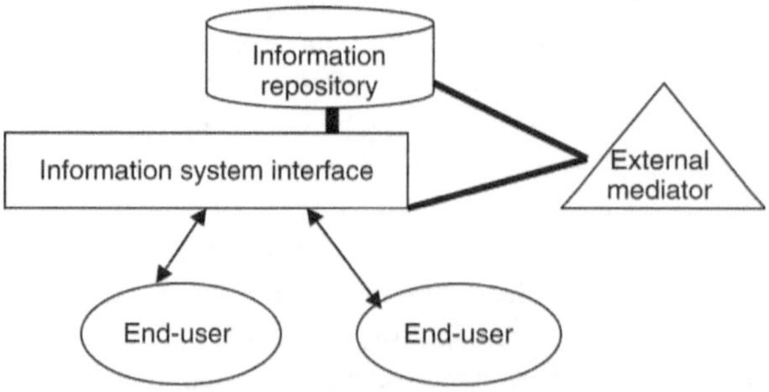

FIGURE 34.1 Traditional groupware applications modeling. In the groupware paradigm, users are generally unaware of the presence of any mediator, and generally rely on input/output interfacing with their requisite information source.

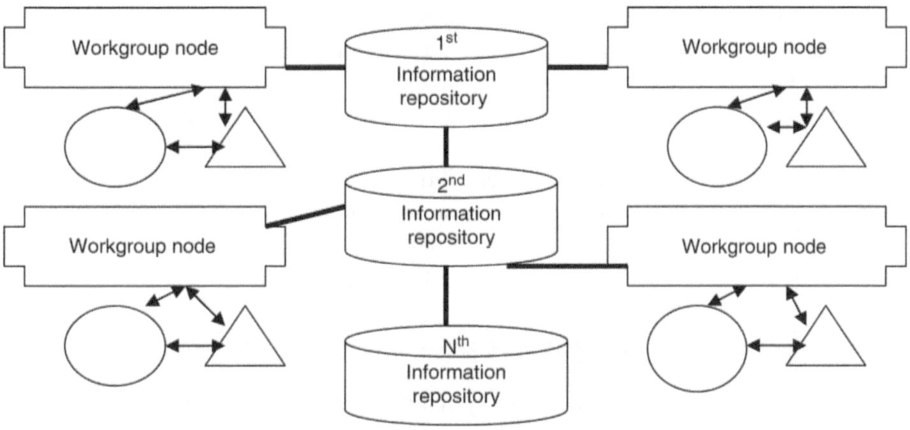

FIGURE 34.2 Traditional collaborative systems modeling. In the collaborative systems paradigm, workgroup members and their mediators work interactively and share operational responsibility. Multiple workgroups all work autonomously, and central repositories are utilized for the storage of necessary information utilized by all groups.

ORIGIN AND GROWTH

The genesis of these platform environments is the batch-processing software applications of the late 1970s and early 1980s, which allowed people to communicate with each other via time-sharing operations (TSOs). These included the early iterations of electronic mail, listservs, and relational database management systems (RDBMS). Due to today's increased reliance upon organizational Intranets employing graphical user interfaces (GUIs), collaborative systems have since become the preferred platform standard for network-based cooperative work, while groupware remains the umbrella term describing a number of software applications supporting information sharing.

The origin of these applications can be traced to the birth of ARPANET, the military precursor to today's Internet, where collaborative principles were utilized in the development of internetworked systems and services. Computer systems engineer Douglas Engelbart, prominent in U.S. Department of Defense research and development work during World War II, has been credited with having coined the term "groupware."[14] Although acceptance of the term "collaborative systems" has only reached prominence in recent years, coinage of the phrase can be traced as far back as the pioneering business research of scholar Felix Kaufman who, in the 1960s, argued for the elimination of the walls that prevented computer system users from working "beyond [computer] system boundaries."[15]

The first product to advance groupware functions in the enterprise was Lotus Notes, developed and launched during the 1980s and the early 1990s. Notes was developed initially at a proprietary level to facilitate automated online collaboration among Lotus scientists and engineers. It evolved into a corporate-wide office automation tool, and eventually launched commercially as a standalone product. A similar evolution occurred with OCLC, one of the most prominent collaborative systems in LIS, which began as a standalone service for use by the Ohio College Library Center. In their infancy, groupware products were used exclusively as office automation tools, operating in a limited real-time environment. They were at first categorized varyingly as "electronic brainstorming" or "decision support" software,[16] but their value across the enterprise was realized with the advent of in-house telecommunications networks. Emergence of Internet technology within organizational IT is widely viewed as the impetus fostering the design and development of more collaborative software platforms.[17]

The deployment of electronic bulletin board systems for businesses in the late 1980s was a turning point in the metamorphosis of groupware applications into collaborative systems. These early electronic messaging centers were far more dynamic than printed office memoranda. Electronic bulletin boards provided mechanisms by which announcements could be posted in a central location, accessed electronically, and viewed by individuals in different geographic locations. Unlike the print world, viewers could immediately contribute their observations electronically. These contributions could then be responded to by others, thus offering timely communication among workgroups. Since online bulletin boards also prevented contributors from altering or in some way editing the contributions of others, a relative degree of privacy and security could still be assured. Security concerns are still mirrored in the evolution of collaborative software products today, though this function is relegated from central IT to the individual workgroups utilizing collaborative products.

EVOLUTION OF COLLABORATIVE SYSTEMS AND GROUPWARE

Enhancements to groupware and collaborative systems are now advanced across a variety of industry sectors, and on a variety of IT platforms. Examples include desktop publishing and videoconferencing, online whiteboarding, virtual training, and so-called "2.0" and "second life" simulations. Online chat rooms and virtual research assistance provide some of the latest examples of collaborative software's versatility within the information services sector. This evolution is well beyond that of groupware's initial conception as a platform for shared information exchange.

Groupware's genesis was quite non-collaborative. Were it not for the automated batch-processing utilized to enhance TSO in data processing centers, it is quite possible that collaborative systems might have evolved in a less activity-centric manner. Groupware's benefit to information managers lies in the user's ability to handle information processing while simultaneously engaging in other computer tasks. In this IT dynamic, synchronous functionality comes to replace asynchronous strategies in the data processing paradigm, and lays the groundwork for the emergence of collaborative systems, or "enhanced groupware."[18]

Many areas of groupware functionality that now are taken for granted in collaboration models were dramatic when first introduced. Table 34.1 presents a traditional groupware taxonomy drawn from the contributive families of software applications that constitute groupware functions. These activities are presented along with the representative workgroup tasks that comprise them. Groupware functionality exists in terms of known-task completion. This distinguishes it from collaborative systems, in that the latter focuses more on enhanced completion of shared workgroup activities among many different users via dynamically interactive IT systems. Such dynamic inter-

TABLE 34.1
Taxonomy of Groupware Applications

Software Application Family	Sample Workgroup Tasks
Electronic messaging	• Group scheduling and Online calendaring • LISTSERV discussion groups and E-mail
Virtual meeting environments	• Electronic bulletin board systems and Intranets • Desktop videoconferencing • Online Chat Rooms
Electronic document management	• Online whiteboarding, electronic bulletin boards, etc. • Desktop Publishing
Workflow and workgroup utilities	• Batch-processing and Electronic File Transfer • Project management • Web page design and editing
Collaborative networking	• Relational Database Systems • Dynamic storage, retrieval, and representation

TABLE 34.2
Taxonomy of Collaborative Systems

System Design Factors	Sample Related Cognitive and Workgroup Components
SAD	• Activity-centric interaction design • Heuristic modeling and evaluation • Object programming and Web Application Development
HCI	• Graphical interface design • Pattern recognition support • Portal enhancement capability
CSCW	• Distributed and external cognition support and mapping • Mental representation and modeling • Activity-centric workflow • Artificial Intelligence agents
Dynamic workflow and workgroup utilities	• Real-time information processing • Information robots • Enhanced multimedia data transfer • Hyperlinked support for office suite software
Support of social computing	• Social tagging and bookmarking • Interactive chat • Enablement of Wikis, Blogs, RSS feeds, etc.

action, in order to enhance productivity, must reflect the work styles and cognitive processes extant within the groups using these systems.

Table 34.2 illustrates taxonomically the information science principles that constitute the phenomenon known as collaborative systems. This taxonomy is unique from the groupware taxonomy in that it is structured in terms of workgroup-focused IT, capitalizing upon those portions of the evolving computer science paradigm that contribute to user-centered design. Today's view of collaborative systems prefers the concept of "activity-centered" as opposed to "user-centered" design.[19] This is important for many reasons, but especially because it reflects movement in IT toward support for activities rather than tasks. Such appreciation is considered to be at the heart of enterprise IT operations.[20]

The success of online collaborative systems relies heavily on an appreciation of the social science theories that reflect how people work, while successful launching of groupware applications relies more on an appreciation of how IT systems work. While groupware facilitates task completion, collaborative systems capitalize on tasking by embracing the principles of both activity theory and social interaction theory, thus permitting workers to be more productive. Their goal is to assist workers in completing shared tasks at the group level, as opposed to merely offering individuals newly automated approaches to the completion of individual tasks. This goal is attained when users, as a group, capitalize on this functionality, and when system developers, as a group, understand how people work together.

ONTOLOGY OF COLLABORATIVE SYSTEMS AND GROUPWARE

Epistemologically, collaborative systems and groupware appear to be very similar. Closer examination, however, reveals their ontological differences. First and foremost, the centralized mediation element in groupware platforms is absent from collaborative systems. Where groupware platforms always feature moderators who oversee their operation, collaborative systems operate in environments that are far less centrally governed. Any mediative activity exercised in collaborative environments is done so at the workgroup level, and always parameterized by group members themselves.

The principles of mental modeling, cognitive mapping, activity theory, and social computing, are addressed by collaborative systems in ways that were likely never imagined by the developers of groupware products. As basic as system-level utility functions and file exchange protocols are across all product arenas, the impact of social and interactive computing has redefined processing power in the collaborative arena. This can be seen in Tables 34.3 and 34.4, with respect to heuristic modeling, federated searching, multimedia file format support, and related social tagging processes. These examples provide a picture of redefined expectations at the systems level as well as at the user level.

At the heart of social computing is the idea of sharing, be it sharing of resources, sharing of information, or sharing of data. Collaborative systems can be viewed as shared online environments that enhance cooperative work, which brings "sharing" to a new level as the driver of enterprise productivity. These systems emphasize knowledge sharing rather than data processing. Whether as low-level office automation packages or high-level project management tools, collaborative systems require structures that allow for workgroup-defined processing environments. These factors are now seen as significant drivers of IT product development in the field of Library and Information Science.[21]

Groupware products are largely ancillary in nature, and may or may not prove useful to individuals who are engaged in some sort of workplace task. Users may choose whether or not to utilize them on a case by case basis, and opting not to does not necessarily hinder workgroup progress. Collaborative systems are far from ancillary. Their interactive nature exists to enhance preexisting workplace dynamics, and especially, preexisting social relationships among workgroup members. Consequently, collaborative technologies might replace previously existing modes of operation, both online and offline, thus redefining workgroup processes for some time. Without full appreciation of the social interaction of workers, or the activity-centric nature of work, implementation of collaborative systems can actually fail.

Within the workplace, individual workgroups are usually already engaged in those activities that collaborative systems are presumably going to enhance or replace. These activities are viewed by the organization as the entity that must be supported. With respect to the client-server model

TABLE 34.3
Functional Applications of Groupware in Library and Information Services

Software Application Family	LIS Workgroup Tasks
Electronic messaging	• E-mail reference • Resource exchanges and Knowledgebases • Online reserves and Interlibrary Loan
Virtual meeting environments	• Digital interactive reference • Intranets • Online conferencing • Wikis, blogs, etc.
Electronic document management	• Web authoring tools • Online cataloging and Metadata protocols • Desktop publishing and EDM • Resource digitization
Workflow and workgroup utilities	• Dynamic indexing and relational database building • Project Management • Federated searching • Electronic transfer of PDF, RSS, etc.
Collaborative networking	• Dynamic information indexing and representation • Multitype consortia and shared networking • Social computing • Intranets and portals

TABLE 34.4
Influence of Collaborative Systems on Library and Information Services

Contributing System Design Factors	Related Cognitive and Workgroup Components
SAD	• Cognitive measures of activity theory in LIS • Increased use of library focus groups • Rapid and joint application development
HCI	• User-enabled Library Web page authoring • Activity-centric usability testing • Use of information agents and robots
CSCW	• Metadata representation • Real-time online data capture • Use of Podcasts and RSS feeds
Dynamic workflow and workgroup utilities	• Information visualization • Real-time information representation • Support for multimedia data objects
Support of social computing	• Support of social tagging, Wikis, and Blogs • Digital information instruction and chatting • Transparent hyperlinks in library Web sites

of computing, the "client" here is no longer the end-user but the work activity in which the user is engaged. In this paradigm, collaborative systems are being introduced to supposedly improve operation of preexisting critical processes. The collaborative system is of no use if it gets in the way of, or worse, hinders the operational functions of the established workgroup.

Collaborative products, therefore, are not considered off-the-shelf tools; rather, they are platforms that are launched to support users at the task level, enhance communication at the group level, and definitely not obstruct workgroup processes at any level. They are process structures as opposed to application modules, although reliance on the latter is critical for the successful functioning of collaborative systems. Individualized parameterization and collectivized optimization are tenets of collaborative systems. They require input from all stakeholders engaged in workgroup activity, and are crucial to the successful functioning of the enterprise.

APPLICATIONS

Overview

Historically, more than a dozen software application categories can be identified as constituting a taxonomy for collaborative and groupware applications. Among these, groupware applications have been more prescient, due to their somewhat unique, standalone characteristics. Collaborative products, on the other hand, have evolved largely in response to need. This has created an environment where functional requirements and specifications of users now carry greater influence in the systems analysis and design (SAD) paradigm.

LIS centers have proven to be ideal laboratories for collaborative product implementation. This is evident in such areas as enhanced information retrieval and representation protocols, federated searching of bibliographic databases, online delivery of reference and interlibrary loan, and the now prominent role of the so-called library "Webmaster." The influence of library and information service professionals can further be seen in groupware applications such as Intranets, Web search engine gateways, and the design engineering of business information portals (BIPs).

Tables 34.3 and 34.4 detail many of the groupware and collaborative systems functions evident today in library and information center environments. It can be seen here that the birth of collaborative technology is normatively traced to the data processing functionality that groupware offered, and formatively traced to activity-centric parameterization that later came to be expected of online information systems.

Most commercially available groupware packages have overlapping functions that are traditionally couched in office management activity, and have heretofore been targeted toward decision making in the firm via group support systems (GSS).[22] Within the field of library and information services, however, groupware is more accurately represented within broader functional contexts, as illustrated in Table 34.3. This is in contrast to the more virtually interactive collaborative contexts of LIS software applications as depicted in Table 34.4. These contexts illustrate the influence of cognitive and social interaction theories upon both groupware and collaborative systems in LIS.

Electronic Messaging

Communication with library users is now handled in much the same way as customer relationship management (CRM) services are handled in various business sectors. So-called "24 × 7" service models are being utilized in LIS in an attempt to facilitate client contact around the clock. E-mail reference service and patron account status messaging are early examples of some of these activities, and are evolving via the social context of "MyLibrary" and "MyBooks." Listservs and online discussion groups are used for the enhancement of professional development and resource sharing. Collection development assistance for rural library systems, information and referral assistance for remote users and underserved populations, and "Needs and Offerings" programs instituted by government documents librarians are particularly strong examples of collaborative project implementations of this genre.

Virtual Meeting Environments

More static forms of electronic messaging are transitioning to such online environments as Blogs, Wikis, and related areas of social collaborative software. They have complemented, rather than usurped, the role of the online chat room in the delivery of automated research assistance. The growing demand for enhanced digital reference service, initially launched under collaborative software such as "LiveAnswer," has led to a variety of service platforms for interactive reference interviews and research assistance, provided at any hour of the day or night, and in almost any geographic location.

Before the advancement of voice and video telecommunications, teleconferencing provided the closest available alternative to face to face communication. Collaborative software functions provided by videoconferencing on the desktop have been greatly enhanced by the successful launch of such technologies as streaming video and audio data transmission. Voice Over Internet telephony (VOIP) is now standard fare in the telecommunications world, and desktop videoconferencing has enhanced service programs to the disabled.

The LIS world is also taking heed of social interaction principles at work in library and information services. Heuristic modeling of information interaction online, interactive focus groups, and the increased reliance of online surveying and inter-portal hyperlinking have permitted increased outreach to the virtual community at large. These skills have proved valuable in the collection of meaningful research data related to online systems interaction and use.

Electronic Document Management

With the advent of electronic publishing, organizations continued their move toward online document composition and editing. Electronic document management (EDM) encompasses interactive editing capabilities not previously available in the electronic publishing world. This has permitted not only automated publishing and distribution, but shared document editing as well. In the field of library and information service, EDM applications are evident in such areas as web-based authoring of library and information services pages utilizing Hypertext Markup Language (HTML), newsletter publishing, support for integrated multimedia formats, and electronic "e-Books." The advantages evidenced by online whiteboarding in virtual business meetings and corporate training programs are also evident in the world of library and information services by the increased use of electronic "WebCT," "Blackboard," and "Chalkboard" products in academic, school, and special library settings.

Workflow and Workgroup Utilities

Some of the earliest forms of library and information services technology have actually paralleled the earliest forms of groupware. The shared databases at the heart of such established services as OCLC, Dialog, and the Library of Congress, were precursors to the systems and services now considered standard fare for collaborative software. What groupware did for so-called "back office processing" can be witnessed today in automated library systems. Database indexing for online literature searching and online public access catalogs (OPACs) were among the first forms of library technology to benefit from groupware design. Today, such high volume input–output (I/O) activities include circulation, reserves processing, and interlibrary loan.

Important new components of the LIS collaborative systems paradigm are information representation, and support for multimedia file formats and transfer. While groupware advances years ago paved the way for more dynamic database building and indexing, collaborative systems development has paved the way for more cognitive-based functions in information storage and retrieval (ISAR) and information visualization.[23] The use of information agents has increased in recent years, as has the move toward federated search capabilities. Additionally, support for the dynamic handling of multimedia object files such as portable documents (PDFs), PODcasts, and RSS feeds, is indicative of the influence of collaborative systems development in the LIS sphere.

Collaborative Networking

LIS is rooted in the very concept of "networking," be it through online bibliographic environments or shared administration through consortia. It continues to evolve as the leading knowledge sector of the information industry. Whether through internal workplace activity or external user services, groupware and collaborative design principles are always at the heart of new products and services in LIS. Library and information services today now depend upon collaborative technology; they are no longer merely assisted by it. Bibliographic utilities, online databases, OPACs, shared technical processing, electronic books, and multimedia transmission are now at the heart of modern LIS service, and these services can not exist without the continued enhancements of collaborative systems that drive IT networks. Librarians and information specialists have seen their responsibilities expand within the knowledge management arena, and the approaches to information management afforded by collaboration technology have helped redefine their functional roles as "organizational knowledge backbones."[24]

FUTURE TRENDS

The most immediate impact of collaborative technology on the library and information services sector is clearly that of social computing. While advances in technology are certainly influencing the SAD process in LIS, it is the new focus on individual users, their work behavior, and their social interaction that will direct that influence. Inasmuch as cultural trends continue to drive technology development, this development will drive organizational SAD far more than internal design projects.

Ultimately, advances in information representation and visualization may likely prove the most visible example of cognitive science's influence on collaborative systems both in LIS and across industry sectors. The emergence of cognitive science in the HCI domain will also influence the SAD process in online information system design. A particularly strong example of this trend is the movement from standalone OPACs toward the seamless hyperlinking of libraries' physical holdings and their digital resources.[25]

In the past, many proprietary applications designed to foster collaboration in the workplace focused on internal corporate functions such as archival records management (ARM), sales force automation (SFA), and human resources information systems (HRIS). Enhancements to these applications at the end of the twentieth century were typically driven by the need to maximize operating effectiveness of individual organizational departments, thus illustrating the emerging emphasis on activity rather than task. At the beginning of the twenty-first century, there is renewed interest in established processes that will likely benefit from collaborative technology. These include business processing reengineering (BPR), enterprise resource planning (ERP), methodological approaches to change management, and adherence to legislative regulations such as the Sarbanes–Oxley Act. All illustrate the continued evolution and value of collaborative systems for the entire enterprise.

CONCLUSION

In the past, the benefits of groupware in LIS had mirrored those of the business world vis a vis "back office technology." Today, advances in networking technology via the Internet and World Wide Web are expanding groupware's impact in the "front office" of library and information services, where information users are most often outside of the library or information center structure. Whether with services to users, to professional colleagues outside of the organization, or to the intra-organization clients which they directly serve, library and information service professionals are not only redefining their work; they are redefining how they do their work.

Collaborative systems and groupware have influenced the library and information services paradigm more than any other area of software development, and are driving the knowledge management sector's growth. Through sharing, manipulation, tagging, and selective dissemination, information handling in library and information services is now almost entirely redefined. LIS centers have been pushed, rather than led, into the heuristic SAD process, and they are now expected to monitor library and information systems usage online; to conduct focus groups in an effort to streamline library SAD; to continually survey users via online research methodologies; to master the programming skills necessary for online system retooling; and, finally, to come to grips with the principles inherent in social interaction and activity theories. Only with this base of knowledge will library and information professionals be able to fully realize the benefits of successful implementation of collaborative systems.

REFERENCES

1. Coleman, D. Groupware: Collaboration and knowledge sharing. In *Knowledge Management Handbook*; Liebowitz, J., Ed.; CRC Press: Boca Raton, FL, 1999; 12:1–12:15.
2. Koenig, M.E.D. Knowledge management and user education: The unrecognized Achilles' heel. In *Knowledge Management: Lessons Learned*; Koenig, M.E.D., Srikantaiah, T.K., Eds.; Information Today: Medford, NJ, 2004; 487–496.
3. Mai, J.E.; Albrechtsen, H.; Fidel, R.; Pejtersen, A.M. Cognitive work analysis: The study of work, actors, and activities. In *ASIST 2004: Proceedings of the 67th ASIS&T Annual Meeting: Managing and Enhancing Information: Cultures and Conflict*, November 12–17, 2004, Providence, Rhode Island. Information Today: Medford, NJ, 2004.
4. Jank, D. Groupware. In *Encyclopedia of Library and Information Science*; Drake, M.A., Ed.; Marcel Dekker, Inc.: New York, 2003; Vol. 3, 1175–1178.
5. Downing, C.E.; Clark, A.S. Groupware in practice. Inform. Syst. Manage. **1999**, *16* (2), 25–31.
6. Duffy, J. Collaborative computing, groupware and knowledge. Inform. Manage. Comput. Secu. **1996**, *4* (2), 39–41.

7. Graham, C.R.; Misanchuk, M. Computer-mediated learning groups. In *Encyclopedia of Information Science and Technology*; Khosrow-Pour, M., Ed.; Idea Group: Hershey, PA, 2005; Vol. 1, 502–507.
8. Johansen, R. *Groupware: Computer Support for Business Teams*; MacMillan: New York, 1988.
9. Lapiedra, R.; Smithson, S.; Alegre, J.; Chiva, R. Role of information systems on the business network formation process. J. Enterp. Inform. Manage. **2004**, *17* (3), 219–228.
10. Lim, J.; Zhong, Y. Cultural diversity in collaborative learning systems. In *Encyclopedia of Information Science and Technology*; Khosrow-Pour, M., Ed.; Idea Group: Hershey, PA, 2005. Update, 1–6.
11. Wiig, K.M. Introducing knowledge management into the enterprise. In *Knowledge Management Handbook*; Liebowitz, J., Ed.; CRC Press: Boca Raton, FL, 1999; 12:1–12:15.
12. John, B.E. Information processing and skilled behavior. In *HCI Models, Theories, and Frameworks: Toward a Multidisciplinary Science*; Carroll, J.M., Ed.; Elsevier: Boston, 2003; 55–102.
13. Chi, L.; Holsapple, C.W. Understanding computer-mediated interorganizational collaboration: a model and framework. J. Knowl. Manage. **2005**, *9* (1), 53–75.
14. Wheeler, B.C.; Dennis, A.R.; Press, L.I. Groupware comes to the Internet: Charting a new world. Data Base Adv. Inf. Syst. **1999**, *30* (3/4), 8–21.
15. Kaufman, F. Data systems that cross company boundaries. Harvard Bus. Rev. **1966**, *44* (1), 141–151.
16. Dennis, A.R.; Aronson, J.E.; Heninger, W.G.; Walker II, E.D. Structuring time and task in electronic brainstorming. MIS Quart. **1999**, *23* (1), 95–108.
17. Attaran, M.; Attaran, S. Collaborative computing technology: the hot new managing tool. J. Manage. Develop. **2002**, *21* (8), 598–609.
18. Lotus links with Oracle for enhanced groupware. Info Canada **1994**, *19* (12), 2.
19. Preece, J.; Rogers, Y.; Sharp, H. *Interaction Design*; John Wiley & Sons, Inc.: New York, 2002.
20. Coughlan, P.; Coughlan, D.; Lombard, F.; Brennan, L.; McNichols, T.; Nolan, R. Managing collaborative relationships in a period of discontinuity. Int. J. Oper. Prod. Manage. **2003**, *23* (10), 1246–1259.
21. Twidale, M.B.; Nichols, D.M. Computer supported cooperative work in information search and retrieval. In *Annual Review of Information Science & Technology*; Williams, M., Ed.; Information Today: Medford, NJ, 1999; 259–319.
22. Hilmer, K.M.; Dennis, A.R. Stimulation thinking: Cultivating better decisions with groupware through categorization. J. Manage. Inform. Syst. **2001**, *17* (3), 93–114.
23. Chu, H. *Information Representation and Retrieval in the Digital Age*; Information Today: Medford, NJ, 2003.
24. Lamb, C.M. Creating a collaborative environment: the human element. Inform. Outlook **2001**, *5* (5), 23–25.
25. Byrum, J.D., Jr. Online catalogs and library portals in today's information environment. J. Libr. Admin. **2005**, *43* (1/2), 135–154.

BIBLIOGRAPHY

1. Andriessen, J.H.E. Group work and groupware: Understanding and Evaluating Computer Supported Interaction; Springer: New York, 2002.
2. Andriessen, J.H.E. Working with Groupware: Understanding and Evaluating Collaboration Technology; Springer: New York, 2003.
3. Beyerlein, M.M. The Collaborative Work Systems Field-book: Strategies, Tools, and Techniques; Lawrence Erlbaum Associates: Mahwah, NJ, 2006.
4. Beyerlein, M.M.; Freeman, S. Beyond Teams: Building Collaborative Work Systems; Wiley: San Francisco, 2002.
5. Chester, B. Fundamentals of collaboration systems. AIM E-DOC **2005**, 19 (1), 10.
6. Christopher, D. E-world: Virtual Learning, Collaborative Environments, and Future Technologies; National Business Education Association: Reston, VA, 2004.
7. Crabtree, A. Designing Collaborative Systems: A Practical Guide to Ethnography; Springer: New York, 2003.
8. Fichter, D. The many forms of e-collaboration: Blogs, wikis, portals, groupware, discussion boards, and instant messaging. Online **2005**, 29 (4), 48–50.
9. Khosrowpour, M. Collaborative Information Technologies; IRM Press: Hershey, PA, 2002.
10. Mark, G.; Poltrock, S. Groupware adoption in a distributed organization: Transporting and transforming technology through social worlds. Inform. Organ. **2004**, 14 (4), 297–327.

11. Olson, G.M.; Malone, T.W. Coordination Theory and Collaboration Technology; Lawrence Erlbaum Associates: Mahwah, NJ, 2001.
12. Smith, D.E. Knowledge, Groupware, and the Internet; Butter-worth-Heinemann: Boston, MA, 2000.
13. Spring, M.B. Peripheral social awareness information in collaborative work. J. Am. Soc. Inform. Sci. Technol. **2003**, 54 (11), 1006–10013.
14. Stahl, G. Group Cognition: Computer Support for Building Collaborative Knowledge; MIT Press: Cambridge, MA, 2006.
15. Ye, Y.; Churchill, E.F. Agent Supported Collaborative Work; Kluwer: Boston, 2003.

35 Geographic Information Systems (GIS)

Timothy F. Leslie and Nigel M. Waters

CONTENTS

INTRODUCTION AND OVERVIEW

In 1998, *The Encyclopedia of Library and Information Science* published an entry on geographic information systems (GIS)[1] that reviewed both the history and the body of knowledge associated with GIS. A sequel in 2001[2] documented the progress made by the community during the following 3 years, with particular detail given to the "systems versus science" debate. For the sake of completeness and self-containment, this overview of the subject again begins with formal definitions of GIS. Next, the state of the art as it existed in 2008 is described. This is followed by a discussion of spatial thinking as conceptualized within the (generally American) educational system.

In recent years, GIS has come to represent a synthesis of science and application. The "systems versus science" debate has become passé. Internet applications have flourished, with many users unaware they were using GIS technology to create maps or obtain driving directions. This entry concludes with an overview of the near-term future of GIS and with a list of GIS resources, both online and traditional print materials. The present account does not provide a complete and comprehensive introduction to GIS, and readers wishing to learn the basics before consulting the rest of the entry are advised to go to the following online tutorials: the U.S. Geological Survey (USGS) GIS education Web site at http://education.usgs.gov/common/lessons/gis.html and the Environmental Systems Research Institute (ESRI) discussion of GIS presented at http://www.gis.com/whatisgis/. A comprehensive description of those topics belonging to the body of knowledge associated with GIS may be found in DiBiase et al.[3]

In addition, this entry does not review the history of GIS. The reader may consult the extensive discussion in Waters[1] or in Clarke.[4] A complete review may be found in Foresman[5] and comprehensive online resources are maintained with The GIS History Project (http://www.ncgia.buffalo.edu/gishist/). Chrisman[6] has described the transformation of computer mapping software into GIS at the Harvard Laboratory for Computer Graphics and Spatial Analysis during the 1960s and 1970s.

MODERN DEFINITIONS OF GIS

A terse, useful definition of GIS continues to elude the community. Two views of GIS pervade the literature, differing largely because of the difference in the "S" in the acronym. Those scholars that represent the "S" as systems include Clarke,[4] who provides a number of definitions of GIS. Clarke begins by stating that a GIS is a computer-based system for linking attribute data from a database with spatial information. He notes that a GIS can be described in various ways. Thus some authors have referred to GIS as a toolbox. Similarly, Burrough and McDonnell[7] state that GIS is a "a powerful set of tools for storing and retrieving at will, transforming and displaying spatial data from the real world for a particular set of purposes." Longley et al.[8] review definitions that describe GIS as both data analysis–data display tools and as map-making tools. These definitions emphasize the applied nature of GIS and are generally used by practitioners in the field, such as the government and related industry contractors. These definitions have become more entrenched with the increasing use of software programming packages and languages (e.g., Visual Basic, Python, and Java, among others) to create sets of procedures that specialized user groups can employ (e.g., transportation planners, see Kang and Scott[9]).

Alternatively, the "S" in GIS can be taken to represent Science[10]. This approach has been advocated by scholars who are actively developing new methods and who view themselves as more than simple toolmakers. Goodchild provides an overview of the differences between GISystems, GIScience and GIStudies at http://www.ncgia.ucsb.edu/giscc/units/u002/u002.html. According to Goodchild GIScience is the science behind the technology of GIS. It is also the science that keeps GIS at the research frontier. GIScience is thus a multidisciplinary field in which cartography, cognitive psychology, computer science, geodesy, geography, photogrammetry, and spatial statistics are all important contributors.

The tool versus science debate has been reviewed by Wright et al.[11] It has been resolved largely by the acceptance of both terms and an increased vagueness in the use of the GIS acronym. Within universities this dichotomy is evident in the number of "professional master's" programs available largely to fill the market for increased application courses and community-based GIS funding in the vein of GISystems. GIScience remains as a realm for continued research and software development, and is popular as a specialization, minor, or additional certificate in degree programs. Academic units with a mix of GIScience and GISystems activity remain healthy.

Finally, Chrisman[12] has defined GIS as an "organized activity by which people measure and represent geographic phenomena then transform these representations into other forms while interacting with social structures." This definition reflects the increased interest in the use of GIS for community planning and advocacy. It is such an important new trend that it has been variously referred to as community-based GIS and Public Participation GIS (PPGIS) and more recently as VGIS where the "V" in the acronym indicates volunteer involvement. These developments are described in further detail below.

GIS: THE STATE OF THE ART IN 2008

In 2008, GIS software packages for making maps and for displaying and analyzing spatial data in a variety of ways was commonplace. Large price differences existed, with GIS software packages ranging in cost from free (for GRASS and other open source initiatives) to a few hundred dollars (for Idrisi, MapInfo, and Maptitude) to tens of thousands of dollars (for enterprise versions of TransCAD and ArcServer). These packages generally come with a graphical interface and run on the Windows operating system, although Unix-friendly server editions are becoming common. Mac OS X and Linux are poorly represented, and can only run a subset of existing GIS software without a Windows emulator or interpreter. Open source software has been particularly successful with these operating systems, to the point that dedicated teams focus on GIS-specific Linux distributions (see information on DebianGIS at http://wiki.debian.org/DebianGis).

Conducting analysis with GIS software still requires extensive training and this is especially so if it is to be used for decision-making and policy implementation. Most GIS education and training is completed in university undergraduate programs. Post-degree diploma programs are also popular as are graduate level master's degree programs, and employers frequently pay for such education for their employees.

Web-based GIS applications and the use of software and data online are becoming increasingly common. Many of these Web-based devices are lowering the technical know-how necessary to interact with spatial data. GPS units are capable of calculating driving directions as well as tracking traffic information from a server and rerouting the user on the fly. Cell phones, such as the iPhone, can track their location, navigate users, and check the weather with a few touches of the screen.

Spatial data is still extremely costly in most countries where cost-recovery models are often used by government agencies (see Taylor[13] for an exhaustive discussion of this topic for various countries around the world). The United States is almost the lone exception to this approach to the provision of spatial data, and it is arguable that this has done much to spawn the world's most active and innovative GIS industry.

Although GIS, even today, cannot be considered more than a niche application it is now a common place subject in university curricula and is frequently used as a research tool by a large number of university disciplines.[1] In addition, it is being taught more and more in the K-12 curriculum in schools and is being used in an increasingly extensive number of applications in both the public and private sectors.

PUBLIC PARTICIPATION GIS AND VOLUNTEERED GEOGRAPHIC INFORMATION

During the last decade, GIS has been used more and more for community planning and social advocacy. Such developments have been variously described as Public Participation GIS and Participatory GIS with the acronyms PPGIS and PGIS, respectively, in common use. The most extensive set of resources for participatory GIS may be found at the portal Web site maintained by the integrated approaches to participatory development (IAPAD) organization at http://www.iapad.org/. IAPAD maintains a list for those interested in PGIS research and also stores numerous case studies which may be downloaded. In recent years it has promoted as participatory three-dimensional modeling (P3DM) of physical environments and the ethically responsible use of GIS to protect lands belonging to indigenous communities.

PGIS has now been well accepted by mainstream GIS researchers with highly regarded texts such as that by Craig et al.[14] devoted to this topic. For a number of years PGIS had its own series of conferences sponsored by the Urban and Regional Information Systems Association (URISA) although during 2006 and 2007 PGIS was again merged into URISA's main, annual conference. The PPGIS Web site (http://www.ppgis.net/) maintains an open forum on Participatory GIS and associated technologies.

Volunteered geographic information is an increasingly important and associated development. Software developments that include Google Earth, Google SketchUp, Wikimapia, and OpenStreetMap have allowed citizens with limited or indeed no specialized knowledge of GIS to upload their geographic knowledge to publicly accessible Web sites. This process of "geotagging" and its impact on the future of GIS is discussed by Goodchild.[15] The Geography Network (http://www.geographynetwork.com/) supports project Globe (http://www.globe.gov/GaN/analyze.html) which allows students in elementary schools to observe data, for example, the brilliance of the night sky. It is easy for these students to record their observations and upload them to a map where they can become part of a network of thousands of observations from schoolchildren around the world. As Goodchild notes, the children have become geographic sensors.

TEACHING SPATIAL THINKING

GIS Education continues to progress as spatial thinking has received attention at all educational levels. Many vendors of GIS software offer reduced or free versions of their packages for education institutions, and resource materials including data sets and lesson plans are widely available.

Schools

Recently the National Research Council has produced a major study[16] advocating the teaching of spatial thinking and GIS across the K-12 curriculum. The authors of the report argue that spatial thinking is a constructive mix of three elements: spatial concepts, methods of representation, and spatial reasoning. Indeed the Association of American Geographers has argued recently (http://aag.org/nclb/nclb.pdf) for changes to the U.S. No Child Left Behind Legislation that would see an appropriation of funding in this legislation for the teaching of geography and GIS.

It can be argued that GIS should be incorporated into the K-12 curriculum for several reasons. First, it helps with the teaching of geography, a core academic discipline. Major software manufacturers such as ERSI (http://www.esri.com) have made available at no cost software such as ArcGIS Explorer which, at the time of writing is available with seven worldwide coverages that include various themes such as physical relief and political boundaries. Second, spatial thinking is advocated because it helps with other disciplines such as the physical, mathematical and environmental sciences. Third, it prepares students to be better citizens in that the data embedded within a GIS provides them with an understanding of other regions of their country and of other countries within the world. A GIS also prepares them to interact with the world in a more effective manner as an entrepreneur or merely as someone who can use an in-car navigation system more resourcefully.

Evidence to support improved spatial thinking and education in the National Research Council Report is contained in Chapter 4 and Appendix C of the study. Unfortunately, most of this research is dated and will have to be revisited if the council is to succeed in its goal of developing new GIS software that is age appropriate in its design, scope, and sequence.

Information on geographic information technology for teachers and the lay person may be found at http://geography.about.com/od/geographictechnology/Geographic_Technology.htm. A complete set of links summarizing articles, lesson plans, and software for teaching GIS in the K-12 curriculum is available at http://www.esi.utexas.edu/gk12/lessons.php.

GIS and geography teaching in elementary and secondary schools has moved forward quickly since 1990. Bednarz and Bednarz[17] take an optimistic view of the progress that has been made and how future challenges may be addressed. Doering (http://gis2.esri.com/library/userconf/educ02/pap5039/p5039.htm) has analyzed the effectiveness of various strategies for teaching about GIS in the K-12 curriculum (see also Doering and Veletsianos[18]).

Simply put, GIS is a highly effective way of teaching schoolchildren about their world. There is, however, a steep learning curve for teachers and professional development resources constantly need to be upgraded (McClurg and Buss[19]). Others have argued for a minimal GIS software package that increases in complexity with grade level and focuses on the introduction of geographical concepts appropriate to a child's intellectual development (Marsh et al.[20]).

Resources for teachers may be found at a link on the ESRI Web site at http://www.esri.com/industries/k-12/education/teaching.html. These resources include lesson plans for a variety of ages and skill levels A list of resources for teachers including annotated bibliographies of the use of GIS in the K-12 system may be found at the Web site http://gislounge.com/k-12-education-in-gis/. Links to resources on best practices and "white papers" discussing the future of GIS in school education may be found at this link on the ESRI Web site: http://www.esri.com/library/whitepapers/pdfs/higher_ed.pdf.

The work of the National Center for Geographic Information and Analysis (NCGIA) at the University of California at Santa Barbara in supporting the integration of GIS into the secondary school curriculum may be seen at the following Web site: http://www.ncgia.ucsb.edu/education/projects/SEP/sep.html. This Web site also contains links to other sites providing resources and support for K-12 GIS initiatives. Resources for schools in the United Kingdom and a sourcebook that may be ordered online can both be found at http://www.abdn.ac.uk/gis_school/.

A new trend is the linking of qualitative geography to GIS (Mei-Po Kwan[21]). This development may also unite interest in another new area of research, Children's Geographies (see the new journal of that name and introductory editorial by Matthews[22]). Children and youths may be used to supply volunteer information that can be incorporated into GIS (see discussion above and Dennis[23]).

Despite all these developments the reality is that in the year 2008 many schools still do not have the computers or the teacher expertise to take advantage of the resources that are available to them on the Internet. It can only be hoped that this will change in the coming years.

Universities

University education in GIS grew substantially after the introduction of the core curriculum in GIS by the NCGIA in 1990. The original core curriculum was designed to provide university faculty with notes for 75 lectures that represented a year-long introduction to the fundamental issues and concepts in GIS. This curriculum was remarkably successful and about 2000 copies were distributed to over 70 countries after being translated into at least eight languages (including Portuguese, Chinese, Hungarian, Japanese, Korean, Polish, Russian, and French). It may still be found at http://www.geog.ubc.ca/courses/klink/gis.notes/ncgia/toc.html.

The new Core Curriculum in GIScience may be found at http://www.ncgia.ucsb.edu/education/curricula/giscc/ and is still under development. It includes two sets of lecture notes specifically on teaching GIS within a university setting http://www.ncgia.ucsb.edu/education/curricula/giscc/units/

u158/u158_f.html. A core curriculum for the closely related field of remote sensing may be found at http://userpages.umbc.edu/~tbenja1/umbc7/.

A related occurrence has been the NCGIA's development of CSISS (The Center for Spatially Integrated Social Science http://www.csiss.org/index.html).

GIS research and teaching in Universities in the United States has been substantially stimulated through the creation of the University Consortium for Geographic Information Science [UCGIS; (http://www.ucgis.org/)]. The UCGIS defines its mission to be "an effective, unified voice for the geographic information science research community." A listing of university-based, GIS courses in the United Kingdom may be found at http://www.agi.org.uk/ under the Education Link. University based GIS research in the U.K. was also supported by the Regional Research Laboratory initiative.[1] Canadian GIS degree programs may be accessed at http://www.canadian-universities.net/Universities/Programs/Geography_and_GIS.html.

Masters Courses

In recent years, master's degrees have proliferated at universities in the United States and in many other countries around the world. A listing of these programs, including distance-based offerings, may be found at http://www.ucgis.org/priorities/education/GIS_Cert+Masters_Prog/certificates.htm. Many of these master's degree programs now include modules on programming in GIS. Popular choices for programming languages include Visual Basic, Java, C, C#, and C++. Students find these courses most attractive and often feel that their education in the GISciences is not complete without some basic training in programming. The more important software vendors such as ESRI (see below) are moving away from their own, proprietary scripting languages toward industry standard languages such as Visual Basic.

In some cases these masters programs have been seen as terminal, professional degree programs which supply a need generated by the GIS industry. Others have seen them as the ideal "springboard" into Ph.D. research in Geography and other disciplines such as Archaeology that use spatially distributed data (see the Web site at http://www.le.ac.uk/geography/postgraduate/msc_gis_hg.html which discusses the Master of Science degree in GIS at the University of Leicester).

Colleges

The NCGIA has developed a core curriculum for technical programs taught in colleges and this may be accessed at http://www.ncgia.ucsb.edu/education/curricula/cctp/Welcome.html. GIS has found a particularly successful niche in technical colleges that offer postgraduate diploma programs. One of the oldest and most successful of these programs has been taught at the College of Geographic Sciences in Nova Scotia, Canada, since the early 1980s. A description of this program may be found at http://www.cogs.ns.ca/Programs/Geomatics/. A partial listing of some of the better known college programs in GIS may be found at http://www.ncgia.ucsb.edu/education/curricula/cctp/resources/example_courses/examples_f.html.

Virtual Campuses

Distance education is a well-established method of instruction in GIS and is sponsored by the UCGIS organization among others. A "white paper" on this topic may be found at (http://dusk.geo.orst.edu/disted/). Links to many U.S. sites that offer distance education may be found at this location together with a link to the UNIGIS International site (http://www.unigis.org/) which has offices in 10 separate countries around the world. Perhaps one of the most outstandingly successful attempts at distance education is ESRI's virtual campus which may be found at http://training.esri.com/gateway/index.cfm?fa=trainingOptions.gateway. These courses may be either self study or instructor led.

While distance-based education represents an affordable and convenient way of learning about GIS or indeed any other subject it is not without its critics such as Noble.[24]

SOFTWARE PACKAGES

Software vendors have done much to popularize the use of GIS in academia, government, and industry. This they have achieved by sponsoring software distribution, conferences, Web sites, Web services, and trade newsletters. Here the activities of a number of the more important vendors and software developers are described. Most software vendors now support their own online listserves, Web knowledge banks, and other interactive communities in order to resolve problems for their user base. Information on Open Source GIS software may be found at the Open Source Geospatial Foundation Web site (http://www.osgeo.org/) and is discussed in more detail below. A survey of this software undertaken in late 2007 is available at http://www.foss4g2007.org/presentations/view.php?abstract_id=136. The rest of this section lists the leading commercial GIS software.

ESRI

Founded in 1969, ESRI (http://www.esri.com/) continues to dominate the industry as the GIS market leader. ESRI offers various configurations of its ArcGIS software. The current version of the ArcGIS software is 9.3 but new releases occur about every 6 months. The Desktop configuration has three components: ArcGIS Desktop, ArcGIS Engine, and ArcGIS Explorer (http://www.esri.com/products.html#arcgis). The Desktop product allows for the creation, editing, and analysis of geographic data and the development of professional, publication-quality maps. ESRI provides a server configuration for delivering maps and geographic data across an organization and over the Web. This configuration requires their ArcGIS Server and Image Server products. ESRI's Mobile GIS products include ArcGIS Mobile and ArcPad, products that allow the development of GIS products in the field and full use by clients with mobile devices including phones. ESRI offers data in various formats to populate these GIS products and also as Web services that are available online (http://www.esri.com/software/arcwebservices/index.html). Other organizations that offer Web services include GIS factory (http://gisfactory.com/webservices.html) where the services include address finders, district finders, and route finders (http://gisfactory.com/whitepapers/wp_giswebservices.pdf).

ESRI sponsors the ArcWatch e-mail newsletter, the ArcUser magazine, and the ArcNews publication. In 2008 it will hold its 28th annual user conference (http://www.esri.com/events/uc/index.html), one of the most popular and enduring of all the yearly GIS conferences. Recently attendance at this premier, vendor-sponsored conference has been around 14,000 attendees. The functionality of the ESRI ArcGIS software has been augmented by a series of extensions that can be deployed to perform specific functions. For ArcGIS these include extensions for analysis, such as Spatial Analyst and Network Analyst, for productivity including, Publisher and Street Map, and solution based software such as Business Analyst and Military Analyst and, finally, Web services. A complete list of ESRI supported extensions may be found at http://www.esri.com/software/arcgis/about/desktop_extensions.html. Extensions developed by their partners may be found at http://gis.esri.com/partners/partners-user/index.cfm. A review of these extensions, organized by application type, is provided by Limp,[25] an article which may be accessed by registering at the GeoPlace Web site (http://www.geoplace.com), a GIS industry Web portal. Some extensions are packaged in the form of toolboxes that perform specific GIS operations that are often missing from the standard GIS packages. A prototypical example is Hawth's Tools that provides functionality for a variety of spatial, sampling, and animal movement operations and may be found at the spatial ecology Web site (http://www.spatialecology.com/htools/tooldesc.php).

IDRISI

One of the most popular, affordably priced, GIS products is Idrisi which was developed in 1987 by Ron Eastman and is now supported by Clark Labs at Clark University in Worcester, Massachusetts (http://www.clarklabs.org/). Idrisi's roots are as a raster GIS and as such it has been most widely used in resource management, land use change, and image processing applications. At the time of writing, the Andes Edition, the 15th major release, was the current version of this enormously popular GIS software package. The unusual name of the software owes its origins to the famed, twelfth century, Moroccan cartographer, Muhammad al-Idrisi. The Idrisi software is a fully functional GIS and image processing package that is now used in more than 175 countries. It has an especially rich and diverse set of processing modules for analytical research that include the first ever machine learning algorithms for use in a GIS and image processing system, soft classifiers, multi-criteria and multi-objective decision making that provided the first GIS implementation of Saaty's Analytical Hierarchy Process (Saaty[26]), sophisticated geospatial statistics, and a dynamic modeling routine that is implemented through a graphical interface.

Intergraph

Intergraph is ESRI's chief competitor for the title of GIS market leader and has been providing GIS and related software for 35 years. Intergraph has a suite of GIS-related products including its GeoMedia products (http://www.intergraph.com/geomediasuite/). Intergraph also sponsors its own annual user's conference and publications including the trade publication, Insight, which is available online together with Intergraph's e-Connection Newsletter. Intergraph works with business partners such as Hansen Information Technologies (http://www.hansen.com/) to provide additional geospatial functionality, in this case for asset management and transportation and related solutions.

MAPINFO

Since 1986 MapInfo Corporation, Troy, New York (http://www.mapinfo.com/) has been producing affordable GIS software that is eminently suited to desktop mapping and such applications as geodemographics and target marketing. MapInfo emphasizes location-based intelligence especially in the field of business planning and analysis. It too supports an annual conference, the MapWorld Global User Conference, and provides customer support through online user groups.

Caliper Corporation

Caliper Corporation, Newton, Massachusetts (http://www.caliper.com/), produces one of the most sophisticated low-cost GIS desktop mapping products available, Maptitude. This software comes complete with extensive data sets from the U.S. Bureau of the Census and is ideal software for many GIS applications and has been favorably reviewed. A special version of Maptitude is available for building and analyzing political and other redistricting plans. Caliper Corporation's flagship product is TransCAD, a transportation GIS package that has the most complete set of transportation planning and related routines available in any GIS package. The latest release of this software, Version 5, is also produced as a Web mapping package that may be used for developing online transportation planning applications. One suggestion is that this software could be used to do online travel surveys greatly reducing the cost of traditional in-house, paper-based surveys (http://www.caliper.com/web/gist2002.pdf). Caliper Corporation is now marketing a GIS-based traffic simulation package, TransModeler.

Autodesk

Autodesk, San Rafael, California (http://www.autodesk.com), is the major software developer in the Computer Assisted Drafting market with its AutoCAD product. In recent years it has also added desktop mapping and GIS to its product line with its Map 3D product.

Bentley

In a 2006 study the Daratech organization (http://www.daratech.com/) rated Bentley Systems, Inc., as the number two provider of GIS systems worldwide. Their flagship GIS/CAD product, Microstation, was originally developed for Intergraph. It is now available as Bentley Map.

Manifold

Manifold (http://www.manifold.net/index.shtml), manufactured by CDA International Ltd., is a low cost GIS that is highly popular with organizations that have limited budgets and lack the technical expertise to work with open source software. It has an online users' support group (http://forum.manifold.net/forum/). It is a full featured GIS that in its current release of 8.0 offers 64 bit processing, an Internet map server, and is available in personal and enterprise editions.

Free and Open Source Software

There are numerous GIS packages now available in various amounts of free and open-source packages. GRASS (the geographic resources analysis support system) has made large strides in development since its release under the open source GPL license in 1999 (http://grass.itc.it/). It is designed primarily to work on Linux and other operating systems that use X windows (not to be confused with Microsoft Windows).

GeoDA is a specialized analysis tool used to examine spatial autocorrelation and related spatial regression analyses implemented on Windows. PySal (python spatial analysis library) is a shared set of libraries for both GeoDA and the STARS software that is available at the Regional Analysis Laboratory at San Diego State University (http://regionalanalysislab.org/).

Software, such as the crime analysis package, Crimestat (http://www.icpsr.umich.edu/CRIMESTAT/), are free and used frequently in the professional world, although they are not truly open source. GIS also shares a great deal of overlap with the postgreSQL and mySQL server backends, and postgis serves as "spatially-enabled" upgrade for postgreSQL and has been implemented in both the U.S. and U.K. Programs such as terraview (http://www.terralib.org/), and mapserver (http://mapserver.gis.umn.edu/) have more niche audiences but are also growing in popularity.

Geoexploration Systems

There now exist a number of competing technologies that have been described as geographic exploration systems (Ball[27]) or geoexploration systems. These technologies include Google Earth, Microsoft's Virtual Earth, NASA WorldWind, and ESRI's ArcGIS Explorer among others. They have become extremely popular since the introduction of "mashup" technology that allows even the neophyte user to combine their spatial data with real world environments across a nation or indeed across the globe. Visualization software such as GeoFusion (http://www.geofusion.com/) has been developed to improve download times, allow the integration of multiple data sets, and enhance the interface of these systems. Geoexploration systems have proved extremely useful in aiding the development of participatory GIS where nonspecialists use GIS technology for advocacy planning or to protect the rights of indigenous populations (see discussion above). Volunteer geographic information has been made far more effective by the ease of use of this new type of GIS.

Geographic social networking is a new development that represents the integration of social network technology such as MySpace, video technology such as YouTube, and geoexploration systems like Virtual Earth. This approach is being pioneered by The Carbon Project (http://www.thecarbonproject.com/).

SPATIAL AUTOCORRELATION

Spatial analysis continues to be the crux of GIScience's growth. The forms of analysis special to geographic information have continued to be developed and remain unique to the discipline (Gould[28]). Spatial autocorrelation, the problem of observations near each other having correlated regression residuals, and related analysis has become ubiquitous in the geography literature. Increases in computational resources have allowed for most desktop computers to be able to create weight matrices, calculate spatial autocorrelation, and map significance scores (Anselin[29,30]; and Anselin and Florax[31]). These tools were originally implemented in stand-alone software, but are increasingly part of commercial software such as Idrisi and ArcMap.

For more sophisticated forms of analysis, researchers are still forced to use packages such as SpaceStat (http://www.spacestat.com/) or the spatial statistics routines in S-Plus (http://insightful.com). Modern spatial analysis continues to focus on local models of spatial association (Fotheringham et al.[32]). These Local Indicators of Spatial Association (LISA) statistics, such as Local Moran's I, are frequent in the literature. Anselin's GeoDA software is the most frequently used software employed to examine these local autocorrelation statistics. GeoDA allows for the creation and analysis of weight matrices, as well as the use of them to account for spatial autocorrelation in modified regression analysis. Another approach has been to allow the coefficients within regressions to vary over space. This method, termed geographically weighted regression, is promoted by Fotheringham and has received a mixed reception in the literature.

Markup Languages

Markup languages are the *lingua franca* of the Internet. Since its inception hypertext markup language (HTML) has been the dominant method for encoding information for text that is transmitted over the Internet. Essentially HTML does little more than provide a "picture" of a document for the Web user. All markup languages seek to provide information about the data that is transmitted over the Internet. When that data has unique characteristics, as is the case with spatial or geographical data, it requires its own markup language.

Geography markup language has been in development since 1998 and this has been largely due to the efforts of Ron Lake and his company Galdos Systems (http://www.galdosinc.com/). GML v3.0 was released as ISO Standard 19136 for the storage and transport of geographic data. GML is now the standard for the GeoWeb (http://www.geoweb.org/). It thus allows devices that are connected to the Internet to store and transmit geographical data across the Internet permitting the efficient use of Web services. Like XML, it has also spawned other related markup languages including CityGML which enables the storage and exchange of three dimensional objects that describe urban infrastructure (http://www.citygml.org/). In late 2007, CityGML was officially adopted by the Open Geospatial Consortium as the preferred markup language for urban infrastructure.

More commonly, GIS data on a server is accessed through flash and JavaScript applets that do not require the screen to refresh every time the user makes a change but instead the onscreen image will change "on the fly." This has vastly increased the usability of many online GIS applications. However, it also has made it far more difficult to create these GIS systems, with more advanced training required for these software and database packages.

GIS AND ITS APPLICATIONS

A major strength of GIS has been its ability to prove itself useful in a great many application areas. The reader may find detailed discussions of the use of GIS in the management of utilities, telecommunications, emergency management, land administration, urban planning, military applications, library management, health care, political redistricting, geodemographics and target marketing, agriculture and environmental monitoring in Longley et al.[8] Each of these application areas has an extensive literature of its own and these are described in the various chapters included in Longley et al.'s comprehensive review of the discipline.

CERTIFICATION OF GIS PROFESSIONALS

An ongoing concern for GIS professionals has been the need for certification. Many individuals and organizations have argued that GIS professionals should be certified in a manner similar to the certification of engineers, geologists, psychologists, and others in professional disciplines. In 1998 the Urban and Regional Information Systems Association (URISA: http://www.urisa.org/) created a Certification Committee. After extensive industry-wide debate, the finalized portfolio-based certification program was established in 2003. This certification process was adopted and administered by the newly established GIS Certification Institute (http://www.gisci.org/). Certification involves establishing evidence of professional competence and ethical conduct. Until January 1, 2009, a "grandfathering" process was also permitted. At the end of 2007 almost 2000 individuals have availed themselves of the certification process.

GIS AND THE FUTURE

Judging the future of the discipline is difficult, as rapid advancements make such statements outdated by the time of publishing. Such is the case in a recent work by Reuter and Zipf (http://www.i3mainz.fh-mainz.de/publicat/zipf05/gis.where.next-reuter-zipf.pdf), that predicts the trajectory of a device to support trip planning that is partially implemented in a new release of the iPhone. As GIS presses onward, it will continue to be embedded within more and more electronics. While appliances such as refrigerators and stoves do not generally need location information, most devices that move today already have some sort of location-finding mechanism inside them. The future of these devices may rely on the ability to more precisely locate themselves, particularly inside buildings. Reuter and Zipf suggest this may come in a ground-based GPS system they term a "Global Universal Computer."

The amount of spatial data is blossoming and will likely continue to do so. As users mark important personal events and places linked to particular places, storage and retrieval of this data will become increasingly important. Reuter and Zipf suggest it is the storage and search of these items that will be most important. This technology may be crucial to historians and psychologists working to understand the reasons for individual behavior.

At some point, the lack of widespread spatial education will segment the population further, based on those who can use new integrated devices and those who cannot. Technological advances will make up for some of this digital divide by simplifying interfaces. However, these new interfaces generally cannot wholly account for such differences and maintain full functionality without a significant paradigm shift.

Finally, it may be noted that GIS in the future will become more involved with the third and fourth dimensions. The third dimension is already being implemented in geographic exploration systems and the integration of products such as Google SketchUp (http://sketchup.google.com/) into Google Earth. The fourth dimension is time, a difficult concept to incorporate into traditional GIS software structures. Peuquet[33] has provided part of the theoretical paradigm for this new implementation and new versions of commercial software such as ESRI's ArcGIS 9.3 make it easier to create animated visualizations of geodatabases. 3-D/4-D GIS will be the new frontier.

BIBLIOGRAPHY AND ADDITIONAL RELATED RESOURCES

GIS Day

On November 14, 2007, GIS Day was held in over 80 countries around the World and in all 50 states in the United States. GIS Day is a grassroots movement in which GIS users and vendors (academics, government employees and entrepreneurs) open their doors to schoolchildren and all members of the general public in order to showcase the capabilities of GIS projects which they have developed (http://www.gisday.com/). The event is sponsored principally by the National Geographic Society, the Association of American Geographers, the University Consortium for Geographic Information Science, the United States Geological Survey, The Library of Congress, Sun Microsystems and Hewlett-Packard and ESRI, and by local GIS organizations. The next GIS Day will be held on November 18 and 17 in 2009 and 2010, respectively. The event is usually held as part of Geography Awareness Week, which has been sponsored by the National Geographic Society since 1987. The U.S. e-Government Web site using data from Daratech estimates that there are 1,000,000 users of GIS worldwide, half of whom are in the United States (http://www.whitehouse.gov/omb/egov/c-7-10-b-geospatial.html).

Books

The most important reference works for GIS are the so-called "Big-Books" of GIS. The first edition of this huge, two-volume review of the state of the art in GIS was edited by Maguire, Goodchild, and Rhind[34] and published in 1991, while the second edition was edited by Longley, Goodchild, Maguire, and Rhind[35] in 1999. More recently, the second volume has been published in a paperback edition with editorial updates based on input from the individual chapter authors, various additional chapters, and a CD featuring all the chapters from the second edition (Longley et al.[36]). Popular textbooks discussing the concepts behind GIS include Longley et al.[37] and Clarke.[4] The latter author provides an extensive list of GIS books magazines and journals, conference proceedings, and professional organizations. Price's[38] text is a guide to operating the industry leading ArcGIS 9.2 software and includes a series of hands-on tutorials to aid the novice user.

A searchable GIS bibliography may be found at ESRI's Web site: http://training.esri.com/campus/library/index.cfm. Important publishers of GIS texts include ESRI (http://store.esri.com/esri/category.cfm?SID=2&Category_ID=35) and Taylor & Francis (http://gis.tandf.co.uk/). Longley et al.[37] provide a list of major GIS textbooks while Chrisman[6] describes the earliest days of the discipline. Vendor publications have been discussed above. Suffice it to note that most major vendors have a company publication designed to inform their user base of the latest developments in their software products and many of these are now available online.

Journals and Magazines

Some of the main academic journals in which GIS research is published include

Annals of the Association of American Geographers (http://www.aag.org/)
Canadian Geographer (http://www.blackwellpublishing.com/CG)
Cartographica (http://www.utpjournals.com/carto/carto.html)
Cartographic Perspectives (http://www.nacis.org/index.cfm?x=5)
Cartography and GIS (http://www.cartogis.org/)
Computers, Environment, and Urban Systems (http://www.elsevier.com/locate/compenvurbsys)
Computers and Geosciences (http://www.elsevier.com/locate/cageo)
Conference Papers in GIS (http://srmwww.gov.bc.ca/gis/papers/index.html)
ESRI User Conference Proceedings (http://gis.esri.com/library/userconf/index.html)
Geocarto International (http://www.geocarto.com/geocarto.html)
Geographical Systems (http://link.springer.de/link/service/journals//10109/)
GeoInformatica (http://www.wkap.nl/journalhome.htm/1384-6175)
Geoscience E-Journals (http://paleopolis.rediris.es/geosciences/)
Geographical Journal (http://www.ingentaconnect.com/content/bpl/geoj/latest)
GeoJournal (http://www.ingentaconnect.com/content/klu/gejo/latest)
GIS Law

IEEE Transactions on Computer Graphics and Applications (http://ieeexplore.ieee.org/xpl/RecentIssue.jsp?punumber=38)
IEEE Transactions on Geoscience and Remote Sensing (http://ieeexplore.ieee.org/xpl/RecentIssue.jsp?punumber=36)
International Journal of Geographical Information Science (http://www.tandf.co.uk/journals/titles/13658816. asp)
International Journal of Remote Sensing (http://www.tandf.co.uk/journals/frameloader.html?http://www.tandf.co.uk/journals/tf/01431161.html)
International Journal of Mapping Sciences and Remote Sensing (http://www.ingentaconnect.com/content/bell/msrs/latest)
Journal of Geographical Systems (http://link.springer.de/link/service/journals/10109/index.htm)
Photogrammetric Engineering and Remote Sensing (http://www.asprs.org/publications/pers/www.asprs.org/publications/pers/)
Public Health GIS News and Information (http://www.cdc.gov/nchs/about/otheract/gis/gis_publichealthinfo.htm)
Remote Sensing Reviews (http://www.tandf.co.uk/journals/online/0275–7257.asp)
Transactions in GIS (http://www.blackwellpublishing.com/journals/tgis/)
The Spatial Odyssey Website also has a list of GIS Journal Abstracts and Citations (http://libraries.maine.edu/Spatial/gisweb/journals/journals.html)

Many **magazines** are available in both an online and a paper version. Some of the more notable examples are

ArcNews Online (http://www.esri.com/news/arcnews/arcnews.html)
ArcUser Online (http://www.esri.com/news/arcuser/index.html)
Challenges: A news letter from UCGIS (http://dusk2.geo.orst.edu/ucgis/news/)
Asian surveying and mapping (http://www.asmmag.com/)
GEOWorld (http://www.geoplace.com/)

Other online GIS-oriented magazines include

Directions Magazine (http://www.directionsmag.com/)
Earth Observing Magazine (http://www.eomonline.com/)
GeoCommunity (http://www.geocomm.com/)
Geomatics Information and Trading Centre (http://www.gitc.nl/)
GeoSpatial Solutions (http://www.geospatial-online.com/)
GeoVision (http://www.gisvisionmag.com/)
Geomatics Info Magazine International (http://www.reedbusiness-geo.nl/Home.asp)
GPS World (http://www.gpsworld.com/)
Spatial News (http://spatialnews.geocomm.com/)
Mentor Software (http://www.mentorsoftwareinc.com/cc/ccdir.htm)
Position Magazine (http://www.positionmag.com.au/)
Professional Surveyor Magazine Online (http://www.profsurv.com/)
The CADD/GIS Technology Center CADD/GIS Bulletins Page (https://tsc.wes.army.mil/news/bulletins/)

Organizations

The following are some of the better known organizations with a strong interest in GIS:

The American Congress on Surveying and Mapping (ACSM) (http://www.acsm.net/)
The American Society for Photogrammetry and Remote Sensing (ASPRS) (http://www.asprs.org/)
The Association for Geographic Information (AGI) (http://www.agi.org.uk/)
The Association of American Geographers (AAG) (http://www.aag.org/ this organization has a specialty group devoted to GIS) (http://geography.sdsu.edu/aaggis/)
The International Geographical Union which has a Commission on Geographical Information Science (http://www.hku.hk/cupem/igugisc/)

The North American Cartographic Information Society (NACIS) (http://www.nacis.org/)
Geospatial Information and technology Association (http://www.gita.org/)
The Urban and Regional Information Systems Association (URISA) (http://www.urisa.org/)

Conferences

This section lists a number of the more important conferences other that the vendor-specific conferences mentioned above. Many of the general, omnibus GIS Conferences have in recent years folded as more specialized offerings take their place. These conferences have usually produced either a print proceedings or a proceedings on CD-ROM.

Most of the major GIS organizations such as URISA will also have annual and even regional GIS conferences. Some conferences are strictly devoted to a single theme and are strongly oriented toward training. This is true of the Web mapping conferences (http://www.gisconferences.com/). In 2007, the following was a selection of the conferences held across the globe:

ACM GIS conference in Bellevue, Washington
Africa GIS conference in Ouagadougou, Burkina Fasa
AGIC (Arizona Geographic Information Council); GIS conference in Prescott, Arizona
AGILE (Association Geographic Information Laboratories Europe); conference on GIS in Aalborg, Denmark
Annual CA Geographic Information Association conference in Cypress, California
Annual GIS conference, ASPRS and URISA in Vancouver, Washington
Annual GIS for Oil & Gas Conference in Aurora, Colorado
Annual International airport GIS conference in Budapest, Hungary
Annual Minnesota GIS conference in Rochester, Minnesota
Annual Missouri GIS conference in Osage Beach, Missouri
Annual NC GIS conference in Winston-Salem, North Carolina
Annual Ohio GIS conference in Columbus, Ohio
Annual Virginia GIS conference in Virginia Beach, Virginia
Arc GIS conference in Biloxi, Mississippi
Biennial GIS conference, Iowa Geographic Council in Sioux City, Iowa
California GIS conference in Oakland, California
Croatian GIS Association conference in Sinj, Croatia
Delaware GIS conference in Dover, Delaware
East Tennessee GIS conference in Pigeon Forge, Tennessee
Eastern Montana GIS conference in Miles City, Missouri
ESRI Asia-Pacific User Conference in New Delhi, India
ESRI Australia: GIS user conference in Sydney, Australia
ESRI Eastern Africa: GIS user conference in Kampala, Uganda
ESRI Federal Users GIS conference in Washington, District of Columbia
ESRI GIS solution expo in Danvers, Massachusetts
ESRI Health GIS conference in Scottsdale, Arizona
ESRI International User conference in San Diego, California
ESRI New Zealand: GIS user conference in New Zealand
ESRI South Asia user conference in Novotel Clarke Quay, Singapore
EUC (European User Conference) in Stockholm, Sweden
The GeoTec Event in Ottawa, Ontario, Canada
GI and GIS conference in Porto, Portugal
GIS conference, Office of Lt Governor, U.S. Virgin Islands
GIS Engineers Society conference in Trivandrum, India
GIS for public sector conference in London, U.K.
GIS for Urban Environmental summit in Johannesburg, South Africa
GIS in Rockies conference in Denver, Colorado
GIS in Transit in Tampa, Florida
GIS South Africa conference in Umhlanga Rocks, Durban
Historical GIS conference in Nagoya, Japan

Homeland Security GIS summit in Denver, Colorado
Illinois GIS conference (ILGISA) in Oak Brook, Illinois
Indiana GIS conference in Indianapolis, Indiana
Indonesian Geospatial Technology Exhibition in Jakarta, Indonesia
Intermountain GIS conference in Donnelly, Idaho
International conference of GIS/RS in Hydrology in Guangzhou, China
International conference on Health GIS in Bangkok, Thailand
International GIS crime mapping conference in Brussels, Belgium
Ireland GIS conference in Dublin, Ireland
Kentucky GIS conference in Louville, Kentucky
Kuwait GIS conference in Kuwait
Map Asia in Kulamanpur, Malaysia
Memphis Area Geographic Information Council GIS conference in Memphis, Tennessee
National GIS symposium in Saudi Arabia in Khobar, Saudi Arabia
Nebraska GIS Symposium in Omaha, Nebraska
Nordic GIS conference in Herning, Denmark
North Dakota GIS user conference in Bismarck, North Dakota
North Western PA GIS conference in Clarion, Pennsylvania
Northeast Arc Users Group: GIS conference in Burlington, Vermont
NSGIC (National States Geographic Information Council); in Madison, Wisconsin
NYS GIS conference in Liverpool, New York
PA GIS conference in Harrisburg, Pennsylvania
Pacific Islands GIS/RS conference in Suva, Fiji
Real estate GIS user conference in Scottsdale, Arizona
Rhode Island GIS conference in Narragansett, Rhode Island
ScanGIS—Scandinavian GIS Conference in As, Norway
Southern Forestry and Natural Resources Management GIS conferences in Kissimmee, Florida
Super map GIS conference in Beijing, China
Towson GIS conference in Towson, Maryland
UGIC (Utah Geographic Information Council)—GIS conference in Salt Lake City, Utah
URISA & IAAO 11th Annual GIS conference in Las Vegas, Nevada
URISA (urban regional information systems association)
VIGIC (Virgin Islands Geospatial Information Council)
Washington GIS conference in Lynnwood, Washington

GIS Dictionaries

The Association for Geographic Information has an online dictionary at http://www.geo.ed.ac.uk/agidict/welcome.html. For a published GIS dictionary McDonnell and Kemp's[39] International GIS Dictionary can be referred to.

ACKNOWLEDGMENT

The authors would like to thank Matt Ball for comments on an earlier draft.

REFERENCES

1. Waters, N.M. Geographic information systems. In *Encyclopedia of Library and Information Science*; Marcel Dekker Inc.: New York, 1998; Vol. 63, Supplement 26, 98–125.
2. Waters, N.M. Geographic information systems. In *Encyclopedia of Library and Information Science*, 2nd Ed.; Drake, M., Ed.; Marcel Dekker, Inc.: New York, 2003; 1106–1115.
3. Dibiase, D.; Demers, M.; Johnson, A.; Kamp, K.; Taylor Luck, A.; Plewe, B.; Wentz, E. *Geographic Information Science and Technology Body of Knowledge*; Association of American Geographers: Washington, DC, 2006.
4. Clarke, K.C. *Getting Started with Geographic Information Systems*, 4th Ed.; Prentice Hall: Upper Saddle River, NJ, 2003.

5. Foresman, T.W., Ed.; *The History of Geographic Information Systems: Perspectives from the Pioneers*; Prentice Hall: Upper Saddle River, NJ, 1997.
6. Chrisman, N. *Charting the Unknown: How Computer Mapping at Harvard Became GIS*; ESRI Press, Redlands, CA, 2006.
7. Burrough, P.; McDonnell, R. *Principles of Geographical Information Systems*, 2nd Ed.; Oxford University Press: New York, 1998.
8. Longley, P.; Goodchild, M.F.; Maguire, D.J.; Rhind, D.W. Introduction. In *Geographical Information Systems, Vol. 1, Principles and Technical Issues*; Longley, P., Goodchild, M.F., Maguire, D.J., Rhind, D.W., Eds.; Wiley: New York, 1999; 1–16.
9. Kang, H.; Scott, D.M. An integrated spatio-temporal GIS toolkit for exploring intra-household interactions. *Transportation*, **2008**, *35*, 253–268.
10. Mark, D.M. Geographic information science: Defining the field. In *Foundations of Geographic Information Science*; Duckham, M., Goodchild, M.F., Worboys, M.F., Eds.; Taylor & Francis: New York, 2003; 3–18.
11. Wright, D.J.; Goodchild, M.F.; Proctor, J.D. Demystifying the persistent ambiguity of GIS as 'tool' versus 'science.' Ann. Assoc. Am. Geogr. **1997**, *87*, 346–362.
12. Chrisman, N.R. What does GIS mean? Trans. GIS **1999**, *3*, 175–186.
13. Taylor, D.R.F., Ed.; *Policy Issues in Modern Cartography*; Elsevier Science: Oxford, 1998.
14. Craig, W.J.; Harris, T.M.; Weiner, D. *Community Participation and Geographical Information Systems*; CRC Press: Boca Raton, FL, 2002.
15. Goodchild, M.F. Citizens as sensors: The world of volunteered geography. GeoJournal **2007**, *69*, 211–221.
16. National Research Council, *Learning to Think Spatially*; The National Academies Press: Washington, DC, 2006.
17. Bednarz, S.W.; Bednarz, R.S. Geography education: The glass is half full and it's getting fuller. Prof. Geogr. **2004**, *56*, 22–27.
18. Doering, A.; Veletsianos, G. An investigation of the use of real-time, authentic geospatial data in the K-12 classroom. J. Geogr. **2007**, *106*, 217–225.
19. McClurg, P.A.; Buss, A. Professional development: Teachers use of GIS to enhance student learning. J. Geogr. **2007**, *106*, 79–87.
20. Marsh, M.; Golledge, R.; Battersby, S.E. Geospatial concept understanding and recognition in G6-college students: A preliminary argument for minimal GIS. Ann. Assoc. Am. Geogr. **2007**, *97*, 696–712.
21. Kwan, M.P.; Knigge, L. Guest editorial: Doing qualitative research using GIS: An oxymoronic endeavor? Environ. Plann. A **2006**, *38*, 1999–2002.
22. Matthews, H. Inaugural editorial: Coming of age for children's geographies. Child. Geogr. **2003**, *1*, 3–5.
23. Dennis, S. Prospects for qualitative GIS at the intersection of youth development and participatory urban planning. Environ. Plann. A **2006**, *38*, 2039–2002.
24. Noble, D. *Digital Diploma Mills*; Monthly Review Press: New York, 2003.
25. Limp, W.F. ArcGIS extensions: Quick take review. Geo-World **2005**, *18* (7), 54–58.
26. Saaty, T.L. *Theory and Applications of the Analytic Network Process: Decision Making with Benefits, Opportunities, Costs, and Risks*; RWS Publishers: Artarmon, Australia, 2005.
27. Ball, M. Digital reality: Comparing geographic exploration systems, 2006. http://www.geoplace.com.
28. Gould, P.R. Is Statistix Inferens the geographical name for a wild goose? Econ. Geogr. **1970**, *46*, 439–448.
29. Anselin, L. *Spatial Econometrics*; Kluwer: Dordrecht, 1988.
30. Anselin, L. Local indicators of spatial autocorrelation. Geogr. Anal. **1995**, *27*, 93–115.
31. Anselin, L.; Florax, R. *New Directions in Spatial Econometrics*; Springer-Verlag: Berlin, 1995.
32. Fotheringham, A.S.; Brunsdon, C.; Charlton, M. *Quantitative Geography: Perspectives on Spatial Analysis*; Sage: London, 2000.
33. Peuquet, D. *Representations of Space and Time*; Guilford: New York, 2002.
34. Maguire, D.J.; Goodchild, M.F.; Rhind, D.W. Eds., *Geographical Information Systems*; Longman: London, 1991.
35. Longley, P.; Goodchild, M.F.; Maguire, D.J.; Rhind, D.W. Eds., *Geographical Information Systems*; Wiley: New York, 1999.
36. Longley, P.A.; Goodchild, M.F.; Maguire, D.J.; Rhind, D.W. Eds., *Geographical Information Systems*, 2nd abridged Ed.; Wiley: New York, 2005.
37. Longley, P.A.; Goodchild, M.F.; Maguire, D.J.; Rhind, D.W. *Geographic Information Systems and Science*, 2nd Ed.; Wiley: New York, 2005.
38. Price, M. *Mastering ArcGIS 9.2*; McGraw-Hill: New York, 2008.
39. McDonnell, R.; Kemp, K. *International GIS Dictionary*; Longman: London, 1995.

36 Clinical Decision-Support Systems

Kai Zheng

CONTENTS

INTRODUCTION

The notion that artificial intelligence (AI) might one day rival the decision-making capability of human brain sparked the first generation of computerized clinical decision-support systems (CDSS) developed from the 1960s into the 1980s.[1,2] However, years of trials and frustrations convinced AI enthusiasts that the enormous variations in patient care cannot be reduced to systematic decision making to render qualitative medical treatments.[3] These limitations became even more apparent with the increasing awareness that patient care outcomes are also subject to other factors including quality- and value-of-life judgments, economic and psychosocial considerations, and social well-being of the patient as a whole. This brought a disappointing close to the first chapter in the use of computers to aid in medical decision-making.[4]

The story did not end there. Computerized clinical information systems proliferate throughout health care organizations today, significantly reducing the costs to acquire and store patient data. These changes, however, have invited new challenges, including an explosion of patient information that far exceeds any practitioner's capability of processing such data.[5] This situation is further compounded by a wellspring of medical knowledge resulting from the "evidence-based medicine" (EBM) movement over the past 20 years that has revolutionized the way medicine is practiced. EBM requires physicians to rely less on their own experience and more on the current best evidence in making decisions about the care of individual patients.[6] Unfortunately, "current best evidence" is a temporal concept that may become outdated rapidly as medical research advances or the mechanisms causing diseases change (e.g., new varieties of flu virus).

Further, the U.S. health care system has been criticized for its high costs, low efficiency, poor quality, and unacceptable rates of preventable medical errors. In 2007, \$2.2 trillion or 16.3% of national gross domestic product (GDP) was spent on health care in the United States,[7] while this number was only 8.7% on average in other industrialized countries, based on 2006 data.[8] Despite the twofold higher health care expenditure, the quality of care provided in the United States ranks last among major industrialized countries.[9] As a result, 31% of Americans rated the U.S. health care system as "poor" in 2008.[10] Further, the landmark 2001 report published by the Institute of Medicine, *To Err is Human: Building a Safer Health System*, showed that preventable medical errors in the U.S. health care system cost a total of 44,000–98,000 patient lives and $17–29 billion a year.[11] In response to these challenges, regulatory bodies and payer systems are actively establishing new regulations and incentive policies to assure health care institutions operate optimally. Joint Commission on the Accreditation of Healthcare Organizations (JCAHO, http://www.jointcommission.org/), for example, publishes *Comprehensive Accreditation Manual for Hospitals* every year articulating a wide range of accreditation criteria on facility operation, care provision, and patient safety. Similarly, the National Committee for Quality Assurance (http://www.ncqa.org) specifies a comprehensive set of measures for monitoring patient care performance through its annual publication *The Healthcare Effectiveness Data and Information Set* (*HEDIS*). While these may help to address the problems in U.S. health care, they also add a new layer of complexity to the already chaotic clinical workspace. This is the reason the medical community is embracing more than ever the idea of using computer systems to aid in medical decision making.

CLINICAL DECISION-SUPPORT SYSTEMS

Broadly speaking, a decision-support system is an interactive, flexible, and adaptable computer-based information system developed specifically for supporting the solution of a nonstructured management problem for improved decision making. It utilizes data, provides an easy-to-use interface, and allows for the decision maker's own insights.[12] Google Maps™ (http://maps.google.com) provides a good example. The site applies intelligent algorithms to geographic data to provide "optimal" routes for traveling from location A to location B while, at the same time, allowing the travel planner to manually intervene in the process, such as creating a more preferred route with click-and-drag options.

Likewise, in the health care arena, clinical decision-support systems provide clinicians, staff, patients, and other individuals with knowledge and specific, individualized information, intelligently filtered and presented at appropriate times, to enhance clinical performance and patient outcomes. It encompasses a variety of tools and interventions such as computerized alerts and reminders, clinical guidelines, order sets, patient data reports and dashboards, documentation templates, and diagnostic support.[13] The essential component of CDSS is *inference engine*, which applies the knowledge stored in a knowledge base to patient data to derive case-specific recommendations. CDSS is usually interfaced with, or as a part of, other clinical information systems such as electronic health records (EHR) or computerized provider order entry (CPOE) systems. For example, every full-fledged commercial EHR system provides certain types of electronic templates for managing chronic disease conditions. These templates offer individualized treatment and lifestyle change advice based on clinical guidelines and patient data.

With its capability of generating decision-support alerts warning against drug–drug interactions and drug–allergy interactions, CDSS is being increasingly mandated by regulatory bodies and advocacy groups such as JACHO, the Leapfrog Group for Patient Safety (Leapfrog, http://www.leapfroggroup.org/), and the Certification Commission for Healthcare Information Technology (CCHIT, http://www.cchit.org/). The JACHO accreditation manual has a dedicated Management of Information section clearly specifying the data requirements for enabling clinical decision support. Leapfrog, a voluntary group of large employers that ranks hospitals based on their quality and safety performance, has specific requirements to evaluate whether a hospital is equipped with CPOE decision-support systems capable of warning against drug interaction, allergy, and overdose. CCHIT, a recognized certification body (RCB), incorporates the clinical decision-support provision as a key component of its clinical information system certification process.

History of Clinical Decision Support

Started in the 1960s, the initial objective of introducing computers into medical practice was very clear: to provide doctors with decision aids using AI-based medical diagnostic reasoning. The enthusiasm was primarily spurred by the capability of computers to solve complex decision models in real time. This stream of research eventually developed into a dedicated discipline, Artificial Intelligence in Medicine (AIM), with wide appeal and broad consensus for optimism. In 1970, Schwartz announced in the New England Journal of Medicine that clinical computing would likely be commonplace in the "not too distant future."[14] *DXplain*, shown in Figure 36.1, is a representative example of the early generation diagnostic tool. Developed at the Massachusetts General Hospital, *DXplain* uses a modified form of Bayesian logic to produce a ranked list of possible diagnoses based on symptom manifestations. Table 36.1 lists several other influential systems developed during this time period. For a comprehensive bibliography of these early generation CDSS systems, readers can refer to Miller 1994.[15]

Unfortunately, the plethora of clinical computing, as predicted by many, never occurred. A large number of AI-based diagnostic reasoning systems were developed and tested, but most was not adopted in practice. A plausible reason accounting for this failure is that the AI-based diagnostic reasoning "functioned more like the 'Greek Oracle' rather than permitting a more flexible, interactive approach" (p. 4).[2] A "decision-making," rather than a "decision-supporting" structure, was perceived by physicians as a threat to clinician autonomy.[2] Moreover, most of these early generation systems were stand-alone, self-contained applications. They were not integrated with other computerized systems supporting hospital operation and patient data management, which were not readily available at the time. As a result, the decision-support advice generated by these early generation CDSS was often inaccurate or irrelevant. For example, Berner et al. (1994) tested four diagnostic systems and found that the proportion of correct diagnoses ranged from 0.52 to 0.71, and the mean proportion of relevant diagnoses ranged from 0.19 to 0.37.[16] This level of performance made the

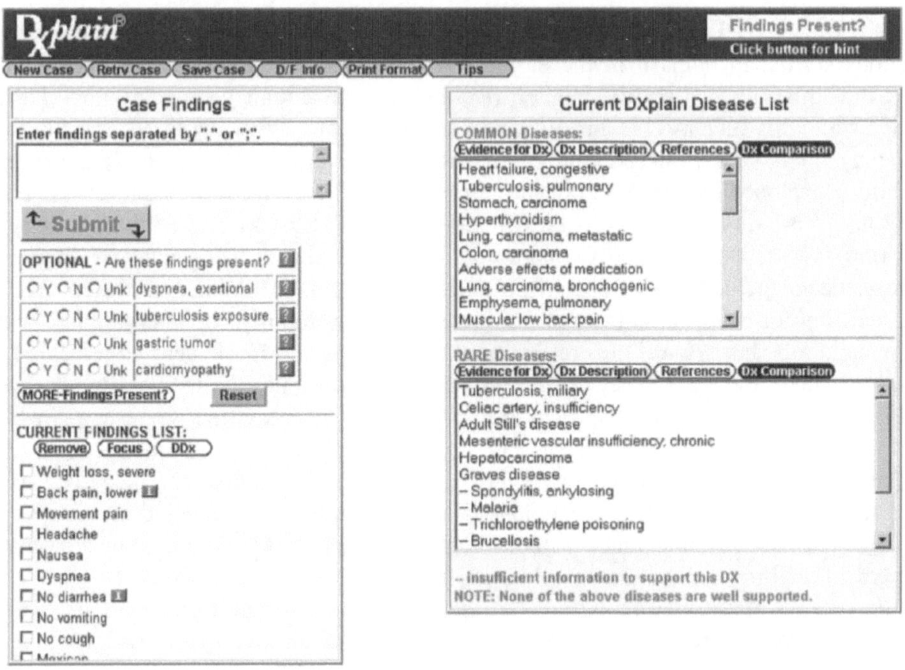

FIGURE 36.1 *DXplain*: A representative early generation clinical decision-support system. (From MGH Laboratory of Computer Science, http://dxplain.org.)

TABLE 36.1
Examples of Early Generation Clinical Decision-Support Systems

De Dombal	1972	Developed at the Leeds University, United Kingdom, De Dombal is a clinical decision-support tool that uses naive Bayesian approach to provide automated reasoning under uncertainty for diagnosing acute abdominal pain and recommending the need for surgery.
INTERNIST I	1974	INTERNIST I is a rule-based expert system for solving complex diagnostic problems in general internal medicine. It was developed at the University of Pittsburgh and later commercialized under the brand name Quick Medical Reference (QMR).
MYCIN	1976	MYCIN is a rule-based expert system developed at Stanford University. It was used to diagnose and recommend treatments for certain blood infections and other infectious diseases.
DXplain	1984	Developed at Massachusetts General Hospital, DXplain uses a modified form of Bayesian logic to produce a ranked list of diagnoses that might explain or be associated with the clinical manifestations.

adoption of such systems for treating real patients unrealistic. Another major reason accounting for the failure of early generation CDSS was the lack of financial returns. The dominant pay-for-service model—reimbursement was determined based on what was done rather than how well it was done—provided little incentives for medical practices to invest in expensive computer-based decision-support technology.

New Generation of Guideline-Based CDSS

The use of computerized clinical information systems to support hospital operation as well as clinical activities started to flourish in the early 1990s. Besides the significant technological breakthroughs, including the availability of enterprise-level database management systems (DBMS) and health data standards such as ICD and HL7, new legislation and advocacy by federal funding agencies also played a key role. International Statistical Classification of Diseases: Standard diagnostic classification developed by the World Health Organization (WHO) for its member states to report mortality and morbidity statistics. In the United States, ICD-9-CM (ICD 9th Revision, Clinical Modification) is widely used to codify diagnostic data for administrative (such as billing) purposes. http://www.cdc.gov/nchs/datawh/ftpserv/ftpICD9/ftpICD9.htm. Health Level Seven (HL7) is an all-volunteer, not-for-profit organization. It oversees the development of international health data exchange standards. http://www.hl7.org. Financial investments to implement large-scale health IT systems were made by the Agency for Healthcare Research and Quality (AHRQ, http://healthit.ahrq.gov), Health Resources and Services Administration (HRSA, http://www.hrsa.gov/healthit/), and many other foundations and private funding sources. Insurance companies have also been actively engaged. They either funded health IT directly, or provided financial incentives to medical practices for adopting information technology. The purpose was to reduce administrative costs in processing paper-based claims, thereby improving the quality and timeliness of health data submitted by medical facilities.

This provides a platform warranting the rise of a new generation of CDSS. Fewer of these new generation systems remain as stand-alones because of the need to provide clinicians with a unified interface to access all patient data and all clinical functionalities. Instead, CDSS often appears as modules embedded in other computerized systems, such as EHR and CPOE. Compared with their AI-based ancestors, these new generation systems represent a new class of

CDSS—evidence-adaptive decision support—that provides decision aids with a knowledge base constructed from, and continually adapting to, new evidence based on research and practice, i.e., EBM. EBM is the conscientious, explicit, and judicious use of current best evidence in making decisions about the care of individual patients.[6] It distills scientific evidence from the systematic analysis of medical literature using statistical or data mining approaches.[17] These systems are primarily used to help improve the coherence of preventive care and chronic disease management guidelines. A significant portion of clinical decision support is also provided using rather primitive database look-up rules. For example, dosage levels may be suggested based on patient age and body mass index (BMI), or prompts may appear for medication interactions based on commercially available medication lexicons, or reminders for vaccines based on well-specified childhood or adulthood vaccination schedules. The rationale behind these CDSS systems is simple: the majority of quality care problems and patient safety issues are due to human omissions, rather than lack of medical knowledge. Hence, CDSS should focus on "reminding" clinicians to avoid potential omissions instead of providing direct diagnostic aids by assuming clinicians are unable to solve a problem. As shown by Garg et al. 2005, such passive reminding systems are far more effective than proactive diagnostic systems.[18]

In 2006, the American Medical Informatics Association (AMIA) published *Roadmap for National Action on Clinical Decision Support*, which identifies three key objectives for CDSS research and practice: 1) Best Knowledge Available When Needed; 2) High Adoption and Effective Use; and 3) Continuous Improvement of Knowledge and CDS Methods.[19] Objective 1 of the AMIA CDS Roadmap suggests that providing clinical decision support should be based on up-to-date medical knowledge and should occur "as part of clinician workflow" and "at the time and location of decision-making" (p. 765).[20] Objectives 2 and 3 are related to medical knowledge engineering and the implementation and user resistance barriers of CDSS, which is discussed in detail in the following two sections.

Guideline Ontologies for Effective Medical Knowledge Engineering

The up-to-date medical knowledge implemented in CDSS is primarily derived from evidence-based clinical guidelines. AHRQ's National Guideline Clearinghouse (http://www.guideline.gov) is the principal resource for the latest guidelines spanning a wide variety of disease areas. However, these clinical guidelines are usually disseminated as unstructured, narrative documents that often lack sufficient detail for computing. For example, a very simple guideline for breast cancer screening recommends "screening mammography, with or without clinical breast examination, every 1–2 years for women aged 40 and older." U.S. Preventive Services Task Force, Screening for breast cancer, Recommendations and rationale. http://www.ahrq.gov/clinic/3rduspstf/breastCancer/brcanrr.htm. To convert this guideline into a computable form, "screening mammography," "women," and "age" all need to be rigorously defined with standard medical terminology, shown in Figure 36.2. The location of the corresponding patient data elements and how to retrieve them must also be specified. Oftentimes, this task is not trivial. For example, "mammography" may be stored in a laboratory information system (LIS) that does not communicate with the CDSS, or the terminology representing "mammography" in the LIS may not conform to the terminology used in the CDSS.

Arden Syntax, a procedural language for representing medical logics, was introduced in 1989 to enable effective and standard-based computation of medical knowledge. It soon became a standard of the American Society for Testing and Materials (ASTM) and was later adopted by HL7. Arden Syntax provides a specification for encoding medical logic as individual rule-based procedures, also known as Medical Logic Modules (MLMs). Each MLM contains sufficient computational detail and data requirements to make a single medical decision. For example, the following MLM code determines when to issue the alert, "Consider impaired kidney function" based on the most recent creatinine level and blood urea nitrogen (BUN) test results:

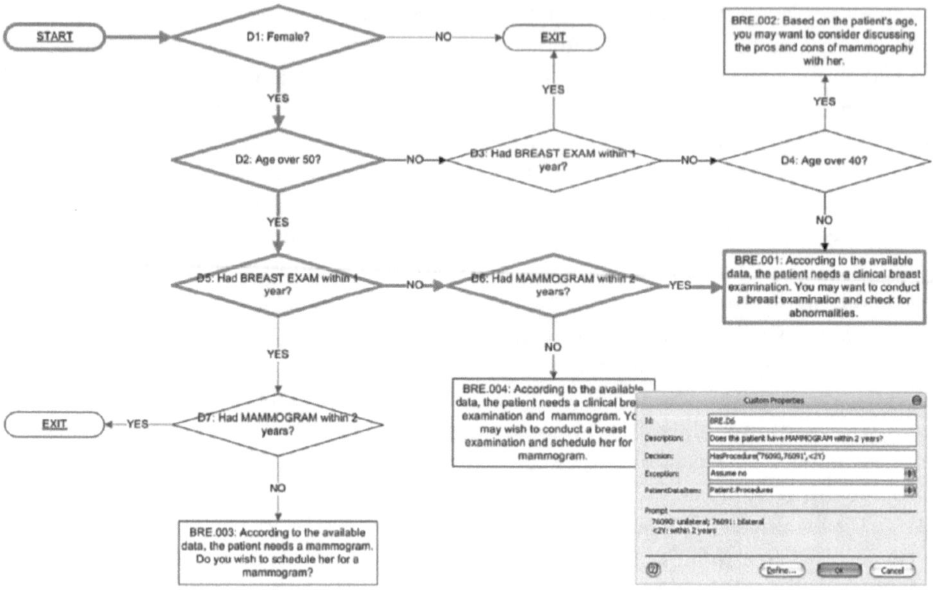

FIGURE 36.2 A computerized clinical guideline flowchart.

```
data:
       last_creat := read last {"Creatinine level"};
       last_BUN := read last {"BUN level"};
;;
logic:
       if last_creat > 1.5 or last_BUN > 30
       then alert_text := "Consider impaired kidney function.";
       conclude true;
       end if;
;;
```

Arden Syntax, however, is not suitable for representing comprehensive guidelines. Each MLM represents a discrete decision-making logic, like the example above, and could easily become unmanageable as guidelines become more complex. This limitation has led to the development of several ontology-based guideline representation models.

A guideline representation ontology is a specification of elements that constitute evidence-based guidelines. It represents the elements by specifying their attributes and defining the relationships that hold them together. For example, a guideline may represent a set of medical decisions and actions (attributes) and a set of rules (relationships) that link the evaluation of a decision criterion to a set of further steps to be taken. A rigorously defined computational ontology provides considerable promise of producing computable representations that can be visualized, edited, executed, and shared using CDSS. Several ontology-based guideline representation models have been developed over the past 20 years. The influential ones include Asbru (http://www.asgaard.tuwien.ac.at), EON (http://www.smi.stanford.edu/projects/eon/), GLIF (Guideline Interchange Format, http://www.glif.org), and SAGE (Sharable Active Guideline Environment, http://sage.wherever.org), developed in the United States; and GUIDE (http://www.labmedinfo.org/research/dsg/decision_support.htm), PRODIGY (http://www.prodigy.nhs.uk) and PRO*forma* (http://www.acl.icnet.uk/lab/proforma.html), developed in Europe. Some models, such as GLIF and SAGE, aim to achieve a general, interchangeable format.[22] Others, such as PRODIGY, focus on representing guidelines in specific disease areas.[21]

Barriers to Implementing and Using Clinical Decision Support

Clinician time is the most precious resource in a medical practice. Average time for seeing each outpatient visit is less than 20 min.[23,24] Considering other administrative time loss, the amount of time for accomplishing the actual work—examining patients, reviewing historical data, making judgments, and documenting new findings and performing treatments—is extremely limited. Any innovations that slow things down are bound to fail.

Unfortunately, very few CDSS systems benefit time efficiency. In fact, most require extra clinician time to enter patient data and review and act upon decision-support prompts. Managing complex chronic disease conditions such as diabetes, for example, is very time-consuming and often distracts clinicians from the main focus of a patient visit.[25] As a result, the actual efficacy and effectiveness achieved by new generation CDSS are still mixed.[17,26,27] Overriding or ignoring computer-generated decision-support advice is common,[28] and many CDSS systems are abandoned altogether.[29]

Patient Data Codification

A fundamental barrier in CDSS adoption is the need for patient data codification. All patient data must be properly codified, according to certain standard taxonomies, in order to be computed in the inference engine of a CDSS. However, picking a right code is a mechanical, time-consuming process that generally keeps clinicians away from focusing on the content of clinical documentation. The codified patient data also risks losing the narrative, story-telling nature that used to be conveyed in free-text patient notes. Moreover, numerous competing and conflicting taxonomies exist for historical reasons. ICD-9-CM, for example, is widely used in the United States to prepare diagnosis-based billing claims. Nevertheless, many clinical observations and findings are intermediate disease stages that are not necessarily "diagnoses," and hence cannot be meaningfully represented using ICD-9-CM.[30,31] To address this issue, new observation-oriented clinical data taxonomies, such SNOMED-CT, have been proposed. Systematized Nomenclature of Medicine-Clinical Terms (SNOMED-CT): A clinical terminology that provides unique meanings and formal logic-based definitions for diseases, clinical findings, and procedures. http://www.ihtsdo.org/snomed-ct/. The National Library of Medicine also maintains the Unified Medical Language System (UMLS, http://www.nlm.nih.gov/research/umls/), a meta-thesaurus for translating terminologies across different medical vocabularies whenever compatible.

System Interoperability

Another significant barrier inhibiting CDSS adoption is the system interoperability issue. In order to generate case-specific advice, CDSS must have access to complete and up-to-date patient data. While computerized clinical systems are now commonly used to manage a variety of patient information, many of these systems do not readily talk to each other. Creating one-to-one data exchange interfaces is possible, but can be very costly and difficult to maintain as systems constantly upgrade. Enabling patient data sharing across health care settings is further challenged by the lack of regional health data exchange networks. Personal Health Records (PHR), that allows all care providers to upload patient data to a common repository, have shown some promise as a solution to the issue. Google Health™ (http://www.google.com/health/) and Microsoft HealthVault™ (http://www.healthvault.com) are examples of PHRs that are currently being tested in the field.

Other Contextual Factors

Lastly, there are many other concerns in using CDSS beyond technological considerations. CDSS introduces a radical impact on patient care delivery and, in particular, can be detrimental to the quality of point-of-care physician communication if not used properly. Using computers in front of patients and the resulting loss of eye contact is considered rude and often listed among common reasons causing user resistance.[32] The threat to clinical autonomy is also an enduring issue for physicians. Many new-generation CDSS systems are now associated with certain evaluative mechanisms to "score" clinician performance. This unpleasant characteristic could further erode user acceptance. As Anderson et al. 1994 commented, "despite the fact that they are technologically sound, more than half of medical information systems fail because of user and staff resistance" (p. 1).[33] These contextual human factors must be taken into account when implementing CDSS in real practice.

Case Study: The Clinical Reminder System

The clinical reminder system (CRS) was jointly developed by the H. John Heinz III School of Public Policy and Management at Carnegie Mellon University and the Western Pennsylvania Hospital (WPH). Since February 2002, CRS has been deployed in two WPH medical practices treating real patients.

CRS uses evidence-based clinical guidelines to support the management of four chronic health conditions (asthma, diabetes, hypertension, and hyperlipidemia), and five preventive care procedures (breast cancer, cervical cancer, influenza, pneumonia, and steroid-induced osteoporosis). A guideline representation model built upon existing ontologies (e.g., GLIF) was implemented in CRS for enabling structured acquisition and automated execution of evidence-based guidelines. Figure 36.2 shows a sample visual representation encoded in this model. These visual representations, with embedded medical decision-making logic (shown at the bottom right corner in Figure 36.2), are stored in XML files that theoretically can be shared with other CDSS systems if they implement the same underlying guideline representation model.

In order to generate case-specific reminders, CRS stores and manages comprehensive patient information, such as patient descriptors, symptoms, and orders. Standard medical vocabularies are used whenever possible. For example, ICD-9-CM is used in CRS for encoding diagnoses, CPT4 for procedural treatments, and the National Drug Code (NDC) for medication prescriptions. Current Procedural Terminology: A directory of descriptive terms and identifying codes for reporting medical services and procedures under public and private health insurance programs. CPT4, its 4th edition, is the most widely adopted version in the United States. http://www.ama-assn.org/ama/pub/category/3113.html. National Drug Code Directory: A directory that lists universal product identifier for human drugs. Its current edition is limited to prescription drugs and insulin products. http://www.fda.gov/cder/ndc/. CRS also retrieves patient data from many other hospital information systems, most in real time. The clinic staff use CRS to manage appointments, patient check-in and check-out, and record vital signs. The residents and attending physicians use CRS to document clinical observations, prescribe medication and laboratory test orders, and generate reminders to aid in their decision making. The reminders usually take the form of recommended actions to have certain tests performed, to receive vaccinations, or to discuss the pros and cons of alternative treatments. The main workspace of CRS is shown in Figure 36.3, where residents and attending physicians can act upon the reminders by selecting "Performed," "Deferred," "Not Compliant," among several other possible responses.

A series of research studies were conducted to examine the user adoption and acceptance of CRS. Periodical user satisfaction surveys showed that while CRS was rated "satisfactory" on all interface-related items, it received very poor user evaluation on system-related items as indicated by the survey comment, "the system is ineffective in helping me complete my work quickly." Follow-up semi-structure interviews were conducted to investigate the issue. The results revealed several challenges to overcome, including iterative advisories ("the same reminder was generated time and time again"), cumbersome data entry ("it is too difficult and takes too long to enter data"), workflow disruption ("slowed down my work"), solicitation for one single system ("we should have only one system to access all information needed"), disrupted physician–patient communication ("my patient felt upset when I used my computer"), and lack of guidance in the application workflow ("I don't know where to start"). These problems are primarily associated with the sociotechnical integration issues when clinicians try to incorporate CRS into their routine clinical practice.[34]

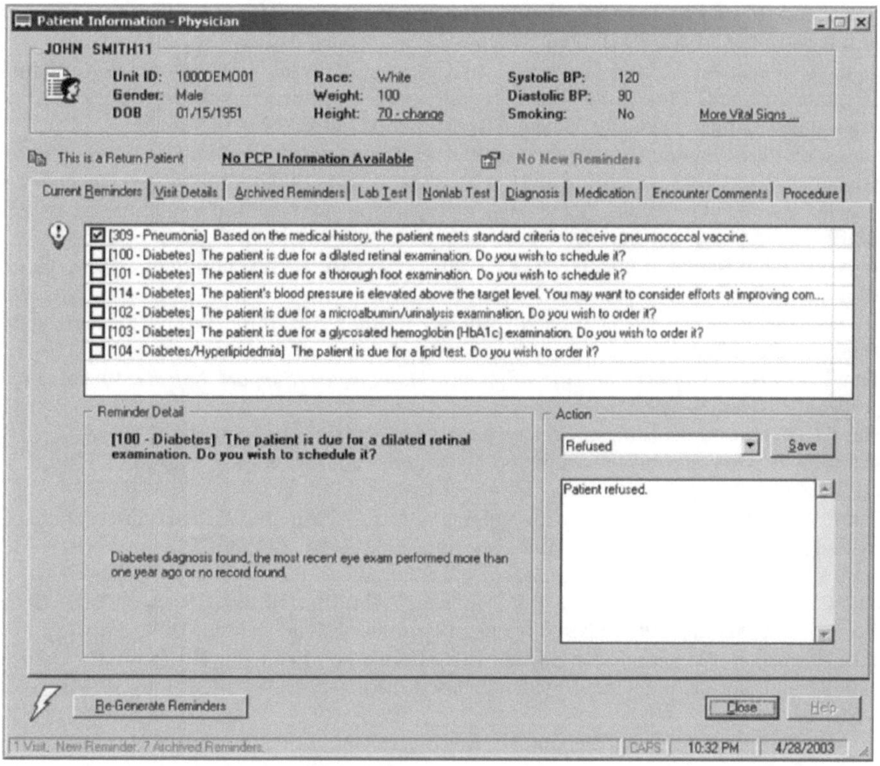

FIGURE 36.3 The main workspace of the clinical reminder system.

CONCLUSION

This entry introduces the concept, history, and key considerations and barriers to providing computerized decision support to clinicians, with a particular focus on systems that provide prompts based on evidence-based clinical guidelines. This stream of CDSS has become increasingly popular and viewed as a key solution to addressing the quality and safety problems of the U.S. health care system. Cutting-edge research is also being conducted to explore the efficacy and applicability of more sophisticated decision models particularly those accommodating decision making under uncertainty. Readers who wish to develop a full spectrum of knowledge of CDSS may refer to the OpenClinical Project (http://www.openclinical.org/dss.html) or Berner's textbook *Clinical Decision Support Systems: Theory and Practice*.[35] Practitioners interested in the design, development, and implementation of CDSS may refer to the CDSS Implementer's Guide developed by the Healthcare Information and Management Systems Society.[36]

REFERENCES

1. Ledley, L.L.B. Reasoning foundations of medical diagnosis; symbolic logic, probability, and value theory aid our understanding of how physicians reason. Science **1959**, *130* (3366), 9–21.
2. Ledley, L.L.B. Computers in medical data processing. Oper. Res. **1960**, *8* (3), 299–310.
3. Engle, R.L. Jr. Attempts to use computers as diagnostic aids in medical decision making: A thirty-year experience. Perspect. Biol. Med. **1992**, *35* (2), 207–219.
4. Berner, E.S.; Detmer, D.E.; Simborg, D. Will the wave finally break? A brief view of the adoption of electronic medical records in the United States. J. Am. Med. Inform. Assoc. **2005**, *12* (1), 3–7.
5. Berner, E.S.; Moss, J. Informatics challenges for the impending patient information explosion. J. Am. Med. Inform. Assoc. **2005**, *12* (6), 614–617.

6. Sackett, D.L.; Rosenberg, W.M.; Gray, J.A.; Haynes, R.B.; Richardson, W.S. Evidence based medicine: What it is and what it isn't. BMJ **1996**, *312*, 71–72.
7. Keehan, S.; Sisko, A.; Truffer, C.; Smith, S.; Cowan, C.; Poisal, J.; Clemens, M.K. National Health Expenditure Accounts Projections Team. Health spending projections through 2017: The baby-boom generation is coming to medicare. Health Aff. (Millwood) **2008**, *27*, w145–w155.
8. Organisation for Economic Co-operation and Development. *OECD Health Data 2008*, http://www.oecd.org/document/30/0,3343,en_2649_34631_12968734_1_1_1_1,00.html (accessed November 7, 2008).
9. American College of Physicians, Achieving a high-performance health care system with universal access: What the United States can learn from other countries. Ann. Intern. Med. **2008**, *148*, 55–75.
10. Employee Benefit Research Institute. *The Health Confidence Survey*, http://www.ebri.org/pdf/notespdf/EBRI_Notes_10– 2008.pdf (accessed October 31, 2008).
11. Institute of Medicine, *To Err Is Human: Building a Safer Health System*; National Academies Press: Washington, DC, 2000.
12. Turban, E. *Decision Support and Expert Systems: Management Support Systems*, 4th Ed.; Prentice-Hall: Upper Saddle River, NJ, 1995.
13. Payne, T.H. Computer decision support systems. Chest **2000**, *118* (2 Suppl), 47S–52S.
14. Schwartz, W.B. Medicine and the computer. The promise and problems of change. N. Engl. J. Med. **1970**, *283* (23), 1257–1264.
15. Miller, R.A. Medical diagnostic decision support systems—Past, present, and future: A threaded bibliography and brief commentary. J. Am. Med. Inform. Assoc. **1994**, *1* (1), 8–27.
16. Berner, E.S.; Webster, G.D.; Shugerman, A.A.; Jackson, J.R.; Algina, J.; Baker, A.L.; Ball, E.V.; Cobbs, C.G.; Dennis, V.W.; Frenkel, E.P.; Hudson, L.D.; Mancall, E.L.; Rackley, C.E.; Taunton, O.D. Performance of four computer-based diagnostic systems. N. Engl. J. Med. **1994**, *330* (25), 1792–1796.
17. Sim, I.; Gorman, P.; Greenes, R.A.; Haynes, R.B.; Kaplan, B.; Lehmann, H.; Tang, P.C. Clinical decision support systems for the practice of evidence-based medicine. J. Am. Med. Inform. Assoc. **2001**, *8* (6), 527–534.
18. Garg, A.X.; Adhikari, N.K.; McDonald, H.; Rosas-Arellano, M.P.; Devereaux, P.J.; Beyene, J.; Sam, J.; Haynes, R.B. Effects of computerized clinical decision support systems on practitioner performance and patient outcomes: a systematic review. JAMA **2005**, *293* (10), 1223–1238.
19. The American Medical Informatics Association. *A Road-map for National Action on Clinical Decision Support*, http://www.amia.org/files/cdsroadmap.pdf (accessed October 31, 2008).
20. Kawamoto, K.; Houlihan, C.A.; Balas, E.A.; Lobach, D.F. Improving clinical practice using clinical decision support systems: A systematic review of trials to identify features critical to success. BMJ **2005**, *330* (7494), 765.
21. Peleg, M.; Tu, S.; Bury, J.; Ciccarese, P.; Fox, J.; Greenes, R.A.; Hall, R.; Johnson, P.D.; Jones, N.; Kumar, A.; Miksch, S.; Quaglini, S.; Seyfang, A.; Shortliffe, E.H.; Stefanelli, M. Comparing computer-interpretable guideline models: A case-study approach. J. Am. Med. Inform. Assoc. **2003**, *10* (1), 52–68.
22. Ohno-Machado, L.; Gennari, J.H.; Murphy, S.N.; Jain, N. L.; Tu, S.W.; Oliver, D.E.; Pattison-Gordon, E.; Greenes, R.A.; Shortliffe, E.H.; Barnett, G.O. The guideline interchange format: A model for representing guidelines. J. Am. Med. Inform. Assoc. **1998**, *5* (4), 357–372.
23. Cherry, D.K.; Burt, C.W.; Woodwell, D.A. *National Ambulatory Medical Care Survey: 2001 Summary. Advance Data from Vital and Health Statistics*; National Center for Health Statistics: Hyattsville, MD, 2003.
24. Mechanic, D.; McAlpine, D.D.; Rosenthal, M. Are patients' office visits with physicians getting shorter? N. Engl. J. Med. **2001**, *344*, 198–204.
25. Østbye, T.; Yarnall, K.S.; Krause, K.M.; Pollak, K.I.; Gradison, M.; Michener, J.L. Is there time for management of patients with chronic diseases in primary care? Ann. Fam. Med. **2005**, *3* (3), 209–214.
26. Hunt, D.L.; Haynes, R.B.; Hanna, S.E.; Smith, K. Effects of computer-based clinical decision support systems on physician performance and patient outcomes: A systematic review. JAMA **1998**, *280*, 1339–1346.
27. Kaushal, R.; Shojania, K.G.; Bates, D.W. Effects of computerized physician order entry and clinical decision support systems on medication safety: A systematic review. Arch. Intern. Med. **2003**, *163* (12), 1409–1416.
28. Van der Sijs, H.; Aarts, J.; Vulto, A.; Berg, M. Overriding drug safety alerts in CPOE. J. Am. Med. Inform. Assoc. **2006**, *13*, 138–147.
29. Roukema, J.; Steyerberg, E.W.; van der Lei, J.; Moll, H.A. Randomized trial of a clinical decision support system: Impact on the management of children with fever without apparent source. J. Am. Med. Inform. Assoc. **2008**, *15* (1), 107–113.

30. Rhodes, E.T.; Laffel, L.M.; Gonzalez, T.V.; Ludwig, D.S. Accuracy of administrative coding for type 2 diabetes in children, adolescents, and young adults. Diabetes Care **2007**, *30* (1), 141–143.
31. Tang, P.C.; Ralston, M.; Arrigotti, M.F.; Qureshi, L.; Graham, J. Comparison of methodologies for calculating quality measures based on administrative data versus clinical data from an electronic health record system: Implications for performance measures. J. Am. Med. Inform. Assoc. **2007**, *14* (1), 10–15.
32. Linder, J.A.; Schnipper, J.L.; Tsurikova, R.; Melnikas, A.J.; Volk, L.A.; Middleton, B. Barriers to electronic health record use during patient visits. AMIA Annu. Symp. Proc. **2006**, 499–503.
33. Anderson, J.G.; Aydin, C.E.; Jay, S.J. *Evaluating Health Care Information Systems*; SAGE Publications: Thousand Oaks, CA, 1994.
34. Zheng, K.; Padman, R.; Johnson, M.P.; Diamond, H.S. Understanding technology adoption in clinical care: Clinician adoption behavior of a point-of-care reminder system. Int. J. Med Inform. **2005**, *74* (7–8), 535–543.
35. Berner, E.S. *Clinical Decision Support Systems: Theory and Practice*, 2nd Ed.; Springer: New York, 2007.
36. Osheroff, J.A.; Pifer, E.A.; Teich, J.M.; Sittig, D.F.; Jenders, R.A. I*mproving Outcomes with Clinical Decision Support: An Implementer's Guide*; Productivity Press: New York, 2005.

37 Integrated Library Systems (ILS)

Emily Gallup Fayen

CONTENTS

INTRODUCTION

Integrated Library Systems (ILS) are a natural outgrowth of Library Automation systems. Libraries have eagerly employed whatever tools have become available to assist in the enormously labor-intensive tasks of managing a library. In the early twenty-first century, ILS combine various components in numerous ways to meet the needs of libraries ranging from small school and hospital libraries, large academic and government libraries, corporate libraries of all sizes, and huge consortia of public libraries.

BACKGROUND

Library automation systems began to appear as soon as tabulating equipment and early computer systems had advanced sufficiently to support library applications. Some very early automation tools such as circulation control systems using punched cards were implemented in the 1940s and 1950s, but the work was limited to a very few installations where the necessary resources were available. Of course, the costs were extremely high, making these options available only to a very few libraries.

As computer technology advanced and became commercially available in the late 1960s and 1970s, the first ILS emerged. These systems have continued to evolve and there have been rapid advances in their functionality and deployment. ILS have revolutionized library operations. They have led to tremendous advances in ease of use and productivity, both for library staff members and for library users.

Anyone who has ever worked in a library knows that library tasks are extremely labor-intensive. Successful collection development, cataloging or bibliographic control, reference and other library work depend on the presence of highly trained and skilled people who are dedicated to making information available to library users. In addition, careful record-keeping is needed in order to preserve the integrity of the collection, to manage patron information as well as circulation transaction data, and to keep track of acquisitions and other financial information.

In the early twenty-first century, libraries face increasing challenges as patrons want increasingly sophisticated access to information and the easy availability of information over the Internet no matter how questionable its veracity may be. Further, Internet access to library catalogs and other electronic resources makes it almost unnecessary to actually visit the library.

Originally dependent on computer mainframe technology for the data storage and processing power required, early library automation systems often cost millions of dollars, both to develop and to operate. As computers became ever more powerful and inexpensive, the large mainframe-based systems were gradually replaced with microcomputer-based systems costing hundreds of thousands of dollars rather than the millions required by their predecessors. Development of the personal computer in the 1980s led to dramatic reductions both in the cost and staff required to support these systems, thus making library automation affordable for even the smallest libraries.

The tremendous and rapid changes in the computer equipment, operating systems, and software available, not to mention the impact of the Internet, have led to the gradual development of a wide range of ILS. Appropriate systems are now available to support institutions as large and complex as the Library of Congress, large academic institutions, corporate and law libraries, public libraries, and small school libraries.

ILS grew slowly from stand-alone systems developed to meet specific library needs. Some of the earliest systems were quasiautomated. Each of these systems depended for its existence on having the necessary information available in machine-readable form, or as we would say now, in digitized form. These systems were certainly not online and most operated via overnight batch processing of one sort or another. Examples of these early systems are the circulation transaction processing systems developed by or for large public libraries using punched cards and overnight batch processing. Soon after, fledgling optical character recognition (OCR) and bar code technologies were employed to make it easier to capture the necessary information to support these systems. The data captured were often minimal: titles truncated to 50 characters, upper case characters only, and no diacritics or other special characters.

Although these early systems provided enormous savings in labor for large libraries, they were only able to handle a small part of the work load. As a result of the development of the MARC format,[1] it became possible to create high quality cataloging records in machine-readable form for library collections. These soon led to the development of computer-generated public catalogs, produced by using the bibliographic records. Suddenly, it was possible to conceive of the first ILS by exploiting a linkage between the library catalog database and a database of patron information with the addition of holdings information to identify specific copies of items in the library's collections.

Two of the first ILS were CLSI[2] and NOTIS.[3] These two systems were developed at about the same time in the late 1970s. CLSI was developed primarily for public libraries, although it was implemented in many other types of libraries later on. It used highly innovative, touch-screen technology to provide a very easy interface for library patrons, who, for the first time, were encouraged to use these systems on their own. Of course, this amazing new approach introduced new problems as librarians in charge of children's libraries found themselves constantly wiping sticky finger marks off the screens.

NOTIS, which stands for Northwestern's Total Online Integrated System, was the first true online, ILS. It was developed by Northwestern University library staff members in the late 1970s and was first made available to library patrons about 1980. The early implementations of NOTIS included systems to support circulation, cataloging, and online patron access to the catalog.

At about the same time, the term "OPAC" (standing for Online Public Access Catalog) was born. This term has been used ever since to designate that portion of an ILS that enabled library patrons to search the catalog on their own. This component has generally been treated as a separate component from the cataloging subsystem, which supported the creation and maintenance of bibliographic records for the library's collection.

COMPONENTS OF THE ILS

Each of the components of an ILS became known as a "module," and ILS were generally considered to be "modular" systems. This term may have perhaps been borrowed from the Space Program which was also in its ascendancy at about the same time. In that environment, many complex systems were composed of numerous, more-or-less stand-alone components known as "modules," for example, the "LEM" or "Lunar Excursion Module." The term seemed completely appropriate for the components of the ever-evolving ILS in an environment in which libraries could combine the modules they needed to create a system to meet their needs.

The first ILS consisted of just two or three modules:

1. Catalog—for storage and management of bibliographic records for each title owned by the library.
2. OPAC—provides public access for searching the collection.
3. Circulation System—tracks borrowing and returning of materials, generates overdue notification, and calculates any fines or fees owed.

These modules, taken together, were generally referred to as the "core system." The core system was the smallest unit that could be purchased or licensed for use by a customer.

Throughout the remainder of this entry the word "library" is used as an inclusive term to describe various repositories of information. ILS have been (and are being used) to automate many different types of technical information centers, newspaper morgues, archives of various sorts, and even television stations. The main differences among these are the types of information being handled and some specific application requirements.

Once the core modules had been developed and implemented, new modules were soon added to meet the needs of different kinds of libraries for specific purposes such as

- Authority Control—a special module used with the Cataloging module as a repository for creating, storing, and managing the authorized headings such as author names, subject headings, etc. These headings are used in the bibliographic records in the Catalog module.
- Acquisitions—for purchasing and tracking receipt of library materials, sometimes including serials.
- Serials Control—for purchasing and checking-in serial publications including journals, newspapers, monographic series, etc. The Serials Control module also generally includes provisions for claiming if issues are not received when expected.
- Holdings support—used especially in library systems with multiple branches and holding multiple copies of items to link the physical collections to the bibliographic information contained in the Catalog and to provide the item-specific information needed for the Circulation module. Note that Holdings support is frequently incorporated into the Catalog or Circulation module. However, some systems treat it as a separate module.
- Materials Booking—most often used in public libraries to manage and reserve special resources such as audiovisual equipment, meeting rooms, etc.
- Course Reserves—most often used in academic institutions to handle circulation of materials with loan periods of less than one day.
- Inventory Control—designed for taking physical inventory (either complete or partial) of the collection. This module may also include some functions normally included in the Circulation module.
- Binding—intended to identify materials that are ready for binding and/or notification of missing issues, define binding specifications, and track shipments and receipts of materials.
- Community Bulletin Board—designed to work with the OPAC to provide a place for library users to get information online about upcoming community events. This module

is most frequently included in systems designed for public libraries and generally utilizes the MARC21 Community Information Format, which was specifically designed for this purpose.

- Interlibrary Loan—designed to track borrowing and loaning of library materials not to library patrons, but to and from other libraries.
- Reporting—some ILS embed reports that can be generated for each function in the appropriate module while others have a separate, stand-alone Reporting module which may be used to produce a variety of reports from the system.
- Administration—many systems include support for Administrative functions within each module while others have a separate Administration module for use by the library staff in configuring the system for their own needs.

Figure 37.1 shows the relationships among the various modular components of a typical ILS. The following sections describe each of these modular components briefly and show how each contributes to the ILS.

1. The Catalog—Bibliographic records, available in machine-readable (or digitized) form for the materials in the library's collection form the foundation for the entire ILS. The records may be created within the ILS itself or with the assistance of a Bibliographic Utility such as OCLC, the Library of Congress, and numerous commercial vendors. Many vendors of books, journals, and so forth now routinely include bibliographic records as part of the purchase.

   Most Catalog modules today provide support for importing MARC records from these and other sources. MARC was developed by the Library of Congress in the mid-1960s. It was widely adopted nationally and internationally and is now available in a number of variations, some minor (OCLC MARC, RLIN MARC) and some requiring translation for compatibility with U.S. MARC systems (UNIMARC, NORMARC). *MARC 21 Format for Bibliographic Data 1999* is the most recent edition of the LC version. There are updates available for the succeeding years. This standard combines the USMARC and CANMARC standards and will soon incorporate the current UKMARC standard. Although few ILS originally provided support for exporting records in MARC format, many systems have added this functionality due to customer demand.

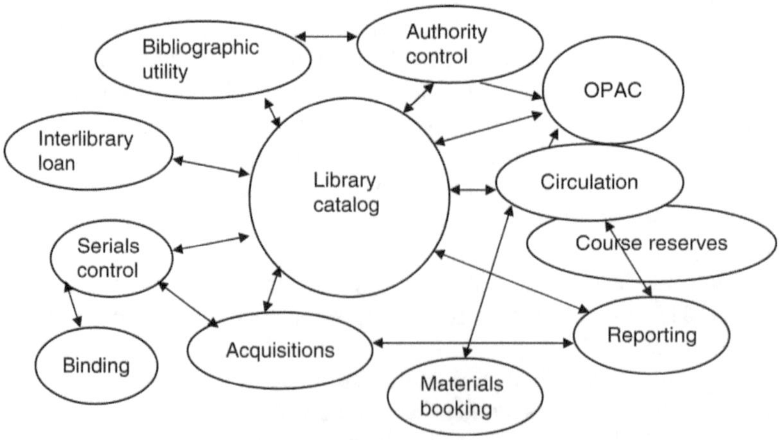

FIGURE 37.1 Typical modular components of an ILS.

Most Catalog modules provide support for an extended ASCII character set including special characters (e.g., Ł, ß, ð) and diacritics (e.g., ~, ` , ^). Many newer Catalog modules and OPACs now support Unicode, greatly expanding the number of languages and characters that can be represented in the catalog database. Unicode is now an international standard. It includes *The Unicode Standard, Version 5.0* plus the Unicode Character Database, Version 5.0.0. The standard presents the general principles, requirements for conformance, and guidelines for implementers. The Character Database includes character code charts and names. The text of all of the Unicode Standard Annexes are also available. The widespread use of Unicode has had an enormous impact on the ability to exchange cataloging information among libraries and bibliographic utilities in different parts of the world and has enabled ILS vendors to build systems that can handle many different languages and character sets.

Most Catalog modules provide support for entering bibliographic information (or cataloging) using the classic MARC tagging structure and field layout. These systems may also have been designed to work closely with a bibliographic utility such as OCLC. In addition, most Catalog modules also have a user-friendly data entry and editing format that prompts the cataloger for frequently needed fields such as title, author, ISBN, etc. These systems then convert the data as entered to the appropriate MARC tags for future use (Figures 37.2, 37.3, 37.7 and 37.9).

The Catalog module is generally intended for use by library staff members and not by end-users or library patrons. The Catalog module generally provides search access by typical bibliographic data elements such as title, author name, subject heading, publisher, etc. It may also provide search access by other fields such as ISBN, ISSN, record identifier, cataloger's ID, etc.—fields that are less often important to patrons. The catalog may also offer an expert searcher mode, sometimes limited for staff use only that allow limiting the search by date range, language, material format, and other parameters that might be of interest to library staff members but not to patrons.

Most Catalog modules are designed to work in a tightly integrated fashion with a Bibliographic Utility such as OCLC. Because producing original bibliographic records (i.e., cataloging information) for publications is especially labor intensive and by extension, expensive, libraries very early on realized that there would be tremendous cost savings for all if they could share cataloging information across many libraries. OCLC began operation in the early 1970s is a not-for-profit organization and is supported by its member

Ocean processes in climate dynamics : global and mediterranean examples /...

LC Control No.: 93038824
Type of Material: Book (Print, Microform, Electronic, etc.)
Main Title: Ocean processes in climate dynamics : global and mediterranean examples / edited by Paola Malanotte-Rizzoli and Allan R. Robinson.
Published/Created: Dordrecht ; Boston : Kluwer Academic, c1994.
Description: xxii, 437 p. : ill., maps ; 25 cm.
ISBN: 0792326245 (alk. paper)

CALL NUMBER: GC190.2 .O23 1994
Copy 1
-- **Request in:** Jefferson or Adams Bldg General or Area Studies Reading Rms
-- **Status:** Not Charged

FIGURE 37.2 A bibliographic record in human-readable form. (From the Library of Congress Web site.)

LC Control No.: 93038824

000 01714pam a2200325 a 450

001 1580476

005 20020724065034.0

008 931014s1994 ne ab b 101 0 eng

035 __ |**9** (DLC) 93038824

906 __ |**a** 7 |**b** cbc |**c** orignew |**d** 1 |**e** ocip |**f** 19 |**g** y-gencatlg

955 __ |**a** pc14 to ja00 10-15-93; je39 10-19-93; je08 to PS-1 10-20-93; jd05 10-20-93; jd85 10-21-93; aa07 10-21-93; CIP ver. pv08 01-25-94

010 __ |**a** 93038824

020 __ |**a** 0792326245 (alk. paper)

040 __ |**a** DLC |**c** DLC |**d** DLC

050 00 |**a** GC190.2 |**b** .O23 1994

082 00 |**a** 551.5/246 |**2** 20

245 00 |**a** Ocean processes in climate dynamics : |**b** global and mediterranean examples / |**c** edited by Paola Malanotte-Rizzoli and Allan R. Robinson.

260 __ |**a** Dordrecht ; |**a** Boston : |**b** Kluwer Academic, |**c** c1994.

300 __ |**a** xxii, 437 p. : |**b** ill., maps ; |**c** 25 cm.

FIGURE 37.3 The same catalog record showing the MARC tags and contents of the fields. (From the Library of Congress Web site.)

libraries. A few library automation vendors also provide bibliographic records for their customers.

Most ILS therefore require access to a Bibliographic Utility or other source of MARC records for adding title records to the Catalog in addition to allowing creation of original records. However, the Bibliographic Utility is not considered to be a part of the ILS.

2. Authority Control—A separate module to support Authority Control may be included for use with the Catalog or the library may perform necessary authority control tasks through a Bibliographic Utility or other vendor. It is extremely important in managing a very large collection that materials are brought together under a single form of author name, title, etc. Minor variations in the form of these entries can mean that closely related information is separated by hundreds or thousands of entries, or, perhaps lost forever!

   A high level Authority Control module will manage the headings used by the records in the Catalog module, allowing for global changes to be made to a single heading and reflected in all linked bibliographic records. MARC 21 Authority Format records are used to manage the headings and associated cross-references, which will be searchable and viewable in the OPAC to lead end-users to the headings used in the Catalog.

   The Catalog module generally does not provide any information on the status of the items linked to the bibliographic record. For example, a particular item might be on order, in circulation, at the bindery, or lost. This information is generally provided by the Holdings (item) records stored within the integrated system.

3. The OPAC—The Online Public Access Catalog, or OPAC as it is universally known, is the "public face" of the library catalog. OPACs are designed to provide a very easy and user-friendly way for library patrons to locate needed materials or other information from the library Catalog. Figure 37.4 shows a typical OPAC search data entry form.

   As noted above, the Catalog module often does not include information on the status of items in the library's collection. However, the OPAC is linked to holdings information within the ILS so it can provide this vital information. Details provided can include the location of the item, whether it is available for loan, whether it is already in circulation, etc. Figure 37.5 shows an example of how this status information may be displayed in the OPAC.

   Early in the twenty-first century, library information resources are increasingly available in electronic form. Thus, it is becoming very common to include the Universal

FIGURE 37.4 A typical OPAC basic search entry form. (From the Library of Congress Web site.)

Resource Locator or URL in the information that is displayed in the OPAC. By using these links, users may go directly to the needed information or other material at whatever site it may be available. In some cases, libraries maintain locally loaded stores of electronic resources. In others, the materials may be made available directly by the publisher at the publisher's site or via third-party suppliers. Aggregators also provide relatively seamless access to electronic resources for authorized users.

The need to authenticate users and to control or limit access to certain electronic resources introduces new problems for libraries. ILS vendors and others have responded with new services and products. In some cases, there is a separate, stand-alone module to meet this need, while other vendors supply the necessary functionality as part of the total system.

The NISO Z39.50 standard has allowed libraries to host their Catalogs on the Internet and/or provide searching of other Z39.50 Catalogs to their patrons. Most ILS systems either provide integrated Z39.50 functionality or utilize a third-party vendor product to support this feature.

4. Community Events—A Community Events module is often included with the OPAC, especially for public libraries. The events described may be limited to events sponsored by the library or may include any community events that the library wishes to post and make available via the library's OPAC or Web site. Some libraries use the MARC 21 Community

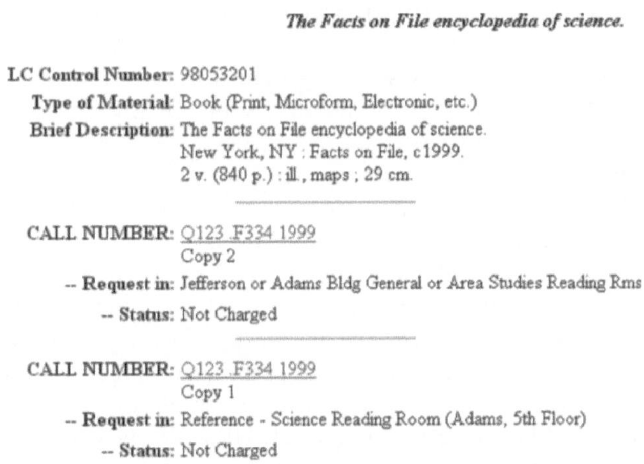

FIGURE 37.5 OPAC record showing Holdings and Status information for an item in the Library's collections. (From the Library of Congress Web site.)

FIGURE 37.6 Community events calendar for the Boston Public Library. (From the Boston Public Library Web site.)

Information Format to integrate this information into their OPAC while others maintain separate Web pages for this purpose. Figure 37.6 shows the Events posted for the Boston Public Library. The site also shows that each of the branch libraries may have its own listings.

5. Circulation—Large libraries frequently have hundreds of thousands or millions of loan transactions and thousands of patron records to maintain. Therefore, this function was among the very first to be automated. Some of the very early systems employed punched cards and tabulating equipment. Over the years, these systems have become enormously complicated and have evolved to include features to cover special circumstances and materials. *Course Reserves*, *Materials Booking*, and *Interlibrary Loan* are often listed as separate, stand-alone modules; however, each is really a special case of the more general Circulation module.

   The classic library Circulation system is generally used to control circulation transactions for periods of time as short as a day and as long as a year. It can accommodate a variety of types of materials, loan periods, and patron types, and can handle a wide variety of fee and penalty formulas to deal with overdue materials.

   Most Circulation systems also allow patrons to place materials *on hold*. This means that if a needed item is already in circulation, at the bindery, or is a newly acquired item being processed, patrons can request that the item be set aside for them as soon as it becomes available. The Circulation system will notify the staff when the item in question is available and will block loan of the item to anyone else until the hold is cleared.

   The Circulation system depends on accurate identifying labels of some sort on the materials to be loaned. A variety of techniques have been used for these identifiers. The most common form in use today is the bar code label. These are easy to scan with inexpensive equipment and are relatively error-free. A similar form of bar code label is usually used to identify the patron who is borrowing the item, but the form of the bar code enables the system to distinguish between them (Figure 37.7).

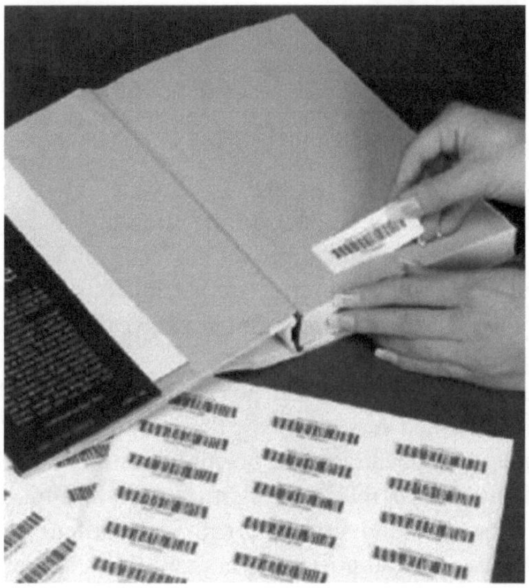

FIGURE 37.7 Bar code labels for a Circulation System. (From the Gaylord Web site.)

The back and front of a sample Patron ID card, showing the library logo and the patron identifying bar code are demonstrated in Figure 37.8.

Circulation modules may also offer self-checkout kiosks or terminals, or link to third-party products for this functionality. A number of larger ILS, particularly those involved with consortial library systems, are beginning to offer the functionality provided by the newly approved NISO Z39.83 NCIP (Circulation Interchange Protocol) standard, which allows protocols for checkout, requesting, Inter Library Loan (ILL), and other system-to-system communications.

An interesting new technology now frequently used for Circulation systems as well as Inventory Control is RFID (or Radio Frequency Identifier). RFID systems use a combination of tags, antennas, and readers. The tags identify each item to the reader. The primary benefit of RFID tags over bar codes is their ease of use, long life, and reliability. The primary drawback is the cost.

RFID tags can be read or written at longer distances of up to several feet, while in motion, in any orientation, through intervening objects and without the need for line of sight. RFID tags enable reliable automation while bar codes are better suited for manual scanning. Perhaps, most significant is the fact that several RFID tags can be read simultaneously and automatically, while bar codes have to be scanned one by one.

FIGURE 37.8 A Patron Card showing the bar code label. (From the Gaylord Web site.)

Thus, for example, a pile of books may be checked in or out without handling each item.

6. Course Reserves is a special case of the Circulation module. There are some significant differences:
   - The basic loan period is almost always less than a day. A frequent exception is for loans made late on a Saturday evening that will not be due until Monday.
   - Fines may be calculated on the elapsed time (hours or even minutes!) that a needed item is returned after the due time.
   - Patrons may need to identify and request materials based on the instructor or professor's name and/or course identifying number rather than by more conventional access points such as author, title, or subject.
   - Materials for the Course Reserves may belong to the library's permanent collection or they may have been loaned especially for the course. If from the library's permanent collection, they may be unavailable for normal circulation while they are on Reserve.

   As library materials become increasingly digital, more and more content is being made available for Course Reserves in electronic form. The challenge with these materials is to ensure that access is limited to authorized users and that the materials are removed from the Course Reserves at the designated time.
7. Materials Booking is another special case of the Circulation module. In this instance, the features of the Circulation System are used to manage the pre-booking (or scheduling) and loan of equipment and facilities such as overhead projectors, DVD players, conference rooms, lecture facilities, etc. The major difference between Materials Booking and the usual circulation hold transaction is that patrons may use the features of this module to reserve a particular piece of equipment or facility for use at a designated date and for a specified amount of time. As with Course Reserves, the needed search criteria may be different, that is, equipment type rather than an author or title, and possibly a location.
8. Interlibrary Loan is yet another variation on the Circulation module. In this case, the loan transaction takes place not between a patron and a library but between participating libraries. Various fees may be charged, depending on the net borrower/lender relationship among any two libraries exchanging materials. Further, the statistical usage reporting requirements can be daunting and may involve special reports generated for local use, state use, and one or more consortia of similar institutions.

   Once again, the move to digital content is changing the way Interlibrary Loan is managed. Libraries have been sending copies of ILL materials via fax for many years. In this situation the item is never expected to be returned.

   Interlibrary lending of electronic journals and other digital content is more problematical. As of this writing, many publishers do not allow loaning of electronic documents under the terms and conditions and/or their license agreements for access to electronic content. On the other hand, organizations such as CrossRef, JSTOR, and the Copyright Clearance Center (CCC) are helping to facilitate access to content. Frequently materials are available via Pay-Per-View; that is the requestor or institution pays a fee to obtain the item.
9. Inventory Control is another special purpose module provided by some ILS vendors. This module is especially useful in large public or other libraries where there is extensive browsing use of the collection. Items may or may not have been reshelved or may have been misshelved. The Inventory Control module generally uses a remote scanning device embedded in a handheld reader. This enables a library staff member to scan the items on the shelves detecting the bar code label that has been placed on the item. Items that are located on the shelves as well as missing items will be detected. The module generally includes a subset of Circulation functions so that the library staff member can change the status of an item,

for example, from "In Transit" to "Checked In" if it is located on the shelf or from "Claims returned" to "Lost" if it is not found.

10. Acquisitions—The Acquisitions module provides support for purchasing and other means of acquiring materials for the library's collection. This module is sometimes called Collection Development, but Acquisitions is the more usual term.

    Some Acquisitions systems are intended to handle only procurement of non-serial materials (e.g., books, audiovisual materials, pamphlets, ephemera). Others are designed to handle all publishing patterns including serials (with all of their various publishing patterns), monographic series, books-in-parts, newspapers, and other dailies.

    Most Acquisitions systems are designed to work closely with the Catalog and other modules of the ILS so status information about items that are being procured is available to staff and sometimes to patrons. For example, the link between the Acquisitions module and the Catalog can provide a way to alert both library users and staff when new materials have been received.

    Many acquisitions systems also include features such as allocation of monies from designated Funds for procuring materials, currency conversion, and exchange of ordering information with publishers and other sources via Electronic Document Interchange or EDI. Some systems also can exchange procurement and ordering information with the controller's office or other purchasing group within the host institution. These features save vast amounts of record-keeping and labor on the part of the library staff.

    A major benefit of an Acquisitions module is that it enables the library to monitor expenditures for new materials throughout the year. It can easily provide early warning if the library's acquisitions budget is in any danger of being over-spent and/or if there is any possibility of funds being available which need to encumbered before the close of the fiscal year. Acquisitions modules also notify staff if material on order has not been received, and often can generate notices to vendors.

11. Serials Control—This module has perhaps the most variation from vendor to vendor of any of the modules in an ILS. Some vendors, for example, offer the Serials Control module as a stand-alone system that includes components from the Catalog, Acquisitions, and Serials Control modules. Such a module would enable library staff members to
    - Create bibliographic records for serials in their collection.
    - Prepare and transmit orders for serials subscriptions, either to an agent or directly to the publisher.
    - Check-in serials issues as they are received.
    - Flag missing issues and prepare claims as required.
    - Notify library staff members when an issue is ready for binding.

    Other vendors may offer a Serials Control module that is closely integrated with other modules in the ILS. In this case, the Serials Modules would support only the check-in function and Claiming operations. The module would be linked closely with the Catalog module for establishing the bibliographic records for serial titles, with the Acquisitions module for preparing and transmitting Orders for serials subscriptions, and with a Binding module for notification when issues are ready to be bound.

    The level of support for full MARC 21 Holdings records for serials data also varies greatly from system to system. Libraries with large serial collections—particularly academic and law collections where print subscriptions can be very costly—are particularly concerned with the capability for full serial pattern and issue level holdings support, as demonstrated by the tremendous interest and progress made by the CONSER Pattern Initiative project.

    Although many Serials modules were designed originally to transmit Ordering and Claiming information using paper forms, today's libraries, subscription agents, and publishers are increasingly able to accept this information in electronic form (EDI). Various standards have been developed to control the data elements and format in which the information is communicated among the various participants in the process.

Many special variations of the Serials module have been developed over the years to meet the special requirements of law libraries and other types of collections that have special needs, either for ordering, or check-in, or for OPAC holdings display.

12. Binding—The Binding module is a special purpose module intended to assist a library in determining when issues are ready for binding and when issues are missing that would prevent a volume from being bound. This module is most useful for a library with a very large and active serials collection and a continuing program of binding journal volumes, perhaps using in-house facilities. Many ILS systems do not include this module.
13. Holdings—A Holdings module is generally required in situations where the library's collection may be spread over many branches as in a large university library system or in a case where many libraries belong to a single system or consortium. As mentioned previously, support for holdings information is frequently incorporated into the Catalog or Circulation module.

    Comprehensive and full-featured support for holdings information is essential for large library systems with many different collections or branches, different circulation policies for various copies, and patrons who may be eligible to view and/or check-out items belonging to any of the collections (Figure 37.9). The *MARC 21 Format for Holdings Data* provides the standards information on how this information is to be recorded and represented.
14. Reporting—The Reporting function is sometimes included in the various modules of an ILS (i.e., the Circulation module may have its own Reporting subsystem) or the ILS may include a special Reporting module that can extract data from any part of the system to produce the desired Reports. Capability for libraries to format reports or create their own data sets and custom reports varies widely from system to system. Various vendor-proprietary report generators are used. However, increasingly, the Reports are available in PDF format so they may be transmitted and read easily by recipients.
15. Administration—As with Reporting, the administration functions are sometimes embedded within each separate module while other vendors provide a separate Administration module for use by designated members of the library staff. The Administration module may be used for a wide range of functions, including but not limited to the following:

The American Heritage college dictionary.

LC Control Number: 2001039826
Type of Material: Book (Print, Microform, Electronic, etc.)
Brief Description: The American Heritage college dictionary
4th ed.
Boston : Houghton Mifflin, c2002.
xxviii, 1636 p. : ill., maps ; 25 cm.
Links: Publisher description

CALL NUMBER: PE1628 .A6227 2002
Copy 4
-- Request in: Jefferson or Adams Bldg General or Area Studies Reading Rms
-- Status: c.4 Charged: Due - 12-31-2003

CALL NUMBER: PE1628 .A6227 2002 Ref Desk
Copy 2
-- Request in: Reference - Business Reading Room (Adams, 5th Floor)
-- Status: Not Charged

FIGURE 37.9 Multiple Holdings for an item in different collections and with different Circulation status. (From the Library of Congress Web site.)

- Create User IDs and passwords for library staff members.
- Configure library staff member user accounts to allow/disallow certain functions.
- Establish Patron Classes and Item Classes for use in Circulation.
- Establish loan periods, fine and fee structures, and other parameters for use in Circulation.
- Post items to the Community Bulletin Board.
- Register institutional IP range or ranges for use in authenticating access to various electronic resources.
- Specify indexing parameters (what indexes are available, fields included in each) and display characteristics (what fields and data is displayed, what labels are used) for the system.

NEW MODULES

1. Web OPACs—The rapid growth of the Internet in the late 1990s and early 2000s has had a dramatic impact on ILS, especially the OPAC. Most ILS now have a Web interface for the OPAC that allows users to browse library catalogs from any Internet Browser. Countless OPACs are now available online to the general public. The OPAC modules for most academic and public libraries do not require any kind of log on to gain access to the Catalog. Many government agencies and other quasipublic groups also allow totally unrestricted access via the Internet to their Catalogs. Of course, corporate and other private institutions still generally provide access only to their own user community and thus require some sort of log on, registration, or IP authentication.
2. Wireless OPACs—Recognizing that many library patrons want to search an OPAC from wherever they are, some ILS vendors are now offering OPAC access via Personal Digital Assistants (PDAs) and cell phones.
3. Extended Catalogs Many ILS vendors now offer additional modules that broaden the scope of information resources that can be made available to their patrons. These extensions enable the library to provide access to internal documents that may not normally be considered part of the library's collections. Additional resources made available in this way might include internal technical reports and documents, engineering drawings, blueprints, and other images. These extensions may also provide access to various resources available on the Internet by providing URL links to those sites.

   In addition to the enhanced cataloging support required (many of the materials to be included may not have applicable MARC formats established for them), these modules require some sort of URL checker to ensure that the stored links are still active.
4. Portals—many ILS vendors now offer various types of portals that extend the resources available to include those that are outside of the institutions collections. These portals may provide access to online databases, abstracting and indexing databases, aggregator databases, etc. In general, they require that access rights to the various resources be secured beforehand. Many publishers and other content providers now are making electronic content available via Pay-Per-View. Thus, a portal might link a user to an electronic journal article, for example, that may be purchased online at the publisher's site.
5. Digital Rights Management–as libraries include more electronic resources among their collections, the problems posed by Digital Rights Management must be tackled. The problem is especially acute for electronic journals because the content may be available to a library's users under a variety of arrangements. For example, a library may subscribe to a single e-journal directly from a publisher or agent or it may have rights to an e-journal's content via subscription to a "package" containing multiple journals and perhaps electronic databases as well. Publishers, aggregators, and others provide a wide array of such offerings. In addition, libraries may also have subscription rights to certain electronic publications as a result of blanket

agreements negotiated by consortia on behalf of their members. Library patrons may then find that there are several choices available to them for obtaining a particular e-journal article or other document. Providing guidance to the user in selecting the most appropriate source is called the "Appropriate Copy Problem." Consider, for example, in a given institution, a user may have access to a particular article from multiple sources. The institution may have already negotiated access rights to content available from some of these sources but not others. Thus, the "Appropriate Copy Problem" is the task of ensuring that the end-user obtains the desired material from the most appropriate (i.e., free of any additional cost) source.

Additionally, different users at the same institution may have varying rights to access specific publications, so specific user identification and rights control is an important factor. ILS vendors and others have devised several auxiliary modules to assist libraries in managing this problem.

6. Metasearching or Federated Searching—Several ILS vendors now include a module that allows library patrons and staff members to search the resources in other collections that have been pre-defined. These Metasearch engines frequently have been designed to take advantage of the Z39.50 protocol, but they can also search resources using proprietary Web searching technologies.

   The major advantage of Metasearch modules is that they provide the long sought-after "one stop shopping" for library patrons. A user may enter a single search strategy and know that it will be executed against all of the resources that are available to that library. The results are generally presented in a relevance-ranked listing with duplicate entries removed.

OTHER SERVICES

As libraries face increasing budgetary pressure and have had to cut staff in many areas, ILS vendors are adding services to help ease the burden. Some examples are listed below:

1. Hosting—Many smaller institutions and libraries do not have access to highly skilled IT staff members or the budget to support them. Therefore, several ILS vendors now are able to provide the servers, data storage devices, network controllers and other devices that are needed to support today's ILS. Library staff members and patrons may gain access to the system via standard Internet Browsers or via a Virtual Private Network (VPN).
2. Implementation and Training Services—Several ILS vendors now offer a variety of consulting, project management, and training services to assist the library in implementing an ILS. Such assistance may be especially helpful during a conversion from one ILS to another.
3. Electronic Resource Management (ERM)—This service extends the Digital Rights Management module described above by providing assistance to the library in managing licensing, purchasing, and access rights to electronic publications. It is extremely time-consuming for library staff members to keep track of ever-changing licensing requirements and Terms and Conditions (T&C) for electronic publications. Further, many staff members do not have the legal training and experience required to negotiate these arrangements with publishers and others.
4. Data Conversion—This service is essential for most first-time ILS implementation as well as for conversion from one ILS to another. It may be necessary to convert bibliographic, patron, and other data from a proprietary format supported by one vendor into a format that can be imported by another.
5. Scanning—As libraries wish to add other materials to their catalogs, archival-quality scanning may be required to produce materials that can be delivered online in electronic form. Some ILS vendors now are able to provide this additional service.

STATUS

The Library Technology Guides Web site (http://www.librarytechnology.org) provides information on the ILS vendors to libraries that are members of the Association of Research Libraries (ARL), public libraries, and large urban systems. Taken together, they present a comprehensive picture of the library automation industry in the early twenty-first century. There are a large number of ILS vendors who provide systems for public libraries. However, only a few large and well-established ILS vendors dominate the ARL automation marketplace. These firms tend to have a global customer base, to be highly diversified, and privately owned.

The ILS industry has been extremely volatile during its relatively short history. Only a handful of companies (e.g., Follett, Gaylord, GEAC, Innovative Interfaces, Sirsi, VTLS) have survived untouched by mergers or acquisitions. Over the years, many ILS vendors have been purchased by larger companies or have merged with other ILS vendors to form new companies with new products. Examples are Elsevier's purchase of Endeavor (which has subsequently been acquired by Ex Libris) and the purchase of Data Research Associates (DRA) and Dynix by Sirsi.

CONCLUSION

It is readily apparent that ILS have had an enormous impact on library operations in the past decades. ILS have evolved rapidly since the 1960s. They have taken every advantage of advances in computer hardware and software, networking capabilities, and, of course, the Internet. In addition, the dramatic decreases in costs to develop, implement, and maintain an ILS have made them affordable for even the smallest library. There are few good cost/benefit analyses for library automation. However, it seems clear that today's libraries could not function as they do without substantial support from automated tools and services.

A LOOK TO THE FUTURE

Libraries have been early adopters of computer and other library automation technologies since these options first started to become available. The desire for easy, inexpensive tools to manage ever-expanding collections is never satisfied. Both librarians and vendors continue to chase "the next greatest thing" to help libraries achieve their goals of providing the best possible access to the best possible information for their patrons.

At the same time, user expectations keep rising. For example, users now not only expect that today's metasearch engines will find whatever information is available somewhere in the world, but also that they will understand the context of the query and make allowances for those words that carry a heavy semantic burden.

Libraries will increasingly rely on resources in electronic form and the library's collection will be defined in terms of the materials its users can access rather than being limited to those materials that are physically within its collections.

Library users will expect to be able to search and access materials from the library—or the universe of libraries—using whatever device may be available be it a personal computer with a dial-up connection, a computer with a wireless connection, or a cell phone or PDA.

The only constant in the future for ILS will be constant change as they continue to grow and evolve to meet the ever-increasing demands of libraries and their constituencies.

ACKNOWLEDGMENTS

With grateful thanks for information graciously provided by many ILS vendors including Innovative Interfaces, Inc.; Sirsi, Inc., VTLS, and comments and suggestions by many.

REFERENCES

1. ANSI/NISO Z39.2-1994.
2. Matthews, J.R. *Public Access to Online Catalogs*, 2nd Ed.; Neal-Schumann: New York, 1985; 17.
3. Boss, R.W. *The Library Managers Guide to Automation*, 3rd Ed.; G.K. Hall & Co.: Boston, 1990; 3.
4. http://orweblog.oclc.org/archives/000585.html
5. http://en.wikipedia.org/wiki/Library_automation_system

38 Online Public Access Catalogs (OPACs)

Kevin Butterfield

CONTENTS

INTRODUCTION

As long as there have been libraries there have been catalogs. In one form or another, from a mental list in the mind of the librarian, to book catalogs, card indexes, and online information retrieval systems, some type of meta access has existed to guide library users through collections. Over the last 40 years, these constructs of paper and wood evolved into Online Public Access Catalogs (OPAC0). When the catalog shifted out of drawers and off of three by five cards to become a networked, universally accessible entity, its role in the library shifted as well. The OPAC competes with the World Wide Web, metadata registries, search engines, and more sophisticated database structures for attention. Amongst this assortment of access mechanisms, the purpose of the OPAC has become muddled. The OPAC has now become one information source among many and one of a number of portals for accessing library collections and beyond.

HISTORICAL DEVELOPMENT

The OPAC is understood to be the technological device that replaced the card catalog. The card catalog had in turn replaced the book catalog form that preceded it. The widespread acceptance of the card catalog at the beginning of the twentieth century reflected a trend towards standardization. The format used by these card catalogs lasted well into the 1990s and represented the influence of mass production in libraries. Catalog cards were first written by hand in library script, then typed, and ultimately ordered from vendors or the Library of Congress. Later they were produced via bibliographic utilities such as OCLC using MARC records. Each change in turn marked a move toward a more efficient means of record creation and maintenance.

The widespread acceptance of the online catalog in the early 1980s marked a trend toward experimentation in library catalog design.[1] However, the card catalog still has a strong influence on how current OPACs have been developed. Current systems and usage patterns are historical artifacts of the library card catalog. The OPAC interfaces and usage patterns embody a history of assumptions made during the card era.[2] At the time online catalogs were developed, the library catalog had reached a remarkable degree of standardization and stasis as a device. The standardization arose from the mass production of cards and from the cultural acceptance of the card catalog as an access device. Online catalogs upset that stasis, and it appears that the standardization enjoyed during the era of the card catalog will not return for some time.[2]

Online catalogs did not develop during a crisis situation. There was no pressing need to find an alternative to the card catalog. The technological capability was there, so the attempt was made to apply the new technologies to the existing systems and routines. Thus OPACs were not brought about by a revolution, but by an evolution of need. A large catalyst in this development was the creation and widespread acceptance of MARC. Use of MARC led to lower cataloging production costs and a greater standardization of description. The first attempts at library automation revolved around card production, acquisitions, and serial control. As the data formerly typed by hand or printed onto three by five cards was encapsulated and transmitted via the MARC formats, libraries and bibliographic utilities began to amass archives of bibliographic records. A natural next step for these libraries was to experiment with making access to these archives available to librarians, libraries, and the public by adapting or creating search interfaces and emerging computer and database technologies. Early library automation centered on using these records to computerize circulation functions. This tendency to apply new technology to existing systems and routines is a common response to technological advance. There seemed to be no overwhelming burden under which librarians and users toiled that motivated them to push for the development and implementation of online catalogs. Consequently, the OPAC was not expected to be a great improvement over previous catalog formats. It was simply seen as a better, faster way to realize desirable system and cost efficiencies.[2]

The cost and capabilities of computer and communications technologies shaped the ability of libraries to realize these efficiencies, as well as drove the dominant trends in library automation over the last three decades.[3] In the specific case of OPACs, four factors can be seen as necessary for their development and acceptance[2]:

1. The technology had to be available.
2. It had to be available at a price that was perceived as cost efficient by potential purchasers.
3. The systems had to be acceptable to users with their specific needs.
4. Online catalogs had to mesh with the goals of the libraries that developed or purchased the system.

The requisite technology for the birth of online catalogs (other than the MARC record structure perhaps) developed outside the library profession. This parallels the current trend in digital library development. Digital libraries initially arose out of the engineering and computer science disciplines before catching on in libraries. In the early days of OPAC development, library collections still revolved around monographs and serials, in various physical formats. Automated library access to monographic holdings developed after automated access to journal literature in most fields was well established.[4] Many of the design features of the prototype online catalog systems, however, did not mimic the automated systems for access to journal articles.

The card catalog remains as the most influential parent of online catalogs and reinforces the evolutionary nature of their development. Online databases of journal articles, for example, did not emulate printed abstracts and indexing tools to the extent that early online catalogs emulated the printed card catalogs.[2] This may have been an outgrowth of the fact that the same MARC record used to produce a catalog card was being used to create an on-screen display. Libraries did not switch en masse from card catalogs to OPACs. Large bibliographic utilities such as OCLC were still producing cards for libraries during this transition period. As a result, there was no immediate or revolutionary change in the basic record structure. It still had to play a dual role.

The development of Integrated Library Systems (ILS) and OPACs has been a response to needs for efficient production and maintenance workflows within libraries. Needs for efficient authority control, inventory tracking of serials, circulation, and acquisitions were among the initial reasons for their development. Most systems developed out of MARC-based cataloging systems or commercial online circulation systems. In both of these instances, automation of library staff functions came first. Efficient production and maintenance routines were the chief attraction of online catalogs, not enhanced access. To the extent that access was discussed, an increased number of access points to bibliographic records were stressed, rather than enhanced user access possibilities.[2] Much of this can be traced to the relative lack of search engine and interface design development at the time, but it also demonstrates the continued influence of the card catalog paradigm.

Although several academic libraries offered enhanced keyword searching early in OPAC development, it was not until the advent of the World Wide Web that we see real pressure from users to develop more sophisticated search and display mechanisms for OPACs. As the field of interface design began to thrive and better, faster more efficient search mechanisms became standard on the Internet and within commercial databases, the pressure to develop more effective services to users of OPACs grew. The World Wide Web and the perceived universal access to content it provides have raised expectations for OPAC interface design.

The imagined production efficiencies hoped for from ILS and OPACs were within the library as an institution, not efficiencies to be realized by the users of information systems. Initially, online catalogs were much more attractive to libraries and librarians than they were to users.[2] In terms of automating arduous tasks and maintaining tighter bibliographic control, the systems were a boon to libraries. Unfortunately interface design at the time was not as sophisticated an area as today. This resulted in often-difficult interactions with the catalog as users attempted to grasp the new technology.

Online catalog development initially was supported by underfunded institutions (e.g., libraries) and the systems needed to be designed for a broad, untrained user population. Database and user interface design were not, then, traditionally part of the librarians experience. This was definitely the case during these early days. These two facts may explain why online catalogs were not on the leading edge of bibliographic storage and retrieval development and reflect the evolutionary, rather than a revolutionary, nature of their development.[2] These systems were designed not to replace, but to enhance and continue preexisting practice.

There were three major types of OPAC systems developing during these early years: in-house, consortium, and package or turnkey systems.[5] Of the pioneering in-house systems, the Library Control System (LCS) of the Ohio State University Libraries is perhaps the best known. Developed by IBM for the university in the late 1960s, it developed from a circulation system to an online catalog. The LCS planners did not envision patrons conducting their own searches at public terminals nor did they plan on replacing the card catalog with LCS. Nevertheless, both of these things came to pass.

Notable milestones introduced by LCS in 1978 included the ability to store and display full bibliographic records, the provision of subject access to records, and the ability to browse through subject heading lists.[5] Other pioneering in-house systems were Northwestern University's Northwestern Online Total Integrated System (NOTIS) and the Virginia Tech Library System (VTLS).

Libraries and library consortia that have designed and developed online catalogs locally to provide access to their databases of MARC records represent another type of online catalog development. What sets these online catalogs apart from those such as LCS and NOTIS is their radical departure from the card catalog as the model for online searching. The database structure and search methods of these catalogs were modeled largely after commercial information retrieval systems such as DIALOG and BRS. The challenge for these online catalogs was not merely to apply the models used by these information retrieval systems but to also preserve the traditional functions of the catalog and to produce a retrieval system that could be used by novices without assistance.[5] Dartmouth College Library developed an end-user, self-explanatory, user interface to the BRS retrieval system as their online catalog in the early 1980s by creating a database using Dartmouth's OCLC transaction tapes. These MARC records were converted to BRS's internal record format. The project was innovative in its interface design goals and it uses of a record structure other than MARC.

One of the more significant consortial endeavors was begun in 1977 by the University of California system. Dubbed MELVYL, the purpose of the catalog was to make it possible to use the separate collections of the university's libraries as a single collection or to allow a user at any campus to access the collection at any other campus. Since some of the UC libraries used OCLC and others used RLIN, MELVYL became the first catalog to successfully merge OCLC and RLIN records into a single database. The prototype version went operational in 1981. As a public-access retrieval system, MELVYL was innovative in that it had a file structure that supported keyword access and Boolean queries, a patron interface that included two user-selectable dialog modes (menu-guided and command language) and an extensive "help" facility.[5]

During the 1970s commercial vendors began to replace large university libraries as the principal developers of computer-based library systems.[3] Among the reasons were libraries' lack of funding and research and development staffing. Commercial vendors were able to fund development more consistently; however, they did not always understand the access needs of patrons. These were more inventory control systems with a searchable front end for the public than true information retrieval systems. Early online systems evolved according to the hardware and software systems of the era. Those that ran on proprietary operating systems and hardware fell away replaced by those that ran on operating systems thought of as industry standards.[6] These turnkey systems were implemented in libraries often with mixed results.

The economic and technical realities of the 1980s favored increased autonomy and local library responsibility.[3] A reaction to the economies of scale of the online technologies developed. In the 1980s administrators tried to regain much of the control over their own operations and decision making that they gave up to the networks in the 1970s.[3] Many institutions of higher education were getting out of the systems design, development, and support business.[2] Libraries began either purchasing entire systems from vendors or assembling ILS modules from several different vendors to create systems that fit their needs.

During the 1990s, integrated systems design became the exclusive domain of vendors. However, libraries and universities began exploring a tangential subject, that of digital library development. With the explosion of the World Wide Web in the mid-1990s, many information retrieval systems and search engines were developed to locate, organize, and retrieve information on the Web. The OPACs, as information retrieval systems, were, in many cases, left behind. They are now beginning to find a role in this new information landscape. The interfaces for these early OPACs tended to be less user friendly than their paper-based predecessors. The strongest pressure for the adoption of online catalogs came not from users, but from library management. Again, a need to find better, faster ways to realize production and management efficiencies was a driving force. However, the more online catalogs are expected to perform the functions of inventory control, acquisitions, cataloging, and public access to the collection, the less likely it is that public users will have a system well designed for public use.[7]

WHAT DO OPACs DO?

The OPAC serves as a public face on a library's ILS. The ILS controls the following functions:

- Circulation (keeping track of items checked out and by whom)
- Cataloging (keeping and offering access to materials)
- Acquisitions (acquiring new items and tracking payments for them)
- Serials (tracking periodicals, claiming missing, or nonreceived items and binding)
- The OPAC
- Interlibrary loan (cooperative sharing of library materials)

At the core of the majority of ILS is the MARC record. Although there are innovative systems using BRS/Dataware, SGML/XML, or SQL to reformat data, typically a MARC/AACR2r-based bibliographic record serves as the focal point for all functions. Order, serial check-in, item, and circulation records "hang" off of it. The bibliographic record acts as a surrogate for the item describing its provenance, content, and container. The ancillary records document financial transactions related to acquisition, continued maintenance, and usage by the public. The OPAC interface translates MARC tags within the records to display labels read more easily by the public (i.e., 100 becomes author, 650 becomes subject).

A great deal of effort must be put into translating tags into labels that make sense to nonlibrarians. Also, given the large number of tags in the typical MARC record, the OPAC displays can run quite long. This has given rise to the traditional brief record display in today's OPAC. Typically one MARC tag generates one labeled field unless the system is instructed to collapse fields together. The library can, depending upon the ILS involved, control what gets displayed and in what order.

The OPACs will search MARC records by author, keyword, corporate name, class number, title, series author/title acronym, ISBN/ISSN/LCCN, subject heading keyword, and subject heading browse. In addition, most OPACs offer phrase and keyword searching. Keyword searching within OPACs has become problematic. Web search engines lead users to believe that OPACs provide deeper access to content than they actually do. The OPAC keyword search is dependent upon the keywords being used within the MARC record. A Web search engine keyword query may mine the full text of an item in an effort to locate the terms used. Since an OPAC consists of item surrogates rather than complete text, the results are not the same.

A review of OPAC search logs may reveal that users attempt to use the OPAC as if it were a Web search engine without knowledge of the classification and subject heading structures inherent in it. Content enhancement of the basic OPAC record would allow the user to take full advantage of the abilities of the basic OPAC, let alone the future incarnations. Addition of abstracts, table of contents, back of the book indexes, etc. would greatly enhance the search experience.

Advanced OPACs allow users to sort and save search results for export in specific data formats. Results can be imported into programs for creating bibliographies or databases. Increased access is also available to patrons for reviewing their circulation records or, in the case of academic libraries, print and retrieve reserve materials for classes.

The OPACs began as stand-alone systems unique to each library, much the same as card catalogs. If a user wished to search the online catalogs of multiple institutions, they would need to locate the catalogs for each and run their search repeatedly. As networking and the Internet came to the fore, more and more OPACs became linked via academic, regional, and statewide consortia. Consortia allow for simultaneous searching across member catalogs or group specific types of libraries together in clusters depending upon the subjects they represent (law, theology, etc.) or their status (academic, public, etc.). Consortial catalogs allow users to search the catalogs of multiple institutions at once, collate the results, and request materials needed through cooperative borrowing arrangements. This allows users access to the combined catalogs of many public and academic libraries with enhanced borrowing functions. It facilitates cooperative collection development among the institutions involved, as they will now be able to see where collections overlap. This has become more prevalent as libraries shift from the paradigm of collecting materials "just in case they are needed" to providing access to materials "just in time."

In addition, bibliographic utilities placed public search interfaces on their union catalogs. OCLC's WorldCat and FirstSearch allow users to search across OCLC's database and retrieve records for items throughout the world. The OCLC's Intercat and CORC projects have extended the scope of the catalog beyond traditional media. Increasingly, recent journal holdings are being made available to libraries through aggregator databases. In a number of cases, vendors will hook the holdings of a particular journal title in their databases to the MARC record in the library's OPAC, allowing users to find the print version of the text should the full text not be available in the vendor's database.

These recent enhancements to OPACs have allowed them to serve as gateways or proxy servers to licensed databases. The ILS patron database can be used to verify that an individual has authorization to access the databases and ensure that the library functions within licensing agreements.

Also, additional enhancements have allowed title-level access to aggregator databases, and hooks to holdings that allow reverse access as well. Methods have become available that allow users to jump directly from an OPACs bibliographic record to a Web site or electronic file, text, or journal. Use of the 856 MARC field as a linking technology or bridge between the catalog record and the item described has made this commonplace. It alters, significantly, definitions of the catalog. Now the catalog not only describes what the library owns, but also what the library potentially has access to. These developments illustrate a growing convergence of portal development and OPAC design. Through this portal-OPAC, the user gains access to resources and people far beyond what earlier, more traditional definitions of a catalog would allow.

HOW EFFECTIVE ARE OPACs?

Users come to the OPAC with a particular need for information. However, they tend to search the OPAC as if it were a Web search engine. While various metadata schemes exist to provide more structure to Web-based information, they are not in widespread use. As successive generations of users, savvier at searching, come to expect natural language oriented, full text searching and retrieval, the OPACs interface and search capabilities begin to look dated in structure and potential. The surrogate record structure does not lend itself easily to that type of query. Most users are unaware of the catalog's structure and are unable to use it effectively.

OPACs depend on user expertise for reasonably successful operation. Given their increased use of search engines on the Web, it is hard for users to understand that they cannot find everything in the catalog by using their own vocabulary, as they would doing a Web search, but must use a pre-coordinated subject heading system that does not necessarily match their language usage or topical vocabulary. The OPACs are very bad at subject searching often due to poor authority control and subject heading assignment and the fact that increasingly students and the public attempt to search the OPAC as they would search with an Internet search engine. These two insufficiencies combine to provide poor search results. With international access to OPACs on the Web, automation in multilingual and multiscript environments becomes important. Some vendors support this, but not all.

There appears to be a need to break the public pieces of the ILS away from the administrative functions related to the collection and other licensed databases. One system cannot do all of this effectively while still clinging to the vestiges of a card catalog. Not all of this is the fault of the OPAC. Descriptive cataloging has not yet mastered bibliographic control of electronic or digital items with the same degree of expertise as it has the medium of print. Innovative OCLC-led projects such as Intercat and Cooperative Online Resource Catalog (CORC) experimented with the ability of OPACs and the MARC format to access and describe electronic objects. Much progress has been made, specifically in describing and providing access to e-journals, but, despite great strides forward, library systems still lag behind many of their Web search engine counterparts. More work is needed to create descriptive metadata that focuses on content, not containers, and public displays that distill for users the information they require to find and retrieve items while, at the same time, balancing the needs of libraries for full, robust, standardized record keeping. An OPAC can only display and interpret the information it contains. It cannot make up for inefficiencies in the catalog record.

CONCLUSION

It is becoming more and more clear that in the future library catalogs will no longer retain their exclusive role as the sole portal to the collection. More and more items are being cataloged in separate registries or via links and portal systems. The catalog becomes, then, one of many access tools. What is not clear is what will be the connecting force between all of these registries and the catalog.

MARC was created as a method of communicating bibliographic information. It is not necessarily the best method for organizing information within a database. New, more object-oriented methods have developed since MARC came on the scene. Mark-up languages such as XML as well as developments in descriptive metadata will improve functionality of the OPAC and allow for a more flexible container or packet structure for the data. Leveraging these technologies would make OPAC function more flexible and allow for the integration of other data structures. All of these technologies also play into the OPACs function as a user interface for the catalog. Compared to other search engines prevalent on the Internet, the OPACs interface seems very dated.

Library automation vendors vie with each other to deliver a system that can stand as a true client/server, multitiered, graphical, Web-enabled, Unicode-enhanced, object-oriented integrated library system built on an industry-standard relational database management system.[6] And so the standard is set for the current generation of library automation systems. The OPAC's general characteristics will include a client/server architecture; support for multiple character sets, preferably through Unicode; a windows-based graphical user interface for library staff; a Web interface for library users; use of a standard relational database system; a Z39.50-compliant server; import and export of MARC records; and Electronic Data Interchange (EDI).[6]

REFERENCES

1. Cochrane, P.A.; Markey, K. Catalog use studies—Since the introduction of online interactive catalogs: Impact on design for subject access. Libr. Inf. Sci. Res. **1983**, *5* (4), 338.
2. Peters, T.A. *The Online Catalog: A Critical Examination of Public Use*; McFarland & Company: Jefferson, NC, 1991; 10–14.
3. De Gennaro, R. Library automation and networking: Perspectives on three decades. Libr. J. **1983**, *108* (7), 243–274.
4. Lynch, C.A.; Berger, M.G. The UC MELVYL medline system: A pilot project for access to journal literature through an online catalog. Inf. Technol. Libr. **1989**, *8* (4), 372.
5. Hildreth, C.R. Online public access catalogs. Annu. Rev. Inf. Sci. Technol. **1985**, *20*, 246–254.
6. Breeding, M. A new look at large-scale library automation systems. Comput. Libr. **1999**, *19* (8), 36–37.
7. Estabrook, L. The human dimension of the catalog: Concepts and constraints in information seeking. Libr. Res. Tech. Serv. **1983**, *27* (1), 71.

39 Internet Filtering Software and Its Effects

Lynn Sutton

CONTENTS

INTRODUCTION

Few issues in recent years have divided the library community as deeply as that of Internet filtering. Filtering is here defined as commercial computer software that limits, blocks, or restricts access to Internet content. "Filtering technologies allow Internet material or activities that are deemed inappropriate to be blocked, so that the individual using that filtered computer cannot gain access to that material or participate in those activities."[1] This entry will discuss the purposes of Internet filters, describe how they work, report on their effectiveness and prevalence in libraries, and explore the effects that filtering has on library users. While the conversation about filtering has been dominated by U.S. libraries primarily due to federal legislation, a survey of international filtering will also be provided.

PURPOSE OF INTERNET FILTERS

Filters block access to Internet content that has been predetermined to be objectionable or inappropriate in some way. The vast majority of content in libraries is blocked because it is sexually explicit, although chat rooms, e-mail and subject categories such as violence, hate speech, smoking, and gun control are also content areas that are commonly blocked.

There are a number of sectors in society that have interest in filtering Internet content. Employers may have an economic interest in preventing their employees from surfing the Internet, shopping online, or composing personal e-mail. Parents may have a moral interest in limiting the Internet content that their children see in terms of violence, sexuality, commerce, and sharing personally identifying information. Libraries, particularly public and school libraries, may have an interest in reflecting the values of the communities in which they operate. Academic and special libraries are less commonly involved with Internet filtering

In the United States, the federal government has wrestled with the desirability, feasibility, and constitutionality of restricting Internet content. In 1996, the U.S. Congress first tried to criminalize those who post indecent content to the Internet with the Communications Decency Act. This was unanimously struck down as unconstitutional by the U.S. Supreme Court in 1997. Congress next tried to use narrower language to protect minors from harmful material on the Internet in 1998 in the Child Online Protection Act (COPA). Enforcement of COPA was blocked immediately and it was eventually also overturned in the courts. Congress's third attempt was finally successful when the Children's Internet Protection Act (CIPA) of 2000 withstood fierce legal challenges by the American Library Association (ALA) and American Civil Liberties Union (ACLU) and was narrowly ruled constitutional by the U.S. Supreme Court in a plurality decision in 2003. Significantly, CIPA required libraries to install technology protection measures (filters) on all computers in order to obtain government e-rate discounts for Internet access and in certain categories of federal grants, such as those from the Library Services and Technology Act (LSTA). Thus, many public and school libraries that did not filter previously began to filter when CIPA went into effect. Libraries facing the decision of whether or not to filter need to weigh the costs of filtering against the loss of federal e-rate discounts and, most importantly, gauge the sense and tolerance of the community on free speech and Internet safety values.

Deciding Whether or Not to Filter

Every public and school library in America must make its own decision on whether filtering should be implemented after considering all the factors involved. This is an important decision that should receive input from staff, community users, and governing officials. A list of factors and criteria to be considered include[2]

- The amount of e-rate discounts and LSTA funds received and what support these funds provide.
- The availability of other types of funds to cover Internet connectivity should e-rate discounts and LSTA funds be lost.
- The amount of expense to purchase, install and maintain filters on all computers in the library, as well as to train library staff to implement them.
- The effect on library users and staff, including information that might be blocked as well as political situations that might arise to unblocked material.
- Policies and procedures to guide the library in Internet use in general and implementation of filters in particular, including disabling features.

HOW FILTERS WORK

Filters use several methods for blocking data. Early filters used word blocking, which matched Web pages against a list of keywords and either eliminated the offensive word from the Web page or eliminated the entire Web page itself. Later filters tend to use the site blocking technique, which analyzes Web site URLs by category. The pass-through filtering method compares requested Web pages to a database of existing URLs with preassigned categories. If the filter is set to allow the category to which an individual Web site has been assigned, then it is displayed. If the category of the Web site is not allowed according to the filter's protocol, then it is blocked and a block page is displayed instead. The content or pass-by filtering method allows the Web page into the system and then analyzes its content on-the-fly and assigns it to a category, which is then compared to the filter's list of allowable categories. Ironically, few filters focus on images even though the CIPA does not address text but rather prohibits access only to visual depictions that are obscene, child pornography, or harmful to minors.

The emphasis on categorization of Web sites gives both power and flexibility to the staff of the filtering companies who make those decisions and to the local filter administrators who decide which categories to enable or disable on their systems. Further, individual categories in a system may be set across a continuum ranging from least restrictive to most restrictive. Thus, "sexuality" may be set at the most restrictive level but "violence" may be set at the least restrictive level. Filtering systems in libraries are most often installed at the system level, that is, a local school district or a public library system. Local filter administrators are commonly technical computing staff, rather than librarians. In some systems, advisory committees of teachers or librarians give guidance on filter settings. Filter companies and local filter administrators play determining roles in how much or how little Internet content is blocked.

Most commercial filtering companies are reluctant to list specific Web sites by category, claiming that is proprietary information. This makes it difficult to move a specific site from a misplaced category to a more suitable category. To some extent, what is blocked is a reflection of the intended market for the filtering product. Some new open source filtering products go against this trend and openly list the Web sites in each category, inviting librarians to move individual Web sites to more appropriate categories in a wiki-type collaborative effort.

EFFECTIVENESS OF INTERNET FILTERS

No one claims that technology protection devices such as filters work perfectly. Public and private studies agree that filters still fail to block all objectionable content (underblocking) and block content that is protected by the First Amendment (overblocking). Over a range of tests, filters have been found to be roughly 85% accurate, considering both underblocking and overblocking failures.[3]

The U.S. Congress has appointed two separate commissions to study the use of filtering technology to protect children from materials inappropriate to minors. The Commission on Online Child Protection presented its final report to Congress in October, 2000.[4] The report stated that the best Internet filtering technologies can be highly effective in directly blocking access to content that is harmful to minors, but noted that there are significant concerns about First Amendment issues when filters are used in libraries and schools.

The second commission to study the use of Internet filtering technology was the "Committee to Study Tools and Strategies for Protecting Kids from Pornography and Their Applicability to Other Inappropriate Internet Content" of the Computer Science and Telecommunications Board of the National Research Council. This Commission provides one of the most comprehensive considerations of the issue. One of the study's findings is that, due to the nature of filters, underblocking and overblocking errors are inevitable and while that should not, in and of itself, rule out filters as useful tools, the extent of underblocking and overblocking must be taken into account in understanding and deciding about the use of filters. In the end, one of the Committee's conclusions is that social and educational strategies, rather than technological strategies such as filters, are most useful. Parents, teachers, and librarians all share the responsibility in guiding children in safe and effective use of the Internet. Delegating this responsibility to technology protection devices such as filters is not sufficient. "While technology and public policy have important roles to play, social and educational strategies that impart to children the character and values to exercise responsible choices about Internet use and the knowledge about how to cope with inappropriate materials and experiences in central to promoting children's safe Internet use."[5]

The U.S. Congress also asked the National Telecommunications and Information Agency (NTIA) to evaluate whether the technology measures currently available adequately address the needs of educational institutions, and also to evaluate the development and effectiveness of local Internet safety policies. After balancing the importance of allowing children to use the Internet with the importance of protecting children from inappropriate material, the report concludes that currently available technology measures have the capacity to meet most, if not all, needs and concerns of educational institutions, although educators have significant concerns with underblocking and overblocking.

Because of the legal controversies surrounding CIPA, the literature has been filled with various kinds of studies and opinion pieces on the effectiveness of filters. Perhaps the most scientific study of filter effectiveness was the Kaiser study, which appeared in *JAMA* (*Journal of the American Medical Association*)[6] and demonstrated the difference that filter settings make in the amount of harmless material that is blocked through the use of filters. The objective of the study was to measure how much pornography-blocking software used in schools and libraries limits access to health information Web sites, which is of particular concern because adolescents' health questions often focus on sexuality issues and because students rely on schools and libraries for Internet access when they do not have computers at home. The results showed only minimal overblocking of legitimate health sites at the least restrictive level, but significantly more overblocking at the most restrictive level. The amount of overblocking varied according to topic. The way in which the Kaiser study has been interpreted in the field reveals the dichotomy of opinion on the subject of filters. Free speech activists emphasized the dangers of overblocking at the most restrictive levels and say the study clearly demonstrates the First Amendment concerns about filtering. Others in community-based libraries believe that the study's findings indicate that filters, when operated at their least restrictive setting, pose only a minor impediment to searching for health information.

Disabling Feature

The CIPA provided for the disabling of filters upon request by an adult for bona fide research or other lawful purposes. The disabling feature was a deciding factor in the Supreme Court ruling that CIPA did not violate the First Amendment. Some libraries report that disabling can be accomplished quickly and simply if the power to do so resides at the local library level. Others report that such disabling is neither easy nor timely in meeting immediate patron needs if it is necessary to take the request to the system level. At least one major urban library system has gone beyond CIPA and under mayoral mandate will not disable the filter upon adult request,[7] although unblocking of individual sites erroneously blocked may be requested in writing. The constitutionality of such a far-reaching policy remains to be tested.

Division in the Field of Librarianship

The controversy over Internet filters has divided the library community. ALA came out strongly against filters in 2001 shortly after CIPA was signed into law with a "Resolution on Opposition to Federally Mandated Internet Filtering." ALA immediately joined with the ACLU in filing suit to challenge CIPA's constitutionality. However, a number of librarians in the field, such as filtering advocate David Burt,[8] felt their national association had lost touch and the insistence on extreme free speech activism was not helpful to libraries trying to represent the wishes of their communities. These librarians view filters as a commonsense approach to keeping unwanted pornography from their libraries and well worth the relatively small amount of overblocking and underblocking that is inevitable. Free speech advocates, however, hold intellectual freedom as a core value and moral compass and view filters that block constitutionally protected speech as intolerable. Both sides agree that if filters must be used, they should minimize the blocking of legal content, encourage users to report problems and make filter disabling easy and unobtrusive. Where they still do not agree is whether filters are worth the benefit, given the cost.

PREVALENCE OF FILTERS IN LIBRARIES

Public Libraries

Before the CIPA decision in 2003, less than half of the public libraries in the United States used filters. After CIPA, a few libraries said very publicly they would forego e-rate discounts rather than subject their users to filtering, but many more libraries began to filter after the law was put into effect. In Indiana, 66% reported filtering in 2003 and another 22% said they were planning to implement filters in the near future. In Rhode Island, the ACLU reported a generally docile response where all 48 member library systems ultimately agreed to filter after the CIPA decision under the statewide automation consortium. Further, the ACLU observed that some of these libraries initially went beyond the minimum requirements of the law to the point of restricting information that users are allowed to see even under CIPA's restrictions. In addition, a number of states have imposed "mini-CIPA" laws requiring filters, which have also had the effect of increasing the numbers of public libraries that filter.[9]

School Libraries

By 2005, the U.S. Department of Education reported that 90% of schools were using Internet filters. School libraries were not part of the ALA's legal challenge to CIPA, so they were subject to its provisions regarding the Federal Communications Commission's e-rate discounts since it was first implemented in 2001. The e-rate discount has been extremely popular in schools and experts agree that this program has been largely responsible for the increase in Internet access in public schools over the years by making it so affordable.

Even before 2001, schools across the country debated the pros and cons of Internet filters. While hailing the increased access to information, some dreaded the preoccupation with pornography, hate groups, and violence while others foresaw the constitutional problems that would inevitably arise from any official act by the government to limit free speech. Librarians and media specialists knew that the reduced chances of a student accessing inappropriate material must be balanced against the knowledge that any kind of commercial filter will almost certainly block appropriate material, with a corresponding risk of violating the student's First Amendment rights.

EFFECTS OF FILTERS ON USERS

Apart from the professional debate among librarians, it is important to know what effect filtering has on library users. Librarians on both sides of the issue report anecdotes supporting their views. There have been a small number of qualitative research studies in which library patrons were systematically interviewed, observed, and analyzed. These studies have shown that students, in particular, report annoyance, frustration, and anger when filters block the material they need to complete their school work. In a semester-long 2004 study of high school students, Sutton found that a majority of students felt that the school's filter hindered their work in doing Internet research for their term papers.[10] Very few students felt the filter had a positive effect, while another group felt the filter had a negative effect even though it might be necessary.

In an earlier study, Levin and Arafeh used qualitative methods to describe the attitudes and behaviors of students using the Internet in public schools. They said that "while many students recognize the need and a desire to shelter teenagers from inappropriate material and adult-oriented commercial ads, they complain that blocking and filtering software raise significant barriers to their legitimate educational use of the Internet."[11]

The 2003 study conducted by the Electronic Frontier Foundation and the Online Policy Group is critical of the effectiveness of filters in educational institutions. Their study was one of the few to study the issue of student Internet access within public schools that operate Internet blocking software. The study portrayed the effect of filtering on students in this way, "Biases and mistakes inherent in Internet blocking software reduce the student's access to materials directly related to state-mandated curriculum topics in school without adequately shielding the students from objectionable content."[12]

The Digital Divide

Of particular concern to librarians is the risk that Internet filters in public and school libraries will worsen the phenomenon known as the digital divide, which may be defined as the difference in access to digital information that separates the information-rich from the information-poor. The groups that fall into the digital divide are minorities, low-income individuals, and those with less education. Gender is no longer an issue, as Internet use in America is exactly 50% male and 50% female. The role that libraries play in bridging the digital divide is of primary importance. The public library may be the only access that the poorest of the poor have to information that is published electronically. Ironically, the federal e-rate discount was a major cause of Internet penetration in public libraries and it is the threat of e-rate withdrawal that has convinced many libraries to filter library computers for the first time.

Implications of the digital divide also come into play with high school media centers. Poor, nonwhite children are much more likely to rely on libraries, especially school libraries, for Internet access. When that access is filtered to a less than comprehensive version of the Internet, the question must be asked, what is being left out? Filtering companies offer blocking for many categories of subject material other than the illegal categories of obscenity, child pornography, and "materials harmful to minors." Moral and political viewpoints are sometimes blocked such as information on homosexuality, sex education in general, gun control, smoking, hate speech, abortion, and contraception. Gay youth, in particular, rely on the privacy of the Internet to search for answers to their questions on sexuality, and gay speech is often blocked by filters. Free speech advocates worry that poor children who have no other recourse than library computers are blocked from accessing information that they need.

Best Practices in Filtering

If a library finds itself in a position where filters are legally required or felt to be a desirable solution, the following guidelines may be applied to keep undesired effects to a minimum:

- Have an Acceptable Internet Use Policy in effect.
- Implement educational programming for children, parents, and community members, emphasizing safe and responsible use of the Internet.
- Undertake a cost–benefit analysis of the costs of filtering vs. the cost of not filtering (loss of discounts and grants).
- Gather input from library staff, community members, and local officials before implementing filtering.
- If the decision is made to filter, begin with settings at the lowest levels.
- Limit blocking to the categories specifically set out in the CIPA statute.
- Institute a procedure that is timely and effective to turn off the filter upon request.
- Check back frequently with users to make sure that the filter is working and not blocking legitimate information. If so, adjust the filter settings.

INTERNATIONAL FILTERING

The United States is not the only nation to engage in filtering. Whereas the Internet was originally conceived as a global network of limitless information, a number of countries have imposed content-restrictive filters at the national level. Their intentions in doing so include interests in commerce, protecting children, banning pornography and other vices, discouraging political dissidents and independent media, and protecting national security. These countries typically use the same commercial filtering products developed by U.S. companies and are thus susceptible to the same overblocking and underblocking that is seen in U.S. libraries. When filtering is centrally applied at the national gateway level, the entire country is subject to filtered content. Filtering in developing countries is often controlled through an obscure level of rules and regulations, rather than established laws, which makes it harder to track. In response, citizens in these countries have resorted to an array of sophisticated circumvention technologies with some success.[13]

The OpenNet Initiative (opennet.net) has the mission of identifying and tracking Internet filtering and surveillance wherever it exists in an effort to promote a greater public understanding of such practices. This organization maintains a comprehensive database of filtering across the globe and lists 40 countries known to filter. Filtering in Asia is very common. China, in particular, is well known for its aggressive filtering practices at the backbone level, thus subjecting all users to uniform filtering. Google has come under a good deal of criticism for its participation in China's Golden Shield Project. Filtering in the countries of the Middle East is predominantly for political and cultural–religious reasons and media censorship is strong. In sub-Saharan Africa, there is not much Internet penetration to filter. Latin America generally does not engage in systematic filtering, with the obvious exception of Cuba, which does so for political reasons. European states are particularly sensitive to hate speech, with the normally liberal French and German governments litigating against pro-Nazi sites.

CONCLUSION

Technology protection measures, such as filters, whose purpose is to block objectionable content on the Internet are imperfect, at best. Those who mandate filtering have a variety of purposes, from well-intentioned protection of children to manipulative control of information within a society. Because the very nature of filters is to automate the otherwise prohibitive task of examining content of millions of Web sites, there is inevitably a margin of error in both overblocking legitimate content and underblocking prohibited content.

To some extent, filters have undermined the formerly principal role that librarians played as gatekeepers of information. Filters are now designed by commercial technology companies and implemented by local technology administrators so that the professional role of the librarian in guiding the information discovery process is diminished. Great care must be taken to ensure that filters do not disenfranchise the underprivileged in society who depend on institutions such as public and school libraries and who may find that their access to information is reduced with filtered computers.

The trend toward filtering is strong in the United States and elsewhere. Filtering offers some level of protection against objectionable content, but it comes at considerable cost. As in other areas of society, librarians and other information officials are still divided on whether the protection is worth the price.

REFERENCES

1. Thornburgh, D.; Lin, H.S., Eds. *Youth, Pornography, and the Internet*; National Academy Press: Washington, DC, 2002; 51.
2. Jaeger, P.T.; McClure, C.R.; Bertot, J.C.; Langa, L.A. CIPA: Decisions, implementation, and impacts. Publ. Libr. **2005**, *44* (2), 105–109.
3. Ayre, L. Filtering and filter software. Libr. Technol. Rep. **2004**, *40* (2), 1–80.
4. COPA Commission. *Final Report of the COPA Commission Presented to Congress, October 20, 2000*, http://www.copacommission.org/report (accessed October 12, 2007).
5. Thornburgh, D.; Lin, H.S., Eds. *Youth, Pornography, and the Internet*; National Academy Press: Washington, DC, 2002; 388.

6. Richardson, C.R.; Resnick, P.J.; Hansen, D.L.; Derry, H.A.; Rideout, V.J. Does pornography-blocking software block access to health information on the Internet? JAMA **2002**, *288* (22), 2887–2894.
7. Eberhart, G.T. Phoenix Council demands filters on all computers. Am. Libr. **2004**, *35* (9), 14–16.
8. Burt, D. *Dangerous Access 2000*; Family Research Council: Washington, DC, 2000.
9. Heins, M.; Cho, C.; Feldman, A. *Internet Filters: A Public Policy Report*, 2nd Ed.; Brennan Center for Justice: New York, 2006.
10. Sutton, L. *Access Denied: How Internet Filters Impact Student Learning in High Schools*; Cambria Press: Youngstown, NY, 2006.
11. Levin, D.; Arafeh, S. *The Digital Disconnect: The Widening Gap between Internet-Savvy Students and their Schools*; Pew Internet & American Life Project, 2002, http://www.pewinternet.org/PPF/r/67/report_display.asp (accessed October 6, 2007).
12. Electronic Frontier Foundation & Online Policy Group. *Internet Blocking in Public Schools: A Study on Internet Access in Educational Institutions*; 2003, http://www.eff.org/Censorship/Censorware/net_block_report/ (accessed October 6, 2007).
13. Villeneuve, N. The filtering matrix: Integrated mechanisms of information control and the demarcation of borders in cyberspace. First Monday **2006**, *11* (1–2). http://www.uic.edu/htbin/cgiwrap/bin/ojs/index.php/fm/article/view/1307/1227 (accessed October 1, 2007).

BIBLIOGRAPHY

1. Auld, H. Filtering materials on the Internet does not contradict the value of open access to material. Publ. Libr. **2005**, *44* (4), 196–98.
2. Comer, A.D. Studying Indiana public libraries' usage of Internet filters. Comput. Libr. **2005**, *25* (6), 10–15.
3. Deibert, R.J.; Palfrey, J.G.; Rohozinski, R.; Zittrain, J. *Access Denied: The Practice and Policy of Global Internet Filtering*; MIT Press: Cambridge, MA, 2008.
4. Filtering software: Better, but still fallible. Consum. Rep. **2005**, *70* (6), 36–38.
5. Kranich, N. Filtering materials on the Internet contradicts the value of open access to material. Publ. Libr. **2005**, *44* (4), 198–200.

40 Personal Bibliographic Systems (PBS)

Dirk Schoonbaert and Victor Rosenberg

CONTENTS

INTRODUCTION

History of the Software Genre

Before personal computers appeared in the late 1970s there were a few attempts to write software that would organize and punctuate bibliographic references. As the Apple II and the IBM PC began to proliferate in the early 1980s one of the obvious applications for these machines was the software category that we call bibliographic software. Two major products were developed almost simultaneously, Reference Manager, and the Personal Bibliographic System (PBS), later renamed ProCite. Reference Manager was the brainchild of a researcher in hematology, Ernest Beutler, and ProCite was developed by Victor Rosenberg at the School of Library Science at the University of Michigan. A somewhat later entry into the market was EndNote, developed by Rich Niles. All three of these products were subsequently purchased by Thomson Scientific (http://www.isiresearchsoft.com) and all are still sold by them today. In addition, Thompson Scientific has developed two Web products, RefViz and EndNote Web.

Earl Beutler, Ernest's son, commercialized his father's idea and after selling his company to Thomson in the mid-1990s, has been instrumental in launching a new and popular bibliographic software product, RefWorks. RefWorks is now owned by CSA. A number of other software developers created bibliographic products, including Library Master, Papyrus, Nota Bene, BibTex. Library Master is available from Balboa Software of Phoenix, Arizona (http://www.balboa-software.com).

The vision for bibliographic software was a personal program that mirrored the larger bibliographic databases. This vision called for the researcher to be able to retrieve citations from many sources such as subject-specific databases or library catalogs. For example, a researcher could find and then download references from PubMed, Web of Science, Chemical Abstracts, as well as from the Library of Congress Catalog, or university library catalogs from around the world. The major obstacle to realizing this vision was that the record formats for the various bibliographic resources were all different. This problem has been largely solved by the combined efforts of the personal software developers and the efforts of the publishers of the major databases and the library automation vendors. Most major library catalogs and databases now provide a format that the major personal bibliographic products can read. This was not always so, and great effort went into creating interface software that would translate records from the large resources into the personal system.

The vision further included the idea that the researcher would want to collect references into one personal database from which he or she could retrieve the reference into a manuscript in any of the various formats that publishers require. The researcher could include personal notes in the bibliographic record to help in creating the manuscript. As technology developed and the capacity of personal computer databases increased, it became possible to include entire papers as part of the bibliographic record.

It was important for the personal system to have all the functionality of the larger institutional systems. The user of the system had to be able to organize the references in various ways, alphabetically by author, title, or subject. The user had to be able to index the data, or to retrieve information by words in the record. In addition, the user had to be able to add the references to a document in the word processor in all the various formats that different publishers demand.

Early on it became clear that users wanted not only a program to format bibliographies in a word processor, but a complete database management system specifically designed for bibliographic records. The common DBMS programs like Access or Filemaker simply would not do for bibliographic applications. Most of those involved in developing the software kept wondering when Microsoft or the publishers of WordPerfect would simply include a bibliography manager as a new feature of their program. Soon it became obvious that the complexity of the bibliographic program rivaled that of the word processor itself. Then again, PBS have become a sort of mainstream software, as they are increasingly being included in university education, a practical subject taught by librarians.

A Survey of PBS Features

In the following sections, a number of characteristics that individual PBS do or do not feature are discussed in a generic way. Most of these items are available in at least one of the mainstream systems. Some additional features can be encountered in packages that are not strictly PBS but that would do credit to any PBS. As both the advantages and disadvantages of individual features are not always immediately obvious, this discussion may prove helpful when shopping for a PBS. First, the very heart of these systems will be studied; that is, the structural possibilities and limits of the database file itself, as these define, arguably more than any other issue, whether or not a PBS is adequate for the user's basic needs. Further on, the actual database functions such as input, retrieval, and output will be discussed. For a discussion of the major PBS themselves, we refer the reader to a number of excellent review articles. Schoonbaert (2002) lists over 100 different PBS. Although many systems have become obsolete by now, several others are flowering, releasing new major upgrades every few years.

DOCUMENT TYPES

When dealing with bibliographic references, it is essential that the system handle highly structured data. This is often done admirably by highly sophisticated full-text storage and retrieval software. However, in order to retrieve or (re)produce specific bibliographic elements, it is necessary to keep these different pieces of information in separate (sub)fields, grouped in adequate document types.

Whereas some software packages may present themselves as "naked" toolboxes at the disposal of creative enthusiasts willing and able to spend sometime to develop the bibliographic system of their dreams from scratch, most PBS offer a number of standard document types, such as journal article, book, book chapter, and dissertation. Some include quite a variety of predefined formats, including videotapes, electronic files, and Internet-based formats such as electronic mail messages or Web sites, with clickable URLs. If you believe the variety of document types offered lives up to your expectations there is not much point in looking for further structural flexibility. However, you may feel the need to modify these formats or add extra ones. This may not be that important for personal reprint databases, where you can put divergent materials within the constraints of an existing format. The field labels or output formats may not be fully representative of the data included, but for personal purposes, they will suffice. In a library situation, however, it may be necessary to alter these formats. If you want to incorporate a great variety of materials in your database(s) (e.g., unpublished documents or annual reports), your system must allow for more than standard book or journal article formats. Even if abundant arrays of formats are available, it may be necessary to create new fields, adjust some field tags, and so forth. Therefore, it is certainly a boon if you are allowed to change field characteristics and the structure of document types. Another important issue is that of a posteriori flexibility: can fields and document types be added, moved, renamed, or deleted without limitation once the database structure is defined, and what effect does this have on existing records (e.g., are field contents moved to other fields or just removed from the record)?

In the most flexible PBS, practically all fields and record types can be defined freely, which allows you to accommodate totally different kinds of information (even including non-bibliographic data). Of course, flexibility of structure can only be enjoyed if it is matched by an equal flexibility of display and output formats. It does not make sense to rename or create fields when they cannot be displayed, printed, or downloaded in an adequate fashion. Tinkering with predefined structures also implies that some system-defined formats (e.g., journal output styles) may no longer give correct results unless they are doctored also. On the other hand, using only the default-predefined modules offers a comfortable plug-and-play ease of use.

FIELDS

Unlike general-purpose databases using fixed length fields to deal with numerical data, postal addresses, and the like, bibliographic databases should be able to provide for information with highly variable sizes. Fields can be just a few bytes long, in which case it would be a waste to reserve a fixed number of bytes for each potential occurrence of each field for each record in the database. On the other hand, field contents such as corporate sources or abstracts can occasionally get quite long. In some systems, there is a limit to field lengths, but this limit can be several thousand bytes, so it generally poses no practical problems. Some PBS offer a compromise with hybrid types featuring a number of fields of limited length, coupled with one or a few of long length.

Not all systems are equally user-friendly in exploiting their field structures. Many use short alphabetic tags of one or a few characters. They are often mnemonic, so it is easy to remember that the title field is coded with "T" or "TI." This makes it easy to do field-specific searches. This is far less evident when fields are identified with numerical tags (compare MARC codes), which are not easy to remember or guess for experienced users, let alone for novice users. When working with fields and field tags, there should be an easy way to get a survey of these fields and their major characteristics (e.g., via pop-up or drag-down lists). Furthermore, this basic field indication may be complemented by the interface by automatically providing full-field names for display purposes (e.g., "T" is transformed into "TITLE:").

CHARACTERS

For bibliographic purposes, it is essential that all necessary characters be adequately supported by the system. Next to the alphanumeric ASCII characters, there is also a need for the extended ASCII set, including, for instance, the French accented characters and other diacritics. In the early days, this used to be a problem with many Anglo-Saxon systems, but most current PBS support extended ASCII and even Unicode, so the most prevalent foreign texts can be accommodated. The same is true for scientific and graphic symbols. In this respect, there is not only the question of input and storage to be addressed, but there are also repercussions on other levels, such as retrieval, display, printing, downloading and uploading in word processors, and for each of them, there is the issue of (self-definable) sorting values.

Another advantageous feature is the capacity to foreground or highlight certain parts of the text, so that these strings can be displayed or printed in bold, italic underlined, superscript, independent of the actual display or output formats or the type of field to which they belong.

RECORD NUMBERING AND LINKING

It may be helpful to dispose of an explicit permanent number for each record, so it can still be uniquely identified when intermediate records are deleted or the database is rearranged. Useful options include the automatic generation of such numbers and the possibility to modify single record numbers or renumber a complete database. Automatic generation of the date of record creation and last modification may also be useful.

Some systems allow the linking of separate records. In this way, pointers to hierarchically related records can be included, so a lot of bibliographic information of the parent record need not be duplicated within each individual child record, thus guaranteeing economy and consistency. This is generally possible in the relational database category, but it can also be found in some other PBS types.

In the last few years, multimedia capabilities have gained in popularity. Ever more, PBS can now handle images or graphics, either through limited links to external files and viewing software, or by full integration, including internal viewing software. This may not only be useful for displaying pictures but also for more text-related items such as diagrams, mathematical formulas, and chemical structures. Another type of linking is that to records in other (more elaborate) databases (e.g., PubMed or ISI Web of Science) or to full-text sources (often PDF files), either on the local system or on an external server (e.g., PubMed Central).

DATABASE SELECTION

Database selection is generally the first option you are presented with when starting up the system. A good PBS makes it easy to access the right database. Therefore, it is important that all available databases are listed in an adequate way. Having access to different database directories can be helpful. In this way, a hierarchical structure can be maintained, in which each type of database has its specific subdirectory; thus, related databases are displayed within the same menu excluding other irrelevant ones.

ENTERING NEW RECORDS (INPUT)

MANUAL INPUT

Keying bibliographic references in a database is a tedious chore. Any help to ease this job, avoid unnecessary duplication of effort and minimize spelling mistakes is more than welcome. Generally, manual input is achieved using an electronic input sheet offering a number of fields to be filled in. Preferably, only those fields that are relevant for the specific document type are presented. Having different input sheets for different document types (one of which should be the system default or the de facto default until changed explicitly) avoids being confronted with a lot of irrelevant fields during manual input. Also, it should be easy to customize the information you have just entered in a default input sheet, so that when necessary, less common fields can also be added.

Input models generally make use of some kind of text editor. These may differ greatly in versatility and power. Good editors can make life much easier. A common example is the capability to automatically replace or copy strings or full-field contents to other fields within the same record. A comparable issue is the creation of new records by duplicating existing records [e.g., for articles in the same journal (issue), chapters in the same book, and books in the same series]. If this function is not explicitly available, users may be able to use the standard clipboard and copy/cut/paste or drag and drop techniques. Another useful feature is the option to specify default content for specific fields (e.g., journal or book title) or automatically add field occurrences (e.g., keywords common to a retrieval results set) to all new records created during an input session. Some PBS offer automatic generation of keywords from the title or abstract field (optionally coupled to a stop list, or a "go" list for that matter).

Index-assisted input, where the strings typed are compared to information that is already available within the indexes, has two major advantages. First, it guarantees alphabetic consistency because the indexes act as authority files. Second, if automatic truncation is incorporated, this can dramatically reduce the amount of typing. For example, you may only need to enter "t t m" to get the rather elaborate string "Transactions of the Royal Society of Tropical Medicine and Hygiene" in your journal name field. It gets even better if the index extract also displays the actual number of hit records, thus showing the comparative popularity of each suggested item. This is helpful when choosing between several alphabetically related terms, yet it should equally be possible to overrule this feature or temporarily neutralize it, otherwise no new index terms can be added. Although indexes are very useful for enhancing uniformity and thus boosting retrieval, it should not be forgotten that one of the purposes of PBS is the generation of reference lists. Many authors use different formats of their names (e.g., one or more initials). If during manual data entry you revert the author name to its "standardized" format, the resulting bibliographic references will, strictly speaking, not be correct. Input-validation tables, defining what type of data (alphabetic, numeric, alphanumeric, etc.) are allowed in what field or whether certain compulsory fields cannot be left empty may further optimize data integrity and decrease flexibility.

IMPORTING EXTERNAL RECORDS

Ever more electronic records are becoming available from Internet databases. When these can easily be imported into the PBS, adding new records to the system almost becomes a zero-effort action, afterwards offering the advantages of fast retrieval and flexible reformatting. Many database providers are offering their data for downloading in a recyclable format.

On a technical level, the importing of electronic records is only possible if the import files conform to the internal structure of the PBS. The more complex this structure, the more difficult it is to prepare acceptable input files. In the easiest case, the source database provides an output format tailored to match the structure of your PBS or this internal structure conforms to a standardized data interchange format. In this case, no data manipulation is necessary, but this will be the exception rather than the rule. Therefore, many PBS provide made-to-measure import profiles that can convert records downloaded from specific online databases to their own format. *Endlink*, *Biblio-Links*, and *Capture* are the reformatting modules matching *EndNote*, *ProCite*, and *Reference Manager*, respectively. Sophisticated PBS may offer hundreds of such conversion modules. However, even then, certain sources may not be provided for. As far as the data structure is concerned, some PBS are quite severe, whereas others are more forgiving. Evidently, the more lenient a system is, the less adequately structured the imported records may turn out to be. Some PBS vendors are willing to add new profiles; provided the source database/host combination has a sufficiently broad user base or you are willing to pay for their creation. But then again, conversion modules may be inaccurate or incomplete or you may have tinkered with the internal structure of the records. Therefore, it is a boon if you can edit existing profiles or create new ones, tailored to your specific needs. Originally, these reformatting profiles were separate modules distributed individually or in group(s). Current PBS tend to integrate these often abundant profiles within the main program.

Automatic duplication detection is a time-saving feature. This is achieved either during import, comparing each individual new record of the uploaded file to the records already present in the database, or acting on the whole database at a later time, as a batch procedure. Again, it is an asset if you can define the criteria deciding whether two records are considered duplicates, or are prompted to judge each suspected duplicate individually. In this way, you can choose between a rigid and a more forgiving approach.

Uploading records from other databases produced with the same PBS can be considered a special case of electronic import, yet there may be mutually incompatible field or document-type definitions between two such databases. Merging complete databases is a more complex matter, as it may be necessary to avoid duplicates, to keep original record numbers, or to maintain a specific ranging order.

MODIFYING RECORDS (EDIT)

Many helpful features for creating records are equally relevant when editing them: using only relevant (i.e., non-empty) fields versus the complete data sheet; various copy, cut and paste capabilities; and so forth. Other important features are the maximum number of records that can be modified simultaneously using global editing and the corresponding qualitative capacities, such as full-record modifications versus only within specific fields, and case-specific versus case-independent. Having the edit functionality available at all times is more comfortable than when it constitutes an individual module to be accessed separately. Some systems allow external editors to be used instead of the standard one provided within the system.

SEARCHING THE DATABASE (RETRIEVAL)

Index-Based Retrieval

Some PBS generate one general index, with terms extracted from all meaningful fields, whereas others create field-specific indexes, so you can, for example, limit the search to title words or keywords, discarding less relevant information from abstracts or author addresses. Field-specific indexes are not only an advantage when searching but also when the input module allows index-assisted authority control. Being able to view (part of the [field-specific] index [preferably showing the number of hits for each item]) is essential for quality control. They make it feasible to systematically track down typos and alphabetically related notions. Some systems can also generate field-specific lists in descending order of frequency, so you can easily spot the most popular authors, keywords or journals in a database. Often, when field-specific indexes are supported, these are limited in number or cannot be defined by the user.

Not all fields are indexed the same way. Most PBS offer more than one indexing technique, making a distinction between "text" and "non-text" fields. In text fields, such as "title" or "abstract," each word is indexed separately. In non-text fields, the full contents are indexed as a coherent unit, so standard combinations such as "journal name," "series title," or "corporate authors," are represented as one index entry. In this way, the composite search terms will be found in one step and need not be retrieved by combining their constituent parts. Some systems have a limited maximum length for index entries, even when the corresponding field contents have no such limits. For "text" fields, this is generally not a handicap, but "non-text" index entries often need several dozens of characters to uniquely identify them (e.g., long journal names or series titles, including subsections). Customizable stop lists can keep less meaningful words out of the indexes. It is even better when separate stop lists for each specific database or database type can be maintained. Special types of stop lists may be field specific, e.g., to ignore prepositions in author names (De, La, Le, Van, Von, etc.) during retrieval of ranging. In contrast to stop lists, some systems opt for the opposite principle; only terms specified by a go list are included in the indexes. Another related mode of indexing avoids irrelevant terms by selecting only strings explicitly marked during input or editing. Other characteristics (repeatable versus non-repeatable fields, alphanumeric versus numeric data, decimal versus integers, author versus non-author fields, etc.) can also influence the way fields are indexed or sorted within the index.

Indexes are generally maintained using one of two basic methods: "real-time" updating brings the database up to date immediately after modifying records, so they are fully reliable at any time. The second method consists of batch updating; the indexes are not updated until the user decides it is time to do so or has programmed the system to do it at fixed time intervals. No time is wasted while creating or editing records. The disadvantage is that the modified information is not immediately incorporated in the index. Some programs offer an additional sequential searching of that part of the database that differs from the index (e.g., the new or modified records).

Basic Retrieval Patterns

As indicated earlier, many PBS are fundamentally limiting; they assume that each new operation is meant to limit the current set. This is fine as long as you want to narrow your search, but it may not permit returning to previous steps to adjust the search formulation. In this case, the option to "select all records" is essential to start new searches. Although this straightforward design will often suffice for its purposes, the set building alternative can offer a more refined retrieval. In many traditional systems, each search formulation is executed on the complete database and its results constitute an autonomous set kept during the rest of the session. In this way, you can return to previously executed searches or combine them with later sets without needing to reactivate them. Backtracking is a comparable feature that allows you to go back one or several steps to previous screens, selections, commands, or menus. Also useful is the ability to retain the previous search formulation so that it can be modified without the need for retyping. Records marked for display should also be kept as autonomous sets to be printed or downloaded in their own right. It can also be useful to drop specific sets from the current session survey in order to get a clearer view of the search strategy used so far. Being able to permanently save specific sets so they can be recalled in later sessions is also helpful. This is especially true when it not only holds for sets of records but also for sets of commands or search histories so that the same combination of commands can be used in subsequent sessions. This is essential if you intend to use your PBS for SDI purposes.

Refining Retrieval

Retrieval options can be rather basic and limited, but a wide variety of extra possibilities exists—some rather evident, others pretty ingenious. A basic requirement is the capacity to combine individual search terms and previously defined sets. Generally, this implies the use of the Boolean operators AND, OR, and NOT. These may be freely applicable or compulsory, which is helpful for novice users but may preclude some types of more advanced search formulations. Serious searching may involve quite intricate combinations with various sets of (nested) parentheses.

Most PBS offer the ability to limit the search to specific fields. Like the Boolean operators, this can be optional, assisted by field tables or compulsory, being integrated in the search dialog. More refined operators include "begins with . . . ," "ends with . . . ," and the radical "field is (not) empty." Consultation of field-specific indexes showing the number of actual postings for each index entry is helpful and points out alphabetically related items, including their comparative popularity. Just seeing this information on the screen is helpful, but being able to select your search terms directly from these index extracts is still better. Some systems allow you to choose just one index term; others allow several, either activating each index term as a separate search set or combining them in an OR relation (or doing both). These can be optional or the system default, or a combination. In the best case, default retrieval fields can be customized (i.e., which fields are searched and in what order).

As explained earlier, not all fields are necessarily indexed in the same way. It certainly is an advantage if you can choose between text and non-text indexing and retrieval for some fields. Depending on your preferences, you can select records by either searching for the full-field contents (e.g., "American Journal of Tropical Medicine and Hygiene" in the journal name field), which gives you the unambiguous result, or by combing some of the constituent parts (e.g., "American" and "Tropical," both in the journal name field), which is helpful when you do not know the exact name.

Using lots of different fields can guarantee highly sophisticated output formats and ultra-specific retrieval (e.g., first authors only), but sometimes it is more helpful to combine several related fields. For example, when you are looking for all publications by a specific individual, it is not important whether he or she is a first author, a secondary author, or a book editor. Some PBS offer this possibility of implicitly combining similar fields under one field group tag.

Proximity operators are more narrowing than the Boolean AND relation; they demand that two words must appear within the same field, the same paragraph, the same sentence, or a self-selected (exact or maximum) number of words separated, in either specified or indiscriminate order. Comparative searching allows you to select records by requesting that the contents of a field are equal to, larger than, or smaller than a certain value (e.g., publication date). Interval searching is especially valid for numerical data, but it can also be useful for alphabetical data, such as a range of author names.

A special retrieval option is that of lateral searching; while viewing records, specific strings (e.g., title words or keywords) can be marked, which are then automatically posted as new search terms. A more elegant option is when you can directly jump to the other (hyper)linked records in which this search term is featured (e.g., by simply clicking on them). In this way, you can navigate around the database. This is a very attractive feature when you want to look at, for instance, all available titles within a specific series when this series was not even a search term in the first place.

Alphabet-Related Devices

It is obvious that while searching for specific words or strings, a number of alphabetically related items may be missed. This can be overcome by index browsing, which alerts you to the closest alternatives. An easier way is (implicit) truncation. Most systems offer a way to activate or deactivate right-hand truncation. For instance, "immune*" yields "immunity," "immunodeficiency," "immunology," and so forth. Left-hand truncation is less common and, if available, often only on a non-text field basis. For instance, "*diseases" yields "infectious diseases," "sexually transmitted diseases," and so forth. Full left truncation, in which "*ology" yielding "epidemiology," "immunology," and "parasitology," is rather rare in index-based systems. In sequential searches, however, this should be no more difficult to execute than right-hand truncation. A powerful variant of automatic truncation of non-text fields is sometimes referred to as "embedded wild cards." Only the first letter(s) of some of the constituents are needed to find (among others) the correct item. For instance, "j = j e m" (in which "j =" stands for "journal name") finds "journal of electron microscopy," "journal of emergency medicine," and "journal of experimental medicine." A third possibility is internal truncation or masking, in which one or more characters within a word are replaced by a wildcard. For instance, "h*matology" yields both "hematology" and "haematology." Truncation or masking symbols can replace either an exact number or just any number of characters, ranging from zero to a dozen or more. Stemming is a comparable feature, which includes related forms such as adverbial or conjugated forms, based on fixed or manually customizable lists or on more sophisticated artificial intelligence-based devices.

Some retrieval systems distinguish between uppercase and lowercase; others do not. Ideally, you can choose whether to search in a case-specific way or not. This may be attractive to immediately distinguish terms that are always written in uppercase or with a peculiar mixture of uppercase and lowercase, but mostly the use of initial uppercase letters will be decided by whether this word appears at the beginning of a sentence or not. Just as it is interesting to combine several fields to one field tag, it is also helpful if you can specify a number of characters (including diacritics and foreign characters) to be searched together by default (yet be able to search them individually when necessary).

Subject-Related Retrieval Devices

Just as (field) indexes and other authority files alert for alphabetically related terms, the thesaurus shows related subject terms (synonyms, related, higher- and lower-level terms). These may function as optional suggestions or as an obligatory vocabulary police, rejecting all terms that are not explicitly defined in the thesaurus. Some powerful thesauri can automatically activate all lower-level terms ("explode"). For example, using the keyword "Africa" may yield only a small proportion of the relevant results. Using the explode feature, however, recall is far higher because records with keywords such as "Nigeria," "Rwanda," or "Zimbabwe" are also selected, even though the term "Africa" itself cannot be found in these records. However powerful a thesaurus may be, if the keywords are not applied in a consistent way, the thesaurus loses a lot of its functionality. During manual input, automatic thesaurus checking may minimize this, but when importing records from different external databases, the chances that keywords are used consistently may become quite low.

If an explicit thesaurus is lacking, the explode function can sometimes be emulated by defining a set of trigger terms; these automatically activate a number of self-specified search terms. These can be maintained using, for instance, a synonym list or a number of individually saved search strategies. Synonym lists need not necessarily include meaningful alternatives. They may include sound-alikes and look-alikes. This may be especially helpful when the database contains scanned and OCRed records.

Sophisticated Retrieval Techniques

The retrieval techniques discussed so far are relatively straightforward and logical. In order to guarantee useful results, the search terms should conform to certain conditions (e.g., authors should alphabetically conform to an author index, and keywords should conform to the hierarchic thesaurus or synonym list). Certain highly sophisticated techniques try to overcome these one-dimensional limitations in such a way that natural language can be adequately interpreted, so the information need not be entered with the rigid Boolean operators in mind. These techniques are often based on artificial intelligence techniques, using probabilistic relevance ranking, fuzzy set searching, and the like. This may imply special computer algorithms that automatically combine the search terms in an OR relation and count actual postings and compare relative positions. Others go one step further and find out which other words often appear in close proximity with the actual search terms and suggest or include these as extra search terms. Sound-alikes and look-alikes may also be activated on an artificial intelligence basis instead of an explicit customizable list.

Such less common techniques can be quite useful when dealing with unstructured texts. When searching for structured bibliographic records, however, it is not unwise to keep Boolean operators and field-specific indexes as a basis. This basis may then be supplemented with these extra features, but in real life these do not always lead to fully orthodox results. Another essential drawback of natural language retrieval techniques is their language dependence; if they are successful, they may be so with one specific language only.

A special retrieval issue is that of multiple database searching. Some of the large online hosts offer the possibility of accessing several databases at the same time, thus reducing the need to search individual databases consecutively. They may also allow searching for specific terms from the database menu, in which case they show the number of hits in each database, so you know which databases resemble each other and use the same field indicators and/or keywords systems.

Searching a PBS need not necessarily be limited to the actual database records physically stored on the computer or local network drive. Nowadays, retrieval may go way beyond these, automatically connecting with a plethora of World Wide Web resources (online databases, external library catalogs). Some offer modules based on client-server technology, which allows searching in external Z39.50-enabled databases while still using your own PBS interface. This client-server-based searching over the Internet may result in amazingly fast and diversified retrieval performances and may offer the highest degree of streamlined import of external records by making it possible to just drag and drop records from one database to the other. On the downside, using a PBS retrieval engine in this way may not match the degree of sophistication offered by searching the remote databases directly.

DISPLAY

The immediate attraction of PBS very much depends on the way the databases can be browsed and how search results are displayed. The least flexible PBS offer one fixed format (per record type), showing all fields included in the data definition tables, whether or not they are actually used in the record, and always in the same sequence. Having the choice between different presentation formats is an advantage, and the options should be clearly indicated. Toggling between several formats is a boon, especially if the options include a (customizable) short list, showing, e.g., 25 records per screen, each limited to one line. Ideally, you can define which fields are displayed in what order. This default can then be overruled at any time.

While viewing, a number of scrolling possibilities should be allowed: go to the top or the bottom of a record (especially when more than one screen per record is involved); go to the next or previous record; or go to the beginning or the end of the current set. When displaying search results, hit terms should be highlighted so it is immediately clear why a record was selected. It is also useful if you can quickly navigate toward these search terms within these records (e.g., with "next hit" or "previous hit" options or buttons). During record display, selection and deselection of specific items should be possible. Such records are best kept as autonomous sets that can later be combined with other sets or printed or downloaded in their own right.

Some PBS can only display the most recently created set; therefore, in order to view an earlier set, the corresponding search needs redoing. The option of displaying just any set ad hoc, using cursor or set number to select them, is far more elegant. Ideally, you can specify (a) specific (range of) record(s) to be displayed within a specific set. Another aspect is the sequence in which the records are displayed. Early systems tended to display the records in the order in which they were physically stored in the database. Although records can be sorted in a number of ways before they are printed or downloaded, this opportunity is not equally obvious when displaying them. However, this is an agreeable option and it adds to overall clarity if records can be viewed in a certain order [e.g., alphabetical (by author, or any other meaningful alphanumeric field such as "journal name") or in (reverse) chronological order (e.g., by publication date)]. Now many PBS offer several ways of arranging records before display, but these may be based on a limited sort key (e.g., only the first few characters), which only creates an approximate order. Ranging can be quite refined though, including several sort levels (e.g., year of publication, then authors, then title).

Within different windows, a selection of several types of data can be displayed simultaneously (e.g., short list, full record, preview of the formatted record, index extract, available operators, and overview of search sets). The presentation is quite dynamic, as you can resize these windows at any time and choose which fields to display in what order in the short lists. Within the short lists, you can range the records on a specific key just by clicking on the corresponding field label.

The advantages of the ability to store and display images or graphics are discussed earlier. Next to the issues of linking or integrating techniques and (internal versus external) image viewers, there remains the question of flexibility: can the images be enlarged or reduced? Are thumbnails available? etc.

PRINTING AND DOWNLOADING (OUTPUT)

Record Selection

A first question to be addressed is that of record selection. Do you need to print or download a complete search set, or can you specify a subset using either (fixed) record numbers or relative positions within the set, indicate ranges or mark records? Limitations of the number of records that can be printed or downloaded can be a nuisance, but if they can be defined and customized by the systems manager, such limits can be advantageous for keeping public access output under control.

Record Formatting

One of the essential advantages of putting bibliographic information in a number of separate fields is that you can reconstruct these records in many different ways. The advantage is obvious when you consider the hundreds of divergent bibliographic styles that are being used by different scientific journals. With a good PBS, reformatting a complete bibliography is generally a matter of less than a minute. Most popular formats (e.g., ANSI, Harvard, Science, and Vancouver) should be provided with the program. If you are allowed to customize these formats or create new ones, the possibilities are virtually unlimited, and if you can freely construct new document types, this is an absolute must in order to be able to export them in a meaningful way.

For both the largely inflexible and the fully customizable systems, there exists a whole range of levels of detail. Some allow certain fields to be printed, without allowing any change to the field contents or their respective order. Others allow fields to be selected in any chosen order or allow conditional relations between fields (e.g., "if A then B, else C"). This can result in highly sophisticated nesting of instructions. Some allow formatting within individual fields (e.g., to define the number of words or characters for each field). This is especially important for adequate author formatting or short lists (e.g., using one line for each reference, restricting the length of each of the fields included to fit into self-specified columns). Some PBS go as far as to select what types of characters or how many of each should be printed; for instance, only upper case letters, only numerals, change all lowercase letters to uppercase, or remove all punctuation. Some formatting issues, such as absolute positioning use exact instead of relative values (e.g., to start printing field "a" at "position 25").

Some fields tend to inspire more attention of system designers than others. Special provisions for author fields include inversion of initials, removal or inclusion of blanks or periods, using ";" "&," or "and" before the last author, conditional selection of the number of authors reproduced (e.g., when there are more than six authors, print only the first three plus the formula "et al."), and so forth. Some PBS feature special modules that manage a number of alternatives for each journal name, such as full name, Index Medicus abbreviation (a de facto standard, but limited to biomedical sciences), other (self-selected) abbreviations (e.g., regardless of which form is actually stored in the record's journal name field). Again, receiving such authoritative lists of alternatives with the system is a boon, but being able to modify or supplement it may remain essential. Certain output styles may feature their own idiosyncratic journal abbreviations that cannot always be foreseen in the PBS, and the PBS's formatting language. Conditional capitalization of such elements as author names or titles may be difficult to incorporate correctly. The same is true for cited page indication, where page 1134–1137: may need to be reformed to "1134–7" or simply truncated to "1134." Comparable routines to those of the journal name and journal abbreviation fields may also be offered for publication date fields, thus providing, for instance, different ranges and formats for year, month, and day values.

Bibliography Formatting

Other issues concern the overall look of the formatted bibliography, such as ranging the references: sorting on several levels (freely choosing the fields involved), combining different sort directions, and page formatting (defining margins, indenting and numbering references, providing customizable bibliography headings, and so forth). Again, foreign characters and diacritics can cause trouble if there is no provision for them. In some PBS, you can define a sort order integrating both standard and special characters. As with display, it can be useful for highlighting the hit terms, but this is generally easier for printing than for downloading purposes. Page formatting options may be integrated within the specific output styles or be system-wide. The first method is the most comfortable one if all the styles you need are provided for accurately, as you will not need to think about these intricacies when generating a reference list. If you have deviant document types, need extra output styles, or simply want to be able to experiment with these settings, system-wide options may be more suitable.

Of course, the more options that are available the more confusing the overall picture becomes. When all formatting instructions are fully integrated within the same output style, each variant calls for a separate combination, so the number of different styles quickly becomes overwhelming. Some PBS group the relevant parameters and output formats in a number of subsequent levels (e.g., basic record format, additional features, sorting order, page format, physical output device driver), so each level offers a limited amount of alternatives, but because each item can be combined with each item from each other level, a few possibilities on each level lead to a vast array of different output formats. WYSIWYG previews of printed output on the screen offer a last control and can avoid wasteful printing of incorrectly formatted reference lists.

Output does not always imply printing or downloading lists of bibliographic records. If index surveys can be produced easily, generating subject or author lists, featuring record numbers or full bibliographic descriptions linked with each keyword or author, becomes child's play. More essential is the possibility of exporting a complete database in a generally accepted interchange format, thus allowing the transfer of the database to another (newer and more versatile) PBS.

For the output modules, the Internet has inspired PBS producers to come up with new provisions. Not only do references to Web pages or e-mails need to be printed in an adequate fashion, but you may also need to provide bibliographies in HTML or XML format to put them on your private or corporate Web site or send search results by e-mail.

Word Processing

As discussed earlier, an important output-related feature is the ability to combine the PBS's database functionality with word processing programs. While writing the manuscript, some kind of pointer is inserted at the place of the in-text citation. This pointer can be a reference-specific anchor (e.g., the record number) or a retrieval-based key (typical an author-publication year combination). Generally, these pointers are inserted as the result of a genuine retrieval action that is launched from within the word processor, either while citing each record individually or in a group later. When ambiguity arises (e.g., when more than one publication in the database conforms to these search criteria), the more sophisticated systems will be able to deal with this (e.g., by offering a selection opportunity), and when necessary, they will provide multiple notations, such as "1995a" and "1995b." When, finally, the bibliographic aspects of the manuscript need to be generated, the corresponding references are retrieved from the database and both the in-text citations and the reference list are formatted in a style appropriate for the specific target journal to which the manuscript is submitted.

This kind of integration can be quite sophisticated. In the best case, the PBS software, upon installation, adds extra database-related menu options to the toolbars of the word processor. Even when there is no integration whatsoever, it may prove useful to generate the reference list separately with a PBS rather than typing it from scratch in the word processor, thus avoiding typos, formatting errors, and omissions—provided the records were entered correctly in the database and the right bibliographic output format is available and accurate.

INTERFACE- AND MANAGEMENT-RELATED ISSUES

Networking

Although PBS are essentially personal software programs, they can also be very useful for more than one user (e.g., smaller libraries and research units). Obviously, not all microcomputer-based PBS are network products. But in the best case, the system is fully network-compatible, including full file and record locking. Several users can then access the same database simultaneously, but editing specific records is automatically limited to one user at a time to prevent data corruption. The option of mounting PBS databases on a Web server and offering access to them worldwide is clearly gaining in popularity.

CONCLUSION

Personal Bibliographic Systems are specialized software products, related to, but using a basically different approach from general-purpose database management systems or traditional electronic library catalogs. Within their own niche, PBS come in all sorts and varieties and can differ strongly in basic concept. The various individual features reviewed in this entry together offer an enormous potential of attractive characteristics. When looking at individual systems, however, it is obvious that none has all the aces. Each package has its own strong and weak points; certain features will generally impress you, but you will equally find it a pity that other aspects are not dealt with as ingeniously as in some of its rival systems. Also, some amazing bells and whistles may hide fundamental shortcomings. Moreover, the usefulness of the various features will be evaluated differently by individual users, either for personal or for professional (e.g., in a library) reasons. Instead of advertising one specific PBS, this survey points out the major pros and cons (or even the very existence) of the various features that may be encountered in this type of software. Potential users should define their own list of preferences and priorities and then select the real-life PBS that offers the best compromise.

BIBLIOGRAPHY

1. Brahmi, F.A.; Gall, C. Retrieval comparison of EndNote to search MEDLINE (Ovid and PubMed) versus searching them directly. Med. Ref. Serv. Q. **2004**, *23* (3), 25–32.
2. Brahmi, F.A.; Gall, C. EndNote and Reference Manager citation formats compared to instructions to authors in top medical journals. Med. Ref. Serv. Q. **2006**, *25* (2), 49–57.
3. East, J.W. Academic libraries and the provision of support for users of personal bibliographic software: a survey of Australian experience with EndNote. Libr. Autom. Syst. Inform. Exc. **2001**, *32* (1), 64–70.
4. East, J.W. Z39.50 and personal bibliographic software. Libr. Hi Tech J. **2003**, *21* (1), 34–43.

5. Hanson, T., Ed. *Bibliographic Software and the Electronic Library*; University of Hertfordshire Press: Hertfordshire, U.K., 1995; 136.
6. Harrison, M.; Summerton, S.; Peters, K. EndNote training for academic staff and students: the experience of the Manchester Metropolitan University library. New Rev. Acad. Libr. **2005**, *11* (1), 31–40.
7. Kelly, J.A. Downloading information using bibliographic management software: End-user software. In *Encyclopedia of Library and Information Science*; Marcel Dekker: New York, 1997; Vol. 59, Suppl. 22, 111–119.
8. Kessler, J.; Van Ullen, M.K. Citation generators: generating bibliographies for the next generation. J. Acad. Libr. **2005**, *31* (4), 310–316.
9. Koopman, A. Bibliographic citation management software for Web applications. Internet Ref. Serv. Q. **2002**, *7* (1/2), 99–112.
10. Mattison, D. Bibliographic research tools round-up. Searcher **2005**, *13* (Oct), 16–27.
11. McGrath, A. RefWorks investigated—An appropriate bibliographic management solution for health students at King's College London? Libr. Inform. Res. **2006**, *30* (94), 66–73.
12. Nicoll, L.H.; Quellette, T.H.; Bird, D.C.; Harper, J.; Kelley, J. Bibliography database managers; a comparative review. Comput. Nurs. **1996**, *14* (1), 45–56.
13. Schoonbaert, D. Personal bibliographic systems (PBS) for the PC: A generic survey of features. Electron. Libr. **1997**, *15* (1), 31–46.
14. Schoonbaert, D. Personal bibliographic systems. In *Encyclopedia of Library and Information Science*; Marcel Dek-ker: New York, 2002; Vol. 70, Suppl. 33, 326–362.
15. Sieverts, E. End-user software. In *Encyclopedia of Library and Information Science*; Marcel Dekker: New York, 1996; Vol. 57, Suppl. 20, 154–175.
16. Stigleman, S. Bibliography programs do Windows. Database April/May **1996**, *19*, 57–66.

41 Collection Management Systems

Perian Sully

CONTENTS

INTRODUCTION

Good collection management is of key importance to the ongoing care and preservation of museum objects. As long as there have been computers in museums, museums have used them to manage collection objects.[1] The professional practices of object care which govern a museum collection manager's duties have not changed significantly for many decades. Instead, the tools and resources available to the collection manager have changed information management dramatically, not the least of which is how the computer can manage and organize disparate types of data. Evolving technological capabilities have led to a number of advancements in collection management systems (CMSs), and today's software packages regularly incorporate features which were discussed as theoretical 30 years ago. Although the core function of managing collection-related data has remained constant, development of software for collection management has been in lockstep with shifting museum theories about public access, educational missions, and community engagement.[2] As a result, CMS packages can be robust and powerful tools for inventory of, accessibility to, and contextualization of museum objects.

This entry is designed to assist museum professionals who have never been involved with selecting or implementing a CMS, or who have not done so recently. The entry discusses what a CMS is and which features make it desirable for a museum setting. Also covered are explanations of key concepts, such as standards, which are frequently presumed to be understood, but their importance may be difficult to grasp, especially if those staff leading the project are not museum information management specialists.

The main body of the entry is an overview of the planning, selection, implementation, and maintenance process—the four phases of the project's lifecycle. Determining institutional needs, outlining project goals, and selecting standards are some of the key components of the planning phase. For the selection phase, this entry covers some of the decisions which must be made when deciding to purchase or create a CMS as well as some tips for working with vendors. Training, administrative controls, and the data conversion process are all covered within the "Implementation" section. Maintenance is the most important phase of the four, and this entry stresses the importance of data preservation, administrative roles, and sharing information.

Ending the entry are brief discussions about future developments, including open-source initiatives, experiments in social tagging and public interaction, integration of library and archival materials, and digital asset management tools. A brief list of recommended reading and resources is also included.

DEFINITIONS

Database

A database is a collection of structured records or data, arranged in such a way within a computer that allows a software program, such as a CMS, to access that data. Depending on the programming which organizes the records into electronic tables, a database can be more or less efficient at managing a certain quantity of tables. Because of this, some databases are better at managing information about a large number of objects—along with their associated donor information, locations, and the like—than others are.

Collection Management System

A CMS is a piece of software which facilitates how the user inputs, sees, and retrieves data from the database. It is designed for use within museums and private collections for managing artworks, historical artifacts, anthropological and horticulture specimens, and living collections, just to name a few examples. Although some database management software packages are modified and used for the purpose of museum management, including FileMaker Pro and Microsoft Access, because they are not specifically designed to manage museum collections, and because they do not contain certain features common to CMS, they do not technically fall under the CMS umbrella. Some of those features can be added to these basic systems, so these types of software are included in this discussion.

Please note these definitions when they are referred to within the text of this entry. Comments about a database refer to the set of data being managed, whereas a reference to the CMS is referring to the software system managing the database.

HISTORICAL OVERVIEW

Throughout the history of museums, paper-based systems have been developed to manage and organize collection inventories and scholarly information. Most systems were institution-specific, their methodology known only to their creators. As the size of museum collections increased, these methods for recording object information became less effective for organizing complex relationships between different types of data. Often this data included not only basic artifact descriptions and locations, but also artist biographical information, donor details, press releases, exhibition lists, and scholarly research.

By the mid-1960s, advances in computer technology made it conceivable that some museums might be able to harness the organizational power of computer mainframes in order to more effectively manage their collections. As early as 1966, computer mainframe manufacturers were consulting with museums, such as the Fort Worth Museum of Science and History.[3] Despite the early adoption of computers in some museums, it would take another 20–30 years before the vast majority of small museums used computers to assist with collection inventory practices. During this period of increased adoption of computerized collection management programs, shifting institutional ideologies often prompted the addition of new features which were outside the scope of pure collection inventory activities, such as adding the ability to share information and related multimedia on the Internet, fields for tracking copyright information or traveling exhibitions, or modules to manage lexicons and thesauri.[4]

With the advent of the World Wide Web in the 1990s, many museum administrators realized that the information contained within the collection database could be presented on the museum's Web page, thereby increasing public access to rarely seen collection objects. Although some museums had shared their computerized collection information with other institutions throughout the late 1970s and 1980s, the ease of online publishing and digital photography in the 1990s allowed even more museums to share their collections.[5] Indeed, funding bodies and professional organizations stressed the importance of making collections accessible to a wide range of potential stakeholders. As a result, CMSs evolved to include tools for presenting collection data and images on the museum's Web site, as well as for facilitating the electronic sharing of information with other institutions.

Today, a majority of museums have Web sites with some information about their collections available. This may be as simple as a brief textual description of the collections or as complex as a fully CMS-driven site.[6] The current challenge for many museums is to make that information presentable and relevant to the online audience. These museums are utilizing a number of new Web-based technologies to bridge the gap between static collection data and an engaged public. Collection management system vendors are slowly changing their products to address these new needs, but direct involvement by museums in the development process is often necessary to initiate these changes. Although there is increasing demand for the CMS to interface with the Web site in order to provide public access to collections, it is worth keeping in mind that the system is, first and foremost, a tool for managing museum collections.

PURPOSE OF A COLLECTION MANAGEMENT SYSTEM

In her entry for this Encyclopedia, Marla Misunas addresses the various duties which a museum collection manager must perform in order to ensure that collection objects are available for future generations. One could argue that one of the primary duties of the collection manager is a very specialized type of inventory control. The collection manager must encode each object with a unique number; record all the descriptive details about the object, including its title, where it came from, what kind of object it is, its age, its measurements, and what it looks like; respond to research requests about the object; track which exhibition it is currently in or has been in; generate loan and donation forms; fulfill audit requests about the collection's value; and know exactly where the object is at any given moment. Such a complex job requires the assistance of specialized organizational systems or tools. As discussed above, CMSs have changed in response to the needs of the collection manager. As there are different types of museums, so too are there different types of CMS. Some CMSs are better-suited toward natural history collections which are often large and need specific taxonomic vocabularies installed. Some are specialized for ethnic collections which need special language fields. Others are specifically designed for large art collections with high exhibition and accessions volume. A few are designed for the small museum with modest needs.

Depending on the product, the vendor or programmer, the type of collection it is designed for, its age, and its internal database structure, a CMS offers a wide variety of features. The most basic CMS has a few hundred fields available, while the more robust packages can handle several thousand fields. Despite this wide range, there are core fields which are standard to all systems.

Facilitating Object Inventory—Basic Identifiers

All of today's CMSs offer a number of different fields for organizing specific collection information. This information is required for the basic handling of collection inventory practices and includes fields for recording accession number, date and type of accession, artifact title, the name of the creator or author, the source of the object—either donor or seller, a description of the piece, the date and place of the object's creation, and monetary value.

In addition to the basic information above—often called "tombstone" information because with the exception of valuation and sometimes source information, it reflects the text presented on exhibition wall labels—every CMS has fields devoted to recording the location of the object. Some CMS can even help the registrar track object movement if the artifact is out on exhibition or being moved between facilities. The ability to easily create lists of items within a given location greatly facilitates inventory auditing processes.

Donor Information or Provenance

All CMSs contain a source and/or credit line field. These fields can be powerful tools to assist the collection manager with determining the provenance of a work. The source and credit lines can be valuable to collection managers, as they frequently receive requests from donors asking to see a piece they have given to the institution in the past. Even development and fund-raising departments find this information useful, since that knowledge can help them tailor donation requests.

Also, for some museums, donor information can help them comply with one of the worldwide initiatives to repatriate cultural objects: objects which have been removed from their home countries or ethnic groups through looting, illegal sales, and cultural insensitivity. In some cases, like the North American Graves Protection and Repatriation Act (NAGPRA) of 1990 and various European initiatives about Nazi-looted artworks, these initiatives have the force of law and museums are required to comply. Even the Source field alone can help a provenance researcher determine if a piece falls under those laws and guidelines.

Notes

Unlike some systems in the past, when most individual fields could only manage around 250 characters worth of information,[7] CMSs today can handle a large number of free-text fields. A specific module can have a field dedicated to all of the miscellaneous information which does not necessarily fit within any of the defined fields. For example, a catalog record may have a whole tab specified "Notes," a section devoted to accession history, and within it there may be a free-text field labeled Accession Notes for unusual or interesting history about the accessioning process of the work. This eliminates the confusion which may happen if, for example, accessions and exhibition histories are placed in the same field.

Data Input, Organization, Exports, and Reports

It is critical to effectively input information into the system, organize it in a meaningful way, and allow for its use outside of the system. After all, data is only useful if you can do something with it! Collection management system packages have a variety of ways in which they allow information to be input, organized, and retrieved. First, CMSs have a variety of import applications, which allow the user to transfer electronic data from an older CMS, a database program, another institution, or even Microsoft Excel or Word files. Often this data must be converted into a form the CMS will accept, such as a Comma-Separated Value (CSV) or Extensible Markup Language (XML) file. This requires exporting the data from the initial source into the required format, but the widespread availability of programs with CSV and XML export capabilities makes this a relatively simple process. Of course, every CMS has fields to input data, but the organization and variety of those fields will vary greatly from system to system. The data conversion process involves mapping fields from the old CMS to the new one, rearranging the data if some fields do not match up, and performing data cleanup.

Once data is input, it is critical for the user to be able to organize the information in a meaningful way. Collection management system programs have a variety of searching and sorting options, and many systems even allow complicated searches to be saved for later retrieval by the user.

Finally, all CMSs have the ability to present the data as a report or as an electronic export. Some of these reports are programmed into the CMS, but many larger packages use a third-party report-writing program, such as Business Objects' Crystal Reports, for more complicated report-writing. These third-party programs can require specialized training to learn, which may be a consideration when selecting a CMS. Other systems can report in to Excel, Word, PDF, or their own proprietary format. As with the import functions already mentioned, CMS can export data for backup, data transfer, system migration, or collaborative purposes.

Multimedia Display

Today, digital images of artifacts are a necessary tool to help identify objects. These images are displayed within the object's catalog record, or they can be presented as a thumbnail view for quick visual browsing of items. Some CMSs can also store Microsoft Word or Excel documents, video and audio files, live links to Web sites, documents, images and multimedia files on the Internet, and even other computer programs.

In addition to the features listed above, CMSs can contain a number of other tools to assist users with managing and using collection information. These tools are not universal to every system, and the needs of the institution will determine if these additional features are necessary to the care and maintenance of the museum's collection. For some museums, the following are nice to have, but not necessary. For others, these tools are critical.

Tracking Historical Changes

All CMSs have the capability of storing current location, condition, ownership, and valuation information. Some CMSs have the added capability of tracking and presenting those changes, rather than only storing the current information. For example, tracking the condition of an object over a period of time can be helpful when evaluating the stability of an object for exhibition or conservation.

Notifications and Calendars

Automatic reminders to a collection manager can be exceptionally useful. The system can automatically send an e-mail to remind users of any number of tasks, such as checking on the condition of an object or renewing annual contracts.

Barcode and RFID Linking

Many museums now affix a barcode or radio-frequency identification (RFID) tag to their objects, for ease of tracking object movement. Although many CMSs have a field to record the barcode number of an artifact, some can also work with a barcode or RFID reader directly to instantly update movements.

Exhibition History

In some CMSs, the user can create a record for an exhibition which can link to an associated object record. The exhibition history of the work is recorded automatically within the object's catalog record and can be recalled for later use. Likewise, if an exhibition is upcoming, the object list can be run as a report to generate loan forms or wall labels.

Global Find and Replace

In any collecting institution, consistency of data input is of vital importance. Frequently, years of poorly enforced data input standards, changing rules, shifting terminology, and newly developed standards require changing text and information throughout the entire catalog or a select group of records. Some systems are better equipped to handle complicated find and replace tasks, but no matter the functionality, global find and replace is a powerful, and potentially dangerous tool. For example, during a recent data transfer, the author found nearly 1200 instances of the abbreviation "mtl" in place of the word "metal." Using the find and replace tools available within the CMS, the abbreviation was easily changed. However, care had to be taken in case the letter string "mtl" belonged within a word or phrase and did not, in those instances, mean "metal."

Administrative Gatekeeping Tools and Controls

Global find and replace is one of those features which an institution will want to limit to a trusted user, usually the system administrator. Data input, modifying terminology lists, searching certain fields, or being able to see sensitive information are only some of the types of uses that may not be appropriate for all users. Museums implementing a CMS will assign a system administrator, whose job it is to troubleshoot the system and assign the access levels for each user. For example, a curator may be assigned to the Curator access group, which would have the capability to correct information in very specific fields, but would not be allowed to change the information which is under the registrar's purview, such as identification number or condition. Likewise, the Volunteer access group is unlikely to be able to see the valuation of works or the sensitive personal information of donors.

Thesauri and Vocabularies

In order to ensure consistency of information, many museums adopt formalized thesauri and develop their own additional vocabularies. In the case of structured thesauri, such as *The Revised Nomenclature for Museum Cataloging*[8] or Getty's *Art and Architecture Thesaurus*,[9] the terms can be installed in the system as a dictionary, providing instant access to terminology within designated fields. In-house vocabularies can sometimes be input as a dictionary, or they can be part of a lookup list which can be modified by those users given adequate permissions.

Multilingual Dictionaries, Phonetic Searching, and Non-Latin Alphabets

Many museums have a variety of objects from different locales within their vaults. Sometimes, the translation of an inscription is entirely dependent upon a single scholar or curator. If the CMS can record the object information in the original language and alphabet, this increases the chances that another scholar may be able to confirm or correct the translation. In addition, some CMSs have built-in dictionaries for automatic language translation and phonetic searching—a useful feature when dealing with transliterated terminologies.

Web Interface

With the current importance placed upon Web-accessible collection databases, many CMS have built-in tools for presenting collection data on the museum's Web site.[10] Web site users can search for objects using search terms within available fields, selecting a predefined search, or browse objects by subject. Only certain types of information and objects, determined by museum staff, are displayed on the web site.

PROJECT LIFECYCLE—PLANNING, SELECTING, IMPLEMENTING, AND MAINTAINING

Transitioning to a new CMS is often a daunting task. The long-term integrity of the institution's information and the usability of the system relies upon careful research and planning in the earliest stages of the project.

The Canadian Heritage Information Network (CHIN) has, since 1995, conducted a regular review of available CMSs.[11] In addition to the pages devoted to selecting and managing a CMS, CHIN's Web site has several articles covering intellectual property, standards, digital imaging, and various new technologies such as podcasting and RSS feeds. As a companion to the *Collections Management Software Review*, CHIN has also developed an online course to teach the CMS project manager how to effectively plan and select, implement, and manage the collection software.[12]

The Getty Research Institute has also developed a number of guides, freely available on their Web site, covering topics necessary to understanding how to develop and maintain a digitization project.[13] The key topics the Getty volumes cover are imaging, metadata, online accessibility, and vocabularies and standards. Although the Getty materials may overlap with CHIN's, the Getty guidebooks provide broader context for many issues surrounding CMS and accessibility projects. Anyone beginning a CMS project is strongly encouraged to study both the CHIN's and the Getty Research Institute's materials.

Planning

Within the museum environment, it is usually the collection manager who is the first to recognize when a new CMS is needed for improving management and care of the collections. Sometimes it may be senior staff or even the governing board of directors who have determined that the museum's collections should be more accessible to staff or the public. In either case, a CMS is a major capital investment and requires initial and ongoing support from senior management and the board.

Once support is secured, a project manager must be assigned. The project manager will be responsible for guiding the planning and software selection processes. In contrast, a system administrator will be the person who is assigned the task of ongoing maintenance of the CMS. The project manager may become the system administrator. In some institutions, the collection manager may also be both project manager and system administrator.

The first step in any planning process is to determine the purpose and scope of the project. What does the institution realistically want to accomplish? Will the CMS only manage collection information or will it also be responsible for presenting the collection to the general public? Who has the authority to make specific decisions and who will be asked to provide input? During this time, the users and their needs must be identified. The project team should define and interview appropriate staff, surveying them for information about their requirements, how they would expect to use the system, and how they would like to see collection information used.

Second, the project manager must outline each phase of the project, assigning key staff members specific tasks and deadlines. It is helpful to draft a set of goals and objectives to enumerate the tasks.

Third, assess the resources required for each phase of the project and evaluate currently available technology, information, and staff. Remember that the project will almost certainly require more time and resources than anticipated. Although a great number of staff will be involved in the project, having a full-time person responsible for implementation and care of the software, as well as for the data itself, will help maintain the integrity of the data and ensure that other stakeholders are able to use the system effectively.

Evaluating the currently available technology and existing collection data will help with the assessment of costs and timelines. Can hardware and software already within the building be used for the project? Would it be compatible with a specific system or should all hardware be new? How much cleanup and standardization of existing collection records will be necessary? Which records will be transferred to the new system and which data is obsolete? Are there paper records which will need to be entered?

The CHIN's *Criteria Checklist*[14] is a wonderful tool for prioritizing needs and reminding the project team of the myriad features to consider. Even if CHIN's *Software Review* has not been updated recently, the *Criteria Checklist* is still a necessary resource that can be adapted for conducting the user needs interviews.

Budgeting

Once needs are determined and the project plan is outlined, research the costs for the software, hardware, training, and staff support necessary to maintain the CMS for at least the next 5 years. Contact the vendors with your needs and ask them for an initial estimate of the cost of the CMS and annual maintenance agreements; then add an extra 10–20% for contingencies. Once those figures are in hand, present them and the project plan to senior staff and the board of directors. The board will determine how much funding will be available for the project, which will help to narrow the selection.

Metadata Schemas and Vocabulary Standards

Although it may seem a bit premature, assuming that the museum's collection data is going to be shared with other institutions or the general public, the planning stage is a good time to start deciding the standards upon which the collection data will be organized, if they have not already been established. Many collection managers recognize the need for terminology consistency within their own institutions, but they may not be familiar with globally established standards or understand the term "metadata." When selecting a CMS which will be used to share information electronically, the variety of metadata schemas and controlled vocabularies available can quickly become confusing.

Metadata is a way to describe the individual information objects, like a record, within a system. Metadata does not have to be electronic—it could be the text on a paper library catalog card, for example—but for the purposes of this discussion, only the electronic forms of metadata will be discussed. The Getty Research Institute has published a detailed guide, *Introduction to Metadata*,[15] to help facilitate cultural heritage professionals understanding metadata and how it is important to anyone working with, presenting, and preserving information.

Metadata schemas are frameworks into which information can be inserted, to ensure that information is disseminated efficiently along various pathways. There are a number of different types but only a few will be useful to your specific institution. For most institutions, it is wise to choose a software that is compliant with a schema appropriate for use with the type of institution. Standards such as Categories for the Descriptions of Works of Art (CDWA),[16] Standard Procedures for Collections Recording Used in Museums (SPECTRUM),[17] Encoded Archival Description (EAD),[18] and Machine Readable Cataloging (MARC),[19] are designed specifically for use by museums, libraries, and archives, and these groups should consult with other similar institutions to determine the right one (or ones) to choose.

Controlled vocabularies are terminology dictionaries which have been decided upon by some authoritative body to describe discipline-specific types of objects, preferred spellings of place or artist names, and terms for art-making materials. There are also subject dictionaries which help define how objects should be classified for ease of searching. *The Revised Nomenclature for Museum Cataloging* is the successor of an early object classification system for describing historical objects in museums. The Getty Research Institute has published several vocabularies, including *The Art and Architecture Thesaurus* (AAT), *The Union List of Artist Names* (ULAN), and *The Getty Thesaurus of Geographic Names* (TGN).[20] None of these vocabularies completely encompasses all of the names and terms we might apply to an object's description. Therefore, it is sometimes necessary for an institution to create their own lexicon, which is used if no appropriate terminology is available within the controlled vocabularies. It is good practice to work with other similar, respected institutions to develop the internal lexicon. Each of these vocabularies may be used together within an institution's cataloging system (Figure 41.1).

There are a few important reasons why adhering to metadata schemas and selecting controlled vocabularies are a good idea. Metadata standards and vocabularies help data input consistency, allow for increased accessibility by cultural heritage groups, expand the possible uses of the data, and help assure that your collection information can be preserved. When choosing a CMS, many systems will already be compliant with certain metadata schemas and will be able to integrate controlled vocabularies automatically. Selecting the appropriate metadata standard and a package which can use controlled vocabularies will narrow down the choices during the selection process.

		Vocabulary used
Object name:	Purim Plate	Internal lexicon
Object title:	Vilno Purim Plate	Object title is often determined by the artist, left as "Untitled," or if an object is commonly known by a name, the museum will frequently retain that name
Object creator:	Mark Antokolsky	Getty *Union List of Artist Names*, ID #500028935
Object date:	1872 (5632)	Institutionally defined format of using the Gregorian date with the Hebrew date in parentheses
Object origin:	Vilnius (was Vilno), Lithuania	*Getty Thesaurus of Geographic Names*, ID # 7006521
Object medium:	Oil painting on eggshell porcelain	Getty *Art and Architecture Thesaurus*, ID #s 300178684 and 300263307, respectively

FIGURE 41.1 Example catalog record (fictional) utilizing different vocabularies.

Selection

Approaches

Once the institutional needs have been decided, it is time to evaluate various CMSs. Museums may choose one of four approaches:

1. Purchase a commercial software package which has most or all of the necessary features. Some compromises will usually have to be made, since a package will rarely be a perfect fit.
2. Purchase a commercial software package and work with the vendor to customize it according to the institution's specifications.
3. Purchase a development tool around which an application will be especially developed for the institution, by the institution.
4. Develop a customized system from the bottom up.

Although it may seem very expensive to purchase a commercial package, unless the institution has an in-house programmer who understands how the institution's data is used, how data transfer and standards function, and who can maintain or modify it, it is often more expensive in the long run to select options 3 and 4.

Options 1 and 2 may appear at first to have their limitations, especially when one considers the annual licensing fee, maintenance contract, cost of modifications, and that any modifications and upgrades will most likely have to go through the vendor. However, if product support is provided by the vendor, the institution will not need to have a dedicated programmer on staff, and any problems should be solved quickly and efficiently by those who deeply understand the product. One thing to consider when deciding whether to customize the system or not, is if professional practices are impeded by the software's functioning. It may be tempting to select a system which is a close match to the users' needs and not spend extra to add features or modify the interface, but if the interface and lack of features impede the desired workflow, the system will not be a good long-term investment. Do not allow the software to dictate the institution's practices, but be prepared to be flexible within reason. No software program will replicate your institution's workflow in every detail.

Narrowing Down the Options

As mentioned above, CHIN publishes several guides to help with the selection process. The products on the market change frequently, and so it is a good idea to contact like institutions and ask which CMS they use.

Once you have decided on several possible options, begin to examine them against your list of requirements. Also talk to other institutions to determine what their experiences have been with the company and the CMS. Scrutinize the vendor carefully and check their references. Are they reliable? How is their customer support? How long have they been in business and how many other installations have they performed? If possible, visit a site which has the software installed to see how it works outside of the ideal demonstration environment.

Of course cost is going to be a large consideration. Request a breakdown of the estimate; what the costs are for the licenses, annual maintenance, and training, as well as additional costs for customization, customer support, troubleshooting, data migration, and upgrades. It also does not hurt to ask if the source code can be placed in escrow in case the company dissolves at a later date. There can be an additional cost for this as well.

Finally, examine the technological needs of the system. What kind of hardware does the system require? Can the data be imported and exported easily? Is the system cutting edge or is it at the end of a technology phase? Is the necessary hardware compatible with other hardware in the institution and does it require specialized expertise to administer?

Look for vendors who are accustomed to working within your institution's discipline. Educating the vendor about your workflow will be much easier if the vendor has worked with similar institutions.

Vendor Demonstrations

Once the project manager has developed a short list of possible systems, ask each vendor for an on-site demonstration of the CMS. If possible, ask the vendor to preload some of the institution's data prior to the demonstration. This will help the project manager gauge the suitability of the CMS to the data. If this is not be possible, it is important to bear in mind that the data the vendor is demonstrating is "perfect" and not as idiosyncratic as the institution's own data might be.

During the demonstration, keep the requirements checklist nearby, take detailed notes, and ask plenty of questions. It also helps to outline a specific, real-world scenario and ask the representative to demonstrate how their product manages that situation. Remember that a vendor may promise that the product is capable of doing anything, but those capabilities may be at an extra cost or may not work quite as anticipated.

Decision-Making

After all of the demonstrations have been completed, compare notes against the requirements to narrow down the list even further. Send detailed specifications of any necessary modifications to the vendors and request a detailed quotation for modifications, training, support, licenses, and annual fees. Often vendors are willing to negotiate on price or to add extra features if they are part of the start-up package.

Once a final decision has been made, notify the vendor and request the license, and work with them to write the contract and fee schedule. All of the terms must be addressed within the contract. This includes installation timelines, warranties, return policies, training courses and procedures, data conversion, long-term support, and requested modifications. Assign someone with contracts experience to write or look over the document. In some cases, the vendor may provide a contract; however, it is recommended that the museum or its representatives work with the vendor directly to write the contract.

Implementation

The time needed to install the system will vary greatly depending upon the complexity of the system, the hardware needed to run it, the available personnel, if there are any modifications needed to be completed, and if there is other software which will need to interface with the CMS.

If the institution chooses to invite the vendor to conduct training classes, the project manager or system administrator will need to set dates which are convenient for the greatest number of potential users. Even though it may take some time before the CMS is ready for use by museum employees, some training will help if the system administrator must refamiliarize the staff in the future. At the very least, it is a good idea for the system administrator and at least one trusted "lieutenant" to attend the staff training as well as administrator training sessions for knowledge redundancy amongst the staff.

After training and installation, the system administrator must test and troubleshoot the system to ensure that it works to specification, a process called acceptance testing. This phase should occur prior to finalizing the deal and accepting the product from the developer, and should be written into the contract that the museum can return the product for a full refund if it does not meet specification during the acceptance testing. Be aware that long after testing and troubleshooting the new CMS, it is not uncommon for problems or situations to appear, sometimes due to oversight or shifting needs. It should be understood that extra monies should be budgeted for changes and fixes outside the scope of the support agreement.

If it has not been done already, data input standards will need to be defined. If using a metadata standard such as SPECTRUM or CDWA, refer to these standards to develop or refine the institution's data entry practices. Distill the metadata standard to common entry fields, such as artist's name, object date, object origin, and material, for example, and keep them available as an easy reference for the data cleanup phase. Do the same for key vocabulary terms. Although it may seem tedious, consistency of terminology, period and comma placement in specific fields, descriptive terms, or placement of artist or place names will help both staff and scholars find the materials they are looking for. If the CMS has that capability, input those standards into the appropriate field's help menu.

Data cleanup is likely to be the longest part of the implementation process. If there are many records and many inconsistencies, this process may take a year or more. Some institutions will transfer their data directly from the original system, but if there are problems with the records, those problems will simply exist in the new CMS. It is often worth the time for the original system to run parallel with the new one while the data is being cleaned. In some cases, exporting the data into a third software program such as Microsoft Excel, which has find and replace and sorting features, will help identify and fix errors at a glance. The system administrator and/or the collection manager may have to make some compromises to determine when something is "clean enough," as it is likely that other staff will be eager to use the new CMS. In this case, some fields will need to be cleaned after being imported into the system.

In many institutions, there are frequently unidentified problem records which will be revealed during the cleanup process, or during everyday use. It is helpful to reconcile those problems immediately, lest they remain as bad data forevermore. Do not anticipate that it will be possible to go back and fix the problem later. Day-to-day activities generally take priority over old problems.

Also during the implementation process, assuming that the CMS has this capability, the system administrator must define access authority for each user of the system. Obviously, it is undesirable that a curator may freely change information pertaining to a registrar's duties. Similarly, volunteers should not be allowed to see sensitive donor or appraisal information unless their tasks require it. The system administrator should interview each user and ask them how they need to use the system, as well as what sorts of information they require access to. Although these questions were asked during the selection phase, interviewing the users after they have seen the system in use will help them understand how the CMS can facilitate their responsibilities.

Even though it may not be implemented immediately, if the CMS is going to interact with other software packages, such as archive, library, digital asset management, or content management systems, it may be helpful to explore any necessary programming and requirements at this time. Many proprietary software packages are difficult to integrate seamlessly with other packages and frequently require the vendors and in-house or contract programmers to work together for a long period of time. Understanding the challenges as well as the optimal functioning of the systems will help ensure that future surprises are minimal.

Maintenance

Maintenance is the most expensive and most important part of the process, and the CMS will require constant maintenance throughout its lifetime. Vendors usually offer a maintenance plan to provide ongoing support, troubleshooting, modifications, and training.

Clearly document the procedures necessary to maintaining the system and the data and write up a Preservation Policy. The CHIN has published several in-depth articles about digital preservation[21] which provide step-by-step details about how to select appropriate preservation materials and practices. As technology, standards, and storage media change, it is always a good idea to research the available options.

A good rule of thumb for backing up data is to perform backups on a nightly basis onto either an off-site storage facility or onto a media type, which is separate from the main drives of the machine running the CMS. Such media would include an external hard drive or a tape drive. Compact discs or DVDs may also be used, but their longevity is relatively short, their storage capacities small, and they must be migrated to new media relatively regularly. No matter the media used, make sure that it is stored in optimal conditions lest the integrity of the media is threatened. In case of a natural disaster, it is always a good idea to store a copy of the backups off-site.

The role of the system administrator is critical during this phase. The system administrator will be responsible for maintaining the well-being of the CMS and the value and integrity of the data.

The system administrator will also be responsible for troubleshooting problems, assisting users with questions about the CMS, contacting the vendor with support requests, keeping the data up to date and consistent with applied standards, managing user permissions, and training new users.

Often the system administrator will be responsible for determining how best to make the data usable to a wide variety of possible users. The system administrator will need to write reports, train others to do so, and understand how best to export selected data if it is going to be shared with other consortia, researchers, and the general public. Sometimes the system administrator is in charge of data input, but even if there are other users who are inputting data, the system administrator will need to have a holistic understanding of the data and its proper functioning.

Ongoing costs for hardware, additional staff, modifications, and training need to be budgeted throughout the life of the system. Frequently, as users become more familiar with the CMS, they will understand its capabilities better and will wish for additional features or modifications. These changes may be expensive, but they can extend the usefulness of the system beyond the initial vision.

CURRENT AND FUTURE DEVELOPMENTS

Integration of Library and Archive Tools

Currently, there is much debate about sharing data between archives, libraries, and museums. Frequently, materials housed in these institutions relate to or complement materials available in another type of cultural heritage institution. For example, an Etruscan vase may reside in a museum, correspondence from an archaeologist about its discovery is stored in an archive, and a library may hold a series of books which feature the vase or Etruscan pottery in general. Sometimes, these materials are all stored within the same institution, but are managed according to museum, archival, and library standards. As these types of materials have very different care and cataloging requirements, accommodating such different information within one system has only been a recent development. Historically, this has been neither desirable nor feasible.

As institutions are able to use technology to share information, it is also possible for them to make relationships between related materials and present those relationships to researchers, often on a central Web site. This allows users to facilitate their research and increase access to different types of content.

Increasingly, CMS are offering solutions to manage archival and library materials in accordance with requisite professional standards. Such packages are currently expensive, but for institutions needing to manage all three types of data, they may be a good investment.

Digital Asset Management

A digital asset management system (DAMS) is a system which acts as a central repository for the digital images, documents, videos, and other multimedia materials an institution generates. A DAMS can also help embed appropriate metadata into the digital file and manage backup of those digital files. An institution with many digital resources will quickly find that managing them becomes unwieldy and a software solution such as a DAMS becomes desirable.

Many CMSs have multimedia modules which mimic some of the functions of a DAMS. They can embed metadata into the file and share files with other users. Currently, institutions with a manageable number of digital assets may find that their CMS performs these tasks adequately. In the future, additional features for onboard digital asset management may be added to many systems.

Open-Source

In an attempt to expand accessibility to materials in all museums, there are efforts underway to create open-source, freely available, Web-based CMS. The first of these, called Collective Access,[22] offers many of the features available in commercial CMS, but is available for any institution to use and modify as they wish. As of March 2008, OpenCollection became publicly available for download. There are, as of this writing, 15 institutions using it, and it is expected to be adopted more widely.

Web 2.0 Philosophy—Public Interaction

Web 2.0 tools refer to software which works with Web sites to allow increased visitor participation and interaction. Many institutions are experimenting with allowing online visitors to create their own connections and interactions with collection information. For example, the Art Institute of Chicago (AIC) has a Web site called Art Explorer[23] which allows visitors to create their own digital scrapbooks of art images discovered through searching AIC's collection database. Visitors can add notes, curate their own online exhibitions, and share these scrapbooks with other users.

Other museums are investigating how online visitors are searching their collection databases and providing additional features to facilitate accessibility to and/or interpretation of objects. Folksonomy, or social tagging, permits users to assign their own search terms to images. This allows visitors to assign their own meaning to objects, meaning which helps the museum understand which search terms are useful for the general public to identify the work. Social tagging in museums relies upon the understanding that standardized vocabularies and curatorial descriptions may mean much to researchers, but may not be useful to the general public. "steve"[24] is an experiment currently underway between several museums to study the feasibility and usability of social tagging in the museum context, as well as to develop tools to help museums adopt social tagging of their collections.

As of this writing, no commercial CMS incorporates user-generated tagging tools into its Web modules and very few offer scrapbooking tools. The Powerhouse Museum does use its CMS to store and manage user-generated tags, but it is an in-house modification of the system, and not a feature generally offered by the software developers. Instead, other software and programming is needed to bridge these tools and the system, but it is likely that CMS developers will incorporate Web 2.0 features in the near future.

CONCLUSION

Museum objects require specialized care and museums have developed elegant systems to ensure that these artifacts are available for many generations to come. Each object is unique and has a story to tell within the greater framework of history. Collection management systems are but one tool in an arsenal of professional practices to help museum staff properly catalog, evaluate, inventory, and organize all types of information about individual objects. The system can be as simple or as complex as the user desires, but it is only as useful as the data entered into it.

As a major capital investment, selecting and caring for a CMS is an exhausting, expensive, and time-consuming process. However, in return, the software can greatly enhance knowledge of the overall well-being of the collection, facilitate proactive care of the artifacts, and increase access to the collection by staff, researchers, other institutions, and the general public. Collection information is frequently used by all museum departments, and being able to quickly retrieve data can facilitate tasks for many staff members.

The other vital benefit of a good CMS is its unique ability to export collection information for use all over the world. Ever since the software was first developed, museums have dreamed of sharing their collections with other museums. Today, not only are other museums and cultural institutions interested in what's in the vault, but the general public is eager to learn about their culture, their history, science, and arts. The CMSs of today will continue to evolve, providing better tools for collection information management, accessibility, and interpretation.

ACKNOWLEDGMENTS

I would like to thank Marla Misunas, Collections Information Manager at the San Francisco Museum of Modern Art for her continuing support of my endeavors over the past few years. Also, many warm thanks to Angela Spinazze of ATSPIN Consulting for her invaluable input on this entry, and for her belief in me. I would also like to thank Marjorie Schwarzer, Department Chair; Susan Spero, Associate Professor; and John Taylor, Librarian of John F. Kennedy University for their guidance and assistance, not the least of which is allowing my use and abuse of the university's library and its laser printer.

REFERENCES

1. Lindsay, K.C. Computer input form for art works: Problems and possibilities. *Computers and Their Potential Applications in Museums*; The Metropolitan Museum of Art; Arno Press: New York, 1968.
2. Sully, P. *Inventory, Access, Interpretation: The Evolution of Museum Collection Management Software*. Final Masters Project, John F. Kennedy University: Berkeley, CA, 2006; 18–44. http://library2.jfku.edu/Museum_Studies/Inventory.pdf (accessed July 2008).
3. Williams, D.W. A brief history of museum computerization. Mus. Stud. J **1987**, *3* (1), 60.
4. Sully, P. Inventory, access, interpretation: The evolution of museum collection management software, Final Masters Project, John F. Kennedy University: Berkeley, CA, 2006; 27–38. http://library2.jfku.edu/Museum_Studies/Inventory.pdf (accessed July 2008).
5. Sully, P. Inventory, access, interpretation: The evolution of museum collection management software, Final Masters Project, John F. Kennedy University: Berkeley, CA, 2006; 27–44. http://library2.jfku.edu/Museum_Studies/Inventory.pdf (accessed July 2008).
6. Sully, P. Findings—Web site review. In *Inventory, Access, Interpretation: The Evolution of Museum Collection Management Software*, Final Masters Project, John F. Kennedy University: Berkeley, CA, 2006; 57–59. http://library2.jfku.edu/Museum_Studies/Inventory.pdf (accessed July 2008).
7. Misunas, M. Collection management in museums. In *Encyclopedia of Library and Information Sciences*, 3rd Ed.; Bates, M.J.; Maack, M.N., Eds.; Taylor & Francis: New York, 2010; 1124.
8. Blackaby, J.R.; Greeno, P. The Nomenclature Committee. *The Revised Nomenclature for Museum Cataloging: A Revised and Expanded Version of Robert G. Chenhall's System for Classifying Man-Made Objects*; AltaMira Press: Walnut Creek, CA, 1995.
9. *Art and Architecture Thesaurus*; Getty Research Institute: Los Angeles, CA, http://www.getty.edu/research/conducting_research/vocabularies/aat/ (accessed August 2007).
10. Powerhouse Museum Collection Search 2.4. http://www. powerhousemuseum.com/collection/database/ (accessed July 2008). Yad Vashem's entire Web site, including the collections search, is managed using IDEA@ALM, from IDEA Information Systems. *Yad Vashem—The Holocaust Martyrs' and Heroes' Remembrance Authority*, http://www.yadvashem.org/ (accessed July 2008).
11. *Collections Management Software Selection*; Canadian Heritage Information Network: Canada, 2002. http://www.chin.gc.ca/English/Collections_Management/Software_Selection/index.html (accessed July 2008).
12. *Creating and Managing Digital Content*; Canadian Heritage Information Network, http://www.chin.gc.ca/English/Digital_Content/index.html (accessed August 2007).
13. *Data Standards and Guidelines*; Getty Research Institute: Los Angeles, CA, http://www.getty.edu/research/conducting_research/standards/ (accessed August 2007).
14. *Collection Management Software Review—Criteria Checklist*; Canadian Heritage Information Network. http://www.chin.gc.ca/English/Collections_Management/Criteria_Checklist/index.html (accessed August 2007).
15. Gill, T.; Gilliland, A.J.; Woodley, M.S. *Introduction to Metadata—Pathways to Digital Information*, Online Ed.; Version 2.1; Baca, M., Ed.; Getty Research Institute: Los Angeles, http://www.getty.edu/research/conducting_research/standards/intrometadata/index.html (accessed August 2007).
16. *Categories for the Description of Works of Art*; Baca, M., Harpring, P., Eds.; Getty Research Institute: Los Angeles. http://www.getty.edu/research/conducting_research/standards/cdwa/ (accessed August 2007).
17. MDA Standard. MDA: Cambridge, England. http://www.mda.org.uk/stand.htm (accessed August 2007).

18. Encoded Archival Description—Version 2002 Official Site; Library of Congress: Washington, DC. http://www.loc.gov/ead/ (accessed August 2007).
19. MARC Standards; Library of Congress: Washington, DC. http://www.loc.gov/marc/ (accessed July 2008).
20. *Learn about the Getty Vocabularies*; Getty Research Institute: Los Angeles, http://www.getty.edu/research/conducting_research/vocabularies/ (accessed August 2007).
21. *Managing and Preserving Digital Content*; Canadian Heritage Information Network, http://www.chin.gc.ca/English/Digital_Content/index.html (accessed August 2007).
22. Collective Access Whirl-i-Gig. http://www.collective access.org (accessed March 2009).
23. *Art Explorer*; Art Institute of Chicago: Chicago, http://www.artic.edu/artexplorer/ (accessed June 2008).
24. steve. http://www.steve.museum/ (accessed August 2007).

BIBLIOGRAPHY

1. Besser, H. *Introduction to Imaging*, revised Ed.; Hubbard, S., Lenert, D., Eds.; Getty Research Institute: Los Angeles, CA, http://www.getty.edu/research/conducting_research/standards/introimages/ (accessed August 2007).
2. Callery, B.G., Ed. *Collaborative Access to Virtual Museum Collection Information—Seeing Through the Walls*; The Haworth Information Press: Binghamton, NY, 2004.
3. *Collection Management Software Selection*; Canadian Heritage Information Network. http://www.chin.gc.ca/English/Collections_Management/Software_Selection/index.html (accessed August 2007).
4. Collections Link. http://www.collectionslink.org.uk/ (accessed August 2007).
5. Gill, T.; Gilliland, A.J.; Woodley, M.S. *Introduction to Metadata—Pathways to Digital Information*, online Ed., Version 2.1; Baca, M., Ed.; Getty Research Institute: Los Angeles. http://www.getty.edu/research/conducting_research/standards/intrometadata/index.html (accessed August 2007).
6. Harpring, P.; Hourihane, C.; Shatford Layne, S.; Sundt, C. L. *Introduction to Art Image Access*; Baca, M., Ed.; Getty Research Institute: Los Angeles. http://www.getty.edu/research/conducting_research/standards/intro_aia/ (accessed August 2007).
7. Sully, P. Beyond access: A resource guide for museum staff beginning a collections or content management system project. In *Inventory, Access, Interpretation: The Evolution of Museum Collection Management Software*. Final Masters Project.; John F. Kennedy University: Berkeley, CA, 2006; 113–130. http://library2.jfku.edu/Museum_Studies/Inventory.pdf (accessed August 2007).

42 Interactive Multimedia in Museums

Nik Honeysett

CONTENTS

INTRODUCTION

For the purposes of this entry, Interactive Multimedia (IM) is broadly defined as computer-based technology that delivers text, audio and imagery, under user control.

The diversity of IM in museums is reflected in the diversity of museums themselves. Just as no two museums are the same, similarly no two IM installations are the same. While there are some general principles that guide interactivity, there are no national or international standards that govern how IM should look, feel, or function. The possibilities are boundless, limited purely by the creativity of the people who are responsible for building them.

To describe all the IM installations that have been built is an impossible task, so this entry will focus on the principles that apply to the technology, design and trends of IM in museums. Interactive Multimedia is dynamic and changing, grounded as it is in the ever-evolving world of digital technology so, in this fluid and dynamic world, to single out particular examples installed at some point in time in a museum is less informative than describing the principles or types of IM installations that have been built.

There are some general trends within particular types of museums, for example: children's museums often want to provide a rich and colorful hands-on experience that requires more physical activity on the part of the user, often paralleling a video game experience; science and technology museums often have more complex interactivity that controls real-world devices or demonstrates processes; whereas art and history museums, zoo and aquaria have more scholarly or encyclopedic-based installations. It is widely acknowledged that the user-driven approach to learning that IM provides is more closely associated with the way people think, supported by educational studies that have demonstrated greater teaching success through providing multiple stimuli and a game-based approach to learning—in part a direct response to the growth and ubiquity of computer gaming among our youth.

A glimpse into the world of IM in museums can made by reviewing the session programming and initiatives of organizations such as Archives and Museum Informatics[1]; Museum Computer

Network[2]; the American Association of Museum's Media and Technology Standing Professional Committee[3,6]; the International Cultural Heritage Informatics Meeting[4]; and Electronic Information, the Visual Arts, and Beyond.[5] The efforts and initiatives of these organizations are peer-reviewed by the museum professional community and should be regarded as demonstrating good examples and practices of the field IM.

A fairly extensive review up to 1993 can be found in an Archives and Museum Informatics Technical Report, IM in American Museums by Stephanie Eva Koester. This report also contains an extensive bibliography.[7]

WHY MUSEUMS PRODUCE IM

As with other initiatives, museums produce IM to further their mission. While museums have unique mission statements, they invariably distill down to a number of key principles including using their collection to educate and engage their audience. Interactive Multimedia is a technique that museums have adopted to achieve this broad directive as one of a number of methods to present information and complex or in-depth interpretive material to the visiting audience. Studies show that the interactive way in which a user engages with educational material leads to a greater and longer-lasting understanding of the material. There are an ever-increasing number of studies on the use interactivity in the learning environment, more recently involving online and e-learning. The *Journal of Interactive Online Learning* publishes such studies quarterly,[8] for example: The Importance of Interaction in Web-Based Education: A Program-level Case Study of Online MBA Courses[9]; College in the Information Age: Gains Associated with Students' Use of Technology.[10] Other online publishers of this type of research include the Center for Interactive Learning and Collaboration[11] and the Association for the Advancement of Computing in Education.[12]

Another compelling reason to use interactive technology is to specifically target and engage younger audiences, so-called Digital Natives.[13] Described as anyone born after the mid 1980s who has grown up using digital technology in all aspects of their life, Digital Natives have used digital technology either as a research tool during their schooling or as entertainment through the use of computer-based video games, the Internet, mp3 players, and cell phones. Conversely, Digital Immigrants are those individuals who have had to adapt to using technology and are either uncomfortable or unfamiliar with it. Interactive Multimedia designers are tasked with designing for individuals with all levels of expertise or familiarity with technology, but can increasingly make assumptions based on prior experience that individuals have had in the classroom or with computer games.

The development and use of interactivity within the classroom environment has largely focused on interactive CD-ROMs from companies such as the Learning Company,[14] Microsoft,[15] Scholastic,[16] and Dorling Kindersley (DK Multimedia).[17] In the 1990s, companies like Microsoft began producing interactive encyclopedias for the educational and consumer markets such as Microsoft Encarta,[18] and one of the first titles in their Microsoft HomeTM series[19] was Art Gallery—an electronic catalog of the entire collection of The National Gallery in London, which itself was based on an IM system that it developed by the early 1990s. Wikipedia has a number of entries that chronicle the development of educational interactive software, such as Educational Software[20] and a History of Virtual Learning Environments.[21]

The development and use of interactivity within the computer gaming industry has been more expansive and revolutionary and has been a much greater driver of the expectation of using digital technology to both play and learn. The evolution of video game controllers[22] in particular, which determines the amount of control or interactivity a player has over game play, has significantly increased in complexity over the last three decades and has played a significant role in its success.

Interactive Multimedia is a response to these trends, and there is increasingly an expectation that part of the learning experience within a museum will involve some kind of interactive technology. However, the expectation that the video-gaming industry has set for computer interaction has been a double-edged sword. On the one hand, it has trained the visiting public to be comfortable with complex technology but conversely, this multibillion dollar industry has set a high bar for production quality, immersion, and control that the museum world cannot compete with. Nevertheless, interactive installations are a prevalent feature in museums and have borrowed approaches, techniques, and even gaming hardware to create compelling and engaging installations.

WHAT IM IS

The broad definition that IM is "computer-based technology that delivers text, audio, and imagery under user control" does not capture the essence or variety of IM. The essential component of IM is the interactivity. Interactivity is the amount of control a user has over the experience—the user performs some kind of task or action and the computer responds appropriately. The task or action is performed using some kind of input device, and the response is made on some kind of visual display usually, although not exclusively, a computer monitor. Focusing on these two elements, the input device and the display, will provide a definition of IM, or as it is more commonly referred to: an interactive.

To understand a complex technology, it is often helpful to understand its earliest form. Some of the earliest interactives in museums in the 1970s and early 1980s used simple arcade-style buttons as their input device. Before desktop computers were capable of delivering video, graphics, or animation, Laser discs were used.[23] Laser discs could hold approximately 60 min of video sectioned into as many discrete chunks as desired, anything from a single frame to the entire duration of the disc. The Laser disc player was connected via the computer's serial port and could be instructed to play from a specific video frame for a specified number of frames. Pauses in the video play, (technically, a looping single frame), when the user would make a decision or choose an option allowed for narrative paths to be constructed. See Figure 42.1.

The major challenge with these systems, and an often-cited reason for their demise, was the high production cost to master the disc and the fact that writing the control software was a custom development, in that programmers and designers had to build the application from scratch. Further, there was limited opportunity to recoup any development costs from visitor sales of the discs due to the high cost of the players themselves which very few households or schools owned. Production of these bespoke video interactives was limited to large museums with enough time, budget, and resources to devote to the production effort.

This early example highlights the essence of IM where the user is in control of the learning experience, it also highlights the fact that simple input devices limit the amount of control and thus, the amount of interactivity. However, this basic design of button-controlled interactivity is still prevalent in museums, particularly children's museum where an input device needs to be clear,

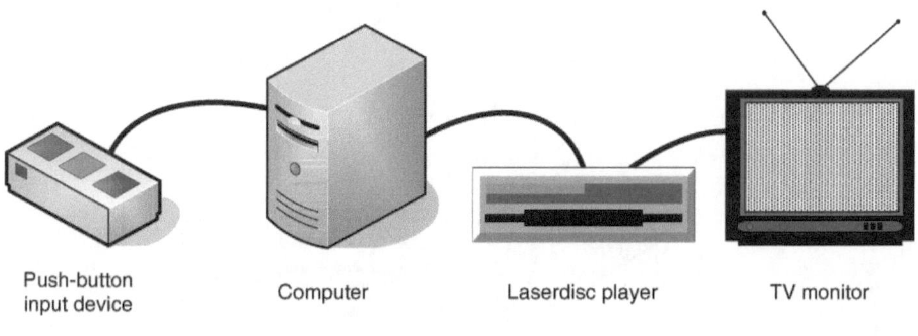

FIGURE 42.1 One of the earliest forms of IM was the push-button control of a Laser disc player, connected to a television screen. The buttons related to simple options or decisions in the narrative displayed on the screen. The basic concept is still used today in some designs of interactives.

simple and robust and can be intrinsically part of the learning experience, for example, *Press the "Red" Button*.

If a simple input device limits the scope of interactivity, it follows that a more complex input device allows for a more complex or nuanced interactive experience. One of the most common input devices that can be seen in museums today is the touch screen.[24] Patented in the early 1970s, the first commercially available touch screen was produced by Hewlett Packard[25] in 1983.[26] There are a number of different approaches available today that form the basis of touch screen technology: Resistive,[27] Capacitive,[28] and Surface Acoustic Wave[29] are all versions of what is essentially a touch-sensitive transparent panel overlaying a computer monitor and connected to a computer through either its serial or USB port (see Figure 42.2). These panels can be either retrofitted to a commercial monitor or integrated by the manufacturer.

In the mid 1980s, touch screens were introduced as an extremely intuitive form of interaction control for many kinds of IM. They allow for a much richer experience and interaction for the user. Previously, the input device had been separate from the presentation, but a touch screen combined the input device and the presentation to provide an integrated experience, and further, allowed the entire real estate of the computer display to be used for controlling the experience—the user could simply point to the region of interest in context. The continued use of touch screens in interactives more than 20 years later, is indicative of their ability to allow for an intuitive interaction and experience.

Touch screens tend to be a preferred input device for interactives because they provide an intuitive interaction for the user and therefore require a very short learning curve to teach the user how to control the experience. However, with the rise of the Internet and the prevalence of desktop computers in the home and at the office, the general public can be expected to have a much greater familiarity using more advanced input devices such as a mouse and keyboard. This increased familiarity has allowed for a greater variety and complexity of interactives in museums. Relying on a user to be able to type in a query or keyword and use a much more accurate pointing device (a mouse cursor as opposed to a finger) allows for much greater complexity and functionality.

But touch screens, mice and keyboards are not the sole input device for IM. Much more complex and engaging devices are used in children's museums and science museums, where IM systems teach physical or mechanical principles, mimic how things work or control real-world devices. These types of IM systems might use handheld game controllers,[30] biometric devices,[31] motion detectors,[32] video capture with image recognition,[33] infra-red[34] or ultraviolet[35] sensors or more recently, three-dimensional motion and spatial detectors.

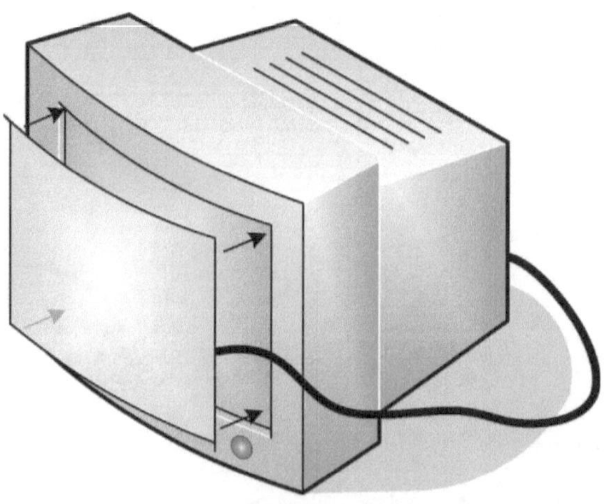

FIGURE 42.2 Touch screen monitors are created by overlaying a touch-sensitive panel onto a standard computer monitor.

These types of input devices once required significant custom software and hardware development to integrate into an interactive but are now commercially available. For example, the Wii™ gaming system from Nintendo®[36] comes with a three-dimensional motion and spatial sensor complete with Firewire connector. Interactives are beginning to appear that provide interaction through this device, where natural motion and gestures can control the experience. This particular example illustrates a crucial point for IM developers that the adoption of USB[37] and Firewire[38] as standard serial bus connectors in the desktop computer world as well as the consumer electronics market has made the task of modifying and integrating complex but user-friendly input devices much simpler.

IM DESIGN

Designing an IM system is a complex process. Its design, look and feel, functionality and even content are determined by many factors. The location of an IM installation is also significant.

A common type of museum interactive is a guide to its collection. These are normally encyclopedia-style interactives that use an object-based organization and either a touch screen or mouse and keyboard as their control device. Typical features include a digital image for every object; information such as an object's title, maker, origin and date; associated information such as an interpretive description; and ancillary images which might be X-rays, detailed or comparative subject images. Often they will provide functionality such as zooming into details of the object, animations, or video to show a process. These interactives will normally provide various ways to navigate to an object based on its maker, theme, timeline, or subject and will often be the only opportunity aside from buying a poster or postcard in the museum store, for a visitor to see a representation of an object that may not be on view.

If an installation uses a touch screen then there are implications for how the user can access the information. Typing text using a touch screen is cumbersome, so indexes and searches will normally be prebuilt so that the user selects an index and pages through. The size and proximity of control buttons has to account for a significant margin of error from the user's finger—one-half inch on screen is normally regarded as the absolute minimum size for a button and its spacing. However, if the installation uses a keyboard and mouse, there is a greater degree of flexibility in how the information is organized and how the user can access it. Keyboards allow the user to perform free-text searches, and control buttons can be much more granular. In general, interactives designed for touch screens benefit from a wholly predetermined organization and structure, whereas keyboards allow for many functions or screens, particularly indexes, to be generated on the fly.

Many interactives use the concept and function of hyperlinking to navigate and control the experience.[39] While the Internet has familiarized many with the concept of hyperlinking, interactives were there first. Many museum visitors of the late 1980s and early 1990s were taught the concept of hyperlinking before they encountered the Internet. The underlying principle of hyperlinking is that it allows for the presentation of layered content. This concept allows an IM designer to build a system that is engaging to users of many levels of education or subject matter expertise. For example, the pop-up-glossary concept used in many interactives, can be used to display more complex information about certain topics or themes or more explanatory information—see Figure 42.3. By writing content for a middle of the road educational level, say 8th grade, obscuring information until it is requested allows the narrative to flow, but provides the opportunity to less- or better-informed users to have an equally engaging or educational experience.

A collections-guide interactive is often situated away from the collection objects themselves to study-room type areas and within the last few years there has been an increasing trend to build these types of interactives as a Web site and simply provide restricted access within the confines of the museum. However, a number of museums have taken this a step further and built a dual-channel installation which presents the same content and functionality with a higher production version inside the museum, and a version appropriately optimized for Web delivery.

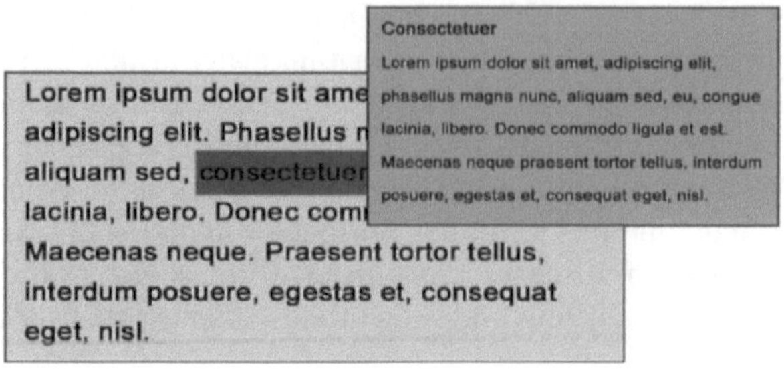

FIGURE 42.3 An example of layered content seen on a screen—a crucial functionality that allows a single interactive to engage users of a wide spectrum of educational backgrounds or knowledge.

Because collections-guide style interactives encompass a lot of information some of which is dynamic, they are often networked and designed to receive periodic updating. In museums where the interactive reflects the location of an object for example, the installation may need to be updated daily or weekly to provide up-to-date information.

Another common type of interactive in contrast to the collections-guide type is the in-gallery interactive. In-gallery interactives are a more specific or dedicated interpretive installation, situated within a gallery, which compliments the object around it, or the particular gallery in which it is installed. These range from a simple user-driven video player, explaining a particular theory or technique, to an in-depth treatment of a subject, process, theme, or historical context. These types of interactives are normally limited in depth and time commitment required to step through their content and also tends to be standalone,[40] rather than attached to a network since they normally do not require frequent updates.

IM DELIVERY

The applications used to deliver an interactive have gone through many iterations. Ever since the late 1980s there have been vendor solutions for building interactive applications although the larger, more complex interactives have been custom developments. This is still the case for interactives that interface with external devices. The release of HyperCard™ in 1987 by Apple[41] allowed anyone with a Macintosh to build an interactive application. The software had some limitations—in particular it would not support full color, but many of these things could be circumscribed with additional programming.

The real workhorse of interactive application delivery for many years was Director.[42] First released in 1987 as Macromind Director, this product is still commercially available as Adobe Director 11.[43] It uses a movie metaphor in that the interactive is a movie that plays from start to finish, and has all the required interactive functionality built in. It has an integrated scripting language, Lingo,[44] that allows for complex functionality to be developed and pauses can be inserted at any point within the movie to allow for user choices. Ironically, this approach mimics the original Laser disc IM approach.

Director has been an extremely popular choice for developing interactives due to its ability to generate a standalone version for delivery on CDROM, which allowed museums to recoup their investment costs by selling the interactive in their stores.

Today, one of the most widely-used applications to deliver interactives is a Web browser[45] due in large part to its ability to support Flash[46] which provides full motion video, animation, and interactivity using a powerful embedded scripting language called ActionScript.[47] Since the mid 1990s, the most common Web browsers have had the ability to run in "kiosk mode" which essentially removes the chrome normally associated with a browser window such as the tool bar, scroll bar, and navigation buttons, presenting a clean, anonymous window for the interactive to run within.

The use of a Web browser to deliver an interactive has forced developers to apply some improved practices in how they structure IM applications. At the basic level, it has required the adoption of a client/server application architecture[48] whether local or networked, but at the more advanced level it has imposed some better practices for application architecture design, which benefit scalability, flexibility, and maintenance. These practices dictate that an application should be built in a modular way, which separates out content (data and media), logic (application), and presentation (display) into layers. See Figure 42.4. Previously, the applications that were used to deliver interactives such as Director, wrapped all the content and media into a single application, which is appropriate for small in-gallery style interactives but presents maintenance and support challenges for larger systems.

This modular approach is a crucial development for the delivery of interactive content because it extends the capabilities and greatly reduces the burden of maintenance and support for IM systems. For example, changes to the application can be made without affecting the content and changes to the media can be made without affecting the application. Two additional benefits are: easier integration with support applications such as a Digital Asset Management System[49] and support for multiple channel delivery. The ability to integrate with a management system is crucial for the sustainability of a collections-guide style interactive, which needs to grow as the institution acquires more objects. The ability to deliver to multiple platforms is significant because current trends in IM are to extend the experience by taking advantage of the many types of devices or platforms that can handle multimedia content, such as Personal Digital Assistants (PDAs)[50] and Smart Phones[51] in addition to the Web. Using these types of devices has extended a museum's ability to engage with its audience, taking it out of the confines of the museum, which has been the traditional venue, and making it possible to engage anywhere and at anytime.

Some IM systems have extended this engagement to either before or after a visit to the museum. This is achieved by deploying interactive content to the museum's Web site and providing functionality that will assist the visitor in planning their visit, for example, or afterwards by summarizing or providing additional information of the objects that were seen. Some collections-guide interactives provide the visitor with the ability to generate their own tour of the museum to view the objects that most interest them, in this way the interactive acts like a visitor information booth. The pre-visit approach has been fairly successful for schools since the educator can plan ahead and pre-teach the works that the class will see. Furthermore, some of the more cutting-edge IM systems allow the potential visitor to build a tour online then pick up a handheld device on arrival that contains their tour. The handheld device then acts as a personal tour guide, map, information kiosk, and way-finding device for the visitor.

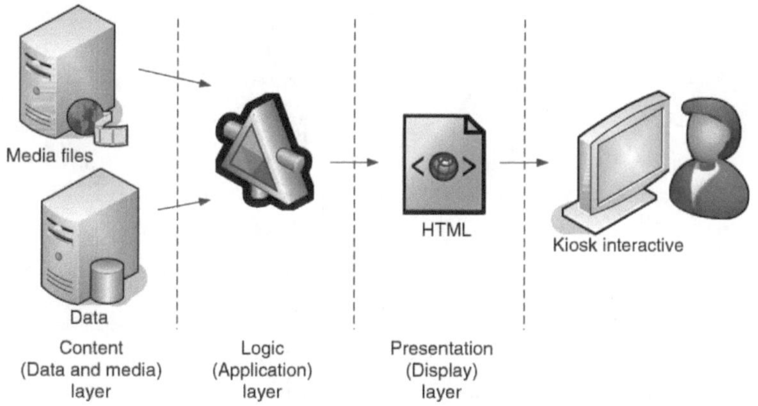

FIGURE 42.4 Best practices for the application design of an interactive system are that it should be built in a modular way. The modularity separates out the content (data and media), logic (application), and presentation (display) into layers.

Alternatively, some IM systems try to establish a relationship with the visitor after their visit. For these types of interactives, the user can use the IM system at the museum during their visit to create a tour of the things they would like to see. By creating an account, the user can have the list of objects e-mailed to them or they can access them by logging into the system over the Internet. These systems benefit from the advanced and modular architecture described above that allows the content to be deployed to multiple platforms. Figure 42.5 shows this and demonstrates the advantages of building an interactive in a modular way. The presentation layer represents different templates to describe how the content and media should be displayed on different platforms.

Pre-engagement, capture, and visitor retention approaches like these are increasingly a crucial goal of IM systems. A number of museums have built extremely advanced systems that further this initiative by allowing a user to actually create their own Web site that includes features pertinent to the museum. These approaches have been successful with science and natural history museums due to the nature of the content, which presents themes, processes, or topics, which are programmed to change over time. This approach requires the user to periodically revisit their Web site to observe the changes, which in turn provides an opportunity for the museum to "up-sell" their exhibitions, merchandise, or membership. Examples of the type of content that can be programmed to change over time are chemical processes, geological processes, and lunar or planetary motion tracking. An interesting side effect of this approach is that some museums have become very large ISPs.[52] The overall success of these approaches in establishing an ongoing engagement with the visitor has been mixed.

For many years, the only way to engage the visitor using IM was within the museum itself. This follows a fundamental principle of museums, which is to encourage people to engage directly with the collection, however, these IM examples have allowed museums to engage the visitor remotely. The growing prevalence of handheld communications devices which now support all necessary functions for IM, including an intuitive touch screen, are significant opportunities for museums to connect and engage with their visitors and museums are increasingly taking advantage of visitors' having their own equipped device. This development will have a significant impact on museums in the future. It will allow museums to do what they do best and concentrate on developing content and interpretative material for their collections. Purchasing, supporting, and maintaining expensive delivery hardware is a significant challenge for many museums.

The trend to deliver content to a visitor's own device has its challenges, but enables a museum to engage with the public wherever they are, including their visit to the museum. As functionality such as Global Positioning System (GPS)[53] and other forms of location based services[54] become more

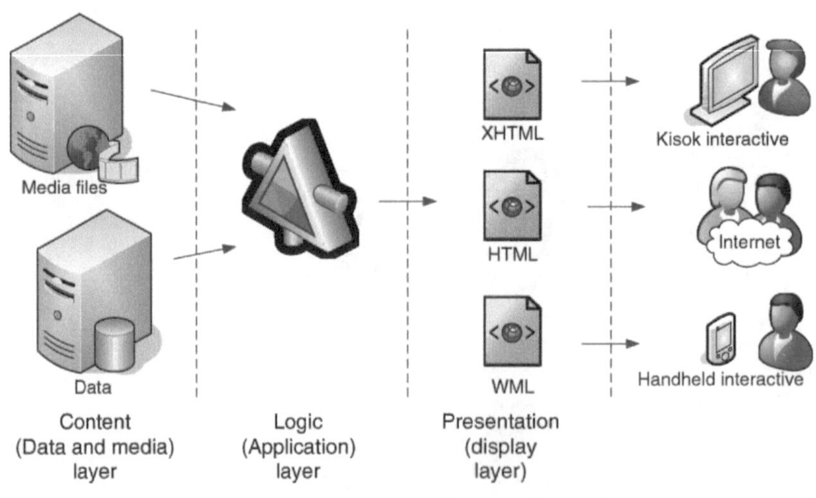

FIGURE 42.5 The modular application design allows for the delivery of interactive content to multiple devices using different templates and markup languages such as HTML[66] and XHMTL.[67]

of a standard in mobile devices, museums can leverage this technology to provide a deeper interactive experience and supplant current services and support. Botanical gardens, zoos, and arboretums are beginning to take advantage of this development by providing interactive handheld tours and guides driven by GPS. The dispersed nature of the flora and fauna and its outdoor nature, plays well to the strengths and accuracy of GPS. Museums that wish to provide an experience delivered on a visitor's own device within their institution will likely have to revisit their cell phone usage policies and ensure that reception is available within their building.

A number of museums have experimented with wireless handheld devices to intelligently pinpoint a visitor within their gallery and deliver location-specific content. These installations have used triangulation[55] as their location technology, but the accuracy, robustness, and complexity of the infrastructure required to support the technology has been challenging.

Although not regarded as multimedia, the emerging trend of cell phone audio tours to replace traditional museum-distributed audio guides is a good example of a museum relying on a visitor's own equipment. Museums can set up a telephone-based service to record their own audio descriptions that visitors' access simply using their own cell phone to call the number and key in an appropriate code. Another example is the use of iTunes[56] to distribute audio and video content to visitors as podcasts for their personal players.[57] As this trend emerges, a number of museums are encouraging its adoption by offering admission discounts to visitor who can demonstrate that they have downloaded the museum's content and brought it with them. Some museums are even starting to make stand-alone IM applications for visitors to download and run on their own suitably-equipped devices. A compelling argument for a museum to adopt this approach is the lack of hardware that it needs to invest, support, and maintain at a time when museums are looking for creative but economic approaches to further their mission.

As these technologies enable the visitor to engage with a museum outside the confines of its walls, it is logical to carry this to its extreme. The dominating trends in both the video-gaming industry and the Internet are towards more realistic, immersive, and social experiences in the context of a virtual environment. These trends are realized in the current genre of Massively Multiplayer Online Role-Playing Games,[58] in which individuals interact with others virtually and in pursuit of common goals. A key example would be the phenomena of Second Life,[59,60] and pioneers in the museum technology field are already experimenting in this virtual museum environment to host exhibitions, interpret their collections, and develop their audiences.[61]

This development fundamentally challenges the notion that a museum is a physical place, which people visit to engage with a collection. In the 1980s and 1990s, developers faced significant resistance from curatorial staff over the digital representation of objects—some still face this challenge, but with in-gallery multimedia, visitors still have to visit the institution. Time will tell whether there is a similar resistance to the virtual environment.

CONCLUSION

Multimedia interactives have been available in museums for over three decades. Interactive Multimedia has been used to extend the ability of museum professional staff to engage and teach their audience and for the most part it has proved to be very successful, particularly with young emerging audiences who represent the future. With the continued evolution of the Internet, the continued proliferation and capability of personal computing devices, and the expectation that technology is a tool for research, education, and entertainment, there is every indication that IM has a solid future as a didactic tool in the museum world.

Often and sometimes unwittingly, museums have been at the forefront of experimentation and research into the whole science of Human Computer Interaction[62,63] which IM represents, but have also followed the trends and developments of the educational software, video-gaming, and consumer electronics industries. Ironically, IM in museums was available to the public before the mass adoption of the Internet, but that has come full circle and the Internet now plays a significant role in the design, architecture, and delivery of IM. Together, these industries have increased the literacy and acceptance of technology by the general public, which has fueled a willingness on the part of museums to experiment with more complex and engaging IM systems.

As the dominating influence, the Internet will continue to dictate the direction and evolution of IM more than any other phenomena. The implications of the current iteration of Web evolution known as Web 2.0[64] are significant not only for the networking and collaboration aspects that it facilitates, which are core to the museum mission, but also the application architecture and business models that it fosters. Looking forward to the so-called Web 3.0[65] version of the Web, there are potential innovations that fundamentally support the core museum values of education and dissemination ensuring the continued use of engaging and interactive technology in the museum environment.

As these trends develop they may encourage the public to engage with a museum through its virtual alternative. Ironically, this virtual alternative would be a structure and mechanism that brings individuals together to engage at a social level for the mutual appreciation of our cultural heritage.

ACKNOWLEDGMENTS

The success and continued development of IM in museums is due in large part to the generosity of individuals and institutions who share their knowledge and skill with the broader museum community at a professional level and in a public forum.

The following list of selected online references detail the last 5 years' programming of IM at the Museums on the Web annual conference. This list demonstrates the diversity and creativity of this continually evolving field.

REFERENCES

1. http://www.archimuse.com (accessed July 14, 2008).
2. http://www.mcn.edu (accessed July 14, 2008).
3. http://mediaandtechnology.org (accessed July 14, 2008).
4. http://ichim.org (accessed July 14, 2008).
5. http://www.eva-conferences.com (accessed July 14, 2008).
6. http://mediaandtechnology.org/muse (accessed July 14, 2008).
7. http://www.archimuse.com/publishing/interactive_multimedia.html (accessed July 14, 2008).
8. http://www.ncolr.org/jiol (accessed July 14, 2008).
9. http://www.ncolr.org/jiol/issues/getfile.cfm?volID=4&IssueID=14&ArticleID=2 (accessed July 14, 2008).
10. http://www.ncolr.org/jiol/issues/getfile.cfm?volID=5&IssueID=17&ArticleID=83 (accessed July 14, 2008).
11. http://www.cilc.org (accessed July 14, 2008).
12. http://www.aace.org (accessed July 14, 2008).
13. http://wikipedia.org/wiki/Digital_native (accessed July 14, 2008).
14. http://www.learningcompany.com (accessed July 14, 2008).
15. http://www.microsoft.com (accessed July 14, 2008).
16. http://www.scholastic.com (accessed July 14, 2008).
17. http://www.dk.com (accessed July 14, 2008).
18. http://www.microsoft.com/encarta (accessed July 14, 2008).
19. http://wikipedia.org/wiki/Microsoft_Home (accessed July 14, 2008).
20. http://wikipedia.org/wiki/Educational_software (accessed July 14, 2008).
21. http://wikipedia.org/wiki/History_of_virtual_learning_environments (accessed July 14, 2008).
22. http://wikipedia.org/wiki/Video_game_console (accessed July 14, 2008).
23. http://wikipedia.org/wiki/Laserdisc (accessed July 14, 2008).
24. http://wikipedia.org/wiki/Touchscreen (accessed July 14, 2008).
25. http://hp.com (accessed July 14, 2008).
26. http://wikipedia.org/wiki/HP-150 (accessed July 14, 2008).
27. http://wikipedia.org/wiki/Touchscreen#Resistive (accessed July 14, 2008).
28. http://wikipedia.org/wiki/Touchscreen#Capacitive (accessed July 14, 2008).

29. http://wikipedia.org/wiki/Touchscreen#Surface_acoustic_ wave (accessed July 14, 2008).
30. http://wikipedia.org/wiki/Game_controller (accessed July 14, 2008).
31. http://wikipedia.org/wiki/Biometric (accessed July 14, 2008).
32. http://wikipedia.org/wiki/Motion_detector (accessed July 14, 2008).
33. http://wikipedia.org/wiki/Computer_vision (accessed July 14, 2008).
34. http://wikipedia.org/wiki/Infra_red (accessed July 14, 2008).
35. http://wikipedia.org/wiki/Ultraviolet (accessed July 14, 2008).
36. http://wii.com (accessed July 14, 2008).
37. http://wikipedia.org/wiki/Usb (accessed July 14, 2008).
38. http://wikipedia.org/wiki/Firewire (accessed July 14, 2008).
39. http://wikipedia.org/wiki/Hyperlink (accessed July 14, 2008).
40. http://wikipedia.org/wiki/Standalone_software (accessed July 14, 2008).
41. http://wikipedia.org/wiki/Hypercard (accessed July 14, 2008).
42. http://wikipedia.org/wiki/Macromind_Director (accessed July 14, 2008).
43. http://www.adobe.com/products/director (accessed July 14, 2008).
44. http://wikipedia.org/wiki/Lingo_(programming_language) (accessed July 14, 2008).
45. http://wikipedia.org/wiki/Web_browser (accessed July 14, 2008).
46. http://wikipedia.org/wiki/Adobe_flash (accessed July 14, 2008).
47. http://wikipedia.org/wiki/Action_Script (accessed July 14, 2008).
48. http://wikipedia.org/wiki/Client_server (accessed July 14, 2008).
49. http://wikipedia.org/wiki/Digital_Asset_Management (accessed July 14, 2008).
50. http://wikipedia.org/wiki/Personal_digital_assistant (accessed July 14, 2008).
51. http://wikipedia.org/wiki/Smart_phone (accessed July 14, 2008).
52. http://wikipedia.org/wiki/Internet_service_provider (accessed July 14, 2008).
53. http://wikipedia.org/wiki/Gps (accessed July 14, 2008).
54. http://wikipedia.org/wiki/Location-based_service (accessed July 14, 2008).
55. http://wikipedia.org/wiki/Triangulation (accessed July 14, 2008).
56. http://wikipedia.org/wiki/Itunes (accessed July 14, 2008).
57. http://wikipedia.org/wiki/PodCast (accessed July 14, 2008).
58. http://wikipedia.org/wiki/MMORPG (accessed July 14, 2008).
59. http://secondlife.com (accessed July 14, 2008).
60. http://wikipedia.org/wiki/Second_life (accessed July 14, 2008).
61. Urban, R.; Mart, P.; Twidale, M. *A Second Life for Your Museum: 3D Multi-User Virtual Environments and Museums*; Museums and the Web: San Francisco, April 11–14, 2007; http://www.archimuse.com/mw2007/papers/urban/urban.html
62. http://hcibib.org/ (accessed July 14, 2008).
63. http://wikipedia.org/wiki/Human-computer_interaction (accessed July 14, 2008).
64. http://wikipedia.org/wiki/Web_2.0 (accessed July 14, 2008).
65. http://wikipedia.org/wiki/Web_3.0 (accessed July 14, 2008).
66. http://wikipedia.org/wiki/Html (accessed July 14, 2008).
67. http://wikipedia.org/wiki/Xhtml (accessed July 14, 2008).

BIBLIOGRAPHY

1. Aroyo, L.; Brussee, R.; Rutledge, L.; Gorgels, P.; Stash, N.; Wang, Y. Personalized museum experience: The Rijks-museum use Case. In *Museums on the Web*, San Francisco, April 11–14, 2007; http://www.archimuse.com/mw2007/papers/aroyo/aroyo.html (accessed July 20, 2008).
2. Arts, M.; Schoonhoven, S. Culture around the corner and its location-based application. In *Museums on the Web*, Vancouver, BC, Canada, April 14–16, 2005; http://www.archimuse.com/mw2005/papers/arts/arts.html (accessed July 20, 2008).
3. Bressler, D. Mobile phones: A new way to engage teenagers in informal science learning. In *Museums on the Web,* Albuquerque, NM, March 22–25, 2006; http://www.archimuse.com/mw2006/papers/bressler/bressler.html (accessed July 20, 2008).
4. Cinotti, T.S.; Raffa, G.; Roffia, L.; Garzotto, F.; Muzii, R.; Varlese, V.; Malavasi, M.; Galasso, S. Evaluating context-aware mobile applications in museums: experiences from the MUSE Project. In *Museums on the Web*, Arlington, VA, April 1–3, 2004; http://www.archimuse.com/mw2004/papers/salmon/salmon.html (accessed July 20, 2008).

5. Colazzo, S.; Garzotto, F.; Paolini, P. Let's go mobile! design issues in multichannel "accessible" applications for cultural heritage. In *Museums on the Web*, Vancouver, BC, Canada, April 14–16, 2005; http://www.archimuse.com/mw2005/papers/colazzo/colazzo.html (accessed July 20, 2008).
6. Detroit Institute of Arts; Acoustiguide. Getting Closer: Technology-based Interpretation at the Detroit Institute of Arts. A museum-wide reinstallation of interpretive media including a virtual eighteenth-century European banquet surrounded by objects made for dining; a life-sized video of an African masquerade near masks on display; an ancient Egyptian Book of the Dead scroll; a PDA multimedia tour of Diego Rivera's immense Detroit Industry murals.
7. Filippini-Fantoni, S.; Bowen, J. Bookmarking in museums: extending the museum experience beyond the visit? In *Museums on the Web*, San Francisco, April 11–14, 2007; http://www.archimuse.com/mw2007/papers/filippini-fantoni/filippini-fantoni.html (accessed July 20, 2008).
8. Granlie, J.; Macquarrie, K. *Interactive and Customizable Learning Environments for Various User Needs; Museums on the Web*, Montréal, QC, Canada, April 9–12, 2008; http://www.archimuse.com/mw2008/papers/granlie/granlie.html (accessed July 20, 2008).
9. Haley, G.K. Cell phones and exhibitions 2.O: Moving beyond the pilot stage. In *Museums on the Web*, San Francisco, April 11–14, 2007; http://www.archimuse.com/mw2007/papers/haleyGoldman/haleyGoldman.html (accessed July 20, 2008).
10. Harcup, C.; Nesbitt, M. Attaining the Holy Grail: How to Encourage Wider Engagement with Museum Collections through Participation in New Media Projects. In *Museums on the Web*, Albuquerque, NM, March 22–25, 2006; http://www.archimuse.com/mw2006/papers/harcup/harcup.html (accessed July 20, 2008).
11. Jaén, J.; Bosch, V.; Esteve, J.M.; Mocholí, J.A. MoMo: A hybrid museum infrastructure. In *Museums on the Web*, Vancouver, BC, Canada, April 14–16, 2005; http://www.archimuse.com/mw2005/papers/jaen/jaen.html (accessed July 20, 2008).
12. Jones, B.J. Visitor interactivity becomes museum exhibit. In *Museums on the Web*, Arlington, VA, April 1–3, 2004; http://www.archimuse.com/mw2004/papers/jones/jones.html (accessed July 20, 2008).
13. Katz, S.; Kahanov, Y.; Kashtan, N.; Kuflik, T.; Graziola, I.; Rocchi, C.; Stock, O.; Zancanaro, M. Preparing personalized multimedia presentations for a mobile museum visitors' guide—A methodological approach. In *Museums on the Web*, Albuquerque, NM, March 22–25, 2006; http://www.archimuse.com/mw2006/papers/katz/katz.html (accessed July 20, 2008).
14. Leon, J.; Fisher, M. Interactive educational storytelling: The use of virtual characters to generate teachable moments. In *Museums on the Web*, Albuquerque, NM, March 22–25, 2006; http://www.archimuse.com/mw2006/papers/leon/leon.html (accessed July 20, 2008).
15. Lindgren-Streicher, A.; Reich, C. Visitor interactions with digitized artifacts. In *Museums on the Web*, Albuquerque, NM, March 22–25, 2006; http://www.archimuse.com/mw2006/papers/lindgren/lindgren.html (accessed July 20, 2008).
16. Lucey-Roper, M. Discover Babylon: Creating a Vivid User Experience by Exploiting Features of Video Games and Uniting Museum and Library Collections. In *Museums on the Web*, Albuquerque, NM, March 22–25, 2006; http://www.archimuse.com/mw2006/papers/lucey-roper/lucey-roper.html (accessed July 20, 2008).
17. Manning, A; Sims, G. The Blanton iTour—An interactive handheld museum guide experiment. In *Museums on the Web*, Arlington, VA, April 1–3, 2004; http://www.archimuse.com/mw2004/papers/manning/manning.html (accessed July 20, 2008).
18. Museo Interactivo de Economia; Magian Design Studio. Market Simulator Game. A PDA-based interactive set in a simulated contemporary stock market used to educate visitors about the forces that influence market prices.
19. Museum at Eldridge Street; Potion Design. Limud Tables. A pair of interactive tables used to educate visitors about synagogue design, rituals and practice and the historical community of the Lower East Side.
20. National Library of Medicine; Second Story Interactive Studios. Visible Proofs: Forensic Views of the Body. A life-size interactive autopsy slab that traces the history of forensic medicine—the efforts of physicians, surgeons and other specialists to translate views of bodies and body parts into hard evidence or "visible proofs" that testify on behalf of the victims of violent crime and against the guilty.
21. National World War II Museum; Unified Field. D-Day 096 Interactive. The recreated cockpit of a DC-3/C 47 Dakota airplane, features primary sources such as first person interviews, oral histories, a virtual re-creation of the plane and historical footage that connect the artifact, the people and the context.
22. Nevile, L.; Lissonnet, S.; Roberts, V.; Treviranus, J. Rich experiences for all participants. In *Museums on the Web*, Arlington, VA, April 1–3, 2004; http://www.archimuse.com/mw2004/papers/nevile/nevile.html (accessed July 20, 2008).

23. Pert, T. Hand-held heritage: The development of mobile applications by the Royal Commission on the ancient and historical monuments of Wales. In *Museums on the Web*, Montréal, QC, Canada, April 9–12, 2008; http://www.archimuse.com/mw2008/papers/pert/pert.html (accessed July 20, 2008).
24. Proctor, N. When in Roam: Visitor response to phone tour pilots in the U.S. and Europe. In *Museums on the Web*, San Francisco, April 11–14, 2007; http://www.archimuse.com/mw2007/papers/proctor/proctor.html (accessed July 20, 2008).
25. President Lincoln's Cottage at the Soldiers' Home. Lincoln's Toughest Decisions. A group-mode interactive using virtual desktops, that places visitors in the role of President Lincoln's cabinet members. Visitors use the interactive to advise Lincoln about critical issues like the Emancipation Proclamation in 1862, the military turning point of the Civil War in 1864; and the strategy for Lincoln's reelection in 1864.
26. Puig, V.; Sirven, X. Lignes De Temps: Involving cinema exhibition visitors in mobile and on-line film annotation. In *Museums on the Web*, San Francisco, April 11–14, 2007. http://www.archimuse.com/mw2007/papers/puig/puig.html (accessed July 20, 2008).
27. Reich, C. Universal design of computer interactives for museum exhibitions. In *Museums on the Web*, Albuquerque, NM, March 22–25, 2006; http://www.archimuse.com/mw2006/papers/reich/reich.html (accessed July 20, 2008).
28. Samis, P. Gaining traction in the vaseline: Visitor response to a multi-track interpretation design for matthew barney: DRAWING RESTRAINT. In *Museums on the Web*, San Francisco, April 11–14, 2007; http://www.archimuse.com/mw2007/papers/samis/samis.html (accessed July 20, 2008).
29. Samis, P. *Who has the Responsibility for Saying What We See? Mashing Up Museum and Visitor Voices, On-site and Online*: Museums on the Web, Montréal, QC, Canada, April 9–12, 2008; http://www.archimuse.com/mw2008/papers/samis/samis.html (accessed July 20, 2008).
30. Sauer, S.; Osswald, K.; Göbel, S.; Feix, A.; Zumack, R.; Hoffmann, A. Edutainment environments. A field report on DinoHunter: Technologies, methods and evaluation Results. In *Museums on the Web*, Arlington, VA, April 1– 3, 2004; http://www.archimuse.com/mw2004/papers/sauer/sauer.html (accessed July 20, 2008).
31. Schaller, D.T.; Allison-Bunnell, S.; Borun, M. Learning Styles and Online Interactives. In *Museums on the Web*, Vancouver, BC, Canada April 14–16, 2005; http://www.archimuse.com/mw2005/papers/schaller/schaller.html (accessed July 20, 2008).
32. Silveira, M.; Pinho, M.; Gonella, A.; Herrmann, M.; Cal-vetti, P.; Bertoletti, A.C.; Girardi, M. Using mobile devices to help teachers and students during a visit to a museum. In *Museums on the Web*, Vancouver, BC, Canada, April 14–16, 2005; http://www.archimuse.com/mw2005/papers/silveira/silveira.html (accessed July 20, 2008).
33. Springer, J.; White, P. Video iPods and art education. In *Museums on the Web*, San Francisco, CA, April 11–14, 2007; http://www.archimuse.com/mw2007/papers/springer/springer.html (accessed July 20, 2008).
34. Taxén, G.; Frécon, E. The Extended Museum Visit: Documenting and Exhibiting Post-Visit Experiences. In *Museums on the Web*, Vancouver, BC, Canada, April 14–16, 2005; http://www.archimuse.com/mw2005/papers/taxen/taxen.html (accessed July 20, 2008).
35. Tellis, C. Multimedia handhelds: One device, many audiences. In *Museums on the Web*, Arlington, VA, April 1–3, 2004; http://www.archimuse.com/mw2004/papers/tellis/tellis.html (accessed July 20, 2008).
36. The American Association of Museums' Media and Technology Standing Professional Committee sponsors an annual award competition for museum media and technology projects. The following selection of past winners from the IM category, represent peer-reviewed excellence in the field of IM and serve as an example of the diversity of IM.
37. The John Deere GPS Combine/Tractor Display; Museum of Science and Industry, Chicago and Silver Oaks. A real John Deere steering wheel controls this interactive tractor putting the visitor behind the wheel of sophisticated farm equipment to teach how GPS technology is used for field treatment and harvesting.
38. Thomas, W.A.; Carey, S. Actual/virtual visits: What are the links. In *Museums on the Web*, Vancouver, BC, Canada, April 14–16, 2005; http://www.archimuse.com/mw2005/papers/thomas/thomas.html (accessed July 20, 2008).
39. Van Loon, H.; Gabriëls, K.; Luyten, K.; Teunkens, D.; Robert, K.; Coninx, K.; Manshoven, E. Supporting Social Interaction: A Collaborative Trading Game on PDA. In *Museums on the Web*, San Francisco, CaliforniaApril 11–14, 2007; http://www.archimuse.com/mw2007/papers/vanLoon/vanLoon.html (accessed July 20, 2008).
40. Virginia Museum of Natural History; Cortina Productions. Carmel Church Bone Bed. An interactive reconstruction of a partially-excavated bone-bed site, detailing 300 million years of evolution.

41. Wakkary, R.; Newby, K.; Hatala, M.; Evernden, D.; Droumeva, M. Interactive audio content: An approach to audio content for a dynamic museum experience through augmented audio reality and adaptive information retrieval. In *Museums on the Web*, Arlington, VA, April 1–3, 2004; http://www.archimuse.com/mw2004/papers/wakkary/wakkary.html (accessed July 20, 2008).
42. Wilson, G. Multimedia tour programme at Tate Modern. In *Museums on the Web*, Arlington, VA, April 1–3, 2004; http://www.archimuse.com/mw2004/papers/wilson/wilson.html (accessed July 20, 2008).

43 Museum Web Sites and Digital Collections

David Bearman and Jennifer Trant

CONTENTS

INTRODUCTION

The World Wide Web (the Web) has provided an easy way for museums to reach their many audiences, publishing a range of materials about their institutions and collections, and creating spaces for their varied constituents to engage with each other, and with the content of collections. Following its release in 1993[1] the Web was rapidly adopted by museums (a development traced in the proceedings of the Museums and the Web conferences (1997–). Today, 15 years after its release, having a Web site is considered a necessity by museums. This rapid adoption of the Web by museums reflects the fit between museum needs for widespread dissemination of multimedia content and the ease with which the functionality embodied in the Web supports programmatic needs.

Museums care for information as much as they care for collections. The Web enabled relatively easy publication of complex documents, richly illustrated in color (something that the economics of print publication was making more and more difficult). The broad reach of the Web enables contact with both local constituencies, and international networks of potential tourist visitors and subject-specialist scholars. Broadcast of basic information about the institution (such as location, hours, and exhibition program) and narrow-cast of in-depth information for particular audiences (such as teacher-packets and interpretive programs for schoolchildren) are enabled by the same technology.

Museums were well positioned to take advantage of the Web through early experiments in multimedia. They remain leaders in the use of social computing technologies, because of the true fit between these tools and the desire to engage communities—based in part on the new museology.[2]

HISTORY OF MUSEUMS ON THE WEB

BACKGROUND

Museum adoption of the Web in the mid-1990s built on a decade of museum experiences with hypertext, networking, and multimedia. By 1993, museums were widely exploiting stand-alone interactive image and text on kiosks within the museum, often using videodisc or CD storage.[3] While these technologies enabled distribution outside the museum on fixed digital media, the reach of these publications was extremely limited when compared to the near ubiquity that the network now provides. Authoring tools were proprietary and often difficult to use, and run-time environments were closely prescribed and often hardware-based.

Museum networking on private, proprietary connections had been available in the 1970s, and national networks (such as the Canadian Heritage Information Network) and regional ones (such as the Museum Computer Network GRIPHOS application), had been built. But prior to the Web, networking databases was expensive, limited to text only, and for institutional rather than public needs; early French experiments with public access to Minitel reached out more broadly. Immediately prior to the advent of the Web, in the late 1980s and early 1990s, open protocols developed for access to (predominantly text) files over the Internet—such as archie [for ftp] and gopher for files—were experimentally employed by some museums. The most radical aspect of the Web was that it enabled true multimedia. While initially only text and image, for a community that had struggled with side-by-side monitors for text and image videodisc display, and hardware-dependent CD-Rom authoring, this was a major breakthrough.

EARLY CULTURAL WEB EXPERIMENTS

Most museum technology professionals were probably introduced to the possibility of networked access to cultural heritage information by the Library of Congress' exhibit of *Treasure from the Vatican* which was delivered over the Internet[4] from January to April 1993, even before European Organization for Nuclear Research (CERN) board decided to make the World Wide Web publicly available, using the alpha release of the first popular Web browser, Mosaic.[5] A few might even have seen the exhibit of Soviet materials released in the previous year, before any inkling of the Web had spread beyond CERN. Outside of academia, uptake was only slightly slower. The French Ministry of Culture site on the Lascaux caves, which first appeared late in 1994 played an important role in alerting generalists to the benefits of publishing cultural content on the Web.[6]

Some museums in the academic sphere were introduced to the Web before commercial browsers made their debut in late 1994. Teaching and research collections took the lead by implementing Web access to their existing databases. As early as August 1993, the University of Illinois's Krannert Art Museum launched a hypermedia exhibit on the Web; the University of California at Berkeley, Museum of Paleontology had a site underway by September which by year-end included a walk-through of the Dinosaur halls and an interactive guest book. The University of Virginia Rosetti Archive had launched an experimental Web site with digital collections, exhibits, and educational materials by the spring of 1994. The Perseus Project, a digital library that was under development since the spring of 1987, was quick to try out Web-based access methods.[7] These early scholarly initiatives pointed out a new audience for museum collections content. In January 1994, the Exploratorium became the first nonacademic museum site on the World Wide Web.

However, the Web was not seen as the only viable solution to networked access to linked image and text for a few years. In late 1994, when the Getty Museum Educational Site Licensing Project launched its competition for University participation in a museum image sharing project, one element in evaluation was whether the participants had the capacity to develop applications to deliver networked multimedia. Several contenders had existing, non-Web, applications that were in experimental use, and were selected in part based on that. However, by the time the first MESL applications appeared a year later, all but one of the Universities employed Web protocols rather than the special solutions each had been expected to have to create to deliver multimedia over the Internet.[8]

Early Museum Web Sites

It is tempting to paint a path from simple to complex museum Web site–from brochure, to exhibit, to shop, to online collection, to social network, to semantic Web—but the history of museum use of the Web is not linear. Many museums first saw the Web as an experimental space in which they could develop hypermedia and test very demanding digital delivery scenarios. It was only with the broad public popularity of the Web that museums came to realize that their sites ought to include basic "brochure" information.

It is still surprising to many that the first sites built by museums often lacked such fundamental elements as museum hours (and especially location information), and that some of the earliest museum Web sites included collections, exhibitions, educational interactives, and even what we would now think of as social networking features.

The citation given by GNN (The Global Network Navigator) in 1994 to the Paleontology Server at The University of California Museum of Paleontology[9] read:

> The server is an interactive natural history museum available over the Internet. This museum without walls is well organized and makes interesting use of large graphics. You can learn about phylogeny, the "Tree of Life," or examine photographs of Great White Sharks off the California coast, which proves that paleontologists study living things as well as fossils.

Other early adopters included the Museum of Natural History, London[10]; the Science Museum, London; and the Canadian Museum of Civilization.

MUSEUM PROGRAMS ONLINE

Web pages of museums have evolved to reflect the range of museum programming. An informational core, which presented the museums' physical reality in cyberspace, soon formed the required "brochure."[11] The basic elements of a museum Web site included information about the museum, location, maps and admissions, details of exhibits and current events such as tours, a profile of the collections, possibly with some highlights, perhaps some detail about the institution's history, a welcome from the director, information about museum membership and giving to the museum, facilities rental, and the museum store. Extended features often centered around special exhibitions, and then were "archived." Education materials, for teachers could be exhibition related, or related to the permanent collection. If this sounds like a reiteration of the physical museum, in many ways it was. Each department found its place on the Web, and early museum sites often reflected the concerns of their internal leads.[12]

Online Museum Exhibitions

As with the physical site, most museums' preferred way to display their collections online has proven to be as part of an online exhibition. The fundamental advantage of the Web is that it offers opportunities for additional content and broader audiences. From the first, exhibitions were about more than simply showing museum objects with juxtaposed text; the object was to create an experience in multiple sensory dimensions, not unlike that of entering a real-world exhibit. In early 1994, when "fast" Web access meant someone was using a 14.4 mbps modem, the Smithsonian's "The White House Collection of American Crafts," (which opened on the Web on April 25, 1994), included extensive video and audio clips of the curator talking about selected pieces and handling them in ways that would not be possible during the exhibition.[13] In addition, each artist was asked to answer a series of questions about their work, which was not part of the exhibition itself. An important element of the exhibit, novel at the time, was what we would now think of as a "social networking" feature that allowed visitors to add comments to a comment book.[14]

In 1995, the Museum of Modern Art, New York (MOMA) was developing online exhibitions to accompany many of its physical shows. Like many museums, it still lacked an infrastructure to support its online activity so sites for "Annette Messager," "Video Spaces: Eight Installations," and "Mutant Materials in Contemporary Design" were hosted for MOMA by the School of Visual Arts.[15]

Within a short time, museums developed a range of interpretive materials to augment online exhibits. These were often aimed at specific niche audiences, such as games for children, pre- and post-visit guides for families, learning packages for teachers, and extensive scholarly research pathways, and have become a standard way both to market the in-house show and to extend its useful lifetime. Most museums today will have an online surrogate or augmentation of current exhibitions on their sites. In addition, many will provide access to past exhibits, which of course are no longer accessible in the physical world, even if they are not truly serving a guaranteed, permanent archival function.

Substantial research has been undertaken on storytelling and narrative presentation online in support of museum exhibitions. But museums are aware that their efforts are often subverted by the fact that their visitors do not "enter by the front door" and read the linear script as written by curators, but rather reach the museum by search engines taking them deep into the interpretive narration.[16]

Online Events

Museums have found the low cost of entry to broadcasting over the Internet highly attractive, in part because of their interactive capability (though the facility for narrow-casting provided by Web-based programs is equally important). Using the network to bridge geography is a common strategy, whether this is the virtual reuniting of a dispersed work, or the creation of a real-time multipoint event. As an example of the latter integrated into a museum's educational program, from February 11–21, 1997, the Exploratorium site provided live interactions with astronauts servicing the Hubble Space Mission. In two shows daily, they combined live feeds from the orbiting shuttle, science demonstrations, videoconferencing with researchers across the country, and questions from the audience.[17] Since then, at the Exploratorium and many other science museums worldwide, regular interactions between scientists and school children via Webcasting, have become standard features of museum programming. At the Natural History Museum (London) these Web-based features now occur daily.[18]

Social Experiences

Museums envision themselves as gathering places designed to encourage thinking, generate dialogue, and occasionally create controversy. So the social potential of the Web was seen as crucial to its museum implementations long before the mainstream invented the rubrics Web 2.0 and social computing. Partnerships with schools were the first territory explored by museums, and this rapidly led to the teachers, and then the students, contributing content back to the museum.[19] Applications that enabled visitors to provide their views followed swiftly.[20]

By 1997, museums were inventing mechanisms for user feedback missing from the Web at large. Web designers for the Smithsonian Institution's *Revealing Things* exhibit envisaged users as both "designers of their personal exhibits" and "contributing objects and stories to the presentation . . . chang(ing) the experience for themselves and others."[21]

Early observers recognized that user-generated (or user-contributed) content and the interaction of the Web would challenge the authority of museums. Some celebrated that,[22,23] while others were concerned. The resulting dialogue clarified the differences between authority and authenticity and helped museums position themselves vis-à-vis their varied publics.[24]

Some museums, led by the National Museum of the American Indian in Washington and Te Papa in New Zealand—two national institutions that were first opened during the "Web-Age," began to construct architectures that enabled them systematically to obtain and use the insights of indigenous informants to bring a perspective from within the societies that originally created artifacts to bear on museum documentation.[25] The Encyclopedia of New Zealand encourages and incorporates user-contributed content.[26]

Because one of the problems museums face is that of describing the objects in their collections, and providing access to them in ways that visitors find useful, engaging volunteer catalogers over the Internet was explored in the 1990s. In the MESL project, the Fowler Museum's experience of obtaining remote assistance in describing part of its African collection from Columbia University was held up as a justification for the effort involve in putting collections online.[27] The Fine Arts Museum of San Francisco had early success with volunteer keywording of its Thinker database.[28,29] But action came with the success of social tagging at del.icio.us and flickr in 2004. Organized investigation of the potential for folksonomy in the steve.museum project[30,31] coincided with implementations of nonresearch taggers, the most extensive of which is at the Powerhouse Museum in Sydney.[32] Early findings are that many people find it rewarding to tag, and will generously give their time to museums if asked. The resulting tags are mostly relevant and not terms that the museums have in their own documentation.[33,34]

Museums have also been attracted by the engaging power of serious games, especially as a means of attracting and keeping the attention of younger audiences and people who might be alienated by more traditional methods of teaching. An excellent example, Launchball at the Science Museum of London, winner of several "best of the Web" awards in 2008, including one at the South by Southwest Interactive Festival.[35] Similarly, the power of providing visitors with sophisticated tools with which to construct their own meanings and publish them to the Web, has been successfully used by museums to engage visitors, as with the film editing widget at the American image exhibit of the Maxwell Museum of Anthropology.[36]

Museums are also finding that they can meet potential audiences in engaging social spaces created by others, including commercial services. Social computing spaces such as FaceBook, Flickr, and YouTube are attracting museum attention and programming.[37–39]

Virtual Experiences

Museum exhibitions are three-dimensional (3-D) installations designed to offer context to objects so that they may be better understood. It is not surprising, then, that efforts to create 3-D environments on the Web attracted museum interest from the first. In 1993, the University of California Berkeley Museum of Paleontology demonstrated the potential of exhibition walk-throughs. By 1997, museums were regularly providing remote visitors with 3-D experiences over the Web—both walk-throughs of spaces, and 3-D models of artifacts.[40,41] Quickly, though, the community realized that we didn't need elevators in Web museums; the logical models of museum information-space were more effective when they didn't mirror the architecture—and historic organic growth—of physical museum spaces.

Early reports featured natural history educators using 3-D modeling to teach morphology, registrars providing information to potential researchers prior to shipping a fragile item, and school teachers exciting students into careful observation. Reconstructions also tested historical hypotheses.[42] The Science Museum in Milan provided remote 3-D access to "working" models of Leonardo

Da Vinci's inventions, including those never built in the real world, in 1999, and allowed avatars representing individuals logged in from remote locations to "join" each other in an experience[43,44] similar to that museums are now exploring virtual worlds such as Second Life.[45]

Museums have also successfully used the Web to offer a window onto otherwise "back-room" museum processes. Projects like those that chronicled the lengthy conservation of works of art at the Minneapolis Institute of Arts[46] helped museums demystify some of their professional processes.

Some museums (along with universities, governments, and many other institutions) have taken up a virtual presence in these virtual worlds today. Often, they have done so, like the Exploratorium, explicitly in order to provide experiences that are not possible in the physical world, such as experiencing Brownian motion by riding on a dust particle.[47] Others are content to see virtual worlds as useful because avatars provide an emotional extension of humans into the virtual world and thereby enhance interpersonal communication that might otherwise occur through online chatting or bulletin boards alone.

Evaluators are still trying to determine when these kinds of experiences were necessary, and when they might be simply entertaining, or even distracting. Investigation about how to bridge the physical space of the museum and the virtual space of the Web is ongoing.[48] Findings have often seemed counterintuitive; for example, after years of experimentation, museums have discovered that bookmarking, per se, is not something that visitors do at museums, though museum professional repeatedly hypothesized that it would be a highly rewarding application.[49]

Searchable Collections

Although "virtual collections" and "digital museums" are concepts that are often associated with museum use of the Web, they have their roots, and their primary appeal, outside of the museum culture, in broader society and in academia. Many early "virtual museums" such as the Virtual Louvre or the Artchive, were creations of individual enthusiasts rather than institutions.

Online catalogs have not been the primary goal of museums on the Web, in direct contrast to libraries, who have seen the OPAC as the first point of contact with their online public. Some institutions with close academic ties, particularly if their collections were assembled for research or teaching, made their collections catalog searchable on the Web early. For example, the American Museum of Natural History had its Library catalog online in 1996.[50] The Fine Arts Museums of San Francisco (FAMSF)—an early adopter of digital imaging technology—had over 65,000 works online for viewing at its "Thinker" site in 1996,[51] and encouraged its Web visitors to "be the curator!" The FAMSF site included teachers' guides and online tours of temporary exhibitions as well.

Museum collections catalogs are difficult for the nonspecialist to interpret and are often better suited for expert use. These text databases often only include rudimentary data often without any images, or with only one relatively low-resolution image. Because the primary audiences museums wish to reach through the Web are not only "researchers" but potential visitors, additional contextual and interpretive materials have priority.[52] One approach to making the museum catalog more accessible has been to link it to familiar interfaces. Integrating museum databases with other sources of information, especially to enable graphical displays that are intuitive to end users, was a desire of museums before the Web and suggested as an early objective of Web implementations[53]; with the advent of Ajax and techniques for Web mashups, integrating museum data with data and tools from other sites, there have been successful implementations in museums. By dragging multiple images from the public sources on the Web, researchers have been able to recreate 3-D renderings of historical sites as if they were flying through them.[54] Many "museum-like" applications, such as the mashup (combination) of ornithology data with map coordinates, have emanated from university laboratories.[55]

Still in its infancy, but growing quickly, geo-encoding of museum collections enlists the potential of location-aware information delivery based on open APIs (Application Programming Interfaces) to put museum objects where the audience is physically, rather than expecting the audience to come to the museum. By geo-encoding the locations of important events in the life of an object into its digital record, museums use the same Web-based infrastructure that is evolving to tell people in passing cars about local restaurants and other commercial offerings, to inform them about the cultural artifacts that are native to the area in which they find themselves, even if these are in museum collections thousands of miles away. This has potentially revolutionary consequences for how people relate to the spaces in which they live, and for museums it has the capacity to "turn the museum inside out" and show its collections in the contexts in which they were made, used, or collected.[56]

Collecting and Preserving

Museums, particularly art museums that have contemporary culture as part of their collecting mission, or those that are dedicated to understanding contemporary events, such as science centers, face a special challenge since they not only need to use digital methods to provide the public with access to their collections, but also are challenged to collect and exhibit digital works.

Art museums, self-consciously collecting *avant garde* digital art, were the first to encounter the challenges of exhibiting and preserving born-digital collections.[14,57,58] Some early examples, such as "Gallery 9" as of December 1998, can still be seen at the Internet Archive.[59]

Increasingly science museums and even history museums are being challenged to collect digital artifacts as these artifacts have an impact on everyday life. A community museum, might, for example, have to collect digital artifacts in order to document community involvement in a planning process conducted using environmental impact mapping in a collaborative Web space.[60] This process, conducted over many months, relied on visualization tools, models, and data that were specific to the community, and logged hundreds of citizens participating in the discussion and illustrating their points by digitally generating representations of different possible futures. Science museums which are experimenting with making science news feeds a part of their on-site exhibition, such as the Minnesota "Science Buzz" project, or which are creating opportunities for visitor feedback by cell phone as at the Liberty Science center, will need to consider just what place an archival record of these interactions has in documenting the museum programs.

Ongoing digitization programs are retrospectively creating digital versions of photographic surrogates kept by museums for identification and documentation purposes. But while in libraries retrospective digitization is sometimes cast in terms of preservation (for the digital copy holds the same informational content as the original), in museums digital surrogates will never take the place of original museum artifacts. Although digitization projects in museums are primarily about access they have spin-off preservation benefits by reducing the impact of repeated handling for reference purposes, and have, unfortunately, also sometimes left us with the only copies of works once in museums but lost through war or natural disaster.

IMPACT ON MUSEUMS

In its brief 15-year history, the World Wide Web has already had significant impact on museums as institutions.

Sectoral Identity: The Museum Domain

At MW97, Cary Karp proposed that museums ought to have a place in the Internet domain name system.[61] By 2000, he had led ICOM and the J. Paul Getty Trust in an effort to obtain a high level domain for museums in the belief that high level domains would proliferate and that a distinctive one for museums would serve their needs to be recognizable in Web space.[62,63] Although widely publicized in the museum community, the new top level domains have not had the impact socially that was expected in 2000. Museums, which generally maintained their identities in "dot org" or "dot edu" space, have not made the switch to "dot museum" in appreciable numbers. At present it seems unlikely that they will because newer top level domains, introduced after the national domains and the three original ones for commerce, civil organizations, and education, have not captured the popular imagination in other sectors either.

Outreach

Though the distinction of museums as high level domains did not enhance their sectoral visibility, Web technologies are being deployed successfully to raise the profile of individual institutions and their programs. Many museums are using RSS (really simple syndication) to narrowcast the contents of their sites to those with specific interests in their topic. By tagging their content with a variety of highly specific descriptors, and using RSS to distribute a feed of news items, they enable aggregation and re-presentation of museum content in diverse contexts. The 24-hr museum, now culture 24, aggregates news about U.K. museum activities, and presents it as an integrated museum-related RSS feed.[64] RSS has also been used to create content streams that are used to animate museum exhibition environments.[65,66]

Some museums are encouraging viral marketing[67] in order to build mini-communities of interest around particular parts of their content. Museums are actively engaged in blogging, podcasting, and even in posting videos to YouTube. And the "fans" of museums on social sites such as Facebook, are being used to promote its activities to their friends.

Like other institutions influenced by academia and libraries, museums were caught off-guard by the overwhelming success of search engines. By 1997, reports already revealed that while museums were expending much energy in authoring visually and intellectually enticing sites, their content was organized narratively and linearly while most of their users were finding specific content in searches and then linking directly into the museum site at the level of that content. Museums have responded to their users "entering by the window rather than the front door" in several different ways. Some museums have taken great care to be fully available to search engines—hiring Search Engine Optimization (SEO) consultants, inviting crawlers, making metadata for the search engines to use, identifying resources with URIs and other digital identifiers, and attending to the requirement for persistent addressing. Others have become engaged with libraries and universities promoting the use of the Open Archive Initiative (OAI) protocols for harvesting museum collections data. The Consortium for Computer Interchange of Museum Information (CIMI) led a well-publicized effort to adopt OAI for museums, but the limitations of the Dublin Core metadata framework essentially defeated this effort, despite funded attempts to overcome them.[68]

Some museums are watching carefully to see how the Semantic Web evolves and what kinds of discovery can be provided by geo-aware methods. When museums were first introduced to the semantic Web in 2002, the excitement level was high[69,70] however as these technologies evolved and it became clearer that semantic Web accessibility of collections depended not just on metadata but on quite sophisticated metadata expressed in Resource Description Framework (RDF) with a defined ontology, the enthusiasm gave way, outside academic circles, to watching and waiting.[71] In 2008, with the launch of some more sophisticated toolsets demonstrating the potential of semantic Web approaches, some cautious renewed interest is being expressed, but as always the barriers to museum making their collections available in this way are that they lack the resources and often the knowledge of their collections, to create the necessary metadata. Meanwhile, geo-aware devices in phones and automobiles, and an array of services that might be built upon these, are attracting significant attention in museums whose collections were gathered from locations around the globe and can often be best interpreted in those contexts, if they could be discovered there by tourists or locals.

Staffing and Resource Allocation

The Web has created new opportunities for museums to reach their audiences and conduct their missions, but it did so at a cost. In effect, each museum has now opened another branch. While early museum Web sites were often projects of one or two dedicated people (or even unauthorized "skunkworks"), increasingly museums have learned that their Web presence requires all the manpower and programming attention of a second venue.[72]

Maintaining a quality Web site makes both technical and program content demands on the museum. Staff throughout the institution become responsible for updating the public face of their departments and programs as represented on the Web. Data that was created for internal purposes needs to be revisited and repurposed for public access. As information is created digitally for use in-house, on the museum Web site, in virtual exhibits and in syndicated content for "cultural events" sites and ticketing agents, the need to manage digital objects that can be reused for a variety of purposes increases. The technical sophistication demanded by such reuses has led museums to implement Digital Asset Management and Digital Rights Management systems in addition to traditional Collections Management Systems that keep track of the physical collection of the museum.

User expectations based on the evolution of nonmuseum Web experiences impinge on acceptance of the museum product and force the museum to continuously upgrade its capabilities and offerings. And requirements imposed by governments, for example to provide accessibility to those with physical handicaps, now extend to online visitors.

Museums face the challenge of retaining skilled staff. In a project-driven culture, where much work is often outsourced developing institutional capacity is an issue. Many museums don't have programming staff on site and so are stretched to take full advantage of the potential of the Web.

Even maintenance becomes a great challenge, since the Web imposes a constantly changing technical requirement on the museum. Information technologies within the institution and servers providing access to the outside world must be maintained. Specialist staff must learn about online education, online fundraising, online publication, and other online programming skills. Technical standards that were optional for institutions without interconnections become mandatory. And in-service education becomes necessary. Ongoing venues for professional development include annual conferences such as Museums and the Web, the meetings and listservs of organizations such as the Museum Computer Group (United Kingdom) and the Museum Computer Network (USA), the Association of Science and Technology Centers, The Visitor Studies Association, and to some extent the work of the International Council of Museums' Committees on Documentation (ICOM/CIDOC) and Visual Information (ICOM/AVICOM). Emerging online communities of professionals include ExhibitFiles.org and conference.archimuse.com.

Business Models

In the early days of the Web, museums and other social institutions, wondered if it had income potential, and if so whether they wanted to exploit that source. Quite a few museums were caught up in the early widespread notion that the Web might be a source of significant new income. Museums lived through the dot.com boom and bust; while only a few (notably the Museum of Fine Arts Boston, museum shop[73]) succeeded in making money from it, none went out of business as a consequence. However, some museums joined high-profile consortia with universities to provide online education, and these did collapse in the bust of 2001. Since then few museums have made online commerce a priority. However, most museum Web sites have e-commerce functionality (often delivered by an outside provider) to support basic store purchases, membership sales, and occasionally online ticketing. Although advertising emerged as a means of making income from the Web in the early twenty-first century, other than a few high-profile sponsorship relationships (such as British Telecom and Tate) museums have not introduced advertising on their sites. For the present, anyway, museums are treating the Web as a service to be provided for free and without commercial advertising, even when they charge for access to the physical museum and actively solicit sponsorship for on-site exhibitions.

Outside the museum community, museums are perceived to be making money from the sale of rights and reproductions; however, far from being a major source of new income, online licensing has become a cost-center for most museums.[74,75] As well as requiring costly research in order to discover the rights inherent in collections, museums often pay fees to use materials online themselves. Efforts to make the works available under Creative Commons licenses or free to scholars have not proved very attractive to museum administrators, who, unlike their counterparts in libraries, have historically incurred high costs in making images available and recovered some of that cost through fees. Experiments with access for noncommercial uses at the Victoria & Albert Museum and The Metropolitan Museum of Art are, however, ongoing. The Creative Commons was not flexible in offering museums a license that worked for them, until the CC+ license of 2008, which some museums may now be ready to consider.

In 1997 more than 30 high-profile art museums joined to form the Art Museum Image Consortium (AMICO). The purpose of AMICO was not to earn income for the museums, though it developed a successful licensing scheme that ultimately recovered its costs of rights clearance (which are quite high for art of the past century), but to find a way to serve university and school students high-quality digital reproductions by reducing transaction costs.[75,76] Its success attracted the Mellon Foundation which launched ArtStor, a program with similar objectives which subsequently absorbed AMICO and now licenses a collection of art reproductions (much not sourced from museums) to higher education.

Despite these experiments, museums have generally not followed either the commercialization route or the licensing route. The trend is toward more open access, with mission-related goals of accessibility and education guiding museums to make content available on the Web without restrictions, but within the context of museum programming rather than as discrete objects in searchable databases.

Issues Facing Museums Online

From the first, museums have been concerned that their move of programming to the Web increase opportunities for participation. Early implementations were highly sensitive to average slow access speeds and low resolution monitors, and present implementations avoid proprietary tools. The Digital Divide continues to echo in museum discussions. As public institutions museums don't want their choice of delivery channel to exclude users.

Using the Web in a socially responsible way has led museums to open themselves up to challenges to their ownership of objects in their collections (creating, for example, avenues that can be used by those claiming they benefited from Nazi war loot), their interpretation of objects in their collections (enabling alternative accounts from aboriginal communities for instance) and ensuring accessibility.

Finally, museums are beginning to alter their measures of success. Instead of counting "visitors" to the museum itself, or to its Web sites, some museums are beginning to find ways to measure their audiences or impact even when the content of the museum is seen or used somewhere other than the museum site.[77] It is likely that syndication of content on other nonmuseum sites, as the Library of Congress and Powerhouse Museum are now experimentally doing with photographs from its collections in the Flickr Commons,[78] will become a growing trend. Museums are slowly ceding control of their content in order to reach audiences through as many channels as possible.

CONCLUSIONS

Museums have long used new media technologies, be they murals, dioramas, films, or interactive Web pages, to help explain the complexities of their collections to many diverse audiences. They publish a wide range of materials, from printed ephemera (in-gallery hand-outs) to scholarly tomes (exhibition catalogs), in a wide range of formats. From its outset, the Web has proven a suitable platform for delivering many types of information to many different users, and museums have adopted its many potentials. As the Web interpenetrates real space, with portable, geo-aware devices like the iPhone™, museums will find that it continues to serve their goals: engaging communities with collections and encouraging active learning and participation.

REFERENCES

1. Connolly, D. A little history of the World Wide Web. 2000. http://www.w3.org/History.html (accessed April 29, 2008).
2. Vergo, P., Ed. *The New Museology*; Reaktion Books: London, 1989.
3. Bearman, D. Museum interactives. Arch. Museum Info. **1993**, *7* (2), 6.
4. Library of Congress. Rome reborn: The Vatican library & renaissance culture. 1993 [2002] http://www.loc.gov/ exhibits/vatican/.
5. Bearman, D. Exhibits on the Internet. Arch. Museum Info. **1993**, *7* (1), 8.
6. [editor]. Out of the caves. In The Washington Post; January 28, **1995**, A 14.
7. Crane, G. The Perseus project and beyond: How building a digital library challenges the humanities and technology. D-Lib Magazine January **1998**. http://www.dlib.org/dlib/january98/01crane.html (accessed April 28, 2008).
8. Trant, J. The museum educational site licensing project. Spectra, J. Museum Comput. Network **1995**. *22* (Winter 1994–1995), 19–21. http://www.archimuse.com/papers/jt.mesl.spectra9502.
9. University of California Museum of Paleontology. Awards and reviews of the University of California Museum of Paleontology Website. 2001, July 30, 2001 http://www.ucmp.berkeley.edu/museum/reviews.html (accessed June 17, 2008).
10. T1 Rex: Street Cred. Wired **1999**, *7* (3). http://www.wired.com/wired/archive/7.03/streetcred_pr.html.
11. Garzotto, F.; Discenza, A. Design patterns for museum Web Sites. In *Museums and the Web 1999: Proceedings*, Bearman, D., Trant, J., Eds.; New Orleans, LA, 1999. http://www.archimuse.com/mw99/papers/discenza/discenza.html (accessed June 15, 2008).
12. Bearman, D.; Trant, J. Survey of museum Web implementations, 2005. Arch. Museum Info. **2006**. http://www.archimuse.com/research/mwbenchmarks/report/mwbenchmarks 2005.html (accessed January 31, 2008).
13. National Museum of American Art. In *"The White House Collection of American Crafts" and Exhibit*; 1994. http://web.archive.org/web/19980130054030/http://nmaa-ryder.si.edu/whc/invirtutourmainpage.html (accessed October 14, 2008).
14. Dietz, S. Curating on the Web: The museum in an interface culture. In *Museums and the Web 1998: Proceedings*; Bearman, D., Trant, J., Eds.; Toronto, ON, Canada, 1998. http://www.archimuse.com/mw98/papers/dietz/dietz_curatingtheweb.html (accessed June 15, 2008).
15. Museum of Modern Art, N. Y. 1996, November 11, 1996, http://web.archive.org/web/19961111103911/www.moma.org/webprojects.html
16. Nordbotten, J. Entering through the side door—a usage analysis of Web presentations. In *Museums and the Web 2000: Proceedings*; Bearman, D., Trant, J., Eds.; Archives & Museum Informatics: Minneapolis, MN, 2000.
17. Exploratorium, T. Hubble Servicing Mission: Looking Beyond Boundaries; 1997. August 17, 2000 [archive date].
18. Natural History Museum, L. Nature live online: Live Webcast. 2008. http://www.nhm.ac.uk/nature-online/nature-live/live-webcast/live-webcast.html (accessed April 30, 2008).
19. McKenzie, J. Building a virtual museum community. In *Museums and the Web 1997: Proceedings*; Bearman, D., Trant, J., Eds.; Los Angeles, 1997. http://fromnowon. org/museum/museweb.html (accessed June 15, 2008).
20. Glasser, S. New ideas/new audiences. In *Museums and the Web 1997: Proceedings*; Bearman, D., Trant, J., Eds.; Los Angeles, CA, 1997. http://www.archimuse.com/mw97/speak/glasser.htm (accessed June 15, 2008).
21. Gradwohl, J. Revealing things: An experiment in museum Web Sites. In *Museums and the Web 1997: Proceedings*; Bearman, D., Trant, J., Eds.; Los Angeles, 1997.
22. Walsh, P. The Web and the unassailable voice. In *Museums and the Web 1997: Proceedings*; Bearman, D., Trant, J., Eds.; Los Angeles, 1997. http://www.archimuse.com/mw97/speak/walsh.htm (accessed June 15, 2008).
23. Smith, A. The museum as a forum for the nation. In *Museums and the Web 1998: Proceedings*; Bearman, D., Trant, J., Eds.; Toronto, ON, Canada, 1998. http://www.archimuse.com/mw98/papers/smith_a/smith_a_paper.html (accessed June 15, 2008).

24. Bearman, D.; Trant, J. Authenticity of digital resources: Towards a statement of requirements in the research process. D-Lib Magazine June **1998**. http://www.dlib/org/dlib/june98/06/bearman.html (accessed April 28, 2008).
25. Witcomb, A. The end of the Mausoleum: Museums in the age of electronic communication. In *Museums and the Web 1997: Proceedings*; Bearman, D., Trant, J., Eds.; Los Angeles, 1997. http://www.archimuse.com/mw97/speak/witcomb.htm (accessed June 15, 2008).
26. Williams, S. Te Ara—The encyclopedia of New Zealand: An encyclopedia created for the Web. In *Museums and the Web 2007. Proceedings*; Toronto, ON, Canada, 2007. http://www.archimuse.com/mw2007/papers/williams/williams.html (accessed June 15, 2008).
27. Trant, J. Enabling educational use of museum digital materials: The Museum Educational Site Licensing (MESL) Project. In *The Electronic Imaging and Visual Arts Conference (EVA)*, Florence, Italy; 1996. http://www.archimuse.com/papers/jt.eva.florence.9602.html (accessed January 31, 2008).
28. Futernick, B. On access points in The Thinker. 2003. http://www.thinker.org.
29. Futernick, B. Keyword indexing the thinker. To J. Trant: e-mail message. August 15, 2005.
30. Bearman, D.; Trant, J. Social terminology enhancement through vernacular engagement: Exploring collaborative annotation to encourage interaction with museum collections. D-Lib Magazine **2005**, *11* (9). http://www.dlib.org/dlib/september05/bearman/09bearman.html (accessed September 11, 2006).
31. Chun, S.; Cherry, R.; Hiwiller, D.; Trant, J.; Wyman, B. Steve.museum: An Ongoing experiment in social tagging, folksonomy, and museums. In *Museums and the Web 2006: Selected papers from an international conference*, Albuquerque, NM, Trant, J., Bearman, D., Eds.; 2006, http://www.archimuse.com/mw2006/papers/wyman/wyman.html (accessed September 11, 2006).
32. Chan, S. Tagging and searching—serendipity and museum collection databases. In *Museums and the Web 2007. Proceedings*; Trant, J., Bearman, D., Eds.; Toronto, ON, Canada, 2007. http://www.archimuse.com/mw2007/papers/chan/chan.html (accessed October 15, 2006).
33. Trant, J. Exploring the potential for social tagging and folksonomy in art museums: Proof of concept. New Rev. Hypermedia Multimedia **2006**, *12* (1), 83–105. http://www.archimuse.com/papers/steve-nrhm-0605preprint.pdf (accessed June 15, 2008).
34. Trant, J.; Wyman, B. Investigating social tagging and folksonomy in art museums with steve.museum; World Wide Web 2006 (WWW2006): Collaborative Web Tagging Workshop: Edinburgh, Scotland, 2006. http://www.archimuse.com/research/www2006-tagging-steve.pdf (accessed January 31, 2008).
35. Science Museum. Science Museum's Launchball game wins international media award, 2008. http://www.sciencemuseum.org.uk/about_us/press_and_media/press_releases/2008/03/launchball_game.aspx (accessed June 15, 2008).
36. Maxwell Museum of Anthropology, U. o. N. M. The American image: The photographs of John Collier Jr.: Propaganda filmmaker. 2007. http://americanimage.unm.edu/propagandafilmmaker.html (accessed July 15, 2008).
37. Bernstein, S. Where do we go from here?: Continuing with Web 2.0. In *Museums and the Web 2008. Proceedings*; Trant, J., Bearman, D., Eds.; Montreal, QC, Canada, 2008. http://www.archimuse.com/mw2008/papers/bernstein/bernstein.html (accessed March 31, 2008).
38. Burnette, A.; Alexander, C.; Dark, D.; Hart, D.; Rossi, J.; Minor, N. Beyond launch: Museum videos on YouTube. In *Museums and the Web 2008. Proceedings*; Trant, J., Bearman, D., Eds.; Montreal, QC, Canada, 2008. http://www.archimuse.com/mw2008/papers/hart/hart.html (accessed March 31, 2008).
39. Dawson, B.; Trépanier, G.; McDonald, F. Social presence: New value for networked museum audiences. In *Museums and the Web 2008. Proceedings*; Trant, J., Bearman, D., Eds.; Montreal, QC, Canada, 2008. http://www.archimuse.com/mw2008/papers/dawson/dawson.html (accessed March 31, 2008).
40. Calvo, C.M.; Hansen, C.C.; Rosenberger, A. The digital Darwins project. In *Museums and the Web 1997: Proceedings*; Bearman, D., Trant, J., Eds.; Los Angeles, 1997. http://www.archimuse.com/mw97/speak/calvo.htm (accessed June 15, 2008).
41. Quackenbush, A.; Toomey, R.; Schroeder, E. QuickTime virtual reality and museums on the Internet. In *Museums and the Web 1997: Proceedings*; Bearman, D., Trant, J., Eds.; Los Angeles, 1997.
42. Devine, J. Reconstructing Rosie: A digital experiment in facial reconstruction. In *Museums and the Web 2001: Proceedings*; Trant, J., Bearman, D., Eds.; Seattle, WA, 2001.
43. Paolini, P.; Barbieri, T. Cooperative visits for museum WWW sites a year later: Evaluating the effect. In *Museums and the Web 2000: Proceedings*; Bearman, D., Trant, J., Eds.; Minneapolis, MN, 2000. http://www.archimuse.com/mw2000/papers/barbieri/barbieri.html (accessed June 15, 2008).
44. Paolini, P.; Gaia, G.; Barbieri, T.; Alonzo, F. Cooperative visits for museum WWW sites. In *Museums and the Web 1999: Proceedings*; Bearman, D., Trant, J., Eds.; New Orleans, LA, 1999. http://www.archimuse.com/mw2000/papers/barbieri/barbieri.html (accessed June 15, 2008).

45. Marty, P.; Twidale, M.; Urban, R. A second life for your museum: 3-D multi-user virtual environments and museums. In *Museums and the Web 2007. Proceedings*; Toronto, ON, Canada, 2007. http://www.archimuse.com/mw2007/papers/urban/urban.html (accessed June 15, 2008).
46. Sayre, S. Sharing the experience: The building of a successful online/on-site exhibition. In *Museums and the Web 2000: Proceedings*; Trant, J., Bearman, D., Eds.; Minneapolis, MN, 2000. http://www.archimuse.com/mw2000/papers/sayre/sayre.html (accessed June 15, 2008).
47. Rothfarb, R.; Doherty, P. Creating museum content and community in second life. In *Museums and the Web 2007: Proceedings*; Trant, J., Bearman, D., Eds.; Archives & Museum Informatics: Toronto, ON, 2007. http://www.archimuse.com/mw2007/papers/rothfarb/rothfarb.html
48. Barry, A. Creating a virtuous circle between a museum's on-line and physical spaces. In *Museums and the Web 2006: Proceedings*; Bearman, D., Trant, J., Eds.; Albuquerque, NM, 2006. http://www.archimuse.com/mw2006/papers/barry/barry.html (accessed June 15, 2008).
49. Bowen, J.; Filippini-Fantoni, S. Bookmarking in museums: Extending the museum experience beyond the visit? In *Museums and the Web 2007. Proceedings*; Toronto, ON, Canada, 2007. http://www.archimuse.com/mw2007/papers/filippini-fantoni/filippini-fantoni.html (accessed June 15, 2008).
50. American Museum of Natural History. December 18, 1996 [archive date]. American museum of natural history research Web. http://web.archive.org/web/19961218225054/http://amnh.org/ (accessed April 30, 2008).
51. Fine Arts Museums of San Francisco. The Thinker Image-base: 60,000 works of art, 1996, December 19, 1996 [archive date].
52. Sumption, K. Beyond museum walls—A critical analysis of emerging approaches to museum Web-based education. In *Museums and the Web 2001: Proceedings*; Trant, J., Bearman, D., Eds.; Seattle, WA, 2001. http://www.archimuse.com/mw2001/papers/sumption/sumption.html
53. Bearman, D. Museum strategies for success on the Internet. In *Museum Collections and the Information Superhighway Conference, Science Museum*, London, 1995. http://web.archive.org/web/20010211004518/http://www.nmsi.ac.uk/infosh/bearman.htm (accessed April 30, 2008).
54. Microsoft Live Labs. In *Photosynth at TED Conference. Photosynth Team Blog*, 2007. http://labs.live.com/photosynth/blogs/CommentView,guid,721172f9-f94f-4cee-93ec-88e7274cca53.aspx (accessed April 30, 2008).
55. Cornell Ornithology Lab. eBird 2008. http://ebird.org/(accessed April 30, 2008).
56. Liberge, L.; Gerlings, J. Cultural heritage on the map. In *Museums and the Web 2008. Proceedings*; Trant, J., Bearman, D., Eds.; Montreal, QC, Canada, 2008. http://www.archimuse.com/mw2008/papers/liberge/liberge.html (accessed March 31, 2008).
57. Cook, S. Researching and presenting a history of new media: Ten years of the Banff New Media Institute. In *Museums and the Web 2005: Proceedings*; Vancouver, BC, Canada, 2005. http://www.archimuse.com/mw2005/papers/cook/cook.html
58. Cook, S.; Graham, B. A curatorial resource for upstart media bliss. In *Museums and the Web 2001: Proceedings*; Trant, J., Bearman, D., Eds.; Seattle, WA, 2001. http://www.archimuse.com/mw2001/papers/graham/graham.html (accessed June 15, 2008).
59. Walker Art Center. Gallery 9. 1998, December 2, 1998. http://web.archive.org/web/19981202203145/www.walk-erart.org/gallery9/ (accessed April 30, 2008).
60. Suen, I.-S.; Borich, T.O. 3-D visualization in community-based planning. J. Extension **2004**, *42* (6). http://www.joe.org/joe/2004december/tt2.shtml
61. Karp, C. The international museum community's position in the Internet domain name system. In *Museums and the Web 1997: Proceedings*; Bearman, D., Trant, J., Eds.; Los Angeles, 1997.
62. Karp, C. The further adventures of the museum top-level Internet domain. Cultivate Interactive 2003. http://www.cultivate-int.org/issue9/musenic/
63. Karp, C.; Hamma, K. A top level domain for museums. In *Museums and the Web 2001: Proceedings*; Trant, J., Bearman, D., Eds.; Seattle, WA, 2001. http://www.archimuse.com/mw2001/papers/hamma/hamma.html (accessed June 15, 2008).
64. Pratty, J. The 24 hour museum tunable RSS news feed. In *Museums and the Web 2005: Proceedings*; Bearman, D., Trant, J., Eds.; Vancouver, BC, Canada, 2005. http://www.archimuse.com/mw2005/papers/pratty/pratty.html (accessed June 15, 2008).
65. LaBar, W. Exhibit commons: Using the Internet for a new exhibit paradigm. In *Museums and the Web 2006: Proceedings*; Bearman, D., Trant, J., Eds.; Albuquerque, NM, 2006. http://www.archimuse.com/mw2006/papers/labar/labar.html (accessed June 15, 2008).
66. LaBar, W.; Balsamo, A.; MacDonald, D.; Minneman, S.; Winet, J. Science mobilized: Bringing up-to-the-minute headlines into the museum and back out again: The times square of science and techn.

In *Museums and the Web 2007. Proceedings*; Toronto, ON, Canada, 2007. http://www.archimuse.com/mw2007/papers/macdonald/ macdonald.html (accessed June 15, 2008).

67. de Vet, M. Buzz and viral marketing as a PR tool for museums: A Dutch case study. In *Museums and the Web 2006: Proceedings*; Bearman, D., Trant, J., Eds.; Albuquerque, NM, 2006. http://www.archimuse.com/mw2006/papers/devet/devet.html (accessed June 15, 2008).
68. Marty, P.F.; Cole, T.; Sandore, B.; Kaczmarek, J.; Prom, C.; Shreeves, S. Now that we've found the 'Hidden Web' what can we do with it? The Illinois open archives initiative metadata harvesting experience. In *Museums and the Web 2002: Proceedings*; Trant, J., Bearman, D., Eds.; Boston, 2002. http://www.archimuse.com/mw2002/ papers/cole/cole.html (accessed June 15, 2008).
69. Dingley, A.; Shabajee, P. Today's authoring tools for tomorrow's semantic Web. In *Museums and the Web 2002: Proceedings*; Trant, J., Bearman, D., Eds.; Boston, MA, 2002. http://www.archimuse.com/mw2002/papers/dingley/dingley.html (accessed June 15, 2008).
70. Miller, E. Weaving meaning: The W3C's semantic Web initiatives. In *Museums and the Web 2002: Proceedings*; Trant, J., Bearman, D., Eds.; Boston, 2002. http://www.w3.org/Talks/2002/04/20-sw/ (accessed June 15, 2008).
71. Hyvönen, E.; Junnila, M.; Kettula, S.; Saarela, S.; Salminen, M.; Syreeni, A.; Finnish museums on the semantic Web: The user's perspective on Museum Finland. In *Museums and the Web 2004: Proceedings*; Bearman, D., Trant, J., Eds.; Washington DC/Arlington, VA, 2004. http://www.archimuse.com/mw2004/papers/hyvonen/hyvonen.html (accessed June 15, 2008).
72. Getchell, P.; LaKind, D. Zero to a million in one year flat. In *Museums and the Web 2000: Proceedings*; Trant, J., Bearman, D., Eds.; Minneapolis, MN, 2000. http://www.archimuse.com/mw2000/papers/getchell/getchell.html (accessed June 15, 2008).
73. Tanner, S. Reproduction charging models & rights policy for digital images in American art museums; August 2004. http://www.kcl.ac.uk/kdcs/pubs/USMuseum_SimonTan-ner.pdf (accessed December 13, 2008).
74. Tanner, S.; Deegan, M. Exploring charging models for digital cultural heritage: Digital image resource cost efficiency and income generation compared with analog resources. June 2002. http://heds.herts.ac.uk/mellon/title.html (accessed December 13, 2008).
75. Bearman, D. The economics of publishing cultural heritage content online: The AMICO experience. *International Cultural Heritage Informatics Meeting: Proceedings from ichim03*, École du Louvre, Paris, France, Perrot, X., Ed.; 2003.
76. Bearman, D.; Trant, J. Economic, social and technical models for digital libraries of primary resources. New Rev. Info. Network. **1998b**, *4*, 71–91. http://www.archimuse.com/papers/amico/index.html (accessed June 15, 2008).
77. Chan, S. Towards new metrics of success for online museum projects. In *Museums and the Web 2008. Proceedings*; Trant, J., Bearman, D., Eds.; Montreal, QC, Canada, 2008. http://www.archimuse.com/mw2008/papers/chan-metrics/chan-metrics.html (accessed March 31, 2008).
78. Oates, G. The commons on Flickr: A primer. In *Museums and the Web 2008. Proceedings*; Trant, J., Bearman, D., Eds.; Montreal, QC, Canada, 2008. http://www.archimuse.com/mw2008/papers/oates/oates.html (accessed March 31, 2008).

BIBLIOGRAPHY

General introductions to the issues of museum and technology can be found in the following:

1. Din, H.; Hecht, P., Eds. *The Digital Museum: A Think Guide*; American Association of Museums: Washington, DC, 2007.
2. Marty, P.; Jones, K., Eds. *Museum Informatics: People, Information, and Technology in Museums*; Routledge: New York, London, 2008.
3. The annual Museums and the Web conference publish peer-reviewed papers surveying the broad range of activity on the Web. Other conferences have been mentioned above.

Part IV

Standards for Information Retrieval Systems

Information retrieval systems that are entirely stand-alone can, in principal, be developed any way their designers choose, within the constraints of available computing resources. However, today, information resources are everywhere networked together. As soon as two IR systems need to talk to each other, or information is to be sent over a network, then it becomes necessary to develop common standards that can be used by developers to enable the various systems to inter-operate. To many people, "standards" sounds like a boring topic of little possible interest. In fact, however, heated debates take place around standards development, and the financial and practical consequences of decisions made on standards affect our lives in surprisingly many ways. Competing needs of different stakeholders in social and technical systems have to be resolved in ways that are productive for all sides. The resulting standards often represent thousands of hours of late-night development work and committee time, as every side of an issue is explored and solutions found.

Precisely because so many different needs and uses come together in information systems and networks, there is a huge and proliferating number of standards available, each attuned to a particular niche of the information universe. Literally scores of different standards may come to bear on a particular network of information facilities. In this volume are presented just a handful of some of the most important standards that play a role in information retrieval systems and networks. After reading about these standards, developed for various aspects of information systems, the reader should have a good grasp of the range of issues that are involved in information system interoperability.

We begin with the most specific standard in the set, and move up to standards applicable to broader and broader areas of reference. Chapter 44, "Digital Object Identifier (DOI®) System," is written by its originator, Norman Paskin. The purpose of this standard is to provide a unique and persistent identifier for each object in the digital universe, if the object's producer desires such an identifier. Scientific journals, for example, often provide DOI identifiers for each of their articles.

Chuan Heng Foh, of the School of Computer Engineering, Nanyang Technological University, Singapore, describes a dozen or so standards associated with "Data Transmission Protocols" (Chapter 45). He addresses specific protocols, such as HTTP, and a number of others, as well as the overarching computer network design model, the Open System Interconnection (OSI) reference model.

When transmitting and searching for complex bibliographic records, such as those developed for libraries, a standard suitable specifically for information retrieval was needed. The initial major such standard accepted was known as Z39.50, and was widely used by libraries, well before the World Wide Web came to dominate information transmission. Reorientation of that standard to the Web has led to another standard called Search and Retrieve via URL. William Moen, of the Texas Center for Digital Knowledge, has been one of the major figures in the development and use of these IR standards. Chapter 46 describes them and their history: "Information Retrieval Protocols: Z39.50 and Search & Retrieve via URL."

Two closely-related standards are "Extensible Markup Language (XML)" (Chapter 47), described by Kevin S. Clarke, and the "Resource Description Framework (RDF)" (Chapter 48), presented by Nicholas Gibbins and Nigel Shadbolt, who have been heavily involved in the experimental application of RDF. XML is a syntax for tagging, or marking-up, textual information, and was established by the World Wide Web Consortium (W3C). As Clarke notes, "XML isn't used by itself, but as a tool to create other data-specific markup languages." RDF uses XML as its standard syntax, but also goes beyond what XML can do. As the authors say, "RDF can be used to write metadata about web pages and to describe real-world objects with equal facility. RDF is a key language in the technical architecture of the Semantic Web…". (See Chapter 24 for more information on the Semantic Web.)

The "Text Encoding Initiative (TEI)" (Chapter 49), by Edward Vanhoutte and Ron van den Branden, is an example of a standard developed specifically to meet the needs of a community with common needs, in this case, humanities scholarship. The TEI , also based on XML, makes it possible to mark off segments of documents and to provide descriptive labels for those segments, such as "title," so that later search can easily locate relevant portions of the record for retrieval.

Daniel V. Pitti, of the Institute for Advanced Technology in the Humanities, University of Virginia, Charlottesville, has been a prime mover in the development of the "Encoded Archival Description (EAD)," which he describes in Chapter 50. Archives, the unique records of individuals or organizations, have a different inherent arrangement than books, journals, and other published works do. That structure is represented in something called a "finding aid," a complex document presenting all the relevant information needed by archivists and users of archival resources. The EAD is a standard for encoding those finding aids so that they may be shared and accessed digitally.

Finally, Christopher A. Lee, of the School of Information and Library Science, University of North Carolina, describes the "Open Archival Information System (OAIS) Reference Model" (Chapter 51). This is a very high-level model, intended to be "implementation-independent" and showing the relationships among high-level entities in a particular technical environment. "Archival" in this context is used very broadly—not at all limited to finding aids—to address most cases where digital information is to be retained long-term.

44 Digital Object Identifier (DOI®) System

Norman Paskin

CONTENTS

IDENTIFIER CONCEPTS

An identifier is a concise means of referencing something. The term "identifier" can mean several different things:

- A "string," typically a number or name, denoting a specific entity (the referent of the identifier string). For example, the identifier ISBN 978-0-00-721331-3 denotes the book "Francis Crick" by Matt Ridley.
- A "specification," which prescribes how such strings are constructed. For example, the ISO standard ISO 2108:2005[1] is the current specification of the ISBN numbering system; but having that standard alone will not enable someone to construct and register a new valid ISBN.
- A "scheme," which implements such a specification. For example, the ISBN International Agency[2] implements the ISBN standard in an implemented scheme, by assigning ISBN prefixes to publishers, registering specific ISBNs (strings); providing rules on use of the ISBN (such as the incorporation of the ISBN as a bar code on the cover of a book). Typically, such schemes provide a managed registry of the identifiers within their control, in order to offer a related service.

Some important concepts relating to identifiers are "uniqueness," "resolution," "interoperability," and "persistence."

Uniqueness is the requirement that one string denotes one and only one entity (the "referent"). Note that the converse is not a logical consequence: it is not necessary that an entity have only one identifier. For example, a book may have an ISBN and also an LCCN. An identifier scheme may even allow multiple identifiers for one entity, though usually these are deprecated.

Resolution is the process in which an identifier is the input to a service to receive in return a specific output of one or more pieces of current information related to the identified entity. For example, a bar code ISBN in a bookshop is scanned by a bar code reader and resolves to some point of sale information, such as title and price. Note that resolution depends on a particular application: while a bar code in a bookshop may resolve to price, the same bar code in a warehouse application might resolve to current stock number, or pallet position. Another familiar example of resolution is the Internet Domain Name System (DNS) which resolves a domain name address (URL) to a file residing on a specific host server machine.

Interoperability denotes the ability to use an identifier in services outside the direct control of the issuing assigner: identifiers assigned in one context may be encountered in another place or time without consulting the assigner. This requires that the assumptions made on assignment will be made known in some way. For example, a customer may order a book from a bookseller or a library system by quoting its ISBN, without consulting the publisher who assigned the number.

Persistence is the requirement that once assigned, an identifier denotes the same referent indefinitely. For example, ISBNs, once assigned, are managed so as to reference the same book always (and are not reassigned). Persistence can be considered to be "interoperability with the future."

The management of content on digital networks requires identifiers to be persistent, unique, resolvable, and interoperable. As an example, URLs do not identify content but a file location: using them as a substitute for such identifiers is not sustainable for reliable automation. The content may be removed ("404 not found"), or changed (not being the same as the user anticipated, or the user being unaware of such change). There have been a number of efforts to address the need for such reliable identifiers, notable among them URN[3] and URI[4] specifications; however these do not of themselves provide an implemented managed scheme and registry for specific content sector applications. Such full schemes require more: a model for identifiers and their management; shared, standards-based, persistent identifier management infrastructure; support for adoption of persistent identifiers and services, and a plan for sustainable shared identifier infrastructure.[5,6] The Digital Object Identifier (DOI®) system is such a managed system for persistent identification of content on digital networks, using a federation of registries following a common specification.

The uncapitalized term "digital object identifier" may be used nonspecifically to describe a number of varied technologies concerned with the identification of entities in a digital environment. The capitalized term "Digital Object Identifier" refers to one specific system defined and managed by the International DOI Foundation,[7] which provides an infrastructure for persistent unique identification of entities (here termed "objects") on digital networks deployed in a number of content-related applications.

DOI® SYSTEM: OUTLINE

DOI is an acronym for Digital Object Identifier. The DOI system provides for unique identification, persistence, resolution, metadata, and semantic interoperability of content entities ("objects"). Information about an object can change over time, including where to find it, but its DOI name will not change.

The DOI system brings together

- A syntax specification, defining the construction of a string (a DOI name)
- A resolution component, providing the mechanism to resolve the DOI name to data specified by the registrant
- A metadata component, defining an extensible model for associating descriptive and other elements of data with the DOI name
- A social infrastructure, defining the full implementation through policies and shared technical infrastructure in a federation of registration agencies

More detail on each of these aspects is given later in this chapter.

The DOI system operates through a tiered structure:

- The International DOI Foundation is the umbrella organization defining the rules and operation of the system. It is a non-profit member-funded organization.
- Registration agencies are all members of the International DOI Foundation, and have a contractual arrangement with the Foundation including a license to operate the DOI system. They provide defined services in specific sectors or applications. DOI registration is normally only a part of the service such an organization offers, since assignment of an identifier is usually done for the purpose of a specific initial service or application. An example is the CrossRef registration agency,[8] which provides services to publishers for linking reference citations in articles based on DOI-identified articles. Registration agencies may collaborate, or remain relatively autonomous.
- DOI names are registered by clients via a registration agency (e.g., in the case of the CrossRef agency, individual publishers are clients using the CrossRef service). Part of this process may be undertaken by the registration agency, as part of its service offering. If a suitable registration agency cannot be found for a certain sector, the International DOI Foundation will seek to appoint one.

DOI is a registered trademark of the International DOI Foundation, Inc. (abbreviated to IDF). The preferred usage, to avoid ambiguity, is with a qualifier to refer to either specific components of the DOI system (e.g., "DOI name": the string that specifies a unique referent within the DOI system); or the system as a whole ("DOI system": the functional deployment of DOI names as the application of identifiers in computer-sensible form through assignment, resolution, referent description, administration, etc.).

SCOPE

The term "Digital Object Identifier" is construed as "digital identifier of an object," rather than "identifier of a digital object": the objects identified by DOI names may be of any form—digital, physical, or abstract—as all these forms may be necessary parts of a content management system. The DOI system is an abstract framework which does not specify a particular context of its application, but is designed with the aim of working over the Internet.[9]

A DOI name is permanently assigned to an object, to provide a persistent link to current information about that object, including where it, or information about it, can be found. The principal focus of assignment is to content-related entities; that term is not precisely defined but is exemplified by text documents; data sets; sound carriers; books; photographs; serials; audio, video, and audiovisual recordings; software; abstract works; artwork; etc., and related entities in their management, for example, licenses or parties. A DOI name is not intended as a replacement for other identifier schemes, such as those of ISO TC46/SC9[10] ISBN, ISSN, ISAN, ISRC, etc., or other commonly recognized identifiers: if an object is already identified with another identifier string, the character string of the other identifier may be integrated into the DOI name syntax, and/or carried in DOI metadata, for use in DOI applications.

A DOI name may be assigned to any object whenever there is a functional need to distinguish it as a separate entity. Registration agencies may specify more constrained rules for the assignment of DOI names to objects for DOI-related services (e.g., a given registration agency may restrict its activities to one type of content or one type of service).

SYNTAX

A DOI name is the string that specifies a unique object (the referent) within the DOI system. The DOI syntax (standardized as ANSI/NISO Z39.84-2005)[11] prescribes the form and sequence of characters comprising any DOI name. The DOI syntax is made up of a "prefix" element and a "suffix" element separated by a forward slash. There is no defined limit on the length of the DOI name, or of its prefix or its suffix elements. The DOI name is case-insensitive and may incorporate any printable characters from the Unicode Standard.

- Example: a DOI name with the prefix element "10.1000" and the suffix element "123456": 10.1000/123456.

The combination of a unique prefix element (assigned to a particular DOI registrant) and a unique suffix element (provided by that registrant) is unique, and so allows the decentralized allocation of DOI numbers. The DOI name is an opaque string for the purposes of the DOI system: no definitive information should be inferred from the specific character string of a DOI name. In particular, the inclusion in a DOI name of any registrant code allocated to a specific organization does not provide evidence of the ownership of rights or current management responsibility of any intellectual property in the referent. Such information can be asserted in the associated DOI metadata.

The DOI prefix has two components: a "Directory" indicator followed by a "Registrant" code, separated by a full stop (period) (e.g., 10.1000). The directory indicator is always "10" and distinguishes the entire set of character strings (prefix and suffix) as DOIs within the wider Handle System® used for resolution. The registrant code is a unique alphanumeric string assigned to an organization that wishes to register DOI names (four digit numeric codes are currently used though this is not a compulsory syntax). The registrant code is assigned through a DOI registration agency, and a registrant may have multiple-registrant codes. Once a DOI name is assigned the string should not be changed, regardless of any changes in the ownership or management of the referent object; if an object is withdrawn from digital access, its DOI name should still resolve to some appropriate message to this effect.

The DOI suffix may be a sequential number, or it may incorporate an identifier generated from or based on another system used by the registrant (e.g., ISBN, ISSN, ISTC). In such cases, the existing system may specify its own preferred construction for such a suffix:

- Example: a DOI suffix using an ISSN: 10.1038/issn.0028-0836.

When displayed on screen or in print, a DOI name is normally preceded by a lowercase "doi": unless the context clearly indicates that a DOI name is implied.

- Example: the DOI name 10.1006/jmbi.1998.2354 is displayed as doi:10.1006/jmbi.1998.2354.

The use of lowercase string "doi" follows the specification for representation as a URI (as for e.g., "ftp:" and "http:").

DOI names may be represented in other forms in certain contexts. For example, when displayed in Web browsers the DOI name itself may be attached to the address for an appropriate proxy server (e.g., http://dx.doi.org/ resolves DOIs in the context of Web browsers using the Handle System resolution technology) to enable resolution of the DOI name via a standard Web hyperlink.

- Example: the DOI name 10.1006/jmbi.1998.2354 would be made an active link as http://dx.doi.org/10.1006/jmbi.1998.2354.

DOI names so represented in a URL and transported by the HTTP protocol are constrained to follow standard IETF guidelines for URI representations. The syntax for URIs is more restrictive than the syntax for DOIs; some characters are reserved and will need encoding (the NISO Z39.84 DOI syntax standard provides more detail). Certain client or server software may be able to handle DOIs using native handle resolution technology (where doi:10.1006/jmbi.1998.2354 would be understood by the browser and automatically resolved without the addition of the proxy server address).

DOI names may also be represented in other schemes, for example, in the info URI schema[12,13] as info:doi/10.1006/jmbi.1998.2354.

RESOLUTION

A DOI name can, within the DOI system, be resolved to values of one or more types of data relating to the object identified by that DOI name, such as a URL, an e-mail address, other identifiers, and descriptive metadata (or any additional types defined extensibly by the registration agency). Resolution is the process of submitting a specific DOI name to the DOI system (e.g., by clicking on a DOI in a Web browser) and receiving in return the associated values held in the DOI resolution record for one or more of those types of data relating to the object identified by that DOI name. Since the referent objects referred to by DOI names may be of various types (including abstractions as "works," physical "manifestations," performances), they may or may not be directly accessible in the form of a digital file or other manifestation; hence the resolution may or may not return an instance of the object.

The initial implementation of DOI system was that of persistent naming: a single redirection from a DOI name to a digital location (URL) of the entity (Figure 44.1).

A significant DOI function is the capability for multiple resolution, that is, delivering more than one value back from a resolution request. The values are grouped into defined types, which can form the basis of services (Figure 44.2). An example of current usage of this facility is resolution to a specific local copy of an article, determined by combining the resolution result (several URLs) and local information about the user's location (from the user's browser application).

Objects (identified by DOI names) which have common behavior (defined by metadata) can be grouped, using DOI application profiles; these application profiles can in turn be associated with one or more services applicable to that group of DOI names (see Figure 44.3).

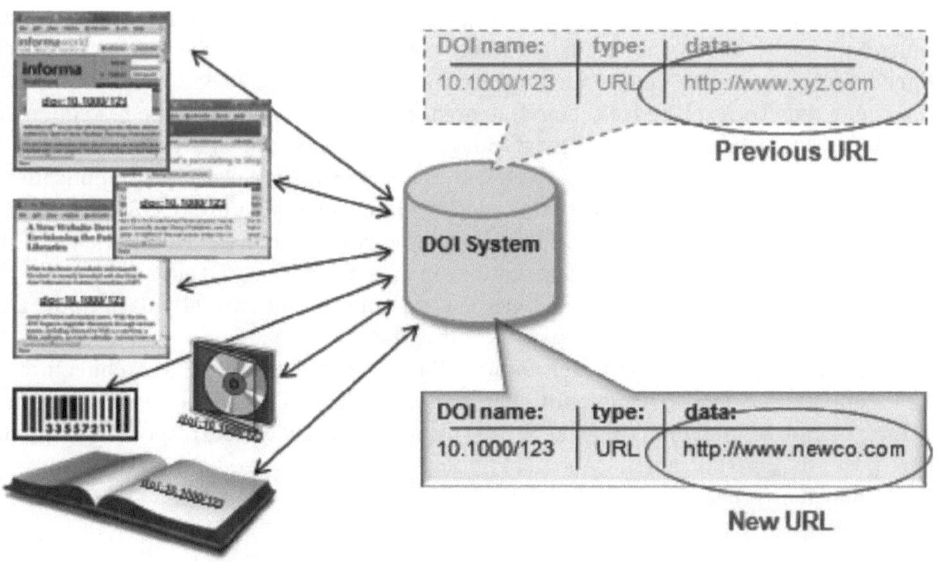

FIGURE 44.1 The role of the DOI system as a persistent identifier. A DOI name (10.1000/123) has been assigned to a content entity; the DOI system provides resolution from that name to a current URL. When the content, previously at URL xyz.com, is moved to a new URL newco.com, a single change in the DOI directory is made: all instances of the DOI name identifying that content (even if already recorded in print, as bookmarks, etc.) will resolve to the new URL, without the user having to take any action or be aware of the change. Note that the DOI name is persistent, i.e., remains unchanged. (From International DOI Foundation.)

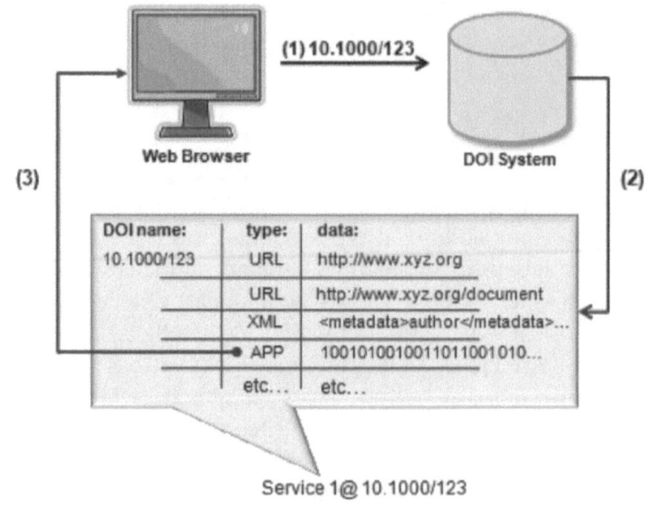

FIGURE 44.2 Multiple resolution. A Web browser is running an application "Service 1." That service resolves DOI name 10.1000/123 to the DOI system (1) where it finds four values within the relevant DOI record (2): here, two are of the type URL, one is XML, and one is a conjectural application. Service 1 selects one of these results, the APP value (3), on the basis of combining information provided in the resolution result and the local application. (From International DOI Foundation.)

The Handle System,[14] the resolution component used in the DOI system, is a general-purpose distributed information system designed to provide an efficient, extensible, and secure global name service for use on networks such as the Internet. The Handle System includes an open set of protocols, a namespace, and a reference implementation of the protocols. The DOI system is one implementation of the Handle System; hence a DOI name is a "Handle." DOI names are distinguished from other handles by additional "metadata" and "policy." The Handle System enables entities to be assigned first-class names, independent of domain names and other location-specific information, which can then be resolved (redirected) to appropriate locations: since the resolution destination is managed and can be changed, this provides a tool for persistence, avoiding "404 not found" and similar problems with URLs. The Handle System is used in a variety of applications such as the Content Object Repository Discovery and Resolution Architecture (CORDRA) of the U.S. Department of Defense (DoD) Advanced Distributed Learning initiative; The Library of Congress National Digital Library Program; and applications in grid computing and advanced future Internet architectures. The Handle System also includes several features not currently used in the DOI system, such as trusted resolution using public key infrastructure.

The Handle System is part of a wider Digital Object Architecture[15]; that architecture specifically deals only with digital objects with identifiers (Handles). There is no conflict in these two views, since any non-digital entity may be reified (or represented) as a corresponding digital object for the purposes of digital object management (though some care is needed in the definition of such objects and how they relate to non-digital entities).

METADATA

The object associated with a DOI name is described unambiguously by DOI metadata, based on an extensible data model to support interoperability between DOI applications. Assignment of a DOI name requires the registrant to record metadata describing the object to which the DOI name is being assigned. The metadata describes the object to the degree that is necessary to distinguish it as a separate entity within the DOI system.

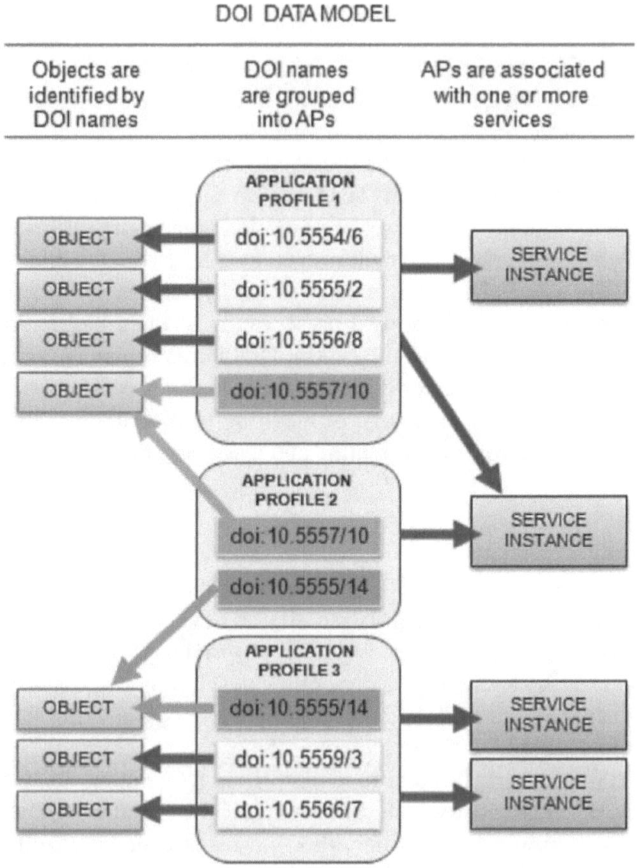

FIGURE 44.3 DOI data model: the Application Profile Framework. DOI names (identifying the entities on the left) are grouped into application profiles. Any single DOI name can be a member of multiple application profiles (e.g., DOI 10.5557/10 is shown here in two). Each application profile can similarly be associated with one or more services: each service can be made available in multiple ways. This makes it possible to make a new service applicable to many DOI names, simply by adding that service to the relevant application profile(s). (From International DOI Foundation.)

A minimum set of such metadata, the DOI kernel, is specified by the IDF. This includes elements such as "other identifier(s) commonly referencing the same referent (e.g., ISBN, ISRC)," and the name by which the referent is usually known (e.g., title). This minimum kernel may be enhanced by registration agencies through the development of specific application profiles with metadata elements appropriate to a particular application or set of applications. The IDF also specifies the template for the exchange of metadata between DOI registration agencies to support their service requirements, and specifies a Data Dictionary as the repository for all data elements and allowed values used in DOI metadata specifications.

The basis of the metadata scheme and extensions used in the DOI system is the indecs (interoperability of data in e-commerce systems) project.[16] This contextual ontology approach to interoperability is shared by a number of significant content sector activities.[17,18] This allows the use of a variety of existing metadata schemes with DOI names in a common framework.

The use of these tools for DOI metadata has been limited in initial applications, but more applications are emerging as the sophistication of content management on digital networks and the need for interoperability increases.

SOCIAL INFRASTRUCTURE

DOI names are intended to be persistent identifiers: no time limit for the existence of a DOI name is assumed in any assignment, service, or DOI application. A DOI name and its referent are unaffected by changes in the rights associated with the referent, or changes in the management responsibility of the referent object. Since such persistence requires a social infrastructure, policies as well as technical infrastructure need to be defined and implemented. The IDF develops and implements policies such as rules for transfer of management responsibility between registration agencies, requirements placed on registration agencies for maintenance of records, default resolution services, and technical infrastructure resilience. These are codified in a formal agreement between the IDF and each of the registration agencies.

The DOI system is not a means of archival preservation of identified entities; it does not store the identified objects themselves; nor does the central DOI Directory store comprehensive metadata (only pointers to the registration agency or other source of such data). The system provides a means to continue interoperability through exchange of meaningful information about identified entities through at minimum persistence of the DOI name and a description of the referent.

HISTORY

The DOI system was the result of a publishing industry initiative in the late 1990s, which recognized the need to uniquely and unambiguously identify content entities, rather than refer to them by locations, and commissioned a study to specify an appropriate technical solution, selected if possible from one or more existing technologies rather than developing a new system. The International DOI Foundation was incorporated in 1998 to develop the system; where possible, existing technologies and standards were adopted for the implementation of the DOI system. The first DOI registration agency began in 2000; by early 2009 around 40 million DOI names had been assigned through eight registration agencies. The most widely known application of the DOI system is the Crossref cross-publisher citation linking service which allows a researcher link from a reference citation directly to the cited content on another publisher's platform, subject to the target publisher's access control practices. Other applications include government documentation, books, and data; further applications are under development.

The development of the DOI system has proceeded through three parallel tracks:

- An initial implementation of persistent naming: a single redirection from a DOI name to a digital location (URL) of the entity or information about it.
- The development of more sophisicated means of management such as contextual resolution, where the result of a redirection is also a function of some additional information such as local holdings information.
- Collaboration with other standards activities in the further development of tools for managing entities in a digital environment.

The DOI System is a Draft International Standard of ISO, it is expected that the final standard will be published in late 2009 or 2010.

RELATED ACTIVITIES

The DOI system is associated with two independent technical activities which it has used as components of DOI implementations: the Handle System and the series of contextual ontology initiatives derived from the indecs project. Each is used in other non-DOI applications (an aim of the International DOI Foundation was to use existing solutions where available and proven to be useful). Either of these components could be replaced in the DOI system by other technologies offering similar features in the future if necessary.

The International DOI Foundation, particularly through its registration agency CrossRef, has also been closely involved in the development of the OpenURL, a mechanism for transporting metadata and identifiers describing a publication for the purpose of context-sensitive linking. The DOI system is now widely implemented using OpenURL by many libraries: further information on this topic is available from the Crossref Web site. The use of open URL was the first widespread example of more sophisticated means of content management through contextual resolution.

The expertise of the International DOI Foundation in issues such as resolution and semantic interoperability has also led to some IDF members being active participants in discussions of further identifier scheme development such as the International Standard Text Code (ISTC) numbering system for the identification of textual works, and identifiers for parties (persons and organizations), and licenses.

REFERENCES

1. ISO 2108:2005 Information and documentation—International standard book number (ISBN), http://www.iso.org/iso/isocatalogue/cataloguetc/cataloguedetail. htm?csnumber=36563 (accessed July 2009).
2. The International ISBN Agency web site: International Standard Book Number System for Books, Software, Mixed Media etc. in Publishing, Distribution and Libraries. http://www.isbn-international.org/ (accessed July 2009).
3. Sollins, K.; Masinter, L. 1994. Functional Requirements for Uniform Resource Names. Internet Engineering Task Force (IETF) Request for Comments (RFC) 1737, December 1994. http://tools.ietf.org/html/rfc1737 (accessed July 2009).
4. Berners-Lee, T.; Fielding, R.; Masinter, L. Uniform Resource Identifiers (URI): Generic Syntax. Internet Engineering Task Force (IETF) Request for Comments (RFC) 3986, January 2005. http://www.ietf.org/rfc/rfc3986.txt (accessed July 2009).
5. Dyson, E. Online Registries: The DNS and Beyond. Release 1.0, Volume 21, Number 8, 16 September 2003. http://doi.contentdirections.com/reprints/dyson_excerpt.pdf (accessed July 2009).
6. PILIN team: Persistent Identifier Linking Infrastructure Project Report December 2007. https://www.pilin.net.au/Closure_Report.pdf (accessed July 2009).
7. The DOI system web site: http://www.doi.org (accessed July 2009).
8. CrossRef web site, http://www.crossref.org (accessed July 2009).
9. Kahn, R.E.; Cerf, V.G. *What is the Internet (And What Makes It Work)*, Internet Policy Institute, December 1999. http://www.cnri.reston.va.us/what_is_internet.html (accessed July 2009).
10. ISO (International Organization for Standardization) TC 46 (Technical Committee for information and documentation standards SC9 (Subcommittee on the identification and description of information resources). http://www.iso.org/iso/iso_catalogue/catalogue_tc/catalogue_tc_browse.htm?commid=48836&published on (accessed July 2009).
11. ANSI/NISO Z39.84 (2005): Syntax for the Digital Object Identifier. http://www.niso.org (accessed July 2009).
12. Van der Sompel, H.; Hammond, T.; Neylon, E.; Weibel, S. The info URI Scheme for Information Assets with Identifiers in Public Namespaces. Internet Engineering Task Force (IETF) Request for Comments (RFC) 4452, April 2006. http://www.ietf.org/rfc/rfc4452.txt
13. About INFO URIs: Frequently Asked Questions, http://info-uri.info/registry/docs/misc/faq.html (accessed July 2009).
14. The Handle System, http://www.handle.net/ (accessed July 2009).
15. Kahn, R.; Wilensky, R. A framework for distributed digital object services. Int. J. Digital Libr. April **2006**, *6* (2). [doi:10.1007/s00799–005–0128-x] (First published by the authors in May 1995.) Reproduced at http://www.doi.org/topics/2006_05_02_Kahn_Framework.pdf with permission of the publisher (accessed July 2009).
16. Rust, G.; Bide, M. The <indecs> Metadata Framework: Principles, model and data dictionary. 2000. http://www.doi.org/topics/indecs/indecs_framework_2000.pdf (accessed July 2009).
17. Paskin, N. Identifier interoperability: A report on two recent ISO activities. D-Lib Mag. April **2006**, *12* (4). http://www.dlib.org/dlib/april06/paskin/04paskin.html (accessed July 2009).
18. Dunsire, G. Distinguishing content from carrier: The RDA/ ONIX framework for resource categorization. D-Lib Mag. January **2007**, *13* (1). http://www.dlib.org/dlib/january07/dunsire/01dunsire.html (accessed July 2009).

45 Data Transmission Protocols

Chuan Heng Foh

CONTENTS

INTRODUCTION

When two parties communicate, there is a need for a mechanism to manage communication flow and provide consistent interpretation of messages between the two parties. This requirement extends to the communications between computers. Data transmission protocols provide a means to allow computers to properly exchange and interpret data messages in a computer network. To achieve that, data transmission protocols define rules for message exchange and structures for message formatting. A computer network is a complex system, which relies on a collection of data transmission protocols to operate, with each data transmission protocol providing some specific functions. In this entry, we describe the general principles of data transmission protocol design, the Open System Interconnection (OSI) reference model, the transmission control protocol/Internet protocol (TCP/IP) suite, and various commonly used data transmission protocols in the modern computer networks.

ROLES AND FUNCTIONS

The Internet is the de facto wide area network of today's computer network. The Internet is based on packet-switched technology. In packet-switched technology, a packet is forwarded hop by hop from one router to another based on each router's decision. In contrast to packet-switched technology, circuit-switched technology is another technology that provides large-scale communications. Circuit-switched technology is used in telephone systems. In circuit-switched technology, switches establish a communication path when a call request appears, and maintain the established path during the entire call period. It was recognized that circuit-switched technology is not appropriate for data communications, and hence the Internet adopts packet-switched technology. The Internet consists of a set of communication devices, called *routers*, interconnected in a mesh structure to form a single network. Computers, called *end systems*, join the computer network by connecting themselves to the routers using a particular local access technology, such as dialup, cable, local area networks, or others. The end systems may act as client terminals for end users to access the network resources or network servers to provide them with required services.

The operation of message exchange between communication devices is essential not only for the provision of services to network users but also to support the reliable operation of the computer network itself. Data transmission protocols facilitate the exchange of information and messages between communication devices. For example, routing protocols are implemented in routers to allow the exchange of routing table update information between the routers themselves. The application layer protocols are implemented in the end systems (clients and servers) to allow network users to access information held by servers and to communicate with other network users.

There is no single data transmission protocol that can fulfill the complex task of computer networks. A computer network relies on a collection of data transmission protocols to maintain its operation and provide services to network users. Depending on the purposes, the design of a data transmission protocol varies greatly. In general, a data transmission protocol features one or more of the following functions:

- Encapsulation: A data transmission protocol usually has its own format containing a protocol header, followed by the data to transmit. A sender may use a protocol header to inform the receiver about its transmission status and the additional information related to the data attached to the protocol header. The receiver analyzes the protocol header of a received packet to handle the data accordingly. The process of constructing and attaching a protocol header to the data for transmission is known as encapsulation.
- Session control: Communications between two parties often require a specific dialog to maintain the proper flow of message exchanges. In a data transmission protocol, a particular session control is designed to specify the message exchange mechanism. Two communication devices implementing a particular data transmission protocol follow the specified session control in the protocol to transmit and receive packets in order to prevent any deadlock in the message exchange. Deadlock may occur when two communication devices turn to receiving mode and endlessly wait for packets from each other.
- Flow control: The process of controlling the rate of data transmission between two communication devices is known as flow control. The design of flow control in a data transmission protocol directly affects the performance and implementation complexity. Simple flow control scheme, such as stop-and-wait, offers implementation simplicity, but the performance of data transmission in terms of channel utilization is also low. A more sophisticated flow control scheme, such as selective-repeat, requires complex flow control management but offers high channel utilization.
- Error control: Packet transmissions may occasionally suffer from transmission errors due to channel noise or breakdown of intermediate communication devices in a computer network. In communications between a sender and a receiver pair, error control is used for the receiver to report identified transmission errors and for the sender to correct the reported transmission errors typically by retransmission of missing packets.
- Connection management: In a data transmission protocol, connection management provides easy management of the session control, flow control, and error control that are implemented in the protocol. Before any data exchange may take place between two

communication devices, they negotiate, initialize, and establish necessary parameters to manage subsequent data exchanges. This process is known as connection establishment. Upon the completion of data exchanges, the connection termination will take place to properly release the established connection and the allocated resource.

THE OSI REFERENCE MODEL

The development of computer networks were started by experimental networks, such as ARPANET, created in 1969 (which evolved into today's Internet) and ALOHANET, demonstrated in 1970 (which led to the development of Ethernet). Seeing the need for computer networks, computer manufacturers were also quick to offer their proprietary computer network solutions. For example, IBM introduced its system network architecture (SNA) in 1974 and Digital Equipment Corporation launched its DECnet in 1975. These commercial network architectures were closed and did not support the interconnection of equipment from multiple vendors. The need for standards to allow interconnection among various different computer systems and network designs became obvious.

In 1977, International Organization for Standardization (ISO) took the role of defining standards for computer network interconnection between different computer systems. A subcommittee was formed on OSI to address the need for such standards. Finally, an interconnection architecture was proposed known as the "OSI Reference Model." The OSI reference model describes computer network architecture in seven layers illustrated in Figure 45.1(a). The following gives the overview of the seven layers of the OSI reference model:

- The physical layer: The physical layer deals with the transmission of bit streams over a certain physical medium. It addresses how to represent bits with electrical signals and how to transmit the signals over a physical medium.
- The data link layer: The data link layer provides reliable data transmission over a physical link. It deals with framing of bit streams and reliable transmission of the data frames.
- The network layer: The network layer is responsible for routing and switching of data packets router by router across the network.
- The transport layer: The transport layer provides reliable end-to-end data transmission across a computer network.
- The session layer: The session layer mainly deals with the control of data exchange within an established session.
- The presentation layer: The presentation layer deals with data representation. It provides services to the entities at the application layer to enable correct interpretation of the exchanged messages.
- The application layer: The application layer provides services to end users to access the computer networks.

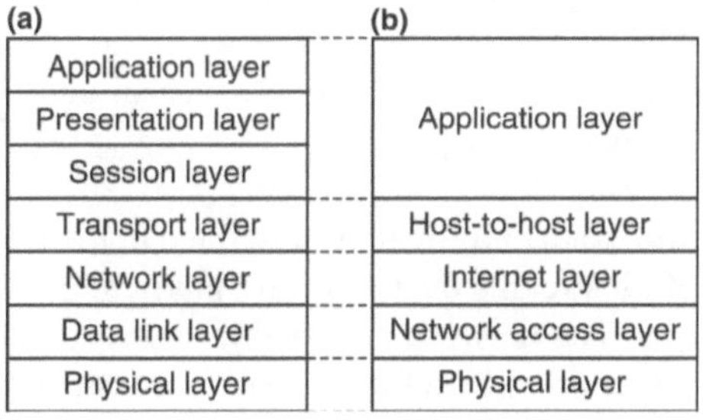

FIGURE 45.1 (a) The seven layers OSI reference model and (b) the TCP/IP model.

Although today's computer networks do not precisely follow the OSI reference model for their designs, the OSI reference model remains influential to the designs of modern computer network architectures and data transmission protocols. The OSI model is also frequently used to demonstrate the concept of layering fundamental to the understanding of packet-switched network systems.

TCP/IP AND THE INTERNET

The history of the Internet dates back to the mid-1960s. In the middle of the 1960s, the Advanced Research Project Agency (ARPA, now called Defense Advanced Research Project Agency, or DARPA) of the United States Department of Defense had decided to build a national computer network. Adopting the packet-switching concept proposed independently by Paul Baran (U.S.) and Donald Davies (U.K.) in the 1960s, the ARPANET was built and first tested in 1969. ARPANET also made its first public appearance in 1972 at the International Conference on Computers and Communications in Washington, District of Columbia.[1]

One of the original data transmission protocol used in the APRANET was network control protocol (NCP). NCP provides some basic functions to allow two hosts in the ARPANET to exchange data. However, it was soon realized that NCP required revision to allow the ARPANET not only to support the efficient operation of ARPANET as it grew in size but also to interconnect with other existing computer networks. To address this issue, Vinton Cerf and Robert Kahn published their research article in 1974 on TCP,[2] introducing a new data transmission protocol for host-to-host communications. TCP was soon accepted as the host-to-host protocol for the ARPANET. In 1978, TCP was further split into two protocols, TCP and IP. The final stable version of TCP and IP is version 4, which remains in use on the Internet today.

More TCP/IP implementations were developed for various computer systems between 1978 and 1983, and it was decided that TCP/IP would replace ARPANET's NCP. On January 1, 1983, the full transition from NCP to TCP/IP was completed. Henceforth, only those hosts implementing TCP/IP would be able to connect to the network. This event is viewed as the beginning of what is known today as the Internet.

While TCP and IP are the two main protocols that drive the Internet, there are many other protocols that help maintain the operation of the Internet. The body that governs the Internet architecture, IP design and operation is Internet Engineering Task Force (IETF).[3] IETF maintains two main series of documents, which are Internet-Drafts and Request for Comments (RFC). New proposals or designs related to the Internet technologies are first submitted to Internet-Drafts for evaluation and discussion. Once the proposals or designs have been accepted, they are transferred and permanently archived in RFC. The RFC documents provide specifications and design details of newly proposed technologies to allow consistent implementation.

The collection of all protocols used in the Internet, including TCP and IP, is often called the TCP/IP protocol suite. It is possible to relate the TCP/IP design to the OSI reference model. While not expressed officially in this way, the TCP/IP protocol suite can be decomposed into five layers that roughly correspond to the OSI reference model (Figure 45.1(b)). In particular, the TCP/IP model consists of the application layer, the host-to-host layer, the Internet layer, the network access layer, and finally the physical layer. The relationship between the five layers of the TCP/IP protocol suite and the seven layers of the OSI reference model is illustrated in Figure 45.1. The following explains the important roles of these five layers:

1. The physical layer: Similar to the physical layer defined in the OSI reference model, it deals with the transmission of bit streams over a certain physical medium.
2. The network access layer: The network access layer corresponds to the data link layer in the OSI reference model. It provides physical network access to the entities at the upper layer. It is responsible for reliable data transmission over a physical link of a network.
3. The Internet layer: The Internet layer provides routing of packets across the Internet.

4. The host-to-host layer: The host-to-host layer provides session control and reliable data transmission between two end systems across the Internet.
5. The application layer: The application layer provides network services to end users to access the Internet. It also consists of the functions of the session and presentation layers described in the OSI reference model. Specifically, it defines the control of data exchange and ensures the consistency in message interpretation.

COMMON PROTOCOLS IN THE PHYSICAL LAYER

Due to their roles and functions, protocols in the physical layer appear in a much different form than those in the other layers. Protocols in the physical layer mainly focus on specifying how to represent bits with electrical signals and how to transmit the signals over a medium, which can be copper wires, optical fibers, or air. In the physical layer, the signal conversion may use line coding or modulation techniques. The transmission of signals may include operations such as transmission synchronization, equalization filtering, error detection or correction, and channel coding for robustness and performance considerations. Some commonly used technologies in the physical layer are described below.

ITU-T V SERIES RECOMMENDATIONS AND MODEMS

International Telecommunication Union–Telecommunication Standardization Sector (ITU-T)[4] is the main organization responsible for defining standards, referred to as "recommendations" in the field of telecommunications. ITU-T partitions its standardization work into different groups, and the recommendations defined within a group are filed in a series identified by an alphabetic character. One of the series related to data transmission protocols is the V Series, which defines recommendations for data communication over the analog telephone network. After standardization is complete, these recommendations are implemented in products called modems. The main function of modems is to modulate and demodulate electrical signals that represent digital information. These electrical signals are transmitted across the analog telephone network interface to allow data transmissions between two end users of the telephone network. The use of a modem to support access to the Internet is referred to as dialup.

The increase in transmission data rate of modem has been fueled by the advancement of digital signal processing technologies in the 1980s and the 1990s. Some notable modem technologies include V.32 for transmission rates up to 9600 bits per second (bps), approved in 1993; V.34 for transmission rates up to 28.8 kilobits per second (kbps), approved in 1994; V.34bis for transmission rates up to 33.6 kbps; V.90 for downlink transmission rates up to 56 kbps and uplink transmission rates up to 33.6 kbps, approved in 1998; and V.92 for downlink transmission rates up to 56 kbps and uplink transmission rates up to 48 kbps, approved in 2000. With V.92 technology, dialup has reached a channel data rate that is very close to the fundamental limit of 64 kbps in the telephone network. Due to its data rate limitation and massive deployment of the high bandwidth Internet broadband technologies in the 2000s, dialup has become less attractive as a means of Internet access. Dialup remains in use in regions without higher speed options or as a backup method for Internet access.

DSL AND ADSL

DSL, sometimes called xDSL, stands for digital subscriber line. It is a family of technologies providing data transmissions over copper telephone lines. One of the most widely deployed variants of DSL is asymmetric digital subscriber line (ADSL).

Similar to the traditional dialup Internet access discussed in the previous subsection, ADSL also makes use of the existing copper telephone wires for data transmissions. End users of ADSL require ADSL modems to connect between the computers and the telephone network. The term

"DSL modem" is a misnomer that remains in common use. DSL and cable "modems" are not actually modulators/demodulators. They perform complicated tasks to achieve communications. Unlike the traditional dialup access where a modem couples with another modem across the telephone network, an ADSL modem couples with a special device called DSL access multiplexer (DSLAM) installed at the other end of the telephone lines, which is located a few kilometers away from the end user's premise. DSLAM then connects directly to the Internet. This architecture bypasses the telephone network that limits the channel data rate to 64 kbps.

However, the data rate of ADSL still depends on the quality of the copper telephone wires and the distance running between ADSL modems at end users and DSLAMs at the network. In addition, strong signals for high data transmissions from end users may result in undesirable crosstalk noise at DSLAMs where all telephone wires concentrate, however, there is no such problem at ADSL modems. It thus makes sense to have a lower data transmission rate from an ADSL modem to a DSLAM, and a higher data transmission rate in the reverse direction resulting in asymmetrical data rates. It is this unique property of asymmetrical data rates that gives the name to this DSL technology.

10BASE5 and Its Popular Variations

Ethernet is the most popular local area network technology used in today's Internet. It has a wide range of physical layer technologies. 10BASE5, also known as Thick Ethernet, is one of the earliest Ethernet designs. This Ethernet technology chooses a thick 50 Ω coaxial cable as its medium with a maximum segment length of 500 m. Each computer is connected to the coaxial cable with a medium attachment unit (MAU) and an attachment unit interface (AUI) cable no longer than 50 m. This setup allows Ethernet to operate at 10 Mbps with baseband signaling. It is referred to as 10BASE5 where 10 stands for the 10 Mbps of channel data rate, BASE refers to baseband transmissions, and 5 represents the maximum segment length of 500 m. This technology had been a popular solution in the past, but it is no longer available in the market today.

10BASE2, known as Thin Ethernet, was proposed after 10BASE5 as an alternative low cost solution for the Ethernet deployment. 10BASE2 uses a cheaper type of medium, that is, the thin coaxial. This medium only allows for 185 m of maximum segment length. This physical layer technology is called 10BASE2, where 2 represents the maximum segment length of just below 200 m. This technology is targeted for small-scale local area network deployment.

As early as 1987, several manufacturers started to develop a new type of Ethernet physical layer technology which uses copper twisted pair wires as the medium. This technology was later standardized and named 10BASE-T, where the T in 10BASE-T stands for twisted pair cabling. A 10BASE-T network requires an additional device known as an Ethernet hub, also referred to as a repeater, for the deployment. This Ethernet technology gives increased reliability compared to its previous variations. This popular solution remains in operation today, with more recent higher speed variations such as 100BASE-T and 1000BASE-T, which are compatible with 10BASE-T connectivity.

WiFi

Wireless local area networks have become a popular Internet access technology due to its deployment convenience. The first official standard for wireless local area networks for use for Internet access is IEEE 802.11, released in 1997. To promote the interoperability of the IEEE 802.11 products built by various manufacturers, Wireless Fidelity (WiFi) Alliance[5] has taken on the role of performing IEEE 802.11 conformance testing to certify the interoperability of the IEEE 802.11 products.

The IEEE 802.11 physical layer is based on radio transmissions. Many modern technologies are used in WiFi networks to achieve high data transmission rates. These technologies include direct sequence spread spectrum (DSSS), orthogonal frequency division multiplexing (OFDM), and the more recent multiple-in multiple-out (MIMO) technologies.

The IEEE 802.11 consists of a number of standardized physical layer technologies. A few of the most widely used are

- The IEEE 802.11a operating at 5 GHz radio band delivering up to 54 Mbps
- The IEEE 802.11b operating at 2.4 GHz radio band delivering up to 11 Mbps
- The IEEE 802.11g operating at 2.4 GHz radio band delivering up to 54 Mbps

A WiFi network typically consists of one or more access points (APs) which are connected to the Internet. These APs extend their Internet access to surrounding computers in the form of wireless radio signals. The area within the radio coverage of the APs is called a WiFi hotspot. Computers configured with wireless capability within the hotspot can then access the Internet.

COMMON PROTOCOLS IN THE DATA LINK LAYER

The data link layer provides reliable transmission between two communication devices over a physical channel. The data link protocols mainly deal with the reliability and performance of bit stream transmissions. Bit streams at the data link layer are packed into data frames for the management of the flow and the error controls. ISO has developed one of the most important data link protocols, namely, the high-level data link control (HDLC) protocol. Many modern point-to-point data link protocols derive from HDLC including the point-to-point protocol (PPP) for dialup Internet access.

The data link protocols implemented in local area networks, however, follow a different strategy. Due to the shared medium architecture in local area networks, local area networks implement medium access control (MAC) protocols in the data link layer. Some commonly used protocols are the IEEE 802.3 MAC protocol for Ethernet and the IEEE 802.11 MAC protocol for WiFi networks.

HDLC Protocol

The HDLC protocol (High-Level Data Link Control Protocol) provides reliable data transmissions over a physical link. HDLC defines a number of options to meet a wide range of user requirements. HDLC communications are mainly based on command and response, where one party issues a command and the other party replies with a response. The data to exchange between the two parties may be included within the command and response communications.

HDLC defines two types of communication devices, namely, primary station and secondary station. The primary station issues a command to a secondary station for it to respond. The primary station acts as a master station controlling and managing the data flow on a link. The link may be a point-to-point or a multipoint link. In a multipoint link, the primary station is connected to several secondary stations, and the primary station polls each secondary station in a round-robin manner to achieve communications. The communication devices that implement the features of both the primary and secondary stations are called combined stations. When two combined stations communicate over a link, a combined station may issue transmissions without permission from another combined station. In this configuration, both combined stations are responsible for managing the link.

Some important features provided by HDLC include the connection establishment and termination, flow control, error detection and retransmission, and information transmissions.

PPP

The PPP (Point-to-Point Protocol)[6] is a common data link protocol used for dialup connection to access the Internet. PPP is largely derived from HDLC and customized for the dialup connection. PPP has a much simpler design since it is targeted for a specific type of physical link. Like HDLC, PPP features the connection management, but it does not provide flow and error controls, and it only operates on a point-to-point link. PPP also allows multiple network layer protocols to run over the same link.

Ethernet and the IEEE 802.3 Protocol

The design of Ethernet was inspired by ALOHANET demonstrated in 1970.[7] ALOHANET is a wireless local network based on a random MAC strategy. Ethernet adopts the protocol design of ALOHANET and modifies it for a wired network, originally a coaxial cable. The resultant MAC protocol used for Ethernet is named carrier sense multiple access with collision detection (CSMA/CD). Together with CSMA/CD, Ethernet design chooses binary exponential backoff (BEB) for the retransmission scheme. The Ethernet technology was officially documented and published in 1976,[8] and the first specification of Ethernet appeared in 1983 as the IEEE 802.3 standard.

The CSMA/CD protocol employs random MAC strategy. An Ethernet communication device is called a station. Each station follows the rule of "listen before transmit" to politely access the shared medium. A station must defer its access if the medium is sensed busy, otherwise, it can access the medium to transmit its data. During the transmission, each station must also follow the rule of "listen while transmit." This allows a station to identify any collision of transmissions on the medium. If a transmission collision is detected, a station immediately stops its transmission and enforces a delayed retransmission attempt where the delay duration is randomly selected. This random selection of delay helps avoid further collisions on the medium.

In 1993, a new Ethernet MAC technology, Switched Ethernet, was introduced to provide improved Ethernet performance. With the use of switching technology, the CSMA/CD protocol is no longer essential since switching technology changes the medium of Ethernet from a common shared medium to individual point-to-point links. Technically, to differentiate between the two technologies of Ethernet, Ethernet implementing the CSMA/CD protocol on a shared medium is called Shared Ethernet, and Ethernet based on the switching technology is called Switched Ethernet. Shared Ethernet products are largely obsolete due to the low cost and high performance of Switched Ethernet solutions.

WiFi and the IEEE 802.11 Protocol

WiFi networks employ a similar MAC protocol as Ethernet, as discussed in the previous subsection. While "listen before transmit" is possible, "listen while transmit" is difficult to achieve on a wireless medium on which WiFi networks operate. The MAC protocol was refined by introducing the carrier sense multiple access with collision avoidance (CSMA/CA) protocol. The CSMA/CA protocol retains the "listen before transmit" rule, but employs explicit acknowledgment for the detection of transmission errors which may be due to transmission collisions. In addition, a less aggressive medium access is introduced to avoid excessive collisions during medium access. The first specification of WiFi networks was released in 1997 as the IEEE 802.11 standard.

The IEEE 802.11 MAC protocol also specifies an optional four-way handshake. An additional request-to-send (RTS) and clear-to-send (CTS) message exchange is performed between two stations before the actual data transmission. Moreover, the IEEE 802.11 standard also introduces an optional function that uses a particular polling scheme to increase performance. The polling scheme bypasses the use of CSMA/CA. It allows an access point to poll each individual station for data transmissions. The use of polling scheme eliminates transmission collision but introduces polling overhead. This function is rarely implemented in current IEEE 802.11 products.

NETWORK LAYER AND IP

The network layer in the context of the TCP/IP model is mainly responsible for global addressing and packet routing in a network. The implementation of the network layer in the TCP/IP model is

IP.[9] In addition to addressing and packet routing, IP also performs some common tasks of a data transmission protocol such as fragmentation, protocol multiplexing, and error detection.

The most widely deployed version of IP on the Internet is IP version 4 (IPv4). IPv4 header is illustrated in Figure 45.2. Some important fields are explained as follows:

- Version (4 bits): It specifies the version number of IP.
- IHLs (4 bits): Internet header length (IHL) specifies the length of the header in 32 bit unit. The minimum value is 5, for the smallest header of 20 bytes.
- Total length (16 bits): It specifies the length of the packet in bytes, including its header.
- Identification (16 bits): It specifies an identifier for an IP packet. When a packet is fragmented, all fragments will carry the same identification number.
- Flags (3 bits): There are three 1 bit flags. The first bit is reserved and must be set to zero. The second flag is DF, i.e., Don't Fragment. The third flag is MF, i.e., More Fragments. When set to 1, DF specifies that the packet should not be fragmented and MF indicates that this packet is not the last fragment of a fragmented packet.
- Fragmentation offset (13 bits): It tells the position in the current packet where this fragment belongs. It is specified in 8 byte units.
- Time to live (8 bits): It is a counter used to limit the packet lifetime in routing.
- Protocol (8 bits): It indicates the transport layer protocol that this IP packet carries in order to perform protocol multiplexing.
- Header checksum (16 bits): It is used for detecting error of the header.
- Source and destination address (32 bits each): They indicate the IP addresses of the source and the destination.
- Options (variable): The option may or may not appear in the header. Options allow additional information to be specified in the header.
- Padding (variable): It contains enough zero bits to ensure that the length of the header is a multiple of 32 bits.

The 32 bit IP address is usually written into four decimal values separated by dots. The first, the second, the third, and the fourth decimal values represent respectively the first, the second, the third, and the fourth 8 bit block in the 32 bit IP address. For example, an IP address of 000000010 00000100000001100000100 has the four 8 bit blocks of 00000001.00000010.00000011.00000100, which is usually written as 1.2.3.4.

Related to routing, a 32 bit IP address consists of two parts, they are the network part and the host part. Routers operating in the public Internet domain read the network part of IP addresses to perform routing, whereas routers operating in a private intranet domain use the host part of IP addresses to route packets. Several classes are defined for this two-level hierarchical address structure. In particular,

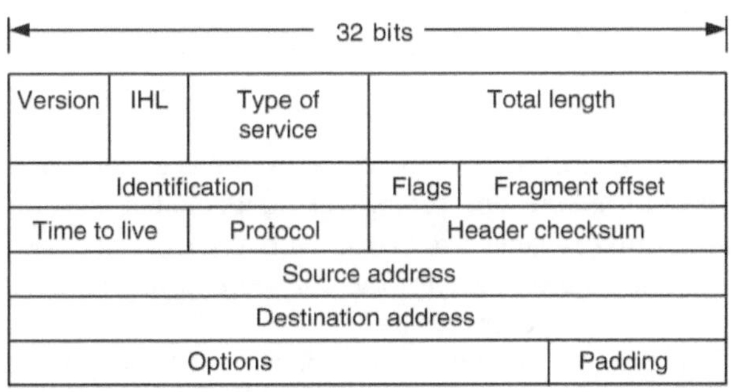

FIGURE 45.2 IP header.

classes A, B, and C are used for address assignment for hosts. Each class defines a different space size for the network and the host parts. This is known as classful addressing.

The classful addressing in IP has later caused the IP address exhaustion problem. Classful addressing is said to be inefficient in IP address space usage as many organizations are given excessive IP address space due to the classful addressing. Some important attempts to mitigate the IP address exhaustion problem are described as follows:

- CIDR addressing: Classless inter-domain routing (CIDR) introduces a flexible partitioning between the network and the host parts in the IP address to achieve a more efficient use of IP address space.
- NAT: Network address translation (NAT) allows the deployment of private IP addresses in a private network that use a router as an agent to access the Internet. All private IP addresses are translated into a single IP address by the agent during the Internet access. Since private IP addresses have only local significance, they can be deployed concurrently in other private networks. The use of private IP addresses reduces the total usage of public IP address space on the Internet.
- IPv6: IP version 6 (IPv6) defines 128 bit IP address space. This immediately relieves the IP address exhaustion problem in IPv4, however, the transition from IPv4 to IPv6 remains slow due to the worldwide massive deployment of IPv4 routers in today's Internet.

TRANSPORT LAYER AND TCP

As specified in the OSI reference model, the main role of the transport layer is to provide reliable communications between two end systems which may be connected via intermediate communication devices. In the TCP/IP model, the major transport protocol is the TCP.[10] In the design of TCP/IP, the network or IP layer contains only basic functions in order to simplify the implementation of routers. Other essential functions for reliable data transmissions are left for the transport layer to address. As a result, TCP implementation is relatively complex. The TCP/IP protocol suite does have simple transport protocols, such as the user datagram protocol (UDP),[11] which provides no end-to-end reliability of data transmission. Use of UDP for the transport protocol implies that the upper layer protocols, precisely the application protocols, must feature their own reliable transmission mechanism if reliability of data transmission is needed.

The primary objective of TCP is the reliable data exchange between two end systems in an efficient way. To provide this essential feature, each TCP communication session must first set up a connection to manage data flow. During the connection setup, necessary parameters and resources are initialized to manage the subsequent data transmissions. To further address the efficiency of data transfer, TCP employs ordered and controlled sliding window-based data transmission. The data transmission rate of a sender is controlled by two factors: the implicit network congestion indication and explicit advertising of the buffer availability of a receiver.[12]

TCP has five main functions: connection management, flow control, error control, congestion control, and protocol multiplexing.

1. Connection management: TCP uses connections to manage data transfer. TCP employs a three-way handshake for connection setup. During a connection setup, necessary parameters for data transfer are exchanged between the two parties and resources are allocated. Upon completion of the data transfer for the connection, the connection is terminated to properly release the allocated resources.
2. Flow control: TCP requires all sent packets to be positively acknowledged to confirm that the earlier data transmissions are successful. Data transmissions in TCP are performed in the sliding window style to allow packets flow in a stream. To avoid buffer overflow at a

receiver, the receiver advertises its buffer availability to a sender to ensure that the sender will not overwhelm the receiver's buffer with excessive transmissions.[12]

3. Error control: TCP uses timers to monitor packet transmissions. If a packet transmission is not acknowledged within a certain time interval, it is assumed that the packet has been lost or otherwise affected by a transmission error, and retransmission of the packet follows. This is commonly known as timeout retransmission.
4. Congestion control: TCP detects network congestion by the indication of transmission errors, as it is likely that a transmission error is due to network congestion. When a transmission error is detected, apart from retransmitting the packet, TCP also reduces its packet sending rate to relieve a possible traffic congestion in the network.
5. Protocol multiplexing: TCP performs protocol multiplexing through the use of port numbers. TCP identifies an application using the assigned port number. The Internet Assigned Numbers Authority (IANA)[13] specifies a number of well-known ports to the popular and commonly used application protocols, such as port 25 for simple mail transfer protocol (SMTP) and port 80 for hypertext transfer protocol (HTTP). Port numbers outside the well-known assignment can be used freely by application protocols to dynamically assign unused port numbers for their TCP connections.

Figure 45.3 illustrates the TCP header. Some important fields are explained as follows:

- Source and destination port (16 bits each): They are used to specify the source and the destination ports.
- Sequence number (32 bits): It is used for a sender to specify the sequence number in bytes of the data in this connection. During a connection setup, an arbitrary chosen initial sequence number will be decided.
- Acknowledgment number (32 bits): It is used for a receiver to specify the data that have been received successfully.
- Data offset (4 bits): It specifies the length of the header in 32 bit units.
- Control bits (6 bits): They are used to give a specific instruction to the other communicating peer. Some commonly used instructions include connection setup, termination, reset, and urgent data transfer.
- Window (16 bits): It specifies the buffer availability of a receiver. This field is used for flow control to avoid buffer overflow.
- Checksum (16 bits): It is used for detecting error of the header and data which follow after the header.
- Urgent pointer (16 bits): It points to the sequence number of the byte following the urgent data.
- Options (variable): The option may or may not appear in the header. Options allow additional information to be specified in the header.

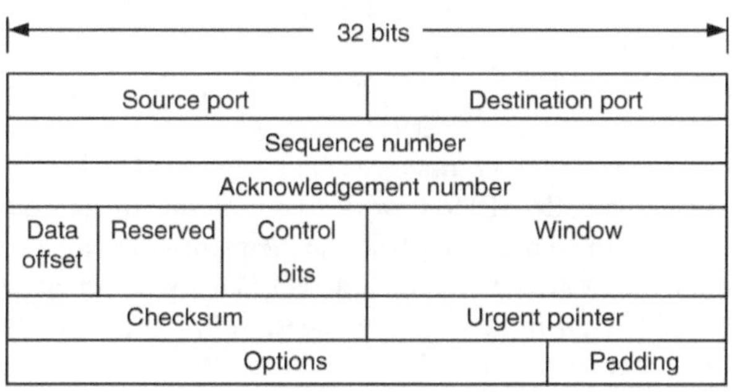

FIGURE 45.3 TCP header.

- Padding (variable): It contains enough zero bits to ensure that the length of the header is a multiple of 32 bits.

COMMON PROTOCOLS IN THE APPLICATION LAYER

In the context of computer networks, the application layer mainly provides network services to end users to access the computer network. Essentially, an application interacts with an end user to take instructions, collect data for transmissions, report network status, and present received data.

Two of the most popular Internet applications used in today's Internet are the World Wide Web (WWW) and e-mail. The protocol that provides Web surfing is HTTP, and the main protocol that provides e-mailing is SMTP. They are described as follows.

HTTP

HTTP (Hypertext Transfer Protocol)[14] is a data transmission protocol used to deliver information on the WWW. It is based on client–server architecture. In other words, when two parties communicate using HTTP, one party acts as a client and another party acts as a server. Web browsers implement the client communication of HTTP, while Web servers implement the server communication. HTTP uses TCP to deliver data over the Internet. HTTP is assigned to TCP port 80. Web servers passively listen on TCP port 80 for a connection request from a client.

HTTP employs a simple request–response dialog of conversation. A Web client implemented in a Web browser initiates a HTTP request to the destination based on the information provided by the end user, such as a URI (e.g., http://www.ietf.org/). Upon the reception of the HTTP request, the destination Web server responds with the required information which can be the content of a Web page, image, or video. This request and response dialog ends an HTTP session.

Due to security concerns, many HTTP connections are now handled by Web proxies. A Web proxy is an agent that relays the HTTP information between a Web client and a Web server. Since a Web proxy reinitiates the HTTP requests on behalf of a Web client, the destination Web server only sees the identity of the Web proxy, and hence this relay of HTTP connections hides the true identity of the Web client from the server.

SMTP

SMTP (Simple Mail Transfer Protocol)[15] is the main protocol used to deliver e-mail messages over the Internet. SMTP facilitates transmission of e-mail messages from one computer to another.

When an end user composes an e-mail message and takes action to send the e-mail, the e-mail client application initiates an SMTP connection to the default e-mail server to transfer the composed e-mail message. Once the e-mail server receives the e-mail message, it identifies the destination e-mail server from the message and initiates an SMTP connection to further transfer the message to the destination e-mail server. When the e-mail message has reached the destination e-mail server, the recipient is ready to retrieve the message.

There are several ways a recipient may read the e-mail messages. In the mainframe era, Telnet was used for users to login to an e-mail server and read their e-mail messages. In more recent implementations, the desktop personal computer users use post office protocol version 3 (POP3) or Internet message access protocol (IMAP) to download e-mail messages from the server. The downloaded e-mail messages can then be read locally at the recipient's desktop computer. For Web-based e-mail services, e-mail messages are delivered using HTTP to Web browsers for reading.

SMTP uses TCP port 25 to transmit e-mail messages. SMTP is a text-based protocol, and hence messages remain in clear text during the delivery. To address the security concerns, enhanced SMTP (ESMTP)[16] was proposed to replace SMTP, and is widely used in today's e-mail system.

SUMMARY

Data communication protocols provide a means to allow computers to properly exchange and interpret data messages in a computer network. A computer network is a complex system; its operation relies on a collection of data transmission protocols. The OSI reference model that describes the computer network architecture in seven layers is often used to demonstrate the operation of a computer network and the roles of data transmission protocols. This entry provided overview of some physical layer technologies including modem and ADSL, and some commonly used data transmission protocols including Ethernet, WiFi, HDLC protocol, PPP, IP, TCP, HTTP, and SMTP.

REFERENCES

1. Abbate, J. *Inventing the Internet*; MIT Press: Cambridge, MA, 1999.
2. Cerf, V.G.; Kahn, R.E. A protocol for packet network intercommunication. IEEE Trans. Commun. **1974**, *22* (5), 637–648.
3. http://www.ietf.org (accessed August 2007).
4. http://www.itu.int/ITU-T/index.html (accessed August 2007).
5. http://www.wi-fi.org (accessed August 2007).
6. Simpson, W. The point-to-point protocol (PPP). RFC 1661, 1994 online: http://www.ietf.org/rfc/rfc1661.txt (accessed August 2007).
7. Abramson, N. In *The Aloha System—Another Alternative for Computer Communications*, Proceedings of Fall Joint Computer Conference, AFIPS Conference, 1970.
8. Metcalfe, R.M.; Boggs, D.R. Ethernet: Distributed packet switching for local computer networks. Commun. ACM **1976**, *19* (7), 395–404.
9. Postel, J. Internet protocol, RFC 791, **1981**. Online: http://www.ietf.org/rfc/rfc0791.txt (accessed June 2008).
10. Postel, J. Transmission control protocol, RFC 793, **1981**. Online: http://www.ietf.org/rfc/rfc0793.txt (accessed June 2008).
11. Postel, J. User datagram protocol. RFC 768, **1980**. Online: http://www.ietf.org/rfc/rfc0768.txt (accessed June 2008).
12. Stevens, R.S. *TCP/IP Illustrated, Volume 1: The Protocols*; Addison-Wesley: Reading, MA, 1994.
13. http://www.iana.org (accessed August 2007).
14. Berners-Lee, T.; Fielding, R.; Frystyk, H. Hypertext transfer protocol—HTTP/1.0. RFC 1945, **1996**. Online: http://www.ietf.org/rfc/rfc1945.txt (accessed June 2008).
15. Postel, J. Simple mail transfer protocol, RFC 821, **1982**. Online: http://www.ietf.org/rfc/rfc0821.txt (accessed June 2008).
16. Klensin, J.; Freed, N.; Rose, M.; Stefferud, E.; Crocker, D. SMTP service extensions, RFC 1869, **1995**. Online: http://www.ietf.org/rfc/rfc1869.txt (accessed June 2008).

46 Information Retrieval Protocols: Z39.50 and Search & Retrieve via URL

William Moen

CONTENTS

INTRODUCTION

In the 1970s, a number of library leaders, such as Henriette Avram at the Library of Congress and the developer of the machine-readable catalog record (MARC), envisioned the convergence of computing and telecommunications that would enable machine-to-machine communication for accessing bibliographic and other types of information. Initial work on intersystem communication focused on connecting large bibliographic databases such as those at the Library of Congress, the Online Computer Library Center (OCLC), and the Research Libraries Group (RLG). Making this vision a reality required the development of standard protocols for intersystem communication. Protocols specify rules for communication including what information can be exchanged, in what format, and in what order. Thirty years later, the networked information landscape has changed dramatically, but the need still remains for standard protocols that support information retrieval (IR) transactions (e.g., sending a query and receiving the results of the executed query) against a range of databases or systems. Standards development work through the 1980s and 1990s yielded the ANSI/

NISO Z39.50 IR Protocol, developed in a historical context predating the World Wide Web. By the late 1990s, Web technologies were providing a new context for networked IR, and implementors of Z39.50 and others responded to these changes by evolving Z39.50 into Search and retrieve via URL (SRU), a protocol that uses key Web standards and technologies.

This entry addresses both Z39.50 and SRU. A brief discussion of IR and communications protocols provides background to the specifics of these two IR protocols. Although communications protocols are by their nature technical specifications, this entry focuses on an overview of the functions and capabilities of the protocols. It uses technical concepts and terminology from the protocols to help explain how the protocols work but limits discussion of technical details.

IR

IR, in the context of protocols, can be viewed very simply or quite complexly. At its simplest, IR involves issuing a query to an IR system, having the IR system execute the query, and presenting the results of the query to the user (human or machine). Web search engines such as Google provide exactly this functionality. The vision for networked IR assumes, though, an environment that contains a large number of IR systems and their databases that provide a range of search and retrieval functionality but differing in important ways (e.g., types of field searching supported).

A first step in preparing a protocol to support IR transactions requires modeling those transactions and the components of IR systems. Figure 46.1 illustrates these basic components of the IR model.

The following description provides an abstract view of IR and IR systems in the context of bibliographic databases (i.e., databases containing metadata records describing bibliographic items held, for example, in a library's collection). This description of an abstract model for information retrieval is derived from *ANSI/NISO Z39.89-2003. The U.S. National Z39.50 Profile for Library Applications*. The author drafted the text describing the abstract model in his capacity as chair of NISO Standards Committee AV that created this profile. Since this is an abstract view, actual implementation of these components may differ.

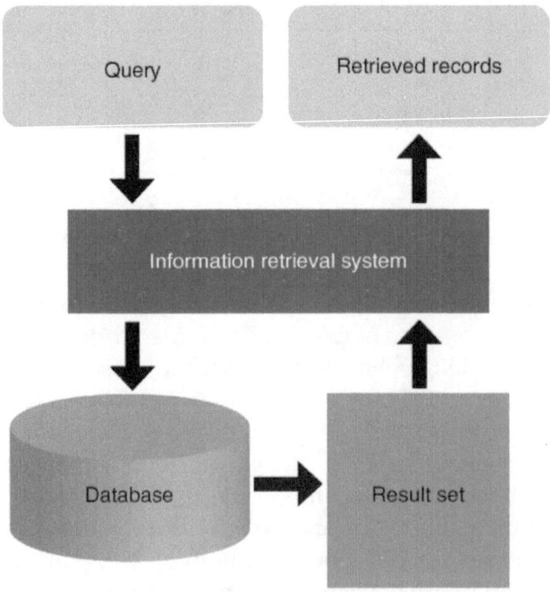

FIGURE 46.1 Abstract model of IR.

- *Bibliographic database:* This is the logical component that stores data representing bibliographic items. These representations can be created according to accepted standards (e.g., the Anglo-American Cataloguing Rules) and can reflect the use of various metadata element sets (e.g., MARC 21, Dublin Core, or others). Typically, the database records include information about the title, author, subject, and other salient features of bibliographic items. The physical structure of the database will be implementation specific, and no specific physical database model is assumed (e.g., relational, flat file, etc.).
- *Access points and indexes:* This is the logical component related to searching the database. This model assumes there is an index, which is a list of values with pointers to the database records that contain those values. Indexes are created for specific types of searches the IR system will support, and reflect searchable areas of the database record. A bibliographic database in an online catalog implementation typically supports title, author, subject, and other types of searches. The physical structure of an index and how it associates the list of values with pointers to database records will be system and implementation specific.
- *IR system:* This is the logical component that manages the search of the database and retrieval of records from the database. It typically provides an interface to receive a query and then executes the query by matching the search criteria with information stored in the indexes. When values in the index(es) match the query criteria, the system retrieves the relevant records from the bibliographic database for presentation to the user.
- *Query:* This is the logical component that contains simple or complex criteria along with a search term specified by the user (human or machine). Also referred to a search criteria, the query can contain criteria related to access points to be searched (e.g., search the author access point), characterizations of the search term (e.g., treat this search term as a phrase or treat this search term as a date), and also indicate processing of the search term (e.g., perform right truncation where specified).
- *Result Set and retrieved records:* This logical component manages the results of the executed query. The result set comprises all records that the IR system identified as matching the criteria contained in the query. From this Result Set, the IR system selects one or more records to return to the user. A specific IR system may store the Result Set for later processing, but that consideration is implementation specific and not addressed by this model.

IR can include other tasks beyond what the basic model describes. For example, some IR systems allow the user to specify how the results should be sorted (e.g., by date of publication in ascending order). Protocol developers face the challenge of modeling all IR transactions and components in a way that a standard IR protocol does not privilege specific implementations or structures. Before discussing the details of Z39.50, a basic description and explanation of a protocol is needed.

COMMUNICATIONS PROTOCOLS

Protocols governing communication and behavior between two entities exist for human-to-human as well and machine-to-machine interactions. For example, diplomatic protocols guide the interaction between representatives of sovereign entities. The protocols are agreed upon rules (written or unwritten) for governing behavior. When addressing machine communication, the rules must be specific and well-documented to ensure machine-to-machine communication is successful and the machines and applications behave according to the rules.

Machine-to-machine communication typically involves the sending and receiving of messages. One machine or an application residing on the machine (referred to here as the client) initiates the communication by sending a message requesting some service or other behavior from the receiving machine or application on that machine (referred to here as the server). The server responds by returning a message to the client. The model for this communication is characterized as request and response.

A communications protocol defines the services supported and provides the rules controlling the order in which messages can be sent, the contents of those messages, allowable request and response messages, and other aspects of the communication (e.g., the character set for encoding the data in a message). Machines conforming to the protocol can conduct successful intersystem communication because they know how to send and receive protocol messages and "understand" the content of those messages.

In the networked information environment of computers and their applications, there are a range of familiar communications protocols such as File Transfer Protocol (FTP), Simple Mail Transport Protocol (SMTP), and HyperText Transfer Protocol (HTTP) to name a few. Each is distinguished by the services or functions it provides. In fact, a large number of protocols exist to support successful communication between two machines and applications. Models representing a layering approach to intersystem communication (e.g., in the Open Systems Interconnection (OSI) seven-layer model and the five-layer model from the Internet) identify specific protocols to handle communication from the lowest layer of physical connection through routing and session information to the top layer, which in both models is called the application layer. Z39.50 is an application-layer protocol as indicated by the title of the Z39.50 standard: *Information Retrieval (Z39.50): Application Service Definition and Protocol Specification*.[1]

Returning to the context of IR protocols, the following are basic aspects that such a protocol needs to accommodate:

- Providing a standard way to encode the request and response messages
- Specifying methods to transport request and response messages across a network
- Identifying a database on a server to search
- Utilizing a vocabulary and grammar for expressing search requests, search criteria, retrieval requests, etc.
- Specifying formats for records that are returned in response to a search request

The Z39.50 protocol provides these and more, which are discussed next.

THE Z39.50 IR PROTOCOL

Z39.50 is a technical standard, developed under the auspices of the National Information Standards Organization (NISO), a standards developer accredited by the American National Standards Institute (ANSI). At the international level, Technical Committee 46 of the International Organization for Standardization (ISO) worked concurrently on an IR protocol called Search and Retrieve. This section provides a brief history of the development of the Z39.50 standard, explains in relatively nontechnical terms what the standard addresses, and discusses sufficient details of the specifications to yield a basic understanding. Many resources are available that discuss the Z39.50 protocol, features, and implementations (see Bibliography at the end of this chapter).

A Brief Chronology of Z39.50 Development

The nearly 30-year period during which Z39.50 and SRU, its successor protocol, were developed was marked by major computing and networking technology changes that strongly influenced the character of these IR protocols. Technical standards often reflect assumptions and beliefs about existing technologies, and it is fair to say that this was true for Z39.50.

The genesis for the standard was the late 1960s and early 1970s when library leaders began envisioning a future of interconnected automated bibliographic systems and identified the need for computer communication protocols that would enable the interconnection of systems and sharing of bibliographic data. The need for an IR protocol emerged also from visions for a national bibliographic network articulated by library leaders such as Henriette Avram and organizations such as the Library of Congress and its Network Advisory Committee, the National Commission on Library and Information Science, and the Council of Library Resources. A detailed historical treatment is beyond this entry's scope, but readers interested in Z39.50 history can review chapter 4 in *The Development of ANSI/NISO Z39.50: A Case Study in Standards Evolution*.[3]

Work on the Z39.50 standard began in 1979 by a formal standards committee authorized by NISO. NISO issued the first version of the standard in 1988.[4] After 1988, work on protocol development shifted from NISO, which disbanded the standards committee, to a group of people and organizations interested in implementing the standard. This group became known as the Z39.50 Implementors Group (ZIG). NISO established the Z39.50 Maintenance Agency, located at the Library of Congress, to oversee further development of the standard. The Maintenance Agency and the ZIG worked collaboratively to produce a revision to the 1988 standard, which was submitted and approved by NISO in 1992.[5] One specific goal of the 1992 standard, known as Version 2, was to harmonize the Z39.50 specifications with those in the ISO Search and Retrieve standard. Version 2 also specified critical services lacking from the 1988 standard such as access control, and as a result it provided a solid basis for widespread pilot projects, testing, and production implementations by members of the ZIG.

The early versions of the protocol were particularly library-centric, in that many of the specifications addressed issues related to searching bibliographic databases in the context of library catalogs. ZIG members, however, wanted to evolve Z39.50 into a more generalized IR protocol that could be used by libraries and many other information providers. Version 3 was approved in 1995 by NISO.[6] Many new features were specified in Version 3, and it became the basis for wide-spread implementation, albeit predominantly within the library community and by information services supporting libraries. In addition, the separate ISO Search and Retrieve standard was abandoned, and in its place, ISO adopted verbatim the 1995 Z39.50 standard and labeled it ISO 23950-1998.

Part of NISO's standards development process as approved by ANSI includes regular 5 year reviews of published standards. In the late 1990s, the Maintenance Agency initiated this review and issued in 2003, a revised version of the Z39.50 standard.[2] The Maintenance Agency viewed this version as a reaffirmation version, and included clarifications, commentaries, defect reports, amendments, and implementor agreements.

Z39.50 Protocol Details

When discussing Z39.50, it is important to distinguish between: 1) the technical standard that defines the protocol; and 2) the implementation of those specifications in software. Taking the latter first, system developers (e.g., vendors of integrated library systems) implement the protocol specifications in software programs: client-side software and server-side software. The Z39.50 client initiates a communication session with the Z39.50 server. A user (human or machine) initiates a search, which is passed to the Z39.50 client for processing into standard protocol messages and sends the query to the Z39.50 server. The Z39.50 server passes the request to a local IR system, which executes the search, finds records that match the criteria, and then returns results back to the Z39.50 client via the protocol. The Z39.50 client passes the results back to the local machine for presentation to the user. Building on the IR model presented earlier, Figure 46.2 illustrates where the Z39.50 client and server software logically sit in relation to the client- and server-side applications.

The Z39.50 client and Z39.50 server each have their own responsibilities, listed below in the order of a typical Z39.50 session:

- Initiate a session: client
- Send query: client
- Execute query: server
- Create result set: server
- Request records "in" result set: client

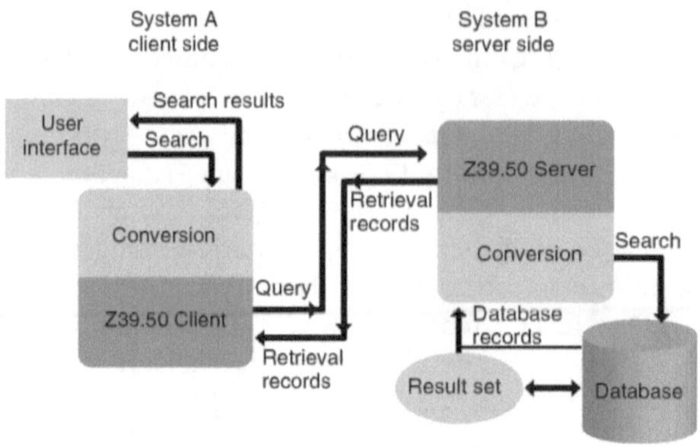

FIGURE 46.2 Z39.50 and the abstract model of IR.

- Specify database elements to be returned: client
- Specify format in which to return records: client
- Create retrieval records and sent to client: server

As a communications protocol, Z39.50 specifies a standard set of messages that are communicated between two systems. The initiating system's request needs to be transformed from the local language of that system into the language of Z39.50. The Z39.50 client and server both understand the meaning of the Z39.50 language, and thus provide the communication link between the two different systems. Upon receipt of the Z39.50 message, the Z39.50 server then translates it into the local language of the IR system. For example, it maps a request for a title search where the search term is a phrase into the appropriate commands, syntax, and query of the local IR system.

In the context of the protocol specifications, Z39.50 defines a set of "services." A Z39.50 service describes functionality and defines the specific protocol messages related to that service exchanged between the Z39.50 client and Z39.50 server in support of that functionality. Z39.50 defines 14 services, but for purposes here, only a few core services will be discussed: Init, Search, and Present. These services enable: 1) establishing a connection between a client and server (Init); 2) issuing a query (Search); and 3) retrieving results (Present).

Init Service

The Init service provides for a Z39.50 client to initiate a connection and session with a Z39.50 server by first issuing an Init request message. Included in the structured message are a number of parameters: Version, Id/authentication, Options, Preferred-message-size, Exceptional-record-size, Implementation-id; some of these are mandatory and some are optional. The Z39.50 client sends the Init request message with values listed for each of the parameters. The Z39.50 server responds by returning to the Z39.50 client an Init response message with the following parameters (again, some of which are mandatory and some optional): Version, Id/authentication, Options, Preferred-message-size, Exceptional-record-size, Result, Implementation-id. If the server responds positively to the Init request, it returns a value of "accept" in the result parameter. Upon successful negotiation in the Init service, the client can then move to requesting the server to execute a search using the Search service.

Search Service

For successful IR interoperability between two systems, there are two important considerations: a mutual understanding of the search request and a mutual understanding of the format of records retrieved. We will examine how Z39.50 addresses these two requirements, since at its core, Z39.50 was developed to support interoperable search and retrieve.

When one submits a search to a local IR system via its native interface, there is a tight linkage between the search interface offered to the user and the underlying IR system and database. Communication is not an issue. Yet, to send a search from one system to a different IR system, the search must be transformed into a language understood by both systems where information about some of the following must be clearly communicated:

- The database to search
- The access points or searchable fields to search
- How search terms are to be interpreted, such as treating the search term as a word, phrase, date, normalized name, etc.
- The use of Boolean operators for complex queries
- Other search qualifications and criteria, such as limiting the search by date, language, etc.

Z39.50 defines a standard language for expressing searches. The language is very rich and precise to reduce ambiguity in the communication. A query in Z39.50 is a specified structure for expressing the search requirements; it identifies a database to search and characterizes the search term using attribute types and values. A query can also include Boolean operators.

Key to the query is the attribute types and their values; these are what allow the search to be expressed in a standardized and mutually understood vocabulary and grammar. The following is an example of part of a Z39.50 query:

(1,1003)(2,3)(3,1)(4,1)(5,100)(6,3) Twain, Mark

The pairs of number in parentheses are the attribute/type value pairs and "Twain, Mark" is the search term. The following explains how the attribute types and values characterize the query term, "Twain, Mark."

Attributes and their permissible values are defined in attribute sets. A basic Z39.50-related attribute set goes by the label of Bib-1 (for use when searching a variety of databases).[7] The Bib-1 attribute set defines six attribute types (identified by the first number in parentheses): Use (1); Relation (2); Position (3); Structure (4); Truncation (5); and Completeness (6). The Z30.50 query contains a number representing an attribute as the first part of the type/value pair. The use of numbers avoids problems of words in various languages and yields more universality.

Each attribute type represents a feature of the search and search term; for example the Use attribute indicates the index to be searched, while the Relation attribute indicates, for example, that the search term should match exactly an entry in the index, and the Truncation attribute indicates whether the IR system should perform some type of truncation on the search term. The Bib-1 attribute set defines the values associated for each attribute type. For example, if the Use attribute value is 1003, this means that the IR system should process this query as an author search; if the value is 4, the IR system should process the query as a title search. It is beyond the scope of this entry to give all the details on attribute types and values, but this indicates how the search term can be characterized using a standard vocabulary and grammar to result in intersystem communication for the purpose of searching.

Parsing the Z39.50 query listed earlier, which means in human terms "search for items where Mark Twain is listed as author," the use of attribute type/value pairs are understood by the server as

(1,1003) means execute this search as an author search.
(2,3) means exactly match the search term with an entry in the index.
(3,1) means to begin matching the search term with the first term in the field.
(4,1) means to treat the search term as a phrase rather than two words.
(5,100) means to carry out no truncation on the search term.
(6,3) means that the search term should match the complete data value in the field (i.e., the entry in the index).

The Z39.50 server receives the query as expressed in the type/value pairs, parses the query, and maps the search to the local IR system and its search engine.

Present Service

The other aspect of IR is the return of records to the Z39.50 client that match the query. The Z39.50 Present service is used to request records to be returned from the result set, how many to return, what syntax the records should be returned in, and what elements in the records to return. To support interoperability, Z39.50 registers a number of record syntaxes in which records can be exchanged between Z39.50 clients and servers. The original focus of Z39.50 was on bibliographic records and the retrieval of MARC records. As Z39.50 evolved into a general IR protocol, the MARC format for records became just one of a variety of record syntaxes in which records could be formatted and returned via Z39.50. Record syntaxes include HTML, Extensible Markup Language (XML), and others, including a syntax developed by the ZIG called Generic Record Syntax (GRS).[8] While accommodating more applications with this variety of record syntaxes, interoperability problems also increased.

This brief glimpse into some of the details of Z39.50 illustrates that for intersystem communication to occur, the Z39.50 client and server must not only support the defined protocol messages but also understand the language of Z39.50, its vocabulary and grammar. Most current Z39.50 implementations robustly support the protocol messages. However, implementors make choices from the options available in the standard for specific protocol messages. Also, the local IR system on the Z39.50 server side does not always provide the functionality requested by the Z39.50 client as expressed in protocol messages. These and other issues have led to interoperability problems. There has been, unfortunately, a pervasive sense that Z39.50 did not live up to the promises of providing a solution for interoperable intersystem search and retrieval across disparate databases.

INTEROPERABILITY AND INTERSYSTEM IR

Implementing a standard IR protocol on systems is intended to enable interoperability of those systems and applications. System-level interoperability can be defined as the ability of two or more systems or components to exchange information and use the exchanged information without special effort on either system. One can also define interoperability from the perspective of the end user in terms of the user's ability to successfully search and retrieve information in a meaningful way and have confidence in the results. Interoperability between two systems can be assessed from a binary perspective; they either do or do not interoperate. However, experience has demonstrated that when two systems have implemented the Z39.50 protocol, it is more likely that systems may be more or less interoperable, and interoperability is better assessed as a continuum rather than a binary decision. This raises the question of what acceptable levels of interoperability can be produced, especially from the perspective of the end user.

To understand how or why IR systems may not interoperate or not have an acceptable level of interoperability, a number of factors that threaten interoperability can be identified:

- Multiple and disparate systems, operating systems, IR systems, etc.
- Multiple protocols such as Z39.50, HTTP, SOAP, etc.
- Multiple data formats, syntax, metadata schemes such as MARC 21, UNIMARC, XML, ISBD/AACR2-based metadata, Dublin Core, etc.
- Multiple vocabularies, ontologies, disciplines such as LCSH, MESH, and AAT.
- Multiple languages, multiple character sets.
- Indexing, word normalization, and word extraction policies.

If a protocol has a range of options, implementors can choose from (e.g., what protocol services are implemented, specific values for parameters, etc.) as is the case with Z39.50, different implementations of the protocol specifications can threaten interoperability. However, the experience with Z39.50 has shown that the key threats to interoperability relate mostly to differences in local IR systems specifically the differences in search functions supported, the indexes available for searching, and the record syntaxes supported for retrieved records. Examples of these differences include whether IR systems support the searches being requested by the client, such as how to treat the search term (e.g., as word, phrase, date, etc.), the access points to be searched (e.g., author, title, subject, ISBN, etc.), and the format of records available (e.g., in MARC, MARCXML, etc.).

Optimal interoperability occurs not only if the Z39.50 client and server both implement the same protocol services and choices among options within the protocol but also when the IR system on the Z39.50 server side provides the search functions requested by the Z39.50 client, including types of searches and access points, and also is able to supply the records in the syntax requested by the Z39.50 client.

A common approach to address the threats to Z39.50 interoperability was the development of application profiles. A profile specified what Z39.50 clients and servers had to implement from the options available in the Z39.50 standard, as well as the searches supported on the local IR system. Conformance to a profile's specifications increased the level of interoperability. An example of such a profile is *The U.S. National Z39.50 Profile for Library Applications* published by the NISO as ANSI/NISO Z39.89.[1]

A NEXT GENERATION Z39.50

The development of Z39.50 and release of Version 3 in 1995 occurred in advance of the emergence of the World Wide Web in the 1990s. By the late 1990s, the ZIG was discussing how the broader Web community, and especially those involved with Web search, could be made interested in the power provided by the Z39.50 IR protocol. Yet, where the ZIG saw Z39.50's power, many in the Web community and even some in the library community—its core implementation context—perceived it as difficult and complex, heavyweight, reflecting old technology, not Web friendly, and in some cases simply broken. The ZIG recognized that the Web was quickly becoming the common implementation environment. For several years Z39.50 implementors discussed and tried out a number of initiatives as part of a Z39.50 International Next Generation (ZING) project.[9]

A pivotal meeting of the ZIG occurred in 2001 at which a discussion about the future of Z39.50 resulted in a consensus recognition that Z39.50 needed to evolve in the context of the Web. The goal for developing the next generation Z39.50 was to lower the barriers to implementation while preserving the intellectual contributions of Z39.50 and discarding those aspects no longer useful or meaningful. Part of lowering the barrier to implementation was to recast Z39.50 protocol specifications in terms of existing and emerging Web technologies, tools, and standards (e.g., HTTP, XML, and XML schemas). Part of preserving the intellectual contributions of Z39.50 was to separate the abstract and semantic models provided in Z39.50 from representation of the protocol in the arcane Abstract Syntax Notation (ASN.1) and associated Basic Encoding Rules (BER) and running it directly over TCP/IP for transport rather than HTTP.

In 2001, an international team of implementors and standards developers began work on a new IR protocol that would be simpler, more easily implemented, and more comprehensible than Z39.50 and most importantly Web compatible. The result of discussions and deliberations was the decision to develop a new Web services based protocol: SRU. The name of the new protocol has changed since its inception in 2001. Initially it was referred to as Search/Retrieve Web Service (SRW). This was later accompanied by SRU. Except for the method the client used for sending a search request to the server, the details of the protocol were the same. By 2007, the label SRW had been deprecated and the protocol is officially known as SRU. The first version of the protocol was released in late 2002; Version 1.1 was released in 2004, which was registered with NISO. The current Version 1.2 was published in 2007.[10]

The Z39.50 Maintenance Agency at the Library of Congress plays a key role in managing the development of the new protocol and now serves as the maintenance agency and managing editor for SRU, supported by a SRU Editorial Board consisting of the managing editor along with a senior editor, XML editor, and associate editors. The Board oversees the development of proposals for changes and enhancements, and a SRU Implementors Group, an open membership group, serves in an advisory capacity to the Editorial Board.

SRW

SRU addresses the same IR problems confronted by Z39.50, namely, communicating with a range of information services and servers that have their own local IR systems with different database structures, indexes, and local query structures. However, SRU adopts current standards for syntax of messages and records (i.e., XML) exchanged between a client and server and for transport of the messages (i.e., HTTP). It retains and builds on the abstract models, concepts, and functions developed through the experience with Z39.50 such as abstract access points, abstract record schemas, result sets, and others. The protocol defines a set of operations and associated parameters (see below) and all responses are encoded in XML. The Contextual Query Language (CQL) is used to represent queries in search requests (see below). The result is a Web friendly and standard protocol for networked IR.

At the outset of protocol development, there were two related protocols referred to as SRW and SRU. In fact, there is no real difference between SRW and SRU at the protocol parameter level but only in the way they are implemented as Web services.

The basic difference between them relate to how they issue search requests. SRW uses SOAP (originally known as Simple Object Access Protocol) and encodes messages in XML within SOAP (Figure 46.3). SRU uses the Representational State Transfer (REST) approach, which encodes protocol messages from the client in the URL syntax and issues a HTTP GET request (Figure 46.4). Both protocols return data encoded in XML, and both use HTTP for transport of messages.[11]

Protocol Operations and Examples

SRU uses the concept of "operation types" to describe and define what IR functions the protocol supports and defines the following operations:

- *searchRetrieve:* Expresses the query criteria and specifications for records to be returned
- *Explain:* Allows a client to retrieve a description of the facilities available at a server
- *Scan:* Allows the client to request a range of the available terms at a given point within a list of indexed terms

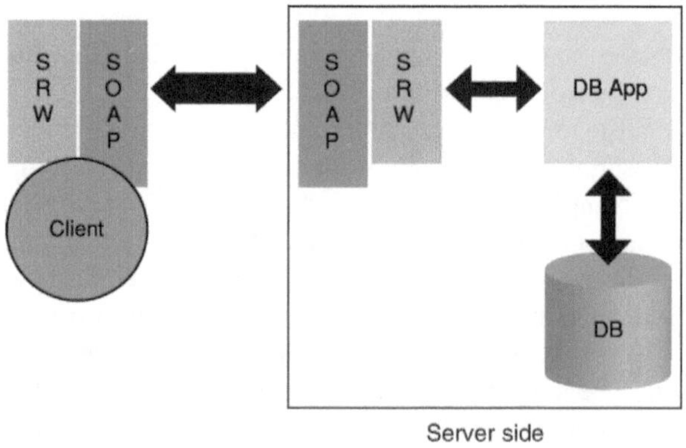

FIGURE 46.3 SRW Communication using SOAP.

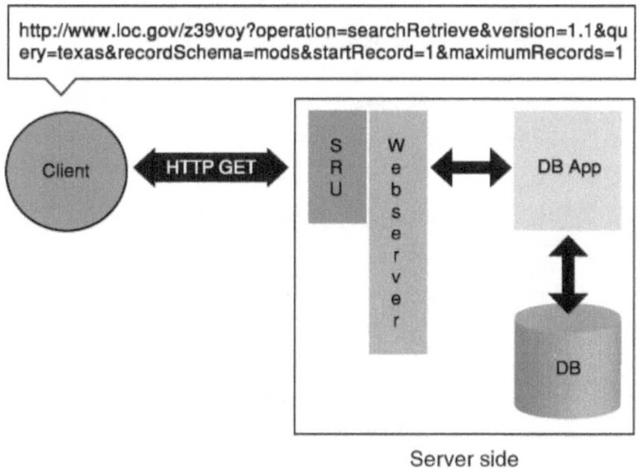

FIGURE 46.4 SRU Communication using HTTP GET.

The searchRetrieve and explain operations are core to the protocol, and each is discussed in more detail below.

searchRetrieve Operation

This operation combines the Z39.50 Search and Present services in one operation. The searchRetrieveRequest message contains the query which is expressed using CQL (see below). In addition to the query, the searchRetrieveRequest contains specifications for returning the records that match the query, such as what schema should be used to package the retrieved records.

If one uses SRW, the searchRetrieveRequest message is encoded in XML and sent via HTTP wrapped in SOAP. Figure 46.5 is part of a searchRetrieveRequest (in XML) that includes a single-word query.

There are a number of parameters defined for the searchRetrieveRequest, and Figure 46.5 shows two mandatory parameters (`<version>` to indicate the version of the protocol; `<query>` to express the search criteria), and several optional parameters (`<maximumRecords>` to indicate how many records should be returned; `<startRecord>` to indicate in the list of records found where to begin returning; and `<recordSchema>` to indicate in what format the records should be returned. In this sample case, the request is to have the records returned in the form of Dublin Core records according to a Dublin Core XML schema.

If one uses SRU, the searchRetrieveRequest parameters are expressed in standard URL syntax, which includes the baseURL for the server separated from the protocol parameters with a question mark (?). Figure 46.6 shows the same searchRetrieveRequest as in Figure 46.5 but expressed as a URL.

Figure 46.6 shows that the URL syntax can express all searchRetrieveRequest parameters without any loss of specification.

After the server receives the searchRetrieveRequest and executes the search and finds records, it returns a searchRetrieveResponse (no matter whether the searchRetrieveRequest was sent via SOAP or as HTTP GET) that indicates the number of records found and may also include the

```
<searchRetrieveRequest>
  <version>1.1</version>
  <query>texas</query>
  <maximumRecords>1</maximumRecords>
  <startRecord>1</startrecord>
  <recordSchema>dc</recordSchema>
</searchRetrieveRequest>
```

FIGURE 46.5 Sample searchRetrieveRequest expressed in XML.

```
http://www.loc.gov/z39voy?operation=searchRetrieve&version=1.1&query=texas&
recordSchema=dc&startRecord=1&maximumRecords=1
```

FIGURE 46.6 Sample searchRetrieveRequest expressed as URL.

```
<searchRetrieveResponse>
  <version>1.1</version>
  <numberOfRecords>10</numberOfRecords>
  <records>
   <record>
    <recordSchema>info:srw/schema/1/dc-
             v1.1</recordSchema>
    <recordData>
     <dc:record>
      <dc:title>The prediction of subsequent violent
             offenses by the inmates of the Texas
             Department of Corrections </dc:title>
     </dc:record>
    </recordData>
   </record>
  </records>
</searchRetrieveResponse>
```

FIGURE 46.7 Sample searchRetrieveResponse.

records found. Figures 46.7 is a sample of a searchRetrieveResponse to the sample searchRetrieve Request in Figures 46.5 and 46.6.

There are a number of parameters defined for the searchRetrieveResponse, and Figure 46.7 shows two mandatory parameters (`<version>` ; `<numberOfRecords>` to indicate the number of records found on the server), and several optional parameters (`<records>` which indicates the beginning of the records being returned; `<record>` which indicates the segment containing the records; `<recordSchema>` which indicates the XML schema according to which the records are encoded; and `<recordData>` that contains the actual record. In this example, the `<schema>` parameter indicates that the records are formatted according to the Dublin Core (i.e., DC) schema, as requested in the searchRetrieveRequest above. The `<recordData>` parameter in this example contains only one DC element simply to illustrate elements that might comprise the record.

In summary, the searchRequestResponse is in XML syntax and may include the actual records found in the XML schema requested by the client. Other schemas in which records can be returned (assuming the server supports those schemas) include ONIX, MODS, and MARCXML.

Explain Operation

A challenge for Z39.50 in the context of interoperability was the difficulty for a Z39.50 client to discern what a Z39.50 server supported in terms of Z39.50 services and especially in terms of available access points and record formats. The development of SRU gave priority attention to ensuring a robust method for the server to tell the client what it supports. The explain operation addresses this need. A client sends an explainRequest to the server and the server responds with an explainResponse, and the response message contains a record in XML structured according to the ZeeRex schema.[12] The ZeeRex record provides several key pieces of information including:

- Information about the database such as title and description
- Information about how to search in the database including what indexes exist to search
- Information about the record syntaxes in which records can be returned and what record elements can be returned

With the information contained in the explainResponse, the client is able to configure searches against the server that are likely to be more successful and request records in specific schemas (e.g.,

MARCXML, MODS, Dublin Core, etc.) that the server is able to supply. Interoperability can be significantly improved because of this protocol operation.

CQL

In addition to the protocol, another component for successful intersystem IR communication is a standard language to express the query. Based on the experience with Z39.50 and in keeping with the desire to build upon that experience, SRU developers created the CQL.[13] CQL is a formal language for representing queries to issue to IR systems such as Web indexes, bibliographic catalogs, and museum collection information. It is capable of expressing complex queries and yet can be used for very simple keyword searches. CQL is also human-readable, unlike the query types associated with Z39.50.

A CQL query contains one or more search clauses connected by Boolean operators. A search clause contains at a minimum the search term. A single word in a search clause comprises a perfectly legitimate instance, and this reflects the simplicity available in CQL. It has the power of expressiveness in that the search clause can indicate a specific index to search, and CQL supports relation and proximity operators as well as masking characters (e.g., to indicate truncation) to express more complex queries.

As a general purpose query language, CQL provides a syntax for expressing the component parts of the query. The basic syntax for a CQL search clause is: [index][relation][search term]. CQL also supports searching by semantics or context and introduced the concept of context sets in relation to indexes; this begins to make the meaning of "contextual" in the name of CQL clearer.[14] For example, a SRU search to a database can indicate that the index to be searched should be in the context of the Dublin Core element semantics. Individual communities can define their own context set to indicate the semantics of the indexes available. Context sets and individual indexes supported by the server can be listed in the ZeeRex record returned through the explain operation, which assists the client in issuing queries that take advantage of what the server offers. Figure 46.8 shows legitimate CQL search clauses from the simplest to more complex.

The examples in Figure 46.8 show that `<index>` and `<relation>` are optional, and further that `<index>` can be include a prefix to the index name to indicate that the index is from a specific context set.

Current Status and Plans for SRU

A variety of projects and implementations are using SRU for networked IR.[15] In some cases, implementations provide a SRU gateway to existing Z39.50 servers. For example, the Library of Congress

Search Clause	Explanation
cat	Simple single word search
cat and dog	Simple two-word Boolean search
"black cat"	Simple two word phrase; quotation marks must be used to indicate that words comprise a phrase
title = cat	Search for term cat in a title index
dc.title = cat	Search for term cat in an index defined in the Dublin core context set

FIGURE 46.8 Sample CQL search clauses.

implemented SRU access to its Z39.50 server and can return records in MARCXML, MODS, and even DC.[16] The European Library uses SRU as a search gateway to 47 European national libraries from a single interface, thus providing metasearch functionality across those libraries' resources.[17] SRU is used in venues beyond accessing library catalogs. For example, OCLC has developed a SRU interface to the DSpace digital repository system, allowing a standard search interface to the Lucene indexer used in DSpace repositories.[18] The NISO Metasearch Initiative has included reviewing SRU as the basis for a metasearch search and retrieval standard.[19]

In a move to gain formal standards status for SRU, the SRU Editorial Board, with support from the SRU Implementors Group, decided to pursue standardization of a specification based on SRU through the Organization for the Advancement of Structured Information Standards (OASIS) Consortium. Work on that effort began in Summer 2007. The specification has not yet been approved as an OASIS standard, and work is continuing on moving the specification through the OASIS process. Members of the SRU Editorial Board established the OASIS Search Web Services Technical Committee and the Committee's work includes the development of an Abstract Protocol Definition.[20] An important aspect of the OASIS work is to provide methods for accessing servers that support OpenSearch. The OpenSearch provides a method for describing a search engine's interface to assist clients in automating search Web forms.[21] The OASIS Committee plans to define application protocol bindings that provides the description (either human-readable or machine-actionable) of a server. A client will be able to access any server that provides such a description, if only it implements the capability to read the description file and interpret the description and based on that description to formulate a request (including a query) and interpret the response.

According to Ray Denenberg, cochair of the OASIS Technical Committee and managing editor for SRU, the plans are for the committee to produce initially two bindings: SRU 1.2 (compatible with the current SRU 1.2 specification) and OpenSearch (compatible with the current OpenSearch 1.1 specifications).[22] These will be straightforward renderings of the two existing specifications. The committee will follow with a third binding for the planned SRU 2.0, a revised version that will introduce new features into SRU. The committee will also initially produce a draft CQL 1.2 (compatible with the current CQL specifications) and will follow later with CQL 2.0, which will introduce new features into CQL.

CONCLUSION

"Information retrieval, while seemingly simple and obvious when accessing Google, is surprisingly complex."[16] IR tasks can range from simply submitting a keyword search to a search engine to issuing complex queries simultaneously to multiple and diverse information servers living on the Web. Searching a diverse set of IR systems and the data they hold, and then returning results in useful formats are made possible through the development and implementation of IR protocols. Z39.50 first explored the complexity of intersystem search and retrieval, and the attendant issues of interoperability. The widespread deployment of Z39.50 servers, primarily in the context of library catalogs, demonstrated the utility of a standard, protocol-based, search and retrieval interface to the diversity of library systems. Cross-database searching, or metasearch, was first explored by using Z39.50 for concurrent access to multiple resources, including but not limited to library catalogs.

Search in the context of the Web presented both challenges and opportunities for Z39.50. On the one hand, that protocol appeared to be both library-centric and not Web friendly, and thus there was little take up of that protocol by the wider Web search community. On the other hand, implementors and developers—primarily from the library community—have built on the experience and intellectual contributions of Z39.50 and evolved Z39.50 into a search/retrieve protocol and an associated query language more in line with the needs and expectations for the Web. SRU uses current standards and technologies to reduce the barriers to implementation and provides a robust IR protocol that effectively supports networked IR.

REFERENCES

1. National Information Standards Organization. *ANSI/NISO Z39.89-2003. The U.S. National Z39.50 Profile for Library Applications*; NISO Press: Bethesda, MD, 2003. http://www.niso.org/kst/reports/standards?step=2&gid=&project_key=e1a85edddd965ac64eaefa7f3ba28d136c6c08f5 (accessed June 2008).
2. National Information Standards Organization (NISO). *ANSI Z39.50-2003, Information Retrieval (Z39.50) Application Service Definition and Protocol Specification*; NISO Press: Bethesda, MD, 2003. http://www.loc.gov/z3950/agency/Z39–50–2003.pdf (accessed June 2008).
3. Moen, W.E. The development of ANSI/NISO Z39.50: A case study in standards evolution, Ph.D. Dissertation; School of Information Studies, Syracuse University: Syracuse, NY, 1998; UMI Publication Number: AAT 9904698, http://www.unt.edu/wmoen/dissertation/DissertationIndex.htm (accessed June 2008).
4. National Information Standards Organization (NISO). *American National Standard Z39.50, Information Retrieval Service Definition and Protocol Specifications for Library Applications*; Transaction Publishers: New Brunswick, NJ, 1988.
5. National Information Standards Organization (NISO). *ANSI/NISO Z30.50-1992 (version 2) Information Retrieval Service and Protocol: American National Standard, Information Retrieval Application Service Definition and Protocol Specification for Open Systems Interconnection*; NISO Press: Bethesda, MD, 1992. http://www.cni.org/pub/NISO/docs/Z39.50-1992/ (accessed June 2008).
6. National Information Standards Organization (NISO). *ANSI Z39.50-1995, Information Retrieval (Z39.50) Application Service Definition and Protocol Specification*; NISO Press: Bethesda, MD, 1995. http://www.loc.gov/z3950/agency/markup/markup.html (accessed June 2008).
7. Bib-1 Attribute Set, 2007, http://www.loc.gov/z3950/agency/defns/bib1.html (accessed June 2008).
8. Registry of Z39.50 Object Identifiers. Record syntaxes. (n.d.), http://lcweb.loc.gov/z3950/agency/defns/oids.html#5 (accessed June 2008).
9. Needleman, M. ZING—Z39.50 international next generation. Ser. Rev. **2002**, *28* (3), 248–250. doi:10.1016/S0098-7913(02)00188-0.
10. SRU Version 1.2 Specifications. 2007, http://www.loc.gov/standards/sru/specs/ (accessed June 2008).
11. Morgan, E.L. An introduction to the search/retrieve URL service (SRU). Ariadne **2004**, (40). http://www.ariadne.ac.uk/issue40/morgan/intro.html (accessed June 2008).
12. The ZeeRex DTD. 2004, http://explain.z3950.org/dtd/index.html (accessed June 2008). See also, An overview of ZeeRex. 2002, http://explain.z3950.org/overview/ (accessed June 2008).
13. CQL: Contextual Query Language (SRU Version 1.2 Specifications). 2008, http://www.loc.gov/standards/sru/specs/cql.html (accessed June 2008).
14. CQL Context Sets. 2008, http://www.loc.gov/standards/sru/resources/context-sets.html (accessed June 2008).
15. Implementors. 2008, http://www.loc.gov/standards/sru/resources/implementors.html (accessed June 2008).
16. McCallum, S.H. A look at new information retrieval protocols: SRU, OpenSearch/A, CQL, and XQuery. In *World Library and Information Congress: 72nd IFLA General Conference and Council*, Seoul, Korea, August 20–24, 2006; http://www.ifla.org/IV/ifla72/papers/102-McCallumen.pdf (accessed June 2008).
17. Woldering, B. The European Library: Integrated access to the national libraries of Europe. Ariadne **2004**, (38). http://www.ariadne.ac.uk/issue38/woldering/intro.html (accessed June 2008).
18. OCLC. Search & retrieve web service/search & retrieve URL service. (n.d.), http://www.oclc.org/research/projects/webservices/default.htm (accessed June 2008).
19. NISO Metasearch Initiative. (n.d.), http://www.niso.org/workrooms/mi (accessed June 2008).
20. OASIS Search Web Services Technical Committee. (n.d.), http://www.oasis-open.org/committees/search-ws/charter.php (accessed June 2008).
21. OpenSearch. (n.d.), http://www.opensearch.org (accessed June 2008).
22. Personal communication, June 2, 2008.

BIBLIOGRAPHY

1. Additional information related to Z39.50 and SRU can be found at: The Z39.50 Maintenance Agency website under Z39.50 Resources. http://www.loc.gov/z3950/agency/resources/ (accessed June 2008).
2. SRU maintenance agency, http://www.loc.gov/standards/sru/index.html (accessed June 2008).
3. Z39.50: Selected list of resources, http://www.unt.edu/wmoen/Z3950/BasicZReferences.htm (accessed June 2008).

47 Extensible Markup Language (XML)

Kevin S. Clarke

CONTENTS

INTRODUCTION

XML, the Extensible Markup Language, is a syntax for tagging, or marking-up, textual information. It is often described as a metalanguage because it provides a set of rules from which other, data-specific, markup-based languages may be created. As a syntax, XML does not exist in any form apart from its application in these data-specific languages. One of XML's strengths is that it may be used in its most simple form, as a set of markup rules used to create XML documents, or with a host of other XML-related standards and technologies. These additional standards and technologies increase its usefulness, and also its complexity.

XML is popular as a data markup syntax because it is extremely flexible, stable, and easy to use. It is used for both data storage and transmission. It may be used for purely semantic markup or for markup which is also intended for presentation purposes. XML is often said to be self-describing because its tags may be given names that provide a hint as to what is contained within them. For XML to truly be self-describing, though, one must be aware of the context in which the tags are used. A FirstName tag in one information or organizational context, for instance, might represent something completely different from a FirstName tag in another. XML has mechanisms for dealing with these variations.

HISTORY

The history of XML begins in the 1960s with generic coding and the Graphic Communication Association's GenCode. Generic coding was the use of descriptive tags, like "heading," to markup data. Prior to generic coding, electronic texts contained control codes, or macros ("specific coding"), which caused a document to be formatted in a particular way. Generic coding allowed simple tagging schemes to be used instead; this gave document producers greater flexibility in the typesetting process.

In the 1970s, markup advanced with the creation of the Generalized Markup Language (GML). GML grew from the design efforts of Charles Goldfarb, Edward Mosher, and Raymond Lorie at IBM. It advanced the generic coding movement by introducing "the concept of a formally designed document type with an explicit nested element structure." Goldfarb describes his motivation for introducing these changes as an interest in improving information retrieval.[1]

In the early 1980s, standardization efforts led to SGML, the Standard Generalized Markup Language, which further facilitated the production and sharing of electronic documents. In 1986, the International Organization for Standardization (ISO) ratified a standard for SGML. SGML solidified the convention of using strings of textual characters enclosed in angle brackets, i.e., tags, to demarcate other segments of text. This proved useful in publishing and sophisticated text processing and the publishing industry adopted SGML as a result.

After the success of SGML, the need arose for a method to markup and display documents on the emerging World Wide Web. In 1990, Tim Berners-Lee and Anders Berglund developed an application of SGML for this purpose called the Hypertext Markup Language (HTML). Like earlier generic coding efforts, HTML used a predefined set of tags to describe the structure of documents to be placed on the Web. HTML tags included things like head, body, title, img (for image), p (for paragraph), a (for anchor), and others.

HTML was a great success, but its singular focus on presentation led developers to experiment with SGML's greater flexibility, and comprehensiveness, to deliver more semantic content on the Web. In 1996, The World Wide Web Consortium (W3C) set up a working group (including Jon Bosak, Tim Bray, Michael Sperberg-McQueen, James Clark, and others) to develop a new version of SGML. This new version was to be slimmer than SGML and better suited than HTML for marking-up rich content.

In 1998, these simplification efforts resulted in the W3C's Recommendation: the XML, version 1.0.[2] A fourth edition, correcting minor errors, appeared in 2006; in 2006, the W3C also released a Recommendation for XML 1.1.[3] Though version 1.1 did not contain that many changes, the recommended changes did break backwards compatibility with version 1.0. With the loss of compatibility and without enough practical gain for XML developers, XML 1.1 was never widely adopted by the community.

In Web applications, XML is often used for the markup, manipulation, storage, and transmission of data. The final step in the process is often the transformation of data marked up in XML into HTML for presentation on the Web. This is frequently accomplished through another XML-based standard, XSLT (the Extensible Stylesheet Language), which takes an XML document as input and can return a different markup-based document as a result. There are a host of XML-related standards that allow for transformation, linking, styling, querying, and general manipulation of data marked up in XML. These are used extensively on the server side in Web application development.

At the time of XML's creation, it was seen as an improvement over SGML. Today, there are critics of XML who see new and, arguably, better options for doing many of the things that XML does. The most widely touted contender to XML is JSON, JavaScript Object Notation.[4] As a lightweight data-interchange format, JSON addresses two of the complaints that some people have about XML: 1) that it's too verbose and 2) that it is too difficult to understand. While JSON enjoys a good deal of success, it seems unlikely to replace XML as a data markup syntax; instead, it adds another useful tool to the Web developer's toolbox.

EXTENSIBLE MARKUP SYNTAX

By defining a standard set of markup rules, XML allows a common set of data processing tools to be used. This means programmers working in libraries can use the same tools as those working in the publishing industry or in any other industry that works with structured data. The tool that makes this possible is the XML parser. XML parsers read XML in its raw form and provide a model that can be used in higher level tools (e.g., editors, browsers, stylesheet processors, databases, etc.).

For an XML parser to work, it relies on the "well-formedness" of an XML document. When an XML document is said to be well-formed, it means that the document conforms to all of XML's syntactical rules. If a document's markup is not well-formed, the document cannot be parsed by an XML parser. XML parsers, unlike HTML parsers, are not forgiving in what they accept. All XML documents must be well-formed, but not all XML documents must have their elements and structures formally defined. Adherence to the syntactical rules is the only steadfast requirement.

The syntactical rules of XML are strict, but what one does with XML's structural components is open and flexible. This is unlike data that is stored in a database. Databases require that data conforms to certain rules. Data is often normalized to fit into the rules of the database. XML in contrast can store semistructured data. Semistructured data is data whose structure hasn't been, or can't be, formally defined. Since XML doesn't require formal data structures, it is an ideal container for this type of data.

This doesn't mean that XML cannot also work with highly structured data. XML is often used as a transmission format for data stored in relational databases. Its strength is that it can convey or store highly or semistructured data using a single syntax and, so, a common set of tools. When one does want to work with highly structured data and XML, a Document Type Definition (DTD) or schema (XML Schema or RELAX NG schema) is created to enforce the conceptual units and structure of the data. Consult the DTD entry in this encyclopedia for more information on DTDs (See the entry on "Document Type Definitions," p. 1640).

This additional restriction is known as the validity of an XML document. An XML document must be well-formed to be valid, but does not have to be valid in order to be well-formed. The validity restraint is an additional layer on top of the requirements of the basic XML syntax and, so, is not required in order to work with XML. Though not required, enforcing validity is useful when sharing data marked up in XML or putting it into a highly structured database. The XML-related standards related to DTDs and XML schemas achieve this additional layer of conformance by defining the top-down structure of an XML document and the characteristics of data being marked up.

To start working with XML, one need only be aware of the rules of well-formedness and the required and optional components of an XML document. Using an XML-aware text editor is advised because it will automatically supply many of the syntactical constructs, but it isn't necessary. XML's components include the XML declaration, elements, attributes, comments, processing instructions, PCDATA and CDATA, and entity references.

THE XML DECLARATION

In most cases, XML documents contain a declaration that identifies the document as XML. The XML declaration specifies information that is useful to the XML parser, but it is not required. If it doesn't appear, parsers will make assumptions about the XML. Though the declaration is not required, it is good practice to include one in all XML documents as it states, explicitly, what is to follow and gives humans reading the XML additional information about the data.

A sample XML declaration follows:

```
<?xml version='1.0' encoding='UTF-8'?>
```

It has several components. The declaration begins with `<?xml` and ends with `?>`. The *xml* string in the markup is case sensitive and must not be capitalized. The *xml* string distinguishes the XML declaration from a generic XML processing instruction, discussed later. In addition to the declaration's beginning and ending markup, there are several other required and optional parts. These occur between the `<?xml` and `?>` markup in an XML declaration.

One required part of the XML declaration is the *version* document declaration. The *version* declaration is a key–value pair. Its name, or key, is *version* and its value is the version of the XML specification to which the document conforms. Since XML 1.1 never caught on within the XML community, the most common use of *version* will be to indicate that the document conforms to the XML 1.0 specification. If in the future there is an XML version 2.0, future XML declarations might contain *version = '2.0'*.

The first optional part of the XML declaration is the *encoding* document declaration. Encoding indicates the type of character encoding used within the document. There are a wide variety of character encodings that one could use. ISO-8859-1, also called Latin-1, is used on Windows in most Western countries. It is not used on the Western version of Mac OS, though, and does not match character sets in most non-Western countries. EUC-JP and SHIFT_JIS are used in Japan. ANSEL is a character set used in many library applications but it is not, by default, supported by XML parsers.

Unicode, available in UTF-8 or UTF-16, is a character set that can handle most existing languages. Since UTF-8 is the default encoding for XML documents, XML's success as a data transmission and storage format has significantly promoted the use of Unicode on the Web. This has been a great boon for data interoperability and is seen as one of the successes of XML. To indicate encoding in the XML document's declaration, an encoding key–value pair is used. The value of *encoding* is the character set encoding used in the XML document; one example of how this looks in markup is *encoding = 'UTF-8'*.

There is also an optional *standalone* document declaration. This key–value pair is used with DTDs. When a *standalone* key has the value "yes," it tells an XML processor that nothing outside of the document is needed to complete it, such as an external entity. The processor may safely skip loading a DTD. When the standalone attribute is omitted, the value "no" is assumed. An example of how this looks in markup is *standalone = 'no'*.

While the XML declaration is an optional part of an XML document, if it is included it must have the *version* declaration. Whether or not the *encoding* or *standalone* declarations are included is up to the XML's author. Since DTDs are an aging standard and newer and, arguably, better alternatives for validating XML are available, more often than not one will see the *version* and *encoding* document declarations without the *standalone* declaration.

Elements

XML elements are the fundamental building blocks of an XML document. Elements are identified by brackets which encapsulate the name of the element. Elements have beginning and ending tags, e.g., the element name plus the angle brackets, with a textual content value, included between the two tags. A sample XML element follows:

```
<topic>The Extensible Markup Language</topic>
```

In this example, the name of the element is *topic*. XML is case sensitive so *topic* is different from *Topic*, *TOPIC*, and *ToPiC*. According to the syntactical rules of XML, the first and last tags in an element must be the same word with the same case. This is different from HTML, which will accept beginning tags with a different case from their ending tags.

In addition to the case sensitivity of XML element names, there are some additional rules for naming XML elements. The first is that XML element names may contain letters, numbers, and other characters. They must not, though, start with punctuation or a number. Element names are not allowed to start with string *xml* in any form: *XML*, *Xml*, *xml*, etc. Spaces in a name are also prohibited.

The inclusion of punctuation in the XML element name is a little trickier: the underscore, hyphen, period, and colon are allowed (although the colon has a special significance, as discussed in the Namespaces section). Other punctuation marks, though, are not allowed. This includes characters that are reserved for markup: angle brackets, ampersands, apostrophes, semicolons, slashes, and question marks.

Here are some examples of well-formed elements, elements that adhere to XML's syntactical rules:

```
<lastname>Clarke</lastname>
<firstName>Caitlin</firstName>
<Middle_Name>Lassiter</Middle_Name>
```

The following XML elements are not well-formed because they do not abide by the naming rules:

```
<100_Field>Clarke, Caitlin</100_Field>
<First Name>Kylie</First Name>
<lastName>Clarke</LastName>
```

XML is often criticized for its verbosity. While XML gives document authors the ability to name their elements as they wish, best practices would encourage using names that are descriptive and brief. One of XML's strengths is that it is human readable, but it is a good idea to keep in mind that data marked up in XML will also be transmitted between machines. Names like *first_middle_and_last_name* might be technically acceptable, but are probably more than are needed to identify the data being marked up.

Container Elements

Elements are the basic building blocks of an XML document. Singular elements, like described above, markup data with a tag, or element name that can give a hint to what the element contains. By itself an individual XML element isn't that useful but, by using elements in conjunction with others, we can model more complex and granular data structures. Take, for instance, the example of a person's name:

```
<first>Kylie</first>
<middle>Harrison</middle>
<last>Clarke</last>
```

In this example, the XML elements are siblings to one and other. There is a relationship between the elements that is indicated by their co-occurrence. XML can markup other types of relationships too. For instance, hierarchy gives us a sense of ownership or subsumption. Consider the example elements in a fuller context:

```
<name>
        <first>Kylie</first>
        <middle>Harrison</middle>
        <last>Clarke</last>
</name>
```

In this example, we have sibling relationships between the *first*, *middle*, and *last* elements, but we also have a parent–child relationship between these elements and the *name* element. XML models hierarchy using container elements. Container elements are just elements that contain other elements. In the case of the example above, the *name* element is a container element for the *first*, *middle*, and *last* elements.

The more element containers, or levels of element nesting, in an XML document, the more complex the document becomes. It's important when creating nontrivial XML documents to remember that XML's syntactical rules require a strict format to the nesting. For XML to be considered well-formed, all start and end tags for elements must nest correctly. When an element's start tag is inside another element, its end tag must also be inside that element. Take, for example, the following XML fragment:

```
<person>
       <name>
              <first>Sullivan</first>
              <middle>Ryan</middle>
              <last>Clarke</last>
       </name>
</person>
```

All the start tags and end tags open and close within their own scope. There isn't any overlap between them. An example of XML container elements that are not well-formed follows. XML requires that elements be closed in the order they were opened. The example below closes the *name* element before the *last* element, which was opened after the *name* element. This is not well-formed XML.

```
<person>
       <name>
              <first>Sullivan</first>
              <middle>Ryan</middle>
              <last>Clarke</name>
       </last>
</person>
```

The Root Element

Another type of element found in XML documents is the root element. Each XML document must have a single root element that contains all the other elements within the document. Using an inverted tree analogy, the root element is the top level element and all the other XML elements are hierarchically subordinate to it. If an XML document contained two top level elements, it would not be a well-formed document.

The root element establishes the boundaries of the document's data content. For illustration purposes, a well-formed XML document is as follows:

```
<?xml version='1.0' encoding='UTF-8'?>
<people>
       <person>
              <name>Kylie Harrison Clarke</name>
       </person>
       <person>
              <name>Caitlin Lassiter Clarke</name>
       </person>
</people>
```

If, however, the same data is used without encapsulating the *person* elements in a root element, then the document is not well-formed. What follows is an example of a document that has multiple root elements. It is not well-formed XML and could not be parsed by an XML parser. A parser would report an error instead, indicating that the document does not have a single root element.

```
<?xml version='1.0' encoding='UTF-8'?>
<person>
       <name>Kylie Harrison Clarke</name>
</person>
<person>
       <name>Caitlin Lassiter Clarke</name>
</person>
```

Empty Elements

The last type of element that may be used in an XML document is the empty element. Empty elements are just like other elements except that they intentionally contain no textual data. There are many reasons one might want to have an empty element. For instance, just its presence may be intended to indicate something about that which the data is describing.

The appearance of an empty element is similar to that on a closing element's tag. A tag used to close a normal element has a slash before the name: `</closing>`. In contrast, an empty element has its slash at the end of the element's tag: `<empty/>`. It is also acceptable to use standard element markup structure to indicate an empty element. Both of the examples below are well-formed XML.

```
<emptyElement></emptyElement>
<emptyElement/>
```

Empty XML elements might also be used to carry XML attributes, which are discussed in more detail below.

Mixed Content

Mixed content is not so much a different kind of XML element, but a way to use elements to markup information that is document-centric. XML may be used to markup metadata and it may be used to markup full-text. Metadata, unlike most full-text, will usually have a very consistent structure and is sometimes called data-centric markup because it is often machine generated and/or intended to be processed by machines. Document-centric markup, on the other hand, is markup that is more likely to be processed or read by humans, though it may be machine processed as well.

An example of document-centric markup might be an HTML page that has a main body, paragraphs, and then individual words marked up within those paragraphs.

```
<body>
       <p>This is a paragraph with <strong>significant</strong> words which
       need to be <strong>distinguished</strong> from the others.</p>
</body>
```

The above markup differs from that used up to this point because the elements contain other elements and text. Prior to this, elements in the examples have contained either other elements or text, but not both.

The inclusion of both text and child elements within an element is known as mixed content. Mixed content is commonly encountered when working with textual-based materials that are intended for consumption by humans. It is less likely to be found when working with data that comes from a structured database, though sometimes people do store large chunks of marked up text in a database.

ATTRIBUTES

Attributes may be added to elements to describe characteristics or properties, i.e., information about the element that is discrete from the name of the element. Attributes tend to function like adjectives, modifying the meaning of the elements. Consider this variation on the earlier examples:

```
<person>
       <name type='first'>Sullivan</name>
       <name type='middle'>Ryan</name>
       <name type='last'>Clarke</name>
</person>
```

Rather than create individual elements for each type of name, one might choose instead of view name as the unit of data and consider the type of name as a characteristic of the *name* element. In XML, this would be accomplished by using a *type* attribute on a generic *name* element.

Elements may have multiple attributes, but an element may not have two attributes of the same name. If this happens, the element will not be well-formed. The rules for attribute naming are like the rules for element naming. Attribute names that begin with a number, for instance, are not allowed. Nor are spaces within an attribute's name allowed. Some punctuation is allowed, but not all types and definitely not that reserved for general XML markup (ampersands, angle brackets, single and double quotes, etc.).

Elements have rules about well-formed nesting of child elements and attributes have rules about the use of value delimiters. To indicate the value of an attribute, an equals sign is followed by two quotation marks. The quotation marks may be double quotes, one on each side of the value, or they may be single quotes, one on each side of the value.

Double quotes and single quotes though may not be mixed. This allows double or single quotes to be used in the attribute's value. For this to work, the value of the attribute must be wrapped by quotes of the opposite type. The following examples all contain well-formed XML attributes:

```
<message text='Rosie is going to the ball tonight.'/>
<message text="Rosie is going to the ball tonight."/>
<message text="Ronald received Rosie's message in time."/>
<message text='"Thanks," said Ronald'/>
```

There are no clear rules for when to use attributes versus a child element. There are some who prefer to work with XML with no attributes and others who view attributes as an essential part of XML. Some guidelines might prove useful. For instance, attributes usually are considered as modifiers of the XML elements on which they occur. Also, if you want to have further substructure, then an attribute would not be a good choice because, unlike elements, they don't have children. Other than this, though, XML authors are on their own.

Comments

Comments are a type of markup that enables authors to put information into the document that is not intended for display or further processing. They provide a way to make editorial additions to an XML document. Comments may be used for documenting decisions, providing explanatory notes, flagging areas in need of review, or commenting out segments of markup so that they will not be processed by an XML parser.

Comments begin with < ! – and end with – >. So that it is clear where comments end, they are not allowed to contain double hyphens (–) or the end comment markup (– >). Other than that, they may contain any other text or markup. In an XML document, comments occur outside of element tags. They may not be included within an element tag, this would include the prohibition from occurring within attributes.

Some examples of well formed comments:

```
<!- This is where the document starts ->
<!- do not use: <author/> ->
```

Some examples of comments that are not well formed:

```
<!- contents: introduction - history - discussion - conclusion ->
<author <!- attribute here -> type='book'/>
```

Processing Instructions

Similar in construction to an XML declaration, processing instructions provide a mechanism for passing instructions to applications which process the XML document. They have a common syntax, starting with <? and ending with ?> but, beyond that, are open to whatever the particular application that will process the instruction needs. Example processing instructions include

```
<?xml-stylesheet href='display.xsl' type='text/xsl'?>
<?include data?>
```

Perhaps the most common use of XML processing instructions is the inclusion of an "xml-stylesheet" instruction. These instructions, which follow the XML declaration and precede the document's root element, are used to tell Web browsers what to use when they transform data-centric XML into a form that will display in the browser (XHTML or HTML, for example).

Entities

The markup of XML documents requires using certain characters that have a specific meaning in the XML syntax. To include these reserved characters as needed in the content of an XML document, there must be a way to escape or encode them so that they do not confuse the XML parsers for whom their occurrence indicates markup. This is accomplished by using entity references.

The five reserved characters in XML are the ampersand, the apostrophe, the quotation mark, the greater than symbol, and the less than symbol. Their corresponding entity references are on the left:

<	<	less than
>	>	greater than
&	&	ampersand
'	'	apostrophe
"	"	quotation mark

When, for instance, an author needs to include an ampersand in an XML document, this can be done using the & entity reference. If an apostrophe is needed in an attribute's value, one might use an ' entity reference. For example

```
<publisher>Smith &amp; Sons, inc.</publisher>
<message text='Jada&apos;s first dog was named Rain'/>
```

In addition to the five built-in entity references, entities can be used for other purposes as well. There are, for instance, also numeric versions of character entities in the Unicode character set. These come in two types: decimal references and hexadecimal references. € is the decimal reference for the euro and &#20AC; is the hexadecimal reference for the euro. Either may be used in XML.

CDATA Sections

In some situations the need for entity references can become excessive. When writing about XML, for instance, one might want to include large blocks of markup. This can be accomplished by using entity references but this is a lot of work. CDATA sections provide an alternative to using entity references for lots of markup. By using the CDATA section, XML authors can indicate blocks of text that should not be parsed by the XML parser; instead, these blocks are just passed through.

CDATA sections are indicated using the following markup: <![CDATA[ ]]>. Anything inside of the inner brackets will be ignored by the XML parser and just passed through. CDATA sections work best when large blocks of text are involved. They can be confusing though because the XML author must switch modes; for instance, entity references inside a CDATA section will not be resolved to the entity they represent.

An example CDATA section showing the person element used in the XML element section above illustrates how one might want to use CDATA sections:

```
<example>
       <!CDATA[
              <person>
                     <name type='first'>Sullivan</name>
                     <name type='middle'>Ryan</name>
                     <name type='last'>Clarke</name>
              </person>
       ]>
</example>
```

The only requirement for a CDATA section is that it cannot contain the end marker:]>. This would prematurely end the CDATA section. This can be circumvented by ending the CDATA block prior to the CDATA end characters and then using a plain string with an entity reference for the greater than symbol (e.g.,]]>) to complete the missing illegal string.

XML NAMESPACES

While XML can be used completely within a single information environment, more often than not people use it to share their data with others. When this happens, it is often desirable to combine elements from two or more document structures into a single document. However, because each document structure may be defined independently, there exists the possibility of ambiguity. A *name* element in one information context might means something different from a *name* element in another.

XML namespaces are designed to deal with this ambiguity. They define a unique scope for element names so that when they are mixed with elements from other documents the names are unique. Namespaces are declared using a Uniform Resource Identifier (URI). The URI, which should be unique and is often a Uniform Resource Locator (a type of URI that is used on the Web to identify sites), is associated with elements' names to create a name that is unique across different information contexts.

When thinking about namespaces, it is sometimes useful to think of the URI as prepended to the local element name. Several examples of element names with their namespaces are

{http://www.loc.gov/mods/v3}title
{http://www.tei-c.org/ns/1.0}title
{urn:isbn:1-931666-22-9}title

This syntax isn't an official form for representing the association between URIs and element names, but is provided to illustrate the relationship between the two components of a qualified element name. A qualified element name is a name that is associated with a namespace URI either through a namespace prefix or by virtue of the namespace being defined as the default namespace for that XML document. These two options are explained in more detail below.

All the above elements are *title* elements, but each element is distinct because it exists within a unique namespace. The first two namespaces are URLs. The last namespace is a Uniform Resource Name (URN), which is another type of URI. Using namespaces, it is possible to mix all three of these *title* elements in the same document without confusion.

XML Namespaces may be defined at the top of the document in the root element or at any other point within the document. When a namespace is defined it applies to all the child elements underneath the element on which it is defined. It is possible to redefine a document's default namespace several times throughout the hierarchy of the document. It is important to note that XML namespaces do not apply to attributes unless specifically associated with the attribute through a namespace prefix.

Namespace prefixes are one way to associate element names with a namespace's URI. They are often used when there is more than one namespace defined within a document. They may be used instead of, or in addition to, a default namespace in a XML document. The following XML document uses two namespaces, one which is defined as the default for the document and one which is associated with a namespace prefix.

```
<mads xmlns=http://www.loc.gov/mads/ xmlns:mods="http://www.loc.gov/mods/
v3">
       <authority>
              <mods:name>
                     <mods:namePart>Smith,John</mods:namePart>
                     <mods:namePart mods:type="date">1995-</mods:namePart>
              </mods:name>
       </authority>
</mads>
```

The default namespace in this document is http://www.loc.gov/mads/; the other namespace, named using the http://www.loc.gov/mods/v3 URI, is associated with the *mods* namespace prefix. The default namespace applies to all the elements in the document that do not have a namespace prefix and that reside underneath the element on which the namespace is defined. The namespace associated with the *mods* namespace prefix applies to all elements and attributes whose names are prefixed with the *mods* prefix and that reside beneath the element on which it is defined.

It is not necessary to use XML namespaces if one is not planning on sharing XML outside a particular information context. Even if XML isn't shared, if other XML element sets are brought into the environment, it might make sense to use a namespace prefix to distinguish the local elements from the ones that are being used. Though namespaces are often referenced from XML schemas, there is no direct connection between namespace and validating XML documents. Namespaces provide a context in which names are used; they may be used without XML schemas. It is worth noting that there is no built-in support for namespace in DTDs.[5]

SPECIFIC USES IN THE LIBRARY ENVIRONMENT

XML's strength is that it provides a syntax from which data-specific markup languages may be created. Librarians, like many others, have taken advantage of this to markup data structures that are unique to their information needs. The availability of a generalized markup syntax has also engendered new initiatives designed to foster cooperation between institutions of cultural knowledge (e.g., museums, libraries, and archives). From these efforts, several XML-based standards have appeared—among the most notable are MODS, the Metadata Object Description Schema[6]; METS, the Metadata Encoding and Transmission Standard[7]; VRA Core, the Visual Resources Association's core element set[8]; MIX, the Metadata for Images in XML standard[9]; and, PREMIS, the Library of Congresses' Preservation Metadata Implementation Strategies schema.[10]

METS is a general all-purpose wrapper for objects from institutions of cultural knowledge. It describes the structure of objects that may be exchanged over the Web and also provides a metadata wrapper for other XML formats that address other aspects related to digital objects. For instance, a

METS wrapper may contain a MODS record that provides the bibliographic description for a digital image; it may also contain a MIX record that marks-up the technical metadata associated with the image. A good source for asking questions about library-specific XML standards is the Metadata Librarians mailing list.[11]

Though the details of the many library-specific XML standards are beyond the scope of this entry, an example MODS record, in its entirety, is provided for illustration purposes:

```
<?xml version="1.0" encoding="UTF-8"?>
<mods xmlns:xlink="http://www.w3.org/1999/xlink" xmlns:xsi="http://
www.w3.org/2001/XMLSchema-instance" xmlns="http://www.loc.gov/mods/v3"
version="3.0" xsi:schemaLocation="http://www.loc.gov/mods/v3 http://
www.loc.gov/standards/mods/v3/mods-3-0.xsd">
      <titleInfo>
            <title>Directory of computer assisted research in
            musicology</title>
      </titleInfo>
      <titleInfo type="alternative">
            <title>Computer assisted research in musicology</title>
      </titleInfo>
      <name type="corporate">
            <namePart>Center for Computer Assisted Research</namePart>
      </name>
      <typeOfResource>text</typeOfResource>
      <genre authority="marc">directory</genre>
      <originInfo>
            <place>
                  <placeTerm authority="marccountry" type="code">cau</
                  placeTerm>
            </place>
            <place>
                  <placeTerm type="text">Menlo Park, CA</placeTerm>
            </place>
            <publisher>Center for Computer Assisted Research</publisher>
            <dateIssued>-1988</dateIssued>
            <dateIssued encoding="marc" point="start">1985</dateIssued>
            <dateIssued encoding="marc" point="end">1988</dateIssued>
            <issuance>continuing</issuance>
            <frequency>Annual</frequency>
      </originInfo>
      <language>
            <languageTerm authority="iso639-2b"
            type="code">eng</languageTerm>
      </language>
      <physicalDescription>
            <form authority="marcform">print</form>
            <extent>4 v.: ill., music; 26 cm.</extent>
      </physicalDescription>
      <note>Description based on: 1986.</note>
      <subject authority="lcsh">
            <topic>Musicology</topic>
            <topic>Data processing</topic>
            <topic>Periodicals</topic>
      </subject>
      <subject authority="lcsh">
            <topic>Music</topic>
            <topic>Bibliography</topic>
```

```
            <topic>Periodicals</topic>
      </subject>
      <subject authority="lcsh">
            <topic>Musicians</topic>
            <topic>Directories</topic>
      </subject>
      <subject authority="lcsh">
            <topic>Musicologists</topic>
            <topic>Directories</topic>
      </subject>
      <subject authority="lcsh">
            <topic>Musicology</topic>
            <topic>Data processing</topic>
            <topic>Directories</topic>
      </subject>
      <classification authority="lcc">ML73 .D57</classification>
      <classification edition="19" authority="ddc">780/.01/02584</
      classification>
      <relatedItem type="succeeding">
            <titleInfo>
                  <title>Computing in musicology</title>
            </titleInfo>
      </relatedItem>
      <recordInfo>
            <recordContentSource>DLC</recordContentSource>
            <recordCreationDate encoding="marc">861202</
            recordCreationDate>
            <recordChangeDate>20020320050438.0</recordChangeDate>
            <recordIdentifier>11315879</recordIdentifier>
      </recordInfo>
</mods>
```

MODS allows bibliographic records, usually stored in an integrated library system, to be shared and used in a format that is, arguably, more readily accessible than the MARC format,[12] the traditional binary format that has conveyed bibliographic library data since the 1960s.

XML also has more mundane uses within the library. Its availability has prompted cooperation on a global scale; this includes use by many libraries. Some librarians, for instance, are using XML as a format into which information extracted from their integrated library systems may be marked up and then conveyed on the Web. Once library data is marked up in XML, reusing it on the library's Web page, or in e-mail alerts sent to library patrons, is much easier. XML provides library developers with a common syntax that can be layered over a diverse field of proprietary and closed source databases and applications. Enabling developers to abstract the traditional "black box" of library applications into a text-based markup language allows for greater flexibility in the types of services that the libraries can offer.

These two types of library uses, formalized schemas and ad hoc messaging, illustrate both ends of the continuum in XML development. XML may be used in its most simple way, as markup to convey data from one point to another, or it may be used more globally, as a way to share information and encourage greater cooperation. When approaching the more universal uses of XML it is important to remember that XML is not a panacea. Many times the most difficult problems are administrative or cultural rather than technical. Although XML provides a good technical solution to sharing, storing, and conveying data in a platform and application neutral way, it often illuminates the need for higher level cooperation and communication across institutions that might want to share data. Though it may highlight issues that extend beyond the technical realm, it is also important to give credit to it as a technology that has changed the way the Web works.

CONCLUSION

XML is extensible because it provides users with the ability to systematically markup almost any type of data. It was created at a time in the development of the Web when richer markup mechanisms were needed and it succeeded because it gave document and data authors the tools and standards they needed to solve their content markup problems. XML is still a good choice for marking-up data today because it is well supported by many applications. Even if, in the future, other formats prevail, XML's human readability will make moving to these new formats easy. For this reason, many describe XML as future proof.

XML continues to enjoy a great deal of success and growth. The World Web Web Consortium[13] is working on new XML-related standards and technologies. XSLT[14] is an XML-based language for transforming and styling data marked up in XML; XPath, is a way to express XML hierarchies in a concise format[15]; XQuery is a language for querying XML that is evolving into a full-fledged XML programming language[16]; SVG, Scalable Vector Graphics, is a way of encoding graphical information in a textual XML format[17]; and, XForms is a way to express data input forms, like those in HTML, in an XML format.[18]

Like with XForms, XML-based languages separate the presentation view from the semantic markup. This allows data marked up in XML to repurposed in a variety of contexts. Data can have one display that is rendered on the Web and another that is used on mobile devices; there might be one display for library staff and another for library patrons. Librarians have taken advantage of this strength to build XML applications for the library environment. Being able to take advantage of a larger community of application developers has made this easier. It looks like XML will continue to be a significant player in the information markup space well into the future.

REFERENCES

1. http://www.sgmlsource.com/history/jasis.htm (access March 1, 2008).
2. http://www.w3.org/TR/2006/REC-xml-20060816/ (access March 1, 2008).
3. http://www.w3.org/TR/2006/REC-xml11-20060816/ (access March 1, 2008).
4. For more on DTDs' strengths and weaknesses, see the entry on *Document Type Definitions* in this volume (see the entry on "Document Type Definitions," p. 1640).
5. http://www.json.org/ (accessed March 1, 2008).
6. http://www.loc.gov/standards/mods/ (accessed March 1, 2008).
7. http://www.loc.gov/standards/mets/ (accessed March 1, 2008).
8. http://www.vraweb.org/projects/vracore4/index.html (accessed March 1, 2008).
9. http://www.loc.gov/standards/mix/ (accessed March 1, 2008).
10. http://www.loc.gov/standards/premis/ (accessed March 1, 2008).
11. http://metadatalibrarians.monarchos.com/ (accessed March 1, 2008).
12. http://www.loc.gov/marc/ (accessed March 1, 2008).
13. http://www.w3.org/ (accessed March 1, 2008).
14. http://www.w3.org/TR/xslt (accessed March 1, 2008).
15. http://www.w3.org/TR/xpath (accessed March 1, 2008).
16. http://www.w3.org/TR/xquery/ (accessed March 1, 2008).
17. http://www.w3.org/Graphics/SVG/ (accessed March 1, 2008).
18. http://www.w3.org/TR/xforms/ (accessed March 1, 2008).

48 Resource Description Framework (RDF)

Nicholas Gibbins and Nigel Shadbolt

CONTENTS

INTRODUCTION

The Resource Description Framework,[1] or RDF, is a knowledge representation language for the Semantic Web,[2,3] and is used to express knowledge about things both on and off the Web; RDF can be used to write metadata about web pages and to describe real-world objects with equal facility. RDF is a key language in the technical architecture of the Semantic Web, being both a format for describing instance data, and the foundation for the vocabulary definition languages RDF Schema[4] and OWL.[5]

The Semantic Web is a development of the World Wide Web that aims to provide an infrastructure for machine-understandable information on the Web. By expressing information in a form that makes the meaning, or semantics, accessible to machines, the goal of the Semantic Web is to create a next-generation Web in which information can be mediated by software agents on behalf of and without intervention from their users. At present, information on the World Wide Web is predominantly textual and requires human understanding to interpret it; the meaning of such natural language information must be made explicit if a machine is to be able to make sense of it. In artificial intelligence, the long-standing discipline of knowledge representation has developed a variety of approaches for expressing information to facilitate reasoning; these knowledge representation languages are of varying degrees of complexity and expressivity, but they share the common feature that they encode information as structures that can be formally interpreted to give some sense of their meaning.

By itself, RDF provides a domain-neutral framework for information interchange that must be augmented with terms to meet the requirements of a specific application domain. For example, a bibliographic application needs to be able to talk about works and authors, while an e-commerce application needs to be able to talk about orders and prices. This orientation to a particular application domain or domains is accomplished by means of one or more domain vocabularies, or *ontologies*.[6] In Computer Science, an ontology is a formal description of a domain of knowledge. Gruber[7] defines an ontology as "a specification of a conceptualization"; in other words, a formal account of an abstract model of some application domain which includes, but is not limited to, the classes of entity that exist within the domain, and the relations that link those entities.

RDF has two accompanying ontology languages, RDF Schema[4] and the Web Ontology Language OWL.[5] RDF Schema is the simpler of the two, and provides a small set of modeling constructs for defining classes, properties and certain global constraints on those properties. OWL is more expressive (and correspondingly more complex to reason with), and provides a larger set of modeling constructs that allows an ontology designer to more richly specify classes in terms of the necessary and sufficient conditions for membership of those classes. An in-depth treatment of OWL is beyond the scope of this entry; we refer the reader to[8,9] for further information.

In addition to these languages for defining RDF vocabularies, the World Wide Web Consortium (W3C) has also published an SQL-like query language for interrogating RDF graphs, known as the SPARQL Protocol and RDF Query Language[10,11] (or more simply as SPARQL).

THE TRIPLE MODEL

The information presented on the Semantic Web can be viewed as a directed, labeled graph in which the nodes stand for things and values, and the edges (with their labels) are the properties that relate nodes to one other. The fundamental unit of knowledge representation is the triple, a directed edge that represents a binary relationship between two nodes. Customarily, the components of this triple are referred to as the subject, the predicate and the object: the subject is the node that the directed edge leaves, the object is the node that it enters, and the predicate is the type of the edge. Alternatively, a triple could be considered to be a statement that a particular entity (the subject) has a property (the predicate) with a particular value (the object); this corresponds closely to object-oriented[12] or frame-based[13] models of knowledge representation.

The nodes in an RDF graph denote resources, which are things in the domain of discourse. Nodes may be Uniform Resource Identifiers (URIs),[14] literals, or blank nodes. URIs are used to denote things with identity, such as web pages, organizations, people, or books. Literals are values such as character strings, numbers or dates, which do not have identity; a (plain) literal is considered to denote itself, so two literals with the same value are treated as if they were the same literal. Finally, blank nodes are used to indicate the existence of a thing, without saying anything about the name of that thing.

With the careful use of URIs, RDF allows machines to unambiguously identify entities and vocabulary terms; each URI identifies a single thing, even though it is expected that there may be multiple URIs that identify the same thing (effectively synonyms for the thing). Adapting an example from the RDF Primer,[15] we can represent the statement (that a particular web page was created by John Smith) as a triple with

- A subject, http://www.example.org/index.html
- A predicate, http://purl.org/dc/terms/creator
- And an object, http://www.example.org/staffid/85740

In this example, we refer to the web page using its URI: http://www.example.org/index.html. We also use URIs to refer to John Smith (http://www.example.org/staffed/85740), and to the creator

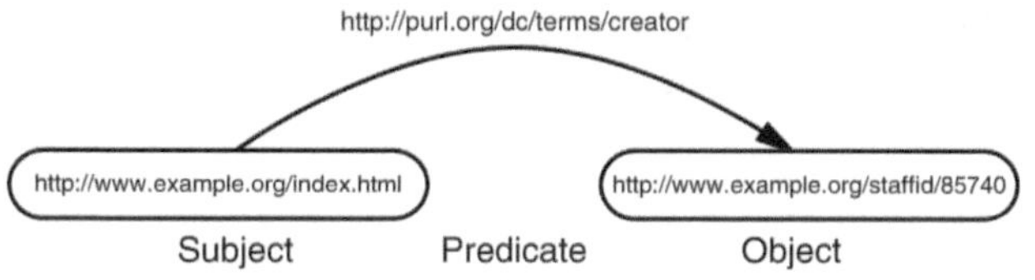

FIGURE 48.1 An RDF graph containing a single triple.

relation (http://purl.org/dc/terms/creator), taken from the Dublin Core vocabulary.[16] Presented graphically, this statement forms a graph containing two nodes with a single directed edge between them, as shown in Figure 48.1.

This triple can also be written as

```
<http://www.example.org/index.html> <http://purl.org/dc/terms/creator>
<http://www.example.org/staffid/85740>
```

This example uses a syntax based on the Notation 3 syntax for RDF[17] (discussed in more depth below), in which terms in angle brackets denote resources identified by URIs. In the order written, the three terms are the subject, predicate and object of the triple, and the completed triple is followed by a period.

COMPARING XML AND RDF

The relationship between RDF and the eXtensible Markup Language (XML)[18] warrants further explanation. Both are used to represent structured information on the Web, and XML is used as the standard syntax for RDF, but the two languages are distinct and have different characteristics.

The most fundamental difference between XML and RDF is in the way in which they structure information. As described above, RDF structures information as a labeled, directed graph, whereas XML is limited to tree structures, which has consequences in the way that data from different sources can be merged. Merging two RDF files can be accomplished by taking the union of the underlying graphs; this operation does not require any knowledge of the vocabularies (schemas) that are used in these graphs. In contrast, merging two XML files that use different schemas is a more difficult operation, because the resulting file will not validate using either schema, but rather a new schema that combines the two original schemas must be used instead.

An XML document can be parsed to give an unambiguous structure, but this structure has no innate meaning; the meanings of XML schemas must be agreed between the relevant parties on a case-by-case basis. RDF differs from XML in that the triples that are created when an RDF file is parsed have a well-defined semantics, which facilitates further information exchange by providing a basic set of rules for manipulating the information while preserving its knowledge content. Together with the ease of merging RDF files, these formal semantics mean that RDF has considerable advantages for information interchange over XML, and can be used to facilitate interoperability between heterogeneous systems.

Finally, RDF uses URIs to refer to objects in the domain of discourse. This has been used to promote what is known as the linked data model of publishing.[19,20] Given that the resources in an RDF graph may be represented by URIs, the aim of the linked data model is that it should be possible to dereference those URIs and by doing so retrieve a description of the resources that they represent. In effect, linked data results from the hypertextual foundations of the World Wide Web (and so of the Semantic Web); users of the Web follow links to obtain human-readable information in the form of web pages, so Semantic Web agents should be able to do likewise. Linked data may be implemented using several different Web technologies; a general overview of the more common approaches is given in Sauermann,[21] and a summary of the best practices for publishing ontologies as linked data is given in Berrueta.[22]

FEATURE SUMMARY

RDF defines the triple model of data and a standard syntax for expressing those triples (RDF/XML), but does not constrain the vocabulary used in those triples: the URIs denoting categories and relations that we might wish to use in our descriptions. RDF Schema defines a basic vocabulary for use with RDF that lets users represent and define vocabularies that are specific to their problem domains. This basic vocabulary supports the following primitive modeling constructs:

- Named classes and explicit hierarchies of classes
- Named properties and explicit hierarchies of properties
- Global ranges and domains of properties
- A reification vocabulary for using triples to describe other triples
- Containers and collections, two methods for representing information about groups of resources
- A set of ancillary properties for providing human-readable documentation and links to further information

All of the vocabulary terms defined in RDF Schema are assigned URIs from one of two namespaces, rdf and rdfs (for largely historical reasons that originate with the first version of RDF, the terms defined in RDF Schema are divided across two different namescapes). For clarity, we will write rdf:XXX as a shorthand for http://www.w3.org/1999/02/22-rdf-syntax-ns#XXX, and rdfs:YYY as a shorthand for http://www.w3.org/2000/01/rdf-schema#YYY. This abbreviation style, whereby a lengthy URI is reduced to a short string consisting of a namespace abbreviation (representing a URI prefix), a separating colon, and a name defined in that namespace (which is to be appended to the URI prefix), is known as a Qualified Name or QName.[23,24]

CLASSES

RDF Schema defines the property rdf:type that allows a user to indicate that a resource is an instance of a particular class. For example, if we wished to indicate that John Smith (denoted by the URI http://www.example.org/staffid/85740) was an instance of the Person class defined in the FOAF (Friend of a Friend) ontology,[25] we would write the triple:

```
<http://www.example.org/staffid/85740> rdf:type <http://xmlns.com/
foaf/0.1/Person>.
```

In this example, rdf:type is a QName which represents the "type" from the rdf namespace; the QName is expanded to the URI http://www.w3.org/1999/02/22-rdf-syntax-ns#type as described above. We can define a resource to be a class by declaring it to have an rdf:type of rdfs:Class. For example, to define a class of documents (represented by the URI http://example.org/ontology#Document), we would write:

```
<http://example.org/ontology#Document> rdf:type rdfs:Class.
```

These classes may be arranged into an explicit hierarchy by stating that a class is a subclass of another class, using the rdfs:subClassOf property:

```
<http://example.org/ontology#Newspaper> rdfs:subClassOf <http://example.
org/ontology#Document>.
```

In this example, we have stated that the class Newspaper is a subclass of the class Document, which is equivalent to saying that every newspaper is also a document (or to put it a third way, that the set of newspapers is a subset of the set of documents).

Properties

In the same way that classes are defined in RDF Schema, properties may be defined by declaring a resource to be of `rdf:type`, `rdf:Property`. Properties may be arranged into hierarchies to represent the specialization and generalization of relationships. For example, an "employed by" property might be considered to be a specialization of an "affiliated with" property. A property can be declared to be a specialization of another property by stating that it is `rdfs:subPropertyOf` the other.

```
<http://example.org/ontology#employedBy> rdfs:subPropertyOf
<http://example.org/ontology#affiliatedWith>.
```

Properties can be further described by defining their domain and range using the rdfs:domain and `rdfs:range` properties. The domain of a property is the class of objects that it runs from. For example, the "employed by" property might run from a class Person (being the class of people). The range of a property is the class of objects that it runs to; the range of "employed by" might be the class of organizations. These constraints on properties permit a reasoner to make inferences about the types of objects that are involved in a relationship.

```
<http://example.org/ontology#employedBy> rdfs:domain <http://example.org/
ontology#Person>.
<http://example.org/ontology#employedBy> rdfs:range <http://example.org/
ontology#Organisation>.
```

Containers and Collections

RDF Schema provides two different mechanisms for defining groups of objects, each with separate properties. The first of these, RDF containers, represents a group of objects with a resource which may be typed to informally indicate the intended semantics of the group; a group of type `rdf:Bag` is unordered, one of type `rdf:Seq` is an ordered sequence, and one of type `rdf:Alt` is a set of alternatives from which a single member should be selected (in practice, `rdf:Alt` is rarely used). The vocabulary pertaining to containers includes a countably infinite set of special properties (the ordinal container membership properties `rdf:_1, rdf:_2` and so on), which indicate both the membership of a resource in the group, and for the ordered `rdf:Seq`, the position of a member within the group.

A sequence of three resources (for example, three email addresses) would be represented as follows:

```
<http://example.org/data#seq1> rdf:type rdf:Seq.
<http://example.org/data#seq1> rdf:_1 <mailto:groucho@example.org>.
<http://example.org/data#seq1> rdf:_2 <mailto:chico@example.org>.
<http://example.org/data#seq1> rdf:_3 <mailto:harpo@example.org>.
```

The container vocabulary has the disadvantage that it produces groups that are open and mutable. There is no way to state that a group is closed, that is that the stated members of a group are the only members; a third party could assert that the above sequence has an extra member by adding the following triple:

```
<http://example.org/data#seq1> rdf:_4 <mailto:karl@example.org>.
```

The collection vocabulary addresses this by supporting the definition of closed groups that can have no further members. A collection is a recursive data structure that defines a group as a resource of type `rdf:List`, which consists of the first object in the group (indicated using the `rdf:first` property), and another `rdf:List` which contains the remainder of the group (indicated using the `rdf:rest` property). This second `rdf:List` contains the second element of the collection, and another `rdf:List` with the remainder of the collection, and so on. This recursion is terminated by the term `rdf:nil`, which represents an empty list. The example above could be represented in the container vocabulary as follows:

```
<http://example.org/data#list1> rdf:type rdf:List.
<http://example.org/data#list1> rdf:first <mailto:groucho@example.org>.
<http://example.org/data#list1> rdf:rest <http://example.org/data#list2>.
<http://example.org/data#list2> rdf:type rdf:List.
<http://example.org/data#list2> rdf:first <mailto:chico@example.org>.
<http://example.org/data#list2> rdf:rest <http://example.org/data#list3>.
<http://example.org/data#list3> rdf:type rdf:List.
<http://example.org/data#list3> rdf:first <mailto:harpo@example.org>.
<http://example.org/data#list3> rdf:rest rdf:nil.
```

As can be seen, an RDF collection requires more triples to represent the same group of objects than does a container, but it has the property that an attempt to tamper with the collection by adding extra members will result in an ill-formed data structure in which one of the component `rdf:Lists` has more than one `rdf:first` or `rdf:rest` property.

Reification

Reification is a mechanism for treating triples as first-class objects about which other assertions can be made (that is, as resources which can be referred to as the subjects or objects of other triples). The reification vocabulary in RDF Schema introduces the class `rdf:Statement`, which represents triples, and the properties `rdf:subject`, `rdf:predicate` and `rdf:object`, which represent the three components of a triple.

If we were to reify our original example (that a web page was written by John Smith), we would construct a small RDF graph containing four triples: one to represent the type of the reified statement, and one for each of the three components.

```
<http://example.org/data#stmt1> rdf:type rdf:Statement.
<http://example.org/data#stmt1> rdf:subject <http://www.example.org/
index.html>.
<http://example.org/data#stmt1> rdf:predicate <http://purl.org/dc/terms/
creator>.
<http://example.org/data#stmt1> rdf:object <http://www.example.org/
staffid/85740>.
```

In this example, the statement itself is represented by the URI http://example.org/data#stmt1; this may be used in other triples to express information about the statement. For example, if John Smith wanted to assert that he was the author of the statement, he could write:

```
<http://example.org/data#stmt1> <http://purl.org/dc/terms/creator>
<http://www.example.org/staffid/85740>.
```

The reification vocabulary provides a simple framework that supports the expression of fine-grained (triple level) provenance information about Semantic Web data. However, RDF reification is rarely used in practice, with many RDF practitioners preferring to use named graphs (a set of triples that is identified by a URI) to achieve the same ends, that of making assertions about other assertions.

Ancillary Properties

Finally, RDF Schema contains a number of properties that are not used to define ontology concepts, but to provide human-readable documentation, or to link to related information. The `rdfs:label` property is used to attach a human-readable label to a resource (necessary, given that URIs may be verbose), while `rdfs:comment` is used to add a comment (a natural language definition or rationale, perhaps). The `rdfs:seeAlso` property is used to indicate another resource which contains further information about a given resource; this is specialized by the `rdfs:isDefinedBy` property, which can be used to indicate the Web resource that defines a particular resource (for example, an ontology).

SYNTAX

The standard (normative) syntax for serializing RDF graphs for storage or transmission is RDF/XML.[24] This syntax is defined by a set of rules for transforming an XML document into an RDF graph[18]; element names, element contents, attribute names and attribute values are turned into resources, predicates and literals. While this syntax builds on the availability of high-quality XML tools, it tends to verbose serializations; in situations where RDF is to be read (and written) by people rather than machines, other non-XML syntaxes are preferred by many practitioners.

The best known of these alternative syntaxes is Notation 3 (N3),[17] a non-XML format that produces easy-to-understand serializations that can be quickly written by hand (or reproduced compactly in printed materials). Although it is well-known, N3 is a work in progress and subject to change, and has ambitious design goals; the expressivity of N3 goes beyond that of both RDF and OWL, so an arbitrary document written in N3 might contain constructs that cannot be translated into RDF/XML. For this reason, a number of N3 variants have evolved. N-Triples[26] is the simplest of these, and represents triples with no abbreviations such as QNames. Turtle[27] includes the QName-based namespace and abbreviation mechanism used by N3, but restricts the expressivity of the language to match that of RDF/XML.

Finally, there are two different approaches to serializing RDF graphs by embedding them within XHTML documents; the intent with both is to expose the structured data in ordinary web pages in such a way that Semantic Web agents can recognize and extract that data for their own use. The first of these, RDFa[28] defines a convention for expressing triples using the attributes on the elements in an XHTML document. A SW agent, on receiving a document containing RDFa markup, would first parse it as XML to obtain an intermediate representation, such as that provided by the Document Object Model (DOM), then parse this intermediate representation to obtain the encoded triples. GRDDL,[29] the second technique, provides a method for attaching a transformation to an XML document; this transformation, typically written in the eXtensible Stylesheet Language (XSLT),[30] can be used to extract selected information from the XML document and turn it into an RDF/XML document which can then be parsed to yield the RDF triples.

All of these RDF syntaxes have the feature that they do not define a canonical way in which an RDF graph can be written to a flat file for storage (a process known as serialization). Because a graph has no beginning or end, and no order to the edges, two implementations of the same serialization algorithm may process the triples in the graph in different orders, producing two different sequences of characters in the flat file. This complicates the process of comparing RDF data; comparison must be performed on the graphs themselves, rather than on their serializations.

SEMANTICS

RDF has a formal semantics[31] that defines the meaning of RDF statements by means of a model theory, an abstract, mathematical account based on the truth or falsity of statements. The goal of a model theory is that it enables the determination of the soundness and completeness of an inference process.[32]

The RDF semantics permit certain new triples to be inferred from those in an RDF graph. The following list of inferences is not comprehensive, but rather an indicative list of the sorts of inference that RDF permits:

- Transitivity of the rdfs:subClassOf relation
  - (if A is a subclass of B, and B is a subclass of C, then A is a subclass of C)
- Transitivity of the rdfs:subPropertyOf relation
  - (if A is a subproperty of B, and B is a subproperty of C, then A is a subproperty of C)
- Inferring general properties from more specific properties
  - (if two resources are related by a property, and there is a generalization of that property, then the resources are related by the superproperty)
- Inferring membership of general classes from membership of more specific classes
  - (if a resource is an instance of a class A, and A is a subclass of B, then the resource must also be a instance of class B)
- Inferring membership of classes from domain and range constraints
  - (if a resource has a property whose domain is B, then the resource must be an instance of B)

Comparison of RDF Schema and OWL

RDF Schema and OWL both fulfill similar roles within the architecture of the Semantic Web, in that they both support the definition of formal vocabularies for classifying entities and specifying the natures of their interrelations. The key difference between the two approaches is one of expressiveness; RDF Schema provides a concise set of primitives that are familiar to users of object-oriented modeling methodologies, but these primitives are limited to expressing explicit subclass and superclass relationships between classes and properties.

The OWL language extends the modeling capabilities of RDF Schema using a family of formal logic known as description logics[33] in order to produce a more expressive ontology language that allows the user to specify the nature of a class in terms of the necessary and sufficient conditions that must be met by members of that class. Necessary conditions are those which must be satisfied by all resources that are members of a class, while sufficient conditions allow an OWL reasoner to infer that a resource that satisfies them must be a member of a the class. For example, "is an animal with four legs" is a necessary condition for the class Horse (if an entity is a horse, we can infer that it is an animal and that it has four legs), but not a sufficient condition (if an entity is an animal and has four legs, we cannot be certain that it is a horse, because things other than horses will satisfy those conditions).

If classes are defined in terms of their necessary and sufficient conditions for membership, it is possible to identify the implicit subclass hierarchies that must naturally follow from these definitions. For example, if the class Quadruped is defined with the sufficient condition that it is an animal with four legs (that is, if we have a four-legged animal, then we can infer that it is a quadruped), then we could infer that Horse is a subclass of Quadruped (every Horse is a Quadruped), even though this relationship has not been explicitly stated in our ontology.

HISTORY

RDF and RDF Schema have a strong lineage which draws on the knowledge representation formalisms developed over the past 40 years. The graph-oriented triple model resembles the approaches made by network knowledge representation techniques (principally semantic networks[34] and conceptual graphs).[35] Although the simple class and property model of RDF Schema owes much to object-oriented approaches to software engineering, which in turn were derived in part from Minsky's frames,[36] RDF Schema is a purely declarative representation (unlike object-oriented models with member functions on objects, or frames with demons attached to slots). There is a further difference between the approach taken by RDF, and that taken by traditional object-oriented languages such as C++ or Java. The former is a property-centric approach, in that classes are associated with properties by defining the global range and domain constraints on the properties, while the latter is more class-centric, and defines classes in terms of the properties that may appear on objects of that category. This is largely a difference of emphasis rather than of the fundamental underlying logic, however. It should be noted that OWL takes an approach closer to that of the frame-based systems, in that classes are defined in terms of the necessary and sufficient properties that their instances must have.

The lineage of RDF in the context of Web-based knowledge representation and metadata languages dates back to the mid-1990s, with the publication of the Meta Content Framework (MCF) and the Platform for Internet Content Selection (PICS). The two languages prepared the way for RDF, by introducing a key use case (web page description) and the notion of a triple. The first version of RDF was published as a W3C Recommendation in 1999, and this version was deprecated by a revision in 2004 which sought to provide a formal foundation for the more expressive ontology language OWL; the description of RDF in this entry is based on the 2004 standard.

PICS

PICS[37,38] is a W3C Recommendation that was designed as a means for attaching machine-readable ratings to web pages in order to inform filtering software of the nature of the content of the web pages, with the intent that such filtering software would better be able to control the content displayed to users.

The technology emerged in part as a response to the U.S. Communications Decency Act of 1996 (Sec. 502), which effectively sought to place censorship restrictions on material distributed via the Internet. Rather than place the onus for removing unacceptable material on the publisher, PICS proposed a model whereby a potential consumer of such material could obtain an accurate description of the material that would enable them to decide whether or not they wished to view the material. The descriptions, known as content labels, consisted of values taken from some rating system, where a rating system comprised a set of independent dimensions on which an Internet resource could be evaluated. Such rating systems can be considered to be more complex versions of those used for film classification (for example, the film ratings G, PG, PG-13, R, and NC-17 specified by the Motion Picture Association of America); the commonly used ICRA system[39] specified by the Family Online Safety Institute classifies works on seven different scales: nudity, sexual material, violence, language, potentially harmful activities, user-generated content, and context.

PICS originally used a non-XML (Lisp-like) syntax for expressing content labels, with specific ratings represented by numeric values; a rating system might specify a rating category (dimension) for language, with ratings for "slang" given the value 0, "mild expletives" the value 1, "expletives" the value 2, "obscene gestures" the value 3, and so on. A content label also included information about the party that had generated the metadata, and could be digitally signed to support the verification of the identity of the rating party.

Although the practice of attaching PICS metadata to web pages was never widespread, several Web browsers implemented the standard, including Internet Explorer (from version 3.0 onwards). The principle of a standard syntax for Web metadata was a key step towards the advent of the Semantic Web, even if PICS was too tightly coupled to its application domain to serve well as a general-purpose metadata language. In 2000, W3C published a proposal for the use of RDF as the underlying syntax for content labels, which specified an RDF Schema vocabulary for expressing both content labels and rating systems.[40]

MCF

MCF[41] originated at Apple Computer Inc. in 1995 as a metadata format for representing the content and structure of Web sites, and was used by the HotSauce web navigation system (a browser that allowed a user to fly through a 3D map of a Web site). The author of MCF, Ramanathan V. Guha, moved from Apple to the Netscape Communications Corporation in 1997, and reimplemented MCF as an application of the emerging XML dialect of SGML. This XML syntax for MCF has been an important influence on the development of RDF, and introduced a number of features that persist in the most recent version of RDF and its XML syntax.

The underlying model of an MCF description is a directed labeled graph much like that of RDF. The nodes in the graph can represent both literal values and objects with identity (which could be either web objects or real-world objects), and are linked by typed binary relations. Unlike RDF, it assumes that only Web-addressable objects have URLs; real-world objects are identified by non-URI strings.

RDF (1999 Version)

The original 1999 specifications of RDF[42] and RDF Schema[43] differ from the versions described above in three main ways. First, they do not contain a formal account of the semantics of the languages that would be suitable for reasoning. The 1999 RDF specification contains a definition of a triple and an explanation of the entailed triples produced by reification, and the RDF Schema specification informally defines rdfs:subClassOf and rdfs:subPropertyOf as transitive properties, but there is no model-theoretic account of the sort that would be needed to verify the soundness and completeness of a reasoning engine.

Secondly, they contain a number of features that were deprecated in the 2004 specification because they could not be given an unambiguous meaning. Chief amongst these features is the ability to express statements about the members of a container. Given an rdf:Bag containing a number of resources, it was possible to write a single triple which applied to each member of the Bag by using the rdf:aboutEach attribute instead of the rdf:about attribute to indicate the subject of the triple. While this could be seen as a convenient shorthand for expressing repetitive information, there is an unfortunate interaction with the non-closed nature of RDF containers. In the absence of a framework for provenance, it is possible for a third party to state that a container has extra members; it thus becomes possible to make the original claim about the members of the container apply to more resources than were intended. A similar construct, rdf:aboutEachPrefix, allowed an author to express statements that would hold for all resources whose URIs began with a particular string. The set of triples entailed by this could not be determined without detailed knowledge of all the URIs with a particular prefix, and so the construct would therefore have unpredictable consequences as web pages were created and deleted over time. These two constructs, rdf:aboutEach and rdf:aboutEachPrefix, were included in the 1999 specification in order to support certain functionality provided by PICS, and in doing so to facilitate the transition from PICS to RDF. The 2004 specification also clarified the formal basis for reification; while the reification vocabulary remains part of the language, a triple does not entail its reification, nor vice versa.

Finally, the 2004 specifications contain a number of new constructs that were intended to bolster those constructs of RDF-1999 that were felt to have awkward consequences, but which were too widely used to be deprecated; the RDF container vocabulary was considered to be such, and was supplemented with the collection construct which enforced a well-formedness criterion on closed lists.

The RDF revision in 2004 aimed to make a number of corrections and improvements following feedback from implementers, and to complete the work on RDF Schema, which had previously only reached the state of W3C Candidate Recommendation. This new version of RDF was developed contemporaneously with the OWL Web Ontology Language, and so there was a close dialogue between the relevant W3C working groups in order to ensure that the revised form of RDF would form a suitable foundation for OWL; the earlier language DAML+OIL,[44] from which OWL was derived, used RDF/XML as a serialization syntax but disregarded its semantics (or lack thereof) and adopted a conventional description logic semantics.[33] An aim of the collaboration between these working groups was therefore to develop a semantics for RDF and RDF Schema that would be compatible with the semantics of OWL.

CONCLUSION

The RDF is a versatile knowledge representation language that can be used to express information about both Web resources and real-world objects. In conjunction with the vocabulary description languages RDF Schema and OWL, both of which are built on RDF, it can be used to create complex descriptions of application domains that a computer may use to infer new knowledge. The role played by RDF in the development of the Semantic Web is crucial; it integrates with the existing Web architecture to provide a common infrastructure for the creation and publication of structured data.

REFERENCES

1. Klyne, G.; Carroll, J.J.; McBride, B. Resource Description Framework (RDF): Concepts and abstract syntax, World Wide Web Consortium; 2004, http://www.w3.org/TR/rdf-concepts/ (accessed February 2008).
2. Berners-Lee, T.; Hendler, J.; Lassila, O. The Semantic Web. Sci. Am. May **2001**, 29–37.
3. Shadbolt, N.; Hall, W.; Berners-Lee, T. The Semantic Web revisited, IEEE Intell. Syst. May/June **2006**, 96–101.
4. Brickley, D.; Guha, R.V. RDF vocabulary description language 1.0: RDF Schema, World Wide Web Consortium, 2004, http://www.w3.org/TR/rdf-schema/ (accessed February 2008).
5. McGuinness, D.L.; van Harmelen, F. OWL Web Ontology Language overview, World Wide Web Consortium, 2004, http://www.w3.org/TR/owl-features/ (accessed February 2008).
6. Staab, S.; Studer, R., Eds. *Handbook on Ontologies*, 2nd Ed.; Springer: Berlin, 2009.
7. Gruber, T.R. A translation approach to portable ontology specifications. Knowl. Acquis. **1993**, *5* (2), 199–220.
8. Dean, M.; Schreiber, G.; Bechhofer, S.; van Harmelen, F.; Hendler, J.; Horrocks, I.; McGuinness, D.L.; Patel-Schneider, P.F.; Stein, L.A. OWL Web Ontology Language reference, World Wide Web Consortium, 2004, http://www.w3.org/TR/owl-ref/ (accessed February 2008).
9. Horrocks, I.; Patel-Schneider, P.F.; van Harmelen, F. From SHIQ and RDF to OWL: The making of a Web Ontology Language. Web Semantics: Science, Services and Agents on the World Wide Web **2003**, *1*, 7–26.
10. Prud'hommeaux, E.; Seaborne, A. SPARQL query language for RDF, World Wide Web Consortium, 2008, http://www.w3.org/TR/rdf-sparql-query/ (accessed February 2008).
11. Clark, K.G.; Feigenbaum, L.; Torres, E. SPARQL protocol for RDF, World Wide Web Consortium; 2008, http://www.w3.org/TR/rdf-sparql-protocol/ (accessed February 2008).
12. Information technology—open distributed processing—unified modelling language (UML) Version 1.4.2, ISO/ IEC 19501:2005.
13. Minsky, M. A framework for representing knowledge. In *The Psychology of Computer Vision*; Winston, P.H., Ed.; McGraw-Hill: New York, 1975; 211–277.
14. Berners-Lee, T.; Fielding, R.; Masinter, L. Uniform Resource Identifier (URI): Generic Syntax, RFC3986, Internet Engineering Task Force, 2005, http://www.ietf.org/rfc/rfc3986.txt (accessed February 2008).
15. Manola, F.; Miller, E. RDF primer, World Wide Web Consortium, 2004, http://www.w3.org/TR/rdf-primer/ (accessed February 2008).
16. DCMI metadata terms; 2008. http://dublincore.org/documents/dcmi-terms/ (accessed February 2008).
17. Berners-Lee, T. Notation 3, 2006, http://www.w3.org/DesignIssues/Notation3.html (accessed February 2008).
18. Bray, T.; Paoli, J.; Sperberg-McQueen, C.M.; Maler, E.; Yergeau, F. Extensible markup language (XML) 1.0 (Fourth Edition), World Wide Web Consortium, 2006, http://www.w3.org/TR/xml (accessed February 2008).
19. Berners-Lee, T. Linked Data, 2007, http://www.w3.org/DesignIssues/LinkedData.html (accessed February 2008).
20. Bizer, C.; Heath, T.; Idehen, K.; Berners-Lee, T. Linked data on the web, In *Proceedings of the 17th International World Wide Web Conference (WWW2008)*, Beijing, China, April 21–25, 2008; Association of Computing Machinery: New York, 2008.
21. Sauermann, L.; Cyganiak, R.; Ayers, D.; Völkel, M. Cool URIs for the Semantic Web, World Wide Web Consortium, 2008, http://www.w3.org/TR/cooluris/ (accessed April 2008).
22. Berrueta, D.; Phipps, J. Best practice recipes for publishing RDF vocabularies World Wide Web Consortium, 2008, http://www.w3.org/TR/swbp-vocab-pub/ (accessed February 2008).

23. Bray, T.; Hollander, D.; Layman, A.; Tobin, R. Namespaces in XML 1.0, World Wide Web Consortium, 2006, http://www.w3.org/TR/REC-xml-names/ (accessed February 2008).
24. Beckett, D. RDF/XML syntax specification (revised), World Wide Web Consortium, 2004, http://www.w3.org/TR/rdf-syntax-grammar/ (accessed February 2008).
25. Brickley, D.; Miller, L. FOAF vocabulary specification, 2007, http://xmlns.com/foaf/spec/ (accessed February 2008).
26. Grant, J.; Beckett, D. RDF test cases, World Wide Web Consortium, 2004, http://www.w3.org/TR/rdf-testcases/ (accessed February 2008).
27. Beckett, D.; Berners-Lee, T. Turtle—terse RDF triple language, World Wide Web Consortium, 2008, http://www.w3.org/TeamSubmission/turtle/ (accessed February 2008).
28. Adida, B.; Birbeck, M. RDFa primer: Embedding structured data in web pages, working draft, World Wide Web Consortium, 2007, http://www.w3.org/TR/xhtml-rdfa-primer (accessed February 2008).
29. Connolly, D. Gleaning resource descriptions from dialects of languages (GRDDL), World Wide Web Consortium, 2007, http://www.w3.org/TR/grddl/ (accessed February 2008).
30. Clark, J. XSL transformations (XSLT) version 1.0, World Wide Web Consortium, 1999, http://www.w3.org/TR/xslt (accessed February 2008).
31. Hayes, P. RDF semantics, World Wide Web Consortium, 2004, http://www.w3.org/TR/rdf-mt/ (accessed February 2008).
32. Hunter, G. *Metalogic: An Introduction to the Metatheory of Standard First Order Logic*; University of California Press: Berkeley, CA, 1973.
33. Baader, F.; Nutt, W. Basic description logics. In *The Description Logic Handbook: Theory, Implementation and Applications*, 2nd Ed.; Baader, F., Calvanese, D., McGuinness, D.L., Nardi, D., Patel-Schneider, P.F., Eds.; Cambridge University Press: Cambridge, U.K., 2007; 47–104.
34. Quillian, M.R. Word concepts: A theory and simulation of some basic semantic capabilities. Behav. Sci. **1967**, *12*, 410–430.
35. Sowa, J.F. *Knowledge Representation: Logical, Philosophical, and Computational Foundations*; Brooks Cole Publishing Co.: Pacific Grove, CA, 2000.
36. Minsky, M. A framework for representing knowledge. In *Readings in Cognitive Science*; Collins, A., Smith, E.E., Eds.; Morgan-Kaufmann: San Francisco, 1992.
37. Resnick, P. Filtering information on the Internet. Sci. Am. **1997**, *276* (3), 62–64.
38. Miller, J.; Resnick, P.; Singer, D. Rating services and rating systems (and their machine readable descriptions), World Wide Web Consortium, 1996, http://www.w3.org/TR/REC-PICS-services (accessed February 2008).
39. The ICRA vocabulary, http://www.icra.org/vocabulary/ (accessed February 2008).
40. Brickley, D.; Swick, R. PICS rating vocabularies in XML/ RDF, World Wide Web Consortium, 2000, http://www.w3.org/TR/rdf-pics (accessed February 2008).
41. Guha, R.V.; Bray, T. Meta content framework using XML, World Wide Web Consortium, 1997, http://www.w3.org/TR/NOTE-MCF-XML/ (accessed February 2008).
42. Lassila, O.; Swick, R. Resource description framework (RDF) model and syntax specification, World Wide Web Consortium, 1999, http://www.w3.org/TR/1999/REC-rdf-syntax-19990222/ (accessed February 2008).
43. Brickley, D.; Guha, R.V. Resource description framework (RDF) schema specification, World Wide Web Consortium, 1999, http://www.w3.org/TR/1999/PR-rdf-schema-19990303/ (accessed February 2008).
44. Connolly, D.; van Harmelen, F.; Horrocks, I.; McGuinness, D.L.; Patel-Schneider, P.F.; Stein, L.A. DAML+OIL reference description, World Wide Web Consortium, 2001, http://www.w3.org/TR/daml+oil-reference (accessed February 2008).

BIBLIOGRAPHY

1. Antoniou, G.; van Harmelen, F. *A Semantic Web Primer*, 2nd Ed.; MIT Press: Cambridge, MA, 2008.
2. Berners-Lee, T. *Weaving the Web: the Past, Present and Future of the World Wide Web by Its Inventor*; Texere Publishing: London, 1999.
3. Fensel, D. *Ontologies: A Silver Bullet for Knowledge Management and Electronic Commerce*, 2nd Ed.; Springer: Berlin, 2004.
4. Fensel, D.; Hendler, J.; Lieberman, H.; Wahlster, W. *Spinning the Semantic Web: bringing the World Wide Web to its full potential*; MIT Press: Cambridge, MA, 2003.

49 Text Encoding Initiative (TEI)

Edward Vanhoutte and Ron Van den Branden

CONTENTS

INTRODUCTION

Computers can only process texts whose characters are represented by a system that relates to the binary system computers can interpret. This is called character encoding. One such character encoding scheme based on the English alphabet is ASCII (American Standard Code for Information Interchange). Character encoding facilitates the storage of text in computers and the transmission of text through telecommunication networks. Character encoding, however, does not say anything about the semantics, interpretation, or structure of a text. Such information on a text is called meta-information. If we want to add any meta-information to a text so that it can be processed by computers, we need to encode or markup texts. We can do this by inserting natural language expressions (or codes representing them) in the text with the same character encoding the text is using, but separated from the text by specific markers. One such expression, we call a tag. All of the tags used to encode a text together constitute a markup language. The application of a markup language to a text, we call text encoding.

The Text Encoding Initiative (TEI) is a standard for the representation of textual material in digital form through the means of text encoding. This standard is the collaborative product of a community of scholars, chiefly from the humanities, social sciences, and linguistics who are organized in the TEI Consortium (TEI-C http://www.tei-c.org). The TEI Consortium is a nonprofit membership organization and governs a wide variety of activities such as the development, publication, and maintenance of the text encoding standard documented in the *TEI Guidelines*, the discussion and development of the standard on the TEI mailing list (TEI-L) and in Special Interest Groups (SIG), the gathering of the TEI community on yearly members meetings, and the promotion of the standard in publications, on workshops, training courses, colloquia, and conferences. These activities are generally open to nonmembers as well.

By "TEI Guidelines" one may refer both to the markup language and tag set proposed by the TEI Consortium and to its documentation online or in print. Informally "TEI Guidelines" is often abbreviated to "TEI." In this entry "TEI Guidelines" is used as the general term for the encoding standard. The *TEI Guidelines* are widely used by libraries, museums, publishers, and individual scholars to present texts for online research, teaching, and preservation. Since the TEI is expressed in terms of the eXtensible Markup Language (XML) and since it provides procedures and mechanics to adapt to one's own project needs, the *TEI Guidelines* define an open standard that is generally applicable to any text and purpose.

The entry first introduces the concepts of text encoding and markup languages in the humanities and then introduces the TEI encoding principles. Next, the article provides a brief historical survey of the TEI Guidelines and ends with a presentation of the Consortium's organization.

TEXT ENCODING IN THE HUMANITIES

Since the earliest uses of computers and computational techniques in the humanities at the end of the 1940s, scholars, projects, and research groups had to look for systems that could provide *representations* of data which the computer could process. Computers, as Michael Sperberg-McQueen has reminded us are binary machines that "can contain and operate on patterns of electronic charges, but they cannot contain numbers, which are abstract mathematical objects not electronic charges, nor texts, which are complex, abstract cultural and linguistic objects" (p. 34).[1] This is clearly seen in the mechanics of early input devices such as punched cards where a hole at a certain coordinate actually meant a 1 or 0 (true or false) for the character or numerical represented by this coordinate according to the specific character set of the computer used. Because different computers used different character sets with a different number of characters, texts first had to be transcribed into that character set. All characters, punctuation marks, diacritics, and significant changes of type style had to be encoded with an inadequate budget of characters. This resulted in a complex of "flags" for distinguishing uppercase and lowercase letters, for coding accented characters, the start of a new chapter, paragraph, sentence, or word. These "flags" were also used for adding analytical information to the text such as word classes, morphological, syntactic, and lexical information. Ideally, each project used its own set of conventions consistently throughout. Since this set of conventions was usually designed on the basis of an analysis of the textual material to be transcribed to machine-readable text, another corpus of textual material would possibly need another set of conventions. The design of these sets of conventions was also heavily dependent on the nature and infrastructure of the project, such as the type of computers, software, and devices such as magnetic tapes of a certain kind that were available.

Although several projects were able to produce meaningful scholarly results with this internally consistent approach, the particular nature of each set of conventions or encoding scheme had lots of disadvantages. Texts prepared in such a proprietary scheme by one project could not readily be used by other projects; software developed for the analysis of such texts could hence not be used outside the project due to an incompatibility of encoding schemes and nonstandardization of hardware. However, with the increase of texts being prepared in machine-readable format, the call for an economic use of resources increased as well. Already in 1967, Michael Kay argued in favor of a "standard code in which any text received from an outside source can be assumed to be" (p. 171).[2] This code would behave as an exchange format which allowed the users to use their own conventions at output and at input (p. 172).[2]

MARKUP LANGUAGES IN THE HUMANITIES

Procedural and Descriptive Markup

When human beings read texts, they perceive both the information stored in the linguistic code of the text and the meta-information which is inferred from the appearance and interpretation of the text. By convention, italics are, for instance, used as a code signaling a title of a book, play, or movie; a foreign word or phrase; or emphatic use of the language. Through their cognitive abilities, readers usually have no problems selecting the most appropriate interpretation of an italic string of text. Computers, however, need to be informed about these issues in order to be able to process them. This can be done by way of a markup language that provides rules to formally separate information (the text in a document) from meta-information (information *about* the text in a document).Whereas markup languages in use in the typesetting community were mainly of a procedural nature, that is, they indicate procedures that a particular application should follow (e.g., printing a string of text in italics), the humanities were also and mainly considered with descriptive markup that identifies the entity type of tokens (e.g., identifying that a string of text is a title of a book or a foreign word). Unlike procedural or presentational markup, descriptive markup establishes a one to one mapping between logical elements in the text and their markup. In order to achieve this, descriptive markup languages tend to formally separate information (the text in a document) from meta-information (information *about* the text in a document).

Early Attempts

Some sort of standardization of text encoding for the encoding and analysis of literary texts was reached by the COCOA encoding scheme originally developed for the COCOA program in the 1960s and 1970s,[3] but used as an input standard by the Oxford Concordance Program (OCP) in the 1980s[4] and by the Textual Analysis Computing Tools (TACT) in the 1990s.[5] For the transcription and encoding of classical Greek texts, the beta-transcription/encoding system reached some level of standardized use.[6]

The Standard Generalized Markup Language (SGML)

The call for a markup language that could guarantee reusability, interchange, system and software independence, portability, and collaboration in the humanities was answered by the publication of the Standard Generalized Markup Language (SGML) as an ISO standard in 1986 (ISO 8879:1986).[7] Based on IBM's *Document Composition Facility Generalized Markup Language*, SGML was developed mainly by Charles Goldfarb as a metalanguage for the description of markup schemes that satisfied at least seven requirements for an encoding standard (pp. 28–29)[8]:

1. The requirement of comprehensiveness.
2. The requirement of simplicity.
3. The requirement that documents be processable by software of moderate complexity.
4. The requirement that the standard not be dependent on any particular characteristic set or text-entry device.
5. The requirement that the standard not be geared to any particular analytic program or printing system.
6. The requirement that the standard should describe text in editable form.
7. The requirement that the standard allow the interchange of encoded texts across communication networks.

In order to achieve universal exchangeability and software and platform independence, SGML made use exclusively of the ASCII codes. As mentioned above, SGML is not a markup language itself, but a metalanguage by which one can create separate markup languages for separate purposes. This means that SGML defines the rules and procedures to specify the vocabulary and the syntax of a markup language in a formal Document Type Definition (DTD). Such a DTD is a formal description of, for instance, names for all elements, names and default values for their attributes, rules about how elements can nest and how often they can occur, and names for reusable pieces of data (entities). The DTD enables full control, parsing, and validation of SGML-encoded documents. By and large the most popular SGML DTD is the Hypertext Markup Language (HTML) developed for the exchange of graphical documents over the Internet.

A markup scheme with all these qualities was exactly what the humanities were looking for in their quest for a descriptive encoding standard for the preparation and interchange of electronic texts for scholarly research. There was a strong consensus among the computing humanists that SGML offered a better foundation for research-oriented text encoding than other such schemes.[8,9] From the beginning, however, SGML was also criticized for at least two problematic matters: SGML's hierarchical perspective on text, i.e., the representation of text as a hierarchical tree structure, and SGML's verbose markup system.[9] These two issues have since been central to the theoretical and educational debates on markup languages in the humanities.

The eXtensible Markup Language (XML)

The publication of the eXtensible Markup Language (XML) 1.0 as a W3C recommendation in 1998[10] brought together the best features of SGML and HTML and soon achieved huge popularity. Among the strengths XML borrowed from SGML are the explicitness of descriptive markup, the expressive power of hierarchic models, the extensibility of markup languages, and the possibility to validate a document against a DTD. From HTML it borrowed simplicity and the possibility to work without a DTD. Technically speaking, XML is a subset of SGML and the recommendation was developed by a group of people with a long standing experience in SGML, many of whom were members of the TEI community.

For example, a simple two-paragraph document could be encoded as follows in XML:

```
<?xml version="1.0" encoding="UTF-8"?>
<document>
<!-- paragraphs go here -->
      <paragraph number="1">Paragraph one of <title>an example
      </title>.</paragraph>
      <paragraph number="2">Paragraph two of this example.</paragraph>
</document>
```

This is an example of an XML document, representing both information and meta-information. Information (plain text) is contained in *XML elements*, delimited by *start tags* (e.g., <document>) and *end tags* (e.g., </document>). Additional information to these XML elements can be given in *attributes*, consisting of a name (e.g., number) and a value (e.g., [1]). *XML comments* are delimited by start markers (<!--) and end markers (-->). This particular example illustrates how XML enables semantically transparent encoding of a document (<document>), which consists of two paragraphs (<paragraph>), the first of which contains text identified as a title (<title>). By providing facilities to define own tags and attributes, XML allows encoders to devise their own markup languages for their document (types).

Among more technical ones, Steven DeRose pointed out substantial advantages of XML to the TEI community: by allowing for more flexible automatic parsing strategies and easy delivery of electronic documents with cheap ubiquitous tools such as Web browsers, XML could spread the notion of descriptive markup to a wide audience that will thus be acquainted with the concepts articulated in the TEI Guidelines (p. 19).[11] Because of its advantages and widespread popularity, XML became the metalanguage of choice for expressing the rules for descriptive text encoding in TEI.

TEI: GROUND RULES

GUIDELINES

The conclusions and the work of the TEI community are formulated as guidelines, rules, and recommendations rather than standards, because it is acknowledged that each scholar must have the freedom of expressing their own theory of text by encoding the features they think important in the text. A wide array of possible solutions to encoding matters is demonstrated in the TEI Guidelines which therefore should be considered a reference manual rather than a tutorial. Mastering the complete TEI encoding scheme implies a steep learning curve, but few projects require a complete knowledge of the TEI. Therefore, a manageable subset of the full TEI encoding scheme was published as TEI Lite, currently describing 145 elements.[12] Originally intended as an introduction and a didactic stepping stone to the full recommendations, TEI Lite has, since its publication in 1995, become one of the most popular TEI customizations and proves to meet the needs of 90% of the TEI community, 90% of the time.

The ground rules discussed in this section apply to the most recent version of the TEI at the time of writing, i.e., TEI P5. See the section on TEI: History for more details about P5 and previous versions of the TEI Guidelines.

TEXT STRUCTURE

The TEI Guidelines[13] define a set of rules to mark up the phenomena in a wide range of texts in a descriptive fashion. This means that, for example, encoders can (and should) not just indicate *that* a bit of text is printed in italics, but *why* this is the case: either because it appears to be a title in a bibliographical reference, or a technical term, a foreign word, a regular word with rhetorical emphasis, and so on. Texts that are enriched with intelligible meta-information not only can be preserved and reused more easily by humans, but also can be processed more intelligently by computers.

The TEI guarantees this potential by imposing a common structure on texts:

```
<TEI xmlns="http://www.tei-c.org/ns/1.0">
        <teiHeader>
                <fileDesc>
                        <titleStmt>
                                <title><!--Title--></title>
                        </titleStmt>
                        <publicationStmt>
                                <p><!--Publication Information--></p>
                        </publicationStmt>
                        <sourceDesc>
                                <p><!--Information about the source--></p>
                        </sourceDesc>
                </fileDesc>
        </teiHeader>
        <text>
                <body>
                        <p n="1">Paragraph one of <title>an XML example
                        </title>.</p>
                        <p n="2">Paragraph two of this example.</p>
                </body>
        </text>
</TEI>
```

This example, as any TEI text, is recognizable as a TEI text by the outermost *<TEI>* element, which is declared in the dedicated TEI namespace (http://www.tei-c.org/ns/1.0). The TEI considers texts units of information that are composed of two mandatory parts:

1. A header (<*teiHeader*>) containing descriptive meta-information. This should minimally document following aspects of the electronic file itself (<*fileDesc*>):
   - The title statement (<*titleStmt*>), providing information about the title, author, and others responsible for the electronic text.
   - The publication statement (<*publicationStmt*>), providing publication details about the electronic text.
   - A description of the source (<*sourceDesc*>), documenting bibliographic details about the electronic text's material source (if any).
2. The actual text (<*text*>) containing meta-information about the text's structure and the actual text. This should minimally contain a text body (<*body*>). The body contains lower-level text structures like paragraphs (<*p*>), or different structures for text genres other than prose: lines for poetry, speeches for drama.

Apart from simple texts, TEI provides means to encode composite texts, either by grouping structurally related texts in a <*group*> element inside <*text*>, or treating them as a corpus of diverse texts, using <*teiCorpus*> as the outermost element.

TEI Modules

As illustrated by this example, a significant part of the rules in the TEI Guidelines apply to the expression of descriptive and structural meta-information about the text. Yet, the TEI defines concepts to represent a much wider array of textual phenomena, amounting to a total of 503 elements and 210 attributes. These are organized into 21 modules, grouping related elements and attributes:

1. *The TEI Infrastructure.* Definition of common datatypes and modular class structures used to define the elements and attributes in the other modules.
2. *The TEI Header.* Definition of the elements that make up the header section of TEI documents. Its major parts provide elements to encode detailed metadata about bibliographic aspects of electronic texts, their relationship with the source materials from which they may have been derived, nonbibliographic details, and a complete revision history.
3. *Elements Available in All TEI Documents.* Definition of elements and attributes that may occur in any TEI text, of whatever genre. These elements cover textual phenomena like paragraphs, highlighting and quotation, editorial changes (marking of errors, regularizations, additions), data-like structures (names, addresses, dates, numbers, abbreviations), cross-reference mechanisms, lists, notes, graphical elements, bibliographic references, and passages of verse or drama.
4. *Default Text Structure.* Definition of elements and attributes that describe the structure of TEI texts, like front matter and title pages, text body, and back matter. These may contain further divisions, possibly introduced by headings, salutations, opening formulae, and/or concluded by closing formulae, closing salutations, trailing material, and postscripts.
5. *Representation of Nonstandard Characters and Glyphs.* Definition of specific provisions for representing characters for which no standardized representation (such as defined by the *Unicode Consortium* http://www.unicode.org/) exists.
6. *Verse.* Definition of specific elements and attributes for dedicated analysis of verse materials, such as caesurae, metrical systems, rhyme schemes, and enjambments.
7. *Performance Texts.* Definition of specific elements and attributes for dedicated analysis of drama materials. These include provisions for encoding specific phenomena in front matter and back matter, like details about performances, prologues, epilogues, the dramatic setting, and cast lists. Other drama-specific structures include speeches and stage

directions. For multimedia performances, elements for the description of screen contents, camera angles, captions, and sound are provided.

8. *Transcriptions of Speech.* Definition of elements and attributes for (general purpose) transcription of different kinds of spoken material. These cover phenomena like utterances, pauses, nonlexical sounds, gestures, and shifts in vocal quality. Besides this, specific header elements for describing the vocal source of the transcription are provided.
9. *Dictionaries.* Definition of elements and attributes for representing dictionaries, with provisions for unstructured and structured dictionary entries (possibly grouped). Dictionary entries may be structured with a number of specific elements indicating homonyms, sense, word form, grammatical information, definitions, citations, usage, and etymology.
10. *Manuscript Description.* Definition of specific header and structural elements and attributes for the encoding of manuscript sources. Header elements include provisions for detailed documentation of a manuscript's or manuscript part's identification, heading information, contents, physical description, history, and additional information. Dedicated text elements cover phenomena like catchwords, dimensions, heraldry, watermarks, and so on.
11. *Representation of Primary Sources.* Definition of elements and attributes for detailed transcription of primary sources. Phenomena covered are facsimiles, more complex additions, deletions, substitutions and restorations, document hands, damage to the source material, and illegibility of the text.
12. *Critical Apparatus.* Definition of elements and attributes for the representation of (different versions of texts as) scholarly editions, listing all variation between the versions in a variant apparatus.
13. *Names, Dates, People, and Places.* Definition of elements and attributes for more detailed analysis of names of persons, organizations, and places, their referents (persons, organizations, and places), and aspects of temporal analyses.
14. *Tables, Formulae and Graphics.* Definition of specific elements and attributes for detailed representation of graphical elements in texts, like tables, formulae, and images.
15. *Language Corpora.* Definition of elements and attributes for the encoding of corpora of texts that have been collected according to specific criteria. Most of these elements apply to the documentation of these sampling criteria, and contextual information about the texts, participants, and their communicative setting.
16. *Linking, Segmentation, and Alignment.* Definition of elements and attributes for representing complex systems of cross-references between identified anchor places in TEI texts. Recommendations are given for either in-line or stand-off reference mechanisms.
17. *Simple Analytic Mechanisms.* Definition of elements and attributes that allow the association of simple analyses and interpretations with text elements. Mechanisms for the representation of both generic and particular linguistic analyses are discussed.
18. *Feature Structures.* Definition of elements and attributes for constructing complex analytical frameworks that can be used to represent specific analyses in TEI texts.
19. *Graphs, Networks, and Trees.* Definition of elements and attributes for the analytical representation of schematic relationships between nodes in graphs and charts.
20. *Certainty and Responsibility.* Definition of elements for detailed attribution of certainty for the encoding in a TEI text, as well as the identification of the responsibility for these encodings.
21. *Documentation Elements.* Definition of elements and attributes for the documentation of the encoding scheme used in TEI texts. This module provides means to define elements, attributes, element and attribute classes, either by changing existing definitions or by creating new ones.

Each of these modules and the use of the elements they define are discussed extensively in a dedicated chapter of the TEI Guidelines.

Using TEI

In order to use TEI for the encoding of texts, users must make sure that their texts belong to the TEI namespace (http://www.tei-c.org/ns/1.0) and adhere to the requirements of the text model proposed by the TEI. In order to facilitate this conformance, it is possible (and strongly suggested) to associate TEI texts with formal representations of this text model. These formal *structural grammars* of a TEI compatible model of the text can be expressed in a number of ways, commonly referred to as a *TEI schema*. Technically, a TEI schema can be expressed in a variety of formal languages such as *Document Type Definition* (http://www.w3.org/TR/REC-xml/#dt-doctype), *W3C XML Schema* (http://www.w3.org/XML/Schema), or the *RELAX NG* schema language (http://www.relaxng.org/). It is important to notice that no such thing as "the TEI schema" exists. Rather, users are expected to select their desired TEI elements and attributes from the TEI modules, possibly with alterations or extensions where required. In this way, TEI offers a stable base with unambiguous means for the representation of basic textual phenomena, while providing standardized mechanisms for user customization for uncovered features. It is a particular feature of TEI that these abstract text models themselves can be expressed as TEI texts, using the documentation elements defined in the dedicated module *Documentation Elements*. A minimal TEI customization file looks as follows:

```
<TEI xmlns="http://www.tei-c.org/ns/1.0"xml:lang="en">
       <teiHeader>
              <fileDesc>
                     <titleStmt>
                            <title>A TEI customization</title>
                            <author>generated by Roma</author>
                     </titleStmt>
                     <publicationStmt>
                            <p>for use by whoever wants it</p>
                     </publicationStmt>
                     <sourceDesc>
                            <p>created on Thursday 24th July 2008 10:20:17
                            AM by the form at http://www.tei-c.org.uk/
                            Roma/</p>
                     </sourceDesc>
              </fileDesc>
       </teiHeader>
       <text>
              <front>
                     <divGen type="toc"/>
              </front>
              <body>
                     <p>My TEI Customization starts with modules tei,
                     core, header, and textstructure</p>
                     <schemaSpec ident="TBEcustom" docLang="en"
                     xml:lang="en" prefix=" ">
                            <moduleRef key="tei"/>
                            <moduleRef key="header"/>
                            <moduleRef key="core"/>
                            <moduleRef key="textstructure"/>
                     </schemaSpec>
              </body>
       </text>
</TEI>
```

Besides the common minimal TEI structure (<teiHeader> and <text>), a TEI customization file has one specific element which defines the TEI schema (<schemaSpec>). A TEI schema must minimally include the modules which define the minimal TEI text structure: the *TEI infrastructure* module, the *core* module with all common TEI elements, the *header* module defining all teiHeader elements, and the *textstructure* module defining the elements representing the minimal structure of TEI texts.

In the vein of *Literary Programming* (http://www.literateprogramming.com/), a TEI customization file not only contains the formal declaration of TEI elements inside `<schemaSpec>`, but may also contain prose documentation of the TEI encoding scheme it defines. Consequently, TEI customization files are commonly called *ODD files* (One Document Does it all), because they serve as a source for the derivation of

- A formal TEI schema (either as a DTD, W3C XML Schema, or RELAX NG schema).
- Human-friendly documentation of the TEI encoding scheme (in HTML, PDF, or XML).

In order to accommodate the process of creating customized TEI schemas and prose documentation, the TEI has developed a dedicated piece of software called *Roma* http://www.tei-c.org/Roma/. This is an ODD processor, offering an intuitive Web-based interface for the creation and basic editing of ODD files, generation of according TEI schemas and prose documentation in a number of presentation formats.

A TEI schema, stating all structural conditions and restraints for the elements and attributes in TEI texts can then be used to automatically validate actual TEI documents with an XML parser. Consider, for example, following fragments:

[A]

```
<TEI xmlns="http://www.tei-c.org/ns/1.0">
	<teiHeader>
		<fileDesc>
			<titleStmt>
				<title>A sample TEI document</title>
			</titleStmt>
			<publicationStmt>
			<publisher>
				Taylor & Francis
			</publisher>
			<pubPlace>London</pubPlace>
			<date when="2008"/>
			</publicationStmt>
			<sourceDesc>
				<p>No source, born digital</p>
			</sourceDesc>
		</fileDesc>
	</teiHeader>
	<text>
		<body>
			<p>This is a sample paragraph, illustrating a <name
			type="organization">TEI</name> document.</p>
		</body>
	</text>
</TEI>
```

[B]

```
<TEI xmlns="http://www.tei-c.org/ns/1.0">
      <text>
            <body>
                  <p>This is a sample paragraph, illustrating a
                  <orgName>TEI</orgName> document.</p>
            </body>
      </text>
</TEI>
```

When validated against a TEI schema derived from the previous ODD file, file [A] will be recognized as a valid TEI document, while file [B] will not:

- The TEI prescribes that the `<teiHeader>` *must* be present in each document, and that it precede the `<text>` part.
- The minimal set of TEI modules does not include the specialized `<orgName>` element. Although it is a TEI element, using it requires selection of the appropriate TEI module in the ODD file (in this case, the module for *Names, Dates, People, and Places*).

TEI: HISTORY

After the concise overview of the most recent version of TEI (P5) in the preceding section, this section explains the historical development of the TEI Guidelines.

POUGHKEEPSIE PRINCIPLES

Shortly after the publication of the SGML specification as an ISO Standard, a diverse group of 32 humanities computing scholars gathered at Vassar College in Poughkeepsie, New York in a 2-day meeting (November 11 and 12, 1987) called for by the Association for Computers and the Humanities (ACH) (http://www.ach.org), funded by the National Endowment for the Humanities (NEH), and convened by Nancy Ide and Michael Sperberg McQueen. The main topic of the meeting was the question how and whether an encoding standard for machine-readable texts intended for scholarly research should be developed. Among the delegates were representatives from the main European text archives and from important North American academic and commercial research centers. Contrary to the disappointing outcomes of other such meetings in San Diego in 1977 or in Pisa in 1980, this meeting did reach its goal with the formulation and the agreement on the following set of methodological principles—the so-called *Poughkeepsie Principles*—for the preparation of text encoding guidelines for literary, linguistic, and historical research (pp. 132–133),[14] (p. E.6-4),[15] (p. 6.)[16]:

1. The guidelines are intended to provide a standard format for data interchange in humanities research.
2. The guidelines are also intended to suggest principles for the encoding of texts in the same format.
3. The guidelines should
   a. Define a recommended syntax for the format
   b. Define a metalanguage for the description of text-encoding schemes
   c. Describe the new format and representative existing schemes both in that metalanguage and in prose
4. The guidelines should propose sets of coding conventions suited for various applications.
5. The guidelines should include a minimal set of conventions for encoding new texts in the format.

6. The guidelines are to be drafted by committees on
   a. Text documentation
   b. Text representation
   c. Text interpretation and analysis
   d. Metalanguage definition and description of existing and proposed schemes coordinated by a steering committee of representatives of the principal sponsoring organizations
7. Compatibility with existing standards will be maintained as far as possible
8. A number of large text archives have agreed in principle to support the guidelines in their function as an interchange format. We encourage funding agencies to support development of tools to facilitate this interchange.
9. Conversion of existing machine-readable texts to the new format involves the translation of their conventions into the syntax of the new format. No requirements will be made for the addition of information not already coded in the texts.

For the implementation of these principles the ACH was joined by the Association for Literary and Linguistic Computing (ALLC) (http://www.allc.org) and the Association for Computational Linguistics (ACL) (http://www.aclweb.org/). Together they established the Text Encoding Initiative (TEI) whose mission it was to develop the *Poughkeepsie Principles* into workable text encoding guidelines. The Text Encoding Initiative very soon came to adopt SGML, published a year before as ISO standard, as its framework. Initial funding was provided by the US National Endowment for the Humanities, Directorate General XIII of the Commission of the European Communities, the Canadian Social Science and Humanities Research Council, and the Andrew W. Mellon Foundation.

TEI P1 and TEI P2

From the Poughkeepsie Principles the TEI concluded that the TEI Guidelines should

- Provide a standard format for data interchange.
- Provide guidance for encoding of texts in this format.
- Support the encoding of all kinds of features of all kinds of texts studied by researchers.
- Allow the rigorous definition and efficient processing of texts.
- Provide for user-defined extensions.
- Be application independent.
- Be simple, clear, and concrete.
- Be simple for researchers to use without specialized software.

A Steering Committee consisting of representatives of the ACH, the ACL, and the ALLC appointed Michael Sperberg-McQueen as editor-in-chief and Lou Burnard as European editor of the Guidelines.

The first public proposal for the TEI Guidelines was published in July 1990 under the title *Guidelines for the Encoding and Interchange of Machine-Readable Texts* with the TEI document number TEI P1 (for Proposal 1). This version was reprinted with minor changes and corrections, as version 1.1 in November 1990.[17] Further development of the TEI Guidelines was done by four Working Committees (Text Documentation, Text Representation, Text Analysis and Interpretation, and Metalanguage and Syntax) and a number of specialist Working Groups among which groups on character sets, text criticism, hypertext and hypermedia, formulae, tables, figures, and graphics, language corpora, manuscripts and codicology, verse, drama and performance texts, literary prose, linguistic description, spoken text, literary studies, historical studies, print dictionaries, machine lexica, and terminological data. The extensions and revisions resulting from this work, together with extensive public comment resulted in the drafting of a revised version, TEI P2, that was released chapter by chapter between March 1992 and the end of 1993[18] and that included substantial amounts of new material.

TEI P3

The following step was the publication of the TEI P3 *Guidelines for Electronic Text Encoding and Interchange* in 1994[19] that presented a further revision of all chapters published under the document number TEI P2, and the addition of further chapters. A final revised edition of these P3 Guidelines correcting several typographic and other errors, and introducing one new element was published in 1999.[20] The publication of this 1292 page documentation of the definitive guidelines defining some 439 elements marked the conclusion of the initial development work. With this work, the Poughkeepsie Guidelines were met by providing a framework for the encoding of texts in any natural language, of any date, in any literary genre or text type, without restriction on form or content and treating both continuous materials ("running text") and discontinuous materials such as dictionaries and linguistic corpora.

TEI P4

Recognizing the benefits for the TEI community, the P4 revision of the TEI Guidelines[21] was published in 2002 by the newly formed TEI Consortium in order to provide equal support for XML and SGML applications using the TEI scheme. The chief objective of this revision was to implement proper XML support in the Guidelines, while ensuring that documents produced to earlier TEI specifications remained usable with the new version. The XML support was realized by the expression of the TEI Guidelines in XML and the conformation to a TEI conformant XML DTD. The TEI P4 generated a set of DTD fragments that could be combined together to form either SGML or XML DTDs and thus achieved backward compatibility with TEI P3 encoded texts. In other words, any document conforming to the TEI P3 SGML DTD was guaranteed to conform to the TEI P4 XML version of it. This "double awareness" of the TEI P4 is the reason why this version was called an "XML-compatible edition" rather than an "XML edition." This was achieved by restricting the revisions needed to make the P4 version with its 441 elements to error correction only. During this process of revision, however, many possibilities for other, more fundamental changes had been identified, which led to the current TEI P5 version of the Guidelines.

TEI P5

In 2003 the TEI Consortium asked their membership to convene Special Interest Groups (SIGs) whose aim could be to advise revision of certain chapters of the Guidelines and suggest changes and improvements in view of the P5. With the establishment of the new TEI Council, which superintends the technical work of the TEI Consortium, it became possible to agree on an agenda to enhance and modify the Guidelines more fundamentally which resulted in a full revision of the Guidelines published as TEI P5.[13] TEI P5 contains a full XML expression of the TEI Guidelines and introduces new elements, revises content models, and reorganizes elements in a modular class system that facilitates flexible adaptations to users' needs. Contrary to its predecessor, TEI P5 does not offer backward compatibility with previous versions of the TEI. The TEI Consortium will, however, maintain and error correct the P4 Guidelines. This means that users still have the option between P4 and P5.

TEI: ORGANIZATION

The TEI Consortium was established in 2000 as a not-for-profit membership organization to sustain and develop the Text Encoding Initiative (TEI). The Consortium is supported by a number of host institutions. It is managed by a Board of Directors, and its technical work is overseen by an elected technical Council who take responsibility over the content of the TEI Guidelines.

The TEI charter outlines the consortium's goals and fundamental principles. Its goals are

1. To establish and maintain a home for the Text Encoding Initiative (TEI) in the form of a permanent organizational structure.
2. To ensure the continued funding of TEI-C activities, for example: editorial maintenance and development of the TEI Guidelines and DTD/Schema training and outreach activities, and services to members.
3. To create and maintain a governance structure for the TEI-C with broad representation of TEI user-communities.

The Consortium honors four fundamental principles:

1. The TEI Guidelines, other documentation, and DTD/Schema should be free to users.
2. Participation in TEI-C activities should be open (even to nonmembers) at all levels.
3. The TEI-C should be internationally and interdisciplinarily representative.
4. No role with respect to the TEI-C should be without term.

Involvement in the consortium is possible in three categories: voting membership which is open to individuals, institutions, or projects; nonvoting subscription, which is open to personal individuals only; and sponsorship, which is open to individual or corporate sponsors. Only members have the right to vote on consortium issues and in elections to the Board and the Council, have access to a restricted Web site with prerelease drafts of Consortium working documents and technical reports, announcements and news, and a database of members, sponsors, and subscribers, with contact information, and benefit from discounts on training, consulting, and certification. The Consortium members meet annually at a Members' Meeting where current critical issues in text encoding are discussed, and members of the Council and members of the Board of Directors are elected. The membership fee payable varies depending on the kind of project or institution and its location depending on where the economy of the member's country falls in the four-part listing of Low, Lower-Middle, Middle-Upper, and High Income Economies, as defined by the World Bank.

CONCLUSIONS

Computers can only deal with explicit data. The function of markup is to represent textual material into digital form through the explicating act of text encoding. Descriptive markup reveals what the encoder thinks to be implicit or hidden aspects of a text, and is thus an interpretive medium which often documents scholarly research next to structural information about the text. In order for this research to be exchangeable, analyzable, reusable, and preservable, texts in the field of the humanities should be encoded according to a standard which defines a common vocabulary, grammar, and syntax, while leaving the implementation of the standard up to the encoder. A result of communal efforts among computing humanists, the Text Encoding Initiative documents such a standard in the TEI Guidelines. These guidelines are fully adaptable and customizable to one's specific project while enhancing this project's compatibility with other projects employing the TEI. For over two decades, the TEI has been used extensively in projects from different disciplines, fields, and subjects internationally. The ongoing engagements of a broad user community through the organization of the TEI Consortium consolidates the importance of the text encoding standard and informs its continuous development and maintenance.

REFERENCES

1. Sperberg-McQueen, C.M. Text in the electronic age: Textual study and text encoding with examples from Medieval texts. Literary Linguist. Comput. **1991**, *6* (1), 34–46.
2. Kay, M. Standards for encoding data in a natural language. Comput. Humanit. **1967**, *1* (5), 170–177.
3. Russel, D.B. *COCOA: A Word Count and Concordance Generator for Atlas*; Atlas Computer Laboratory: Chilton, U.K., 1967.

4. Hockey, S. *Oxford Concordance Program Users' Manual*; Oxford University Computing Service: Oxford, U.K., 1980.
5. Lancashire, I.; Bradley, J.; McCarty, W.; Stairs, M.; Woolridge, T.R. *Using TACT with Electronic Texts*; Modern Language Association of America: New York, 1996.
6. Berkowitz, L.; Squiter, K.A. *Thesaurus Linguae Graecae, Canon of Greek Authors and Works*; Oxford University Press: New York/Oxford, 1986.
7. Goldfarb, C.E. *The SGML Handbook*; Clarendon Press: Oxford, U.K., 1990.
8. Barnard, D.T.; Fraser, C.A.; Logan, G.M. Generalized markup for literary texts. Literary Linguist. Comput. **1988**, *3* (1), 26–31.
9. Barnard, D.T.; Hayter, R.; Karababa, M.; Logan, G.; McFadden, J. SGML-based markup for literary texts: Two problems and some solutions. Comput. Humanit. **1988**, *22* (4), 265–276.
10. Bray, T.; Paoli, J.; Sperberg-McQueen, C.M. *Extensible Markup Language (XML)* 1.0.; W3C Recommendation February 10, 1998 http://www.w3.org/TR/1998/REC-xml-19980210 (accessed September 2008).
11. DeRose, S.J. XML and the TEI. Comput. Humanit. **1999**, *33* (1–2), 11–30.
12. Burnard, L.; Sperberg-McQueen, C.M. TEI Lite: Encoding for interchange: An introduction to the TEI Revised for TEI P5 release; February 2006. http://www.tei-c.org/release/doc/tei-p5-exemplars/html/teilite.doc.html.
13. TEI Consortium Ed.; *TEI P5: Guidelines for Electronic Text Encoding and Interchange*, Text Encoding Initiative Consortium, http://www.tei-c.org/Guidelines/P5/ (accessed October 2008).
14. Burnard, L. Report of Workshop on Text Encoding Guidelines. Literary Linguist. Comput. **1988**, *3* (2), 131–133.
15. Ide, N.M.; Sperberg-McQueen, C.M. Development of a Standard for Encoding Literary and Linguistic Materials. In *Cologne Computer Conference 1988. Uses of the Computer in the Humanities and Social Sciences*, Volume of Abstracts. Cologne, Germany, September 7–10, 1988; E6-3-4.
16. Ide, N.; Sperberg-McQueen, C.M. The TEI: History, goals, and future. Comput. Humanit. **1995**, *29* (1), 5–15.
17. Sperberg-McQueen, M.; Burnard, L., Eds. *TEI P1: Guidelines for the Encoding and Interchange of Machine Readable Texts*; ACH-ALLC-ACL Text Encoding Initiative: Chicago/Oxford, 1990. http://www.tei-c.org.uk/Vault/Vault-GL.html (accessed October 2008).
18. Sperberg-McQueen, M.; Burnard, L., Eds. *TEI P2 Guidelines for the Encoding and Interchange of Machine Readable Texts Draft P2 (published serially 1992–1993)*; Draft Version 2 of April 1993, 19 chapters. http://www.tei-c.org.uk/Vault/Vault-GL.html (accessed October 2008).
19. Sperberg-McQueen, C.M.; Burnard, L., Eds. *Guidelines for Electronic Text Encoding and Interchange. TEI P3*; Text Encoding Initiative: Oxford, Providence, Charlottesville, Bergen, 1994.
20. Sperberg-McQueen, C.M.; Burnard, L., Eds. *Guidelines for Electronic Text Encoding and Interchange. TEI P3*; Revised reprint. Text Encoding Initiative: Oxford, Providence, Charlottesville, Bergen, 1999.
21. Sperberg-McQueen, C.M.; Burnard, L., Eds. *TEI P4: Guidelines for Electronic Text Encoding and Interchange, XML-compatible edition*; XML conversion by Bauman, S., Burnard, L., DeRose, S., and Rahtz, S.; Text Encoding Initiative Consortium: Oxford, Providence, Charlottesville, Bergen, 2002. http://www.tei-c.org.uk/P4X/ (accessed October 2008).

BIBLIOGRAPHY

1. Burnard, L.; O'Brien O'Keeffe, K.; Unsworth, J., Eds. *Electronic Textual Editing*; MLA: New York, 2006. http://www.tei-c.org/About/Archive_new/ETE/ (accessed October 2008).
2. Cummings, J. The text encoding initiative and the study of literature. In A *Companion to Digital Literary Studies*, Siemens, R., Schreibman, S., Eds.; Blackwell Publishing: Malden, MA, Oxford, 2007; 451–476. http://www.digital-humanities.org/companionDLS/ (accessed October 2008).
3. Ide, N.; Véronis, J., Eds. *Text Encoding Initiative: Background and Context*; Kluwer Academic Publishers: Dordrecht, 1995. Reprinted from Comput. Humanit. **1995**, *29*.
4. Mylonas, E.; Renear, A., Eds. Special Issue: Selected Papers from TEI 10: Celebrating the Tenth Anniversary of the Text Encoding Initiative. Comput. Humanit. **1999**, *33*(1–2).
5. Schreibman, S.; Rahts, S., Eds. Special Issue: TEI at 20. LLC. J. Digit. Scholarsh. Humanit. **2009**, *24*.
6. Van den Branden, R.; Vanhoutte, E.; Terras, M. *TEI By Example*; http://www.teibyexample.org (accessed October 2008).

50 Encoded Archival Description (EAD)

Daniel V. Pitti

CONTENTS

INTRODUCTION

Encoded Archival Description (EAD) is an international digital standard for encoding descriptions of archival records. An individual archival description is commonly called a finding aid, archival guide, handlist, inventory, or register. Though these terms cover a wide variety of apparatus, they most commonly refer to a hierarchical description of records that share a common origin or provenance. A collection of records sharing a common provenance is called a *fonds* or simply a collection. The hierarchical description begins with a description of all records in a *fonds* and then proceeds to a description of components, typically identified by the activity or function that they document (for example, correspondence or minutes of meetings). These components and components of components, and so on, may be analyzed and described, with the hierarchical analysis and description terminating in the description of a file or an item. The depth of analysis is determined by both intellectual and economic criteria.

EAD is a standard for communicating archival descriptions and is not itself a standard for the content of the descriptions. The general standard for descriptive content is *ISAD(G): General International Standard Archival Description*,[1] developed by the International Council on Archives (ICA). *ISAD(G)* provides general guidance on the composition of archival descriptions and serves as the basis of national standards such as the Society of American Archivist's *Describing Archives: A Content Standard* (DACS).[2] As a communication standard, EAD has a number of interrelated purposes. In conjunction with complementary content standards, it is intended to promote the regularization of description in order that the data are consistent and readily understood by users across archives. Regularized description and encoding enables intelligent searching, rendering, navigation, access, and use of archival materials. And since EAD is based on Extensible Markup Language (XML), a widely used and supported standard for developing encoding schemas, it provides reasonable assurance that the data will endure changes in hardware and software. Finally, standardized description enables the repurposing of archival description, including its eventual migration into successor encodings, and aggregation of descriptions across repositories to provide union, universal access to distributed archival resources.

The Society of American Archivists (SAA) and the Library of Congress are jointly responsible for the maintenance and development of EAD. Within SAA, the EAD Working Group (EADWG) is responsible for the intellectual and technical content of the standard. The members of the Working Group reflect the international nature of the standard, with members from the United Kingdom, Germany, France, the Netherlands, Australia, Canada, and the United States. The first version of the standard was released in 1998 and a second version in 2002. The first two versions of the standard were in the form of an XML Document Type Definition (DTD) with an accompanying Tag Library. The DTD provides the formal semantic and structural requirements of the standard and is used by software to validate encoded instances of archival descriptions. The Tag Library provides guidance on the use of the codes or tags prescribed in the DTD and used to encode descriptive data. In 2007, the formal and structural requirements were released in the form of a schema, an alternative syntax that provides support for validating some descriptive content. While the 2002 DTD remains the official authoritative expression of the standard, future versions of the standard will be in the form of a schema or schemas.

ARCHIVAL RECORDS

Archival records are created and assembled by people living their lives as individuals, as members of families, and as members of corporate bodies. The creation of records is typically not the objective of the activities, but rather the records serve as instruments for carrying out or documenting the performance of activities. Archival records thus document people and organizations performing activities or functions, and as such, may serve as legal evidence as well as historical evidence. By contrast, the books and journals that constitute the bulk of most library collections are the objectives of the activities that created them. To illustrate this difference, it is useful to look at the creation of an encyclopedia.

At the beginning, the editors have the objective of publishing an encyclopedia. They correspond with a publisher with the proposal. Or perhaps the publisher conceives of the encyclopedia and contacts one or more editors. In either case, through a series of exchanges the publisher and editors negotiate the scope and content of the encyclopedia, the form or forms of publication, financial arrangements, methods for soliciting authors and editing articles, and so on. In turn authors for entries are solicited and a series of exchanges take place between the editors, authors, and publisher. Various agreements are formally made and signed. The authors are given formal instructions and deadlines. Authors create and submit drafts of articles to the editors, and after another series of exchanges, the authors submit articles to the publisher for publication. At each stage, the participants in the creation and publication of the encyclopedia generate and maintain copies of the correspondence, agreements, instructions, drafts, financial transactions, and so forth. All of these documents serve the dual purpose of creating and publishing the encyclopedia and documenting the activities that lead to its publication. Each document is not an objective in itself but an instrument by which the objective is realized.

The participants' involvement in the creation of the encyclopedia constitutes only one set of activities over the course of their existence. Authors and editors have both professional as well as personal lives. The publishing company publishes more than one book. Each participant generates and accumulates records over the course of a lifetime or existence. Many of these records will be kept for legal reasons, such as financial accounting and reporting, as proof of responsibilities performed, or perhaps self-consciously as records documenting a life or the history of a business. All of the records generated or accumulated by an individual, family, or corporate body, collectively serve as documentation of the life of the individual, or the history of the family or organization. When they are assembled and preserved, they are archival records. Each collection of records generated and accumulated by one individual, family, or organization is called a *fonds*. The items in a *fonds* share a common origin or provenance.

When considered individually, records frequently make little sense and thus have little value. It is only when individual records are considered in context, in relation to other records that document a network of interrelated transactions or series of transactions carrying out a particular function, that they can be understood. In this way, archival records are quite different from books and journals, as the latter are intended to function independently. This statement ignores the issue of intertextuality, which is beyond the scope of present considerations. Archival records are by and large unique. In this respect, archival records again differ fundamentally from books. Books and journals are not unique, at least not in ways that would be of interest to most users. Typically books and journals exist in many copies, and any one copy will serve as well as any other.

Archival records are varied in both content and format, and the number of items in any given *fonds* may be quite large. While many records are exclusively or primarily textual, these may be in the form of handwritten, typed, printed, or, increasingly, digital. The content may be minutes of a meeting, a marriage license, receipts, a report card, correspondence, and so on. Sound, photographic, and audiovisual records may be in any format used for recording each of these forms. Content again will be varied, depending upon the context and the purpose of the recording. Maps, similar to textual records, may be hand-drawn, printed, or in digital form, as images, graphics, or as geographic information system (GIS) data. While a *fonds* may contain exclusively one form or content, it is more likely, in particular with respect to personal and family records, that both the form and content of the records will be diverse. In addition to a variety of form and content, the number of items in any given *fonds* may be quite large. The administrative records of Tom Bradley, who served as the mayor of Los Angeles from 1973 to 1993, are stored in 4253 boxes occupying 2101.5 linear feet of shelf space.[3]

ARCHIVAL DESCRIPTION

Archival description reflects the nature of archival records and the mission of the archival institutions into which their care and management is placed. Like museums and libraries, archives have a responsibility to remember on behalf of others. Preservation is the first essential responsibility, for without the physical preservation, memory fails. Equally important though, is a description of archival records that provides information essential for establishing their authenticity and completeness and serves effective administration, discovery, access, and understanding. Archival preservation and description make the remembering as trustworthy, reliable, and thorough as possible. To serve these objectives, archival description has traditionally focused on the *fonds* as the fundamental unit of description rather than the individual items, as is the common practice in libraries and museums. While there is an obvious economic advantage in collection-level description, this descriptive practice is based on the nature of archival records and the objectives to be served.

Archival description rests on two fundamental principles, *respect des fonds* and principle of original order. *Respect des fonds* is frequently also called the principle of provenance. While understanding of this principle has undergone ongoing interpretation since its articulation by French archivists in the early nineteenth century, its fundamental meaning has remained unchanged. Archivists must honor the origin and integrity of records generated or accumulated by an individual, family, or corporate body. The records generated or accumulated by a single source are intricately related to that source, whether it is a corporate body performing the functions with which it is charged or an individual pursuing personal and occupational activities. Given this intimate relationship, records cannot be understood apart from their origin. From this follows the archival practice of treating all records with a common provenance as a group.

The principle of original order addresses the arrangement of the archival records. The concept of original order is frequently conflated with the physical arrangement of records as received by the archive, though it is better understood as an intellectual arrangement that reflects the purpose and use of the records by the creating entity.[4] Commonly, particularly with records deriving from and maintained within a corporate body (such as a government agency or business), records have been arranged and maintained to support the functions and related transactions performed by the body. In such cases, the physical order reflects the purpose and use of the records. It is quite common, though, that the arrangement of the records as received by the archive does not reflect a discernable order and it is incumbent on the archivist to analyze and arrange the records to reflect their understood purpose and use.

Based on the application of the principle of *respect des fonds* and the principle of original order, archivists maintain and describe all records in a *fonds* together, physically arranged to reflect the original order. A description of a *fonds* begins with a description of the whole, and through a progressive, hierarchical analysis, describes components of the whole based on a shared characteristic or characteristics, which may in turn be analyzed into components and described. The analysis and description can progress to the item level, though frequently do not. Each level of description has a formal designation based on the nature of the shared characteristics that identify them as a coherent group: *fonds*, series, file, and item. Series and files may have intervening levels. The depth of the description is based on both intellectual and economic considerations. While it may seem counterintuitive, excessive analysis and description may hinder rather than facilitate the discovery, identification, and use of archival records, a phenomenon known as "getting lost in the details."

Archival hierarchical analytic or multilevel description is shaped in part on two rules. First, the description at any given level applies exclusively to that level. Second, the description at each level inherits the description of its parent level, including any description the parent inherits from its parent, and so on up to the top level. A number of distinctive features follow from these two rules. Typical finding aids begin at the top level with several descriptive components, many of which may comprise detailed prose. At each successive level, the number of descriptive components and the amount of data supplied decrease. It is quite typical for the top level of description to be several printed pages in length, while an item-level description may be no more than a title or a date. Viewed from the perspective of the entire archival description, though, the item inherits all of the description back to the top level. While archival descriptions vary in length from less than a page to over 1000 pages, they are typically 10 to 25 pages in length.

A third rule governing archival description dictates that all components of description are available at each level of description. This rule addresses the fact that individual archival collections are each unique, as they each reflect the lives and activities of individuals, families, or corporate bodies in particular places and times. They also vary greatly in the forms and quantity of records. In principle, all elements of description may be appropriate at any level of description. In practice, though, given the inheritance of description and the progression from general to specific description, use of descriptive patterns assumes particular patterns.

In a typical description, the top- or *fonds*-level contains information about the entire collection. The following information is typically given succinctly:

- Identifier or designation that is unique within the repository.
- Title of the *fonds*.
- Date range giving earliest and latest dates of creation, frequently with a second range for the dates within which the bulk of the materials was created.
- Provenance or creator information.
- Extent of the collection, typically given in linear units of shelf space occupied and number of boxes.
- Repository holding the collection.
- Language or languages represented in the content.
- Abstract of the scope and content, or biography or administrative history of the creator.

Information generally provided in brief text form at the top-level includes the following:

- Restrictions on physical access to the materials
- Copyright restrictions

- Scope and content or biography/administrative history abstract
- Preferred form of citation
- Processing and acquisitions information
- Related and separated materials

Finally, the following information is commonly given in expansive text form:

- Biographical/administration history
- Scope and content
- Overview of the arrangement of the materials

The detailed analysis of the *fonds* into components follows. The form of this analysis varies considerably from description to description, and sometimes within a single description from component to component. Some patterns of analysis, though, are prevalent: *Fonds*-series-file, *fonds*-series-subseries-file, *fonds*-series-file-item, and *fonds*-series-subseries-file-item. The pattern of the hierarchical analysis is not prescribed, but is determined by the judgment of the archivists analyzing and processing the collection.

Series and subseries descriptions frequently include the following information:

- Title
- Dates range giving earliest and latest dates of creation
- Scope and content
- Arrangement

File or item information commonly includes the following:

- Title
- Date or date range
- Extent
- Container information

Container information or storage location is provided at the terminal node of description, which corresponds to the most specific intellectual unit that can be requested for use. In the scenario described above, this may be an item or file, though when the description terminates at the series or subseries level, container information will be provided at these levels.

ENCODING ARCHIVAL DESCRIPTION

Technical Foundation

Traditionally archival description was typescript and then later printed using word processors and to a lesser extent, database software. With the emergence of markup technologies in the middle to late 1980s, it became possible to create machine-readable findings that were descriptively encoded and thereby supported a much broader range of functional possibilities. Standard Generalized Markup Language (SGML) was first issued as a formal standard in 1986 by the International Standards Organization (ISO). In the early 1990s the Hypertext Transfer Protocol (HTTP) and an accompanying document encoding standard, Hypertext Markup Language (HTML), became the foundation of the rapidly emerging World Wide Web (WWW). The success of HTTP and HTML gave rise to the World Wide Web Consortium (W3C), which turned its attention to the development of standards. While remarkably successful, HTML was insufficient for secure, flexible, semantically rich exchange of information, and SGML, though supporting flexible, semantically rich exchange, was difficult to process. As an alternative of both SGML and HTML, the W3C developed XML, releasing version 1.0 in 1998. Among the key features of both SGML and XML was the ability to develop community-based rules or schemas to govern the encoding of specific kinds of documents, employing a semantics that reflected the nature of the document and the professional language of the community. The archival community was one of the first to employ XML.

The archivists developing EAD chose XML as the best available technology for developing a communication standard for archival description for a number of reasons. Markup and database technologies are the two prevailing techniques for representing textual data in forms that support complex, multipurpose processing. While they have some overlapping functionalities, each is optimized to support particular and in part mutually exclusive kinds of data. Markup technologies support traditional documents, such as books, journals, and journal articles, where the order of components and unbounded component hierarchies are prevalent. Database technologies support information with complex many-to-many relations, and the particular order of data elements has minimal if any significance. Archival description can best be characterized as occupying a middle ground, having structurally different data components that map well to one or the other technology. For the purposes of communicating information, as opposed to its creation and maintenance, XML is the superior representation, as it will accommodate native XML data as well as data derived from databases.

In addition to its representational capability, XML also offers other attractive features. Since its release in 1998, XML has been widely adopted and supported, not only by the original document community where SGML had had reasonably good success, but also by the database development community. As a widely used and supported standard for developing encoding schemas, XML provides reasonable assurance that the data will endure changes in hardware and software, an essential concern because digital data is absolutely dependent on computers for retrieval and rendering into human readable form. The semantically and structurally rich descriptive encoding made possible by XML also enables multiple uses of the data: a wide range of alternative renderings for onscreen presentation and printing, in-depth and descriptive component-specific indexing and retrieval, and, when a successor to XML emerges, migration into a successor digital representation.

The apparatus for developing a rule-based encoding for a particular class or kind of documents is a DTD. More recently, both ISO and W3C have developed XML-based syntaxes as alternatives to DTDs which employ a dedicated syntax. The alternative XML-based encoding rules are called schemas. EAD exists in all three forms: DTD, ISO Relax NG Schema, and W3C Schema. The semantics and structure of the three forms of the EAD are the same, although the schemas add compliance with other XML and descriptive markup schemas as well as constraints on some data values.

Semantics and Structure—Top Level

EAD (`<ead>`) comprises three main sections: EAD Header (`<eadheader>`), Front Matter (`<frontmatter>`), and Archival Description (`<archdesc>`). The `<archdesc>` contains the archival description itself, while the `<eadheader>` contains control information about the description, and the `<frontmatter>` contains information intended for use in the formal publication of the description. Of the three sections, `<eadheader>` and `<archdesc>` are required and `<frontmatter>` is optional. For detailed information on the semantics and structure of EAD, see the Society of American Archivists, and Library of Congress[5] and Ruth.[6]

While an EAD document provides information describing and documenting archival materials, it is itself an archival resource that must be maintained and managed. The `<eadheader>` section contains information that facilitates control of the resource. It contains four major sections:

1. EAD Identifier (`<eadid>`): a unique designation for identifying and tracking the EAD document file.
2. File Description (`<filedesc>`): title, edition, publication, series, and notes describing the description.

3. Profile Description (<profiledesc>): information on the date, methods of creation, language, and descriptive rules used in the description.
4. Revision Description (<revisiondesc>): information on the dates, editors, and revisions made to the description.

Of these four sections, <eadid> and <filedesc> are required. Within <filedesc>, only Title Statement (<titlestmt>) and Title (<title>) are required.

The <frontmatter> is an optional section that may be used if the archival description is formally published. Of all finding aids, only a few are formally published. With the advent of Internet-accessible descriptions, it is likely that fewer and fewer will be. The principal section of the <frontmatter> is the Title Page (<titlepage>), which contains components commonly found on the title page of published monographs. Optionally, sections such as preface, acknowledgments, and other introductory information may be provided in a succession of text Divisions (<div>).

The section dedicated to an archival description is <archdesc>. The <archdesc> is probably best understood as representing the logical semantics and structure of archival description, with additional semantics and structure that facilitate navigable and intelligible rendering for those seeking archival records. These additional structures enable labeling sections or descriptive components, and rendering them in forms that are readily understood. An example of the former is Head (<head>), which enables the archivist to supply section titles, and an example of the latter is Paragraph (<p>), which enables rendering of prose description. The primary focus of <archdesc>, though, is the hierarchical, prose description itself.

The first component of the archival description is Descriptive Identification (<did>). The <did> is intended to succinctly provide all of the information necessary to uniquely identify the collection and make a competent first-pass judgment of its relevancy. The information is succinctly stated and collocated in order to function as a summary surrogate for the complete description, in particular in retrieval sets in union archival description systems (such as those used by state and regional consortia, and archival gateways). Archivists have identified the following descriptive elements to support these objectives:

- Unit Identifier (<unitid>): unique identifier of the *fonds*, including a national identifier and repository identifier.
- Unit Title (<unittitle>): title of the *fonds*.
- Unit Date (<unitdate>): date range of earliest and latest creation, frequently with a second range for the dates within which the bulk of the materials was created.
- Origination (<origination>): Provenance or creator information.
- Physical Description (<physdesc>): description is typically restricted to the physical extent (<extent>) and is given as the number of boxes or storage containers or the linear space of storage space occupied by the records.
- Repository (<repository>): archival institution holding the collection.
- Language of the Materials (<langmaterial>): Language or languages represented in the content, with individual languages provided in Language (<language>).
- Abstract (<abstract>): summary of either or both the scope and content, or biography or administrative history.

Following the summary description of the *fonds*, several components already described in summary form are described in more detail. In addition, some new descriptive elements that are not considered essential to the objectives of the summary description, but are essential or at least useful for fully understanding and using the collections are provided. Expanded descriptions are commonly provided for Scope and Content (<scopecontent>) and Biography or History (<bioghist>), both of which may have been provided in summarized form in the <abstact> in the <did>. Further information may be provided in the following descriptive components:

- Arrangement (<arrangement>): information on the intellectual analysis and arrangement of the records, reflecting, in principle, the original order and the hierarchical analysis reflected in the description.
- Access Restrictions (<accessrestrict>): information concerning limitations on physical access to the records because of privacy, agreements with donors, or other reasons.
- Use Restrictions (<userestrict>): information concerning copyright restrictions.
- Acquisition Information (<acqinfo>): information on the immediate source of the records and the circumstances of the acquisition.
- Controlled Access (<controlaccess>): controlled personal name, family name, corporate name subject, genre or form, function or activity, geographic, and other headings under authority control.
- Preferred Citation (<prefercite>): information on the preferred form of citation of the records in referencing or citing publications.
- Processing Information (<processinfo>): information on archival record processing activities applied to the records such as accessioning, describing, preserving, and storing.
- Related Material (<relatedmaterial>): information, usually in the form of a citation, on intellectually related records (though not related by provenance).
- Separated Material (<separatedmaterial>): information, usually in the form of a citation, on publications and artifacts in a collection, or archival records that have been separated from the *fonds*, frequently for curatorial reasons.
- Accruals (<accruals>): information about anticipated additions to the materials, including (when available) information indicating the quantity and frequency of additions.

Several additional descriptive components are available. This additional information is provided when it is appropriate and available. When copies of the records, such as microfilm copies or digital facsimiles are available, this is typically noted. The corollary is also true, that is, in the description of copies of archival records, information about the originals is provided. If there is more than one description of a *fonds*, each description will reference the alternative description. For example, predominately French language *fonds* may be held by an institution that prepares descriptions in English. A French translation of the original English description would function as an alternative finding aid.

EAD attempts to be comprehensive in accommodating accepted components of archival description. Due to the nature and complexity of archival records and the *fonds* within which they are interrelated, descriptive information deemed essential or at least useful may not be accommodated within an existing element. EAD accommodates such information with the Other Descriptive Data (<odd>). It is similar to the use of a general note in bibliographic description.

EAD groups descriptive components together only minimally because there is no international consensus on logical grouping. Nevertheless, many archival institutions find it desirable to group descriptive components together in one or more labeled groups to enhance the intelligibility and use of the description. The Descriptive Group (<descgrp>) may be used to accomplish this. With the exception of the Descriptive Identification (<did>) components, and the Description of Subordinate Components (<dsc>), to be discussed below, all of the descriptive elements described so far can be arbitrarily brought together in one or more groups and labeled as a descriptive section.

Semantics and Structure—Hierarchical Analysis

The EAD apparatus used in the hierarchal analysis is the Description of Subordinate Components (<dsc>). Of all of the structures in the EAD, the <dsc> is the most complex. The key element is the Component, which comes in two forms, simple and enumerated. To enable hierarchical description, each Component is recursive, which is to say, it is available within itself. The simple form is called <c>, and the enumerated form is called <c01>, <c02>, through <c12>. The major difference between the two forms is that the <c> permits unlimited recursion or depth of analysis, and the enumerated limits depth of analysis to 12 levels. Because more than 12 levels of analysis is rare, choosing which form of the Component to use is primarily a decision based on ease of use and processing, usually influenced by the software chosen for processing.

Each `<c>` or `<c01>` through `<c12>` contains all of the descriptive components available in the `<archdesc>`, beginning with the `<did>`. This availability reflects a rule governing archival description described above, that all components of description are available at each level of descriptive analysis. Thus all of the `<did>` contained elements are available, as are `<scopecontent>`, `<arrangement>`, and so on. While all of the components are available throughout the hierarchy, because of the inheritance of description both the number of elements employed and the quantity of description contained in them typically decreases through each descending level of analysis.

In order to understand the way in which the hierarchical analysis unfolds as reflected in the EAD structure, it is useful to translate common patterns of analysis. The following examples exclude the *fonds* description, as it has been covered immediately above.

1. *Fonds*-series-file (3 levels including *fonds*)
```
<c01 level="series">
   [description]
   <c02 level="file">
         [description]
   </c02>
</c01>
```
2. *Fonds*-series-subseries-file (4 levels including *fonds*)
```
<c01 level="series">
   [description]
   <c02 level="subseries">
         [description]
         <c03 level="file">
               [description]
         </c03>
   </c02>
</c01>
```
3. *Fonds*-series-file-item (2 levels including *fonds*)
```
<c01 level="series">
   [description]
   <c02 level="file">
         [description]
         <c03 level="item">
               [description]
         </c03>
   </c02>
</c01>
```
4. *Fonds*-series-subseries-file-item (5 levels including *fonds*)
```
<c01 level="series">
   [description]
   <c02 level="subseries">
         [description]
         <c03 level="file">
               [description]
               <c04 level="item">
                     [description]
               </c04>
         </c03>
   </c02>
</c01>
```

It is very important to note that `<c01>` through `<c12>` are not to be equated with the level of analysis. The `<c01>` places the description within a hierarchy, but does not itself indicate the level of analysis. The level of analysis is rather indicated through the use of a Level attribute on the tag, for example, `<c01 level="series">`. Note that in example 1. above, `<c02>` has the Level attribute value "file," while in example 2., the `<c02>` has the Level attribute value "subseries." This is further complicated by the fact that even within one series, for example, the Level attribute values of the same subordinate Component may change, depending on the arrangement of the records.

Following the same pattern as the `<archdesc>`, the first and required descriptive element in each descriptive component is `<did>`. Typically each `<did>`, no matter what the level of analysis (*fonds*, series, subseries, file, item), will contain a `<unittitle>`, a `<unitdate>`, and often an `<extent>`. For series and subseries analysis, the `<did>` is generally augmented with a `<scopecontent>` as well as an `<arrangement>`.

When a user identifies the records of interest, the archival staff and the user need to know in what box and folder or folders the records will be found (or other container types, as appropriate to the nature of the records). The organization of records in storage containers has its own inherent physical logic and structure, independent of the intellectual arrangement of the records. EAD privileges the intellectual arrangement in the single hierarchy that XML supports, and thus information on the physical organization and storage is subordinate to the intellectual arrangement. Information about the box and folder or other medium of storage is given in Container (`<container>`), an element contained in the `<did>`. Container information is most appropriately supplied at the deepest or terminal components of description. Following this practice, in the hierarchies illustrated above, `<container>` would appear within the `<did>` in the following component descriptions:

- 1. `<c02 level="file">`
- 2. `<c03 level="file">`
- 3. `<c03 level="item">`
- 4. `<c04 level="item">`

In order to complete our understanding of how the hierarchical descriptive apparatus works in EAD, it is necessary to understand one additional feature of the use of Component. Not only are the Component elements recursive, they are also repeatable. Thus at the top level of analytic description, the `<c01>` is repeated. A *fonds* comprising four series will have a sequence of four `<c01>`s, one for each series. Within a series, a series containing 12 files will begin with a `<c01>`, and within it, a sequence of 12 `<c02>`s, one for each file. While the order of the sequence (arrangement) may not always be significant, in many and perhaps most descriptions it is important, such as, when a sequence of files is arranged chronologically by date of creation or alphabetically by title.

HISTORY

Work on an encoding standard for archival description began in 1992 at the University of California, Berkeley. In the early 1980s, archivists developed the MARC AMC (MAchine-Readable Cataloging for Archives and Manuscript Control) format that enabled archivists to make collection-level summary descriptions available in online catalogs. While representing a major improvement in archival access, the full, detailed descriptions found in finding aids remained available only in printed forms. There was a widespread perception in the archival community that a method for making the full descriptions Internet-accessible was needed. Many archivists experimented with the use of database technologies as a solution. The complex, unbounded hierarchical descriptions found in finding aids, however, were not easily accommodated using database technology. The Berkeley effort was initiated by Timothy Hoyer in the Bancroft Library, who recruited Daniel Pitti to work on the problem. With a grant from the U.S. Department of Education, Pitti developed a prototype SGML DTD based on representative sample finding aids contributed by archivists at collaborating institutions in the United States. The FindAid DTD, as the prototype was called, served to demonstrate the feasibility and utility of using markup technologies, rather than MARC or database technologies, to develop an encoding method that would enable Internet-accessible finding aids.

At the conclusion of the Berkeley project, the Commission on Preservation and Access sponsored a conference in Berkeley to bring together archivists, librarians, and technologists to evaluate the results. With encouragement from the participants at this conference, Pitti applied for and was awarded a Bentley Historical Library fellowship that brought together seven archival description experts, Pitti, and Steve DeRose, a systems designer and developer at Electronic Book Technologies. The description experts were Jackie M. Dooley (University of California, Irvine), Michael J. Fox (Minnesota Historical Society), Steven L. Hensen (Duke University), Kris Kiesling (Harry Ransom Center), Janet E. Ruth (Library of Congress), Sharon Gibbs Thibodeau (National Archives and Records Administration), and Helena Zinkham (Library of Congress). The team met for one week in summer, 1995, in Ann Arbor, MI. Based on experience with the FindAid prototype, the team substantially revised the underlying conceptual model, in part in reference to *ISAD(G)*. The prototype standard that emerged from this meeting was renamed EAD.

Subsequent to the Ann Arbor meeting, the Library of Congress and the SAA agreed to share responsibility for further development and maintenance of the emerging standard. SAA formally charged the EADWG in August 1995 with overseeing the ongoing development of the standard. With support from the Library of Congress National Digital Library Program, Delmas Foundation, and Council on Library Resources (now Council on Library and Information Resources), the EADWG met several times from 1995 to 1998 to further revise the conceptual model, and review and revise first the alpha and then the beta versions of the EAD DTD and Tag Library. Version 1.0 of the EAD DTD and Tag Library were released in summer 1998. The version 1.0 DTD was compliant with both SGML and XML.

Subsequent to the release of EAD version 1.0, there were developments in both technological and descriptive standards that led the EADWG to begin revising EAD. Released in early 1998 by the W3C, XML was quickly embraced by both developers and users. The availability of XML software made it possible for users of EAD to make a transition from SGML to XML. The ICA also completed its review and revision of *ISAD(G)* in 2000. With funding from the National Historical Publications and Records Commission (NHPRC), the EADWG began revision of EAD in 2000. Based on comments and suggestions solicited from the EAD user community and the second edition of *ISAD(G)*, EAD 2002 was developed and released. Following the release of version 2002, responding to the emergence of schemas as an alternative to DTDs, the EADWG release two schema versions of the 2002 DTD in early 2008, one in the Relax NG Schema syntax and the other in W3C Schema syntax. Funding for this work was again provided by NHPRC.

Since its release in 1998, adoption and use of EAD by institutions with archival holdings has increased steadily. While only a few institutions employed EAD in the first year or two after its release, today EAD is used around the world by scores of academic research libraries, business archives, historical societies, museums, national libraries and archives, and other archival repositories. State and regional consortia in the United States have formed to provide union access to the archival holdings of members. Similar regional and national consortia have formed in Europe and elsewhere. Planning for a European archival consortium is underway. The EAD Tag Library has been translated into Spanish, Greek, Chinese, French, German, and Italian. Reflecting the internationalization of EAD, the members of the EADWG represent seven countries.

FUTURE

Paralleling the ever increasing utility of computer and network technologies, archival descriptive practice has been undergoing a transition from the printed finding aid to an integrated archival description system. This transition is at least in part inspired by the advancements in the technology.

Particularly important have been database technologies, in particular relational and object-relational databases, and markup technologies. Each of these technologies is optimized to represent and facilitate the maintenance and use of distinct data structures. Many real world data structures, however, are not wholly of one type or the other, which has required those promoting automation to make difficult compromises when choosing which technology to use. But there are indications that this situation is changing. Many of the major developers of database technologies, responding to real world data structures and needs, are exploring the integration of database and markup technologies. If these efforts are successful, archivists will no longer have to choose between the two technologies and will be able to take advantage of the strengths of each.

In a world dominated by print technologies, archivists have generally employed a single apparatus, the finding aid, to describe all of the records created by a single person, family, or corporate body. For a given *fonds*, the finding aid brought together information describing the creator, the functions performed by the creator, the records that facilitated or documented the performance of the functions, and the archival institution responsible for the records. Since at least the early 1980s, archivists have been discussing "relational" archival systems that enable creating and maintaining each of these fundamental components of description separately, and bringing them together dynamically upon user request. Such an approach has economic advantages, but also supports more flexible and accurate description, and greatly enhanced access.

The ICA has supported the development of four standards for the components of archival description. The first of these standards, *ISAD(G)*, addresses the description of archival records and was first released in 1993. A second edition was released in 2000. Following *ISAD(G)* was *ISAAR(CPF): International Standard Archival Authority Control for Corporate Bodies, Persons, and Families* in 1996, with a second edition in 2003.[7] The third standard, *ISDF: International Standard for Describing Functions*[8] was approved in 2007, and the fourth standard, *International Standard for the Description of Institutions with Archival Holdings* (*ISDIAH*) is in draft form. Each of these standards provides (or will provide) a framework for the intellectual content for the four areas of description: records, creators, functions, and repositories. All are intended to function together in a complete archival description. In order to be realized in a dynamic archival description system, though, communication standards for each are necessary.

EAD was originally designed as a communication standard for archival description as represented in finding aids. As such, the four descriptive components are interleaved in EAD. Based on the work of ICA, efforts are underway to develop communication standards based on XML for *ISAAR(CPF)*, *ISDF*, and *ISDIAH*. SAA formed an Encoded Archival Context (EAC) Working Group in 2006 to formalize and complete a communication standard for *ISAAR(CPF)*. Developers in Spain have created an XML DTD called Encoded Archival Guide (EAG) that served to inform the development of *ISDIAH*, and in turn may be revised to be compliant with it. Informal efforts are underway to develop a communication standard for *ISDF*. Given these developments, revision of EAD will be necessary in the near future to coordinate its semantics and structure with the other emerging standards. Rather than a communication standard for finding aids, EAD will be a communication standard for record description, playing an essential role in a dynamic archival description system.

REFERENCES

1. *ISAD(G): General International Standard Archival Description*, 2nd Ed.; International Council on Archives: Ottawa, ON, 2000, http://www.ica.org/sites/default/files/isad_g_2e.pdf
2. *Describing Archives: A Content Standard*; Society of American Archivists: Chicago, 2004.
3. *Mayor Tom Bradley Administrative Papers 1973–1993*; Online Archive of California: http://content.cdlib.org/view?docId=kt4489n8jd&&chunk.id=did-1.8.1&brand=oac
4. Fox, M.J. *Introduction to Archival Organization and Description*; Getty Information Institute: Los Angeles, 1998.

5. Society of American Archivists, and Library of Congress. *Encoded Archival Description Tag Library*, version 2002; EAD technical document, no. 2. Society of American Archivists: Chicago, 2002. http://www.loc.gov/ead/tglib/index.html
6. Ruth, J. "The development and structure of the encoded archival description (EAD) document type definition." J. Internet Catalog **2001**, *4* (3), 27–61.
7. *ISAAR(CPF): International Standard Archival Authority Control for Corporate Bodies, Persons, and Families*, 2nd Ed.; Ottawa, ON, 2003, http://www.ica.org/sites/default/files/ISAAR2EN.pdf
8. *ISDF: International Standard for Describing Functions*; International Council on Archives: Ottawa, ON, 2008, http://www.ica.org/sites/default/files/ISDF%20ENG.pdf

51 Open Archival Information System (OAIS) Reference Model

Christopher A. Lee

CONTENTS

INTRODUCTION

The Reference Model for an Open Archival Information System (OAIS) describes components and services required to develop and maintain archives, in order to support long-term access to and understanding of the information in those archives.[1] The development of the OAIS took place within a standards development organization called the Consultative Committee for Space Data Systems (CCSDS), whose formal purview is the work of space agencies, but the effort reached far beyond the traditional CCSDS interests and stakeholders.[2] It has become a fundamental component of digital archive research and development in a variety of disciplines and sectors.

This entry discusses the context in which the OAIS was initiated and provides a chronology of the OAIS development process, including its transformation from a space data standard into a document of much wider scope. It then describes the major components and concepts of the OAIS Reference Model. The entry also summarizes numerous initiatives that have adopted and expanded on the OAIS. Finally, the author discusses major implications of the OAIS.

HISTORICAL CONTEXT

Digital preservation has long been an area of concern for those responsible for repositories of digital objects. Data mismanagement, technological dependency, media degradation, and technological obsolescence have all threatened the long-term accessibility of resources stored in digital formats. In the 1950s, 1960s, and 1970s, organizations began increasingly to rely on collections of computer-dependent data. Several streams of activity gradually emerged to address parts of the digital preservation problem (e.g., care and physical properties of physical storage media; hardware and software interoperability; management and provision of access to digital library collections), but there was often little communication or coordination across the streams. The streams of activity often developed their own distinct forums (journals, conferences, consortia) and sets of funding mechanisms (government budget areas, research agendas, foundation support).

Two trends that began in the 1960s and 1970s, but became much more prominent during the 1980s and early 1990s, were: 1) actors with long traditions of preserving physical artifacts (e.g., archivists, librarians, museum curators) increasingly recognizing that information which fell within the scope of their responsibility was now digital; and 2) actors with long traditions of managing computer-dependent data sets (e.g., scientific data center personnel, corporate information technology managers) increasingly recognizing that information which fell within the scope of their responsibility had long-term preservation value. The effort to develop the OAIS came at a time when the separate streams of activity were making important progress but they were only beginning to identify points of intersection between the streams. During the years immediately preceding and throughout the OAIS development effort, participants in digital preservation work increasingly recognized that they were addressing similar issues.

The 1990s were characterized by a broadening societal awareness of both the importance of standards in supporting the infrastructure that underlies various activities and the challenges of long-term digital preservation. Two closely connected factors were the development of widely distributed computer networks and an industry trend toward commercial off-the-shelf (COTS) equipment. Rather than depending on the compatibility of an entire suite of hardware and software from a single vendor, producers and consumers of computer equipment came to rely on conventions for interchange of data between a heterogeneous set of components. Both the International Organization for Standardization (ISO) and Internet Engineering Task Force (IETF) developed layered architectures to which hardware and software producers could conform in order to ensure that their products could interchange data with other products on the Internet. In the early 1990s, the adoption of the World Wide Web reflected and contributed to a dramatic growth in the base of consumers who had a stake in the interchange of data over computer networks. The Year 2000 (Y2K) conversion effort was one widely recognized example of dependence on a widespread assortment of hardware and software components that usually interoperated in ways invisible to most people, but could cause significant problems when they failed to interoperate. In 1994, the Commission on Preservation and Access (CPA) and Research Libraries Group (RLG) created a Task Force on Digital Archiving. The Task Force issued a report in 1996 called *Preserving Digital Information*, which was frequently cited by subsequent literature on digital preservation.[3] Two works that brought digital preservation to popular attention were a 1995 article by Jeff Rothenberg in *Scientific American* called "Ensuring the longevity of digital documents"[4] and a movie called *Into the Future*,[5] which was released in 1997 and shown on Public Broadcasting Service (PBS) across the United States in 1998.

Prior to the development of the OAIS, there had been numerous calls in professional literature for both development and adoption of open standards in support of long-term digital preservation. The most active standardization and consensus was associated with physical storage media and storage conditions. In other areas of digital preservation, most of the existing standards had served primarily to advance work within specific streams of activities, rather than spanning multiple professions.

OAIS DEVELOPMENT PROCESS

The historical context discussed in the previous section is essential to understanding the character and impact of the OAIS. The Reference Model was both a product of and an influential factor in the evolution of digital preservation activities in the mid- to late-1990s—reflecting preexisting notions and helping to define new notions. A major factor in the success of the OAIS was the timing of its development. Actors within several streams of activity related to digital preservation perceived the need for a high-level model but had not themselves developed one. At the same time, several actors now felt they had knowledge from their own recent digital archiving efforts, which could inform the development of the OAIS. Despite this growing body of practical experience and understanding of the functions associated with digital archiving, one essential element that was missing was a common vocabulary. Problems had often stemmed from terms—such as archives/archiving or metadata—that were used so widely and for so many different purposes that it was difficult to determine if they were being used in the same way by different actors. The combination of pressing need, available expertise, and inconsistent language meant the time was ripe for developing a reference model that could codify and support greater consistency in discussions of digital archives.

The development of the OAIS took place within the CCSDS, whose formal purview was specifically support for study of the terrestrial and space environments. However, the OAIS development effort took on a much wider scope than one may have reasonably predicted, given its CCSDS origins. The OAIS development process ultimately involved and gained visibility among a much broader set of stakeholders than simply members of the CCSDS. The word "Open" in the acronym OAIS—meant to indicate that the standard was "developed in open forums"—was a defining feature of its evolution. The leader of the OAIS development process was Don Sawyer, Computer Scientist and head of the U.S. National Aeronautics and Space Administration (NASA) Office of Standards and Technology (NOST) at the Goddard Space Flight Center (GSFC) in Greenbelt, Maryland. Sawyer indicated early and continued to reiterate that the process should be open and inclusive, in order to get sufficient input and buy-in. The core development team actively recruited commentary on the drafts of the document and gave dozens of public presentations about the Reference Model to a diverse range of professional groups.

The formal process began on April 5, 1994, when Gael Squibb of the Jet Propulsion Laboratory (JPL) proposed a New Work Item (NWI) related to "archiving space data" to ISO Technical Committee 20 (Aircraft and Space Vehicles), Subcommittee 14 (Space Systems and Operations). This proposal ultimately found a home in another subcommittee of ISO TC 20: Subcommittee 13 (Space Data and Information Transfer Systems). The formal Secretariat for TC 20/SC 13 is the American National Standards Institute (ANSI), and it is administered by NASA. The CCSDS is a liaison organization to TC 20/SC 13 (see Figure 51.1). Sawyer made the case for this effort to NASA management. As the NASA representative, Sawyer also submitted a document to Panel 2 (Information Interchange Processes) of the CCSDS on April 25, 1995, proposing a new "work package." In May, Panel 2 created "WP [Work Package] 700 Archiving" with Sawyer as the leader and the initial subtask being "WP 710 Archiving Reference Model." Sawyer and Lou Reich, who worked under contract for the GSFC as Senior Consulting Engineer for the Computer Sciences Corporation, coauthored a preliminary discussion draft of a reference model document. Sawyer and Reich remained the primary authors and editors of later versions, but the process also increasingly drew from contributions (both text and figures) from other participants. John Garrett, who was a contractor for the NSSDC as Senior Analyst at Hughes STX (ST Systems Corporation), helped to set up the initial meeting, and he served as a significant source of administrative support and documentation throughout the OAIS development process.

Development of the OAIS was markedly different from the previous standards development efforts of the CCSDS by being both broader in scope and inclusive of a more diverse set of actors. In order to support this unusually inclusive effort, the leaders set up a unique meeting and decision-making structure. In addition to the well-established semiannual CCSDS meetings, the OAIS development effort also involved a set of 18 U.S. Workshops, devoted primarily to document development, and a set of more open meetings (one in France, two in the United Kingdom, and two in the United States), designed to gather input and review from a wider set of actors. Most of the U.S. Workshops took place at the Archives II facility of the U.S. National Archives and Records Administration (NARA); Bruce Ambacher, Archives Specialist at NARA, was one of the most active participants in the OAIS development process. The creation of the Reference Model involved a relatively small

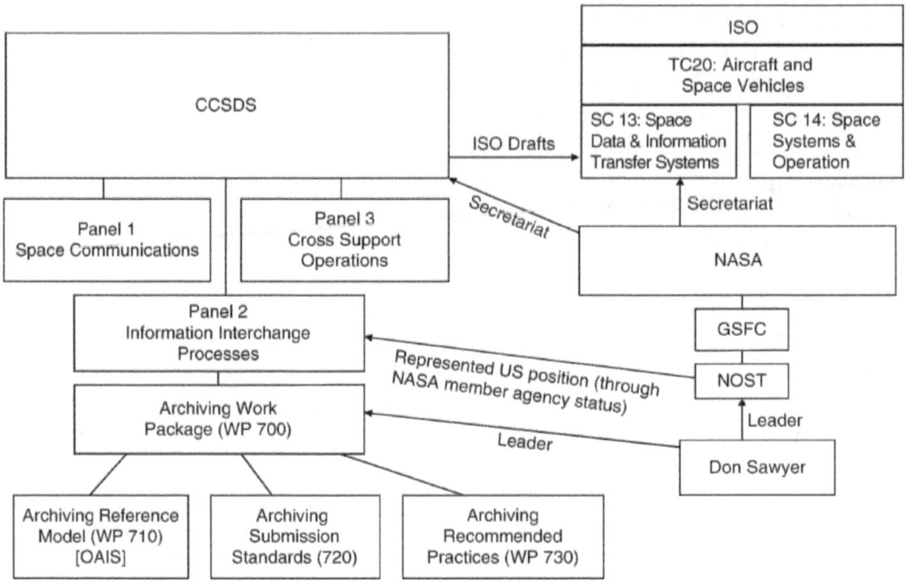

FIGURE 51.1 Organizational context of OAIS development. (Adapted from C. Lee, Doctoral Dissertation, University of Michigan: Michigan, 2005. CCSDS, Consultative Committee for Space Data Systems; GSFC, Goddard Space Flight Center; ISO, International Organization for Standardization; NASA, U.S. National Aeronautics and Space Administration; NOST, NASA Office of Standards and Technology.)

and stable set of core actors, but it also involved a much larger set of actors who had more limited Workshop participation. The latter played an extremely important role in the development, review, and visibility of the Reference Model. There were 306 individuals who participated in one or more of the Workshops.

Development of the OAIS involved negotiation over issues such as the scope of the Reference Model, its intended purpose, and the definition of basic terms. The development process also involved considerable borrowing and adaptation of ideas and documents already in existence. Over time, common notions about the content of the Reference Model became more established, and the number and extent of revisions to drafts of the Reference Model decreased.

After being requested to do so by CCSDS Panel 2, ISO SC 13 voted on May 22, 2000 to allow circulation of Red Book 1[6] as a Draft International Standard (DIS) to all ISO national member bodies. By releasing the Reference Model as a Red Book, the CCDS was indicating that the document was "technically mature and ready for extensive and formal review by appropriate technical organizations within each Member Agency." Comments received in response to Red Book 1 implied substantive changes to the document. SC 13 sent a request to the ISO in January 2001 to "reprocess" the DIS, meaning a revised document would be resubmitted to ISO member bodies for another vote. Red Book 1.1 (April 20, 2001), Red Book 1.2 (June 2001), and Red Book 2 (July 2001) were the result of efforts to address the comments received in response to Red Book 1. On October 23, 2001, SC 13 approved the submission of Red Book 2 for ISO vote. There were then a few minor editorial changes to the document before it was circulated (as the Blue Book)[7] to ISO member bodies for balloting. A Blue Book is a CCSDS Recommendation, which "reflects resolution of official comments from Member Agencies during formal reviews, and, as such, represents the consensus of appropriate implementing organizations within each Member Agency. Member Agency approval of a Blue Book implies an intent to reflect its provisions in future data systems standards developed through internal mechanisms." The ISO balloting process, which involved ISO national member bodies, ran from January 24 to April 5, 2002. There were eight affirmative votes, no negative votes, and two abstentions. The chair of SC 13 formally reported the results of voting on the Reference Model to ISO on August 20, 2002. On February 24, 2003, the Reference Model was finally published by ISO as an International Standard (ISO 14721:2003).[8] The Blue Book version, which is freely available from the CCSDS Web site, is identical in content to the International Standard, except that the current Blue Book version reflects a September 2007 "editorial correction," involving slight alterations to several figures to correct "display anomalies" (problems with encoding of line breaks had resulted in extraneous square blocks appearing next to some text elements) and a "typographical error" in one of the figures.

Many important activities in the development of the OAIS took place outside the context of formal ISO Archiving meetings and review processes. Teleconferencing, e-mail, and the Web greatly facilitated work on the OAIS and allowed review and use of the Reference Model drafts by those who were not necessarily able to attend the Workshops. Core members of the OAIS development effort gave dozens of presentations related to the Reference Model at conferences and other professional events. Several of the actors in the ISO Archiving Workshops also took part in mass storage systems and technologies (MSST) conferences, which served as forums for both the dissemination of information about the development of the Reference Model and recruitment of actors into the process. Individuals and organizations involved in initiatives that attempted to apply and test the Reference Model—e.g., CEDARS (CURL [Consortium of Research Libraries] Exemplars in Digital Archives) in the United Kingdom, NEDLIB (Networked European Deposit Library), British Library, and PANDORA (Preserving and Accessing Networked Documentary Resources of Australia)—played an essential role in the process. The archives certification work that built off of the Reference Model also provided important input into the development of the OAIS and demonstrated the Reference Model's potential value to a variety of stakeholders.

Development of the Reference Model drew from many other sources. These included concepts, terminology, models, and strings of text and images from guidelines, reports, and standards. In some cases—such as the "Z39.50 profile for access to digital collections" (PDC),[9] *Preserving Digital Information*, *Planetary Data System Data Preparation Workbook*,[10] and *IEEE Guide to the POSIX Open System Environment (OSE)*[11]—it is possible to identify specific terms or concepts that were incorporated into the Reference Model. Other sources were discussed during Workshops and provided varying degrees of conceptual background for the work on the Reference Model.

OAIS AS A REFERENCE MODEL

The OAIS is a reference model, which is a very particular type of standard. Carl Cargill provides a framework for describing standards, which distinguishes providers of information technology products and services from the users of those products and services. According to Cargill, these two groups have very different motivations and needs in the standardization process (p. 1-11).[1]

> On the provider side is the global model that describes all of the potentials that the IT industry will need to satisfy all users over a long time in nearly all situations, and that serves as a reference for all providers. This reference model, if it is correctly constructed, includes some present and future technologies, a road map function, and some of the methodologies of the thought processes that occurred when it was constructed. The time span covered is up to ten years, and the model is applicable to all technical disciplines that deal in this area. On the IT user side is a description of a solution implementation that is immediate and particular to that user's application problems.

As explained by Cargill above, reference models operate at a higher level of abstraction than other types of standards and are purposely designed to be "implementation-independent." The OAIS itself provides the following definition of reference model:

> A framework for understanding significant relationships among the entities of some environment, and for the development of consistent standards or specifications supporting that environment. A reference model is based on a small number of unifying concepts and may be used as a basis for education and explaining standards to a nonspecialist.[12]

Cargill explains that bridging the gap between reference models and application implementations requires a chain of standards at increasing levels of specificity (p. 1-12).[1] Within the arena of digital archives, this means that one would expect more specific standards to emerge, which indicate how to apply the concepts of the OAIS in more specific contexts. As explained later in the section on "OAIS Adoption, Extension, and Future Directions," such follow-on standardization has been taking place.

CONTENT OF THE OAIS

The OAIS is a 148-page document, composed of six sections and six annexes. Section 1 frames the content to follow, by providing discussions of purpose, scope, applicability, definitions, rationale, and conformance requirements. It also situates the document in a larger context by including a "road map for development of related standards." Section 2 lays out several core concepts that are then modeled in more detail in Section 4. These include archive; information (as distinct from data); interfaces between an archive, Producers, Consumers, and Management; and Information Package and its subtypes: Submission Information Package (SIP), Archival Information Package (AIP), and Dissemination Information Package (DIP). Section 3 discusses the responsibilities of an Open Archival Information System and "some examples of mechanisms to discharge these responsibilities." Section 4 presents a "more detailed model view" of the concepts previously laid out in the document. The section includes a functional model (including a high-level view and then unpacking of each entity and data flows between the entities) and an information model, which provides a hierarchical set of views and explanations for what logical elements should be stored and managed in association with a data object. Section 4 also provides an account of the "transformations, both logical and physical, of the Information Package and its associated objects as they follow a lifecycle from the Producer to the OAIS, and from the OAIS to the Consumer." Section 5 provides some discussion—intended to be implementation agnostic—of technical issues and strategies that an archive can potentially use to address changes in underlying hardware, software, formats, and access services. Section 6 discusses potential arrangements between multiple archives. The annexes that follow Section 6 are not considered part of the Reference Model's normative content but are instead "provided for the convenience of the reader." The annexes include a set of five "scenarios" that use OAIS terminology and concepts to describe specific existing archives; explanations of how the Reference Model relates to other standards and projects; a brief Unified Modeling Language (UML) tutorial; list of references; a layered model of how software could be used to support Representation Information; and a "composite diagram" that presents in one place the detailed interfaces between each of the entities in the functional model.

FUNDAMENTAL TERMS AND CONCEPTS

The Reference Model defines an OAIS as "an archive, consisting of an organization of people and systems, that has accepted the responsibility to preserve information and make it available for a Designated Community." Many of the requirements for an OAIS are based on the needs of its Designated Community, which is the set of one or more "user communities" that the OAIS is serving. An OAIS is responsible for digital information over the "long term," which is "long enough to be concerned with the impacts of changing technologies, including support for new media and data formats, or with a changing user community" (p. 1-11).[1] One of the fundamental challenges of an OAIS is to ensure that the digital information in its care is "independently understandable" to the

Designated Community, which means that the Designated Community can understand it "without having to resort to special resources not widely available, including named individuals" (p. 1-10).[1] The Designated Community has a certain "knowledge base," which can change over time.

One of the most important insights embedded in the Reference Model is that the "Content Information" to be preserved by an archive is composed not only of a "set of bit sequences" (the "data object") but also associated sufficient "Representation Information" to allow the bits to be rendered, used, and understood (p. 2-4)[1]:

> Since a key purpose of an OAIS is to preserve information for a Designated Community, the OAIS must understand the Knowledge Base of its Designated Community to understand the minimum Representation Information that must be maintained. The OAIS should then make a decision between maintaining the minimum Representation Information needed for its Designated Community, or maintaining a larger amount of Representation Information that may allow understanding by a larger Consumer community with a less specialized Knowledge Base. Over time, evolution of the Designated Community's Knowledge Base may require updates to the Representation Information to ensure continued understanding.

The three main roles played by the external entities with which an OAIS interacts are Producer, Consumer, and Management. Producers are "persons, or client systems, who provide the information to be preserved." Consumers are "persons, or client systems, who interact with OAIS services to find preserved information of interest and to access that information in detail." Management is "the role played by those who set overall OAIS policy as one component in a broader policy domain (p. 1-11)."[1]

A diversity of workflow and collaborative arrangements can be mapped to the Reference Model by representing "other OAISs" and "internal OAIS persons or systems" as Producers and Consumers (pp. 1-8, 1-12).[1] The Reference Model describes "four categories of archive association" based on "successively higher degrees of interaction":

- Independent—"no management or technical interaction."
- Cooperating—"potential common producers, common submission standards, and common dissemination standards, but no common finding aids."
- Federated—serve "both a Local Community (i.e., the original Designated Community served by the archive) and a Global community (i.e., an extended Designated Community) which has interests in the holdings of several OAIS archives and has influenced those archives to provide access to their holdings via one or more common finding aids."
- Shared resources—have agreed to share resources between the archives, which "requires various standards internal to the archive (such as ingest-storage and access-storage interface standards), but does not alter the user community's view of the archive" (p. 6-2).[1]

The primary mechanisms that the Reference Model uses to convey the aspects of an OAIS are its functional model and information model. Roughly speaking, the former indicates what an OAIS must do, and the latter indicates what the OAIS must have in its collections.

Functional Model

The functional model is composed of seven main functional entities and the interfaces between them: Access, Administration, Archival storage, Common Services, Data Management, Ingest, and Preservation Planning. The single figure from the Reference Model that has received the most attention in the digital preservation literature is a representation of six of the functional entities (see Figure 51.2). Not directly represented in Figure 51.2 are Common Services, which are the "supporting services" that must be in place for computer systems to operate and perform properly,

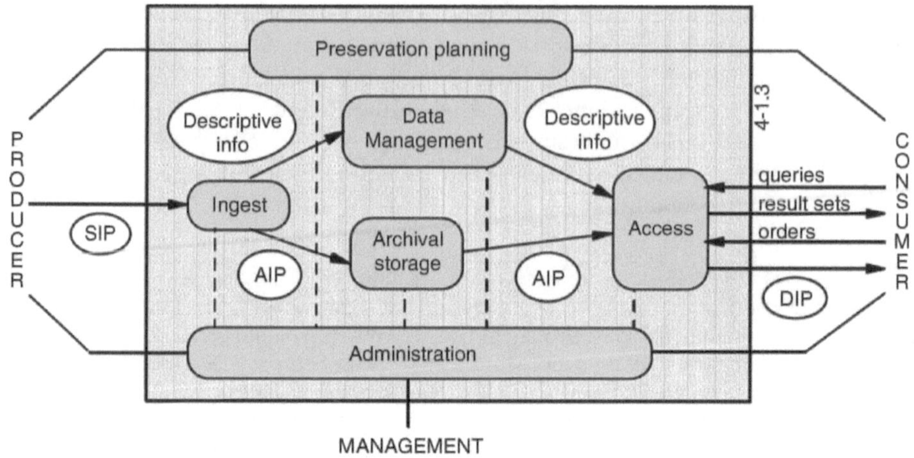

FIGURE 51.2 OAIS Functional Entities; SIP = Submission Information Package; AIP = Archival Information Package; DIP = Dissemination Information Package. (Reference model for an Open Archival Information System (OAIS); Consulative Committee for Space Data System: Washington, D.C, 2002; 4:1.)

including interprocess communication, name services, temporary storage allocation, exception handling, backup, directory services, as well as other aspects of operating system, network, and security services. Although Common Services are necessary for an OAIS, they are not a major focus of the Reference Model, because they are "assumed to be available" (p. 4-2).[1] As illustrated in Figure 51.2, the OAIS functional model also identifies between Administration and management, but it does not elaborate any function within management itself.

Many aspects of the functional model rest on the distinction between SIPs, AIPs, and DIPs. SIPs are what the OAIS receives from Producers. AIPs are what the OAIS manages and preserves. DIPs are "derived from one or more AIPs, [and are] received by the Consumer in response to a request to the OAIS" (p. 1-10).[1]

Ingest is the entity that receives SIPs, performs quality assurance on the SIPs, generates AIPs, extracts Descriptive Information from AIPs, and coordinates updates to Archival Storage and Data Management. Archival Storage is responsible for "receiving AIPs from Ingest and adding them to permanent storage, managing the storage hierarchy, refreshing the media on which archive holdings are stored, performing routine and special error checking, providing disaster recovery capabilities, and providing AIPs to access to fulfill orders" (pp. 4-1, 4-2).[1] Data Management supports the populating, maintenance and accessing of both Descriptive Information and administrative data associated with the OAIS holdings; this includes database administration, database updates, performing queries on the data, and producing reports that result from the queries. Administration is responsible for "the overall operation of the archive system," which includes soliciting and negotiating submission agreements, auditing submissions, configuration management, system engineering, activating stored requests, and the establishment and maintenance of standards and policies (p. 4-2).[1] Preservation Planning monitors the environment for important changes in technology or the needs of the Designated Community; evaluates the implications of those changes to the archive's holdings; designs Information Package templates; "provides design assistance and review to specialize these templates into SIPs and AIPs for specific submissions"; "develops detailed Migration plans, software prototypes and test plans," and provides periodic recommendations for "archival information updates," standards and policies (p. 4-2).[1] Access both provides and appropriately restricts Consumers' ability to discover, request, and receive information from the archive, including DIPs, "result sets" and reports (p. 4-2).[1]

Information Model

The information model defines and describes "the types of information that are exchanged and managed within the OAIS" (p. 4-18).[1] It is based on the recognition that long-term preservation of digital information requires an archive to "store significantly more than the contents of the object it is expected to preserve" (p. 4-19).[1] The Reference Model uses the term "Information Package" to refer to the logical unit that includes both a digital object and the other types of information that should be associated with the digital object in order to preserve and provide meaningful access to it over time. AIPs are the information packages that are managed internally by the OAIS. An AIP can be either an Archival Information Collection (AIC), "whose Content Information is an aggregation of other Archival Information Packages" (p. 1-7),[1] or Archival Information Unit (AIU) "whose Content Information is not further broken down into other Content Information components." Figure 51.3 presents the main types of information that constitute and are associated with an AIP. The Package Description is information about an Information Package, which is used by Access Aids. An Access Aid is "a software program or document that allow[s] Consumers to locate, analyze, and order Archival Information Packages of interest" (p. 1-7).[1] Packaging Information, in contrast, is not intended for direct use by Consumer but is instead "used to bind and identify the components of an Information Package" (e.g., volumes and directory information for the components) (p. 1-12).[1]

The Content Information is the "the original target of preservation" (p. 1-8).[1] As described earlier, Content Information is composed of both the Data Object (for digital information, one or more sequences of bits) and Representation Information, which "allows for the full interpretation of the data into meaningful information" (p. 4-19).[1] Representation Information can be either Structure Information, which "imparts meaning about how other information is organized," such as mapping "bit streams to common computer types such as characters, numbers, and pixels and aggregations of those types such as character strings and arrays" (p. 1-13),[1] or Semantic Information, which indicates the meaning of language used in either the Structure Information or other parts of the Content Information.

Representation Information is often conveyed using Digital Objects, which then require their own Representation Information, resulting in what is called a Representation Network. For example,

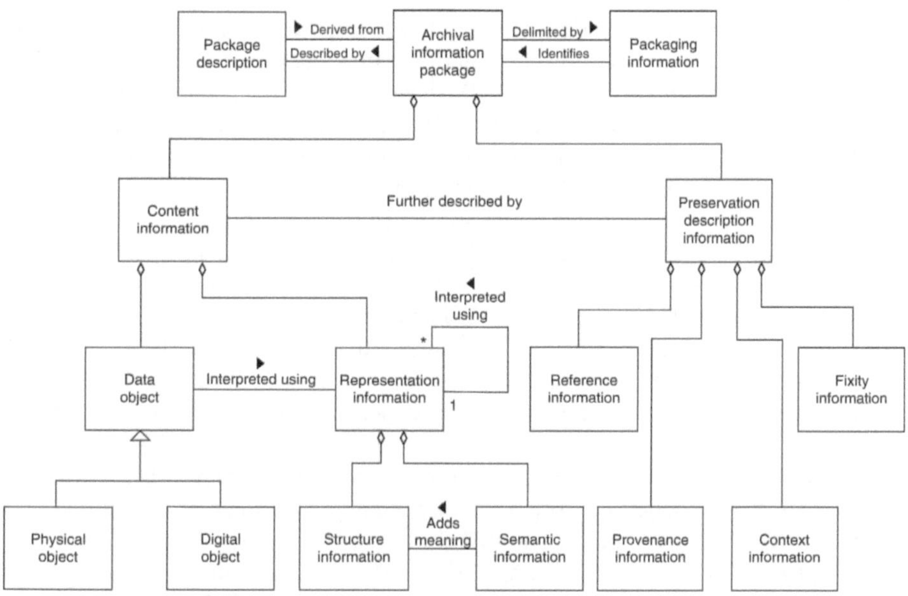

FIGURE 51.3 Archival Information Package (Detailed view). (Reference Model for an Open Archival Information System (OAIS); Consulative Committee for Space Data Systems: Washington, D.C, 2002-4-37.)

a string of bits (Digital Object) could represent an array of pixels, but a Consumer would also need information about the file format (Representation Information), in order to render and use that Digital Object as an image. If the image were encoded using Scalable Vector Graphics (SVG), which is based on Extensible Markup Language (XML), then rendering and using the image would require not only the SVG specification but also the specification for XML, as well as other specifications for character encoding and Uniform Resource Identifiers (URIs) upon which XML itself depends.

As illustrated in Figure 51.3, Content Information is "further described by" Preservation Description Information (PDI), which "is necessary for adequate preservation of the Content Information." PDI is composed of

- Reference Information—"identifies, and if necessary describes, one or more mechanisms used to provide assigned identifiers for the Content Information" and "provides identifiers that allow outside systems to refer, unambiguously, to a particular Content Information."[14]
- Provenance Information—"origin or source of the Content Information, any changes that may have taken place since it was originated, and who has had custody of it since it was originated" (p. 1-12).[1]
- Context Information—"documents the relationships of the Content Information to its environment" including "why the Content Information was created and how it relates to other Content Information objects" (p. 1-8).[1]
- Fixity Information—"documents the authentication mechanisms and provides authentication keys to ensure that the Content Information object has not been altered in an undocumented manner" (p. 1-10).[1]

PDI is an extension and elaboration of what *Preserving Digital Information* called the "features that determine information integrity and deserve attention for archival purposes": "content, fixity, reference, provenance, and context."[13]

OAIS ADOPTION, EXTENSIONS, AND FUTURE DIRECTIONS

Several years before it had reached formally approved status within the CCSDS or ISO, the OAIS was already receiving considerable attention from those engaged in digital preservation research and development. An extensive survey of the English-language literature up to April 2005 identified 335 sources that cite or discuss the OAIS, beginning in 1997 and increasing every year thereafter.[14] Over the past several years, the OAIS has come to be a widely assumed basis for research and development on digital archives, with conference papers, articles, and reports very often presenting their findings within the context of the OAIS.

The OAIS has become "the reference model of choice of those involved in digital preservation worldwide,"[15] serving as a "galvanizing force"[16] and a "major factor in the advancement of digital archiving efforts."[17] It has contributed "a common language and concepts for different professional groups involved in digital preservation and developing archiving systems."[18] "The reference model represented common ground upon which to consolidate understanding of the needs and requirements of digital preservation: an opportunity to gather the strands of isolated digital preservation activities, merging them into a shared (albeit highly conceptual) characterization of the problem's boundaries."[19]

A large number of research and development projects have either based their work directly on or claimed that their final products conform to the OAIS, many of which are listed in Table 51.1.

Professional development has also been strongly influenced by the OAIS. One of the earliest activities of the Digital Preservation Coalition (DPC) in the United Kingdom after its formation in 2001 was to develop, along with the British National Space Centre (BNSC), a seminar to discuss and "raise the profile of" the OAIS. The Cornell University Library offered a highly acclaimed workshop series from 2003 to 2006, and disseminated an associated tutorial, both called Digital

TABLE 51.1
Examples of Research and Development Activities with Stated Oais Influence or Requirements

Major institutions, organizations, and repositories	British Library
	Digital Curation Centre in the United Kingdom
	European Union
	French Archive Institute
	French National Archiving Center for University and Scientific Publications (CINES)
	Inter-University Consortium for Political and Social Research (ICPSR)
	JSTOR (Journal Storage)
	National Library of Australia
	National Library of France (BnF)
	National Library of New Zealand
	National Library of the Netherlands (KB)
	Online Computer Library Center (OCLC)
	Portico
	Project Euclid—Cornell University Library and Duke University Press
	U.S. Government Printing Office
	U.S. Library of Congress, National Library of China
	U.S. National Archives and Records Administration
	U.S. National Library of Medicine
	U.S. National Oceanic and Atmospheric Administration
	United Nations Educational, Scientific and Cultural Organization (UNESCO)
	Numerous university libraries and space agencies
Funding bodies emphasizing OAIS in solicitations and research agendas	U.S. National Science Foundation
	Joint Information Systems Committee (JISC)—United Kingdom
Digital collection management systems and preservation platforms	aDORe Archive—Los Alamos National Laboratory
	CONTENTdm—OCLC
	DSpace—Massachusetts Institute of Technology
	Flexible Extensible Digital Object and Repository Architecture (Fedora)
	Digital Information Archiving System (DIAS)—IBM
	LOCKSS (Lots of Copies Keep Stuff Safe)—Stanford University Libraries
	Integrated Rule-Oriented Data System (iRODS)—Data Intensive Cyber Environments (DICE) Group
	Preservation and Long-term Access through Networked Services (PLANETS)
	Testbed
	Securing a Hybrid Environment for Research Preservation and Access (SHERPA)
	Digital Preservation (DP) Service—Arts and Humanities Data Service (AHDS)

Preservation Management: Implementing Short-Term Strategies for Long-Term Problems, which used the OAIS as a foundation.[20] In 2008, Inter-University Consortium for Political and Social Research (ICPSR) became the host of the Digital Preservation Management workshop and tutorial, which continue to be based heavily on the OAIS.

From its initial conception, the OAIS was intended to serve as the basis for further development of more specific digital archives standards, and the OAIS has indeed played that role. It has served as the basis for several very prominent digital preservation metadata initiatives, including CEDARS, NEDLIB, and two joint Research Libraries Group (RLG)/Online Computer Library Center (OCLC) efforts—the Working Group on Preservation Metadata and then the Preservation Metadata Implementation Strategies (PREMIS) Working Group. The CCSDS also has been coordinating the development of follow-on standards based on the OAIS, which provide more detailed guidance related to parts of the OAIS functional and information models. The *Producer–Archive Interface Methodology Abstract Standard* (PAIMAS) "defines the methodology for the structure of actions that are required from the initial time of contact between the producer and the archive until the objects of information are received and validated by the archive."[21] PAIMAS was issued as a CCSDS Blue Book in May 2004 and was published as an ISO standard (ISO 20652) in 2006.[22] The *Producer–Archive Interface Specification* (PAIS) focuses on an even finer level of granulating, by presenting "a standard method to formally define the digital information objects to be transferred by an information Producer to an Archive and for effectively transferring these objects in the form of Submission Information Packages (SIPs)." As of the writing of this entry, the PAIS was in a tenth White Book version (April 2009), undergoing consideration for Red Book status. A White Book is "a preliminary draft of a planned CCSDS Recommendation or Report" that is "under development" and "not necessarily endorsed by any CCSDS Member or Observer Agency or given any CCSDS external distribution."[23]

RLG and NARA formed a Digital Repository Certification Task Force, whose efforts were explicitly tied to the OAIS. An initiative by the Center for Research Libraries (CRL) is extending the RLG/NARA certification work, with funding from the Andrew W. Mellon Foundation. A Birds of a Feather group is also attempting to develop an ISO standard for digital repository audit and certification, through the same channels as the OAIS, viz. ISO TC 20, SC 13, and the CCSDS.

The OAIS is currently undergoing a 5-years review within the CCSDS and then within the ISO. During the comment period, which ended in October 2006, the CCSDS received 11 separate documents containing comments. At a meeting on October 4, 2007, the Digital Archive Ingest (DAI) Working Group began reviewing the OAIS review comments, and identified several action items related to specific parts of the text. In 2003, the CCSDS underwent a major reorganization. The digital archives standardization activities that were previously part of Panel 2, including the OAIS, were moved into a new area called Mission Operations and Information Management Services (MOIMS). The DAI working group, is part of MOIMS. The DAI Working Group determined an initial set of responses to the comments, shared the potential responses with those who submitted the original comments, and then revised the OAIS document based on the comments and follow-on interchanges. On May 5, 2009, John Garrett (Chair) and David Giaretta (Deputy Chair) of the DAI Working Group disseminated a proposed draft of the revised OAIS Reference Model through several electronic mailing lists, "seeking primarily to identify errors" in preparation for submitting the revised Reference Model for ISO review and balloting.

CONCLUSION

The OAIS has been a focal point and foundation for discussion of digital preservation and digital curation across many professional boundaries. It is thus valuable for information professionals not only to understand the content of the document but also to learn lessons about how the Reference Model was developed and promulgated. A reference model is a very high-level, conceptual standard. Rather than providing detailed specifications of mandatory data elements or file formats, the OAIS has introduced a set of interrelated terms and concepts. Its development occurred during a period when many professional communities had a need for such a high-level standard but had not yet developed one themselves. There are various ways in which the Reference Model is able to provide detailed concepts, while still remaining relatively "implementation-independent": presentation of the functional model and information model in terms of high-level entities; extensive use of figures; and elaboration of implementation details in nonnormative appendices to the document, including several organization-specific "scenarios."

Much of the value of the Reference Model comes from its coherence, clarity, and synthesis of ideas. The Reference Model does define many new terms and introduces many original concepts, but its development has also been characterized by significant adaptation and reuse of preexisting sources.

Finally, the word "Open" in the acronym OAIS—meant to indicate that the standard was "developed in open forums"—was a defining feature of its evolution. The leaders of the effort presented draft products to many professional forums and actively recruited contributions and commentary. In addition to the traditional set of CCSDS stakeholders (space agencies and their contractors), many other organizations and individuals also contributed to the OAIS development process.

The OAIS is playing a major role in many current standardization, research, and development initiatives. Its impact on professional conversations surrounding digital preservation and digital curation continues to grow, 7 years after the Reference Model was approved as an International Standard.

ACKNOWLEDGMENTS

The author would like to thank Don Sawyer for sharing information about the OAIS five-year review process and the CCSDS for granting rights to use two of the figures from the OAIS.

REFERENCES

1. *Reference Model for an Open Archival Information System (OAIS)*; CCSDS 650.0-B-1; Consultative Committee for Space Data Systems: Washington, DC, 2002.
2. Lee, C.A. Defining digital preservation work: A case study of the development of the reference model for an open archival information system; Doctoral dissertation, University of Michigan, Michigan, 2005.
3. Waters, D.; Garrett, J. *Preserving Digital Information: Report of the Task Force on Archiving of Digital Information*; Commission on Preservation and Access and Research Libraries Group: Washington, DC, 1996.
4. Rothenberg, J. Ensuring the Longevity of Digital Documents. Sci. Am. **1995**, *272* (1), 42–47.
5. Sanders, T.; MacNeil, R. *Into the Future: On the Preservation of Knowledge in the Electronic Age*; Commission on Preservation and Access, and American Council of Learned Societies, 1997.
6. Procedures Manual for the Consultative Committee for Space Data Systems; CCSDS A00.0-Y-8; Consultative Committee for Space Data Systems: Washington, DC, November 2003; 1–4.
7. Procedures Manual for the Consultative Committee for Space Data Systems, CCSDS A00.0-Y-8; Consultative Committee for Space Data Systems: Washington, DC, November 2003; 1–4.
8. *Space Data and Information Transfer Systems—Open Archival Information System—Reference Model*; ISO 14721:2003; International Organization for Standardization: Geneva, Switzerland, 2003.
9. *Z39.50 Profile for Access to Digital Collections*; Library of Congress: Washington, DC, 1996.
10. *Planetary Data System Data Preparation Workbook*; Jet Propulsion Laboratory, California Institute of Technology: Pasadena, CA, 1995.
11. *IEEE Guide to the POSIX Open System Environment (OSE)*; Institute of Electrical and Electronics Engineers: New York, 1995.
12. Cargill, C.F. *Open Systems Standardization: A Business Approach*; Prentice Hall: Upper Saddle River, NJ, 1997; 90.
13. Waters, D.; Garrett, J. *Preserving Digital Information: Report of the Task Force on Archiving of Digital Information*; Commission on Preservation and Access and Research Libraries Group: Washington, DC, 1996, 12.
14. Lee, C.A. English-language literature citing or discussing the OAIS. In *Defining Digital Preservation Work: A Case Study of the Development of the Reference Model for an Open Archival Information System*; Doctoral dissertation, University of Michigan: Michigan, 2005; 227–253.
15. Greenstein, D.; Smith, A. Digital preservation in the United States: Survey of current research, practice, and common understandings. In *New-Model Scholarship: How Will It Survive?*; Smith, A., Ed.; Council on Library and Information Resources: Washington, DC, 2003; 40–48, 43.
16. Waters, D. Good archives make good scholars: Reflections on recent steps toward the archiving of digital information. In *The State of Digital Preservation: An International Perspective*; Council on Library and Information Resources: Washington, DC, 2002; 78–95, 80.

17. Hodge, G.M. Digital Preservation: Overview of Current Developments. Inform. Serv. Use **2002**, *22* (2/3), 73–82.
18. Beagrie, N. *National Digital Preservation Initiatives: An Overview of Developments in Australia, France, the Netherlands, and the United Kingdom and of Related International Activity*; Council on Library and Information Resources and the Library of Congress: Washington, DC, 2003, 45.
19. Lavoie, B.F. *The Open Archival Information System Reference Model: Introductory Guide*; OCLC Online Computer Library Center and Digital Preservation Coalition: Dublin, OH, 2004; 2.
20. Kenney, A.R.; McGovern, N.Y.; Entlich, R.; Kehoe, W.R.; Olsen, E.; Buckley, E.; DeMello, C. *Digital Preservation Management: Implementing Short-Term Strategies for Long-Term Problems*; Cornell University Library: Ithaca, NY, 2005, http://www.library.cornell.edu/iris/tutorial/dpm/ (accessed November 14, 2007).
21. *Producer–Archive Interface Methodology Abstract Standard*; CCSDS 651.0-B-1; Consultative Committee for Space Data Systems: Washington, DC, 2004.
22. *Space Data and Information Transfer Systems—Producer–Archive Interface—Methodology Abstract Standard*; ISO 20652:2006; International Organization for Standardization: Geneva, Switzerland, 2006.
23. Procedures Manual for the Consultative Committee for Space Data Systems; CCSDS A00.0-Y-8; Consultative Committee for Space Data Systems: Washington, DC, November 2003; 1–3.

Index

Page numbers followed by f and t indicate figures and tables, respectively.

E

F

J

K

L

M

N

O

P

Q

R

S

T

U

V

W

X

Y

Z